THE OXFORD HANDBOOK OF

DIGITAL ETHICS

THE OXFORD HANDBOOK OF

DIGITAL ETHICS

Edited by

CARISSA VÉLIZ

OXFORD
UNIVERSITY PRESS

OXFORD
UNIVERSITY PRESS

Great Clarendon Street, Oxford, OX2 6DP,
United Kingdom

Oxford University Press is a department of the University of Oxford.
It furthers the University's objective of excellence in research, scholarship,
and education by publishing worldwide. Oxford is a registered trade mark of
Oxford University Press in the UK and in certain other countries

Published in the United States of America by Oxford University Press
198 Madison Avenue, New York, NY 10016, United States of America

British Library Cataloguing in Publication Data
Data available

Library of Congress Control Number: 2023937489

ISBN 978-0-19-885781-5

DOI: 10.1093/oxfordhb/9780198857815.001.0001

Printed and bound by
CPI Group (UK) Ltd, Croydon, CR0 4YY

CONTENTS

PART III. FRIENDSHIP, LOVE, AND SEX

PART IV. ETHICAL DESIGN
OF TECHNOLOGY

PART V. JUSTICE AND FAIRNESS

PART VI. HEALTH

PART VII. PRIVACY AND SECURITY

PART VIII. THE FUTURE

Contributors

Mark Alfano, Associate Professor, Department of Philosophy, Macquarie University

Dean Cocking, Research Fellow, Digital Ethics Centre

Rowan Cruft, Professor of Philosophy, University of Stirling

John Danaher, Senior Lecturer, School of Law, University of Galway

Thomas Douglas, Professor of Applied Philosophy, Oxford Uehiro Centre for Practical Ethics, Faculty of Philosophy, University of Oxford

Brian D. Earp, Senior Research Fellow in Moral Psychology, Oxford Uehiro Centre for Practical Ethics, University of Oxford

Lily Frank, Assistant Professor, Philosophy and Ethics Group, Department of Industrial Engineering & Innovation Sciences, Eindhoven University of Technology

Iason Gabriel, Staff Research Scientist, Ethics Research Team, DeepMind

Vafa Ghazavi, Executive Director, Research and Policy, James Martin Institute for Public Policy

Alberto Giubilini, Senior Research Fellow, Oxford Uehiro Centre for Practical Ethics; Wellcome Centre for Ethics and Humanities, University of Oxford

Katerina Hadjimatheou, Senior Lecturer, University of Essex

Daniel R. Harris, PhD candidate, Philosophy Department, McGill University

Lisa Herzog, Professor of Political Philosophy, Faculty of Philosophy, University of Groningen

Johannes Himmelreich, Assistant Professor of Public Administration and International Affairs, Maxwell School of Citizenship and Public Affairs at Syracuse University

Jeffrey W. Howard, Associate Professor of Political Philosophy and Public Policy, University College London

Marcello Ienca, Professor of Ethics of AI and Neuroscience, TU München

Geoff Keeling, Research Scientist, Google

Michiel Kemmer, Student, Applied Ethics Master's, Utrecht University

Michal Klincewicz, Assistant Professor, Department of Cognitive Science and Artificial Intelligence, Tilburg University

Holly Lawford-Smith, Associate Professor in Political Philosophy, School of Historical and Philosophical Studies, University of Melbourne

Brenda Leong, Partner, BNH.AI

Neil Levy, Professor of Philosophy, Macquarie University

Kasper Lippert-Rasmussen, Professor of Political Theory, Department of Political Science, University of Aarhus

Kevin Macnish, Consulting Senior Manager, Sopra Steria

Andrei Marmor, Jacob Gould Schurman Professor of Philosophy and Law, Cornell University

Jessica Megarry, Postdoctoral Research Fellow in Geoprivacy, Queensland University of Technology

Francesca Minerva, Researcher, Faculty of Philosophy, University of Milan–Università Statale Milano

Abhishek Mishra, DPhil in Philosophy, University of Oxford; Engagement Manager, Faculty

Brent Mittelstadt, Associate Professor, Oxford Internet Institute, University of Oxford

Vincent C. Müller, A. v. Humboldt Professor for Theory and Ethics of AI, Friedrich-Alexander Universität Erlangen-Nürnberg

Lauritz Aastrup Munch, Postdoc, Department of Philosophy and History of Ideas, Aarhus University

Christopher Nathan, Research Fellow, University of Warwick

Sven Nyholm, Professor of the Ethics of Artificial Intelligence, Faculty of Philosophy, Philosophy of Science and Religious Studies, Ludwig Maximilian University of Munich

Rune Nyrup, Senior Research Fellow, Leverhulme Centre for the Future of Intelligence, University of Cambridge

Elizabeth O'Neill, Assistant Professor, Philosophy and Ethics, Eindhoven University of Technology

Rebecca Roache, Senior Lecturer in Philosophy, Department of Politics, International Relations, and Philosophy, Royal Holloway, University of London

Michael Robillard has held prior academic appointments at the University of Oxford, University of Notre Dame, and the U.S. Naval Academy

Julian Savulescu, Chen Su Lan Centennial Professor in Medical Ethics, Centre for Biomedical Ethics, National University of Singapore

Evan Selinger, Professor of Philosophy, Rochester Institute of Technology

Rob Simpson, Associate Professor, Department of Philosophy, University College London

Robert Sparrow, Professor of Philosophy, Monash University

Aksel Sterri, Primary Investigator of a three-year postdoctoral research grant from the Norwegian Research Council (2021–2024); Research Associate, Department of Government, Harvard University

Emily Sullivan, Assistant Professor, Eindhoven University of Technology; Eindhoven Artificial Intelligence Systems Institute

Laura Specker Sullivan, Assistant Professor, Department of Philosophy, Fordham University

Krista K. Thomason, Associate Professor of Philosophy, Department of Philosophy, Swarthmore College

Shannon Vallor, Baillie Gifford Chair in the Ethics of Data and Artificial Intelligence, University of Edinburgh

Jeroen van der Ham, Associate Professor, Design and Analysis of Communication Systems group, University of Twente

Effy Vayena, Professor of Bioethics, Department of Health Sciences and Technology, Institute of Translational Medicine, ETH Zurich

Carissa Véliz, Associate Professor at the Institute for Ethics in AI and the Faculty of Philosophy, University of Oxford

Karina Vold, Assistant Professor, Institute for the History and Philosophy of Science and Technology, University of Toronto

James Williams, Former Google Advertising Strategist, Oxford-Trained Philosopher

INTRODUCTION

CARISSA VÉLIZ

THE HANDBOOK

THE last decade witnessed a drastic change in attitudes concerning the digital: from tech hype to techlash. Scandals such as the Cambridge Analytica affair, and questionable practices related to algorithmic decision-making, the commodification of personal data, and the design of persuasive technologies have resulted in anxiety about the digital age. As concern has grown, more has been written inside and outside academia about the rights and wrongs of all things digital. Much of what has been written about digital ethics or AI ethics, however, has not been produced under the purview of practical ethics. This volume seeks to remedy that.

The ambition for *The Oxford Handbook of Digital Ethics* is to be the ultimate source for state-of-the-art scholarship in the emerging field of digital ethics. The book offers a rigorous, research-oriented, comprehensive, and up-to-date academic view of the discipline from the perspective of practical ethics.

Although the handbook is firmly grounded in philosophy and practical ethics, it draws from and aspires to contribute to related fields, including computer science, engineering, public policy, law, science and technology studies, anthropology, sociology, and media and information studies. While academic, it is nonetheless accessible for a broader public, introducing some of the most important challenges society is facing in relation to digital technologies: from fake news, online shaming, and trolling to questions of friendship, love, and sex in the digital age; from the ethics of persuasive technology, AI and value alignment, and concerns about fairness to issues related to cybersecurity, privacy, and surveillance; from health and AI to concerns about the future of work and democracy, and more.

The Title

The title of his handbook could have substituted 'digital ethics' with 'AI ethics', 'data ethics', or 'computer ethics'.

The field of computer ethics has a history going back at least to the 1970s. While today's work on digital ethics is a close younger cousin of that work, it is not a direct descendant in the topics it covers or the approach it takes. Furthermore, many of the ethical issues today are more about how people interact with technology than about computers per se. A search for the term 'computer ethics' on Google's Ngram Viewer reveals that the term rocketed in the 1980s, peaked in 2006, and seems to be falling into disuse, although it is still a more commonly used term than 'digital ethics' or 'AI ethics'. Perhaps its decline is partly explained by our ceasing to think of digital technologies such as smartphones and smartwatches as computers, even though they are arguably more of a computer than they are a phone or a watch. 'Computer ethics' puts the emphasis on machines, but the machines are increasingly becoming invisible to us.

The term 'AI ethics', in contrast, is growing in popularity. However, even though AI (artificial intelligence) is indisputably one of the main characters of the digital age, the term is slightly misleading. Much of the ethical problems arise from technologies that are not AI. Sometimes it's a badly designed spreadsheet that causes the problem, or intrusive data collection. Similarly, 'data ethics' emphasizes a vital element of the digital technological toolbox, but only one element. The problem of the future of work, for instance, does not obviously fit under the umbrella of data ethics.

The term 'digital ethics' aims to encompass AI ethics, data ethics, and other more specific areas of research like robot ethics. It refers to the study within practical ethics of the issues that arise in the design, implementation, and interaction with digital technologies. 'Digital' includes whatever has been translated into ones and zeros (the building blocks of code); it involves or is related to the use of computing, and stands in opposition to the world of the analogue. Although 'digital' makes indirect reference to data (binary digits represent data), it goes well beyond it and reminds us of the contrast with the analogue, and how those differences have ethical implications. Social media posts, for instance, are able to spread so rapidly by virtue of their being digital. If we had to copy each message by hand, as we used to with analogue technology, fake news and public shaming would be less of a problem.

The Emergence of Digital Ethics

Even though there has always been a component of practical ethics in ethics —the branch of philosophy dedicated to the question of how we ought to live— it did not come into its own as a subdiscipline within academic philosophy until the 1970s. Practical ethics reflects on and attempts to suggest solutions to the moral dilemmas that individuals and societies face in everyday life. It deals with questions related to matters of life and death, healthcare, the environment, business, and now, digital technologies.

One of the crucial elements that played a part in the consolidation of practical ethics as a subdiscipline was the progress of medical ethics. In turn, two factors contributed to the development of medical ethics: scandals and new technology. Medical scandals such as the Tuskegee Syphilis Experiment —in which researchers did not treat subjects with syphilis for decades despite treatment being available— highlighted the need to establish ethical standards and regulation. In addition, new technology was confronting healthcare professionals with ethical conundrums for which there were no obvious solutions. The mechanical ventilator, for instance, faced doctors with warm, heart-beating bodies whose brain was no longer working but whose organs could be procured for transplantation; that forced a rethink of the concept of death and the development of the ethics of organ transplantation. In short, medical ethics took off because there were practical demands that needed to be met, and it was clear that the burden should not lie solely on the shoulders of healthcare professionals whose expertise is in keeping people healthy, not resolving ethical dilemmas.

In a matter of a few years, medical ethics went from being a somewhat obscure interest to becoming a thriving subdiscipline with its own academic journals, anthologies, specialized programmes, degrees, and practices. When I was studying practical ethics as an undergraduate, I felt a pang of wistfulness thinking about the pioneers of medical ethics. How exciting it must have been, I thought, to be a philosopher and be called upon to give answers to novel real-life problems that needed urgent solutions. Little did I know.

Today, digital ethics is encountering both scandals —leaks, hacks, misuse of data, and sexist and racist algorithms— and new technologies that are creating ethical dilemmas. Digital ethics has much to learn from medical ethics—from its successes as well as its failures. But digital ethics spans a much broader horizon which includes not only public policy but political philosophy and geopolitics. One of the characteristics of the digital that makes it so powerful is that it can scale incredibly quickly, which creates systemic effects. When most offices around the world use the same algorithm or a version of the same algorithm, the impact of the design of that algorithm can be enormous. Furthermore, data and AI are being used as pawns and knights in the global game of geopolitical chess. In addition to being more political, the digital context is also more dominated by private forces. Arguably, one of the shortfalls of medical ethics has been its failure to curb some of big pharma's bad practices. The challenge society faces with big tech is even more formidable.

For all its faults, however, half a century after the establishment of medical ethics, medical ethics codes and best practices are well established, there are hardly any hospitals around the world without an ethics committee, and almost no healthcare students graduating without some sense of the issues at stake in medical ethics. All of it has contributed to avoiding much unnecessary suffering. We should expect nothing less of digital ethics in the next few decades.

One of the roles of ethics is to supply a grounding for good regulation and the development of best practices. Even though big tech often refers to its developments as 'inevitable', no technology is inevitable, and every device we have ever invented could have had a different design. Once something is invented, marketed, and is successful, however, it can remain in usage for a long time, even if it has been shown to be detrimental to people's health and wellbeing, and even when better alternatives are possible (e.g. gasoline and diesel cars). That is why building ethics into the very fundamentals of digital design is of vital importance. If we get things right from the start, we can have a huge positive impact on people's chances of having a good life now and in the future. If we fail to think through the ethical implications of the digital technologies we are developing now, we could be hampered by toxic consequences for decades to come.

Digital ethics is becoming mainstream for good reason. It is here to stay. Our ways of life, democracies, and wellbeing depend on how well we think through it and implement it. *The Oxford Handbook of Digital Ethics* is intended as a cornerstone in this work.

Acknowledgements

My thanks to all the authors of *The Oxford Handbook of Digital Ethics* for producing such outstanding contributions, for their perseverance (especially through the pandemic), and their patience. I'm thankful to Peter Momtchiloff, Philosophy Editor at Oxford University Press, for his patience as well, and for trusting me with this project. Thank you to the Oxford Uehiro Centre for Practical Ethics, and especially to Julian Savulescu and Roger Crisp, for having provided me with the perfect academic platform from which to do research in practical ethics. Thank you to the University of Oxford for having the foresight and ambition to found the Institute for Ethics in AI, and for allowing me to be a part of it. My gratitude to all the members of the Institute for their support. And thank you to the Principal, Fellows, and Scholars of Hertford College for being my academic home.

PART I

ETHICAL THEORIES AND DIGITAL ETHICS

....

CHAPTER 1

THE HISTORY OF
DIGITAL ETHICS

....

VINCENT C. MÜLLER

INTRODUCTION

THE history of digital *ethics* as a field was strongly shaped by the development and use of digital *technologies* in society. This digital ethics often mirror the ethical concerns of the pre-digital technologies that were replaced, but in more recent times, digital technologies have also posed questions that are truly new. When 'data processing' became a more common activity in industry and public administration in the 1960s, the concerns of ethicists were old issues like *privacy, data security*, and *power* through information access. Today, digital ethics involves old issues that took on a new quality due to digital technology, such as *surveillance, news*, or *dating*, but it also covers new issues that did not exist at all, such as *automated weapons, search engines, automated decision-making*, and *existential risk from artificial intelligence (AI)*.

The terms used to name the expanding discipline have also changed over time: we started with 'computer ethics' (Bynum 2001; Johnson 1985; Vacura 2015), then more abstract terms like 'information ethics' were proposed (Floridi 1999), and now some use the term 'digital ethics' (Capurro 2010), as this Handbook does. We also have digital ethics for particular areas, such as 'the ethics of AI', 'data ethics', 'robot ethics', etc.

There are reasons for these changes: 'computer ethics' now sounds dated because it focuses attention on the machines, which made good sense when they were visible, big boxes but began to make less sense when many technical devices invisibly included computing and the location of the processor became irrelevant. The more ambitious notion of 'information ethics' involves a digital ontology (Capurro 2006) and faces a significant challenge to explain the role of the notion of 'information'; see (Floridi 1999) versus (Floridi and Taddeo 2016). Also, the term 'information ethics' is sometimes used in contexts in which information is not computed, for example, in 'library and information science'. Occasionally, one hears the term 'cyberethics' (Spinello 2020), which specifically deals with the connected 'cyberspace'—probably now an outdated term, at least outside the military. In this confusion, some people use 'digital' as the new term, which captures the most relevant phenomena and moves away from the machinery to their use. One might argue that the process of 'computing' is still fundamental but that we will probably soon care less about whether a device uses computing (analogue or digital)—like we do not care much which energy source the engine in a car uses. The notion of 'data' will continue to make sense, but, in the future, I suspect that terms like 'computing' and 'digital' will just merge into 'technology'.

Given that this Handbook already has articles on the current state of the art, this article tries to provide historical context, both in debates during the early days of information technology (IT) from the 1940s to the 1970s, when IT was an expensive technology available only in well-funded central 'computation centres'; then roughly the 1980s to the early 2000s, with networked personal computers entering offices and households; finally, the past fifteen years or so with 'smart' phones and other 'smart' devices being used privately—for new purposes that emerge with the devices.

This article is structured around two ideas, namely, that (a) technology drives ethics and (b) many issues that are now part of 'digital ethics' predate digital technology. There is a certain tension between these two ideas, however, so the discussion will try to disentangle when and in what sense 'technology drives ethics' (e.g. by posing new problems, by revealing old ones, or even by effecting ethical change) and when that 'drive' is specific to 'digital' (computing) technology. I start on the assumption that (b) is true, thus the article must begin before the invention of digital technology, in fact, even before the invention of writing. We will return to these two ideas in the conclusion.

I propose to divide history into three main sections: pre-digital modernity (before the invention of digital technology), digital modernity (with digital technology but analogue lives), and digital post-modernity (with digital technology and digital lives). The hope is that this organization matches the social developments of these periods, but I make no claim that the terminology used here is congruent with a standard history of digital society. In each section, we will briefly look at the technology and then at digital ethics. Finally, it may be mentioned that there are significant research desiderata in the field; a detailed history of digital ethics, and indeed of applied or practical ethics, is yet to be written.

Pre-digital modernity: Talking and writing

Technology and society

A fair proportion of the concerns of classical digital ethics are about informational privacy, information security, power through information, etc. These issues existed long before the computing age, in fact before writing was invented—after all, they also feature in village gossip.

One significant step in this timeline, however, was the beginning of symbols and iconic representations from cave paintings onwards (cf. Sassoon and Gaur 1997). These allowed records that do not immediately vanish to be maintained, as speech does, some of which can be transported to another place. It may be useful to differentiate (a) representation *for* someone, or *intentional representation*, and (b) *representation per se*, when something represents something else because that is its function in a system (assuming this is possible without intentional states). The word 'tree', pronounced by someone, is an intentional representation (type 1); the non-linguistic representation of a tree in the brain of an organism that sees the tree is a non-intentional representation (type 2) (Müller 2007). Evidently, one major step that is relevant for digital ethics was the invention and use of *writing*—for the representation of natural language but also for mathematics and other purposes. Symbols in writing are already digital; that is, they have a sharp boundary with no intermediate stages (something is either an 'A' or a 'B', it cannot be a bit of both) and they are perfectly reproducible—one can write the exact same word or sentence more than once.

In a further step, the replication of writing and images in print multiplies the impact that goes with that writing—what is printed can be transported, remembered, and read by many people. It can become more easily part of the cultural heritage. A further major step is the transmission of speech and symbols over large distances and then to larger audiences through telegraph, mail, radio, and TV. Suddenly, a single person speaking could be heard and even seen by millions of others around the globe, even in real time.

Ethics

There is a significant body of ethical and legal discussion on pre-digital information handling, especially after the invention of writing, printing, and mass communication. Much of it is still the law today, such as the privacy of letters and other written communication, the press laws, and laws on libel (defamation). The privacy of letters was legally protected in the early days of postal services in the early eighteenth century, for example, in the 'Prussian New Postal Order' of 1712 (Matthias 1812: 54). Remarkably, several of these laws have lost their teeth in the digital era without explicit legal change. For example, email is often not protected by the privacy of letters, and online publications are often not covered by press law.

The central issue of privacy, often connected with 'data protection', started around 1900 (Warren and Brandeis 1890), developed into a field (Hoffman 1973; Martin 1973; Westin 1968) and is still a central topic of discussion today; from classical surveillance (Macnish 2017), governance (Bennett and Raab 2003), and ethical analysis (Roessler 2017; van den Hoven et al. 2020) to analysis for activism (Véliz 2020). This is an area where the law has not caught up with technical developments in such a way that the original intentions could be maintained—it is not even clear that these intentions are still politically desired.

The power of information and misinformation was well understood after the invention of printing but especially after the invention of mass media like radio and TV and their use in propaganda—media studies and media ethics became standard academic fields after the Second World War. Media ethics is still an important aspect of digital ethics (Ess 2014), especially the aspect of the 'public sphere' (Habermas 1962).

Apart from this tradition of more 'societal' ethics, there is a more 'personal' kind of ethics of *professional responsibility* that started in this area—and had an impact in the digital era. The influential *Institute of Electrical and Electronics Engineers* (IEEE, initially American Institute of Electrical Engineers, AIEE) adopted its first 'Principles of Professional Conduct for the Guidance of the Electrical Engineer' in 1912 (AIEE 1912). 'Engineering ethics' is thus older than ethics of computing—but, interestingly, the electrical and telephone industries in the United States managed to get an exception to the demand that engineers hold a professional licence (PE). This move may have had a far-reaching impact into the computer science of today, which usually does not see itself as a discipline of engineering, and bound by the ethos of engineers—though there are computer scientists that would want to achieve recognition as a profession and thus the ethos of 'being a good engineer' (in many countries, engineering has high status and computer science degrees are 'diplomas in engineering').

Up to this point, we see the main ethical themes of privacy and data security, power of information, and professional responsibility.

DIGITAL MODERNITY: DIGITAL ETHICS IN IT

Technology and society

As a rough starting point in this part of the timeline, one should take the first design for a universal computer with Babbage's 'analytic engine' in about 1840; the first actual universal computer was feasible only when computers could use electronic parts, starting with Zuse's Z3 in 1941, followed by the independently developed ENIAC in 1945, and the Manchester Mark I in 1949 and then many more machines, mostly due to military funding (Ifrah 1981). All major computers since then have been electronic universal digital computers with stored programs. Shortly after the Second World War came the beginnings of the science of 'informatics' with 'cybernetics' (Ashby 1956; Wiener 1948) and C.E. Shannon's 'A Mathematical Theory of Communication' (Shannon 1948). In 1956, J. McCarthy, M.L. Minsky, N. Rochester, and C.E. Shannon organized the Dartmouth conference on 'Artificial Intelligence', thus coining the term (McCarthy et al. 1955). Less than ten years later, H. Simon predicted, 'Machines will be capable, within 20 years, of doing any work that a man can do' (Simon 1965: 96). In 1971, integrated processor (microprocessor) computers started, with all integrated circuits in one micro-chip. This technology effectively started the modern computer era. Up to that point, computers had been big and very expensive devices, only used by large corporations, research centres, or public entities for 'data processing'; from the 1980s, 'personal computers' were possible (and had to be labelled as such).

Ray Kurzweil has put the development from the Second World War to the present with characteristic panache:

> Computers started out as large remote machines in air-conditioned rooms tended by white coated technicians. Subsequently they moved onto our desks, then under our arms, and now in our pockets. Soon, we'll routinely put them inside our bodies and brains. Ultimately we will become more nonbiological than biological.
>
> (Kurzweil 2002)

Ethics

Professional ethics

The first discussions about ethics and computers in digital modernity were about the personal ethics of the people who work professionally in computing—what they should or should not do. In that phase, a computer scientist was an expert, rather like a doctor or a mechanical engineer, and the question arose whether the new 'profession' needed ethics. These early discussions of computer ethics often had a certain tinge of moralizing, of having discovered an area of life that had escaped the attention of ethicists so far, but where immorality, or at least some impact on society, looms. In contrast to this, professional ethics today often take the more positive approach that practitioners face ethical problems that expert analysis might help to resolve. This suspicion of immorality was often supported by the view of practitioners that our technology is neutral and our aims laudable, thus 'ethics' is not needed—a naïve view one finds even today.

The early attempts at professional ethics moved into computer science quite early in the discipline; for example, the US *Association for Computing Machinery* (ACM) adopted 'Guidelines for Professional Conduct in Information Processing; in 1966 and Donn Parker pushed this agenda in his discipline in the ensuing years (Parker 1968). The current version is called the 'ACM Code of Ethics and Professional Conduct' (ACM 2018).

Responsible technology

The use of nuclear (atomic) bombs in the Second World War and the discussion about the risk of generating electricity in nuclear power stations from the late 1950s fuelled the increasing concern about the limits of technology in the 1960s. This political development is closely connected to the political developments in 'the generation of 1968' on the political left in Europe and the United States. The 'Club of Rome' was and is a group of high-level politicians, scientists, and industry leaders that deals with the basic, long-term problems of humankind. In 1972, it published the highly influential book, *The Limits to Growth: A Report for the Club of Rome's Project on the Predicament of Mankind* (Club of Rome 1972). It argued that the industrialized world was on an unsustainable trajectory of economic growth, using up finite resources (e.g. oil, minerals, farmable land) and increasing pollution, with the background of an increasing world population. These were the views of a radical minority at the time, and even today they are still far from commonplace.

This report and other similar discussions fuelled a generally more critical view of technology and the growth it enables. They led to a field of 'technology assessment' in terms of long-term impacts that has also dealt with information technologies (Grunwald 2002). This area of the social sciences is influential in political consulting and has several academic institutes (e.g. the Karlsruhe Institute of Technology). At the same time, a more political angle of technology is taken in the field of 'Science and Technology Studies' (STS), which is now a sizable academic field with degree programmes, journals, and conferences. As books like *The Ethics of Invention* (Jasanoff 2016) show, concerns in STS are often quite similar to those in ethics, though typically with a more 'critical' and more empirical approach. Despite these agreements, STS approaches have remained oddly separate from the ethics of computing.

Concerns about *sustainable development*, especially with respect to the environment, have been prominent on the political agenda for about forty years and they are now a central policy aim in most countries, at least officially. In 2015, the United Nations adopted the '2030 Agenda for Sustainable Development' (United Nations 2015) with seventeen 'Sustainable Development Goals'. These goals are now quite influential; for example, they guide the current development of official European Union policy on AI. The seventeen goals are: (1) no poverty; (2) zero hunger; (3) good health and well-being; (4) quality education; (5) gender equality; (6) clean water and sanitation; (7) affordable and clean energy; (8) decent work and economic growth; (9) industry, innovation, and infrastructure; (10) reducing inequality; (11) sustainable cities and communities; (12) responsible consumption and production; (13) climate action; (14) life below water; (15) life on land; (16) peace, justice, and strong institutions, and (17) partnerships for the Goals.

Control

It had also been understood by some that science and engineering generally pose ethical problems. The prominent physicist, C.F. v. Weizsäcker predicted in 1968 that computer technology will fundamentally transform our lives in the coming decades (Weizsäcker 1968). Weizsäcker asked how we can have individual freedom in such a world, 'i.e. freedom from the control of anonymous powers' (439). At the end of his article, he demands a Hippocratic oath for scientists. Soon after, Weizsäcker became the founding Director of the famous *Max Planck Institute for Research into the Life in a Scientific-Technical World*, co-directed by Jürgen Habermas since 1971. At that time, there was clearly a sense with major state funders that these issues deserved their own research institute.

In the United States, the ACM had a Special Interest Group 'Computers & Society' (SIGCAS) from 1969—it is still a significant actor today and still publishes the journal *Computers and Society*. Norbert Wiener had warned of AI even before the term was coined (see Bynum 2008: 26–30; 2015). In *Cybernetics*, Wiener wrote:

> […] we are already in a position to construct artificial machines of almost any degree of elaborateness of performance. Long before Nagasaki and the public awareness of the atomic bomb, it had occurred to me that we were here in the presence of another social potentiality of unheard-of importance for good and for evil.
>
> (Wiener 1948: 28)

Note that the atomic bomb was a starting point for a critical view on technology in his case, too. In his later book, *The Human Use of Human Beings*, he warns of manipulation:

> […] such machines, though helpless by themselves, may be used by a human being or a block of human beings to increase their control over the rest of the race or that political leaders may attempt to control their populations by means not of machines themselves but through political techniques as narrow and indifferent to human possibility as if they had, in fact, been conceived mechanically.
>
> (Wiener 1950)

Thus, in this phase, professional responsibility gains prominence as an issue, the notion of *control* through information and machinery comes up as a theme, and there is a general concern about the longer-term impacts of technology.

POST-MODERNITY

Technology and society

In this part of the timeline, from 1980 to today (2021), I will use a typical university student in a wealthy European country as an illustration. I think this timeline is useful because it is easy to forget how the availability and use of computers have changed in the past decades and even the past few years. (If this text is read a few years after writing, it will seem quaintly old-fashioned.) We will see that this is the phase in which computers enter peoples' lives and digital ethics becomes a discipline.

In the first half of the 1980s, a student would have seen a 'personal computer' (PC) in a business context, and towards the end of the 1980s they would probably own one. These PCs were not connected to a network, unless on university premises, so data exchange was through floppy disks. Floppy disks held 360KB, later 720 KB and 1.44 MB;

if the PC had a hard drive at all, it would hold ca. 20–120 MB. After 1990, if private PCs had network connections, that would be through modem dial-in on analogue telephone lines that would mainly serve links to others in the same network (e.g. CompuServe or AOL), allowing email and file-transfer protocol (ftp). Around the same time, personal computers moved from a command-line to a graphic interface, first on MacOS, then on MS Windows and UNIX. Students would use electrical typewriters or university-owned computers for their writing until *ca.* the year 2000, and often even later. The first worldwide web (WWW) page came online in 1990 and institutional web pages became common in the late 1990s; around the same time a dial-in internet connection at home through a modem became affordable, and Google was founded (1998). After 2000, it became common for a student to have a computer at home with an internet connection, though file exchanges would still be mostly via physical data carriers. By *ca.* 2010, the internet connection would be 'always on' and fast enough for frequent use of www pages, and video; by *ca.* 2019, it would be fully digital (ISDN, ASDL, ...) and its files would often be stored in the 'cloud', that is, spaces somewhere on the internet. Fibre-optic lines started to be used around 2020. With the COVID-19 pandemic over 2020–2022, cooperative work online through live video became common.

Mobile phones (cell phones) became commonly affordable by students in the late 1990s, but these were just phones, increasingly miniaturized. The first 'smart' phone, the iPhone, was introduced in 2007. Around 2015, a typical student would own such a smartphone and would use that phone mostly for things other than calls; essentially as a portable tablet computer with wi-fi capability (but it would be called a 'phone', not a 'computer'). After 2015, the typical smartphone would be connected to the internet at all times (with 3G). The frequent use of the web-over-phone internet became affordable around 2018/2019 (with 4G), so around 2020 video calls and online teaching became possible and useful.

The students born after *ca.* 1980 (i.e. at university from around 2020) are often called 'digital natives', meaning that their teenage and adult lives took place when digital information processing was commonplace. To digital natives, pre-digital technologies like print, radio, or television, feel 'old', while for the previous generations, digital technologies feel 'new'. This generational difference may also be one of the few cases where technological change drives actual ethical change, for example, in that digital natives are not worried about privacy in the way older generations are.

Together with smartphones, we now (2022) also begin to have other 'smart' devices that incorporate computers and are connected to the internet (soon with 5G), especially portables, TVs, cars, and homes—also known as the 'Internet of Things' (IoT). 'Smart' superstructures like grids, cities, and roads are being deployed. Sensors with digital output are becoming ubiquitous. In addition, a large part of our lives is digital (and thus does not need to be captured by sensors), much of it conducted through commercial platforms and 'social media' systems. All these developments enable a surveillance economy where data is a valuable commodity (as discussed in other chapters in this Handbook).

While a 'computer' was easily recognized as a physical box until *ca.* 2010, it is now incorporated into a host of devices and systems and often not perceived as such; perhaps even designed not to be noticed (e.g. in order to collect data). Much of computing has become a transparent technology in our daily lives: we use it without special learning and do not notice its existence or that computing takes place: 'The most profound technologies are those that disappear' (Weiser 1991: 94).

For the purposes of digital ethics, the crucial developments of our students were the move from computers 'somewhere else' to their own PC (*ca.* 1990), the use of the WWW (*ca.* 1995) and their smartphone (*ca.* 2015); the current development is the move to computing as a 'transparent technology'.

Ethics

Establishment

The first phase of digital ethics, or computer ethics, was the effort in the 1980s and 1990s to establish that there *is* such a thing or that there *should be* such a thing—both within philosophy or applied ethics and within computer science, especially the curriculum of computer science at universities. This 'establishment' is of significant importance for the academic field since, once 'ethics' is an established component of degrees in computer science and related disciplines, there is a labour market for academic teachers, a demand for writing textbooks and articles, etc. (Bynum 2010). It is not an accident that the field was established beyond 'professional ethics' and general societal concerns around the same time as the move of computers from labs to offices and homes occurred.

The first use of 'computer ethics' was probably by Deborah Johnson in her paper 'Computer Ethics: New Study Area for Engineering Science Students', where she remarked, 'Computer professionals are beginning to look toward codes of ethics and legislation to control the use of software' (Johnson 1978). Sometimes (Bynum 2001), it is Walter Maner who is credited with the first use for 'ethical problems aggravated, transformed or created by computer technology' (Maner 1980). Again, professional ethics seems to have been the forerunner for computer ethics, generally.

A few years later, with fundamental publications like James H. [Jim] Moor's 'What is Computer Ethics?' (Moor 1985), the first textbook (Johnson 1985), and three anthologies with established publishers (Blackwell, MIT Press, Columbia University Press), one can speak of an established small discipline (Moor and Bynum 2002). The two texts by Moor and Johnson are still the most cited works in the discipline, together with classic texts on privacy, such as (Warren and Brandeis 1890) and (Westin 1968). As (Tavani 1999) shows, in the next fifteen years there was a steady flow of monographs, textbooks, and anthologies. In the 1990s, 'ethics' started to gain a place in many computer science curricula.

In terms of *themes*, we have the classical ones (privacy, information power, professional ethics, impact of technology) and we now have increasing confidence that there is 'something unique' here. Maner says, 'I have tried to show that there are issues and problems that are unique to computer ethics. For all of these issues, there was an essential involvement of computing technology. Except for this technology, these issues would not have arisen, or would not have arisen in their highly altered form' (Maner 1996).

We now get a wider notion of digital ethics that includes issues which *only* come up in ethics of *robotics and AI*, for example, manipulation, automated decision-making, transparency, bias, autonomous systems, existential risk, etc. (Müller 2020). The relationship between robots or AI systems and humans had already been discussed in Putnam's classic paper 'Robots: Machines or Artificially Created Life?' (Putnam 1964) and it has seen a revival in the discussion of singularity (Kurzweil 1999) and existential risk from AI (Bostrom 2014).

Digital ethics now covers the human *digital life*, online and with computing devices— both on an individual level and as a society, for example, social networks (Vallor 2016). As a result, this handbook includes themes like human–robot interaction, online interaction, fake news, online relationships, advisory systems, transparency and explainability, discrimination, nudging, cybersecurity, and existential risk—in other words, the digital life is prominently discussed here; something that would not have happened even five years ago.

Institutional

The journal *Metaphilosophy*, founded by T.W. Bynum and R. Reese in 1970, first published articles on computer ethics in the mid-1980s. The journal *Minds and Machines,* founded by James Fetzer in 1991, started publishing ethics papers under the editorship of James H. Moor (2001–2010). The conference series ETHICOMP (1995) and the European Council of the Paint, Printing Ink and Artists' Colours Industry (CEPE) (1997) started in Europe, and specialized journals were established: the *Journal of Information Ethics* (1992), *Science and Engineering Ethics* (1995), *Ethics and Information Technology* (1999), and *Philosophy & Technology* (2010). The conferences on 'Computing and Philosophy' (CAP), since 1986 in North America, later in Europe and Asia, united to the International Association for Computing and Philosophy (IACAP) in 2011 and increasingly have a strong division on ethical issues; as do the Society for the Study of Artificial Intelligence and the Simulation of Behaviour (AISB) (in the UK) and the Philosophy and Theory of Artificial Intelligence (PT-AI).

Within the academic field of philosophy, applied ethics and digital ethics have remained firmly marginal or specialist even now, with very few presentations at mainstream conferences, publications in mainstream journals, or posts in mainstream departments. As far as I can tell, no paper on digital ethics has appeared in places like the *Journal of Philosophy, Mind, Philosophical Review, Philosophy & Public Affairs* or *Ethics* to this day—while, significantly, there are papers on this topic in *Science, Nature,* or *Artificial Intelligence.* Practically orientated fields in philosophy are treated largely as the poor and slightly embarrassing cousin who has to work for a living rather than having old money in the bank. In traditional philosophy, what counts as 'a problem' is still mostly defined through tradition rather than permitting a problem to enter philosophy from the outside. Cementing this situation, few of these 'practical' fields have the ambi-tion to have a real influence on traditional philosophy; but this is changing, and I would venture that this influence will be strong in the decades to come. It is interesting to note that the citation counts of academics in computing ethics and theory have surpassed those of comparable philosophers in related traditional areas, and similar trends are happening now with journals. One data point: as of 2020, the average article in *Mind* is cited twice within four years, while the average article in *Minds and Machines* is cited three times within four years—the number for the latter journal doubled in three years.[1]

Several prominent philosophers have worked on theoretical issues around AI and computing (e.g. Dennett, Dreyfus, Fodor, Haugeland, Searle), typically with a foun-dation of their careers in related areas of philosophy, such as philosophy of mind, philosophy of language, or logic. This also applies to Jim Moor, who was one of the first people in digital ethics to hold a professorship at a reputed general university (Dartmouth College). Still, the specialized researchers in the field were at marginal institutions or doing digital ethics on the side. This changed slowly; for example, sev-eral technical universities had professors working in digital ethics relatively early on; the Technical Universities in the Netherlands founded a 4TU Centre for Ethics and Technology in 2007 (Delft, Eindhoven, Twente, and Wageningen). In the past decade, Floridi and Bostrom were appointed to professorships at Oxford, at the Oxford Internet Institute (OII) and the Future of Humanity Institute (FHI). Coeckelbergh was appointed to a chair at the philosophy department in Vienna in 2015 (where Hrachovec was already active). A few more people were and are active in philosophical issues of 'new media', for example, Ch. Ess, who moved to Oslo in 2012. The ethics of AI became a field only quite recently, with the first conference in 2012 (Artificial General Intelligence (AGI)-Impacts), but it now has its own institutes at many mainstream universities.

In other words, only five years ago, almost all scholars in digital ethics were at institutions marginal to mainstream philosophy. It is only in those last couple of years that digital ethics is becoming mainstream; many more jobs are advertised, senior positions are available to people in the field, younger faculties are picking up on the topic, and more established faculties at established institutions are beginning to deem these matters worthy of their attention. That development is rapidly gaining pace now.

I expect that mainstream philosophy will quickly pick up digital ethics in the coming years—the subject has shown itself to be mature and fruitful for classical philosophical issues, and there is an obvious societal demand and significant funding opportunities. Probably there is also some hype already. In the classic notion of a 'hype cycle' for the expectations from a new technology, the development is supposed to go through several phases: After its beginnings at the 'technology trigger', it gains more and more attention, reaching a 'peak of inflated expectations', after which a more critical evaluation begins and the expectations go down, eventually reaching a 'trough of disillusionment'. From there, a realistic evaluation shows that there is some use, so we get the 'slope of enlight-enment' and eventually the technology settles on a 'plateau of productivity' and becomes mainstream. The *Gartner Hype Cycle for AI, 2019* (Goasduff 2019) sees digital ethics itself at the 'peak of inflated expectations' ... meaning that it is downhill from here, for some time, until we hopefully reach the 'plateau of productivity'. (My own view is that this is wrong since we are seeing the beginnings of AI policy and stronger digital ethics now.)

Future

The state of the art at the present and an outlook into the future are given in the chapters of this Handbook. Moor saw a bright future even twenty years ago: 'The future of computer ethics: You ain't seen nothin' yet!' (Moor 2001), and he followed up with a programmatic plea for 'machine ethics' (Moor 2006). Moor opens the former article with the bold statement:

> Computer ethics is a growth area. My prediction is that ethical problems generated by computers and information technology in general will abound for the foreseeable future. Moreover, we will continue to regard these issues as problems of computer ethics even though the ubiquitous computing devices themselves may tend to disappear into our clothing, our walls, our vehicles, our appliances, and ourselves.
>
> (Moor 2001: 89)

The prediction has undoubtedly held up until now. The ethics of the design and use of computers is clearly an area of very high societal importance and we would do well to catch problems early on—this is something we failed to do in the area of privacy (Véliz 2020) and some hope that we will do in the area of AI (Müller 2020).

However, as Moor mentions, there is also a very different possible line that was developed around the same time: Bynum reports on an unpublished talk by Deborah G. Johnson with the title 'Computer Ethics in the 21st Century' at the 1999 ETHICOMP conference:

> On Johnson's view, as information technology becomes very commonplace—as it gets integrated and absorbed into our everyday surroundings and is perceived simply as an aspect of ordinary life—we may no longer notice its presence. At that point, we would no longer need a term like 'computer ethics' to single out a subset of ethical issues arising from the use of information technology. Computer technology would be absorbed into the fabric of life, and computer ethics would thus be effectively absorbed into ordinary ethics.
>
> (Bynum 2001: 111ff) (cf. Johnson 2004)

On Johnson's view, we will have applied ethics and the ethics will concern most themes, such as 'information privacy' or 'how to behave in a romantic relationship' (Nyholm et al. 2022)—and much of this will be taking places with or through computing devices, but it will not matter (even though many things will remain that cannot be done without such devices). In other words, the 'drive' of technology we have seen in this history will come to a close, and the technology will become transparent. This transparency will likely have ethical problems itself—it enables surveillance and manipulation. If Johnson is right, however, we will soon have the situation that all too much is digital and transparent, and thus digital ethics is in danger of disappearing into general applied ethics.

In Molière's play, this bourgeois who wants to become a gentleman tells his 'philosophy master':

> Oh dear! For more than forty years I have been speaking prose while knowing nothing of it, and I am most obliged to you for telling me so.
> Molière, *Le Bourgeois gentilhomme* (Act II) 1670

CONCLUSION AND QUESTIONS

One feature that is characteristic of the new developments in digital ethics and in applied philosophy generally is how a problem becomes a problem worth investigating. In traditional philosophy, the criterion is often that there already exists a discussion in the past noting that there is something philosophically *interesting* about it, something unresolved. Thus, typically, we do not need to ask again whether that problem is worth discussing or whether it relies on assumptions we should not make (so we will find people who seriously ask whether Leibniz or Locke was right on the origin of ideas, for example). In digital ethics, what counts as a problem also includes the demand to be philosophically *interesting*, but more importantly, whether it has *relevance*. Quite often, this means that the problem first surfaces in fields other than philosophy. The initially dominant approach of *professional ethics* had a touch of 'policing' about it, of checking that everyone behaves—that moralizing gives ethics a bad name and it typically comes too late. More modern digital ethics tries to make people sensitive in the design process ('ethics by design') and to pick up problems where people really do not know what the ethically right thing to do is—these are the proper ethical problems that deserve our attention.

For the relation between ethics and computer ethics, Moor seemed right in this prediction:

> The development of ethical theory in computer ethics is sometimes overstated and sometimes understated. The overstatement suggests that computer ethics will produce a new ethical theory quite apart from traditional ethical notions. The understatement suggests that computer ethics will disappear into ordinary ethics. The truth, I predict, will be found in the middle [...] My prediction is that ethical theory in the future will be recognizable but reconfigured because of work done in computer ethics during the coming century.
> (Moor 2001: 91)

In my view, philosophers must do more than *export* an expertise from philosophy or ethics to practical problems: we must also *import* insights from these debates back to philosophy. The field of digital ethics can feed largely on societal demand and the real impact philosophical insights can have in this area, but in order to secure its place within philosophy, we must show that the work is both technically serious and has real potential to shed light on traditional issues. As an example, consider the question of when an artificial agent truly *is* an agent that is responsible for their actions—that discussion seems to provide a new angle to the debates on agency that traditionally focused on human beings. We can now ask the conceptual question anew and provide evidence from experiments with *making* things, rather than from passive observation.

Nearly 250 years ago, Immanuel Kant stated that the four main questions of philosophy are: '1. What can I know? 2. What should I do? 3. What can I hope for? 4. What is the human?' (Kant 1956/1800: 26) (questions 1–3 in Kant 1956/1781: A805 and B33). The philosophical reflection on digital technology contributes to all four of these.

ACKNOWLEDGEMENTS

I am grateful to Karsten Weber and Eleftheria Deltsou for useful comments and to Carissa Véliz, Guido Löhr, Maximilian Karge, and Jeff White for detailed reviewing.

NOTE

1. See https://www.scimagojr.com, accessed 8 August 2022.

REFERENCES

ACM (Association for Computing Machinery) (2018), 'ACM Code of Ethics and Professional Conduct', https://ethics.acm.org, accessed 8 August 2022.

AIEE (American Institute of Electrical Engineers) (1912), 'Principles of Professional Conduct for the Guidance of the Electrical Engineer', *Transactions of the American Institute of Electrical Engineers*, 31.

Ashby, W.R. (1956), *An Introduction to Cybernetics* (Eastford, CT: Martino Fine Books).

Bennett, C.J., and Raab, C. (2003), *The Governance of Privacy: Policy Instruments in Global Perspective*, 3rd 2017 edn (Cambridge, MA: MIT Press).

Bostrom, N. (2014), *Superintelligence: Paths, Dangers, Strategies* (Oxford: Oxford University Press).

Bynum, T.W. (2001), 'Computer Ethics: Its Birth and Its Future', *Ethics and Information Technology* 3(2), 109–112.

Bynum, T.W. (2008), 'Milestones in the History of Information and Computer Ethics', in K.E. Himma and H.T. Tavani (eds), *The Handbook of Information and Computer Ethics* (New York: Wiley), 25–48.

Bynum, T.W. (2010), 'The Historical Roots of Information and Computer Ethics', in L. Floridi (ed.), *The Cambridge Handbook of Information and Computer Ethics* (Cambridge: Cambridge University Press), 20–38, https://www.cambridge.org/core/books/cambridge-handbook-of-information-and-computer-ethics/AA0E1E64AE997C80FABD3657FD8F6CA8, accessed 8 August 2022.

Bynum, T.W. (2015), 'Computer and Information Ethics', *The Stanford Encyclopedia of Philosophy* (*Summer 2018 Edition*) (Stanford, CA: CLSI). https://plato.stanford.edu/archives/sum2018/entries/ethics-computer, accessed 8 August 2022.

Capurro, R. (2006), 'Towards an Ontological Foundation of Information Ethics', *Ethics and Information Technology* 8(4), 175–186.

Capurro, R. (2010), 'Digital Ethics', in Academy of Korean Studies (ed.), *Civilization and Peace* (Seoul : The Academy of Korean Studies), 203–214, http://www.capurro.de/korea.html, accessed 8 August 2022.

Club of Rome (1972), *The Limits to Growth* (New York: Potomac Associates).

Ess, C. (2014), *Digital Media Ethics*, 2nd edn (Cambridge: Polity Press).

Floridi, L. (1999), 'Information Ethics: On the Philosophical Foundation of Computer Ethics', *Ethics and Information Technology* 1(1), 33–52.

Floridi, L., and Taddeo, M. (2016), 'What is Data Ethics?', *Philosophical Transactions of the Royal Society A*, 374(2083).

Goasduff, L. (2019), 'Top Trends on the Gartner Hype Cycle for Artificial Intelligence, 2019', 12 September, https://www.gartner.com/smarterwithgartner/top-trends-on-the-gartner-hype-cycle-for-artificial-intelligence-2019, accessed 8 August 2022.

Grunwald, A. (2002), *Technikfolgenabschätzung—eine Einführung* (Berlin: Edition Sigma).

Habermas, J. (1962), *Strukturwandel der Öffentlichkeit. Untersuchungen zu einer Kategorie der bürgerlichen Gesellschaft* (Neuwied and Berlin: Luchterhand).

Hoffman, L.J. (1973), *Security and Privacy in Computer Systems* (Los Angeles, CA: Melville Publications).

Ifrah, G. (1981), *Histoire Universelle des Chiffres* (Paris: Editions Seghers).

Jasanoff, S. (2016), *The Ethics of Invention: Technology and the Human Future* (New York: Norton).

Johnson, D.G. (1978), 'Computer Ethics: New Study Area for Engineering Science Students', *Professional Engineer* 48(8), 32–34.

Johnson, D.G. (1985), *Computer Ethics* (Englewood Cliffs, NJ: Prentice Hall).

Johnson, D.G. (2004), 'Computer Ethics', in L. Floridi (ed.), *The Blackwell Guide to the Philosophy of Computing and Information* (Oxford: Blackwell), 65–74.

Kant, I. (1956/1781), *Kritik der Reinen Vernunft*, ed. W. Weischedel, A/B edn (Werkausgabe III & IV; Frankfurt: Suhrkamp).

Kant, I. (1956/1800), *Logik*, ed. W. Weischedel (Werkausgabe VI; Frankfurt: Suhrkamp).

Kurzweil, R. (1999), *The Age of Spiritual Machines: When Computers Exceed Human Intelligence* (London: Penguin).

Kurzweil, R. (2002), 'We Are Becoming Cyborgs', 15 March, http://www.kurzweilai.net/we-are-becoming-cyborgs, accessed 8 August 2022.

Macnish, K. (2017), *The Ethics of Surveillance: An Introduction* (London: Routledge).

Maner, W. (1980), *Starter Kit in Computer Ethics* (Hyde Park, New York: Helvetia Press and the National Information and Resource Center for Teaching Philosophy).

Maner, W. (1996), 'Unique Ethical Problems in Information Technology', *Science and Engineering Ethics* 2(2), 137–154.

Martin, J. (1973), *Security, Accuracy, and Privacy in Computer Systems* (Englewood Cliffs, NJ: Prentice-Hall).

Matthias, W.H. (1812), *Darstellung des Postwesens in den Königlich Ppreußischen Staaten* (Berlin: Selbstverlag).

McCarthy, J., Minsky, M., Rochester, N., and Shannon, C.E. (1955), 'A Proposal for the Dartmouth Summer Research Project on Artificial Intelligence', 31 August, http://www-formal.stanford.edu/jmc/history/dartmouth/dartmouth.html, accessed 8 August 2022.

Moor, J.H. (1985), 'What is Computer Ethics?', *Metaphilosophy*, 16(4), 266–275.

Moor, J.H. (2001), 'The Future of Computer Ethics: You Ain't Seen Nothin' Yet!', *Ethics and Information Technology* 3(2), 89–91.

Moor, J.H. (2006), 'The Nature, Importance, and Difficulty of Machine Ethics', *IEEE Intelligent Systems*, 21(4), 18–21.

Moor, J.H., and Bynum, T.W. (2002), *Cyberphilosophy: The Intersection of Philosophy and Computing* (Oxford: Blackwell).

Müller, V.C. (2007), 'Is There a Future for AI without Representation?', *Minds and Machines* 17(1), 101–115.

Müller, V.C. (2020), 'Ethics of Artificial Intelligence and Robotics', in E.N. Zalta (ed.), *Stanford Encyclopedia of Philosophy* (Summer 2020; Palo Alto, CA: CSLI, Stanford University), 1–70, https://plato.stanford.edu/entries/ethics-ai, accessed 8 August 2022.

Nyholm, S., Danaher, J., and Earp, B.D. (2022), 'The Technological Future of Love', in A. Grahle, N. McKeever, and J. Sanders (eds), *Philosophy of Love in the Past, Present, and Future* (London: Routledge), 224–239.

Parker, D.B. (1968), 'Rules of Ethics in Information Processing', *Communicaitions of the ACM* 11, 198–201.

Putnam, H. (1964), 'Robots: Machines or Artificially Created Life?', *Mind, Language and Reality, Philosophical Papers II*, repr. 1975 (Cambridge: Cambridge University Press), 386–407.

Roessler, B. (2017), 'Privacy as a Human Right', *Proceedings of the Aristotelian Society*, 2(CXVII), 187–206.

Sassoon, R., and Gaur, A. (1997), *Signs, Symbols and Icons: Pre-History of the Computer Age* (Exeter: Intellect Books).

Shannon, C.E. (1948), 'A Mathematical Theory of Communication', *Bell Systems Technical Journal*, 27(July, October), 379–423, 623–656.

Simon, H. (1965), *The Shape of Automation for Men and Management* (New York: Harper & Row).

Spinello, R.A. (2020), *Cyberethics: Morality and Law in Cyberspace* (Burlington, Mass: Jones & Bartlett Learning).

Tavani, H.T. (1999), 'Computer Ethics Textbooks: A Thirty-Year Retrospective', *ACM SIGCAS Computers and Society* (September), 26–31.

United Nations (2015), 'The 2030 Agenda for Sustainable Development', https://sustainabledevelopment.un.org/post2015/transformingourworld, accessed 8 August 2022.

Vacura, M. (2015), 'The History of Computer Ethics and Its Future Challenges', *Information Technology and Society Interaction and Independence (IDIMT 2015)* (Vienna), 325–333.

Vallor, S. (2016), 'Social Networking and Ethics', in E. N. Zalta (ed.), *The Stanford Encyclopedia of Philosophy*, Summer 2016 edn, https://plato.stanford.edu/entries/ethics-social-networking, accessed 8 August 2022.

van den Hoven, J., Blaauw, M., Pieters, W., and Warnier, M. (2020), 'Privacy and Information Technology', in E.N. Zalta (ed.), *The Stanford Encyclopedia of Philosophy*, Summer 2020 edn, https://plato.stanford.edu/archives/sum2020/entries/it-privacy, accessed 8 August 2022.

Véliz, C. (2020), *Privacy is Power* (London: Penguin).

Warren, S.D., and Brandeis, L.D. (1890), 'The Right to Privacy', *Harvard Law Review* 4(5), 193–220.

Weiser, M. (1991), 'The Computer for the 21st Century', *Scientific American* 265(3), 94–104.

Weizsäcker, C.F. v. (1968), 'Die Wissenschaft als Ethisches Problem', *Physikalische Blätter*, 10, 433–441.

Westin, A.F. (1968), 'Privacy and Freedom', *Washington & Lee Law Review* 25(166), 101–106.

Wiener, N. (1948), *Cybernetics: Or Control and Communication in the Animal and the Machine*, 2nd. edn 1961 (Cambridge, MA: MIT Press).

Wiener, N. (1950), *The Human Use of Human Beings* (Boston, MA: Houghton Mifflin).

CHAPTER 2

....

VIRTUES IN THE
DIGITAL AGE

....

SHANNON VALLOR

INTRODUCTION
....

THE earliest systematic applications of ethical theory and practice to the digital domain were primarily rooted either in consequentialist or deontological approaches to morality, with notions of virtue and character relegated to a marginal role at best. Yet, in the past decade there has been a noticeable shift towards virtue ethics as a constructive lens for understanding the complex and evolving relationship between digital technologies and the 'good', especially when the latter is framed not in terms of particular acts and outcomes but in terms of the broader conditions of human flourishing and character.

As will be explored in the next section, virtue ethics represents a wide range of traditions and philosophies ranging from classical to contemporary and stretching around the globe. But it brings to digital ethics important conceptual and practical resources lacking in consequentialist and deontological frameworks. Those frameworks remain useful, if limited, tools for digital ethics in many contexts, and virtue ethics has its own limitations, some of which are explored at length in this chapter. Yet, virtue ethics has features which seem uniquely suited to our digital age—most notably, a way of talking about how our digital practices change *us* and our own moral capabilities and restructure the very social environments that nurture and allow us to exercise those capabilities. It also offers the contextual sensitivity and adaptability needed to accommodate the rapidly changing and increasingly complex and interdependent landscape of digital affordances that new technologies are creating.

More so than at any other time in history, our technological creativity is enabling entirely new kinds of action with increasingly uncertain and incalculable consequences—from near-instantaneous communication across vast distances to billions of people, to the selective manipulation of the human genome, to the re-engineering of our planet's atmosphere and climate. We need a way of thinking about and enacting our moral responsibilities that adapts well to novel and uncertain conditions; that is, we need *practical wisdom* and an ethic that fosters the moral practices that can produce it.

It is precisely for these reasons that virtue ethics has become an increasingly popular frame for ethicists struggling with the complex and rapidly shifting dynamics of the digital transformation of modern industrial societies. Early examples of applying virtue ethics to the digital domain arose in the context of professional computing ethics: James Moor's 'If Aristotle Were a Computing Professional' (1998) and Frances Grodzinsky's 'The Practitioner from Within: Revisiting the Virtues' (1999), both for the ACM *SIGCAS Computers and Society* journal, were notably influential contributions. Soon, virtue ethics began to be a lens through which not only the computing professional but also the technologies themselves and their morally significant affordances were explored. This dovetailed with a rising scholarly interest in the problem of the *good life* in relation to technology, which had been neglected by utilitarian and deontological narratives about the rightness or permissibility of particular technology-enabled actions.[1] Virtue ethics has since been applied to the analysis of computer games (Sicart 2005), social media platforms and other digital media (Ess 2010, 2013; Vallor 2010, 2012; Wong 2013; Elder 2014), care robots for the elderly (Vallor 2011), military robots (Sparrow 2013; Sullins 2010; Vallor 2013), chatbots (Elder 2019), cyberbullying (Harrison 2015), online trolling (Cohen 2017), artificially intelligent agents (Wallach and Allen 2009; Coeckelbergh 2010; Tonkens 2012; Fröding and Peterson 2020; Wallach and Vallor 2020), engineering education (Pierrakos et al. 2019), and data visualization (Correll 2019).

Yet, virtue ethics, particularly in its classical and modern forms, is no panacea for the woes of digital societies. Its limitations, as acknowledged in the next section, are not insignificant, even if it remains arguably better adapted to the complexities of the digital sphere than many other forms of ethical theory and practice. In the third section of this chapter, I explore a growing stress fracture in the coherence of a virtue-based approach to digital ethics, namely, the acute challenge presented by two diverging norms of global digital culture: the liberal ideal of ethical digital practices as enabling individual self-determination and its antagonist, a communitarian ideal in which ethical digital practices sustain a shared life of social harmony and unity. In the final section, I show how the apparent insolubility of this conflict may reveal the true value of virtue ethics as a confrontation with our moral *unknowing*, one that reveals the necessary task of imagining and constructing a new path to sustainable human flourishing in a digital age.

THE VIRTUES OF A DIGITAL VIRTUE ETHIC

While virtue ethics is a collective tag for a diverse constellation of moral philosophies cutting across cultural and historical lines, each motivating very different normative judgements of digitally mediated phenomena, there are some notable shared advantages of a virtue-ethical approach to digital ethics. First and foremost among these, virtue ethics pays close attention to the moral characteristics of individual agents and communities, and in particular, how these characteristics (such as honesty, humility, courage, compassion, and practical wisdom) can be developed or degraded by exposure to various kinds of actions and environments. Thus, virtue ethics is highly attuned to and uniquely prepared to incorporate facts about the transformative effects of digital environments and technologies on us as moral agents. Virtue ethics recognizes that we are not just actors facing isolated choices but subjects-in-formation constantly being acted upon by digital phenomena in ways that alter our own moral habits, dispositions, and capabilities. It dovetails neatly with the longstanding view in the philosophy of technology that human persons and societies are co-shaped by their technologies in morally and politically significant ways (Verbeek 2011).

This offers a helpful contrast with a consequentialist approach to digital ethics, in which the characteristics of the agent are generally excluded in favour of a focus upon the specific goods or harms most likely to be realized by particular actions the agent might take in the digital domain. Initially, digital moral hazards seemed ready-made for analysis through the lens of utilitarianism or, in the narrower context of business and organizational ethics, related forms of cost–benefit analysis (CBA) adapted to ethical 'risk management'. Such approaches also appear to lend themselves more readily to computationally friendly methods of quantitative analysis, in which potential harms and benefits of a particular course of action can be tallied on a ledger, appropriately adjusted for scale and likelihood of impact, and optimized for a net beneficial outcome. The highly controversial philanthropic movements known as effective altruism and longtermism, which increasingly focus on digital futures, embody this promise to reduce moral judgment to a utilitarian calculus. Of course, these approaches to digital ethics inherit all of consequentialism's usual troubles, from the risk of neglecting unquantifiable harms and benefits to the fact that when properly applied, a robust utilitarian ethic commands far more demanding sacrifices than many moral agents will find reasonable. Utilitarianism is also widely understood to be insensitive to the incontrovertible demands of justice and the moral rights of the individual, as demonstrated in countless popular depictions of Phillipa Foot's trolley problem and in fiction such as Ursula Le Guin's *The Ones Who Walk Away from Omelas* (1975).

Perhaps most problematic for a consequentialist *digital* ethics is the fact that the scale, complexity, novelty, and systemic interdependence of digital phenomena make the long-term, global consequences of many courses of action either incalculable (predicting the future is already hard but predicting a digital future harder still!) or over-reliant on questionable priors of the agent (which are likely to favour the agent's easiest or most attractive choice). Of course, as John Stuart Mill (1864) reminds us, any system of ethics may be proved to work poorly 'if we suppose universal idiocy to be conjoined with it' (35). While consequentialism is certainly a fallible instrument for ethical reasoning in the digital domain, in environments with relatively familiar dynamics and clearly constrained choices, it is often still of considerable value. Yet, in many digital contexts, these dynamics are anything *but* familiar and predictable. They often seem *random*. A given social media post might get three likes or it might go viral and shift the global conversation overnight. It might provoke a war, or save a life, or bring down a company.

These outcomes could not be more opaque to *ex ante* consequentialist analysis. How could the author of an amusing 2021 Reddit post about a buttered orange cat in the workplace guess that within weeks they would have a massive Twitter platform for Jorts the Cat, now a powerful new icon of the American labour movement (Morrow 2022)? Yet, the original thread, silly as the story was, struck many as a parable about the virtues of compassion, moderation, acceptance, and accommodation of our limitations and differences, while gently pushing back against a co-worker's extreme moral overreach (by accusing her co-worker of 'ethnic stereotyping' of a cat, not to mention buttering said cat in an ill-advised attempt to teach it self-cleaning habits). The point is that in many digital environments, modelling virtues of character and prudential judgement is a more reliable guide to flourishing than predicting net consequences. Thus, virtue ethics' primary action guidance—what it tells us to *do*—is largely preparatory: to practice building specific traits of moral excellence into one's habits of digital behaviour and to cultivate practical judgement in reading the shifting moral dynamics of digital environments.

Virtue ethics *does* take action outcomes as relevant to particular moral choices. However, it does so in more limited and locally tractable ways than consequentialism, focusing on how our actions affect those with whom we share meaningful relationships and life projects. When more global effects are considered, they do not predict specific consequences but alignment with a broad moral pattern or 'shape of life'. Accounts such as Aristotle's consider the action's general compatibility with *eudaimonia*, a flourishing and happy life. A virtuous action will typically be strongly associated with a known pattern of living well and doing well with others, and a vicious action will typically be negatively associated with human flourishing. For example, a habit of using digital tools to spread rumours and conspiracy theories is not only individually vicious in its deceptiveness and recklessness, but it also weakens the social conditions for honest politics and thus is broadly incompatible with *eudaimonia* as shared human flourishing.

Similarly, *teleological* accounts such as that of Confucian virtue ethics judge the compatibility of the action with a certain ideal pattern of social and political affairs (the *Dao* or Way). The worry, of course, is that such accounts rest on local and historical conceptions of the good life that may be outmoded and impossible for modern digital societies to enact. Worse, these 'ideal' configurations may, from our present moral understanding, be objectively unjust, as with Aristotle's exclusion of women and non-Greeks from lives of political virtue. Hence, recent attempts to employ the structural tools of classical virtue ethics to construct more just and sustainable visions of human flourishing in a digital age (Brey et al. 2012; Vallor 2016).

Virtue ethics also enjoys notable advantages in digital contexts over deontological, rule-based approaches to moral decision-making. Deontological theories appeal to fixed, general rules of moral action, which typically must be formulated at a level of high abstraction in order to have universal applicability. Thus, we find in modern European moral philosophies the common appeal to Immanuel Kant's categorical imperative, whether formulated in terms of universal rational consistency (always act as you can will it generally done) or as a universal respect for the dignity and moral autonomy of persons (always treat others as an end in themselves and never *merely* as a means to your ends).

We also find professionalized versions of deontology in codes of computing ethics that prescribe rules and duties of general application, such as 'avoid harm', 'be fair', and 'respect privacy' (Association for Computing Machinery 2018: 1.2–1.6). The problem with this approach to digital ethics is twofold. First, most deontological frameworks give us no rigorous and reliable method to reconcile conflicting duties, or cases in which there is more than one way to follow all the rules, or, far more commonly, no way to follow them all. How do I determine which duties are most important to satisfy? What do I do when the best way to follow one rule (say, to respect users' privacy) appears by all lights to be incompatible with another (such as ensuring transparency or promoting fairness)? Attempts to construct deontological systems that rank duties or values to resolve such conflicts have been made, although these are not widely viewed as successful. But the far more problematic nature of deontological frameworks is their relative insensitivity to moral context and particularity.

Virtue ethics holds a rule-governed ethic to be plainly incompatible with the varied texture of human moral life as a social reality. In a critique that strikes equally hard at the core of both consequentialist and deontological understandings, Aristotle reminds us in Book One of the *Nicomachean Ethics* that the domain of human action is simply not amenable to perfect fixity or precision either in the description or prescription of social life—not because we are incapable of it but because these are the wrong standards: they distort or neglect the objective reality of the subject matter. Asking ethics to transcend context and social particularity is like asking the science of biology to transcend the phenomenon of life. You can, of course, try it (the ever-popular modern quest to reduce all biological science to non-biological phenomena) but it's a rather quixotic effort and it always leaves you talking about something *else*.

This is the case for all attempts to remove particularity from ethics. What is right for me or us to do depends very much on who I am/we are, what we are capable of, which particular relationships hang in the balance of our action, what our environment offers as support or impediment, what we need, what particular others in our sphere of action need, what historical and political meaning this action signifies for our community, and what other moral agents around us are willing and able to do *with* us.

In the digital domain, for example, relationships of power and inequality are extremely salient for moral action, leading to norms that rightly differ from those that would apply in an idealized egalitarian context. Consider the power asymmetries highlighted in the widely recognized moral distinction between 'punching up' in online contexts and 'punching down'. A tenured white professor publicly shaming a graduate student from a minoritized and excluded ethnic group for a social media post that indulges a common stereotype of whiteness (say, a snarky social media post about 'Karens'), is not identical in moral meaning to a graduate student who exposes a tenured white professor's post that indulges historical stereotypes about immigrant students. Likewise, information that an honest person would readily disclose in an offline public setting can be morally vicious to share in a digital environment, where data-mining, stalking, and profiling risks can warrant an honest person's deliberate acts of obfuscation to shield themselves and others (entering a wrong birthdate, misstating one's gender, giving a false hometown or false name of one's companions). Similarly, a virtuous person who mounts a justifiably indignant response to an unprovoked verbal attack in public will often rightly temper that outrage if that same attack transpires in an online public space where trolls routinely seek to provoke anger for their own self-gratification. Hence, the digital relevance of Aristotle's injunction that virtue in relation to anger requires the ability 'to be angry with the right person, and to the right degree, and at the right time, and for the right purpose, and in the right way' (Aristotle 2009: 1108b).

The degrees and forms of moral particularism inherent to different varieties of virtue ethics vary but most articulate the need for a well-developed contextual sensitivity and non-rigidity of the agent in making judgements that embody the virtue of practical wisdom. The flip side of this strength can, of course, be framed as a weakness. Contextual sensitivity means that virtue ethics appears unable to provide specific prescriptions for action in advance. What prescriptions can be offered end up looking very much like the high-level abstractions of deontology—be *virtuous*, be honest, just, kind, courageous, wise, etc. What that looks like in practice for a given moral agent, however, seems to be something that can only become evident in situ. While we can offer a plausible explanation after the fact of why a particular action was virtuous, given all the salient contextual factors, what we are looking for from an *applied* digital ethics in particular is effective action *guidance*. We want to know what we should do *before* we are presented with the moment of choice.

Fortunately, we can borrow Mill's injunction here to respond to this objection. While it is true that each moral situation is unique, and the need for spontaneous moral adjustment of our usual practice must always be granted as a possibility and given appropriate latitude,[2] we do have sufficient accumulated experience in the domain of human action (and now, in digitally mediated domains) to form strong and generally reliable moral heuristics concerning the expected shape of virtuous actions in digital environments. Only if we imagine someone deprived of access to prior moral experience does the artificial problem arise of an agent having to construct each moral judgement *ex nihilo*. What virtue ethics allows that deontology does not, is that what is, as a general rule, morally permissible may sometimes be wrong to do—and, for a unique configuration of moral reasons, not reducible to another rule specified in advance.

Consider, for example, the data-sharing scandal involving Crisis Text Line, a not-for-profit organization that provided confidential mental health crisis interventions via a free text service. After it was revealed by the media outlet *Politico* (Levine 2022) that Crisis Text Line had been sharing its chat logs with its for-profit spin-off Loris, to help it to build an artificial intelligence (AI) product for companies to improve the performance of their customer service agents, an intense public outcry ensued. The company was caught off guard, as it had, in its own self-understanding, complied with all of the legal *and* ethical requirements of data-sharing. Forced to terminate the data-sharing arrangement a scant three days later, the company's bafflement remained evident in its public statement: 'We understand that you don't want Crisis Text Line to share any data with Loris, *even though the data is handled securely, anonymized and scrubbed of person-ally identifiable information*' (Handel 2022, emphasis added).

The company was following 'the rules' as it understood them, and indeed its practice mirrored many other accepted data-sharing agreements in the health and social services domain. Nevertheless, there was, among data ethicists, a clear consensus that Crisis Text Line had violated moral norms, and Danah Boyd, a widely esteemed member of its advisory board, immediately expressed regret for her endorsement of the arrangement (Boyd 2022). Yet, its obvious wrongness is not traceable to a clear violation of any universal rule of data-sharing, and the company used common privacy-preserving techniques to mitigate harmful consequences. Instead, seeing the wrongness of the arrangement required the virtue of practical reason or *phronesis*: a cultivated sensitivity to the total moral situation in all its particularity, which, in this case, brought together a unique confluence of morally salient facts: the extreme vulnerability of the user population, which included suicidal youth and adults; the volunteer service of counsellors, who were unaware that their donated sessions would be used for commercial profit; and the discordant irony of a company using desperate people's cries for help and the generosity of those who help them to market a product to 'boost empathy AND bottom line' for its corporate clients, as Loris' website boasted (Levine 2022).

The contextual particularity of virtue ethics is therefore no vice but a reflection of the fact that moral performances are more akin to acts of perceptual or aesthetic *attunement* than to calculation or logical deduction from first principles. A more robust objection to virtue ethics is the worry that it is parochial and fundamentally conservative, given its heavy reliance on moral exemplars. If our models for virtue, those from whom we learn the appropriate moral patterns, are always already recognized as virtuous in my society, this seems to inhibit moral growth, creativity, and social learning. Fortunately, rich accounts of moral learning in accounts such as those of Kongzi and Mengzi (Confucius and Mencius in Latinized form) make it clear that exemplars are themselves enabled by virtue to continue to grow and deepen their moral insights in ways that provide a powerful engine for social learning and reformist critique of conventional norms. Still, the conservatism explicit in many modern attempts at character education for 'traditional' virtues[3] reminds us that, as Kongzi and Mengzi noted, there remains a real danger that a 'semblance of virtue'—the so-called 'village honest man' of rigid and superficial moral convention (Yearley 1990: 67–68)—will be mistaken for the real thing.

A related worry is that virtue ethics lends itself too easily to moral relativism, insofar as the content of virtue seems to be defined *internally*, by community consensus on what and who counts as excellent (MacIntyre 1984). How, then, do we avoid the conclusion that virtue is simply whatever model of social excellence a given digital community happens to endorse, no matter how morally repugnant it may appear to us? There are several available replies to this worry, but the most common rests on the naturalistic foundation of contemporary neo-Aristotelian theories. As argued in Foot's *Natural Goodness* (2000) and by others, including Nussbaum (1988), Hursthouse (1999), and Annas (2005), there exist certain fundamental needs and capabilities of the human person as a social and rational animal. A human animal cannot sustainably and fully flourish with others unless most if not all of these natural needs are satisfied and our basic capabilities allowed to develop and be exercised.

In the same way that a hardy, adaptable plant can flourish in many different locales (but not on the lunar surface or in an ocean trench), the adaptable and intelligent human animal can therefore flourish in a broad variety of cultures and social arrangements, but some such arrangements will be simply incompatible with shared human flourishing. An oppressive authoritarian state, for example, will routinely fail to meet its citizens' natural human needs for secure affiliative bonds of social trust and care, and since these are not mere desires but fundamental preconditions of human physical, psychological, and cognitive health, they function as objective constraints upon social models of virtue. Likewise, a society such as that of which Aristotle approves, in which women and ethnic minorities are excluded from public life and education—and thus prevented from fully developing and exercising their natural capabilities as rational and social animals—can rightly be judged as having been objectively vicious in that regard. Such naturalistic foundations are not unique to neo-Aristotelian accounts of virtue; for example, Mengzi is noted for his parable of Ox Mountain, a barren place where nothing will grow; he likens it to corrupt social conditions of poverty, cruelty, and depredation that objectively inhibit the successful cultivation and exercise of human virtue.[4]

Yet another objection is the 'situationist' critique that virtue ethics is premised upon an objectively incorrect theory of moral psychology (Harman 1999). This critique holds that character traits and (and thus character itself) either do not exist or are so weak in their practical force that they make little difference to moral behaviour. The situationist holds that external circumstances (the social situation) and internal fluctuations (such as my mood) tend to determine our moral behaviour far more than any robust internal dispositions such as courage or honesty. While it is hardly controversial that human behaviour is influenced by our environment and our internal states, the claim that virtues are typically rare or weak is not a direct challenge to all forms of virtue ethics.

Aristotle is well known for the view that excellence of character is difficult to achieve and hence relatively rare and certainly not the norm. Unlike Aristotle, Mengzi holds the view that moral excellence is widely attainable in the human family, but, as noted above in the fable of Ox Mountain, he observes that members of unjust societies are routinely denied the material, social, and political conditions necessary to nurture and sustain its development. Given that many of the empirical studies used to support situationist critiques show evidence of moral outliers who do seem to resist situational manipulation or disruption of their character (Kamtekar 2004; Wright et al. 2021), there is scant evidence in the literature that contradicts the moral psychology behind virtue ethics. What the response to the situationist critique does demonstrate is the importance of creating social structures and political conditions that are more conducive to human moral development than those common to many modern industrial societies, a task often ignored by social programmes of character education that adopt an excessively responsibilized view of individual or family character formation.

This observation leads to a final critique of virtue ethics that squarely strikes its target and provides a critical opportunity for moral philosophers and applied ethicists to address: virtue ethics remains narrowly and excessively focused on the character of persons rather than groups and societies. The criticism is that virtue ethics relies too much on the ideal of the individual moral hero or exemplar who provides a pattern for others to imitate and model their own moral development. What is missing is an account of the domain of *collective moral action and learning*, which is more than the sum of individual actions or learning paths but rather a joint exercise of moral capability. While accounts of collective virtue (Fricker 2010; Byerly and Byerly 2016) have been developed, they have yet to be applied effectively to digital ethics. Such an account is particularly vital in the contemporary digital domain, in which actions and moral communication are spread across increasingly non-local and disparate communities. It is also underscored by the COVID-19 pandemic, the climate change emergency, and other global challenges and calamities that directly challenge models of local action and responsibility. How can we cultivate the new digital capabilities and habits needed to deliberate and act as a human family to protect the future of our species and this planet while also remaining situated as persons within our own cultural and regional contexts of meaning?

This question incorporates the most pressing challenge for virtue ethics in a digital age. As the next section argues, digital life's bridging of cultures and geographies has forced a collision between two distinct visions of the good life that seem to be incompatible, and yet the digital public sphere must begin to enable at least a minimally shared conception of human flourishing in order for practically wise and effectively coordinated responses to humanity's existential challenges to emerge.

THE DIGITAL COLLISION OF LIBERAL AND COMMUNITARIAN VIRTUE

The digital transformations of twenty-first-century human sociality and the post-Cold War rise of new global existential challenges for human flourishing have jointly reawakened a long-simmering tension in moral and political philosophy between liberal and communitarian visions of the good life. This tension presents a challenge for contemporary digital ethics, and, as I will show, the challenge is more acute for a virtue-based digital ethic than for the alternatives. Before I explain why, it will help to quickly review the state of play in contemporary political philosophy.

Among the notable distinctions between the moral traditions of Anglo-European philosophy and other moral traditions—including many Asian, African, and indigenous American philosophies—is the anchoring of the former in a liberal value framework. Modern liberal thought, rooted in Enlightenment moral and political philosophies from Locke to Kant, Smith, Mill, and others, has powerfully influenced how Anglo-European thinkers conceive of moral agency and the primary goods to be realized or protected by moral and political action. Contemporary moral, political, and economic philosophies from Hayek (1960), Rawls (1971), and Nozick (1974) to Kymlicka

(1989), Nussbaum (1997), and Dworkin (2000) have attempted to outline the proper commitments of a liberal view.

Liberal philosophies vary widely in their views of the appropriate powers of the state, the nature and justification of private property, the rightful limits of personal freedom for the individual, and how to enjoy effective yet politically liberal institutions in light of ineradicable value conflicts and value pluralism. Yet, as a corpus and influence upon twenty-first-century digital cultures, they generally cohere in two key commitments:

- the view that rational autonomy (in practice, the capacity of each individual to exercise reflective and unconstrained choice in the domains of belief, value, and action) is a primary and universal good to be preserved and enhanced by moral, political, and economic life;
- the view that value propositions or claims that legitimately constrain the freedom of the individual agent must be able to be freely and rationally endorsed by the agent.

Critics of these and a number of other liberal commitments, who defend various alternative conceptions of political society and agency, are typically captured under the umbrella of *communitarian* thought. Contemporary communitarian thinkers range from Anglo-European philosophers who defend traditionalist and/or relational conceptions of the moral agent and the political good (Sandel 1982; Walzer 1983; MacIntyre 1984; Taylor 1989) to neo-Confucian thinkers and others articulating the philosophical foundations of non-liberal moral and political norms from without the Anglo-European tradition (Bell 2006; Chan 2014; Bai 2019).

While the roots of communitarianism lack a singular philosophical and cultural legacy of the sort that underpins modern liberalism, the common thread linking communitarian philosophies is a view of the human good as inseparable from the good of community life. Traditional communitarians focus on human flourishing as anchored in and sustained by familiar spheres of community that are largely consistent across human experience: the family, the state or civic community, the spiritual or religious community, and the workplace. Contemporary versions of communitarian thought offer a more expansive typology that includes, in addition to communities of place, communities of memory and psychological communities (Bell 1993).

Communitarians hold not *merely* that humans flourish only in and through community (a view which the great majority of liberal thinkers share) but that human personhood and identity, including our capacities for belief, thought, and action, are constituted only in and through community life and the network of relationships that bind us to others in care and obligation. Thus, the 'autonomous individual' as conceived in many liberal philosophies is viewed by communitarians as a harmful fiction, even when framed only as a regulative ideal. For such an ideal seems to encourage individuals to detach their self-conception and their intellectual, moral, and political lives from the very ground that sustains them and makes them valuable.

Critics label communitarianism as unacceptably susceptible to authoritarianism, stagnant conservatism, and oppression, particularly of minorities or others who transgress the shared values of their given communities (Young 1990). Many contemporary communitarians answer these charges by articulating views of communitarian life that aim to be compatible with democratic institutions, human rights, and considerable, if bounded, tolerance for individual diversity, value pluralism, social critique, and personal liberties (Shun and Wong 2004). Attempts to reconcile some of the tensions between liberal and communitarian political philosophy, or at least to show that we can safely preserve many of the commendable features of one within the frame of the other (Raz 1987; Kymlicka 1989; Macedo 1990; Ihara 2004; Nussbaum 2011) have been received with varying degrees of enthusiasm.

Liberalism and communitarianism are agnostic regarding the traditional classifications of ethical theory—there exist consequentialist, deontological, and virtue-based interpretations and moral justifications of each. Yet, virtue theorists are uniquely pressed on this decisive political question, for a holistic conception or discernible pattern or shape of human political flourishing is, as noted earlier, fairly foundational in most virtue traditions. A contemporary virtue theorist must therefore have *something quite specific to say* about what human political flourishing looks like in a digitally mediated world.

A utilitarian consequentialist might well regard certain political configurations as more conducive to the general happiness, but they could also be agnostic, treating as a contingent and undetermined matter the question of which political arrangements will be more productive of general hedonic satisfaction. A deontological approach does not offer this flexibility, but, arguably, the political question has already been decided in advance by one's given deontological frame. A deontological ethic that commands inviolable respect for individual autonomy, such as Kant's, demands a liberal frame, while a deontological frame that commands selfless fulfilment of social or religious duty, such as the ethic of Hindu philosophy, seems to straightforwardly require a communitarian politics.

Contemporary virtue theories cannot be as agnostic as the utilitarian may be on the question of the political good because unlike a psychological state like pleasure, a virtue such as 'justice' must be cashed out in a thick description of excellent political habits and judgements of the virtuous citizen. Neither, however, can the contemporary virtue ethicist rely upon a pre-given answer to the question of whether liberal or communitarian political arrangements are more conducive to a flourishing digital society.

While deontological norms are typically framed as universal and ahistorically fixed, virtue is always relative to a particular environment in which one hopes to flourish with others. Even if Aristotle *had* been wholly correct about the nature of virtue in ancient Athenian society,[5] we could not flourish together today by replicating the patterns and exemplars he articulated. The size, structure, composition, material affordances and challenges of twenty-first-century environments are simply too different for us to be able to flourish by mimicking the habits and dispositions of fifth-century Athenian men.

Thus, contemporary virtue theorists (excluding those few who adopt an ahistorical, universalist, and thick conception of the good life) are in a distinctly difficult position. They must *invent*, as a new ground, a satisfactory account of the specific patterns of human excellence—including political excellence—that can best meet the unique challenges of flourishing sustainably together in a digitally mediated environment that is radically unlike any our species has dwelled in previously, and furthermore, that is *changing* at unprecedented speeds and scales.

As an example of this difficulty, consider the increasingly acute problem of online disinformation. If one is wedded to a liberal frame that commits one to privileging individual autonomy and freedoms as well as cosmopolitan aims of tolerance, this is a hard problem. Paradoxes of tolerance (Popper 2020/1945) suggest that even the basic freedom to profess and disseminate one's views may need to be constrained in cases in which enabling such expression is likely to inhibit or obstruct *others'* access to basic freedoms. Yet, such constraint cannot be allowed to erect barriers to the new ideas and critical pressures necessary for an open society. This problem predates the internet, of course, but the internet makes it far worse because speech that might have been a self-contained or remediable harm in a pre-digital medium—such as a rumour about a quack cure for a virus or a false claim about the violent intentions of a minoritized group—can online rapidly become a life-threatening conspiracy theory rooted in the minds of millions, or mutate in days into a thousand divergent and newly sourced variations that no single expert narrative can counter.

The problem defies easy and clean solutions; however, the deontological frame at least provides the criteria for an *acceptable* solution. If the frame is wedded to a liberal philosophy rooted in respect for the autonomy of persons, then this will be the value that dictates which online expressions of disinformation and their attendant harms we must permit and which we must not. A deontological frame that is wedded to a communitarian standard of permissible conduct may address the challenge very differently, again, under the guidance of the pre-eminent rule(s). This divergence has led to a number of worries by scholars and media pundits that we are facing a decisive collision between these two ethical frames of the digital future. In Anglo-European media, it is framed as a battle to preserve the liberal ideal of free, diverse, and open cosmopolitan societies from the threat posed by the authoritarian and closed digital society favoured in countries like China, where digital tools are simply extensions of the State's mandate to enforce a singular and harmonious vision of the good life. In China, of course, the narrative is turned on its head but framed in similarly oppositional terms. And deontology can't save us because the particular fixed principles and values we are committed to in advance already determine which vision of human flourishing we can countenance.

What is the utilitarian to make of this looming collision of incommensurable digital futures? Let's first return to the problem of online disinformation. The utilitarian will also encounter this problem as a significant practical challenge, for it is difficult to quantify and project the scale and duration of the pain that online conspiracies will foster. After all, some conspiracy theories simmer for generations, while others flare and die out quickly. It can also be difficult to weigh the positive hedonic value of conspiracy theories and disinformation—it is precisely because reading and sharing these gives many users a significant hedonic boost that the internet has become so saturated with them. Finally, it is hard to predict whether a particular policy of suppression—whether taken by a social media platform or by governments or other bodies—will make the internet a more or less enjoyable place to be in the long run, much less predict its net hedonic consequences beyond the digital realm.

This problem is recreated at a global scale when we frame things as a contest between liberal and communitarian visions of the digital future. The utilitarian can, unlike, the deontologist, avail themselves of the possibility that some people are simply happiest in fractious but free liberal societies while others are happier in communitarian harmony, and allow for both visions to co-exist. However, many utilitarians presume that there exists some ground truth about what social conditions are optimal for the broad enjoyment of human pleasure and are unlikely to be satisfied with a globe sundered by two competing and incommensurable views of social happiness. Moreover, various material, economic, and cultural pressures make it practically difficult to maintain this incommensurability in practice. Digital networks demonstrate a global affordance for connectivity, exchange, and standardization at scale. Hence, the widespread perception among pundits that 'something has to give', that is, that future digital societies will need to coalesce around one or the other political ideal but not both. So, like the deontologist, the utilitarian confronts particular and general problems of digital ethics that are very difficult to solve. Yet, like the deontologist, a utilitarian already knows what tools they must use to do it.

The virtue ethicist, on the other hand, is in a far more difficult position. Virtue ethics, as noted earlier, is distinct from principle and rule-based ethics as a result of its intrinsic groundedness in the successful flourishing of a particular way of life. It cannot exist as a rootless, abstract, ahistorical philosophy based on the elevation of any singular value or set of values, whether that be autonomy, dignity, pleasure, or duty. For this reason, its responses to the ethical challenges of today's digital transformations cannot be simply mapped from a pre-given value hierarchy. They must be tied to a preferred form or style of human life, and herein lies the difficulty—and, as I will argue later, the opportunity. First, let me explain what is meant by a 'style of life' in this context and why the virtue ethicist cannot simply map ethical answers to digital dilemmas from within an existing normative frame.

Living virtuously means crafting and adopting a coherent and successful *moral style* of living within a given community and set of practices, as Alasdair MacIntyre (1984) and others have noted.[6] While Aristotle identifies *eudaimonia* as the highest moral good, what moderns have unhelpfully translated as 'happiness' is not, in fact, a psychological state to be optimized as the utilitarian will aim to do. Rather, *eudaimonia just is* the particular style of successful Athenian living that Aristotle's account of the virtues describes. *Eudaimonia*—human flourishing, in more adequate English translations—is the pattern that should be visible throughout the life of any Athenian man deservedly known for his political and personal nobility. The virtues of courage, magnanimity, honesty, justice, and wisdom cannot be grasped as *Aristotle* meant them without knowing quite a bit about the particular style of living that would be adopted by such men.

Even the universal guidance to 'seek the mean' in every action becomes quickly contextualized in such a way that one could not know what the mean envisioned by

Aristotle *was* in any given case without recognizing the particular style of elite Athenian living that Aristotle is asking our virtues to enable. For example, to find the Aristotelian mean of amiability—the state between obsequiousness and surliness—in a given inter-action, one would have to know a great deal about the cultural norms operative in an-cient Athenian society. An amiable French banker instantaneously transported from today's world to the Athenian agora would have absolutely no clue what the 'mean' of amiability demanded as a smiling stranger approached.

This notion of a cohesive style of living is even more explicit in the Confucian virtue tradition, in which the concept of the *Dao* ('the Way') is the controlling one. The *Dao* is the only normative pattern of human affairs (seen as co-extensive with a cosmic pattern) that *works*, in the view of Confucians. The *Dao* is viewed by Confucians, internally, as a universal and ahistorical style of living well with others, not one to be altered or tested. But from the standpoint of our present, most contemporary virtue ethicists see both Aristotle and Confucius as articulating particular historical and temporal styles of *local* flourishing that, whatever their merits may have been, and whatever portions may still carry over into our lives, are not immune from critique or revision. For virtue ethicists who adopt some form of moral realism (consistent with pluralism), the normative styles celebrated by Aristotle and Confucius are subject to critique even relative to the moral realities of their own time and place. They are certainly subject to critique and revision relative to the demands of *our* new time and places—in particular, those created by a diverse global network of *digital* publics in which humans must now seek to jointly flourish.

This malleability is both a challenge and an opportunity. It is also consistent with how virtue traditions have developed and branched over time. Indeed, both 'neo-Aristotelian' virtue ethics and 'neo-Confucian' virtue ethics have made very substan-tive alterations to the thick content of the respective accounts in ways that are directly responsive to particular historical, cultural, and environmental changes over the millennia. For example, neo-Confucian writings were powerfully shaped by the cul-tural inroads of Buddhism and Taoism in China, and, in responding to such changes, neo-Confucians incorporated both new ideas and new practices into the ideal style of Confucian living, such as Wang Yangming's sixteenth-century articulation of *jingzuo* as a form of meditative knowing. Even more fundamental reforms to Aristotle's vision of human flourishing are standard in contemporary neo-Aristotelian ethics which must guide us in a world where women are routinely (if not yet universally) granted moral and political standing and which must therefore seek to expel the embedded misogyny of the base view.[7]

What are the implications for the application of virtue ethics to digitally mediated societies? The first is that the most perplexing and novel moral challenges presented by digital life cannot be safely resolved by simply mapping the correct answers from a fixed principle or rule-based value hierarchy since (for the virtue ethicist) this is not how practical ethics is properly understood in any case. However, the virtue ethicist is in a tricky position because neither can these answers be readily mapped from an existing fixed pattern of virtuous living as would be the case for a wide range of more familiar moral dilemmas, such as whether or not to be troubled to rescue a stranger's child about to meet an unhappy end.[8]

Fortunately, virtue ethics incorporates in the concept of practical wisdom (in Greek, *phronēsis*) a capability to respond well to novel moral circumstances. Much of the creative moral thinking we do involves adapting a familiar pattern. We solve the problem analogically, with prudent adjustments for the salient differences. We say, for example, 'this new harm (internet addiction) is relevantly like a known harm (drug addiction), except in certain relevant respects (the internet, unlike drugs, is an essential social tool that we cannot outlaw)'. So, we craft an appropriate moral policy that largely follows a known pattern (e.g. encouraging practices of moderation and self-restraint in young people while increasing pressure on platforms and developers to eschew addictive designs and provide more counter-addiction tools). This is not really a form of moral invention so much as it is moral *extension*, seeing that the moral pattern encompasses a new fact, or one previously unappreciated for its moral salience. As Mencius/Mengzi explained to the morally challenged King Xuan, 'what you need to do is simply take that [heart/*xin*] which is here and apply it over there' (Mencius 1970: 1A7).[9]

What is more challenging for the virtue ethicist are features of digital life that increasingly *do* require robust moral invention. The first wave of visible digital harms—cyberbullying, cyberstalking, internet addiction—mirrored older harms and readily yielded to the kind of analogical *phronēsis* described earlier. But newer waves of digital transformations are reshaping the very structures and rhythms of social life and institutions, to which our familiar moral patterns are geared. For example, machine agency—from AI assistants to predictive autonomous decision systems—is transforming not only the range of our moral choices but also the field of moral action itself. In the final section, I show how this deep challenge to the analogical extension of familiar moral patterns forces us into a long overdue rethinking of the basic shapes of moral life—perhaps enabling us to deploy the most creative capabilities of practical wisdom to reconcile the stale and arguably unsustainable modern opposition between liberal and communitarian visions of the good life.

BEYOND LIBERAL AND COMMUNITARIAN VIRTUE

The widespread commercial viability of AI applications driven by advances in machine learning has brought with it a new wave of artificial agents that perform in ways which substantially surpass the capabilities of previous generations of digital agents and assistants. Earlier versions of virtual agents (from Microsoft's near universally ridiculed 'Clippy' to even more detested automated call centre agents that forced users to navigate unintuitive and inflexible decision trees until they found themselves back at the start and gave up) failed to approach the most basic expectations of artificial agency set by twentieth-century science fiction. However, newer tools such as Amazon Echo's Alexa and Apple's Siri, and the most recent advances in large language models, are beginning to show us what it might be like to have artificial agents in the not-too-distant future that actively participate in our social milieu, in ways that would, in any other era, have constituted an *interpersonal* connection with reciprocal expectations and duties of care.

Dylan Wittkower (2021) has argued that Alexa and other digital assistants are already forcing us into a peculiar and novel relational configuration with them, insofar as we are required, by virtue of their design and functionalities, to habitually anticipate, navigate, and respond to intentional states of these machines—beliefs, attitudes, and desires— that they *do not have*. The ethical implications of such relations are already difficult to tease out, but these implications will only become more challenging to articulate as our de facto interpersonal engagements with and dependencies upon machine *nonpersons* become deeper and further extended through human communities on a global scale. Of course, this presumes that artificial agency will continue to be integrated into our workplaces, public spaces, and homes, and yet a politics or ethics of *refusal* is still conceivable (Ganesh and Moss 2022). Nevertheless, let's imagine what happens if these developments are not refused. What kind of ethical thinking will we need to navigate that future?

I argue that this is a future in which remaining bound to traditional modes of analogical thinking presents a significant danger and in which we might be better advised to rethink the norms of moral and political community from the ground up, relying on the creative moral capacities of mature *phronēsis*. Let me explain. A Kantian ethic grounded in liberal philosophical thinking about the moral community will tend to regard only the class of autonomous moral agents—that is, persons we can reason with and hold responsible for their actions—as moral patients to whom we owe unconditional respect and who possess certain moral *rights* by virtue of this autonomy. Alexa today has neither the capacity to reason well with us nor any capability of bearing moral responsibility. But as Wittkower notes, users are already having to think *habitually* of Alexa as having many states it *does not have*—specific beliefs about us and the world, wishes to hear something spoken in a certain way, expectations of our response. What happens when artificial agents are sufficiently capable and embedded as actors in our societies that we have to habitually *think of them* as having not only beliefs and attitudes but also reasons-responsive goals and moral responsibilities, even though these are merely a functional illusion just as Alexa's 'wishes' are today? Do we treat them as moral patients or not?

A rights-based framework anchored in liberal conceptions of society will either have to deny such agents any moral status whatsoever, treating them as mere 'tools' to be exploited, or begin to entertain some conception of 'robot rights'. On a Kantian ethical view, for example, there are no gradations of moral personhood—there are persons and there are things but nothing in between. Indeed, this particular philosophical debate has already begun, to the great consternation of many and the great enthusiasm of others (Coeckelbergh 2010; Bryson 2010; Gunkel 2018; Birhane and van Dijk 2020). And yet this debate seems to lock us into an unhelpful frame. It is psychologically and sociologically implausible, not to mention morally problematic, to envision a future in which we depend upon and interact with machine agents daily as skilled collaborators and helpful co-workers while simultaneously regarding them as mindless tools to be exploited.

Those in favour of taking the idea of robot rights seriously, such as Mark Coeckelbergh and David Gunkel, assert that such a relation to artificial agents would be undesirable or untenable for humans—probably both—and they are probably correct on this narrow point. They also rely heavily on the analogical argument that treating robots or other artificial agents as mindless tools to be exploited should be morally suspect because we already know that treating people that way is wrong, and we have a history of immorally excusing such wrongs by arbitrarily saying, 'Well, that group (of agents) just aren't the kind of beings that have or deserve rights.'

But those who regard the concept of robot rights as a philosophical near-obscenity argue that the solution *cannot* be to grant moral or legal rights—the full protection of which are still denied to the lion's share of the human family (e.g. women, the poor, and racialized and/or minoritized communities), not to mention non-human animals—to mindless, non-sentient assemblages of silicon and plastic just because we now happen to find it economically and culturally useful to insert these entities into more intimate roles within our social environments and relations. First, it creates a dangerously false equivalence between persons and non-persons (Birhane and van Dijk 2020). This false equivalence encourages us to slip from an ideal stance of moral regard based on the absolute worth and equal dignity of persons to a stance in which all it takes to earn moral regard is to usefully perform certain economic and social *functions* of persons. This view also entails that the billions of humans who are systematically excluded by unjust hierarchies from performing equivalently valued economic and social roles may continue to be morally and politically neglected, as they have been. Alternatively, it suggests that the status of personhood is not a fact but a gift to be bestowed by those privileged enough to have never had their humanity questioned. As Abeba Birhane and Jelle van Dijk (2020) observe, 'The line of reasoning runs the risk of developing into: "The women and slaves we liberated should not complain if we, enlightened men, decide to liberate some more!" ' (209).

The liberal frame thus seems to leave us in an unsatisfactory position with respect to the moral status of machine agency. For while those who object to robot rights are well justified in doing so, the question remains, 'How then can we rightly situate and treat machine agents within our day-to-day lives, when they occupy vital interpersonal roles?' This is why Joanna Bryson (2010) has suggested abstaining from designing machines to occupy these roles in forms or ways that would create this risk of moral-ontological confusion. Better to keep them in familiar, non-personal roles that do not encourage the kind of projected experience that Wittkower notes we already find ourselves compelled to perform. Even if we replace her problematic selection of the category of 'slave' with a more benign role label, however, Bryson's move would arguably require stripping machines of any capacity that might be called social, and this medicine may be stronger than Bryson realizes, requiring a near-blanket refusal of AI in all but a few highly delimited spheres of action. The path of refusal, of course, is still open. But there are many good reasons to welcome future worlds with artificial agents in them; is refusal our only or best option?

Perhaps a communitarian frame will do better? Indeed, a kind of communitarian frame has already informed the arguments of those who seriously entertain the prospect of 'robot rights' on the basis of a *relational* ethic (Coeckelbergh 2010). The idea here is that moral status does not arise from a quality within individuals, as the liberal frame would have it, but rather arises *between* them; that is, morality is relational to the core. There are a number of communitarian ethics in which a relational notion of selfhood or personhood is embedded. For example, Confucian ethics is widely understood to take the family and the State to be the morally primary entities, from which moral duties to individual persons are then derived on the basis of their relations to the primary entities. One can see, then, that a communitarian ethic might lend itself to granting moral status to machines insofar as they can occupy the right kinds of relations to the primary entities and perform the rights kinds of duties for and with them. Again, if we rely upon the analogical frame, we are pushed to this conclusion. If machines embody the same interpersonal roles and perform the same duties that grant human beings their moral status as persons, why should we not extend it to them?

This solution also falls apart, however, when one considers that, even in Confucian ethics, there is an important and non-substitutable role for moral reciprocity of persons, which is grounded in an affective moral sincerity or care that machine agents of the sort we are considering will still lack. If we go back to Mengzi's instructions to King Xuan, he did not tell him that it was enough to simply perform the right duties to his people and continue to feel nothing. He told the King that he needed to extend his *xin—his* loving concern, which the King could already feel for his animals—to his subjects. Moreover, it is the case in Confucian thought that the subjects of the King must feel a similar emotional bond with their King in order to rightly live. The 'Way' is not just a mechanical pattern but an affective and cognitive one as well. This is why Confucius vigorously rejected the kind of functional moral success embodied by what he called the 'village honest person'—the rigid (*gu*) morality of the person who does the right things reliably, as called for by their role, just as their neighbours and fellow citizens expect and want but without any internal moral sincerity or motivation and also without the flexible, aesthetic capability of moral invention that is demanded for novel and complex situations (Yearley 1990: 67–68). Given that artificial sentience is nowhere on the horizon, artificial agents of the near future, even if they acquire functional moral competence in well-defined contexts, will be no better than the 'village honest person', and thus we find ourselves again in a bind. From a relational communitarian stance, personhood falls out of interpersonal relations and duties that machines may soon perform routinely. And yet, for at least many communitarian frames (for Confucianism is not alone in its affective anchors), to grant moral personhood to affectively empty machines is to deny the heart—literally—of moral meaning.

What if we accepted that neither a liberal nor a communitarian frame can easily make sense of a social fabric in which artificial agents are interwoven as a new kind of thread? Is there another way forward? Are the familiar dichotomies of person and thing, or individual agent and community, or autonomy and interdependence, really as fixed as we are liable to envision? Might our dominant moral and political patterns, which have often served us well but increasingly fail us in practice, simply be *worn out, no longer fitting* the new social bodies that must take shape in a resource-depleted, information-saturated, and rapidly warming world where 8 billion humans must find unprecedented ways to flourish together?

What if we used our moral courage and humility to admit this shortcoming and, if not clear the deck of our existing moral patterns and analogies, at least create a bit more open space to explore *in between* them? What if the human family could be free to start a set of new moral conversations not only about how we choose to relate to technology but also to one another? Most importantly, how might those conversations avoid retracing the familiar patterns of injustice and exploitation that have constrained our imaginations of human flourishing thus far? The most promising scenario for this new kind of moral freedom involves ensuring that these conversations not only include but are also facilitated by voices that have been routinely excluded from the moral conversations of previous traditions that led us to this stale impasse. For such conversations to succeed, contributors will need to bring to the table many virtues: courage, compassion, honesty, patience, humility, justice, and care. But perhaps *moral imagination* is the virtue we need to cultivate most of all. Virtue ethics is a powerful frame for digital ethics not because it already has the answers we need but because it is the one frame that clearly does *not*, that makes most evident that those answers do not yet exist and will not exist until we learn to write them together within radically new relations of equity, solidarity, justice, and resolute love.

CONCLUSION

New digital dilemmas such as those generated by artificial agency are pushing at the ageing, splintering joints of our existing moral and political conceptions of the good life. They show us that neither the liberal nor the communitarian frames can, by themselves, point us reliably forward to futures with new technology that will not *only* be justified and sustainable but also able to supply the *joy* that good lives promise. From brain–computer interfaces, to the global spread of customized reality/disinformation bubbles, to the techno-social challenges of meeting Sustainable Development Goals on a planet made less hospitable to humans by the year, we are increasingly called to enact our capabilities for *original* moral thinking in a way that, I fear, philosophers in recent years have not adequately answered. The philosophical patterns of the past were built to suit worlds that no longer exist. What virtue ethics can offer us today is not a study of the various historical patterns of past modes of human flourishing that could be carried over into a digitally mediated world. What it really offers us, as I have argued elsewhere (2016), is a set of shared moral *practices* for cultivating within our communities the creative capacity to invent entirely new patterns of flourishing, ones better suited to the futures we must build.

Notes

1. See (Brey et al. 2012), a collection of essays based on an international conference devoted to this theme in 2007. The theme of the 'good life' brings to applied technology ethics the same shift towards a normative focus on virtue and flourishing that is often attributed to G.E.M. Anscombe (1958) in the domain of moral philosophy.
2. See Vallor (2016: ch. 5, section 2) on the necessary flexibility of prudential judgement.
3. See Jerome and Kisby (2019) for critiques of character education as a force of conservativism.
4. See Mencius (1970: 6A8) and the fable of Ox Mountain.
5. He was *not* correct, having excluded the moral agency of well over half of the Athenian adult population (including women and non-Greek men) from eligibility.
6. The aesthetic implication of 'style' is intentional here; the notion of an aesthetic dimension of moral performance is most explicit in Confucian virtue ethics but holds generally in the notion of the person whose virtue is lived authentically through the expression of a characteristic unity, integrity, or harmonious style; see Gier (2001).
7. There is a question here, of course, of how neo-Aristotelians can know that the full incorporation of women into the moral community is in fact *good* or *right* unless they make an appeal to some deeper normative standard than Aristotle was able to give (e.g. a utilitarian or deontological standard). The options range from pointing out that Aristotle's view rests on demonstrable falsehoods about women (and non-Greeks), and thus that the defect is internally remediable, to accepting a certain degree of moral anti-realism or relativism, to accepting that virtue ethics must be buttressed by some deeper but still virtue-compatible normative theory, such as Martha Nussbaum's capabilities approach or a feminist ethic of care.
8. This, of course, is the scenario appealed by Mencius (1970: 2A6) as evidencing a universal moral pattern inscribed in the heart-mind (*xin*) of every fully formed human person.
9. See Nivison (1980: 746) on the connection in Mencius between analogical moral extension of a reasoning pattern and moral extension of affective capacity.

References

Annas, J. (2005), 'Virtue Ethics: What Kind of Naturalism?', in S.M. Gardiner, ed., *Virtue Ethics, Old and New* (Ithaca, NY: Cornell University Press), 11–29.

Anscombe, G.E.M. (1958), 'Modern Moral Philosophy', *Philosophy* 33: 1–19.

Aristotle (2009), *The Nicomachean Ethics*, trans. D. Ross (Oxford: Oxford University Press).

Association for Computing Machinery (2018), 'ACM Code of Ethics and Professional Conduct', https://www.acm.org/code-of-ethics, accessed 8 August 2022.

Bai, T. (2019), *Against Political Equality: The Confucian Case* (Princeton, NJ: Princeton University Press).

Bell, D. (1993), *Communitarianism and Its Critics* (Oxford: Oxford University Press).

Bell, D. (2006), *Beyond Liberal Democracy: Political Thinking for an East Asian Context* (Princeton, NJ: Princeton University Press).

Birhane, A. and van Dijk, J. (2020), 'Robot Rights? Let's Talk about Human Welfare Instead', in *2020 AAAI/ACM Conference on AI, Ethics, and Society (AIES '20)*, F7–8 February (New York: ACM), 207–213, https://doi.org/10.1145/3375627.3375855, accessed 8 August 2022.

Boyd, D. (2022), 'Crisis Text Line, from my perspective', *Medium*, 31 January, http://www.zepho ria.org/thoughts/archives/2022/01/31/crisis-text-line-from-my-perspective.html, accessed 8 August 2022.

Brey, P., Briggle, A., and Spence, E. (2012), *The Good Life in a Technological Age* (New York: Routledge).

Bryson, J.J. (2010), 'Robots Should Be Slaves', *Close Engagements with Artificial Companions: Key Social, Psychological, Ethical and Design Issues*, 63–74.

Byerly, T.R., and Byerly, M. (2016), 'Collective Virtue', Journal *of Value Inquiry* 50, 33–50, https://doi.org/10.1007/s10790-015-9484-y, accessed 8 August 2022.

Chan, J. (2014), *Confucian Perfectionism: A Political Philosophy for Modern Times* (Princeton, NJ: Princeton University Press).

Coeckelbergh, M. (2010), 'Robot Rights? Towards a Social-Relational Justification of Moral Consideration', *Ethics and Information Technology* 12(3), 209–221.

Cohen, D.H. (2017), 'The Virtuous Troll: Argumentative Virtues in the Age of (Technologically Enhanced) Argumentative Pluralism', *Philosophy and Technology* 30, 179–189, https://doi. org/10.1007/s13347-016-0226-2, accessed 8 August 2022.

Correll, M. (2019), 'Ethical Dimensions of Visualization Research', *CHI '19: Proceedings of the 2019 CHI Conference on Human Factors in Computing Systems*, May, Paper No. 188, 1–13, https://doi.org/10.1145/3290605.3300418, accessed 8 August 2022.

Dworkin, R. 2000. *Sovereign Virtue: The Theory and Practice of Equality* (Cambridge, MA: Harvard University Press).

Elder, A. (2014), 'Excellent Online Friendships: An Aristotelian Defense of Social Media', *Ethics & Information Technology* 16(4), 287–297.

Elder, A. (2019), 'Conversation from Beyond the Grave? A Neo-Confucian Ethics of Chatbots of the Dead', *Journal of Applied Philosophy* 37(1), 73–88.

Ess, C. (2010), 'Trust and New Communication Technologies: Vicious Circles, Virtuous Circles, Possible Futures', *Knowledge, Technology and Policy* 23(3–4), 287–305.

Ess, C. (2013), *Digital Media Ethics*, 2nd edn (Cambridge: Polity).

Foot, P. (2000), *Natural Goodness* (Oxford: Oxford University Press).

Fricker, M. (2010), 'Can There Be Institutional Virtues?', in T. Szabo Gendler and J. Hawthorne (ed.), *Oxford Studies in Epistemology 3* (Oxford: Oxford University Press), 235–252.

Fröding, B., and Peterson, M. (2020), 'Friendly AI', *Ethics and Information Technology*, 23, 207–214, https://doi.org/10.1007/s10676-020-09556-w, accessed 8 August 2022.

Ganesh, M. I., and Moss, E. (2022). Resistance and refusal to algorithmic harms: Varieties of 'knowledge projects'. Media International Australia, 183(1), 90–106.

Gier, N.F. (2001), 'The Dancing *Ru*: A Confucian Aesthetics of Virtue', *Philosophy East and West* 51(2), 280–305.

Grodzinsky, F. (1999), 'The Practitioner from Within: Revisiting the Virtues', *Computers and Society* 29(1), 9–15.

Gunkel, D. (2018), *Robot Rights* (Cambridge, MA: MIT Press).

Handel, J. (2022), 'Crisis Text Line Ends Data-Sharing Relationship with For-Profit Spinoff', *Politico*, 31 January, https://www.politico.com/news/2022/01/31/crisis-text-line-ends-data-sharing-00004001, accessed 8 August 2022.

Harman, G. (1999), 'Moral Philosophy Meets Social Psychology: Virtue Ethics and the Fundamental Attribution Error', in *Proceedings of the Aristotelian Society*, New Series, 99 (Oxford: Oxford University Press), 315–331.

Harrison, T. (2015), 'Virtuous Reality: Moral Theory and Research into Cyber-Bullying', *Ethics and Information Technology* 17(4), 275–283.

Hayek, F. (1960), *The Constitution of Liberty* (Chicago, IL: University of Chicago Press).

Hursthouse, R. (1999), *On Virtue Ethics* (Oxford: Oxford University Press).

Ihara, C. (2004), 'Are Individual Rights Necessary? A Confucian Perspective', in Kwong-loi Shun and David B. Wong (eds), *Confucian Ethics: A Comparative Study of Self, Autonomy, and Community* (Cambridge: Cambridge University Press), 11–30.

Jerome, L., and Kisby, B. (2019), *The Rise of Character Education in Britain: Heroes, Dragons and the Myths of Character* (Cham: Palgrave MacMillan).

Kamtekar, R. (2004), 'Situationism and Virtue Ethics on the Content of Our Character', *Ethics* 114(3), 458–491.

Kymlicka, W. (1989), *Liberalism, Community and Culture* (Oxford: Oxford University Press).

Le Guin, U.K. (1975), 'The Ones Who Walk Away From Omelas', in *The Wind's Twelve Quarters* (New York: Harper & Row), 275–284.

Levine, A.S. (2022), 'Suicide Hotline Shares Data with For-Profit Spinoff, Raising Ethical Questions', *Politico*, 28 January, https://www.politico.com/news/2022/01/28/suicide-hotline-silicon-valley-privacy-debates-00002617, accessed 8 August 2022.

Macedo, S. (1990), *Liberal Virtues: Citizenship, Virtue and Community in Liberal Constitutionalism* (Oxford: Clarendon Press).

MacIntyre, A. (1984), *After Virtue* (Paris: University of Notre Dame Press).

Mencius (1970), *Mencius*, trans. D.C. Lau (London: Penguin).

Mill, J.S. (1864), *Utilitarianism*, 2nd edn (London: Longman, Green, Longman, Roberts and Green).

Moor, J. (1998), 'If Aristotle Were a Computing Professional', *Computers and Society* 28(3), 13–16.

Morrow, A. 2022. 'How a Beloved Orange Tabby Cat Became a Voice for America's Union Workers', *CNN Business*, 17 February, https://amp.cnn.com/cnn/2022/02/17/business/jorts-cat-unions-labor-movement/index.html, accessed 8 August 2022.

Nivison, D. (1980), 'Two Roots or One?', *Proceedings and Addresses of the American Philosophical Association* 53(6), 739–761.

Nozick, R. (1974), *Anarchy, State and Utopia* (New York: Basic Books).

Nussbaum, M. (2011), 'Perfectionist Liberalism and Political Liberalism', *Philosophy & Public Affairs* 39, 3–45.

Nussbaum, M.C. (1988), 'Non-Relative Virtues: An Aristotelian Approach', *Midwest Studies in Philosophy* 13(1), 32–53.

Nussbaum, M.C. (1997), 'Capabilities and Human Rights', *Fordham Law Review* 66, 273–300.

Pierrakos, O., Prentice, M., Silverglate, C., Lamb, M., De-maske, A., and Smout, R. (2019), 'Reimagining Engineering Ethics: From Ethics Education to Character Education', in *2019 IEEE Frontiers in Education Conference* (FIE), 1–9, https://doi.org/10.1109/FIE43999.2019.9028690, accessed 8 August 2022.

Popper, K. (2020/1945). *The Open Society and Its Enemies* (Princeton, NJ: Princeton University Press).

Rawls, J. (1971), *A Theory of Justice* (Cambridge, MA: Harvard University Press).

Raz, J. (1987), 'Autonomy, Toleration and the Harm Principle', in R. Gavison (ed.), *Issues in Contemporary Legal Philosophy* (Oxford: Oxford University Press), 313–333.

Sandel, M. (1982), *Liberalism and the Limits of Justice* (Cambridge: Cambridge University Press).

Sicart, M. (2005), 'Game, Player, Ethics: A Virtue Ethics Approach to Computer Games', *International Review of Information Ethics* 4, 13–18.

Shun, K.-L., and Wong, D.B. (eds), (2004), *Confucian Ethics: A Comparative Study of Self, Autonomy, and Community* (Cambridge: Cambridge University Press).

Sparrow, R. (2013), 'War without Virtue?', in Strawser, B.J. (eds), *Killing by Remote Control* (New York: Oxford University Press), 84–105.

Sullins, J. (2010), 'RoboWarfare: Can Robots Be More Ethical Than Humans on the Battlefield?', *Ethics and Information Technology* 12(3), 263–275.

Taylor, C. (1989), *Sources of the Self: The Making of the Modern Identity* (Cambridge, MA: Harvard University Press).

Tonkens, R. (2012), 'Out of Character: On the Creation of Virtuous Machines', *Ethics and Information Technology* 14(2), 137–149.

Vallor, S. (2010), 'Social Networking Technology and the Virtues', *Ethics and Information Technology* 12(2), 157–170.

Vallor, S. (2011), 'Carebots and Caregivers: Sustaining the Ethical Ideal of Care in the Twenty-First Century', *Philosophy and Technology* 24(3), 251–268, https://doi.org/10.1007/s13347-011-0015-x, accessed 8 August 2022.

Vallor, S. (2012), 'Flourishing on Facebook: Virtue Friendship and New Social Media', *Ethics and Information Technology* 14(3), 185–199.

Vallor, S. (2013), 'Armed Robots and Military Virtue', in L. Floridi and M. Taddeo (eds), *The Ethics of Information Warfare* (New York: Springer), 169–185.

Vallor, S. (2016), *Technology and the Virtues: A Philosophical Guide to a Future Worth Wanting* (New York: Oxford University Press).

Verbeek, P.-P. (2011), *Moralizing Technology: Understanding and Designing the Morality of Things* (Chicago, IL: University of Chicago Press).

Wallach, W., and Allen, C. (2009), *Moral Machines: Teaching Robots Right from Wrong* (New York: Oxford University Press).

Wallach, W., and Vallor, S. (2020), 'Moral Machines: From Value Alignment to Embodied Virtue', in M. Liao (ed.), *Ethics of Artificial Intelligence* (New York: Oxford University Press), 383–412.

Walzer, M. (1983), *Spheres of Justice: A Defense of Pluralism and Equality* (New York: Basic Books).

Wittkower, D.E. (2021), 'What Is It Like to Be a Bot?', in S. Vallor (ed.), *Oxford Handbook of the Philosophy of Technology* (New York: Oxford University Press), 358–373.

Wong, P.-H. (2013), 'Confucian Social Media: An Oxymoron?', *Dao* 12(3), 283–296.

Wright, J.C., Warren, M.T., and Snow, N.E. (2021), *Understanding Virtue: Theory and Measurement* (New York: Oxford University Press).

Yearley, L. (1990), *Mencius and Aquinas: Theories of Virtue and Conceptions of Courage.* (Albany, NY: SUNY Press).

Young, I.M. (1990), *Justice and the Politics of Difference* (Princeton, NJ: Princeton University Press).

CHAPTER 3

THE ETHICS OF HUMAN-ROBOT INTERACTION AND TRADITIONAL MORAL THEORIES

SVEN NYHOLM

INTRODUCTION

SELF-DRIVING cars chauffeuring us around, military robots helping to fight wars, logistics robots moving boxes around in warehouses, robotic vacuum cleaners and lawn movers cleaning up after us and keeping backyards neat, humanoid sex robots being advertised as a new form of intimate partner, and so on and so forth (Royakkers and Van Est 2016). More and more areas of life are having robots with more or less advanced artificial intelligence introduced into them—so much so that the robot ethicist David Gunkel muses that we are 'in the midst of a robot invasion' (Gunkel 2018, 2019). This proliferation of robots raises new types of ethical questions. For example, what if a self-driving car detects that a crash is unavoidable and that all options open to it will involve harming human beings? What should the car do (Nyholm 2018a–b)? Is it ever permissible to use autonomous weapons systems in war, which are specifically designed to kill human beings and select their own targets (Sparrow 2016; Purves et al. 2015)? What if a robot—for example, a sex robot—is designed to look and act like a human being? Does the resemblance mean that we should treat that robot with any of the moral consideration we should show to human beings (Eskens 2017; Danaher 2019)?

In general, there are two main kinds of questions here. On the one hand, how should robots and other machines be made to behave around human beings? On the other hand, how should human beings conduct themselves around robots and other machines with advanced forms of artificial intelligence? We can call the branch of digital ethics that confronts these two questions *the ethics of human–robot interaction* (Nyholm 2020). The aim of this chapter is to discuss whether, and to what extent, traditional moral theory—including specific theories such as utilitarianism, Kantianism, and virtue ethics—can be useful when we try to approach the questions that arise within the new ethics of human–robot interaction.

Many authors who discuss the ethics of human–robot interaction have turned to the traditional moral theories in their work. For example, proponents of so-called 'machine ethics' have theorized that we can create artificial moral agents that conduct themselves based on the principles espoused by traditional moral theories (e.g. Anderson and Anderson 2007, 2010, 2011; Powers 2011; Wallach and Allen 2009). And writers discussing whether machines should ever be accorded moral consideration or rights have asked what the traditional moral theories imply about that issue (e.g. Coeckelbergh 2010a; Gunkel 2018; Gordon 2020a).

There is a general problem with this tempting project of applying traditional moral theory to the ethics of human–robot interaction, however: traditional moral theories all developed long before robots and artificial intelligence (AI) existed. In particular, they developed with human–human interaction in mind, not with human–robot interaction—or, more generally, human–machine interaction—in mind (Nyholm 2020: ch. 2; see Turner 2019 and Weaver 2013 for a similar argument in the context of the law). In what follows, I explore some ways in which this problem creates challenges and difficulties for the temptation to approach the ethics of human–robot interaction using traditional moral theory.

Specifically, I consider difficulties relating to the notions of moral obligation and moral virtue, and the properties that traditional moral theories associate with having moral standing. These all seem better suited for ethics relating to human–human interaction and are ill-suited for the ethics of human–robot interaction. One possible conclusion is that we need, as Gunkel suggests, to 'think otherwise', that is, to look for some new kind of ethical theorizing (Gunkel 2018). Even so, I end with some reflections about how traditional moral theory might best be applied in the ethics of human–robot interaction if we want to keep using the traditional moral theories when we grapple with the new ethics of human–robot interaction. The usefulness of the traditional moral theories in the ethics of human–robot interaction depends, I will argue, on who we take the relevant moral agents and patients to be.

AGENTS AND PATIENTS

In 2015, *CNN Edition* ran a story with the headline 'Is it Cruel to Kick a Robot Dog?' (Parke 2015). This was a story about a robot created by the company Boston Dynamics. The four-legged robot, nicknamed 'Spot', looks like a dog. Another distinguishing feature of this particular robot is how good it is at keeping its balance. To illustrate this ability, a video released by Boston Dynamics shows Spot walking up some stairs and running on a treadmill. Later in the video, in order to further illustrate how stable Spot is, some Boston Dynamics engineers are shown kicking Spot. Sure enough, Spot does not fall over when kicked. Many viewers of this video, however, lost part of their composure when they saw Spot being kicked. CNN reported that people made comments such as 'Kicking a dog, even a robot dog, just seems wrong' and 'Poor Spot!' (Parke 2015; cf. Coeckelbergh 2018).

This story helps to illustrate a distinction that is useful to draw in this context. Following Luciano Floridi and others, I will use the terminology whereby we think of ethics as involving both *moral agents* and *moral patients* (Floridi 2011). In the just-summarized news story, a robot is, interestingly, seemingly portrayed in the role of a moral patient; that is, it is portrayed in the role of somebody against whom we can act rightly or wrongly. The Boston Dynamics engineers kicking the robot dog, in contrast, are viewed as moral agents. They are viewed as agents who are able to act rightly or wrongly and who can be held responsible for their conduct. The question of whether it is cruel to kick robot dogs, in other words, takes seriously the idea that robots can be moral patients against whom human moral agents can act in cruel ways (Coeckelbergh 2018; Danaher 2019; cf. Friedman 2020).

A more common way of introducing robots or other machines into the domain of ethics is via the idea of them as potentially playing the role of moral agents. As mentioned in the Introduction, there is a whole field of research called 'machine ethics' whose main aim is to investigate the prospect of creating machines—robots, computers, or whatever—that can function as moral agents of some significant kind (Wallach and Allen 2009, Anderson and Anderson 2011). Some of the more modest machine ethics researchers focus on what James Moor calls 'implicit moral agents', that is, agents whose patterns of behaviour merely conform to what certain moral principles might recommend that they do (Moor 2006). Others—like Michael Anderson and Susan Leigh Anderson (2007, 2010)—have a much more ambitious goal. They want to create what Moor calls 'explicit moral agents'. This expression refers to agents whose behaviour does not merely conform to what moral principles might recommend, but who also are able to engage in decision-making that is explicitly guided by ethical principles (Moor 2006).[1]

Self-driving cars and military robots are common examples of artificially intelligent machines that defenders of machine ethics claim need to be made into a form of moral agent. Why? Because these machines will be functionally autonomous, and potentially dangerous; that is, they will operate for certain periods of time on their own, without direct human steering. They will interact with human beings in ways that are sometimes risky, occasionally creating life-and-death situations. Accordingly, the machines may be put in situations—crash scenarios in the case of self-driving cars or battles in the case of military robots—in which the machines seemingly need to make life-and-death decisions (Wallach and Allen 2009; Goodall 2014).

Defenders of the programme of machine ethics claim that because of such considerations, we ought to design these machines in ways that make them into 'artificial moral agents' (Wallach and Allen 2009; Anderson and Anderson 2011).[2] So here we have a case that is significantly different from the one considered above. While a robot is the supposed moral patient and human beings the moral agents in the example with Spot the robot dog above, in the cases of self-driving cars and military robots, human beings would be the moral patients and certain robots the supposed moral agents.

A fascinating question to reflect on is whether there could ever be any realistic scenarios in which robots would be both the only relevant moral agents and the patients involved. In science fiction, we could easily imagine such a scenario. For example, what if the robots C3PO and R2D2 in the *Star Wars* movies got into a fight and treated each other in immoral ways? In real life, however, such scenarios seem less realistic.

When it comes to the ethics of human–robot interaction, it is important to reflect carefully on the different ways in which we can think about who or what can be moral agents and patients. One possible view—the one that I have in effect just illustrated—is that in addition to human beings, robots and other machines can also be both moral agents and moral patients (e.g. Gunkel 2012, 2018; Gordon 2020a). A second possible view is that while robots and other machines can be a form of moral agent (albeit perhaps a less advanced form of moral agent than humans can be), they cannot and should not be regarded as moral patients. Floridi, for example, seems to be an example of an author who holds that sort of view. In his writings, Floridi takes the idea of machines as artificial moral agents very seriously. Yet, he thinks that they are not moral patients, but that they can be seen as a kind of 'slave' to us human beings (Floridi 2011, 2017).

A third—and less common—view would be that while robots can be moral patients, they cannot be moral agents. Some of John Danaher's different writings on the ethics of technology suggest that he might be someone who would take this view. Danaher has one paper in which he argues that autonomous robots might give rise to 'retribution gaps', since they are not responsible moral agents that are fit to be punished in case they act wrongly (Danaher 2016). But in more recent writings, Danaher argues that if machines behave like people or animals that we view as moral patients, we should also regard those machines as moral patients (Danaher 2019, 2020). On this type of view—whether or not it is a view Danaher would, on reflection, endorse—while humans can be both moral agents and patients, robots can be moral patients but not moral agents.

A fourth and final view is that only human beings can be moral agents and that only human beings (as well as some non-human animals) can be moral patients (cf. Bryson 2018).[3] On this view, when we create machines that are made to conduct themselves around human beings in certain ways, there are always certain human beings (e.g. the designers or users) who are the relevant moral agents (see e.g. Van Wynsberghe and Robbins 2018). And if there are ever any reasons to act in ways that appear to show moral consideration for robots, the real moral patients are actually certain human beings. For example, the real moral patients could be people who might be offended or otherwise negatively impacted unless the robots in question are treated in ways that appear to show moral consideration for those robots (Darling 2017; Friedman 2020; cf. Nyholm 2020: ch. 8).

We have a spectrum of four views here, then. At one extreme, there is the view that in the ethics of human–robot interaction, robots can be considered both as agents and patients. At the other extreme, there is the view that ultimately, only human beings can be considered as the relevant agents and patients when we think about how robots should be made to function around human beings and how human beings should conduct themselves around robots. Between these two extremes there are views on which robots could be either only moral agents or only moral patients. With these basic distinctions introduced, we can move on to discuss traditional ethical theory. What would influential canonical philosophers such as—or authors following in the footsteps of—Aristotle, Hume, Bentham and Mill, and Kant say about this topic?

TRADITIONAL ETHICAL THEORY

When we think about the ethics of human–robot interaction, it is tempting to turn to traditional ethical theory as a source of ideas and inspiration. After all, when we study moral philosophy, we typically first learn about traditional ethical theories such as utilitarianism, Kantianism, and virtue ethics (see, e.g. Driver 2007). We usually also learn about attempts to apply these theories within different domains of practical ethics, such as bioethics and animal ethics. So, it is only natural to think that these kinds of theories would also be useful to apply to this novel topic of human–robot interaction, not least because in ordinary common sense, we are concerned with things such as the consequences of actions, respect for people's dignity, and the development of good character traits. Those are the sorts of considerations that the traditional moral theories place at the centre of their accounts of how we should live our lives and conduct ourselves around other human beings (Suikkanen 2014). Utilitarian—or more broadly consequentialist—theories focus on the consequences of people's actions. Kantian ethics concerns itself with how to properly show respect for human dignity and the principles we act on. And virtue ethical theories are about what character traits people should try to cultivate (Driver 2007).

When it comes to whether it is a good idea to carry over the traditional ethical theories into the new domain of the ethics of human–robot interaction, two related complications or challenges immediately come to mind. These both concern the fact that the traditional ethical theories are—first and foremost—theories of the ethics of human–human interaction rather than human–technology interaction (Nyholm 2020: ch. 2).[4]

First, as mentioned in the Introduction, most of the traditional ethical theory that we learn about when we study ethics developed before anybody was concerned with human–robot interaction. Virtue ethical theory first made its appearance during classical antiquity (Crisp and Slote 1997). Broadly speaking, consequentialist and so-called deontological ethical theories[5] started to develop throughout the Enlightenment. Immanuel Kant developed his influential ethical theory in the last decades of the eighteenth century (Kant 2012). The origin of utilitarian can be traced to the middle of the eighteenth century, first by Christian authors like William Paley and Joseph Priestly, and later by secular authors like Jeremy Bentham and John Stuart Mill (Darwall 1995). This was all before anyone had any reason to think about whether robots and other technologies with AI could potentially be thought of as moral agents or patients. Since traditional ethical theory developed with human–human interaction in mind, we should be careful about assuming that this body of theory will carry over in a smooth way to the context of human–robot interaction.

The second consideration I want to highlight in this section is that the traditional ethical theories involve numerous different ideas and theoretical assumptions about human beings and human nature (Driver 2007). They are, to use an expression from John Rawls, typically 'comprehensive theories' (Rawls 1993). Those who import the traditional ethical theories into the context of human–robot interaction sometimes appear to truncate these theories to single principles that can be formulated in one short sentence—for example, 'Maximize happiness, minimize suffering!', 'Act on principles that can be made into universal laws!', or 'Develop these virtues!'—and then ask whether these principles can be programmed into the AI of robots. There is an issue with this decontextualization, however. The issue is that behind the snappy bumper-sticker summaries of the traditional moral theories, there are typically comprehensive theories of human nature, rationality, the human condition, moral psychology, etc. that help to motivate why the canonical authors who proposed these theories arrived at the ethical conclusions and suggestions that they did.

In the following three sections, I zoom in on three common themes reoccurring in much of traditional moral theory. I will relate those themes to the prospects of human–robot interaction ethics of the sort that regards robots as potentially being both moral agents and patients. In particular, I will discuss some common ideas about moral obligation, moral virtue, and what it is to be benefitted in a morally relevant way. In each case, we will find that it is not easy to directly carry these ideas from traditional ethical theory over into the new context of the ethics of human–robot interaction.

Moral obligation

Imagine that a self-driving car carrying one person is heading towards a tunnel. The self-driving car detects that, for whatever reason, its brakes have suddenly stopped working. The car also detects that there are five people walking on the narrow road inside of the tunnel. Since the car's brakes are malfunctioning, the car seems to face two options. It can either drive into the tunnel and ram into the five people in there, potentially killing or seriously injuring them, or it can swerve and crash into the side of the tunnel, potentially killing or seriously injuring the person inside the car. What should the car do?

This case—which I borrow from Jason Millar (2014)—is of the sort that is sometimes used to motivate the need to design moral agency or decision-making capacities into self-driving cars. The car appears to face a moral dilemma similar to the sorts of dilemmas associated with the so-called trolley problem.[6] And so, it is argued, the car needs to be able to make a moral decision about what to do in this situation and others like it. (Keeling 2020; cf. Nyholm and Smids 2016) Indeed, some researchers in behavioural economics and social psychology take this sort of case so seriously that they have created a worldwide research project to track and catalogue ordinary people's intuitions about various trolley problem-inspired cases (Bonnefon et al. 2016). The idea behind that research programme is that in addition to whatever input traditional ethical theory can provide us with, we also need to survey the world's population about what self-driving cars should do (Awad et al. 2018). That way, programmers tasked with programming moral decision-making algorithms into self-driving cars will have lots of input about what is morally relevant in the kinds of accident scenarios one can imagine that self-driving cars might potentially face (Awad et al. 2020; for a critical perspective, see Harris 2020; cf. Nyholm 2018a).

Suppose now that we have a view about what sorts of 'decision' self-driving cars ought morally to make in different kinds of risky or otherwise morally loaded situations. Suppose also that we somehow managed to programme those moral rules into self-driving cars.[7] Have we then created moral agents of a sort that are recognizable from the perspective of traditional moral theories?

One symptom that we would have done so would be that we had managed to create an agent who would be under an obligation to act in certain ways, or whose duty it would be to so act (Darwall 2004). That is to say, traditional moral theory associates moral dilemmas and moral decision-making with moral obligation. Moral agents are portrayed by the traditional moral theories as having certain obligations. It is not just that it would be nice or a good thing if the moral agents acted in certain ways. This requirement raises the question of whether a self-driving car—or any other realistic type of robot—would be under an obligation to act in the ways in which we might think they should act (cf. Talbot et al. 2017).

It might be thought that it is primarily in Kantian or other deontological theories that obligations or duties are prominent (see, e.g. Floridi 2011: 203). However, one of the most canonical statements of how ethical theory deals with obligations rather than mere expediency comes from a utilitarian. Famously, John Stuart Mill writes:

> We do not call anything wrong, unless we mean to imply that a person ought to be punished in some way or other for doing it; if not by law, by the opinion of his fellow-creatures; if not by opinion, by the reproaches of his own conscience. This seems the real turning point of the distinction between morality and simple expediency. It is a part of the notion of Duty in every one of its forms, that a person may rightfully be compelled to fulfil it. Duty is a thing which may be exacted from a person, as one exacts a debt. Unless we think that it may be exacted from him, we do not call it his duty.
>
> (Mill 2001: 48–49)

Could a self-driving car sensibly be punished or blamed for any of its actions or omissions (Danaher 2016)? Could a self-driving car or any other robot suffer a guilty conscience in case it fails to act as it should (Sparrow 2007)? If not, the just-described way of thinking about moral obligation in the quote from Mill indicates that the self-driving car could not have any duties or obligations.

Suppose that we think the right decision in the above-described tunnel case would be for the car to swerve to the side and endanger the person in the car rather than to drive into the tunnel and endanger the five people in the tunnel. Unless the self-driving car could sensibly be punished or blamed, or unless it would be possible for it to feel guilty about its actions, it could not be a moral obligation or duty for the self-driving car to act in any way rather than in any other way (Nyholm 2020: ch. 7). If this self-driving car were nevertheless considered a moral agent, it would be a moral agent without any obligations. From the point of view of traditional moral theory, that is an idea that does not make much sense.

MORAL VIRTUE

It might be replied that being a good moral agent in the sense of doing what one is obligated to do is not the only way to be a good moral agent that we find in traditional moral theory. Not all traditional moral theories are centrally concerned with duties and the idea of moral obligation (Darwall 1995). Another way of being good, according to some traditional ethical theories, is to have certain virtues (Hursthouse 1999). Could robots have virtues and thereby be moral agents in that sense? This will, of course, depend on what we understand virtues to be. Perhaps the most widely discussed conception of what virtues are is derived from the work of Aristotle (1999). But there are also other theories, for example, the one that David Hume (1983) put forward in his *An Enquiry concerning the Principles of Morals*. Let us briefly consider both of these theories of virtue. We can start with Hume's theory and then consider Aristotle's theory, which is more demanding in nature.

Hume has a simple and neat theory of what virtue is. His whole theory of virtue in the *Enquiry* is contained in two key distinctions. To begin with, according to Hume, a virtue is always some characteristic of the person who has the virtue. The first key distinction Hume then draws is between personal characteristics that are useful and ones that are agreeable in themselves. The second key distinction is between personal characteristics that benefit oneself and ones that benefit others. All virtues, on this way of thinking, are personal characteristics that are useful to ourselves, useful to others, agreeable to ourselves, or agreeable to others. Of course, some personal characteristics might have more than one of these features.

What about Aristotle? A virtue, on the Aristotelian view, is some habit or personal disposition that is associated with human flourishing and that is admirable to others (Aristotle 1999). This type of habit involves a disposition to do the right thing, at the right time, to the right degree, and for the right reasons. It is, typically, a middle path between two extremes. Courage, for example, is a disposition that lies between cowardice, on the one hand, and foolhardiness, on the other hand. Moreover, in order to act on any particular virtues, it is also important—according to Aristotle—to have a set of other virtues as well. This is called the 'unity of the virtues' thesis (Crisp and Slote 1997). For example, in order for a person to be courageous in the right way, they also need to be just, wise, prudent, and so on. Without these other virtues, a person cannot have the virtue of courage in the right way that we associate with human flourishing. Or so Aristotle famously argues.

Moreover, the Aristotelian ideal of virtue is, as Philip Pettit puts it, a 'robustly demanding' ideal (Pettit 2015). It requires that we are disposed to do the rights sorts of things for the right reasons, not just in cases in which it is easy and convenient, but also in cases in which it is more challenging and less convenient for us to do so. If we only act correctly when it is easy and convenient, but are not robustly disposed to do the right thing across a wider range of circumstances, we do not truly possess the types of dispositions that Aristotelian ethics understands the virtues as being (Alfano 2013a).

Could robots have virtues and be moral agents? Could they have virtues in the sense Hume describes, or in the sense described in Aristotelian ethics (cf. Nyholm 2020: ch. 7)? A first challenge when it comes to whether robots could have virtues in the sense Hume describes is that virtues are supposed to be certain personal characteristics—namely, personal characteristics that are useful or agreeable in themselves either to ourselves or to others. It might be thought, to begin with, that it makes no sense to think of robots or other machines as having any personal characteristics. Only persons, it might be thought, have those.[8]

It might be easier, though, for a robot to be useful or agreeable to people. For example, a robotic vacuum cleaner such as the Roomba robot might be useful to its owners and thereby have a virtue in a somewhat minimalistic and watered-down sense (Sung et al. 2007). Some other robots might be entertaining and agreeable, and might therefore be seen as having a type of virtue. Nor does a technological artefact need to be a robot in order to potentially be useful or agreeable to people. A tool might have the 'virtue', in a loose sense, of making it easy to get the job done, and a chair the virtue of being comfortable to sit in. However, none of these examples come close to being virtues of the sort we expect in moral agents. There is a difference in kind between being, say, a sharp knife or an efficient lawnmower and being a just or compassionate person.

It is even more unrealistic to imagine a robot that would have any virtues in the demanding sense described by Aristotle (Nyholm 2020: ch. 7). Could a robot be disposed to do the right thing, at the right times, and for the right reasons? Could it have a unity of virtues by not just having one, but a whole set of virtues that reinforce and support each other? Is it realistic to imagine a robot that is robustly disposed to do the right thing, not just in situations in which it is 'easy' for the robot, but across a wider range of possible circumstances that might arise?

Robots and other technologies with AI are typically only good at one task, in a very controlled environment (Royakkers and Van Est 2016). It is hard to imagine any realistic robot with a robust disposition that would enable it to do the right sorts of things in a stable way across a wide range of circumstances. And, moreover, according to Duncan

Purves, Ryan Jenkins, and Bradley J. Strawser, robots cannot act for reasons. They cannot act for reasons because this requires the possession of certain forms of mental state that we do not typically attribute to robots (Purves et al. 2015; see also Talbot et al. 2017 and Brey 2014). If that is right, robots cannot act rightly, for the right reasons, to the right degree, etc. in the sense that virtuous agents are supposed to.

It seems best to conclude that if robots can be said to have virtues in any sense, it would be in a rather watered-down and minimalistic sense. Indeed, as many critics of virtue ethics argue, and as some defenders of virtue ethics themselves admit, it is even hard for human beings to qualify as having virtues in the sense described by Aristotle because having virtues is a very demanding ideal (Alfano 2013b; Pettit 2015). Virtue is something human beings can realistically aspire to. But it is something that it is much less realistic to aspire to create in robots.

Different ways of being
A MORAL PATIENT

Let us return now to the example above of a robot dog being kicked and people reacting to this in a negative way (Parke 2015). That many people spontaneously perceive something problematic about kicking a robot that looks and behaves like a dog suggests that we should reflect on whether it might make sense to cast robots in the role of moral patients (Coeckelbergh 2010a–b, 2018). Presumably, people's reactions would be even stronger if the robots being kicked looked and behaved like human beings.

In the previous sections, we looked at what traditional ethical theory associates with moral agency. Let us now switch over to looking at what traditional ethical theory associates with moral patients (see e.g. Driver 2007). What sorts of things do the traditional theories see as most relevant in order for somebody to be a moral patient with a moral status that we need to take into consideration? Can we imagine realistic robots that have any of those properties? If not, then what should we conclude about whether it ever makes sense to regard robots and other machines as moral patients?

First, in the virtue ethical tradition, the main moral patients associated with the actions of the moral agents were often the moral agents themselves (see various contributions in Crisp and Slote 1997). That is to say, the person who was considered the main beneficiary of the development and exercise of the virtues was the agent herself. This is certainly the case in Aristotle's theory, for example, which is centred around the idea of 'eudaimonia' or human flourishing (Aristotle 1999). By developing the virtues, we flourish as human beings. Another example is the way in which the topic of justice is approached in Plato's *Republic* (2007). The main question in that book is: in what ways does it benefit an agent to develop the virtue of justice? Plato argues that it is both instrumentally and non-instrumentally good for the agent to develop the virtue of justice. Again, the main moral patient in focus is the moral agent herself.

In Kantian ethics, the self and other human beings are treated on a par in terms of who are the main moral patients that moral agents ought to concern themselves with (Kant 2012). In utilitarian moral theory, the self is a possible moral patient—since our own happiness can be positively or adversely affected by our actions. But the main moral patients usually considered within utilitarian moral philosophy are other human beings, as well as other sentient beings (Bentham 1996; Mill 2001).

I have already mentioned that the capacity for human flourishing is what is treated as the key thing to focus on in virtue ethics. In Kantian ethics, in turn, the main basis associated with moral patiency is the possession of practical reason and a will. In utilitarian theory, the main object of concern in a moral patient is their sensibility to pleasure and pain (Bentham 1996; Mill 2001). We benefit moral patients within virtue ethical theory by promoting their flourishing. We show moral consideration within Kantian ethical theory by having respect for persons and their dignity (e.g. by seeking their consent before treating them in certain ways) (Kant 2012). And we show moral consideration according to utilitarians by relieving pain and suffering, and by promoting the happiness of others.

Utilitarian philosophers have long emphasized that their theory can include non-human animals in the class of moral patients, since animals can also feel pleasure and pain (see, e.g. Bentham 1996). It is nevertheless clear that all of these theories developed with human beings in mind as the paradigmatic moral patients to be taken into consideration. The theories home in on typically human properties when they describe what makes someone a moral patient. Accordingly, when some authors have recently explored whether it might ever make sense to include robots among those who we think of as moral patients, they have often concluded either of two things: that we have to wait for the arrival of much more sophisticated robots in the far-off future before we can view machines as moral patients, or that traditional moral theories do not lend support to the idea that robots can be moral patients.

Eric Schwitzgebel and Mara Garza (2015) take the former approach. They argue that since (a) we should treat like cases alike; and (b) it is, in principle, possible to imagine future robots with sophisticated enough AI that they would have the capacities we associate with human moral patients, we should conclude that in the future, there might eventually be robots whom we should treat as moral patients for the same reasons that we treat human beings as moral patients.

Romy Eskens (2017), in contrast, takes the latter approach. In particular, she considers the case of sex robots and the question of whether there should be a moral requirement to seek their consent before one has sex with them. Eskens argues that this depends on whether sex robots can have the sort of properties that Kantian and utilitarian theories associate with moral patients. Do the robots have practical reason and a will ('sapiens'), or a capacity for pleasure or pain ('sentience')? No, Eskens suggests. In the case of human beings, it would be rape to have sex with someone without their consent. In the case of robots, they lack moral status because they lack sapiens and sentience, Eskens argues. Therefore, they are not moral patients who would be raped if people had sex with them without their consent. (For two other perspectives on this particular issue, see Frank and Nyholm 2017 and Sparrow 2017.)

In general, since robots cannot achieve human flourishing, lack practical reason and a will, and do not experience pleasure and pain, traditional moral theories seemingly imply that robots cannot be moral patients for the reasons that human beings can be moral patients. If we want to explore the possibility of regarding robots and other machines as potential moral patients, the traditional moral theories are not going to be of much help.

TWO DIFFERENT WAYS OF CONCEIVING OF THE ETHICS OF HUMAN–ROBOT INTERACTION AND ITS RELATION TO TRADITIONAL MORAL THEORIES

The issues briefly discussed in the sections above can all be explored in much greater detail. I and others have done so elsewhere (see, e.g. Anderson and Anderson 2011; Gunkel 2018; Nyholm 2020). But I hope that even this quick discussion of these different topics helps to show that we seem to face the following choice. If we want to make use of the traditional moral theories when we approach the issues that confront us within the ethics of human–robot interaction, we should understand human beings as being the main moral agents and patients in question. (Of course, we can also consider non-human animals as being among the moral patients to take into account.) Or if we want to start exploring ways in which robots and other machines with AI might become moral agents and patients, then we need to look elsewhere than what I have been calling the traditional moral theories in order to find solid theoretical grounding for this project.

Let me briefly comment on the two options I just sketched. How, it might first be asked, could human beings be both the main moral agents and main moral patients if our questions are about how robots should be made to behave around human beings and about how human beings should conduct themselves around robots? For example, if we are asking how self-driving cars should be programmed to deal with accident scenarios, then we should not think of the self-driving cars themselves as being the moral agents whose decisions should be guided by moral theories. Rather, we should think of whoever decides on how the self-driving cars should behave as being the moral agents whose decision-making should be guided by the principles and ideals associated with traditional moral theories (cf. Nyholm 2018a).

For example, a utilitarian might say that it is not the self-driving car that should make decisions aimed to promote happiness and relieve suffering. Rather, it is whoever is programming or otherwise making decisions about self-driving cars who should make decisions that promote happiness and relieve suffering. According to Kantian ethics, it is not the self-driving car that should respect others or adopt a set of principles it would be willing to lay down as universal laws. It is rather the person deciding how the self-driving car should behave who should respect others and conduct him or herself on the basis of principles they would be willing to lay down as universal laws. Likewise, if anyone should try to cultivate and exemplify virtues, it is the human beings making decisions about how robots will treat people, and not the robots themselves.

Consider next the issue of how people should behave around robots. If human beings (and some animals) are ultimately seen as the only moral patients, then whether we should ever treat robots in any way that appears to show moral consideration for those robots will depend on whether there are any human beings (or any animals) whose moral interests we might respect by acting in ways that seemingly show moral consideration for the robots. For example, we may fail to show proper respect for real dogs if we are prepared to kick a robot dog. We could certainly be thought to not show proper respect for human beings if we want to create robotic copies of them and then treat those robotic replicas in seemingly disrespectful ways (Nyholm 2020: ch. 8).

By avoiding treating robots in certain ways, we might also train ourselves to avoid treating human beings in those ways (Darling 2017). Just as Kant argued that we might make ourselves cruel towards human beings by being cruel towards animals, it might also be argued that we might potentially end up being cruel towards human beings if we get in the habit of behaving in what appears to be cruel ways towards robots. Similarly, Robert Sparrow (2020) argues that we might undermine our own virtue and develop vices if we treat robots in ways in which it would be vicious to treat human beings. Thus, in order to stay on the path of virtue and avoid vice, it might be that we should avoid acting in what appears to be vicious ways when we interact with robots (cf. Friedman 2020).

In other words, it is perfectly possible to reflect on how robots should behave around humans and how humans should behave around robots while viewing human beings (and non-human animals) as being the only relevant moral agents and patients. But what if we want to also start thinking of robots as potentially being both moral agents and moral patients? How should we then relate our reflections to the traditional moral theories?

Of course, it should be noted that not everyone will agree with me that the traditional moral theories do not show a great deal of promise as a theoretical basis for reflections about robots as moral agents and patients. It might also be objected that the discussion above has assumed much more agreement among the traditional moral theories than there really is, and that some existing moral theories might lend themselves better than others to being applied to human–robot interaction. In particular, when it comes to robots envisioned as potential moral agents, I should point out that some theorists think that traditional moral theories have much more to offer than I have made things appear above (see, e.g. Floridi 2011; Powers 2011; and other contributions in Anderson and Anderson 2011). Many authors working in the field of machine ethics think that we can create artificial moral agents that follow the principles spelled out by the traditional moral theories. Some theorists—such as Michael Anderson and Susan Leigh Anderson, and Ronald Arkin—even think that robots are likely to eventually become better moral agents than human beings can be, as judged from the perspective of the traditional moral theories (Anderson and Anderson 2010; Arkin 2010). I want to note, though, that this is a point of view that has received a lot of critical push-back. John-Stewart Gordon (2020b), to take one example, argues that much theorizing within machine ethics involves 'rookie mistakes' regarding how the traditional moral theories should be applied and how the theories should be understood in the first place (see also Purves et al. 2015).

But I will not get into that debate here. What I rather want to mention is the way in which some other authors have chosen to respond to the issue of whether traditional moral theories can be useful if we start taking seriously the idea of robots as agents and patients. What I have in mind is the point of view associated in particular with Mark Coeckelbergh (2010a) and David Gunkel (2018). According to them, we should take seriously the idea of robots as both moral agents and patients. However, doing so requires, as Gunkel likes to put it, that we start 'thinking otherwise' (Gunkel 2018).

What he means is that we need to explore non-traditional types of ethical theory when thinking about what it might mean for robots to be moral agents and patients. Coeckelbergh and Gunkel are both interested in motivating what they call a 'relational turn' that moral theorizing might take. According to this approach, our focus should be less on the capacities and features of moral agents and patients, and instead more on what kinds of relations and interactions there can be between human beings, robots, and other technologies. The traditional moral theories, according to Coeckelbergh and Gunkel, are too focused on moral agents and patients considered in isolation and judged on the basis of their individual features. According to them, we should instead focus on the ways in which robots and other machines might come to have a 'social presence' by being brought into our homes, by being able to respond to us, and by being able to evoke certain social responses in us (Coeckelbergh 2010a–b, 2018; Gunkel 2018). If we changed our theoretical focus in this way, we would take what Coeckelbergh and Gunkel call a 'relational turn'.[9]

CONCLUDING REMARKS

I have suggested that when we start introducing robots and other technologies equipped with different forms of AI into different domains of life, new ethical questions arise. New questions arise about, on the one hand, how these machines should be made to behave around human beings and, on the other hand, how human beings should behave around these machines. Whether we can use traditional ethical theory in reflection on human–robot interaction depends on who we consider the relevant moral agents and patients to be, since these theories were developed with human beings in mind as the paradigmatic moral agents and patients.

One possible way to go here, which I will end by suggesting, is the following. Perhaps we can stick with the traditional moral theories when we think about the ethics of human–robot interaction with a focus on human beings as the moral agents and patients that we are concerning ourselves with. At the same time, we should also take seriously the idea that robots might one day become moral agents and patients. For them, we might then need to 'think otherwise', to use Gunkel's phrase. That is to say, if and when we start reflecting on what it might be for robots to be moral agents and patients, we may need new ethical theories to think about them. This way, the ethics of human–robot interaction can partly be based on traditional ethical theory—viz. when it considers human beings as moral agents and patients—and partly based on some other, possibly new form of ethical theorizing—viz. when it considers robots as moral agents and patients.

It might be objected here that moral theory is supposed to be universal and apply equally to all (whether it is humans, angels, aliens, animals, or whatever creatures we might be talking about). Universality implies that moral theory should also apply equally to human beings and robots, and that we cannot have one theory for one and another theory for the other. To this objection I respond that, on the one hand, we typically relativize what duties we think moral agents have to their capacities ('ought implies can'), so that, for example, mature adults are regarded as having different moral duties than children. On the other hand, we also relativize what protection, care, or rights we think moral patients should have to their capacities or situation, so that, for example, the vulnerable or the sick should get different treatment than others, all of which is compatible with the principle of treating like cases alike. Since human beings and robots are not like cases, the idea that we should not treat them alike, either in theory or in practice, does not conflict with the idea of moral universality, at least not if we take moral universality to be captured most importantly by the idea of treating like cases alike.

So long as we stick to the old moral agents and patients that philosophers have already been theorizing about for a very long time, we can make use of traditional ethical theories developed specifically to apply to those agents and patients. But once we start introducing new potential moral agents and patients of a radically different nature than the old ones, new, non-traditional theories might be needed.

ACKNOWLEDGEMENTS

Many thanks to Carissa Veliz and an anonymous reviewer for their helpful comments and suggestions. My work on this chapter is part of the research programme 'Ethics of Socially Disruptive Technologies', which is funded through the Gravitation programme of the Dutch Ministry of Education, Culture, and Science and the Netherlands Organisation for Scientific Research (NWO grant no. 024.004.031).

NOTES

1. The distinction Moor makes is similar to Kant's distinction between merely 'acting in accordance with duty' and 'acting from duty' (Kant 2012).
2. Some authors even claim that artificial moral agents will be better moral agents than human beings are able to be (Arkin 2010). The reason given for this is that while humans have

emotions that can lead us to react in morally problematic ways, machines lack emotions and can be guided by moral principles alone in a purely non-emotional way. For a contrasting point of view, according to which the lack of emotion makes machines less like moral agents and more like 'psychopaths', see Coeckelbergh (2010b).

3. I should note here that Joanna Bryson's view, as I understand it, is not that robots could not be moral agents or patients. It is rather that we should not create robots that might have an ambiguous moral status that might lead some people to regard them incorrectly as moral agents or patients (Bryson 2010, 2018).

4. It might be objected here that some of the traditional moral theories seek to distil the essence of morality in a way that does not necessarily need to be human-centric in nature. In particular, Kant might come to mind as somebody seeking to formulate an ethical theory applying to all possible rational beings, and not only human beings. In response to this, I would point out that even Kant appeals to common human experience when he tries to defend his moral theory. See, e.g. sections one and three of Kant (2012) or Kant's discussion of what he calls the 'fact of reason' in Kant (2015). Moreover, when he tries to spell out the substantive implications of his moral theory in his biggest book on moral philosophy, *The Metaphysics of Morals*, Kant spends the first half of the book ('The Doctrine of Right') on human political institutions and the second half of the book ('The Doctrine of Virtue') on his ideas about human moral virtue (see Kant 1996). This helps to illustrate that even those traditional moral philosophers who ostensibly try to avoid a strongly human-centric approach have nevertheless tended to be primarily focused on humans and human–human interaction in their writings.

5. The expression 'deontology' actually comes from a utilitarian, Jeremy Bentham, who used this expression to refer to the 'science of duty' and named one of his last books about utilitarianism *Deontology* (see Bentham 1983). These days, however, the expression 'deontological ethics' is typically used to refer to non-utilitarian ethical theories of a more broadly Kant-inspired sort, which focus on things such as moral rights and principles prescribing certain general duties (e.g. not to lie, not to kill, not to break promises, etc.) (see Driver 2007 and Suikkanen 2014).

6. The trolley problem is an expression associated with a set of philosophical thought experiments devised in the 1960s and 1980s by Philippa Foot and Judith Jarvis Thomson. In those thought experiments, a runaway train or trolley car is about to hit and kill five people. But we can save those five people, either by redirecting the train onto a separate track where one person would be hit by the train or by pushing a large person in front of the train. Depending on what variation of that case is considered, people typically have different intuitions about what the right thing to do is, and the puzzle of making sense of these different judgements is what is referred to as the trolley problem (see Foot 1967; Thomson 1985; Kamm 2015).

7. It is worth mentioning here that many authors doubt that it is possible to programme moral principles into machines in any sensible way. One problem that is often highlighted is that the application of moral principles to actual situations requires a capacity for judgement that it is hard, if not impossible, to design into machines (see, e.g. Purves et al. 2015 and Harris 2020).

8. That being said, it should be noted that some view robots as having a personality. Some American soldiers in Iraq got very attached to a bomb disposal robot they called 'Boomer', and some of them claimed that the robot had 'developed a personality of his own' (Garber 2013).

9. To be more precise, it is traditional Western ethical theories that are too focused on agents and patients in isolation and their individual capacities and features, according to Coeckelbergh and Gunkel. According to their reading of some non-Western ethical frameworks, other traditions of ethical theorizing—such as certain Eastern perspectives—have traditionally taken a much more relationally focused approach (see, e.g. Coeckelbergh 2010a: 216). For a similar argument about the ethics of human–robot interaction that appeals to another non-Western tradition (namely, the Southern African ubuntu approach to ethics), which is also strongly focused on relations and interactions among members of the moral community, see Wareham 2020.

REFERENCES

Alfano, Mark (2013a), 'Identifying and Defending the Hard Core of Virtue Ethics', *Journal of Philosophical Research* 38, 233–260.

Alfano, Mark (2013b), *Character as a Moral Fiction* (Cambridge: Cambridge University Press).

Anderson, Michael, and Anderson, Susan Leigh (2007), 'Machine Ethics: Creating an Ethical Intelligent Agent', *AI Magazine* 28(4), 15–26.

Anderson, Michael, and Anderson, Susan Leigh (2010), 'Robot Be Good: A Call for Ethical Autonomous Machines', *Scientific American* 303(4), 72–77.

Anderson, Michael, and Anderson, Susan Leigh, eds (2011), *Machine Ethics* (Cambridge: Cambridge University Press).

Aristotle (1999), *Nicomachean Ethics*, transl. Terence H. Irwin (Indianapolis, IN: Hackett).

Arkin, Ronald (2010), 'The Case for Ethical Autonomy in Unmanned Systems', *Journal of Military Ethics* 9(4), 332–341.

Awad, Edward, Dsouza, Sohan, Kim, Richard, Shulz, Jonathan, Henrich, Joseph, Shariff, Azim et al. (2018), 'The Moral Machine Experiment', *Nature* 563, 59–64.

Awad, Edward, Dsouza, Sohan, Bonnefon, Jean-Francois, Shariff, Azim, and Rahwan, Iyad (2020), 'Crowdsourcing Moral Machines', *Communications of the ACM* 63(3), 48–55.

Bentham, Jeremy (1983), *The Collected Works of Jeremy Bentham: Deontology. Together with a Table of Springs of Action and the Article on Utilitarianism* (Oxford: Clarendon).

Bentham, Jeremy (1996), *The Collected Works of Jeremy Bentham: Introduction to the Principles of Morals and Legislation* (Oxford: Clarendon).

Bonnefon, Jean-Francois., Shariff, Azim, and Rahwan, Iyad (2016),' The Social Dilemma of Autonomous Vehicles', *Science* 352(6293), 1573–1576.

Brey, Philip (2014), 'From Moral Agents to Moral Factors: The Structural Ethics Approach', in Peter Kroes and Peter-Paul Verbeek, eds, *The Moral Status of Technical Artifacts* (Berlin: Springer), 125–142.

Bryson, Joanna (2010), 'Robots Should Be Slaves', in Yorick Wilks, ed., *Close Engagements with Artificial Agents* (Amsterdam: John Benjamins Publishing Co.), 63–74.

Bryson, Joanna (2018), 'Patiency is Not a Virtue: The Design of Intelligent Systems and Systems of Ethics', *Ethics and Information Technology* 10(1), 15–26.

Coeckelbergh, Mark (2010a), 'Robot Rights? Towards a Social-Relational Justification of Moral Consideration', *Ethics and Information Technology* 12(3), 209–221.

Coeckelbergh, Mark (2010b), 'Moral Appearances: Emotions, Robots, and Human Morality', *Ethics and Information Technology*, 12(3), 235–241.

Coeckelberg, Mark (2018), 'Why Care about Robots? Empathy, Moral Standing, and the Language of Suffering', *Kairos. Journal of Philosophy & Society* 20, 141–158.

Crisp, Roger, and Slote, Michael (1997), *Virtue Ethics* (Oxford: Oxford University Press).

Danaher, John (2016), 'Robots, Law, and the Retribution Gap', *Ethics and Information Technology* 18(4), 299–309.

Danaher, John (2019), 'Welcoming Robots into the Moral Circle: A Defense of Ethical Behaviorism', *Science and Engineering Ethics*, doi: https://doi.org/10.1007/s11948-019-00119-x.

Danaher, John (2020), 'Robot Betrayal: A Guide to the Ethics of Robotic Deception', *Ethics and Information Technology*, https://link.springer.com/article/10.1007/s10676-019-09520-3, accessed 5 August 2021.

Darling, Kate (2017). "Who's Johnny?' Anthropological Framing in Human–Robot Interaction, Integration, and Policy', in Patrick Lin, Keith Abney, and Ryan Jenkins, eds, *Robot Ethics 2.0: From Autonomous Cars to Artificial Intelligence* (Oxford: Oxford University Press), 173–192.

Darwall, Stephen (1995), *The British Moralists and the Internal 'Ought': 1640–1740* (Cambridge: Cambridge University Press).

Darwall, Stephen (2004), *The Second Person Standpoint* (Cambridge, MA: Harvard University Press).

Driver, Julia (2007), *Ethics: The Fundamentals* (Oxford: Blackwell).

Eskens, Romy (2017), 'Is Sex with Robots Rape?', *Journal of Practical Ethics* 5(2): 62–76.

Floridi, Luciano (2011), 'On the Morality of Artificial Agents', in Michael Anderson and Susan Lee Anderson, eds, *Machine Ethics* (Cambridge: Cambridge University Press), 184–212.

Floridi, Luciano (2017), 'Roman Law Offers a Better Guide to Robot Rights than Sci-Fi', *Financial Times*, https://www.ft.com/content/99d60326-f85d-11e6-bd4e-68d53499ed71, accessed 5 August 2021.

Foot, Philippa (1967), 'The Problem of Abortion and the Doctrine of Double Effect', *Oxford Review* 5, 5–15.

Frank, Lily, and Nyholm, Sven (2017), 'Robot Sex and Consent: Is Consent to Sex between a Human and a Robot Conceivable, Possible, and Desirable?', *Artificial Intelligence and Law* 25(3), 305–323.

Friedman, Cindy (2020), 'Human–Robot Moral Relations: Human Interactants as Moral Patients of Their Own Agential Moral Actions Towards Robots', in Aurona Gerber, ed., *Artificial Intelligence Research* (Berlin: Springer), 3–20.

Garber, Megan (2013), 'Funerals for Fallen Robots', *The Atlantic*, https://www.theatlantic.com/technology/archive/2013/09/funerals-for-fallen-robots/279861/, accessed 5 August 2021.

Goodall, Noah J. (2014), 'Ethical Decision Making During Automated Vehicle Crashes', *Transportation Research Record: Journal of the Transportation Research Board*, 2424, 58–65.

Gordon, John-Stewart (2020a), 'What Do We Owe to Intelligent Robots?', *AI & Society* 35, 209–223.

Gordon, John-Stewart (2020b), 'Building Moral Robots: Ethical Pitfalls and Challenges', *Science and Engineering Ethics* 26(1), 141–157.

Gunkel, David (2012), *The Machine Question* (Cambridge, MA: The MIT Press).

Gunkel, David (2018), *Robot Rights* (Cambridge, MA: The MIT Press).

Gunkel, David (2019), *How to Survive a Robot Invasion* (London: Routledge).

Harris, John (2020), 'The Immoral Machine', *Cambridge Quarterly of Healthcare Ethics*, 29(1), 71–79.

Hume, David (1983), *An Enquiry concerning the Principles of Morals*, ed. J. B. Schneewind (Indianapolis, IN: Hackett).

Hursthouse, Rosalind (1999), *On Virtue Ethics* (Oxford: Oxford University Press).

Kamm, Francis (2015), *The Trolley Mysteries* (Oxford: Oxford University Press).

Kant, Immanuel (1996), *The Metaphysics of Morals*, ed. Mary Gregor (Cambridge: Cambridge University Press).

Kant, Immanuel (2012), *Immanuel Kant: Groundwork of the Metaphysics of Morals, A German-English Edition*, ed. Mary Gregor and Jens Timmermann (Cambridge: Cambridge University Press).

Kant, Immanuel (2015), *Critique of Practical Reason*, ed. Reath Andrews (Cambridge: Cambridge University Press).

Keeling, Geoff (2020), 'Why Trolley Problems Matter for the Ethics of Automated Vehicles', *Science and Engineering Ethics* 26(1), 293–307.

Mill, John Stuart (2001), *Utilitarianism*, 2nd edn, ed. George Sher (Indianapolis, IN: Hackett).

Millar, Jason (2014), 'An Ethical Dilemma: When Robot Cars Must Kill, Who Should Pick the Victim?', *Robohub*, https://robohub.org/an-ethical-dilemma-when-robot-cars-must-kill-who-should-pick-the-victim/, accessed 5 August 2021.

Moor, James (2006), 'The Nature, Importance, and Difficulty of Machine Ethics', *IEEE Intelligent Systems* 21, 18–21.

Nyholm, Sven (2018a), 'The Ethics of Crashes with Self-Driving Cars: A Roadmap, I', *Philosophy Compass*, e12507.

Nyholm, Sven (2018b), 'The Ethics of Crashes with Self-Driving Cars: A Roadmap, II', *Philosophy Compass*, e12506.

Nyholm, Sven (2020), *Humans and Robots: Ethics, Agency, and Anthropomorphism* (London: Rowman & Littlefield International).

Nyholm, Sven and Smids, Jilles (2016), 'The Ethics of Accident-Algorithms for Self-Driving Cars: An Applied Trolley Problem?', *Ethical Theory and Moral Practice* 19(5), 1275–1289.

Parke, Phoebe (2015), 'Is It Cruel to Kick a Robot Dog?', *CNN Edition*, https://edition.cnn.com/2015/02/13/tech/spot-robot-dog-google/index.html, accessed 5 August 2021.

Pettit, Philip (2015), *The Robust Demands of the Good: Ethics with Attachment, Virtue, and Respect* (Oxford: Oxford University Press).

Plato (2007): *The Republic* (London: Penguin).

Powers, Thomas M. (2011), 'Prospects for a Kantian Machine', in Michael Anderson and Susan Lee Anderson, eds, *Machine Ethics* (Cambridge: Cambridge University Press), 464–475.

Purves, Duncan, Jenkins, Ryan, and Strawser, Bradley James (2015), 'Autonomous Machines, Moral Judgment, and Acting for the Right Reasons', *Ethical Theory and Moral Practice* 18(4), 851–872.

Rawls, John (1993), *Political Liberalism* (New York: Columbia University Press).

Royakkers, Lamber, and Van Est, Rinie (2016), *Just Ordinary Robots: Automation from Love to War* (Boca Raton, FL: CRC Press).

Schwitzgebel, Eric, and Garza, Mara (2015), 'A Defense of the Rights of Artificial Intelligences', *Midwest Studies in Philosophy* 39(1), 98–119.

Sparrow, Robert (2007), 'Killer Robots', *Journal of Applied Philosophy* 24 (1), 62–77.

Sparrow, Robert (2016), 'Robots and Respect: Assessing the Case against Autonomous Weapons Systems', *Ethics & International Affairs* 30(1), 93–116.

Sparrow, Robert (2017), 'Robots, Rapte, and Representation', *International Journal of Social Robotics* 9(4), 465–477.

Sparrow, Robert (2020), 'Virtue and Vice in Our Relationships with Robots: Is there an Asymmetry and How Might it be Explained?', *International Journal of Social Robotics*, https://link.springer.com/article/10.1007/s12369-020-00631-2, accessed 5 August 2021.

Suikkanen, Jussi (2014), *This is Ethics: An Introduction* (Oxford: Wiley-Blackwell).

Sung, Ja-Young, Guo, Lan, Grinter, Rebecca E., and Christensen, Henrik I. (2007), '"My Roomba is Rambo": Intimate Home Appliances', in John Krumm, Gregory D. Abowd, Aruna Seneviratne, and Thomas Strang, eds, *UbiComp 2007: Ubiquitous Computing* (Berlin: Springer), 145–162.

Talbot, Brian, Jenkins, Ryan, and Purves, Duncan (2017), 'When Robots Should Do the Wrong Thing', in Patrick Lin, Keith Abney, and Ryan Jenkins, eds, *Robot Ethics 2.0: From Autonomous Cars to Artificial Intelligence* (Oxford: Oxford University Press), 258–273.

Thomson, Judith Jarvis (1985), 'The Trolley Problem', *Yale Law Review* 94(5), 1395–1415.

Turner, Jacob (2019), *Robot Rules: Regulating Artificial Intelligence* (Cham: Palgrave MacMillan).

Van Wynsberghe, Aimee, and Robbins, Scott (2018), 'Critiquing the Reasons for Making Artificial Moral Agents', *Science and Engineering Ethics* 25(3), 719–735.

Wallach, Wendell, and Allen, Colin (2009), *Moral Machines: Teaching Machines Right from Wrong* (Oxford: Oxford University Press).

Wareham, C. S. (2020), 'Artificial Intelligence and African Conceptions of Personhood', *Ethics and Information Technology*, doi: 10.1007/s10676-020-09541-3.

Weaver, John Frank (2013), *Robots Are People Too: How Siri, Google Car, and Artificial Intelligence Will Force Us to Change Our Laws* (Santa Barbara, CA: Praeger).

....

CHAPTER 4

IS THERE A RIGHT TO INTERNET ACCESS?

....

ROWAN CRUFT

INTRODUCTION

....

SOME claim that access to the internet is a moral right, perhaps a human right; others claim that there is also a moral right to remain offline. The two claims are not inconsistent, but both are challenged by government policies that, for instance, require voter registration or disability benefits to be claimed online, or that provide distinctive arenas for online democratic participation through petitions. Do these policies either directly, or through third-party effects, violate the human rights of those who choose web-free lives, or who cannot afford internet access? This chapter will assess whether the ideas of 'rights' and 'human rights' are useful moral–legal concepts for getting to grips with these issues. The values in this area—democratic participation, freedom of speech, privacy, the idea of a welfare state—are often understood in terms of rights, but they are also often taken more communally, as morally grounded fundamentally by their role in constituting an open society that serves us all collectively. Rights approaches highlight the individual as a party who is 'wronged' when a duty is violated. This chapter defends a rights-based approach to moral questions about internet access – as one useful approach among others. The chapter explores the practical implications of this approach for policy and law, including human rights law, focusing especially on the extent to which people can justifiably be compelled to become 'netizens' and the ways in which web exclusions should be understood as wronging those who are excluded.

IN DEFENCE OF HUMAN RIGHTS
TO CONTINGENT MODERN GOODS

....

Is there a human right to internet access? Is there a human right to remain offline if one chooses? We should start by rejecting a common way of dismissing these claims. The common dismissal maintains that because human rights are universal, there can be no human rights to the provision of contingent modern goods. One version of this dismissal sees human rights as timeless, held by all humans at any time. Because medieval farmers or Stone Age hunters clearly lacked a right to internet access, we must also lack such a right, at least if it is taken as a *human right*—says this line of argument.[1] We can find a similar argument even if we reject the timelessness claim: if human rights are held universally by all humans *in modern conditions* (Raz 2015: 224–225), it can still seem implausible to say that my elderly retired neighbour who has a very decent life, yet has never used a computer, holds a right to internet access, or that the people in North Sentinel Island hold such a right; so it cannot be a *human right* because not all humans hold it.

We should resist this line of argument. Instead, quite specific, technical human rights can be justified as rights to the means to ensure that particular right-holders are secured with more abstractly specified goods—abstractly specified goods to which all hold human rights. For example, in some places, a right to a polling station within walking distance might be a human right, if it is our local chosen way to ensure respect for people's universal human right to political participation; in other places, access to online polling, or to transport to a distant polling station, might be human rights specifying that same general human right to political participation. Similarly, under modern conditions, a right to in vitro fertilization (IVF) treatment might be a human right in some societies, but not in others, in which the goods of parenthood are as readily available to non-biological parents (Tasioulas 2015: 61). If internet access is to be a human right, it will be either a necessary means, or else a good important local (but contingent) means chosen for the fulfilment of more fundamental abstract human rights, such as the universal right to be able to play a full part in one's community's life. So conceived, putative human rights to internet access, or to remain offline, are not undermined by their non-universality and contingency.

We will see that there is a notable distinction here: between specific rights that are *uniquely necessary* means to fulfilling more fundamental human rights in modern conditions, and those that are *our chosen* way of fulfilling such human rights, where other options would also have been possible and might be chosen by others. Internet access falls into the latter class, I will argue—but that need not undermine its status as a human right, so long as internet access is a specially effective, central means to fulfil fundamental human rights in modern conditions.

THREE WAYS OF JUSTIFYING RIGHTS

We have yet to establish that there are indeed human rights in this area. Is the language of human rights appropriate here? Is the language of *rights* appropriate here, even before we ask whether it is a *human* right subject to the universality requirements just mentioned? A Hohfeldian claim-right to internet access would be constituted by duties on others: duties to supply internet access and not to impede it, duties whose violation specifically wrongs *the right-holder*.[2] A claim-right to remain offline would be similar: constituted by duties not to compel people to go online, whose violation wrongs those people. Are we correct to think of internet access as the kind of good the impeding or non-providing of which wrongs specific people? Would we do better to think of it as an 'undirected' wrong, the violation of which means that the duty-bearer has *done wrong* without *wronging anyone in particular*? Failure to play one's part within a team game can sometimes look like an 'undirected' wrong, as can harms to the natural environment, or breaking the rules of some scheme of collective action that serves the common good, such as a parking violation.[3] In each case, I think it is debatable whether the language of rights and directed duty might not still be appropriate—doesn't one wrong one's fellow team members, nature, and one's community in the three cases mentioned?

In this chapter, I make the case that the language of rights does have a morally justified role to play in the morality of internet access.[4] There are three ways one might argue for this view. First, one might see internet access (and/or the chance to remain offline) as something to which a legal right is morally justified, but for reasons unrelated to prior natural or moral rights. Such an approach can be found in the justifications of systems of rights and duties created to serve efficiency, beauty, or other collectively conceived social goals, perhaps on 'tragedy of the commons' grounds. Examples might include a town's system of parking regulations, or the rights created by an electromagnetic spectrum auction, or the rights held by business corporations. If the goods justifying the creation and maintenance of such legal rights are not themselves fundamentally a matter of moral or natural right, then in my view, the case for the relevant created legal duties and rules taking a rights-type form will be rather limited. It will depend on instrumental considerations about how allowing parties to conceive particular duty-entailed actions as 'mine by right' and 'demandable in my name' serves the relevant grounding good (e.g. efficiency, public entertainment). I have argued elsewhere that there is rarely a strong case for regulations so grounded—that is, grounded on goods that are not themselves rights—to qualify as rights (Cruft 2019: 73–74, 162–163, and ch. 13). Undirected duties whose violation does not wrong a particular party tend to do just as well at serving any particular rights-independent goods one might choose. Undirected duties or rules can be as readily and firmly enforced, their violation can be as closely associated with shame and blame, and they can regulate matters with as wide a range of content, as directed duties correlating with rights (Feinberg 1970; Ihara 2004; Cruft 2019: 73–74, 162–163, and ch. 13). Allowing a party to conceive what a duty requires as 'theirs', 'demandable on their own behalf', might perhaps sometimes make for better policing of the duty. But I think that in the absence of prior natural or moral rights for law or convention to operationalize, there is rarely a clear instrumental case for creating legal–conventional rights rather than undirected duties.

Instead, to justify normative structures taking a rights-type form, one does better to show that such structures either themselves constitute pre-legal natural or moral rights or are legal or conventional creations that operationalize or determine such pre-legal rights. In the latter case, the justification for the relevant legal rule taking a rights-type form is that this is necessary to reflect the form of the moral or natural right on which it is based. In the typology at the start of the previous paragraph, these two approaches are the second and third ways to argue for the appropriateness of the language of rights in relation to internet access, alongside the first outlined in the paragraph above.

The second way maintains that internet access—perhaps including remaining offline—is itself a pre-legal moral right, in the sense of a right that exists independently of whether it has been created, or indeed recognized, by anyone: what I think we could reasonably call a 'natural right', so long as we remember that this does not necessarily mean a right that would exist in some asocial state of nature, or that is created for us by God, or that is held universally by all human beings; instead, it just means a right whose existence and rights-type structure is independent of acts of deliberate human creation, and is in that respect recognition-independent.

For internet access to be a pre-legal or natural right, it would need to exist as a right—in the modern context, and not necessarily universally—whether or not anyone recognizes that it exists. 'Recognition' does not here mean respect for the right in the sense of fulfilling it, but rather belief in the right's existence. Pre-legal or natural moral rights exist independently of people's belief in them. In my view, we clearly hold such pre-legal rights not to be tortured, to education, to political participation, and in context we hold more specific, non-universal pre-legal rights, such as my right that you call for an ambulance when I fall over and injure myself in front of you: I hold this right even if, because of my lowly social status, say, neither of us believe I do. If internet access is a pre-legal moral right in this sense, that will be because, in the modern context, people hold rights to internet access (and perhaps to remain offline) independently of whether anyone believes they do, or has intentionally created such a right.[5]

The third way to justify norms requiring internet access taking a rights-type form maintains that while internet access is fundamentally a legally or conventionally created right, it is one that we have good reason to choose to create as our way of operationalizing certain pre-legal natural or moral rights. This is not the same as the case in which a right to internet access is in context uniquely *necessary* for securing pre-legal natural or moral rights. The latter case falls under my second approach above: if free access to the internet is the *only* way to secure certain pre-legal rights, then such access is in this context itself required by natural–moral right—just as calling for an ambulance might be in context required by natural–moral right. By contrast, the third approach sees internet access as our local *chosen* way of operationalizing certain natural–moral rights, such as a nat-ural right to legitimate government. On this approach, a rights-type structure through created law or convention reflects the fact that we have chosen internet access as our way of giving determinate form to relevant pre-legal natural–moral rights. If there were no pre-legal *rights* underlying our decision to provide internet access, then—as in the first way above—the case for giving the resultant legal or conventional structures a rights-type form would be significantly diminished, turning on difficult instrumental questions about how far thinking in terms of rights helps achieve the underlying values here. But if the underlying values are themselves pre-legal natural or moral rights, we have a stronger case for seeing the operationalizing law as a matter of rights, even if (unlike on the second approach) such law is not strictly necessary to ensure respect for the relevant pre-legal rights.

My case for internet access as a human right will be based predominantly on this 'third way': we have good reason to choose to institute legal and conventional rights protecting internet access, and because this reason is primarily to do with the protection of underlying fundamental pre-legal rights (broadly, to political participation and legitimate power), our chosen legal–conventional protection should take a rights-type structure. But I will also argue that if enough societies have already chosen to institute internet access as a right, that could leave those who remain with no real choice: in context, they *must* secure internet access for their members, and this will be a contextually generated natural right like the right to have an ambulance called for one.

AN ACCOUNT OF NATURAL MORAL RIGHTS

Because both my second and third 'ways' to justify a right to internet access draw on the idea of fundamental pre-legal natural or moral rights, I need to explain what such things might be. In my view, there is a moral or natural claim-right for a particular party (individual or group) to internet access only if that party's good plays a significant part on its own in morally grounding duties to provide or not impede such access for that party. The theory of natural rights underpinning this view is quite controversial, and embodies prior work. It amounts to the thought that Raz's Interest Theory of rights-in-general— the view that a party holds a right if, and only if, that party's interests ground duties— actually gives an account of natural or moral rights, and not of all rights, as Raz claims.[6] Before looking at critics of this claim, I will say a little in its support.

The idea is that if a party's good really is important enough largely on its own to ground the existence of moral duties independently of whether anyone chooses to create such duties, then this duty-grounding importance is best registered by drawing attention to the party whose good is so important, as one who can claim on their own behalf that which the duty requires, and as one who is wronged if the duty is violated. This is what the rights concept does: it highlights the relevant party as one who can claim the duty on their own behalf, and is wronged if the duty is violated; such highlighting only occurs 'naturally', I believe, when that party's good is the ground of the duty. So understood, natural–moral rights reflect Rawls's insight about the 'separateness of persons': natural–moral rights register the independent duty-grounding importance of the good of a particular person, the importance of that person's good as a generator of duties relatively independently of how it interacts with the good of others or of the wider group (Rawls 1971: 27).

If this framework is correct, then do natural, recognition-independent rights include a right to internet access, and/or to remain offline? The theory just outlined tells us that, to answer this question, we need to examine the relative importance of individual interests in such access vis-a-vis competing individual interests and other more collective or less individually situated goods—and we need to examine whether the relevant individual interests could on their own require internet access for their bearers.

Before getting into these questions, we should note the controversiality of my claims about natural or moral pre-legal rights. There are many theories of what rights are. My own view is unusual in taking Raz's account as accurate for *natural or pre-legal moral claim-rights*, while adopting a broader view of claim-rights in general as *duties demandable on the right-holder's behalf*. My account argues that a duty is naturally, pre-legally demandable on behalf of a particular party (who thereby qualifies as a natural right-holder) when, and only when, that party's interests morally ground the duty in question. And it also argues that we can construct legal or conventional demandability on a right-holder's behalf more or less whenever we wish through promising or law, including independently of the right-holder's interests.

Of course, there are alternative views of what claim-rights are. I will here mention the range of theories: note that these are not just theories of natural–moral rights, but of rights in general. Non-Razian versions of the 'Interest Theory' argue that I hold a claim-right if, and only if, my interests are necessarily *served* by a duty's fulfilment, whether or not they are the moral *ground* for the duty (MacCormick 1982; Kramer 1998, 2010). A rival 'Will Theory' maintains that I hold a claim-right if, and only if, I hold powers of control over a duty (Hart 1955; Steiner 1994). The 'Demand Theory' maintains that I hold a claim-right if, and only if, I hold power to demand a duty's fulfilment (Feinberg 1970; Skorupski 2010; Gilbert 2018). There is also an ingenious 'Hybrid Theory' in which rights are held by those whose interests ground their level of control over a duty (Sreenivasan 2005), and an insightful 'Kind-Desire Theory' in which rights are held by those who necessarily want a duty's fulfilment given their kind (Wenar 2013). And I have recently developed my own account of claim-rights in general: as any duty that formally requires its bearer to conceive some party (who is thereby identified as the right-holder) second-personally as the object of the duty-bearer's action; this, I argue, is what it is for a duty to be *demandable distinctively on that party's behalf* in the way that the party's rights make possible (Cruft 2019: Pt I).

Each theory offers a different account of the special way in which being a right-holder makes a duty owed to one, and thereby makes one the special focus of the duty, wrongable when it is violated. This is not the place to compare these theories in detail.[7] Each account has major attractions but also problems, some of which are very famous: for instance, the Will Theory seems to exclude parties who are incapable of controlling duties, such as animals or babies, from being right-holders. One of the deepest problems arises from the fact that we can, through law and social convention, create legal–conventional rights anywhere, with almost any content, whenever we want to do so and are in an appropriate position of law-creating power—and many of these created rights can be morally justified. There are of course some conceptual limits on what law can create: it is doubtful that the colour blue could be a right-holder, or that rubbish bins could hold rights, even if law-makers tried to create rights for these entities. Nonetheless, I think law-makers can create rights for any conceptually appropriate party, just as readily as they can create legal duties for such a party. If this is correct and if, as I believe, rights are duties demandable distinctively on a particular party's behalf (the party who is the right-holder), then such a demandability structure can be justifiably created independently of whether it serves the right-holder's prior interests or independent kind-based desires, or endows the right holder's will with control over others' duties. To deny this—as the Interest, Will, Hybrid and Kind-Desire Theories of rights do—overlooks our ability to create the relevant structure of demandability where we want through law or convention. Further, the demandability structure distinctive of right-holding must be specifically demandability *on the right-holder's behalf*. Many duties can be justifiably demanded by third parties (e.g. regulatory bodies) on behalf of others, and the standard Demand Theory over-inclusively fails to distinguish these cases.

The central point for the moment is that we need an account of legal and conventional rights that respects our ability to create them where we want, but we also need to note—from the previous section —that the strongest case for such creation of legal rules justifiably to take a rights-type form is when our legal and conventional rights specify or operationalize prior pre-legal natural–moral rights. And, in my view, the best account of the latter is as duties grounded morally by the right-holder's good: duties morally generated by a particular party's interests independently of the wider good, in a way that reflects what Rawls calls the 'separateness of persons'. Many theorists dispute this, some by denying the possibility of natural rights altogether,[8] others by seeking to ground natural–moral rights as spheres of freedom morally grounded in the importance of equal freedom.[9] I am sceptical of these views. It seems to me that the distinctive asymmetrical normative relation in which rights consist—one that demands action of a duty-bearer while giving special status to the right holder as a formally passive party—is best accounted for, if found in natural morality, by the Razian idea of a demand springing from the practical importance for the duty-bearer of the right-holder's good. The forthcoming sections are based on these assumptions.

THE CASE FOR NATURAL MORAL RIGHTS SERVED BY INTERNET ACCESS

Suppose the foregoing is correct. Does the individual in the modern world sometimes hold a powerful enough interest in being provided with internet access, or in being able to remain offline, for that interest to work largely on its own to ground duties in others, perhaps including the state, to respect or support it? If so, then this interest will ground a pre-legal moral or natural right. Or alternatively, are there related interests grounding pre-legal natural moral rights in the area, for the serving of which internet access might be among our best chosen (if not unique) means? If the answer to either question is 'Yes', then I will argue that internet access could qualify as a 'human right' if it is also appropriately globally demandable. If the answer to either question is 'No', then whether we should invoke the language of rights will depend on the instrumental considerations—about legal rights with no 'underlying' natural rights—mentioned in the second paragraph of the earlier section titled 'Three ways of justifying rights'.

My view is that there are powerful enough individual interests in the offing to ground pre-legal rights—to legitimate power and political participation—for which internet access is a prominent, especially valuable, but not uniquely necessary means in the modern context. I discuss these interests and the way they ground a human right to internet access here before discussing the values of remaining offline. The case for a right to internet access in the modern world is made by Reglitz. He outlines three fundamental individual interests that, in my view, ground pre-legal moral or natural rights and that in the modern world either require or are powerfully served, in a transformative way, by internet access:

> (a) It is necessary for individuals to meaningfully influence global players who make global rules; (b) In an increasingly global and virtual world, [internet access] is already uniquely effective for the realisation of important political human rights (free speech, free association, and information); and (c) If it would be governed appropriately, [internet access] would be extremely effective in protecting other basic human rights (i.e. life, liberty, and freedom from torture).
>
> (Reglitz 2020: 314–315)

Reglitz argues that these three interests are so important, and the costs of meeting them are so comparatively affordable, that they work to ground what I would call a pre-legal moral or natural right to internet access in the modern world. Reglitz goes on to argue that this right is politically demandable in a way that qualifies it as a *human* right; I return to this idea in a later section (titled 'Human rights as "everyone's business"'). I endorse Reglitz's argument, with the important qualification that I do not think the interests he cites make a right to internet access strictly *necessary*, but rather a strongly advisable social choice. Thus, I do not see internet access as itself a pre-legal natural or moral right, even just in the modern context for appropriately placed people. Instead, I will argue that it would be wise to choose it as our contingent means for respecting certain other pre-legal natural rights: those to do with political participation and legitimacy that Reglitz mentions.

Let us look in more detail at the interests Reglitz outlines; he seems correct in writing as follows:

> The first justification of the human right to free internet access is that without such access many individuals lack a meaningful way to hold accountable supranational rule-makers and to influence supranational institutions. 'Offline' options of lobbying global rule-makers are available, e.g. in traditional forms of non-virtual resistance (such as rallies). However, such protests are by nature 'local' and even such local forms of protest increasingly require internet access to access relevant information, raise awareness, and coordinate action. If individuals lack internet access, they are at a structural disadvantage to global players who negotiate international treaties and laws with the help of internet communication. Moreover, without internet access it

is harder for individuals to stay informed about the issues at stake in supranational negotiations and to effectively organise internationally to hold international rule-makers accountable.

(Reglitz 2020: 318)

In support of this claim, Reglitz notes the centrality of internet protest in contesting negotiation of the Transatlantic Trade and Investment Partnership, and the centrality of such protests against the actions of multinational corporations. We can also focus on related global institutions, including the United Nations' own human rights institutions, as similarly needing to be held to account by the individuals ultimately governed by them (via their control over states) in a way that internet access allows, and offline options do not. Without such access, individuals will be dominated by illegitimate institutions: for their legitimacy, the rules of international trade, the power of multinational corporations, and the agencies of international law all require an inclusive global public sphere to hold them to account, a sphere in which all individuals can, in principle, participate as equals. The internet seems essential to the provision of such a global public sphere.

But, as Reglitz recognizes, many older media also seem to allow individuals to communicate in ways that in principle address everyone globally: publishing a book, joining a demonstration, issuing a pamphlet, or writing a letter to a paper. Such communications could be directed merely at some local audience, but they could also be addressed to everyone, and their mode of production in principle leaves it possible that they could reach anyone, unlike that of an unrecorded public speech or protest, whose direct reach is limited by how many can get close enough to hear or see. But the internet seems at a big advantage compared to all these methods. First, it offers direct, immediate access to a much larger group. Second, participation as a communicator is not subject to the judgements of gatekeeping editors—as in newspaper or book publications. In addition, opportunities for direct response by one's addressees, and thus for dialogue, are much more readily available online.

But we should not pretend that the internet is already a global public sphere. Maybe some of those who remain offline have chosen to do so, and could join the internet public sphere if they wished, but this is certainly not true of all. Further, some class and political stratification by modes of internet communication is discernible, as in newspaper consumption—and there is the problem of echo chambers. In addition, there are internet gatekeepers in place of traditional editors: not just the disembodied algorithms of search engines, but also social media content moderators and state gatekeepers such as the firewall governing internet access in China.[10]

Nonetheless, internet access does seem to be the closest we can get to a global public sphere with contemporary technology. Securing ready and equal access to it, along with further rights to freedom of communication and impartial gatekeepers, will be an important necessary step towards the kind of public sphere required for the legitimacy of international and multinational institutions. A *rights* approach to internet access seems to be justified by this line of argument because each individual has a powerful interest in living under legitimate institutions: an interest sufficient to place any institution that wields power over that person under natural–moral duties to allow them sufficient say in control of that power for that power's control over them to be minimally legitimate. This means that the moral duties that power-wielders are under to provide and support the kind of public sphere necessary for their legitimacy qualify as duties appropriately conceivable in rights terms: duties whose violation counts as a pre-legal or natural wronging of the parties who are, by the violation, denied a say in control over the relevant power.[11]

If the public sphere necessary for legitimate global institutions *uniquely required* internet access, then we would have an argument for a natural moral right to internet access in a world with global institutions. But is internet access strictly *needed* for the relevant public sphere? I return to this question in the next section. Before then, note that I have focused so far on Reglitz's first ground for a right to internet access: as a means for individuals to hold global power to account through what I have called a 'global public sphere'. As Reglitz notes, it is rather unclear how anything other than widespread internet access could constitute such a global public sphere with current technology. By contrast, internet access seems rather *less necessary* for securing the goods at the heart of Reglitz's second and third grounds for internet access rights: these goods are, on the one hand, our fundamental political rights, and, on the other, further human rights, such as the right not to be tortured or the right to food. Reglitz makes a strong case that my having internet access is in the modern context especially effective at ensuring my fundamental political rights and my further human rights (Reglitz 2020: 319–321). In addition to those just mentioned, we could add rights to education, to health (including mental health), to economic freedom, and rights to an environment in which one can engage in romantic relationships, as further fundamental rights well served by the internet, but for which the internet is not strictly necessary.[12]

As noted earlier, the fact that internet access is only an *effective* rather than a strictly *necessary* means to the important goods outlined does not undermine its status as something that, in the contemporary context, we might have a right to: as wisely chosen means to further pre-legal natural rights. For example, as regards our right to political participation, this seems true: political participation—having a say in how one's community is run, and having it in some sense as an equal participant—seems to me an especially important, and especially deep, unavoidable human interest. Even those with no personal interest or aptitude for such participation need to be *able* to participate as equals if they choose to do so. This is, of course, partly because of political participation's relation to the interest already discussed: the interest in living under legitimate power. But the interest in political participation also has an independent life of its own: how we live and act together is absolutely central to each person's well-being (even that of the hermit), even before we turn to questions of legitimacy. I contend that each individual's interest in their own political participation is sufficient to ground duties on others (including the state) to enable such participation, relatively independently of whether this would serve the wider common good.[13] Political participation is therefore a pre-legal moral or natural right for everyone. And in the modern context, internet access seems especially conducive to such participation, largely for reasons already mentioned about the directness of internet participation, the absence of traditional editorial gatekeepers, and the ease of reply.

Tomalty voices a similar argument, focused on freedom of expression and association—though she goes on to deny that it grounds a genuine human right to internet access:

> Exactly what constitutes *adequate* opportunity and ability to exercise one's freedom of expression and association is an important and difficult question; but in view of the tremendous importance of the internet it seems reasonable to hold that to prevent someone from accessing the internet is to deprive her of adequate opportunities to exercise her freedom of expression and association.
>
> (Tomalty 2017)

Tomalty certainly thinks that there is a pre-legal natural human right to freedom of expression and association for which legal rights to internet access are especially important. But she goes on to conclude, tentatively, that internet technology is too likely to be superseded very quickly in its rights-serving role for it to qualify as a human right. Equally tentatively, I disagree with her assessment, and discuss some of her concerns in the next section—but I do endorse her general approach, in which the tightness or looseness of the empirical relation between internet access and deeper needs is central to its status as a human right. Note that in addition to the arguments discussed so far, many of our other human rights also seem to be well served by internet participation, as Reglitz claims (2020: 319–321).

The costs of making internet access a right

The comparatively loose relationship between internet access and the goods that ground a right to it prompts the following questions. Do we want to 'solidify' or 'firm up' the internet as our particular solution to the problems of legitimizing global institutions, securing political freedoms and wider human rights? In doing so, might we unwittingly make it harder to achieve better new technological solutions through the 'path dependency' of having chosen internet access as our means to solve them?[14] Might we even accidentally preserve particular problems to which internet access is the solution—for example, by shoring up global institutions by making them legitimate, and thereby reducing the case for dismantling them?

Note how these problems do not arise for rights to things that are strictly necessary in all realistic contexts for securing unavoidable fundamental goods. In securing a right against torture, we do not thereby unwittingly make it harder to secure alternative torture-involving ways of protecting people from the distinctive pain and destruction of torture—for there can be no ways of protecting you from torture that nonetheless involve torturing you.[15] Similarly, in securing your right to education by teaching you to read, we do not thereby unwittingly make it harder to institute non-educative solutions to your need for literacy. For no non-educative ways of teaching you to read are realistically possible in a world anything like ours.[16]

For less necessary human goods, though, such questions do arise. I worry that if we accept Reglitz's case for a right to internet access, we might rule out alternative ways of securing participation in a global public sphere that do not come with the costs to the individual and society of internet participation. I don't know what these alternative ways might be; I can't imagine them, but this failure of imagination seems just that, a failure of imagination, rather than a bumping up against impossibility, as in the case of trying to imagine non-educative ways of fulfilling the needs that education meets. Nonetheless, this inability to imagine alternative non-internet ways of securing a global public sphere is a reason to think that, in the current context, this worry has rather little force, and that Reglitz's arguments can stand. But we need to be aware of the worry. One thing I can imagine—because history shows the possibility—is the non-existence of the global institutions that generate Reglitz's first case for a right to internet access. Without global institutions, we would not need a global public sphere to legitimate them, even if it would be extremely useful for other purposes.

A rather similar worry strikes me in relation to Reglitz's second and third cases for the right to internet access. These cases observe that internet access is an especially effective way of securing our prior human rights to political participation and the further wide range of human rights (against torture, to health care, and so on). The worry is that even if this is true, institutionalizing internet access as our way of securing these further rights could make it harder for us to be open to alternative technological ways of meeting these rights that have advantages over internet access. Once again, I cannot imagine what these alternative ways will be, and this is why I think the worry does not undermine Reglitz's case. Tomalty disagrees because she is readier to envisage the superseding of internet technology in which it is no longer an effective means to serving human rights—but possibly even an impediment. But I find it hard to imagine this situation.

One response to these concerns would be to retreat to a more general, abstractly specified right—perhaps a right to whatever particular technological access at a time is important to securing the fundamental pre-legal rights that we have identified as crucially served by internet access. Note that very little would be gained by talk of a right to what is technologically *necessary* for respecting the fundamental rights in question, for what is necessary for respect for them is already required by them as rights, independently of talk of a further right to 'what is necessary'. But we might think that a rather general right to what is technologically *important, if not necessary,* for the relevant pre-legal rights would be helpful. I shall not assess this proposal here. It seems to me possibly attractive but also unhelpfully vague. It is consistent with the existence of a more specific right to internet access, and my main focus is on that. But we should note that my case for internet access could, as technology changes, turn into a case for some new technology in ten years' time, for example.

To get clearer about whether there should be specific rights to internet access, grounded in the importance of such access in serving further pre-legal rights (even though the internet is not strictly *necessary* to serve them), we need to think about the costs of the internet approach. Reglitz gives careful consideration to the financial costs of providing the technology in a means-tested way so that those who cannot currently afford it are able to access the internet (Reglitz 2020: 325); he also notes the affordability of removing further barriers, such as literacy. I think we should add to this discussion the non-financial costs to the internet user of this particular way of securing global legitimacy, political participation, and further human rights. One cost is the effect on the human attention span; others include loss of privacy and risks of identity theft and harassment. Another is the creation and magnification of new communities of interest—the famous echo chambers. Another is that the relative ease of participation that makes internet access so attractive for the reasons outlined can also itself be seen as a sort of cost. The great accessibility of public participation makes it harder for an individual to justify retreating from the public sphere; yet such retreat to a low-pressure private sphere for slow, imaginative thinking is often necessary, not only for individual mental health but also for autonomy and the development of the most creative and thoughtful ideas, ideas most valuable in the public sphere.[17]

This last concern about costs reflects a particular feature of the right to internet access, as brought out by Reglitz's first and second defence. This is that—as provider of a public sphere in which global legitimacy can be secured, and in which political participation can be pursued—the right to internet access is a *right protecting fulfilment of a duty*: specifically, a right that makes it more possible for one to fulfil one's duty to hold global institutions to account, and one's duty to participate in political debate. Political participation, and holding power to account, would be very important individual interests even if they were not also duties. But they are nonetheless also duties: duties we owe to our fellow citizens, duties to help fulfil their further right to live under legitimate power.

This right to political participation does not, in my view, entail duties falling on everyone individually: it is not that everyone has to devote much of their energies to political debate and to fighting against abuses by global or local institutions. But the community at large has to do it, and the community's general duty does entail some duties to contribute borne by everyone, and further duties that particular individuals must take on (Cruft 2019: 149–162). This is what I mean by seeing the right to internet access as a right protecting fulfilment of a duty. Rights to education, health care, or life have aspects of this feature too: fulfilling these rights for an individual helps that individual fulfil their duties. But political participation and holding power to account are interests whose importance depends more significantly on their being ways of fulfilling prior duties. If the legitimacy of power did not matter, I would still benefit instrumentally by being able to participate politically and hold power to account; but because legitimacy is very important, my interest in political participation includes a central interest in playing my part within the community's duties to hold power to account.

This point means that we should pay special attention to how instituting a right to internet access would affect our ability to fulfil our duties of political participation. If internet access makes political participation much easier, but at the expense of damaging the quality of our participation, then we might find that the reasons in favour of the right are matched by reasons against. I have some sympathy with this concern, though I do not think ultimately that it succeeds against the right. My sympathy arises from the worry that ease of political participation can result in unthinking hasty participation crowding out more considered positions. I also worry that the very knowledge that one could participate easily can make it harder to foster the kind of safe space for creative utopian thinking that would generate the most imaginatively radical new ideas.[18] But perhaps these concerns just reveal me to be a product of the pre-internet era.

A further worry, arising again from the rather loose connection between internet access and the fundamental interests and prior moral rights it serves, is as follows. Because internet access is, I think, not uniquely necessary as the only admissible way a society can choose to fulfil the rights it serves (rights to be subject to legitimate power, rights to political participation, and further human rights), internet access's status as a right fits the 'third way' outlined in my earlier section, 'Three ways of justifying rights'. The right to internet access is a chosen normative construction, one that we should choose, and one that should take the form of a right because it is our chosen way of meeting underlying pre-legal moral rights. But if internet access is a chosen way of fulfilling more fundamental rights, in that it would have been morally permissible to choose alternative technological solutions to the problems that the internet solves, alternative solutions that similarly provide for a global public sphere with equality of participation, then who is the group that makes this choice? If most societies have already chosen it, we might find that we cannot choose otherwise if we want to fulfil the relevant pre-legal moral rights. But then there will still be some group—perhaps the group who, by joining others, tips the rest of humanity into a position in which they have to choose it if they want their political participation and legitimacy—who it turns out will have been able to make the decision for us. And should they choose it? On balance, in the modern world, I think they, and we, should. But this choice—whether to adopt internet access as our rights-protected means to fulfil important pre-legal rights, and whether to adopt this even as a 'tipping point' that will compel others to follow us—turns on difficult empirical questions about the (unimaginable) alternatives, and about the costs in terms of the stifling of creativity, the dissipating of attention, privacy losses, and other cyber threats, as outlined above. (I agree with Reglitz that the direct financial costs of providing the infrastructure are insufficient to tell against it.)[19]

HUMAN RIGHTS AS 'EVERYONE'S BUSINESS'

Even if internet access readily available for all is, as argued earlier, something that we should choose to institute as a way of giving form to prior natural moral rights, it does not yet follow that it is a *human* right. It should be a *right*, in recognition of the rights-type structure of the moral considerations that ground it. But I follow many theorists in thinking that a human right is more than simply a legal right grounded on pre-legal moral rights. Human rights law makes the *state* (and perhaps other members of the 'international community')[20] the primary bearer of duties correlating with human rights, and hence the primary agent capable of violating them. And many theorists have stressed human rights' political dimension, as rights whose fulfilment is demandable internationally.[21]

There are many rival versions of these statist and international-demandability criteria on something's being a human right. I will not adjudicate between them, but I will note that at least a weak version of such a criterion seems plausible to me, as a matter of how we use the 'human rights' concept. At a minimum, a *human* right must be permissibly morally demandable on the right-holder's behalf by anyone anywhere: with regard to a human right held by any particular person, *anyone* (state or individual) is permitted to demand that it be respected by those for whom it entails duties. The duty-bearer cannot permissibly claim that 'this is none of your business'—in the way that one can with regard to certain other pre-legal moral rights, such as those definitive of romantic relationships.[22]

It seems that the rights to hold power to account, to political participation, and the further human rights that internet access rights are founded upon, are clearly 'public' in the manner just sketched: that is, it seems very plausible to say that, *ceteris paribus*, anyone is morally permitted to demand, on behalf of a given right-holder, that their state provide them with internet access as a means to such account-holding, participation, and other rights. One need not be the right-holder's compatriot, family member, or in any other way related to the right-holder to have the standing to demand that the duty-bearer respect and ensure their political participation—if need be, through securing internet access. One has standing to demand that human rights be respected, simply as a fellow human being alongside the right-holder. States also have such standing to demand this of other states—that they respect and ensure their members' political participation through providing internet access.[23]

This is not to say that military intervention to uphold the right would be justified.[24] But the right is not a 'private' matter between the state and its citizens or within some smaller group. That a right to internet access is morally the business of everyone, demandable by everyone, *ceteris paribus*, qualifies internet access as a human right: it is a *right* because we should choose it as our way of fulfilling pre-legal natural moral rights (to political participation, etc.) grounded on powerful duty-grounding interests, and it is a *human* right because these interests give the right a fundamentally public dimension as everyone's business.

A RIGHT TO REMAIN OFFLINE?

In earlier sections, I suggested that the unimaginability of alternatives that are anything like as effective as universal internet access in serving the important interests (grounding

pre-legal natural moral rights) that Reglitz highlights is, ultimately, strong ground in favour of a right to internet access. But because of its costs to the individual, its optionality,
and the fact that it fixes a particular way as the standard way in which one fulfils one's
duties to hold power to account, it will be important to offer plausible options for those
who wish to remain offline. How far should such provision run? It should certainly be
offered to those who *cannot help* remaining offline, but if internet access is secured for
all, then what about those who *choose* to remain offline?

We do not always feel the need to provide for those who choose permissible
exceptions to standard practices: for example, we do not provide freedom of movement
to those who choose not to wear clothes. So why should we bother offering forms of political participation or other human rights to those who choose not to use our adopted
best effective means—internet access—for achieving these important rights, especially when the people in question are capable of using these means? Perhaps internet
access is different here, partly because its costs are quite high, in terms of the impact
on individual attention, creativity, privacy, and other risks.[25] And the cost of providing
alternatives (e.g. enabling state benefits to be claimed 'offline') is fairly low—partly because we still have in place much infrastructure from the pre-internet age. In addition, it
is sensible to retain these offline options as back-up, in case we lose the internet one day,
even if temporarily (e.g. as a result of a massive cyberattack).[26]

Much turns on empirical questions about these costs. For now, I simply record my
sense that, from a rights perspective, the importance of allowing people to remain offline will depend partly on how 'freely' internet access is made available, but that being
able to remain offline is also significantly important in its own right: even if internet
access is readily freely available, the cost of engaging in it means that there is also a
rights-based case (grounded in the individual's interest) for enabling offline opt-outs.
And this opens a whole new topic: how far important right-grounding interests can justify expensive exceptions to common practices.[27] Even human rights are not absolute,
and can sometimes be justifiably infringed for the greater good—but this cannot just be
when the balance of interests would be best served by ignoring the right. The expense of
allowing people a real option to choosing a life offline (e.g. by not requiring online registration to vote or participate in other ways in society) is, I suspect, one we have to bear
even when everyone has internet access readily available. But to make this case fully
would require a new chapter.

CONCLUSION

In this chapter, I have explained the place I see for rights and human rights within our
moral and legal thinking. I have argued that the interests served by internet access give
us some reason to take this as a human right—not a necessary one, but one that we
should choose as an important and uniquely effective means to fulfilling prior natural
moral human rights in the modern world.

Notes

1. See the discussion at Beitz (2009: 57); Cruft et al. (2015: 6–7); and Tomalty (2017).
2. On Hohfeld's analytical framework, see Wenar (2020: s. 2.1) and Hohfeld (1964).
3. For this claim in relation to games, see Ihara (2004: 11–13); on the idea that environmental legislation can treat animals as 'raw materials for wrongdoing' rather than wrongable beings, see Thompson (2004: 372).
4. I will focus on claim-rights, but the language of rights is also appropriate because Hohfeldian privileges, powers, and immunities capture aspects of our moral relation to internet access. I focus on claim-rights as a core position in the attribution of rights (Cruft 2019: 5–6, 83–84).
5. On this account, promissory rights are not pre-legal or natural—promising is, rather, a case of two-person law-making; its 'directed' structure as *rights*-creating (rather than merely creating *undirected* duties) is nonetheless recognition-independent, reflecting the directed addressive nature of the act of promising (Cruft 2019: 132).
6. See Raz (1986: ch. 7); for defence of Raz's view as an account specifically of natural rights, see Cruft (2019: ch. 7); see also Tasioulas (2015).
7. For a summary comparison, see Cruft (2013); for a fuller treatment, see Cruft (2019: Pt I). See also Wenar 2013 and 2020.
8. Famously Bentham (1987 [1789]).
9. See, e.g. Hart (1955), Steiner (1994) and many Kantian approaches.
10. See, e.g. Moore (2018: 237–241).
11. Note that this would ground a right to 'free' internet access in whatever sense of 'freedom' was needed to ensure that each person had sufficient genuinely realizable opportunity to participate in the global public sphere for that person's duty-grounding interest in the legitimacy of the relevant institutions to be met. This requirement might well be compatible with regulation of internet content and costs.
12. Thanks to Carissa Véliz for pressing me on these further goods.
13. My interest in political participation is important enough on its own to ground duties in others, even though Raz is correct to claim:

   If I were to choose between living in a society which enjoys freedom of expression, but not having the right myself, or enjoying the right in a society which does not have it, I would have no hesitation in judging that my own personal interest is better served by the first option. (1994: 54).

   Despite the greater value of others' participation vis-à-vis my own, my interest in being able to participate through expression myself is nonetheless of duty-grounding importance.
14. Hints of this concern are evident in Tomalty (2017). She writes:

   It is impractical to have international laws that constantly need to be updated. As such, legal human rights not only need to be of great importance now, but also for the foreseeable future. So the lightning-fast pace of technological progress makes the internet, and consequently a legal right to it, much more precarious.

   I see this as partly a concern that a legal human right to internet access could shortly—as technology changes—become an impediment to rather than a support for our pre-legal natural rights.

15. I set aside complicated (and contrived) cases in which torturing you now could reduce your risk of future torture.
16. This is not to deny that our current practices of education close off options for better education, and options for meeting other human rights, for example, to equality of opportunity. (Thanks to Carissa Véliz for this point.) My point in the main text is just that practices which are, at core, educative seem unavoidable for meeting our rights to education. By contrast, the internet is not unavoidable for meeting the right-grounding needs it serves.
17. Thanks to Natalie Ashton for discussion of the importance of what she calls 'epistemic respite', and the difficulty of finding it in the digital age.
18. In the UK academic context, my worry about the pressures of knowing how easily one can access the public sphere in order to do one's duty is akin to a worry about the pressure to show the impact of academic work on wider society: too much such pressure, coupled with ease of access, counterproductively makes more difficult the more imaginative academic work that could have the most impact in the long run.
19. See Reglitz 2020: 325.
20. See the analysis in Lafont (2012), in which she argues that human rights practice takes them to be binding on the 'international community', where this includes—but is not limited to—states.
21. See, e.g. Beitz (2009); Raz (2015).
22. Here I follow Waldron (2018); for a view of human rights that rejects this 'public' requirement and allows, for instance, rights that one's friends not lie to one to qualify as human rights, see Gewirth (1982: 56).
23. This is not to say that such standing is indefeasible: one can sometimes lose such standing by violating rights oneself, and this is one prominent reason why former or current colonizing powers lack proper standing to insist on global respect for human rights.
24. As in over-extreme interpretations of the 'political' conception of human rights in Rawls (1999).
25. Might one say the same about clothes? Costs are high in terms of the relation to social perceptions of body image.
26. Thanks to Carissa Véliz for this point.
27. See, e.g. debates about minority language rights or religious exceptions in multicultural societies.

References

Beitz, Charles R. (2009), *The Idea of Human Rights* (Oxford: Oxford University Press).

Bentham, Jeremy (1987 [1789]), 'Anarchical Fallacies', in Jeremy Waldron, ed., *'Nonsense upon Stilts': Bentham, Burke, and Marx on the Rights of Man* (London: Methuen), 29–76.

Cruft, Rowan (2013), 'Introduction', Symposium on Rights and the Direction of Duties, *Ethics* 123, 195–201.

Cruft, Rowan (2019), *Human Rights, Ownership, and the Individual* (Oxford: Oxford University Press).

Cruft, Rowan, Liao, S. Matthew, and Renzo, Massimo (2015), 'The Philosophical Foundations of Human Rights: An Overview', in Rowan Cruft, S. Matthew Liao, and Massimo Renzo, eds, *Philosophical Foundations of Human Rights* (Oxford: Oxford University Press), 1–41.

Feinberg, Joel (1970), 'The Nature and Value of Rights', *Journal of Value Inquiry* 4, 243–257.

Gewirth, Alan (1982), *Human Rights: Essays on Justifications and Applications* (Chicago, IL: University of Chicago Press).

Gilbert, Margaret (2018), *Rights and Demands* (Oxford: Oxford University Press).

Hart, H. L. A. (1955), 'Are There Any Natural Rights?', *Philosophical Review* 64, 175–191.

Hohfeld, Wesley N. (1964), *Fundamental Legal Conceptions*, ed. Walter.W. Cook (New Haven, CT: Yale University Press) [reprinted from Yale Law Journal 1913 and 1917].

Ihara, Craig K. (2004), 'Are Individual Rights Necessary? A Confucian Perspective', in Kwong-loi Shun and David B. Wong, eds, *Confucian Ethics: A Comparative Study of Self, Autonomy, and Community* (Cambridge: Cambridge University Press), 11–30.

Kramer, Matthew H. (1998), 'Rights without Trimmings', in Matthew H. Kramer, N. E. Simmonds, and Hillel Steiner, *A Debate Over Rights: Philosophical Enquiries* (Oxford: Oxford University Press), 7–112.

Kramer, Matthew H. 2010. 'Refining the Interest Theory of Rights', *American Journal of Jurisprudence* 55, 31–39.

Lafont, Cristina (2012), *Global Governance and Human Rights* (Amsterdam: Van Gorcum).

MacCormick, Neil (1982), *Legal Right and Social Democracy: Essays in Legal and Political Philosophy* (Oxford: Clarendon).

Moore, Martin (2018), *Democracy Hacked: Political Turmoil and Information Warfare in the Digital Age* (London: OneWorld).

Rawls, John (1971), *A Theory of Justice* (Oxford: Blackwell).

Rawls, John (1999), *The Law of Peoples with 'The Idea of Public Reason Revisited'* (Cambridge, MA: Harvard University Press).

Raz, Joseph (1986), *The Morality of Freedom* (Oxford: Clarendon).

Raz, Joseph (1994), 'Rights and Individual Well-Being', in *Ethics in the Public Domain* (Oxford: Oxford University Press), 44–59.

Raz, Joseph (2015), 'Human Rights in the Emerging World Order', in Rowan Cruft, S. Matthew Liao, and Massimo Renzo, eds, *Philosophical Foundations of Human Rights* (Oxford: Oxford University Press), 217–231.

Reglitz, Merten (2020), 'The Human Right to Free Internet Access', *Journal of Applied Philosophy* 37, 314–331.

Skorupski, John (2010), *The Domain of Reasons* (Oxford: Oxford University Press).

Sreenivasan, Gopal (2005), 'A Hybrid Theory of Claim-Rights', *Oxford Journal of Legal Studies* 25, 257–274.

Steiner, Hillel (1994), *An Essay on Rights* (Oxford: Blackwell).

Tasioulas, John (2015), 'On the Foundations of Human Rights', in Rowan Cruft, S. Matthew Liao, and Massimo Renzo, eds, *Philosophical Foundations of Human Rights* (Oxford: Oxford University Press), 47–70.

Thompson, Michael (2004), 'What is It to Wrong Someone? A Puzzle about Justice', in R. J. Wallace, Phillip Pettit, Samuel Scheffler, and Michael Smith, eds, *Reason and Value: Themes from the Moral Philosophy of Joseph Raz* (Oxford: Oxford University Press), 333–84.

Tomalty, Jesse (2017), 'Is There a Human Right to Internet Access?', *Philosophy Now* 118.

Waldron, Jeremy (2018), 'Human Rights: A Critique of the Raz/Rawls Approach', in Adam Etinson, ed., *Human Rights: Moral or Political?* (Oxford: Oxford University Press), 117–144.

Wenar, Leif (2013), 'The Nature of Claim-Rights', *Ethics* 123, 202–229.

Wenar, Leif (2020), 'Rights', in Edward N. Zalta, ed., *The Stanford Encyclopedia of Philosophy*, Spring edn (Stanford, CA: CLSI), https://plato.stanford.edu/archives/spr2020/entries/rights/, accessed 24 January 2022.

PART II

SOCIAL MEDIA AND FREE SPEECH

CHAPTER 5

A NORMATIVE FRAMEWORK FOR SHARING INFORMATION ONLINE

EMILY SULLIVAN AND MARK ALFANO

INTRODUCTION

THE vast majority of what any individual knows depends on chains and networks of testimony stretching outwards socially and backwards temporally. Our knowledge has accumulated over the course of years, decades, centuries, and even millennia. Each talk exchange is an opportunity to extend and enrich this vast testimonial network, which is—with the exception of a few isolated tribes—almost fully connected around the globe. Moreover, since the invention of the internet, both the speed and the fidelity of transmission have increased dramatically. Despite these exciting developments, the epistemology of testimony has made modest progress in addressing its inherently social components. The paradigm case of testimony in the philosophical literature consists of the transmission of knowledge from *exactly one* person to *exactly one* other person, neglecting proximal and (even more so) distal social sources of knowledge. In this chapter, we draw on resources from multiple disciplines to explore the differences among various modes of communication and the social epistemic consequences of these differences. We highlight several key parameters of different testimonial regimes, including *fidelity*, *velocity*, *traceability*, *demoticization*, and *anonymization*. Online communication is characterized by extremely high fidelity, velocity, traceability, and demoticization (where demoticization differs from democratization in referring to increased access of the people to communication networks but not necessarily to any institutional process that would represent or express the general will).[1] For this reason, the epistemic norms that ought to govern online communication may differ in interesting and important ways from the epistemic norms that have traditionally governed other testimonial regimes such as oral tradition, handwriting, and print media. While other norms, such as those protecting people's privacy and tamping down on hate speech, are no doubt important, our focus in this chapter will be on the distinctively epistemic norms that ought to govern the sharing of information online. We believe that this topic has clear ethical and political implications, as illustrated by the weaponization of conspiracy theories to motivate the deadly siege of the US Capitol on 6 January 2021: when people are systematically deceived, for instance by accepting the QAnon conspiracy theory, they are liable to act out in ethically and politically heinous ways.

A BRIEF HISTORY OF TESTIMONIAL NETWORKS

Few philosophers, even in social epistemology, have moved beyond the hearer–speaker dyad. For example, some have considered what it means for *groups* to testify (Tollefsen 2007; Lackey 2015, 2018). And in the philosophy of science, others have started to explore which network structures are conducive to sharing knowledge within idealized communities of scientific researchers through agent-based modelling (Holman and Bruner 2015; Rosenstock et al. 2015; Weatherall et al. 2019; Zollman 2007, 2010). Little attention has been paid to the evaluation of testimonial networks consisting of both experts and non-experts in non-ideal settings. In philosophy, Coady (1992) briefly considers the influence of network structure on the transmission of historical knowledge. However, he does not identify formal network features or structures that are likely to produce epistemic goods (e.g. knowledge, justification, understanding) and avoid epistemic ills (e.g. ignorance, unjustified beliefs, misunderstandings, acceptance of conspiracy theories). More recently, Sullivan et al. (2019, 2020) showed that some online social networks are ill suited to deliver the wisdom of crowds.

Researchers in other fields offer a broader perspective. In sociology, Senturk (2005) addresses the structure of the *hadith* transmission network from Muhammad's contemporaries to subsequent generations. This is arguably the longest extant intergenerational testimonial network of its sort, spanning 610 CE–1505 CE. Senturk shows that participants in this network, known as *huffaz* (roughly 'ones who memorize and protect' *ahadith*), aimed to learn *ahadith* from other *huffaz* with the shortest paths back to the prophet and his companions. In the terminology we use below, this means that the *huffaz* saw themselves as playing the role of epistemic conduits, and that they attempted to minimize the length of epistemic geodesics (minimum number of hops through the network) in the *hadith* transmission network.

In anthropology, Blong (1982) shows that oral legends passed down through generations of Papua New Guineans accurately record a catastrophic volcanic eruption that occurred centuries prior. And in literary studies, researchers have pointed out that bards (like *huffaz*) were professional memorizers and reciters of important pieces of language. Lord (1960; see also Parry 1971) argues that bards and other singers of epic poetry from Homer to the present did not memorize whole poems verbatim. Instead, they memorized themes and formulas (important, memorable phrases that employ a particular rhythmic pattern, for example, 'Ajax with his shield like a wall'), which they creatively recombined in each successive recitation of the epic. Lord contends that the transmission methods associated with oral versus written transmission make an important difference to how language is preserved over time. Essentially, the shift from the spoken to the written word increases fidelity. At the same time, this tectonic shift poses a threat to the creativity of professional memorizers and reciters. And by demoticizing the transition process, writing and mass literacy have the potential to destroy the livelihoods of these professionals.

These processes continued to accelerate with the shift from the written to the printed word after the development of Gutenberg's printing press. Copying errors introduced by medieval monks could be largely eliminated by the use of the printing press, though it did not produce transmittable copies with perfect fidelity. Even more recently, the invention of the internet has made it possible in many cases to quickly and automatically track back a piece of testimony to its original source. At the same time, the unregulated way in which online knowledge is recorded and transmitted has led to a seemingly intractable problem of citogenesis, in which track-backs among dynamic webpages such as Wikipedia entries lead one in a loop rather than back to any genuine original source (Sterzer et al. 2008; Saez-Trumper 2019).

In what follows, we identify several key parameters that describe testimonial networks (e.g. fidelity and demoticization), and how the online information environment is shaped by these parameters, leading to changes in our epistemic responsibilities and which sorts of dispositions we ought to cultivate if we want to promote the spread of knowledge and avoid the spread of error. We then discuss how these parameters could inform individual epistemic norms and institutional norms surrounding information sharing in the online context.

KEY PARAMETERS OF TESTIMONIAL NETWORKS

There are several parameters that can describe information flow in a testimonial network. These parameters range from the speed of information flows to whether the structure of the network creates bottlenecks to information flow. In this chapter, we focus on the following five parameters and their impact on epistemic norms of testimony in the online context:

Fidelity The similarity that message, m', has to the original or transmitted message, m. Fidelity can be understood in terms of semantic, linguistic, or orthographic similarity.

Velocity The speed of message transmission.

Traceability The ease with which it is possible for a receiver of m' to trace m' back to m.

Demoticization The proportion of those in the network who are able to transmit messages. The mechanism that determines who in the network is able to transmit messages.

Anonymization The degree to which the identity of individuals transmitting messages in the network is publicly known to each other member of the network.[2]

Fidelity

As information moves through a network, it can get more or less distorted or noisy along the way (Shannon 1948). Fidelity measures the extent to which noise or decay occurs. The way information is shared, or the medium that information is shared through, can impact the type of information stored and shared. For example, greater processing power allows for sending complex messages that otherwise would have needed to be condensed.[3] As such, technology, along with the type of testimonial network, can impact fidelity. As mentioned above in 'A brief history of testimonial networks', the printing press increased fidelity by eliminating many typographical errors when transmitting messages. Social media platforms increase fidelity even further through their share functions, which create digital copies of the original message.

The content of a message can be more or less similar to the original message both in terms of its semantic content and in terms of its linguistic features. For example, a message may have the same words as another message but have different semantic content, or a message may have different words but express the same semantic content. For example, a message translated into a different language will not have linguistic fidelity but may hold onto its semantic fidelity (and such translation services are increasingly being automated online). Shortened messages can also have semantic fidelity. In the context of online information sharing, messages are broadcast to large numbers of people very quickly. While linguistic fidelity remains high, increased spread allows for context shifting in which the meaning and function of the message evolves as it moves through the network, resulting in semantic fidelity decay while linguistic fidelity remains intact (Sullivan 2019). The epistemic climate on social media platforms, Twitter (now in the process of rebranding to X) in particular, becomes a series of overhearers engaging in context shifting, due in part to short messages, but also due to the sheer number of people that messages can travel through. Linguistic fidelity can be easy to measure with the right tools, but the degree of semantic fidelity is considerably more difficult because the pragmatic context of utterance matters (Lackey 2006). The pragmatic context can sometimes be difficult enough for the average person to identify, and is an especially complicated problem for automated algorithms. As a result, algorithms that aim to filter messages are often trained on linguistic similarity, which can miss important semantic trends and shifts.

It may seem as though increased fidelity in a network makes the network epistemically better than one with decreased fidelity. After all, higher fidelity means less room for miscommunication and misunderstandings. However, sometimes message decay can have epistemic benefits. For example, information decay can be useful in collective systems by disrupting gridlock and promoting cooperation (Shirado and Christakis 2017). There is even evidence in schools of fish that decreased fidelity can prevent the spread of false alarms (Rosenthal et al. 2015). If we take the spread of misinformation and disinformation as a type of false alarm, then perhaps it is the increased fidelity of messages in the online environment that is in part to blame for our current epistemic landscape, in which rumours and misinformation spread faster than truth (Vosoughi et al. 2018, Levy, 'Fake News: Rebuilding the Epistemic Landscape', this volume).

Velocity

Message fidelity is also impacted by *velocity*, that is, how quickly messages are transmitted throughout the network. Testimonial networks found in early human communication involved slow and noisy travel. As a result of a low velocity, information degraded or changed as it moved through the network. For example, early battlefield communication suffered from low velocity, and armies with more efficient means of sending messages had an advantage over their enemy while operating under the fog of war (Clausewitz 1832/1989). The internet affords almost instantaneous transfer of messages. This speed can help preserve message fidelity since there is essentially no time in between the sharing and receiving of a message for the message to change.

Increased velocity not only benefits message fidelity; there are other benefits to the faster spread of messages. In an emergency situation such as a wildfire or flood, the speed with which messages can be propagated can save lives. High-velocity networks also level the epistemic playing field among agents in the network. Information can be powerful, and in a slow-moving network, those who get information first can have advantage over those who receive it later. Thus, a network with increased velocity creates a more egalitarian epistemic environment in some respects.

Increased velocity can also come with epistemic downsides. There is evidence linking high-speed message flow with overwhelming cognitive processes or leading to less accurate decisions (Tversky and Kahneman 1974; Chittka et al. 2009). When there are too many messages coming in quickly, it is not possible for each one to be fact-checked or even paid attention to. There needs to be some mechanism for filtering important messages from unimportant messages. However, left to our own devices, we human beings often rely on 'system 1' processing that relies on heuristics and biases that can lead us astray (Kahneman 2011). High velocity itself also puts pressure on the network not to slow down. This can lead to a lack of due diligence in fact-checking or tracing back the message to authenticate it. Agents may feel rushed in making their decisions on whether to spread a piece of information to keep up with underlying flow trends. Utilizing automated algorithms as a means of filtering information can reduce cognitive overload, but algorithms come with their own biases, which often recapitulate—or even exacerbate—human biases, resulting in systematic bias across the whole network. When individuals in the network filter for themselves, there may be an increased likelihood that individuals introduce message diversity due to different interests and perspectives; however, algorithms run the risk of shutting out important messages entirely.

Traceability

Traceability concerns the ease with which it is possible for a receiver of m' to trace m' back to m. Traceability is important for verifying the accuracy and authentication of messages, contributing to the epistemic health of a network. The more difficult a message is to trace back to its original source, the harder it will be for the message to be assessed on its epistemic credentials. In networks in which there are few actors who are able to transmit messages, especially if the network has low velocity, traceability is likely to be easier to achieve. However, in a high-velocity network in which there are numerous active information-sharers, the thread of a message can get lost in the sea of interconnections (especially when screen-capping, photoshop, blocking, and other technologies enter the scene). Amplification farms that repost content from other pages, either with or without the original source name, have significantly decreased traceability on social media platforms. An increasing number of these amplification farms repost the same content under a different source name, creating the appearance that the content has originated from many places instead of just one (Burke 2018; Nyhan 2019). In regular offline environments, if the same message comes from a variety of sources, that signals its importance and reliability; however, this epistemic heuristic only makes sense if the messages are genuinely sprouting up from independent sources. Increased traceability allows for knowing whether our epistemic heuristics about sources continue to hold true in the current network, or whether they need to be revised in some way.

While social media technology has in many ways hindered traceability, there are possible technological fixes. Introducing technological architectures that authenticate and keep a record of message sharing can increase traceability. For example, blockchain architectures provide an immutable and decentralized ledger with an authentication process. Blockchain is used primarily in currencies and financial transactions such as Bitcoin (Nakamoto 2008). However, the underlying concept of an immutable ledger for message sharing may be attractive for epistemic reasons.

Demoticization

Who in the network is able to transmit messages? How much training/certification is required for someone to be given the ability to transmit messages? Demoticization tracks the proportion of those in the network who are able to transmit messages, and the ease with which they are able to gain this status. Historically, technology has played a role in increasing the demoticization of testimonial networks. The printing press not only increased the fidelity of messages flowing through contemporary testimonial networks, but it also increased demoticization by expanding who could own *and publish* books. However, even though more people could own and publish books, the publishing system was not fully demoticized, since gatekeepers prevented most from getting their books published and would give only certain people or organizations the rights to distribution, limiting access to many.

Social media in turn has created a highly demoticized system of message sharing by eliminating gatekeepers. Accounts can be created in minutes with very little oversight of the content of shared messages. We all now serve as editors, choosing which messages to pass on and influencing the content that those in our immediate network see. The public acting as editor has even begun to bleed over into more traditional media outlets. For example, in 2017 the *New York Times* decided to eliminate their public editor. A public editor acts as a liaison to the public and seeks to uphold ethical journalistic practices at the paper, balancing the interests of the public with the interests of journalists. The *Times* decided that, instead of a public editor, the public itself could directly be the judges of quality and informativeness. Comment boards were opened up and journalists were advised to read these comments to learn how to better do their jobs. While there is still editorial oversight for the content of the paper, it is the public at large who votes on what is worth reading and what is considered newsworthy with their shares and other forms of engagement. Critics argue that this move opens up the *Times* to promoting more click-bait and lower-quality articles (Lind 2017).

As with the other network parameters discussed above, there are epistemic advantages and disadvantages to the increased demoticization of our testimonial networks. A more open system for information sharing allows those from historically disenfranchised groups to contribute to the shared knowledge of the network. It can also increase the diversity of the topics that are discussed. If more people are engaged in content creation and content sharing, then a variety of content should make it through at least portions of the network, since each person has his or her own editorial sense. However, there are also costs to increased demoticization. When everyone is an editor, there is no centralized check or filter to content. This means there can be a flood of disinformation and conspiracy theorizing, since there is no central body fact-checking or eliminating such information. The repercussions of a lack of epistemic oversight is showcased across social media with the increased prevalence of flat earthers and anti-vaccine advocates, not to mention the deluge of misinformation associated with the QAnon conspiracy theory. Importantly, disinformation in a highly demoticized network can come both from bad actors (e.g. spooks, grifters) and those who are well intentioned but lack the required expertise (e.g. aunts, uncles, tech bros on Medium).

Moreover, because of the aforementioned problems stemming from high velocity and the sheer number of messages propagating throughout contemporary networks, along with increased demoticization, the need for message filtering becomes even more pressing. Each individual cannot possibly attend to all the messages in a careful way. Instead of using more traditional gatekeeping methods for quality checks, such as needing to be a member of a professional organization or a newspaper editor, the network relies on other ways of filtering content. For example, celebrities have enjoyed a greater degree of epistemic power in social networks online (Archer et al. 2020), and studies consistently find that the Gini coefficient of the contemporary attention economy is approximately 0.90 (van Mierlo et al. 2016; Quintana et al. under review), a level that would be predictive of revolution if the resource in question were income (MacCulloch 2005). People rely on those whom they trust or are in the public eye to determine what is important information for them. However, celebrities are not necessarily epistemically qualified to determine what is important or truthful (Dennis et al. under review). Again, we see the negative side effects that celebrity power has with regard to the anti-vaccine movement (Freed et al. 2011).

There are other means of filtering messages that rely less on heuristics and shortcuts made by individuals. For instance, filtering algorithms are prevalent on social media platforms. However, the way they work is typically opaque to those in the network. Typically, these algorithms are not optimized to promote truth or other epistemic values, but rather are developed to promote message engagement to drive advertising revenue. Until quite recently, in the face of the COVID-19 pandemic and Donald Trump's promotion of dangerous electoral disinformation, Facebook even went as far as to actively avoid making epistemic decisions on content (e.g. refusing to fact-check political advertisements (Ortutay and Anderson 2020)). Social media platforms do not see themselves as media or news providers but as a social network connectors, akin to the community bulletin board in a café. Unfortunately, given the monopolistic position that social media platforms occupy in our economy, they are unlikely to change their business model on their own. As of the writing of this chapter, just three companies account for nearly 90 per cent of global market share. Facebook alone enjoys 64.22 per cent, plus another 7.05 per cent from Instagram (which Facebook owns). Twitter enjoys 13.96 per cent, and YouTube 3.79 per cent (Alfano and Sullivan forthcoming). Regulation could help by classifying social media companies as news agencies and holding them to the standards that other news agencies face, in regard to fact-checking content, or by forcing them to move away from the current attention-economy business model towards one that is more consistent with epistemic norms.[4] However, notice that any centralized mechanism that restricts the messages within the network cuts down on demoticization. A tension thus exists between epistemic values and network demoticization.

Anonymization

Anonymization measures the degree to which the identity of individuals transmitting messages in the network can be determined by others. It ranges from no anonymization to pseudonymization to full anonymization. Anonymization, as with the other network parameters, has both epistemic upsides and downsides. The upsides are similar to those seen with demoticization. If sources of information or those who merely transmit messages can remain anonymous, then sensitive information, such as whistleblowing, leaking to the press, and behind-the-scenes gossip, can be introduced in the network that might otherwise be kept silent (Alfano and Robinson 2017). People may fear retaliation for spreading certain true information and thus refrain from sharing it, even if they have the ability to do so.[5] Thus, a level of anonymization can improve the epistemic standing of the network by introducing important information that would otherwise never be reported.

The downsides of anonymization also mirror the downsides of demoticization. Anonymization reduces the social costs of producing low-quality information or sharing misinformation. If there is no social risk to transmitting a message, then there is less need to be epistemically diligent. Thus, the removal of filters and a high level of demoticization, coupled with a high level of anonymization, can perpetuate the rapid distribution of false information in a network (Véliz 2019).

Translating parameters into epistemic norms

It should be clear from the previous section that we can consider each network parameter on its own, but they also influence each other in complex ways. Velocity can impact fidelity, anonymization has an impact on traceability and demoticization, and so on. Due to the interconnected nature of these network parameters, we propose a virtue theoretic approach to epistemic norms for online information sharing. However, we should note that this approach does not presuppose that knowledge can be defined or analysed in terms of epistemic virtues, and much of the following could, we suspect, be made compatible with an alternative approach centred on maximizing epistemic goods (consequentialism) or respecting epistemic rights (deontology).

Conduits and epistemic norms

One aspect that is different in epistemic networks that we find online compared to ordinary cases of testimony often considered by epistemologists is that there are more than two testimonial roles. In an ordinary case of testimony, there is the *source* of the message and the *receiver* of the message. We submit that there is a third possible epistemic role, someone simply passing messages across the network, that is, a *conduit*. Conduits pass on information from sources (or from other conduits).[6] Thus, they are not content creators or sources, though they sometimes comment on content that they pass along to others. Moreover, conduits are not mere receivers of information. A receiver of information is someone who listens for incoming messages and perhaps is looking for a specific message, but a receiver need not pass on this information. Conduits, on the other hand, receive messages *and* pass them on (Sullivan and Alfano forthcoming; Sullivan et al. 2020).

The question concerning epistemic norms and the responsibility of online information sharing is largely a question concerning the epistemically responsible or virtuous behaviour of a conduit, where epistemic virtues are understood as whatever dispositions tend to contribute to the acquisition, spread, and maintenance of knowledge while epistemic vices are understood as whatever dispositions tend to undermine the acquisition, spread, and maintenance of knowledge. It is a question about passing information along through the network, not necessarily about content creation or merely being on the receiving end of messages. Thus, our focus here is on the epistemic responsibility of conduits. In the next section, we articulate more institutional norms that can also mitigate some of the epistemic problems of the online information landscape.

Maintaining knowledge in a social epistemic environment requires distinct considerations. First, once we move beyond the speaker–hearer dyad, network structure plays a role in the way information is spread throughout the network. There has been interesting work in agent-based modelling that looks at testimonial network structures at the level of the whole network, suggesting that certain types of structures are epistemically better than others, at least for certain purposes (e.g. Zollman 2007). However, individual agents in the network also need to bear in mind their surrounding network structure in order to be epistemically responsible or virtuous conduits (Sullivan and Alfano forthcoming; Sullivan et al. 2020).

In previous work, we identified three central classes of virtues that are required to be a good epistemic agent in a social network: monitoring, adjusting, and restructuring (Sullivan and Alfano forthcoming). These virtues also apply specifically to conduits within networks on social media platforms concerning when to virtuously share information. *Monitoring* virtues cover what is needed for agents to attend to the structure of their network. It is only through monitoring paths of information flow that one can see whether the sources they are relying on are independent from each other or not. For example, if a piece of information is shared by multiple people in your network, you have prima facie evidence that this information is important and reliable. However, if you trace back the origin of this message to only one original biased source, then the fact that multiple people amplified the message should not increase your confidence in the information. On the contrary, it should make you question whether your network structure has enough independent sources (Sullivan et al. 2020). A conduit blindly contributing to the amplification of information from a single biased source reduces the epistemic quality of the network overall.

One reason for monitoring one's network is so that one can more accurately judge how to calibrate and adjust one's credence in sources and pieces of information, not only in order to adjust belief formation, but also in order to decide when to take on the conduit role and pass the information along. *Adjusting* virtues are those that govern this decision. One specific factor in the decision to become a conduit should be based on how independent your sources are. For those that find themselves in a network structure that relies on only one or two sources, it may be foolhardy to amplify these messages, if there are no countervailing reasons to suspect the information is reliable. As such, monitoring virtues also involve monitoring the epistemic roles and track records of those in the network. Do my sources have a reliable track record, or do they often provide false or misleading information? Are my sources independent, or are they themselves conduits simply amplifying the messages of others? Adjusting virtues in turn govern your sharing behaviour based on this information. In the former case, there is good reason to share information, but in the latter case refraining from passing along the message could be the more responsible action.

Being a responsible or virtuous conduit also means taking action to *restructure* your network if the current one is too severely flawed. This could involve seeking out new sources (especially trusted sources such as established newspapers), no longer listening to sources one had previously trusted, or effecting more distal changes in the structure of the network. Doing this well depends on sufficiently successful monitoring and the motivation and capacity to identify efficient and effective changes that one has the power to enact. It might be that the nature of the network is so far gone that the epistemically responsible thing to do is either remove oneself from the network (Levy 2017) or to no longer engage in the conduit role. Moreover, while in an ideal world conduits would do their epistemic due diligence in developing the dispositions necessary to share information in a epistemically responsible way, in reality it can involve a lot of time and effort, such that only a small number of actors in the network are able to become responsible conduits. This creates a trade-off between demoticization and epistemically responsible agents. If only a small number of actors function as conduits in an epistemically responsible way, then the network cannot be fully demotic and epistemically successful at the same time.

Another feature of online testimonial networks is that epistemic virtues should not just be understood as localized within the individual. As with ethical virtues, epistemic virtues can be *other-regarding* (Kawall 2002; Fricker 2007). After all, the role of the conduit is to pass on information in the network to the benefit or hindrance of others. Other-regarding considerations should both be directed towards specific individuals (e.g. the conduit's inner circle) and the health of the network as a whole. Indeed, there are some things that individuals can do to help mitigate the epistemic problems that come with fidelity, velocity, traceability, demoticization, and anonymization. One of the problems with maintaining fidelity in online networks is that the same message can take on different semantic meanings because of context shifting. One response to this problem is for conduits to refrain from passing along messages that would change the semantic fidelity of the original message when shared in a particular context, and also to refrain from sharing messages with a low level of semantic fidelity to their originals. For example, satirical posts are likely candidates of context shifting. Some people will interpret the message as being informative instead of non-informative.[7] Conduits should take care that they are not sharing a satirical message in a way that could be interpreted by others as informative. Conduits, then, might even have the responsibility to clearly state that the message is not informative. This responsibility can increase for a specific conduit, depending on the position the specific conduit has in the network. Do their messages tend to propagate far through the network? Or do the messages tend to spread only to a few? However, this heuristic regarding *current* network position can only take us so far. The viral nature of platforms means that any message can propagate far through the network even if there was no reasonable indication it would do so beforehand. If a given network has a low level of traceability, then fidelity checks will be hard to perform. In the absence of sufficient traceability, conduits again should think twice about passing along a message without adequately tracing and contextualizing it.

As discussed above in 'Key parameters of testimonial networks', high-velocity networks come with the drawback of eliminating the space for fact-checking and can lead to cognitive overload and poor decisions about what to believe and what to share. Individual conduits can help to mitigate these issues by intentionally slowing down the speed of information flow simply by waiting before sending. A conduit can take time to trace back the message, checking source reliability against an alternative, independent source as a way of delaying. Delaying messages could be especially important for breaking news from unverified sources. Retraction in general can be ineffective (Ecker et al. 2011), especially in online environments. In such environments, conduits have a greater responsibility to get things right the first time, whereas in other social network environments in which retraction is effective, delaying messages might not be as important.

Due to the high level of demoticization on social media platforms, conduits need to take their role as public editor seriously. They should work to cultivate virtues that are conducive to responsible filtering. For example, not giving celebrity voices undue epistemic power and making sure that the expert voices amplified are actually experts in the specific topic of the message seems prudent. Even though social media platforms are egalitarian in terms of how message sharing operates (i.e. everyone shares a message in the same way), these platforms are not egalitarian in terms of epistemic power (as illustrated by the Gini coefficient of the attention economy mentioned above in the section on 'Demoticization'). People who are seen as celebrities or experts have much more influence on others, with more weight attached to the messages they share. Moreover, those in the network whose messages are more likely to spread far throughout the network because of their network position have more epistemic power. Following up on sociological work by Conway and Oreskes (2010), network simulations have shown that a determined propagandist in a testimonial network is often capable of shifting the opinions of many others (Weatherall et al. 2019). So even in the absence of a centralized system that controls epistemic power in online networks, unequal power structures can emerge. Conduits should do well to monitor these power relations and do what they can by choosing which messages they share in a way that would distribute epistemic power along epistemic lines instead of perpetuating epistemically poor patterns of information flow.

Institutional norms

Many of the problems associated with the network parameters discussed in the section on 'Key parameters of testimonial networks' cannot be solved merely by individuals developing conduit virtues. Change must be made on an institutional level in the form of regulation, oversight, education, and developing new technological tools to mitigate some of the problems. Rini (2017) likewise argues that individual epistemic dispositions and virtues are inadequate to address the problem of misinformation, and that targeting the structure of epistemic institutions such as social media platforms is necessary.

It is the design of social media platforms themselves that can play a role in perpetuating false and misleading information. Platforms play an active role in perpetuating some of the network parameters discussed in this chapter in a way that hinders epistemic goals. The functionality that allows immediate and quantifiable social feedback through likes and shares can amplify the velocity of sharing and works to prioritize certain types of content. For example, Brady et al. (forthcoming) discuss the propensity of sharing morally charged content and Vosoughi et al. (2018) discuss the propensity of people sharing news that tends to inspire fear, disgust, and surprise, which is often associated with false news. This problem is exacerbated by another common feature of social media platforms: displaying the number of times an article has already been shared by others. Research suggests that people are up to seven times more likely to share content online when they see others are already doing so (Bakshy et al. 2015). Platforms are also known to delay the like and share count of particular posts to give the appearance of continued engagement throughout the day (Morgans 2017). This has the added benefit that users check the platform more regularly.

Social media platforms are also designed to encourage as many connections as possible (Arfini et al. 2018), which means that any time an individual shares something it will be spread further than if the connections were more limited. In network simulations of highly connected networks, failures of epistemic competence are demonstrated (Hahn et al. 2020), along with bandwagoning effects (e.g. O'Connor and Weatherall 2019; Zollman 2007). While individual epistemic dispositions matter for sharing information online, several of the problems with social media platforms come from the conflict between financial goals and our various normative goals (Zuboff 2019). For example, Alfano and Sullivan (forthcoming) argue that social media platforms are natural monopolies, which explains the business models of these companies and the reluctance to adapt to growing ethical and epistemic concerns (though the recent banning of Donald Trump from the vast majority of social networks may signal a welcome, if inadequate, change).

In the remainder of this section, we articulate institutional changes affecting the five network parameters discussed in the section 'Key parameters of testimonial networks', with the hope of mitigating some of the problems with online information sharing. Recall that one of the problems with message fidelity in online environments is that semantic fidelity is hard to measure and yet can change rapidly in a highly connected and high-velocity network. Automated algorithms, if developed to identify semantic fidelity, may help to mitigate this problem. However, since algorithms can be biased, these algorithms should be subject to oversight. Users of the platforms should have some understanding of how information is flagged and filtered. Regulatory agencies should have access to algorithms to oversee whether they respect privacy and protected classes. Social media platforms also have a responsibility to track linguistic similarity. Sometimes small changes to the words of a message can alter meanings, giving the message, at first glance, the appearance of being reliable even if it was changed to represent a falsehood. As of this writing, we are not aware of any pressure on social media platforms to track message fidelity.

The central problem arising from high-velocity networks is that they can overwhelm cognitive processes and leave little room for fact-checking and proper gatekeeping. Again, there are institutional changes that could mitigate these issues. For example, platforms already engage in altering the actual timeline of posts, likes, and shares. However, they engage in these delaying tactics in order to increase engagement and their profit margins. Delaying messages that are indicative of rumours or false and misleading information could help to reduce the spread of such problematic messages. The delaying tactic could be implemented while the platform is able to engage in more direct fact-checking or authentication. It is important to note, though, that fact-checking can be difficult during emergencies and with developing stories. Care must be taken when engaging in delaying tactics that vital life-saving information is not delayed. Furthermore, content moderation in general is not an easy problem to solve. A recent report found that content moderators for Facebook often end up believing the very conspiracy theories they are meant to screen (Newton 2019). Moreover, the working conditions for moderators is poor, with workers suffering from post-traumatic stress disorder (PTSD), given the type of content they need to screen. Developing labour regulations around content moderation is an important first step to any acceptable solution.

Traceability is also an important issue in large, interconnected networks. Social media platforms have well-known problems with amplification and troll farms that distort where a message originated from. If platforms were able to make progress on fidelity, it could come with gains in traceability. Moreover, more vigilant oversight of amplification and troll farms could help to remove bad actors from the network. Given the monopolistic character of these platforms, such oversight might need to come from regulatory agencies and not simply be done internally by the company. Another avenue for a technological solution, as mentioned above, could include the introduction of an immutable ledger that would keep track of messages and how they changed. Including an authentication mechanism to the ledger could also make strides towards identifying amplification farms.

Above, in the section on 'Demoticization', we discussed how highly demoticized networks remove some gatekeeping mechanisms. In highly connected and high-velocity networks, some form of filtering or gatekeeping is necessary. Without a centralized mechanism, individuals will use their own heuristics, which may not be epistemically virtuous. For example, celebrities have large amounts of epistemic influence on social media platforms. Platforms also contribute to promoting content by allowing sponsored posts and advertising. For example, on Instagram, advertising can go unnoticed because so-called influencers are paid behind the scenes to promote a product, which gives a misleading impression to other users. Even though everyone in the network has the same ability to post and share information, severe power imbalances emerge. Not everyone in the network has equal access to amplification. Amplification algorithms are designed with the platform's business model in mind. Requiring social media platforms to be transparent about their amplification methods and classifying social media companies as news agencies, forcing them to move away from the current attention-economy business model, would be a start to mitigating these issues.

Finally, consider anonymization. Some level of anonymization is desirable in any epistemic network because it creates the environment for information to be shared that might not otherwise be shared (e.g. whistleblowing). However, allowing unlimited anonymous or pseudonymous accounts can degrade the epistemic quality of the network due to the lack of reputational risk. Véliz (2019) suggests a variety of approaches to pseudonyms that could ensure that reputation still does its essential work. One such suggestion is for people to have a certain number of pseudonyms that are traced by a third party in the event of either ethical or epistemic misconduct. How to best handle trade-offs between the freedom and epistemic benefits of anonymization, while still securing reputational accountability, is a difficult problem. One thing is clear, though: there need to be institution-wide solutions that go beyond shutting down one troll or bot at a time.

CONCLUSION

In this chapter, we identified five network parameters that can be used to describe online testimonial networks: fidelity, velocity, traceability, demoticization, and anonymization. We explored the epistemic benefits and drawbacks of increasing each of these measures. We then used these insights to help inform individual and institutional epistemic norms for online information sharing. In the case of the individuals, we focused on what it would mean to be an epistemically virtuous *conduit*, that is, someone who takes on the role of message passing in a social network. In the case of institutional norms, we identified that social media platforms could institute institution-wide changes in order to combat false and misleading information. However, given their business structure and profit motive, it seems that such institutional changes need to come from regulation.

NOTES

1. Thanks to an anonymous reviewer for suggesting that we switch from speaking of democratization to speaking of demoticization. While the word is a bit cumbersome, we find that it better expresses the ideas articulated in this chapter.
2. While other network parameters may also be important for norms of testimony, for the purposes of this chapter, we restrict our scope to focusing on the five identified here.
3. See Szathmary and Smith (1995) for an example from biology.

4. Companies can be quite motivated to spend a lot of resources monitoring content if there are commercial interests at stake. For example, tracking copyright infringement is not seen as burdensome, even though it takes considerable resources and technical sophistication.

5. An example of retaliation for whistleblowing might be seen in the developing case of three doctors mysteriously falling out of windows in Russia after speaking out about the medical conditions there surrounding COVID-19 (Ilyushina 2020). URL <https://edit ion.cnn.com/2020/05/04/europe/russia-medical-workers-windows-intl/index.html>. Accessed 1 October 2021.

6. The line between a conduit and a source is not always clear-cut. If a conduit substantially changes a message before sending it along, then the conduit could also be considered a source. In this chapter, we stick to cases of conduits that do not intentionally change the messages they receive.

7. See, e.g. https://literallyunbelievable.tumblr.com/, accessed 11 August 2021.

References

Alfano, M., and Robinson, B. (2017), 'Gossip as a Burdened Virtue', *Ethical Theory and Moral Practice* 20, 473–482.

Alfano, M., and Sullivan, E. (forthcoming), 'Online Trust and Distrust', in Michael Hannon and Jeroen de Ridder, eds, *Routledge Handbook of Political Epistemology* (London: Routledge).

Archer, A., Cawston, A., Matheson, B., and Geuskens, M. (2020), 'Celebrity, Democracy, and Epistemic Power', *Perspectives on Politics* 18(1), 27–42.

Arfini, S., Bertolotti, T., and Magnani, L. (2018), 'The Diffusion of Ignorance in On-Line Communities', *International Journal of Technoethics* 9(1), 37–50.

Bakshy E., Messing, S., and Adamic, L.. (2015), 'Exposure to Ideologically Diverse News and Opinion on Facebook', *Science* 348, 1130

Blong, R. J. (1982), *The Time of Darkness: Local Legends and Volcanic Reality in Papua New Guinea* (Washington, DC: University of Washington Press).

Brady, W., Crocket, M., and Van Bavel, J. (forthcoming), 'The MAD Model of Moral Contagion. The Role of Motivation, Attention and Design in the Spread of Moralized Content Online', *Perspectives on Psychological Science*.

Burke, T. (2018), 'How America's Largest Local TV Owner Turned Its News Anchors Into Soldiers in Trump's War on the Media', *Deadspin*, https://theconcourse.deadspin.com/how-americas-largest-local-tv-owner-turned-its-news-anc-1824233490, accessed 11 August 2021.

Chittka, L., Skorupski, P., and Raine, N. E. (2009), 'Speed–Accuracy Trade-offs in Animal Decision Making', *Trends in Ecology & Evolution* 24(7), 400–407.

Clausewit, C. (1832/1989), *Vom Kriege [On War]* (Princeton, NJ: Princeton University Press).

Coady, C. A. J. (1992), *Testimony: A Philosophical Study* (Oxford: Oxford University Press).

Conway, E., and Oreskes, N. (2010), *Merchants of Doubt* (London: Bloomsbury).

Dennis, M., Alfano, M., and Archer, A. (under review), 'The Uses and Disadvantages of Celebrity for Pandemic Response.

Ecker, U. K., Lewandowsky, S., Swire, B., and Chang, D. (2011), 'Correcting False Information in Memory: Manipulating the Strength of Misinformation Encoding and Its Retraction', *Psychonomic Bulletin & Review* 18(3), 570–578.

Freed, Gary L., Clark, Sarah J., Butchart, Amy T., Singer, Dianne C., and Davis, Matthew M. (2011), 'Sources and Perceived Credibility of Vaccine-Safety Information for Parents', *Pediatrics* 127(1), 107–112.

Fricker, M. (2007), *Epistemic Injustice: Power and the Ethics of Knowing* (Oxford: Oxford University Press).

Hahn, U., Hansen, J. U., & Olsson, E. (2020). Truth tracking performance of social networks: How connectivity and clustering can make groups less competent. *Synthese*, 197, 1511–1541.

Holman, B., and Bruner, J. P. (2015), 'The Problem of Intransigently Biased Agents', *Philosophy of Science* 82(5), 956–968.

Ilyushina, M. (2020). Three Russian doctors fall from hospital windows, raising questions amid coronavirus pandemic. *CNN*. url = < https://edition.cnn.com/2020/05/04/europe/rus sia-medical-workers-windows-intl/index.html >. Accessed 1 October 2021.

Kahneman, D. (2011), *Thinking, Fast and Slow* (London: Macmillan).

Kawall, J. (2002), 'Other-Regarding Epistemic Virtues', *Ratio* 15(3), 257–275.

Lackey, Jennifer (2006), 'The Nature of Testimony', *Pacific Philosophical Quarterly* 87(2), 177–197.

Lackey, Jennifer A. (2015), 'A Deflationary Account of Group Testimony', in Jennifer Lackey, ed, *Essays in Collective Epistemology*. (Oxford: Oxford University Press), 64–94.

Lackey, J. (2018), 'Group Assertion', *Erkenntnis* 83(1), 21–42.

Levy, Neil. (2017), 'The Bad News About Fake News.' *Social Epistemology Review and Reply Collective* 6(8), 20–36.

Lind, D. (2017), 'The New York Times Is Getting Rid of Its Public Editor for Exactly the Wrong Reasons', Vox, https://www.vox.com/2017/5/31/15719278/public-editor-liz-spayd-new-york-times., accessed 11 August 2021.

Lord, A. (1960), *The Singer of Tales* (Cambridge, MA: Harvard University Press).

MacCulloch, R. (2005), 'Income Inequality and the Taste for Revolution', *Journal of Law and Economics* 48(1), 93–123.

van Mierlo, T., Hyatt, D., and Ching, A. (2016), 'Employing the Gini Coefficient to Measure Participation Inequality in Treatment-Focused Digital Health Social Networks', *Network Modeling and Analysis in Health Informatics and Bioinformatics* 5(32), 1–10.

Morgans, J. (2017), 'Your Addiction to Social Media Is No Accident', Vice News, https://www.vice.com/en_us/article/vv5jkb/the-secret-ways-social-media-is-built-for-addiction, accessed 11 August 2021.

Nakamoto, S. (2008), 'Bitcoin: A Peer-to-Peer Electronic Cash System'. *Decentralized Business Review*.

Newton, C. (2019), 'The Trauma Floor', *The Verge*, https://www.theverge.com/2019/2/25/18229 714/cognizant-facebook-content-moderator-interviews-trauma-working-conditions-ariz ona., accessed 11 August 2021.

Nyhan, B. (2019), 'Americans Trust Local News. That Belief Is Being Exploited', *New York Times*, https://www.nytimes.com/2019/10/31/upshot/fake-local-news.html, accessed 11 August 2021.

O'Connor, C. and Weatherall, J. (2019), *The Misinformation Age*. (New Haven, CT: Yale University Press).

Ortutay, B., and Anderson, M. (2020), 'Facebook Again Refuses to Ban Political Ads, Even False Ones', *AP News*, https://apnews.com/90e5e81f501346f8779cb2f8b8880d9c, accessed 11 August 2021.

Parry, M. (1971), *The Making of Homeric Verse: The Collected Papers of Milman Parry*, Ed. A. Parry (Oxford: Oxford University Press).

Quintana, I. O., Klein, C., Cheong, M., Sullivan, E., Reimann, R., and Alfano, M. (under review), 'The Evolution of Vaccine Discourse and Communities on Twitter during COVID-19'.

Rini, R. (2017), 'Fake News and Partisan Epistemology', *Kennedy Institute of Ethics Journal* 27(S2), 43–64.

Rosenstock, S., Bruner, J., and O'Connor, C. (2015), 'In Epistemic Networks, Is Less Really More?', *Philosophy of Science* 84(2), 234–252.

Rosenthal, S., Twomey, C. R., Hartnett A. T., Wu H. S., and Couzin I. D. (2015), 'Revealing the Hidden 732 Networks of Interaction in Mobile Animal Groups Allows Prediction of Complex Behavioral Contagion', *Proceedings of the National Academy of Sciences* 112(15), 4690–4695.

Saez-Trumper, D. (2019), 'Online Disinformation and the Role of Wikipedia', https://arxiv.org/abs/1910.12596, accessed 11 August 2021.

Senturk, R. (2005), *Narrative Social Structure: Anatomy of the Hadith Transmission Network, 610-1505* (Stanford, CA: Stanford University Press).

Shannon, C. E. (1948), 'A Mathematical Theory of Communication', *Bell System Technical Journal* 27(3), 379–423.

Shirado, H., and Christakis, N. A. (2017), 'Locally Noisy Autonomous Agents Improve Global Human Coordination in Network Experiments', *Nature* 545(7654), 370–374.

Sterzer, M., McDuff, P., and Flasz, J. (2008), 'Note to File—the Challenge of Centralized Control Faced by the Intelligence Function in Afghanistan', *Canadian Army Journal* 11(2), 96–100.

Sullivan, E. (2019), 'Beyond Testimony: When Online Information Sharing Is Not Testifying', *Social Epistemology Review and Reply Collective* 8(10), 20–24.

Sullivan, E., and Alfano, M. (forthcoming), 'Vectors of Epistemic Insecurity', in Ian James Kidd, Heather Battaly, and Quassim Cassam, eds, *Vice Epistemology: Theory and Practice* (London: Routledge).

Sullivan, E., Sondag, M., Rutter, I., Meulemans, W., Cunningham, S., Speckmann, B., et al. (2019), 'Can Real Social Epistemic Networks Deliver the Wisdom of Crowds?', in T. Lombrozo, J. Knobe, and S. Nichols, eds, *Oxford Studies in Experimental Philosophy*. (Oxford: Oxford University Press), 29–63.

Sullivan, E., Sondag, M., Rutter, I., Meulemans, W., Cunningham, S., Speckmann, B., et al. (2020), 'Vulnerability in Social Epistemic Networks', *International Journal of Philosophical Studies* 28(5), 731–753.

Szathmary, E. and Maynard Smith, J. (1995), 'The major evolutionary transitions.' *Nature* 374, 227–232.

Tollefsen, D. (2007), 'Group Testimony', *Social Epistemology* 21(3), 299–311.

Tversky, A., and Kahneman, D. (1974), 'Judgment under Uncertainty: Heuristics and Biases', *Science (New York, NY)* 185(4157), 1124–1131.

Véliz, C. (2019), 'Online Masquerade: Redesigning the Internet for Free Speech through the Use of Pseudonyms', *Journal of Applied Philosophy* 36(4), 643–658.

Vosoughi, S., Roy, D., and Aral, S. (2018), 'The Spread of True and False News Online', *Science* 359, 1146–1151.

Weatherall, J., O'Connor, C., and Bruner, J. (2019), 'How to Beat Science and Influence People: Policymakers and Propaganda in Epistemic Networks', *British Journal for the Philosophy of Science* 71(4), 1157–1186.

Zollman, K. J. (2007), 'The Communication Structure of Epistemic Communities', *Philosophy of Science* 74(5), 574–587.

Zollman, K. J. (2010), 'The Epistemic Benefit of Transient Diversity', *Erkenntnis* 72(1), 17.

Zuboff, S. (2019), *The Age of Surveillance Capitalism: The Fight for a Human Future at the New Frontier of Power* (New York: Profile Books).

CHAPTER 6

FAKE NEWS

Rebuilding the Epistemic Landscape

NEIL LEVY

INTRODUCTION

BEGINNING around 2014, new technology enabled the resurgence of an old phenomenon: the widespread dissemination of fabricated news stories. Partially fabricated stories were characteristic of the 'yellow journalism' of the late nineteenth century, and even such heroes of American history as Benjamin Franklin and John Adams deliberately faked news stories (Parkinson 2016). Franklin, for example, produced a fake issue of a real American newspaper, in order to embed a story about native Americans having been employed by the English crown to scalp innocent people on a mass scale. Franklin disseminated the fake issue and succeeded in having the invented story reported in a number of (real) newspapers.

This sordid episode in American history has multiple contemporary echoes, from the indifference to truth and the racism it manifested through to its success in gaining a measure of legitimacy by having the story reported by a number of reputable sources. Even the medium, the copying of a real Boston newspaper, echoes the way in which contemporary purveyors of fake news mimic the layout of more reputable media outlets and often use a URL that suggests legitimacy (e.g. 'news-cnn.com', intended to borrow the legitimacy of the real *Cable News Network* (*CNN*)). But contemporary fake news has a prevalence and a reach that Franklin or William Randolph Hearst could only dream of. Fake news on Twitter, for example, may reach people faster and spread further than real news (Vosoughi et al. 2018). Produced and disseminated by hundreds of individuals motivated by advertising dollars or directly paid for, amplified by dupes, bots, and a number of media outlets indifferent to truth and eager to swing debates (Benkler et al. 2018), fake news is no longer an episodic phenomenon or one that typically has little influence. It has been credited with swinging the Brexit referendum (Grice 2017) in the United Kingdom and the 2016 election of Donald Trump in the United States (Gunther et al. 2018).

Its significance makes a response to it an urgent political and social priority. Fake news also confronts us with a range of ethical issues. A full ethical assessment of the significance of fake news and of possible responses to its rise would need to cover a number of problems and possible solutions. Distinct ethical issues arise with regard to the individual user, networks of users (e.g. friends), social media companies, and the individuals and institutions that regulate them. Even if we focus on just one element of this complex web, say, the individual user, there are a number of different problems to consider. Is the consumption or the sharing of fake news the manifestation of a vice (and, if so, which vice)? Is the behaviour blameworthy, and, if so, what kind or kinds of blame (epistemic, prudential, moral ... and each of these fractionates in turn) are at issue? Is sharing fake news permissible when it is explicitly tagged as such? And so on.

In this chapter, I focus on issues centred around the effects of fake news on what we might call our epistemic environment. By 'epistemic environment', I mean those features of the social and institutional world that influence us in our belief formation in a way that is *general* with regard to the content of the belief formed; that is, I am not concerned with the features of our environment that allow us to form beliefs about, say, cats—like the presence or absence of cats in our vicinity—but with features of that environment that allow us to generate accurate beliefs in general, or at least across a range of domains. Forming accurate beliefs is essential for our flourishing because we can make good decisions only in the light of accurate information. For instance, I can satisfy my hunger only if I know which stuff in my environment is edible and how it can be procured and prepared. If my epistemic environment is unfavourable (for instance, if it contains predators who mimic food, or liars who seek to mislead me with regard to which items are palatable), then I will find it difficult to satisfy my hunger.

In this chapter, I argue that fake news corrupts our epistemic environment in a way that has not been widely appreciated. Fake news often leaves us epistemically adrift. Rather than believing the false narratives it spreads, we find ourselves sceptical of all narratives. I will argue that the epistemic corrosion induced by fake news may usefully be understood as the result of bringing about what I will call a flattening of the epistemic landscape, constituted by the loss of cues to credibility; this flattening, in turn, can be understood as a loss of higher-order evidence. I will then propose possible responses to the flattening of the epistemic landscape and evaluate their ethical permissibility.

WHAT IS FAKE NEWS AND SHOULD WE BE CONCERNED BY IT?

Much of the current philosophical literature on fake news aims at defining it. *News* is, roughly, reporting of purported facts of broad interest about the world. *Fake* news would seem to be news that is not true (Gelfert 2018). But lack of truth does not seem sufficient for (apparent) attempts at reporting to qualify as fake news (Jaster and Lanius

2018). Donald Trump loves to characterize *CNN* and *The New York Times* as 'fake news', but even when these media organizations get things wrong (as, of course, they do from time to time), they do not count as fake news. Equally, *The Onion* and other satirical newspapers do not count as fake news.

Instead, what distinguishes fake news from genuine is at least in part its aim. Fake news purveyors either seek to deceive—aiming to convince audiences that the world is, in some respect, different from how it actually is—or they are indifferent to the truth because they are motivated almost entirely by financial considerations. Frankfurt (2009) famously defined 'bullshit' as assertion made without regard to truth. Several philosophers have suggested that fake news is closer to bullshit than to lies: its purveyors are often indifferent to truth, rather than seeking to deceive. For Mukerji (2018), fake news is dissimulated bullshit: it is bullshit that is passed off as news. Of course, people's intentions are hidden, and we might disagree about the intentions of a particular person or organization. However, attention to the *processes* whereby stories are generated helps to settle such disputes. Real news is produced following certain journalistic norms for truth-seeking and reporting; fake news ignores these norms (Pepp et al. 2019).

Of course, reputable news organizations (or individual reporters at such organizations) sometimes seek to deceive too, and are almost always motivated in part by financial considerations. The difference is one of degree, with the most reputable media organizations being very much more sensitive to truth (either because they care about its value or because their business model depends on a high reputation for credibility) than are typical purveyors of fake news. For instance, Donald Trump's favourite example of fake news, *The New York Times* is given a reliability score of 47 by the respected *Ad Fontes Media* organization, while *Fox News* cable TV is given 23, *Breitbart* 20.5 and *Infowars* 12. Whatever their motivation, reliable news organizations use a process that leads to significantly more reliable reports than those who aim to deceive or are indifferent to the truth.

Several philosophers have pointed to a current lack of clarity over the nature of fake news, and the way in which the accusation may be weaponized against any report that the person who uses the charge does not like, to argue that we should drop talk of fake news altogether (Coady 2019; Habgood-Coote 2019). Coady compares 'fake news' to 'conspiracy theories', noting that the latter term has been used to dismiss theories simply on the grounds that they postulate a conspiracy, even in the face of plentiful evidence that conspiracies have been, and continue to be, powerful forces in history. There is, however, an important difference between the two. The accusation that something is 'just a conspiracy theory' points to an uncontested feature of a purported explanation—that it postulates a conspiracy—to downgrade its epistemic standing. The fact that this move has powerful rhetorical force might indeed be a reason to avoid talking about conspiracy theories (though, as my own use of the term below indicates, I do not believe the argument to show that, all things considered, we are better off without it). But the accusation that something is fake news just labels it. It does not constitute an argument of any sort. If we were to succeed in banning the label, those who want to reject stories would use a different label: it's propaganda, it's lies, it's rubbish (Brown 2019). The only thing we would have accomplished is to remove a reminder that unreliable claims are more prevalent today than in the past.

Further, opponents of the term exaggerate the extent to which there is disagreement over the nature of fake news, and therefore the extent to which it may be contested for nefarious purposes (Brown 2019). Coady (2019) and Habgood-Coote (2019) provide us with a salutary reminder that in politically sensitive arenas like this one, theorists have a special obligation to take care to ensure that they do not inadvertently provide tools for those who aim to spread disinformation or to take advantage of it. But they do not provide a strong reason to reject the term 'fake news' altogether.

The importance of an unpolluted epistemic environment

A favourable epistemic environment is important for many reasons; here, I am especially concerned with its political significance. An unpolluted epistemic environment is important to the proper functioning of democracies. In democracies, voters are given the power directly or indirectly to decide the most important policy issues that face the nation: how much taxation there will be and how it will be spent, whether the country will pursue peace or war, whether it will protect human rights or violate them, and so on. While a great deal of ink has been spilled on the democratic deficit (the numerous ways in which actual democracies and their institutions fall short of the principle that important decisions should be subject to democratic deliberation), it is indisputably true that well-functioning democracies leave many decisions subject to some degree of democratic control. But for democratic control to be exercised responsibly and effectively, voters must be adequately informed. For instance, they must have a basic understanding of the direction in which different parties would take the country, if not of the details of the policies they would implement (see Brennan (2016) for a summary of evidence that we tend to fall very short of the latter). Such an understanding requires a favourable epistemic environment.

In recognition of the importance of the epistemic environment to a decent life, most countries have a range of laws that aim to minimize what I have elsewhere called epistemic pollution (Levy 2018a). Epistemic pollutants are features of the epistemic environment that (accidentally or by design) make it difficult to form accurate beliefs. For example, a soft drinks manufacturer may deliberately give its product a name and a label that mimics a well-known brand, making it more difficult to distinguish its product from the familiar one, or a purveyor of expensive and unproven 'miracle cures' for terminal illnesses might pay a diploma mill to give them a spurious accreditation and a predatory journal to publish their 'research', thus gaining an aura of scientific respectability and lowering the guard of those who are desperate. Legislative countermeasures include trademark laws, which reduce the capacity of the unscrupulous to mimic familiar brands, and laws against deceptive advertising. Beyond the law, institutional responses to epistemic pollution include the accreditation of universities by organizations set up for that purpose and formal and informal mechanisms for distinguishing reputable academic journals from disreputable ones. Yellow journalism declined as journalism professionalized and was able to self-regulate (Benkler et al. 2018). But contemporary fake news is produced anonymously, circulates outside traditional channels, and is able to mimic real news. It escapes these attempts at environmental clean-up.

If fake news is an environmental pollutant, what are its effects on consumers and on the epistemic landscape more generally? It is to these questions that I turn next.

FAKE NEWS AND FALSE BELIEF

The obvious epistemic worry about fake news is that it is a pollutant of the same general kind as deceptive advertising. Though as we saw, fake news need not be motivated by an intention to deceive, it nevertheless largely consists in false claims. The obvious ill effect of such claims is an increase in false beliefs. Since adequate information is essential to the functioning of democratic decision-making, fake news is bad—on this model—because it leads people to have false beliefs.

This concern has some merit. Almost certainly, some people are sometimes taken in by fake news, and sometimes for long enough for this to have a consequential effect on their behaviour. For instance, the person who infamously fired three shots at Comet Pizza while investigating claims that it contained dungeons where children were abused by leading members of the Democratic Party (Siddiqui and Svrluga 2016) clearly believed (or had a significant credence) that nefarious activities were taking place there. Similarly, a number of Sandy Hook 'truthers'—conspiracy theorists, who allege that the mass shooting was a false flag operation—have subjected parents who lost children at the elementary school not only to online trolling, but also to threats delivered in person (Robles 2016). This pattern has been replicated with survivors and relatives of survivors of other mass shootings (Raphelson 2018). Moreover, people often *report* that they believe fake news. For instance, approximately one-third of Americans report believing the 'Birther' conspiracy theory, according to which Barack Obama was not born in the United States (Uscinski and Parent 2014).

However, there is strong evidence that surveys like these overestimate the true extent of belief in fake news. It is important, first, to recognize that survey responses are often constructed on the spot: rather than report their pre-existing beliefs, people generate an answer to a question they may never before have considered (Zaller and Feldman 1992). As a consequence, surveys may play a role in *producing* the beliefs that they report. Respondents answer the question they are asked not only by bringing to mind prior beliefs, but also by using (often partisan) heuristics or motivated reasoning ('Do I believe Hilary Clinton gave uranium to Russia in return for donations to the Clinton Foundation? That sounds like the kind of thing she'd do, so I will answer yes'). They may not be confident of the answer they report, and it may be forgotten by them soon after-wards (alternatively, they may continue to believe it, but only because they were asked by the survey).

Moreover, there is direct evidence that a significant proportion of responses are the product of *expressive responding* (Berinsky 2017)—when people give a response, not to report their beliefs, but to express support for a policy, party, or person. Thus, people may report '*I believe that Hilary Clinton gave uranium to Russia*' not because they be-lieve that she did but because they want to express their dislike of her (Bullock and Lenz 2019). The most persuasive demonstration that expressive responding plays a significant role in response to questions like these comes from a recent paper by Schaffner and Luks (2018). They took advantage of the then current controversy over crowd sizes at Trump's inauguration to conduct a study. Members of the Trump administration had claimed, falsely, that the crowd had been the biggest ever (notoriously, Kellyanne Conway introduced the phrase 'alternative facts' in defending these claims). Schaffner and Luks gave participants photographs of the crowds at Obama's inauguration in 2009 and at Trump's and asked, simply, which photo depicted a bigger crowd. They relied on the fact that the controversy was current to ensure that many participants would recognize the photos, and hypothesized that this knowledge would affect their responses. This hy-pothesis proved correct: while only a very small proportion of non-voters and Clinton voters picked the photo of the Trump inauguration as depicting the larger crowd (3 and 2 per cent, respectively), 15 per cent of Trump voters picked the photo of his inaugur-ation as depicting a larger crowd.

Since the crowd at the Obama inauguration was very obviously bigger than the crowd at the Trump inauguration, it is not plausible that Trump voters genuinely believed that the photo they chose depicted a larger crowd. It is far more plausible that they were engaged in expressive responding: in choosing that photo, they expressed their support for Trump. This evidence dovetails with other data which suggests that some responses to polls are expressive, rather than veridical reports of beliefs. There is evidence that incentivizing accuracy reduces the partisan gap on survey responses. For instance, while Republicans and Democrats often report diverging beliefs about factual matters like the unemployment rate, in ways that reflect partisan biases (e.g. they assess the economy as worse when the president belongs to the opposite party), incentivizing accuracy leads to a substantial decrease in bias in these reports (Bullock et al. 2015; Prior et al. 2015).

The evidence concerning the *extent* of expressive responding remains mixed. Schaffner and Luks argue that the 15 per cent figure likely underestimates the extent of expressive responding: some participants would have been unaware of the controversy and it is likely that even some of those who were aware failed to recognize the photos or grasp their relevance to the controversy. While Bullock et al. (2015) succeeded en-tirely in eliminating partisan response using a mix of methods, Berinsky (2017) found little evidence of expressive responding using time (i.e. more rapid completion of the study) as an incentive. Taken together, however, the evidence strongly suggests that a substantial number of people report attitudes that do not reflect their real beliefs when they recognize an opportunity to express support for a political position by reporting a different attitude. The extent of expressive responding may be larger than is suggested by the decrease in partisan response produced by incentivization: monetary incentives may offer more extreme partisans an opportunity to send a stronger signal of support. Such partisans may be resistant to incentives of the kind that experimenters can afford to provide.

No doubt some people come to believe the fake news they read, and some maintain their belief long enough for it to guide their actions. But we should be very careful not to exaggerate the extent to which this phenomenon occurs. While our fellow citizens may claim to believe a range of things that are very implausible (e.g. that the Clintons have had people who might have revealed their corruption assassinated, or even more bizarre fantasies), many of those who report such beliefs are engaged in some mix of trolling and expressive responding. Insofar as it succeeds in duping some people, for some time, fake news is epistemically polluting, but it has ill effects beyond that, and these ill effects may be much more serious.

FLATTENING THE EPISTEMIC LANDSCAPE

Up until now, I have been using the metaphor of the epistemic environment. Let me now introduce a new metaphor. There are many sources of information in our epistemic environment. We accord greater credibility to some than to others. Think of more credible sources as rises in the epistemic landscape. Those sources to which we assign a great deal of credibility are peaks. Those we regard as just as likely to be wrong as right represent the ground level in the landscape. There may be depressions, or even valleys: they are sources that are more likely to be wrong than right (and which we can therefore utilize as sources of information by raising our credence in the negation of what they assert). These sources of information may be individuals or institutions (your mother; the American Medical Association; Fox News) non-human animals (you may think the flight of crows foretells the future, as the Romans apparently did, or perhaps you learn about the onset of spring from the song of the cuckoo), and so on. Whatever the source, the greater the credibility appropriately given to it, the higher the peak in the epistemic landscape it represents.

Peaks in the epistemic landscape are absolutely central to the proper functioning of our epistemic agency. We cannot evaluate each and every claim for ourselves. Some claims we cannot evaluate because they are reports about events far from us, in time or space, and we cannot check for ourselves. Others we cannot evaluate because we lack the expertise. It is important to emphasize that the epistemic labour of human beings is, and always has been, *distributed* across multiple agents (Levy 2019a; Levy and Alfano 2019). For the entire history of our species, we have been dependent on one another for knowledge: we have always lacked the expertise to evaluate all the knowledge claims circulating in our group, and crucial to our flourishing, for ourselves. Because epistemic labour is distributed and because we rely on one another for reports about distant times and places, we are epistemically dependent on testimony. Most of what we know, we know because we have been told. But we can rely on testimony only if we have cues on the basis of which to filter it. There are multiple competing sources of testimony in the epistemic environment. Given that we encounter many competing claims we cannot evaluate for ourselves, we rely on cues to credibility to distinguish reliable from unreliable reports; that is, we depend on the peaks and troughs of the epistemic landscape for much of our knowledge. The most serious effect of fake news may be its pernicious effects on this epistemic landscape.

In their analysis of the effects of fake news on the 2016 presidential election, Benkler et al. (2018) find little evidence that fake news explains the Trump victory by itself. Russian fake news was effective only because it was amplified by a right-wing media ecosystem that had two characteristics: (a) it was and is relatively self-contained; and (b) it was already engaging in tactics similar to those of the new Russia-based fake news. This media ecosystem was and is self-contained in that consumption patterns on the right involve sampling from fake news and an ecosystem centred on Breitbart and similar unreliable sources, with little sampling from more reliable sources, whereas consumption patterns on the left are broader-ranging and include more reliable mainstream media sources. At least as importantly, this ecosystem pursued much the same aim as Russian fake news: disorientation, rather than inducing false belief (note that this claim provides further support for the view that fake news is closer to bullshit than to lies).

Even prior to the Russian initiative, the right-wing media ecosystem produced and echoed conspiracy theories and similarly unbelievable claims about the Sandy Hook mass shooting, false flag operations and the like. These bizarre claims are not designed to be believed. They are designed to disorientate. As Benkler et al. argue, these claims:

> seem so ludicrously implausible that it is difficult to imagine that they are in fact intended to make people believe them, rather than simply to create a profound disorientation and disconnect from any sense that there is anyone who actually 'knows the truth.' Left with nothing but this anomic disorientation, audiences can no longer tell truth from fiction, even if they want to. They are left with nothing but to choose statements that are ideologically congenial or mark them as members of the tribe. And in a world in which there is no truth, the most entertaining conspiracy theory will often win
>
> (Benkler et al. 2018: 37)

Disorientation is produced not by bizarre claims on their own, but by the fact that they are apparently taken seriously by those with epistemic standing. Infamously, Alex Jones's *Infowars* show promoted the Sandy Hook conspiracy (Associated Press 2019). But it is not only unreliable (though relied upon) sources that appear to take them seriously. Major newspapers devote considerable attention to such conspiracies, in an attempt to debunk them, and may thereby inadvertently lend them a degree of legitimacy.

Of course, were the claims so obviously ludicrous that no one could possibly believe them, they would not produce disorientation. Those conspiracy theories and bizarre theories are not designed to be believed, but they are not entirely unbelievable (for their target audience) either. They occupy a penumbra of plausibility. There is a large body of experimental evidence showing that much of what we accept we do not really under-stand. From evolution (Shtulman 2015), to how zippers work (Rozenblit and Keil 2002), to the basics of the political processes (Brennan 2016), our opinions frequently fail to be backed up by even basic understanding. This kind of ignorance is probably adaptive: it allows for better and more flexible deference to epistemic experts (Levy 2018b). But it also leaves us epistemically vulnerable. We cannot be brought to believe just anything; we filter messages for plausibility (Mercier 2017). But something need only be plaus-ible enough, and widely promulgated enough, to be taken seriously enough to produce disorientation (in his chapter in this volume, 'Privacy in Social Media', Andrei Marmor describes another way in which social media might blur the boundary between fact and fiction, which may contribute to disorientation).

Disorientation seems to be a primary goal of propaganda aimed at Russians them-selves by state-linked agencies. For example, Russian state media reported as fact a var-iety of conflicting explanations for the downing of Malaysia Airlines Flight 17, without attempting to reconcile them. Flight 17 was brought down by the Americans to frame Russia, *and* it was brought down by accident in a failed attack on Vladimir Putin's pri-vate jet, *and* it was brought down by Russian forces who knew that it was not a scheduled passenger plane at all. Benkler et al. (2018: 36) quote Peter Pomerantsev's observa-tion that these conflicting narratives do not aim to convince viewers of some state-sanctioned narrative, 'but rather to leave them confused, paranoid, and passive—living in a Kremlin-controlled virtual reality that can no longer be mediated or debated by any appeal to "truth"'.

The era of fake news is sometimes described as a 'post-truth' age. To the extent to which we live in such an age, the flattening of the epistemic landscape is part of the cause. Insofar as fake news succeeds in disorientating us, it renders all sources of information suspect. An explanation of an event, or even the report that some event occurred, is rap-idly countered by another, which decries the first as fake news, and it in turn is countered by yet a third narrative. Those who have lost contact with, or trust in, the mainstream media no longer have a means of choosing between these narratives. In this environ-ment, expressive responding can reign: if agents have no way of adjudicating between narratives with regard to their truth values, then why not choose to repeat and assert belief in the best—most congenial—story? Here, the best story is likely to be the one that casts oneself and those with whom one identifies in the best light and one's opponents in the worst.

Suppose this analysis is on the right track. How should we respond to the problem of fake news? In a recent paper, Regina Rini put forward a similar diagnosis of the problem of fake news and proposed a response (Rini 2021). In an earlier paper, Rini (2017) had argued that the best response to the spread of fake news is tightening up online norms of assertion: if we were to eliminate the ambiguities surrounding posts, for instance (is reposting endorsement or not?) we would be able to hold one another to account for spreading fake news and people would exercise more care to check veracity before posting or sharing a post. She is now pessimistic about this response, in part because she believes that, given that people use social media for diversion, they cannot be expected to have an appetite for epistemic care. Rather than advocate the strategy she now calls *disarming* the threat (by changing testimonial norms), she now advocates nothing less than *detonation*: we should become universally sceptical about claims made on social media, according them no credibility at all.

In effect, Rini embraces the flattening of the epistemic landscape that (she herself argues) has been a major consequence of the advent of fake news on a large scale. She sees this flattening as relatively less threatening than I do, I suspect, because her diagnosis has as a central element one feature about which I remain agnostic. She suggests that a principal effect of the dissemination of fake news is a decrease in the trust citizens have in one another because each of us knows that many of our fellow citizens are vectors for the spread of lies. As she suggests, trust is essential to the functioning of democracies, so if this is the case, the worry is serious. So far, there does not seem to be much evidence that fake news is contributing to any such decline, but the claim is plausible. If a corrosive decrease in trust is really a consequence of seeing one another as vectors for the spread of misinformation, then her solution may succeed in arresting it. While I may come to distrust you because you spread lies, I will not come to distrust you because you spread articles from *The Onion*. The difference is that in the latter case, but not the former, I do not see you as purporting to provide information about the world. If we detonate, and see all claims made on social media as akin to the presentation of links to *Onion* articles, we will not come to distrust one another on account of our social media content.

While arresting the decrease in trust would be beneficial, Rini's solution leaves unaddressed the more narrowly epistemic problems on which I have focused. We need not only a certain level of trust in one another to function as democratic citizens, but also reliable information about the world and our own society, and about the options that face us as democratic deliberators. If there is a response to fake news available that would not require us to sacrifice so much in the way of epistemic value for the sake of trust, we ought to embrace it.

In any case, I am sceptical that Rini's detonation strategy would succeed. Social media is used routinely to make assertions. People report the daily events of their lives (*that I have a new job; that it's my youngest's first day at school; that I am on holiday in Majorca*) and they report their opinions (*that Boris Johnson will not solve the UK's problems; that this product is better than that*). Making these assertions is a major function of social media, and we cannot expect people either to desist from making them or to come to make them, or to receive them, as fictions akin to an *Onion* article. Moreover, social media is now a very large source of straight news: indeed, Americans who have social media as their primary source of news outnumber those who rely on newspapers (Shearer 2018). For the detonation strategy to succeed, either people would have to cease using social media for these purposes (which seems unlikely), or they would have to be selectively sceptical. I do not see any way in which people can reasonably be expected to adopt the sceptical attitude to the right set of claims; indeed, I am sceptical that there is any way to demarcate potentially fake news from either straight news or from routine assertions we make on social media about our lives.

Fortunately, there is an alternative to both detonation and disarming (of the sort Rini envisages). Developing this alternative will require a different way of conceptualizing the epistemic landscape.

FAKE NEWS AND HIGHER-ORDER EVIDENCE

One way to understand the corrosive effects of fake news on our epistemic environment is through the frame of higher-order evidence. First-order evidence is evidence that directly bears on the truth or falsity of a particular proposition. The pattern of blood spatter in the room is evidence that the killer used a knife; the fingerprints on the light switch are evidence that the killer was the butler. Higher-order evidence is evidence about our evidence. In epistemology, the main focus of debates about higher-order evidence has been the reliability of the agents who assess the evidence: in particular, on how disagreement can constitute a source of higher-order evidence—if someone who I have good reason to believe is just as reliable as me disagrees with me, I have some reason to reduce my confidence (see Matheson, 2015 for discussion). But different sorts of higher-order evidence are equally epistemically significant.

Higher-order evidence is ubiquitous. We routinely modulate the credibility we give a claim by reference not (only) to its content, but also to its source or its context because source and context provide us with indispensable higher-order evidence. Content matters, of course. If you are feeling unwell and someone diagnoses you with Dutch elm disease, you probably will not be convinced (if you know that Dutch elm disease is exclusively a disease of trees). But source and context matter independently of content. If someone were to tell you, more plausibly, that you have Lyme disease, you would probably be more convinced if your informant had a medical degree than if he or she were an accountant. The degree constitutes higher-order evidence for the content of the claim. Context matters too: if you hear that someone with a Ph.D. in a branch of medicine gave a talk at the local sports club, claiming that the new flu vaccine is dangerous, you will probably be less worried about getting the vaccine than if you hear that he or she gave the talk at the local university (and more worried still if the university is an especially prestigious one). The platform itself provides higher-order evidence in favour of the content of the claims made (Levy 2019b).

So-called newspapers of record used to be widely regarded as credible by both left and right. Today, trust in mainstream media is declining across the spectrum, but more markedly on the right than the left (Verma et al. 2018). Declining trust in the mainstream media can be modelled as a flattening of the epistemic landscape: where there were peaks, there are now hillocks, or a plain, or for some people, perhaps, even a valley (perhaps there are some individuals for whom the fact that *the New York Times says p* is a reason to think not-p; for most people, it is plausible to think, credibility has not been reduced all the way to zero, let alone below zero). At the same time, trust in fake news has increased for the same individuals who have lowest trust in mainstream media. That is, at any rate, a reasonable inference from the fact that as trust in mainstream media has declined on the right, trust in fake news has risen (Verma et al. 2018). For these people, the epistemic landscape is very much flatter than was previously the case. To put it another way, they have fewer sources that both produce, and are seen by them to produce, strong higher-order evidence for their beliefs.

It might be objected that introducing the language of higher-order evidence adds nothing to our understanding of the epistemic environment, over and above what the language of peaks and valleys enabled. In fact, the new terminology is useful because it emphasises *evidence*, and a focus on evidence enables a clearer understanding of the ethics of responding to the problem of fake news. In brief: whereas intervening to change the heights of features in an epistemic landscape might reasonably be thought to be unacceptably paternalistic (i.e. treating competent adults in an infantilizing way by making decisions on their behalf), intervening to produce evidence, or to remove misleading evidence, cannot reasonably be thought to be unacceptably paternalistic. Understanding the epistemic landscape in terms of higher-order evidence gives us a better sense of the *permissible* options we have to respond to the problem of fake news.

It is paternalistic to substitute one's own judgement for that of another. This kind of paternalistic substitution is warranted under certain conditions—when the person is temporarily or permanently unable to make the decision for themselves (it is not paternalistic to make decisions for young children, in spheres in which they lack the competence to decide for themselves)—but paternalism with regard to competent agents, within the sphere of their competence, is widely seen as unacceptable. Control of the epistemic environment might be seen as epistemic paternalism (or authoritarian). For instance, suppressing arguments against the consensus view on evolution might improve people's epistemic position (for, after all, the consensus view on evolution is true), but it nevertheless might be seen as infantilizing people. While epistemic paternalism is sometimes acceptable (Ahlstrom-Vij 2013), embracing it is a cost to any theory in terms of plausibility and the extent to which it can be expected to win over people.

If, however, peaks in an epistemic landscape are appropriately thought of as providing higher-order evidence, then certain ways of controlling the epistemic environment might not count as epistemically paternalistic. Elsewhere, I have argued that there are grounds for refusing certain speakers a platform on the basis that provision of a platform generates higher-order evidence in favour of the claims speakers make, or even claims with which they are associated, and we should avoid generating misleading evidence (Levy 2019b). Analogously, there may be good reasons to control the epistemic environment, to the extent to which doing so avoids generating misleading higher-order evidence and instead generates reliable higher-order evidence.

It is not paternalistic to avoid the generation of misleading evidence. While it may be paternalistic to prevent people from hearing the claims of creationists for themselves, it is surely ethically (and epistemically) permissible to deny creationists the opportunity to generate *higher-order evidence*—that is, misleading evidence of its credibility—in favour of their views. Indeed, we do this routinely: for instance, a university administration which learns that a faculty member intends to give a talk on a controversial topic might take steps to ensure that he or she is not taken to represent the university. One reason, of course, is to dissociate the university from the content of the views, but another is to ensure that he or she is not given the credibility that comes through association with the university. Whether or not he or she is taken to speak *for* the university, the fact of being a faculty member *of* the university is higher-order evidence for the credibility of his or her views (especially, but not only, when speaking within the realm of his or her expertise) and a disclaimer from the university reduces the strength of this higher-order evidence. Just as it is not paternalistic to take steps to stop the generation of higher-order evidence, it is not paternalistic to generate higher-order evidence. Were the university to have the speaker introduced by the Dean, the speaker's claims would be seen to be endorsed, and the higher-order evidence thus generated would lend the claims added credibility.

Similarly, we may permissibly act to suppress (what would otherwise be) misleading higher-order evidence. Suppose you have invited a guest speaker to address your students in an auditorium. Half an hour before she is due to speak, you notice that the backdrop includes a banner left over from a previous event, sponsored by the prestigious National Academy. Of course, you do not act paternalistically if you remove it (in fact, you may have a duty to remove it because the society may not want to be associated with the event and, in any case, you do not have their consent to being linked to it). In removing it, you suppress what would otherwise be misleading higher-order evidence in favour of the speaker's claims. Such suppression of misleading evidence is surely acceptable: while it might be epistemically paternalistic to suppress evidence that already exists, there is no duty to ensure that it exists. (If there were such a duty, how could we act on it, given that the space of implied claims is indefinitely large?)

Just as it is not paternalistic to act to avoid the generation of higher-order evidence, it is not paternalistic to ensure that reliable higher-order evidence is generated. You surely do not act paternalistically if you swap the National Academy banner for another that displays the insignia of the sponsoring society. You might thereby be generating higher-order evidence (of a different kind and strength) in favour of the speaker's claims, insofar as your new banner implies endorsement of him or her and recognition of his or her credentials. It is unsurprising that it is not paternalistic either to avoid the generation of misleading higher-order evidence or to act to ensure that reliable higher-order evidence is generated, since higher-order evidence is evidence, and it is not paternalistic to avoid generating misleading evidence (for instance, to carefully check one's sources before one publishes an article) or to take care to generate reliable evidence (by trying to assert only claims that are warranted, for instance).

The flattening of the epistemic landscape brought about by fake news represents the loss of sources of good-quality higher-order evidence. Because higher-order evidence is evidence, we have good reason to respond by rebuilding the peaks and troughs of the epistemic landscape, ensuring that we have reliable cues for credibility. Such a response is (ceteris paribus, of course) ethically permissible: at least it is not unacceptably epistemically paternalistic, so if it meets other tests for permissibility, it is, all things considered, permissible.

Of course, it is much easier to say that we ought to restore the epistemic landscape than actually to do it. How can we ensure that there are, and are known to be, reliable sources of higher-order evidence, which can orientate people in this landscape? How can we combat fake news?

RESTORING THE TOPOGRAPHY

The problem represented by fake news can only be understood from a multidisciplinary perspective. It is at once a problem (or a set of problems) for political science, media studies, sociology, computer science, law, and philosophy, and other disciplines besides. Responding to the problem, too, requires a multidisciplinary approach, and philosophers may need to take a back seat in this arena. Nevertheless, in this section I will venture a suggestion.

If the analysis above is on the right track, there is an urgent need to restore peaks to the epistemic landscape. We should aim at an epistemic environment in which people can safely weight the credibility of various sources of competing claims. This is no small task in a fractured epistemic environment, in which trust in all sources is falling. We face a bootstrapping problem: how can we bring people to trust a source or sources when we can expect them to be sceptical of any claim we might make that such and such a source is credible? It is easier to destroy trust than to restore it, and especially hard to restore it when there are few sources left taken to be credible to which we can appeal.

I suggest we start small. We might aim to establish a stock of claims that will be accepted as common knowledge across the political spectrum. Insofar as that is the aim, starting small is more or less built in: the more expansive the set of claims, the more contested some of them will be, and if some are contested, the reliability of the stock as a whole will be under threat. One way to establish this stock is by inaugurating a fact-check website staffed by people with a broad and representative range of political biases. Unlike existing fact-check websites, which aim to keep up with current events and check a wide variety of facts (and whose credibility accordingly suffers partisan attacks), this new site would accredit a small number of facts—at least initially, until a sufficient degree of trust has been restored. Each accredited fact would be checked by a panel of experts, with diverse political allegiances (that, too, would limit the number and range of facts that could be accredited). All claims up for reasonable (perhaps even unreasonable) political debate would fail this bipartisan check and therefore would not receive accreditation.

While this project is limited in its ambition, it would be able to play a role in re-establishing a common reality, which would then serve as an accepted background for political debates. A number of claims that are regularly denied in fake news would be accredited: *that Barack Obama was born in the United States; that the Sandy Hook shooting took place and twenty-six people died; that the Mueller Report neither exonerated President Trump nor provided actionable evidence of collusion.* Other claims, which we might like accredited (on the grounds that the evidence in their favour is overwhelming) might be denied accreditation: for instance, right-wing fact-checkers might refuse to accredit *'climate change is human-induced and a serious threat'* (our 'white list' must, in any case, be extremely conservative in what it accepts, to avoid a reduction in its broad credibility). However, we should expect them to agree to accredit *'the vast majority of experts believe that climate change is human-induced and a serious threat'*, and that would be significant epistemic progress (only 42 per cent of Americans recognize that the vast majority of climate scientists accept this consensus view (Hahn et al. 2016) and there is evidence that this false belief plays an important role in the rejection of the science (S. L. van der Linden et al. 2015; S. van der Linden et al. 2019)).

If we succeeded in establishing a broadly credible fact-checking site (ideally, funded by backers with diverse partisan leanings), we would have taken an important step towards rebuilding an epistemic landscape in which we safely place our trust in some sources. Such a stock of common knowledge could be expected to radiate out: other sources of information would have to conform their claims to it or lose credibility. One result might be that some sources come to be seen as troughs in the epistemic landscape, insofar as they make claims inconsistent with the local peak. Others would, of course, adapt, limiting their false claims to those on which the fact-checking site is silent. Perhaps in so adapting, they would limit and eventually undermine the usefulness of the common stock of claims. Perhaps the panel would rapidly come to be seen as partisan by one or both sides and would lose credibility. I propose the panel as an experiment worth undertaking, with some realistic chance of establishing a common, albeit narrow, reality for at least some period of time. Other proposals, in particular proposals by those with greater expertise in policy and in media than I have, would be welcome. We may need to experiment with a variety of options to slow the erosion of peaks in our epistemic landscape.

We cannot solve the problem of fake news—of restoring the topography—in one step, or any time soon. But establishing a common stock of claims would be an important first step. Over time, we can expect the stock to expand. Eventually, we may hope, reference to this single peak may play a role in restoring a variegated epistemic landscape, in which there are a number of competing sources of information in which people can reasonably trust.

CONCLUSION

In this chapter, I have suggested that fake news is epistemically corrosive, insofar as it brings about a loss of higher-order evidence. Given that we are epistemically limited beings who are pervasively dependent on testimony for much of our most important knowledge, the loss of higher-order evidence leaves us epistemically adrift. It threatens our capacity to make good decisions and thereby threatens the foundations of democracy.

I have suggested that we ought to respond to the problem of fake news by restoring peaks to the epistemic landscape. I have (tentatively) ventured a more specific proposal for how this might be done: by establishing a fact-checking site that would accredit those claims that could pass the test of bipartisan fact-checking. I argued that while the range of such facts would be much narrower than we might like, it might constitute an important first step toward restoring a more complex epistemic landscape, in which we are able to trust a variety of competing sources.

Obviously, the suggested response is sketchy. It remains to be seen whether it is practical and whether it would have a significant enough effect on our epistemic environment to warrant the effort it involves. Perhaps there might be more effective ways to restore the epistemic landscape: those with expertise in other areas might identify problems with my proposal that I have not seen and put forward better alternatives. Perhaps it is too late: trust in one another and in a common epistemic world has been lost to such an extent that neither bipartisan fact-checking nor any other restorative project can succeed, even on the (initially) small scale suggested here. Once trust is lost, it hard to restore: the time to start is therefore *now* (since we cannot start yesterday).[1]

NOTE

1. I am grateful to Carissa Véliz and an anonymous reviewer for helpful comments. Work on this paper was supported by grants from the Australian Research Council (DP180102384) and the European Research Council ERC (Grant number 819757).

REFERENCES

Ahlstrom-Vij, Kristoffer (2013), *Epistemic Paternalism*. (Houndmills, Basingstoke, Hampshire; New York: Palgrave Macmillan).

Associated Press (2019), 'Conspiracy Theorist Alex Jones Ordered to Pay $100,000 in Sandy Hook Case', *The Guardian*, 31 December. https://www.theguardian.com/us-news/2019/dec/31/alex-jones-pay-sandy-hook-conspiracy-theory

Benkler, Yochai, Faris, Robert, and Roberts, Hal (2018), *Network Propaganda: Manipulation, Disinformation, and Radicalization in American Politics* (Oxford; New York: Oxford University Press).

Berinsky, Adam. J. (2017), 'Telling the Truth about Believing the Lies? Evidence for the Limited Prevalence of Expressive Survey Responding', *Journal of Politics* 80(1), 211–224, doi: https://doi.org/10.1086/694258.

Brennan, Jason (2016), *Against Democracy* (Princeton, NJ: Princeton University Press).

Brown, Étienne. (2019), '"Fake News" and Conceptual Ethics', *Journal of Ethics and Social Philosophy*, 16/2, doi: https://doi.org/10.26556/jesp.v16i2.648.

Bullock, John G., Gerber, Alan S., Hill, Seth J., and Huber, Gregory A. (2015), 'Partisan Bias in Factual Beliefs about Politics', *Quarterly Journal of Political Science* 10(4), 519–578, doi: https://doi.org/10.1561/100.00014074.

Bullock, John G., and Lenz, Gabriel (2019), 'Partisan Bias in Surveys', *Annual Review of Political Science*, 22/1, 325–342, doi: https://doi.org/10.1146/annurev-polisci-051117-050904.

Coady, David (2019), 'The Trouble with "Fake News"', *Social Epistemology Review and Reply Collective*, https://social-epistemology.com/2019/10/07/the-trouble-with-fake-news-david-coady/, accessed 11 August 2021.

Frankfurt, Harry G. (2009), *On Bullshit* (Princeton, NJ: Princeton University Press).

Gelfert, Axel (2018), 'Fake News: A Definition', *Informal Logic* 38(1), 84–117, doi: https://doi.org/10.22329/il.v38i1.5068.

Grice, Andrew (2017), 'Fake News Handed Brexiteers the Referendum—and Now They Have No Idea What They're Doing', *The Independent*, 18 January http://www.independent.co.uk/voices/michael-gove-boris-johnson-brexit-eurosceptic-press-theresa-may-a7533806.html

Gunther, Richard, Beck, Paul A., and Nisbet, Erik C. (2018), 'Fake News Did Have a Significant Impact on the Vote in the 2016 Election: Original Full-Length Version with Methodological Appendix'. Working paper. https://cpb-us-w2.wpmucdn.com/u.osu.edu/dist/d/12059/files/2015/03/Fake-News-Piece-for-The-Conversation-with-methodological-appendix-11do ni9.pdf

Habgood-Coote, Joshua (2019), 'Stop Talking about Fake News!', *Inquiry: An Interdisciplinary Journal of Philosophy* 62(9–10), 1033–1065, doi: https://doi.org/10.1080/0020174x.2018.1508363.

Hahn, Ulrike, Harris, Adam J. L., and Corner, Adam (2016), 'Public Reception of Climate Science: Coherence, Reliability, and Independence', *Topics in Cognitive Science* 8(1), 180–195, doi: https://doi.org/10.1111/tops.12173.

Jaster, Romy, and Lanius, David (2018), 'What Is Fake News?', *Versus* 2(127), 202–227.

Levy, Neil (2018a), 'Taking Responsibility for Health in an Epistemically Polluted Environment', *Theoretical Medicine and Bioethics* 39(2), 123–141, doi: https://doi.org/10.1007/s11 017-018-9444-1.

Levy, Neil (2018b), 'You Meta Believe It', *European Journal of Philosophy* 26(2), 814–826, doi: https://doi.org/10.1111/ejop.12344.

Levy, Neil (2019a), 'Due Deference to Denialism: Explaining Ordinary People's Rejection of Established Scientific Findings', *Synthese* 196(1), 313–327.

Levy, Neil (2019b), 'No Platforming and Higher-Order Evidence, or Anti-Anti-No-Platforming', *Journal of the American Philosophical Association*, 5(4), 487–502.

Levy, Neil, and Alfano, Mark (2019), 'Knowledge from Vice: Deeply Social Epistemology', *Mind*, doi: https://doi.org/10.1093/mind/fzz017.

van der Linden, Sander L., Leiserowitz, Anthony A., Feinberg, Geoffrey D., and Maibach, Edward W. (2015), 'The Scientific Consensus on Climate Change as a Gateway Belief: Experimental Evidence', *PLOS ONE*, 10(2), e0118489, doi: https://doi.org/10.1371/journal.pone.0118489.

van der Linden, Sander, Leiserowitz, Anthony, and Maibach, Edward (2019), 'The Gateway Belief Model: A Large-Scale Replication', *Journal of Environmental Psychology* 62, 49–58, doi: https://doi.org/.1016/j.jenvp.2019.01.009.

Matheson, Jonathan (2015), *The Epistemic Significance of Disagreement* (New York: Palgrave Macmillan).

Mercier, Hugo (2017), 'How Gullible Are We? A Review of the Evidence from Psychology and Social Science', *Review of General Psychology*, 21(2), 103–122.

Mukerji, Nikil (2018), 'What is Fake News?', *Ergo: An Open Access Journal of Philosophy* 5, 923–946, doi: https://doi.org/10.3998/ergo.12405314.0005.035.

Parkinson, Robert G. (2016), 'Fake News? That's a Very Old Story', *Washington Post*, 25 November. https://www.washingtonpost.com/opinions/fake-news-thats-a-very-old-story/

2016/11/25/c8b1f3d4-b330-11e6-8616-52b15787add0_story.html?noredirect=on&utm_t
erm=.66b05188be20

Pepp, Jessica, Michaelson, Eliot, and Sterken, Rachel K. (2019), 'What's New about Fake News?', *Journal of Ethics and Social Philosophy* 16/2, doi: https://doi.org/10.26556/jesp.v16i2.629.

Prior, Markus, Sood, Gaurav, and Khanna, Kabir (2015), 'You Cannot Be Serious: The Impact of Accuracy Incentives on Partisan Bias in Reports of Economic Perceptions', *Quarterly Journal of Political Science* 10(4), 489–518, doi: https://doi.org/10.1561/100.00014127.

Raphelson, Samantha (2018), 'Survivors of Mass Shootings Face Renewed Trauma from Conspiracy Theorists', *NPR.org*, https://www.npr.org/2018/03/20/595213740/survivors-of-mass-shootings-face-renewed-trauma-from-conspiracy-theorists, accessed 11 August 2021.

Rini, Regina (2017), 'Fake News and Partisan Epistemology', *Kennedy Institute of Ethics Journal* 27(S2), 43–64, doi: 10.1353/ken.2017.0025.

Rini, Regina (2021), 'Democratic Testimony and Weaponized Skepticism', in M. Hannon and E. Edenberg, eds, *Political Epistemology* (Oxford: Oxford University Press), 31–48.

Robles, Frances (2016), 'Florida Woman Is Charged with Threatening Sandy Hook Parent', *New York Times*, 7 December. https://www.nytimes.com/2016/12/07/us/florida-woman-is-charged-with-threatening-sandy-hook-parent.html

Rozenblit, Leonid, and Keil, Frank (2002), 'The Misunderstood Limits of Folk Science: An Illusion of Explanatory Depth', *Cognitive Science* 26(5), 521–562, doi: https://doi.org/10.1207/s15516709cog2605_1.

Schaffner, Brian F., and Luks, Samantha (2018), 'Misinformation or Expressive Responding? What an Inauguration Crowd Can Tell Us about the Source of Political Misinformation in Surveys', *Political Opinion Quarterly* 82(1), 135–147.

Shearer, Elisa (2018), 'Social Media Outpaces Print Newspapers in the U.S. as a News Source', https://www.pewresearch.org/fact-tank/2018/12/10/social-media-outpaces-print-newspapers-in-the-u-s-as-a-news-source/, accessed 11 August 2021.

Shtulman, Andrew (2015), 'How Lay Cognition Constrains Scientific Cognition', *Philosophy Compass* 10(11), 785–798, doi: https://doi.org/10.1111/phc3.12260.

Siddiqui, Faiz, and Svrluga, Susan (2016), 'N.C. Man Told Police He Went to D.C. Pizzeria with Gun to Investigate Conspiracy Theory', *Washington Post*, 12 May. https://www.washingtonpost.com/news/local/wp/2016/12/04/d-c-police-respond-to-report-of-a-man-with-a-gun-at-comet-ping-pong-restaurant/?utm_term=.e506b32f69dd

Uscinski, Joseph E., and Parent, Joseph M. (2014), *American Conspiracy Theories* (Oxford: Oxford University Press).

Verma, Nitin, Fleischmann, Kenneth R., and Koltai, Kolina S. (2018), 'Demographic Factors and Trust in Different News Sources', *Proceedings of the Association for Information Science and Technology*, 55(1), 524–533, doi: https://doi.org/10.1002/pra2.2018.14505501057.

Vosoughi, Soroush, Roy, Deb, and Aral, Sinan (2018), 'The Spread of True and False News Online', *Science* 359(6380), 1146–1151, doi: https://doi.org/10.1126/science.aap9559.

Zaller, John, and Feldman, Stanley (1992), 'A Simple Theory of the Survey Response: Answering Questions versus Revealing Preferences', *American Journal of Political Science* 36(3), 579, doi: https://doi.org/10.2307/2111583.

CHAPTER 7

WHAT'S WRONG WITH TROLLING?

REBECCA ROACHE

INTRODUCTION

INTERNET trolls are the bane of our online lives. They distract and annoy us by making provocative, and sometimes cruel, comments that derail our debates. They sour the atmosphere by making the forum, website, or online community we are using an unpleasant place to be. Trolls often act anonymously, using online identities that cannot easily be linked with their offline, real-life identity. When they do not act anonymously, they tend to direct their trolling efforts towards people whose opinion they do not value, sometimes acting in groups with other trolls, or they troll in such a way that they retain plausible deniability.

Sometimes, trolls act in ways that are clearly objectionable by well-established standards that pre-date online interactions. These ways include bullying and making threats. But sometimes trolls simply annoy people and disrupt others' interactions in ways that tend not to happen offline. We lack an established ethical framework for evaluating behaviour like this, which I call *low-key trolling*. I draw on Joel Feinberg's work on offence, and on the literature on silencing and epistemic injustice, to show that low-key trolling is ethically objectionable because of its effects on the people trolled; effects which are disproportionately felt by people from vulnerable and oppressed groups.

A SPECTRUM OF TROLLING

'Trolling' is a broad term. It is difficult to identify any feature shared by all instances of trolling. Examples include posting controversial, provocative comments in response to a blog post, news article, or social media post disrupting debates by trying to engage participants in a tangential discussion; insulting others or making accusations (especially unfair, rude, or otherwise inappropriate ones); and mocking people, usually in ways that would be rude or otherwise inappropriate offline.

Trolling can be benign and even humorous. One of the first uses of the term referred to seasoned users of the alt.folklore.urban group in the early 1990s, who would post about an already well-discussed topic in a bid to engage unwitting new users in debate for the amusement of seasoned users. This is not obviously objectionable. If the behaviour is short-lived and the target is subsequently welcomed, it is little more than a benign initiation ritual.

Deliberately wasting people's time and attention is an important feature of trolling, and defines a subspecies of trolling known as *sealioning*. In an experimental epistemology paper studying online debates, Emily Sullivan and her co-authors describe sealioning as '[i]ncessant, bad-faith invitations to engage in debate' (2020: 55). Sealions are superficially polite, and their engagement with their targets is 'bad faith' because they do not have any genuine interest in debating. Instead, their apparent politeness is a tool to make it difficult for the target to disengage without appearing unreasonable or rude. Sealions' primary purpose is to annoy their targets and to waste their time and attention; though if accused of trolling, they can deny behaving objectionably and claim instead to have a legitimate interest in the debate they are attempting to propagate. Bailey Poland, in *Haters*, her book on online harassment, writes that sealions were first described during the 2014 'Gamergate' controversy, when it became common for trolls to use sealion tactics en masse to harass female video game developers (Poland 2016: 144–145). The term derives from a *Wondermark* comic that depicted a sealion pestering a woman with repeated and intrusive attempts to enter into debate (Malki 2014).

Not all trolling involves wasting people's time, or even attempts to interact with its target. A 2018 article in *Indy100* entitled 'How Google is Excellently Trolling Flat Earthers' described how, if you typed 'I'm a flat earther' into Google Translate, the French translation was for a time given as 'Je suis un fou' ('I am an idiot') (Waters 2018). Various other publications referred to this feature of Google translate, along with similar instances directed at flat earthers, as trolling (Best 2018; Hale 2018; Pearlman 2018). The approving tone of these reports expresses a view of the trolling as non-objectionable. We will return to this later.

Other instances of trolling are more sinister. Gamergate saw female video game developers harassed, doxed (having personal information publicized), and threatened with rape, injury, and death via various online platforms. The attacks caused some targets to flee their homes, cancel public appearances, and resign from their jobs. Gamergate is frequently referred to as an instance of trolling (Biggs 2014; Malone 2017; Marcotte 2018). Trolling is also a central aspect of the racist, misogynistic, right-wing, alt-right movement. The political scientist George Hawley has described the alt-right as 'an outgrowth of internet troll culture' (Hawley 2017: 4), and its supporters have used trolling to stir up hatred for women, non-whites, gays, and other oppressed groups (Signorile 2016). More recently, the British TV presenter Caroline Flack took her own life in 2020; an event that has been widely blamed on the trolling she experienced over many years, including during her vulnerable final months while she was battling serious personal problems (BBC News 2020; Fogarty 2020; Saunders 2020).

There is significant overlap between 'trolling' and related terms such as 'flaming', 'griefing', and 'shitposting'; notwithstanding the copious online articles arguing for distinctions between them. I will not get into the taxonomy of these terms, nor will I engage in any serious conceptual analysis—a task which risks being quickly doomed to irrelevance, given that our use of terms like this is liable to change as online interactions change, which can happen with the introduction of new platforms, or (as with Gamergate) when a particular online conflict makes the news, highlighting previously overlooked behaviour and establishing new norms. Rather than trying to identify necessary and sufficient conditions of trolling, I will focus my discussion on actual examples of behaviour that is widely agreed to count as trolling.

Trolling that drives people from their homes, their jobs, and to their deaths is in a different league to trolling that involves pestering participants of online discussions. Harassing or threatening people and inciting hatred are clearly unethical, and there are established offline precedents for dealing with them. I will not focus on these obviously sinister sorts of trolling here. Instead, I will focus on trolling that is less obviously harmful, and that either does not have obvious offline correlates about which we have firm ethical intuitions or it has offline correlates that tend not to be regarded as problematic in the way that their online equivalents are. These milder forms of trolling include behaviour such as sealioning, mockery, derailing discussions, unfair accusations, and so on. I will call these forms of trolling *low-key trolling*.

LOW-KEY TROLLING, ONLINE AND OFFLINE

We might be wary of claiming that low-key trolling is unethical, but it is clearly impolite. Yet acts like making irrelevant contributions to a debate that one has joined uninvited or responding with deliberately provocative comments to someone else's views do not cause big problems offline. Nobody was debating the ethics of this sort of behaviour, or coining terms like *troll* and *sealion* before it started happening online. Why is it that trolling is so often discussed as a problem these days when similar behaviour offline slipped under the radar for centuries?

The answer is that various factors contribute to how problematic we view certain behaviour. These factors typically combine in different ways online and offline, with the result that the behaviour characteristic of low-key trolling is more problematic online than offline. Let's introduce a framework to help us make judgements about how objectionable certain behaviours are. In his extensive study on offensive behaviour, the legal philosopher Joel Feinberg drew on nuisance law to gauge the extent to which offensive behaviour is objectionable. He remarks, 'We demand protection from nuisances when we think of ourselves as *trapped* by them, and we think it unfair that we should pay the cost in inconvenience that is required to escape them' (Feinberg 1984: 5). He argues that the seriousness of offensiveness depends on three factors: how intense and long-lasting the unpleasant experience of the offended person (assuming that the person is not abnormally sensitive to offence), how easy it is to avoid the offensive behaviour, and whether or not the witnesses willingly took the risk of being offended. These factors must be weighed against the importance of the behaviour to the person behaving offensively and the social value of freedom of expression, whether the behaviour could be moved to a place and time where it would cause less offence, and the extent to which the behaviour is motivated by spite.[1]

These latter considerations evoke remarks commonly made in discussions of trolling. People accused of trolling—particularly those on the political right—often appeal to the value of freedom of speech in attempting to defend their right to say what they like. It is common, too, for trolls to point out that those whom they target are occupying a public space, which they could have chosen not to enter and are free to leave. We will return to both of these points later. Let's first take a closer look at low-key trolling in light of the framework provided by Feinberg.

First, Feinberg considers the intensity and longevity of the unpleasant experience of the offended person. One way in which low-key trolling might produce more intense and long-lasting unpleasant experiences than comparable behaviour offline is for the former to be more common than the latter. Repeated objectionable behaviour is more serious than a one-off instance. As Feinberg notes, 'The single mosquito bite is simply too trivial a thing. A swarm of mosquitos, on the other hand, biting continuously as they relentlessly pursue their victim, is quite another thing' (Feinberg 1984: 277).

There is good reason to think that low-key trolling is more common online than comparable behaviour offline. We have a name for it, after all. Before the internet, people disrupted others' discussions and made unfair accusations, but nobody united these behaviours under a single concept—unless it was a general concept like 'being rude' or 'wasting people's time'.[2] That we noticed and named the behaviour only after experiencing it online suggests that it is more common online than offline. This makes sense, since it is more comfortable and convenient to troll than to engage in comparable behaviour offline. Online, trolls are spared the discomfort of confronting face-to-face the negative reactions that their behaviour provokes in others. One reason is that trolls often act anonymously. Psychologists have found that people are more likely to engage in antisocial behaviour under conditions of anonymity (Nogami and Takai 2008). This lack of restraint when communicating online is known as *online disinhibition effect* (Suler 2004; Lapidot-Lefler and Barak 2012; Casale et al. 2014). Online disinhibition results not just from anonymity and the associated reduced accountability, but also from asynchronous communication (i.e. the delay between one's comments to others and their responses) and lack of eye contact. Its effects are not always negative—online disinhibition can make us emotionally more open, which can be beneficial (Lapidot-Lefler and Barak 2015)—but it helps to explain why trolling and other antisocial behaviour is more common online than offline.[3]

What of Feinberg's second factor; the issue of how easy it is to avoid the offensive behaviour? Whether objectionable behaviour is difficult to avoid, along with whether it is repeated, affects how we conceptualize it. A person who criticizes us unjustly—a behaviour characteristic of low-key trolling—behaves only mildly objectionably if the behaviour is not repeated, or not objectionably at all (perhaps they genuinely believe the criticism to be warranted). But if they make a habit of unjust criticism, their behaviour is more objectionable, and in some contexts it can constitute bullying. This might happen if they are a work colleague, a classmate, or a fellow sports club member—contexts where it is difficult to avoid them. We can find employment elsewhere, move to a different school, or leave our sports club, but these ways of avoiding bullying are unacceptably burdensome to the victim. Instead, we typically expect employers, schools, and clubs to prevent bullying. The law requires employers to take reasonable steps to prevent bullying and makes them culpable for not doing so.[4] Analogous responsibilities fall upon schools.[5] Sporting clubs and organizations generally have anti-bullying policies too. Online, people targeted by trolls can escape it by avoiding the venues where it happens, but this too is unacceptably burdensome to the target, who becomes excluded from an environment that they value.

Feinberg's third factor determining the seriousness of offensive behaviour considers whether the target willingly took the risk of being offended. Some online platforms have a reputation for being beloved of trolls. Is a person who knows a platform to be replete with trolls and chooses to use it anyway justified in complaining about those who troll them? The answer, I think, is: it depends. In many cases, a user of a platform has little ground to object to the established norms governing interactions on that platform, when those norms apply to everyone. But such a user does have reason to object when other users of the platform target specific groups or individuals for trolling, even if the user knew that there was a risk of such behaviour when choosing to use the platform.

As an analogy, consider banter. Banter involves teasing and trading insults with one's social group in a light-hearted, non-malicious way, and can promote bonding. Behaviour that constitutes acceptable banter in some contexts can be offensive in other contexts. Someone who chooses to join an environment, such as a sports club, knowing that banter is part of the culture, and who subsequently objects to it, might be thought unreasonable. This is because changing the aspects of the club to which they object would change a central aspect of the club's culture, and we might think that it would have been better for such a person not to have joined a club whose culture they found objectionable, especially if existing members value the culture. However, if a person who joins a club knowing that its culture includes banter is targeted for insults more often than others, or if the insults directed towards them are more hurtful than those directed towards others, then this person can reasonably object.[6] In this case, changing the aspects of the club to which the target objects does not necessitate changing a central part of the club's culture; it merely entails treating the target in the way that other members are treated. Likewise, we might think that someone who chooses to use an online platform knowing that it is characterized by certain sorts of interactions is unjustified in complaining about such interactions, yet would be justified were they or others disproportionately targeted for unpleasant interactions. We will see below that it is indeed the case that trolling disproportionately targets certain groups.

Sometimes, of course, the established norms of a group are objectionable regardless of context and even when applied equally to everyone; for example, where groups consisting solely of white men have a culture of racism or misogyny. Anyone has cause to object to such a culture, regardless of whether they willingly exposed themselves to it.

Let's consider what Feinberg argues must be weighed against the three factors just discussed. The first is the importance of the objectionable behaviour to the actor, and the wider value of freedom of expression. It is common to hear complaints from the political right about political correctness: restrictions on what people can say in order to avoid harming or offending others. There is room for debate about what should happen in borderline cases where it is unclear whether free speech or protecting people from harm or offence should prevail. But trolling is not a borderline case. Trolling typically involves behaviour that, offline, would be contrary to established norms of politeness. Offline, people tend to regulate their own behaviour in accordance with those norms; online, as we have seen, people are disinhibited. When people's online anonymity is reduced, such as by being required to register before commenting in a platform, trolling is reduced even without censorship or other restrictions on freedom of expression (Santana 2014; Bartlett et al. 2016).[7] This tendency of trolls to regulate their own behaviour demonstrates that, unless it can be done under conditions of anonymity, many trolls themselves value trolling less highly than they value the social norms that prohibit it.

The second consideration that Feinberg believes may mitigate the seriousness of objectionable behaviour is whether it could be moved to a place and time where it would cause less offence. For example, a person who disturbs fellow hotel guests by talking on a mobile phone late at night in the corridor outside people's bedrooms behaves more objectionably if they could reduce the disturbance by entering their own bedroom (but do not) than if they have no option than to conduct their conversation in the corridor. This consideration simply does not apply to trolling. Trolling is not a behaviour that has value to trolls independently of the annoyance and inconvenience it causes.

Feinberg's final mitigating consideration is the extent to which the objectionable behaviour is motivated by spite. By this, he means '[o]ffending the senses or sensibilities of others simply for the sake of doing so' (1984: 41). Low-key trolling very often has this character. However, a caution from Feinberg is relevant here. He notes that offensive behaviour motivated entirely by spite can be hard to distinguish from instances of what Donald Vandeveer has called *conscientious offences*: behaviour designed to 'provoke and upset' and 'to shock the complacent into a reevaluation of their position' (Vandeveer 1979: 187). Contemporary examples include public mass breastfeeding protests and gay mass kissing protests that are sometimes organized in response to discrimination against nursing mothers or gays. Conscientious offences involve causing offence not for its own sake but for some other, more benign end, such as drawing attention to some political issue that one believes to be important. Vandeveer observes that furthering one's aims through offending others is more likely to attract media attention than doing so inoffensively, and that makes it more likely that protesters will 'get a hearing' (1979: 187).

Trolling is sometimes used in this way: a person might engage in low-key trolling in an online forum for misogynists, causing annoyance and inconvenience not for their own sake, but to sabotage a space in which hateful ideas are encouraged. Since protest speech is an important part of free speech, any efforts to condemn or suppress spiteful trolls should avoid automatically also condemning or suppressing conscientiously motivated trolls—a requirement that will likely be challenging to implement. This challenge is made more difficult by the fact that many objectionable trolls (like many protesters off-line) may claim to be conscientiously motivated: examples include trolls who target feminists because they sincerely believe that women are inferior to men and should not demand rights to which they are not entitled. Annoyance and inconvenience are not the ultimate goals of such a troll; rather, they are tools used to oppress feminists—but trolling in the service of repugnant values is hardly any more acceptable than trolling for its own sake.

These reflections help to show how trolling can be objectionable even when it is low key, that is, even when the individual instances of trolling appear trivial. Feinberg's analysis helps us to gauge the seriousness of offensive behaviour and helps us understand why the behaviour characteristic of low-key trolling is more of a problem online than offline, but there is more to say about why low-key trolling is objectionable. In the next section, I argue that low-key trolling, when it is embedded in the general culture of on-line communities, can be a form of silencing.

TROLLING AND SILENCING

The concept of silencing, in the relevant sense, was first described by the feminist legal scholar Catharine MacKinnon, who claimed that pornography silences women (MacKinnon 1987, 1993). It was further developed by the philosophers Jennifer Hornsby and Rae Langton, drawing on John Langshaw Austin's speech act theory. Austin (1962) distinguished between a locutionary act (the act of uttering words with particular meanings), a perlocutionary act (the act of bringing about a particular effect through one's utterance, such as convincing someone of a particular view, or preventing someone from doing something), and an illocutionary act (the act one performs in virtue of uttering particular words; for example, by uttering the words 'I promise to come to your party', one performs the act of making a promise). Langton (1993) argued that there are forms of silencing corresponding to each of these forms of speech act. A person can be locutionarily silenced by being prevented from speaking, whether through being gagged, intimidated, or some other way. A person is perlocutionarily silenced when their words are prevented from having their intended effects. Langton argues that one way in which pornography silences women is by undermining the effectiveness of women's saying 'No' to sex; in other words, pornography makes it more likely that women who try to refuse to have sex will be forced to have sex. A person is illocutionarily silenced by being prevented from performing the acts they intend to perform through uttering particular words. Langton argues that pornography illocutionarily silences women by encouraging the view that a woman's saying 'No' to sex does not constitute a refusal to have sex.

Low-key trolling is commonly used to effect all of these forms of silencing.

Locutionary silencing

Sometimes, people stop using social media as a result of their being targeted by trolls. Such people have been locutionarily silenced: literally prevented from speaking on the platform in question. Locutionary silencing can be harmful: think of the hostage whose gag prevents them from calling for help, or the political activist who is arrested for criticism of the government. Other cases of locutionary silencing are beneficial. We value privacy laws that prevent the organizations holding our data from sharing it freely; we also value the social norms against talking loudly in cinemas. Between the extremes of harmful and beneficial locutionary silencing are cases which are objectionable, but not seriously so. If you and I are talking on the phone and you locutionarily silence me by hanging up while I'm mid-sentence, I will object to your behaviour, but I might forgive it, especially if you later apologize.

As we have seen, however, behaviour that is unconcerning when it occurs just once can become much more concerning when it is repeated. If you regularly hang up on me while I'm speaking, I am likely to feel more seriously wronged by you, and my attempts to communicate with you will be significantly disrupted. If other people also make a habit of cutting me off when I'm trying to speak, I may be dissuaded from attempting to speak at all; an effect that Kristie Dotson (2011) has called *testimonial smothering*. In off-line contexts, we would view this sort of persistent locutionary silencing of a person as a serious moral wrong.

What if something similar happens online? If a culture of trolling results in certain people restricting what they say or avoiding certain platforms in order to avoid trolls, those people are locutionarily silenced. Even low-key trolling can have this effect if it happens regularly, and it is objectionable as a result. What makes it objectionable is the silencing effect on the target.

Victims of trolling are locutionarily silenced not only by trolls; the general culture of online discussion also risks locutionarily silencing them. The ubiquitous advice, 'Don't feed the trolls', tells us that responding to trolls encourages them to continue, and that victims of trolling can best deal with trolls by ignoring them, which causes them to stop and move on. The view that trolls are sustained by the engagement of their victims is reflected in the explicit advice of alt-right troll Andrew Anglin, whose website *Daily Stormer* takes its name from *Der Stürmer*, the pro-Nazi propaganda tabloid whose style was so embarrassingly crude that several senior Nazi officials, including Joseph Goebbels and Hermann Göring, tried to ban it (United States Holocauset Memorial Museum (n.d.); Zelnhefer (n.d.)). In a 'style guide' produced by Anglin for fellow neo-Nazis who might publish online content under his name, and which was leaked to the public in 2017, Anglin includes the following trolling advice in a section entitled 'All publicity is good publicity':

> We should always be on the lookout for any opportunity to grab media attention. It's all good. No matter what. The most obvious way to do this is to troll public figures and get them to whine about it. I keep thinking this will stop working eventually, but it just never does.[8]

So influential is the 'Don't feed the trolls' advice that it comprises the title of a highly publicised, celebrity- and politician-backed report by the Center for Countering Digital Hate (Center for Countering Digital Hate 2019).[9] There is some evidence that trolls will give up if ignored, although ignoring them leads some to troll even more aggressively (Craker and March 2016). However, even when it works, following the 'Don't feed the trolls' advice is not without cost. It can be difficult and stressful to disengage politely from trolls; a fact exploited by sealions. Further, 'Don't feed the trolls' encourages the attitude that anyone who does not remain silent in the face of a trolling attack is responsible for its continuation. This attitude is illustrated in the Center for Countering Digital Hate's 2019 report, which highlighted as unhelpful the outraged response to the United Kingdom Independence Party (UKIP) candidate Carl Benjamin's comments about whether he might rape Labour MP Jess Phillips. The report advises ignoring remarks like Benjamin's because responding might 'amplify' trolls' voices. Not only does this constitute an attempt to locutionarily silence victims of trolling, but it implicitly claims that people who respond to trolls bear some causal responsibility for any continued trolling.

Responding to trolls does often cause them to continue. However, for many, it is a short, easy inference from observing that trolling victims who do not remain silent are *causally* responsible for their own continued trolling to concluding that they are *morally* responsible—that is, blameworthy—for it.[10] This inference is invalid: being causally responsible for some objectionable behaviour does not entail that one is morally responsible for it.[11] Without clarification on this issue, 'Don't feed the trolls' risks fomenting a culture of inappropriate victim-blaming and locutionary silencing, in which victims who want to escape blame for being targeted by trolls had better remain silent. To avoid this result, those who advocate not feeding trolls should take care to emphasize the distinction between causal and moral responsibility and recognize that while those who do not heed this advice may find themselves targeted by more trolling, the victim is not to blame for this result. This distinction is important because it is overly demanding to insist that trolling victims always remain silent in the face of unjust, hurtful, insulting, or simply annoying verbal attacks. It can require unusually strong self-control to refrain from responding to such attacks. This is recognized in law: provocation is a criminal defence in a number of jurisdictions.[12] Further, it is widely held that people have a *right of reply* or *right of correction* following public criticism or inaccurate accusations. In some countries, this is a legal or constitutional right.[13] Targets of unfair criticism might reasonably fear that by failing to exercise this right, they implicitly admit that the criticism has merit. It is important that victims of trolling who wish to continue to use a platform and who choose not to remain silent in the face of often unfair attacks designed to provoke a response are not seen as blameworthy for the attacks they suffer as a consequence.

Perlocutionary silencing

Trolling can involve perlocutionary silencing. Adherents of right-wing politics, and especially members of the alt-right, use a range of terms to dismiss concerns about equality and justice. One such term is *snowflake*, which has had various pejorative uses over the years.[14] Its current use originated in efforts by people on the political right to characterize and dismiss the concerns of those on the left, who (in the opinion of users of the term) ought to be less sensitive about views that they find objectionable. It was popularized by Steve Bannon, former US President Donald Trump's former chief strategist and former executive chairman of the far-right website, *Breitbart*. The term has become so widely used on social media that many people sympathetic to 'snowflake' concerns have begun to reappropriate the term by self-labelling as snowflakes and by using it to describe overly sensitive right-wingers.

'Snowflake' is not the only dismissive term used by right-wingers. *Libtard*, *SJW* (an abbreviation of 'social justice warrior'), and *crybaby* are also common. Nor do adherents of right-wing politics have a monopoly on vocabulary to characterize and dismiss the concerns of their political opponents: *gammon*, *boomer*, and *white male* are used by liberals in this way. Using terms like these to dismiss certain concerns is a form of perlocutionary silencing because it is intended to prevent certain speech from having its intended effect, and it does so *ad hominem*, by expressing that the speaker is not somebody worth listening to, rather than by engaging with the content of what the speaker says. Responding to a person's views by labelling them as 'snowflake' or 'gammon' indicates that these views can be disregarded by others without heeding, engaging with, or debating them. Since heeding, engaging with, or debating their views tends to be precisely the effect that the speaker intends their words to have, being labelled with these terms perlocutionarily silences the speaker.

If we subscribe to Jonathan Haidt's view of moral reasoning, according to which we arrive at our moral judgements based on emotion and use reason primarily to justify existing moral beliefs, the dismissive behaviour described here is an example of a more general phenomenon. According to Haidt (2012), it is a mistake to attempt to change the views of one's political opponents by using reason; one needs, instead, to appeal to their emotions. The expressed views of one's opponents are, as a result, easy to dismiss when they fail to engage with one's emotions. Haidt argues that humans tend towards *groupishness*: we are inclined to promote the interests of our group and to compete with other groups, which motivates us to resist the views of our opponents and promote the views of our own group. For Haidt, these considerations explain why people of different political persuasions can argue without ever agreeing, even when failing to agree has significant costs for all parties. This problem is exacerbated when political disagreements are moved online because expressing moral outrage comes with fewer costs and more benefits online than offline (Crockett 2017). Additionally, 'the way so-cial media turns so much communication into a public performance' (Haidt and Rose-Stockwell 2019) means that individuals often have more to gain by scoring points against their opponents than by engaging with them. It is, then, unsurprising that dismissing one's opponents by using a term—'snowflake' or 'gammon'—that neutralizes the effects of their arguments while also enabling one to signal solidarity with fellow users of the term is so common in online interactions.

Illocutionary silencing

Right-wing trolls have developed a form of illocutionary silencing. The term *virtue signalling* was popularized by James Bartholomew in the conservative magazine *The Spectator* in 2015, and it has been widely adopted on social media. Virtue signalling, as understood by those who use the term as an insult, is the act of insincerely communicating moral concern because one wants to appear more virtuous than one really is, in order to impress some group of people. We tend to dislike this sort of be-haviour, which in pre-social-media days we would simply label hypocritical.[15] However, it has become common for right-wing trolls to dismiss *any* liberal attempt to com-municate moral concern as virtue signalling. This is a form of illocutionary silencing. A person who is accused of virtue signalling in response to their attempt to (say) urge people to take racism more seriously is painted as not being concerned about racism at all; rather, they are simply trying to impress an audience. The illocutionary act that they intended to perform via their utterance—the act of *urging people to take racism more seriously*—is not recognized as such an act, and therefore it is not such an act.[16]

Suspecting apparently morally concerned people of mere virtue signalling is not without grounds. The psychologist Molly Crockett has argued that expressing moral outrage online has fewer costs and more benefits than doing so offline. Offline, one risks retaliation, whereas online the risk is much lower, given that people often find them-selves addressing 'echo chambers' of people with similar views (Crockett 2017: 770). Online, too, one can 'hide in a crowd', and can avoid witnessing face-to-face the effects of one's words on those whom one is criticizing, which are costs associated with expressing moral outrage offline (Crockett 2017: 770). On the other hand, the 'reputational rewards' that one enjoys as a result of signalling one's moral principles to an approving audience are magnified online, since there are more onlookers than there typically are offline (Crockett 2017: 770). As a result, it is reasonable to expect that insincerely expressing moral concern in order to secure reputational rewards—that is, virtue signalling—is more common online than offline.

Bartholomew was, as a result, on to something. Virtue signalling really happens, and is probably more common online than offline. However, rarely is it possible to infer re-liably that the moral outrage a person expresses online is insincere; consequently, it is rarely possible to distinguish mere virtue signallers from those who are genuinely mor-ally concerned. The right-wing trolls who have adopted this term, however, need not be concerned about this. They have another motivation for accusing their opponents of virtue signalling: doing so excuses them from having to engage with their opponents. By accusing a seemingly morally outraged person of virtue signalling, one refuses to recognize them as morally outraged, which means that there is no moral outrage with which one need engage.

Other terms also effect illocutionary silencing, including *troll*. A person may appear to be encouraging others to engage in debate, but if they are actually a troll, they are simply saying whatever they think will provoke a certain response from others. If they are not in fact trolling, but really *are* attempting to encourage others to engage in debate, being labelled a troll will make it more likely that they are not recognized as doing this, which in turn means that they will fail to do it. Being accused of trolling when one is not trolling, then, involves being illocutionarily silenced. It is not uncommon for trolls to attack others by accusing them of trolling; a practice that *Urban Dictionary* has called 'reverse trolling' (xselectivex 2011).

TROLLING, SILENCING, AND INJUSTICE

Rae Langton observed:

> The ability to perform speech acts of certain kinds can be a mark of political power. To put the point crudely: powerful people can generally do more, say more, and have their speech count for more than can the powerless. If you are powerful, there are more things you can do with your words.
>
> (Langton 1993: 298–299)

The forms of silencing we have discussed disempower the silenced by restricting the things they can do. Jason Stanley argues that, used in political debate, silencing is a form of propaganda. It is used to advance a particular political agenda while suppressing dissenting voices and the opportunity for debate. In doing so, the perspectives of certain groups are 'invisible'. Addressing this issue at the level of political decision-making, Stanley explains:

> If the perspectives of a group are invisible to everyone else, their interests are not weighted in the forming of laws … If the members of the excluded group are without property, they will remain so; if they are without political power, they will remain so as well.
>
> (Stanley 2015: 115).

That low-key trolling can constitute silencing is ethically concerning. But if trolling disproportionately targets certain groups, it is additionally concerning, for the reasons mentioned above by Langton and Stanley. This is exactly what is happening. A 2019 investigation by the UK government found that young people are more likely than older people to be victims of trolling, and that women are more likely than men to be trolled (Centre for Strategy & Evaluation Services 2019). Research conducted by Amnesty International in 2017 found that women of colour are especially likely to be victims of trolling (Amnesty International 2018). In a 2016 *Time* article entitled 'How Trolls Are Ruining the Internet', Joel Stein surveyed his journalist colleagues and provides the following picture that, whilst informal, reflects the wider data:

> When sites are overrun by trolls, they drown out the voices of women, ethnic and re- ligious minorities, gays—anyone who might feel vulnerable. Young people in these groups assume trolling is a normal part of life online and therefore self-censor. An anonymous poll of the writers at TIME found that 80% had avoided discussing a par- ticular topic because they feared the online response. The same percentage consider online harassment a regular part of their jobs. Nearly half the women on staff have considered quitting journalism because of hatred they've faced online, although none of the men had. Their comments included 'I've been raged at with religious slurs, had people track down my parents and call them at home, had my body parts inquired about.'
>
> (Stein 2016)

Social media tend to be viewed as a free-speech democracy. Yet the picture that emerges is that they are spaces where the voices of certain groups are suppressed. This constitutes what Miranda Fricker has called *epistemic injustice*: a harm suffered by people whose testimony is not given sufficient credence due to others' prejudices (Fricker 2007).[17] The result is that the experiences and perspectives of certain groups are under-recognized.

But don't some voices deserve to be silenced? Consider the example of right-wing troll Milo Yiannopoulos, who, in 2016, was permanently banned from Twitter. Twitter—which in 2023 was rebranded as X—did not specify exactly what Yiannopoulos had done wrong, but the ban occurred in the course of Twitter's crackdown on the sexist, racist abuse of *Ghostbusters* actor Leslie Jones, which Yiannopoulos had played a leading role in encouraging (Ohlheiser 2016). Twitter locutionarily silenced Yiannopoulos by banning him, which both he and his followers resented. Yiannopoulos, whose foray into film criticism comprised a *Breitbart* review of *Ghostbusters* entitled 'Teenage Boys with Tits', attacked Jones for complaining about the abuse. He posted 'If at first you don't succeed (because your work is terrible), play the victim', and 'EVERYONE GETS HATE MAIL FFS' (cited in Hunt 2016). Yiannopoulos and Jones both referred to free speech when discussing the ban. Jones tweeted, 'Twitter I understand you got free speech I get it. But there has to be some guidelines when you let spread like that' (cited in Woolf 2016). Yiannopoulos was quoted in *Breitbart*, 'This is the end for Twitter. Anyone who cares about free speech has been sent a clear message: you're not welcome on Twitter' (cited in Hunt 2016).

More recently, in January 2021, outgoing US President Donald Trump was banned from Twitter after his tweets in the wake of violence from his supporters in the run-up to the inauguration of his successor, Joe Biden, fell foul of Twitter's 'Glorification of Violence' policy (Twitter Inc. 2021). While Trump's ban was meant to be permanent, he was allowed back on the platform in 2022 following its purchase by Elon Musk.

What should we make of cases like the social media bans of Yiannopoulos and Trump? Free speech is valuable, but it competes with other values. In decisions about which values should prevail, it is common to invoke John Stuart Mill's harm principle: 'the only purpose for which power can be rightfully exercised over any member of a civilized community, against his will, is to prevent harm to others' (Mill 1863: 23). Joel Feinberg has argued that the harm principle should be supplemented with an 'offense principle': some forms of expression can permissibly be restricted because they are very offensive (Feinberg 1984). In some cases, it is unclear whether a form of expression is sufficiently harmful or offensive to warrant restriction. However, neither a Yiannopoulos ban nor the Trump ban are unclear cases. The behaviour to which Jones was subjected by Yiannopoulos on Twitter constitutes bullying, according to a long-established conception of bullying that originates in offline contexts. Similarly, Twitter's 'Glorification of Violence' policy at the time of Trump's ban resembled international law against incitement of violence, which has been in force for over half a century.[18] Yiannopoulos and Trump therefore deserved to be silenced.

What about cases of silencing that are not comparable to bullying or incitement of violence? Recall Google's 'trolling' of flat-earthers, in which Google Translate temporarily rendered 'I'm a flat-earther' as 'Je suis un fou'. We might reasonably expect this to encourage people to discredit the pronouncements of those who identify themselves as flat-earthers, which constitutes perlocutionary silencing of flat-earthers. In an important sense, this case of silencing is unconcerning. Someone who believes the earth to be flat is insufficiently attentive to overwhelming evidence that the earth is not flat, which expresses a general tendency to be under-attentive to relevant evidence when forming beliefs. Other things being equal, it is appropriate to be more sceptical of claims by flat-earthers than of non-flat-earthers' claims, since the former are less likely to be true than the latter. This makes perlocutionary silencing of flat-earthers epistemically appropriate. Perlocutionarily silencing them prevents their claims from having their intended effect of convincing an audience of the claims; since flat-earthers are not reliable sources of knowledge, it is undesirable that they should succeed in this aim. By contrast, when we perlocutionarily silence our opponents using words like 'snowflake' and 'gammon', we typically do so in the absence of evidence that our opponent is an unreliable source of knowledge; indeed, such words are often used to dismiss one's opponent without considering the evidence they might adduce in support of their claims. What makes perlocutionary silencing an epistemically appropriate response to flat-earthers looks to be absent in the perlocutionary silencing of our political opponents.

However, judging one's opponent to be rationally flawed, even sincerely and on solid evidence, is not always a reliable guide to whether it is epistemically appropriate to perlocutionarily silence them. According to the contrast I have sketched, our disagreement with flat-earthers is supported by evidence that they are rationally flawed, whereas our disagreement with our political opponents is based on groupishness; consequently, it is epistemically appropriate to perlocutionarily silence the former but not the latter.

But this contrast is not so clear cut. Our attitudes towards flat-earthers are not devoid of groupishness. That the internet is replete with memes mocking flat-earthers indicates that not only are they regarded as epistemically irresponsible, but also as *not one of us*. Conversely, the groupishness of our political attitudes does not preclude judgements about our opponents' reliability as knowers. Our political opponents often diverge from us in their fundamental moral beliefs, which can lead us to judge them morally flawed. This judgement was famously expressed by Elizabeth Anscombe:

> But if someone really thinks, *in advance*, that it is open to question whether such an action as procuring the judicial execution of the innocent should be quite excluded from consideration—I do not want to argue with him; he shows a corrupt mind.
> (Anscombe 1981: 17)

Anscombe's attitude is controversial, but it is sincere and reflective. Jesse Prinz expresses something similar when he writes, 'Suppose … that you say discrimination is not morally wrong. The best I can do is stare at you incredulously. If you think discrimination is not wrong, then we are constituted differently' (Prinz 2007: 124).

It is often true that we are correct in our sincere, considered judgements that those who express certain views are morally or rationally corrupt; but those judgements are not always reliable. History is replete with examples of various groups, including women and Black people, being inappropriately silenced because they were wrongly thought morally or rationally flawed by people who were apparently sincere in these judgements. In considering who to protect and who to suppress in our online interactions, we should be aware of the potential danger of wronging people by inappropriately silencing them when we get things wrong.

SHAPING ONLINE NORMS

It is beyond the scope of this chapter to explore and evaluate specific practical measures for online platforms and regulators to protect people from the harms that can result from trolling. But let me suggest a broad direction to take. We have noted that behaviour characteristic of low-key trolling is more of a problem online than offline. Whatever the explanation for that, it is notable that while our norms of offline social interaction have developed over many years, with the result that they are highly nuanced, things are different online. Consider the following example. Offline, if a person wanders alone into a public place (say, a public park on a warm day, where many groups of people are gathered), various factors determine how socially acceptable it is to approach and converse with the people gathered there. If one of the groups comprises people wearing t-shirts prominently emblazoned with a political slogan, who look like they have just come from a public protest, approaching the group to talk about the political issue in question is acceptable—although even then much depends on *how* one approaches them (aggressively versus tentatively, walking into the middle of the group versus addressing them from the edges, and so on). By contrast, attempting to strike up a conversation with a couple who are sitting closely and kissing is likely to be regarded as strange. As a result, while the park is a public place in the sense that anyone is free to enter it, various norms govern the social interactions between the users of the park. Even socially adept people struggle at times to navigate such norms: consider the discomfort of walking alone into a social or professional event at which one is expected to mingle but where one does not know anyone well and faces the challenge of non-intrusively initiating a conversation with people who have already formed themselves into groups. In our offline lives, we use various cues to help us work out whether and how we may interact with someone: body language, volume of speech, mode of dress, even background features like how furniture is arranged or the volume of background music.

Things are different online. Online, there are some gradations between private so-cial settings and public ones (sometimes, we are able to restrict our audience, and on some sites discussion is explicitly or otherwise expected to focus on a particular topic, despite being publicly accessible), but the gradations are much less nuanced than those offline. Further, what nuance there is can be more difficult to read, since many cues that can help us judge whether and how we may join offline discussions are not available online. Many techniques for extricating ourselves inoffensively from an offline conver-sation, too, do not apply online. None of this entails that it is impossible to develop such nuance, cues, and techniques online. Factors like the look of a website, the way the dis-cussion is structured on a page, whether a publicly accessible site is promoted in a way that encourages others to join and interact, whether users are forced to use their real names, how much personal information they are able to share with other users, whether users are able to control who sees their information and comments—all of these, to varying extents, guide online interaction. However, the relative youth of even the most well-established platforms means that, for the most part, the factors that shape our on-line interactions have not translated into social norms that we have internalized and connected with emotionally, and which consequently lead us to regulate our own be-haviour. There are more opportunities for social faux pas offline than online. Currently, many trolls exploit this: they take the view that if a debate is publicly visible, they are entitled to join it, and they apparently do not feel the sense of awkwardness that would arise from joining offline publicly visible debates at which they are unwelcome, such as those occurring between diners at a table in a restaurant or between lovers sitting in a park. Were they to feel that sense of awkwardness when joining online discussions at which they are unwelcome, we could expect them to be dissuaded from doing so.

With norms of online interaction still in their infancy, there are opportunities to shape them to discourage trolling, and to make it as emotionally uncomfortable to troll online as it is to engage in comparable behaviour offline. Online disinhibition means that it is more difficult to make people feel uncomfortable about online bad behaviour than offline bad behaviour—but it is not impossible. Consider the embarrassment that most of us would experience if, while viewing our ex-partner's new wedding photos on Facebook, we accidentally reacted to one of them with the 'crying' emoji. This shows that despite being relatively new, we have internalized and emotionally connected with the norms around Facebook reactions. Even anonymously, we are not beyond being emotionally affected by our online interactions: it can be frustrating to lose a debate about an issue one cares about, even when one participates using a pseudonym. There are, then, ways of getting people to invest emotionally in their online interactions; exploiting this in order to encourage people to regulate their own behaviour is likely to be a promising strategy for discouraging trolling.

One possible strategy could involve cooperation across various websites to require that users have available only a limited number of online identities, each of which is linked to a publicly accessible user profile, which includes details of which websites a particular identity has commented on and details of any bans or suspensions from websites. Who is using a particular online identity, and what their other online identities are, should not be publicly available—this is important in order to allow users to maintain anonymity and to enable, say, a person who regularly comments on political news stories to join an online alcoholism support group without fear that their different online guises could be linked by fellow internet users. Perhaps users could have the option of exchanging any of their online identities for a new one, but only relatively infrequently; say, once a year. Since, under a system like this, online identities would be less disposable than they currently are, there is reason to hope that internet users would be more emotionally invested in their online identities, and that this would dissuade them from antisocial behaviour. Such a system would not be without problems—for example, banning a user from a site would have greater consequences than it currently does, which would place more power in the hands of those making decisions about bans, which may be inappropriate—but there is reason to be optimistic about overcoming those problems. A system in which people are more invested in their online identities than they currently often are would, after all, make the online world more similar to the offline world than it currently is; and we have had centuries of experience dealing with antisocial behaviour offline.

Conclusion

I have argued that low-key trolling, which involves behaving online in ways that are often viewed as little more than irritating offline, is ethically concerning. Using Feinberg's framework for assessing the seriousness of offensive behaviour, I argued that there is reason to view low-key trolling as more seriously objectionable than comparable behaviour offline. I've also drawn on the literature on silencing and epistemic injustice to articulate what is objectionable about low-key trolling. Low-key trolling tends to be objectionable because of its silencing effect on those targeted by it and because it tends disproportionately to target vulnerable and oppressed groups. I have suggested that considering how emerging norms of online interaction might be shaped to encourage users to invest emotionally in interacting respectfully online is a promising strategy for reducing trolling.

Acknowledgements

I am grateful to Carissa Veliz, Clare Moriarty, and an anonymous reviewer for helpful comments on an earlier draft of this chapter.

Notes

1. Summarized from Feinberg (1984: 26).
2. Of course, having coined the term 'trolling', it is now common to use the term to refer to certain offline behaviours.
3. In some cases, non-anonymity increases aggressive behaviour online. Katja Rost and colleagues find that in online firestorms—defined as 'potentially devastating storms of emotional and aggressive outrage'—non-anonymous individuals are more aggressive than anonymous ones (Rost et al. 2016). Further, former US President Donald Trump—until recently the world's best-known troll—trolled non-anonymously prior to his ban from Twitter and Facebook in January 2021. He embraced the troll label, having remarked 'We like to troll' at a rally in March 2020 (Smith 2020). These observations do not undermine the claim that anonymity generally exacerbates trolling, however. First, the non-anonymous firestorm participants studied by Rost and colleagues were not trolls. They were aggressive in the course of reinforcing social norms, which is by definition socially valuable. Trolls, by contrast, do not generally act to achieve a socially valuable end. Second, whilst Trump clearly used social media to cause disruption or annoyance, he lacked the incentives that push the average troll towards anonymity. His politically and financially powerful position made him mostly immune from the negative consequences that face the average troll if identified. Further, some have hypothesized that he trolled in order to fulfil certain political objectives, including distracting his opponents and the media; these objectives would be harder to achieve anonymously (Tumulty 2019; York 2020).
4. UK employees who resign following bullying that their employer has not taken sufficient action to prevent can sue their employers for constructive dismissal; in US law, such employers can be held liable for enabling a hostile work environment.
5. UK schools are required by law to implement anti-bullying measures. Protection from bullying is weaker in US schools, where civil rights law prevents bullying on the basis of membership of protected groups (e.g. certain ethnic groups, religion, sexual orientation), but not all cases of bullying fall into this category.
6. This is not uncommon. Many have observed that there is a fine and frequently crossed line between banter and bullying. See, e.g. Salin (2003) and Espelage (2008).
7. There is, however, some evidence that the relationship between anonymity and online anti-social behaviour is more complex than I have presented it here. Rösner and Krämer (2016) found that, at least in some contexts, anonymity does not predict aggressive wording, although it does predict the likelihood that commenters will conform to a norm of aggressive commenting.
8. Due to the nature of this text, a full citation is not provided here.
9. For an article about its high-profile announcement see Young (2019).
10. See, e.g. Desmet et al. (2012); Weber et al. (2013); Scott et al. (2019); Scott et al. (2020).
11. Consider the following analogy. All victims of theft bear some causal responsibility for the theft, since had they not owned the stolen item, it would not have been stolen. But this does

not entail that victims of theft are thereby morally responsible—that is, blameworthy—for the theft.

12. For an overview, a history, and a philosophical analysis of provocation in law, see Horder (1992).

13. The Brazilian constitution guarantees a right of reply (Presidência da República, Casa Civil, Subchefia para Assuntos Jurídicosis 1988: Título II, Capítulo I, Art. 5.V), as does the European Union (Council of Europe Committee of Ministers 1974). The United Nations recognizes an 'International Right of Correction' (United Nations 1962). A similar right is recognized in various countries, including Germany, Austria, Switzerland, France, and the United States; it also forms part of the editorial policy of various organizations, including the BBC and the Federal Communications Commission (FCC).

14. For an overview, see Merriam-Webster (n.d.).

15. Neil Levy (2021) argues that virtue signalling is an important part of morality because signalling one's moral beliefs plays an important role in enabling social cooperation. He remarks that '[g]ood signals are hard to fake, because they are costly, self-validating or involuntary' (2020, unpaginated); for example, '[r]egular attendance at religious services is costly, insofar as it requires forgoing more immediately rewarding activities'. A person who regularly attends religious services signals their devotion in a way that is hard to fake, and this provides their community with evidence of their devotion, which may be important in others' decisions about whether to cooperate with this person. 'Virtue signalling', used pejoratively by Bartholomew and others, involves *mere* signalling: the thought is that those they accuse of virtue signalling are faking their signals; something that is easier to do online compared to offline. Justin Tosi and Brandon Warmke discuss *moral grandstanding*, which is roughly identical to this sense of virtue signalling. Someone who engages in moral grandstanding does not necessarily fail to hold the moral views they express, but their motivation for expressing those views is to cause others to view them as morally respectable. Tosi and Warmke view moral grandstanding, and therefore virtue signalling, as concerning because 'to grandstand is to turn one's contribution to public discourse into a vanity project' (Tosi and Warmke 2016: 199).

16. A key point here is the notion of *uptake*. Langton (1993) and Hornsby and Langton (1998) argue that in order for illocution to occur (in certain circumstances), the audience must recognize that the speaker intends, by their utterance, to perform a certain illocutionary act. Whether uptake is required for illocution has been disputed (see, e.g. Bird 2002); however, I will not discuss this here.

17. While this terminology is associated with Fricker, Rachel McKinnon points out that this and similar phenomena have long been discussed among Black feminist writers (McKinnon 2016).

18. Twitter's 'Glorification of Violence' policy prohibited 'content that glorifies acts of violence in a way that may inspire others to replicate those violent acts and cause real offline harm, or events where members of a protected group were the primary targets or victims' (Twitter Inc. 2019). The United Nations' International Covenant on Civil and Political Rights states that '[a]ny advocacy of national, racial or religious hatred that constitutes incitement to discrimination, hostility or violence shall be prohibited by law' (United Nations General Assembly 1966: art. 20). Twitter/X's policy on violence was updated following Elon Musk's purchase of the platform to remove reference to protected groups (X Corp. 2023).

REFERENCES

Amnesty International (2018), 'Toxic Twitter: Violence and Abuse against Women Online', https://www.amnesty.org/en/latest/research/2018/03/online-violence-against-women-chapter-1/, accessed 24 January 2022.

Anscombe, Gertrude Elizabeth M. (1981), *Metaphysics and the Philosophy of Mind (The Collected Philosophical Papers of G. E. M. Anscombe)*, Vol. 2 (Minneapolis, MIN: University of Minnesota Press).

Austin, John L. (1962), *How to Do Things with Words: The William James Lectures delivered at Harvard University in 1955* (Oxford: Clarendon Press).

Bartholomew, James (2015), 'Easy Virtue', *The Spectator* 18, 18 April, https://www.spectator.co.uk/article/easy-virtue, accessed 24 January 2022.

Bartlett, Christopher P., Gentile, Douglas A., and Chew, Chelsea (2016), 'Predicting Cyberbullying from Anonymity', *Psychology of Popular Media* 5(2), 171–180.

BBC News (2020), 'Caroline Flack: Laura Whitmore Attacks Trolls over Friend's Death', 16 February, https://www.bbc.co.uk/news/entertainment-arts-51522618, accessed 24 January 2022.

Best, Shivali (2018), 'Woops! Hilarious "Error" Sees Flat Earth Believers Trolled by Google Translate', 4 June, https://www.mirror.co.uk/science/woops-hilarious-error-sees-flat-12643826, accessed 24 January 2022.

Biggs, John (2014), '#Gamergate is the Future of Troll Politics', *Tech Crunch*, 20 October, https://techcrunch.com/2014/10/20/gamergate-is-the-future-of-troll-politics/, accessed 24 January 2022.

Bird, Alexander (2002), 'Illocutionary Silencing', *Pacific Philosophical Quarterly* 83(1), 1–15.

Casale, Silvia, Fiovaranti, Guilia, and Caplan, Scott (2014), 'Online Disinhibition: Precursors and Outcomes', *Journal of Media Psychology* 27, 170–177.

Center for Countering Digital Hate (2019), 'Don't Feed the Trolls: How to Deal with Hate on Social Media', https://counterhate.com/research/dont-feed-the-trolls/, accessed 5 October 2022.

Centre for Strategy & Evaluation Services (2019), 'Rapid Evidence Assessment: The Prevalence and Impact of Online Trolling', *Department for Digital, Culture, Media and Sport*, Reference No: 101030, https://assets.publishing.service.gov.uk/government/uploads/system/uploads/attachment_data/file/811449/DCMS_REA_Online_trolling_.pdf, accessed 24 January 2022.

Council of Europe Committee of Ministers (1974), 'On the Right of Reply—Position of the Individual in Relation to the Press', *Resolution 74*, 26, 2 July, https://rm.coe.int/CoERMPublicCommonSearchServices/DisplayDCTMContent?documentId=09000016805048e1, accessed 24 January 2022.

Craker, Naoimi, and March, Evita (2016), 'The Dark Side of Facebook: The Dark Tetrad, Negative Social Potency, and Trolling Behaviours', *Personality and Individual Differences* 102 (November), 79–84.

Crockett, Molly J. (2017), 'Moral Outrage in the Digital Age', *Nature Human Behavior* 1, 769–771.

Desmet, Ann, Bastiaensens, Sara, Van Cleemput, Katrien, Poels, Karolien, Vandebosch, Heidi, and De Bourdeaudhuij, Ilse (2012), 'Mobilizing Bystanders of Cyberbullying: An Exploratory Study into Behavioural Determinants of Defending the Victim', *Annual Review of Cybertherapy and Telemedicine* 181, 58–63.

Dotson, Kristie (2011), 'Tracking Epistemic Violence, Tracking Practices of Silencing', *Hypatia* 26(2), 236–257.

Espilage, Dorothy L., and Swearer, Susan (2008), 'Addressing Research Gaps in the Intersection between Homophobia and Bullying', *School Psychology Review* 37(2), 155–159.

Feinberg, Joel (1984), *Offense to Others* (New York: Oxford University Press).

Fogarty, Shelagh (2020), 'Richard Bacon Opens Up in a Moving Interview about Caroline Flack and Online Trolling', *LBC*, 17 February, https://www.lbc.co.uk/radio/presenters/shelagh-fogarty/richard-bacon-opens-up-about-caroline-flack/, accessed 24 January 2022.

Fricker, Miranda (2007), *Epistemic Justice: Power and the Ethics of Knowing* (Oxford: Oxford University Press).

Haidt, Jonathan (2012), *The Righteous Mind* (New York: Pantheon).

Haidt, Jonathan, and Rose-Stockwell, Tobias (2019), 'The Dark Psychology of Social Networks', *The Atlantic*, December, https://www.theatlantic.com/magazine/archive/2019/12/social-media-democracy/600763/, accessed 24 January 2022.

Hale, Tom (2018), 'Google Translate is Hilariously Trolling Flat-Earthers', *IFL Science!*, 31 May, https://www.iflscience.com/technology/google-translate-is-hilariously-trolling-flatearthers/, accessed 24 January 2022.

Hawley, George (2017), *Making Sense of the Alt-Right* (New York: Columbia University Press).

Horder, Jeremy (1992), *Provocation and Responsibility* (Oxford: Oxford University Press).

Hornsby, Jennifer, and Langton, Rae (1998), 'Free Speech and Illocution', *Legal Theory* 4(1), 21–37.

Hunt, Elle (2016), 'Milo Yiannopoulos, Rightwing Writer, Permanently Banned from Twitter', *The Guardian*, 20 July, https://www.theguardian.com/technology/2016/jul/20/milo-yiannopoulos-nero-permanently-banned-twitter, accessed 24 January 2022.

Langton, Rae (1993), 'Speech Acts and Unspeakable Acts', *Philosophy and Public Affairs* 22(4), 293–330.

Lapidot-Lefler, Noam, and Barak, Azy (2012), 'Effects of Anonymity, Invisibility, and Lack of Eye-Contact on Toxic Online Disinhibition', *Computers in Human Behavior* 28(2), 434–443.

Lapidot-Lefler, Noam, and Barak, Azyy (2015), 'The Benign Online Disinhibition Effect: Could Situational Factors Induce Self-Disclosure and Prosocial Behaviors?', *Cyberpsychology: Journal of Psychosocial Research on Cyberspace* 9(2), 20–38.

Levy, Neil (2021), 'Virtue Signalling is Virtuous', *Synthese* 198, 9545–9562.

Malki, David (2014), 'The Terrible Sea Lion', *Wondermark* #1062, 14 September, http://wondermark.com/1k62/, accessed 24 January 2022.

MacKinnon, Catharine A. (1987), *Feminism Unmodified: Discourses on Life and Law* (Cambridge, MA: Harvard University Press).

MacKinnon, Catharine A. (1993), *Only Words* (Cambridge, MA: Harvard University Press).

Malone, Noreen (2017), 'Zoë and the Trolls', *New York Magazine*, 24 July, https://nymag.com/intelligencer/2017/07/zoe-quinn-surviving-gamergate.html, accessed 24 January 2022.

Marcotte, A. (2018), *Troll Nation: How The Right Became Trump-Worshipping Monsters Set On Rat-F*cking Liberals, America, and Truth Itself* (Cleveland, OH: Hot Books).

McKinnon, Rachel (2016), 'Epistemic Injustice', *Philosophy Compass* 11(8), 437–446.

Merriam-Webster (n.d.), 'No, "Snowflake" as a Slang Term Did Not Begin with "Fight Club"', *Words We're Watching*, https://www.merriam-webster.com/words-at-play/the-less-lovely-side-of-snowflake, accessed 24 January 2022.

Mill, John S. (1863), *On Liberty* (Boston, MA: Ticknor Fields).

Nogami, Tatsuya, and Takai, Jiro (2008), 'Effects of Anonymity on Antisocial Behaviour Committed by Individuals', *Psychological Reports* 102(1), 119–130.

Ohlheiser, Abby (2016), 'Just How Offensive Did Milo Yiannopoulos Have to Be to Get Banned from Twitter?', *The Washington Post*, 21 July, https://www.washingtonpost.com/news/the-intersect/wp/2016/07/21/what-it-takes-to-get-banned-from-twitter/, accessed 24 January 2022.

Pearlmen, Mischa (2018), 'Google Trolls Flat Earthers by Adding New Feature to Google Maps', *Lad Bible*, 3 August, https://www.ladbible.com/technology/news-awesome-technology-google-trolls-flat-earthers-by-adding-new-feature-to-google-maps-20180803, accessed 24 January 2022.

Poland, B. (2016), Haters: Harassment, Abuse, and Violence Online (Lincoln, NE: University of Nebraska Press).

Presidência da República Casa Civil Subchefia para Assuntos Jurídicos (1988), *Constituição da República Federativa do Brasil*, https://www.stf.jus.br/arquivo/cms/publicacaoLegislacaoAnotada/anexo/constituicao.pdf, accessed 5 October 2022.

Prinz, Jesse (2007), *The Emotional Construction of Morals* (Oxford: Oxford University Press).

Rösner, Leonie, and Krämer, Nicole C. (2016), 'Verbal Venting in the Social Web: Effects of Anonymity and Group Norms on Aggressive Language Use in Online Comments', *Social Media + Society* 2(3), 1–13.

Rost, Katja, Stahel, Lea, and Frey, Bruno S. (2016), 'Digital Social Norm Enforcement: Online Firestorms in Social Media', *PLoS ONE* 11(6), e0155923.

Salin, Denise (2003), 'Ways of Explaining Workplace Bullying: A Review of Enabling, Motivating and Precipitating Structures and Processes in the Work Environment', *Human Relations* 56(10), 1213–1232.

Santana, Arthur D. (2014), 'Virtuous or Vitriolic: The Effect of Anonymity on Civility in Online Newspaper Reader Comment Boards', *Journalism Practice* 8(1), 18–33.

Saunders, Josh (2020), 'Caroline Flack: Heartbreaking Way Ex-Love Island Host Hit Back at Vicious Trolls Online', *Express*, 18 February, https://www.express.co.uk/celebrity-news/1243774/caroline-flack-dead-trolls-comments-online-suicide-love-island-spt, accessed 24 January 2022.

Scott, Graham G., Wiencierz, Stacey, and Hand, Christopher J. (2019), 'The Volume and Source of Cyberabuse Influences Victim Blame and Perceptions of Attractiveness', *Computers in Human Behavior* 92, 119–127.

Scott, Graham G., Brodie, Zara P., Wilson, Megan J., Ivory, Lucy, Hand, Christopher J., and Sereno, Sara C. (2020), 'Celebrity Abuse on Twitter: The Impact of Tweet Valence, Volume of Abuse, and Dark Triad Personality Factors on Victim Blaming and Perceptions of Severity', *Computers in Human Behavior* 103, 109–119.

Signorile, Michelangelo (2016), 'Donald Trump's Hate-Fueled, Alt-Right Army Hates "Faggots" Too', *Huffpost*, 20 September, https://www.huffingtonpost.co.uk/entry/donald-trumps-hate-fueled-alt-right-army-hates-faggots-too_n_57e11904e4b04a1497b67558, accessed 24 January 2022.

Smith, David (2020), '"We Like to Troll": Trump Tries to Steal Spotlight on Eve of Super Tuesday', *The Guardian*, 3 March, https://www.theguardian.com/us-news/2020/mar/02/donald-trump-super-tuesday-rally-north-carolina, accessed 24 January 2022.

Stanley, Jason (2015), *How Propaganda Works* (Princeton, NJ: Princeton University Press).

Stein, Joel (2016), 'How Trolls Are Ruining the Internet', *Time*, 18 August, https://time.com/magazine/us/4457098/august-29th-2016-vol-188-no-8-u-s/, accessed 24 January 2022.

Suler, John (2004), 'The Online Disinhibition Effect', *CyberPsychology & Behavior* 7(3), 321–326.

Sullivan, Emily, Sondag, Max, Rutter, Ignaz, Meulemans, Wouter, Cunningham, Scott, Speckmann, Bettina, and Alfano, Mark (2020), 'Can Real Social Epistemic Networks Deliver the Wisdom of Crowds?', in Tania Lombrozo, Joshua Knobe, and Shaun Nichols, eds, *Oxford Studies in Experimental Philosophy*, Vol. 3 (Oxford: Oxford University Press), 29–63.

Tosi, Justin, and Warmke, Brandon (2016), 'Moral Grandstanding', *Philosophy & Public Affairs* 44(3), 197–217.

Tumulty, Karen (2019), 'Trump is Trolling Us Again. Stop Falling for It', *The Washington Post*, 6 May, https://www.washingtonpost.com/opinions/trump-is-trolling-us-again-stop-falling-for-it/2019/05/06/09679ae0-7009-11e9-8be0-ca575670e91c_story.html, accessed 24 January 2022.

Twitter Inc. (2019), 'Glorification of Violence Policy', *Help Center*, March, https://help.twitter.com/en/rules-and-policies/glorification-of-violence, accessed 24 January 2022.

Twitter Inc. (2021), 'Permanent Suspension of @realDonaldTrump', *Twitter Blog*, 8 January, https://blog.twitter.com/en_us/topics/company/2020/suspension.html, accessed 24 January 2022.

United Nations (1962), 'Convention on the International Right of Correction', *U.N.T.S.* 435, 191, http://hrlibrary.umn.edu/instree/u1circ.htm, accessed 24 January 2022.

United Nations General Assembly (1966), 'International Covenant on Civil and Political Rights', *Treaty Series* 999, https://www.ohchr.org/en/professionalinterest/pages/ccpr.aspx, accessed 24 January 2022.

United States Holocaust Memorial Museum (n.d.), 'Julius Streicher: Biography', *Holocaust Encyclopedia*, https://encyclopedia.ushmm.org/content/en/article/julius-streicher-biography, accessed 24 January 2022.

Vandeveer, Donald (1979), 'Coercive Restraint of Offensive Actions', *Philosophy & Public Affairs* 8(2), 175–193.

Waters, Lowenna (2018), 'How Google is Excellently Trolling Flat Earthers', *Indy100*, 30 May, https://www.indy100.com/article/google-translate-flat-earth-troll-prank-im-a-flat-earther-australia-gravity-8375821, accessed 24 January 2022.

Weber, Mathias, Ziegele, Marc, and Schnauber, Anna (2013), 'Blaming the Victim: The Effects of Extraversion and Information Disclosure on Guilt Attributions in Cyberbullying', *Cyberpsychology, Behavior, and Social Networking* 16(4), 254–259.

Woolf, Nicky (2016), 'Leslie Jones Bombarded with Racist Tweets after Ghostbusters Opens', *The Guardian*, 19 July, https://www.theguardian.com/culture/2016/jul/18/leslie-jones-racist-tweets-ghostbusters, accessed 24 January 2022.

X Corp. (2023), 'Violent Speech Policy', Help Center, https://help.twitter.com/en/rules-and-policies/violent-speech#:~:text=You%20may%20not%20glorify%2C%20praise,glorifying%20animal%20abuse%20or%20cruelty, accessed 11 August 2023.

xselectivex (2011), 'Reverse Trolling', *Urban Dictionary*, https://www.urbandictionary.com/define.php?term=Reverse%20Trolling, accessed 24 January 2022.

York, Byron (2020), 'Trump Trolling for Fun and Profit', *Daily Herald*, 10 May, https://www.dailyherald.com/discuss/20200510/trump-trolling-for-fun-and-profit, accessed 24 January 2022.

Young, Sarah (2019), 'Sadiq Khan, Gary Lineker, and Rachel Riley Pledge to Fight Online Hate by Silencing Trolls', *Independent*, 16 September, https://www.independent.co.uk/life-style/online-trolls-social-media-abuse-campaign-celebrities-sadiq-khan-gary-lineker-rachel-riley-a9106916.html, accessed 24 January 2022.

Zelnhefer, Siegfried (n.d.), 'Der Stürmer. Deutsches Wochenblatt zum Kampf um die Wahrheit', *Historisches Lexikon Bayerns*, https://www.historisches-lexikon-bayerns.de/Lexi kon/Der_St%C3%BCrmer._Deutsches_Wochenblatt_zum_Kampf_um_die_Wahrheit, accessed 24 January 2022.

CHAPTER 8

....

THE MORAL RISKS OF ONLINE SHAMING

....

KRISTA K. THOMASON

INTRODUCTION

....

SHAMING practices are not new. Evidence of shaming practices can be found in ancient and pre-modern societies in many parts of the globe (Stearns 2017: ch. 2). Given shaming's long history, the prevalence of online shaming should not be surprising. The technology involved has shifted quickly and sometimes dramatically, but online shaming seems to follow it wherever it goes. Chatrooms, fan forums, blogs, and social media platforms can all provide examples of shaming. It seems that as long as we have been online, we have been finding ways to digitally shame each other.

Let me begin with a brief survey of the current literature about online shaming. Philosophical work on online shaming is not as extensive as one might think, given how the topic captures public attention. Perhaps fittingly, philosophers who have written about online shaming have done so for online media outlets. For example, both Beard (2016) and Raicu (2016) have discussed the moral problems with shaming in brief public pieces. Beard presents four common arguments in favour of shaming and then raises possible problems with them. His main goal is to examine 'the internal logic of mass online shaming' (2016). Raicu warns against online shaming because it resembles vigilantism and because it quickly becomes disproportionate to the original wrong (2016). Although these pieces are helpful and informative, since they appear in short-form essays, the arguments presented are brief. Two books written for popular audiences have thorough discussions of online shaming: Jon Ronson's *So You've Been Publicly Shamed* (2015) and Jennifer Jacquet's *Is Shame Necessary? New Uses for an Old Tool* (2015). Ronson is a journalist and a documentary filmmaker, and his book explores the downsides of online shaming by interviewing people who have been its targets. Jacquet's view is more optimistic; she describes shaming as a 'delicate and sometimes dangerous' tool that can help us solve problems (2015: 26). As an environmental studies scholar, many of Jacquet's arguments involve the shaming of corporations or organizations, so it is unclear how well her account applies to individual cases (2015: 174). Philosophers have written about the role of the emotion of shame in democratic politics and their arguments can be instructive in thinking about online shaming. Nussbaum (2004) and Locke (2007), for example, are sceptical of the value of shame in political life, while Tarnopolsky (2004) draws on Plato to defend it.

More recently, Norlock (2017), Billingham and Parr (2019), and Adkins (2019) have tackled online shaming directly. Norlock situates online shaming in the context of' imaginal relationships' (2017: 188). Our presence on social media proliferates online relationships. Because we are at a distance from the people with whom we interact on these platforms, we imaginatively fill in the context of those relationships (2017: 189–190). For example, people who shame online often construct the object of their shaming to be a person in a position of power who needs to be 'taken down a peg', even if that turns out not to be true (2017: 192). Norlock argues that we should be more cognizant of the ways that imaginal online relationships can affect us in real life in positive and negative ways (2017: 194). Billingham and Parr draw on John Locke's work to argue that online shaming can be an important informal social sanction, especially for racist and sexist behaviour (2019: 5–7). Online shaming can play the 'reparative' and 'restraint' roles that Locke assigns to punishment in the state of nature: it can lead the shamed person to make amends and it can deter others from engaging in the same behaviour (2019: 6). By contrast, Adkins calls into question the assumption that online shaming for sexism is as effective as it appears. She argues that some incidents of online shaming for sexist behaviour result in a 'shame backlash' against the shamers (2019: 77). On Adkins' view, successful shaming requires that the shamer has epistemic and social authority in the community, which most members of marginalized groups do not possess (2019: 82–83).

I will draw on this work as well as some related literature for the purposes of this chapter. Here, I wish to identify and articulate the risks of shaming. The risks that I have in mind are moral and political risks: shaming threatens to undermine some of our moral commitments or political goals. Given the risks and given that there are alternative and comparable strategies, even if shaming can be effective, we have good reason to avoid it.

Let me set some initial parameters for this chapter. My primary focus is online shaming that occurs between individuals. As such, I will not directly address cases in which individuals try to shame corporations or organizations. I also will not directly address shaming legal punishments because these cases introduce questions about the justification of punishment and the relationship between citizens and the state. My primary examples will involve the kind of shaming that occurs online, which means that in these cases most people are shamed for types of speech. I will sometimes refer to these remarks as 'actions' or 'misdeeds'. I do not make a sharp distinction between speech and action, although I recognize some may argue that shaming is justified for one and not the other.

WHAT IS SHAMING?

To explore questions about online shaming, we have to first understand what shaming is. 'Shaming' is a broad term that often encompasses (at least) the following things: *feelings of shame, shaming practices*, and *stigmatizing* (Thomason 2018: ch, 5). Philosophers draw distinctions between these concepts differently. For example, Tarnopolsky distinguishes between the 'occurrent experience of shame' and 'acts of shaming' (2004: 475). Roughly, Tarnopolsky's distinction tracks the difference between feelings of shame and shaming practices. Adkins (2019) and Nussbaum (2004) draw a close connection between shaming practices and stigmatizing. As Adkins writes, shaming is a 'stigmatizing judgment, where an actor or group condemns another actor or group for failing to adhere to a shared ideal or norm' (2019: 77). Shaming practices, feelings of shame, and stigmatizing are, of course, related concepts. Yet because they can all occur independently from each other, it is a mistake to theorize them together.

Although it is reasonable to think that an act of shaming is meant to induce feelings of shame, there is no necessary connection between the two. Shaming someone might not make that person feel shame. He or she might think that someone's attempt to shame them is laughable and dismiss it as ridiculous. Members of stigmatized groups might embrace that membership and celebrate it rather than feel shame about the stigma. The movement to fight 'slut-shaming'—the stigmatizing of women for having multiple sex partners—is an example of an unashamed response to both shaming and stigmatization (Poole 2013). Feelings of shame can also arise when we are neither shamed nor stigmatized. Philosophers are divided on the question of whether an actual or imagined audience is required to experience feelings of shame (Taylor 1985; Velleman 2001; Calhoun 2004; Deonna et. al. 2012; Thomason 2015, 2018). Shaming and stigmatizing, by contrast, seem to require an audience. Shaming also should not be confused with cases in which we use the phrase 'Shame on you' in conversation. Often, 'Shame on you' is a stand-in for 'You have done a bad thing' or 'You should feel bad about yourself for what you have done' (Thomason 2015: 18). We can, of course, try to induce feelings of shame in others, but shaming practices are only sometimes undertaken for this purpose.

The kind of shaming that occurs online is usually an act of shaming or an instance of a shaming practice. To get a better sense of what shaming is, consider one of the most famous cases of shaming: Hester Prynne from *The Scarlet Letter* (Hawthorne 1850/2003). Hester is a member of a Puritan community during the 1600s and is forced to wear the scarlet letter on her clothing because she has an affair that produces a child. Hester's shaming is complicated: it is simultaneously a legal penalty, a tool to get her to confess the name of her lover, and the public display of her sin, both for her own sake and for the sake of the community. It is this final aspect of her shaming that illustrates the key features of the practice. Philosophers have noted that a certain kind of publicity is central to shaming (Jacquet 2015; Thomason 2018; Adkins 2019; Billingham and Parr 2019). Shaming practices require what I have called the 'marshalling of communal attention' (Thomason 2018: 181). In order to shame someone, her flaw or offense must be pointed out to others. Of course, not all shaming happens in large public forums. We can shame others in front of a handful of people, but the practice assumes an audience who is there to see the shamed person's flaw or misdeed (Adkins 2019: 77). In wearing the scarlet letter, Hester is meant to be a 'living sermon against sin' (Hawthorne 1850/2003: 58); that is, the scarlet letter is meant to draw the community's attention to her.

What is the purpose of marshalling communal attention towards the shamed person? There are generally two motivations for shaming. First, we might say that shaming is meant *to inspire self-consciousness or self-awareness* (Tarnopolsky 2004; Thomason 2018; Billingham and Parr 2019). We can see this in Hester's shaming: it is meant to make her appreciate the seriousness of her sin. As such, her shaming is meant to inspire a change of heart or moral self-reflection. Second, shaming is meant to *send a message of condemnation on behalf of and to the community* (Nussbaum 2004; Tarnopolsky 2004; Norlock 2017; Thomason 2018; Adkins 2019; Billingham and Parr 2019). I am using the term 'community' in a loose sense here. 'Community' can refer to a small group, a group of peers, or, in the case of social media, members of the online community. In Hester's case, shaming is a form of censure that tells her she has done something that her community finds unacceptable; she has failed to live up to or take seriously the values of that her community holds dear. Additionally, Hester serves as an example of what not to do for the benefit of onlookers. Her shaming is not just directed at her, but it is also directed at her peers. The rest of the village receives the message that this behaviour is unwelcome or prohibited. Shaming is thus an expression of condemnation both from and to the rest of the group.

The question that is the focus of most of the literature on online shaming is whether this practice is morally good or morally justifiable. We should be careful here to distinguish the efficacy of shaming from the ethics of shaming. For example, Jacquet's (2015) arguments in favour of shaming are mostly arguments claiming that it is a powerful tool in shaping the behaviour of powerful corporations. We might grant her conclusion and yet nonetheless argue that online shaming is unjustified for other reasons. Compare such arguments to arguments that punishing the innocent effectively deters crime: this may be true, but it would not automatically license the conclusion that such measures are morally justified. Philosophers are divided on the issue of effectiveness. Adkins argues that online shaming can produce shame backlashes, which may diminish its effectiveness (2019: 76). By contrast, Billingham and Parr cite cases of shaming that led offenders to apologize, make amends, and change their future behaviour (2019: 1–2). Questions of shaming's effectiveness are certainly relevant to its justifiability. If some argue that we should use shaming because it is an effective way to police community norms, and yet it turns out not to be effective, we ought to rethink its use. Nevertheless, I will focus most of this chapter on questions of justifiability apart from effectiveness; that is, even if we assume that shaming is effective, the controversy over its justifiability is not settled.

THE CASE IN FAVOUR OF SHAMING

Let us first construct the case in favour of online shaming. When and why might shaming be a good thing to do? Shaming online is pervasive, and people are shamed for a wide range of alleged offences. Optimists about online shaming do not defend every instance of it. Typically, they argue that the most compelling candidate for good shaming is shaming directed towards racist and sexist behaviour (Jacquet 2015; Thomason 2018; Adkins 2019; Billingham and Parr 2019). Since this is taken to be a strong candidate for justified shaming, I will focus on these types of cases. Supporters of shaming argue that it is an important tool in helping to uphold and enforce community norms and values. As Billingham and Parr put it, 'public shaming provides a way that we can express our endorsement of valuable social norms, thus strengthening our shared sense of commitment to those norms, and the values that they promote or respect' (2019: 7). Social media platforms are most often the places where we see the 'calling out' of racist and sexist behaviour, though shaming practices need not be confined to social media. Any online forum where there is a recognizable community and where communication is visible to its users is a place where shaming can occur.

To get a sense of how an episode of online shaming works, consider the case of Hank and Adria from Jon Ronson's book, *So You've Been Publicly Shamed* (2015). At a technology conference, Hank made a joke (containing a sexual innuendo) to another male friend during one of the presentations (Ronson 2015: 114–115). Adria was sitting one row in front of the two men and heard the joke. She turned around, took their picture and posted it to her social media account with a message indicating what Hank had joked: 'Not cool. Jokes about forking repo's in a sexual way and 'big' dongles right behind me' (2015: 114). Adria was reposted thousands of times. She then wrote a blog post explaining why she had done it: 'Yesterday I publicly called out a group of guys at the PyCon conference who were not being respectful to the community ... Yesterday the future of programming was on the line and I made myself heard' (2015: 115–116).

Notice that Adria articulates two common motivations for shaming identified in the previous section ('What is shaming?'). Adria wants Hank to realize that his joke was offensive (self-awareness), and she wants the rest of the tech community to realize that jokes like his do not reflect the values that the community should stand for (sending a message of community condemnation). She marshals communal attention by posting Hank's joke to her social media. In doing so, she invites the community to likewise judge the joke as offensive. She intends for them to join her in condemning it and to refrain from making similar jokes.

Online shaming in cases like this seems positive for a number of reasons. Consider first how it inspires self-awareness in the offender. Racism and sexism are morally offensive and the people who express racist and sexist remarks are doing something morally disrespectful. Shaming is therefore a way of showing the people making these comments that they have done or said something disrespectful (Billingham and Parr 2019: 6). If people make such remarks online, the fact that other members of the community can 'call them out' for it might inspire the self-reflection they need to realize what they said was wrong and make appropriate amends. Being subject to public criticism for racism or sexism should, at the very least, make someone think twice about doing it again. Also, shaming people for these sorts of remarks can allow others to stand up for people who have been subject to this kind of invective and allow the targets of the invective to communicate their offence. As Billingham and Parr put it, 'shaming helps to protect potential victims against future violations' (2019: 7). According to arguments like these, shaming functions as another kind of moral criticism or condemnation. In the same way that I would object to a sexist joke made in my presence, online shaming is a way of objecting to offensive online communication.

Additionally, shaming can act as a form of condemnation when other kinds of consequences are unavailable or not forthcoming (Jacquet 2015: 106; Billingham and Parr 2019: 5–6). Sexism and racism expressed online are often unpunished and unacknowledged. Women of all races are routinely told that they are overreacting or imagining things when they report misogyny online. Similarly, complaints of racism made by people of colour are either treated as not serious or as imagined. Philosopher George Yancy, for example, was targeted with racist abuse after he wrote an opinion piece on racism called 'Dear White America' for the *New York Times* (Evans and Yancy 2016). Shaming provides the targets of abuse with a way of showing that these things in fact occur and that they are not just 'making it up'.

Finally, shaming for racism and sexism allows the community to uphold the values it cares about. In this way, it functions as a sanction that can empower vulnerable members of the community. Shaming is one of the few strategies that the community can use to regulate the behaviour of its members—social media is free and open to everyone, and the platforms cannot (or perhaps will not) shut down profiles of people who say offensive things that stop short of threats. Because any member of the online community can call the community's attention, each person can be a standard bearer for community values (Etzioni 1999: 47; Solove 2007: 92; Jacquet 2015: 26). At its best, then, shaming is a tool that can help to shape communities according to morally desirable norms. As Arneson puts it, 'A society that strives to be just cannot dispense with tools that help get the job done' (2007: 32).

THE MORAL RISKS OF SHAMING

Many philosophers have expressed scepticism about the promise of online shaming, and objections to the practice take a variety of forms. Here I have divided them into three broad risks: the risk of disproportionality, the risk to co-deliberation, and the risk to creating safe communities.

Risk of disproportionality

One of the problems with online shaming is that the negative attention the shamed person receives is often far worse or more sustained than the harm or offense caused by the original misdeed. A commonly cited example is the case of Justine Sacco. Sacco was a public relations manager for a magazine. In December of 2013, she was flying from the United States to South Africa to visit family and posted the following joke on social media: 'Going to Africa. Hope I don't get AIDS. Just kidding. I'm white!' (Ronson 2015: 68). Although Sacco meant for the joke to be an ironic commentary on the obliviousness of Americans, her audience did not read it that way (2015: 78). Her joke was reposted thousands of times and she became a trending topic. When she landed in South Africa, people followed her through the airport, snapped her photo, and posted it to social media (2015: 71–72). She eventually lost her job, suffered from insomnia, and had trouble meeting new people because Google search results continued to link her to the incident (2015: 79–80).

Shaming sceptics point to cases like this one to show that online shaming can have much larger effects than it appears (Solove 2007: 95–96; Norlock 2017: 188–189; Thomason 2018: 192; Billingham and Parr 2019: 2). There are two senses of disproportionality to which critics object. First, the shamed person receives far more negative attention than he or she deserves. Second, online shaming can have lasting or permanent effects that it should not have. To use Sacco as an example, even if we grant that her joke was offensive, having thousands of strangers condemn her for it is excessive. Moreover, in person, one offensive joke would not be sufficient grounds to fire someone from a job, nor would it license being followed and having one's photo taken by strangers. The consequences she suffered were too harsh given the nature of her offence. Additionally, sceptics of online shaming often follow the objections presented by Nussbaum, who argues that shaming stigmatizes another person as having a 'spoiled identity' (2004: 230). On her view, shaming sends the message to the offender and to the community that the offender is irredeemable and is no longer welcome as part of the community. This kind of permanent stain is incompatible with the belief that the shamed person is of equal worth and dignity (2004: 239).

Optimists about online shaming have responded to worries about proportionality. First, they argue that online shaming is only justified when the shamed person has culpably violated a serious moral norm (Billingham and Parr 2019: 8–9). This provision would prohibit online shaming that is mere bullying or revenge (Solove 2007: 98). Second, they argue that online shaming must be reintegrative: there must be a way for the shamed person to make amends or return to the community (Billingham and Parr 2019: 10–11; Solove 2007: 95). Although instituting reintegrative shaming online is difficult, philosophers have argued that greater awareness of the dangers and effects of shaming might help to dampen its negative effects (Norlock 2017: 193–194; Billingham and Parr 2019: 13). Additionally, philosophers have argued that shamers bear responsibility for ensuring that they are shaming in morally justifiable ways. Shamers ought to better consider the well-being of the target of their shame (Norlock 2017: 194). As Billingham and Parr put it, 'Those who accuse others of violating social norms should be willing to listen to the other side of the story and consider whether their criticisms might be misplaced' (2019: 14). Sceptics argue that such responses paint an overly rosy picture of online communication. We might hope that people will behave better on social media, but experience tells us not to expect it.

Some have advocated for a technical solution to the problems with online shaming. For example, Basak et. al. (2019) designed an application called BlockShame, which would be used on social media to limit online shaming. BlockShame uses an algorithm to detect shaming posts and automatically block the shamer who sends them (2019: 217–218). Since one of the problems with online shaming is its context sensitivity, it is unclear whether an algorithm would be sophisticated enough to detect shaming reliably. Although the ethics and technology of online communication can surely present novel solutions to online shaming, it is unclear whether those solutions will satisfy sceptics. Optimists think that online shaming can be justified, provided it is done well, and mitigating concerns about disproportionality may help to show that it can be done well. Yet there are sceptics who will reject online shaming no matter how well it is done. Those rejections likely stem from the concerns that extend beyond disproportionality.

Risk to co-deliberation

The second risk is what I will call the risk to co-deliberation. There are two types of co-deliberation I will examine here: epistemic co-deliberation and moral co-deliberation.

Levy's chapter in this volume, 'Fake News: Rebuilding the Epistemic Landscape', discusses the negative effect that fake news has on our epistemic landscape. Although the objections to shaming are usually moral, some sceptics are concerned that shaming might have similar negative effects. These objections are broadly Millian in nature. In chapter 2 of *On Liberty*, John Stuart Mill makes his famous case that suppressing views—even those we believe to be false and offensive—is illegitimate on two grounds: 'We can never be sure the opinion we are stifling is a false opinion, and if we are sure, stifling it would be an evil still' (1859/2003: 88). Proper pursuit of truth, in Mill's view, is a collective endeavour that requires free and open conversation. It is only 'by discussion and experience' that we are able to correct our mistakes in reasoning and our false beliefs (1859/2003: 90). Sceptics will argue that shaming can be a form of suppressing free and open conversation. The target of online shaming is the object of communal condemnation and is typically prevented from further participating in the conversation. Further, when other people witness instances of online shaming, they may be less willing to speak their minds. Online shaming may therefore have a 'chilling effect' on speech (Billingham and Parr 2019: 12). According to Mill, the chilling of speech makes us worse off epistemically: not only will we lose the opportunity to learn from others and test our own opinions against theirs, but we also risk holding our own views as 'dead dogma, not a living truth' (1859/2003: 103).

We can see a possible example of the negative effects of shaming in online echo chambers. As Nguyen argues, echo chambers are epistemic communities that create a disparity of trust between members and non-members: members of echo chambers portray non-members as unreliable or dishonest (2020: 146). Once non-members are the objects of distrust, the members of the echo chamber become more impervious to any claims or evidence that contradict their beliefs (2020: 147). Shaming might be used as a way to discredit certain voices within a community and create echo chambers. In drawing communal attention to the shamed person's flaw or misdeed, others tend to see the shamed person as defined by that flaw or misdeed (Thomason 2018: 205–206). If the shamed person is seen as flawed on the whole, he or she is more likely to be dismissed or discredited. Sceptics may claim that widespread use of shaming can create echo chambers and damage our abilities to hear opposing views.

Optimists will respond that free expression does not entail freedom from criticism, but we must ask whether shaming is simply another form of criticism. To explore this question, let us now turn to the second risk: the risk to moral co-deliberation. On the surface, it appears that online shaming is simply another form of moral criticism or moral communication. Tarnopolsky argues in favour of shaming on these grounds because it causes a 'potentially salutatory discomfort' in which someone comes to a newfound self-awareness (2004: 479). This kind of moral communication is most familiar in interpersonal cases. Suppose I have said something hurtful to a friend and others have witnessed the incident. Someone might say something to me along the lines of, 'How would you like it if she said that to you?' This person is attempting to get me to realize or appreciate that what I said was hurtful by getting me to see my words differently than I currently see them. She is hoping that, if I come to see my words differently, this realization will lead me to perhaps apologize or at least lead me to stop saying similar hurtful things (Thomason 2018: 179). If sexist and racist speech—whether in person or online—is wrong or hurtful, online shaming seems to be no more controversial than other kinds of negative attention we direct towards anyone who commits a moral wrong (Billingham and Parr 2019: 8–9).

Yet there is a difference between shaming and other kinds of moral communication: shaming requires the marshalling of communal attention (Thomason 2018; Adkins 2019; Billingham and Parr 2019). We can—and often do—communicate disapproval to those who are disrespectful without drawing the attention of others. In interpersonal communication, we direct our disapproval directly to the offending party. If, for example, someone makes an offensive joke in my presence, I might object and say, 'That is not funny.' By contrast, shaming publicizes the person's wrongdoing and calls on other people to direct disapproval to the offending party. In the case of the offensive joke, I would shame the offending party by calling out to a group of people, 'This person just made an offensive joke.' In typical interpersonal communication, we do not put the offending party on display merely by protesting her actions or comments. The publicity or drawing of communal attention distinguishes shaming from regular moral communication. In light of this, sceptics worry that shaming communicates with others in ways that are morally problematic.

Some philosophers phrase this concern as a lack of due process. For example, Nussbaum argues that shaming is akin to 'justice by the mob', which is not 'deliberative, impartial or neutral' (Nussbaum 2004: 234). Solove objects that 'There are no rules and procedures to ensure that the internet norm police are accurate in their assessments of who should be deemed blameworthy' (2007: 97). Others talk about this risk in terms of the context-sensitivity of norms. Billingham and Parr warn that what will count as a norm violation is dependent on a particular social context (2019: 8–9). Norlock makes a similar point about the nature of jokes online—a joke is a 'social thing' that has to be taken up as such in order to count as a joke (2017: 192). In offline communication, norms vary with our social context and it is not always clear when someone violates those norms. Online communication exacerbates this problem. For example, social media posts are generally short and do not invite nuanced distinctions. As Roache shows in this volume ('What's Wrong with Trolling?'), activities like trolling rely on sarcasm, intentional insincerity, and bad faith arguments. We often struggle to discern the basic meaning and intent of online communication. Sceptics will argue that, since it is hard to tell what norms apply to online communication and when those norms have been violated, we are rarely (if ever) in a position to know whether someone deserves to be shamed.

Underlying both of these concerns is a certain conception of moral communication: a moral community must discover together which moral norms are authoritative through a process of co-deliberation (Scanlon 1998; Calhoun 2000, 2004; Walker 2007). As Walker argues, moral life is 'a continuing negotiation *among* people' (2007: 67, emphasis original). We do not, in other words, come to have moral knowledge of either our own or others' behaviour without 'collaboration and communication in identifying moral problems and resolving them' (Walker 2007: 61). As moral co-deliberators, we figure out together where moral obligations, responsibilities, and violations lie. To be able to receive and offer moral evaluations, we operate with a 'presumption in favour of accounting to others and trying to go on in shared terms' (Walker 2007: 69). In other words, we see each other as part of a moral conversation the terms of which are not unilaterally dictated and the point of which is to come to collective decisions about how to live together.

Shaming is in tension with this picture of moral co-deliberation. To see this, let us look more closely at the way shaming is supposed to communicate. Shaming is supposed to inspire moral self-reflection because it is unpleasant and uncomfortable for the shamed person to be the target of people's anger. As such, shaming relies on what Scanlon calls a 'sanction' model of moral criticism (1998: 268). The painful weight of public disapproval is a negative consequence for bad behaviour. Notice, however, that the sanction model of moral criticism does not directly aim to get the shamed person to appreciate what was hurtful or disrespectful about his or her remarks. The weight of disapproval sends the message that these remarks were out of bounds, but the disapproval does not by itself communicate why they were out of bounds. Also, the shamed person is offered no opportunities to respond to the negative attention. Shaming does not presume *mutual* accountability; it presumes that the shamed person is accountable to the group and not the other way around (Billingham and Parr 2019: 14). Particularly on social media, the shamed person is expected to simply accept the disapproval and preferably apologize rather than try to respond to the charges. The shamed person is offered no say in the process of hammering out whether or not his or her remarks were offensive or out of bounds. If we are truly committed to the idea that moral life consists in ongoing negotiation, we are not licensed to unilaterally exclude others from participating in the negotiation process, even when they have said or done something wrong—as Walker puts it, this negotiation 'occurs in real time' (2007: 71). Similar to the risk of epistemic co-deliberation, the marshalling of negative attention that is central to shaming typically has the effect of simply silencing the shamed person. Shaming is risky because it closes off the negotiation process that is essential for working out our moral understandings. It is, of course, possible for shaming in some ideal situations to be compatible with co-deliberation, but sceptics will say that in practice this compatibility is unlikely.

One could object that the targets of shaming do not deserve to be treated as co-deliberators because they refuse to recognize the standing of others as co-deliberators. As Billingham and Parr argue, the strongest cases for online shaming are directed towards people who express racist and sexist views (2019: 8). Is there no place for forms of social sanction within the co-deliberative model, especially when the violations are serious? Why not sanction people who flagrantly refuse to treat marginalized groups as co-participants? As Arneson argues, shaming is a response to a 'failure to comply' with norms that we think are valuable and important (2007: 38). According to this position, shaming is a way of enforcing anti-racist and anti-sexist norms that the community has already decided to uphold.

Although this argument is compelling, it relies on the claim that our moral norms have already been decided and that violations of them are easy to identify. If we are committed to moral co-deliberation, exactly when norm violations occur will be a matter of debate and negotiation. Since morality is an ongoing practice of negotiation, the boundaries of moral violations are contestable—as Walker puts it, there is no 'pure core of moral knowledge' (2007: 73). This is not to say that there are no moral violations, but a commitment to morality as co-deliberative requires that we are ready to articulate our reasons for thinking that a violation has taken place and ready to respond to those who disagree. Only through moral protest and renegotiation is such behaviour finally seen as disrespectful. It is tempting to think that if an online user makes an offensive remark, we are licensed to shame him or her rather than draw them into conversation because in making an offensive remark they have demonstrated that they are 'on the wrong side'. Yet if morality is co-deliberative and there is no pure core of moral knowledge, we cannot determine who has the wrong views without the process of negotiation. Being a co-deliberator is not conditional on having the right views. Determining which views are right and which are wrong is something we must figure out together. As such, being open to challenge is something all members of the moral community must accept.

Moral conversation is—and often should be—uncomfortable and difficult. Of course, the targets of abusive rhetoric do not have to listen to it and engage with the person hurling it (Hill 2000; Bell 2013). If, for example, someone defends themselves against sexist comments and the person making those comments refuses to stop or to listen, he or she is well within their rights to withdraw from the conversation. Being open to challenge and negotiation does not amount to an obligation to talk to someone who mistreats you. Yet we can maintain these positions while at the same time claiming that when we do engage in moral dialogue we should do so in a way that does not presume we are right. Since shaming operates as a sanction, we are not merely objecting to or challenging someone else's behaviour; we are punishing it. The problem is not that we are never in a position to morally judge others because we never have enough information. The problem is with shaming and not with moral criticism.

Even if we accept that ruling out shaming need not rule out all forms of moral criticism, online moral communication is difficult to do well. The public nature of social media platforms makes online moral criticism without shaming difficult. An exchange that starts out a moral criticism can become shaming if many users repost or share the exchange. All conversations have the potential to turn into public spectacles. We are left with a considerable challenge. Online communication may not lend itself to healthy, respectful moral conversation, but more and more conversations are happening online. If moving all moral criticism offline is not a viable option, philosophers need to do more work in the ethics of online communication.

The risks to creating safe communities

One of the powerful arguments in favour of shaming is that it helps shape our communities to be more welcoming to members of marginalized groups. On this view, we need to make public the behaviour that violates the values of the community to make clear what the community's values are. The public element of shaming is essential to this task. It is only by holding up racist or sexist behaviour that we are able to show everyone that such behaviour is out of bounds. If we do not 'call out' this behaviour, we are condoning it or we are complicit in allowing it to continue. Bell, for example, states the position this way: 'To respond civilly to [a racist person] is to risk condoning the [vices] they express, thereby further damaging moral relations' (2013: 219). If we allow people to say racist or sexist things online, we are allowing them to violate the values of the community and, in turn, we are failing in our own obligations to uphold those values. According to arguments like these, shaming is an important tool for creating communities that are properly anti-racist and anti-sexist and therefore safer for members of marginalized groups (Arneson 2007: 51; Adkins 2019: 78; Billingham and Parr 2019: 7).

The first question to ask is whether shaming is necessary to accomplish the task of creating safer communities. In the argument above, there is a false equivalence made between condemning behaviour and shaming a person who engages in that behaviour (Thomason 2018: 202–203). If I fail to shame my fellow community members when I discover they have not upheld some value, it does not follow that I have no other options. I can speak out about the importance of the value in general without shaming individual people who do not uphold it. In order to ensure that our communities embody the values we want them to, it is important to make clear which behaviour is acceptable and which is unacceptable, but we do so by focusing on the behaviour rather than the people who engage in it. To see how this might work, consider the following: some women have started posting misogynistic messages they receive from online dating sites, but they exclude the names and photos of the men who send them (Dewey 2015; Levy 2015). In these cases, women are trying to draw people's attention to the types of harassment they receive rather than to the harassers. We may, of course, think that harassers and abusers do not deserve to be shielded in this way. Giving harassers a taste of their own medicine is no doubt 'pleasurable and therapeutic' for those who have encountered them (Locke 2007: 156). Yet this conclusion does not count in favour of shaming them unless giving harassers and abusers a taste of their own medicine is helping to improve women's online experience. We have to ask whether engaging in this kind of shaming is creating the kind of community we want: is shaming misogynists actually making online platforms safer and more welcoming to women? Here is one of the cases in which the effectiveness of shaming and its justifiability overlap. If shaming does not make the online community safer, then it may not be justified on these grounds. Adkins provides reasons to think that shaming does not accomplish this task. She points to at least two high-profile examples of a shame backlash (2019: 83). Two different women took to an online platform to shame sexist behaviour within their professional communities (2019: 81). As a result, they 'became the objects of sustained, public, and shaming scrutiny' (2019: 83). According to Adkins, shaming requires that one has credibility and competence to speak on behalf of one's community (2019: 86). Since women are often not seen as legitimate members of their community, they are seen as lacking this credibility and competence. Women who 'risk speaking up and challenging bad behaviour are themselves the focus of sustained shaming, and those who wish to speak up in the future are implicitly cautioned against doing so' (2019: 86). If members of marginalized groups are likely to face shame backlash, it is unclear whether shaming will work to make online communities safer for them.

Even if shame backlashes were not a problem, we may still wonder whether shaming creates a welcoming environment. Etzioni argues that one of the upsides to shame is that it is 'democratic' (1999: 47); that is, anyone in the community can shame anyone else, so all members of the community can enforce its values. Sceptics of shaming will argue that what Etzioni identifies as an advantage can quickly become a disadvantage (Thomason 2018: 203–204). One of the risks is that the community can quickly become one that is moralizing (Driver 2005: 138). Moralizing takes several forms, but here moralizing refers to an objectionable form of perfectionism. As Driver writes, 'When one accepts the values [of the community], there is a sense that one may be slacking off in not supporting those values whenever and wherever one can do so' (2005: 141). The trouble is that enforcing community values becomes a way of publicly expressing one's commitment to those values. The more I am ready to shame the behaviour of other online patrons, the more committed to our values I appear. Especially online, there is an expectation that people must 'weigh in' or 'make a statement' about any troubling incident within the community. Failure to do so is often read as a half-hearted commitment to the community's values. When we require people to call out violations of community values to prove that they adhere to those values, we engender an atmosphere of objectionable moral perfectionism. Additionally, if publicly 'calling out' bad behaviour is seen as a sign of one's commitment to the values, there is the risk of moral grandstanding (Tosi and Warmke: 2016). Moral grandstanding occurs when 'one makes a contribution to moral discourse that aims to convince others that one is "morally respectable"' (2016: 199). The public element of shaming makes this risk particularly salient. First, shamers might be more apt to shame so that they can be recognized by others as pillars of the community for enforcing values. Second, as Tosi and Warmke point out, grandstanding often involves the phenomenon of 'ramping up', in which people make increasingly strong moral claims in an exchange (2016: 205). If enforcing the community's values showcases one's good character, then the harshness of one's condemnation will further reinforce the appearance of that good character. Sceptics will argue that the 'democratic' nature of shaming turns us all into moral police.

Shaming is often touted as a way of protecting marginalized groups, but shaming may turn out to create an environment that is more precarious for them. Adkins points out that marginalized people may face a shaming backlash from the dominant group (2019). Tessman argues that similar hierarchies can exist within marginalized groups, which can give rise to what she calls 'dangerous loyalty' (2005: 133). Although loyalty is often treated as a virtue, especially in feminist and anti-racist movements, Tessman argues that dangerous loyalty can 'present an impediment to a political resister's own flourishing' and fail to bring about 'the goals of the very community that serves as an object of loyalty' (2005: 134–135). Tessman provides the example of Chicana feminists who are seen as betraying racial liberation struggles when they are critical of Chicano masculinity (2005: 138). Individuals who are committed to liberation struggles are often labelled as traitors when they choose to reject 'hegemonic beliefs and practices' within the marginalized group that are damaging either to them as individuals or to the goals of liberation (2005: 135). In Tessman's view, dangerous loyalty often arises in communities in which 'identity and politics are closely tied' (2005: 136).

Using shaming as a way to uphold community values creates the conditions for dangerous loyalty. Since shaming requires collective negative attention, initiating and participating in shaming becomes one of the ways that community members display to others their own commitment to the values. As such, relying on this kind of enforcement both requires and encourages public displays of loyalty. These displays of loyalty are similar to the problems with moral grandstanding: members of the liberatory group will face increased pressure to appear the most committed to the cause. The demand for public displays of loyalty, however, frequently undermines internal criticism of the values of the community. As Tessman points out, some 'feminist communities and racialized communities of colour have fallen into the mistake of silencing internal dissent, for they have tended to portray departures from the communities' hegemonic beliefs and practices ... as reprehensible acts of treason' (2005: 144). Any community that identifies itself with certain values, but does not also allow for critique of those values or different ways of expressing those values runs the risk of inculcating dangerous loyalty. If upholding values is too strongly equated with enforcing values, the space of critique and dissent might become so narrow that critique and dissent start to look like violations of the values and thus fair targets for shaming. People who are already vulnerable may be put in a position of further vulnerability if they decide to be critical of the values of the community. Even if shaming effectively changes racist and sexist behaviour, it may do so by enforcing particular views about what racism and sexism are, which can be harmful to the vulnerable populations it is meant to protect. Additionally, the risk to epistemic co-deliberation re-emerges here. If certain views about racism and sexism become too dominant in public discourse, the conversation surrounding them may become impoverished. Dogmatic or rigid views about racism and sexism may prevent communities from addressing behaviour that does not immediately fit the categories on which they rely and from coming to new understandings about the categories.

ALTERNATIVES TO SHAMING

In this final section, I want to identify some of the goods that shaming is meant to accomplish and suggest that we can come about them by other means. Shaming seems attractive because it appears to be a tactic that (a) is a way of defending people who are vulnerable to online abuse; and (b) calls attention to actions that violate community values.

As I have argued above, shaming may not improve the situation of marginalized people as much as we think. Still, some might argue that shaming is sometimes our only defence. When members of marginalized groups are abused, often no one does anything about it. Shaming seems like the only way to get people to pay attention to what is happening. Clementine Ford, for example, a weekly columnist for *Daily Life*, posted screen shots of abusive comments from men on her Facebook page. She explained her actions in an interview by saying: 'These men don't get to just go around leaving these kinds of comments and attempting to degrade women just for the hell of it. Why should they get away with it? Why should there be no consequences at all for them?' (Levy 2015). Ford's claims clearly reflect her frustration that no one takes misogynistic abuse seriously, and it is only once she starts shaming that her abusers face any sort of consequences for their actions. In this case, however, we only shame because nothing else works. We shame because we think that abusers 'should not get away with it'. The underlying problem is that there are often no mechanisms in place on online platforms for marginalized people to stop abuse. As such, reforming reporting policies and terms-of-use policies is key to protecting vulnerable members of the community. In addition, we can ensure that vulnerable groups have supportive enclaves to which they can turn for help. We can take abuse seriously and protect people from it without shaming.

The other main draw of shaming is that it allows members of marginalized groups opportunities to make visible the online abuse that they face. Just as we sometimes conflate shaming and moral criticism, here I think we conflate visibility and shaming. There are ways to shine a light on this kind of abuse without shaming people who engage in it. For example, in 2016 a sports podcast posted a video in which male sports writers read examples of abusive misogynistic comments that their female colleagues received on-line. Even though the abusers were not named, the video was picked up by major news organizations and was viewed over three million times on YouTube (Willingham 2016; Dunlap 2016; Curtis 2016). This strategy both makes visible the kind of misogyny that women face online and serves as a critique of the online sports community. The video asks viewers to imagine what it might be like to say such abusive things to someone's face rather than firing off a hateful social media post from a distance. Projects like this inspire a community to reflect on its own practices, while simultaneously revealing that the community is not living up to the values that it could or should have. Campaigns to increase the visibility of misogyny and racism help show that our communities often are not what we take them to be and can start conversations about what our values are, but we do not have to engage in shaming to accomplish these important tasks.

CONCLUSION

The strategies I have suggested in this chapter are part of a forward-looking, rather than a backward-looking, approach to positively shaping our communities. Since shaming is a reactive strategy, it takes place largely as a response to occurrences of wrongdoing. It is therefore less likely to address or change the background conditions that lead to wrongdoing in the first place. Additionally, shaming may not be a response to wrongdoing that will create the sort of communities we want to live in. If we want people to see the importance of certain values, will punishing them for not expressing those values accomplish this task? Instead of relying on social sanctions we might be better off trying to model the values that we think are important. As Locke puts it, rather than 'focusing on shaming those who shame us, let's make films, tell stories, tend parks, paint murals, open farmers' markets, build schools and universities, support clinics, and foster misfit salons' (2007: 159). In order to uphold the value of anti-sexism, for example, I can promote positive signs of respect for women, I can praise people who treat women with respect, and I can work for policy changes that help women combat the sexism they face. Arguments against shaming often sound like high-minded calls for politeness, but sceptics argue that the concerns run much deeper. Even if shaming seems like a good way to enforce anti-racist and anti-sexist values, it may put at risk the very kinds of communities we want to create.

REFERENCES

Adkins, K. (2019). 'When Shaming Is Shameful: Double Standards in Online Shame Backlashes', *Hypatia* 34, 76–97.

Arneson, R. (2007), 'Shame, Stigma, and Disgust in the Decent Society', *Journal of Ethics* 11, 31–63.

Basak, R, Sural, S., Ganguly, N., and Ghosh, S. K. (2019), 'Online Public Shaming on Twitter: Detection, Analysis, and Mitigation', *IEEE Transactions on Computational Social Systems* 6(2), 208–220.

Beard, M. (2016), '4 Arguments for Ethical Online Shaming (and 4 Problems with Them)', *The Conversation*, 18 May, https://theconversation.com/4-arguments-for-ethical-online-shaming-and-4-problems-with-them-59662., accessed 11 August 2021.

Bell, M. (2013), *Hard Feelings* (New York: Oxford University Press).

Billingham, P., and Parr, T. (2019), 'Online Public Shaming: Virtues and Vices', *Journal of Social Philosophy* (Early view December) 1, 1–20, doi: https://doi.org/10.1111/josp.12308.

Calhoun, C. (2000), 'The Virtue of Civility', *Philosophy and Public Affairs* 29, 251–275.

Calhoun, C. (2004), 'An Apology for Moral Shame', *Journal of Political Philosophy* 12, 127–146.

Curtis, C. (2016), 'Men Read Terrible Tweets to Female Sportswriters in Eye-Opening PSA,' *USA Today*, 26 April 26, http://ftw.usatoday.com/2016/04/sarah-spain-julie-dicaro-harassing-tweets-video, accessed 11 August 2021.

Deonna, J., Rodogno, R., and Teroni, F. (2012), *In Defence of Shame: The Faces of an Emotion* (New York: Oxford University Press).

Dewey, C. (2015), 'Can Online Shaming Shut Down the Internet's Most Skin-Crawly Creeps?', *Washington Post*, 16 September, https://www.washingtonpost.com/news/theintersect/wp/2015/09/16/can-online-shaming-shut-down-the-internets-most-skin-crawly-creeps/, accessed 11 August 2021.

Driver, J. (2005), 'Moralism', *Journal of Applied Philosophy* 22, 137–151.

Dunlap, T. (2016), 'Men Read Hate Tweets Sent to Female Sports Journalists', *People Magazine*, 28 April, http://www.people.com/article/men-read-mean-tweets-female-sports-anchors, accessed 11 August 2021.

Etzioni, A. (1999), 'Back to the Pillory?', *The American Scholar* 6(3), 43–50.

Evans, B., and Yancy, G. (2016), 'The Perils of Being a Black Philosopher', *New York Times*, 18 April, http://opinionator.blogs.nytimes.com/author/george-yancy/?_r=0, accessed 11 August 2021.

Hawthorne, N. (1850/2003), *The Scarlett Letter* (London: Penguin Books).

Hill, T. E., Jr (2000), 'Must Respect Be Earned?', in *Respect, Pluralism, and Justice: Kantian Perspectives* (New York: Oxford University Press), 87–118.

Jacquet, J. (2015), *Is Shame Necessary? New Uses for an Old Tool* (New York: Pantheon).

Levy, M. (2015), 'Hotel Worker Michael Nolan Sacked over Facebook Post to Clementine Ford', *The Sydney Morning Herald*, 1 December, http://www.smh.com.au/national/hotel-worker-michael-nolan-sacked-over-facebook-post-to-clementine-ford-20151130-glc1y4.html., accessed 11 August 2021.

Locke, J. (2007), 'Shame and the Future of Feminism', *Hypatia* 22, 146–162.

Mill, J. S. (1859/2003), *On Liberty* (New Haven, CT: Yale University Press).

Nguyen, C. T. (2020), 'Echo Chambers and Epistemic Bubbles', *Episteme* 17, 141–161.

Norlock, K. (2017), 'Online Shaming', *Social Philosophy Today* 33, 187–197.

Nussbaum, M. (2004), Hiding from Humanity: Disgust, Shame, and the Law (Princeton, NJ: Princeton University Press).

Poole, E. (2013), 'Hey Girls, Did You Know? Slut-Shaming on the Internet Needs to Stop', *University of San Francisco Law Review* 48, 221–260.

Raicu, I. (2016), 'On the Ethics of Online Shaming', *ABC*, 25 February, http://www.abc.net.au/religion/articles/2016/02/25/4413372.htm, accessed 11 August 2021.

Ronson, J. (2015), *So You've Been Publicly Shamed* (New York: Riverhead Books of the Penguin Books Group).

Scanlon, T. M. (1998), *What We Owe to Each Other* (Cambridge, MA: Harvard University Press).

Solove, D. (2007), *The Future of Reputation: Gossip, Rumour, and Privacy on the Internet* (New Haven, CT: Yale University Press).

Stearns, P. N. (2017), *Shame: A Brief History* (Urbana, IL; Chicago, IL; Springfield, OR: University of Illinois Press).

Tarnopolsky, C. (2004), 'Prudes, Perverts, and Tyrants: Plato and the Contemporary Politics of Shame' *Political Theory* 30, 468–494.

Taylor, G. (1985), *Pride, Shame, and Guilt* (Oxford: Oxford University Press

Tessman, L. (2005), *Burdened Virtues: Virtue Ethics for Liberatory Struggles* (New York: Oxford University Press).

Thomason, K. K. (2015), 'Shame, Violence, and Morality', *Philosophy and Phenomenological Research* 91, 1–24.

Thomason, K. K. (2018), *Naked: The Dark Side of Shame and Moral Life* (New York: Oxford University Press).

Tosi, J., and Warmke, B. (2016), 'Moral Grandstanding', *Philosophy & Public Affairs* 44, 197–217.

Velleman, J. D. (2001), 'The Genesis of Shame', *Philosophy and Public Affairs* 30, 27–52.

Walker, M. U. (2007), *Moral Understandings: A Feminist Study in Ethics* (New York: Oxford University Press).

Willingham, A. J. (2016), 'Brutal Video is Leaving Sport Twitter Speechless', *CNN*, 26 April, http://www.cnn.com/2016/04/26/us/women-journalists-target-of-offensive-tweets/, accessed 11 August 2021.

CHAPTER 9

IS THERE COLLECTIVE RESPONSIBILITY FOR MISOGYNY PERPETRATED ON SOCIAL MEDIA?

HOLLY LAWFORD-SMITH AND JESSICA MEGARRY

WOMEN AND SOCIAL MEDIA

SOCIAL media is by now a ubiquitous part of many people's lives. But women and men do not have the same experience online. First, the platforms tend to have been designed and maintained by men. Second, social media usage is gendered: users tend to skew male on some platforms (e.g. Twitter, Reddit, and LinkedIn), and skew female on others (e.g. Pinterest, Instagram, and Facebook) (Perrin and Anderson 2019).[1] And third, women tend to face disproportionate amounts of harassment and abuse (see discussion in Citron 2014; Jane 2014; Megarry 2014). Things are different on different platforms, depending on whether interactions are generally public (Twitter, Reddit) or private (Facebook, Instagram); local (particular Facebook groups or Reddit threads) or global (Twitter, Instagram, Facebook, Reddit).

We want to make a start on the more general question of whether there is collective responsibility for harm perpetrated online by asking about a specific type of harm in a specific type of online context. We will focus on social media platforms that tend to be used in a way that is public and global, and we will focus on the harm of misogyny. By 'misogyny', we mean expressions of negative beliefs about women, and of beliefs about women's 'difference' that cast women as inferior to men. For example, negative beliefs might include believing that women exist to serve men, physically, sexually, and/or emotionally (Pateman 1988; Frye 1983; Dworkin 2008), that they lack reason, or that they are closer to nature; hierarchical beliefs might include thinking that sex roles are complementary but the masculine is the superior role (see further discussion in Clack

1999: 1–5). Twitter is the actual platform that typifies the phenomenon we are interested in, so we will have the most to say about it. But our discussion is intended to generalize to other platforms with a similar structure, both actual and possible, and to other disadvantaged social groups.[2]

In 2019, Twitter had 330 million monthly users and 152 million daily users—34 per cent of these people were female and 66 per cent were male (Omnicore 2020). One explanation for this sex discrepancy in usage might be the differential experience that men and women have on the platform. In 2018, the three most prominent female politicians in Scotland spoke out about the death and rape threats they had received over Twitter (BBC 2018).

In Amnesty International's 2018 report *Toxic Twitter*, multiple study results revealed harmful impacts on women. A survey of 162 women revealed that 62 per cent had experienced abuse on Twitter. A machine learning analysis of tweets directed at British female MPs active on Twitter found that 2.9 per cent of tweets in a roughly five-month period were abusive. (A later study by two researchers at the University of Liverpool looked at incivility and gendered content directed at female MPs over a fourteen-day period, and found that female MPs 'were more likely to receive generally uncivil tweets, tweets with stereotypes about their identity, and tweets questioning their position as politicians than male MPs'. They also found tweets demonizing and objectifying female MPs, and tweets containing misogynistic abuse (Southern and Harmer 2021)). A cross-country study polling women from eight countries—the UK, the United States, Spain, Denmark, Italy, Sweden, Poland, and New Zealand—found that 23 per cent of women across social media, including but not limited to Twitter, had experienced abuse or harassment. Of those who had experienced abuse or harassment, for 26 per cent it was threats of physical or sexual assault, for 46 per cent it was misogynistic or sexist comments (as opposed to more generally abusive language), and 76 per cent had made changes to the way they used social media as a result (Amnesty 2018). This suggests that the abuse of women online has had a 'silencing or censoring effect' on women (Dhrodia 2017).

Amnesty International's conclusion, as is clear from the title of their report, was that Twitter is a toxic place for women. They wrote that Twitter was 'failing in its responsibility to respect women's rights online by inadequately investigating and responding to reports of violence and abuse in a transparent manner' (Amnesty 2018: ch. 1). It would seem that Twitter in fact agrees with this accusation; a member of the Twitter General Council said back in 2015 that 'voices are silenced because they are afraid to speak up', meaning that abuse on the platform had impacts on people's freedom of expression. In March 2018, Twitter wrote to Amnesty claiming to have made a number of changes in the past year-and-a-half, although as we will discuss later, some of these changes actually made things *worse* rather than better for (some) women. Many women have had temporary suspensions or permanent bans of their Twitter accounts for violating 'Hateful conduct' policies put in place to protect women and other marginalized groups.[3]

What causes women to have this negative experience on Twitter and platforms like it? It might seem fairly obvious that it is individuals, choosing to use a technology that is in itself neither positive nor negative but which depends entirely on the use to which it is put. When an angry young man decides to tweet a misogynistic comment out to a Member of Parliament, he is responsible for that decision. If we want to hold someone accountable, it should be him. But things are not so simple: many states do not have laws that protect women from such speech (whether hate speech, vilification, or anti-discrimination laws), and even in those that do, the process involved in getting a prosecution, especially when the source account is anonymous, is arduous and unlikely to succeed. And in many cases, short of rape and death threats, the abuse that women receive can be less about any single tweet and more about the cumulative effect of many such tweets arriving on a daily basis.

Experiencing a dogpile (say, an account with a high number of followers retweets something of yours and makes a derisive comment, which directs many of that person's followers to reply to you or tag you into similarly negative tweets) is unpleasant because of the volume of communication and its quality, and often it is the case that no one tweet (save the original retweet) makes much of a difference. How are we to think about what women are owed on social media platforms, given these complications?

IS THERE INDIVIDUAL RESPONSIBILITY FOR MISOGYNY ON TWITTER?

There are many ways to carve up an individual woman's 'experience' on Twitter, from single notifications at the most fine-grained level (a tweet that tags you; a reply; a retweet; a retweet with a comment; a 'like'), through the cluster of reactions to a single event or tweet of hers (say she is in the news that day, or she tweets something that attracts widespread attention), through to her day on Twitter (her week, month, year). Which of these we choose makes a difference to who caused it, and who is involved when there is a question of responsibility if that unit of experience was harmful to her. Say it affected her mood, caused her to seek legal advice, made her feel unsafe at work or in a public setting, caused stress and anxiety, etc. (at worst, such abuse has been argued to have played a contributing role in individual women's suicides; at best, it is just unpleasant—see further discussion in Gorman 2019). For anything other than a single notification, the cause will involve multiple individuals.

There is a lively literature on the question of how to think about responsibility for jointly caused outcomes. Philosophers have been interested in a range of cases in which unilateral individual actions do not seem to cause any harm alone, but 'add up' together with others' similar actions to cause outcomes that are harmful. Four central applications of this discussion have been voting (e.g. Brennan and Lomasky 1993; Beerbohm 2012; Brennan 2016), global labour injustice (Kagan 2011; Nefsky 2012; Lawford-Smith 2018), global poverty (Barry and Øverland 2016), and climate change (Broome 2012; Hiller 2011; Kingston and Sinnott-Armstrong 2018) (see also discussion in Lawford-Smith and Tuckwell 2020). In a voting case, for example, individuals cause unilateral independent votes for their preferred political candidate (or refuse to vote, or spoil the ballot, etc.), and it is almost never the case that any of these single individual votes makes the difference to who wins or loses the election. In almost every election, the margin of difference for who wins the election is significantly greater than one vote. So we can say, no single individual vote makes a difference to the election outcome. However, when all the enfranchised citizens of a country vote (or refuse to vote, etc.) there is an outcome that their actions *taken together* cause, namely, the electing of a particular candidate.

Philosophers have also been interested in cases that work slightly differently, either because individual actions are not quite so unilateral and independent or because individual actions do some harm. Consider a loosely connected online group of men interested in perceived social harms to men (e.g. men's greater likelihood of suicide, outcomes for men in custody battles). When some of these men make #notallmen or #whataboutmen interventions into feminist discourse, they are not acting in a way that can be fairly described as unilateral and independent. They influence one another and they take inspiration from the shared commitments of their online communities (e.g. particular Reddit forums or Facebook groups). Still, they are not highly organized in the sense that they have formal leaders or formalized decision-making procedures, or in the sense that when any one of them acts he does so with the authority of the rest of the group. No one acts 'in the group's name', even if others may interpret any actions of such individuals *as* actions undertaken on behalf of the group. One man's tweet may have such offensive content as to count as a harm in its own right, while other men's tweets may not.

These differences are all relevant when it comes to the way in which Twitter can be toxic for women. Consider what happened to Charlotte Dawson, an Australian female celebrity who was open about her struggle with depression. Dawson was routinely subject to online bullying and harassment of a misogynist nature, which some of those close to her took to be a contributing cause in her eventual suicide (see discussion in Gorman 2019).

Let us imagine two different individuals involved in the harassment of Dawson, both of which are templates for persons who in fact participated. The first is not in any particular online or offline networks or communities that would take a special interest in Dawson, but simply comes across one of her tweets, finds it worthy of objection or ridicule for whatever reason, and tweets about it. Perhaps he quote-tweets[4] her with a scathing comment, perhaps he simply replies to her original tweet in a nasty way. Maybe he does this on multiple occasions, maybe just once.

The second person is part of a Facebook group whose members advocate for a return to traditional sex roles, and whose members routinely post about women in Australian public life in degrading and dehumanizing ways. Suppose Dawson is one of these women. This individual comes across one of Dawson's tweets *because* someone in the Facebook group posts about it. The men in the group compete with each other to post more and more vile comments under her tweet. Because they are networked in with each other on Twitter, when one retweets or replies it shows up to the others and they are able to expand on each other's efforts.

Neither of these cases are like the individual voter in the election that is won by a margin bigger than one vote. In the election, the single vote does no good, and does no harm either. In the case of misogynistic tweeting, one reply or retweet is generally felt as a negative by the person being targeted, even if this negative is fairly minor. It does a small amount of harm, comparable perhaps to an ordinary micro-aggression (see discussion in McTernan 2018). In this sense, a better parallel is to a poverty relief case. Suppose a workplace is running a fundraiser for people in need after a climate disaster. It asks its twenty employees for donations of $5 each, which will provide one meal for a hungry child, and offers to quadruple the donations if they reach $100. And suppose further that no employee donates. In this case, each employee does some small amount of harm by not donating $5 (denying one meal to a hungry person), but the whole group does quite a bit of harm by not enabling the provision of *eighty* meals (more than the sum of the individual contributions). The differences between the cases are in (a) whether the individual tweeters act unilaterally and independently, and (b) whether the individual tweets do more harm together than each does alone.

In the case of the first 'template' harasser they do; in the case of the second, they do not. A good way to think about the second case is in terms of individuals acting 're-sponsively' (Held 1970; Collins 2013; see also discussion in Lawford-Smith 2015). In Stephanie Collins' example, a group of beachgoers previously unknown to one another are mutually responsive in the event of a drowning, in a way that allows them to coord-inate in using a lifeboat to rescue a drowning swimmer. The men in the Facebook group are responsive to one another.

Some have tried to bypass the question of individual contributions, given that they seem to make no difference or minimal difference, and what really matters is the com-parative weight of the *cumulative* outcome (e.g. the outcome of an election, workers' suffering in sweatshops, the global poor remaining poor, the deaths and suffering wreaked by climate change; we might add to this list, the psychological and emotional suffering of those who are bullied online). Christian Barry and Gerhard Øverland, Garrett Cullity, and Peter Singer all assign responsibility for global poverty to 'the affluent' (Barry and Øverland 2016; Cullity 2004; Singer 2009); Martha Nussbaum assigns responsibility for providing capabilities to 'humanity' (Nussbaum 2007); Bill Wringe assigns obligations to satisfy positive rights to subsistence to 'the global col-lective' (Wringe 2005, 2014); the 'Responsibility to Protect' doctrine assigns respon-sibility for intervention to protect against serious human rights violations to 'the international community' (United Nations 2009).[5] So we could similarly assign respon-sibility for misogyny on Twitter to 'misogynists of Twitter', or similar.

But these arguments are flawed. There cannot be group-level responsibility or culp-ability when there is not group-level agency, and no such groups come even close to meeting conditions for collective agency (Lawford-Smith 2015, 2019). Such conditions generally require group-level beliefs, desires, values, and decision-making procedures (see e.g. Gilbert 1989; Pettit and Schweikard 2006; List and Pettit 2011; Bratman

2014). A shared interest in treating women with contempt does not meet that bar. Responsiveness between those who share that interest may implicate each in what the other does, but it cannot create a group that is a genuine author of an action that brings about cumulative harm. We still do not have a route to responsibility for the cumulative effects of misogyny on social media.

The preceding discussion establishes that while there are two different ways that individuals might be implicated in misogyny on Twitter, first by acting unilaterally, second by acting responsively, both in a way that has cumulative effects on women in the aggregate, neither are sufficient to collective agential action, and so are dead ends for generating collective responsibility or culpability for online misogyny. This is true except in the extreme circumstances in which a discrete individual action on Twitter is itself above a threshold such that it can be argued to cause harm in its own right. Some commentary will count as hate speech or vilification and thus meet this standard, so there will be some cases of original tweets, replies, and retweets with comments that count as harmful in their own right. But 'likes' and retweets are not good candidates for this; these contribute to the aggregate effect of online misogyny that a given woman experiences, but they do not generally 'register' morally when taken in isolation (or if they do, they are such low-level bads that we generally have more important things to worry about).

Setting these exceptional cases aside, it looks like individual responsibility for misogyny on Twitter is not particularly viable, and nor is collective responsibility, at least when the collective is the group of users who cause the harm together. Are we out of options? We think not; if we cannot talk about the individuals who use the platform, we can talk about the platform itself. There are two different ways to approach this idea. One is to think about Twitter as having a custodial role, as the agent responsible for crafting an online environment that minimizes harm, in much the same way the government might be responsible for creating laws that force businesses to limit their carbon emissions. The other is to think about Twitter as a culpable agent, which has at a number of different points in the past, right up to the present, made decisions that have directly caused the incidence of misogyny on their platform. Whereas emissions decisions, and therefore climate change, occur in a landscape that no one in particular designed, misogyny on Twitter occurs in a landscape that *Twitter* designed, and maintains, and therefore is responsible for. Because we think we can make this stronger latter argument, we will not pursue the former option (but it remains for those to explore who are not convinced by our argument).

Is there collective responsibility for misogyny on Twitter?

Should we shift responsibility for misogyny on Twitter onto the platform itself? We think we can make a good case for this, given that Twitter, since its inception, has made a series of choices that render it culpable. But before we get there, let us anticipate and answer an obvious objection to this approach, namely that Twitter is not *morally* responsible for anything, and also explain why we have chosen not to take a free speech approach to making our case.

One way to sidestep the claim that Twitter is culpable for misogyny on its platform is to deny that Twitter is culpable for *anything*, short of breaking the law.[6] Because it is a platform, not a publisher, it is not responsible for the content of what its users publish. And as a private rather than a public entity, it is not bound by the democratic ideals that govern the media or other sites of public democratic deliberation. As a commercial entity, Twitter is free to implement—or not implement—any rules that it likes; individuals who choose to use its service are also free to say whatever they like within the parameters of those rules.

However, society does regularly accept that ethical constraints should be placed upon commercial entities. Consider privately owned media outlets. Citizens generally acknowledge that the media plays a key role in democratic societies, ideally as a watchdog of democratic institutions and processes, as a key channel of public political discourse, and as a vehicle for reporting public sentiment back to those in positions of power (McNair 2017). When media are perceived as unfairly representing groups or individuals, they can be pressured to reform. One example is the regular backlash against media reporting of 'African gangs' by the Australian press (Wahlquist 2018). Another is the British feminist campaign 'No More Page 3', which aimed to convince *The Sun* newspaper to stop printing topless photos of women (Glozer & McCarthy 2021). Activists argued that the photos objectify women, expose children to nudity, and damage the integrity of the media. Following a petition, a loss of advertising revenue, and twenty universities deciding to boycott the masthead, *The Sun*—a company that had been publishing regular topless photos of women since 1970—quietly dropped the feature in 2015. Twitter too, despite its early claims to be 'the free speech arm of the free speech party', eventually bowed to public and legal pressure and introduced rules around acceptable user content (which we discuss further below) (Jeong 2016). These examples (not to mention the considerable amount of work on corporate social responsibility done within business ethics—see overview in Moriarty 2016) demonstrate that corporate entities are part of the moral landscape, subject to both legal and moral sanctioning.

Although we could situate our argument for why Twitter is culpable for misogyny on its platform in relation to free speech concerns, we have chosen not to do so. Twitter is distinct from other social media platforms because it is supposed to be the place for global, public deliberation, the 'source for what's happening in the world' (according to its own marketing). In principle, anyone can contact anyone on the platform (although it is possible to have a locked account and only interact with approved followers, an option which some people make use of periodically to avoid abuse). If Twitter is a global deliberative democratic platform,[7] in other words, Twitter's actions (or lack thereof) have directly contributed to denying women the opportunity for freedom of expression and global political participation, which can impact the outcome of international debates.

Claims for the right to free speech, beginning with John Stuart Mill, have been premised upon the idea that truth, or at least the best ideas, will emerge triumphant via a process of rational deliberation. According to this logic, there is deliberative value in an online free speech platform because global deliberation can act as a vehicle for social progress. Framed in this way, Twitter is culpable for misogyny on its platform *because* this misogyny affects women's political participation and thus distorts democratic processes (and potentially also democratic outcomes).

But feminist concerns with free speech rationales, more general concerns about whether corporate entities are well-positioned to be the facilitators of global democratic debate, and worries about whether social media does more harm than good when it comes to democratic deliberation, all make this a not entirely persuasive rationale for Twitter's culpability.

Feminist critics have argued that the idea that the most rational ideas will emerge triumphant through a process of deliberation fails to adequately consider women's social situation and submerges existing power relations between women and men beneath the assumption that our current understandings of the concepts of reason and rationality are politically neutral. The ability to decide what is reasonable and rational denotes an instance of gendered power politics that often works in favour of those who are already in power (see discussion in Kohn 2000). This does not mean that we need to completely discard the concept of reason;[8] rather, it is to point out that the idea that women's viewpoints will automatically be taken seriously in public debate, if only we can secure their participation, does not pay enough attention to the workings of male power. The concepts of reason and rationality have always posed a particular danger for women because women's adherence to normative femininity ensures that they will be viewed as irrational, and their viewpoints delegitimized (Spender 1980). Feminist philosophers have also complicated the ideal of free speech on the basis that it is not equally available to everyone in a society (Langton 1993; McLellan 2010). Some argue that free speech ideals can be better reconstrued as *fair speech* ideals (McLellan 2010). Taking this approach opens up space for constraints on some speech (such as the harassment or the vilification of certain groups, as well as more minor episodes of misogyny) to be seen as compatible with free speech ideals, that is, in ensuring genuine free speech for all.

Alongside these feminist concerns, serious doubts have also been raised in relation to the ability of corporate multinational social media platforms to advance democratic deliberation. Some scholars have argued that current digital trends, such as surveillance and state-based silencing of dissenters, the intimidation of journalists and other public figures, academic self-censorship, and women avoiding digital political discussions out of fear of violent reprisal, all represent severe barriers to free speech ideals (Véliz 2019).

While it is possible that some of these very serious issues might be able to be addressed via certain reforms, critics have also raised serious questions regarding whether global digital deliberation is doing more harm than good, acting to distort democratic goals instead of facilitating them (Bimber and Gil de Zúñger 2020; Kulwin 2018). The American influence on the Irish #RepealThe8th abortion referendum and electoral manipulation via social media during the Donald Trump presidency campaign provide just two examples of instances in which 'global debate' can be seen to be hindering rather than helping the local discussion.

In the Irish case, @repeal_shield was set up in order to block anti-choicers who shared grisly images of aborted foetuses in order to guilt and shame pro-choicers. When the referendum ended, the creator did an analysis of the accounts it blocked (it blocked 16,000 and analysed 13,474 active in the few days prior to the referendum).[9] One of the more interesting findings was that a significant proportion—about 70 per cent—of the blocked accounts were from the United States and Canada, and not from Ireland itself. This statistic is perhaps unsurprising because many people in those countries feel strongly about the abortion issue (on the anti-choice side). But it is also a distortion of democracy—the Irish people were using Twitter as a tool for democratic debate and discussion about change to a law that affected *them*, and were having to deal with emotional blackmail from people who *are not* directly affected by their laws. International deliberation can therefore lead to significant distortion when countries with large populations and strong views pile into local debates.

Instead of grounding our case in free speech considerations, we locate Twitter's culpability in the recognition that both its actions and its failures to take action have impeded women's ability to participate meaningfully in social and political debate. As the case above demonstrates, international relations now play out via Twitter, which further supports our claim that Twitter is not merely a commercial entity, but is rather a social and political institution whose architecture and policies produce real-world effects for women. Nonetheless, rather than arguing that Twitter has duties to make its platform more democratically legitimate vis-à-vis free speech concerns, we think that the stronger argument here is that Twitter owes women something because Twitter has a monopoly, not only in facilitating digital dialogue between citizens (which is likely to be a flawed pursuit), but as the primary online space for career advancement and garnering attention or visibility under the conditions of contemporary neoliberalism.

Twitter is now an indispensable tool for participating in one's society (Véliz 2019), and it plays a 'major role in American's everyday lives' (Rantilla 2020). Many people use Twitter professionally and in a social movement context, and Twitter is where they are likely to find their colleagues and peers. Although we would argue this drive should be subject to critique,[10] Twitter participation is not a take-it-or-leave-it option for many people today. This is even more the case since the lockdown associated with the COVID-19 pandemic has pushed white-collar workers in particular to further embrace digital engagement for professional purposes. It is important to consider that often, digital visibility and the creation of digital connections via Twitter are *most* important for precarious workers, as well as those from marginalized social groups, such as women. For example, early-career academic Crystal Abidin has discussed how junior researchers work within 'a cult of digital sociability' in which:

> Young scholars like myself are constantly being told to establish the visibility of our portfolios in order to secure academic jobs that are increasingly competitive, scarce, and precarious. As the systems of visibility and status symbols of what counts

as a 'successful' researcher develop over the years … [it] is often crassly measured through digital visibility and quantifiable metrics including citation rates, article downloads, media coverage, and even 'alt-metrics' on social media.

(Abdin 2019: 32)

Twitter, by this account, matters; and the platform has—and any platforms like it have—a responsibility to its users in terms of equal-access considerations.

Collective responsibility: the social media platform

There are three points at which Twitter can be taken to have culpability in the matter of misogyny on its platform. It is helpful to consider these because they can inform our thinking about what social media platforms more generally owe to women. The first is a lack of safeguarding at the platform's inception; the second is not taking sufficient action, even when reports of misogyny on the platform were well known; the third is that when it did finally intervene, it did so in a way that interfered with an open discussion at the heart of feminist politics (and therefore likely to be of crucial importance to at least some women).

At its inception, Twitter did not implement safeguards to deal with misogyny. Such safeguards could have included banning content such as misogynistic slurs and the sharing of pornographic or sexually violent images, prohibiting the creation of anonymous accounts, and taking action to prevent pile-on behaviour. Twitter made no mention of *any rules* until 2009, and by this time the platform already had 5 million users (Jeong 2016). In designing a mixed-sex global platform for discussion, Twitter (or any structurally similar platform) might have recognized that women face structural obstacles to participating and are routinely discriminated against.

Ignorance is no excuse here. Misogyny, and its effects on women, were already widely known and studied phenomena at the time. While the widespread adoption of machine-mediated communication 'transformed the web as increasing numbers of people signed up to corporate services such as Facebook, Google, and Twitter' (Richardson 2019: 118), misogyny did not emerge with social media. Offline, the use of new technologies to terrorize women (such as the landline telephone, as well as camera-equipped mobile devices) was well documented, as was the vilification of female public figures (see discussion in Megarry 2020). Early internet communication research had also established that women's experiences of digital space were fundamentally distinct from men's (Herring 1993, 1996). Demonstrating how the internet emerged from the male-dominated industries of the military and academia, several feminist theorists had also argued that online norms developed alongside the hyper-masculine domination of the medium from its inception (Citron 2009; Hawthorne and Klein 1999). Not only did Twitter provide a platform in which already existing forms of abusive speech could be freely directed towards women, but it also enabled new harms via the extension of surveillance opportunities, search functionalities, and unharnessed media distribution practices (see discussion in Megarry 2018, 2020).

As additional experiences of violence against women on Twitter became more widely publicly known, both anecdotally and via media and non-governmental organization (NGO) reports, Twitter still did very little. First-hand accounts of Twitter abuse were well circulated in the public sphere prior to the publication of the Amnesty International report in 2018. The year 2013 was particularly notable. Twitter was still publicly clinging to its libertarian stance: it implemented rules that stated, 'You may not engage in targeted abuse or harassment', but it did nothing in terms of preventing a wider climate of misogyny. Following widespread campaigns of Twitter abuse waged against British public figures such as feminist campaigner Caroline Criado Perez, academic Mary Beard, and politicians including Stella Creasy and Louise Mensch, which led to widespread public outrage and the jailing of three perpetrators, Twitter added a 'report abuse' button. Sarah Jeong has argued that these attacks against high-profile British women demonstrate 'how poorly equipped Twitter was to deal with harassment' (Jeong 2016). While spam had been easy to flag on the platform via the click of a button, reporting abuse involved women finding a separate web form and filling it out to document *each* example of abuse. There was thus no way to easily report pile-on behaviour. According to Jeong, this oversight denoted 'cold indifference … or at the very least, unthinking negligence' (Jeong 2016). Twitter failed to take sufficient action when it should have done.

From 2015 onwards, and off the back of the 2014 Gamergate phenomenon,[11] Twitter changed its rhetoric around its role as a free speech platform, and began to publicly emphasize its duty towards protecting its more vulnerable users. Thus, Twitter now acknowledged that it could, and should, try to improve the experiences of women. It began by altering its rules to prevent pornographic backgrounds, profile pictures, and headers, as well as excessively violent media, and it banned revenge pornography (Jeong 2016). Significantly, Twitter also introduced a 'hateful conduct' policy that stated:

> You may not promote violence against or directly attack or threaten other people on the basis of race, ethnicity, national origin, caste, sexual orientation, gender, gender identity, religious affiliation, age, disability, or serious disease. We also do not allow accounts whose primary purpose is inciting harm towards others on the basis of these categories.[12]

This policy not only banned direct attacks, but also captured indirect threats. On the surface, this looked like a good shift, which could significantly improve women's experiences.

However, the new policy has in fact provided a new means of negatively impacting women's participation. Mass reporting can lead to accounts being suspended, even when they have not broken the rules. Tweets that offend can be reported, which— when successful—means that the tweet must be deleted. Automated appeal procedures make it unlikely that these issues will be rectified.[13] When questioned by the US Senate Judiciary Committee in April 2019 as to whether it censors some users and speech, Twitter (along with representatives from Facebook and Google) denied the allegation and responded that such a claim 'was antithetical to our commitment to free expression' (Rantilla 2020: 162). Contrary to this response from Twitter, women have used the hashtag #DeboostedFeminist to describe how Twitter has algorithmically intervened in democratic debate by shadow banning and deboosting their accounts. A shadow ban is when an account is left active, but any content posted by the user does not appear across timelines or in search feeds.

Deboosting is similar; making sure that the user's content is not promoted ('boosted'). On Facebook, accounts using the livestream function might be modified so that followers do not get notifications of the stream, and the stream does not appear if they go to that page. On Twitter, users report that accounts may not appear in search results, followers stop receiving notifications of tweets, and only a limited number of users can follow their Periscope streams (see discussions of deboosting and shadow banning in Rantilla 2020; Koebler and Cox 2019). Because these practices impact upon what content is seen by users across the platform and what content can be searched for, they significantly distort debate. They impede the affected women's ability to use Twitter as a digital networking tool and stop women from locating likeminded accounts and content, thereby harming their freedom of (virtual) association and expression.

A supporter of Twitter might object at this point, and say that interfering with (virtual) freedom of association and expression by removing comments, removing accounts, and not promoting content, when that content *is harmful*, is a good thing. There is always a balance to be struck between regulating speech in a way that allows maximal participation and allowing unchecked free speech in a way that means some people won't be able to (or won't want to) participate. We wrote about this issue in the section 'Is there collective responsibility for misogyny on Twitter?'. Feminists cannot consistently support regulation when it facilitates their participation and oppose it when it facilitates *another* group's participation by placing restrictions on feminists. Either there is regulation or there isn't. This is a fair point, but our attribution of culpability to Twitter is not that they have regulated online discourse *per se* in a way that impacts women, but that they have *overstepped* in their regulation of online discourse in a way that is *unfairly limiting* of women's speech—particularly feminist speech.

Consider the following example. There is a widespread social consensus that anthropogenic climate change is happening. But there is disagreement over exactly what we should be doing about it. Suppose there are two groups campaigning for different measures, both gaining significant social support (although one with much *more* support than the other). The first group says that climate change is an issue for governments, so individuals' duties stop at voting for a political party with a 'green' agenda. The second group says that climate change is an issue for the people, so individuals' duties include reducing personal emissions as much as possible and carbon-offsetting the rest; and encouraging friends, family, and colleagues to do the same. And suppose that debate tends to get pretty heated between these two groups because each feels the other is saying the wrong thing about an issue that is, politically, an emergency.

Twitter might decide that, in the interests of maximum participation, it will not allow certain kinds of content, for example, slurs or offensive words used by members of the one group against the other, or comments that dehumanize or incite hatred against members of either group. (It might do this for both groups, or it might just do this for the group that is non-dominant). So far, no problem.

But suppose, conversely, that Twitter decides that the second group's position *is right*, and starts counting as 'Hateful Conduct' tweets by members of the first group that discourage people from taking personal action. We think this would be objectionable. It is not *Twitter's* place—or the place of any other commercial social media platform—to interfere in global or local democratic deliberation in order to settle an outcome of an open debate in advance. Given Twitter's size and reach, this kind of interference can be expected to have a significant impact on the debate. As imperfect a space for democratic deliberation as such platforms may be, there is little doubt that such deliberation does in fact play out there. This makes the question of interference crucially important.

As moral and political issues become settled and gain widespread acceptance, this type of interference against dissenters *may* become more acceptable. But note that while gay marriage has majority acceptance in many countries, Twitter is not trying to regulate the speech of those who oppose it for religious reasons. It may regulate speech that is homophobic in a way that counts as hateful, but this is not the same thing as regulating the content of an ongoing disagreement, even when those who disagree are in a minority. What if there is ongoing disagreement about what counts as hateful, so that the line between these two is unclear? For one example, there is ongoing disagreement at the moment over whether stating genital preferences (i.e. a preference for one set of genitals over another in sex or dating) is transphobic. One group says it is, another group says that this claim is itself *homophobic*. Suppose both parties to the disagreement claim that the other's speech is transphobic/homophobic in a way that counts as hateful.

In this case, we suggest asking several further questions. Does the speech of either side plausibly incite real physical violence against the disagreed-with social group, or *risk* inciting real violence through the use of dehumanizing language, or the denial of the moral equality of persons?[14] If it does, it should be restricted. Are both groups disadvantaged in some way, or is one, all things considered, socially/culturally dominant? If the latter, there may be a case for restriction, especially when that speech is subordinating (e.g. mainstream pornography). Does one side claim a greater quantity or magnitude of hurt feelings, psychological harm, or being driven off the platform or out of the debate? If so, are these responses reasonable, or plausibly explained by a lack of resilience of the side with the greater quantity/magnitude of these types of outcomes (see discussion in Lukianhoff and Haidt 2018)? If the latter, there is *not* a good case for restricting it: it is a principle of liberal democracy that we should not be held hostage to others' offence-taking. Is regulation of the disagreement zero sum, such that improving the situation of one disadvantaged group requires worsening the situation of another? Trans people and same-sex-attracted (or both-sex-attracted) people are both disadvantaged social groups, so there is no overall gain for social justice from making one better off *at the expense of* the other. Social media platforms should not regulate speech in these kinds of cases; they should err on the side of non-interference.

CONCLUSION

Public discussion has erred on the side of thinking that Twitter is a corporation and it can run its platform as it sees fit within the constraints of the law. But this ignores the interaction between corporate platforms and public deliberative spaces. Twitter's policy on the protection of some voices at the expense of others needs to be developed in a way that is sensitive to the equal participation of multiple marginalized communities within states where the platform provides a central venue for debate.

Social media platforms should not confuse the limiting of speech for reasons of maximal participation with the *settling* of open questions. The latter is not their place. Preventing real physical harm, or reducing the risk of it, is a good reason to restrict speech; pandering to a lack of resilience, or distributing restrictions in an *ad hoc* way in zero-sum cases, is not.

NOTES

1. Note that these examples are specific to the United States and may be different for global usage.
2. For a discussion focused on Reddit, see Massanari (2015).
3. It is hard to get reliable data on suspensions and bans because Twitter is not transparent about this information. In one response to Amnesty International, Twitter evaded their request for transparent data by writing that such data 'can be both uninformative and potentially misleading' (Amnesty International 2018; see also discussion in Gorman 2019).
4. Quote-tweeting is retweeting but adding a comment. The person who is being retweeted gets a notification of this. An alternative which does not notify the original tweeter is to screenshot the tweet and post it with a comment. Some people do this routinely, so as to not attract a person's followers, or to avoid giving them traffic, or to avoid being reported. But it is also a method that demonstrates that the virtue-signalling and moral grandstanding goods that come from denouncing others can be achieved without actually targeting those others.
5. An alternative to arguing for group-based responsibility in such situations is to argue to ratchet up individual responsibility somehow. In the case of aggregate-level Twitter misogyny, this could involve talking about individuals' complicity in what they do together with others (see, e.g. Kutz 2007; Lepora and Goodin 2013), or about the *indirect consequences* of their actions (e.g. in licensing others to do the same). In their paper 'Interconnected Blameworthiness', Stephanie Collins and Neils de Haan make a good case for enhanced individual responsibility (Collins and de Haan 2021).

6. We have already flagged the problem that many nation states do not recognize the vilification of women as a category of hate speech. This renders the legal concept of hate speech an insufficient vehicle for addressing the online experiences of women because patriarchal societies often do not recognize vilification of a person based on sex as a social harm. Another problem with holding Twitter to legal account is that Twitter operates across international borders, and nation states have been slow to impose any limitations of the actions of digital giants such as Twitter, Facebook, YouTube, and Google.

7. To be clear, we're not advocating for democratic deliberation to 'go digital'; we are merely noting that some democratic deliberation does in fact take place on digital platforms, including Twitter, so striving to make them better spaces to serve that end is a worthwhile goal (see also discussion in both Jeffrey Howard, 'Extreme Speech, Democratic Deliberation, and Social Media' and Johannes Himmelreich, 'Should We Automate Democracy', in this volume; and May Thorseth (2006, 2008).

8. Kohn also does not seek to discard the concepts of reason and rationality completely; she thinks that 'they are crucial for the fair administration of existing judicial and political norms' (Kohn 2000: 426). Her point, rather, is that 'centering deliberation' in democratic political theory can obscure historical injustices and perpetuate existing inequalities.

9. See https://twitter.com/hazel_ok/status/999502988564750336?s=21, accessed 11 August 2021.

10. There are significant issues with digital visibility and safety from a female perspective. For example, Ginger Gorman talks about the moment when, having become a target for online abuse, she realized that she had location services turned on for her tweets, 'and you could just about pinpoint our house on Google Maps'. She says, 'That night [my husband Don and I] both lay awake in bed wondering if our children were in danger' (Gorman 2019: 10). Another issue more generally is that, while norms of neoliberal self-governance urge employees to cultivate a 'digital self-brand' across platforms, the trade-off between the significant labour involved in this pursuit and the economic benefits for workers remains opaque (see discussion in Scolere et al. 2018).

11. Gamergate was sparked by the public shaming of games developer Zöe Quinn, by her then-partner Eron Gjoni. Quinn and other women who critiqued masculine gaming culture (notably vlogger Anita Sarkeesian), as well as women working in the gaming industry, were then subjected to a cascade of anonymous online abuse from self-styled defenders of sexism in gaming (see discussion in Megarry 2018).

12. See https://help.twitter.com/en/rules-and-policies/hateful-conduct-policy, accessed 11 August 2021.

13. Considerations of online harm and cyber violence usually present further technological development as the only possible solution (Simpson 2014: 273–274), yet employing more human moderators would make it easier for women to get through to a person when reporting abuse and would also facilitate fairer dispute resolution processes. Twitter would then be obliged to offer these employees fair renumeration, as well as safe work spaces and work practices geared around harm minimization, such as adequate access to psychological services.

14. This is the difference between saying, for example, 'Sexual orientation is innate so claims about transphobia or exclusion are unjustified' and 'Anyone who denies that sexual orientation is innate is subhuman garbage.'

REFERENCES

Abidin, Crystal (2019), 'Tacit Labours of Digital Social Research as an Early Career Researcher', *Journal of Digital Social Research*, 1/1, 31–34ç.

Amnesty International (2018), *Toxic Twitter—A Toxic Place For Women*, https://www.amnesty.org/en/latest/research/2018/03/online-violence-against-women-chapter-1/, accessed 11 August 2021.

Barry, Christian, and Øverland, Gerhard (2016), *Responding to Global Poverty* (Cambridge: Cambridge University Press).

BBC News (2018), 'Female Politicians Speak Out over Twitter Abuse', *bbc.com*, 21 March, https://www.bbc.com/news/uk-scotland-scotland-politics-43479004, accessed 11 August 2021.

Beerbohm, Eric (2012), *In Our Name: The Ethics of Democracy* (Princeton, NJ: Princeton University Press).

Bimber, Bruce, and Gile de Zúñger, Homero (2020), 'The Unedited Public Sphere', *New Media & Society*, 22(4), 700–715.

Bratman, Michael (2014), *Shared Agency: A Planning Theory of Acting Together* (Oxford: Oxford University Press).

Brennan, Geoff., and Lomasky, Lauren (1993), *Democracy and Decision: The Pure Theory of Electoral Preference* (New York: Cambridge University Press).

Brennan, Jason (2016), 'The Ethics and Rationality of Voting', *Stanford Encyclopedia of Philosophy*, 28 July.

Broome, John (2012), *Climate Matters* (New York: W. W. Norton).

Citron, Danielle (2009), 'Cyber Civil Rights', *Boston University Law Review*, 89, 62–125.

Citron, Danielle (2014), *Hate Crimes in Cyberspace* (Cambridge, MA: Harvard University Press).

Clack, Beverley, ed. (1999), *Misogyny in the Western Philosophical Tradition: A Reader* (Abingdon: Routledge).

Collins, Stephanie (2013), 'Collectives' Duties and Collectivization Duties', *Australasian Journal of Philosophy* 91/2, 231–248.

Collins, Stephanie, and de Haan, Niels (2021), 'Interconnected Blameworthiness', *The Monist* 104(2), 195–209.

Cullity, Garrett (2004), *The Moral Demands of Affluence* (Oxford: Clarendon Press).

Dhrodia, Azmina (2017), 'Unsocial Media: The Real Toll of Online Abuse against Women', *Amnesty Global Insights on Medium*, 20 November, https://medium.com/amnesty-insights/unsocial-media-the-real-toll-of-online-abuse-against-women-37134ddab3f4 accessed 1st September 2021.

Dworkin, Andrea (2008), *Intercourse* (New York: Basic Books).

Frye, Marilyn (1983), *The Politics of Reality* (New York: Crossing Press).

Gilbert, Margaret (1989), *On Social Facts* (Abingdon: Routledge).

Glozer, Sarah, and McCarthy, Lauren (2021), 'No More Page 3: How a feminist collective took on a media behemoth to challenge everyday sexism', *The Conversation*, March 8th 2021.

Gorman, Ginger (2019), *Troll Hunting* (Melbourne: Hardie Grant Books).

Hawthorne, Susan, and Klein, Renate (1999), *Cyberfeminism: Connectivity, Critique and Creativity* (North Melbourne: Spinifex Press).

Held, Virginia (1970), 'Can a Random Collective of Individuals Be Morally Responsible?', *Journal of Philosophy* 68/14, 471–481.

Herring, Susan (1993), 'Gender and Democracy in Computer-Mediated Communication', *Electronic Journal of Communication* 3(2), 476–489.

Herring, Susan (1996), 'Gender Differences in CMC: Bringing Familiar Baggage to the New Frontier', in Victor Vitanza, ed., *CyberReader* (Boston, MA: Allyn & Bacon), 144–154.

Hiller, Avram (2011), 'Climate Change and Individual Responsibility', *The Monist* 94(3), 349–368.

Jane, Emma (2014), '"Your an Ugly Whorish Slut": Understanding E-Bile', *Feminist Media Studies* 14(4), 531–546.

Jeong, Sarah (2016), 'The History of Twitter's Rules', *Vice*, 15 January, https://www.vice.com/en/article/z43xw3/the-history-of-twitters-rules accessed 1st September 2021.

Kagan, Shelly (2011), 'Do I Make a Difference?', *Philosophy & Public Affairs* 39(2), 105–141.

Kingston, Ewan., and Sinnott-Armstrong, Walter. (2018), 'What's Wrong with Joyguzzling?', *Ethical Theory and Moral Practice* 21(1), 169–186.

Koebler, Jason, and Cox, Joseph (2019), 'How Twitter Sees Itself', *Vice*, 8 October, https://www.vice.com/en/article/a35nbj/twitter-content-moderation accessed 1st September 2021.

Kohn, Margaret (2000), 'Language, Power and Persuasion: Towards a Critique of Deliberative Democracy', *Constellations: An International Journal of Critical and Democratic Theory* 7(3), 408–429.

Kulwin, Noah (2018), 'The Internet Apologies …', *New York Magazine*, 16 April.

Kutz, Christopher (2007), *Complicity* (Cambridge: Cambridge University Press).

Langton, Rae (1993), 'Speech Acts and Unspeakable Acts', *Philosophy & Public Affairs* 22(4), 292–330.

Lawford-Smith, Holly (2015), 'What 'We'?', *Journal of Social Ontology* 1(2), 225–249.

Lawford-Smith, Holly (2018), 'Does Purchasing Make Consumers Complicit in Global Labour Injustice?', *Res Publica* 24(3), 319–338.

Lawford-Smith, Holly (2019), *Not In Their Name* (Oxford: Oxford University Press).

Lawford-Smith, Holly, and Tuckwell, William (2020), 'Act Consequentialism and the No-Difference Challenge', *Oxford Handbook of Consequentialism* (Oxford: Oxford University Press).

Lepora, Chiara, and Goodin, Robert (2013), *Complicity and Compromise* (Oxford: Oxford University Press).

List, Christian, and Pettit, Philip (2011), *Group Agency: The Possibility, Design, and Status of Corporate Agents* (Oxford: Oxford University Press).

Lukianoff, Greg, and Haidt, Jonathan (2018), *The Coddling of the American Mind* (London: Penguin Books).

Massanari, Adrienne (2015), '#Gamergate and the Fappening: How Reddit's Algorithm, Governance, and Culture Support Toxic Technocultures', *New Media and Society* 19(3), 329–346.

McLellan, Betty (2010), *Unspeakable: A Feminist Ethic of Speech* (Townsville, QLD: Otherwise Publications).

McNair, Brian (2017), *An Introduction to Political Communication*, 6th edn (London: Routledge).

McTernan, Emily (2018), 'Microaggressions, Equality, and Social Practices', *Journal of Political Philosophy* 26(3), 261–281.

Megarry, Jessica (2014), 'Online Incivility or Sexual Harassment: Conceptualising Women's Experiences in the Digital Age', *Women's Studies International Forum*, 47, 46–55.

Megarry, Jessica (2018), 'Under the Watchful Eyes of Men: Theorising the Implications of Male Surveillance Practices for Feminist Activism on Social Media', *Feminist Media Studies*, 18(6), 1070–1085.

Megarry, Jessica (2020), *The Limitations of Social Media Feminism: No Space of Our Own* (London: Palgrave Macmillan).

Moriarty, Jeffrey (2016), 'Business Ethics', *Stanford Encyclopedia of Philosophy*, 17 November, https://plato.stanford.edu/entries/ethics-business/ accessed 1st September 2021.

Nefsky, Julia (2012), 'Consequentialism and the Problem of Collective Harm: A Reply to Kagan', *Philosophy & Public Affairs* 39(4), 364–395.

Nussbaum, Martha (2007), *Frontiers of Justice* (Cambridge, MA: Harvard University Press).

Omnicore (2020), 'Twitter by the Numbers: Stats, Demographics, and Fun Facts', 10 February, https://www.omnicoreagency.com/twitter-statistics/ accessed 1st September 2021.

Pateman, Carole (1988), *The Sexual Contract* (Stanford, CA: Stanford University Press).

Perrin, Andrew, and Anderson, Monica (2019), 'Share of U.S. Adults Using Social Media, Including Facebook, Is Mostly Unchanged since 2018', Pew Research Centre, 10 April, https://www.pewresearch.org/fact-tank/2019/04/10/share-of-u-s-adults-using-social-media-including-facebook-is-mostly-unchanged-since-2018/, accessed 11 August 2021.

Pettit, Philip, and Schweikard, David (2006), 'Joint Actions and Group Agents', *Philosophy of the Social Sciences* 36(1), 18–39.

Rantilla, Kelly (2020), 'Social Media and Monopoly', *Ohio Northern University Law Review* 46, 161–179.

Richardson, Kathleen (2019), 'The Business of Ethics, Robotics and Artificial Intelligence', in Teresa Heffernan, ed., *Cyborg Futures: Cross Disciplinary Perspectives on Artificial Intelligence and Robots* (Cham: Palgrave Macmillan), 113–126.

Scolere, Leah, Pruchniewska, Urszula, and Duffy, Brooke Erin (2018), 'Constructing the Platform-Specific Self-Brand: The Labor of Social Media Promotion', *Social Media + Society* 4(3), 1–11.

Singer, Peter (2009), *The Life You Can Save* (New York: Random House).

Simpson, Brian (2014), 'Tracking Children, Constructing Fear: GPS and the Manufacture of Family Safety', *Information and Communications Technology Law* 23(3), 273–285.

Southern, Rosalynd, and Harmer, Emily (2021), 'Twitter, Incivility and "Everyday" Gendered Othering: An Analysis of Tweets Sent to UK Members of Parliament', *Social Science Computer Review*, 39(2), 259–275.

Spender, Dale (1980), *Man Made Language* (Sydney: Pandora).

Thorseth, May (2006), 'Worldwide Deliberation and Public Use of Reason Online', *Ethics and Information Technology* 8(4), 243–252.

Thorseth, May (2008), 'Reflective Judgement and Enlarged Thinking Online', *Ethics and Information Technology* 10(4), 221–231.

United Nations (2009), 'Implementing the Responsibility to Protect: Report of the Secretary General', 12 January, https://www.un.org/ruleoflaw/blog/document/report-of-the-secret ary-general-implementing-the-responsibility-to-protect/ accessed 1st September 2021.

Véliz, Carissa (2019), 'Online Masquerade: Redesigning the Internet for Free Speech through the Use of Pseudonyms', *Journal of Applied Philosophy* 36(4), 643–658.

Wahlquist, Calla (2018), 'Is Melbourne in the Grip of African Crime Gangs? The Facts behind the Lurid Headlines', *The Guardian*, 3 January.

Wringe, Bill (2005), 'Needs, Rights, and Collective Obligations', *Royal Institute of Philosophy Supplement* 80, 187–206.

Wringe, Bill (2014), 'From Global Collective Obligations to Institutional Obligations', *Midwest Studies in Philosophy* XXXVIII, 171–186.

CHAPTER 10

EXTREME SPEECH, DEMOCRATIC DELIBERATION, AND SOCIAL MEDIA

JEFFREY W. HOWARD

INTRODUCTION

DELIBERATION among citizens is a touchstone of contemporary normative democratic theory. For better or worse, online networks are now the principal site of civic deliberation. What the coffee house was to the public sphere in the eighteenth century (Habermas 1962), social media surely is to the twenty-first. Peer-to-peer sharing platforms have achieved an amplification of ordinary citizens' voices in a manner unthinkable just a few years ago. In everyone's pocket is a device enabling countless encounters with one's fellow citizens, on anything and everything of public political concern. Citizens who, in an earlier era, would have had their views on some policy matter heard by just their neighbours can now find their speech re-tweeted to millions.

The fact that social networks constitute a central site of democratic discourse seems to militate against the legal regulation of speech on these platforms. A central commitment of deliberative democracy is precisely that it ought to be an open exchange of citizens' authentic convictions. This democratic argument looms large in the scholarly literature on freedom of speech, sitting prominently alongside a raft of other arguments that aim to protect citizens' right to express their viewpoints (and hear the viewpoints of others). From this position, it seems to follow that *indirectly* suppressing citizens' speech—by legally commanding social media companies to do so through their content moderation practices—cannot be morally justified.

Yet the very amplification of varied voices that social media make possible—and that fuels optimistic sentiments about the democratizing power of the internet—has a dark side. Hateful speakers, hostile to the values of free and equal citizenship that underpin liberal democracy, can weaponize these platforms to cause a wide variety of harms. Racist conspiracy theories have inspired mass shootings around the globe, just as on-line sermons advocating religious extremism have encouraged suicide attacks. Given the state's duty to protect its citizens from wrongful harm, cases like these motivate the argument for restricting extreme speech on social media—controversially, by requiring social media companies to purge such content from their platforms.

This chapter examines the state of the debate on the fraught question of whether ex-treme speech should be suppressed or otherwise legally combatted on social media, or whether doing so would be incompatible with fundamental principles of democracy and free speech. I begin by reviewing the argument that freedom of expression, properly understood, protects a wide range of extreme speech, such as terrorist incitement and hate speech. Central to this discussion is the aforementioned thesis that *because* social media constitute a crucial venue of democratic discourse, it is all the more important that citizens be free to express their views, however noxious.

The next section turns to the moral and legal responsibilities of social media companies regarding extreme speech. Even if, as I believe, individual speakers have no right to propa-gate extremist content online (such that individual criminal or civil liability for such speech could, in principle, be justified), it does not follow that social media companies should be legally subjected to a duty to remove such content. A recurrent complaint is that because social media networks are mere platforms on which users post their own content, it would be perverse to hold these companies responsible as if they were publishers. After exploring the extremely young philosophical debate on this difficult question, I explore various philo-sophical challenges that arise in the course of specifying an adequate regulatory model.

The final section then explores what measures there are for combatting extreme speech online beyond the legal regulation of social media networks. One ubiquitous suggestion in the scholarly literature on freedom of expression—one with deep affinities with the ideal of democratic deliberation—is that the best way to combat extreme speech is not to ban it, but rather to argue back through *counter-speech*. This proposal raises the question of who, exactly, ought to argue back against extremist voices, how they ought to go about it, and why it is reasonable to demand of them that they do it. I explore both state-centric and citizen-centric responses to this question in the scholarly literature. And I discuss how to think about the policy choice between banning extremist content and permitting it so it can be challenged.

TOO EXTREME FOR DEMOCRATIC DISCOURSE? EXTREME SPEECH AND THE RIGHT TO FREEDOM OF EXPRESSION

Before we can assess what moral duties social media companies might have to combat extreme speech, we need to assess its normative status. Is it the kind of speech that is protected by the moral right to freedom of expression? If so, then while private companies may decide that it has no place on their platforms, they cannot be forced by law to suppress it. Thus, before we can turn to the issue of what social media companies can be forced to do, one needs to set the stage for that discussion by rehearsing a set of debates over the limits of free speech.

Few believe that freedom of speech is *absolute*; all accept that some speech—be it soliciting a hitman to kill one's nemesis, or intentionally libelling a private citizen to destroy his reputation and livelihood—does not fall under the protective ambit of the right to freedom of expression. Yet liberal democracies disagree about whether speech that exhibits contempt for the values of liberal democracy itself—so-called *extreme speech*—is protected by a properly constituted principle of free speech.[1]

What is extreme speech? The phrase is a common one in the scholarly literature (e.g. Weinstein and Hare 2009), naming speech that expresses hostility to basic commitments of liberal democracy. The most basic subcategory of extreme speech is speech that incites violence and other serious violations of fundamental rights—what I have elsewhere called *dangerous speech* (Howard 2019b; following Benesch 2012). In the UK, for example, there is legislation forbidding the encouragement of terrorism (even implicitly, through speech 'glorifying' past terrorist acts) (Barendt 2009; Choudhury 2009). Under this law, British citizens have been arrested for tweeting praise of the Islamic State of Iraq and Syria (ISIS) and Al-Qaeda (Press Association 2016). Contrast this with the United States, where the Supreme Court has held, since 1969, that speech advocating criminal violence and other lawbreaking is constitutionally protected as free speech—except in emergency cases, in which speech is *intended* and *likely* to lead *imminently* to illegal conduct (*Brandenburg v. Ohio* 395 U.S. 444, 1969). Because online content seldom incites violence *imminently*, as there is time for the audience to ponder whether to act on its exhortations, vast swaths of terrorist propaganda is held protected in the United States (see Tsesis 2017, who thinks this is partly mistaken, for discussion).

The same divergence between democracies is on display with respect to the overlapping subcategory of so-called *hate speech*, that is, expressions of hatred toward vulnerable groups.[2] I call it an *overlapping* category, since a principal reason to be concerned about hate speech is precisely that it can inspire violence (see Howard 2019a: 104, 2019b)—though the empirical assumption on which this hypothesis rests is controversial (Heinze 2016: 125ff). This is only one rationale for restricting hate speech, where harm is caused via an intervening agent. But hate speech can also cause harm directly (see Schauer 1993 for this distinction). For example, some hate speech takes the form of intimidating threats or harassment, constituting an especially objectionable form of such speech (Delgado 1982; Howard 2019a: 101–102). Further, hate speech directly communicated to vulnerable groups can also be objectionable because it undermines the assurance of dignity and equal standing (Waldron 2012). The internet contains both forms of hate speech, and has a distinctive capacity to propel and prolong their harms when contrasted with offline hate speech. (For discussion of the distinctive power of hate speech online, see Tsesis 2001; Delgado and Stefanic 2014; Cohen-Almagor 2015; Brown 2018).

Notwithstanding the harms it may cause, is extreme speech protected by the moral right to free speech?[3] The standard way to answer this question is to review the arguments that serve to justify the moral right to free speech, and then ask whether those arguments count in favour of including extreme speech within the right's ambit (Howard 2019a: 96). For the purposes of this entry, I will focus on arguments that relate to democracy, and in particular that appeal to the idea of *democratic legitimacy*. I suggest that these arguments do not supply decisive protection for extreme speech; we would not wrong democratic citizens by restricting extreme speech on social media.

According to deliberative democrats, the legitimacy of laws flows from the fact that those laws were conceived in a process of open debate among citizens (e. g. Cohen 1989; Habermas 1992). This debate has both non-instrumental and instrumental value (Gutmann and Thompson 2004). The non-instrumental value of the deliberation inheres in the value of respecting our fellow citizens' equal moral status. By permitting one another to speak—and listening to one another—on questions of public concern, we respect each other as possessing the capacity for judgement over complex questions of public concern. Further, we respect each other as agents who are entitled to a justification for the coercion that is exercised over us. The instrumental value of deliberation inheres in the way it improves the quality of policy outcomes—for example, by enabling decision-making to incorporate the diversity of citizens' perspectives (Landemore 2012).

An apparent implication of this view is that the *legitimacy* of democratic decisions—by which we might mean either the permissibility of their enforcement, or their morally binding, authoritative status—is attenuated as more citizens are prevented from expressing their convictions (however wrongheaded) in democratic discourse. This view has been defended, in subtly different forms, by a wide array of scholars (Brettschneider 2012; Heinze 2016; Heyman 2009, Meiklejohn 1948, 1960; Post 1991, 2009, 2011; Sunstein 1993; Weinstein 2009). On this view, contributions to public discourse cannot be supressed simply because of their hateful or extreme character. As Ronald Dworkin puts the point, 'The majority has no right to impose its will on someone who is forbidden to raise a voice in protest or argument or objection before the decision is taken' (2009: vii). If social media are together a central forum of democratic discourse, then, it follows that governmentally imposed, viewpoint-based restrictions on what can be said on these platforms are undemocratic.

What should we make of this family of arguments? Consider the non-instrumental variation of the argument first. One possible reply is to grant that limiting extreme speech diminishes the democratic character of a polity, but to insist that this loss can be justified. Perhaps we *pro tanto* wrong extreme speakers by suppressing their speech, or indeed wrong *all citizens*, given everybody's interest in maximal democratic legitimacy, but this, all things considered, can be justified, given the comparable importance of preventing serious harm. So, for example, when we stop terrorists from advocating terrorism by enacting statutes restricting such advocacy, we do something wrong, but it might be justified nonetheless.[4]

Another possible reply is that even if limiting extreme speech diminishes democracy, this need not commit any *pro tanto* wrong at all, as not all instances of democracy have non-instrumental value (Beerbohm 2012: 36). So, for example, Jonathan Quong notes that when we are determining whether a moral right protects a particular action, we must 'ask whether the particular act that is alleged to be protected by a right is consistent with the overall moral ideal which the system of rights is meant to uphold' (2010: 308; see also Waldron 1989: 518). Because extreme speech expresses hostility towards the system of rights, on this view, it is not protected. A similar strategy, which I have defended, asks whether the moral right in question—in this case, democratic citizens' rights to express extreme speech—is compatible with moral duties that democratic citizens have (Howard 2019b: 232). So, for example, if democratic citizens have duties *not* to advocate for the violation of other citizens' fundamental rights, then these duties constrain what moral rights they have.

Even if we grant that *speakers* have no right to express extreme speech, it may be that efforts to suppress such speech wrong its prospective *listeners*. According to one influential theory, 'a legitimate government is one whose authority citizens can recognize while still regarding themselves as equal, autonomous, rational agents' (Scanlon 1972: 214). This view does not mean that no speech can ever be restricted; but it does rule out certain *justifications* for restricting speech. As T. M. Scanlon argues, 'those justifications are illegitimate which appeal to the fact that it would be a bad thing if the view communicated by certain acts of expression were to become generally believed' (1972: 209; see also Dworkin 1996: 200). While seldom explicitly connected to the idea of deliberative democracy, this argument articulates the deliberative democrat's central concern about legitimacy: that if the state has rigged what ideas were allowed to be aired in a deliberation prior to a law's passage, the legitimacy of that law is called into serious question.

Yet this argument, too, faces important objections (so much so that Scanlon largely rejected it; 1979: 532ff). The most significant objection is that autonomous citizens *also* have an interest in avoiding the wide variety of harms that extreme speech can cause (Amdur 1980: 299; Brison 1998: 329). It is not clear why the interest in being respected as an autonomous thinker ought to have priority over this other weighty interest (for further discussion, see Howard 2019a: 97, 2019b: 236).

There are other reasons for why listeners may value exposure to extreme speech— not because of any deontological constraint on state power, but because of putative benefits that might flow from such exposure. This brings me to the *instrumental* version of the democratic legitimacy argument. The central point here is that by enabling a wide variety of voices' perspectives to enter the democratic discourse, it is thereby epistemically enriched, leading to better policy outcomes. This militates in favour of a truly capacious public discourse, but does it require an unlimited one? One reply here is to deny that extreme speech genuinely contributes to the epistemic value of public discourse; there is little to learn from engagement with neo-Nazis and white supremacists (*pace* Mill 1859/1978, who insisted that there was much to gain from our 'collision with error').[5] This point seems especially apt on social media, where a preponderance of those exposed to extremist views are those *already sympathetic to them*, and so inclined to visit the relevant websites, chat rooms, and pages (see Sunstein 2017).

But even if there *is* considerable epistemic value by permitting extreme views to be aired, this value is not infinite. Surely, we should accept some kind of trade-off between whatever epistemic value is achieved by permitting extreme speech and the obvious value of protecting citizens from the various harms such speech can inspire (Howard 2019a: 244).

Some deliberative democrats are likely to offer the following rejoinder: we cannot identify *ex ante* which views are true and which truths are false; a central point of deliberation is to precisely separate the wheat from the chaff. But this is why the most plausible characterization of extreme speech will pick out only that content whose falsehood is *beyond reasonable dispute*—for example, white supremacism. So, for example, when we're concerned about speech that endangers others by advocating the violation of their moral rights, it is proper to focus only on violations of rights that are properly incontrovertible (Howard 2019b: 215), that is, that no one could reasonably deny counts as a genuine violation of a genuine moral right. This means that citizens would retain broad scope to advocate views within the ambit of reasonable disagreement, but not to harm citizens by inciting rights violations outside of that ambit.[6]

I have inspected some of the most prevalent arguments in the free speech literature that connect to the political autonomy of democratic citizens. Importantly, I have not discussed all of them; for example, I have not discussed the powerful theory developed by Seana Shiffrin, who argues that freedom of expression traces to our fundamental interests as thinkers (2014; for discussion, see Scanlon 2011).[7] Nor have I dealt with the fact that while deliberative democracy is generally an account of the proper nature of public discourse within a nation state, social media is inherently global—a fact that raises a host of complications. Still, I have established two crucial points: that the scholarly literature is far from settled on the question of whether extremist speech must be permitted into democratic discourse; and that there are several powerful reasons on offer to think that it should not, such that democratic citizens would not be wronged by such content's removal from social media. Whether social media platforms are morally obligated to remove such content—and whether such obligations should be enforced through law—are further questions, depending on further moral considerations, to which I now turn.

PLATFORMING HATE: ON THE DUTIES OF SOCIAL MEDIA COMPANIES

Should social media platforms be required to suppress extreme content? It will not suffice simply to point out that such platforms are managed by private corporations that accordingly have a right to do whatever they wish. The idea that private corporations are appropriately saddled with various legal duties not to contribute to unjustified harm to the broader public is nothing new; just consider the raft of regulations corporations face with respect to environmental protection. Nor is it anything new to suppose that corporations should be obligated to look after the well-being of those who are using its products. Corporations—whether they are conceived as bona fide group agents or simply fictitious agents—are duty-bound to refrain from perpetrating wrongful harms, just like individual agents.

In the case of harmful speech on social media, controversy arises because corporations do not *directly* cause harm through their services; rather, they *enable others* to cause harms by supplying them with a platform through which to cause them. Especially significant is the fact that technology companies do not (typically) *intend* that users deploy their platforms to incite terrorism or racist hatred. One way to defend the legal immunity of social platforms for users' illegal posts, then, is to argue that they are simply 'like a billboard: anybody can sign or display anything on it' (Koltay 2019: 157). They are, in this way, privately owned versions of Speakers' Corner in Hyde Park, where anyone can show up to say whatever they want. If those who show up engage speech that is illegal, then *they* may be prosecuted or sued for saying it, but the owner of the platform is not to be held responsible. In stark opposition this 'no liability' view is the thesis that social media networks are akin to either traditional media companies or book publishers, such that they are jointly responsible with users for illegal content. So, just as a publishing house can be sued alongside an author for a book's defamatory content, perhaps social media platforms could be liable alongside users for the illegal extreme speech they post.[8]

Both models are unattractive. The first 'no liability' model is defective because it relies upon mistaken views about a widely discussed philosophical idea known as *intervening agency*. A standard view is that if I act in a certain way, and this leads to harm only because of the intervening decisions of a responsible agent, then this fact (usually) immunizes me from moral responsibility. Yet this seems to me to be false; just consider cases in which someone sells an automatic weapon to someone who foreseeably plans to use it to violate others' rights. When I foreseeably cause harm to innocents through the conduct of others, I am accountable for these decisions and can be blamed for them (Tadros 2016). I have argued elsewhere that this moral truth applies to speech, just as it applies to all conduct (Howard 2019b: 216–217).

It might be replied that so long as the speaker does not *intend* for any intervening agent to engage in wrongful harm, he or she is off the hook. But this cannot be right; a lack of intention is seldom sufficient to immunize a party from moral responsibility (as our intuitions about selling weapons suggests). Leading philosophical work on complicity (understood as causally contributing to the wrongs of others) holds that, to be (*pro tanto*) wrongfully complicit in the wrong of another, one need not *intend* to aid the primary wrongdoer in his or her wrongful project. Rather, it is enough that one knew, or ought to have known, that one was causally contributing to its realization (Lepora and Goodin 2013: 83). (Given the ubiquity of journalistic reporting on the problems of extreme speech on social media, and platforms' efforts to limit extreme content on their networks *voluntarily*, it would appear that this knowledge condition is satisfied.) Such a view offers a rationale for the current 'notice-and-takedown' approach currently

prevalent in the European Union, whereby platforms are required to remove illegal content of which they are notified.[9] This is not necessarily the right regulatory model (more
on that below), but it reflects the insight that it is perfectly possible to aid and abet the
wrongs of another unintentionally.[10]

But the 'publisher' model is defective, too. Simply because social media companies
might be complicit in the wrongs perpetrated by users (e.g., by providing a platform
for the incitement of violence), it does not follow that social media companies are *co-
principals* in these wrongs. Social media companies are not publishers in the traditional
sense; Facebook plainly does not publish the content placed on it by its several billion
users in anything like the way the *New York Times* publishes its editorials—authoring
and standing by their content—or the way in which Penguin Random House publishes
its books—vouching for their merit, and while not necessarily endorsing their content,
suggesting that their content is worth one's time and money. Were regulations to treat
social media firms like publishers, they would need to engage in extraordinary levels of
so-called 'upload filtering'—screening all content for all potential legal issues before it
ever hit the internet. This would radically alter the nature of social media, potentially for
the worse.

We should likely opt, then, for a middle ground in how we are to conceive of social
media networks—not neutral platforms, nor proper publishers. But what? Even if social media companies are not publishers, there is a sense in which they are nevertheless
a new kind of *editor*. As Tim Berners-Lee, the inventor of the World Wide Web, put it,
commenting on what is presently the world's largest social media network: 'Facebook
makes billions of editorial decisions every day ... The fact that these decisions are being
made by algorithms rather than human editors doesn't make Facebook any less responsible ...' (Lee 2016). To be sure, as Koltay notes, a platform is not a *fully fledged* editor;
'it does not initiate or commission the production of content'. Yet 'it is an editor in the
sense that it makes decisions concerning pieces of content and filters, removes content
or keeps it available. It also controls all communications through the platform. All in
all, it is clearly not neutral toward content' (Koltay 2019: 189). It is plausible to think of
social media networks neither as platforms, nor as publishers, but rather as *curators* (cf.
Herman 2016).

This leads to the question: what are the moral constraints on curating users' content, and how should they be enforced? Consider the natural habitat of this term: an
art gallery. Imagine a peculiar kind of enormous 'open' art gallery, where members of
the public are free to display their art, in their millions. Based on its knowledge of visitors' preferences, it directs them to the sections of the gallery that are likely to command
their attention the most, giving grander spaces to those artworks that attract the greatest
interest. Now suppose that artwork inciting hatred (e.g. racist propaganda art) is illegal.
It seems plausible that the gallery should make a reasonable effort to limit the display
of this art—making a reasonable effort to identify it (e.g. investigating complaints) and
removing it in an expeditious manner upon discovering it. The duty to do so would
simply be the duty not to be complicit in the harms such hateful content inspires, by
providing a platform to do it.

If this *curator model* is right, everything hangs on what it is reasonable to expect curators to do. What, exactly, is it reasonable to expect social media companies to do to combat extreme speech? At the time of publication, there is a flurry of political debate on exactly this topic. I am writing this entry shortly after Germany has enacted a law that ramps up the 'notice-and-takedown' mechanism with respect to hate speech (*Netzwerkdurchsetzungsgesetz*, or NetzDG), which requires a robust complaints mechanism requiring companies to remove 'manifestly unlawful' content within twenty-four hours or risk fines up €50 million. The UK is presently contemplating its own legislation to saddle social media companies with a 'duty of care', whereby companies must 'take reasonable steps to keep users safe' (UK Government 2019)—to be specified by a government regulatory body, such as Ofcom, the telecommunications regulator. So, just as amusement parks must pursue various precautionary measures to keep visitors safe, so, too, should online networks (Woods and Perrin 2019). This legislation has provoked fierce debate, and at the time of writing it is difficult to predict what the final law will involve (for discussion, see Woods 2019; Nash 2019; Tambini 2019; see Theil 2019 for a comparison of UK and German approaches). These real-world developments will no doubt provoke further philosophical reflection on what, exactly, a duty of care is and what it demands[11] (e.g. see Herstein 2010, for reflection on that general issue).

What is striking is that, in academia, philosophers have scarcely weighed in; those who are making the greatest contribution at present are (theoretically minded) lawyers, especially scholars of media law (e.g. Rowbottom 2018b: 341ff; Koltay 2019; PoKempner 2019). But there are central philosophical questions here that require greater attention from the philosophical community. A central topic of burgeoning debate, I suspect, will concern the role of artificial intelligence (AI) in content moderation. If using AI is the only efficient way to take down large quantities of extreme content, we face the challenge that highly imperfect algorithmic moderation processes are likely to be either *overinclusive*—taking down more content than we would want—or *underinclusive*— taking down less, or indeed both in different respects (see Douek 2021 for related discussion). This, then, raises a wide set of important questions about what collateral costs of speech restrictions (e.g. reduction in the amount of sarcasm on the internet) it would be reasonable to expect citizens to bear. While I seek to address such questions in my future work, there is little philosophical attention to them at present.

Another important question concerns whether social media networks *themselves* enjoy expressive rights that immunize them from interference. The fact that social media networks are not neutral—that they inevitably take responsibility for the algorithms that determine what content is promoted or quieted—has a particular interesting implication. To the extent that social media firms *do* share some of the properties of publishers or editors, they may be entitled to the protections of freedom of speech and freedom of the press. As Koltay notes, 'In a sense, its news feed is Facebook's "opinion" on what its users might be most interested in and how the platform's business interests could be best served in that context. If a platform has an opinion, it is afforded protection under the constitutional rules.' Of course, that does not mean the platforms are allowed to enable any speech they like; it still means that their speech 'may also be subject to restriction, pursuant to applicable legal principles' (2019: 159). But an intriguing upshot of this view is that *if* a certain category of speech is protected as free speech for users, it would be impermissible for the state to require social media companies to suppress it. Indeed, we should be very suspicious of requiring social media companies to suppress speech that individual users have a legal right to express.

In reply, it may be a mistake to view a social media company as a merely private entity entitled to express 'its' own views. This is partly because of doubts about the expressive rights of corporations. But more fundamentally, social networks have enormous power over the public discourse (Klonick 2018). The nexus of social media is clearly part of what Rawls called *the basic structure* of society, given that 'its effects are so profound and pervasive' (Rawls 1971/1999: 82) on the shape of democratic deliberation. Suppose a social network started to ban the expression of certain religious or political views on the grounds that it disfavoured the view. Given the role of these networks in curating the democratic discourse of contemporary societies, there is a powerful argument for thinking that *the same* free speech principles that bind governments should also regulate social media platforms (see Jackson 2014 for discussion).[12] Those inclined to view social media networks as a kind of communications utility, albeit privately owned as a legal matter, would be inclined to support such a position (see Lentz 2011 for related discussion). In my view, there is nothing *morally* incompatible with viewing these networks as a public utility while also requiring them to remove extreme speech (even though this would raise constitutional issues in the United States).

The final philosophical puzzle that remains unsolved concerns the issue of *asymmetric enforcement of duties*. It seems clear that we are entering a world in which the *primary* way in which extreme speech is combatted is by removing it on social media, rather than prosecuting the extreme speakers themselves. This raises a worry: shouldn't the initial speakers be held accountable if anyone is? In reply, it must be noted that even if speakers *initiate* extreme content by posting it, it is social media platforms that enable its widespread dissemination. Further, there may be something morally desirable about a world in which social media companies limit the dissemination of extreme speech, but individual citizens are nevertheless free to express it. As Jacob Rowbottom notes, this is, in part, a matter of efficiency; given the huge amount of illegal content, 'it is easier to ask a gatekeeper to control the flow of such content than to bring a legal action against each individual publisher' (Rowbottom 2018a: 2). But a more principled worry is that prosecuting individual speakers for each and every extreme statement—however careless—will disproportionately interfere in public discourse and undermine conversation (Rowbottom 2012). What is more, insofar as we think there is *some* interest to engage in extreme speech (even if not weighty enough to justify a moral right, as I have argued in Howard 2019b), permitting such speech—but then requiring intermediaries to limit its dissemination—'may strike a balance between the free flow of conversation and any potential harm' (Rowbottom 2018b: 2). The upshot, then, would be that while individual speakers *do* have moral duties to refrain from posting extreme content, we would refrain from enforcing these duties directly.

In closing, I should note that there are exceptions to the general trend of increasing social media regulation, which raise their own philosophical complications. In the United States, restricting extreme speech on social media will not be so straightforward. Even if Section 230 of the Communications Decency Act were altered in various ways to make platforms liable for illegal speech posted by users (e.g. libel), extreme speech is mostly legal in the United States. And it is highly unlikely that this fact will change any time soon; as mentioned, the prevailing interpretation of the First Amendment to the US Constitution protects extreme speech except in cases of imminent harm (though cf. Tsesis 2017).[13] Even so, many media networks are nevertheless taking it upon themselves to remove extreme content *voluntarily*. As Koltay puts it, 'This means the enforcement of a "pseudo legal system", with its own code, case law, sanctions ... taking place in a privately owned virtual space' (2019: 3). We have reason to be concerned about the prospect of what republican political theorists term *domination* by these entities (Pettit 2012); if these social media firms are going to become the *real* arbiters of what people are permitted to say in the public sphere, a question arises as to whether they enjoy the right kind of *legitimacy* to wield this form of power. If public discourse is to be curtailed to prevent harm, perhaps it should be done by a legitimate democratic state, or by no one at all.

THE ETHICS OF ONLINE COUNTER-SPEECH

What else might be done to combat extreme speech on social media? A recurrent suggestion in the scholarly literature on free speech—indeed, for some, a rationale for free speech itself—appeals to the importance of *counter-speech*. As Justice Louis Brandeis of the US Supreme Court put it, reflecting on the best way to confront speech that is harmful or otherwise disagreeable: '[T]he remedy to be applied is more speech, not enforced silence' (*Whitney v. California* 274 U.S. 357 (1927)). In other words, rather than suppress extreme speech, we need to *argue back against it*. This strategy is an especially fitting one in the context of a deliberative democracy, in which public deliberation (followed by voting) among citizens and their representatives is the default mechanism for dealing with disagreement. And while deliberative democrats tend to suggest that the main substance of their disagreement is *reasonable* disagreement about what justice requires, there is no reason why *unreasonable* disagreements (in which one side is manifestly mistaken) should not also be dealt with through the same strategy. This section explores the moral status of this strategy of response.

Why might counter-speech be preferred to the use of legal coercion? The traditional argument in defence of counter-speech is simply that it is the only option morally available. If the moral right to free speech protects extreme speech, as many philosophers contend, then counter-speech is the only recourse we have left to combat the harms such speech can generate. As discussed above, I am not convinced that this traditional argument succeeds. However, simply because extreme speech is unprotected by the moral right to free speech does not automatically mean that we should prefer the coercive use of state power to peaceful alternatives. A better reason to prefer counter-speech, I have proposed, appeals to the philosophical *principle of necessity*, familiar from the ethics of self-defence (Howard 2019b: 248ff). According to the necessity principle, one ought to avert a threat using the least amount of harm or force, *ceteris paribus*. So, if police can successfully deescalate a dangerous situation through *talking*, they should do that rather than deploying violence. Likewise, if one can attain an important social goal without deploying the coercive power of the state, then *ceteris paribus* we ought to prefer the non-coercive strategy.

Ceteris paribus is an important qualification here. If counter-speech is a significantly less effective strategy, or if it is morally unreasonable to demand that the relevant counter-speakers engage in the requisite counter-speech, then the use of law may turn out to be preferable, after all. An adequate defence of counter-speech thus must attend to the issues of *who* ought to engage in counter-speech, *why* it is reasonable to demand that they undertake, and *how* they ought to undertake it in order to be both ethical and effective (Howard 2019c). I will discuss these issues in turn.

Start with the question of *who* should engage in counter-speech. One possibility is *the state*. Challenging the false dichotomy that the state must either ban extreme content or otherwise sit back and let it proliferate unchecked, Corey Brettschneider argues that the state ought to take on the central role of engaging in counter-speech against extreme views (2012). According to his account of 'democratic persuasion', Brettschneider contends that the state should endeavour to persuade citizens in the grip of extremist views 'to adopt the values of equal citizenship' (2012: 72). In the digital era, this kind of counter-speech could come in many different forms; we might imagine the state recording YouTube videos defending the values of the freedom and equality, or publicizing politicians' speeches doing so on its social media channels. It is tempting to see this as a form of propaganda, though when deployed in the service of just end, we might instead see it as a form of what Jason Stanley has called 'civil rhetoric' (2015).

What is the argument for insisting that the state ought to engage in counter-speech against extreme views? For Brettschneider, the argument appeals to the idea that *if* the state sat back and did nothing in the face of extremist speech, its silence would constitute a form of *complicity* (2012: 71). We might also appeal to the state's obligation to reduce the likelihood of the wrongful harms such extreme speech can inspire—the very same obligation underpinning the case for banning such speech (Howard 2019b). Further, in the case of extreme speech that directly attacks the dignity of vulnerable citizens (of the sort that concerns Waldron 2012), we might think that state counter-speech can more effectively *block* such dignitarian harm by authoritatively affirming the dignity of the attacked citizens (Lepoutre 2017).

Even if state speech is useful in upholding the dignity of citizens who are directly smeared by hate speech, and even if it plays some role in dissuading susceptible citizens from embracing hateful views, it has its limits. Most notably, the liberal state is unlikely to be successful at convincing those in the grip of anti-liberal ideologies to abandon their deeply held convictions (Howard 2019c).

That the state is unlikely to convince opponents naturally leads to the suggestion that *citizens* ought to take up the task of engaging in counter-speech (though, of course, the state could support them in this role in various ways; see Gelber 2012). There have been a variety of attempts in the scholarly literature along these lines. Focusing on the problem of religiously inspired terrorism, Clayton and Stevens argue that liberal adherents to a particular religion ought to engage with those in the grip of an intolerant version of that same religion, since they are those best positioned to persuade (2014: 75). Relatedly, Micah Schwartzman has defended the practice of what Rawls called 'reasoning from conjecture', whereby citizens reason *as if* they shared the argumentative starting points of their interlocutors (2012; cf. Badano and Nuti 2020). In other work, focusing on the problem of right-wing xenophobic populism, Badano and Nuti (2018) defend the claim that citizens have a 'duty of pressure' to try to dissuade their fellows from populist views. And I have argued that all citizens in any position to talk someone out of a dangerous view have powerful reason to do so (2019c).

What is the justification of requiring ordinary citizens to engage in counter-speech, given its difficulties? Some authors have appealed to the *natural duty of justice* (Clayton and Stevens 2014: 81), the moral requirement to support and help advance just institutions. In a similar spirit, others have appealed to the *liberal principle of legitimacy*, which requires citizens to deploy public reason in their engagements with one another on matters of law and policy (Badano and Nuti 2018: 148). I have offered what I take to be a more austere argument, which simply appeals to the natural moral *duty to rescue* others from harm when one can do so at reasonable cost to oneself (Howard 2019c).

One reason to worry about saddling ordinary citizens with duties to engage in counter-speech is that it suggests that even the *victims* of extreme speech have duties to argue back against the speech that degrades and endangers them—which seems unfair (Maitra and McGowan 2012: 9). A possible reply is to argue that even victims of injustice have duties to resist their own oppression (Hay 2011). But a more plausible reply is to recognize that any duty's existence is sensitive to costs; if it is extremely demanding for victims of extreme speech to engage in counter-speech, then it cannot reasonably be required of them (Howard 2019c).

If citizens have moral duties to engage in counter-speech, what do these duties require of them in the digital era? The answer to this question is, to put it mildly, unclear. For example, consider extreme speech propagated on white supremacist websites, chat rooms, or threads. A principal danger of such speech is that it will inspire violence against non-whites. So how should we combat it? Should anti-racists infiltrate these chat rooms, subtly inserting seeds of doubt—or engaging in outright counterargument? The difficulty of answering such questions is compounded by the fact that it is unclear what kinds of counter-speech are actually effective at achieving their aim (see Lepoutre 2019 for relevant discussion). In cases in which the aim is to protect the dignity of vulnerable groups by standing up for them, thereby 'blocking' the hateful speech (Langton 2018; Lepoutre 2017), the aim is achieved just in case the communication is successful. But when the aim of the counter-speech is to change hearts and minds, to persuade susceptible listeners or hardened extremists to reject extremist views, it is simply an open empirical question what strategies are most effective. (For relevant empirical discussion on counter-speech generally, see Benesch et al. 2016 and Brown 2016, and for particular attention to strategies for the online context, see Gagliardone et al. 2015).

Much of the important work left to be done is indeed philosophical. For example, even if *publicly shaming* illiberal citizens on the internet were an effective way of standing up for liberal values, there remain important questions about whether it is morally permissible (see Billingham and Parr 2020). But as with so many applied normative topics, much of the important work that is yet to be done is not strictly philosophical, but rather empirical. This is why it is all the more important that philosophers engage with social scientists, to learn from but also crucially to inform their research agendas. With respect to the issue of online counter-speech, it is vital that we secure an evidence base with which to adjudicate whether online counter-speech is or is not an effective remedy. This is vital precisely because, if counter-speech is not effective, or if it is simply too difficult to do it effectively given constraints on people's time and resources, this could justify a recourse to legal measures.[14]

I sincerely hope this conclusion is false, and that we can indeed combat the harms on social media—as Justice Brandeis hoped for the offline world—with 'more speech'. It is never ideal when a liberal society cracks down on speech, even justifiably, and there is always the risk that it will counter-productively play into extremists' hands (Howard 2019b: 245). As with so many thorny problems in the burgeoning field of digital ethics, we are staring down the precipice at an uncertain new world.

ACKNOWLEDGEMENTS

I am grateful to the Leverhulme Trust for research funding and to Carissa Véliz and an anonymous reviewer for helpful comments.

NOTES

1. I assume, for the sake of this entry, that such a free speech principle is defensible in the first place. Some scholars doubt this (see Alexander 2005, though cf. Kendrick 2017).
2. There is much debate about how to define hate speech, which I do not pursue here; for some varying approaches, see Brison (1998: 313); Brown 2017a, 2017b; Quong 2010: 305n; Waldron 2012: 8–9).
3. I will largely focus on the categories of terrorist advocacy and hate speech, as they are the most pernicious forms of dangerous speech online and raise the thorniest free speech issues. Violent pornography is yet another much-discussed category, which also raises difficult free speech issues (see Scoccia 1996). And there are other forms of dangerous speech online, too, such as recipes for building bombs and instructions on how to commit crimes effectively (see Schauer 2019).
4. This possibility is implied by Heinze (2016); he notes that democratic legitimacy sometimes needs to be compromised to achieve fundamental governmental aims, such as security—though he doubts that this is ever empirically necessary in longstanding stable, prosperous democracies. For related discussion, see Reid (2020).

5. The thesis that the truth is bound to prevail through an open 'marketplace of ideas'—a view strongly associated with Mill, albeit controversially (Gordon 1997)—has been highly discredited in light of the huge empirical literature on cognitive bias. For a terrific review of the relevarnont empirical literature, see Bambauer (2006).

6. This leaves open the important question of what counts as expressing a view. For example, does it qualify as sharing extreme content to 'like' someone else's post sharing that content, thereby promoting it in one's feed? For discussion, see Koltay (2019: 148).

7. My own view is that it is possible to interpret Shiffrin's theory in a manner compatible with restricting extremist speech; for this argument, see Howard (2019b: 228–230). One important implication of Shiffrin's view is that *insincere* speech (e.g. by bots or those deliberately sewing discord by spewing inauthentic hateful sentiments) is largely unprotected by free speech, and so, in principle, permissibly regulated.

8. It is precisely on the condition that social media platforms refrain from exerting strong control over users' speech that they are, at the time of this publication, granted considerable immunity for users' illegal speech by the widely disputed Section 230 of the Communications Decency Act in the United States. For philosophical reflection on Section 230, see Franks (2019).

9. This is spelled out in Article 14 of the Electronic Commerce Directive. A notice-and-takedown approach presently applies in the United States as well, but is largely limited to issues of copyright infringement, as per the Digital Millennium Copyright Act. Notice-and-takedown also characterizes the controversial Network Enforcement Act in Germany (*Netzwerkdurchsetzungsgesetz*), enacted in 2017.

10. The discourse of complicity is not typically used in conjunction with this debate, but I believe it is a plausible framework within which to capture the nature of the wrong as a moral matter. Whether we should think of social media companies as *genuine legal accomplices* in the crimes committed by their users, such that they could be criminally prosecuted for some new inchoate offence ('criminal platforming'), is a further policy question.

11. One promising proposal is that content flagged as extreme by artificial intelligence could be 'quarantined' prior to its review by human moderators—whereby prospective viewers would be notified before seeing it that it is potentially hateful (Ullmann and Tomalin 2020).

12. The idea that social media networks have positive responsibilities not simply to take down harmful speech, but also to keep up legitimate speech is certainly reflected in the popular backlash to cases in which networks remove clearly valuable content, as when Facebook mistakenly removed a famous photograph from the Vietnam War; see https://www.theg uardian.com/technology/2016/sep/09/facebook-reinstates-napalm-girl-photo, accessed 11 August 2021.

13. Different complications are raised by the fact that authoritarian countries have pushed for clearly excessive and impermissible regulation of social media companies (e.g. demanding them to remove content critical of state policy). If the price of doing business in an authoritarian country is to serve as a tool for the repression of citizens' legitimate speech, this is too great a cost.

14. While I have focused on citizens' counter-speech in this section, it is also possible for social media companies themselves to engage in counter-speech (e.g. by putting warning labels around certain content indicating that it violates their community standards). In the case of extreme speech that comes in the form of misinformation, companies can also post links to fact-checking websites. And companies can also combine counter-speech with other methods, such as when Twitter places extreme speech behind an interstitial screen,

forcing users to click through to see it and limiting the possibility of re-tweeting without comments. This occurred in response to US President Donald Trump's claim—'When the looting starts, the shooting starts', which was interpreted as an incendiary threat against Black Lives Matter protesters (see Hern 2020).

REFERENCES

Alexander, Larry (2005), *Is There a Right to Freedom of Expression?* (Cambridge: Cambridge University Press).

Amdur, Robert (1980), 'Scanlon on Freedom of Expression', *Philosophy & Public Affairs* 9, 287–300.

Badano, Gabriele, and Nuti, Alasia (2018), 'Under Pressure: Political Liberalism, the Rise of Unreasonableness, and the Complexity of Containment', *Journal of Political Philosophy*, 26, 145–168.

Badano, Gabriele, and Nuti, Alasia. (2020), 'The Limits of Conjecture: Political Liberalism, Counter-Radicalisation and Unreasonable Religious Views', *Ethnicities* 20, 293–311.

Bambauer, Derek E. (2006), 'Shopping Badly: Cognitive Biases, Communications, and the Fallacy of the Marketplace of Ideas', *University of Colorado Law Review* 77, 649–710.

Barendt, Eric (2009), 'Incitement to, and Glorification of, Terrorism', in James Weinstein and Ivan Hare, eds, *Extreme Speech and Democracy* (Oxford: Oxford University Press), 445–462.

Beerbohm, Eric (2012), *In Our Name: The Ethics of Democracy* (Princeton, NJ: Princeton University Press).

Benesch, Susan (2012), 'Dangerous Speech: A Proposal to Prevent Group Violence', World Policy Institute, 12 January, https://worldpolicy.org/wp-content/uploads/2016/01/Danger ous-Speech-Guidelines-Benesch-January-2012.pdf., accessed 11 August 2021.

Benesch, Susan, Ruths, Derek, Dillon, Kelly P., Saleem, Haji Mohammad, and Wright, Lucas (2016), 'Considerations for Successful Counterspeech', Dangerous Speech Project, https://dangerousspeech.org/considerations-for-successful-counterspeech, accessed 11 August 2021.

Brettschneider, Corey (2012), *When the State Speaks, What Should It Say?* (Princeton, NJ: Princeton University Press).

Brison, Susan (1998), 'The Autonomy Defense of Free Speech', *Ethics* 108, 312–339.

Billingham, Paul, and Parr, T. (2020), 'Enforcing Social Norms: The Morality of Public Shaming', *European Journal of Philosophy*, doi: https://doi.org/10.1111/ejop.12543.

Brown, Alexander (2017a), 'What Is Hate Speech? Part 1: The Myth of Hate', *Law & Philosophy* 36, 419–468.

Brown, Alexander (2017b), 'What Is Hate Speech? Part 2: Family Resemblances', *Law & Philosophy* 36, 561–613.

Brown, Alexander (2018), 'What Is So Special about Online (as Opposed to Offline) Hate Speech?', *Ethnicities* 18, 297–326.

Brown, Rachel (2016), *Defusing Hate: A Strategic Communication Guide to Counteract Dangerous Speech* (Washington, DC: US Holocaust Memorial Museum).

Choudhary, Tufyal (2009), 'The Terrorism Act 2006: Discouraging Terrorism', in James Weinstein and Ivan Hare, eds, *Extreme Speech and Democracy* (Oxford: Oxford University Press), 463–487.

Clayton, Matthew, and Stevens, David (2014), 'When God Commands Disobedience: Political Liberalism and Unreasonable Religions', *Res Publica* 20, 65–84.

Cohen, Joshua (1989), 'Deliberation and Democratic Legitimacy', in Alan Hamlin and Philip Pettit, eds, *The Good Polity* (Oxford: Basil Blackwell), 17–34.

Cohen-Almagor, Raphael (2015), *Confronting the Internet's Dark Side: Moral and Social Responsibility on the Free Highway* (Cambridge: Cambridge University Press).

Delgado, Richard (1982), 'Words that Wound: A Tort Action for Racial Insults, Epithets, and Name-Calling', *Harvard Civil Rights–Civil Liberties Law Review* 17, 133–181.

Delgado, Richard, and Stefanic, Jean (2014), 'Hate Speech in Cyberspace', *Wake Forest Law Review* 49, 319–343.

Douek, Evelyn (2021), 'Governing Online Speech: From "Posts-as-Trumps" to Proportionality and Probability', *Columbia Law Review* 121, 759–834.

Dworkin, Ronald (1996), *Freedom's Law: The Moral Reading of the American Constitution* (Oxford: Oxford University Press).

Dworkin, Ronald (2009), 'Forward', in James Weinstein and Ivan Hare, eds, *Extreme Speech and Democracy* (Oxford: Oxford University Press), 123–138.

Franks, Mary Ann (2019), ' "Not Where Bodies Live": The Abstraction of Internet Expression', in Susan Brison and Katherine Gelber, eds, *Free Speech in the Digital Age* (Oxford: Oxford University Press), 137–149.

Gagliardone, Iginio; Gal, Danit; Alves, Thiago; and Martinez, Gabriela (2015), *Countering Online Hate Speech* (New York: UNESCO).

Gelber, Katherine (2012), 'Reconceptualizing Counterspeech in Hate Speech Policy (with a Focus on Australia)', in Michael Herz and Peter Molnar, eds, *The Content and Context of Hate Speech: Rethinking Regulation and Responses* (Cambridge: Cambridge University Press), 198–216.

Gordon, Jill (1997), 'John Stuart Mill and the "Marketplace of Ideas" ', *Social Theory & Practice*, 23, 235–249.

Gutmann, Amy, and Thompson, Dennis (2004), *Why Deliberative Democracy?* (Princeton, NJ: Princeton University Press).

Habermas, Jürgen (1962), *The Structural Transformation of the Public Sphere* (Cambridge, MA: Polity Press).

Habermas, Jürgen (1992), *Between Facts and Norms* (Cambridge, MA: MIT Press).

Hay, Carol (2011), 'The obligation to Resist Oppression', *Journal of Social Philosophy* 42, 21–45.

Heinze, Eric (2016), *Hate Speech and Democratic Citizenship* (Oxford: Oxford University Press).

Herrman, John (2016), 'Social Media Finds New Role as News and Entertainment Curator', *New York Times*, https://www.nytimes.com/2016/05/16/technology/social-media-finds-new-roles-as-news-and-entertainment-curators.html, accessed 11 August 2021.

Hern, Alex (2020), 'Twitter Hides Donal Trump Tweet for "Glorifying Violence" ', *The Guardian*, https://www.theguardian.com/technology/2020/may/29/twitter-hides-donald-trump-tweet-glorifying-violence, accessed 11 August 2021.

Herstein, Ori (2010), 'Responsibility in Negligence: Why the Duty to Care Is Not a Duty "To Try" ', *Canadian Journal of Law and Jurisprudence* 23, 403–428.

Heyman, Steven (2009), 'Hate Speech, Public Discourse, and the First Amendment', in James Weinstein and Ivan Hare, eds, *Extreme Speech and Democracy* (Oxford: Oxford University Press), 123–138.

Howard, Jeffrey W. (2019a), 'Free Speech and Hate Speech', *Annual Review of Political Science* 22, 93–109.

Howard Jeffrey W. (2019b), 'Dangerous Speech', *Philosophy & Public Affairs* 47, 208–254.

Howard, Jeffrey W. (2019c), 'Terror, Hate, and the Demands of Counter-Speech', *British Journal of Political Science*, doi: https://doi.org/10.1017/S000712341900053X.

Jackson, Benjamin F. (2014), 'Censorship and Freedom of Expression in the Age of Facebook', *New Mexico Law Review* 44, 121–167.

Kendrick, Leslie (2017), 'Free Speech as a Special Right', *Philosophy & Public Affairs* 45, 87–117.

Klonick, Kate (2018), 'The New Governors: The People, Rules, and Processes Governing Online Speech', *Harvard Law Review* 131, 1599–1670.

Koltay, András (2019), *New Media and Freedom of Expression* (Oxford: Hart Publishing).

Langton, Rae (2018), 'Blocking As Counter-Speech', in Daniel Fogal, Daniel W. Harris, and Matt Moss, eds, *New Work on Speech Acts* (New York: Oxford University Press), 144–164.

Landemore, Hélène (2012), *Democratic Reason* (Princeton, NJ: Princeton University Press).

Lee, Timothy B. (2016), 'Mark Zuckerberg Is in Denial about How Facebook is Harming Our Politics', *Vox*, https://www.vox.com/new-money/2016/11/6/13509854/facebook-politics-news-bad., accessed 11 August 2021.

Lentz, Roberta (2011), 'Regulation as Linguistic Engineering', in Robin Mansell and Marc Raboy, eds, *The Handbook of Global Media and Communication Policy* (Oxford: Blackwell), 432–448.

Lepora, Chiara, and Goodin, Robert E. (2013), *On Complicity and Compromise* (Oxford: Oxford University Press).

Lepoutre, Maxime (2017), 'Hate Speech in Public Discourse: A Pessimistic Defense of Counter-Speech', *Social Theory and Practice* 43, 851–885.

Lepoutre, Maxime (2019), 'Can "More Speech" Counter Ignorance Speech?', *Journal of Ethics and Social Philosophy* 16, 155–191.

Maitra, Ishani and McGowan, Mary Kate (2012), 'Introduction', in Ishani Maitra and Mary Kate McGowan, eds, *Speech and Harm: Controversies Over Free Speech* (Oxford: Oxford University Press), 1–23.

Meiklejohn, Alexander (1948), *Free Speech and Its Relation to Self-Government* (New York: Harper and Brothers).

Meiklejohn, Alexander (1960), *Political Freedom* (New York: Harper and Brothers).

Mill, John Stuart (1859/1978), *On Liberty*, ed. Elizabeth Rapaport (Indianapolis, IN: Hackett).

Nash, Victoria (2019), 'Revise and Resubmit? Reviewing the 2019 Online Harms White Paper', *Journal of Media Law* 11, 18–27.

Pettit, Philip (2012), *On the People's Terms* (Cambridge: Cambridge University Press).

PoKempner, Dinah (2019), 'Regulating Online Speech: Keeping Humans, and Human Rights, at the Core', in Susan Brison and Katherine Gelber, eds, *Free Speech in the Digital Age* (Oxford: Oxford University Press), 224–245.

Post, Robert (1991), 'Racist Speech, Democracy, and the First Amendment', *William Mary Law Review* 32, 267–327.

Post, Robert (2009), 'Hate Speech', in James Weinstein and Ivan Hare, eds, *Extreme Speech and Democracy* (Oxford: Oxford University Press), 123–138.

Post, Robert (2011), 'Participatory Democracy as a Theory of Free Speech: A Reply', *Virginia Law Review* 97, 617–632.

Press Association (2016), 'Security Guard Jailed for Five Years over Tweets Glorifying Isis', *The Guardian*, https://www.theguardian.com/uk-news/2016/apr/28/security-guard-moham med-moshin-ameen-jailed-for-five-years-over-tweets-glorifying-isis., accessed 11 August 2021.

Quong, Jonathan (2010), *Liberalism without Perfection* (Oxford: Oxford University Press).

Rawls, John (1971/1999), *A Theory of Justice* (Cambridge, MA: Harvard University Press).

Reid, Andrew (2020), 'Does Regulating Hate Speech Undermine Democratic Legitimacy? A Cautious "No"', *Res Publica* 26, 181–199.

Rowbottom, Jacob (2012), 'To Rant, Vent and Converse', *Cambridge Law Journal* 71, 355–383.

Rowbottom, Jacob (2018a), 'Written Evidence on Internet Regulation to the House of Lords Communications Committee', http://data.parliament.uk/writtenevidence/committeeevide nce.svc/evidencedocument/communications-committee/the-internet-to-regulate-or-not- to-regulate/written/82636.pdf., accessed 11 August 2021.

Rowbottom, Jacob (2018b), *Media Law* (Oxford: Hart Publishing).

Scanlon, Thomas M. (1972), 'A Theory of Freedom of Expression', *Philosophy & Public Affairs* 1, 204–226.

Scanlon, T.M. (1979), 'Freedom of Expression and Categories of Expression', *University of Pittsburgh Law Review* 40, 519–550.

Scanlon, T. M. (2011), 'Comment on Shiffrin's Thinker-Based Approach to Freedom of Speech', *Constitutional Commentary* 27, 327–335.

Schauer, F. (1993), 'The Phenomenology of Speech and Harm', *Ethics* 103(4), 6350–6653.

Schauer, Frederocl (2019), 'Recipes, Plans, Instructions, and the Free Speech Implications of Words that Are Tools', in Susan Brison and Katherine Gelber, eds, *Free Speech in the Digital Age* (Oxford: Oxford University Press), 74–87.

Schwartzman, Micah (2012), 'The Ethics of Reasoning from Conjecture', *Journal of Moral Philosophy* 9(4), 521–544.

Scoccia, Danny (1996), 'Can Liberals Support a Ban on Violent Pornography?', *Ethics* 106, 776–799.

Shiffrin, Seana (2014), *Speech Matters* (Princeton, NJ: Princeton University Press).

Stanley, Jason (2015), *How Propaganda Works* (Princeton, NJ: Princeton University Press).

Sunstein, Cass (1993), *Democracy and the Problem of Free Speech* (New York: Free Press).

Sunstein, Cass (2017), *# Republic: Divided Democracy in the Age of Social Media* (Princeton, NJ: Princeton University).

Tadros, Victor (2016), 'Permissibility in a World of Wrongdoing', *Philosophy & Public Affairs* 44, 101–132.

Tambini, Damian (2019), 'The Differentiated Duty of Care: A Response to the Online Harms White Paper', *Journal of Media Law* 11, 28–40.

Theil, Stefan (2019), 'The Online Harms White Paper: Comparing the UK and German Approaches to Regulation', *Journal of Media Law* 11, 41–51.

Tsesis, Alexander (2001), 'Hate in Cyberspace: Regulating Hate Speech on the Internet', *San Diego Law Review* 38, 817.

Tsesis, Alexander (2017), 'Social Media Accountability for Terrorist Propaganda', *Fordham Law Review* 86, 605–631.

UK Government (2019), 'Online Harms White Paper', https://www.gov.uk/government/consul tations/online-harms-white-paper/online-harms-white-paper, accessed 11 August 2021.

Ullman, Stefanie, and Tomalin, Marcus (2020), 'Quarantining Online Hate Speech: Technical and Ethical Perspectives', *Ethics and Information Technology* 22, 69–80.

Waldron, Jeremy (1989), 'Rights in Conflict', *Ethics* 99, 503–519.

Waldron, Jeremy (2012), *The Harm in Hate Speech* (Cambridge, MA: Harvard University Press).

Weinstein, James, and Hare, Ivan, eds (2009), *Extreme Speech and Democracy* (Oxford: Oxford University Press).

Weinstein, James (2009), 'Extreme Speech, Public Order, and Democracy: Lessons from The Masses', in James Weinstein and Ivan Hare, eds, *Extreme Speech and Democracy* (Oxford: Oxford University Press),

Woods, Lorna (2019), 'The Duty of Care in the Online Harms White Paper', *Journal of Media Law* 11, 6–17.

Woods, Lorna, and Perrin, William (2019), *Online Harm Reduction: A Statutory Duty of Care and Regulator* (Dunfermline: Carnegie UK).

PART III

FRIENDSHIP, LOVE, AND SEX

CHAPTER 11

··

FRIENDSHIP ONLINE

··

DEAN COCKING

I didn't mean what I said last night ... that was just online ... You know
I had to say it.

> (Online bully *whispers* to her best friend the next day at school)

INTRODUCTION

···

OVER the past twenty years, research investigating the nature and value of online
friendship has become central to discussions concerning the impact of online technology upon our lives. In the early days of the information revolution, the pursuit of
friendship online was something of a novelty. With the rise of the online social revolution, the promotion and pursuit of friendship online has become core business of
the internet and part of the friendships and social lives of most of us. In this chapter,
I provide an overview of the burgeoning contemporary research concerning online
friendship and of the main themes, since Aristotle, on the nature and value of friendship.
I aim to provide some substantial fresh research for future analyses and much of the
overview work will be presented as I do so.

A central question of discussions regarding online friendships has been whether
the pursuit of true friendship can proceed purely online. In recent years, many
have argued that it can, and that success depends upon the moral character of those
involved, that is, upon their being highly virtuous (Briggle 2008; Vallor 2012, 2016;
Elder 2014). Moreover, many regard the technology itself as (relatively) normatively
neutral. Indeed, many argue that internet technology is 'just a tool' for communication. As such, the impact upon our values of this tool for communication depends
upon how we are using it, not upon the nature of the technology itself (Vogels et al.
2020; Dorsey 2021).

In this chapter I argue against both views. The first view misunderstands the nature of moral character, overstating the capacities of individuals (even otherwise highly virtuous ones) to achieve the virtuous life, underappreciating the role of others and the various features of the world around the individual in enabling and sustaining their virtue. The second view, regarding internet communication as simply a communication tool, is also too simplistic (and optimistic) an approach to moral education and maintenance. Investigating living online highlights in spectacular fashion the deep dependence of much of our valuing and values upon the multidimensional nature of self-expression and communication (and the broader moral framework) of our traditional worlds. It highlights the fragility of individual virtue and values, seemingly easily, and often very dramatically, undermined by failures of understanding and guidance when the moral demands, expectations, and sensibilities of our traditional social worlds are blurred or blocked from view.

Many are worried about the fate of a range of values as we increasingly live our lives online. As corporate and political organizations collect and harvest their 'plutonium' of online data about what makes us tick, many political scientists and observers are worried about the fate of democracy. We now seem vulnerable to manipulation and misinformation more than ever. Hence, the approximation to something like a 'reasonably informed citizen' upon which representative democracy depends now seems especially at risk (see, e.g. Mössner and Kitcher 2017). In the same way, many social scientists and commentators are worried about the fate of our personal lives. Many worry, for instance, that while we have more 'social connection' in our new online worlds than previously imaginable, we are seemingly lonelier than ever. As Sherry Turkle describes, we are 'maximally connected' but 'alone together' (2011). Similarly, on the basis of a large research project concerning how social media influences education and psychological development, Howard Gardner and Katie Davis describe how young people's sense of self is being weakened, making them (even) more insecure, overly focused on their online likes, visits, and self-promotion (Gardner and Davis 2013: 75–86).

The meeting of our relational needs and interests in personal life depends upon our being engaged with one another, in communication and shared activity, in ways that give our needs and interests traction.[1] In general, having fulfilling social lives notably involves the rich, face-to-face dynamic of plural modes of self-expression, communication, and activity that we have built upon for centuries. Our social media platforms, such as Facebook, Instagram and Twitter, flatline much of this territory, leaving us with a blunt choice regarding self-expression and communication. Either we express aspects of ourselves, and so present ourselves for (potentially enormous) public attention concerning these aspects of ourselves, or we give them no public expression at all. As a result, much of the moral universe we have built upon our traditional multidimensional communication landscape is lost or distorted online.

The fate of intimacy online, as the complexity and nuance of public self-expression and shared activity is flatlined on our social media platforms, mirrors the fate of privacy online. We cannot expose ourselves online but expect to have our privacy respected, for instance, by others abiding by a convention to 'put things aside', to not make our exposure the focus of their attention, like we used to be able to do in the pre-internet world. As Thomas Nagel (1998) and Ervin Goffman (1959) have shown, such public spaces for self-expression where things expressed can be put aside, not made the focus of explicit attention, and can be expected to be so, are very important in many ways. For instance, this kind of nuance and plurality in how we may engage in public communication helps us to flag and pick out the attitudes and conduct for which someone might be more and less responsible, that is, the attitudes and conduct that they have more and less voluntarily chosen to present for our engagement. These different kinds of public self-expression and our use of conventions for communication in regard them are also crucial for our developing expressions of self and identity. When younger, for instance, we can practise and 'try out' expressions of self in the public realm and make mistakes without too much attention and condemnation.

Online, however, we must choose to conceal ourselves altogether or choose to risk exposing ourselves to significant (including negative) public attention and comment.[2] We may well be far better off in these worlds, therefore, with a great deal more concealment and less exposure (Véliz 2021). Nevertheless, to the extent that we live in such worlds we will be far worse off with regard to privacy, having lost much of privacy in public and the valuable forms of social connection such relational forms of respect for one another's privacy (in public) brings.

I begin the story of worries for the fate of friendship with some detailed discussion of one of the most longstanding and notable of relational problems among young people as we live online: the different forms and prevalence of online bullying. In the following section, I focus on the nature of friendship, highlighting how friendship addresses legitimate needs, interests, and claims that are common across our nature; generates and sustains many further ones; and how the enabling of this kind of shared activity (often) crucially depends upon the nature of our settings. The focus is on a particular kind of (ideal) friendship: what Aristotle describes as our *companion friends*, in contrast to the 'lesser' (not bad) friendships of pleasure or utility (Aristotle 1980: 'Friendship', Bk V111). I begin with a widely discussed aspect of Aristotle's account, the contribution of companion friendship to self-knowledge.

The question of whether or not such self-knowledge can be achieved online has been a focus of discussions about the prospects of friendship online in recent years. There are variants on this theme and some further developments that I discuss in the following section. I suggest, however (and develop throughout this chapter), a broader approach. An approach that focuses more attention both on analysing the nature and normative impact of online settings upon our valuing, and on understanding the nature of our relational needs, interests, and claims in companion friendship.

In the final section, I describe how the plural and nuanced communication landscape of our traditional worlds enables us to engage in communication and shared activity in 'louder and quieter' ways, and how this multidimensional territory gives life to and sustains important relational connections common to companion friendship.

ONLINE BULLY AND SCHOOLYARD FRIEND

I attended a funeral eighteen years ago for the teenage daughter of a friend. Her daughter had committed suicide as the result of bullying from a barrage of abusive and shaming phone texts. Most of this bullying came from her friendship group and revolved around a very ordinary aspect of teenage life—her interest in a boy and the competing interest of another girl. Her friends were in a state of shock at the funeral, not only because of the awful occasion, but because they had been pulled out of their thoughtlessness by a sudden, stark awareness of the role they had played in causing their friend's suicide. They were normal kids, and this occurred just before the social media revolution. None of them had any idea of how harmful their texts were, certainly not in terms of the cumulative and pervasive harm they inflicted.

That was eighteen years ago. Texting by mobile phone around the clock was still something very new. Young people, only just developing their moral compass, were especially vulnerable to being clueless about what they were doing. Since then, most of us have become all too aware of online bullying. The problem has been widely studied, and there are support and advocacy organizations, along with educational programmes throughout schools, and anti-bullying messaging across government agencies and mass media around the world. Nevertheless, it continues to flourish.[3] In one of many recent tragedies, the father of a girl bullied to death online echoed precisely what I had seen nearly two decades ago: '(to those) who thought this was a joke ... come to our service and witness the complete devastation you have created'.[4]

So why are we so stuck where we started? Aristotle thought 'argument', or more formal lessons and instruction, such as one might get from school and through media, was rather lame in being able to move us to be good (1980: Book X, 9). Thus, for Aristotle, in so far as current instruction about the dangers of online discourse is of more explicit instruction of the 'do's and do not's' and appeals to reason and our 'better selves', it will not be very effective. We also need to create and support virtue, or virtuous character, by focusing far more on providing the infrastructure for both personal and civic life that enables and maintains inclinations towards the good (our love of what is good). In particular, we need to do so by inculcating and supporting habits in people to want to behave in good ways.[5] Otherwise, without their already being inclined toward (or, open to seeing) the good, arguments about why they should behave in ways that are good will not be well understood. As Aristotle explains:

> the soul of the student must first have been cultivated by means of habits for noble joy and noble hatred, like earth which is to nourish the seed. For he who lives as passion directs will not hear argument that dissuades him, nor understand it if he does ... the character, then, must somehow be there already with a kinship to virtue, loving what is noble and hating what is base.
>
> (Aristotle 1980: Book X, 9, 1179b23–34)

Commonly, however, the problem of online bullying, like many antisocial problems online, is not that users have suffered a notable lack of moral education in their lives, whether in terms of cultivating the right inclinations or receiving the right moral instruction. Many online bullies are raised in (relatively) morally functional and supportive worlds within which they clearly understand that bullying is wrong and have little inclination for it. Moreover, nowadays, unlike more than nearly two decades ago, they do not lack moral education about the problem of bullying online. How and why, then, do those who are not bullies offline continue to become bullies online? How do we explain the ongoing moral failures undertaken in the communication territory of social media by otherwise relatively well-inclined, competent moral agents?[6]

One way in which obfuscation of our moral knowledge in revolutionary technological environments could be explained is by pointing to the creation of significant 'interpretive flexibility' within these environments (Bijker et al. 2012). Additional and distinctive moral uncertainty often appears with the onset of revolutionary technology. When we are so unfamiliar with the options the technology presents, our understanding of what it all means can be especially open to variant interpretations. In time, as we get more familiar with the nature of our new world, the range of plausible interpretations we can help ourselves to closes up and understanding becomes more settled, widely shared, and clear.[7]

This kind of explanation, however, can no longer help us too much with regard to online bullying since the 'newness' of the technology is no longer the issue. Even more striking, there is no lack of education about the problems and risks of the technology. As mentioned above, this is also true for the persistence of many other negatives of life online. For instance, nowadays many people 'know' about various privacy risks. Nevertheless, many of these people 'in the know' *behave* as if they do not know when they get online (Debatin et al. 2009). Most of us are by now well aware of a wide range of relational wrongdoing flourishing online, such as shaming, blaming, and humiliation, and are well aware of how these can escalate, get out of proportion, become a witch-hunt, and do great damage. Yet, like bullying and undermining one another's privacy (including doing so to oneself), in spite of such widespread public knowledge, these online problems continue to flourish.

Another, currently quite influential, explanation for how users seemingly lose their moral compass online is that they become addicted to the short-term rewards of likes, clicks, attention, and so forth designed into social media platforms. (For a variety of disturbing and interesting cases described in terms of addiction online, see Aitken 2016.) Addiction no doubt is an issue, and unlike interpretive flexibility, provides an explanation for the apparent ongoing failure of reason despite experience online and education about online evils. At best, however, addiction can be only a part of the story.

Short-term rewards, along with short-term attitudes generally, of oneself and others, present problems in all sorts of ways absent anything to do with addiction. For instance, my focus on relentlessly getting positive re-enforcement about myself from others is a problem. It means, for example, that I never give myself the time and space to consider my faults, to be honest about myself, to adjust expectations, and to make some progress. However, my conduct and the problem with it might arise from all sorts of psychic states and efforts, for example, that I am insecure, or shallow, or because I am doing my best, however misguided, to self-improve. We need an explanation for the obscuring of our values by the territory of online self-expression and communication that is both deeper and broader than problems of addiction.

Often, we can show 'knowledge' of moral territory, and of how to behave accordingly, but our actual behaviour tells a different story. We may even be able to pass quite stringent tests, show a good knowledge of the issues, and of obligations and permissions with regard them, but not 'walk the talk'. We may simply be going along with the rhetoric and using it to cover the reality of our selfishness or ill will. However, failures to apply our moral knowledge are often not about being selfish or immoral, nor our 'talk' simply a smoke screen for our lesser selves. Many young people who engage in online bullying are not especially selfish or driven by ill will. Instead, quite normal desires, needs, and attitudes, such as wanting to stay in the swim of their social milieu, are commonly at play (for a contrary view of one kind of case, see Martha Nussbaum's account of sexist bullying in terms of hate crime, 2010).

While such peer pressure and how it can send young people astray is hardly anything new, the design and milieu of online social media platforms has introduced various additional and distinctive ways to undermine and obscure moral sensibilities. Facebook, Instagram, and Twitter, for instance, all limit self-expression and communication to the presentation of images and text. In turn, users immersed in these communication environments become especially vulnerable to understanding themselves and others in the limited, often distorted, terms of posted images and text. As a result, many users lose sight of one another as subjective moral beings and (otherwise loud and clear) concomitant moral understandings about how to treat one another.

One mother told me her daughter's online bully and schoolyard friend whispered to her daughter back at school: 'I didn't mean what I said last night ... that was just online ... You know I had to say it.' Once back at school she seemed to recognize that what she thought was acceptable discourse online was not okay back at school. At the same time, however, she felt enabled and expected by the online milieu to behave as she did and thought that her friend should understand this—it was 'just online'. The problem of the altered territory of online social worlds, therefore, is not just that the territory is so unfamiliar, or that we are suffering an abnormality, such as addiction. These problems are certainly issues, but the more fundamental issue is the dysfunctional nature of the territory itself, how the communication territory of social media platforms obscures application of our moral knowledge and undermines our capacities to appreciate value.

This obfuscation occurs in a similar way to how features of the territory upon which many (modern) wars are fought presents what the military describe as the 'fog of war'. Here, they are describing a changed landscape, in which, for instance, it is especially difficult to tell friend from foe, and how this obfuscation undermines applying relevant moral knowledge, such as that it is impermissible to target civilians. While this territory is certainly additionally morally problematic when first encountered, the nature of the territory itself—not being able to tell friend from foe—remains a fundamental problem.

The schoolyard friend gives two closely connected explanations of her online bullying: the need to 'fit in' with her online social milieu and the very different norms of social discourse in this milieu. The obfuscation of her online bullying produced by the alteration in social discourse occurs in an analogous way to the obfuscation created in the military case. In both kinds of cases, the moral fog descends to obscure the application of moral knowledge due to altered territory of self-presentation and communication. In the military case, the altered territory means our enemies present as civilians, or even friends. On social media, the altered territory means, for example, that even our 'friends' have limited and distorted expression qua 'persons', and so we may be led to treat them as less than persons, such as legitimate targets for abuse.

Nowadays, the contrast between offline and online terrain has mostly gone—we live in an online world. Most 'friendships' people have online are also ones they have offline. One might have supposed, then, that even if social media platforms distort or do not allow certain kinds of self-expression or communication that are needed for friendship, our traditional worlds nevertheless do, so we can correct distortions and make up for losses. Moreover, there is a variety of online media and resources in wide use nowadays providing much more information for everyone about everyone, including many reality checks about one another (on the ever-increasing worlds of social media and resources online, and the variety of positive forms of friendship this may bring, see Kaliarnta 2016). Thus, whatever 'moral fog' might be created within certain online social worlds, both the range of online media and resources we use, along with our location in our traditional worlds, might be thought to provide the clarity to lift any moral fog caused by particular online social worlds.

Unfortunately, the case of 'online bully and schoolyard friend' shows we have significant reason to worry about things going the other way. Schoolyard bullies in our traditional worlds have always been common. Here, however, our schoolyard friend has become our bully. Moreover, the case is a very representative one, highlighting the problem and puzzle of how non-bullies become bullies online. Thus, instead of being corrected by the moral force of our traditional worlds and the 'fog' being lifted (indeed, despite significant, additional education efforts across our online and offline worlds aiming to do so), the problem has spread from online worlds to wreak additional havoc in our traditional worlds. It may be a social disaster (rather than, or as well as, a corrective balance) that we now live in an online world, or that most online friendships are now ones that are also conducted offline.

Young people are only developing their understanding of themselves and their relations with others and the world. How these understandings develop will largely depend upon what they get from their environment—the prevailing attitudes, judgments, norms, conventions and rules of the game. If they increasingly grow up online, they will be especially vulnerable to taking on and adapting to the design and milieu of their online social environment. While living online may be causing damage across our social worlds, we can imagine, nevertheless, a future in which we have transcended online evils, such as online bullying. The online social revolution is in its infancy, and the future of technologically mediated social life may well be far better designed and regulated.

Hence, we might imagine the problems of bullying, trolls, shaming, demonizing and so forth to be a problem of 'finding our feet' and playing catch up with the technology.

However, as the case of 'online bully and schoolyard friend' also shows, we should not let our imaginations give us too much comfort. For, while we may know better and can do better, we have a strong record of managing to stay stuck where we started or ending up somewhere worse.[8] If we are to progress towards a better world of technologically mediated social lives, we also need to better understand and address our propensities to stay stuck or devolve morally.

We can, however, still *imagine* an online future transcending the current regular diet of online evils. Would we then be free to pursue friendship online? Is there anything intrinsic to communication online that presents structural barriers to friendship? Philip Kitcher thinks so:

> Suppose the internet becomes as safe and well-mannered as you like. Cyberbullying, sexual predation, revenge porn, cruel pranks, all become things of the past. Yet the pressure to advertise oneself positively on social media remains, and even intensifies ... (offline) interactions are typically less frequent and shorter than those through which friendships of the kinds most admired are developed and sustained ... some *dimensions* of friendship become rarer. The spate of online chat doesn't offer much opportunity for serious exploration of goals, for thinking through uncertain prospects together, for providing and receiving aid or consolation, for sharing the deepest joys. When an intimate friendship has already been formed, contact online can provide resources for maintaining it ... What strikes me as less clear is how multi-dimensional intimacy is achieved without shared experiences, without episodes of standing together against some common threat, without the moments when troubles are confessed and advice is sought. The world I have imagined has banished online evil. Despite that, it is a world in which one of the most valuable aspects of human life has been reduced and cheapened.
>
> (Kitcher 2021: 5)

To determine what reason we might have, if any, to worry about the fate of friendship in an online world, it will be helpful to focus and raise our understanding across a few fronts: the nature of friendship, identifying and evaluating our relational needs and interests, and perhaps most of all, the nature of our capacities to appreciate value and sustain our values (and virtue). We should then be in a better position to investigate whether limitations or distortions online undermine friendship and other values. Let us begin by asking: what is friendship and why do we need it?

FRIENDSHIP, OUR NATURE AND SETTINGS

One well-known answer from Aristotle to these questions is the contribution friends make to one another's self-knowledge: 'If, then, it is pleasant to know oneself, and it is not possible to know this without having someone else for a friend, the self-sufficing man will require friendship in order to know himself' (1915: 1213a20–1213b). The 'self-sufficing' character Aristotle has in mind is someone self-sufficing in virtue, someone able to create and sustain their own state of virtue. Such a character is, of course, an ideal whose capacities with regard to their own virtue go way beyond ours. We may be morally resilient (good at sustaining our moral compass in difficult terrain) and morally creative (good at coming up with helpful and non-harmful ways of regarding and treating others). Certainly, these may be important guiding ideals for us. Also, however, not only are there limits on how resilient and creative individuals might be, but we also very much need one another across both fronts. Thus, self-sufficiency in virtue does not make much sense. At least, the ideal is quite a limited one, one that needs to be balanced by very different, sometimes conflicting, relational ideals concerned with how we might better support and contribute to one another's flourishing. For Aristotle, the ideal of friendship takes centre stage here and the development of our self-knowledge is one way in which it does so.

Aristotle's ethics has been the wellspring for most philosophical discussions of friendship and of what might be important and distinctively valuable about it. Of the many things he writes about friendship, one of his most commonly cited views is that ideal friendship, the best of companion friendships, exists between those who are virtuous. The mutual recognition of one another's virtue, it is often claimed, provides the grounds and characterizes the kind of intimacy, deep affection, trust, loyalty, and so on that is found in excellent companion friendships (Sherman 1993).

Aristotle did allow that those less than virtuous could be friends (1980: Bk VIII, 1, 1154b34–1155a25). He also thought that those unequal in virtue and fortune could be friends (there must be mutual love for one another, see, for instance, on how slaves and non-slaves could be friends in this way, 1980: Bk VIII, 12, 1161a30–b). In any case, however, we can imagine ways in which the virtue of friends could contribute to one another's self-knowledge. Sherman, for example, points to how recognized similarity in virtue can contribute to self-knowledge by providing moral role models for one another (1993: 105–106). Some point to the mutual enhancement of one another's moral sensibilities that comes with recognition of one another's virtue (Thomas 1989: 147). John Cooper highlights how virtuous friends provide objective views of one another (1980: 322–333). Marilyn Friedman points to how friends can correct the biases of our limited subjective perspectives (1993).

Beyond his appeal to the self-knowledge friendship provides, Aristotle also seems to regard shared activity as more broadly valuable, as a wider wellspring for the expression and creation of value: 'If it's a fine thing, as it is, to do good when one has the goods of fortune, to whom will he do good? And with whom will he live?' (1915: 1213a 26–28; for extended discussion, see also Aristotle 1980: Bk. IX, 9, 1169a35–1170b20). On this approach, concern about the prospects of friendship online would have a broader focus on how communication and shared activity found in companion friendship enables our capacities for value appreciation and gives expression to, and generates a range of, relational values (on shared activity, see, for instance, Cooper 1980). How then, might we imagine the shared activity of friendship to enable our valuing and generate values (and virtue) beyond merely communicating knowledge?

As with our consideration of the self-knowledge friendship provides, one way to gauge the value of friendship is to identify some key needs and interests we have but which are beyond our own individual capacities to create or sustain, and then show how they are met by the shared activity of friendship. I have suggested elsewhere (Cocking 2014) that one good way to see how some of our fundamental needs, interests, and related values are *not* met when we change the territory of communication and shared activity is by reflecting upon Plato's presentation of Glaucon's tale of the Ring of Gyges, albeit in a somewhat atypical way (Plato, *Republic*: Book 11, 359b–360b).

In the tale, when we put on this ring, we become invisible, thus being able to escape censure and run amok with impunity. Accordingly, the tale seems to raise the question: do our reasons for being moral really just reduce to self-interest, that is, avoiding punishment? Also, however, we can imagine how terrible it would be if we were reasonably happy, good people, with a life grounded in relationships of mutual love with family and friends, and we were somehow stuck with this ring. Now your family and friends cannot see you. I have suggested that this would make the ring a tragic curse, given the loss and distortion of the rich, ongoing dynamic of communication and shared activity that it would seem to bring. Suppose, however, that things are not so extreme, that not so much is lost and distorted. Your loved ones can now see you and hear you— but only online. Things will be better, since others can now see and hear you. However, you are still not there, not only to touch physically (as if that would not be enough), but to communicate and share activity at the dinner table, in the garden, and everywhere else. It may well be better than being invisible, but, surely, the finger would have to go.

Many of those who argue that there are no decisive structural barriers presented by online communication to pursuing and achieving friendship purely online claim to do so from an Aristotelian perspective. It is clear, however, that Aristotle thought that even exemplars of virtue, brought up well to both understand and love the good, will need a broader morally 'supportive' social world around them to help create and sustain their virtue. As we have seen, they cannot be 'self-sufficient' in virtue. In addition to needing friends for self-knowledge, however, Aristotle also thought that they need a well-developed suite of laws, regulations, social conventions, and various informal mechanisms, including of punishment and censure, to inform and nurture their understanding and love for the good. Also, since they are not perfect in virtue, they will need the support of this broader social system to help reign in the less-than-perfect aspects of themselves (1980: Book X, 9, 1179b39–46).

FRIENDSHIP ONLINE

Twenty years ago, in *Unreal Friends*, Steve Matthews and I argued that friendship online pursued solely through text-based communication could not achieve real friendship

(Cocking and Matthews 2000). The problems identified were limits and distortions of self-expression and communication that ordinarily informs friendship and provide grounds for the relational identity we construct in it. The distortion and limitation highlighted was the primacy given to one's own chosen, controlled, and so more voluntary self-presentations in providing the grounds for interaction in purely text-based communication. Less conscious and voluntary aspects of one another, we argued, are lost or minimized online, and as a result so too are many aspects of our conduct and psychology upon which the interpretive shared activity of friendship proceeds. For instance, that our friend is ungenerous or easy-going emerges, say, when out socially, or at work, often without our friend's more voluntary testimony.

As noted in the introduction, much philosophical discussion of friendship online has focused on whether it is possible to achieve friendship in purely online contexts. The issue of limits and distortions on less chosen and voluntary self-expression, and of the more complex, nuanced, and richer communication we have in our traditional worlds has been a main arena for investigating the question. For some, our less conscious and voluntary aspects of self and our related interaction with one another need not be of any necessary, special import to intimacy. Indeed, for some, even the early online social contexts of text-only communication can deliver the deep and rich knowledge of and connection between one another that features in friendship.

In reply to *Unreal Friends*, for instance, Adam Briggle highlights how our traditional worlds are also full of limits and distortions in self-expression and communication, including ones generated by the less-than-voluntary aspects of one another. As a result, he writes, the 'distance' of virtual communication can liberate us, enabling our 'real' selves to flourish away from the falseness, lack of focused attention, and shallowness that can accompany our offline lives (Briggle 2008: 72). In a representative statement, he writes, 'the fate of online friendships depends at least as much on the people involved as it does on the tools used' (2008: 73).

Nicholas Munn also argues that friendship pursued solely online is possible. However, this is not because there are no real losses in self-expression, nor barriers to knowledge of one another online, or because whatever losses or barriers there are, our individual virtue can prevail. In fact, for Munn, online text, picture, and video communication platforms, such as Facebook, Twitter, and Instagram, cannot deliver close friendship. They fail because they are primarily about facilitating acts of communication, rather than forums for shared activity, and it is shared activity, he argues, that is crucial for friendship: it is 'the act of engaging in shared activity, rather than the medium in which that activity is engaged in, which is the crucial determinant of friendship development' (Munn 2012: 8–9). Unlike our social media platforms, however, the immersive worlds of massively multiplayer online role-playing games, he contends, are primarily about engaging in shared activity. Moreover, this shared activity gives our less chosen and conscious aspects of self far more expression than social media platforms, since we unavoidably reveal such aspects of ourselves in our immersive game playing. Thus, he argues, these communication mediums can provide the richer shared activity commonly featuring in friendship.

For Aristotle, governance by reason is central to valuable shared activity. Thus, it is needs and interests that are permissible or that we ought to develop and pursue that will be the focus of the kind of shared activity important to friendship. The shared activity of the vicious or that is corrupting of virtue, or that is a complete waste of our time does not meet, or undermines, the needs and interests it is (rationally) desirable for us to have. Such shared activity, therefore, is without value or bad. On the other hand, the rationally governed shared activity of friendship addresses many of our (legitimate and worthwhile) needs and interests concerning intimacy. However, even if we consider only self-knowledge, it is hard to see how the shared activity of playing games together online could suffice to deliver (even this aspect of) companion friendship. The broad and deep contributions to self-understanding commonly claimed of companion friendship plainly go well beyond whatever contributions the shared activity of playing games together online might bring (which, nevertheless, may have some value and create and sustain some of our intimate relational needs and interests).

Many writers now seem to agree that while social media platforms may present limits and barriers, the virtuous will do well enough at navigating any limits and distortions of information and shared activity to achieve friendship purely online. Alexis Elder argues that 'social media poses no threat to the richness and particularity of friendship ... Users will be best positioned to enjoy excellent friendships online if they show appropriate sensitivity to social context and some skill at handling complex social exchanges ... not so different from the skill set that benefits any other friendship' (2014: 290; see also Vallor 2012 and 2016). Certainly, it is true, as Briggle suggests, that our face-to-face worlds are often limiting, dysfunctional, and oppressive. As a result, it can also be true in various ways that people might be better off pursuing their lives elsewhere, such as online, or with a pen pal. We may be in prison, for example, and a terrific pen pal may provide an honest, insightful, and rich dialogue that we come to reciprocate. Over time, this may deliver genuine affection and some of the development of intersubjective identity that features in friendship. Thus, for example, we both may recognize and run with each other's openness to one another's interests and ways of seeing things; the dynamic builds and so too do the desires, reasons, and self we come to create together. (On how friends creatively interpret one another, beyond providing virtuous role models, objective self-knowledge, and so forth, see my 'drawing' view of friendship (Cocking and Kennett 1998; Cocking and Kennett 2000; Cocking 2007; Cocking 2014).)

Nevertheless, would it not be better if we were able to communicate face-to-face, and have the limits and any distortions of our communication as penfriends removed? Sometimes it might not be better. Perhaps after meeting the penfriend in person you soon discover you cannot stand one another. In some cases, because of the person (they may have physical or psychological difficulties) or their circumstances (they may be isolated), technologically filtered communication may be as good as it gets. Particular cases aside, however, we would not generally want companion friendship to be so hostage to such limits and distortions. Very virtuous people may do very well despite them. However, it is hard to see how they would not do a great deal better without forces undermining fundamental capacities for self-expression, communication, and shared activity.

Robert Frank, for instance, highlights how our emotional responses are crucial for signalling commitment, and how the plurality of expression in face-to-face activity gives us more reliable information about one another in this regard (Frank 2004). Barbro Froding and Martin Peterson (2012) highlight how the limited information we have about one another online (confined to more voluntary expressions and less spontaneous and diverse shared activity) means we only get parts of one another to admire, love, and trust. We do not get the whole person. Thus, the mutual love and admiration based upon recognizing one another's virtue that marks the Aristotelian ideal of companion friendship, they argue, is out of reach online. We simply don't get enough information about one another for the more complete recognition of one another's virtue upon which the more complete love and admiration of companion friendship is based (Froding and Peterson 2012; see also McFall 2012).

Still, many others, in addition to Briggle, Vallor, and Elder, disagree and argue for the prospects of Aristotelian friendship online. Bulow and Felix, for instance, argue that the Aristotelian requirement of (ideal) companion friendship that it holds between those who are equals (in virtue) can, depending upon circumstances, be met online, and in many cases much better than in the circumstances of someone's offline world (Bulow and Felix 2016). Kristjansson (2019) supports the prospects of Aristotelian companion friendship online by arguing that the ever-developing sophistication of modern technologically mediated communication gives us many more options than were ever available for penfriends. Many penfriends, nevertheless, have been thought real friends. Indeed, some penfriends have been regarded great friends, as having achieved deep intimacy. Kristjansson gives a few cases, but the most discussed is the relationship between penfriends Voltaire and Catherine the Great. Thus, increasingly, we will have far more reason to regard 'e-pals' (online friendships) as genuine friendships, than we ever had for penfriends (who, nevertheless, we thought did well qua friendship).

It remains true, however, that there are limits and distortions *internal* to the nature of online or purely text-based communication, which in turn limit and distort self-expression, communication, and shared activity with regard to our capacities for value appreciation and some of our important relational values.[9] In order to illustrate more clearly how the pursuit of ideal companion friendship (or something closer to it) depends upon the nuanced complexity of communication in our traditional worlds, I now describe some specific ways in which this communication landscape has enabled the pursuit of important relational connections and values that are unavailable (or far less so) online.

'DON'T SAY IT OUT LOUD'

We all know that even if we think something is true, that does not make it a good idea to say it 'out loud'. Indeed, sometimes, not only should we say nothing at all, but we should also try and not let what we are thinking be communicated at all, such as through non-verbal expressions. For example, I might be disappointed in my child, or have negative thoughts about how they have behaved, and the most important consideration be that I give no expression to this due to the damage it would do to their self-esteem. On the other hand, it is also (often) very important that we are able to give our thoughts, feelings, and desires *appropriate* public expression. Indeed, without such communication possibilities, various relational interests and needs could not get off the ground. Our traditional worlds provide the nuanced communication that enables the appropriateness of expression that these relational connections so desperately need.

When, for example, tragedy strikes with the death of a loved one and we need to give one another deep emotional support, various 'quieter' forms of communication will feature prominently. In such disasters, we commonly support one another mostly by being with one another. Many things may need communicating, but often not by saying anything at all and rarely by saying things 'out loud'. We largely monitor one another quietly, tailor our interaction accordingly, and try to protect and support each other without making any of this loud and clear, too conscious and obvious. We may need to be left more to our own thoughts, given more of our own 'space', but more than ever we may need to *not* be alone, to be in communication with one another, but in quieter ways.

We should not say, or perhaps even express at all, certain negative things about our children, when doing so would badly damage their self-esteem. Also, of course, it is very important that we are all located within a public space where our children can make their mistakes, express faults, and we can be witness so that we may support and guide them (without showing disappointment and other negative reactions). It is also important that we are able to communicate and share activity in public together, but without making much comment about one another's conduct, as a way to protect and preserve other values (beyond the cases mentioned earlier of respecting privacy in public or enabling the 'trials and errors' of the developing moral agent).

Often, for instance, we do not want our loved ones to become too aware of themselves, so that we may protect valuable forms of expression from the crushing effects of self-consciousness. We do this all the time with our children, not making them self-conscious of their nakedness, how they mangle their words, their efforts to play sport, create art, tell a joke, or make a point in front of adults. However, it does not stop there. We cherish many things about one another's 'mature' self that we (mostly) keep to ourselves lest we spoil the value that their unself-conscious expression brings. I notice, for example, that my (adult) friend is waxing lyrical about the wonder of trains, or happily immersed in building a pretend train track around his house. I also notice how the nature of his excited, remarkably comprehensive dialogue about trains, or the nature of his 'doing something he really loves' is partly, at least, due to (and characterized by) his being blissfully unaware of himself as so ebullient or happily immersed. In order not to spoil the party (this time at least), I leave it that way and say nothing 'out loud', thereby protecting the valuable forms of self-expression and activity enabled by his lack of self-consciousness.[10]

Our navigation of the terrain of our plural modes of self-expression and communication (with the aid of some 'maps' in the form of longstanding conventions) enables us to express and address many of our limitations, potentialities, strengths, vulnerabilities, weaknesses, and more generally our relational needs and interests. On the limitation and weakness side, for example, are our needs for inclusion, to not be overly shamed and blamed, our proneness to error, need for protection, our defensiveness, self-consciousness, and innocence.

As described earlier, our inhabiting the very different realms of public and private life provides one important locus of the multidimensional terrain for communication and shared activity that features in our traditional worlds. Our varied modes of communication and shared activity often proceed in terms of this contrast, such as in the case of the 'schoolyard friend'. Recall, back at school, the next day, where quieter communication is available, the schoolyard friend *whispered* her comments. She was able to make them privately, indeed secretly, unrecorded words between the two of them, thereby enabling her comments, and whatever value or disvalue they express, to be made at all. The nature and value of 'louder and quieter' varieties of communication and shared activity, however, goes beyond the locus of the public and private realms. The failure of social media platforms, such as Facebook and Twitter, to enable a spectrum of 'more and less' public exposure (along with well-regulated conventions guiding their use) has, in itself, presented significant, well-documented problems, quite apart from, or in addition to, any problems for privacy.

The structure of a typical kind of case, for instance, is that someone has committed a wrong that may well deserve some public exposure and censure, but that does not deserve anything like the overexposure and unconstrained censure that is unleashed online. Thus, the problem of inappropriate kinds and degrees of negative reactive attitudes need not be so much about privacy violations, or that people were not entitled to this information about us. Privacy violations are often involved, but the more general, primary problem concerns overexposure and censure, whether or not privacy violations are involved and part of the injustice. The injustice of the overexposure, for example, is often caused by *how* one is exposed online, such as by a frenzy of shame (often by complete strangers)[11] that the online publicity and milieu has generated, and this being readily available, with images, stories, and comments that really 'shout it out loud'. (For many awful cases of shaming online, see, Ronson 2015.) The multidimensional terrain of our traditional worlds for *public* self-expression, communication, and shared activity is, therefore, itself (without reference or contrast to privacy) an important locus of relational connections and values.[12]

The development of our intersubjective selves in communication contexts without this plurality of self-expression, communication, and shared activity (along with the absence of a relatively functional backgrounding moral world) is thereby limiting and distorting of our capacities to be moral agents. In the case of the pursuit of companion friendship online, we are less able to express, develop, and properly engage with one another's relational needs, interests, and demands, and so create and sustain a suite of relational values.

Conclusion

The ubiquity of social media gives us special cause to worry about the kinds of self-expression and communication it enables. We now live in an online world, and while our offline moral universe may provide some much-needed balance and correction, cases like 'online bully and schoolyard friend' show that things are also going the other way. As many other kinds of cases also show, the moral reality checks of our traditional worlds commonly lose out in the moral fog created online.

Now that the pursuit of personal relationships online is, to lesser and greater extents, ubiquitous across the lives of most, the limiting and distorting impacts of the online medium threaten our capacities for value appreciation and various aspects of our relational values. Beyond friendship, important aspects of respect for privacy, civility, and autonomy commonly get lost and undermined. Indeed, the basic capacity of moral agency to 'treat like cases alike' is routinely disabled by the limiting and perverting effects of the medium and its milieu (such as is also shown by the online bully's failure to recognize her conduct as bullying while online). Our moral worlds, our capacities to practise our hard-won moral understandings and conventions, are fragile.

Many are discussing options about how to better use what we have, and how to improve what we have, that is, how to design software that is more value-sensitive. In the former arena, for instance, Elder suggests that the varied tools across social media platforms that we have to 'unfriend' and disconnect from others, rather than lead us to regard others as too easily disposable, can actually be better used to improve civic discourse online (2020). Some of the other medium and milieu problems, such as the dominance of short-term attention and rewards (likes, clicks, views) and self-other competitive comparisons are also getting some corrective attention. Recently, for instance, Instagram removed from public view how many 'likes' a post gets to help address the competitive problem of social life online.

We need appropriate territory for moral understanding to get traction and be guiding. Even if such improved territory for moral discourse online is developed, however, it is hard to see how it could accommodate the rich and plural territory of offline inter-subjective self-expression and communication, along with the regulatory support and force of the broader social settings that help generate and support our relational needs, interests, claims, and values.[13]

One helpful way forward for better value-sensitive design of computer-mediated communication would be to receive more guidance by the understandings we have about moral education and maintenance from our traditional lives and worlds. Living online, however, highlights some significant problems for standard accounts of moral education and maintenance. Moral education, for instance, has long held self-conceit (i.e. rampant self-interest; see Kant 1996) as the culprit of our moral corruption. While it often is, it often is not. The case of the online bully and schoolyard friend, along with many others, illustrates how problems of moral fog commonly arise and undermine our moral capacities without any aid from self-conceit. We can remain stuck where we started, or end up somewhere worse, even when we otherwise (when out of the dysfunctional terrain) do know better, can do better, and are inclined to do so. Aristotle's account of moral education in terms of requiring knowledge, ability, and love of the good for virtue remains compelling (1980: Book X, 9). However, the various wellsprings of moral fog commonly demonstrate how we can still fall short. Moral education, therefore, also needs to focus a great deal more on understanding such failures.

The future design of online social worlds should also give greater acknowledgement to the limits of the terrain created for communication and shared activity. Accordingly, in addition to value-sensitive online design drawing upon a deeper and broader understanding of how our relational values are enabled and sustained, future design for social life in an online world should also focus on improving (rather than replacing) our engagement in the complex, nuanced terrain of communication and shared activity of our traditional worlds.[14]

Acknowledgements

For their very helpful comments on earlier drafts and for related discussions, many thanks to Kylie Cocking, Roger Crisp, Philip Kitcher, Justin Oakley, Jeroen van den Hoven, Carissa Veliz, and three anonymous referees.

Notes

1. I mean here, as I do throughout where I mention needs, interests, and claims, our *legitimate* relational needs and interests, such as for strong emotional ties with one another. I do not mean 'any old' needs and interests, nor to raise any alarms of a naturalistic fallacy, sliding (simply and quickly) from describing how things happen to be to what we ought to do. Thanks to an anonymous reviewer for raising such concerns.
2. I am imagining here the lack of the convention to 'put things aside' in online public spaces, not talking to a close friend one-to-one online. In our traditional worlds, of course, people may not abide by such conventions and we may just as well be subject to humiliation and abuse. As noted below, however, online our abusers may be great in numbers, their abuse may carry on 24/7, our 'mistakes' may be available for comment indefinitely, and all of this negative public attention can largely go unchecked.
3. Across the school system in Australia, for example, we have embedded e-safety programmes. Nevertheless, online bullying remains a significant problem. Certainly, educators involved in school pastoral care and well-being programmes commonly testify that online problems of bullying, harassment, and so on, are among their main problems. Many of the figures we do have indicate that online bullying remains a significant problem in many young people's lives—around one-quarter is a common figure for the number of young people who have been bullied online. The pursuit of social life online has changed and escalated how people can be bullied—by whom, how many, and how often. While bullying is one of the more recognized and addressed of online problems, I am not

suggesting that we do not need more study and data, for instance, in regard to prevalence and shifts in types of bullying, concerning who becomes a bully and why, and responses that work. An anonymous referee has suggested that my presentation of the problem of online bullying is limited to an 'anglophone', especially Australian, context and does not apply to Scandinavia. I think it is (at least) clear that the problem of online bullying is widespread (enough) and that it is different in various ways (as just noted above) from traditional bullying. For some, however, the problem has been overrated (see Olweus 2012).

4. I refer here to the case of Amy 'Dolly' Everett, a fourteen-year-old girl well known on Australian television (see, e.g. BBC News 2018).

5. Many read the 'inculcating of habits' as the developing of instincts that bypass reason. Quite the contrary. Aristotle emphasizes the role of reason in directing and regulating our inclinations. Thus, we come to find pleasure and pain in the right places, that is, where these places are truly pleasurable and painful. I owe all of these points to Roger Crisp. Aristotle argues that without this role of reason in forming our habits, our habits will become indifferent and resistant to reason.

6. A key problem is that the 'infrastructure' mentioned above is not there online. As I indicate in the conclusion, the 'moral fog' account I sketch below aims to shed further light on how this absence leads people astray.

7. 'Interpretive flexibility' applied to technological artefacts has been widely discussed, along with different ways in which it might occur, such as because of insufficient evidence and knowledge or due to their being multiple explanations of the evidence. I owe my understanding, as described above, of how the concept can apply in *normative* ways, to Jeroen van den Hoven. This use of 'interpretive flexibility' (no doubt in a few senses) provides a compelling explanation of how moral uncertainty often emerges with the new possibilities brought by technological revolutions. As I go on to argue, however, there is also a further problem of moral fog created by the territory itself. This problem is not that there are alternate plausible interpretations or that there is not sufficient evidence to know what to make of things. Rather, the problem concerns how the territory 'pushes our buttons' (often legitimate needs and interests, such as needing to fit in to a milieu) to lead us to act badly, and the absence of a suite of moral guides and forms of censure to help direct us the other way.

8. The obfuscation about climate change is a spectacular contemporary example of moral fog. A strong evidence base of the problem, along with publicity about it, has been around for at least fifty years or so.

9. At the same time, of course, due to certain psychological aspects of the individuals involved, or because of the circumstances of their offline worlds, or due to some mix of the two, the relational needs and interests of particular individuals may do better online, or perhaps with a penfriend.

10. If such forms of self-expression and of relating to one another deliver on relational needs, interests, and values in our shared lives, then this suggests that Plato was wrong about (or overstated) the pursuit of knowledge as the road to individual virtue and the good life. Thanks to Roger Crisp for pointing out this connection to me.

11. Thanks to Carissa Veliz for suggesting this to me.

12. Just as well, our varied kinds of 'louder and quieter' forms of public communication and shared activity goes beyond the realms and contrasts characterized by what is more and less voluntary and what is more and less conscious. Routinely, our use of 'quieter' modes for communicating is, for instance, both very conscious and voluntary, such as where we raise the eyebrow or give one another all sorts of 'looks'.

13. Short, of course, of such possibilities as future VR that does provide a grand replication of the territory. Thanks to Carissa Veliz for reminding me of such possibilities.

14. Thanks again to Carissa Veliz for suggesting that I recommend more engagement offline and for the many improvements provided by her editing.

References

Aitken, Mary (2016), *The Cyber Effect: A Pioneering Cyberpsychologist Explains How Human Behaviour Changes Online* (London: John Murray).

Aristotle. Magna Moralia (1915), *The Works of Aristotle*, ed. William David Ross (Oxford: Clarendon Press).

Aristotle (1980), *The Nicomachean Ethics*, trans. W. D. Ross (Oxford: Oxford University Press).

BBC News (2018), 'Akubra Girl Dolly's Bullying Suicide Shocks Australia', BBC, 13 January 2018.

Bijker, E. W., Bijker, Weibe E., Hughes, Thomas Parke, and Pinch, Trevor J. eds (2012), *The Social Construction of Technological Systems: New Directions in the Sociology and History of Technology* (Cambridge, MA: MIT Press).

Briggle, Adam (2008), 'Real Friends: How the Internet Can Foster Friendship', *Ethics and Information Technology* 10, 71–79.

Bulow, William, and Felix, Catherine (2016), 'On Friendship between Online Equals', *Philosophy and Technology* 29, 21–34.

Cocking, Dean (2007), 'Plural Selves and Relational Identity: Privacy and Intimacy Online', in John Weckert and Jeroen van den Hoven, eds, *Moral Philosophy and Information Technology* (New York: Cambridge University Press), 123–141.

Cocking, Dean (2014), 'Aristotle, Friendship and Virtue', *Revue Internationale de Philosophie*, Societe Belge de Philosophie, 1, 83–90.

Cocking, Dean, and Kennett, Jeanette (1998), 'Friendship and the Self', *Ethics* 108(3), 502–527.

Cocking, Dean, and Kennett, Jeanette (2000), 'Friendship and Moral Danger', *Journal of Philosophy* XCV11(5), 278–296.

Cocking, Dean, and Matthews, Steve (2000), 'Unreal Friends', *Ethics and Information Technology* 2, 223–231.

Cooper, John M. (1980), 'Aristotle on Friendship', in Amelia Oksenberg Rorty, ed., *Essays on Aristotle's Ethics* (Berkeley, CA: University of California Press), 322–333.

Debatin, B., Lovejoy, Jeanette P., Horn, Annamaria, and Hughes, Brittany N. (2009), 'Facebook and Online Privacy: Attitudes, Behaviours and Unintended Consequences', *Journal of Computer-Mediated Communication* 15(1), 83–108.

Dorsey, Dale (2021), 'Moral Intensifiers and the Efficiency of Communication', *Journal of Practical Ethics*.

Elder, Alexis (2014), 'Excellent Online Friendships: An Aristotelian Defence of Social Media', *Ethics of Information Technology* 16 (4), 287–297.

Elder, Alexis (2020), 'The Interpersonal is Political: Unfriending to Promote Civic Discourse on Social Media', *Ethics of Information Technology* 22, 15–24.

Frank, Robert H. (2004), *What Price the Moral High Ground? Ethical Dilemmas in Competitive Environments* (Princeton, NJ: Princeton University Press).

Friedman, Marilyn (1993), *What Are Friends For? Feminist Perspectives on Personal Relationships and Moral Theory* (Ithaca, NY: Cornell University Press).

Froding, Barbro, and Peterson, Martin (2012), 'Why Virtual Friendship Is No Genuine Friendship', *Ethics of Information Technology* 14, 201–207.

Gardner, Howard, and Davis, Katie (2013), *The App generation. How Today's Youth Navigate Identity, Intimacy, and Imagination in a Digital World* (New Haven, CT: Yale University Press).

Goffman, Ervin (1959), *The Presentation of Self in Everyday Life* (New York: Doubleday Anchor).

Kaliarnta, Sofia (2016), 'Using Aristotle's Theory of Friendship to Classify Online Friendships: A Critical Counterview', *Ethics of Information Technology* 18(2), 65–79.

Kant, Immanuel (1996), 'Religion within the Boundaries of Mere Reason', in Allen W. Wood and George Di Giovanni, trans. and eds, *Religion and Rational Theology* (Cambridge: Cambridge University Press), 39–216.

Kitcher, Philip (2021), 'Losing Your Way in the Fog: Reflections on *Evil Online*', *Journal of Practical Ethics* 9(2), doi: https://doi.org/10.3998/jpe.2378.

Kristjansson, Kristjan (2019), 'Online Aristotelian Character Friendship as an Augmented Form of Penpalship', *Philosophy and Technology* 34(2), 289–307.

McFall, T. Michael (2012), 'Real Character Friends: Aristotelian Friendship, Living Together and Technology', *Ethics of Information Technology* 14, 221–230.

Mössner, Nicola, and Kitcher, Philip (2017), 'Knowledge, Democracy, and the Internet', *Minerva* 55, 1–24.

Munn, J. Nicholas (2012), 'The Reality of Friendship within Immersive Virtual Worlds', *Ethics of Information Technology* 14, 1–10.

Nagel, Thomas (1998), 'Concealment and Exposure', *Philosophy and Public Affairs* 27(1), 3–30.

Nussbaum, Martha (2010), 'Internet Misogyny and Objectification', in Saul Levmore and Martha C. Nussbaum, eds, *The Offensive Internet* (Cambridge, MA: Harvard University Press), 68–88.

Olweus, Can D. (2012), 'Cyber-Bullying: An Overrated Phenomenon?', *European Journal of Developmental Psychology* 9(5), 520–538

Plato, *The Republic*, 2007, Desmond Lee (trans) (Penguin, U.K.)

Ronson, Jon (2015), *So You've Been Publicly Shamed?* (London: Picador, PanMacmillan).

Sherman, Nancy (1993), 'Aristotle and the Shared Life', in Neera Kapur Badhwar, ed., *Friendship: A Philosophical Reader* (Ithaca, NY: Cornell University Press), 91–107.

Thomas, Laurence (1989), *Living Morally: A Psychology of Moral Character* (Philadelphia, IL: Temple University Press).

Turkle, Sherry (2011), *Alone Together: Why We Expect More from Technology and Less from Each Other* (New York: Basic Books).

Vallor, Shannon (2012), 'Flourishing on Facebook: Virtue Friendship and New Social Media', *Ethics and Information Technology* 14(3), 185–199.

Vallor, Shannon (2016), *Technology and the Virtues: A Philosophical Guide to a Future Worth Wanting* (Oxford: Oxford University Press).

Veliz, Carissa (2021), 'Self-Presentation and Privacy Online', *Journal of Practical Ethics*.

Vogels, Emily A., Rainie, Lee, and Anderson, Janna (2020), ' "Tech Is (Just) a Tool": Experts Predict More Digital Innovation by 2030 Aimed at Enhancing Democracy', Pew Research Center, https://www.pewresearch.org/internet/2020/06/30/tech-is-just-a-tool, accessed 12 August 2021.

CHAPTER 12

THE MORAL RIGHTS AND WRONGS OF ONLINE DATING AND HOOK-UPS

LILY FRANK AND MICHAŁ KLINCEWICZ

INTRODUCTION

DATING and hook-up applications (DHAs), such as Tinder or Grindr, or websites, such as Snapchat or Instagram, have increased by 18.4 per cent as compared to the same period in 2019 (Kats 2020). The way people are using these platforms has also changed as compared to pre-COVID-19 pandemic times, especially when we look at interaction through DHAs themselves before meeting in person or the phenomenon of 'virtual dates' (Kornath 2020). The pandemic has only sharpened the focus on the already wide-spread phenomenon of the technological mediation of sex, dating, and love.[1] DHAs can change—or have already changed—the norms, expectations, and values associated with sex and dating (Arias et al. 2017, See also Wachter-Boettcher 2017). This is not surprising for anyone familiar with the history or philosophy of technology. From economic activity to family relations, from transportation to food, technology transforms our beliefs, values, and behaviours. From an ethical perspective, it is essential to begin to examine whether these changes are welcome or troubling in the realm of sex, dating, and love.

We divide the chapter into four sections. In the next section, 'Dating and hook-up technologies: the current landscape', we survey DHAs and describe the technological affordances that mediate dating, sex, and love for their users. This is important in understanding how DHAs can influence values. In the third section, 'New moral wrongs', we present and evaluate three areas of moral concern with respect to these affordances, adopting a pluralistic approach to normative ethical theory. We specifically focus on the new kinds of moral wrongs that DHAs introduce and their potential consequences on the norms that govern relationships in general. First, we discuss the phenomenon of catfishing, which is misrepresenting one's identity, often radically, in online romantic and sexual relationships or profiles. Second, we consider new forms of, and the prevalence of, harassment in DHAs. We try to answer the question of whether this harassment is different from what existed in pre-DHA times and, if so, what the crucial morally troubling difference is. Third, we focus on the gamification and commodification of interaction, sex, and relationships that is facilitated by DHAs and whether gamification in this context is morally problematic. In the fourth section, 'Ethics by design', we outline some prominent approaches to ethics by design and highlight the challenges of applying these approaches to DHAs. In the final section, 'Future research directions', we speculate about avenues for future research, suggesting some of the potential soft impacts of DHAs and accompanying techno-moral change that may need immediate attention.

DATING AND HOOK-UP TECHNOLOGIES: THE CURRENT LANDSCAPE

The DHA market is expected to be worth $9.2 billion by 2025 and the scale of its ecosystem is truly enormous. There are currently over 1,500 DHAs.[2] The most popular (Badoo) boasts 200 million users.[3] Distinct DHAs cater to various demographics (Christian singles, the polyamorous, etc.) and target people looking for special kinds of relationships (one-night stands, friendship, long-term relationships, infidelity, etc.). DHAs also vary depending on the way they allow and encourage their users to interact (video, messaging, or pre-written texts all the way to virtual reality and tele-dildonics), what their subscription model involves (free, tiered subscriptions for different features, exclusive/application based), and the algorithms used to create matches between users. This is not by any means an exhaustive categorization of the dimensions along which DHAs can vary.

Each one of the broad dimensions of DHA design creates unique affordances that can have ethical significance. An affordance 'refers to the range of functions and constraints that an object provides for, and places upon, structurally situated subjects' (Davis and Chouinard 2016: 241). Affordances can enable and facilitate certain behaviour, beliefs, and attitudes and also make it difficult or impossible to have others. As Donald A. Norman points out, although a chair can also be carried, a chair 'affords sitting' (Norman 1988). By extension, a DHA that allows its users to communicate via webcams introduces the affordance for non-verbal communication through facial expressions and body language and facilitates using tone and emotion to colour the content of one's expressions. It also creates the affordance for unwanted nude exposure.

The mechanics and features that create DHA affordances are typically informed at least in part by the business models of the companies that develop them. Adding webcam communication to a DHA is a business decision driven by a particular business model and if there is no fungible benefit of adding that feature, then a decision to include it will likely result in profit loss. The most successful DHAs are typically those that can monetize their users' attention through features or by adding advertisements or premium features in the application, for example by making webcam communication available only to 'premium' members, who must pay a monthly fee. Importantly, finding the right fit between the business model, features, and affordances and not necessarily its ability to facilitate dating, intimacy, or relationships, is the ultimate measure of success of a DHA. Some DHAs may even tacitly depend on their users continuing to use them so not finding a permanent relationship, which would put them outside of the DHA eco-system. A business model that banks on creating affordances to form long-term stable relationships would lead to a business failure without distinct streams of revenue.

While DHAs all come with their own affordances, business models, and features, many have common mechanics that put them into a category. First, there is a matrix of potential partners. Second, there is a matching mechanism. Third, there is a mech-anism to take the match beyond the DHA to an off-line meeting. The matrix usually presents profiles, which can include user-generated pictures, text, and categories, while the matching mechanism is typically a behind-the-scenes algorithm that takes as input profile features from the matrix and some sort of input from users. The most common mechanism for user input is a digital button or form that allows users to unilaterally engage with profiles presented in the matrix. There is also sometimes a ranking mech-anism, which determines which profiles are presented to any one user. In small and niche DHAs, the ranking mechanism is usually very simple since browsing through all the relevant profiles does not take that much effort. In the largest DHAs, however, like Badoo or Tinder, the matching mechanism is typically complex and proprietary, some-times even taking advantage of artificial intelligence techniques. Finally, once a match is made, an affordance for more direct communication opens up in the DHA, typically in the form of an online messaging system akin to email or more direct means.

How these three mechanisms are implemented is also to some extent a function of the business model of the company that owns the DHA. For example, on the one hand, a DHA business model that relies on large numbers of members in which differently priced memberships determine levels of potential access would largely focus on the ranking algorithm that determines which profiles make it into the matrix. A business model that relies on advertising would, on the other hand, focus on the way in which the matrix is presented to leave room for advertisements and on increasing the time spent using the DHA itself. Successful DHAs will also take advantage of market and demographic research and sometimes insights from social and behavioural sciences to create an implementation of the business model that will generate the greatest profit. Importantly, again, none of this will have much to do with actual dating, hooking up, or relationships, which typically take place outside of the DHA itself. The implementa-tion of the basic mechanics of DHAs is primarily determined by the need to monetize attention and/or keep users coming back.

Nonetheless, the implicit failure that is built into the promise of DHAs has to be care-fully managed. A user that figures out that a DHA is stringing them along to make a profit without leading to any dates, sex, or relationships isn't likely to continue using it. So, if the DHA has enough features to maintain the illusion of possible success or simply knows how to appeal to people that are potential long-term users, it can be successful without having to negotiate this tension. One way of doing the former is to make the user more interested in gaming the mechanics of the application than in actual meetings off-line. To reach this end, many DHA developers use techniques from gambling to effect-ively hook their users into loops of reward and disappointment similar to slot machines in a casino or loot boxes in video games (Klincewicz et al. 2022). One way of doing the latter is to explicitly target a demographic that is least likely to look for stable, long-term relationships. While the very existence of these mechanisms and business models could be considered a moral wrong, we remain neutral about it here. Instead, we focus on the way in which DHAs generate affordances for potential moral wrongs.

New moral wrongs

Deception and trust

In a recent case featured on the reality TV show *Catfished*, after over a year of an intense online relationship which started on a dating app, British hairdresser Alex wanted to meet Matt, his fiancé, in person. After a televized investigation, it was revealed that Matt was a woman who was engaging in the relationship as an act of revenge against Alex. She met Alex once and he had called her 'boring'. She explained that she needed to teach him a lesson.[4] Nev Schulman, documentary filmmaker and host of the *Catfished*, was himself deceived for months while in a long-distance romantic relationship through Facebook. He believed he was talking to a nineteen-year-old artist but was actually communicating with a middle-aged housewife who was struggling with mental illness.[5] These cases are extreme but by no means uncommon. It is also true that deception is not a new phenom-enon in the context of romantic or sexual relationships. What is unique about deception mediated by the internet is the extent to which someone can misrepresent themselves (from age to gender, physical appearance, geographical location, etc.) and the length of time for which someone can continue the charade. This is perhaps also why romantic deception online has its own pleonasm: catfishing.

There are at least four different kinds of catfishing: (a) the scammer impersonates someone else in order to extract gifts, money, or other favours from their victim; (b) the scammer wishes to torment, exact revenge upon, or monitor the victim by developing a fake relationship with them online; (c) the scammer hides their identity because of in-security about possible rejection of their romantic advances; or (d) the scammer wishes to explore what it would feel like to be someone else more generally. Although there is little empirical research on catfishing, we assume that all forms of it will fall into a spectrum in one of these four broad categories. Version (a) is clearly criminal, so not as philosophically interesting and (b) is morally wrong but relatively easy to understand from a moral perspective by analogy to cases of revenge outside of a DHA. Categories (c) and (d) present interesting material for philosophical analysis. In category (c) the perpetrator disguises or invents their online identity with the misguided intention of creating a genuine connection with their victim via a fake profile. In (d), whatever moral harm may take place is offset by possibly positive consequences like self-discovery, development of empathy, or simply better insight into other people.

People who engage in (c) and (d) seem to have a wide range of reasons for their deception, including exploration and seeking out their sexual identity. However, ongoing research from the Psychology Department at the University of Queensland, Australia, finds that many people who admit to those forms of catfishing identify as having low self-esteem and insecurity, wish to show themselves as more sexually attractive, or have the desire to explore same-sex relationships with a heterosexual partner.[6] While these are similar to the reasons that people may deceive in real life (IRL), the reasons people deceive online are also often importantly different. Catfishing typically 'occurs when the culprit assumes someone else's identity, typically by creating false online profiles' (Simmons and Lee 2020: 350). Assuming a fake identity online is beyond live action role-playing a different person in a chance encounter or a date: it can result in long-term relationships that happen entirely online.

On the one hand, the moral wrongness of catfishing in categories (c) and (d) can be illuminated by standard ethical theories and the harms created by deception in general. These are wide ranging, from undermining willingness to trust, to creating psychological trauma, to loss of opportunities for the victim. Depending on the extent of the (virtual) sexual contact that the perpetrator and victim engage, catfishing can be further analysed using the notion of sexual consent (Dougherty 2013, 2021). Dougherty argues that if one party lies or mispresents themselves to a potential sexual partner and that person would not have had sex (or a relationship) with them if they had not been deceived, then this constitutes non-consensual sex (or a relationship). Deceptive non-consensual sex (or relationship) is a serious moral wrong and 'a grave affront to their sexual autonomy' (2013: 743). This particular moral wrongness of catfishing can also come in degrees.

Perhaps on a first date someone may exaggerate their status or insinuate they are wealthy: so what? Similarly, feigning an interest in something the other person is enthusiastic about, like sports, or simply passing it over in silence, while deceptive, is not clearly morally problematic. Moral wrongs this light and this forgivable also exist online. For example, photographs are often staged, edited, or presented as contemporary while in fact they are quite old. While these may be morally innocuous, things become more troubling once things like age, wealth, origin, race, gender, or biological sex become a part of an edited version of oneself to potential matches. If these things become the basis for a relationship or marriage, then we have a case of lack of sexual consent or even criminal fraud. DHA deception in the romantic context is on a similar continuum with using staged photographs on one end and catfishing at the other extreme. The one difference is that catfishing online is not illegal and can last much longer.

However, the model on which online romantic deception is on the same continuum with IRL romantic deception does not account for the special features that distinguish online deception from IRL deception. As Nyholm and Frank have argued (2017), a key part of the western romantic notion of love has to do with individuals being attached to a particular unique person, including both their good and bad qualities. It would be inconsistent with most of our conceptions of love, or even true friendship, if we were willing to 'trade in' our lover or friend for a better, younger, smarter, wealthier version of them. In addition to valuing the unique particularity of the other person, love also has a diachronic component (Kolodny 2003). People developing loving or intimate relationships, whether face to face or online, build a shared history, including shared experiences, which constitute, at least in part, the nature of their relationship. For example, in stories of couples in which one person is afflicted with extreme memory loss, part of their tragedy is that despite an ongoing attachment in the present moment, one of the persons is no longer able to draw on those shared experiences. And indeed, one of the moral wrongs that catfishing inflicts is that, by facilitating long-term deception, it undermines this shared history-building in two significant ways. First, it puts in question the authenticity of shared experiences of joy or intimacy. Second, it can disrupt the narrative of the relationship itself by being potentially destroyed by the true identity of the catfisher coming to light. Once the victim discovers that their understanding of the narrative of the relationship is based on falsehoods, this will typically negatively impact the victim's way of understanding themselves and their life. As a consequence, the narrative of the catfished relationship is rewritten as a story of victimhood.

That said, the striking thing about catfishing is that the victims (and often the perpetrators) experience a real and meaningful connection to each other while the ruse is ongoing, sometimes spending months or even years in frequent communication. In other words, the unique connection between individuals does exist but only online. One wonders whether or not the same phenomenology exists in cases of IRL romantic deception. If someone misrepresents themselves for the length of a relationship by hiding some important fact, say, that someone is married to another person, with children, one construal of the situation may involve the deceived perceiving the relationship to be altogether invalid and no reciprocal connection having been ever established.[7] Or, maybe not. This is the inverse of the situation in which a perfect duplicate of our friend or partner is substituted and we find ourselves wondering whether this is indeed the person that figures in our relationship. We have the special connection but no duplicate.

Harassment and consent

Quickly sharing explicit sexual images is a unique affordance introduced by the internet in general and DHAs in particular. These are not always welcome. Colloquially known as the 'dick pic', the sharing and receiving of unsolicited explicit images and texts is very common, with a 2017 study showing that 50 per cent of millennial women have received these images.[8] The phenomenon has recently begun a subject of empirical inquiry into motivations for and impacts on recipients of these materials (see, e.g. Oswald et al. 2020; Marcotte et al. 2020) and web developer Kelsey Bressler is reportedly developing an artificial intelligence (AI) application that can filter out these images as an add-on to dating apps and social media.[9]

In a wide variety of contexts, from submission to the rule of law in a nation state, to sexual contact, to participation in medical research, consent is understood as a morally transformative act (Wethheimer 2000). It can be given explicitly, as in signing a form to agree to take an experimental form of chemotherapy, or implicitly, as in holding out one's arm in the physician's office to submit to a blood draw. In the political, sexual, and medical contexts, the boundaries of what kinds of actions require consent and in what form consent must be expressed are contested. But across contexts, the moral signifi-cance and transformative power of consent is grounded (at least in the Western philo-sophical tradition) in the arguably Kantian moral demand for respect for individual autonomy, free choice, and self-determination (Kant 2012/1785; Wood 1999). Like the act of indecent exposure on a subway train or in a park, sending an unwanted genital image seems to be a prima facie moral wrong because it involves someone in a sexual activity without their consent. Should we then categorize sending an unsolicited genital image as the same level of moral wrong as indecent exposure? One reason for thinking exchanging a digital image is different and potentially less morally problematic is that it does not carry the threat of immediate sexual violence in the way that a live-in-person exposure would. However, in-person indecent exposure is criminalized in many places and usually occurs in a public setting, whereas sharing these images digitally is not criminalized and can intrude on one at any time in one's private space.

To further complicate the ethics of the 'dick-pic', we should further consider the dy-namics of sexual consent. Perhaps *mere* consent to receive such images that is created by the affordance in a DHA or by joining the internet ecosystem in general is too weak a moral standard. One way to extend the notion of sexual consent is by borrowing from the work of feminist legal scholars and philosophers who have argued that rape should not be defined merely by absence of consent (MacKinnon 2005; Anderson 2005). Instead, moral and legal sex should be defined by other communicative standards that show it is welcome, freely wanted, or openly discussed and negotiated. 'Dick pics' vio-late this more restrictive notion of consent. And they are not the only type of unwanted or unsolicited content that users of dating apps receive. As Jane, Mantilla, Brown, Reed, and Messing documented, harassment in the form of insulting or abusive messages is widespread on dating platforms, especially when people (mostly men) experience re-jection (Jane 2016; Mantilla 2015; Brown et al. 2018). These people lash out, looking for ways to intimidate, harass, and demean others beyond just sending unwelcome sexual content.

Some of this abuse, as well as the phenomena of 'dick pics' may be explained by the widely researched online disinhibition effect (Suler 2004, 2016): 'people tend to do and say things in cyberspace that they would not ordinarily say or do in the face to face world' (Suler 2016: 96). This psychological phenomenon is often taken to explain many forms of cyberbullying as well as the willingness to freely share personal information online. Given this tendency, DHA users have to pay special attention to what and how they communicate through the platforms lest they bring about a barrage of disinhibited responses. On the one hand, designers of the DHAs and the corporations that own them should also take the online disinhibition effect into account in how they moderate content. If affordance for abuse, violation of communicative standards, and breach of consent is an affordance that a DHA creates on account of its business model or its wilful ignorance of the problem, then it is ultimately responsible for the harm that it brings about (predominantly to women).

Commodification and gamification

The online environment has also brought about what can best be characterized as the gamification of intimate relations. Gamification is a design strategy that intentionally introduces elements of digital quantification of winning and losing into a domain of human activity that previously did not have these elements represented digitally. For example, the gamification of academic publishing introduced citation counts, the h-index, etc., and platforms, such as Google Scholar, or Scopus, where these metrics can be used to rank individual scholars. Academic research can then be seen and experienced as a competition for most points relative to other players in the same game.

Gamification is an important tool in the repertoire of designers of technology for behaviour change or persuasive technologies (AlMarshedi et al. 2017). For example, designers of technology for health-related behaviour change, especially fitness apps and wearables, include in-app competitions for steps taken during a twenty-four-hour period, creating success badges, and unlocking virtual 'achievements'. Behaviour change psychology explains that these techniques aim to motivate users to engage in activities (like exercise) by triggering both extrinsic and intrinsic sources of motivation (Ryan and Deci 2000; AlMarshedi et al. 2017). When one is extrinsically motivated to do something, one is doing it to achieve an outcome separable from the activity itself; as a behaviour change strategy, this is an effective way to get someone to begin an undesirable or neutral activity. When one is intrinsically motivated, one engages in the activity for its own sake, the joy or fulfilment it provides (Deci and Ryan 1985; Ryan and Deci 2000).

Online-mediated intimacy now also involves elements of gamification, many of which are explicitly implemented to increase customer engagement (Rocha Santos 2018; Eisingerich et al. 2019; Isisag 2019).[10] In popular media, Tinder, with its unique swiping feature, is touted as having 'gamified love'. More obvious gamified features can be found in the app Bagel Meets Coffee, in which users must earn the app's currency of coffee beans to unlock special features, including access to users with whom they have not matched.[11] Beans can be purchases but can also be earned by getting your friends to join the app or sharing about the app on social media. One of the main reasons for gamification in online dating is business models that depend on capturing users' attention and time. These models assume that turning courtship into what is essentially a video game of probabilities and bets could capture enough attention to sometimes even be a substitute for actual dating. App users can spend time liking each other's pictures and matching within the ecosystem of ever-changing internet platforms at the expense of spending time outside of the ecosystem interacting with each other.

On the other hand, app users can fully embrace the logic of probabilities and bets and thereby limit app-mediated interactions to a minimum, focusing exclusively on the pay-out of a rendezvous. This leads to brutal efficiency and has had the consequence of normalizing behaviours that were not typical in pre-internet courtship. Among these is ghosting, that is, unilateral halt to an interaction without explanation; breadcrumbing, that is, a strategy of keeping a potential mate in emotional limbo by giving the minimal amount of attention necessary to keep them interested but at the same time focusing one's attention on someone else; and submarining, that is, re-establishing contact with someone who was an object of one's ghosting. What do we make of the morality of these behaviours?

Tsjalling Swierstra (2013) and colleagues distinguish between soft and hard techno-logical impacts (See also Swierstra, Stemerding, and Boenink 2009; Swierstra and Te Molder 2012). The hard impacts of technologies are quantifiable and involve noncontroversial values (e.g. avoiding physical harm or environmental destruction), whereas soft technological impacts are not obviously positive or negative because they often involve destabilization of existing values and norms (Swierstra, Stemerding, and Boenink 2009; Swierstra and Te Molder 2012). The normalization of the practice of ghosting (and others) illustrates a soft impact of DHAs (LeFebvre et al. 2019). Whether or not this normalization is an efficient or even respectful means of communicating dis-interest in pursuing further contact or an unkind and dehumanizing part of dating is up for debate, partly because as we use the technologies our expectations and values in the domain are changing. So, to fully answer the question about the moral dimension of the soft impact of ghosting we would need to actually collect longitudinal data about users and find a measure of something like relationship satisfaction that is independent of the specific values that are presently violated by ghosting and compare these results to a measure of that same variable once ghosting becomes fully integrated into what is considered normal behaviour. To complicate the matter further, there is evidence that one's pre-existing beliefs about how successful relationships are formed, whether they depend on 'destiny' or hard work, impacts on whether one finds ghosting behaviour morally permissible (Freedman et al. 2019). So, to put it bluntly, the moral status of these soft impacts is hostage to many other things. That said, while empirical research into these phenomena is ongoing, it is already clear that online dating has brought major changes in the way in which people in industrialized societies socialize with each other and in the norms that govern their behaviour.

ETHICS BY DESIGN

DHAs can be designed to take stakeholder values into account. And not only the values of employees and shareholder of the DHAs but also their users. However, taking user values into account is difficult, given the variety of people using DHAs, the various interests they have in using DHAs, and what they may hope to get out of them. What makes this especially difficult is that values that people hold about love, sex, and dating are contested, both in private and public spheres, and that they may be changing as the result of the continued and widespread use of DHAs. Compare this situation to that of values that are involved with the use of medical technologies: autonomy, justice, non-maleficence, and beneficence. We do not have a similar stable list for values that have to do with sex, love, or relationships. In sex and relationships, things are less straightforward. Finally, ethically designing DHAs requires making predictions about the long-term impacts of their widespread use. Happily, these challenges have been addressed by work in other domains of the ethics of technology and we will borrow from that literature to provide some answers to these questions.

Technologies present the world, our options for action, and even ourselves to us in specific ways depending on how they are designed and how we end up using them. They thus have the potential to reify or undermine certain values (Van den Hoven et al. 2015). Multiple 'ethics by design' approaches acknowledge the role that technologies have in shaping the way we think and behave in morally relevant ways and attempt to guide designers through a process of becoming aware of this relationship and intentionally translating certain values into their designs (see, e.g. Friedman 1996; Flanagan and Nissenbaum 2009; Friedman et al. 2002; Friedman and Hendry 2019; Borning and Muller 2012). Some approaches aim to guide designers in focusing on designing for a specific value that is particularly relevant to the technology in question or the population that will use the technology, for example, design for privacy (Warnier et al. 2015), inclusivity (Keates 2015), care (Van Wynsberghe 2013), sustainability (Wever and Vogtländer 2015), or attention (Williams, this volume). A leading approach is value-sensitive design (VSD), which incorporates stakeholder analysis and conceptual ethical analysis into the design process from the very beginning (Friedman et al. 2002; Friedman and Hendry 2019). VSD and other ethics-by-design approaches have also been subject to considerable criticisms, which VSD scholars have met with proposed solutions. In the following paragraph, we highlight three such criticisms that are particularly relevant to applying VSD approaches to DHAs and that compound each other. We then consider two possible responses.

First is the challenge of conflicting values. When creating a DHA that incorporates stakeholder values, how should designers make trade-offs between incompatible values or values that cannot both be equally realized in design specifications (Manders-Huits 2011; Jacobs and Huldtgren 2018)? For example, users of an online dating platform may value honesty and transparency and also, at the same time, privacy and individualized control over which information they share. The method of VSD does not offer any specific guidance on how to resolve such a conflict.

A second and related problem is aggregation, which applies specifically to cases in which designers attempt to take user well-being into account. The problem 'arises due to the fact that a design does not affect the well-being of just one person, but rather that of a range of people' (Van de Poel 2014: 296). If we assume some kind of pluralism about well-being, that is, that different people hold different conceptions of the good life, which includes having different and sometimes incommensurable prudential values, then it becomes very difficult to design technology with the value of well-being in mind because it may simultaneously promote and thwart different people's conception of sexual or romantic well-being. For example, the user who is a simple hedonist may value a DHA that facilitates frequent short-term and low-effort sexual encounters while another user values the DHA that facilitates the cultivation of long-lasting relationships based on friendship and shared pursuits.

The third relevant criticism of VSD is that it uncritically incorporates stakeholder values into design, thereby assuming that the stakeholders value what they *should* actually value and ignoring the possibility that they may hold values that are immoral or that undermine their own well-being or the well-being of others (Manders-Huits 2011; Jacobs and Huldtgren 2018). Some user stakeholders of DHAs may value efficiency in matching with other users. This could be embodied in the design by creating an interface that is almost all image rather than being text-based or include options to filter one's results along very narrow perimeters (e.g. weight, race, age). Arguably, the 'swiping' right or left feature of Tinder has this effect. Although users may value efficiency in their selection of partners, perhaps this value is actually problematic from the perspective of respect for human dignity, equality, or flourishing through meaningful relationships.

It is beyond the scope of this chapter to offer detailed solutions to these challenges so we will briefly mention some possible solutions (See Vickery, et al. 2018). Jacobs and Huldtgren (2018) have argued that both the problems of value conflicts and uncritical acceptance of stakeholder values can be resolved by coupling value-sensitive design with a substantive first-order ethical theory (Kantianism, utilitarianism, etc.). Such a theory would provide a value hierarchy and method for dealing with clashing values or norms. In such a version of VSD, stakeholder values would no longer function as the only normative input into the design process. Stakeholder values can be scrutinized in light of a set of normative commitments stemming from the ethical theory. In response to the aggregation problem, Van de Poel suggests segmenting the population for which one is designing into groups that 'share a comprehensive goal or a vision of the good life' (van de Poel 2014: 303; See also Van de Poel 2013).

To some extent, these solutions can be seen in the way various DHAs attempt to cater to different segments of the population who are assumed to share common values or conceptions of sexual or romantic well-being. Although we do not know whether VSD played any role in its development, the location-based dating and friendship app Bumble can illustrate some of these solutions. Bumble identifies itself as the 'feminist alternative' dating app and the founder explicitly claims to work to upend patriarchal heteronormative dating culture (Bumble 2015). For man–woman in app matches, the woman has to initiate contact in order for the man to be able to contact her, thus reducing the unwanted contact women experience and putting women in a position of control. The app has also designed features to reduce catfishing and ghosting through photo verification tools and time limits on how long men can take in responding to women with whom they have matched and with whom they have been talking.

VSD could also play a role in developing alternative business models for DHAs that explicitly nudge people to consider the amount of time and attention they spend using them or models that more robustly respect user autonomy. Although VSD is an involved process requiring design expertise and empirical research, two examples can indicate the types of changes that are possible. Designer Tristan Harris's Center for Humane Technology and the Time Well Spent movement emphasize informing people about the features of digital technologies that keep us mindlessly clicking and have negative impacts on our psychological health. Building profitable DHAs that emphasize mindful and healthy engagement might find traction with populations that are aware of the deleterious impacts of many digital technologies. Informed consent is often offered as a panacea for all kinds of potential technologically mediated harms, violations, or privacy issues. As many have observed, the standard 'clickwrap' or 'click-through' agreements that we constantly sign to gain access to a mobile service or site are extremely ineffective at providing users with meaningful information about the risks and benefits of sharing data or using a service (Obar and Oeldorf-Hirsch 2018). But there is an emerging area of research on alternative models for digital consent (see, e.g. Loosman (2020) on consent to m-health apps, Wee et al. (2013) on dynamic consent, and Tiffin (2018) on tiered consent). Creative reimaging of consent to use DHAs that actually respects user autonomy rather than merely providing legal coverage to the company might involve frequent check-ins with users on the ways in which the DHA might be impacting their behaviour or feedback on the amount of time users are engaging with the app per day, similar to Apple's 'Screen Time' feature, which gives you information on your screen use and tools to help you change your behaviour.

FUTURE RESEARCH DIRECTIONS

Future research in the domain of DHAs is likely to expand in several possible directions as intimacy, sex, and love continue to be further mediated by technology. We argue that this research should pay special attention to soft impacts (Klincewicz and Frank 2018; Nyholm et al. 2022). Several topics that we have not discussed in this chapter but deserve attention involve the soft impacts of DHAs. One of these has to do with discrimination and preference expression. Some mobile dating platforms allow for sorting through potential matches along various parameters, including religion, ethnicity, race, and sexual and gender identity, among others.[12] Of course, these preferences could be expressed and acted upon without the use of DHAs, but several of the technology's features, including filtering by these categories, makes it easier to do so. The ethics of disclosing this information (gender identity, race, etc.) and selecting potential partners based on it is a controversial and emerging area of research. The use of these features has led some thinkers to interrogate the ways in which dating or sexual preferences, which may seem at first glance merely aesthetic or at least morally neutral, can be informed and influenced by morally problematic unconscious biases and assumptions or by unarticulated discriminatory beliefs. For example, philosopher Veronica Ivy has claimed on her Twitter account that having a preference for particular types of genitals in the person one is seeking to date is an expression of transphobia. Brynn Tannehill (2019) in the *Advocate,* among other online magazines has discussed this topic. On the complex issue of disclosure of transgender identity and genital preference, see, for example, Fernandez and Birnholtz (2019) and Bettcher (2007). In their recent book *The Dating Divide: Race and Desire in the Era of Online Romance* (2021), Vaughan, Lundquist, and Lin argue that 'digital-sexual racism' has emerged as a consequence of several features of DHAs (anonymity, digital disinhibition, etc.) used in a society with background conditions of racial inequality in the United States. On the issue of race and ethnicity, see also Mitchell and Wells (2018); Zheng (2016), and Callander et al. (2015) on racialized preferences and fetishization in online dating.

Another area for future philosophical analysis is the variety of new types of relationships that are facilitated by the affordances of DHAs. For example, some apps like Grindr or Skout are specifically focused on geographical proximity, using the phone's GPS to enable users to connect with potential partners in their immediate vicinity. Sharing some intimate information (e.g. in the case of Grindr, HIV status is often shared) through these apps with those in one's vicinity comes with a sacrifice of privacy and potentially safety. In response, hacks like the faking of one's GPS location have been developed by users: is this a form of catfishing? At the other end of the spectrum, some DHAs allow users to widen their search nationally or globally. This seems particularly valuable for people who live in isolated areas or have very specific or uncommon preferences for partners and for those who are seeking a relationship that will be conducted mostly or entirely online. Increasing numbers of people are either in or are open to and participating in long-distance relationships.

In the United States, DHAs are the main way that heterosexuals form relationships (Rosenfeld et al. 2019). In this chapter, we have introduced some of the key features of DHAs and three of the potential new or altered kinds of moral wrongs they facilitate: the catfishing, the unsolicited dick pic, and ghosting. We have also highlighted some of the broader trends that foster these new wrongs, including commodification, gamification, and disinhibition. The incursion of technology into the realm or dating, sex, and even love is not entirely new, nor are its potentially socially or morally transformative impacts. Arguably, the birth control pill, the mechanical vibrator, widely available pornography, or even the newspaper personal advertisement are all cases in which technological developments or new uses for pre-existing technologies had these impacts. Digital DHAs can be seen as part of this lineage, yet they are uniquely ubiquitous and embedded in smart phone and computer technology, which is an unavoidable part of many of aspects of our lives already: work, entertainment, socializing, education, and consumption. For these reasons, they merit special moral consideration and demand further empirical and conceptual research, especially on their soft impacts, their disruptive potential, and how they can be intentionally designed to promote specific values.

Notes

1. For a contemporary elaboration on mediation theory, see: Verbeek (2006, 2008, 2011, 2015).
2. See https://blog.marketresearch.com/dating-services-industry-in-2016-and-beyond, accessed 24 April 2022.
3. See https://tech.eu/news/badoo-200-million-users, accessed 24 April 2022.
4. See https://www.ladbible.com/entertainment/weird-mans-boyfriend-of-a-year-turns-out-to-be-woman-seeking-revenge-20210715, accessed 24 April 2022.
5. See https://abcnews.go.com/2020/catfish-woman-angela-wesselman-twisted-cyber-romance-abc/story?id=11831583, accessed 24 April 2022.
6. See https://phys.org/news/2018-07-catfish-people-onlineit-money.html, accessed 24 April 2022.
7. The authors cannot find anything but anecdotal evidence to support that one experience is more common than others.
8. See https://today.yougov.com/topics/lifestyle/articles-reports/2017/10/09/53-millennial-women-have-received-dick-pic, accessed 24 April 2022.
9. It is important to note here that receiving unsolicited explicit images is not limited to users of DHAs—people, especially women, who use any social media platforms are exposed to this content.
10. For a discussion of digital gamification in the context of relationships, see: Danaher et al. (2018). And for a response, Klincewicz and Frank (2018: 27–28).
11. See https://coffeemeetsbagel.zendesk.com/hc/en-us/articles/360017441574-What-are-beans-, accessed 24 April 2022.
12. According to Hunte (2020), Tinder has promised to remove the race feature in the future.

References

Almarshedi, Alaa, Wanick, Vanissa, Wills, Gary B., and Ranchhod, Ashok (2017), 'Gamification and Behaviours', in Stefan Stieglitz, Christoph Lattemann, Susanne Robra-Bissantz, Rüdiger Zarnekow, Tobias Brockmann, eds, *Gamification* (Berlin: Springer), 9–29.

Anderson, Michelle (2005), 'Negotiating Sex', *Southern California Law Review* 78, 1401–1438.

Arias, V. Santiago, Punyanunt-Carter, Narissa, and Wrench, Jason S. (2017), 'Future Directions for Swiping Right: The Impact of Modern Technology on Dating', in Narissra M. Punyanunt-Carter, Jason S. Wrench, eds, *The Impact of Social Media in Modern Romantic Relationships* (Maryland: Lexington Books), 259–272.

Bettcher, Talia Mae (2007), 'Evil Deceivers and Make-Believers: On Transphobic Violence and the Politics of Illusion', *Hypatia* 22(3), 43–65.

Borning, Allan, and Muller, Michael (2012), 'Next Steps for Value Sensitive Design', in Joseph A. Konstan, ed, *Proceedings of the SIGCHI Conference on Human Factors in Computing Systems* (New York: Association for Computing Machinery), 1125–1134.

Brown, Megan Lindsay, Reed, Lauren A., and Messing, Jill Theresa (2018), 'Technology-based Abuse: Intimate Partner Violence and the Use of Information Communication Technologies', in Jacqueline Ryan Vickery, Tracy Everbach, eds, *Mediating Misogyny*. (Cham: Palgrave Macmillan), 209–227.

Bumble, (2015), 'Meet the Tinder Co-Founder Trying to Change Online Dating Forever', *Vanity Fair*. 7 August 2015. https://www.vanityfair.com/culture/2015/08/bumble-app-whit

ney-wolfe?epik=djoyJnU9cTloao1FYmdtbnY3Mm1ZeFVZcVUzUmVmNoJWNjJ1TWcmc
DowJm49bTZpZlNOcEk4SjB1OVVnUkhNdU5QdyZoPUFBQUFBRoxBTm1n.

Denton Callander, Newman, Christy E., and Holt, Martin (2015), 'Is Sexual Racism Really
    Racism? Distinguishing Attitudes toward Sexual Racism and Generic Racism among Gay
    and Bisexual Men', *Archives of Sexual Behavior* 44(7), 1991–2000.

Danaher, John, Nyholm, Sven, and Earp, Brian. (2018), 'The Quantified Relationship', *American
    Journal of Bioethics* 18(2), 3–19.

Davis, Jenny L., and Chouinard, James B. (2016), 'Theorizing Affordances: From Request to
    Refuse', *Bulletin of Science, Technology & Society* 36(4), 241–248.

Deci, Edward L., and Ryan, Richard M. (1985), *Intrinsic Motivation and Self-determination in
    Human Behavior* (Boston, MA: Springer).

Dougherty, Tom (2013), 'Sex, Lies, and Consent', *Ethics* 123(4), 717–744.

Dougherty, Tom (2021), 'Sexual Misconduct on a Scale: Gravity, Coercion, and Consent', *Ethics*
    131(2), 319–344.

Eisingerich, Andreas B., Marchand, André, Fritze, Martin P., and Dong, Lin (2019), "Hook vs.
    Hope: How to Enhance Customer Engagement through Gamification", *International Journal
    of Research in Marketing* 36(2), 200–215.

Fernandez, Julia R., and Jeremy Birnholtz (2019), ' "I Don't Want Them to Not Know"
    Investigating Decisions to Disclose Transgender Identity on Dating Platforms', *Proceedings
    of the ACM on Human–Computer Interaction*, ACM Conference on Computer-Supported
    Cooperative Work and Social Computing 3, 1–21.

Flanagan, Mary, Howe, Daniel, and Nissenbaum, Helen (2009), 'Embodying Values in
    Technology: Theory and Practice', in Jeroen van den Hoven and John Weckert, eds,
    Information Technology and Moral Philosophy (Cambridge: Cambridge University Press),
    322–253.

Freedman, Gili, Powell, Darcey N., Le, Benjamin, Williams, Kipling D. (2019), 'Ghosting and
    Destiny: Implicit Theories of Relationships Predict Beliefs about Ghosting', *Journal of Social
    and Personal Relationships* 36(3), 905–924.

Friedman, Batya. (1996), 'Value-Sensitive Design', *Interactions* 3(6), 16–23.

Friedman, Batya, Kahn, Peter, and Borning, Alan. (2002), *Value Sensitive Design: Theory and
    Methods*, *University of Washington technical report* 2: 12.

Friedman, B., and Hendry, D. G. (2019), *Value Sensitive Design: Shaping Technology with Moral
    Imagination* (Cambridge, Massachusetts: MIT Press).

Hunte, Ben (2020), 'Grindr Has Promised to Remove the "Ethnicity Filter," But Has Not Yet
    Done So', https://www.bbc.com/news/technology-53192465, accessed 24 April 2022.

Isisag, Anil (2019), 'Mobile Dating Apps and the Intensive Marketization of Dating:
    Gamification as a Marketizing Apparatus', in Rajesh Bagchi, Lauren Block, and Leonard Lee,
    eds, *Advances in Consumer Research*, Volume 47, (Duluth, MN: Association for Consumer
    Research), 135–141.

Jacobs, Naomi, and Huldtgren, Alina (2018), 'Why Value Sensitive Design Needs Ethical
    Commitments', *Ethics and Information Technology*, 23(1), 23–26.

Jane, Emma A. (2016), *Misogyny Online: A Short (and Brutish) History* (London: Sage
    Publications).

Kant, Immanuel (2012/1785), *Groundwork of the Metaphysics of Morals*, ed. and trans. M.
    Gregor and J. Timmermann (Cambridge: Cambridge University Press).

Kats, Rima (2020), 'Love in the Time of the Coronavirus: How Dating is Becoming More
    Virtual Amid the Pandemic', *Business Insider*, https://www.businessinsider.com/dat

ing-apps-growing-becoming-more-virtual-amid-pandemic-2020-9?international= true&r=US&IR=T, accessed 24 April 2022.

Keates, Simeon 2015, Design for the value of inclusiveness', in Jeroen van den Hoven, Pieter E. Vermaas, and Ibo van de Poel, eds, *Handbook of Ethics, Values, and Technological Design: Sources, Theory, Values and Application Domains* (Dordrecht: Springer), 383–402.

Kornath, Sarah (2020) , 'What the Pandemic Has Done for Dating', *The Atlantic*, 31 December 2020. https://www.theatlantic.com/ideas/archive/2020/12/what-pandemic-has-done-dat ing/617502/, accessed 2 July 2022.

Klincewicz, Michał and Frank, Lily (2018), 'Swiping Left on the Quantified Relationship: Exploring the Potential Soft Impacts', *American Journal of Bioethics* 18(2), 27–28.

Klincewicz, Michał, Frank, Lily E. and Jane, Emma (2022), 'The Ethics of Matching: Hookup Apps and Online Dating', in Lori Watson, Clare Chambers, Brian D. Earp, eds, *The Routledge Handbook of Philosophy of Sex and Sexuality* (New York: Routledge).

Kolodny, Niko (2003), 'Love as Valuing a Relationship', *Philosophical Review* 112(2), 135–189.

LeFebvre, Leah E., Allen, Mike, Rasner, Ryan D., Garstad, Shelby, Wilms, Aleksander, and Parrish Callie (2019), 'Ghosting in Emerging Adults' Romantic Relationships: The Digital Dissolution Disappearance Strategy', *Imagination, Cognition and Personality* 39(2), 125–150.

Loosman, Iris (2020), '10 Rethinking Consent in mHealth:(A) Moment to Process', in *Aging Between Participation and Simulation* (Berlin/Boston: De Gruyter), 159–170.

MacKinnon, Catharine (2005), *Women's Lives, Men's Laws* (Cambridge, MA: Harvard University Press).

Manders-Huits, Noëmi (2011), 'What Values in Design? The Challenge of Incorporating Moral Values into Design', *Science and Engineering Ethics* 17(2), 271–287.

Mantilla, Karla (2015), *Gendertrolling: How Misogyny Went Viral: How Misogyny Went Viral* (Santa Barbara: ABC–CLIO).

Marcotte, Alexandra S., Gesselman, Amanda N., Fisher, Helen E., and Garcia, Justin R. (2020), 'Women's and Men's Reactions to Receiving Unsolicited Genital Images from Men', *Journal of Sex Research* 58(4), 1–10.

Mitchell, Megan, and Wells, Mark (2018), 'Race, Romantic Attraction, and Dating', *Ethical Theory and Moral Practice* 21(4), 945–961.

Norman, Donald A. (1988), *The Psychology of Everyday Things* (New York: Basic Books).

Nyholm, Sven, Danaher, John, and Earp, Brian D. (2022), 'The Technological Future of Love', in N. McKeever, A. Grahle, and J. Saunders, eds, *Love: Past, Present, and Future* (Abingdon and New York: Routledge).

Nyholm, Sven and Frank, Lily (2017), 'From Sex Robots to Love Robots: Is Mutual Love with a Robot Possible?' in John Danaher and Neil McArthur, eds, *Robot Sex: Social and Ethical Implications* (Cambridge, Massachusetts: MIT Press), 219–245.

Obar, Jonathan A., and Oeldorf-Hirsch, Anne (2018), 'The Clickwrap: A Political Economic Mechanism for Manufacturing Consent on Social Media', *Social Media+Society* 4(3), 2056305118784770.

Oswald, Flora, Lopes, Alex, Skoda, Kaylee, Hesse, Cassandra L., and Pedersen, Cory L. (2020), 'I'll Show You Mine So You'll Show Me Yours: Motivations and Personality Variables in Photographic Exhibitionism', *Journal of Sex Research* 57(5), 597–609.

Ryan, Richard M., and Deci, Edward L. (2000), 'Self-determination theory and the facilitation of intrinsic motivation, social development, and well-being'. *American psychologist* 55(1), 68.

Rocha Santos, P.C., (2018), *Gamification of Love: A Case Study of Tinder in Oslo* (Master's Thesis), https://www.duo.uio.no/handle/10852/64406, accessed 2 July 2022.

Rosenfeld, Michael J., Thomas, Reuben J., and Hausen, Sonia (2019), 'Disintermediating Your Friends: How Online Dating in the United States Displaces Other Ways of Meeting', *Proceedings of the National Academy of Sciences* 116(36), 17753–17758.

Simmons, Mariah, and Lee, Joon Suuk (2020), 'Catfishing: A Look into Online Dating and Impersonation', in Gabriele Meiselwitz, ed, *International Conference on Human–Computer Interaction* (Cham: Springer), 349–358.

Suler, John (2004), 'The Online Disinhibition Effect', *Cyberpsychology & Behavior* 7(3), 321–326.

Suler, John R. (2016), *Psychology of the Digital Age: Humans Become Electric* (Cambridge: Cambridge University Press).

Swierstra, Tsjalling (2013), 'Nanotechnology and Techno-Moral Change', *Ethics & Politics* 15(1), 200–219.

Swierstra, Tsjalling, and Hedwig Frederica Maria te Molder (2012), 'Risk and Soft Impacts', in Sabine Roeser, Rafaela Hillerbrand, Per Sandin, and Martin Peterson, eds, *Handbook of Risk Theory: Epistemology, Decision Theory, Ethics, and Social Implications of Risk* (Dordrecht: Springer), 1049–1066.

Swierstra, Tsjalling, Stemerding, Dirk, and Boenink, Marianne (2009), 'Exploring Techno-Moral Change: The Case of the Obesity Pill', in Paul Sollie and Marcus Duwell, eds, *Evaluating New Technologies* (Dordrecht: Springer Netherlands), 119–138.

Tannehill, Brynn (2019), 'Is Refusing to Date Trans People Transphobic?' *Advocate*, (14 December 2019), https://www.advocate.com/commentary/2019/12/14/refusing-date-trans-people-transphobic, accessed 2 July 2022.

Tiffin, Nicki (2018), 'Tiered Informed Consent: Respecting Autonomy, Agency and Individuality in Africa', *BMJ Global Health* 3(6), e001249.

van den Hoven, Jeroen, Vermaas, Pieter E., van de Poel, Ibo (2015), 'Design for Values: An Introduction', in Jeroen van den Hoven, Pieter E. Vermaas, Ibo van de Poel, eds, *Handbook of Ethics, Values, and Technological Design: Sources, Theory, Values and Application Domains*, (Dordrecht: Springer), 1–7.

Van de Poel, Ibo (2013), 'Translating Values into Design Requirements', in David E. Goldberg, Diane P. Michelfelder, Natasha McCarthy, eds, *Philosophy and engineering: Reflections on Practice, Principles and Process* (Dordrecht: Springer), 253–266.

Van de Poel, Ibo (2014), 'Conflicting Values in Design for Values', in Jeroen van den Hoven, Pieter E. Vermaas, and Ibo van de Poel, eds, *Handbook of Ethics, Values, and Technological Design* (Dordrecht: Springer), 89–116.

Van Wynsberghe, Amy (2013), 'A Method for Integrating Ethics into the Design of Robots', *Industrial Robot: An International Journal* 40(5), 433–440. https://doi.org/10.1108/IR-12-2012-451

Vaughan Curington, Celeste, Hickes Lundquist, Jennifer, Lin, Ken-Hou (2021), *The Dating Divide: Race and Desire in the Era of Online Romance* (Oakland, California: University of California Press).

Verbeek, Peter Paul (2006), 'Materializing Morality: Design Ethics and Technological Mediation', *Science, Technology, & Human Values* 31(3), 361–380.

Verbeek, Peter Paul (2008), 'Obstetric Ultrasound and the Technological Mediation of Morality: A Postphenomenological Analysis', *Human Studies* 31(1), 11–26.

Verbeek, Peter Paul (2011), *Moralizing Technology: Understanding and Designing the Morality of Things* (Chicago, IL: University of Chicago Press).

Verbeek, Peter-Paul (2015), 'Cover Story: Beyond Interaction: A Short Introduction to Mediation Theory', *Interactions* 22(3), 26–31.

Vickery, Jacqueline Ryan, Everbach, Tracy, Blackwell, Lindsay, Franks, Mary Anne, Friedman, Barbara, Gibbons, Sheila, Gillespie, Tarleton, and Massanari, Adrienne (2018), 'Conclusion: What Can We Do about Mediated Misogyny?', in Jacqueline Ryan Vickery and Tracy Everbach, eds, *Mediating Misogyny* (Cham: Palgrave Macmillan), 389–412.

Wachter-Boettcher, Sara (2017), *Technically Wrong: Sexist Apps, Biased Algorithms, and Other Threats of Toxic Tech* (New York: WW Norton & Company).

Warnier, Martijn, Dechesne, Francien, and Brazier, Frances (2015), 'Design for the Value of Privacy', in Jeroen van den Hoven, Pieter E. Vermaas, and Ibo van de Poel, eds, *Handbook of Ethics, Values, and Technological Design: Sources, Theory, Values and Application Domains* (Dordrecht: Springer): 431–445.

Wee, Richman, Henaghan, Mark, and Winship, Ingrid (2013), 'Ethics: Dynamic Consent in the Digital Age of Biology: Online Initiatives and Regulatory Considerations', *Journal of Primary Health Care* 5(4), 341–347.

Wertheimer, Alan (2000), 'What is Consent? And is It Important?', *Buffalo Criminal Law Review* 3(2), 557–583.

Wever, Renee, and Vogtländer, Joost (2015), 'Design for the Value of Sustainability', in Jeroen van den Hoven, Pieter E. Vermaas, and Ibo van de Poel, eds, *Handbook of Ethics, Values, and Technological Design: Sources, Theory, Values and Application Domains* (Dordrecht: Springer), 513–549.

Wood, Allen W. (1999), *Kant's Ethical Thought* (Cambridge: Cambridge University Press).

Zheng, Robin (2016), 'Why Yellow Fever Isn't Flattering: A Case against Racial Fetishes', *Journal of the American Philosophical Association* 2(3), 400–419.

CHAPTER 13

THE ETHICS OF SEX ROBOTS

AKSEL STERRI AND BRIAN D. EARP

INTRODUCTION

WITH rapid advances in robot technology and artificial intelligence (AI), sex robots, or sexbots for short, are expected to become much more popular than the sex 'dolls' currently on the market.

Some proponents of sexbots, such as Neil McArthur (2017), argue that as long as no one with moral standing is harmed, people should be free to do as they like in their own bedroom (or indeed anywhere else). David Levy (2007) envisions a healthy future for human–robot sexual relations. According to Levy, sexbots will provide a positive outlet for sexual desires and will, over time, become fine-tuned to the preferences of their users. Nevertheless, many worry that sexbots will not be so ethically innocent. There is something chilling about the very idea of a sexual servant—even a technological one—that is always ready and willing to satisfy one's desires, whatsoever they may be. As Jeannie Suk Gersen (2019: 1798) states: 'In the context of sex robots, the idea of forced servitude is especially disturbing because, for many people, the sexual realm is a site of our deepest ideals and fears about personal autonomy and personal relationships.'

Some ethical worries about sexbots relate to scenarios that may never materialize. In the popular TV series *Westworld*, extreme forms of cruelty are on constant display, including what is by all appearances the forcible rape of robots who are indistinguishable from humans and who may well be sentient and even capable of forming and acting on life plans.[1] For the purposes of this chapter, we will set aside such concerns and assume that sexbots of the future will be non-sentient and lack moral standing. They will be neither moral victims nor moral agents; that is, we will assume that sexbots are 'mere' machines that are reliably identifiable as such, despite their human-like appearance and behaviour. Under these stipulations, sexbots themselves can no more be harmed, morally speaking, than your dishwasher. As we will explore, however, there may still be something wrong about the production, distribution, or use of such sexbots.

One kind of wrong could have to do with likely (or at least potential) effects on users. Another has to do with such effects on society: our seemingly private actions may have wider implications for the communities of which we are a part. There may also be intrinsic wrongs associated with sexbot use, depending on one's views on the nature of sex and sexual activity, and the relationship between human beings and inanimate objects more generally.

Supposing it *is* wrong for human beings to engage sexually with robots, what then? Should sexbots be banned? We will discuss arguments in favour of prohibition, as well as arguments against it. We will also explore the possibility that sexbots could be, on balance, good for society if appropriately regulated, and that human–robot sex could be ethical. We explore the prospect of a harm reduction approach to sexbot regulation, analogous to the approach that has been considered for drugs and sex work. Is there a way for regulators to steer the development and use of sexbot technology in a direction that would maximize its benefits and minimize its harms, both for the user and for society at large?

WHAT IS A SEX ROBOT?

A sexbot is a robot that is designed and manufactured primarily for the purpose of being used for sexual gratification. In this chapter, we consider sexbots with four particular features: (1) they are shaped like human beings and have an overall human-like appearance; (2) they move in ways that are relevant for sexual interactions of various kinds; (3) they are embodied (rather than, say, holographic); and (4) they have AI of a sufficiently sophisticated level to allow the user to communicate with the robot, at least in a rudimentary way.[2] The human appearance sets sexbots apart from *sex toys*, such as vibrators, fleshlights, dildos, etc. The ability to move and interact with users sets them apart from *sex dolls*. And their embodiment sets them apart from *virtual reality sex*.

How likely, and how soon, are we to confront the existence of humanoid sexbots? The company Realbotix, which for several years has produced sex dolls, suggests that such sexbots are highly likely in the reasonably near future: 'We're working to create the next generation of the well-known anatomically correct RealDolls, which we intend to blend with Artificial Intelligence, Robotics, touch sensors, internal heaters, virtual and augmented reality interfaces.' These new bots, they continue, 'will have an animated face synchronized with an application that users can talk to and interact with [and] will have the ability to listen, remember, and talk naturally, like a living person. They will have hyper-realistic features, warmth, and sensors that react to touch' (RealBotix 2020).

There are three types of sexbots that have received the most attention in the ethics literature. The first type is a female sexbot with features that are stereotypical of mainstream pornography. The sex dolls that are currently on the market mirror, as one author puts it, 'a strong Eurocentric male gaze', such that 'their design takes semantic coding and stereotyping along hegemonic gender lines to the extreme, basically reducing "robot

companions" to large-breasted Barbie dolls with glimpses of artificial intelligence'
(Kubes 2019: 3). The prospect of doubling down on this gaze and associated attitudes
or expectations from mainstream pornography (widely understood to be harmful and
misogynistic) is one of the leading worries that has been raised about sexbots. The concern is that these attitudes and expectations will be reinforced in the minds of users,
which, in addition to being potentially objectionable in its own right, may also increase
the likelihood of tangible harms to others, in particular women (e.g. by encouraging
users to think of women as objects to be sexually exploited, rather than as equal partners
in a sexual encounter). This worry is a central issue in both the *Campaign against Sex
Robots*, spearheaded by the anthropologist Kathleen Richardson (2015),[3] and in Robert
Sparrow's chapter, 'How Robots Have Politics', in this volume.

The second type of sexbot that has received the most attention is the type that is
designed to be 'raped' (i.e. to simulate resistance to sexual advances and a lack of consent). The rudimentary sexbot Roxxxy, for example, comes with different personalities.
One of them is 'Frigid Farrah', which is described by the manufacturer as an entity
that is 'very reserved and does not always like to engage in intimate activities' (Brown
2019: 112). It has been argued that Frigid Farrah could be used to satisfy rape fantasies—
or to encourage such fantasies in the first place—and that this would be harmful to the
moral character of the people who engage in such acts, while likely contributing to negative effects on society at large (Danaher 2017a; Sparrow 2017).

The third type of sexbot is the type that is designed to look like a prepubescent child
(a child sexbot, for short). While some, such as roboticist Robert Arkin (quoted in
Hill 2014), have proposed that child sexbots could ethically be used in the treatment
of paedophilia (and thus reduce the likelihood of adult sexual contact with actual children), others are afraid that such sexbots would only serve to sexualize children, leading
to more, not less, abuse (Danaher 2019b; Strikwerda 2017).

These three types of sexbots, insofar as they are (or continue to be) developed, raise
important, and partially dissociable, ethical concerns. In their current form, the robots
are not much more sophisticated than dolls. However, given the rapid pace of technological innovation, including in such areas as artificial speech, touch, and affect, it is
reasonable to expect that these robots will, within the next few decades, or even sooner,
become much more human-like along the four dimensions we listed above.

VALUE FROM SEXBOTS

The prospect of human-like sexbots raises several worries. It might seem unthinkable that they could add any real value to society. But as the hypothetical use of such
sexbots in treating paedophilia might suggest, there could potentially be some good
associated with their development in certain cases. The main good that some authors
have suggested sexbots would allow is that more people could have (at least some kind
of) sex.[4] This is not a trivial issue. On some views, sex is not a luxury; rather, it is a central

ingredient in many people's conception of a good life (Jecker 2020). Sex of different kinds can facilitate extraordinary pleasure, vulnerability, exploration, and positive bodily awareness; and under the right conditions, it may have beneficial implications for physical and mental health (Brody 2010; Diamond and Huebner 2012; Kashdan et al. 2014).[5] That many people who desire sex are unable to experience it thus seems lamentable. Insofar as sexbots could provide at least some of the goods of sex to those who would otherwise be unable to access such goods, their availability would be a source of considerable value. On this view, we have at least a prima facie reason to favour their production, distribution, and use (Danaher 2020).

We can distinguish different ways in which sexbots could be valuable. One sort of value they might bring is in the *treatment* of recognized sexual dysfunctions or disadvantages; the other is in the pursuit of *enhanced* sexual pleasure or enjoyment, potentially going beyond what is currently achievable for most people.

Ezio Di Nucci (2017), Neil McArthur (2017), Jeannie Gersen (2019), David Levy (2007, 2011), and Nancy Jecker (2020), discuss various ways in which sexbots could be used for treatment. Di Nucci (2017) argues that some people, including those with certain disabilities, may find it prohibitively difficult to find a willing sexual partner. Given that sex is so important for most people, Di Nucci argues, sexbots could be used to fulfil the strong desire for sex that someone in this situation may have. People with relevant disabilities are not the only ones who may struggle to find a willing sexual partner, however.[6] As suggested by McArthur (2017), in countries such as India and China, a skewed sex ratio imbalance (more males than females born each year), coupled with powerful cultural expectations of monogamy, may prevent a sizable number of men from finding a partner. The same difficulty may face people in prisons or in the military, or others who, for various reasons, cannot find a willing sexual partner for shorter or longer stretches of time (Gersen 2019). For people with rare sexual preferences, sexbots might be the only available (or perhaps the only ethical) way of having those preferences fulfilled. For these groups, sexbots may serve as a (potentially suboptimal) replacement for sex with humans under the relevant circumstances.

Sexbots might also have value insofar as they could be used to help some people have sex (or better sex) with humans. As McArthur (2017: 40) points out: 'People with severe anxiety surrounding performance or body image, an incidence of sexual trauma (such as rape or incest), adults with limited or no experience, or people who have transitioned from one sex to another, may find that their anxieties about sex inhibit their ability to form [intimate] relationships.' Sexbots could potentially help people in such situations gain greater self-acceptance and sexual skill or confidence, which, in turn, might help them to prepare for positive human sexual relationships. In such a case, access to sexual learning via a sexbot partner might be considered a form of psychosexual treatment.

What about people who fall more squarely within the (statistically) normal range of sexual capacity and experience? Might access to sexbots help them to have better sexual experiences and become even better sexual partners to their fellow human beings? Within the context of relationships, sexbots could be designed to give feedback to improve sensitivity to a partner's likes and dislikes. Sexbots might also be used in a manner that is similar to, but goes beyond, the way that many people currently use sex toys, namely, to spice up their sex lives. For example, a sexbot might allow a couple to have a threesome without involving other human partners (Gersen 2019). Sexbots could also help couples to deal with discrepancies in sexual desire by facilitating a potentially more fulfilling alternative to masturbation. Indeed, insofar as mismatched sexual desire between a couple is contributing to the likelihood of an otherwise avoidable—and undesirable—breakup or divorce, consensual use of a sexbot by one or both partners may reduce this likelihood (McArthur 2017).

In principle, therefore, sexbots could facilitate, supplement, treat, or possibly even enhance ethical sex between human beings (which is almost universally recognized as a good). That being said, sexbots might also in some cases replace sex between human beings. So-called 'digisexuals' prefer robots as sex partners because they favour the 'company' of inanimate objects (McArthur and Twist 2017). Insofar as digisexuals can be considered to have a sexual orientation towards robots, it would likely be valuable for them to be able to act on their orientation with a desired object/partner (Danaher 2020).

Having canvassed some of the potential goods associated with sexbots, we can explore in more detail the arguments that have been levied against them. We will begin with the argument that there is something intrinsically wrong with having sex with a robot and go on to discuss whether, even if it is not intrinsically wrong, it may still be harmful, on balance, to the user (or others) to have sex with robots.

Intrinsic wrong

Can it be wrong to have sex with a robot? We have stipulated that sexbots will lack moral standing, so it seems that *they* could not be wronged by such sex.[7] But it might still be true that robots are among the things it is morally unacceptable for us to sexually desire, much less engage with in a sexual manner.

The view that there are at least some kinds of entities that should not be 'sexualized'—even as objects of private, unacted-upon desire—has some precedence. Most people think of children and non-human animals this way, for example. They think it is wrong even to *want* to have sex with a child or non-human animal, even if one does not actually follow through on this desire. One explanation for such a view is that certain desires are wrong in themselves by virtue of being perverted (roughly, morally corrupted deviations from something's original or proper purpose).[8] In Thomas Nagel's (1969) account of sexual perversions, inspired by Jean-Paul Sartre's (1956) analysis of sexual desire in *Being and Nothingness*, Nagel includes sex with inanimate objects alongside 'intercourse with animals [and] infants' as examples of such perversions. 'If the object is not [even] alive, the experience is', in his view, 'reduced entirely to an awareness of one's own sexual embodiment' (Nagel 1969: 12, 14).[9] This reduction, he thinks, is something that is morally troubling in its own right.

Objections to certain kinds of sexual activities on the basis of their alleged perversity come in strong and weak variants. The strong version of Nagel's account of sexual perversion is what David Benatar (2002) calls the *Significance View*: 'for sex to be morally acceptable, it must be an expression of (romantic) love [signifying] feelings of affection that are commensurate with the intimacy of sexual activity'. On this view, 'a sexual union can be acceptable only if it reflects the reciprocal love and affection of the parties to that union' (Benatar 2002: 182). The advantage of such a view is that it is able to explain several interconnected phenomena: (a) the special status that sex is often taken to have; (b) why sex against a person's will is almost universally regarded as an especially egregious violation of their personhood or dignity; and (c) why it would be wrong to have sex with children or non-human animals (i.e. it would be, among other things, non-reciprocal, where reciprocity requires a certain kind of equal standing). This view also entails that sex with robots is outside the boundaries of what is morally acceptable.

There are some difficulties with this view, however. One is that it seems to imply that so-called 'casual' sex is morally impermissible on the grounds that it does not (usually) reflect mutual love between the partners. But casual sex, if mutually desired and consented to, is a practice that many people see as acceptable or even, under the right conditions, good. As Sascha Settegast (2018: 388) argues: 'Successfully engaging in a "lovely fling" may, on occasion... result in feelings of general benevolence—that such an intimate, positive experience of affirmation and community is in fact possible with otherwise strangers.' The Significance View also seems to exclude masturbation with sex toys, insofar as this can be considered a kind of sex with an inanimate object. Taken together, these implications make the Significance View seem much less plausible as an account of why certain forms of sex are permissible and some are not.

The weak version of Nagel's theory, which seems to reflect his own position, might be called the *Gradient View*. This view does not seek to create a clear demarcation line between permissible and non-permissible forms of sex. Rather, on this view, the degree to which a sexual act is a perversion tracks just one aspect of its potential goodness: the less perverted an act is, all else being equal, the better it is, and the more perverted, the worse. Insofar as sex with a robot is a perversion, then, it could on this view be regarded as morally worse than consensual sex with an adult human being without necessarily being impermissible. Indeed, although perversions are morally worse than non-perversions according to this perspective, they may nevertheless be better than nothing. This is Nagel's (1969) own view:

> Even if perverted sex is to that extent not so good as it might be, bad sex is generally better than none at all. This should not be controversial: it seems to hold for other important matters, like food, music, literature, and society. In the end, one must choose from among the available alternatives, whether their availability depends on the environment or on one's own constitution. And the alternatives have to be fairly grim before it becomes rational to opt for nothing.
>
> (1969: 17)

Framed in terms of the value that sex provides for the person in question, the weak, 'gradient' version of the sexual perversion objection opens up the possibility that sex with robots may be valuable for individuals who struggle to have ethical, much less good, sex with human beings. Even if robot sex is suboptimal, that is, it may nevertheless be better than nothing. Moreover, if sexbots could be used to help some people connect better with their human sexual partners, such perversion would (on this view) be instrumental to the achievement of non-perverted, and hence more valuable, forms of sex. Finally, although perverted sex is, in one respect, worse, it could still, on balance, be equal to or even better than some instances of non-perverted sex, so long as other redeeming features are present which outweigh the badness of the perversion, such as a much more pleasurable experience overall.

Assuming that the use of sexbots could, at least in some cases, survive the weaker (and we think more plausible) version of the 'perversion' objection, what other moral objections might be raised? One is the potential harm that such use would cause to the user's moral character.

HARM TO MORAL CHARACTER

An argument against sexbots, raised by Robert Sparrow (2017), Litska Strikwerda (2017), and John Danaher (2017a, 2017c), among others, is that the use of sexbots would causally corrupt—or constitute corruption of—the user's moral character. This concern applies especially to the use of child sexbots and (other) robots used to simulate rape. Someone who takes pleasure in 'raping' a robot that is made to represent a child or a non-consenting (typically female) adult will, according to this view, show a profound deficiency in their moral sensibilities, either because such pleasure entails a desire to harm or show serious disrespect to children or women, or because it reveals a lack of sensitivity to a highly likely moral interpretation of one's behaviour.

Now, one possibility is that such an argument rests on a conflation of symptom and cause. 'Even though such rape is really just the representation of rape', Sparrow (2017: 473) argues, taking pleasure in such an activity 'reveals [the user] to be sexist, intemperate, and cruel'.[10] However, if the use of child sexbots or (other) rape robots only *reveals* that the user has an impermissible attitude towards vulnerable human beings, it is not clear how such use could, on its own, constitute a further wrong or harm. Rather, it would be a powerful source of information about the deficient moral character the user already has.

A more plausible reading of this argument is that simulating rape with a robot would not only reveal a bad moral character, but would also causally contribute to, or exacerbate, its badness. Those who have sex with robots will likely imagine themselves to be partaking in the real-world equivalent of such sex. Danaher (2017a) argues that this possibility is particularly worrisome in the case of engagement with robots compared to other forms of virtual engagement. A person could be so fully immersed in the simulated rape of a robot that the difference between representation and reality disappears.[11]

Alternatively, it could be argued that there is an important distinction between a representation and that which is represented. Gert Gooskens (2010), for example, draws on the work of Edmund Husserl to argue that there always will be a psychological distance between what is represented and what is real. When one looks at a photograph of a friend, one is not directly perceiving one's friend: 'it is only *as if* I do' (Gooskens 2010: 66). The same is true, Gooksen argues, for all representations.[12]

Who is right? Do people desire the real-world equivalent of that which is represented within a fantasy or is there a disconnection between the two? Consider so-called rape 'play' (i.e. mutually desired and consensual simulation of rape) as an analogy. Many women and men have fantasies about being raped or raping others (Bivona and Critelli 2009; Critelli and Bivona, 2008). Suppose, then, that two consenting adults engage in rape play. Some may argue that such role play is inherently repugnant, given how many people suffer from sexual violence. For instance, they may argue that the role play amounts to 'making light' of such suffering. However, interpretive context matters. Without further evidence, it would be a leap to conclude that such consenting adults in fact desire to rape another human being or to be raped, much less that they endorse rape in real life.[13] Moreover, people who engage in bondage, discipline, dominance, and/or submission (BDSM) may intentionally inflict pain on another human being as a part of a sexual encounter. However, it does not follow from this that they desire sexualized torture in general (Airaksinen 2018). By analogy, it seems plausible to conclude that desiring to engage in simulated rape with a robot does not, on its own, entail that one desires to rape a sentient human being.

Nevertheless, it may still be true that to engage in certain acts requires an objectionable lack of moral sensitivity. If one simulates rape with a child sexbot, for example, one must be able to 'bracket' certain vital norms surrounding impermissible, indeed, repugnant, sex in our society. The sheer capacity to do this with an entity that cannot give meta-consent (as may be given for certain BDSM activities, for instance), or indeed any kind of consent, may indicate that one has a defective moral character.[14] And actually engaging in the simulated rape may reinforce the defect (which would be bad in itself), as well as erode behavioural inhibitions towards such rape in real life (which would be instrumentally bad).

INDIRECT HARMS

The notion of instrumental badness can be applied more generally. One worry is that the widespread use of sexbots could cause indirect harms, including undermining important moral norms that regulate sex between humans. By buying and using sexbots, users would uphold, and potentially normalize, a social practice in which robots with certain characteristics were produced and sold in stores or online. This social practice might be interpreted by others in ways that users cannot control and may not intend (Sparrow 2017).[15] Such interpretations, in turn, could change the norms regarding human sexual behaviour for the worse.

One possibility is that objectionable norms concerning attitudes towards, and ultimately treatment of, women would be reinforced. Currently, sex dolls and rudimentary sexbots are made to portray women as submissive, sexualized, and always 'available'. Sinziana Gutiu (2012: 2) argues that sexbots will thus contribute to the belief that women are sexual objects who should be ready to satisfy men at any time: 'By circumventing any need for consent, sex robots eliminate the need for communication, mutual respect and compromise in the sexual relationship'. Gutiu is concerned that such non-consensual sex will 'affect men's ability to identify and understand consent in sexual interactions with women'. In short, sexbots may serve to undermine women's ability to have their boundaries and desires readily recognized and thus respected (see also Sparrow 2017: 471).[16]

Florence Gildea and Kathleen Richardson (2017) similarly argue that sexbots 'represent a step backwards by perpetuating objectification and hence blurring distinctions between sex, masturbation and rape'. Richardson (2015: 292), who makes a parallel with prostitution central to her opposition to sexbots, argues that 'the development of sex robots will further reinforce relations of power that do not recognize both parties as human subjects'.

In the context of child pornography, Suzanne Ozt (2009: 105) argues that legalization of such content is 'objectifying children as sexual objects or resources for unbridled exploitation, [which] may promote the reduction of children to this status'. The idea is that the production, distribution, and use of sexbots (like certain pornographic content) may increase the sexualization of children and women in society, making it more difficult for them to live fulfilling lives. If children or women see themselves as (predominately) sexual objects, this may also make them more vulnerable to harmful and unwanted sexual encounters.

It should be noted that these objections point to possible empirical effects that may or may not materialize. These possibilities should nevertheless be taken very seriously. As it is, it is an uphill battle to move societal norms around sex towards greater mutuality and respect, focusing on the need to ensure consent[17] and to be sensitive to the needs and desires of one's sexual partner(s) (Danaher 2017c; Gildea and Richardson 2017). If sexbots of the sort that are currently envisioned become widely available, this may create the impression that non-consensual sex is a preference that one can be justified in satisfying. In fact, as Sparrow argues in his chapter in this volume, there is a deeper bind. If sexbots are designed in a way that allows simulated rape, this may signal or express that it is permissible to engage in non-consensual sex. However, if female sexbots are designed to always simulate consent, this may express that women should be perpetually ready to satisfy men's sexual desires.[18] In either case, the expressive significance of the sexbots is problematic, and there is an unknown further risk that it will indirectly contribute to an increase in sexual violence (see also Sparrow 2017).

HARM REDUCTION

As can be seen, there are multiple potential risks associated with the development, production, and use of humanoid sexbots. These risks have led some opponents of sexbots, such as Richardson, to favour their outright prohibition. Sparrow also leans in this direction. Although Sparrow (2017: 475) concedes that there may be some benefits involved in allowing sexbots, he argues that, 'given the importance of the goal of gender equality and of a rape-free society, […] it may well turn out to be the case that there is no ethical way to design sexbots modelled on women' (for further discussion, see Nyholm forthcoming). Others, such as Gutiu (2012), Arkin (quoted in Hill 2014), and Danaher (2017c, 2019a), favour regulating the production and distribution of sexbots. What might such regulation look like from the perspective of harm reduction?

Harm reduction as an ethical framework has been applied to several contested commodities or activities, such as drugs and prostitution or sex work (Mac and Smith 2018; Ritter and Cameron 2006; Single 1995; Bioethicists and Allied Professionals for Drug Policy Reform 2021). The inspiration for such a framework can be traced to Jeremy Bentham's writings in the eighteenth and nineteenth centuries (see, e.g. Bentham 1789/ 2007). Bentham's progressive proposals regarding homosexuality arguably constituted an early instance of a harm reduction approach (1785/1978). Instead of engaging with debates about whether homosexuality might be intrinsically immoral, Bentham proposed that society should ask a simple question: Does homosexual sex harm anyone and will a ban lead to less harm? If the answer to either one of these questions is 'No', then people should, he believed, be legally free to pursue whatever activities they found meaningful or which gave them pleasure. Could such an approach be applied to the case of sexbots?

The harm reduction framework depends on three ideas: first, that prohibition is not always the most efficient or effective means of reducing even genuinely harmful outcomes of a given activity; second, that harms may not be *linearly* connected to the activity: more of the activity does not necessarily mean more harm, and how harmful something is depends on how it is used and what the alternatives are; and third, that we should think not only about the potential harms of allowing some activity, but also to the potential harms of prohibition, while giving due consideration to the potential benefits of the activity (in light of what could plausibly be achieved through responsible regulation) (Earp et al. 2014; Single 1995).

Consider the example of people who are addicted to heroin. Research strongly suggests that making the drug safely available to such individuals reduces harm, without increasing overall drug use (Ferri et al. 2011; Strang et al. 2015). This phenomenon could be explained by safer consumption practices, reduction in the perceived need for criminal behaviour, and freeing up time, resources, and mental capacity which the individual can use to get their life in order, which in turn reduces the underlying cause(s) of their addiction (Ferri et al. 2011; Strang et al. 2015). In this case, avoiding outright prohibition appears to allow the turning of many regulatory dials to promote benefits and discourage harms (Earp et al. 2021). The way that many countries have regulated tobacco and alcohol may be another example of success by this approach. Taxes and restrictions on sale and consumption seem to be effective in preventing harmful overuse (Bader et al. 2011; Wagenaar et al. 2009).

Let us now apply these lessons to sexbots. First, as we have seen, there are several potential harms and benefits that the availability and use of sexbots may bring about. There is thus at least a prima facie reason to try to reap the benefits at the smallest cost possible. Sexbots for treatment and remedial purposes, or to help humans improve their sexual practices with each other, are probably the least controversial. If sexbots could be designed to allow the practicing of positive and respectful sexual habits, they might increase the likelihood of people achieving a more optimal version of the good(s) of sex. Insofar as there are other ways of practicing such habits, however, that do not carry the risks associated with sexbots, then those other means should likely be preferred.

The harms involved in the production, distribution, and use of sexbots are to a large degree contingent on how people interpret the practice, which depends on how these activities are situated within the public awareness. To encourage the plausibly beneficial, and discourage the plausibly harmful, uses of sexbots, it may be prudent to ban certain kinds of advertisements or in other ways regulate how sexbots are designed and sold, instead of banning their production altogether. In addition, certain *kinds* of sexbots could be banned, such as those that allow the simulation of rape, while therapeutic sexbots could perhaps be permitted, available only to those who are appropriately licensed in their use.[19]

When we think about how to alleviate the harms involved in allowing sexbots, we also need to keep in mind what they could replace. Levy (2011) has argued that sexbots could replace human prostitution and perhaps also pornography, which might be an improvement over the current situation. It seems plausible that the putatively harmful effects of representing women as enjoying acts 'that are objectifying, degrading, or even physically injurious', as Anne W. Eaton (2007: 682) argues, are more likely or more profound when the women in question are humans, rather than robots (as long as one can tell them apart).

What about child sexbots? Arkin is among the few who have argued that a harm reduction model should be adopted for such sexbots. He is interested in how child sexbots might be used to prevent the abuse of real human children. 'Child-like robots could', Arkin suggests, 'be used for pedophiles the way methadone is used to treat drug addicts' (quoted in Hill 2014).[20]

Whether sexbots would in fact replace prostitution, pornography, and child sex abuse, are, of course, unresolved empirical questions. Richardson (2015: 291) expresses doubts that 'sex robots could help to reduce prostitution... If an artificial substitute [in the form of pornography] reduced the need to buy sex, there would be a reduction in prostitution, but no such correlation is found.' Acknowledging such empirical uncertainty, Danaher (2017c) has proposed that an empirical approach be taken, in which experiments could be conducted, in certain contexts, to produce the knowledge needed to proceed. Gutiu (2012: 22), who is critical of sexbots, similarly raises the possibility of further research: '[s]ex robots could provide an opportunity to understand and correct violent and demeaning attitudes towards women. If regulated, sex robots could provide a means of researching the roots of sex and intimacy for both genders, demystifying female sexuality, and addressing the roots of women's oppression.'

CONCLUSION

Even if sexbots never become sentient, we have good reasons to be concerned with their production, distribution, and use. Our seemingly private activities have social meanings that we do not necessarily intend, but which can be harmful to others. Sex can both be beautiful and valuable—and ugly or profoundly harmful. We therefore need strong ethical norms to guide human sexual behaviour, regardless of the existence of sexbots. Interaction with new technologies could plausibly improve our sexual relationships, or make things worse (see Nyholm et al. forthcoming, for a theoretical overview). In this chapter, we have explored some ways in which a harm reduction framework may have the potential to bring about the alleged benefits of sexbots with a minimum of associated harms. But whatever approach is taken, the goal should be to ensure that our relationships with robots conduce to, rather than detract from, the equitable flourishing of our fellow human beings.

NOTES

1. For contributions to the debate about sentient robots, see John Danaher (2019c), Robert Sparrow (2004), Paul Bloom and Sam Harris (2018), Steve Petersen (2017), Joanna J. Bryson (2010), and Lily Frank and Sven Nyholm (2017).
2. The third feature, its embodiment in physical space, distinguishes this definition from Danaher's (2017b: 4–5).
3. For a detailed analysis of this campaign, see Danaher et al. (2017).
4. It is philosophically controversial what sorts of activities 'count' as sex (as opposed to, say, masturbation) (see, e.g. Gupta forthcoming). We will not attempt to settle that controversy here. For those who are committed to the view that there can be no such thing as 'sex' with a robot, perhaps because they view sex as something that is only possible between members of an organic species, the word 'sexlike' or 'pseudosex' can be substituted where relevant in what follows.
5. For a critical discussion of discourses around sex as a health-promoting activity, see Kristina Gupta (2011). For an argument that sex robots might promote *unhealthy* sexual practices or attitudes, see Brian D. Earp and Katarzyna Grunt-Mejer (2020).
6. Of course, many people with disabilities of all kinds do *not* struggle to find willing sexual partners, unless one defines 'disability' in this context in a circular way to mean 'sexually disabled' (which refers not to the physical lack of capacity to have a certain kind sexual experience, but rather the inability to find a willing sexual partner). For further discussion, see Brian D. Earp and Ole Martin Moen (2016).

7. Against this view, someone might argue that certain objects, such as a work of art, or even some machines, can be worthy of respect. Certainly, if someone were to destroy one of the most astonishing expressions of human ingenuity, it would not seem sufficient, from a moral perspective, for the person to respond by saying it was 'just a machine'. There are various ways one could attempt to make sense of this moral intuition (e.g. if disrespect is shown in this case, it is to the inventor or builder of the machine rather than to the machine itself); however, we will not pursue this digression further.

8. We are indebted to McArthur (2017) for the references to Thomas Nagel's and David Benatar's writings in this area.

9. For an alternative view, according to which even a non-mobile mannequin may (at least potentially) be appropriately considered an object of love or desire, see Gupta (2016).

10. Similarly, Danaher (2017a: 86) argues that sex with such robots 'directly expresses a deficient moral character because [the user desires] real-world rape and child sexual abuse'.

11. Gert Gooskens (2010), Morgan Luck (2009), Ole Martin Moen and Aksel B. Sterri (2018), and Jeannie Gersen (2019), are among those who have questioned whether engaging in (or desiring) behaviour with a robot—behaviour that would be harmful or wrongful if done to a human—shows that one desires to do the same thing to an actual sentient being.

12. The reference to Gooskens is indebted to Danaher (2017a).

13. An objection to this view is that rape play, even in the special context of BDSM, may involve a kind of endorsement of dominant behaviour that could have negative externalities.

14. There may be some narrow (theoretical) exceptions. Moen and Sterri (2018: 375), for instance, argue that if paedophiles—who have not chosen to be sexually attracted to children—were to use child sexbots to satisfy their desires, this could be virtuous insofar as such use was necessary and intended to avoid the pursuit of sexual contact with real human children. Whether there is any substantial proportion of paedophiles for whom such use would be (practically) necessary and intended in this way is an empirical question to which we do not know the answer.

15. For sentences or utterances in a language, the relevant community is the set of speakers fluent in that language. For actions or social practices, the relevant group is less clearly defined, but 'the community' or 'society' are the most plausible reference points.

16. For discussions of the silencing effects of pornography, see Rae Langton (1993) and Catharine A. MacKinnon (1995).

17. However, see the recent work of Quill R. Kukla (2018) and Joseph J. Fischel (2019), both of whom argue that there is much more to good sex than the 'mere' securing of consent, such that new models focused on more positive exploration and expression of desire are needed.

18. Sparrow's bind does not demonstrate that sex robots necessarily will be harmful. It shows that the option of having robots where rape can be simulated and where such simulation is impossible *may* both have harmful effects.

19. However, as Moen and Sterri (2018) point out, such licensing practices could also reduce uptake and therefore be less effective in reducing harms than a less regulated market. We are grateful for being reminded of this possibility by an anonymous reviewer.

20. Moen and Sterri (2018) suggest that regulation of child sexbots might be pursued in such a way that paedophiles would have to agree to take part in carefully controlled experiments to gain access to them. In that way, it might be possible to learn how to deal more effectively with paedophilia, and perhaps gain insights into (disordered) sexual desire more generally. Danaher (2019b), by contrast, favours outright prohibition of child sexbots

over an experimental, harm reduction approach in which sexbots are made available in a regulated way. Danaher's reasons are that science is too flawed to establish a consensus about the effects of using such sexbots and that it is implausible that paedophiles will offend less when they have access to them. We do not aim to settle this debate here.

References

Airaksinen, Timo (2018), 'The Language of Pain: A Philosophical Study of BDSM', *SAGE Open* 8(2), doi: https://doi.org/10.1177/2158244018771730.

Bader, Pearl, Boisclair, David, and Ferrence, Roberta (2011), 'Effects of Tobacco Taxation and Pricing on Smoking Behavior in High Risk Populations: A Knowledge Synthesis', *International Journal of Environmental Research and Public Health* 8(11), 4118–4139, doi: https://doi.org/10.3390/ijerph8114118.

Benatar, David (2002), 'Two Views of Sexual Ethics: Promiscuity, Pedophilia, and Rape', *Public Affairs Quarterly* 16(3), 191–201, http://www.jstor.org/stable/40441324, accessed 12 August 2021.

Bentham, Jeremy (1785/1978), 'Offences against One's Self', *Journal of Homosexuality* 3(4), 389–406, doi: https://doi.org/10.1300/J082v03n04_07.

Bentham, Jeremy (1789/2007), *An Introduction to the Principles of Morals and Legislation* (Mineola, NY: Dover Publications).

Bivona, Jenny M., and Critelli, Joseph W. (2009), 'The Nature of Women's Rape Fantasies: An Analysis of Prevalence, Frequency, and Contents', *Journal of Sex Research*, 46(1), 33–45, doi: https://doi.org/10.1080/00224490802624406.

Bloom, Paul, and Harris, Sam (2018), 'It's Westworld. What's Wrong with Cruelty to Robots?', *New York Times*, 23 April, https://www.nytimes.com/2018/04/23/opinion/westworld-conscious-robots-morality.html, accessed 12 August 2021.

Brody, Stuart (2010), 'The Relative Health Benefits of Different Sexual Activities', *Journal of Sexual Medicine* 7(4, Part 1), 1336–1361, doi: https://doi.org/10.1111/j.1743-6109.2009.01677.x.

Brown, Christina (2019), 'Sex Robots, Representation, and the Female Experience', *The American Papers* 37, 105–118, https://amst.fullerton.edu/students/Final%20AP%202019%20PMG%20PRESS.pdf#page=105, accessed 1 September 2021.

Bryson, Joanna J. (2010), 'Robots Should Be Slaves', in Yorick Wilks, ed., *Close Engagements with Artificial Companions: Key Social, Psychological, Ethical and Design Issues* (Amsterdam: John Benjamins Publishing Co.), 63–74.

Critelli, Joseph W., and Bivona, Jenny M. (2008), 'Women's Erotic Rape Fantasies: An Evaluation of Theory and Research', *Journal of Sex Research* 45(1), 57–70, doi: https://doi.org/10.1080/00224490701808191.

Danaher, John (2017a), 'Robotic Rape and Robotic Child Sexual Abuse: Should They Be Criminalised?', *Criminal Law and Philosophy* 11(1), 71–95, doi: https://doi.org/10.1007/s11572-014-9362-x.

Danaher, John (2017b), 'Should We Be Thinking about Sex Robots?', in John Danaher and Neil McArthur, eds, *Robot Sex: Social Implications and Ethical Implications* (Cambridge, MA: MIT Press), 3–14.

Danaher, John (2017c), 'The Symbolic-Consequences Argument in the Sex Robot Debate', in John Danaher and Neil McArthur, eds, *Robot Sex: Social and Ethical Implications* (Cambridge, MA: MIT Press), 103–131.

Danaher, John (2019a), 'Building Better Sex Robots: Lessons from Feminist Pornography', in Yuefang Zhou and Martin H. Fischer, eds, *AI Love You: Developments in Human–Robot Intimate Relationships* (Cham: Springer International Publishing), 133–147.

Danaher, John (2019b), 'Regulating Child Sex Robots: Restriction or Experimentation?', *Medical Law Review* 27(4), 553–575, doi: https://doi.org/10.1093/medlaw/fwz002.

Danaher, John (2019c), 'Welcoming Robots into the Moral Circle: A Defence of Ethical Behaviourism', *Science and Engineering Ethics*, doi: 10.1007/s11948-019-00119-x.

Danaher, John (2020), 'Sexuality', in Markus Dubber, Frank Pasquale, and Sunit Das, eds, *Oxford Handbook of the Ethics of Artificial Intelligence* (Oxford: Oxford University Press), 404–417.

Danaher, John, Earp, Brian D., and Sandberg, Anders (2017), 'Should We Campaign against Sex Robots?', in John Danaher and Neil McArthur, eds, *Robot Sex: Social and Ethical Implications* (Cambridge, MA: MIT Press), 47–71.

Di Nucci, Ezio (2017), 'Sex Robots and the Rights of the Disabled', in John Danaher and Neil McArthur, eds, *Robot Sex: Social and Ethical Implications* (Cambridge, MA: MIT Press), 73–88.

Diamond, Lisa M., and Huebner, David M. (2012), 'Is Good Sex Good for You? Rethinking Sexuality and Health', *Social and Personality Psychology Compass* 6(1), 54–69, doi: https://doi.org/10.1111/j.1751-9004.2011.00408.x.

Earp, Brian D., and Grunt-Mejer, Katarzyna (2020), 'Robots and Sexual Ethics', *Journal of Medical Ethics* 47(1), 1–2, doi: https://doi.org/10.1136/medethics-2020-107153.

Earp, Brian D., Lewis, Jonathan, Hart, Carl L., and Bioethicists and Allied Professionals for Drug Policy Reform (2021), 'Racial Justice Requires Ending the War on Drugs', *American Journal of Bioethics*, 21(4), 4-19 doi: https://doi.org/10.1080/15265161.2020.1861364.

Earp, Brian D., and Moen, Ole Martin (2016), 'Paying for Sex—Only for People with Disabilities?', *Journal of Medical Ethics* 42(1), 54–56, doi: https://doi.org/10.1136/medethics-2015-103064.

Earp, Brian D., Sandberg, Anders, and Savulescu, J. (2014), 'Brave New Love: The Threat of High-Tech "Conversion" Therapy and the Bio-Oppression of Sexual Minorities', *AJOB Neuroscience* 5(1), 4–12, doi: https://doi.org/10.1080/21507740.2013.863242.

Eaton, Anne W. (2007), 'A Sensible Antiporn Feminism', *Ethics* 117, 674–715, doi: https://doi.org/10.1086/519226.

Ferri, Marica, Davoli, Marina, and Perucci, Carlo A. (2011), 'Heroin Maintenance for Chronic Heroin-Dependent Individuals', *Cochrane Database of Systematic Reviews* 12(1), 1–55, doi: https://doi.org/10.1002/14651858.CD003410.pub4.

Fischel, Joseph J. (2019), *Screw Consent: A Better Politics of Sexual Justice* (Berkeley, CA: University of California Press).

Frank, Lily, and Nyholm, Sven (2017), 'Robot Sex and Consent: Is Consent to Sex between a Robot and a Human Conceivable, Possible, and Desirable?', *Artificial Intelligence and Law* 25(3), 305–323, doi: https://doi.org/10.1007/s10506-017-9212-y.

Gersen, Jeannie S. (2019), 'Sex Lex Machina and Artificial Intelligence', *Columbia Law Review* 119(7), 1793–1810, doi: https://doi.org/10.2307/26810849.

Gildea, Florence, and Richardson, Kathleen (2017), 'Sex Robots: Why We Should Be Concerned', *Campaign against Sex Robots*, 12 May, https://spsc.pt/index.php/2017/05/05/sex-robots-why-we-should-be-concerned/, accessed 1 September 2021.

Gooskens, Gert (2010), 'The Ethical Status of Virtual Actions', *Ethical Perspectives* 17, 59–78, doi: https://doi.org/10.2143/EP.17.1.2046957.

Gupta, Kristina (2011), '"Screw Health": Representations of Sex as a Health-Promoting Activity in Medical and Popular Literature', *Journal of Medical Humanities* 32(2), 127–140, doi: https://doi.org/0.1007/s10912-010-9129-x.

Gupta, Kristina (2016), 'Why Not a Mannequin?: Questioning the Need to Draw Boundaries around Love When Considering the Ethics of "Love-Altering" Technologies', *Philosophy, Psychiatry, & Psychology* 23(2), 97–100, doi: https://doi.org/10.1353/ppp.2016.0008.

Gupta, Kristina (forthcoming), 'What Is a Sexual Act?', in Brian D. Earp, C. Chambers, and L. Watson, eds, *Routledge Handbook on Philosophy of Sex and Sexuality* (London: Routledge).

Gutiu, Sinziana (2012), 'Sex Robots and Roboticization of Consent', Paper presented at the We Robot Conference, http://robots.law.miami.edu/wp-content/uploads/2012/01/Gutiu-Roboticization_of_Consent.pdf, accessed 12 August 2021.

Hill, Kashmir (2014), 'Are Child Sex-Robots Inevitable?', *Forbes*, https://www.forbes.com/sites/kashmirhill/2014/07/14/are-child-sex-robots-inevitable/#519f9bb7e460, accessed 1 September 2021.

Jecker, Nancy S. (2020), 'Nothing to Be Ashamed of: Sex Robots for Older Adults with Disabilities', *Journal of Medical Ethics* 47(1), 26–32, doi: https://doi.org/10.1136/medethics-2020-106645.

Kashdan, Todd B., Adams, Leah M., Farmer, Antonina S., Ferssizidis, Patty, McKnight, Patrick E., and Nezlek, John B. (2014), 'Sexual Healing: Daily Diary Investigation of the Benefits of Intimate and Pleasurable Sexual Activity in Socially Anxious Adults', *Archives of Sexual Behavior* 43(7), 1417–1429, doi: https://doi.org/10.1007/s10508-013-0171-4.

Kubes, Tanja (2019), 'New Materialist Perspectives on Sex Robots. A Feminist Dystopia/Utopia?', *Social Sciences* 8(224), 1–14, doi: https://doi.org/10.3390/socsci8080224.

Kukla, Quill R. (2018), 'That's What She Said: The Language of Sexual Negotiation', *Ethics* 129(1), 70–97, doi: https://doi.org/10.1086/698733.

Langton, Rae (1993), 'Speech Acts and Unspeakable Acts', *Philosophy & Public Affairs* 22(4), 293–330, http://www.jstor.org/stable/2265469, accessed 12 August 2021.

Levy, David (2007), *Love and Sex with Robots: The Evolution of Human–Robot Relationships* (New York: Harper Collins).

Levy, David (2011), 'Robot Ethics: The Ethical and Social Implications of Robotics), in Patrick Lin, Keith Abney, and George A. Bekey, eds, *Robot Ethics: The Ethical and Social Implications of Robotics* (Cambridge, MA: MIT Press), 223–231.

Luck, Morgan (2009), 'The Gamer's Dilemma: An Analysis of the Arguments for the Moral Distinction between Virtual Murder and Virtual Paedophilia', *Ethics and Information Technology* 11(1), 31–36, doi: https://doi.org/10.1007/s10676-008-9168-4.

Mac, Juno, and Smith, Molly E. (2018), *Revolting Prostitutes: The Fight for Sex Workers' Rights* (London: Verso).

MacKinnon, Catharine A. (1995), *Only Words* (London: Harper Collins).

McArthur, Neil (2017), 'The Case for Sexbots', in John Danaher and Neil McArthur, eds, *Robot Sex: Social and Ethical Implications* (Cambridge, MA: MIT Press), 31–45.

McArthur, Neil, & Twist, Mackie L. C. (2017), The Rise of Digisexuality: Therapeutic Challenges and Possibilities. *Sexual and Relationship Therapy*, 32(3–4), 334–344. doi:10.1080/14681994.2017.1397950

Moen, Ole Martin, and Sterri, Aksel B. (2018), 'Pedophilia and Computer-Generated Child Pornography', in David Boonin, ed., *The Palgrave Handbook of Philosophy and Public Policy* (Cham: Springer International Publishing), 369–381.

Nagel, Thomas (1969), 'Sexual Perversion', *Journal of Philosophy* 66(1), 5–17, doi: https://doi.org/10.2307/2024152.

Nyholm, Sven (forthcoming), 'The Ethics of Humanoid Sex Robots', in Brian D. Earp, Clare Chambers, and Lori Watson, eds, *Routledge Handbook on Philosophy of Sex and Sexuality* (London: Routledge).

Nyholm, Sven, Danaher, John, and Earp, Brian D. (forthcoming), 'The Technological Future of Love', in: Natasha McKeever, Andre Grahle, and Joe Saunders, eds, *Love: Past, Present, and Future*.

Ozt, Suzanne (2009), *Child Pornography and Sexual Grooming: Legal and Societal Responses* (Cambridge: Cambridge University Press).

Petersen, Steve (2017), 'Is It Good for Them Too? Ethical Concern for the Sexbots', in John Danaher and Neil McArthur, eds, *Robot Sex: Social and Ethical Implications* (Cambridge, MA: MIT Press), 155–171.

RealBotix (2020), 'FAQ', *RealBotix*, https://realbotix.com/FAQ#q1, accessed 12 August 2021.

Richardson, Kathleen (2015), 'The Asymmetrical "Relationship": Parallels between Prostitution and the Development of Sex Robots', *SIGCAS Computers & Society* 45(3), 290–293, doi: https://doi.org/10.1145/2874239.2874281.

Ritter, Alison, and Cameron, Jacqui (2006), 'A Review of the Efficacy and Effectiveness of Harm Reduction Strategies for Alcohol, Tobacco and Illicit Drugs', *Drug and Alcohol Review* 25(6), 611–624, doi: https://doi.org/10.1080/09595230600944529.

Sartre, Jean-Paul (1956), *Being and Nothingness*, trans. H. E. Barnes (New York: Philosophical Library).

Settegast, Sascha (2018), 'Prostitution and the Good of Sex', *Social Theory and Practice* 44(3), 377–403, http://www.jstor.org/stable/44987073, accessed 12 August 2021.

Single, Eric (1995), 'Defining Harm Reduction', *Drug and Alcohol Review* 14(3), 287–290, doi: https://doi.org/10.1080/09595239500185371.

Sparrow, Robert (2004), 'The Turing Triage Test', *Ethics and Information Technology* 6(4), 203–213, doi: https://doi.org/10.1007/s10676-004-6491-2.

Sparrow, Robert (2017), 'Robots, Rape, and Representation', *International Journal of Social Robotics* 9(4), 465–477, doi: https://doi.org/10.2139/ssrn.2044797.

Strang, John, Groshkova, Teodora, Uchtenhagen, Ambros, van den Brink, Wim, Haasen, Christian, Schechter, Martin T. et al. (2015), 'Heroin on Trial: Systematic Review and Meta-Analysis of Randomised Trials of Diamorphine-Prescribing as Treatment for Refractory Heroin Addiction', *British Journal of Psychiatry* 207(1), 5–14, doi: https://doi.org/10.1192/bjp.bp.114.149195.

Strikwerda, Litska (2017), 'Legal and Moral Implications of Child Sex Robots', in John Danaher and Neil McArthur, eds, *Robot Sex: Social and Ethical Implications* (Cambridge, MA: MIT Press), 133–151.

Wagenaar, Alexander C., Salois, Matthew J., and Komro, Kelli A. (2009), 'Effects of Beverage Alcohol Price and Tax Levels on Drinking: A Meta-Analysis of 1003 Estimates from 112 Studies', *Addiction* 104(2), 179–190, doi: https://doi.org/10.1111/j.1360-0443.2008.02438.x.

CHAPTER 14

THE ETHICS OF VIRTUAL SEXUAL ASSAULT

JOHN DANAHER

INTRODUCTION

Roblox is an online gaming platform—or 'imagination platform' according to its developers—that allows users to create their own games. Players using the platform interact via onscreen avatars with a cartoonish, distinctively 'blocky' appearance. Roblox has more than 100 million active monthly users (Alexander 2019) and its stated mission is to 'bring the world together through play'.[1]

In June of 2018, Amber Petersen was reading to her seven-year-old daughter, while the latter played Roblox on her iPad. At one point, Amber's daughter interrupted her to show her what was happening in her game. Amber was shocked by what she saw. In a Facebook post describing the incident (with some accompanying screenshots), Amber claimed that her daughter's Roblox avatar was 'violently gang-raped' by two male avatars.[2] They grabbed her daughter's avatar and forced it to engage in simulated sex acts in a virtual playground. Amber had taken precautions to limit the number of features her daughter could enable on Roblox, but the platform does feature some 'adult' content and her daughter was unfortunately the victim of a malicious user. The makers of Roblox reacted quickly and banned the user permanently from the platform.

Shocking though this may be, the Roblox 'gang rape' is not unprecedented. Unwanted sexual interactions are now widespread in digital and virtual environments. Some of these interactions take place in open-ended, user-generated environments such as Roblox or Facebook Spaces; some take place within specific games, such as World of Warcraft, Drunkn Bar Fight, or QuiVR (Cortese 2019; Cortese and Zeller 2020). The frequency of such incidents raises a number of important questions. Are these interactions unethical or do the ordinary rules of ethics not apply in virtual environments? If they are unethical, then how unethical are they? Are they equivalent to real-world incidents of sexual assault or are they somehow less serious? If they are less serious, how exactly should they be classified and understood?

In this chapter, I take up these questions and try to offer some answers. I do so in four main stages. First, I review some examples of unwanted sexual interactions in virtual environments, consider how widespread the phenomenon might be, and address how best to define and classify them. Second, I offer an initial argument for viewing such incidents as serious moral wrongs. This argument focuses on both the unwanted and the harmful nature of such incidents. More specifically, it focuses on how such interactions might violate someone's right to sexual autonomy and/or cause them serious harm. Third, I defend this argument from three major objections: the 'it's not real' objection, the 'it's just a game' objection, and the 'unrestricted consent' objection. Fourth, and finally, I consider how, if this argument is correct, we should classify such incidents. More precisely, I review two possible approaches to classifying them: (a) treating them as equivalent to real-world sexual assault; or (b) adopting a graduated scale of seriousness in which some might be equivalent to real-world sexual assault and some are less serious, depending on the precise nature of the virtual interaction. I end the chapter by considering some potential solutions to the problem of unwanted virtual sexual interactions.

THE PREVALENCE OF VIRTUAL
SEXUAL ASSAULT

How prevalent are unwanted sexual interactions in virtual environments? There are two main sources of evidence that can help us answer this question: (a) documented incidents; and (b) surveys.

Let's consider the documented incidents first. These are cases in which the victims of such interactions have reported their experiences, usually in some online media platform. The Roblox example is one. There are several other famous cases that are worth mentioning. Reviewing them helps to give a sense of how widespread and diverse the phenomenon is. Here are some of the better-known examples.

The Lambda Moo 'rape'—this incident took place in the early 1990s and is possibly the first documented case of virtual 'rape'. (I put this in scare quotes for the time being; we will return to the issue of the appropriate name for such incidents later in this chapter.) It was discussed in Julian Dibbell's book *My Tiny Life* (1998) and occurred in the text-based virtual world LambdaMoo. As described by Dibbell, the incident involved one character (Mr Bungle) creating a 'Voodoo Doll' program that allowed him to control the avatars of two other female characters and force them to engage in text-based sexual interactions. Dibbell followed up with the women involved and explained that one of them was particularly traumatized by the incident (Dibbell 1998; Strikwerda 2015; Danaher 2018).

The Second Life rape(s)—Second Life is an open-ended virtual world in which people can create 3D-rendered avatars that interact with one another in complex social environments. It was quite popular in the early 2000s and still exists today. Sexual activity is very common on the platform and sometimes includes unwanted sexual activity or virtual 'rape'. In 2007, the Belgian police decided to investigate an alleged 'rape' that took place on the platform. No charges were brought on the basis of that incident, but similar incidents have been documented by other users of Second Life (Duranske 2007; Lynn 2007).

The QuiVR virtual groping—in 2016, the journalist Jordan Belamire (a pseudonym) wrote a widely reported piece in which she described being virtually groped while playing the virtual reality (VR) game QuiVR. This is an archery game played using a head-mounted display (i.e. a set of goggles that projects 3D images directly onto the user's retinas) and so, unlike two previous incidents, involves an 'immersive' virtual environment. In her case, Belamire was approached by another player in the game environment. This player proceeded to reach out and grab at where her breasts would have been in the real world (Belamire 2016).

The Altspace unwanted kissing—Altspace is a social VR app that can be accessed using an immersive, head-mounted display. It is not a game platform; it's simply a place in which people can 'hang out' virtually—like a sophisticated chat room. In 2016, the journalist Taylor Lorenz and her colleague Alexis Kleinman both reported receiving unwanted 'kisses' when they tried to use the app. The unwanted sexual behaviour was subsequently shut down by a moderator. Similar incidents have been reported by other users (Lorenz 2016).

Sexual harassment in Rec Room—somewhat similar to Roblox, Rec Room is an immersive VR platform that allows users to create and play various games together. In 2017, the Facebook VR researcher Michelle Cortese was on a VR field trip with her colleagues. They were due to play paintball on Rec Room. While waiting for others to arrive, an unknown male user 'dumped' virtual water bottles on her and screamed 'Wet t-shirt contest!' while chasing her around a room. Subsequent to this, Cortese did a public art exhibition in which she exposed herself to the risk of repeated sexual overtures and advances in the social app VR Chat and displayed the experiences to members of the public (Cortese 2019). The intention was to give a vivid depiction of the potential frequency of sexual harassment in virtual spaces.

The list could continue.[3] Hopefully these cases are enough to get a sense of what can happen on these platforms.

What about survey data on the prevalence of such incidents? Jessica Outlaw has performed two studies on this topic. In one, conducted with Beth Duckles, she carried out detailed interviews with thirteen 'tech-savvy' women (Outlaw and Duckles 2017). She found that most of these women reported fear of sexual harassment or unwanted sexual attention as a major barrier to their use of VR platforms. Furthermore, several had actually experienced unwanted sexual attention when using these platform and some of them went out of their way to adopt non-gendered avatars in order to avoid attracting attention. Subsequently, Outlaw conducted a survey of over 600 users of VR platforms and found that 49 per cent of women and 36 per cent of men had experienced at least one incident of sexual harassment (Outlaw 2018). Users also reported other forms of harassment such as racist or homophobic comments. In a similar vein, Sparrow et al. (2019) found that players of online multiplayer games had come to expect some level of abuse and harassment when playing these games. Indeed, although they thought this behaviour was wrong, they had adopted an attitude of almost learned helplessness in response to it (i.e. they believed that they were unable to do anything to control the problem). This is consistent with PEW Research Center findings suggesting that 40 per cent of Americans have been victims of some form of online harassment.[4]

None of this is surprising. Technology has long been used to facilitate sexual interactions, both wanted and unwanted. The prevalence of pornography and cybersex on the internet is common knowledge. Furthermore, sexual harassment and unwanted sexual contact are common in the real world. Consequently, it's not surprising to find that this bad behaviour should transfer online.

But how exactly should we understand these incidents of unwanted sexual interactions in digital and virtual environments? How are they best defined? Some are clearly and unproblematically forms of sexual harassment: menacing, unwanted sexual communications or attention directed at specific persons. Although sexual harassment often must occur in a work environment in order to be legally recognized, colloquially it can be understood to occur in other environments and this can now include virtual environments. Are any of the incidents more than sexual harassment? In past work, I have favoured classifying at least some of them—especifically those that involve enacting or representing sexual contact—as incidents of 'virtual sexual assault' (Danaher 2018; Strikwerda 2015). But this might be thought a problematic designation since it implies an equivalency between these incidents and real-world sexual assault (a topic discussed towards the end of this chapter). Avoiding this equivalency, Lucy Sparrow (2019) has suggested that we refer to them using the more descriptive and neutral term 'UDESI' (unwanted, digitally enacted sexual interactions). This proposal has some merit, particularly if our goal is to scientifically study these incidents as a novel social phenomenon. Nevertheless, as I will argue below, it may fail to do justice to the seriousness of these incidents by failing to grant them some level of equivalency with ordinary sexual assault. For now, I will stick to describing them as unwanted virtual sexual interactions, occasionally adopting the terms 'virtual sexual assault' or 'harassment' as seems appropriate.

More important than terminology, however, is understanding how these incidents arise. If you look at the list of examples given, you can immediately see that there are some differences between them. Some involve simulated or virtual touching and some do not; some involve users wearing immersive, head-mounted displays, whereas others do not; some involve social platforms and some involve games. Are there any shared properties across all these incidents? I have a suggestion. The one thing they all seem to share is that instead of involving direct physical contact between people they each involve a sexual interaction performed via some virtual representation (or avatar). It is these avatars that are used to facilitate sexual communication or engage in representations of sexual acts. In a previous article, building upon work done by Johnny Søraker (2010) and Litska Strikwerda (2015), I have argued this *action-via-a-representation* is perhaps the key defining feature of all these incidents.

Beyond that, it may be worth classifying and distinguishing between these incidents along a number of different dimensions. For example, we could classify them depending on the degree of immersion they involve. This might be based on the intuition that there is something prima facie different about using a controller to manipulate an on-screen avatar versus actually embodying that avatar through an immersive headset. In the former case, there is more separation between what happens to you and what happens to your virtual representation; thus, the potential harm that results from the incident might be reduced. Whether that intuition holds up to closer scrutiny is something that we will need to consider in more detail in what follows.

We could also classify them depending on whether or not they involve game environments. The intuition behind this strategy is that different ethical rules apply to games versus other kinds of interactions. As the Dutch historian Johan Huizinga noted in his famous study of play in human culture, games seem to take place inside a 'magic circle' in which the ordinary moral rules are suspended (Huizinga 1949). There is some prima facie support for this idea. After all, we tolerate conduct as part of games and sports that we ordinarily would never tolerate outside of those games. For example, conduct that would ordinarily meet the legal definition of physical assault or battery is a normal feature of sports such as boxing and rugby. Whether this makes any difference to virtual sexual interactions is another topic that we will need to consider in more detail in what follows, but it is worth noting that the idea that video games exist inside a magic circle has been promoted by game designers and theorists (Zimmerman and Salen 2003).

Finally, we could classify them depending on who exactly is the perpetrator and who is the victim of the unwanted sexual interaction. To this point, and throughout all the examples discussed, the assumption has been that both the victims and perpetrators are real human beings that happen to be acting via virtual representations. But, of course, this may not be the case. Some virtual environments feature artificial characters, who operate according to the rules of a computer program. These characters could, potentially, be both victims and perpetrators of virtual sexual assault. Indeed, I will discuss some examples of this below. Considering these different possibilities is interesting because it raises significant questions about the nature of wrongdoing and responsibility. Can an artificial character be held morally responsible for carrying out a virtual sexual assault? Or does the blame rest with the programmer of that character? Should we care about what people do to wholly artificial characters? If they cannot be moral victims of our actions, if they feel nothing and cannot be harmed, then is it permissible to act out all manner of immoral fantasies on them?

In what follows, I will largely (though not completely) ignore the complexities that arise from cases in which artificial characters are the victims or perpetrators of virtual sexual assault. I do so not because I think these issues are unimportant but because they have been the major focus of my past writings on this topic. To briefly summarize my views: I think that at least some forms of sexual assault that are carried out on artificial characters are morally impermissible, particularly if the artificial character represents a child (Danaher 2017a, 2018, 2019); I also think that it may be permissible to hold the designers of artificial characters responsible for their virtual actions, if certain conditions are met (Danaher 2018). That said, I also believe that there could be cases in which there is no suitably culpable moral agent to hold responsible for the actions of artificial characters (Danaher 2016). And I am not the only one to defend these views. For example, Robert Sparrow (2017) and Stephanie Patridge (2010, 2013) have both argued that representations of rape and sexual assault can be morally problematic. There is also a rich and varied debate about the appropriate take on responsibility for artificial, autonomous systems (Matthias 2004; Danaher 2016; Nyholm 2018; Santoni de Sio and van den Hoven 2018).

THE MORAL WRONGNESS OF VIRTUAL SEXUAL ASSAULT

What is it that makes an action wrong? There are many answers to that question but for present purposes we can consider two common ones corresponding, roughly, with the deontological and consequentialist schools of normative ethics: (a) the action violates someone else's rights; and/or (b) the action causes, or at least has the potential to cause, non-trivial harm to another. Accepting these are the two fundamental criteria of wrongness, a simple argument can be made in favour of the view that unwanted virtual sexual interactions are a serious wrong, as follows:

(1) If an action violates someone else's rights *and/or* causes (or has the potential to cause) them non-trivial harm, then that action is a serious moral wrong.
(2) Unwanted virtual sexual interactions violate someone's rights (specifically their right to sexual autonomy) and/or have the potential to cause them significant harm.
(3) Therefore, unwanted virtual sexual interactions are a serious moral wrong.

Is this argument any good? I presume the first premise is relatively uncontroversial even though it is complicated. The first premise appeals to both deontological and consequentialist theories of moral wrongdoing. It holds that an action is wrong if it violates someone's rights, or if it causes non-trivial harm, or has the potential to cause non-trivial harm. In what follows, I will consider how both examples of wrongdoing might arise in cases of virtual sexual assault. There are, of course, questions to be asked about what counts as a 'right' and what counts as 'harm'. Answers to those questions have provoked centuries of philosophical debate. That said, there are paradigmatic cases of both that are uncontroversial. As I hope to make clear in what follows, the application of both concepts to this particular argument would seem to fall within the paradigmatic range of cases, namely, the right to sexual autonomy and the physical and psychological trauma that can result from unwanted sexual interactions.

The one aspect of the first premise that may raise a few eyebrows is the bit stating that if an action 'has the potential to cause non-trivial harm' it counts as a serious moral wrong. Why is this included? The answer lies in how we categorize wrongful conduct in advance of that conduct actually taking place. People differ in how much harm they suffer at the hands of others. Some people are physically more resilient than others; some people are psychologically more resilient. Sometimes we can reliably predict who is likely to suffer more harm as a result of a particular action. For example, punching a child in the face is likely to result in more harm than punching Mike Tyson (in his prime) in the face. We could factor such predictions into our classification of wrongful actions. But we don't always have the capacity to predict the likely outcome and it would be unethical to run an experimental test of harmfulness for every possible case. This is particularly true in the case of actions that are known to cause psychological harm. There is a wide degree of variability in how psychologically traumatizing people find different experiences. Some people brush them off with relative ease; others suffer from years of post-traumatic stress disorder (PTSD) and depression. Since we cannot know for sure how victims will react in each and every case, and since we can never fully control the consequences of our actions, we have to work with reasonable estimates of the likely harmfulness of our actions. Consequently, it seems legitimate to say that if an action has the potential to result in non-trivial harm it is a serious moral wrong.

What about premise (2)? This might be a little bit more controversial than premise (1) but a strong prima facie case can be made in its favour. First, all the examples of unwanted sexual interactions discussed in the previous section would seem to involve a violation of the victim's right to autonomy in general and sexual autonomy in particular. None of the people in question appear to have invited or desired sexual attention or interactions. They were either playing non-sexual games or participating in general, non-specific social interactions. Other users of the virtual platforms imposed sexual communications and contact on them against their will. In modern liberal societies, we tend see liberty or autonomy as a foundational right (Gaus 2010). On some classic accounts of this basic liberty right, this includes a set of claim-rights against others to forbear from interfering with one's actions or choices, providing these actions and choices do not infringe someone else's rights, and unless there is consent to those actions (Wenar 2020; Mack 2018). That said, some violations of autonomy are tolerated more than others. This is inevitable given that it is impossible to live in a society and have one's autonomy respected at all times. We are, almost inevitably, constantly bumping into and interacting with each other. We don't always consent to these interactions. Nevertheless, most societies place particular emphasis on sexual autonomy as an area of individual choice that deserves the utmost respect. This has not always been true—violations of sexual autonomy for women, in particular, have been historically normalized in many cultures—but it certainly appears to be true nowadays, with increasing criticism and scorn poured on those who violate sexual autonomy. Perhaps this is because the potential harm caused by a violation can be significant, and perhaps it is because it is relatively easy to respect sexual autonomy: unlike casually bumping into someone on an crowded train, you have to go out of your way to violate someone's sexual autonomy. Violations of sexual autonomy are thus treated with particular seriousness and a failure to procure consent prior to a sexual interaction is a serious wrong. In a moment, I will consider whether there is some reason to think that consent can be implied from the participation in certain virtual activities or whether there is reason to be less protective of sexual autonomy in virtual spaces. For the time being, however, I conclude that there is a strong prima facie case for thinking that unwanted sexual interactions in virtual spaces violate the right to sexual autonomy because they violate the consent requirement.

Second, unwanted sexual interactions in virtual spaces would seem to have the potential to do serious harm. In the absence of haptics, a type of technology that enables the transmission of touch at a distance via virtual representations, they do not involve physical harm, but they do seem to involve psychological harm. How do we know this? Well, we have the reports from the victims themselves. As mentioned previously, Julian Dibbell interviewed one of the victims of the LambdaMoo virtual 'rape' for his article on the topic (Dibbell 1998). She was crying and claimed to have been traumatized by the event. Consider also the testimony of Michelle Cortese, whose experiences of sexual harassment in VR were also described above. A past victim of sexual violence, Cortese (2019) says that her experiences were triggering of her past trauma:

> ... I panicked. I innately sensed a familiar knee-jerk reaction to an incoming assault. My heart sank. The air evaporated from my lungs. I froze. I braced.
> ... I braced, for nothing.
> My body responded to virtual stimuli with real-life survivalism [reference omitted]. Ashamed of my emotional lapse and VR noob reaction, I kept on playing like everything was fine.[5]

Again, none of this should be particularly surprising. There are now ample case reports and studies done on the effects of cyberbullying and cyberharassment which suggest that they can be every bit as psychologically harmful as their real-world equivalents (e.g. Hamm et al. 2015). Since unwanted sexual interactions in virtual environments are similar in nature to both of these actions, it is reasonable to suppose that they have the potential to do non-trivial harm.

There is, however, an important question to be asked as to whether harm is a relevant consideration when it comes to understanding sexual wrongs. It is worth noting that when we legally define crimes such as sexual assault and rape, we rarely make any reference to the harmfulness of those actions. This is different from our approach to physical assault, which is often legally categorized based on the degrees of harm it causes (i.e. assault, assault causing harm, assault causing grievous harm, and so on). If we take these legal classifications seriously, then it would appear that we care about sexual assault, legally speaking, because it is a violation of sexual autonomy and not necessarily because it is harmful, even though it may be.[6] As such, this discussion of the harmfulness of virtual sexual assault or harassment might seem to be surplus to requirements. Nevertheless, I include it here for two reasons. First, if it is the case that these interactions have the potential to do non-trivial harm, then this provides an additional reason to treat them as serious moral wrongs. In other words, their potential harmfulness bolsters the argument I wish to make. Second, including some analysis of harm helps to head off a potential criticism of the argument, namely that they are less important because they are not 'real'.

It is to this criticism and others that I now turn.

THREE OBJECTIONS TO THE MORAL WRONGNESS ARGUMENT

In this section, I consider three objections to the argument given in the previous section: (a) the 'it's not real' objection; (b) the 'it's just a game' objection; and (c) the 'unrestricted consent' objection.

The 'it's not real' objection

The first objection is simply that unwanted virtual sexual interactions should not be viewed as serious moral wrongs because they are not real, or at least they are *less real* than other kinds of unwanted sexual interactions, and so don't carry the same moral weight. This objection could be run in two different ways. It could be run as a general objection to the claim that virtual sexual interactions are morally significant. It could also be run as a more nuanced objection to the claim that virtual sexual interactions carry as much weight as their real-world equivalents. I take up the latter possibility in the final section of this chapter. For now, I focus on the former, more general, version of the objection.

From the outset, this objection does not seem very plausible. The claim that virtual interactions are not 'real' and so don't carry the same weight as real physical interactions will seem odd to anyone living in the digital age. The mere fact that an interaction takes place via a virtual representation of some kind (text-based or visual) does not make it less real. We live an increasing portion of our lives via virtual avatars. We communicate with colleagues and friends via our profiles on email and social media all the time. But nobody would claim that these communications and interactions are, consequently, unreal or lacking moral weight. The interactions are certainly missing some of the properties we associate with interactions in the physical world. We cannot (yet, anyway) smell one another in virtual fora, and, in the absence of haptics, we cannot touch each other. Nevertheless, we can hear each other, and see each other, and have real effects on one another's lives. What someone says in a virtual chatroom can really hurt my feelings;

what my boss says to me via email can have real effects on my employment duties, and so on. To claim that this whole swathe of our lives is not real or carries no moral weight would be absurd.

A more plausible version of the objection might claim that by adding an extra representational layer to our virtual interactions we make them *less real*. Consider two people chatting via a videoconferencing app. Presumably, most people would accept that their communications are real in some morally important sense. But now suppose that instead of using unfiltered video to communicate they use cartoon avatars. In other words, they don a virtual skin or costume for the duration of the interaction. Someone might argue that donning the virtual skin turns what would be an ordinary and morally weighty interaction into one that is more akin to make believe or fantasy. This may tip over into the 'it's just a game' objection that I will consider in a moment. That said, at an initial glance, and absent some other rules or norms to suggest that ordinary moral rules should be suspended when we communicate via cartoon avatars, it's not clear why donning the virtual skin makes the interaction any less morally weighty.

It is worth underscoring this point by considering the empirical work that has been done on the blurred boundaries between what happens to digitally encoded virtual avatars and what happens to real, physical people. In recent years, a spate of research studies have been carried out on how people relate to their virtual avatars and how what happens to those avatars can have serious and lasting effects on those people. For example, research has revealed that people can have significant 'self-presence' with their virtual avatars. In other words, they can come to associate themselves with their avatars in a strong way, viewing their avatars as a core part of their identity. This can occur with non-immersive VR avatars, such as those found in Second Life, as well as with more immersive forms using head-mounted displays. For example, research performed by Elizabeth Behm-Morawitz (2013) on 279 Second Life users found that the degree of presence felt towards the virtual self had an effect on offline health, appearance, and well-being. Similarly, research by Nick Yee and Jeremy Bailenson, on what they call the *Proteus effect*, suggests that people conform to the expectations of their virtual avatars (Yee, Bailenson, and Ducheneaut 2007). For example, people embodied in taller virtual avatars tended to be more aggressive than those embodied in shorter avatars. This basic research paradigm has been followed by other researchers, who have found that the appearance and behaviour of virtual avatars can have lasting effects on real-world, offline behaviour. Those who embody elderly avatars have been found to save more for retirement (Hershfield et al. 2011) and those who embody superhero avatars tend to be more altruistic (Rosenberg et al. 2013). Furthermore, in a wide-ranging review of the empirical literature, Slater and Sanchez-Vives (2016) document how VR is now being used to train offline behaviour—for example, using VR as a surgical training tool in medicine has become commonplace—and to treat psychological disorders—for example, people now use VR exposure therapy for victims of PTSD. All this evidence points to an intimate connection between the virtual world and reality, and shows how actions in the virtual world can have real 'extravirtual' effects (Søraker 2010).

In addition, and perhaps most crucially from the present perspective, there is considerable evidence to suggest that people in VR environments can experience what is happening to them as 'real' and not simply as some form of make-believe. This feeling that a virtual experience is real is possible because the human brain already constructs a virtual model of the real world based on a handful of perceptual cues (Slater and Sanchez-Vives 2016). Virtual reality environments, artificial and unrealistic though they may sometimes seem to be, can exploit this feature of human cognition and trick us into thinking that unusual things are really happening to us in virtual environments. Some of the experimental results are quite dramatic. For instance, research by Blanke and Metzinger (2009) (see also Metzinger 2009a) has shown that it is possible to trick people into thinking they are occupying a different body (and, more generally, to have a virtual 'out-of-body experience'). Similarly, a series of so-called 'pit studies', in which subjects stand on a platform raised just over an inch off the floor while wearing a head-mounted display that projects the image of standing on the edge of a pit or canyon into their eyes, has shown that people can be convinced that they are in danger of falling a long way in a VR environment. The subjects know that they are in no danger but experience increased physical stress nonetheless (Meehan et al. 2002; Madary and Metzinger 2016). Again, these studies suggest that experiences in VR are not unreal and have the potential of causing non-trivial harm to their subjects.

It is important that this point is not misunderstood. I am not claiming that there are no differences between virtual interactions and interactions in the physical world. There are. The aforementioned absence of physical contact is one of them and could have important implications for how we classify or understand the magnitude of the wrong inherent in unwanted virtual sexual interactions. This is one of the issues I take up in more detail in the next section of this chapter. Similarly, virtual interactions could involve interactions with artificial characters, who might be thought to lack the capacity to be moral victims. This could also make a difference to the moral character of any virtual interactions in which they might be involved. Nevertheless, none of these differences should be taken to imply that virtual interactions, as a whole, carry no moral weight. They do and they can, particularly when they involve humans interacting via virtual avatars. To dismiss their moral salience because they are 'not real' or 'less real' is not persuasive.

The 'it's just a game' objection

Related to the previous objection is the 'it's just a game' objection. This objection builds on the aforementioned idea that virtual interactions are a species of fantasy role play or game and adds the claim that the ordinary rules of morality do not apply as a result. We have already encountered some reasons to reject this objection but it is worth giving it a fair hearing. There is, after all, something to it. Many games do involve the suspension of ordinary moral rules (Huizinga 1949; Zimmerman and Salen 2003). Earlier I gave the example of sports such as boxing and rugby. These sports sanction what would ordinarily be called physical assault. There are many other examples. For instance, some board games and games of chance, such as Poker and Diplomacy, encourage players to engage in forms of deception and bluffing that would ordinarily be deemed immoral. Doing so is part of the fun of the game.

The notion that games represent an amoral space is a view that is particularly compelling when we turn to the world of video games. There are now all manner of games that encourage players to engage in simulations of actions that, if they occurred in the real world, would be deemed serious moral wrongs. For instance, games like *Hitman* or *Assassin's Creed* or *Grand Theft Auto* all routinely encourage acts of extreme violence, criminality, and cruelty as part of their game play (Luck 2009; Luck and Ellerby 2013; Gooskens 2010; Patridge 2013; Ostritsch 2017; Tillson 2018).

Furthermore, the suspension of ordinary moral rules is not just something that applies to games; it also applies to all manner of fictional activities. Many plays and movies depict acts of physical and sexual violence. Are they immoral for doing so? There is a debate about this, but the reality is that we often treat fiction that depicts immoral acts with great respect. For example, we regularly reward actors who take on the parts of serial killers, psychopaths, and dictators. Think about Joaquin Phoenix in the *Joker*, Daniel Day-Lewis in *There Will Be Blood*, Charlize Theron in *Monster*, and Anthony Hopkins in *Silence of the Lambs*. Each of them won an Oscar for depicting a psychopath or serial killer. We find their depiction of these characters psychologically and emotionally compelling and we don't think they do anything morally wrong by pretending to be serial killers or sexual sadists (Gooskens 2010).

Could something similar not be true of actions in virtual environments? Could they all be deemed a kind of gameplay or make-believe? There are three points to made in response to this objection. First, not all unwanted virtual sexual interactions take place in game-like environments or occur as part of some fantasy/make-believe. Some of the examples given earlier did involve games, for example the archery game in QuiVR and the paintballing game in Rec Room, but in neither of these cases was the unsolicited sexual interaction part of the underlying structure or purpose of the game. It was something added on by malicious users of the game platform. So even if we did accept that game worlds have their own internal ethics, unsolicited sexual interactions would not always be included among the things that ought be tolerated by that internal ethics. Most of the other examples involved open-ended socializing in VR. While there may be an element of fantasy and make-believe to these forms of socializing, and while some online platforms have their own community norms and standards, those norms typically do not tolerate unsolicited sexual interactions, nor are they always transparent to users. Certainly, in the examples cited above, none of the users of the relevant platforms thought that unsolicited sexual interactions were acceptable, even if they did anticipate them to some extent.

Second, even if these interactions did occur within environments in which unsolicited sexual interactions were encouraged, tolerated, or part of the underlying game structure, it is not clear that this would save them from moral reproach. Although we do sometimes tolerate the suspension of ordinary moral rules within games, there are limits to how much we are willing to do this. Extreme or risky violence is rarely tolerated in games that permit rough physical contact. You cannot deliberately snap someone's neck in a game of rugby. And knowledge about dangerous, post-game effects of such physical contact can alter our moral attitude towards games. Fear of permanent brain damage arising from repeated concussion, and the social costs this has both to the affected individuals and their families, have, for example, changed some people's attitudes towards sports such as boxing and American football in recent years. This has, in turn, affected some of the internal rules of such sports (heightening safety protocols and equipment rules). That virtual interactions can have harmful and lasting real-world effects (as documented above) may give us reason to think that we shouldn't tolerate any suspension of the ordinary moral rules when it comes to unwanted sexual interactions.

It is important to bear in mind that this point is not the same as the typical 'effects' argument that is made in relation to exposure to violent or sexually explicit media. I am not claiming here simply that acting out a sexually violent fantasy can have negative downstream effects for our interactions with other people. As I have suggested elsewhere, I am sceptical about our capacity to adequately research such effects (Danaher 2017b; Danaher 2019). What I am arguing instead is that acting out these fantasies can be *immediately* and *intrinsically* harmful, in the sense that they can corrupt or undermine one's moral psychology and character, that these harms are not obviously compensated for by other gains, and that they *may* have other negative repercussions. Others have made this point too, suggesting that video games can be a training ground for the moral virtues, and game designers should pay attention to these possibilities when creating the game structure (Sicart 2009).

Third, and finally, immoral sexual interactions within games or other fantasy realms are not as easily tolerated as other kinds of immorality within games and fantasy realms. This topic has been the subject of much debate in the literature on the ethics of video games. Stephanie Patridge (2010, 2013), for example, has argued that a game player who enjoys and tolerates the immoral sexual actions depicted in games such as *Custer's Revenge* and *Rapelay*—both games that encourage users to engage in represented acts of sexual assault and violence—is displaying a troubling insensitivity to the moral meaning of such representations. Her view is that we are, consequently, within our rights to question their moral character. This is an argument that I and others, such as Robert Sparrow, have applied to the adjacent debate concerning acts of sexual assault and violence towards sex robots (Danaher 2017a; Sparrow 2017—and see also the chapter in this volume by Sterri and Earp, on 'The Ethics of Sex Robots' for more).

The philosopher Morgan Luck (2009) has also noted the odd inconsistency in our attitudes towards sexual immorality in video games and crafted it into something he calls the 'gamer's dilemma'. According to this dilemma, most people seem to think it is immoral to depict and play a game involving acts of virtual child sexual abuse, but most people are tolerant of acts of virtual murder and physical torture. Luck claims that it is very difficult to reconcile these two attitudes. You should either tolerate both or accept both. Luck's formulation of the gamer's dilemma has generated a small cottage industry of replies since it was first published (Luck and Ellerby 2013; Patridge 2013). The details of those replies need not detain us here. What is noteworthy about them, however, is that most contributors to the debate accept the starting position that representing and engaging in acts of virtual child sexual abuse is immoral. This stance is backed up by studies of users of virtual social platforms such as Second Life, who generally see sexual 'ageplay' (when adult users of the platform play at being children engaging in sexual acts) as something that transgresses or lies at the extreme edge of what is acceptable on the platform (Reeves 2018). This supports the notion that there is something different about virtual sexual immorality in most people's minds. Furthermore, it is worth noting that this debate about virtual sexual immorality usually concerns actions carried out by game players against wholly artificial characters, not human-controlled avatars. Whatever objections people might have to those actions would seem to apply *a fortiori* to cases involving human-controlled victims.

The typical counterexample to the suggestion that role-playing sexual violence or assault is morally problematic is, of course, the world of BDSM. To outsiders, practitioners of BDSM appear to tolerate and encourage sexual violence and to endorse fantasies of domination and submission that run contrary to our norms of consent. But this is not a true counterexample, since the BDSM community typically adopts a complex ethical code grounded in explicit consent and a clear statement of boundaries (Nielsen 2010). People who step outside those boundaries or ignore consent are doing something immoral even within the community norms of BDSM. This is very different from tolerating unsolicited sexual interactions in a virtual environment.

In sum, as Ostritsch notes in his discussion of the amorality of games and fiction, 'amoralist reasoning … implausibly severs all ties between the fictional and the non-fictional' (Ostritsch 2017: 122). It does not make sense to sever such ties with the virtual world, particularly given that more and more of us are living more and more of our lives through virtual avatars.

The 'unrestricted consent' objection

One final objection to the claim that unwanted virtual sexual interactions are serious moral wrongs concerns the possibility that people consent to those interactions by participating in certain virtual games or VR social platforms. In other words, these are not 'unwanted' sexual interactions at all. People are consenting to them by entering VR platforms, thereby removing any hint of immorality. Presumably, the idea here would be that either (a) people who use these VR platforms should know that they are liable to be exposed to this kind of experience, hence by using them they signal consent to an un-restricted set of sexual interactions; or (b) because it is relatively easy to withdraw from a virtual environment (take off your headset or switch off your computer), anyone who stays inside a virtual environment knowing that they are at risk of experiencing an un-wanted sexual interaction is signalling consent by failing to withdraw.

This objection should not detain us for too long. As I have noted in past writings on this topic, this objection comes up frequently in conversations and talks that I have given about the topic of virtual sexual assault, but it seems highly implausible (Danaher 2018). To put it bluntly, it is a virtual equivalent of the 'asking for it' defence one sometimes hears in real-world cases of sexual assault and rape. It places the onus on the victim of a sexual assault to communicate non-consent and not on the perpetrator to elicit affirmative consent. Although there was a time when consent was readily inferred by courts and tribunals from non-verbal behaviour, the ethical and legal consensus seems to be shifting away from this norm (Dougherty 2013, 2015). It is unfair to force a victim to communicate their resistance to sexual assault or to 'run away' from a sexual aggressor. They may feel afraid or shocked or otherwise psychologically incapable of doing so. This is true even in virtual environments. Both Jordan Belamire and Michelle Cortese, for example, reported finding themselves initially 'frozen' and in a state of shock when they were subjected to virtual sexual assault. Requiring victims to remove themselves from virtual environments if they don't want to be subjected to sexual interactions would be unfair for an additional reason: it would mean that they are effectively excluded from these environments. Since many of the victims of virtual sexual assault are women, and since these virtual environments are becoming more common and integrated into our daily lives, this exclusion would just perpetuate a social injustice.

WHAT TYPE OF MORAL WRONG IS IT?

If the argument defended above is successful, then an unwanted virtual sexual interaction should be viewed as a serious moral wrong, which raises a follow-up question: what kind of moral wrong? We usually organize our moral wrongs into graduated hierarchies. This is most commonly, but not only, reflected in the criminal law. In other words, some wrongs are taken to be more serious than others. Giving someone a dead leg might be a form of physical assault, for example, but it is not as serious as beating a person to death with an iron bar. These graduated hierarchies are typically incorporated into the legal punishments we attach to different wrongs. For example, minor assault is defined differently from, and attracts a lower penalty than, intentional murder.

This is also true when it comes to sexual wrongs. Most legal jurisdictions around the world distinguish between rape and other kinds of sexual assault or non-consensual sexual activity. Rape is usually deemed the most serious kind of sexual wrong, with some additional gradations introduced for more serious forms of rape such as child rape and statutory rape. Sexual assault is a lesser kind of sexual wrong, and can come in various grades too. If we are to fit unwanted virtual sexual interactions into this graduated hierarchy, then where should we fit it? Is it less serious than rape? Is it a form of common sexual assault? Or is it something entirely sui generis?

In some ways, the simplest answer is to say that it *is* sui generis. It is a new phenomenon, made possible by new developments in technology, and should be treated as its own thing. To some extent, the present chapter has worked from the presumption that it is sui generis. After all, if it is just another form of sexual assault and no different from the ones with which we are familiar, it wouldn't need a separate chapter dedicated to it in a book like this. Following this approach, we should analyse virtual sexual assault on its own terms and, if we wish to criminalize it or legally ban it, then we should create a separate and novel category of legal offence to address it.

But, of course, treating it as a sui generis phenomenon would be to miss the point of much of the preceding discussion. The argument for moral wrongness and the subsequent analysis of objections to that argument hinges largely on drawing out the analogies between unwanted virtual sexual interactions and other kinds of moral wrongs, including specifically sexual wrongs. So it is at least worth asking whether we can just subsume this new phenomenon within the existing categories of rape and sexual assault. When we attempt to do this, two possibilities appear to arise.

First, we could view unwanted virtual sexual interactions as essentially the same as rape and sexual assault. To do this, however, we would probably need to argue for a new understanding of rape and sexual assault. In most countries, both of these offences are defined in such a way that they require physical contact between the parties. Consider, for example, the definitions of rape and sexual assault in the English and Welsh Sexual Offences Act 2003. Under section 1 of that act, rape is defined as an offence that requires penetration, by a penis, of the vagina, anus, or mouth of another person (section 2 builds on this in creating an offence of 'penetrative sexual assault' that covers non-penile penetration of the vagina or anus). Under section 3 of that act, sexual assault is defined in a way that it requires physical touching. Given that virtual sexual interactions tend to lack this element of physical touching (though see the qualification below), they could not count as subtypes of rape or sexual assault.

Nevertheless, there is some reason to think that this physicalist paradigm ought to be abandoned. Human sexuality is a complex thing. People can experience sexual arousal and response in the absence of direct physical contact. Instead of focusing on physical contact as being the defining feature of sexual assault, we could, perhaps, focus on violations of sexual autonomy or sexual agency as being the defining feature (Danaher 2018 takes up this idea). If sexual activity can extend into the virtual world (and the prevalence of 'cybersex' and other kinds of virtual sexual activity would support this idea), then it is possible to have one's sexual agency undermined and compromised through these sexual acts. A non-consensual virtual sexual act could then count as a form of sexual assault and may perhaps rise to a level of seriousness that justifies calling it 'rape'. This suggestion is not as outlandish as it might first sound. There are some countries that have moved away from the traditional, physicalist paradigm—with its obsessive focus on what bits go where—when legally defining rape. For example, under Chapter 6, section 1 of the Swedish Penal Code, rape can occur without physical penetration.[7] This recently led to a man being convicted of rape for encouraging children to engage in sexual activity via a webcam.[8]

What if you are not persuaded by this proposal and think that we should stick with the physicalist paradigm? Does that mean that unwanted virtual sexual interactions can never count as rape or sexual assault? Not necessarily. There are haptic technologies that allow for touch, including sexual touch, to be transmitted via the internet. The world of 'teledildonics', for example, involves the creation of smart sex toys that allow people to engage in physically immersive forms of cybersex. It is possible to combine the use of teledildonics with immersive VR.[9] If users of teledildonics have their interfaces hacked by malicious actors or are deceived into interacting sexually with someone with whom they did not consent to such interactions, then we may have cases of unwanted virtual sex that count as a genuine form of rape and sexual assault. Other forms of unwanted virtual sex—that do not involve the use of teledildonics—could then be treated as a separate category of moral and legal wrong. That said, it is worth bearing in mind that, even if they are not emphasized in the definitions of the offences, there are risks associated with physical sexual contact that do not arise with virtual sexual contact, for example, sexually transmitted diseases and unwanted pregnancies. These risks may warrant differential treatment.

CONCLUSION

In this chapter, I have analysed the phenomenon of unwanted virtual sexual interaction, described some of the forms it can take, and looked at some evidence suggesting that it is quite prevalent. I have argued that it counts as a serious moral wrong from both deontological and consequentialist perspectives because it violates rights and can cause harm. I have argued that the objections to this view are not persuasive. I have also suggested that there is reason to treat these unwanted sexual interactions as a new type of sexual assault and rape, and not simply as a sui generis category of sexual wrongdoing.

One final issue that is worth addressing is what can be done about this new form of sexual wrongdoing. Three possibilities suggest themselves. First, and most importantly, designers of VR technologies and platforms have a major responsibility here. They create the possibilities for unwanted sexual actions within their virtual platforms and so they have a duty to work hard to ensure that people are not subjected to unwanted sexual interactions in VR spaces. In this regard, the proposals from Cortese and Zeller (2020) should be taken seriously. They argue that there are ways to build 'consent' into the design of VR apps by creating features that allow users to control who they interact with, under what terms, and enable easy withdrawal from threatening spaces. More drastically, we could demand that designers prevent all forms of sexualized interaction in virtual spaces. Admittedly, this may be practically difficult in some cases, and may have a moral cost insofar as it could prevent desired VR sexual interactions; nevertheless, there are presumably some kinds of VR platform (e.g. game worlds populated primarily by children) where designing out the possibility of sexual contact is appropriate. Second, where sexual interactions are possible or desirable, there should be strong community standards that outlaw or ban unwanted sexual interactions in virtual spaces. These standards should be monitored and enforced by moderators of these virtual spaces.

This is already being done, to some extent (as is clear from some of the stories discussed earlier on) but it is an important line of defence and should not be neglected. Third, and as implied above, there is a role for legal regulation of VR spaces. In particular, the criminal law should not treat what happens in VR spaces as somehow different or peripheral to its mission. Legislators and legal reformers should work to include virtual sexual wrongdoing within the scope of the law.

NOTES

1. 'The Story of Roblox', video available on YouTube, https://youtu.be/VL6rYNmfrjM, accessed 30 September 2021.
2. The original Facebook post recounting the incident is no longer available but reports of Amber's Facebook post are available at: https://globalnews.ca/news/4316449/roblox-gang-rape-7-year-old-girl/; https://www.bbc.com/news/technology-44697788; and https://knowyourmeme.com/memes/events/roblox-gang-rape, accessed 30 September 2021. It is not clear what the 'gang rape' consisted of, but from the photos accompanying Amber's post, it appears to have involved one of the male avatars pushing her daughter's avatar's head down towards his crotch/groin and holding it there in order to simulate oral sex. The avatars appear to have been clothed throughout the simulated gang rape.
3. Other incidents are documented in detail here: https://www.adl.org/resources/reports/hate-in-social-virtual-reality#sexism-racism-and-anti-semitism-in-social-vr-today, accessed 30 September 2021.
4. Details of this research are available here: http://assets.pewresearch.org/wp-content/uploads/sites/14/2017/07/10151519/PI_2017.07.11_Online-Harassment_FINAL.pdf, accessed 30 September 2021.
5. The text comes from this *Medium* post https://medium.com/@ellecortese/virtual-healing-bf2b5f0cbf51, accessed 30 September 2021.
6. Definitions and approaches can vary cross-jurisdictionally. Some legal definitions of sexual offences could include a reference to harmfulness, and some judges or juries can take harmfulness into consideration when assessing guilt and, more commonly, appropriate punishments. The point here is simply that it is rare for the core sexual offences (rape and sexual assault) to require harm to the victim in order to be legally recognized. They sometimes require force on the part of the perpetrator, but that is not the same thing as harm to the victim and, again, very different to how physical assault offences are classified.
7. An English language translation of the Swedish criminal code can be found here: https://www.government.se/498621/contentassets/7a2dcae0787e465e9a2431554b5eab03/the-swedish-criminal-code.pdf, accessed 30 September 2021.
8. See Cole 2017 - https://www.vice.com/en_us/article/pazyn7/in-a-first-a-man-is-charged-for-rape-over-the-internet, accessed 30 September 2021. This non-physicalist approach to defining sexual assault could also have implications for how we view something like revenge porn (or, to give it its more euphemistic name, the 'non-consensual sharing of intimate images'). Sharing such images non-consensually could also be viewed as a violation of sexual agency and autonomy.
9. The Dutch company Kiiroo makes a range of such devices. See https://www.kiiroo.com/ (accessed 30 September 2021) for more.

REFERENCES

Alexander, Julie (2019), 'Roblox Surpasses Minecraft with 100 Million Monthly Players', *The Verge*, 2 August, https://www.theverge.com/2019/8/2/20752225/roblox-100-million-users-minecraft-youtube-twitch-pewdiepie-keemstar, accessed 30 September 2021.

Behm-Morawitz, Elizabeth (2013), 'Mirrored Selves: The Influence of Self-Presence in a Virtual World on Health, Appearance, and Well-Being', *Computers in Human Behavior* 29(1), 119–128.

Belamire, Jordan (2016), 'My First Virtual Reality Groping', *Medium: Athena Talks*, 5 October, https://medium.com/athena-talks/my-first-virtual-reality-sexual-assault-2330410b62ee, accessed 30 September 2021.

Blanke, Olaf, and Metzinger, Thomas (2009), 'Full-Body Illusions and Minimal Phenomenal Selfhood', *Trends in Cognitive Science* 13, 7–13, doi: https://doi.org/10.1016/j.tics.2008.10.003.

Cole, Samantha (2017), 'In a First, a Man Is Charged for Rape Over the Internet', *Vice*, 1 December, https://www.vice.com/en_us/article/pazyn7/in-a-first-a-man-is-charged-for-rape-over-the-internet, accessed 30 September 2021.

Cortese, Michelle (2019), 'Virtual_ Healing', *Medium*, 18 November, https://medium.com/@ellecortese/virtual-healing-bf2b5f0cbf51, accessed 30 September 2021.

Cortese, Michelle and Zeller, Andrea (2020), 'Designing Safe Spaces for Virtual Reality: Ethics in Design and Communication', in Andrew DeRosa and Laura Scherling, eds, *Ethics in Design and Communication* (London: Bloomsbury Academic Press).

Danaher, John (2016), 'Robots, Law and the Retribution Gap', *Ethics and Information Technology* 18, 299–309.

Danaher, John (2017a), 'Robotic Rape and Robotic Child Sexual Abuse: Should They Be Criminalized?', *Criminal Law and Philosophy*, 11(1), 71–95.

Danaher, John (2017b), 'The Symbolic-Consequences Argument in the Sex Robot Debate', in J. Danaher and N. McArthur (eds), *Robot Sex: Social and Ethical Implications* (Cambridge, MA: MIT Press).

Danaher, John (2018), 'The Law and Ethics of Virtual Assault', in W. Barfield and M. Blitz (eds), *The Law of Virtual and Augmented Reality* (Cheltenham: Edward Elgar).

Danaher, John (2019), 'Regulating Child Sex Robots: Restriction or Experimentation?', *Medical Law Review* 27, 553–575.

Dibbell, Julian (1998), 'A Rape in Cyberspace: How an Evil Clown, a Haitian Trickster Spirit, Two Wizards, and a Cast of Dozens Turned a Database into a Society', in Ian Dibbell, ed., *My Tiny Life* (New York: Holt).

Dougherty, Tom (2013), 'Sex, Lies and Consent', 123(4), *Ethics*, 717–744.

Dougherty, Tom (2015), 'Yes Means Yes: Communication as Consent', *Philosophy and Public Affairs* 43(3), 224–253.

Duranske, Benjamin (2007), 'Reader Roundtable: "Virtual Rape Claim Brings Belgian Police to Second Life"', *Virtually Blind*, 24 April 2007, http://virtuallyblind.com/2007/04/24/open-roundtable-allegations-of-virtual-rape-bring-belgian-police-to-second-life/, accessed 30 September 2021.

Gaus, Gerald (2010). *The Order of Public Reason.* (Cambridge: Cambridge University Press).

Gooskens, Geert (2010), 'The Ethical Status of Virtual Actions', *Ethical Perspectives* 17(1), 59–78.

Hamm Michele., Newton, Amanda., Chisholm, Annabritt, Shulhan, Jocelyn, Milne, Andrea and Sundar, Purnima, et al. (2015), 'Prevalence and Effect of Cyberbullying on Children and

Young People: A Scoping Review of Social Media Studies', *JAMA Pediatrics* 169(8), 770–777, doi: https://doi.org/10.1001/jamapediatrics.2015.0944.

Hershfield, Hal, Goldstein, Daniel, Sharpe, William, Fox, Jesse, Yeykelis, Leo, Carstensen, Laura, et al. (2011), 'Increasing Saving Behavior through Age-Progressed Renderings of the Future Self', *Journal of Marketing Research* 48, S23–S37, doi: https://doi.org/10.1509%2Fj mkr.48.SPL.S23.

Huizinga, Johan (1949), *Homo Ludens: A Study of the Play Element in Human Culture* (London: Routledge and Kegan Paul).

Lorenz, Taylor (2016), 'Virtual Reality Is Full of Assholes Who Sexually Harass Me. Here's Why I Keep Going Back', *Mic*, 26 May, https://www.mic.com/articles/144470/sexual-harassment-in-virtual-reality, accessed 30 September 2021.

Luck, Morgan (2009), 'The Gamer's Dilemma: An Analysis of the Arguments for the Distinction between Virtual Murder and Virtual Paedophilia', *Ethics and Information Technology* 11, 31–36.

Luck, Morgan, and Ellerby, Nathan (2013), 'Has Bartel Resolved the Gamer's Dilemma?', *Ethics and Information Technology* 15, 229–233.

Lynn, Regina (2007), 'Virtual Rape Is Traumatic But Is It a Crime?', *Wired Magazine*, 4 May.

Mack, Eric (2018), 'Robert Nozick's Political Philosophy', in Edward N. Zalta, ed., *The Stanford Encyclopedia of Philosophy* (Summer 2018 edn), https://plato.stanford.edu/archives/sum2018/entries/nozick-political, accessed 30 September 2021.

Madary, Michael, and Metzinger, Thomas. K (2016), 'Real Virtuality: A Code of Ethical Conduct. Recommendations for Good Scientific Practice and the Consumers of VR-Technology', *Frontiers in Robitics and AI* 3, 3, doi: https://doi.org/10.3389/frobt.2016.00003.

Matthias, Andreas (2004), 'The Responsibility Gap: Ascribing Responsibility for the Actions of Learning Automata', *Ethics Information Technology* 6, 175–183, doi: https://doi.org/10.1007/s10676-004-3422-1.

Meehan, Michael, Insko, Brent, Whitton, Mary, and Brooks, Frederick (2002), 'Physiological Measures of Presence in Stressful Virtual Environments', *ACM Transactions on Graphics* 21, 645–652, doi: https://doi.org/10.1145/566654.566630.

Metzinger, Thomas (2009a), *The Ego Tunnel. The Science of the Mind and the Myth of the Self* (New York: Basic Books).

Nielsen, Morten Ebbe Juul (2010), 'Safe, Sane, and Consensual—Consent and the Ethics of BDSM', *International Journal of Applied Philosophy* 24(2), 265–288.

Nyholm, Sven (2018), 'Attributing Agency to Automated Systems: Reflections on Human–Robot Collaborations and Responsibility-Loci', *Science and Engineering Ethics* 24, 1201–1219.

Ostritsch, Sebastian (2017), 'The Amoralist Challenge to Gaming and the Gamer's Moral Obligation', *Ethics and Information Technology* 19(2), 117–128.

Outlaw, Jessica (2018), 'Virtual Harassment: The Social Experience of 600+ Regular VR Users', https://drive.google.com/file/d/1afFQJN6QAwmeZdGcRj9R4ohVr00ZNO4a/view, accessed 30 September 2021.

Outlaw, Jessica, and Duckles, Beth (2017), 'Why Women Don't Like Social Virtual Reality: A Study of Safety, Usability and Self Expression in Social VR', https://extendedmind.io/social-vr, accessed 30 September 2021.

Patridge, Stephanie (2010), 'The Incorrigible Social Meaning of Video Game Imagery', *Ethics and Information Technology* 13(4), 303–312.

Patridge, Stephanie (2013), 'Pornography, Ethics and Video Games', *Ethics and Information Technology* 15(1), 25–34.

Reeves, Carla (2018), 'The Virtual Simulation of Child Sexual Abuse: Online Gameworld Users' Views, Understanding and Responses to Sexual Ageplay', *Ethics and Information Technology* 20(2), 101–113, doi: http://doi.org/10.1007/s10676-018-9449-5.

Rosenberg, Robin, Baughman, Shawnee, and Bailenson, Jeremy (2013), 'Virtual Superheroes: Using Superpowers in Virtual Reality to Encourage Prosocial Behavior', *PLoS ONE* 8, e55003, doi: https://doi.org/10.1371/journal.pone.0055003.

Santoni de Sio, Filippo., and van den Hoven, Jeroen (2018), 'Meaningful Human Control over Autonomous Systems: A Philosophical Account', *Frontiers in Robotics and AI* 5, 73, doi: http://doi.org/10.3389/frobt.2018.00015.

Sicart, Miguel (2009), *The Ethics of Computer Games* (Cambridge: Massachusetts Institute of Technology Press).

Slater, Mel, and Sanchez-Vives, Maria V (2016), 'Enhancing Our Lives with Immersive Virtual Reality', *Frontiers in Robotics and AI* 3, 74, doi: https://doi.org/10.3389/frobt.2016.00074.

Søraker, Johnny (2010), *The Value of Virtual Worlds and Entities—A Philosophical Analysis of Virtual Worlds and Their Impact on Well-Being* (Inskamp: Enschede).

Sparrow, Lucy (2019), 'The Moral (Im)permissibility of Groping in Virtual Reality Games', *Proceedings of DiGRAA 2019, What's Next?*, http://digraa.org/wp-content/uploads/2019/01/DIGRAA_2019_paper_9.pdf, accessed 30 September 2021.

Sparrow, Robert (2017), 'Robots, Rape, and Representation', *International Journal of Social Robotics* 9, 465–477, doi: https://doi.org/10.1007/s12369-017-0413-z.

Sparrow, Lucy, Gibbs, Martin, and Arnold, Michael (2019), 'Apathetic Villagers and the Trolls Who Love Them', doi: https://doi.org/10.1145/3369457.3369514.

Strikwerda, Litska (2015), 'Present and Past Instances of Virtual Rape in Light of Three Categories of Legal Philosophical Theories of Rape', *Philosophy and Technology* 28(4), 491–510.

Tillson, John (2018), 'Is It Distinctively Wrong to Simulate Wrongdoing?', *Ethics and Information Technology*, doi: https://doi.org/10.1007/s10676-018-9463-7.

Wenar, Leif (2020), 'Rights', in Edward N. Zalta, ed., *The Stanford Encyclopedia of Philosophy*, https://plato.stanford.edu/archives/spr2021/entries/rights/, accessed 30 September 2021.

Yee, Nick, Bailenson, Jeremy, and Ducheneaut, Nicolas (2007), 'The Proteus Effect. The Effect of Transformed Self-Representation on Behavior', *Human Communication Research* 33, 271–290, doi: https://doi.org/10.1111/j.1468-2958.2007.00299.x.

Zimmerman, Eric, and Salen, Katie. (2003), *Rules of Play: Game Design Fundamentals* (Cambridge, MA: MIT Press).

PART IV

ETHICAL DESIGN
OF TECHNOLOGY

CHAPTER 15

....

ETHICAL DIMENSIONS OF PERSUASIVE TECHNOLOGY

....

JAMES WILLIAMS

INTRODUCTION

....

PERSUASION is as old as humanity. It is one of the most prevalent and consequential forms of interaction. Its pathways of influence span the conscious and unconscious, rational and nonrational, verbal and nonverbal. Its nature and ethics have been debated since antiquity. However, as networked digital technologies have rapidly transformed our capacities for managing information and attention, they have amplified and extended the means of persuasion in unprecedented ways. These technological advancements have occurred in tandem with advances in the understanding of human psychology and decision making, knowledge of which has been increasingly brought to bear on their design and deployment. The proliferation and power of these new forms of technological persuasion have brought fresh attention to age-old ethical questions about persuasion and raised other ones which are newly salient.

The ethics of persuasive technology intersects with many other areas of applied ethics, yet it also raises distinctive ethical considerations in its own right. Issues of persuasion may coexist with ethical issues that stem from the nature of a technology, for example, its reliance on automation, machine learning, or robotics. Similarly, the ethics of persuasive technology may overlap with ethical issues that emerge from the particular application domain of a technology's usage, such as in health, education, or advertising. Yet, persuasive technologies also present unique ethical considerations of their own which arise from the persuasion *per se*—considerations that broadly pertain to issues of autonomy. While the ethics of persuasive technologies remains an emerging area of study, scholarly attention to the issues it presents has advanced briskly in recent years. Research in the area has broadly been concerned with clarifying the ethical issues persuasive technologies raise and bringing ethical thinking to bear on their design.

In this chapter, I provide an overview of the high-level issues in this area by addressing three questions. First, what counts as a 'persuasive' technology? Second, what are the main ethical issues raised by persuasive technologies? Third, what major questions loom on the horizon for the ethics of persuasive technology?

WHAT IS A 'PERSUASIVE' TECHNOLOGY?

A toy tiger encourages a two-year-old to exercise. A mobile app hooks a teenager into loops of constant status-checking. An advertising platform's algorithmic logic nudges a father to buy a new lawnmower (for more on digital nudging, see Ienca and Vayena, this volume). A home-care robot reminds an elderly woman to take her evening medicine. A self-driving taxi offers its occupant a discount for stopping at a nearby fast-food restaurant to get a milkshake.

There is a particular class of digital technology, only recently emergent in our lives, that as yet has no consensus term. It overlaps with but is not coextensive with design that has been described in terms of 'nudging', 'gamification', 'behaviour change', 'dark patterns', 'smart' technology, and many other descriptors. It has also become common to describe these technologies as 'persuasive' technologies. While this term is not wholly satisfactory, it is sufficient to enable a high-level ethical discussion of this domain (and is much preferable to hastily concocting another ill-considered neologism).

What does it mean to describe a technology as 'persuasive'? At its most basic level, the label is a metaphor drawn from the domain of interpersonal communication which emphasizes similarities between a technology's operation and human capacities of influence, much as the term 'artificial intelligence' does with capacities of pattern recognition, logic, attention, and other aspects of human intelligence. If we adapt an early definition of artificial intelligence given by McCarthy and colleagues in 1955 (McCarthy et al. 2006), we might say that a persuasive technology is one which is 'behaving in ways that would be considered' persuasive 'if a human were so behaving'. While this is a useful starting point, when we turn to specific cases, the lines of comparison between technological persuasion and interpersonal persuasion quickly become hard to draw. And, of course, this anthropomorphic definition does not clarify the central definitional question of what counts as persuasion in the first place.

There is a wide sense in which any technology can be described as 'persuasive' by virtue of its mere influence. That is not the kind of persuasiveness I am interested in here. That common form of influence relates to questions of a technology's 'affordances', 'biases', or 'intentionality' and is an important subject of analysis in its own right—one that has widely been recognized as morally salient (Winner 1980; Borgmann 1987; Latour 1992, Floridi and Sanders 2004; Verbeek 2011). A slightly narrower sense of 'persuasive', though one that is still too wide for our purposes here, involves technologies that are designed *intentionally* to influence. Similarly, to be a 'persuasive' technology, it is not sufficient that a technology merely *enable* persuasion, for example, a forum or email client that allows users to send persuasive messages to one another. In other words, a persuasive technology is persuasive because of its form, not because of its content.

Here it is particularly important to distinguish between persuasive technology as a category of technology and Persuasive Technology as a field of study. In the early years of the twenty-first century, B.J. Fogg's (Fogg 2002; Fogg et al. 2007) work in applying novel insights from behavioural psychology to the design and analysis of personal computing technologies catalysed an interdisciplinary subfield known as Persuasive Technology. (Hereafter, to avoid confusion I will capitalize the term Persuasive Technology when referring to the field and use lower case when referring to the type of technology.) In the years since, the field has proved useful for advancing research into persuasive technologies across application domains and disciplinary boundaries as well as bringing attention to the mechanisms of influence common to these systems (Fogg 2002; Oinas-Kukkonen and Harjumaa 2008).

Within the field of Persuasive Technology, the term 'persuasive technology' has broadly been defined by the presence of three necessary conditions: there must be (a) an intention on the part of its designers to (b) change, reinforce, or otherwise shape human behaviour, attitudes, or both, in (c) a manner that is not coercive. Condition (a) seems overly restrictive of the agents behind a technology but is salvageable if we interpret 'designers' to mean not the narrow set of agents, such as programmers and user-interface designers, who design the technology in a hands-on manner but rather interpret the term more broadly to mean any agent with a substantial influence on the resulting design. This could include leaders of an organization, those who set higher-level goals (such as business models or other organizational priorities), or similar agents who exercise systemic influence rather than direct influence on the design. Condition (b) is, for our purposes, broadly unobjectionable. The third condition, however—the requirement that a persuasive technology be noncoercive—presents three problems. First, it amounts to a negative definition of 'persuasiveness', framing it not in terms of what it is but in terms of what it is not. Second, the nature of coercion remains a subject of considerable debate, especially when (a) the force in question is nonphysical in nature and (b) the psychological avenues of influence are nonrational in nature, both of which are often the case in the context of digital technology design. Finally, the requirement that persuasive technology not coerce—regardless of how one defines coercion—is ultimately a normative condition masquerading as a descriptive one. As far as I am aware, there is no separate category of 'coercive technology' under analysis anywhere, and if a technology does coerce its user, it arguably merits more critical and ethical attention and therefore greater inclusion in the set of technologies under consideration, not less. Ultimately, the noncoercion condition is an artefact of the dual nature of the field of Persuasive Technology, which is concerned with not only enabling analysis of technologies but also informing their design. The exhortation to not coerce is an admirable normative heuristic for avoiding many types of morally objectionable design, but, as a constraint on definition and analytical scope, it ought to be jettisoned.

There is one more important aspect of persuasive technology that has gone unaddressed by definitions to date: the system's assessment of success at producing the desired effect, that is, the measurement of the outcome and its comparison with the system's persuasive goal. Importantly, to achieve effective assessment of persuasive success the outcome must be measured at an equal or greater degree of specificity as the representation of the persuasive goal. For example, if you are using a mobile app designed to persuade you to exercise every day, but it only measures whether you have opened the app at any time in the past month, then it would not count as a 'persuasive' technology.

We can therefore define a persuasive technology as: any sociotechnical system via which an intentional agent or agents intervenes, in a manner substantially involving digital technology, to effect a particular transformation in the experience, thought, or behaviour of a subject or subjects and measures the outcome of that intervention at a level of specificity sufficient to determine whether the transformation has occurred.

While not a paragon of simplicity, this definition seems conceptually sound. At any rate, it is sufficient; it is unnecessary to seek laser-like precision in our definition of persuasive technology in order to proceed with a discussion of its ethical dimensions.

WHAT ETHICAL ISSUES ARE RAISED BY PERSUASIVE TECHNOLOGIES?

Because persuasion is ubiquitous in human life, persuasive technologies may intersect with many ethical considerations. Here I am interested in those ethical issues that arise specifically from the enhanced persuasiveness *per se* rather than secondary aspects which support or otherwise accompany increased persuasiveness. These secondary aspects may include, among other things, the technology's digital nature, considerations specific to a particular application domain, the role of user attributes or behaviour, or the political economy of the technology's influence in society. While many of these secondary aspects may have great ethical importance, the issues they present—which include questions of privacy, consent, or fairness, to name but a few—are already subjects of focused critical discussion in this volume and elsewhere. Furthermore, these secondary issues are so numerous that if we were to undertake an inventory and analysis of them it would require a book of its own.

Within the field of Persuasive Technology (PT), ethics remains a relatively understudied aspect of the literature (Oinas-Kukkonen 2010; Kight and Gram-Hansen 2019). Much attention to PT ethics has occurred in the context of design. Berdichevsky and Neuenschwander (1999) suggested a set of eight ethical principles for PT design using a rule-based utilitarian framework that culminated in the 'Golden Rule of Persuasion', which suggests that 'the creators of a persuasive technology should never seek to persuade a person or persons of something they themselves would not consent to be persuaded to do'. Spahn (2011) theorized about the application of discourse ethics, and Kaptein and Eckles (2010) elaborated the use of reflective equilibrium in a PT context. Oinas-Kukkonen (2010) argued that key ethics research needs in PT included better understanding of the role of user consent, one's awareness of the persuasive process, and the role of tasks or goals in the design of persuasion as well as the importance of factors such as culture or gender in designing persuasion for user autonomy.

Broadly speaking, the ethical considerations that arise from a technology's persuasiveness per se concern questions of autonomy. Autonomy is a central component in many philosophical conceptions of well-being. It may be conceived in terms of reasons (Kant), an individual's motivational hierarchy (e.g. Frankfurt, Dworkin), or one's 'self-authorship' (Raz 1986), among other conceptions. In the context of persuasive technologies, autonomy has been identified as a particularly important ethical consideration (Smids 2012; Spahn 2011; Oinas-Kukkonen 2010; Verbeek 2009). In addition, special autonomy considerations arise in the context of use by children as well as vulnerable people (Jacobs 2020).

It may be useful to consider some of the key ethical issues raised by persuasive technologies in terms of two broad themes that are important for most conceptions of autonomy: (a) freedom of thought and attention and (b) freedom of action. These two categories are not mutually exclusive—in practice, they may and often do co-occur—but rather are two angles of analysis on the kinds of undue claims persuasive technologies may be seen to make on a person's autonomy.

Freedom of thought and attention

Freedom of thought is widely understood as necessary for autonomy and is enumerated as a fundamental freedom in Article 18 of the Universal Declaration of Human Rights (United Nations General Assembly 1948). In *On Liberty*, Mill (1989 [1859]) writes that the 'appropriate region of human liberty ... comprises, first, the inward domain of consciousness', which includes 'liberty of thought and feeling; absolute freedom of opinion and sentiment on all subjects, practical or speculative'. Importantly, these freedoms pertain to not only the content but also the manner of one's inner life: they include not merely the freedom to determine one's beliefs, desires, or volitions, but also to direct the workings of one's thought as they see fit. In particular, attention has been described as the basis of conscious thought as well as will (James 1890). The 'attention economy' (Lanham 2006) that now exists to capture and monetize human attention underlies the creation of many persuasive technologies. Many dominant platforms today optimize their services to maximize users' time and 'engagement' with the system in order to sell access to their attention to other parties (e.g. in the form of advertising) as their primary business model. What is ultimately being sold in these cases is the chance to shape the minds and wills of users.

Four key themes that relate to persuasive technologies and freedom of thought are: distraction, reflection, capacity depletion, and nonrational avenues of influence.

Distraction, or the direction of a person's attention away from task- or goal-salient information, is a common effect of persuasive technology. It may occur as an interruption, for instance, from an automated notification on a mobile device, or as a message from another person who was prompted to send it in order to increase their engagement with the service. The effect of associating a distractor with a reward has attentional effects that last well beyond that specific situation (Itthipuripat et al. 2019). Exposure to repeated notifications can even create mental habits that train users to interrupt themselves later when the technological influences are not present (Mark et al. 2008).

When a distractor directs a person's attention away from effective consideration and processing of internal information, it may undermine their reflection. Reflection is an important component of autonomy, for example, in the formation of second-order desires and volitions (Frankfurt 1988). A persuasive technology may deploy external stimuli (i.e. perceptual information) that compete with reflective information, thereby crowding out opportunities for reflection.

A persuasive technology may drain a person's cognitive capacity, such as working memory or willpower, as well. For example, in *The Morality of Freedom*, Raz (1986) gives the example of 'The Hounded Woman' to describe how capacity depletion threatens autonomy:

> A person finds herself on a small desert island. She shares the island with a fierce carnivorous animal which perpetually hunts for her. Her mental stamina, her intellectual ingenuity, her will power and her physical resources are taxed to their limits by her struggle to remain alive. She never has a chance to do or even to think of anything other than how to escape from the beast.

The Hounded Woman lacks personal autonomy because she lacks 'an adequate range of options to choose from'. Importantly, the 'lacking' here does not mean the absence of a range of options existing in the world but rather the inability to give attention to them. This case is analogous to the way a persuasive technology might relentlessly compete for or otherwise pursue a user's attention in its desire to optimize their engagement with it. (Of course, Raz's example is far more extreme in that the woman's life is in immediate danger, but the principle at work is the same.) Influencing via capacity depletion relates to the wider issue of using nonrational avenues of influence generally, for example, the exploitation of psychological biases or vulnerabilities (Smids 2012; Spahn 2011; Oinas-Kukkonen 2010; Verbeek 2009). Such biases include loss aversion (e.g. 'fear of missing out'), social comparison, the status quo bias, framing effects, appeals to consistency or scarcity, and many others (Kahneman 2011; Fogg et al. 2007). One particular group of biases widely exploited by persuasive technologies involves the psychology of reward and surprise. When a technology seeks to maximize a user's engagement with it, it can often be extremely effective to randomize the delivery of some type of reward that the user experiences. For instance, in a video game, this could take the form of randomizing the value and number of items that the player finds in loot boxes (in-game containers that the player's character opens) or randomizing posts in the infinite scrolling feed on a social media site. These mechanisms of reward and surprise are, of course, the same ones that underlie the compulsive nature of gambling, machine gambling in particular (Schüll 2012).

Freedom of action

Technologies designed to change people's behaviour may raise a wide range of issues related to freedom of action. Four key considerations I wish to address here are: coercion, manipulation, deception, and habituation.

As noted earlier, coercion is often explicitly excluded in definitions of persuasive technology. This exclusion is praiseworthy insofar as it is intended as a normative nudge for practitioners, but its presence ultimately hinders clear philosophical and ethical analysis of persuasive technologies. This is particularly so given the uncertainty regarding whether, and if so how, the concept of coercion can be meaningfully applied to influence that is nonrational in nature. For example, Smids (2012) argues that a car's persistent, incessant beeping aimed at causing the driver to fasten their seatbelt constitutes a type of coercion in the way it wears down their capacity for self-control. This example is particularly useful not only because it reminds us that in some cases coercion may be morally obligatory, but also because it emphasizes that, even if coercive mechanisms are apparent to the user, they may still influence via indirect means.

Like coercion, manipulation is a category of influence widely seen to pose threats to autonomy not only in the context of persuasive technologies but also in wider discussions about 'big data' (Schroeder and Cowls 2014), decision architecture (Sunstein 2015), and human interaction in general (Kane, 1996; Pereboom, 2001). While there is broad disagreement about what the criteria for manipulation are, the definition given by Pennock (1972) captures its most common elements: it is influencing a person 'by controlling the content and supply of information' in such a way that the person is not aware of the manipulation (Powers 2007; Strauss 1991; Kane 1996; Pereboom 2001; Smids 2012). Blumenthal-Barby (2014) further describes it as a form of 'nonargumentative influence', and Susser et al. (2019) describe it as intentionally hidden influence.

In persuasive technologies, design often has a special incentive to deceive the user. Such deceptive design is often described in terms of 'dark patterns', that is, design patterns that serve to trick or mislead a user in the direction of some desired outcome. Especially prevalent on e-commerce websites, dark patterns occur in a wide range of persuasive technologies (Mathur et al. 2019; Gray et al. 2018). In discussion of recommendation algorithms, Seaver (2019) usefully suggests the metaphor of 'traps' as a framework for understanding the design. Personification of artificial agents also presents a wide range of new avenues for the deployment of dark patterns, as has been discussed with, for example, the 'cuteness' of the design of some robots (Lacey and Caudwell 2019).

Habituation is one of the most common goals of persuasive design. One of the most prevalent methods for creating user habits is via strategic use of reward mechanisms. Randomizing the reward schedule for a given action increases the number of times a person is likely to take that action (Ferster and Skinner 1957). Eyal (2013) identifies variable rewards as a crucial step in the process of creating habits and 'hooking' users on a product. This is an underlying mechanism at work behind 'infinite' scrolling feeds of information such as those employed by Twitter, Facebook, Pinterest, and countless other news, social, and entertainment websites. It is often referred to as the 'slot machine' effect because it is the foundational psychological mechanism on which the machine gambling industry relies and which generates for them over $1 billion in revenue every day in the United States alone (Rivlin 2007). The compulsive and at times even addictive effects that these designs have on users can often be severely debilitating (Schüll 2012).

WHAT ARE THE MAJOR QUESTIONS FOR THE FUTURE OF PERSUASIVE TECHNOLOGY ETHICS?

As far as autonomy is concerned, two main categories of concern loom large on the horizon of persuasive technology ethics: (1) how to mitigate the risks that persuasive technologies pose to autonomy and (2) how to use persuasive technology as a way of enhancing autonomy. Within each category, three broad layers of questions exist that pertain to (a) the design and deployment of persuasive technologies, (b) the incentives and other upstream determinants that influence their design, and (c) linguistic, conceptual, and other cultural dimensions that shape our understanding of persuasive technologies.

When it comes to mitigating potential injuries to users' freedom of thought and action, at the level of design, there are many significant questions pertaining to the ethical acceptability of appealing to nonrational and/or nonconscious avenues of persuasion. For instance, are there certain vulnerable parts of our cognition that ought to receive special protection from persuasive attempts in the same way that certain vulnerable parts of our bodies may require special protection from physical harms? At the level of upstream determinants of design, there are major questions to be addressed involving the reformation of business models in a way that respects users' attention and will. And at the level of linguistic and conceptual dimensions that shape how we understand persuasive technology, a major project looms in clarifying and advancing the vocabulary for the myriad varieties of influence, especially as they pertain to nonrational avenues of persuasion. For example, where do the boundaries lie between different forms of influence such as manipulation, suggestion, coercion, exhortation, etc.? In particular, how can these boundaries be better clarified with reference to the morally salient factors that distinguish them?

Ultimately, the aim for persuasive technology ethics should be to transcend questions of harm minimization and pursue the positive enhancement of people's autonomy. At the level of design, this may involve advancing the technological awareness of and sensitivity to users' tasks and goals. It could also entail the use of counter-technologies to mitigate distractions, for example, whether they arise from other technologies or some other external source. Examples may include, for instance, a web browser plug-in that blocks ads or a word processor with a 'focus mode' that blocks out interruptions from other distracting programmes on the user's computer. At the level of upstream determinants of design, key questions include how business models can be created that make it valuable for design to enhance users' autonomy rather than simply not crossing a line in undermining it. Finally, at the level of how we think and talk about persuasive technologies, one could imagine the proliferation of validated metaphors of beneficent influence such as a 'coach', 'guide', 'buddy', 'partner' and so on. I deliberately use the qualification 'validated' here because it would seem particularly important for these metaphors of persuasive nuance not to themselves become tools of undue persuasion (e.g. mere corporate marketing tools or the basis for 'greenwashing' efforts) by merely being able to say, rather than having to verify, that they are in fact on the side of the user. To mitigate such deceptive use, one could imagine the development of a vocabulary and set of expectations for such persuasive metaphors which would enable users to explicitly and confidently delegate aspects of their autonomy to persuasive systems.

Looking into the future, there will be no shortage of substantive ethical questions about persuasive technologies in need of attention any time soon. As these technologies become ever more ubiquitous and indispensable in our lives, attention to their ethical dimensions—which extend into numerous areas well beyond the ones I have briefly surveyed here—will become all the more essential for promoting the well-being of users, designers, and society as a whole.

Conclusion

The ethics of persuasive technology is an emerging field with unique significance and urgency across a wide range of domains. Success in this area will depend on not only advancing the ethical analysis but also clarifying the philosophical landscape that underlies and enables it. That philosophical landscape includes questions of the varieties of forms of influence, in particular, the varieties of nonrational pathways of influence.

Since time immemorial, a great deal of the success of our individual and collective lives has depended on the success of persuasive engagements. In our time, digital technologies have dramatically extended our capacities of persuasion in ways that stand to amplify the harms as well as benefits, depending on the nature of the design. The ethics of persuasive technology, though a young area of work, is poised to inform these technologies' design if, moving forward, it can receive attention that is commensurate with its significance. Informing design in this way will be essential if we are to realize the promise of these technologies, which, if conceived correctly, we can use to persuade ourselves in better ways, and towards better ends.

References

Berdichevsky, Daniel, and Neuenschwander, Erik (1999), 'Toward an Ethics of Persuasive Technology', *Communications of the ACM* 42(5), 51–58.

Blumenthal-Barby, Jennifer S. (2014), 'A Framework for Assessing the Moral Status of "Manipulation"', in Christian Coons and Michael Weber, eds, *Manipulation: Theory and Practice* (Oxford: Oxford University Press), 121–134.

Borgmann, Albert (1987), *Technology and the Character of Contemporary Life: A Philosophical Inquiry* (Chicago, IL: University of Chicago Press).

Eyal, Nir (2013), *Hooked: A Guide to Building Habit-Forming Products* (CreateSpace).

Ferster, Charles B., and Skinner, Burrhus F. (1957), *Schedules of Reinforcement* (New York, NY: Appleton-Century-Crofts).

Floridi, Luciano, and Sanders, John W. (2004), 'On the Morality of Artificial Agents', *Minds and Machines* 14(3), 349–379.

Fogg, Brian J. (2002), 'Persuasive Technology: Using Computers to Change What We Think and Do', *Ubiquity* December, 5.

Fogg, Brian J., Cuellar, Gregory, and Danielson, David (2007), 'Motivating, Influencing, and Persuading Users', in Andrew Sears and Julie A. Jacko, eds, *The Human–Computer Interaction Handbook* (CRC press), 159–172.

Frankfurt, Harry G. (1988), *The Importance of What We Care About: Philosophical Essays* (Cambridge: Cambridge University Press).

Gray, Colin M., Kou, Yubo, Battles, Bryan, Hoggatt, Joseph, and Toombs, Austin L. (2018), 'The Dark (Patterns) Side of UX Design', *Proceedings of the 2018 CHI Conference on Human Factors in Computing Systems April*, 1–14.

Itthipuripat, Sirawaj, Vo, Vy A., Sprague, Thomas C., and Serences, John T. (2019), 'Value-Driven Attentional Capture Enhances Distractor Representations in Early Visual Cortex', *PLoS Biology* 17(8), e3000186.

Jacobs, Naomi (2020), 'Two Ethical Concerns about the Use of Persuasive Technology for Vulnerable People', *Bioethics* 34(5), 519–526.

James, William (1890), *The Principles of Psychology* (New York: Henry Holt and Company).

Kahneman, D. (2011), *Thinking, Fast and Slow* (New York: Farrar, Straus and Giroux).

Kane, Robert (1996), *The Significance of Free Will* (New York: Oxford University Press).

Kaptein, Maurits, and Eckles, Dean (2010), 'Selecting Effective Means to Any End: Futures and Ethics of Persuasion Profiling', in *International Conference on Persuasive Technology* (Berlin, Heidelberg: Springer), 82–93.

Kight, Raymond, and Gram-Hansen, Sandra B. (2019), 'Do Ethics Matter in Persuasive Technology?', in Harri Oinas-Kukkonen, Khin Than Win, Evangelos Karapanos, Pasi Karppinen, and Eleni Kyza, eds, *International Conference on Persuasive Technology* (Cham: Springer), 143–155.

Lacey, Cherie, and Caudwell, Catherine (2019), 'Cuteness as a "Dark Pattern" in Home Robots', in *2019 14th ACM/IEEE International Conference on Human–Robot Interaction (HRI)* (Institute of Electrical and Electronics Engineers), 374–381.

Lanham, Richard A. (2006), *The Economics of Attention: Style and Substance in the Age of Information* (Chicago, IL: University of Chicago Press).

Latour, Bruno (1992), 'Where Are the Missing Masses? The Sociology of a Few Mundane Artifacts', in Wiebe E. Bijker and John Law, eds, *Shaping Technology/Building Society: Studies in Sociotechnical Change*, Vol. 1 (Cambridge, MA: MIT Press), 225–258.

Mark, Gloria, Gudith, Daniela, and Klocke, Ulrich (2008), 'The Cost of Interrupted Work: More Speed and Stress', in *Proceedings of the SIGCHI Conference on Human Factors in Computing Systems* (ACM), 107–110.

Mathur, Arunesh, Acar, Gunes, Friedman, Michael J., Lucherini, Elena, Mayer, Jonathan, Chetty, Marshini, and Narayanan, Arvind (2019), 'Dark Patterns at Scale: Findings from a Crawl of 11K Shopping Websites', *Proceedings of the ACM on Human–Computer Interaction* 3, 1–32.

McCarthy, John, Minsky, Marvin L., Rochester, Nathaniel, and Shannon, Claude E. (2006), 'A Proposal for the Dartmouth Summer Research Project on Artificial Intelligence, August 31, 1955', *AI Magazine* 27(4), 12.

Mill, John S. (1989 [1859]), *JS Mill: 'On Liberty' and Other Writings* (Cambridge: Cambridge University Press).

Oinas-Kukkonen, Harri (2010), 'Behavior Change Support Systems: A Research Model and Agenda', in *International Conference on Persuasive Technology*, 4–14.

Oinas-Kukkonen, Harri, and Harjumaa, Marja (2008), 'A Systematic Framework for Designing and Evaluating Persuasive Systems', in *International Conference on Persuasive Technology*, 164–176.

Pennock, Joland R. (1972), 'Coercion: An Overview', in *Coercion* (New York: Routledge), 1–15.

Pereboom, Derk (2001), *Living without Free Will* (Cambridge: Cambridge University Press).

Powers, Penny (2007), 'Persuasion and Coercion: A Critical Review of Philosophical and Empirical Approaches', *HEC Forum*, 19(2), 125–143.

Raz, Joseph (1986), *The Morality of Freedom* (Oxford: Clarendon Press).

Rivlin, Gary (2007), 'Slot Machines for the Young and Active', *New York Times*, 15 March, http://www.nytimes.com/2007/12/10/business/10slots.html, accessed 6 September 2022.

Schroeder, Ralph, and Cowls, Josh (2014), 'Big Data, Ethics, and the Social Implications of Knowledge Production', in *Proceedings of KDD Data Ethics Workshop*, Vol. 24, 1–4.

Schüll, Natasha D. (2012), *Addiction by Design: Machine Gambling in Las Vegas* (Princeton, NJ: Princeton University Press).

Seaver, Nick (2019), 'Captivating Algorithms: Recommender Systems as Traps', *Journal of Material Culture* 24(4), 421–436.

Smids, Jilles (2012), 'The Voluntariness of Persuasive Technology', in *International Conference on Persuasive Technology, Persuasive Technology. Design for Health and Safety*, 123–132.

Spahn, Andreas (2011), 'And Lead Us (Not) into Persuasion … ? Persuasive Technology and the Ethics of Communication', *Science and Engineering Ethics* 18, 633–650.

Strauss, David A. (1991), 'Persuasion, Autonomy, and Freedom of Expression', *Columbia Law Review* 91(2), 334–371.

Sunstein, Cass R. (2015), 'Nudging and Choice Architecture: Ethical Considerations', Yale Journal on Regulation, Forthcoming, Harvard John M. Olin Discussion Paper Series Discussion Paper No. 809, January.

Susser, Daniel, Roessler, Beate, and Nissenbaum, Helen (2019), 'Technology, Autonomy, and Manipulation', *Internet Policy Review* 8(2), 22.

United Nations General Assembly (1948), 'Universal Declaration of Human Rights', *UN General Assembly* 302(2), 14–25.

Verbeek, Peter-Paul (2009), 'Ambient Intelligence and Persuasive Technology: The Blurring Boundaries between Human and Technology', *Nanoethics* 3(3), 231–242.

Verbeek, Peter-Paul (2011), *Moralizing Technology: Understanding and Designing the Morality of Things* (Chicago, IL: University of Chicago Press).

Winner, Langdon (1980), 'Do Artifacts Have Politics?', *Daedalus* 109(1), 121–136.

....

CHAPTER 16

HOW ROBOTS HAVE POLITICS

....

ROBERT SPARROW

INTRODUCTION

....

IN an influential essay, published in the 1980s, philosopher of technology Langdon Winner (1980), asked, 'Do artefacts have politics?' His answer, confirmed by sub-sequent decades of science and technology studies, was a resounding 'Yes!' Artefacts have political choices embedded in their design and entrench these politics in their applications. Moreover, because technologies are better suited to serving some ends rather than others, artefacts shape the societies in which they are developed by shaping the circumstances of their own use. In this chapter, I will explore *how* robots have politics and how those politics are relevant to their ethics. I will suggest that, for a number of reasons, robots have *more* politics than do other sorts of artefacts.

ROBOTS, POLITICS, ETHICS

....

Robots differ from most of the other digital technologies discussed in this collection by virtue of being orientated towards the physical world. We might say that they are 'embodied computers'. A more workaday definition has it that they are programmable machines capable of interacting with their physical environment (Lin et al. 2011). Robots are computers with actuators. Some authorities suggest that they must be cap-able of 'complex actions' (Ben-Ari and Mondada 2018). Notice that entirely remotely controlled machines will not count as robots according to this definition, while some devices that people don't normally think of as being robots, such as automatic teller machines, dishwashers, and washing machines, may, depending upon where we set the bar for 'complex'. The lack of precision in this definition foregrounds the fact that 'robot' is a social, rather than a natural, category, defined by a history of use rather than by any distinctive features of its application.

Politics is about power: it is about who gets what, when, and how (Lasswell 1950). It is about who gets to make decisions and who gets ordered about. It is about the ability of some people to make choices that shape the choices of others. The more sophisticated our analysis of politics, the better our understanding of the way robots have it. In particular, Foucauldian analyses of power and its relationship to knowledge (Foucault 1991) undoubtedly have much to offer discussions of the relationship between the designers of robots, robots themselves, and the uses of robots. This would be a profitable line for future enquiry. However, for the sake of the current discussion, it will suffice to proceed with the traditional political science definition proffered here, as it is sufficient to generate and illuminate a large number of ethical and political questions about the design and uses of robots.

An understanding of the politics of robots is necessary in order to formulate an adequate account of the ethical issues they raise. The appropriate distribution of power is itself an ethical question (Sparrow 2023). The range of policy options available to shape, or regulate, the uptake and uses of robots is also determined, in part, by the political interests at stake in the various alternatives, as well as by the extent to which robots lend themselves to serving these. As we shall see, many of the ethical controversies about social robots turn on questions about the politics of representation as these are raised by robots.

Technologies and politics

The question as to whether artefacts have politics or not is in many ways the key dispute between two influential and popular accounts of the relation between technologies and their users.

Technological determinists argue that history is driven by—determined by—technologies themselves or perhaps by the process of technological development (Marx and Smith 1994). Perhaps the most famous expression of technological determinism was Karl Marx's claim, in *The Poverty of Philosophy*, that 'The handmill gives you society with the feudal lord: the steam-mill, society with the industrial capitalist' (Marx 1969: 109). However, technological determinism is by no means confined to—or even most popular on—the Left. Whenever you hear a politician or a tech mogul suggest that 'the future is coming and we need to get ready for it', they are invoking technological determinism.

If technological determinism gives too much power to technology, the most popular alternative gives too little. Engineers will often insist that 'technology is neutral'. The same sentiment animates the claim that 'Guns don't kill, people do.'

Winner argued that neither of these claims about technology is true. Instead, technologies shape their uses, and the societies in which they are used, without entirely determining either of these things. Technologies 'have politics' in at least two ways.

First, they are the products of the circumstances in which they are developed and are often developed in order to try to advance particular political agendas (Winner 1980).

For instance, the digital technologies that play such a pronounced role in daily life today have been developed by a remarkably small number of wealthy global corporations, which overwhelmingly employ a particular type of person (i.e. [mostly] male engineers). Moreover, they are structured by design choices to privilege certain values over others and to establish certain sorts of relationships between people, which are inherently political. We might think of this phenomenon as technologies being 'given' or at least 'inheriting' politics. Human beings shape technologies through the choices that they make when they are first being developed. Once these choices have been made, we may not be able to 'unmake' them. For instance, when societies embraced the automobile, it led to an urban geography and a distribution of population in the suburbs, to which all future proposed transport solutions must respond.

The second way in which technologies have politics is more subtle and more controversial. Particular technologies are good for doing some things and bad for others. Although Winner himself did not express his point this way, technologies have 'affordances' (Norman 1988). An affordance is what a technology makes possible but also what it makes impossible, as well as what it encourages those who use it to believe to be possible or impossible (Davis and Chouinard 2016). To a person with a hammer, everything looks like a nail. A hammer has limited utility for picking one's teeth, or cushioning one's head while sleeping, or for eating. It is little wonder that hammers are mainly used for hitting things. A pistol fits in the hand so as to be pointed and it frames a target in its sights at the same time as it guides the user's finger to the trigger. It is good for shooting and shooting is good for killing and little else. This facility for some uses and resistance to others means that technologies shape the activities of those who use them. In many cases, the influence that a technology exerts on its users will itself have implications for relations between people; that is to say, it will be political.

Winner was not the last word on the relationship between technology and politics and a vigorous debate has continued in science and technology studies concerning the extent to which technologies 'themselves' should be thought of as having politics and the extent to which these politics might be a function of their social and/or historical context (Joerges 1999; Feenberg 2010). Nevertheless, it is fair to say that the subsequent discussion has, for the most part, involved various refinements or reformulations of Winner's key insights rather than a rejection of them (Verbeek 2011). Again, I have chosen to frame my discussion using Winner's analysis, rather than some of the more sophisticated more recent analyses, for the sake of the clarity of the discussion and because the problematic that Winner set out is sufficient to progress arguments about the ethics of the design of robots a long way beyond the existing state of the art.

ROBOTS AND THEIR AFFORDANCES

An important reason why robots have more politics than other technologies is that they have more—and more complex—affordances than other technologies. Robots combine the complexity of computers with the materiality of tools. Their sophistication means that they can be used to do many different things in many different circumstances, while their materiality means that their affordances are sometimes very pronounced. For instance, if a robot cannot pick up objects of a certain class or certain shape because of the nature of its manipulators, this will place very definite limits on the use of the robot. What it can do with what it can pick up, though, may be any number of things, which will depend on choices made by the designer.

The claim that robots have more affordances than other tools does need to be made with some care. Every technology makes some input to every possible use scenario. That is to say, the shape of a hammer, for instance, is relevant to—and makes a hammer more or less useful for—any task one could imagine. What is different about robots, though, is that because of the flexibility of the technology, robots will often make *different*, consciously considered, contributions to a much wider variety of use scenarios. Designers of robots have to think about how their robot might serve—or discourage—users who may desire to do any number of different things with the robot. In doing so, they must make assumptions about the bodies and capabilities of users and about the environments in which the robots will function. These assumptions are then 'built into' the robot.

One striking example of the import of the affordances of robots may be found in the debate about the impact of armed drones on international conflicts.[1] Remotely piloted aircraft, like the United States' Predator and Reaper drones, allow the states that can field them an unprecedented power to intervene in the affairs of other nations without putting the lives of their own soldiers at risk (Singer 2009). Yet despite their technological sophistication, these weapons are very good for doing two things only. They have high-powered cameras and systems for intercepting electronic communications, which are great for surveillance. They can be used to kill people, either directly with the missiles and bombs they carry or by illuminating the target with a laser target designator in order that a missile or bomb launched from another system may strike it more accurately. However, they are unable to do anything more than that. Importantly, they do not allow those who operate them to dig a ditch or build a hospital or have a conversation with a villager.[2] Consequently, they have limited utility for nation-building or for winning hearts and minds (Sparrow 2009a). It should hardly come as a surprise then that the United States has adopted a policy of targeted killing in response to insurgent movements rather than attempting a more ambitious—but arguably more productive— political engagement with them. The absence of risk to the operator also allows—even encourages—states to deploy and use drones in situations in which they would not deploy manned platforms, which in turn elevates the risk of accidental war (Sparrow 2009b). Possession of drones also makes it more tempting for governments to resort to the use of force to try to impose their will on other nations by reducing the chance of a public backlash when troops sent overseas return in body bags (Enemark 2013; Kaag and Kreps 2014). In all these ways, the affordances of the technology arguably determine its use and thus its political significance.

The affordances of drones are also relevant to the discussion of the ethics of their use on a smaller scale. A major source of ethical discomfort about drones is the fact that they facilitate 'risk-free' killing. This capacity to distance the operators from their targets is itself one of the key affordances of drones (Strawser 2010). That the operators are not at risk seems to imply that they cannot demonstrate courage, which has been a source of some dismay in military circles (Kirkpatrick 2015; The Economist 2014). There has also been some discussion of whether the operators can demonstrate or cultivate other virtues that have previously been held to be central to the role-morality of a 'warrior' (Sparrow 2013; Sparrow 2015). Perhaps in response to the difficulty of showing that the operation of drones requires physical courage, there has also been increased attention paid to the possibility that operators require moral courage to operate drones and to evidence that suggests that they may suffer post-traumatic stress syndrome (Enemark 2019; Lee 2018). It seems likely that the gap between what operators see—which may include war crimes and other horrific scenes—and what they can do to intervene in events itself plays a central role in generating stress amongst the operators of drones (Sparrow 2009a).

The politics of the technology also plays a central role in the debate about the development of autonomous weapon systems. Again, critics worry that by removing human oversight entirely these weapons make killing easier and war more likely (Singer 2009; Human Rights Watch 2012). One particularly worrying prospect is that, owing to the lack of risk to the operator, these weapons will be placed in more aggressive force postures, increasing the risk of accidental war and opening up the possibility that wars will be started by decisions made by machines. Both critics and defenders of these systems have responded by suggesting that they should remain under 'meaningful human control' at all times (Article 36 2014; Santoni and Van den Hoven 2018; Scharre 2018). Unfortunately, the fact that these machines can operate without direct human supervision almost guarantees that they will do so. Any attempt to maintain a human being in the loop would vitiate most of the advantages of autonomy. Once they reach a certain level of sophistication, robotic weapons operating autonomously will outperform—and therefore defeat—robots that need to communicate with a human operator while in combat (Adams 2001; Sparrow and Lucas 2016). Paying attention to the way in which the affordances of these machines will shape their use lends force to the idea that a prohibition on the development of machines with this capacity would be the only way to address the risk of accidental war they are likely to create.

Finally, a similar dynamic is present in discussions of the future of transport once it becomes possible for cars to operate without direct human supervision. As driverless vehicle technology has become more sophisticated, it has become obvious that a problematic stage in the development of this technology is when it is good enough to be relied upon in most situations but not perfect. Human beings struggle to pay attention to a task that they are not actively engaged in, which means that it is not plausible to rely upon human beings to resume control of the vehicle when the driving task exceeds the capacities of the autonomous drive system (Endsley 2017; Shladover 2016). The only safe driverless vehicles will be those that exceed the performance of human beings across the range of driving situations they are likely to encounter and which do not rely upon the human driver to take control at speed. However, once driverless vehicles are safer for third parties than vehicles driven by human beings, it looks as though it will be unethical for a human being to be in control of a vehicle on a public road (Sparrow and Howard 2017). Removing human beings from control of the vehicles in which they travel in turn is highly likely to alter their relationship with the vehicle, including discouraging private ownership (Masoud and Jayakrishnan 2016). In this way, the affordances of this technology are likely to drive a series of significant changes in how people travel and thus in the transport system as a whole.

Robots and representation

Another reason why robots have more politics than other artefacts is that they will often have a 'representational content'. In part this is because the very idea of a robot already comes loaded with so many expectations as a result of the history of representations of robots in film and literature. The origins of the word robot, in Capek's play 'RUR' (1999) connect it to ideas about artificial persons, labour, and slavery, which associations it has carried ever since (Hampton 2015; Morrell 2015). Unsurprisingly, fears about robots replacing human beings in various roles are endemic to debates about the future of robotics.

However, the other reason why robots have representational content relates to their embodiment. Robots often 'look like' something—an animal, a person, or a 'robot'—and this resemblance communicates ideas about their function, potential, and role. Indeed, it turns out that people tend to place robots in social categories and to attribute both identity and personality to them (Duffy 2003; Lee et al. 2006; Tay et al. 2014). Designers of robots have in turn been quick to use this fact to their advantage. For instance, engineers have made robots modelled on dogs (Fujita 2001) or seals (Shibata et al. 2001) in order to mobilize people's affective responses to these animals in their encounter with the robot. Humanoid and other social robots are given faces with big eyes and exaggerated expressiveness, again so that robots can use their 'faces' to communicate with human beings (Breazeal 2003). The capacity of robots to convey meaning through their bodies and 'facial' expressions is essential to the functionality of social robots.

The moment robots represent things (or people), they participate in—and may be evaluated on the basis of—a politics of representation. In some cases, ethical questions may arise concerning the way in which the designers of robots use their capacity to represent things to achieve their goals; that is to say, that robots represent anything at all may be problematic. In other cases, the way in which robots represent people (in particular) may be problematic.

The use of the capacity of robots to represent things has been controversial in several contexts in which it has thought to be deceptive (Boden et al. 2017; Sharkey and Sharkey 2020; Sullins 2012). For instance, some engineers have developed, or have proposed developing, companion robots for aged care settings, which look to rely on older people treating the robot as if it were a real animal (Sparrow 2002). Deceiving people, even for their own benefit, is *prima facie* unethical. More generally, social robots seem to rely upon people responding to them as though they have capacities that they do not have. For instance, if I look forward to being greeted by a robot because I think that it is pleased to see me, then it seems as though I have been tricked into a response that I would not have had, had I been fully conscious that the robot has no feelings at all.[3] In these sorts of applications, it is the fact that the robot is referring to—represents— something that is not a robot (an animal, a smiling person) that is ethically problematic.

Two other ethical controversies involve the *way* that robots represent people.

Predictably, as robots have become more sophisticated, some engineers have turned to designing sex robots. Perhaps equally predictably, philosophers interested in ro- botics, and also the media, have been quick to discuss the ethics of sex robots (Danaher and MacArthur 2017; Kubes 2019; Levy 2008; Sullins 2012; Whitby 2012; see also Sterri and Earp, this volume).

One obvious—and key—question about sex robots concerns how they represent women (Richardson 2015). Sex robots will convey ideas about how women look, or should look, and also ideas about how women should behave. Both seem problem- atic. Sex robots—indeed 'female' robots generally—participate in and reinforce a fa- miliar set of sexist stereotypes about women's bodies: big lips and big breasts abound (Kubes 2019). They also risk reducing women to their bodies and/or to their sexuality. Indeed, at a deeper level, in building an object in the image of a woman, the designers of sex robots risk implying that women are objects (Richardson 2016). Building an ob- ject in the image of a woman for the purposes of sex, then, might—not unreasonably— be taken to imply that women are fundamentally sex objects, or at least that the most important thing about women is that men can have sex with them. Similarly, when it comes to the behavioural repertoire of sex robots, they are good for only one thing. The fact that sex robots are always available for sex might be thought to express the idea that women are—or should be—always available to satisfy the sexual desires of men (Gutiu 2016).

As well as the argument about what sex robots represent, there is also a question about what sex *with* robots represents. If sex robots represent women, then sex with a robot arguably represents sex with a woman. However, it seems highly unlikely that the users of sex robots will ask the robot for consent before they have sex with it, in which case sex with the robot will arguably represent sex with a woman without consent—and thus rape. Alternatively, if the robot is programmed always to explicitly say yes to sex or we interpret sex with a robot as representing sex with a consenting woman, then, again, sex robots represent women as always available for sex (Sparrow 2017).

None of this seems especially egalitarian and all of it seems ripe for—and has come in for—criticism. One set of worries relates to the implications of such stereotypes for be- haviour. Will sex robots encourage men to treat women like objects? Will they make it the case that men are more likely to rape women (Danaher 2017)? Another set of worries concerns what these stereotypes communicate or express (Richardson 2016; Sparrow 2017). Reducing women to their bodies or suggesting that they are always available for sex is arguably sexist and disrespectful, even if it doesn't alter the behaviour of men in the way that the media effects argument suggests.

A salient response to these concerns about the politics of the representation of women by robots is to point out that sex robots seem no different, in these various regards, from representations of women in other media, most obviously pornography, but also much film and cinema advertising. For the most part, the 1960s and 1970s feminist argument that these sorts of representations are unethical appears to have been lost in most parts of the world today; or, at least, such images are still being made and consumed without much evidence of controversy. Moreover, later waves of feminists have questioned previous generations' criticisms of pornography and sex work. 'Sex positive' feminism celebrates sex, female desire, and women's bodies (Rubin 1984). It is certainly open to someone who is sympathetic to these commitments to insist that they should extend to include robots.

This argument by analogy with other forms of media might be resisted, though, by insisting that the fact that robots are embodied, mobile, and share three-dimensional space with us means that representation functions differently in the case of robots.

As intimated above, there is some evidence to suggest that people unconsciously respond to robots as though the robots were alive (Bartneck et al. 2009; Fink 2012; Krach et al. 2008; Reeves and Nass 1998). It might, therefore, be argued that our interactions with robots have more power to shape our behaviour than our interactions with other forms of media. This is, indeed, a claim that engineers have sometimes made in favour of the use of robots in educational contexts (Belpaeme et al. 2018). If it is true, then, as well as advertising the educational virtues of robots, engineers should be aware of the possibility that some robots might teach the wrong lessons, perhaps even contrary to the intentions of their designers, by virtue of the way they represent people. Certainly, we would have grounds to look again, more critically, at the way in which sex robots represent women. Whether the empirical premise about the causal powers of robots is true or not is, of course, another question. One can only hope that more careful research with robots, with properly designed studies, will resolve the question one way or another in the future.

Alternatively, it might be argued that even if robots do not have more power to shape behaviour than other forms of media, their embodied and mobile nature means that they communicate, or express, *more*—or communicate or express things in a different way—than do other media forms. I am not aware of this argument being made in the literature in a fashion that clearly distinguishes it from the claim that robots have more power to influence the behaviour of those who interact with them than do other media. Nevertheless, it is clearly a logical possibility. One might, for instance, argue that the amount of labour and technological ingenuity required to build a robot means that the choices of designers deserve more scrutiny, or to be taken more seriously than do the choices made by the authors of more disposable cultural artefacts (Sparrow 2017).[4] One might argue that the fact that we are primed by evolution to treat moving things as though they are alive means that we are less capable of critically interrogating the messages they communicate. Even if this doesn't mean that we are more likely to be influenced by them in terms of our behaviour, it might mean that they have more power to offend or to express sentiments that we would normally want to evaluate ethically. Finally, a more subtle—and more interesting—claim would be that representation works differently in robots than in other media because robots are icons of a particularly potent sort. For instance, while someone might say of a photo that represents a woman with large breasts that 'the woman in the photo has large breasts', we tend to say of, for instance, a sex robot that *it* has large breasts rather than that it *represents* a woman with large breasts. This tendency of the signifier and the signified to become entangled in the body of the robot might in turn be held to mean that robots communicate more than other media.

While (most) sex robots represent women, humanoid robots in general seem to represent people more generally as well. Ethical questions also arise here.

As with other forms of media, one question concerns who gets to be represented. Most humanoid robots have white surfaces; where they have 'skin', this is almost always 'white' skin. While it is an empirical matter whether this means that people treat robots as though they are White, it strongly suggests that most robots represent White people (Bartneck et al. 2018: Sparrow 2019). Moreover, because race is socially constructed, to 'have' race is just to be treated according to a racial schema. Thus, if people *do* treat robots differently on the basis of their surface colours, robots really *will* have race (Sparrow 2020). The vast majority of humanoid robots will turn out to be White.[5]

However, as I noted above in 'Robots and representation', historically, robots were slaves. Even today, we expect robots to be designed to serve human beings. Humanoid robots, then, represent people who are slaves—indeed, they represent people *as* slaves. This seems ethically problematic in itself. Just as one might worry about the impact that sex bots might have on the way that men treat women, one might worry about the impact that humanoid robots have on the way that we all treat each other. Just as one might worry about the messages that sex robots communicate about women, one might worry about the messages that humanoid robots communicate about people.

The historical association between robots and slaves also complexifies the race politics of robots (Chude-Sokei 2016). Although their surfaces will usually code them as White, their nature as slaves codes them as Black. Which of these codings will triumph in any particular context is an empirical matter, highly deserving of further study (Sparrow 2019). Either way, though, representing people as slaves seems highly problematic.

THE POLITICS OF DESIGN

The politics—and thus ethics—that robots have by virtue of what they represent is a matter of public knowledge. Indeed, it is a function of what the public think about them. As we have seen, in many—but not all, insofar as it is sometimes a function of the behaviour of robots— cases it exists at the surface of the robot. However, some of the affordances, and thus the politics, of robots will not be obvious to the user. The choices made by engineers will often have consequences for the options available to the users of robots in ways that are very unlikely to be transparent to those who use or encounter them. The more we interact with robots, the more the nature of our activities and our relationships with other people will be shaped by the decisions of those who design the robots with which we interact.

Another important set of ethical and political questions therefore arises regarding the design of robots and who gets to design them. Whose interests will robots serve? The relative lack of diversity in the engineering profession, and in the senior executive of the universities and corporations that are funding research into robotics, makes these questions especially pressing. Sex robots are being designed by men, despite women arguably having a greater unmet need for sexual satisfaction (Mahar et al. 2020). An enormous amount of robotics research is being funded by the military, or at least dedicated to military purposes, despite the many other human needs that robots might be designed to serve (Sparrow 2012). Robots for use in mine clearing and drug delivery in the global South are being designed by engineers from the global North. My own experience visiting robotics labs and attending robotics conferences suggests that robots for aged care are being built by young people trying to answer the question, 'How can robots help the elderly?' rather than 'What do older people need?' or even 'What technologies could improve the lives of older people?': answers to these latter questions might not include robots. One might well wonder how appropriate it is to have members of each group designing robots in each case. Not only do these dynamics risk the design of robots that fail to serve the needs of their intended user group, but they also invite questions about the right of the designers of robots to be exercising power over the lives of their users in this way.

Indeed, there is a danger that the design relationship is fundamentally authoritarian. Designers make choices that shape the experiences of, and the choices available to, users, and users have very limited capacity to influence these. In some applications of robots, users may be able to express opinions on the design by the choices they make as consumers. However, the market is a poor substitute for ethical and political deliberation, and the outcomes of markets often differ in a number of reasonably well-known ways from those that would emerge from democratic political discussions (Sen 1977). Moreover, in many cases the users of robots will not have any choice in whether to engage with the robot or not and will certainly not be responsible for deciding whether or not to buy it. In order to try to address, or at least reduce, the asymmetry in the relationship between the designers and users of robots, many engineers are now turning to ideas about user-centred, participatory, or value-centred design.

No matter who designs robots, or how, we will also need to ask how they will alter relations between people, and who will be empowered and disempowered as a result of these changes.[6]

One issue concerns access to, and control over, the information collected and generated by robots. Many robots, especially social robots, should be expected to generate and store a large amount of information about their interactions with users and thus about their users themselves. Access to this information will grant knowledge of, and some degree of power over, users. Debates about privacy, consent, and control over information will therefore be central to determining the ethical uses of robots (Calo 2012).

A key question in determining the implications of robots for the distribution of political power, which is also of broader ethical interest, is who—if anyone—will be responsible for the outcomes of the operations of robots. Holding someone responsible for something is an exercise of power, which attempts to shape the choices of the responsible party. For that matter, to have responsibility for something is, in most cases, to have the power to make choices about it.[7] When robots rely on machine learning, it may seem that this opens a 'responsibility gap' such that it is no longer appropriate to hold the designers or operators of the robots responsible for the consequences of 'its' actions, which they could neither predict nor control (Matthias 2004; Sparrow 2007). While many people have this intuition, it turns out to be hard to support without attributing a form of moral agency to machines, which they are unlikely to have until they become full moral persons (Sparrow 2021). At the very least, legal responsibility for the consequences of the operations of robots may be assigned to either the designers or operators. It is also plausible to think that both the operators and the designers of robots share moral responsibility for the outcomes of their operations by virtue of knowingly exposing their users to the risks that the robot may go awry, even if—as may sometimes be the case—they do not know how likely this is or what form it might take (Noorman 2014).

Another question, which looms large in relation to many applications of robots, concerns what happens to those whose labours are no longer required because a robot can do their job better, or at least cheaper. Fears of technologically generated unemployment have long haunted discussions of robots and have re-emerged with a vengeance in the past decade (Brynjolfsson and McAfee 2014; Danaher 2019; Danaher, this volume; Ford 2015; Susskind and Susskind 2015). Clearly, robots—or things that should be recognized as robots—have already put many people out of work, on assembly lines, in laundries, and in printing, for instance. However, technological change has always led to changes in the nature of work, including the elimination of some jobs: the question is what happens to those people who used to do those jobs. Do they—or at least the same number of other people—find new work? Predicting the future is a mug's game and philosophers have no special insight here. It is possible to find people, seemingly equally well qualified, predicting that robots will radically decrease the demand for human labour (Brynjolfsson and McAfee 2014; Danaher 2019; Ford 2015; Susskind and Susskind 2015) and that robots will simply change the nature of the work people do, with little impact on the overall rate of employment (Malone 2018: 273–281). Where philosophers can, perhaps, make some contribution is in adjudicating the justice of the various proposals that have been put forward to address the social and economic consequences of widespread technologically generated unemployment, should it occur. Thus, for instance, the suggestion that governments should respond to the rise of robots by introducing a universal basic income raises questions in political philosophy, about economic rights and distributive justice, and in ethics, about the role played by labour in a good human life, as much as it does in economics and social policy. As will be discussed further below, one of those questions concerns the justice of the designers and manufacturers of robots possessing or exercising the power to put tens of thousands of people out of work.

RESISTING ROBOTS

Because they shape social relationships, the design of robots and the regulations that make them possible are important sites of political contestation. Robots encounter resistance—and rightly so.

One place where this resistance has been very pronounced is, again, in public concerns about 'killer robots'. The prospect of autonomous weapon systems capable of choosing and attacking targets without direct human oversight has met with—I believe understandable—public hostility. This is despite the fact that it has proved remarkably hard to explain what precisely is wrong with sending a robot—rather than, for instance, using a bomb or cruise missile—to kill someone (Skerker et al. 2020; Sparrow 2016a). Nevertheless, there is, I believe, an emerging—and inevitably, appropriately, contested—body of opinion that insists that all human beings have a 'right not to be killed by a robot' (Asaro 2012; Human Rights Watch 2012). This argument, as well as a multiplicity of other arguments about the capacities and implications of autonomous weapon systems, have been taken up by the Campaign to Stop Killer Robots (2020). As a result of this campaign, and the earlier activities of the International Committee for Robot Arms Control, there are now ongoing arms control discussions about the possibility of international regulation, or even prohibition, of lethal autonomous weapons systems, in the United Nations Convention on Certain Conventional Weapons processes.

Similarly, feminist concerns about the implications of sex robots have resulted in a high-profile Campaign against Sex Robots. As surveyed above in the section 'Robots and representation', critics have argued that the way sex robots represent women is either inherently disrespectful or likely to have various pernicious consequences. Some authors have also worried that the development of robots will ultimately discourage people from seeking out and enjoying more meaningful relationships with other human beings (Sparrow and Sparrow 2006; Turkle 2011), a possibility that might be thought to be especially disturbing if the relationships being replaced are intimate ones (Gutiu 2016). Interestingly, one thing *almost* everybody agrees on is that the manufacture and sale of sex robots in the form of young children would be unethical.[8] Whether it is possible to reconcile this intuition with the moral permissibility of the design and use of sex robots modelled on women remains to be determined.

There is also an emerging debate about the nature of the future made possible by the development of autonomous vehicles. Early discussions of driverless vehicles touted their capacity to produce environmental benefits by reducing the vehicle fleet (Fagnant and Kockelman 2015). Once cars become capable of driving themselves, it will make little sense to own a private vehicle. When one is not using one's own car, it could be out generating an income by transporting other people for a fare. However, if one's car is transporting other people most of the time, it makes just as much sense to outsource the expenses involved in maintaining it to a third party and pay for it only when one needs it. For these reasons, many pundits expect that the development of driverless vehicles will lead to the rise of a mobility as a service model, wherein a few providers offer access to fleets of driverless vehicles to consumers who purchase trips using their mobile phones, on the model of Lyfft or Uber (Burns 2013; Zimmer 2016). Unfortunately, it is now recognized that the advent of driverless vehicles may have some perverse, and environmentally destructive, consequences. Those vehicles that do exist will spend a much greater proportion of time on the roads, thus potentially increasing congestion (Cohen and Cavoli 2019). More importantly, it is likely to lead to an increase in the total kilometres travelled: because vehicles that would otherwise have been parked may remain on the road searching for fares; because the number of people for whom travel by car is an option will increase dramatically the moment one does not need to own one (or be able to drive); and, because people are likely to be willing to tolerate longer commutes if they can do something other than drive while they are en route (Harper et al. 2016). Thus, the environmental consequences of the widespread uptake of autonomous vehicles are potentially disastrous (Morrow III et al. 2014; Pernestål et al. 2020). An alternative future would, then, involve a massive reinvestment in public transport infrastructure and particularly trains, with fleets of shared autonomous minibuses being employed to solve the 'last mile' problem by transporting people from their starting point to the train station and from the train station to their final destination (Sparrow and Howard 2017).

Finally, although it is yet to arise to the level of a public controversy, there is an argument to be had about the use of robots in aged care settings. In particular, robots might be used to supplement—rather than replace—human care and to allow people to remain in their homes for longer. However, there are both economic and design reasons to fear that robots will instead lead to an increase in the institutionalization of older persons and a decrease in human contact, to the detriment of the welfare of older persons (Sparrow and Sparrow 2006). If robots are to make a positive contribution to aged care, then it will be vital to have a vigorous debate about the appropriate mechanisms to prevent them leading to an increase in the social isolation of the elderly (Sparrow 2016b).

Robots, revolution, and rights

How concerned we should be about the politics of robots, and especially the question of who gets to determine these, will depend on how large a role we think robots will play in the future. In this context, it is striking that many pundits proclaim that robotics and artificial intelligence (AI) are poised to bring about a technological revolution, which will radically reshape the social and economic fabric of modern societies.

Indeed, a number of authors have argued that they constitute an existential threat to the human species (Barrat 2013; Bostrom 2014). For instance, famously, the 'father of AI', Marvin Minsky, is reported to have said, as early as 1970, 'Once the computers get control, we might never get it back ... if we're lucky they might decide to keep us as pets' (quoted in Darrach 1970). The abstract of Verner Vinge's influential essay, 'The Coming Technological Singularity', included the ominous prediction that 'Within thirty years, we will have the technological means to create superhuman intelligence. Shortly after, the human era will be ended' (Vinge 1993). Bill Joy included robots as one of the reasons 'Why the future doesn't need us' (Joy 2000). Less pessimistically, although only slightly less dramatically, any number of authors have predicted massive social and economic disruption due to robots (Brynjolfsson and McAfee 2014; Danaher 2019; Ford 2015; Susskind and Susskind 2015).

Whenever one hears technologists waxing lyrical about our digital future, heralding a 'Fourth industrial revolution', or warning of our impending demise at the hands of robots, one should consider how people would respond if they heard someone making the same claims about a political revolution. Imagine that you are watching the evening news, when the television goes on the fritz. A pirate television broadcast appears on the screen. In it, a bearded revolutionary holding an AK-47 says that his organization intends to bring about the same social and political changes that tech pundits predict will result from future developments in robotics. His group is, he announces, planning a revolution that will radically change the way people live over the next two decades. He and his comrades will put millions of people out of work. He will centralize political power in his own hands and in the hands of a few other people like him. They may even, he admits, have to risk killing us all in order to be able to bring about the benefits of their revolution. A quick Google search reveals that his organization is overwhelmingly made up of young men who have graduated from Stanford, Massachusetts Institute of Technology, or Carnegie Mellon. At no point does he mention elections or the possibility that people might balk at his plans.

How many people do you think would, on hearing such a broadcast, simply shrug? Most people would at least feel that they deserve a say in the plans of this group. Many would demand it. I can see no reason why our response to purported technological revolutions should be any different. If robots are going to reshape our lives, then it is vitally important that the principles according to which they are designed are determined democratically. Recognizing that robots have politics is the first step in the struggle to shape the politics of robots and, thus, the future.

ACKNOWLEDGEMENTS

I would like to thank Michael Flood for assistance with locating relevant sources and Carisa Veliz for comments and suggestions. Joshua Hatherley helped to prepare the paper for publication.

NOTES

1. It is worth observing that drones are only partially robots according to the definition set out above. To the extent that they are remotely piloted, they are not robots. However, modern drones also have some capacity to carry out complex actions, such as travelling to waypoints, or flying figure-of-eights, autonomously, which means that it is not entirely inaccurate to think of them as robots. Certainly, the public and philosophical debate about the ethics of robotic warfare has included drones in its conception of robots.
2. Robots can be used to broadcast messages via loudspeakers but, as yet, have little capacity to replicate the affordances of face-to-face conversation. It is possible that some of these functionalities will be added to remotely operated ground vehicles in the future.
3. Note that there are other ways in which robots might involve deception. For instance, designers or manufacturers might explicitly advertise their robot as having capacities that it does not in fact have. Such deception in advertising is also unethical but is hardly confined to robots.
4. An obvious objection to this line of argument is that some artists, for instance, filmmakers and novelists, may spend more time, and put more thought into, producing their films or novels than any engineer puts into building a robot. It does, however, seem plausible that this argument might succeed in distinguishing sex robots from other forms of pornography.
5. Stephen Cave and Kanta Dihal (2020) argue that this is also true of AI more generally.
6. Of course, one group who will be empowered is precisely those who design robots.
7. 'In most cases' because in some cases involving strict liability, people may be held responsible for matters over which they had no control.
8. Inevitably, some authors have defended the design and use of sex robots modelled on children (see, for instance, Moen and Sterri 2018). Given the legal restrictions on the production and ownership of even CGI-generated images of the sexual abuse of children, this argument seems highly unlikely to win the day with the broader public.

REFERENCES

Adams, Thomas K. (2001), 'Future Warfare and the Decline of Human Decision Making', *Parameters* 31(4), 57–71.
Article 36 (2014), 'Key Areas for Debate on Autonomous Weapons Systems: Memorandum for Delegates at the Convention on Certain Conventional Weapons (CCW) Meeting of Experts on Lethal Autonomous Weapons Systems (LAWS)', http://www.article36.org/wp-content/uploads/2014/05/A36-CCW-May-2014.pdf, accessed 9 August 2021.
Asaro, Peter (2012), 'On Banning Autonomous Weapon Systems: Human Rights, Automation, and the Dehumanization of Lethal Decision-Making', *International Review of the Red Cross* 94(886), 687–709.
Barrat, James (2013), *Our Final Invention: Artificial Intelligence and the End of the Human Era* (New York: St Martin's Press).
Bartneck, Christoph, Kanda, Takayuki, Mubin, Omar, and Al Mahmud, Abdullah (2009). 'Does the Design of a Robot Influence Its Animacy and Perceived Intelligence?', *International Journal of Social Robotics* 1(2), 195–204.
Bartneck, Christoph, Yogeeswaran, Kumar, Min Ser, Qi, Woodward, Graeme, Sparrow, Robert, Wang, Siheng, et al. (2018), 'Robots and Racism', in Takayuki Kanda and Selma Šabanović,

eds, HRI '18: Proceedings of the 2018 ACM/IEEE International Conference on Human–Robot Interaction (New York: ACM), 196–204, doi: https://doi.org/10.1145/3171221.3171260.

Belpaeme, Tony, Kennedy, James, Ramachandran, Aditi, Scassellati, Brian, and Tanaka, Fumihide (2018), 'Social Robots for Education: A Review', *Science Robotics* 3(21), eaat5954.

Ben-Ari, Mordechai, and Mondada, Francesco (2018), 'Robots and Their Applications', in Mordechai Ben-Ari and Francesco Mondada, eds, *Elements of Robotics* (Cham: Springer International Publishing), 1–20.

Boden, Margaret, Bryson, Joanna, Caldwell, Darwin, Dautenhahn, Kerstin, Edwards, Lilian, Kember, Sarah, et al. (2017), 'Principles of Robotics: Regulating Robots in the Real World', *Connection Science* 29(2), 124–129.

Bostrom, Nick (2014), *Superintelligence: Paths, Dangers, Strategies* (Oxford: Oxford University Press).

Breazeal, Cynthia (2003), 'Emotion and Sociable Humanoid Robots', *International Journal of Human-Computer Studies* 59(1–2), 119–155.

Brynjolfsson, Erik, and McAfee, Andrew (2014), *The Second Machine Age: Work, Progress, and Prosperity in a Time of Brilliant Technologies* (New York: W. W. Norton & Co.).

Burns, Lawrence D. (2013), 'Sustainable Mobility: A Vision of Our Transport Future', *Nature* 497 (7448), 181–182.

Calo, M. Ryan (2012), 'Robots and Privacy', in Patrick Lin, Keith Abney, and George A. Bekey, eds, *Robot Ethics: The Ethical and Social Implications of Robotics* (Cambridge, MA; London: The MIT Press), 187–201.

Campaign to Stop Killer Robots (2020), 'A Growing Global Coalition', https://www.stopkillerrobots.org/about/, accessed 9 August 2021.

Capek, Karel (1999), 'R.U.R.', in *Four Plays*, transl. Peter Majer and Cathy Porter (London: Methuen Drama), 1–99.

Cave, Stephen, and Dihal, Kanta (2020), 'The Whiteness of AI', *Philosophy & Technology* 33(4), 685–703.

Chude-Sokei, Louis (2016), *The Sound of Culture: Diaspora and Black Technopoetics* (Middletown, CT: Wesleyan University Press).

Cohen, Tom, and Cavoli, Clémence (2019), 'Automated Vehicles: Exploring Possible Consequences of Government (non)Intervention for Congestion and Accessibility', *Transport Reviews* 39(1), 129–151.

Danaher, John (2017), 'Robotic Rape and Robotic Child Sexual Abuse: Should They Be Criminalised?', *Criminal Law and Philosophy* 11(1), 71–95.

Danaher, John (2019), *Automation and Utopia: Human Flourishing in a World without Work* (Harvard, MA: Harvard University Press).

Danaher, John (2023), 'The Future of Jobs', in Véliz, Carissa, ed, *Oxford Handbook of Digital Ethics* (in press).

Danaher, John, and Macarthur, Neil, eds (2017), *Robot Sex: Social and Ethical Implications* (Cambridge, MA; London: The MIT Press).

Darrach, Brad (1970), 'Meet Shakey, the First Electronic Person', *Life Magazine*, 20 November, 58–68.

Davis, Jenny L., and Chouinard, James B. (2016), 'Theorizing Affordances: From Request to Refuse', *Bulletin of Science, Technology & Society* 36(4), 241–248.

Duffy, Brian R. (2003), 'Anthropomorphism and the Social Robot', *Robotics and Autonomous Systems* 42(3–4), 177–190.

Endsley, Mica R. (2017), 'From Here to Autonomy: Lessons Learned from Human–Automation Research', *Human Factors* 59(1), 5–27.

Enemark, Christian (2013), *Armed Drones and the Ethics of War: Military Virtue in a Post-Heroic Age* (London: Routledge).

Enemark, Christian (2019), 'Drones, Risk, and Moral Injury', *Critical Military Studies* 5(2), 150–167.

Fagnant, Daniel J., and Kockelman, Kara (2015), 'Preparing a Nation for Autonomous Vehicles: Opportunities, Barriers and Policy Recommendations', *Transportation Research Part A: Policy and Practice* 77, 167–181.

Feenberg, Andrew (2010), *Between Reason and Experience: Essays in Technology and Modernity* (Cambridge, MA: MIT Press).

Fink, Julia (2012), 'Anthropomorphism and Human Likeness in the Design of Robots and Human–Robot Interaction', in *ICSR'12: Proceedings of the 4th international conference on Social Robotics* (Berlin; Heidelberg: Springer,), 199–208.

Ford, Martin (2015), *Rise of the Robots: Technology and the Threat of a Jobless Future* (New York: Basic Books).

Foucault, Michel (1991), *Discipline and Punish: The Birth of the Prison* (London; Ringwood, Vic.: Penguin Books).

Fujita, Masahiro (2001), 'AIBO: Toward the Era of Digital Creatures', *International Journal of Robotics Research* 20(10), 781–794.

Gutiu, Sinziana M. (2016), 'The Roboticization of Consent', in Ryan Calo, Michael Froomkin, and Ian Kerr, eds, *Robot Law* (Cheltenham: Edward Elgar), 186–212.

Hampton, Gerome J. (2015), *Imagining Slaves and Robots in Literature, Film, and Popular Culture: Reinventing Yesterday's Slave with Tomorrow's Robot* (London: Lexington Books).

Harper, Corey D., Hendrickson, Chris T., Mangones, Sonia, and Samaras, Constantine (2016), 'Estimating Potential Increases in Travel with Autonomous Vehicles for the Non-Driving, Elderly and People with Travel-Restrictive Medical Conditions', *Transportation Research Part C: Emerging Technologies* 72, 1–9.

Human Rights Watch (2012), *Losing Humanity: The Case against Killer Robots*, https://www.hrw.org/report/2012/11/19/losing-humanity/case-against-killer-robots, accessed 9 August 2021.

Joerges, Bernward (1999), 'Do Politics Have Artefacts?', *Social Studies of Science* 29(3), 411–431.

Joy, Bill (2000), 'Why the Future Doesn't Need Us', *WIRED*, 4 January, https://www.wired.com/2000/04/joy-2/, accessed 18 March, 2020.

Kaag, John, and Kreps, Sarah (2014), *Drone Warfare* (Cambridge; Malden, MA: Polity).

Kirkpatrick, Jesse (2015), 'Drones and the Martial Virtue Courage', *Journal of Military Ethics* 14, 202–219.

Krach, Sören, Hegel, Frank, Wrede, Britta, Sagerer, Gerhard, Binkofski, Ferdinand, and Kircher, Tilo (2008), 'Can Machines Think? Interaction and Perspective Taking with Robots Investigated Via FMRI', *Plos One* 3(7), e2597.

Kubes, Tanja (2019), 'New Materialist Perspectives on Sex Robots. A Feminist Dystopia/Utopia?', *Social Sciences* 8(8), 224–236.

Lasswell, Harold D. (1950), *Politics, Who Gets What, When, How* (New York: Peter Smith).

Lee, Kwan Min, Peng, Wei, Jin, Seung-A., and Yan, Chang (2006), 'Can Robots Manifest Personality? An Empirical Test of Personality Recognition, Social Responses, and Social Presence in Human–Robot Interaction', *Journal of Communication* 56(4), 754–772.

Lee, Peter (2018), *Reaper Force—Inside Britain's Drone Wars* (London: John Blake Publishing).

Levy, David (2008), *Love and Sex with Robots* (New York: Harper Perennial).

Lin, Patrick, Abney, Keith, and Bekey, George (2011), 'Robot Ethics: Mapping the Issues for a Mechanized World', *Artificial Intelligence* 175(5–6), 942–949.

Mahar, Elizabeth A., Mintz, Laurie B., and Akers, Brianna M. (2020), 'Orgasm Equality: Scientific Findings and Societal Implications', *Current Sexual Health Reports* 12, 24–32.

Malone, Thomas W. (2018), *Superminds: The Surprising Power of People and Computers Thinking Together* (London: Oneworld Publications).

Marx, Karl (1969), *The Poverty of Philosophy* (New York: International Publishers).

Marx, Leo, and Smith, Merritt Roe (1994), *Does Technology Drive History? The Dilemma of Technological Determinism* (Cambridge, MA: MIT Press).

Masoud, Neda, and Jayakrishnan, R. (2016), 'Formulations for Optimal Shared Ownership and Use of Autonomous or Driverless Vehicles', in *Proceedings of the Transportation Research Board 95th Annual Meeting*, (Washington, DC: Transportation Research Board), 1–17.

Matthias, Andreas (2004), 'The Responsibility Gap: Ascribing Responsibility for the Actions of Learning Automata', *Ethics and Information Technology* 6(3), 175–183.

Moen, Ole Martin, and Sterri, Aksel Braanen (2018), 'Pedophilia and Computer-Generated Child Pornography', in David Boonin, ed., *The Palgrave Handbook of Philosophy and Public Policy* (London: Palgrave Macmillan), 369–381.

Morrell, Sascha (2015), 'Zombies, Robots, Race, and Modern Labour', *Affirmations: Of the Modern* 2(2), 101–134.

Morrow III, William R., Greenblatt, Jeffery B., Sturges, Andrew, Saxena, Samveg, Gopal, Anand, Millstein, Dev, et al. (2014), 'Key Factors Influencing Autonomous Vehicles' Energy and Environmental Outcome', in Gereon Meyer and Sven Beiker, eds, *Road Vehicle Automation* (Cham: Springer International Publishing), 127–135.

Noorman, Merel (2014), 'Responsibility Practices and Unmanned Military Technologies', *Science and Engineering Ethics* 20(3), 809–826.

Norman, Donald A. (1988), *The Psychology of Everyday Things* (New York: Basic Books).

Pernestål, Anna, Engholm, Albin, Kristoffersson, Ida, and Hammes, Johanna Jussila (2020), 'The Impacts of Automated Vehicles on the Transport System and How to Create Policies that Target Sustainable Development Goals', in Alexander Paulsson and Claus Hedegaard Sørensen, eds, *Shaping Smart Mobility Futures: Governance and Policy Instruments in times of Sustainability Transitions* (United Kingdom: Emerald Publishing Ltd).

Reeves, Byron, and Nass, Clifford Ivar (1998), *The Media Equation: How People Treat Computers, Television, and New Media Like Real People and Places* (Stanford, CA: CSLI Publications).

Richardson, Kathleen (2015), 'The "Asymmetrical Relationship": Parallels between Prostitution and the Development of Sex Robots', ACM *SIGCAS Computers and Society* 45(3), 290–293.

Richardson, Kathleen (2016), 'Sex Robot Matters: Slavery, the Prostituted, and the Rights of Machines', *IEEE Technology and Society Magazine* 35(2), 46–53.

Rubin, Gayle (1984), 'Thinking Sex: Notes for a Radical Theory of the Politics of Sexuality', in Carole S. Vance, ed., *Pleasure and Danger: Exploring Female Sexuality* (Boston, MA; London; Melbourne; Henley: Routledge and Kegan Paul), 267–319.

Santoni de Sio, Filippo, and Van den Hoven, Jeroen (2018), 'Meaningful Human Control over Autonomous Systems: A Philosophical Account', *Frontiers in Robotics and AI* 5(15), doi: https://doi.org/10.3389/Frobt.2018.00015.

Scharre, Paul (2018), *Army of None* (New York; London: W. W. Norton & Co.).

Sen, Amartya K. (1977), 'Rational Fools: A Critique of the Behavioral Foundations of Economic Theory', *Philosophy and Public Affairs* 6(4), 317–344.

Sharkey, Amanda, and Sharkey, Noel (2020), 'We Need to Talk about Deception in Social Robotics!', *Ethics and Information Technology* 11 November 2020, doi: https://doi.org/10.1007/s10676-020-09573-9.

Shibata, Takanori, Mitsui, Teruaki, Wada, Kazuyoshi, Touda, Akihiro, Kumasaka, Takayuki, Yagami, Kazumi, et al. (2001), 'Mental Commit Robot and Its Application to Therapy of Children', in *2001 Proceedings of the IEEE/ASME International Conference on Advanced Intelligent Mechatronics*, Vol. 2 (Como: IEEE), 1053–1058.

Shladover, Steven (2016), 'The Truth about "Self-Driving" Cars', *Scientific American* 314(6), 52–57.

Singer, Peter W. (2009), *Wired for War: The Robotics Revolution and Conflict in the Twenty-First Century* (New York: Penguin Press).

Skerker, Michael, Purves, Duncan, and Jenkins, Ryan (2020), 'Autonomous Weapons Systems and the Moral Equality of Combatants', *Ethics and Information Technology*, 23 February, doi: https://doi.org/10.1007/s10676-020-09528-0.

Sparrow, Robert (2002), 'The March of the Robot Dogs', *Ethics and Information Technology* 4(4), 305–318.

Sparrow, Robert (2007), 'Killer Robots', *Journal of Applied Philosophy* 24(1), 62–77.

Sparrow, Robert (2009a), 'Building a Better Warbot: Ethical Issues in the Design of Unmanned Systems for Military Applications', *Science and Engineering Ethics* 15(2), 169–187.

Sparrow, Robert (2009b), 'Predators or Plowshares? Arms Control of Robotic Weapons', *IEEE Technology and Society* 28(1), 25–29.

Sparrow, Robert (2012), 'Just Say No' to Drones', *IEEE Technology and Society* 31(1), 56–63.

Sparrow, Robert (2013), 'War without Virtue?', in Bradley Jay Strawser, ed., *Killing by Remote Control* (Oxford; New York: Oxford University Press), 84–105.

Sparrow, Robert (2015), 'Drones, Courage, and Military Culture', in George R. Lucas, Jr, ed., *Routledge Handbook of Military Ethics* (Oxford; New York: Routledge), 380–394.

Sparrow, Robert (2016a), 'Robots and Respect: Assessing the Case against Autonomous Weapon Systems', *Ethics and International Affairs* 30(1), 93–116.

Sparrow, Robert (2016b), 'Robots in Aged Care: A Dystopian Future?', *AI and Society* 31(4), 445–454.

Sparrow, Robert (2017), 'Robots, Rape, and Representation', *International Journal of Social Robotics* 9(4), 465–477.

Sparrow, Robert (2019), 'Do Robots Have Race? Race, Social Construction, and HRI', *IEEE Robotics and Automation Magazine*, 29 October, doi: https://doi.org/10.1109/MRA.2019.2927372.

Sparrow, Robert (2020), 'Robotics Has a Race Problem', *Science, Technology, and Human Values* 45(3), 538–560.

Sparrow, Robert (2021), 'Why Machines Cannot Be Moral', *AI & Society: Journal of Knowledge, Culture and Communication*, 21 January, doi: https://doi.org/10.1007/s00146-020-01132-6.

Sparrow, Robert (2023), 'Technology Ethics Assessment: Politicising the "Socratic Approach"', *Business Ethics, the Environment & Responsibility* 32(2), 454–466.

Sparrow, Robert, and Howard, Mark (2017), 'When Human Beings Are Like Drunk Robots: Driverless Vehicles, Ethics, and the Future of Transport', *Transportation Research Part C* 80, 206–215.

Sparrow, Robert, and Lucas, Jr, George (2016), 'When Robots Rule the Waves?', *Naval War College Review* 69(4), 49–78.

Sparrow, Robert, and Sparrow, Linda (2006), 'In the Hands of Machines? The Future of Aged Care', *Minds and Machines* 16, 141–161.

Strawser, Bradley J. (2010), 'Moral Predators: The Duty to Employ Uninhabited Aerial Vehicles', *Journal of Military Ethics* 9(4), 342–368.

Sterri, Aksel Braanen, and Earp, Brian D. (2023), 'The Ethics of Sex Robots', in Véliz, Carissa, ed, *Oxford Handbook of Digital Ethics* (in press).

Sullins, John P. (2012), 'Robots, Love, and Sex: The Ethics of Building a Love Machine', *IEEE Transactions on Affective Computing* 3(4), 398–409.

Susskind, Richard, and Susskind, Daniel (2015), *The Future of the Professions: How Technology Will Transform the Work of Human Experts* (Oxford: Oxford University Press).

Tay, Benedict, Jung, Younbo and Park, Taezoon (2014), 'When Stereotypes Meet Robots: The Double-Edged Sword of Robot Gender and Personality in Human–Robot Interaction', *Computers in Human Behavior* 38, 75–84.

The Economist (2014), 'Medals for Drone Pilots? The Fraught Debate over How to Honour Cyber-Warriors', *The Economist*, 29 March, 33.

Turkle, Sherry (2011), *Alone Together: Why We Expect More from Technology and Less from Each Other* (New York: Basic Books).

Verbeek, Peter-Paul (2011), *Moralizing Technology: Understanding and Designing the Morality of Things* (Chicago, IL: University of Chicago Press).

Vinge, Vernor (1993), 'The Coming Technological Singularity', *Whole Earth Review* 81, 88–95.

Whitby, Blay (2012), 'Do You Want a Robot Lover? The Ethics of Caring Technologies', in Patrick Lin, Keith Abney, and George A. Bekey, eds, *Robot Ethics: The Ethical and Social Implications of Robotics* (Cambridge, MA; London: MIT Press), 233–248.

Winner, Langdon (1980), 'Do Artifacts Have Politics?', *Daedalus* 109(1),121–136.

Zimmer, John (2016), 'The Third Transportation Revolution: Lyft's Vision for the Next Ten Years and Beyond', *Medium*, 18 September, https://medium.com/@johnzimmer/the-third-transportation-revolution-27860f05fa91#.6msd20ja6, accessed 9 August 2021.

CHAPTER 17

....

ETHICAL ISSUES WITH ARTIFICIAL ETHICS ASSISTANTS

....

ELIZABETH O'NEILL, MICHAL KLINCEWICZ, AND MICHIEL KEMMER

INTRODUCTION

FLORA is in a restaurant, chatting with a group of friends, when the conversation turns to climate change, animal welfare, and diet. By the time the waiter asks her what she'd like for lunch, Flora finds herself at a loss, unsure what to order. The locally sourced roast beef? The chicken, likely from a factory farm? Salmon? The vegan quinoa? Usually, she orders whatever sounds most appetizing. But she's just heard a lot of strongly held, conflicting views on what food choices are best for the environment and the well-being of animals. She'd like to do the right thing, and she cares about animals and the environment. However, she isn't sure what option would be best. For one thing, she's missing a lot of information that seems relevant for her decision. She wonders whether fish feel pain, how the chickens were treated, and which dish took the most resources to produce. She'd also like to know what the best arguments are for and against positions like vegetarianism. After listening to some of her friends, she's even begun to question some of her deeper values and normative beliefs like her assumption that ecosystems have only instrumental value.

What to have for lunch is just one of the many ordinary purchasing and consumption decisions we face every day. In many of these situations, we are missing information that we think might be relevant, and we haven't had a chance to fully think through the question, yet we have to make a choice. With the advent of big data and recent developments in artificial intelligence (AI) research, is there some way that computer systems could help us with this kind of decision?

Recently, a number of philosophers and computer scientists have proposed that technologies employing AI could be used to improve human moral reasoning and decision-making (Borenstein and Arkin 2016; Giubilini and Savulescu 2018; Klincewicz 2016; Savulescu and Maslen 2015; Formosa and Ryan 2021; Lara 2021; Sinnott-Armstrong and Skorburg 2021).[1] We will focus on just one part of this AI-aided moral improvement question: the case of the individual who wants to improve their morality, where what constitutes an improvement is evaluated by the individual's own values.[2] We will refer to the technology of interest in this chapter as the 'artificial ethics assistant' (AEA)—an AI system that is designed and used with the aim of improving human moral cognition.[3] We look primarily at the use of AEAs to influence purchasing and consumption decisions made by individuals; we set aside discussion of the many other possible uses of AI technologies to aid moral decision-making.[4]

If Flora were presented with an AEA, with the promise that it would help her make more moral consumer decisions, or perhaps more specifically, decisions that better align with her core moral values, would she have reason to use it? In comparison with other approaches to moral improvement, attempts to use AI technology to improve moral cognition make several potential ethical questions and problems salient. This chapter examines a selection of such problems. We begin by distinguishing three broad areas in which an individual might think their own moral reasoning and decision-making could be improved. We then sketch why one might think that AI tools could be used to support moral improvement in those areas. Finally, we discuss some of the ethical issues that AEAs might raise, looking in particular at three under-appreciated problems posed by the use of AI for moral self-improvement, namely, reliance on sensitive moral data, the inescapability of outside influences on AEAs, and AEA usage prompting the user to adopt beliefs and make decisions without adequate reasons.

MORAL SELF-IMPROVEMENT

When considering the topic of artificial ethics advisors, there is an essential preliminary question to ask: what would it mean to improve one's own moral reasoning and moral decision-making capacities?[5] Given conflicting conceptions of morality, different people have ideas of moral improvement that diverge in substance—one person thinks moral improvement involves increasing compassion; another person thinks it involves increasing devotion to family or loyalty to the country.[6] One can distinguish several aspects of moral cognition that an individual with nearly any set of values might believe could be improved.[7] One may think:

(1) One's actions, character, or other evaluable states or attributes[8] fall short of one's values and what one believes one ought to do. One admits one is sometimes

hypocritical or that one suffers from weak self-discipline. For instance, even if Flora concluded that she ought to be a vegetarian, she may be so tempted by the thought of the delicious roast beef sandwich that she orders this option despite her moral belief.

(2) One sometimes misjudges or is uncertain about what the right thing to do is, given one's values, in a particular situation. Pressure or lack of time can lead to logical errors or to a failure to consider all the information that one ordinarily believes is relevant. One might be missing information or one might have false beliefs about the non-normative features of a particular situation (perhaps Flora incorrectly thinks that the locally sourced beef has a smaller carbon footprint than imported salmon) or about relevant non-normative features of the world more generally (such as whether fish can suffer as much as farm animals). It could be due to thought patterns that one considers to be biased—Flora may tend to have more sympathy for cows than chickens yet view this tendency as a bias. Even if one is confident in one's moral beliefs and values, there is room for things to go wrong when applying them to a particular case and forming a judgement about what to do.

(3) One may also be uncertain about some fundamental moral questions or one may recognize a possibility that one is mistaken in some of one's core moral beliefs and values (or in one's understanding of them).[9] Individuals sometimes look back and think that they have been mistaken about what is right and wrong; people's moral priorities sometimes shift over time. Listening to her friend describe the plight of factory farm animals, Flora might come to think that she has made a moral mistake in the past by weighting human welfare as so much more important than animal welfare.

If one sets out to improve one's morality, then, one may do so with the aim of improving in any of these three areas—roughly, one may aim to align actions or character with moral judgements, aim to align moral judgements about particular cases with one's core moral commitments, or aim to either improve or better understand one's core moral commitments. There are many traditional tools for moral self-improvement that address aims (1)–(3). These include reflection, prayer and other religious practices, the study of texts, soliciting and following the advice of others, imitating people we admire, building up habits, structuring our environments to avoid temptations, and so on. More recently, philosophers have suggested the possibility of moral bioenhancement—the use of biomedical technologies, such as pharmacological, genetic, or neural interventions, for moral enhancement (Persson and Savulescu 2012). An AEA, if it performed as promised, would add a different kind of tool for moral self-improvement. At the same time, the use of AI for moral improvement poses a distinct set of potential ethical problems. In this chapter, we focus primarily on AEAs that could be used to advance aim 2, leaving discussion of the other aims for future work.

How could AI technology be used
to improve moral cognition?

AI, interpreted broadly, is already being used to support reasoning and decision-making in a variety of contexts: for instance, to guide decisions about whether to admit patients into intensive care; to assist predictions about how likely a defendant is to re-offend; and to assist predictions about whether one investment or another is more likely to produce a profit (Phillips-Wren 2012). Furthermore, AI is used in e-commerce, where product rankings or chatbots help customers in making decisions. AI is also used as part of expert systems that automate decisions for pilots, doctors, and in other domains (Liebowitz 2019). Given these already existing systems, it is not implausible that the use of AI to supplement reasoning and decision-making will gradually encroach on more canonically moral domains in the near future. It is also possible that, as some philosophers have been advocating, efforts will be made to develop AI systems explicitly designed to support human moral capacities (see Whitby 2011).

Perhaps the most technologically feasible version of a personal AEA in the near term would be a recommender system that takes into account factors that the user considers moral. Recommender systems are at the heart of popular music streaming services, such as Spotify, and online shopping platforms, such as Amazon. One can easily imagine similar systems that generate purchasing or consumption recommendations in a process that incorporates information about users' values.[10] For instance, if one wants to avoid listening to White supremacist bands or to songs with misogynistic lyrics, one can imagine a music streaming recommendation system accommodating this preference.[11]

There are also a number of systems that provide users with information pertinent to advancing particular kinds of values within specific contexts, such as apps that supply information about restaurant options,[12] household products,[13] and clothing companies (Hansson 2017). And there are robo-advisor systems that make investment recommendations that take into account whether the user wants to avoid investing in particular industries such as in weapons or tobacco. However, no existing systems allow the user to personalize recommendations or information on the basis of moral values in a fine-grained way.

With regard to more advanced systems that could supply personalized ethics assistance, there are many technical questions about how the systems could acquire information about users' values. Here are some possibilities:

- the user completes surveys in which they indicate what they take to be their priorities, which considerations they believe are morally relevant in particular situations (c.f. Sinnott-Armstrong and Skorburg 2021: 9–14), or what their moral judgements are about particular scenarios (Giubilini and Savulescu 2018: 174–175). One might think of these surveys as much more elaborate versions of the Moral Foundations Questionnaire (Graham et al. 2013) or the questions asked in the Moral Machine experiment (Awad et al. 2018), which uses thought experiments to find patterns underlying moral judgements;[14]

- the AI system asks the person specific questions to fill in gaps in the system's model of the person's moral views;
- the AI system observes the person's choices and behaviour and infers desires, preferences, and values on the basis of them (Etzioni and Etzioni 2016);
- the AI system observes the person's choices and behaviour together with the choices and behaviour of others and infers desires, preferences, and values on the basis of correlations at the population level (Giubilini and Savulescu 2018).
- the person gives the AI system feedback on its judgements and recommendations, for example, as in some forms of inverse reinforcement learning (Ng and Russell 2000; Hadfield-Menell et al. 2016) or reward modelling (Leike et al. 2018);

Some of these are quite futuristic; current efforts to do this sort of thing are very rudimentary. Nonetheless, it may eventually be possible to represent much of an individual's moral world view outside of that person's mind.

Suppose, then, that systems have been created that are capable of acquiring a picture of the user's moral functioning and world view (or some subdomain within these) for the purpose of helping the user to improve their moral reasoning and decision-making. Such systems could conceivably influence an individual's moral cognition in a number of ways. One distinction is between preparatory assistance, on the one hand, which is any influence on the user in advance of their consideration of the case or moral question of interest, and, on the other hand, on-the-spot content-specific assistance with particular moral questions or cases.[15]

At the *preparatory* stage of assistance, the AEA might play an advisory role or a training role. When giving *on-the-spot* assistance, during the duration of the user's deliberation on a particular question, the system could play an advisory role or it could play a function facilitation role. In an *advisory role,* the AEA provides information and recommendations, offered for consideration within the user's reasoning process. In advance, the advising AEA could give information about the process of moral reasoning, for instance, and recommendations on how to prepare to make better decisions when one faces a case or moral question; on the spot, the advising AEA could give information and recommendations specific to particular cases or particular moral questions such as about what to value. A *trainer* supplies training that permits the user to improve some moral capacity; this role is specific to preparatory assistance.[16] *Function facilitation* occurs on the spot, over the course of one's consideration of a particular moral question, when the system helps one exercise some capacity such as the detection of morally relevant features of a situation or generation of possible options for action.

Preparatory assistance: Advice and training

One type of preparatory assistance is procedural assistance, which aims to improve one's moral deliberation processes (Paulo 2018).[17] Schaefer and Savulescu (2019: 73) propose that increasing 'logical competence, conceptual understanding, empirical competence, openness, empathy and bias' would be a way to improve the quality of moral decisions of individuals no matter their antecedent values. Another potential target for procedural assistance would be affective perspective-taking—the ability to recognize or infer the emotional states of others (Klincewicz et al. 2018). Via advice and training, the system could also help one develop dispositions for reflection (Giubilini and Savulescu 2018: 179) or for engaging in various stoic practices (Klincewicz 2019). The AEA could also help train one's own capacities for recognizing situations that (one believes) raise moral issues and for more quickly or reliably noticing features of a situation that one considers after reflection to be morally relevant (e.g. by training affective perspective-taking).

In addition to procedural assistance, an AEA might assist in advance of particular cases by helping us better understand our own moral views. For instance, the AI system might find patterns in our judgements about cases so as to identify the underlying norms and principles we subscribe to and the core values we are most concerned with. The advisor might also identify conflicts between an individual's moral world view and their actions or identify apparent conflicts within an individual's moral belief system. Making these things explicit may prompt reflection on whether these are the norms, principles, and values one wants to endorse. We call this the AEA's *moral psychologist function*.

The AEA could also prompt the user to increase the completeness of their moral world view—for instance, by giving them new cases to consider, such as cases they might be likely to encounter in the future in our profession, so that the user thinks about them in advance with the idea that this puts the user in a better position to analyse and develop views about similar cases when they are encountered in reality. In addition, the AEA could simply provide facts that can become a part of background information relevant to future moral decision-making.

On-the-spot assistance: On-the-spot advice and facilitation

During the time when the individual is considering a particular moral question or case, the AEA could supply support by facilitating the functioning of component parts of one's moral deliberation process. If the user has already formed a tentative moral judgement on a particular question, the AEA may weigh in with an assessment of whether the judgement is consistent with one's deeper values and other commitments.[18] Savulescu and Maslen's proposed *moral reasoning prompter* would help the individual think through a moral decision by prompting the individual through some (personalizable and possibly adapting) reasoning procedure. They list some example questions for this process, such as 'Would the act involve crossing a line you promised yourself or another you wouldn't cross?' and 'Do you think you will feel shame or remorse if you go ahead with the act?' (Savulescu and Maslen 2015: 87).[19] With information about the principles or considerations underlying one's judgements (or other people's judgements), the AEA could help with the moral reasoning process by collecting and presenting to the user a range of arguments or considerations that might be offered for and against particular options for action. Lara and Deckers propose a 'Socratic Assistant', with which the user would 'deliberate in dialogue' to subject the user's beliefs to 'conditions of empirical, logical and ethical rigour' (Lara and Deckers 2019: 8);[20] Seville and Field suggest that AI systems could play a devil's advocate role in moral reasoning (Seville and Field 2000). For Flora, who wants to decide whether to become a vegetarian or a vegan or continue eating meat, the AEA could provide arguments for each of these positions, generating them on the basis of her antecedent values. If Flora is a utilitarian, the AEA could provide utilitarian arguments for these diets.

An AEA could remind one of the facts or analogous cases that one usually considers relevant for a given kind of moral question but that one may fail to think about at the moment. It could draw one's attention to features of the situation that one believes are relevant but that one does not always attend to or adequately consider. Suppose Flora is visiting her grandmother and wondering about whether to eat the grilled chicken that her grandmother has lovingly prepared: it might be helpful for the ethics adviser to remind Flora to think about how her grandmother may feel if she refuses the meal, given that on previous, similar occasions Flora has regretted failing to consider the cook's feelings.

Another function that is relevant when the individual is in the midst of considering a case is that of the 'moral environment monitor' (Savulescu and Maslen 2015), which monitors general factors that cause the individual to reason better or worse. These might include things like stress level, sleep deprivation, hormone levels, possible influence by unwanted emotions, etc. On the spot, the system could alert the individual if they are making a decision in a less optimal condition—for example, so that the individual could postpone the decision or take steps to counteract the effects of the non-optimal environment. (If an AEA were to supply information about these patterns in *advance* of the individual considering the particular case or question, then it would be playing a preparatory role—for example, if it recommended that the user ensure that particular conditions are in place before making decisions. And, if the effect of the environment monitor over the long term was that the user learned when they were better at moral decision-making and adjusted their moral deliberation process accordingly, the result would be an enduring procedural enhancement.)

More directly, the AEA might supply advice on what means would fulfil one's ends. Supposing Flora has decided to minimize the number of meat products she consumes, the AI system might assist her lunch decision by screening all the meal options based on whether they include meat. If Flora were thinking more long term, making a decision about where to live, she might be interested in which areas are most conducive to a vegetarian lifestyle; the system might then advise her in a way that allows her to change her social and environmental context so that it is easier to maintain her vegetarianism. Along these lines, Savulescu and Maslen propose the *moral organizer* (Savulescu and Maslen 2015: 86), which may identify ways in which the person could meet their goal or alert them to the fact that they have not yet met the goal—thus aiding them on the spot in the ongoing process of reasoning about how one can meet one's goal.

More fundamentally, AEAs might provide advice—recommendations or information—meant to prompt changes to people's ends or their interpretations of their ends—their core moral beliefs and values. For example, working from premises that the user already accepts or would be likely to accept if they considered them, the AI system could identify, for the user's consideration, a range of arguments for and against possible core moral beliefs and values (Klincewicz 2016: 180; Lara and Deckers 2019: 9). The AI system might have gathered those arguments from other human beings (e.g. from philosophical texts) or it may have generated them itself. The arguments could proceed by appealing to non-moral values (e.g. epistemic values such as coherence) that the individual holds; or they could appeal to metaethical or conceptual arguments (e.g. an argument appealing to the nature of action or obligation).

What kind of arguments would work for this function would depend on what beliefs the user already has. For instance, one type of information potentially relevant for changing one's ends would be information about the morality of others—their judgements about cases, their concepts, the types of considerations they believe to be relevant, the weight they put on different considerations, and so on. Depending on the question, one might be interested in the beliefs of people in one's profession, one's parents and friends, religious leaders, or the entire population. In the moral domain, the reason this information would be of interest is that the user may consider other people's moral beliefs to be information that bears in some way on what they ought to believe (c.f. Chituc and Sinnott-Armstrong 2020: 273) or ought to take into account. To that end, the AEA could deliver Flora a compendium of commonly held moral beliefs about a vegetarian diet among people with whom she shares other moral views, for example.

In addition to offering direct advice on one's ends, the AEA might facilitate one's reasoning about one's ends—for instance, the system could guide the user through the reasoning or discernment processes recommended by particular traditions. If the user believes that a particular approach to ethical reasoning and decision-making is right (e.g. Jewish tradition, or virtue ethics, or something else), the system could help guide the individual through reasoning and decision-making processes from those traditions to help them modify or reinterpret their core values.[21]

ETHICAL RISKS AND PROBLEMS

Given the wide variety of moral functions that could be handed off to an AEA, identifying all the potential ethical issues associated with the use of ostensible AEAs would require much more than one chapter. In addition, which ethical problems may arise depends substantially on what form AEAs might take. Here, we focus on three problems that are worth considering for a broad range of AEAs for moral self-improvement, all of which are tied to their use of AI: (a) the risks associated with AEA reliance on information about the user's own moral psychology; (b) the risks associated with outside influences on AEAs and the possibility that an AEA will not accomplish its function; and (c) the risks associated with taking the AEA's advice without having adequate reasons. After discussing these problems, we briefly discuss some of the problems that have come up in the literature on moral bioenhancement that also appear applicable to the AEA case.[22]

The sensitivity of moral data

Given the complexity of human moral reasoning and psychology, for an AEA to be effective it would likely require substantial information about the world, the cases the user encounters, and the user. In particular, in order to advise the user in a personalized way, an AEA would need *moral data* about that individual: information about the individual's values and beliefs, and possibly even quite an in-depth model of that individual's moral psychology. Information about an individual's values (moral, political, personal, etc.), let alone information about the underlying patterns in a person's moral psychology, which the individual is not even aware of themselves, can be highly sensitive (cf. Christen et al. 2015 on 'morality mining'). Thus, one of the distinguishing ethical issues associated with AEAs, in contrast to other moral improvement interventions, is the risk introduced by its likely reliance on large quantities of detailed, sensitive moral data.

Each of the AEA's various interactions with the individual's moral data—elicitation, aggregation, storage, processing, creation (based on inferences from other data), possible sharing, and use—introduce risks for the user.[23] Furthermore, the creation of AEA technology, long before it reaches the user, may require a process in which AI systems learn moral concepts and construct models of moral world views; such a process would itself likely require the collection and processing of moral data from many people. Then, during use, if the AEA system is updated based on information about others or if one of its functions is to provide the user information about the values and opinions of others, risks arise for all the individuals whose moral information is collected and transferred— such information may flow or be used in ways that violate rights or are otherwise problematic.[24] Additional risks arise from the identification of patterns in moral views across individuals that enable further inferences, including inferences about groups and uninvolved individuals (on the issue of group privacy, see Floridi 2014; Taylor et al. 2016; Loi and Christen 2019; Veliz 2020, ch. 3; on privacy interdependencies, see Humbert et al. 2019 and Barocas and Levy 2020). The use of AEAs by some individuals could expose (probabilistic) information about non-users that enables predictions about non-users' likely moral views or dispositions based on other available information about them. This opens the door for dangerous discrimination against both historically marginalized groups and previously unrecognized groups that become salient as a result of newly discovered moral psychological patterns (see Taylor 2016 on algorithmic groupings).

Why is moral data so sensitive? Information about the individual AEA user—which might include information about the user's intentions, past actions, judgements about controversial cases, and so on—would be of great interest to many people, such as prospective employers, spouses, landlords, security services, loan providers, governments, etc. Imagine a landlord interested to know whether a prospective renter has little regard for property rights; a person interested in whether their fiancée secretly thinks that occasional cheating is not so bad; a parent concerned with whether a babysitter will be a bad influence. Such parties might even claim to have a legitimate interest in accessing this data under some circumstances. Morality is central to identity (Strohminger and Nichols 2014), and the topics that people tend to consider questions of morality are frequently high-stakes. Importantly, people tend to be less tolerant of those they disagree with on moral matters than of those they disagree with on other matters (Skitka et al. 2005; Wright et al. 2008). Individuals' moral data would also be of great interest to people concerned with rule violations and punishment, such as divorce attorneys, law enforcement, juries, etc. In addition, any system that relies on valuable personal data runs a risk of leakages and attacks. We can imagine AEA user data being repurposed for a variety of illegal and malicious ends—moral data used for blackmail, exposing political dissidents, manipulating targets, etc.

Historically, information about individuals' moral values has only been accessible to others in a piecemeal way, for example, via self-disclosure, rumour, behaviour, and other indirect indicators.[25] We have laws and norms that regulate our interactions with such information—in many countries, for instance, closely related data, such as religious affiliation and voting record, is subject to various protections. Digitalizing moral data at the scale an AEA would require introduces substantial hazards—it would harvest some of the most significant information about individuals that there is. It is difficult to anticipate all the ways in which storehouses of presumed-reliable information about individuals' moral world views might alter our social world. Think of friendships made untenable by one person's repugnance at the moral views of the other, moral purity tests for employment, deeper polarization and segregation between groups on the basis of moral views, and moral inquisitions.

Some of the risks associated with moral data can perhaps be addressed by engineering solutions that prevent repurposing or hacking, other technological tools, new social norms, and legal instruments that regulate moral data and the development of purported AEAs. But pending substantial developments along these lines, for the sake of social functioning there is reason to be wary of highly personalized AEA, given their likely reliance on massive amounts of moral data.

The inescapability of outside influences on AEAs

A worry for any ostensible moral enhancement intervention is that it will fail to perform its purported function and, on top of that, that the user might not recognize the failure. Let us distinguish two possible characterizations of the AEA's function. One is the *individual value alignment function*: the system helps the user better align their moral judgements and decisions with their core moral values (cf. Christian 2020; Boddington 2021). However, if the user's core moral values are completely misguided, it could be that efforts to increase alignment will not result in moral improvement and may indeed result in moral worsening. Thus, there is another characterization of the AEA's function to consider, which we will label the *moral improvement function*: the system helps the person improve their moral judgements and decisions, simpliciter. For a user whose core moral values are roughly on track, performing the individual value alignment function may have the result that the system also performs the moral improvement function. For the user whose values are completely misguided, the AEA would presumably need to influence the user's core moral values (or their interpretation) if it is to fulfil the moral improvement function. Since the moral improvement function lies beyond the scope of this chapter, we are concerned here with the possible function failure of an intervention designed to perform individual value alignment and in particular with the low probability that the user would be able to assess whether the system will perform its purported function.

In practice, an AEA cannot be fully personalized: the values of others will invariably influence the design of the system in ways that no user could fully reconstruct (cf. Serafimova 2020). Although the system may take the user's moral views as input, and though it could even be designed to change over time on the basis of the user's input, the initial design of the system and its parts (unless the user were to design the entire system from scratch) comes from elsewhere. For an AEA to come into being, some set of individuals must design it, construct it, advertise it, etc. The creation and availability of such technology is influenced by economic and political structures as well as many other individuals' interests and values; whatever advice or guidance the system provides the user will be partly determined by the choices of the designers of the system, the institution that built it, standards organizations, and others (Frank and Klincewicz 2016).

At minimum, the variety of ostensible AEAs that the interested user may encounter is constrained. As with any computer system, those options that do become available will be the product of a vast number of value-laden design decisions, many of which the user will not be aware of or able to inspect (Friedman and Nissenbaum 1996; Nissenbaum 2001). Among other things, there is the unavoidable challenge of the system needing to select some format in which to present options and information, given the existence of order effects and other presentation factors that affect reasoning. The result may be that the AEA systematically biases or restricts the scope of morally relevant actions that the user considers; it might 'imprison us within a certain zone of agency' (Danaher 2018: 18). There is also the possibility that the use of an AEA, though not intended (by designers or users) to change one's core values, nonetheless does. Using an AEA could then be a 'transformative experience' (Paul 2014), producing a shift in one's values.[26] As many philosophers have observed, even ordinary technology can mediate values and change the values of its users without their awareness (Bergen and Verbeek 2021). The reverse problem is also a potential worry—that a user who interacts with the system will change less over time than they would have had they conducted their moral deliberation without the system; that the system will constrict the moral growth of the user.

In addition to unintended influence, there are critical concerns related to intentional bias, manipulation, paternalism, and social control. If such systems are created by people with an agenda or partisan interests, there will be incentives to design them in ways that nudge or otherwise influence users' choices or even their core moral views. Hidden influence is a risk associated with decision support systems generally (Susser 2019) and would be especially pressing in a context in which the system is used with the aim of moral improvement.

There are serious reasons to doubt that a user could ever adequately confirm that an AEA is successfully accomplishing the individual value alignment function. This is so despite the fact that, for the most part, the user of the AEA system in the scenario we have imagined is an active rather than passive participant in the moral improvement process. In an active moral enhancement intervention, at least as discussed by Focquaert and Schermer (2015), the intervention requires conscious mental participation on the part of the subject. The AEA that we have considered intervenes by offering information and recommendations, which the user may accept or disregard; training, which presumably requires the user's conscious participation; and function facilitation, which we will assume here occurs only with the user's active involvement. The user has an idea of how the AEA is influencing them; and the user may cease using the AEA at any time. Nonetheless, even for the best-case scenario that we have sketched, in practice there remains a high probability that the system will promote values other than the user's and that the user will not be able to identify the ways in which the design decisions or interference of others is exerting an influence on their moral reasoning. Among the causes of this epistemic difficulty is the complexity and opacity of the system, which we discuss in the next section. Thus, there is an ethical risk associated with the purported AEA failing to perform its individual value alignment function and causing the user whose moral convictions are mostly on track to morally worsen.

Moral advice without adequate reasons

One of the worries about moral bioenhancement is that, even if it changes some aspects of an individual's morality for the better (whether their dispositions, actions, beliefs, or something else), if the user did not make that change on the basis of adequate reasons, that change may be less than praiseworthy or may not constitute a moral improvement overall. This kind of issue shows up in a particularly important form for the AEA, given that it would likely employ machine learning, which tends to be highly opaque (Burrell 2016; Goodman and Flaxman 2017; Arrieta et al. 2020). The problem arises most directly when the AEA acts as an advisor providing recommendations.

Suppose the AEA system were to recommend a course of action that would increase the alignment of the individual's reasoning and decision-making with their core moral values. The user does this but lacks adequate reasons for the change (e.g. it may be that the user's only reason in favour of the change is the fact that it is AEA-recommended). The user is unable to independently identify adequate reasons for their behaviour, and the AEA is not able to supply the user with adequate reasons in support of its recommendation. The result of this attempt to use an AEA for moral improvement would be that the user obtains beliefs and reaches decisions without being in possession of or being capable of formulating reasons for those beliefs and decisions. If, as a number of philosophers think, there is inherent or instrumental value in the human agent being in possession of or able to supply reasons for their judgements, actions, and so on, this is a problem.

For instance, Nickel (2001) argues that there is a 'recognition requirement' for moral action. On his view, to act in a moral way one must act on the basis of a recognition of what morality requires: 'morality requires one to act from an understanding of moral claims, and therefore to have an understanding of moral claims that are relevant to action' (257). Having a full understanding of a moral claim is 'a matter of having a grasp of the relevant reasons bearing on action, or in other words, having a grasp of the justificatory basis of the claim' (259). On this view, then, if an AEA cannot supply the user with adequate reasons for its recommendation, there is a risk that one will be left without an understanding of the moral claim so that, even if one acts on the basis of it, one's action will not be moral.

Suppose that in the situation in which Flora is trying to decide whether to eat the meat dish her grandmother has prepared, the best action to take, given the circumstances, Flora's core values, and so on, would be to eat the dish. If Flora takes this action solely on the basis of the AEA's recommendation, without recognition of the morally relevant features of the situation (without recognizing, say, that she should be appreciative of her grandmother's efforts or that accepting the dish would convey respect, etc.), then her action might not be a moral action. Furthermore, lacking a full understanding of the moral conclusion that she has obtained from the AEA puts Flora in a less than optimal position going forward; facing similar situations in the future, Flora will be no more capable of reasoning about what to do than she was before she consulted the AEA about how to respond to her grandmother.

There may be some circumstances in which it is permissible to defer to the moral testimony of another human being—perhaps in low-stakes circumstances, in situations in which one obtains advice about how to implement shared values, or when 'we know that we're unable to resolve a difficult moral issue and reasonably expect that others can do better' (Mogensen 2017: 263). However, deferring to the advice of an AEA may be different—the AEA, or our relationship with it, may be missing some element on which our usual deference relationships depend. This could be so, for instance, if the permissibility of deference to human testimony rests on the fact that human beings can be held responsible for their testimony. The AEA might not be the sort of thing that can be punished or adequately held to account for its claims or recommendations (Floridi 2016; Nyholm 2018).

By contrast, if the AEA could help the user to acquire adequate reasons for making the change that the system recommends, the user would not be epistemically dependent on the AEA's advice itself; the AEA might have played a critical causal role in facilitating the user's acquisition of reasons (and user dependence on that facilitation could raise its own ethical problems), but the user's beliefs or decisions would rest on the reasons that the user has acquired over the course of their interaction with the AEA.

What are the prospects that the AEA could not only advise but could also help the user acquire adequate reasons for accepting the AEA's claim or following its recommendation? A natural place to start would be for the AEA to share information about what prompted its advice. Unfortunately, the computational processes of an AI system that could function as an AEA would invariably be complex, likely so complex that no human being would be capable of understanding them. Even for existing machine-learning systems, the factors that prompt the system to generate outputs are not easily translated into familiar human concepts, let alone moral concepts that might provide the building blocks for articulating reasons. Substantial efforts are currently underway to create explainable AI systems (see the discussion in, e.g. Mittelstadt et al. 2016; Goldenfein 2019; Martin 2019), but some are pessimistic about how far such techniques can take us (see, e.g. Rudin 2019).

In sum, one concern about AEAs that provide moral advice is that they may prompt the user to make changes—acquire beliefs, take actions, and so on—without adequate reasons. This may undermine the moral worth of the user's actions. Although a user like Flora might have had noble motivation for using an AEA in the first place (namely, acting more morally), if she is left without reasons for the system's recommendations, following its advice may leave her less morally worthy.

Additional problems

Many of the potential ethical problems associated with moral bioenhancement efforts may also be applicable for AEAs. One general issue has to do with the fact that using new technologies to interfere with a complex system like human moral tradition and practice risks causing significant bad consequences we cannot predict beforehand. Despite the flowering of empirical research on moral cognition in the past few decades, we still know only a fraction of what there is to know about how moral cognition works—including how hormones and other chemicals, situational factors, and so on, affect reasoning; and how moral world views develop and change. Furthermore, both the functioning and development of moral cognition depends crucially on one's environment and one's interactions with others. Supposing that we could successfully create AI systems that could perform the individual value alignment function, there are still numerous risks associated with use of such a computer system.

For instance, suppose we were using an AEA to reduce inconsistencies in our own moral belief systems—it may well be that some inconsistencies in one's moral beliefs are useful somehow; maybe becoming more consistent would reduce flexibility, creativity, or other qualities that undergird well-functioning moral cognition. For instance, it could be that being as free as we currently are to fall short of our moral standards permits us to keep our standards high. If an AEA were to point out the inconsistencies in our actions and beliefs too frequently, we might respond in a potentially perverse way by lowering our standards. Giubilini and Savulescu (2018: 174) mention this issue, discussing the possibility that one might start out as a strict utilitarian, but in the face of the AI system's recommended actions, such as donating half one's income to charity, say, one might begin to think that strict utilitarianism is too demanding a theory. This weakening of standards might not constitute an improvement.

Another class of unintended consequence has to do with the potential for problematic dependence (Danaher 2018). One incarnation of this problem is the potential for moral deskilling (Vallor 2015). We would want to anticipate whether the use of AEAs would cause us to lose our own abilities to perform essential moral cognitive tasks. We would also want to know whether our own ability to perform that task is instrumentally valuable, such as for reasons of robustness, or intrinsically valuable. Similar concerns already exist in domains of human activity where the introduction of computing tools permanently changes people's cognition. These unintended consequences that AEAs introduce may be difficult to undo. Of course, it is an empirical question whether AEAs would worsen our ability to independently perform whatever cognitive tasks they take over, but when it comes to moral decision-making, such a technology should not be unleashed until we have good evidence that it does not.

However, preparatory assistance, including procedural assistance, is less likely to raise this worry than some of the other assistance that the AEA might provide. Preparatory assistance aims to help us improve skills and obtain information (with the idea that the user retains that information for future use or develops judgements on the basis of that information that are available for future use).

We should also worry about effects such as general alienation from other people and a loss of the social aspects of moral practice—for instance, threats to moral collaboration and discussion due to greater reliance on technology during the process of moral reasoning and decision-making. Among other things, some people think that coming to an ethical agreement via direct social interaction is an intrinsically valuable part of human morality. Social groups are often distinguished by their moral values, and their cohesion often depends on norms that regulate and punish transgressions. The widespread use of personalized AEAs for moral self-improvement may effectively dampen the societal role of moral practice.

Depending on how we interact with AEAs—for example, which moral cognition tasks we outsource entirely, which we perform using AEAs as cognitive extensions (Hernández-Orallo and Vold 2019)—and how reliant we become on them, AEAs may threaten some core component of what we take to be human nature; this is a concern that some have also had about some forms of moral bioenhancement (Cohen 2006; Sandel 2004). There is a worry about whether these interventions would undermine our self-understanding as human beings, as some authors argue moral bioenhancement may do (Elliott 2014; Danaher 2019; Kraemer 2011), or undermine human dignity (Fukuyama 2003; Cohen 2006; Giubilini and Sanyal 2015). A closely related potential problem is the possibility that the AEA could undermine freedom of will or action or, more generally, freedom of mind: some have argued that pharmacological, genetic, or direct neural interventions would impose a limit on these capacities (Bublitz 2016: 94) and that these interventions interfere with our freedom to morally fall (Harris 2011; DeGrazia 2014; Pugh 2019). An AEA may similarly challenge this freedom, especially if such devices could cause permanent changes in our moral world view or ensure, in a way that circumvents our agency, that we always act in accordance with our values.

We may also have certain obligations related to moral reasoning that the use of an AEA would prevent us from discharging. For instance, there may be something morally wrong in Flora failing to spontaneously, independently consider the well-being of her grandmother when making a decision about whether to accept the food she offers. One may argue that this is ultimately a function that she is obliged to perform herself, without the prompting of a computer system.

Another recurring type of worry about enhancement interventions has to do with problems that arise if a substantial portion of the population uses the technology. In the context of moral cognition, widespread changes to our reasoning and decision-making process could produce homogenization at the group level, which might be a problem, for example, if it limits the potential for moral progress at the societal level (Schaefer 2015). For the personalized AEA that we have discussed, one might worry more about polarization and radicalization than homogenization, but the latter is also a risk, particularly if there are common patterns of influence in the way that AEAs affect users' moral cognition.

CONCLUSION

In this chapter, we have analysed three of the risks raised by individual use of purported AEAs, each of which applies to a range of systems designed to provide personalized assistance for individual moral reasoning in the near term. We focused on the hazards associated with reliance on moral data, outside influence on the design of AEAs, and the possibility of the AEA user adopting beliefs and making decisions without sufficient reasons. Each of these is a problem that is difficult to avoid with AEAs. To provide specific, personalized, moral assistance with a broad enough scope to be interesting, an AI system presumably requires vast quantities of moral data. Likewise, at least some outside influence on the substance of AEA advice, via design decisions and other constraints, cannot be avoided. Finally, it remains to be seen to what extent the opacity of complex machine-learning systems can be overcome and to what extent such systems will be able to assist users in acquiring adequate reasons for beliefs and decisions influenced by the AI system. Thus, we consider these three problems to be rather serious obstacles for the hope that AI systems might be harnessed for the purpose of helping individuals who wish to improve their own moral functioning.

ACKNOWLEDGEMENTS

Thanks to audiences at a Cornell Tech Digital Life Initiative seminar, a TU/e Center for Humans and Technology Research Meeting on Artificial Moral Agents, and CEPE 2019 for comments on earlier versions of this paper. E.O.'s research on this paper has been supported by the Netherlands Organisation for Scientific Research under grant number 016.Veni.195.513; the Ethics of Socially Disruptive Technologies research programme, funded through the Gravitation programme of the Dutch Ministry of Education, Culture, and Science and the Netherlands Organisation for Scientific Research under grant number 024.004.031; a fellowship at the Cornell Tech Digital Life Initiative NSF Grant #SES-1650589 (PI: Helen Nissenbaum); and a visit to the Simons Institute at the University of California, Berkeley.

NOTES

1. Much of this discussion has been presented in terms of enhancement. In contrast with past debates about human enhancement, though, which are generally concerned with improving a trait beyond what is normal or typical for some population, the question of moral enhancement is at least sometimes treated as including any sort of moral improvement, even if it does not surpass the normal or typical (e.g. DeGrazia 2014). We are concerned with improvement broadly, not just enhancement in the narrow sense, so to make that explicit we will use the term 'improvement' rather than 'enhancement' (see also Klincewicz 2019).

   For additional discussion on the question of whether machines can aid human moral reasoning and decision-making, see Cave et al. (2019: 568); Boddington (2021).
2. We will not rely on a principled distinction between moral and non-moral values; we pragmatically count an individual's value as a moral value if that individual considers it to be a moral value.
3. We use this term in place of Giubilini and Savulescu (2018)'s 'artificial moral advisor' first, to avoid ambiguity about whether the AI system *itself* is moral/ethical and, second, because we want to consider not only AI systems that give advice but also those that provide assistance in other ways. (See Danaher (2018) for discussion on the ethics of AI assistants generally.) Throughout the chapter, we use the terms 'ethical' and 'moral' interchangeably.
4. A few examples of other types of uses that we will not discuss are: moral decision-making as a group (e.g. at the family, company, or city level) and moral decision-making by individuals who are in special positions, such as politicians, doctors, or designers.
5. Many people have highlighted the importance of this question within debates on moral enhancement; see, e.g. Shook (2012), DeGrazia (2014); Beck (2015), Young (2018).
6. For some discussion on this problem for moral enhancement see, e.g. Paulo (2018); de Sio and van den Hoven (2018). Indeed, one of the biggest hazards associated with ostensible moral improvement via technology is the prospect of some people using such technologies to impose their values on others with different values. Numerous people have addressed various aspects of this important topic, including, e.g. Sparrow (2014) and Paulo and Bublitz (2019).
7. There are also other approaches one could take to carve up the types of ways one might seek to morally improve. For instance, Shook (2012) distinguishes five ways in which one might morally improve; DeGrazia (2014) distinguishes three ways—motivational improvement, improved insight, and behavioural improvement.

8. For instance, one's intentions, motivations, and emotional reactions.

9. Some might dispute whether an agent can coherently or rationally believe that some unspecified subset of their own core moral beliefs and values might be wrong; this may raise an issue like the preface paradox. Nonetheless, (descriptively) at least some individuals have this belief.

10. Manolios et al. (2019) investigate the possibility that music recommendations might be based on personal values (see also Tang and Winoto 2016).

11. In reality, some internet services that use recommendation algorithms have attempted to remove content containing, for instance, hate speech (Hern 2018).

12. Giubilini and Savulescu (2018: 174) discuss an app, the Humane Eating Project, that promises to provide guidance on where to eat if one wants to avoid supporting animal cruelty.

13. For a number of years, the internet service GoodGuide supplied information about whether a product meets various standards, such as 'Leaping Bunny Certified', indicating lack of animal testing (O'Rourke and Ringer, 2016).

14. See also Conitzer et al. (2017); Freedman et al. (2020).

15. The distinction we are drawing between preparatory and on-the-spot assistance is a simplification: of course, people do not deliberate on a single moral question or case without interruption until they reach a conclusion. As a rough-and-ready distinction, however, it is useful.

16. Whether a given act of assistance is preparatory or on-the-spot is defined with reference to a particular moral question. In general, as one is considering a particular question, one cannot be trained to better deliberate about that particular question. (One might make an exception for a very lengthy period of deliberation over the course of which one's deliberation capacities could improve.) Any given instance of deliberation can be part of one's training in advance of future consideration of further cases.

17. See Schaefer and Savulescu (2017, 2019); see Paulo (2018) for discussion of procedural moral enhancement. Paulo (2018) argues that procedural moral enhancement amounts to *moral epistemic* enhancement.

18. For instance, Peterson (2017) suggests an approach to ethical reasoning that one could imagine a computer implementing to help an individual evaluate their own moral consistency. The method involves identifying principles that best explain paradigm moral cases, assessing moral similarity between cases, and ascertaining what principle to apply to a new case by assessing which paradigm case the new case most closely resembles, morally. Suppose that the AEA possesses a model of the human's moral views, which represents the human's moral views geometrically in a 'moral space' of principles and cases as Peterson's describes. Suppose also that the system has learned to predict with some degree of reliability the human's pairwise moral similarity judgements between new cases and paradigm cases. The AEA could then indicate to the human the presence of a possible inconsistency in the human's view, in cases where the human's judgement about a new case diverges from what the AEA predicted the human would judge, on the basis of the AEA's prediction of the human's pairwise moral similarity judgements between the new case and paradigm cases and the AEA's knowledge of what principle is associated with each paradigm moral case.

19. For this intervention to be pertinent in the context of self-improvement, the user would have to consider these to be questions that are conducive to moral improvement or would need to believe more generally that the AEA's prompting method is conducive to moral improvement.

20. They emphasize, though, that the ultimate aim of the system would be to help the user get better at doing this reasoning on their own. This system, then, would be providing on-the-spot assistance as well as preparatory assistance for future cases.

21. Another possibility is that the system guides the user through other (non-reasoning) kinds of processes that can change one's ends or one's understanding of one's ends, such as meditation or life-transition traditions that involve hallucination-inducing drugs. (See Earp (2018) on the possible relevance of psychedelic interventions for moral enhancement).

22. Many potential ethical problems have already been identified for efforts to use technologies, particularly biomedical and genetic technology, for moral enhancement. For useful review, see Raus et al. (2014) and Specker et al. (2014).

23. Also see Milano et al. (2020) on privacy risks associated with recommender systems, and Kreitmair (2019: 158–159) on privacy worries related to direct-to-consumer neurotechnologies.

24. Federated learning (see, e.g. Yang et al. 2019) would be one strategy for reducing the transmission of specific information about individuals; it remains to be seen what form this might take and how much it would help in addressing the risks associated with sensitive moral data.

25. Already, digital technologies are changing this—for instance, some indication of values can be inferred using social media data, though such efforts are both patchy and noisy (Kosinski et al. 2013; Olteanu et al. 2019).

26. On this type of phenomenon, see Alfano et al. (2021)'s analysis of YouTube recommender systems as causing transformative experiences that may lead to radicalization.

References

Alfano, Mark, Ebrahimi Fard, Amir, Carter, J. Adam, Clutton, Peter, and Klein, Colin (2021), 'Technologically Scaffolded Atypical Cognition: The Case of YouTube's Recommender System', *Synthese* 199(1–2), 835–858, doi: https://doi.org/10.1007/s11229-020-02724-x.

Arrieta, Alejandro Barredo, Díaz-Rodríguez, Natalia, Del Ser, Javier, Bennetot, Adrien, Tabik, Siham, Barbado, Alberto, et al. (2020), 'Explainable Artificial Intelligence (XAI): Concepts, Taxonomies, Opportunities and Challenges toward Responsible AI', *Information Fusion* 58, 82–115, doi: https://doi.org/10.48550/arXiv.1910.10045.

Awad, Edmond, Dsouza, Sohan, Kim, Richard, Schulz, Jonathan, Henrich, Joseph, Shariff, Azim, et al. (2018), 'The Moral Machine Experiment', *Nature* 563(7729), 59–64, doi: https://doi.org/10.1038/s41586-018-0637-6.

Barocas, Solon, and Levy, Karen (2020), 'Privacy Dependencies', *Washington Law Review* 95(2), 555–616.

Beck, Birgit (2015), 'Conceptual and Practical Problems of Moral Enhancement', *Bioethics* 29(4), 233–240, doi: https://doi.org/10.1111/bioe.12090.

Bergen, Jan Peter, and Verbeek, Peter-Paul (2021), 'To-Do Is to Be: Foucault, Levinas, and Technologically Mediated Subjectivation', *Philosophy and Technology* 34(2), 325–348, doi: https://doi.org/10.1007/s13347-019-00390-7.

Boddington, Paula (2021), 'AI and Moral Thinking: How Can We Live Well with Machines to Enhance Our Moral Agency?', *AI and Ethics* 1(2), 109–111.

Borenstein, Jason, and Arkin, Ron (2016), 'Robotic Nudges: The Ethics of Engineering a More Socially Just Human Being', *Science and Engineering Ethics* 22(1), 31–46.

Bublitz, Christoph (2016), 'Moral Enhancement and Mental Freedom', *Journal of Applied Philosophy* 33(1), 88–106, doi: https://doi.org/10.1111/japp.12108.

Burrell, Jenna (2016), 'How the Machine "Thinks": Understanding Opacity in Machine Learning Algorithms', *Big Data and Society* 3(1), doi: https://doi.org/10.1177/2053951715622512.

Cave, Stephen, Nyrup, Rune, Vold, Karina, and Weller, Adrian (2019), 'Motivations and Risks of Machine Ethics', *Proceedings of the IEEE* 107(3), 562–574, doi: https://10.1109/JPROC.2018.2865996.

Chituc, Vladimir, and Sinnott-Armstrong, Walter (2020), 'Moral Conformity and Its Philosophical Lessons', *Philosophical Psychology* 33(2), 262–282, doi: https://doi.org/10.1080/09515089.2020.1719395.

Christen, Markus, Alfano, Mark, Bangerter, Endre, and Lapsley, Daniel (2015), 'Ethical Issues of "Morality Mining": Moral Identity as a Focus of Data Mining', in *Human Rights and Ethics: Concepts, Methodologies, Tools, and Applications* (Hershey, PA: IGI Global), 1146–1166.

Christian, Brian (2020), *The Alignment Problem: Machine Learning and Human Values* (New York: WW Norton & Company).

Cohen, Eric (2006), 'Conservative Bioethics and the Search for Wisdom', *Hastings Center Report* 36(1), 44–56, doi: https://doi.org/10.1353/hcr.2006.0004.

Conitzer, Vincent, Sinnott-Armstrong, Walter, Borg, Jana Schiach, Deng, Yuan, and Kramer, Max (2017), 'Moral Decision Making Frameworks for Artificial Intelligence', *Proceedings of the 31st Association for the Advancement of Artificial Intelligence (AAAI-17) Conference on Artificial Intelligence*, 4831–4835.

Danaher, John (2018), 'Toward an Ethics of AI Assistants: An Initial Framework', *Philosophy and Technology* 31(4), 629–653, doi: https://doi.org/10.1007/s13347-018-0317-3.

Danaher, John (2019), 'Why Internal Moral Enhancement Might Be Politically Better Than External Moral Enhancement', *Neuroethics* 12(1), 39–54, doi: https://doi.org/10.1007/s12152-016-9273-8.

de Sio, Filippo Santoni, and van den Hoven, Jeroen (2018), 'Meaningful Human Control over Autonomous Systems: A Philosophical Account', *Frontiers in Robotics and AI*, 28 February, doi: https://doi.org/10.3389/frobt.2018.00015.

DeGrazia, David (2014), 'Moral Enhancement, Freedom, and What We (Should) Value in Moral Behaviour', *Journal of Medical Ethics* 40(6), 361–368, doi: https://doi.org/10.1136/medethics-2012-101157.

Earp, Brian D. (2018), 'Psychedelic Moral Enhancement', *Royal Institute of Philosophy Supplements* 83, 415–439, doi: https://doi.org/10.1017/s1358246118000474.

Elliott, Carl (2014), *A Philosophical Disease: Bioethics, Culture, and Identity* (New York: Routledge), doi: https://doi.org/10.4324/9781315822150.

Etzioni, Amitai, and Etzioni, Oren (2016), 'AI Assisted Ethics', *Ethics and Information Technology* 18(2), 149–156, doi: https://doi.org/10.1007/s10676-016-9400-6.

Floridi, Luciano (2014), 'Open Data, Data Protection, and Group Privacy', *Philosophy & Technology* 27(1), 1–3.

Floridi, Luciano (2016), 'Faultless Responsibility: On the Nature and Allocation of Moral Responsibility for Distributed Moral Actions', *Philosophical Transactions of the Royal Society A, Mathematical, Physical and Engineering Sciences* 374(2083), doi: https://doi.org/10.1098/rsta.2016.0112.

Focquaert, Farah, and Schermer, Maartje (2015), 'Moral Enhancement: Do Means Matter Morally?', *Neuroethics* 8(2), 139–151, doi: https://doi.org/10.1007/s12152-015-9230-y.

Formosa, Paul, and Ryan, Malcolm (2021), 'Making Moral Machines: Why We Need Artificial Moral Agents', *AI and Society* 36(3), 839–851.

Frank, Lily, and Klincewicz, Michał (2016), 'Metaethics in Context of Engineering Ethical and Moral Systems', Association for the Advancement of Artificial Intelligence (AAAI-16) Spring Symposium Series.

Freedman, Rachel, Borg, Jana Schiach, Sinnott-Armstrong, Walter, Dickerson, John P., and Conitzer, Vincent (2020), 'Adapting a Kidney Exchange Algorithm to Align with Human Values', *Artificial Intelligence* 283, doi: https://doi.org/10.1016/j.artint.2020.103261.

Friedman, Batya, and Nissenbaum, Helen (1996), 'Bias in Computer Systems', *ACM Transactions in Information Systems* 14(3), 330–347, doi: https://doi.org/10.1145/230538.230561.

Fukuyama, Francis (2003), *Our Posthuman Future: Consequences of the Biotechnology Revolution* (New York: Farrar, Straus and Giroux).

Giubilini, Alberto, and Sanyal, Sagar (2015), 'The Ethics of Human Enhancement', *Philosophy Compass* 10(4), 233–243, doi: https://doi.org/10.1111/phc3.12208.

Giubilini, Alberto, and Savulescu, Julian (2018), 'The Artificial Moral Advisor. The "Ideal Observer" Meets Artificial Intelligence', *Philosophy & Technology* 31(2), 169–188, doi: https://doi.org/10.1007/s13347-017-0285-z.

Goldenfein, Jake (2019), 'Algorithmic Transparency and Decision-Making Accountability: Thoughts for Buying Machine Learning Algorithms' in Cliff Bertram, Adriana Nugent, and Asher Gibson, eds, *Closer to the Machine: Technical, Social, and Legal Aspects of AI* (Melbourne: Office of the Victorian Information Commissioner), 41–61.

Goodman, Bryce, and Flaxman, Seth (2017), 'European Union Regulations on Algorithmic Decision Making and a "Right to Explanation"', *AI Magazine* 38(3), 50–57, doi: https://doi.org/10.1609/aimag.v38i3.2741.

Graham, Jesse, Haidt, Jonathan, Koleva, Sena, Motyl, Matt, Iyer, Ravi, Wojcik, Sean P., et al. (2013), 'Moral Foundations Theory: The Pragmatic Validity of Moral Pluralism', *Advances in Experimental Social Psychology* 47, 55–130, doi: https://doi.org/10.1016/B978-0-12-407 236-7.00002-4.

Hadfield-Menell, Dylan, Dragan, Anca, Abbeel, Pieter, and Russell, Stuart J. (2016), 'Cooperative Inverse Reinforcement Learning', *Advances in Neural Information Processing Systems* 29, 1–9.

Hansson, Lena (2017), 'Promoting Ethical Consumption: The Construction of Smartphone Apps as "Ethical" Choice Prescribers', in Franck Cochoy, Johan Hagberg, Magdalena Petersson McIntyre, and Niklas Söram, eds, *Digitalizing Consumption: How Devices Shape Consumer Culture* (London: Routledge), 270, doi: https://doi.org/10.4324/9781315647883.

Harris, John (2011), 'Moral Enhancement and Freedom', *Bioethics* 25(2), 102–111.

Hern, Alex (2018), 'Facebook, Apply, YouTube and Spotify ban Infowars' Alex Jones', *The Guardian*. https://www.theguardian.com/technology/2018/aug/06/apple-removes-podca sts-infowars-alex-jones, accessed 24 April 2022.

Hernández-Orallo, José, and Vold, Karina (2019), 'AI Extenders: The Ethical and Societal Implications of Humans Cognitively Extended by AI', *AIES '19: Proceedings of the 2019 AAAI/ACM Conference on AI, Ethics, and Society*, 507–513, doi: https://doi.org/10.1145/3306 618.3314238.

Humbert, Mathias, Trubert, Benjamin, and Huguenin, Kévin (2019), 'A Survey on Interdependent Privacy', *ACM Computing Surveys (CSUR)* 52(6), 1–40.

Klincewicz, Michał (2016), 'Artificial Intelligence as a Means to Moral Enhancement', *Studies in Logic, Grammar and Rhetoric* 48(61), doi: https://doi.org/10.1515/slgr-2016-0061.

Klincewicz, Michał (2019), 'Robotic Nudges for Moral Improvement', *Techné: Research in Philosophy and Technology* 23(3), 425–455, doi: https://doi.org/10.5840/techne2019122109.

Klincewicz, Michał, Frank, Lily E., and Sokólska, Marta (2018), 'Drugs and Hugs: Stimulating Moral Dispositions as a Method of Moral Enhancement', *Royal Institute of Philosophy Supplements* 83, 329–350, doi: https://doi.org/10.1017/s1358246118000437.

Kosinski, Michal, Stillwell, David, and Graepel, Thore (2013), 'Private Traits and Attributes Are Predictable from Digital Records of Human Behavior', *Proceedings of the National Academy of Sciences of the United States of America* 110(15), 5802–5805, doi: https://doi.org/10.1073/pnas.1218772110.

Kraemer, Felicitas (2011), 'Authenticity Anyone? The Enhancement of Emotions via Neuro-Psychopharmacology', *Neuroethics* 4, 51–64, doi: https://doi.org/10.1007/s12152-010-9075-3.

Kreitmair, Karola V. (2019), 'Dimensions of Ethical Direct-to-Consumer Neurotechnologies', *AJOB Neuroscience* 10(4), 152–166.

Lara, Francisco (2021), 'Why a Virtual Assistant for Moral Enhancement When We Could Have a Socrates?', *Science and Engineering Ethics* 27(4), 1–27.

Lara, Francisco, and Deckers, Jan (2019), 'Artificial Intelligence as a Socratic Assistant for Moral Enhancement', *Neuroethics* 13, 275–287, doi: https://doi.org/10.1007/s12152-019-09401-y.

Leike, Jan, Krueger, David, Everitt, Tom, Martic, Miljan, Maini, Vishal, and Legg, Shane (2018), 'Scalable Agent Alignment via Reward Modeling: A Research Direction', arXiv Preprint, arXiv1811.07871.

Liebowitz, Jay (2019), *The Handbook of Applied Expert Systems* (Boca Raton: cRc Press).

Loi, Michele, and Christen, Markus (2019), 'Two Concepts of Group Privacy', *Philosophy & Technology* 33(2), 207–224.

Manolios, Sandy, Hanjalic, Alan, and Liem, Cynthia C.S. (2019), 'The Influence of Personal Values on Music Taste: Towards Value-Based Music Recommendations', *RecSys '19: Proceedings of the 13th ACM Conference on Recommender Systems*, 10 September, 501–505, doi: https://doi.org/10.1145/3298689.3347021.

Martin, Kristen (2019), 'Ethical Implications and Accountability of Algorithms', *Journal of Business Ethics* 160(4), 835–850, doi: https://doi.org/10.1007/s10551-018-3921-3.

Milano, Silvia, Taddeo, Mariarosaria, and Floridi, Luciano (2020), 'Recommender Systems and Their Ethical Challenges', *AI and Society* 35(4), 957–967, doi: https://doi.org/10.1007/s00146-020-00950-y.

Mittelstadt, Brent Daniel, Allo, Patrick, Taddeo, Mariarosaria, Wachter, Sandra, and Floridi, Luciano (2016), 'The Ethics of Algorithms: Mapping the Debate', *Big Data and Society* 3(2), 1–21, doi: https://doi.org/10.1177/2053951716679679.

Mogensen, Andreas L. (2017), 'Moral Testimony Pessimism and the Uncertain Value of Authenticity', *Philosophy and Phenomenological Research* 95(2), 261–284, doi: https://doi.org/10.1111/phpr.12255.

Ng, Andrew Y., and Russell, Stuart J. (2000), 'Algorithms for Inverse Reinforcement Learning', *Proceedings of the Seventeenth International Conference on Machine Learning*, June, 663–670.

Nickel, Philip (2001), 'Moral Testimony and Its Authority', *Ethical Theory of Moral Practice* 4, 253–266, doi: https://doi.org/10.1023/A:1011843723057.

Nissenbaum, Helen (2001), 'How Computer Systems Embody Values', *Computer* 34(3), 120–119, doi: https://doi.org/10.1109/2.910905.

Nyholm, Sven (2018), 'Attributing Agency to Automated Systems: Reflections on Human–Robot Collaborations and Responsibility-Loci', *Science and Engineering Ethics* 24, 1201–1219, doi: https://doi.org/10.1007/s11948-017-9943-x.

O'Rourke, Dara, and Ringer, Abraham (2016), 'The Impact of Sustainability Information on Consumer Decision Making', *Journal of Industrial Ecology* 20(4), 882–892, doi: https://doi.org/10.1111/jiec.12310.

Olteanu, Alexandra, Castillo, Carlos, Diaz, Fernando, and Kıcıman, Emre (2019), 'Social Data: Biases, Methodological Pitfalls, and Ethical Boundaries', *Frontiers in Big Data*, 11 July, doi: https://doi.org/10.3389/fdata.2019.00013.

Paul, Laurie A. (2014), *Transformative Experience* (Oxford: Oxford University Press).

Paulo, Norbert (2018), 'Moral-Epistemic Enhancement', *Royal Institute of Philosophy Supplements* 83, 165–188.

Paulo, Norbert, and Bublitz, Christoph (2019), 'Introduction: Political Implications of Moral Enhancement', *Neuroethics* 12(1), 1–3, doi: https://doi.org/10.1007/s12152-018-9352-0.

Persson, Ingmar, and Savulescu, Julian (2012), *Unfit for the Future: The Need for Moral Enhancement* (Oxford: Oxford University Press).

Peterson, Martin (2017), *The Ethics of Technology: A Geometric Analysis of Five Moral Principles* (Oxford: Oxford University Press).

Phillips-Wren, Gloria (2012), 'AI Tools in Decision Making Support Systems: A Review', *International Journal on Artificial Intelligence Tools* 21(2), 1240005, doi: https://doi.org/10.1142/S0218213012400052.

Pugh, Jonathan (2019), 'Moral Bio-Enhancement, Freedom, Value and the Parity Principle', *Topoi* 38, 73–86, doi: https://doi.org/10.1007/s11245-017-9482-8.

Raus, Kasper, Focquaert, Farah, Schermer, Maartje, Specker, Jona, and Sterckx, Sigrid (2014), 'On Defining Moral Enhancement: A Clarificatory Taxonomy', *Neuroethics* 7(3), 263–273, doi: https://doi.org/10.1007/s12152-014-9205-4.

Rudin, Cynthia (2019), 'Stop Explaining Black Box Machine Learning Models for High Stakes Decisions and Use Interpretable Models Instead', *Nature Machine Intelligence* 1(5), 206–215.

Sandel, Michael J. (2004), 'The Case against Perfection: What's Wrong with Designer Children, Bionic Athletes, and Genetic Engineering', *Atlantic Monthly* 293(3), 50–54, 56–60, 62.

Savulescu, J., and Maslen, H. (2015), 'Moral Enhancement and Artificial Intelligence: Moral AI?', in Jan Romportl, Eva Zackova, and Jozef Kelemen, eds, *Beyond Artificial Intelligence. Topics in Intelligent Engineering and Informatics*, Vol 9 (Heidelberg: Springer), 79–95.

Schaefer, G. Owen (2015), 'Direct vs. Indirect Moral Enhancement', *Kennedy Institute of Ethics Journal* 25(3), 261–289, doi: https://doi.org/10.1353/ken.2015.0016.

Schaefer, G. Owen, and Savulescu, Julian (2017), 'Better Minds, Better Morals: A Procedural Guide to Better Judgment', *Journal of Posthuman Studies: Philosophy, Technology, Media* 1(1), 26–43.

Schaefer, G. Owen, and Savulescu, Julian (2019), 'Procedural Moral Enhancement', *Neuroethics* 12, 73–84, doi: https://doi.org/10.1007/s12152-016-9258-7.

Serafimova, Silviya (2020), 'Whose Morality? Which Rationality? Challenging Artificial Intelligence as a Remedy for the Lack of Moral Enhancement', *Nature: Humanities and Social Sciences Communications* 7(1), 1–10.

Seville, Helen, and Field, Debora (2000), 'What Can AI Do for Ethics?', *AISB Quarterly* 104, 31–34.

Shook, John R. (2012), 'Neuroethics and the Possible Types of Moral Enhancement', *AJOB Neuroscience* 3(4), 3–14, doi: https://doi.org/10.1080/21507740.2012.712602.

Sinnott-Armstrong, Walter and Skorburg, Joshua A. (2021), 'How AI Can Aid Bioethics', *Journal of Practical Ethics* 9(1), doi: https://doi.org/10.3998/jpe.1175.

Skitka, Linda J., Bauman, Christopher W., and Sargis, Edward G. (2005), 'Moral Conviction: Another Contributor to Attitude Strength or Something More?', *Personality and Social Psychology Bulletin* 88(6), 895–917, doi: https://doi.org/10.1037/0022-3514.88.6.895.

Sparrow, Robert (2014), 'Egalitarianism and Moral Bioenhancement', *American Journal of Bioethics* 14(4), 20–28, doi: https://doi.org/10.1080/15265161.2014.889241.

Specker, Jona, Focquaert, Farah, Raus, Kasper, Sterckx, Sigrid, and Schermer, Maartje (2014), 'The Ethical Desirability of Moral Bioenhancement: A Review of Reasons', *BMC Medical Ethics* 15, doi: https://doi.org/10.1186/1472-6939-15-67.

Strohminger, Nina, and Nichols, Shaun (2014), 'The Essential Moral Self', *Cognition* 131(1), 159–171, doi: https://doi.org/10.1016/j.cognition.2013.12.005.

Susser, Daniel (2019), 'Invisible Influence: Artificial Intelligence and the Ethics of Adaptive Choice Architectures', *AIES '19: Proceedings of the 2019 AAAI/ACM Conference on AI, Ethics, and Society*, January, 403–408, doi: https://doi.org/10.1145/3306618.3314286.

Tang, Tiffany Y., and Winoto, Pineta (2016), 'I Should Not Recommend It to You Even If You Will Like It: The Ethics of Recommender Systems', *New Review of Hypermedia and Multimedia* 22(1–2), 111–138, doi: https://doi.org/10.1080/13614568.2015.1052099.

Taylor, Linnet (2016), 'Safety in Numbers? Group Privacy and Big Data Analytics in the Developing World', in Linnet Taylor, Luciano Floridi, and Bart van der Sloot, eds, *Group Privacy: New Challenges of Data Technologies*, Vol. 126 (Cham: Springer), doi: https://doi.org/10.1007/978-3-319-46608-8.

Taylor, Linnet, Floridi, Luciano, and van der Sloot, Bart, eds (2016), *Group Privacy: New Challenges of Data Technologies*, Vol. 126 (Cham: Springer).

Vallor, Shannon (2015), 'Moral Deskilling and Upskilling in a New Machine Age: Reflections on the Ambiguous Future of Character', *Philosophy and Technology* 28, 107–124, doi: https://doi.org/10.1007/s13347-014-0156-9.

Veliz, Carissa (2020), *Privacy is Power* (London: Penguin; Bantam Press).

Whitby, Blay (2011), 'On Computable Morality: An Examination of Machines', in Michael Anderson and Susan Leigh Anderson, eds, Machine Ethics (Cambridge: Cambridge University Press), 138–150.

Wright, Jennifer Cole, Cullum, Jerry, and Schwab, Nicholas (2008), 'The Cognitive and Affective Dimensions of Moral Conviction: Implications for Attitudinal and Behavioral Measures of Interpersonal Tolerance', *Personality and Psychology Bulletin* 34(11), doi: https://doi.org/10.1177/0146167208322557.

Yang, Qiang, Liu, Yang, Chen, Tianjian, and Tong, Yongxin (2019), 'Federated Machine Learning: Concept and Applications', *ACM Transactions on Intelligent Systems and Technology* 10(2), 1–19, doi: https://doi.org/10.1145/3298981.

Young, Garry (2018), 'How Would We Know If Moral Enhancement Had Occurred?', *Journal of Speculative Philosophy* 32(4), 587–606, doi: https://doi.org/10.5325/jspecphil.32.4.0587.

CHAPTER 18

···

THE CHALLENGE OF VALUE ALIGNMENT

From Fairer Algorithms to AI Safety

···

IASON GABRIEL AND VAFA GHAZAVI

INTRODUCTION

···

THERE has long been a view among observers of artificial intelligence (AI) research, often expressed in science fiction, that it poses a distinctive moral challenge. This idea has been articulated in a number of ways, ranging from the notion that AI might take a 'treacherous turn' and act in ways that are opposed to the interests of its human operators, to deeper questions about the impact of AI on our understanding of human identity, emotions, and relationships. Yet over the past decade, with the growth of more powerful and socially embedded AI technologies, discussion of these questions has become increasingly mainstream. Among topics that have commanded the most serious attention, the challenge of 'value alignment' stands out. It centres upon the question of how to ensure that AI systems are properly aligned with human values and how to guarantee that AI technology remains properly amenable to human control. In 1960, the mathematician and founder of cybernetics, Norbert Wiener, articulated a version of this challenge when he wrote that, 'If we use, to achieve our purposes, a mechanical agency with whose operation we cannot efficiently interfere ... we had better be quite sure that the purpose put into the machine is the purpose which we really desire' (1960: 1358). More recently, the prominent AI researcher Stuart Russell has warned that we suffer from a failure of value alignment when we 'perhaps inadvertently, imbue machines with objectives that are imperfectly aligned with our own' (2019: 137).

This chapter explores the questions posed by AI and alignment with human values in more detail. It begins by looking at foundational questions about the relationship between technology and value. Far from existing in a vacuum, we note that there has long been interest in, and concern about, the potential of technology to 'lock in' different values and kinds of authority relationship. Moreover, recognition of this fact has often been accompanied by an understanding that it places a degree of responsibility on designers and recognition that we need specific methodologies to help align technology with visions of the social good that receive widespread endorsement. With this framework in place, the second part of the chapter looks at the question of AI technology in more detail. In particular, we ask: is there something special about AI that makes questions about value more complicated or acute? Here, we answer in the affirmative: while there are clear continuities with technologies that have come before, the combination of intelligence and autonomy demonstrated by modern AI systems gives rise to new challenges. This is true both from a normative perspective, given that we are able to encode a richer set of values in AI systems than in more simple artefacts, and also from a technological perspective—where greater scope of action and intelligence create new challenges from the perspective of alignment and control. The third part of this chapter looks at work being undertaken by technical AI researchers to address the challenge of alignment over the long run and at discussions taking place within that community. Finally, with this understanding in place, we return to earlier observations about the relationship between technology and value, and ask how this philosophical and sociological work might contribute to our understanding of AI alignment. In this context, we note that while most technical discussion of alignment focuses on one-person-one-agent scenarios, we also need to think seriously about social value alignment. This would involve aligning AI systems with a range of different voices and perspectives.

TECHNOLOGY AND VALUES

Although the challenge of value alignment has arisen first and foremost in discussion of AI systems, the notion that technology has a moral valence and moral consequences has a long intellectual lineage. From a philosophical vantage point, value generally refers to what ought to be promoted in the world, encompassing concepts such as autonomy, justice, care, well-being, and virtue. This normative conception of value has deep philosophical roots, and can be contrasted with instrumental value used to price goods in markets (Anderson 1993; Satz 2010). Outside philosophy, there is also considerable intellectual inquiry into the relationship between technology and values. In the context of technological design, a working definition of 'value' has been offered by Friedman and Hendry as 'what is important to people in their lives, with a focus on ethics and morality' (2019: 24). Moreover, the entire interdisciplinary field of science and technology studies (STS) builds upon the insight that values tend to be embedded in technologies, with ramifications for technologists and society, including through the impact on norms and ways of life. As Sheila Jasanoff puts it, 'far from being independent of human desire and intention, [technologies] are subservient to social forces all the way through' (2016: 18). Beyond this, technological artefacts have the potential to 'lock in' or manifest certain values in a variety of ways.

One famous example of this phenomenon can be found in Langdon Winner's seminal article, 'Do Artifacts Have Politics?' (1980). In it, he cites the case of Robert Moses, whose twentieth-century designs for New York City contributed to deepening racial stratification by creating low-hanging bridges that limited public transport flows from poorer, predominantly non-White neighbourhoods to more affluent public spaces.[1] Another example of 'design with a purpose' can be found in the city plans of Baron Haussman, who redesigned the streets of Paris after the events of the French revolution, so that it contained open boulevards that facilitated troop movement and suppressed the possibility of protest (Scott 1998 [2020]). In these ways, technical artefacts may have 'political properties' embodying specific forms of power and authority. Moreover, Winner suggests that there is a temptation, with the creation of powerful tools, for the ends to be adapted to the means (rather than the other way around) and for technologies to draw forth certain modes of social organization. In the context of discussions around AI, Yuval Harari has recently made a version of this argument, suggesting that the need for large datasets and computer power favours centralized forms of political authority and governance (2018).[2]

Viewed from a philosophical vantage point, it should also be clear that technology and value are intimately connected. Crucially, technological artefacts, whether in the form of transport systems, medical innovations, communications devices, energy facility design, or the development of home computers, shape and influence the choice architecture within which individual decisions are subsequently made. This fact is easily obscured by an agent-centric view of ethics. However, it should be clear, upon reflection, that new technologies make some outcomes more likely and some outcomes less likely to occur, that they create new possibilities, and that their creation will sometimes exclude certain possibilities from being realized altogether. In this sense, technology often has a profound effect on the states of affairs that we are able to access on an individual or collective basis, and on the states of affairs that we are likely to pursue. Thus, regardless of the metaethical stance we take, including our view about where value ultimately resides, no technology of scale will be 'value neutral' in the sense of leaving this balance of possible outcomes unaffected.[3]

This insight about what we term the 'technology–value nexus' has a number of important consequences. First, it suggests that technologists are themselves engaged in a world-making activity and that a level of responsibility necessarily attaches to the process of technical innovation and design. For even if Heidegger (1954 [2013]) is correct, and the cumulative growth of technology ultimately represents an 'enframing' or drawing forth of possibilities that are hard to fully foreshadow or understand, some measure of foresight is possible—creating the opportunity for responsible agency and direction in this domain. Second, in order to discharge this responsibility successfully, and guard against moral error, we need methods to ensure that the design of technology is congruent not only with the personal moral beliefs of designers or engineers, but also with a vision of flourishing that is widely endorsed and sensitive to the needs of different communities.[4] Since the early 1990s, an approach known as 'value-sensitive design', which draws on fields such as anthropology, human–computer interaction, philosophy, and software engineering, has actively sought to bring values into techno-logical processes (Friedman and Hendry 2019).[5] Key methods for doing so include techniques such as stakeholder analysis and citizen consultation, both of which empha-size the importance of including the perspective of those who are significantly affected by technological innovation (Martin et al. 2020). Third, it suggests that technologists need to think seriously about these questions early on, including whether to develop certain technologies at all. It is almost always beneficial to exercise ethical foresight at this point, when there is greater latitude of choice and before various path-dependencies have set in.

Is AI special?

With this understanding in place, we can now ask whether AI is 'special' when considered from the standpoint of the technology–value nexus. Is AI just like the other technological artefacts we have mentioned, or does it differ in some important way? To make progress on this question, we start with a brief overview of what AI is, or has come to mean, at the present moment. Building upon this foundation, we then consider what unique properties AI systems might possess.

What is AI?

The term 'artificial intelligence' commonly refers both to a quality of computerized systems and to a set of techniques used to achieve this capability, most often machine learning (ML). 'Intelligence' can be understood in this context to refer to an agent's ability to adapt and 'achieve goals in a wide range of environments' (Legg and Hutter 2007: 402). This instrumental conception of intelligence represents only one view drawn from a family of definitions one might endorse (Dignum 2019; Cave 2020). However, within the vocabulary of computer science, 'artificial intelligence' tends to refer pri-marily to models or agents that perceive their environment and make decisions that maximize the chance of achieving a goal. Indeed, Stuart Russell articulates this view clearly when he writes that 'machines are intelligent *to the extent* that their actions can be expected to achieve their objectives' (2019: 19).

   In this context, ML refers to a family of statistical or algorithmic approaches that can be used to train a model so that it learns to perform intelligent actions—sometimes from scratch. The discipline of ML encompasses a variety of different approaches. One branch called 'supervised learning' focuses on training a model to identify and respond to patterns in labelled datasets. Supervised learning is at the heart of many real-world applications of AI, including automated image recognition, disease diagnosis, the devel-opment of financial trading strategies, and the creation of job recommendation systems. 'Unsupervised learning', by way of contrast, aims to uncover patterns in unlabelled data and to perform tasks, such as the discovery of fraudulent transactions, on that basis. When run on sufficiently powerful hardware, both techniques allow models to learn from experience without using explicit instructions. In this regard, ML systems differ from earlier 'expert system' models such as the Chess-playing computer Deep Blue, which relied upon an intricate set of hand-crafted rules and instructions to defeat the reigning Chess champion Garry Kasparov in 1996. Innovations in ML, the collection of vast datasets, and the growth of computing power have together fostered many recent AI breakthroughs.

Looking forward, one particularly promising approach for more advanced forms of AI is reinforcement learning (RL). RL agents usually contain four key elements: a policy which defines the agent's way of behaving at a given time, a reward signal which defines its goal, a value function which estimates the long-term value of different states of affairs, and a model of the environment which allows the agent to make predictions about how the environment will respond to its decisions (Sutton and Barto 2018: 6–7). RL agents then learn what to do by trying to maximize a numerical reward signal that they receive from their environment. They do this by engaging in exploration and revising their policies along the way. Sophisticated RL agents have proved particularly adept at game-playing, mastering the ancient Chinese board game of Go (which had previously been thought to be computationally intractable because of the vast number of possible moves), as well as real-time computer strategy games such as *Defence of the Ancients (DOTA)* and *StarCraft II*.

The potential uniqueness of AI systems

Many of these innovations are impressive in their own right. However, when considered from the standpoint of the technology–value nexus, do they represent some fundamental departure from previous systems or a significant point of differentiation? In many ways, the answer is no. Concerns over injustice, safety, and unintended consequences exist for ML algorithms as they do for other technologies. Moreover, the central challenge discussed so far, which centres on the potential for technology to lock in or manifest a particular set of values, has clearly spilled over into the domain of ML, where it is usually discussed under the guise of 'algorithmic bias'.

Recent analysis has identified numerous cases where algorithmic tools or models have come to reflect forms of bias that arise from the data they were trained on—or from the way that data was curated and labelled. In the case of natural language processing, algorithms learned to associate certain job types with gender stereotypes, leading to biased predictions that disadvantaged women. Historically compromised data has also led to racially biased recommendations in the context of the criminal justice system, both when it comes to parole recommendations and with predictive policing (Angwin et al. 2016; Lum and Isaac 2016). And there are many examples of ML systems performing worse for minorities or groups who sit at the intersection of different forms of disadvantage. In particular, automated facial analysis algorithms (Buolamwini and Gebru 2018) and health-care diagnostics (Obermeyer et al. 2019) have tended to perform poorly for women and non-White sections of the population. When these decision-making systems are used in socially important contexts such as the allocation of health care, education, or credit, they can compound disadvantage by obscuring its origin, extending its influence over time, and creating forms of automated discrimination that are difficult to address (Eubanks 2018). Moreover, in each case, there is a clear sense that the technologies are not aligned with key values such as the requirements of fairness, or with what we as a society want them to do. Thus, they embody what we might term 'social value misalignment'. To address these shortcomings, there is now an active fairness, accountability, and transparency research community (Benjamin 2019; Selbst et al. 2019; Abebe et al. 2020).

At the same time, the fact that this is an emergent field of academic study testifies to the fact that these problems are often particularly acute for AI, and that, moreover, there are certain features of AI systems that make the task of social value alignment distinctive and particularly challenging. Indeed, the moral questions raised by AI alignment are *not simply* those that are intrinsic to the creation of large-scale technological systems or technologies that occupy public roles, functions, and places. Some of these unique challenges are to do with the complexity and opacity of the systems involved: once an algorithmic model has been trained, it can be hard to say why it decided upon the action or recommendation it arrived at. Others challenges are more precisely tied to the notion of machine intelligence and autonomy in decision-making—to the idea that AI systems can make decisions or choices that are more meaningful than those encountered by technologies in the past.

To see this clearly, we can start by noting that simple technological artefacts, such as hammers or pencils, are not able to respond to their environment, let alone make decisions. Against this backdrop, Daniel Dennett suggests that even the existence of a simple 'switch' that can be turned on and off by some environmental change marks a *degree of freedom*, which is 'a level of interactivity that can be influenced and needs to be controlled' (2003: 162). More complicated artefacts have additional degrees of freedom in cases where 'there is an ensemble of possibilities of one kind or another, and which of these possibilities is actual at any time depends on whatever function or switch controls this degree of freedom' (Dennett 2003: 162). As these switches or nodes proliferate, they form 'larger switching networks, the degrees of freedom multiply dizzyingly, and issues of control grow complex and nonlinear' (Dennett 2003: 162). For Dennett, these properties are evidenced by biological organisms of sufficient complexity, including humans. However, they are also found in the networks used by AI researchers to create models that learn from their environment and optimize for objectives. As a consequence of this design feature, artificial agents can learn new mappings between inputs and outputs, coming up with solutions (or failure modes) that sometimes surprise their human designers.

Partly as a consequence of this freedom, it is possible to 'load' a richer set of values into AI systems than with more simple artefacts. This can be seen, for example, in the case of self-driving cars that have to navigate the world successfully while managing complex trade-offs in emergency situations. It is also reflected by the fact that the behaviour of AI systems is best understood by adopting what Dennett terms 'the intentional stance' (1987; 2009). Whereas it is possible to understand the behaviour of simple artefacts either by reference to mechanical explanations or design principles, it is most useful to think of AI systems as rational agents that have goals and intentions.[6] Moreover, whereas simple artefacts can 'be seen to derive their meaning from their functional goals in our practices, and hence not to have any intrinsic meaning independent of our meaning', AI systems have trajectories that 'can unfold without any direct dependence on us, their creators, and whose discriminations give their internal states a sort of meaning to them that may be unknown and not in our service' (Dennett 2009: 343). Indeed, as these systems make decisions previously reserved as the domain of human control, we are led to ask questions about where responsibility for these behaviours ultimately resides and how to ensure they are subject to meaningful control.

One answer to the first question has been provided by Floridi and Sanders, who argue that AI systems can also be 'moral agents' (2004). As with Dennett, the level of abstraction needed to analyse their behaviour plays a central role in the argument. Indeed, for these authors, the (a) interactivity, (b) autonomy, and (c) adaptability of AI systems make it possible for them to have this status (Floridi and Sanders 2004: 357–358). In this context, interactivity indicates that an agent and its environment can act upon each other. Autonomy 'means that the agent is able to change state without direct response to interaction', meaning 'it can perform internal transitions to change its state', which gives it 'a certain degree of complexity and independence from its environment' (Floridi and Sanders 2004: 357–358). Adaptability refers to the agent's potential, through interactions, to change the 'transition rules' by which it changes state. Taken together, these properties mean that an agent can learn its own mode of operation based on experience, and could, according to Floridi and Sanders, be made accountable for moral action.

However, even without this strong claim about moral responsibility, it seems clear that AI models have agential properties that manifest to a higher degree than in non-AI systems. This insight has implications for the kind of normative questions we can meaningfully ask about AI. For example, we can ask: which principle of values should we encode in AI—and who has the right to make these decisions, given that we live in a pluralistic world that is full of competing conceptions of value (Gabriel 2020)? Can AI be made so that it is kind or compassionate? Can it demonstrate care for human beings and sentient life? In this case, the moral qualities of 'compassion' or 'care' refer not to a subset of decisions made within a defined action space, but rather to a standing disposition, to a set of counterfactual truths about what an agent would do across a variety of circumstances and contextual variations.[7] Questions of this kind make little sense for simpler technologies. At most, we might ask whether a car, transport system, or simple computer program was *designed* in a way that demonstrated compassion or concern for users and non-users of the technology. But with AI systems, the locus of meaningful analysis shifts to the qualities of the agents themselves.

TECHNICAL APPROACHES
TO VALUE ALIGNMENT

If the preceding analysis is correct, then the alignment of powerful AI systems requires interdisciplinary collaboration. We need a clearer understanding both of the goal of alignment *and also* of the technical means available to us for implementing solutions. In this regard, technical research can provide us with a more precise understanding of the challenges we face with AI and about the kind of answers that are useful. Meanwhile, from the philosophical community and the public, we need further direction and guidance about the goals of alignment and about the meaning of properly aligned AI. In the spirit of mutual endeavour, this section looks at technical aspects of the alignment challenge, including methodologies for achieving AI alignment, concrete problems encountered to date, and proposals about how to ensure that AI systems stay aligned even if their intelligence one day significantly exceeds our own.

Top-down and bottom-up approaches

When it comes to strategies for creating value-aligned AI, Wallach and Allen distinguish between 'top-down' and 'bottom-up' approaches (2009). Top-down approaches to alignment start by identifying an appropriate moral theory to align with and then designing algorithms that are capable of implementing it. With this approach, the designer explicitly sets an objective for the machine from the outset based on some moral principle or theory which they would like to operationalize. By way of contrast, bottom-up approaches do not require the specification of a full moral framework. Instead, they focus upon the creation of environments or feedback mechanisms that enable agents to learn from human behaviour and be rewarded for morally praiseworthy conduct. Each approach brings with it technical and normative challenges.

To start with, top-down approaches are based on the possibility that ethical principles or rules can be explicitly stated, that these principles can be expressed in computer code, and that following these principles constitutes ethical action (Wallach and Allen 2009: 83). The relevant ethical principles could derive from religious ideals, moral codes, culturally endorsed values, or philosophical systems (Allen et al. 2005: 150). This approach to alignment has also been explored in science fiction, with Isaac Asimov's *Three Laws of Robotics* serving as a classic illustration. The rules he proposed (a) banned robots from injuring humans; (b) insisted they obey humans—except where this would violate (a); and (c) stipulated that a robot must protect its own existence—as long as this didn't violate (a) or (b).

If it can be made to work, a top-down approach has certain advantages: the rules it relies upon could in principle be widely known and understood—and they could be designed to target undesirable behaviours (such as killing or stealing). However, as

Asimov's stories illustrate, rules can also come into conflict with each other, producing 'computationally intractable situations unless there is some further principle or rule for resolving the conflict' (Allen et al. 2005: 150). More importantly still, this approach appears to require us to identify and specify the correct moral framework for AI up front. If this is the case, then it forces us onto the horns of a dilemma: either we must proceed on the basis of our own personal moral beliefs (which could easily be mistaken) or we need to identify public principles for AI that are, in practice, difficult to come by. So far, variants of utilitarianism have tended to be the preferred option for engineers, given the apparent compatibility of the theory with optimization-based learning (Roff 2020; Russell 2019). Yet this trajectory is problematic if our ultimate goal is social value alignment (i.e. for the alignment of AI systems with values that are widely endorsed).

In the light of how hard it is to identify and encode appropriate moral goals, some researchers have instead pursued a 'bottom-up' approach to alignment that seeks to infer human preferences about values from observed behaviour or feedback. In fact, there is a specific branch of RL called inverse reinforcement learning (IRL) which appears well suited to the task. IRL systems do not directly specify the reward function that the agent aims to maximize. Rather, in these models, the reward function is treated as an unknown which must be ascertained by the artificial agent. More precisely, the agent is presented with datasets (including potentially very large ones), environments, or set of examples (such as the conduct of human experts), and focuses on 'the problem of extracting a reward function given observed, optimal behaviour' (Ng and Russell 2000: 663). The goal of the exercise is then to infer or understand human preferences through observation and to align with them, rather than pursuing an independently specified goal or outcomes.

However, the bottom-up approach to value alignment also encounters challenges. In certain respects it tends to be more *opaque* than in ML systems, where the reward is clearly specified. With IRL, even if the agent appears to be acting in a moral manner, it will be hard to know what precisely it has learned from the dataset or examples we have shown it. Moreover, important normative questions still need to be addressed (Gabriel 2020). As the fairness, accountability, and transparency research community has demonstrated, the salient question immediately becomes what data to train the system on, how to justify this choice, and how to ensure that what the model learns is free from unjustifiable bias.

One interesting data-point for bottom-up approaches comes from the 'Moral Machine' experiment which crowd-sourced the intuitions of millions of people about moral trade-offs encountered by autonomous vehicles (Awad et al. 2018). Ultimately, the result of the study was inconclusive, despite its scale. What it revealed was a set of noisy preferences in this area, some obvious tendencies (e.g. to value many lives over fewer lives), and some ethical variation across cultures, including a propensity to accord more ethical weight to the lives of higher-status individuals in poorer countries. The study therefore raises deep questions about the coherence of everyday moral beliefs and perspectives across populations, and also about the value of an empirical approach to value selection, given that certain views (e.g. those concerning social status) are widely endorsed but hard to justify from an ethical vantage point.

Concrete problems

In practice, AI systems that have been deployed in the world or in training environments have also encountered a number of difficulties that bear upon alignment. At their root sit a number of attributes that we have already mentioned: autonomy, intelligence, and powerful optimization-based learning. In particular, there is concern that the elements may combine in ways that lead the goal of an AI system, as established by its reward function, to diverge from its human operator's true goal or intention (Christiano 2018; Leike et al. 2018). As ML systems become more powerful, there are at least four specific challenges that AI researchers need to overcome (Amodei et al. 2016; Everitt 2018).

The first challenge is *reward hacking* or *reward corruption*. This problem arises when an artificial agent manages to maximize the numerical reward it receives by finding un-anticipated shortcuts or corrupting the feedback system (Ring and Orseau 2011; Everitt et al. 2021). One famous example of this occurred when an RL agent was trained to play the computer game *CoastRunners*. In this case, an agent that had been trained to maxi-mize its score looped around and around in circles ad infinitum, crashing into obstacles, collecting points, and achieving a high score—all without finishing the race, which is what it was really meant to do (Clark and Amodei 2016). To address this challenge, researchers have considered a number of options. Everitt et al. (2017) propose two strategies for promoting aligned behaviour: engineers can provide the agent with richer data so that it avoids mistakes arising from 'systemic sensory error', and they can blunt some of the force of reward hacking when it stems from strong forms of optimization by focusing on a random sample of top-tier outcomes instead of a single, specific objective. Other important approaches include building agents that always entertain a degree of uncertainty about their true reward, something that creates an incentive to consult human operators and ensure that their current policy is still on track (Hadfield-Menell et al. 2016; Russell 2019).

The second challenge is that even if the agent aims for the right goal or outcome, it may simply take the most efficient path to that goal and not factor in *negative side effects*. To avoid this outcome, researchers have focused on ways to ensure that artificial agents are not significantly disruptive, when compared to a counterfactual baseline, and also that they demonstrate 'conservatism' in this regard by minimizing irreversible changes to the environment (Krakovna 2018; Turner et al. 2019). More advanced approaches aim to ensure that agents really understand the meaning of the instructions they are given—including assumptions about outcomes to avoid—by drawing upon contract theory (Hadfield-Menell and Hadfield 2018). The key here is to provide agents with access to 'substantial amounts of external structure' that supplements and fills in any gaps that are left by explicit statements of the goal.

Third, in order to learn successful policies, agents need to engage in a process of exploration where they try different things and receive feedback from the environment. As a consequence, we need to make sure that agents *explore the world in a safe way* and that they do not make costly mistakes while doing so. Often, it makes sense to train agents in simulation and allow them to make mistakes in a contained setting. However, an important element of alignment research centres upon testing agents and ensuring that they are able to perform well in the wild.

Finally, there is the challenge of how to assess and *evaluate complex agent behaviour*. We have already noted that algorithms are often opaque, leading some commentators to use the metaphor of a 'black box' (Pasquale 2015). These qualities are particularly challenging in social and legal contexts, where those affected are entitled to an explanation of why decisions were taken. However, a related problem also occurs at the micro-level when it comes to training and evaluating artificial agents. Usually, this process requires a lot of feedback that is costly to give, in terms of time and attention. As a consequence, designers may use more simple proxies to evaluate agent behaviour. For example, we might check only for visible dirt when evaluating the performance of a cleaning robot, rather than checking under surfaces or doing a full evaluation. However, these proxies then make it more likely that the agent will drift off track or engage in faulty behaviour. This challenge becomes more complicated still when we think about training and interacting with very advanced artificial agents.

Highly advanced AI

Looking forward, a number of theorists have suggested that AI systems are likely to become more powerful in the future. Stuart Russell describes the 'ultimate goal' of AI research as the discovery of a general-purpose 'method that is applicable across all problem types and works effectively for large and difficult instances while making very few assumptions' (2019: 46). Among experts working in this area, AI that matches or exceeds human-level intelligence across different domains is often referred to as 'artificial general intelligence' (AGI). This notion is closely related to—and sometimes equated with—the idea of 'superintelligence', which Nick Bostrom defines as 'any intellect that greatly exceeds the cognitive performance of humans in virtually all domains of interest' (2014 [2017]: 26).

Importantly, while the creation of superintelligence could, presumably, unlock great benefits for humanity, Bostrom has argued that it also poses an existential risk in cases where its objectives are not aligned with our own (Bostrom 2014 [2017]). Moreover, catastrophic outcomes need not be the result of malice on the part of the agent or its designers: rather, they could be a by-product of other tendencies or inclinations that such an agent might have. At the cornerstone of Bostrom's argument sits the *orthogonality thesis*, which holds that any level of intelligence is compatible with any goal. If it is correct, then we should not expect there to be any correlation between how intelligent a machine is and how closely it is aligned with our values. More specifically, the capacity for instrumental rationality—that AI systems exemplify to a high degree—does not equate to alignment with certain substantive goals or outcomes. In this regard, Bostrom is at odds with Derek Parfit (2011) and Peter Singer (2011), who hope that substantive moral insight might result from the capacity for instrumental reason, and has more in common with David Hume, who held that instrumental rationality is compatible with any final end (1739–40 [2000]).

Moreover, both Bostrom and Russell defend a version of the *instrumental convergence thesis*, which predicts that AGI would display instrumental goals of self-improvement, self-preservation, and resource acquisition in pursuit of its goals, even if this is to the disadvantage of human beings. As Russell points out, 'any entity that has a definite objective will automatically act as if it also has instrumental goals' (2019: 141–142). One such instrumental goal is for the machine to stay switched on so it can fulfil other objectives (the 'off-switch problem'); others might be acquiring money or pursuing 'resource objectives' such as computing power, algorithms, and knowledge, since these are 'useful for achieving any overarching objective' (Hadfield-Menell et al. 2017). The problem, Russell suggests, is that 'the acquisition process will continue without limit', thereby necessarily creating a conflict with human interests and needs (Russell 2019: 141–142). As with more prosaic examples of reward-hacking, Russell's solution is to ensure that AGI is *uncertain* about its true objectives so that it exhibits 'a kind of humility', exemplified in behaviour such as deferring to humans and allowing itself to be switched off.

Finally, even if the previous two challenges can be surmounted there is still a challenge around the *intelligibility and supervision* of AGI. The central question here is how to provide scalable advice and direction to an entity whose capabilities, knowledge, and action space are, in certain respects, beyond our comprehension. Most approaches to this task aim to break down the normative evaluation of agent behaviour into smaller tasks, so that humans can then add up their evaluations and arrive at an overall judgement—even when artificial agents are pursuing complex goals on a vast scale. In this context, *reward modelling* is a set of techniques for supplementing RL with a learned reward function, trained with human oversight and monitoring (Leike et al. 2018). In 'recursive reward modelling', the artificial agent is specifically incentivized to help its human instructor better define goals for the AI to pursue, enabling more effective evaluation of the agent's behaviour even as it scales up. Recursive reward modelling is an example of *iterated amplification*, an approach that trains the AI progressively by breaking down a task into simpler sub-tasks (Christiano et al. 2018). Finally, *safety via debate* is a modified version of iterated amplification which involves training systems that debate with each other, competing to provide true answers to human operators (Irving et al. 2018). Given a question or proposed action, two AI agents take turns making short statements, enabling a human judge to decide which gave the most useful information.

THE FUNDAMENTAL RELEVANCE OF VALUE

We have now covered a significant amount of ground, from the technology–value nexus, to the properties of AI systems, to research into agents whose capabilities might one day significantly exceed our own. With this architecture in place, are there any new insights that we can draw upon for the purpose of AI alignment? In particular, can long-standing discussion of the relationship between technology, values, and society, help to illuminate this debate? We believe it can, both in terms of alignment's ultimate goals and in terms of how these outcomes should be brought about.

Given the understanding of intelligence used in this domain, artificial agents will necessarily pursue *some* goal or objective. This then raises normative questions about *what* kind of goal or objective AI systems should be designed to pursue. Within the AI research community there are three prominent answers to the question, 'Alignment with what?' The first approach focuses on alignment with *instructions*, aiming to include as much safety or value-preserving information as possible in the orders that the AI system receives. Russell (2019) refers to this as the 'standard model'. However, he points out that instructions may be understood very literally by agents that lack contextual understanding, and that this could have negative consequences—with the story of King Midas serving as an illustration. This risk has led some researchers to focus instead on creating agents that behave in accordance with the user's true *intentions*. Indeed, this locus for alignment sits at the heart of the reward-modelling approach discussed earlier, and also lends weight to the notion of using contract theory to ensure that AI understands the implied meaning of terms (Hadfield-Menell and Hadfield 2018). A third approach, which is endorsed by Russell among others, aims to align artificial agents with *human preferences*, something that might be achieved using IRL.

However, viewed from the standpoint of the technology–value nexus, there is clear potential for a gap to open up between each of these loci for alignment and the values or states of affairs that a technology ultimately helps us to realize. After all, instructions, intentions, and preferences, can all be misinformed, irrational, or unethical, in which case their promotion by AI would lead to bad states of affairs. The aspiration to create agents that are aligned with values—which is to say, the full spectrum of things that we should promote or engage with—opens up a number of questions about how this could be done.

Additionally, alignment research has tended to focus on aligning AI with the instructions, intentions, or preferences, of a single human operator. In part because of the sizable technical challenges we have considered, discussion of alignment has tended to centre upon scenarios that are 'one-to-one' rather than 'one-to-many'. As a consequence, less attention has been paid to the question of how these various elements can be integrated or made to work on a society-wide, or even global, basis. To the extent that these questions have arisen for more general AI systems, there have been two main kinds of proposal: one of which focuses on social choice theory (Prasad 2018; Baum 2020) and the other of which focuses on the possibility of ideal convergence between different perspectives and opinions (Yudkowsky 2004). The first approach has been studied extensively in the domain of welfare economics and voting systems. It looks at how to aggregate information from individual people into collective judgements. In the context of value alignment, Stuart Armstrong (2019) has argued that these approaches could be used to systematically synthesize different types of human preference (including basic preferences about the world and meta-preferences) into a utility function that would then guide agent behaviour. The second approach has been discussed by Eliezer Yudkowsky (2004), who suggests that AI could be designed to align with our 'coherent extrapolated volition'. This goal represents an idealized version of what we would want 'if we knew more, thought faster, were more the people we wished we were, and had grown up farther together' (2004).

However, this focus on 'one-to-one' versions of alignment and emphasis on preference aggregation potentially elide important aspects of the alignment question. To start with, a fuller appreciation of the social consequences of technology, and the way in which it shapes our own choice architecture, points towards a need for richer and more democratic forms of AI alignment. To achieve what we have termed 'social value alignment' of the kind often advocated for by the fairness, accountability, and transparency community, AI systems ultimately need to embody principles that are widely endorsed by those who have their lives affected—and sometimes powerfully so—by these technologies.

Alignment with instructions and intentions, or the capability to understand human preferences, may still be an important stepping stone towards this goal. However, the richer ideal of social value alignment itself presses us to engage with a new set of challenges, including the challenge of moral uncertainty (i.e. the fact that we are often unsure what action or theory is morally right) and the challenge of moral pluralism (i.e. the fact that people ascribe to a variety of different reasonable views and perspectives). Taken together, these elements mean that we are unlikely to persuade everyone about the truth of a single moral theory using evidence and reason alone (Rawls 1993 [2005]). As a consequence, if we are to avoid a situation in which some people simply impose their views on others, then AI alignment necessarily has a social and political dimension: we need to collectively come up with principles or values that we agree are appropriate for this purpose (Gabriel 2020).

In practice, many public and private bodies have sought to come up with principles for AI systems. These ethics guidelines tend to converge around the values of 'transparency, justice and fairness, non-maleficence, responsibility and privacy' (Jobin et al. 2019). However, they have also led to a well-founded concern that the voices included in these processes are not truly representative of affected parties. Some researchers have argued, for instance, that high-level AI values statements tend to promote a 'limited, technologically deterministic, expert-driven view', setting the terms of debate in a way that makes 'some conversations about ethical design possible while forestalling alternative visions' (Greene et al. 2019: 2122). Indeed, the prominent AI researcher Shakir Mohamed has expressed concern that AI research is currently 'localised' and '[w]ithin restricted geographies and people' (2018). He writes that, 'We [AI researchers] rely on inherited thinking and sets of unquestioned values; we reinforce selective histories; we fail to consider our technology's impacts and the possibility of alternative paths; we consider our work to be universally beneficial, needed and welcomed' (2018).

Moving forward, these considerations point towards the need for a deepening conversation about the nature of AI alignment, including what it means for agents to be socially aligned in different contexts. If the technology comes to have increasingly global reach, then one aspiration might be to build alignment around principles that are subject to a 'global overlapping consensus' (Gabriel 2020). These principles would foreground commonalities between diverse systems of thought and could, in principle, be endorsed by the wide range of people who these technologies affect.[8] However, consensus of this kind needs to be the result of deep and inclusive discussion if it is to have real value (Shahriari and Shahriari 2017). This is for two reasons. First, those affected have a right to contribute to discussions about technologies that have a profound effect on them. The legitimacy of the resulting principles depends upon antecedent recognition of the right to speak about and influence these matters. Second, regarding the epistemic value of the principles themselves, it is important to remember that no individual has a complete monopoly on the truth. In this regard, it is far more likely that J. S. Mill was correct when he suggested that everyone only has access to a part of it (Mill 1859 [2006]: 53). By creating an open and properly inclusive discourse around AI ethics, we create space for new considerations to come to light, something that should lead to a richer, more complete set of guidelines and principles over the long run.

CONCLUSION

This chapter has sought to situate questions around AI alignment within the wider discussion of the relationship between technology and value. We have suggested that the connection between technology and value is best understood through the impact technological artefacts have on our ability and inclination to access various states of affairs. We also argued that this relationship is potentially more complex and salient for AI than it is for simple technological artefacts, given that new agents or models embody greater degrees of freedom and can be loaded with thicker values than was true of objects in the past. Indeed, when it comes to the evaluation of AI systems, we look not only for guarantees that AI artefacts were *designed* in ways that demonstrate care or compassion, but also for AI systems to evidence these qualities themselves. This shift in the locus of evaluation reflects the fact that AI systems are often best understood from the 'intentional stance', a perspective that allows for the possibility that they have qualities of the relevant kind.

Looking forward, this combination of agency and intelligence gives rise to challenges that the technical AI community seeks to address. These matters are rightfully the focus of serious research efforts, given that the challenges could potentially scale to more powerful systems. At the same time, they should not overshadow the question of what values AI systems should ultimately be aligned with. Ultimately, we need to reach beyond alignment with a single human operator and think about what it means for AI technology to be *socially value aligned*. These questions are already being thought about and addressed by the fairness, accountability, and transparency community, creating a significant opportunity for feedback and mutual learning (Crawford and Calo, 2016; Corbett-Davies and Sharad, 2018). More generally, these observations highlight the importance of interdisciplinary approaches for value alignment efforts. As a relatively new area of moral and technical inquiry, there is an opportunity to harness different branches of knowledge as part of a broad and inclusive research agenda. They point also to the need for technologists and policy-makers to stay attuned to their social context and stakeholders, even as the AI systems they build become more capable. Considerations of fair process and epistemic virtue point towards the need for a properly inclusive discussion around the ethics of AI alignment.

NOTES

1. This was also a problem in other cities in the United States. For example, the Interstate 20 in Atlanta was deliberately plotted, in the words of Mayor Bill Hartsfield, to serve as 'the boundary between the white and Negro communities'. Black neighborhoods, he hoped, would be hemmed in on one side of the new expressway, while White neighborhoods on the other side of it would be 'protected' (Kruse 2019).
2. For a contrasting view, see Andrew Trask et al. (2020).
3. This claim holds true both for person-affecting and non-person-affecting theories of value (Parfit 1997).
4. Admittedly, this claim rests on a set of prevailing metaethical views which allow for the possibility of moral error. Certain forms of anti-foundational metaethics or error theory dispute this claim. Yet, a more interesting question still concerns what happens when society as a whole is in a state of error. What should we say about the design of technology then? Are there ways that entire societies can uncover moral blind spots and ensure that they do not carry over into the design of AI systems? These questions take us into the domain of what Allen Buchanan terms 'social moral epistemology' (2002). In his view, there are certain institutions and social practices that society may adopt that reduce the risk of systematic moral error.
5. Indeed, the discipline of value-sensitive design has engaged with AI from its beginnings (Friedman and Kahn 1992).
6. This then leads to the heavily disputed question of whether these artefacts can *really* be said to have goals and intentions. Dennet suggests that they can. Against this view, one might argue that these artefacts do not obviously have the quality of possessing 'mind'. Both perspectives are compatible with the view we are advancing here.
7. This idea that the quality of compassion should be treated as a fixed disposition draws heavily upon the notion of a 'virtue' used in virtue ethics. As Rosalind Hursthouse writes on this point, 'Given that the virtuous disposition is multi-track, no virtue ethicist would dream of making "the fundamental attribution error" and ascribing honesty or charity to someone on the basis of a single honest or charitable action or even a series of them' (2006: 102).
8. The challenge of ensuring that different voices are properly heard has parallels in information ethics, which draws a distinction between a 'mono-cultural view of ethics' that claims exclusive validity, and a 'transcultural ethics' arising from intercultural dialogue (Capurro 2007). It also resonates with concerns raised by feminist epistemologists working on the philosophy of science, including the downplaying of certain cognitive styles and modes of knowledge, and the production of technologies that reinforce gender and other social hierarchies (Anderson 2015).

References

Abebe, Rediet, Abebe, Rediet, Solon Barocas, Jon Kleingberg, Karen Levy, Manish Raghavan, and David G. Robinson (2020), 'Roles for Computing in Social Change', *Proceedings of the 2020 Conference on Fairness, Accountability, and Transparency January*, 252–260.

Allen, Colin, Iva Smit, and Wendell Wallach (2005), 'Artificial Morality: Top-Down, Bottom-Up, and Hybrid Approaches', *Ethics and Information Technology* 7, 149–155.

Amodei, Dario, Chris Olah, Jacob Steinhardt, Paul Christiano, John Schulman, and Dan Mane (2016), 'Concrete Problems in AI Safety', *Proceedings of the AAAI Workshop on Artificial Intelligence* Safety, arXiv, 1606.06565.

Anderson, Elizabeth (1993), *Value in Ethics and Economics* (Cambridge, MA and London: Harvard University Press).

Anderson, Elizabeth (2015), 'Feminist Epistemology and Philosophy of Science', in *Stanford Encyclopedia of Philosophy*, https://plato.stanford.edu/entries/feminism-epistemology/, accessed 30 September 2021.

Angwin, Julia, Jeff Larson, Surya Mattu, and Lauren Kirchner (2016), 'Machine Bias', *ProPublica*, 23 May, https://www.propublica.org/article/machine-bias-risk-assessments-in-criminal-sentencing, accessed 30 September 2021.

Armstrong, Stuart (2019), 'Research Agenda v0.9: Synthesising a Human's Preferences into a Utility Function', *AI Alignment Forum*, 17 June, https://www.alignmentforum.org/posts/CSEdLLEkap2pubjof/research-agenda-v0-9-synthesising-a-human-s-preferences-into-1#fnref-wPj8aGxtWBoDNTAof-2, accessed 30 September 2021.

Awad, Edmond, Sohan Dsouza, Richard Kim, Jonathan Schulz, Joseph Henrich, Azim Shariff, Jean-François Bonnefon, and Iyad Rahwan, (2018), 'The Moral Machine Experiment', *Nature* 563(7729), 59–64.

Baum, Seth (2020), 'Social Choice Ethics in Artificial Intelligence', *AI & Society*, 35, 165–179.

Benjamin, Ruha (2019), *Race After Technology: Abolitionist Tools for the New Jim Code* (Cambridge: Polity Press).

Bostrom, Nick (2014 [2017]), *Superintelligence: Paths, Dangers, Strategies* (Oxford: Oxford University Press).

Buchanan, Allen (2002), 'Social Moral Epistemology', *Social Philosophy and Policy* 19(2), 126–152.

Buolamwini, Joy, and Timnit Gebru (2018), 'Gender Shades: Intersectional Accuracy Disparities in Commercial Gender Classification', Conference on Fairness, Accountability, and Transparency, *Proceedings of Machine Learning Research* 81, 1–15.

Capurro, Rafael (2007), 'Intercultural Information Ethics', in Johannes Frühbauer, Thomas Hausmanninger, and Rafael Capurro, eds, *Localizing the Internet. Ethical Aspects in Intercultural Perspective* (Munich: Fink), 21–38.

Cave, Stephen (2020), 'The Problem with Intelligence: Its Value-Laden History and the Future of AI', Proceedings of the AAAI/ACM Conference on AI, Ethics, and Society, February, 29–35.

Christiano, Paul (2018), 'Clarifying "AI Alignment"', *Medium*, 7 April, https://ai-alignment.com/clarifying-ai-alignment-cec47cd69dd6, accessed 30 September 2021.

Christiano, Paul, Buck Shlegeris and Dario Amodei (2018), 'Supervising Strong Learners by Amplifying Weak Experts', *Proceedings of the AAAI Workshop on Artificial Intelligence Safety*, arXiv, 1810.08575.

Clark, Jack, and Dario Amodei (2016), 'Faulty Reward Functions in the Wild', https://blog.ope
nai.com/faulty-reward-functions, accessed 30 September 2021.

Corbett-Davies, Sam, and Sharad Goel (2018), 'The Measure and Mismeasure of Fairness: A
Critical Review of Fair Machine Learning', arXiv, 1808.00023.

Crawford, Kate, and Ryan Calo (2016), 'There Is a Blind Spot in AI Research', *Nature*
538(October), 312–313.

Dennett, Daniel C. (1987), *The Intentional Stance* (Cambridge, MA: MIT Press).

Dennett, Daniel C. (2003), *Freedom Evolves* (New York: Viking).

Dennett, Daniel C. (2009), 'Intentional Systems Theory', in Brian P. McLaughlin, Ansgar
Beckermann, and Sven Walter, eds, *The Oxford Handbook of Philosophy of Mind* (Oxford:
Oxford University Press), 339–350.

Dignum, Virginia (2019), *Responsible Artificial Intelligence: How to Develop and Use AI in a
Responsible Way* (Switzerland: Springer Nature).

Eubanks, Virginia (2018), *Automating Inequality: How High-Tech Tools Profile, Police, and
Punish the Poor* (New York, NY: St Martin's Press).

Everitt, Tom (2018), 'Towards Safe Artificial General Intelligence', doctoral thesis, Australian
National University, https://openresearch-repository.anu.edu.au/handle/1885/164227, accessed
30 September 2021.

Everitt, Tom, Marcus Hutter, Ramana Kumar, and Victoria Krakovna (2021), 'Reward tam-
pering problems and solutions in reinforcement learning: a causal influence diagram perspective', *Synthese* 198, 6435–6467.

Everitt, Tom, Victoria Krakovna, Laurent Orseau, Marcus Hutter, and Shane Legg (2017),
'Reinforcement Learning with Corrupted Reward Signal', International Joint Conference on
Artificial Intelligence arXiv, 1705.08417, 4705–4713.

Floridi, Luciano, and J.W. Sanders (2004), 'On the Morality of Artificial Agents', *Minds and
Machine* 14, 349–379.

Friedman, Batya, and David G. Hendry (2019), *Value Sensitive Design: Shaping Technology with
Moral Imagination* (Cambridge, MA and London: The MIT Press).

Friedman, Batya, and Peter Kahn (1992), 'Human Agency and Responsible Computing:
Implications for Computer System Design', *Journal of Systems and Software* 17(1): 7–14.

Gabriel, Iason (2020), 'Artificial Intelligence, Values, and Alignment', *Minds and Machines*,
30(3): 411–437.

Greene, Daniel, Anna Hoffmann, and Luke Star (2019), 'Better, Nicer, Clearer, Fairer: A Critical
Assessment of the Movement for Ethical Artificial Intelligence and Machine Learning',
Proceedings of the 52nd Hawaii International Conference on System Sciences, 2122–2131.

Hadfield-Menell, Dylan, and Gillian K. Hadfield (2018), 'Incomplete Contracting and AI
Alignment', https://arxiv.org/abs/1804.04268, accessed 30 September 2021.

Hadfield-Menell, Dylan, Anca Dragan, Pieter Abbeel, and Stuart Russell (2016), 'Cooperative
Inverse Reinforcement Learning', arXiv, 1606.03137.

Hadfield-Menell, Anca Dragan, Pieter Abbeel, and Stuart J. Russell (2017), 'The Off-Switch
Game', https://arxiv.org/abs/1611.08219, accessed 30 September 2021.

Harari, Yuval Noah (2018) 'Why technology favors tyranny', *The Atlantic*, 322(3): 64–70.

Heidegger], Martin (1954 [2013]), *The Question Concerning Technology: and Other Essays*
(New York, NY: Harper Perennial).

Hume, David (1739–40 [2000]), *A Treatise of Human Nature* (Oxford: Oxford University
Press).

Hursthouse, Rosalind (2006), 'Are Virtues the Proper Starting Point for Morality?', in James Lawrence Dreier, ed, *Contemporary Debates in Moral Theory* (Malden, MA: Blackwell), 99–112.

Irving, Geoffrey, Paul Christiano, and Dario Amodei (2018), 'AI Safety via Debate', arXiv, 1805.00899

Jasanoff, Sheila (2016), *The Ethics of Invention: Technology and the Human Future* (New York and London: W.W. Norton and Company).

Jobin, Anna, Marcello Ienca, and Effy Vayena (2019), 'Artificial Intelligence: The Global Landscape of Ethics Guidelines', *Nature Machine Intelligence* 1(September), 389–399.

Krakovna, Victoria, Laurent Orseau, Ramana Kumar, Miljan Martic, and Shane Legg (2018), 'Penalizing Side Effects Using Stepwise Relative Reachability', https://arxiv.org/abs/1806.01186

Kruse, Kevin M. (2019), 'How Segregation Caused Your Traffic Jam', *New York Times*, 14 August.

Legg, Shane, and Marcus Hutter (2007), 'Universal Intelligence: A Definition of Machine Intelligence', *Minds & Machines* 17(4), 391–444.

Leike, Jan, David Krueger, Tom Everitt, Miljan Martic, Vishal Maini, and Shane Legg (2018), 'Scalable Agent Alignment via Reward Modeling: A Research Direction', arXiv, 1811.07871.

Lum, Kristian, and William Isaac (2016), 'To Predict and Serve?', *Significance* 13(5), 14–19.

Martin Jr, Donald, Vinod Prabhakaran, Jill A. Kuhlberg, Andrew Smart, and William S. Isaac (2020), 'Participatory Problem Formulation for Fairer Machine Learning through Community Based System Dynamics', arXiv, 2005.07572.

Mill, John Stuart (2006), *On Liberty and the Subjection of Women* (London: Penguin).

Mohamed, Shakir (2018), 'Decolonising Artificial Intelligence', *The Spectator: Shakir's Machine Learning Blog*, 11 October, http://blog.shakirm.com/2018/10/decolonising-artificial-intelligence/, accessed 30 September 2021.

Ng, Andrew Y., and Stuart J. Russell (2000), 'Algorithms for Inverse Reinforcement Learning', *'00 Proceedings of the Seventeenth International Conference on Machine Learning*, 663–670.

Obermeyer, Ziad, Brian Powers, Christine Vogeli, and Sendhil Mullainathan (2019), 'Dissecting Racial Bias in an Algorithm Used to Manage the Health of Populations', *Science* 366(6464), 447–453.

Parfit, Derek (1997), 'Equality and Priority', *Ratio* 10(3), 202–221.

Parfit, Derek (2011), *On What Matters*, Vol. 1 (Oxford: Oxford University Press).

Pasquale, Frank (2015), *The Black Box Society: The Secret Algorithms That Control Money and Information* (Cambridge, MA: Harvard University Press).

Prasad, Mahendra (2018), 'Social Choice and the Value Alignment Problem', in Roman V. Yampolskiy, ed., *Artificial Intelligence Safety and Security* (New York: Taylor and Francis), 291–314.

Rawls, John (1993 [2005]), *Political Liberalism* (New York: Columbia University Press).

Ring, Mark, and Laurent Orseau (2011), 'Delusion, Survival, and Intelligent Agents', in *International Conference on Artificial General Intelligence*, 11–22

Roff, Heather M. (2020), 'Expected Utilitarianism', arXiv, 2008.07321.

Russell, Stuart (2019), *Human Compatible: Artificial Intelligence and the Problem of Control* (London: Allen Lane).

Satz, Debra (2010), *Why Some Things Should Not Be for Sale* (Oxford: Oxford University Press).

Scott, James C. (1998 [2020]), *Seeing Like a State: How Certain Schemes to Improve the Human Condition Have Failed* (New Haven, CT: Yale University Press).

Selbst, Andrew D., boyd, danah, Friedler, Sorelle A., Venkatasubramanian, Suresh, and Vertesi, Janet (2019), 'Fairness and Abstraction in Sociotechnical Systems', *FAT* '19: Conference on Fairness, Accountability, and Transparency*, 29–31 January, ACM, New York, 59–68.

Shahriari, Kyarash, and Mana Shahriari (2017), 'IEEE Standard Review—Ethically Aligned Design: A Vision for Prioritizing Human Wellbeing with Artificial Intelligence and Autonomous Systems', in *2017 IEEE Canada International Humanitarian Technology Conference*, 197–201.

Singer, Peter (2011), *The Expanding Circle: Ethics, Evolution, and Moral Progress* (Princeton, NJ: Princeton University Press).

Sutton, Richard S., and Andrew G. Barto (2018), *Reinforcement Learning: An Introduction*, 2nd edn (Cambridge, MA and London: The MIT Press).

Trask, Andrew, Emma Bluemke, Ben Garfinkel, Claudia Ghezzou Cuervas-Mons, and Allan Dafoe (2020), 'Beyond Privacy Trade-Offs with Structured Transparency', arXiv, 2012.08347.

Turner, Alexander Matt, Neale Ratzlaff, and Prasad Tadepalli (2019), 'Avoiding Side Effects in Complex Environments', arXiv 2006.06547.

Wallach, Wendell, and Colin Allen (2009), *Moral Machines: Teaching Robots Right from Wrong* (Oxford: Oxford University Press).

Wiener, Norbert (1960), 'Some Moral and Technical Consequences of Automation', *Science* 131, 1355–1358.

Winner, Langdon (1980), 'Do Artifacts Have Politics?', *Daedalus* 109(1), 121–136.

Yudkowsky, Eliezer (2004), *Coherent Extrapolated Volition* (Berkeley, CA: Machine Intelligence Research Institute).

CHAPTER 19

DIGITAL NUDGING

Exploring the Ethical Boundaries

MARCELLO IENCA AND EFFY VAYENA

NUDGING IN THE PRE-DIGITAL WORLD

THE scientific usage of the word 'nudge' dates back to the late 1990s, when it was first introduced in the fields of cybernetics and cognitive science by scholars such as James Wilk and D.J. Stewart. In its original formulation, *nudge* was defined as a micro-targeted design geared towards a specific user group, regardless of the intended intervention's scale (Wilk 1999; Stewart 2000). The notion of nudge was significantly expanded and further popularized in a homonymous book written by economist Richard Thaler and legal scholar Cass Sunstein in 2008. In this book, the two scholars defined a 'nudge' as 'any aspect of the choice architecture that alters people's behaviour in a predictable way without forbidding any options or significantly changing their economic incentives' (Thaler and Sunstein 2009). As such, nudges differ from other interventions aimed at achieving behavioural change, such as mandates and bans via hard law or interventions which alter the economic incentives and disincentives (Sunstein 2014). Accordingly, nudging is the act of leveraging non-mandatory and non-financial interventions that steer people in particular directions. Proponents of nudging (sometimes also called *nudge theory*) argue that these interventions are cost-effective because they can promote a certain behavioural goal without thereby requiring the long process of passing new legislation or creating specific economic incentives (Sunstein 2015a).

Since its early formulations, nudging was considered a viable strategy to promote public health (Marteau et al. 2011). In fact, authors argued that nudges could be designed to predictably alter people's lifestyle and health-related behaviour via non-mandatory modifications of their choice architecture (Sunstein 2014). In this manner, individually unhealthy or collectively harmful behaviours could be disincentivized and replaced with healthier and less harmful ones. For example, Sunstein listed the following public-health-orientated nudges: graphic warnings for cigarettes, nutrition facts panels on food, guides for healthy eating, and making healthy foods more visible and accessible in stores or dining halls (Sunstein 2014). What these seemingly diverse interventions have in common is their objective to predictably alter people's lifestyle or health-related choices in order to reduce the prevalence of unhealthy behaviour (respectively, smoking and unhealthy diet) without mandates, bans, or modifications of economic incentives (e.g. taxing cigarettes or unhealthy foods). Internationally, policies aimed at 'nudging smokers' have proven effective in reducing smoking behaviour and associate morbidity (Sunstein 2015b). Various types of nudges have also been employed to reduce vaccine hesitancy and increase vaccine uptake. For example, social feedback interventions involving communication and moderate rewarding may increase individuals' willingness to act in the group's interest and thereby enhance vaccine uptake (Korn et al. 2018). Similar outcomes have also been pursued by changing the default mode of domain-specific vaccination, for example, influenza vaccination for health workers (Lehmann et al. 2016), from an opt-in to an opt-out model. Based on these kinds of findings, Giubilini and colleagues have argued that such default effect should be used to increase vaccination rates among children in schools and day-care facilities (Giubilini et al. 2019).

The successful use of nudges to improve health outcomes is not limited to patient health behaviour but also applies to the behaviour of health professionals. Caris et al. (2018) have shown that behavioural nudges, displayed as posters, can increase the use of alcohol-based hand rub and thereby improve hand hygiene in hospital wards (Caris et al. 2018), which is paramount in preventing health-care-associated infection. Similarly, Meeker et al. (2014) have shown that displaying poster-sized commitment letters in examination rooms (featuring clinician photographs and signatures stating their commitment to avoid inappropriate antibiotic prescribing) could reduce the inappropriate or unnecessary prescribing rate of antibiotics for acute respiratory infections (Meeker et al. 2014) and increase the rate of guideline-concordant prescribing.

COGNITIVE BIASES AND THE ETHICS OF NUDGING

The use of nudges to steer behaviour, especially health behaviour, has sparked ethical controversy. The main reason for that stems from the fact that nudges are prima facie in conflict with two critical components of personal autonomy: informed consent and free will. Nudges, in fact, are typically administered without the explicit consent— sometimes even without the conscious awareness—of the actors involved. This conflicts with the duty to obtain an informed consent from research participants and patients, which is a critical ethical requirement in both biomedical research ethics and clinical care (Emanuel et al. 2000; Beauchamp and Childress 2001). Furthermore, nudges are inherently designed to restrict a person's ability to choose between different courses of action unimpeded (Omoregie 2015) because they modify a person's choice architecture in manners that obstacle certain courses of actions, while promoting others. Successful nudges influence free will by making certain choices harder to make and reduce thereby the probability of certain courses of action.

Due to this latter aspect, nudges are widely considered 'paternalistic' interventions because they influence people's behaviour to make choices that are considered good for them, even when these choices are undesired by the individual actor (Cohen 2013). In some cases, nudges are purposively designed with the paternalistic aim of protecting people from themselves (e.g. nudging smokers). Proponents of nudge theory do not object to the paternalistic nature of nudging but argue that nudges belong to a distinct class of paternalistic interventions in which liberty and freedom of choice are preserved. Thaler and Sunstein have called this type of paternalism 'libertarian paternalism' (Thaler and Sunstein 2009). Compared to traditional paternalism, those who make use of nudges do not restrict the freedom and responsibilities of individual actors, even though they steer their behaviour in their supposed interested, because individual actors retain the possibility to act otherwise. For example, a nudge which involves displaying healthier food in more visible compartments does not eliminate a person's freedom to buy a less healthy food, but simply makes that choice more difficult to make, hence less probable to happen. Compared to legally binding paternalistic prescriptions, such as making certain unhealthy substances (e.g. illicit drugs) illegal, nudges do not entirely eliminate freedom of choice but simply interfere with a person's ability to make free and unimpeded decisions by introducing modifications of the choice architecture that make certain courses of action less likely than others.

Many authors, such as Vallgårda, consider this reply unsatisfying and regard libertarian paternalism as an oxymoron (Vallgårda 2012). However, nudge theorists object that a certain choice architecture pre-exists chronologically and ontologically before every choice, regardless of whether actors are aware of it or not. In other words, proponents of nudges argue that there is no such thing as an absolutely free choice because there is no such thing as an absolutely neutral choice architecture. Choice architectures, in contrast, are always predetermined by environmental, social, and other external factors. Nudges exploit the non-neutrality of choice architectures for the public good. To go back to our example, it is inevitable that some food item has to come first at the cafeteria. We can choose which one in multiple ways, for example: randomly, by prioritizing customers top-picked products based on previous purchase history, or by prioritizing the healthier option. According to nudge theorists, prioritizing the healthier option is the most effective and ethically sensible choice. In the clinical domain, an analogous example is McNeil and colleagues' model of eliciting patient preferences via mode of information disclosure. In their example, a doctor who needs to secure a patient's consent to an intervention considered in the patient's best interest could present first the intervention's success rates, as opposed to the complementary failure rates (McNeil et al. 1982). Also in this case, one of the two pieces of information has to come first. By choosing one of two equally precise modes of information, disclosure based on the patient's expected health outcomes is considered more sensible compared to a random information disclosure strategy.

Although dominant in the ethics of nudging, the debate over the paternalistic versus non-paternalistic nature of nudges leaves open a deeper challenge. Even if we accept the inevitability of choice architectures and the greater degree of freedom enabled by nudges compared to mandatory regulation, one ethically crucial aspect remains overlooked. In randomly permuted choice architectures, no one is under anyone's control. Nudges, in contrast, allow some actors to exert a certain degree of control of other actors' choices and behaviour. Furthermore, compared to mandatory regulation, nudges appear more invisible, less easy to monitor (Wilkinson 2013), and potentially more likely to elude accountability. These two considerations shift ethical salience from the issue of paternalism to another, more subtle, autonomy-thwarting challenge: manipulation. This latter challenge arises from a twofold fact. First, nudges allow certain actors to exert some degree of invisible and hard-to-monitor control over other actors. Second, they do so by exploiting those actors' cognitive weaknesses and flawed methods of reasoning. It has been noted, in fact, that the success of nudges highly depends on their ability to covertly target hardwired weaknesses of human perception and cognition, especially cognitive biases and decision heuristics (Cohen 2013; Wilkinson 2013).

Cognitive biases are a class of errors in information processing—sometimes also described as patterns of deviation from logical thought—that occur when people are perceiving, elaborating, and interpreting information in the world around them. Nudges can exploit several subclasses of cognitive biases, depending on the phase of the cognitive process at which they occur, especially memory biases, attribution biases, decision-making biases, and behavioural biases (see Table 19.1).

Based on this observation, authors have argued that the 'exploitation of imperfections in human judgment and decision-making ... [is] prima facie as threatening to liberty, broadly understood, as overt coercion' (Hausman and Welch 2010). This is because such purposive exploitation of cognitive deficiencies is inherently manipulative (Wilkinson 2013) and exerts an influence on people's behaviour 'by illegitimately perpetuating bad reasoning' (Cohen 2013) and fostering irrationality, even when it is done with a positive intent. Cohen has elegantly portrayed this problem by referring to the biblical injunction against 'placing a stumbling block before the blind' (Leviticus 19:14), namely, against the deliberate exploitation of someone's weakness or vulnerability.

Considerations of this kind have added a new, fundamental component to the ethics of nudging. Nudges should be ethically assessed based not just on their paternalistic nature but also, and most importantly, based on their potential for manipulation. Susser, Roessler, and Nissenbaum define *manipulation* as 'hidden or covert influence' (Susser et al. 2019). According to this definition, it appears that although nudges could be less detrimental to freedom of choice compared to mandatory regulation (because they may be less restrictive of someone's choice architecture compared to outright bans), they are inherently more manipulative. In fact, while mandatory regulation in liberal democracies operates publicly and transparently (laws are written, publicly promulgated, and auditable), nudges are covert, opaque, and difficult to audit. This observation has led authors to argue that manipulation, by default, 'bypasses the exercise of autonomy' (Blumenthal-Barby and Burroughs 2012).

Table 19.1 Examples of cognitive biases exploited by nudges

Subclass	Bias type	Description	Relevant nudges
Memory bias	Von Restorff effect	When multiple homogeneous stimuli are presented, the stimulus that differs from the rest is more likely to be remembered	Making one or more items visually stick out compared to other items
Memory bias	Primacy and recency effect	Items near the end or at the beginning of a sequence are the easiest to recall; items in the middle are the least likely to be recalled	Placing preferred items at the end or at the beginning of a sequence; placing undesired items in the middle of a sequence
Memory bias	Picture superiority effect	Concepts learned by viewing pictures are more easily and frequently recalled than concepts that are learned in written form	Using pictures, videos, and other visual techniques to induce compliance
Decision-making bias	Zero-sum bias	A situation is incorrectly perceived to be like a zero-sum game	Presenting the gains of a certain choice independently from the losses
Decision-making bias	Selection bias	Tendency to notice something more when something else causes us to be more aware of it	Eliciting stimuli that can increase someone's awareness about a certain item
Decision-making bias	Bandwagon effect	The tendency to do or believe things because many other people do or believe the same (herd behaviour)	Creating fake social media accounts via bots that hold a certain view in order to induce real human users to hold that same view
Attribution bias	In-group bias	The tendency for people to give preferential treatment to others they perceive to be members of their own groups	Increasing empathy by prompting people to consider a certain moral problem as if a family member was involved

DIGITAL NUDGING: INTRODUCING
THE CONCEPT

With the advent of the digital era, following especially the widespread penetration of smartphones and other personal digital devices, many nudges became digitized, that is, mediated, or even enabled, by digital systems.

Digital nudging is the umbrella term used to describe this broad socio-technical trend involving the delivery of nudges via digital tools. Digital nudging can be defined both in a narrow and in a broad sense. Digital nudging in the narrow sense is the 'use of user-interface design elements to guide people's behaviour in digital choice environments' (Weinmann et al. 2016). In contrast, digital nudging in the broad sense involves the design and deployment of digital technology (not just user interfaces) to predictably alter people's choices and behaviour in either a digital or physical (online or offline) choice environment. According to the narrow definition, both the intervention (i.e. the targeted alteration of the choice architecture) and the environment in which the actor behaves have to be in digital format. According to the broad definition, only the intervention is required to be in digital format and it may affect an actor's behaviour even outside the digital or online environment. In this chapter, we focus on digital nudging in the broad sense, although some examples of narrow-sense digital nudges will be provided.

Many digital nudges resemble analogue ones to the extent that they are simple, well-intentioned, and designed to steer human decision-making towards healthier, safer, or otherwise publicly desirable behaviour. Narrow-sense nudges, for instance, have proven effective in steering people's behaviour towards more privacy-conscious and secure online behaviour. For example, social media company Facebook used a popup dinosaur as a narrow-sense nudge to let their users know that they had not updated their privacy settings. This reportedly led more than three-quarters of users who saw the dinosaur to complete their privacy check-up (Renaud and Zimmermann 2018). With a similar privacy-enhancing objective, Grossklags et al. (2010) found that by providing certain ancillary information to users, they could impact their decisions to install anti-virus or use firewalls (Grossklags et al. 2010). Digital nudges in the broad sense attempt to leverage online technology to achieve positive outcomes that outlast online behaviour and extend to offline life. For example, wearable devices and associated applications such as Upright Pro and Lumo Lift Posture Activity Tracker are embedded with sensors capable of detecting bad posture and send a vibration each time users slouch. Another mobile app called Sobriety Counter helps users to stop drinking alcohol by employing motivational nudges such as estimating the money a user saves by abstaining from alcohol consumption (a practice also called *teetotalism*).

Some digital nudges, however, deviate from the analogue standard as they happen to be deployed without a clear positive intent in terms of public health, security, or other form of common good. Most importantly, some digital nudges could even operate against the end-user best interest. This possibility was anticipated by Thaler and Sunstain, who called these kind of interventions 'evil nudges' (Thaler and Sunstein 2009). Evil nudges can occur also in the analogue world. For example, supermarkets may display junk food at more visible locations than fruits and vegetables to improve their expected financial gains if junk foods are observed to generate a higher revenue for the vendor compared to healthier products. However, the digital domain facilitates the design and deployment of potentially manipulative and ethically questionable nudges. The reason for that stems from five distinctive features of digital nudges compared to analogue ones:

- artificial choice architecture;
- self-interest and lack of public vetting;

- data availability and ubiquity;
- system opacity;
- novel channels and scale of influence.

These features are described in the next section, with particular emphasis on their ethical salience. Finally, we provide an analysis of conceptual and normative tools that may be useful to navigate the ethical complexity of digital nudging and demarcate its ethical boundaries.

DISTINCTIVE FEATURES OF
DIGITAL NUDGING

In her book, *The Age of Surveillance Capitalism* (2019), Shoshana Zuboff warns against the use of information technology to steer what she calls 'behaviour modification', arguing that the pervasiveness of digital tools, and their centrality to the functioning of the modern information society, cause an unprecedented spectrum of manipulative risks. In a similar fashion, Susser, Roessler, and Nissenbaum argued that 'information technology is uniquely suited to facilitating manipulative influences' (Susser et al. 2019). In the following, we attempt to characterize five distinctive (although not exhaustive) features of digital environments, which increase the magnitude of ethical significance of digital nudges compared to analogue ones.

Artificial choice architecture

Compared to the analogue world, in the digital world, there is no such a thing as a human-independent choice architecture that is generated by random environmental and social factors. Digital spaces such as websites, search engines, mobile applications, etc., as well as their hardware counterparts, are always artificial and human-made, and hence inescapably reflect the design choices of certain human actors (e.g. the software developers). Human-made choice architectures exist, as we have seen in the supermarket example, also in the analogue world. However, in the digital world, they are inherently and inescapably artificial. In digital spaces, the context in which users make decisions is always pre-organized in a certain manner by some actors. In other words, there is no choice to be made between an engineered and a non-engineered choice architecture because digital technologies and online services are always engineered and predesigned. This inherent feature of digital technologies undermines Sunstein's distinction between 'spontaneous order' and 'conscious design' (Sunstein 2015a) and makes the inevitability argument about choice architectures redundant. In Wilkinson's words, there is no scenario where no one is under anyone else's control (Wilkinson 2013). This implies that a certain risk of digital manipulation (also called 'online manipulation') is inherent in the use of digital tools. This risk is exacerbated by the fact that digital online content is typically personalized, that is, customized to a specific user or user-group. Depending on the degree of personalization, digital nudges may not only steer user behaviour in a certain direction but even undermine their ability to act otherwise.

Self-interest and lack of public vetting

While analogue nudges are largely designed and deployed by public actors such as governmental agencies for the promotion of the public good (e.g. public health), digital nudges are often developed by private actors who may be motivated by self-interest. One reason for that is that digital spaces (also called online spaces) only rarely qualify as public spaces, that is, publicly owned services that are accessible to all by default. The online ecosystem is heavily populated by private spaces, that is, privately owned services whose underlying interest and reason of existence is not promoting the collective good but achieving monetary gain (an attitude known in economics as 'profit motive') and competitive advantage over other actors. Mainstream microeconomic theory posits that pursuing profit and increasing net worth are indeed the ultimate goal of a business. Self-interest and profit motive are therefore more common among private than public actors. As the digital ecosystem is dominated by private actors, self-interest and private motive are more frequently associated with digital than analogue nudges. Furthermore, digital nudges are less publicly vetted than analogue ones.

Some popular online spaces, such as the social network Facebook, may appear prima facie public because they are accessible free of charge and without subscription fees to their users. Nonetheless, these spaces are owned by private corporations, subject to the company's discretional terms of service (which, among other things, entail a transfer of intellectual property rights) and, most importantly, depend on advertising for revenue. Such dependency on advertising for revenue characterizes the business model of most dominant information technology companies, including Amazon, Google, Alibaba, and Tencent. In order to maximize their profit motive, companies like Meta have a competitive interest in indefinitely increasing the amount of time that its users spend on the platform. Accordingly, they have a competitive interest in delivering digital nudges to steer users towards compulsive and persistent engagement on the platform, even despite adverse consequences. Such compulsive engagement is typically pursued through digital nudges that enable repeated exposure to a rewarding or reinforcing stimulus and thereby persistently hack user attention. Psychologists consider such system of rewarding and reinforcing stimuli as potentially addictive, and list social media use as a potential gateway to behavioural addiction (Andreassen et al. 2012). Popular examples of digital nudges aimed at steering compulsive and persistent user behaviour on a digital platform for profit motive include:

- *infinite scroll and auto refill*: automatic loading in of new content, without requiring any specific action, prompt, or request from users. This nudge is implemented on digital platforms such as Facebook, Instagram, and Twitter;

- *autoplay*: automatic playing of music or video content without requiring any specific action, prompt, or request from users. This nudge is implemented on digital
platforms such as Facebook, Instagram, and YouTube;
- *badges*: awards linked to engagement with the platform. This nudge is used
on digital platforms such as Facebook and, most notably, Snapchat, where it is
implemented in the form of the Snapstreak badges, which mark how long two users
have exchanged daily interactions.

The aim of these three types of digital nudges is hijacking user attention in order to
prolong their engagement on the platform and thereby maximize the company's
advertisement-induced revenue, even though such compulsive engagement may be detrimental to the user's mental and physical well-being. As such, they steer user behaviour
away from what is in the user's best interest. This marks a second prominent difference
between popular digital nudges and the classic, well-being-promoting analogue nudges
described in the previous section. Furthermore, self-interested private actors, such as
social media companies, have been observed to often elude public vetting and democratic accountability, which raises concerns about the public vetting and accountability
of the digital nudges administered on their platforms (Zuboff 2019).

Data availability and ubiquity

Due to exponential increase in data volume and storage capacity, the digital world is
now irrigated by an unprecedented quantity of data flows that can be further analysed
computationally at high velocity. This characteristic, usually referred to as *big data*
(Lynch 2008; Vayena and Blasimme 2017; Ienca et al. 2018b), determines that digital
nudges can be designed based on more extensive and granular information about their
targeted actors compared to analogue ones. Among other things, digital tools can now
keep personal records of a person's daily life—a phenomenon known as lifelogging—
and increase the variety and comprehensiveness of datasets related to human activities.
Due to growing technology adoption and lowering hardware costs (Lunney et al. 2016),
digital quantification technologies such as this are now accessible to a large segment of
the population. While the first generation of wearable devices and mobile tools could
collect data and provide insights only related to a small portion of human physiology
and physical activity, chiefly mobility (e.g. daily steps and physical position), novel
applications can now record a broader variety of human activities and underlying
processes, including processes related to a person's mental or psychological domain,
such as their preferences and choices (e.g. likes on Facebook or purchase history on
Amazon). This increased availability of data does not regard only the quantity of data,
but also their variety. In recent years, digital technologies for self-quantification have
expanded not only in number but also in variety to include data sources that could previously be collected exclusively via medical devices such as podometrics, heartbeat
rate, electroencephalography, autonomic function, sleep patterns, etc. (Dimitrov 2016;

McLeod et al. 2016; Webster et al. 2017; Ienca et al. 2018a; Coates McCall et al. 2019). Further, smartphone-sensing and wearable-sensing methods have improved in quality and reliability, now permitting a fine-grained, continuous, and unobtrusive collection of psychologically and socially relevant data such as speaking rates in conversation, tone of utterances, frequency of social interactions, ambient conversations, responses to cognitive tasks, 3D navigation outcomes, sleep patterns, purchase preferences, etc. (Harari et al. 2016).

This increased availability of digitally collected information can be used to create more precise, user-tailored nudges based on a detailed account of their physiology, personality traits, beliefs, attitudes, preferences, and lifestyles. Further, this information can be used to prospectively segment a certain user population according to those characteristics (a process known as 'psychographic segmentation'). This potential for customizing nudges to targeted users or to prospectively segmented groups marks a third important distinctive trait of digital nudges. While some degree of customization and psychographic segmentation can be achieved also in the context of analog nudges, the unprecedented quantity and variety of digital data clearly marks a different order of magnitude and entails a much greater potential for behavioural influence.

System opacity

As the digital ecosystem, especially the online world, is primarily populated by profit-motivated private actors, the way through which digital nudges are designed and administered is not always transparent but often covered under closed-source software or other intellectual property restrictions. In those systems, no universal access to, or universal redistribution of, the product's design or blueprint is provided. This implies that end users are unable to review and modify the source code, design, or blueprint. A main consequence of this technical and legal regime is that end users who are targeted by digital nudges, such as content personalization or attention-hijacking plugins, do not have the ability to review the process through which they are being nudged. This risk is exacerbated by the increasing use of artificial intelligence (AI)-driven software in data analytics. While most digital nudges follow simple analytic logic ('If user performs action X, they are likely to perform action Y'), an increasing amount of digital nudging is administered using machine learning algorithms, especially deep learning (LeCun et al. 2015). AI models are increasingly allowing us to derive insights about a person's mental domain. For example, smartphone apps can be used to infer a person's cognitive status from their responses to gamified cognitive tasks, such as 3D virtual navigation (Morgan 2016). Further, convolutional neural networks (CNNs)—a type of network architecture for deep learning—have proven effective to take in non-verbal cues from facial emotions and detect emotions from human facial images (Lawrence et al. 1997; Matsugu et al. 2003). This information can be used to deliver nudges based on a more detailed understanding of a person's cognition and emotions, including their cognitive biases and emotional weaknesses. Due to their multilayered configuration, however, deep learning algorithms are often considered types of 'black box AI', that is, models whose inputs and operations are not visible nor explainable in logical or mechanistic format to the user or another interested party. Given their impenetrable and opaque nature, using such algorithms in digital nudging exacerbates the threat to transparency described above. Digital nudges are not just contingently invisible (e.g. undetected by a certain actor at a certain time) but ontologically invisible, as they cannot be explained by any human actor, not even their creators. This dual system opacity (closed source and black box) of digital tools exacerbates the threat to transparency caused by digital nudges compared to analogue ones.

Novel channels and scale of influence

Digital technologies do not simply enable a differently motivated, informationally greater, and less transparent basis for nudging, but also novel modes of behavioural influence. This is largely due to the intrusive, ubiquitous, and computationally complex nature of digital tools. As we have seen before, digital nudges can exploit users' decision-making vulnerabilities to steer them into acting against their interests (or, at least, acting in the interests of the service provider). This mode of influence is increasingly enabled by the so-called *dark patterns* in user experience design, such as requiring automatically renewing paid subscriptions that begin after an initial free trial period. In parallel, microtargeting techniques for psychometric segmentation allow identification of end users prone to specific emotional or cognitive traits (Anon 2018; Ienca and Vayena 2018). Such techniques are often deployed for personalized advertising or political messaging, and are purposively designed to evade users' psychological defence mechanisms, which makes the users vulnerable to manipulation (Patel et al. 2012; Fiske and Hauser 2014; Susser et al. 2019). As Yeung put it, these techniques can generate 'highly personalised choice environment[s]'—decision-making contexts in which the vulnerabilities catalogued through pervasive digital surveillance are put to work in an effort to influence our choices (2017: 122). Online tools such as search engines have also been observed to elicit previously unknown cognitive biases such as the 'Google effect' or 'digital amnesia', namely, a memory bias involving a tendency to forget information that can be found readily online by using internet search engines (Sparrow et al. 2011). Self-learning algorithms, furthermore, can provide additional resources to purposively influence behaviour in ways that remain undetected by the user. This is particularly the case for AI algorithms embedded in systems that operate in close proximity to the human user such as smartphones, wearable devices, and brain–computer interfaces. Finally, consumer-available digital technologies can be used not only to 'read' information about a person but also to 'write' it, that is, to purposively influence a person's mental states, behaviour, and their underlying processes either directly via mechanisms such as biofeedback and neuromodulation, or indirectly (Flöel 2014). Some of these systems incorporate AI components within a closed-loop architecture, which is often bioadaptive (or neuroadaptive if interfaced with the nervous system), that is, automatically adaptive to an estimate of the user's body function or mindset (Zander et al. 2016). It has been observed that such intelligent systems can have a profound influence on a person's autonomy and agency (Kellmeyer et al. 2016; Ienca and Andorno 2017), and even create uncertainty about whether a certain behaviour has been intended by the human user or induced by the technical components (Klaming and Haselager 2013; Clausen et al. 2017).

Finally, digital technologies can not only enable new modes of influence but do so in greater scale. For example, in 2014, Facebook conducted a colossal online psycho-social experiment with researchers at Cornell University on 689,003 unaware users, in which they provided experimental evidence of massive-scale emotional contagion through social networks. The study results showed that by algorithmically modifying the users' newsfeeds, it is possible to induce changes in their emotions—a phenomenon that was labelled 'emotional contagion' (Kramer et al. 2014). In particular, when positive expressions were reduced on the newsfeed, users produced fewer positive posts and more negative posts. In contrast, when negative expressions were reduced on the newsfeed, the opposite pattern occurred. The possibility of using online data to algorithmically predict and influence human behaviour in a manner that circumvents users' awareness of such influence has been further corroborated by the so-called 'Cambridge Analytica' scandal. Using an intermediary app, a data brokerage and political consulting firm called Cambridge Analytica was able to harvest large data volumes—over 87 million raw profiles—and use big data analytics to create psychographic profiles in order to subsequently target users with customized digital ads and other manipulative information. According to some observers, this massive data analytics tactic might have been used to purposively swing election campaigns around the world (Rathi 2019). This scandal spurred researchers to discuss the need to update data ethics standards (Anon 2018; Ienca and Vayena 2018). These examples show that manipulation in the digital world can occur not only through novel channels but also on a more massive scale. This is ethically challenging because it implies that many more people can be influenced via the same nudge, often with little oversight.

DEFINING THE ETHICAL BOUNDARIES OF DIGITAL NUDGING

The analysis above indicates that the core ethical challenge of digital nudging is its expanded potential for autonomy-thwarting manipulation. Manipulation, as we have seen, is autonomy-thwarting because it exerts influence in a hidden or covert manner and purposively exploits people's cognitive weakness and vulnerabilities. By exploiting cognitive biases and other psychological or informational vulnerabilities with greater intensity, precision, and opacity, digital nudges are 'ideal vehicles for manipulation' (Susser et al. 2019). This type of influence is *non-rational* (Wood 2014) because it does not involve logical reasoning, conscious reflection, persuasion, or rational decision-making. In contrast, it operates in a manner that exploits cognitive deficiencies and thereby circumvents people's deliberative decision-making abilities.

For this reason, defining the ethical boundaries of digital nudging implies, first and foremost, drawing a demarcation line between rational and non-rational influence. It is worth noting, however, that the rational and the non-rational are not binary, all-or-nothing categories. They are best represented as continuously variable quantities that depend on the extent to which each digital nudge is capable of engaging with a user's cognitive abilities, especially with their capacity for conscious perception, logical reasoning, and rational decision-making. Digital nudges that make themselves visible to a person's cognitive defences and engage with a person's cognitive capacities are, *ceteris paribus*, ethically preferable over those designed to be invisible to a person's cognitive defences and to circumvent cognitive capacities.

Promoting rational over non-rational influence requires two complementary actions and moral obligations. One is exposing, mitigating, and in some cases eliminating, non-rational influence via technology-enabled manipulation. The specular action and corresponding moral obligation is enhancing personal autonomy and its conceptual characterization. Each of these two actions and obligations will be discussed in the following.

Exposing and mitigating non-rational influence

By definition, in order to mitigate the impact of behavioural influence through non-rational means, it is necessary to design a digital nudge in a manner that is detectable by and engages with human rationality. This can be done by implementing design requirements that mitigate the key feature of manipulation: its state of being covert or hidden. These design requirements may concern different features or phases of development of digital nudges, such as data collection, data processing, and post-administration monitoring of behavioural effects.

At the level of data collection, non-rational influence can be mitigated by employing transparent data collection practices, such as explicitly informing users that information is being collected from them, what kind of information is being collected, and for which purposes. The European Union's General Data Protection Regulation (GDPR) states, at Articles 13 and 14, a number of requirements for data collection, such as disclosing the identity of the data controller, the purposes for which the data are being collected, the legitimate interest pursued by the controller, and whether the controller intends to transfer data to third parties. The GDPR also mandates (recital 58) that such information is disclosed to the data subject in a manner that can be detected and comprehended by a person's cognitive abilities, which entails the following requirements: conciseness, ease of access, understandability, clarity, and simplicity of language. The same recital requires, when appropriate, to use visualization to increase comprehension. It is worth highlighting that human cognitive abilities are characterized by significant interpersonal variability. Therefore, strings of information that appear clear and understandable to one user may not be clear and understandable to another user. This is particularly relevant in the context of data collected from children or older adults with cognitive deficits, as these user groups are likely to experience greater difficulty when reading data use agreements. According to recital 58 of the GDPR, data collection from children merits specific protection. Such protections are particularly relevant for digital platforms such as Facebook and Instagram, as they allow minors between thirteen and eighteen to operate on the platform, and hence to be subject to personalized content, attention-hijacking practices, psychographic segmentation, and all other forms of non-rational influence.

At the level of data processing, non-rational influence can be mitigated by employing transparent data-processing practices, such as disclosing the system's design and blueprint and making the source code open to free access and inspection. Whenever intellectual property restrictions are impossible to be lifted, established mechanisms for ex ante and post hoc inspection such as audits can increase the transparency of the data processing. Further, transparency can be enhanced via methods and techniques aimed at solving the black box problem (also called the 'interpretability problem') of AI. These methods and techniques are generally clustered under the umbrella term 'explainable AI' and involve machine learning models whose outputs can be understood by average human experts (Holzinger 2018). It is worth noting that in the context of both data collection and processing, minimizing non-rational influence does not always require full transparency. Disclosing disproportionate amounts of information, in fact, could overcome a person's cognitive defences in an opposite way, by causing informational overload (Bawden and Robinson 2009). On the other hand, however, oversimplification could mislead users by hiding undesirable attributes of the system. In order to mitigate non-rational influence, digital nudges need to strike a trade-off between interpretability and completeness of an explanation.

Finally, non-rational influence can be mitigated by implementing tools and measures to monitor the behavioural effects of a digital nudge after it is administered. For example, Andreassen and colleagues have developed a scale to assess users' addiction to Facebook. The scale was constructed based on previous standardized self-report scales and measures six core elements of addiction: salience, mood modification, tolerance, withdrawal, conflict, and relapse (Andreassen et al. 2012).

Enhancing autonomy in the digital world

Exposing and mitigating technology-enabled non-rational influence entails primarily actions that should be performed by technology developers and deployers (i.e. the *nudgers*) and the corresponding moral obligations of those actors. The complementary duty is preserving and promoting the rights of end users (i.e. those being *nudged*), in particular their autonomy. Susser, Roessler, and Nissenbaum have argued that the key challenge raised by digital nudging transcends the simple mitigation of online manipulation, but they require a discussion on 'how to strengthen autonomy in the digital age'

(Susser et al. 2019). Doing so, however, requires a closer examination of the notion of personal autonomy in the digital ecosystem as well as of the predominant vehicles used for its preservation.

The notion of autonomy pertains to the right and ability of an individual to make decisions, engage with information, and choose courses of action in a manner that is meaningfully independent from external factors such as third-party influence, coercion, or environmental pressures (including those from the social environment). Autonomy as an ability presupposes the prerequisite of having a system of cognitive defences that allows people to filter the flow of information and make conscious and competent decisions about their own life. Autonomy as a right presupposes the prerequisite of having a system of procedures that enable people to exercise autonomy as an ability.

One of the most important procedures in place to ensure autonomy is consent. For example, O'Neill has argued that 'the point of consent procedures is to limit deception and coercion [...]'; hence, they should be designed to give people 'control over the amount of information they receive and opportunity to rescind consent already given'(O'Neill 2003). In the digital ecosystem, however, online service providers typically act in the opposite manner as they constrain end users' control over the type and amount of information they receive and from which they collect. Based on this observation, Vayena, Mastroianni, and Kahn have argued that 'conventional informed consent models are ill suited because they were not conceived in the context of the evolving applications and functionalities of social media that enable innovative research designs' (Vayena et al. 2013). Other authors have attributed the same fate to other autonomy-preserving procedures such as the privacy notice—often nicknamed 'notice-and-consent'—that is, the predominant tool for notifying individuals about information flows and data practices (Yeung 2017). Empirical evidence has corroborated these pessimistic stances, showing that such procedures are ignored by most online users, and hence appear unsuitable to enable a meaningful protection (Obar and Oeldorf-Hirsch 2016). Based on such evidence, a German court ruled in 2018 that there is no guarantee that people are sufficiently informed about Facebook's privacy-related options before registering for the service, which can undermine informed consent (Fountoukakos et al. 2019; Srinivasan 2019).

Due to their potential influence at a non-rational or pre-rational level of information processing, digital nudges urge a reflection on personal autonomy at a more antecedent level than conventional procedures such as informed consent and privacy notices. In fact, these procedures require, by definition, a process of deliberate decision-making by the user based on their conscious and rational processing of information. As we have seen, digital nudges may, in contrast, operate below the threshold of rational deliberation by exploiting the cognitive weaknesses of the human mind. Therefore, in order to address the ethical challenge of digital nudges, especially their unprecedented potential for manipulation, one would require protections that do not presuppose the exercise of rational faculties but rather protect those faculties by default.

Three main proposals have been made, in recent years, to develop strengthened accounts of personal autonomy that entail a broader, chronologically antecedent and cognition-preserving form of protection from manipulation. These are: freedom of thought (Bublitz 2014; Lavazza 2018), mental integrity (Ienca and Andorno 2017; Lavazza 2018), and cognitive liberty (Sententia 2004; Bublitz 2014; Ienca and Andorno 2017; Wolpe 2017). These three notions will now be characterized.

Freedom of thought

The notion of freedom of thought goes back to the Ancient Greek and Judaeo-Christian tradition and has pervaded a significant portion of the history of philosophy and political doctrines through the work of, among others, Epicurus, Socrates, Plato, de Montaigne, Spinoza, Bruno, Locke, and Mill. Throughout this tradition, freedom of thought has often been characterized as a negative freedom from external influence or manipulation. For example. in the first epistle to the Corinthians, Paul of Tarsus wrote 'For why should my freedom [eleutheria] be judged by another's conscience?' (Robertson and Plummer 1914). Sixteen centuries later, John Milton wrote 'Thou canst not touch the freedom of my mind' to express the capacity of one of his characters to protect her mental freedom from external manipulation (Milton 1858). Freedom of thought is usually considered the essential justification of other freedoms, such as freedom of choice, freedom of speech, freedom of press, and freedom of religion. In a US Supreme Court case from 1937 (*Palko v. Connecticut*, 302 U.S. 319), Justice Benjamin Cardozo reasoned that freedom of thought 'is the matrix, the indispensable condition, of nearly every other form of freedom'. Besides permeating the history of ideas, the notion of freedom of thought has been progressively incorporated into international human rights law. Most notably, Article 19 of the Universal Declaration of Human Rights (drafted in 1948) and Article 9(1) of the European Convention on Human Rights (drafted in 1950) prescribe that 'Everyone has the right to freedom of thought, conscience and religion; this right includes freedom to change his religion or belief and freedom, either alone or in community with others and in public or private, to manifest his religion or belief, in worship, teaching, practice and observance.' Freedom of thought is guaranteed also under Article 10(1) of the Charter of Fundamental Rights of the European Union (drafted in 2000). Both conventions characterize freedom of thought in both a narrow and a broad sense.

Freedom of thought in the narrow sense involves the protection of human cognition, especially thinking and reasoning, from external manipulation. Freedom of thought in the broad sense encompasses a number of protections for all behavioural externalizations of human cognition such as speech, religion, and the press. While freedom of thought in the broad sense has been recurrently invoked in human history (typically in response to censorship and propaganda strategies rolled out by totalitarian governments such as Nazi Germany, Stalin's Soviet Union, Pol Pot's Cambodia, and Pinochet's Chile), calls for protecting freedom of thought in the narrow sense are scant. Authors have speculated that the lack of such calls for the direct protection of the internal cognitive and affective domain may be due to the insufficient capacity of pre-digital technology to exert any significant direct manipulation of that domain

(Ienca and Andorno 2017). However, as digital technology and AI increasingly expand the frequency, efficacy, and variety of manipulative activities, enforcing the protection of freedom of thought in the narrow sense may offer a suitable normative ground for enhancing autonomy and thereby preventing manipulation.

Mental integrity

The right to mental integrity is recognized under Article 3 of the European Union Charter of Fundamental Rights, which states that 'everyone has the right to respect for his or her physical and mental integrity'. Ligthart, Meynen, and Douglas have recently conducted a meticulous doctrinal analysis and concluded that a right to mental integrity is recognized also by the Grand Chamber of the European Court of Human Rights (ECtHR), where it is associated with issues of mental health, reputation, and honour (Ligthart et al. 2021). In spite of its international recognition, however, mental integrity has so far eluded a unanimous definition. Ienca and Andorno defined it as the normative protection from 'the unauthorized alteration of a person's neural computation and potentially resulting in direct harm to the victim' (Ienca and Andorno 2017).

Lavazza expanded this definition into 'the individual's mastery of his mental states and his brain data so that, without his consent, no one can read, spread, or alter such states and data in order to condition the individual in any way' (Lavazza 2018). The problem with this latter definition, however, is its reliance on the mechanism of consent. As we have seen in the previous section, the conceptual justification and practical effectiveness of consent practices as autonomy-promoting mechanisms are significantly challenged in the context of digital nudges. The merit of Lavazza's contribution, however, lies in its provision of a 'technical principle for the protection of mental integrity', which is described as 'a functional limitation that should be incorporated into any devices capable of interfering with mental integrity' (Lavazza 2018). While the analysis of Ienca and Andorno as well as Lavazza is primarily focused on invasive or non-invasive neurotechnologies, Ligthart, Meynen, and Douglas highlighted that mental integrity can be challenged also by persuasive technologies that do not interface someone's neural domain.

Cognitive liberty

Strictly connected to freedom of thought and mental integrity is the notion of *cognitive liberty*, often also referred to as the 'right to mental self-determination', namely, the freedom of an individual to control their own cognitive processes. As such, cognitive liberty resembles the notion of freedom of thought. Not surprisingly, Sententia (2004) presented cognitive liberty as a conceptual extension of freedom of thought that 'takes into account the power we now have, and increasingly will have to monitor and manipulate cognitive function'. Cognitive liberty is not a recognized right in any international human rights treaties but has gained strong ethical recognition in countries such as the United States and Switzerland (Ienca and Andorno 2017; Farahany 2019). Furthermore, it is recognized in international soft-law instruments such as the Organisation for Economic Co-operation and Development's 'Recommendation on Responsible Innovation in Neurotechnology' (Organisation for Economic Co-operation and Development-Council 2019). Just like freedom of thought, it is argued to be the principle underlying a number of recognized rights. As argued elsewhere (Ienca and Andorno 2017), cognitive liberty is a multidimensional concept. Bublitz recognizes at least three 'interrelated but not identical dimensions' (Bublitz 2014: 251). These are: (a) the liberty to change one's mind or to choose whether and by which means to change one's mind; (b) the protection of interventions into other minds to protect mental integrity; and (c) the ethical and legal obligation to promoting cognitive liberty. These three dimensions configure cognitive liberty as a complex right which involves the prerequisites of both negative and positive liberties in Berlin's sense (Berlin 1959): the negative liberty of making choices about one's own cognitive domain in the absence of external obstacles, barriers, or prohibitions; the negative liberty of exercising one's own right to mental integrity in the absence of constrains or violations from corporations, criminal agents, or the government; and finally, the positive liberty of having the possibility of acting in such a way as to take control of one's mental life.

Conclusion

With the widespread adoption of digital technologies and their pervasive role in modern societies, nudges are being increasingly administered through digital technology. While the ethics of analogue nudging has been largely debated in public health ethics, the ethical implications of nudging via digital technology have often eluded systematic scrutiny. This chapter has explored and critically demarcated the ethical boundaries of digital nudging. By comparing digital nudges with analogue ones, we identified five distinctive (although not exhaustive) features of digital environments, which increase the magnitude of ethical significance of digital nudges compared to analogue ones. These are the human-made nature of any choice architecture in the digital space, the increased volume and variety of data available, the frequent self-interest of actors operating in the digital arena, the internal opacity of data processing systems, and the emergence of novel modes of behavioural influence. Based on this analysis, we concluded that digital nudges are characterized by an unprecedented potential for non-rational behavioural influence and manipulation. In fact, they can be effectively designed to circumvent a user's cognitive abilities, especially their capacity for conscious perception, logical reasoning, and rational decision-making. In general terms, we argued that digital nudges that make themselves visible to a person's cognitive defences and engage with a person's cognitive capacities are, *ceteris paribus*, ethically preferable over those designed to be invisible to a person's cognitive defences and to circumvent cognitive capacities. However, promoting rational over non-rational influence requires two complementary actions and moral obligations. One is exposing and mitigating non-rational influence via technology-enabled manipulation. The specular action and moral obligation is enhancing personal autonomy and its conceptual characterization. For this reason, in the concluding section of this manuscript, we reviewed a number of procedural mechanisms that could be implemented to detect and mitigate non-rational influence and manipulation, as well as three normative principles that could enhance personal autonomy in the digital ecosystem, namely, freedom of thought, mental integrity, and cognitive liberty.

REFERENCES

Andreassen, Cecilie Schou, Torsheim, Torbjørn, Scott Brunborg, Geir, and Pallesen, Ståle (2012), 'Development of a Facebook Addiction Scale', *Psychological Reports* 110, 501–517.

Anon. (2018), 'Cambridge Analytica Controversy Must Spur Researchers to Update Data Ethics' *Nature*, 555, 559–560.

Bawden, David, and Robinson, Lyn (2009), 'The Dark Side of Information: Overload, Anxiety and Other Paradoxes and Pathologies', *Journal of Information Science* 35, 180–191.

Beauchamp, Tom L., and Childress, James F. (2001), *Principles of Biomedical Ethics* (New York: Oxford University Press).

Blumenthal-Barby, Jennifer Swindell, and Burroughs, Hadley (2012), 'Seeking Better Health Care Outcomes: The Ethics of Using the "Nudge"', *American Journal of Bioethics* 12, 1–10.

Bublitz, Christoph (2014), 'Cognitive Liberty or the International Human Right to Freedom of Thought', in *Handbook of Neuroethics* (Dordrecht: Springer), 1309–1333.

Caris, M.G., Labuschagne, H.A., Dekker, M., Kramer, M.H.H., van Agtmael, M.A., and Vandenbroucke-Grauls, C.M.J.E. (2018), 'Nudging to Improve Hand Hygiene', *Journal of Hospital Infection* 98, 352–358.

Clausen, Jens, Fetz, Eberhard, Donoghue, John, Ushiba, Junichi, Spörhase, Ulrike, Chandler, Jennifer, et al. (2017), 'Help, Hope, and Hype: Ethical Dimensions of Neuroprosthetics', *Science* 356, 1338–1339.

Coates McCall, Lau, Iris Chloe, Minielly, Nicole, and Illes, Judy (2019), 'Owning Ethical Innovation: Claims about Commercial Wearable Brain Technologies', *Neuron* 102, 728–731.

Cohen, Shlomo (2013), 'Nudging and Informed Consent', *American Journal of Bioethics* 13, 3–11.

Dimitrov, Dimiter V. (2016), 'Medical Internet of Things and Big Data in Healthcare', *Healthcare Informatics Research* 22, 156–163.

Emanuel, E.J., Wendler, D., and Grady, C. (2000), 'What Makes Clinical Research Ethical?', *Journal of the American Medical Association* 283, 2701–2711.

Farahany, Nita A. (2019), 'The Costs of Changing Our Minds', *Emory Law Journal* 69, 75.

Fiske, Susan T., and Hauser, Robert M. (2014), 'Protecting Human Research Participants in the Age of Big Data', *Proceedings of the National Academy of Sciences* 111, 13675.

Flöel, Agnes (2014), 'tDCS-Enhanced Motor and Cognitive Function in Neurological Diseases', *Neuroimage* 85, 934–947.

Fountoukakos, Nuys, Kyriakos, Penz, Marcel Juliana, and Rowland, Peter (2019), 'The German FCO's Decision against Facebook: A First Step Towards the Creation of Digital House Rules?', *Competition Law Journal* 18, 55–65.

Giubilini, Alberto, Caviola, Lucius, Maslen, Hannah, Douglas, Thomas, Nussberger, Anne-Marie, Faber, Nadira, et al. (2019), 'Nudging Immunity: The Case for Vaccinating Children in School and Day Care by Default', in *Hec Forum* (Springer), 325–44.

Grossklags, Jens, Johnson, Benjamin, and Christin, Nicolas (2010), 'When Information Improves Information Security', in *International Conference on Financial Cryptography and Data Security* (Springer), 416–23.

Harari, Gabriella M., Lane, Nicholas D., Wang, Rui, Crosier, Benjamin S., Campbell, Andrew T., and Gosling, Samuel D. (2016), 'Using Smartphones to Collect Behavioral Data in Psychological Science: Opportunities, Practical Considerations, and Challenges', *Perspectives on Psychological Science: A Journal of the Association for Psychological Science* 11, 838–854.

Hausman, Daniel M, and Welch, Brynn (2010), 'Debate: To Nudge or Not to Nudge', *Journal of Political Philosophy* 18, 123–136.

Holzinger, Andreas (2018), 'From Machine Learning to Explainable AI', in *2018 World Symposium on Digital Intelligence for Systems and Machines (DISA)* (Institute of Electrical and Electronics Engineers), 55–66.

Ienca, Marcello, and Andorno, R. (2017), 'Towards New Human Rights in the Age of Neuroscience and Neurotechnology', *Life Sciences, Society and Policy* 13, 5.

Ienca, Marcello, and Vayena, Effy (2018), 'Cambridge Analytica and Online Manipulation', *Scientific American* 30.

Ienca, Marcello, Haselager, Pim, and Emanuel, Ezekiel J. (2018a), 'Brain Leaks and Consumer Neurotechnology', *Nature Biotechnology* 36, 805–810.

Ienca, Marcello, Ferretti, Agata, Hurst, Samia, Puhan, Milo, Lovis, Christian, and Vayena, Effy (2018b), 'Considerations for Ethics Review of Big Data Health Research: A Scoping Review', *PLoS ONE* 13, e0204937.

Kellmeyer, Philipp, Cochrane, Thomas, Müller, Oliver, Mitchell, Christine, Ball, Tonio, Fins, Joseph J., et al. (2016), 'The Effects of Closed-Loop Medical Devices on the Autonomy and Accountability of Persons and Systems', *Cambridge Quarterly of Healthcare Ethics* 25, 623–633.

Klaming, Laura, and Haselager, Pim (2013), 'Did My Brain Implant Make Me Do It? Questions Raised by DBS Regarding Psychological Continuity, Responsibility for Action and Mental Competence', *Neuroethics* 6, 527–539.

Korn, Lars, Betsch, Cornelia, Böhm, Robert, and Meier, Nicolas W. (2018), 'Social Nudging: The Effect of Social Feedback Interventions on Vaccine Uptake', *Health Psychology* 37, 1045.

Kramer, Adam D.I., Guillory, Jamie E., and Hancock, Jeffrey T. (2014), 'Experimental Evidence of Massive-Scale Emotional Contagion through Social Networks', *Proceedings of the National Academy of Sciences*, 201320040.

Lavazza, Andrea (2018), 'Freedom of Thought and Mental Integrity: The Moral Requirements for Any Neural Prosthesis', *Frontiers in Neuroscience* 12, 82.

Lawrence, Steve, Giles, C. Lee, Tsoi, Ah Chung, and Back, Andrew D. (1997), 'Face Recognition: A Convolutional Neural-Network Approach', *IEEE Transactions on Neural Networks* 8, 98–113.

LeCun, Yann, Bengio, Yoshua, and Hinton, Geoffrey (2015), 'Deep Learning', *Nature* 521, 436–444.

Lehmann, Birthe A., Chapman, Gretchen B., Franssen, Frits M.E., Kok, Gerjo, and Ruiter, Robert A.C. (2016), 'Changing the Default to Promote Influenza Vaccination among Health Care Workers', *Vaccine* 34, 1389–1392.

Ligthart, Sjors, Meynen, Gerben, and Douglas, Thomas (2021), 'Persuasive Technologies and the Right to Mental Liberty', in M. Ienca, O. Pollicino, E. Stefanini, L. Liguori, and R.

Andorno, eds, *The Cambridge Handbook of Life Science, Information Technology and Human Rights* (Cambridge: Cambridge University Press).

Lunney, Abbey, Cunningham, Nicole R., and Eastin, Matthew S. (2016), 'Wearable Fitness Technology: A Structural Investigation into Acceptance and Perceived Fitness Outcomes', *Computers in Human Behavior* 65, 114–120.

Lynch, Clifford (2008), 'Big Data: How Do Your Data Grow?', *Nature* 455, 28.

Marteau, Theresa M., Ogilvie, David, Roland, Martin, Suhrcke, Marc, and Kelly, Michael P. (2011), 'Judging Nudging: Can Nudging Improve Population Health?', *British Medical Journal* 342, d228.

Matsugu, Masakazu, Mori, Katsuhiko, Mitari, Yusuke, and Kaneda, Yuji (2003), 'Subject Independent Facial Expression Recognition with Robust Face Detection Using a Convolutional Neural Network', *Neural Networks* 16, 555–559.

McLeod, A., Bochniewicz, E.M., Lum, P.S., Holley, R.J., Emmer, G., and Dromerick, A.W. (2016), 'Using Wearable Sensors and Machine Learning Models to Separate Functional Upper Extremity Use from Walking-Associated Arm Movements', *Archives of Physical Medicine and Rehabilitation* 97, 224–231.

McNeil, Barbara J., Pauker, Stephen G., Sox Jr, Harold C., and Tversky, Amos (1982), 'On the Elicitation of Preferences for Alternative Therapies', *New England Journal of Medicine* 306, 1259–1262.

Meeker, Daniella, Knight, Tara K., Friedberg, Mark W., Linder, Jeffrey A., Goldstein, Noah J., Fox, Craig R., Rothfeld, Alan, Diaz, Guillermo, and Doctor, Jason N. (2014), 'Nudging Guideline-Concordant Antibiotic Prescribing: A Randomized Clinical Trial', *JAMA Internal Medicine* 174, 425–431.

Milton, John (1858), *Comus: A Mask by John Milton* (London: Routledge).

Morgan, Jules (2016), 'Gaming for Dementia Research: A Quest to Save the Brain', *The Lancet Neurology* 15, 1313.

O'Neill, Onora (2003), 'Some Limits of Informed Consent', *Journal of Medical Ethics* 29, 4.

Obar, Jonathan A., and Oeldorf-Hirsch, Anne (2016), 'The Biggest Lie on the Internet: Ignoring the Privacy Policies and Terms of Service Policies of Social Networking Services'.

Omoregie, Jesse (2015), *Freewill: The Degree of Freedom Within* (AuthorHouse).

Organisation for Economic Co-operation and Development-Council (2019), 'OECD Recommendation on Responsible Innovation in Neurotechnology'.

Patel, A., Taghavi, M., Celestino, J., Latih, R., and Zin, A.M. (2012), 'Safety Measures for Social Computing in Wiki Learning Environment', *International Journal of Information Security and Privacy* 6, 1–15.

Rathi, Rahul (2019), 'Effect of Cambridge Analytica's Facebook Ads on the 2016 US Presidential Election', *Towards Data Science*.

Renaud, Karen, and Zimmermann, Verena (2018), 'Ethical Guidelines for Nudging in Information Security and Privacy', *International Journal of Human–Computer Studies* 120, 22–35.

Robertson, Archibald Thomas, and Plummer, Alfred (1914), *First Epistle of St. Paul to the Corinthians* (T. & T. Clark).

Sententia, Wrye (2004), 'Neuroethical Considerations: Cognitive Liberty and Converging Technologies for Improving Human Cognition', *Annals of the New York Academy of Sciences* 1013, 221–228.

Sparrow, Betsy, Liu, Jenny, and Wegner, Daniel M. (2011), 'Google Effects on Memory: Cognitive Consequences of Having Information at Our Fingertips', *Science* 333, 776.

Srinivasan, Dina (2019), 'The Antitrust Case against Facebook: A Monopolist's Journey Towards Pervasive Surveillance in Spite of Consumers' Preference for Privacy', *Berkeley Business Law Journal* 16, 39.

Stewart, D.J. (2000), 'The Ternary Analysis of Work and Working Organisations', Kybernetes.

Sunstein, Cass R. (2014), 'Nudging: A Very Short Guide', *Journal of Consumer Policy* 37, 583–588.

Sunstein, Cass R. (2015a), 'The Ethics of Nudging', *Yale Journal on Regulation* 32, 413.

Sunstein, Cass R. (2015b), 'Nudging Smokers', *New England Journal of Medicine* 372, 2150–2151.

Susser, Daniel, Roessler, Beate, and Nissenbaum, Helen (2019), 'Technology, Autonomy, and Manipulation', *Internet Policy Review* 8.

Thaler, Richard H., and Sunstein, Cass R. (2009), *Nudge: Improving Decisions about Health, Wealth, and Happiness* (Penguin).

Vallgårda, Signild (2012), 'Nudge—a New and Better Way to Improve Health?', *Health Policy* 104, 200–203.

Vayena, Effy, and Blasimme, A. (2017), 'Biomedical Big Data: New Models of Control over Access, Use and Governance', *Journal of Bioethical Inquiry*.

Vayena, Effy, Mastroianni, Anna, and Kahn, Jeffrey (2013), 'Caught in the Web: Informed Consent for Online Health Research', *Science Translational Medicine* 5, 173fs6.

Webster, Elizabeth, Sukaviriya, Noi, Chang, H.-Y., and Kozloski, James (2017), 'Predicting Cognitive States from Wearable Recordings of Autonomic Function', *IBM Journal of Research and Development* 61(2), 1–2, 11.

Weinmann, Markus, Schneider, Christoph, and vom Brocke, Jan (2016), 'Digital Nudging', *Business & Information Systems Engineering* 58, 433–436.

Wilk, James (1999), 'Mind, Nature and the Emerging Science of Change: An Introduction to Metamorphology', in *Metadebates on Science* (Springer).

Wilkinson, T. Martin (2013), 'Nudging and Manipulation', *Political Studies* 61, 341–355.

Wolpe, Paul Root (2017), 'Neuroprivacy and Cognitive Liberty' in *The Routledge Handbook of Neuroethics* (Routledge).

Wood, Allen W. (2014), 'Coercion, Manipulation, Exploitation', *Manipulation: Theory and Practice*, 17–50.

Yeung, Karen (2017), ''Hypernudge': Big Data as a Mode of Regulation by Design', *Information, Communication & Society* 20, 118–136.

Zander, Thorsten O., Krol, Laurens R., Birbaumer, Niels P., and Gramann, Klaus (2016), 'Neuroadaptive Technology Enables Implicit Cursor Control Based on Medial Prefrontal Cortex Activity', *Proceedings of the National Academy of Sciences* 113, 14898–14903.

Zuboff, Shoshana (2019), *The Age of Surveillance Capitalism: The Fight for a Human Future at the New Frontier of Power* (Profile Books).

CHAPTER 20

....

INTERPRETABILITY AND TRANSPARENCY IN ARTIFICIAL INTELLIGENCE

....

BRENT MITTELSTADT

INTRODUCTION

....

ARTIFICIAL intelligence (AI) challenges our notions of accountability in both familiar and new ways. Systems we are increasingly entrusting with life-changing decisions and recommendations (e.g. employment, parole, and creditworthiness) have their foundation in our technological past but are now digital, distributed, and often imperceptible. When important decisions are taken which affect the livelihood and well-being of people, one expects that their rationale or reasons can be understood.

Compared to human and organizational decision-making, AI poses a unique challenge in this regard. The internal state of a trained machine learning model can consist of millions of features connected in a complex web of dependent behaviours. Conveying this internal state and dependencies in a humanly comprehensible way is extremely challenging (Burrell 2016; Lipton 2016). How AI systems make decisions may thus be too complex for human beings to thoroughly understand their full decision-making criteria or rationale. Despite the difficulty of explaining the 'black box' of AI, transparency remains one of the most common principles cited in AI ethics frameworks produced internationally by public–private partnerships, AI companies, civil society organizations, and governments (Jobin et al. 2019).

Given these constraints and the importance attached to understanding how AI works (Mittelstadt et al. 2019), it is reasonable to ask how the functionality and behaviour of AI systems can be explained in a meaningful and useful way. This chapter aims to answer precisely this question. The chapter proceeds in six parts. Key terminology, concepts, and motivations behind AI interpretability and transparency are first discussed. Next, two sets of methods are examined: interpretability methods designed to explain and approximate AI functionality and behaviour and transparency frameworks meant to help assess and provide information about the development, governance, and potential impact of training datasets, models, and specific applications. The chapter then turns to prior work on explanations in the philosophy of science and what this work can reveal about how to evaluate the utility and quality of different approaches to interpretability and transparency. Finally, the chapter closes with a discussion of open challenges currently facing AI interpretability and transparency.

Background

To survey interpretability and transparency in AI, it is essential to distinguish, as far as possible, a set of closely related and overlapping terms. Broadly agreed definitions and boundaries for terms such as 'interpretability', 'transparency', 'explanation', and 'explainability' do not yet exist in the field. As a result, the conventions adopted here may not be universal and may contradict other work.

Nonetheless, we can begin to unpack the topic of explaining AI by examining the different types of questions we may ask about AI systems to make them understandable.

How does an AI system or model function? How was a specific output produced by an AI system?

These are questions of *interpretability*. Questions of interpretability address the internal *functionality* or external *behaviour* of an AI system (see below for further explanation of this distinction). A fully interpretable model is one which is human comprehensible, meaning that a human can understand the full set of causes of a given output (Lisboa 2013; Miller 2019). Poorly interpretable models 'are opaque in the sense that if one is a recipient of the output of the algorithm (the classification decision), rarely does one have any concrete sense of how or why a particular classification has been arrived at from inputs' (Burrell 2016: 1). Interpretability can also be defined in terms of the predictability of the model; a model is interpretable if a well-informed person could consistently predict its outputs and behaviours (Kim et al. 2016). Questions of model behaviour narrowly address how a particular output or behaviour of the model occurred.[1] However, model behaviour can also be broadly interpreted to include effects on reliant institutions and users and their AI-influenced decisions; for example, how a physician's diagnosis was influenced by an expert system's recommendation, are also relevant (High Level Expert Group on Artificial Intelligence 2019: 18).

How was an AI system designed and tested? How is it governed?

These are questions of *transparency*. Unlike interpretability, transparency does not address the functionality or behaviour of the AI system itself but rather the processes involved in its design, development, testing, deployment, and regulation. Transparency principally requires information about the institutions and people that create and use

AI systems as well as the regulatory and governance structures that control both the institutions and systems. Here, interpretability play a supplementary but supportive role. Interpretable models or explanations of specific decisions taken by a system may, for example, be needed for regulators to effectively audit AI and ensure that regulatory requirements are being met in each context of use.

What information is required to investigate the behaviour of AI systems?

This is a question of *traceability*. To audit the behaviour of AI systems, certain evidence is needed, which can include 'data sets and the processes that yield the AI system's decision, including those of data gathering and data labelling as well as the algorithms used' (High Level Expert Group on Artificial Intelligence 2019: 18). This data needs to be consistently recorded as the system operates for effective governance to be feasible. Traceability is thus a fundamental requirement for post hoc auditing and explanations of model behaviour; without the right data, explanations cannot be computed after a model has produced a decision or other output (Mittelstadt et al. 2016). Traceability is, however, outside of the scope of this chapter, which is limited to surveying the landscape of methods for AI interpretability and transparency.

The value of interpretability and transparency

As these questions indicate, interpretability and transparency can be valued for many reasons in AI. Interpretability is not a universal necessity in AI. In low-risk scenarios in which errors have little to no impact or in which predictive performance is the sole concern, knowing how a model *functions* or a particular decision was reached may be irrelevant to the problem being solved. However, in many cases, it may be insufficient to merely receive a reliable prediction; rather, understanding how the prediction was made may also be necessary to reliably solve the problem at hand (Doshi-Velez and Kim 2017; Molnar 2020).

In philosophy of science, 'understanding' is treated as an intrinsic good of explanation (Lipton 2001). Understanding how a model *functions* can be inherently valuable for the sake of scientific discovery, human curiosity, and meaning-making (Molnar 2020). These intrinsic goods can be distinguished from the instrumental value of interpretability and transparency in AI as they support goods such as: (a) implementing accountability and auditing mechanisms; (b) complying with relevant legislation and enabling users to exercise legal rights (Doshi-Velez and Kim 2017; Wachter et al. 2017); (c) debugging and refining models (Kulesza et al. 2015); (d) detecting bias and dangerous behaviours; (e) assessing the societal impact of AI (Mittelstadt et al. 2016; Wachter et al. 2020); (f) encouraging user trust (Citron and Pasquale 2014; Ribeiro et al. 2016; Zarsky 2013); and (g) supporting human workers and institutions to work more effectively with AI systems (Rudin 2019a; Samek et al. 2017). Of course, these instrumental goods need to be balanced in practice against the alleged risks of opening systems to public scrutiny, including risks to intellectual property and commercial secrets, potential gaming of decision-making systems, and exploitation of user trust with deceptive or false explanations (Burrell 2016; Mittelstadt et al. 2019; Wachter et al. 2018).

In a recent report, the UK Information Commissioner's Office and Alan Turing Institute distinguish between six categories of explanations of AI systems (Information Commissioner's Office, The Alan Turing Institute 2020: 20) according to what is being explained. Specifically, explanations can address (a) the *rationale* for a decision; (b) the *responsibility* for the system's development, management, usage, and user redress; and (c) what and how *data* has been used to reach a decision; as well as steps taken to consider (d) *fairness*; (e) *safety and performance*; and (f) the social *impact* of the decision-making process. This taxonomy speaks to common interests underlying requests for explanations of AI models and decisions. Data explanations, for example, can provide details on the data used to train a model, including its source, collection method, assessments of its quality and gaps, and methods used to clean and standardize the data. Impact explanations can provide individuals with information regarding the potential impact of a system on their interests and opportunities, which can inform their decision to 'use' the system or provide a starting point for investigating the impact of the system across relevant populations (Mittelstadt 2016; Sandvig et al. 2014). These types of explanations can likewise be highly valuable for researchers working with machine learning to evaluate the epistemological validity, robustness, and limitations of models and systems (Franzke et al. 2020: 36–46; Mittelstadt et al. 2019). Standardized forms of disclosure (see the section 'Evaluating the quality of explanations') can provide consistency across such explanations.

There are thus many motivators for making AI more understandable. As these different goods suggest, interpretability and transparency can serve many different stakeholders and interests. Explanations can be offered to expert developers, professionals working in tandem with a system (Berendt and Preibusch 2017), and to individuals or groups affected by a system's outputs (Mantelero 2016; Mittelstadt 2017; Wachter and Mittelstadt 2019). Understanding the different potential goods and risks of interpretability, as well as the needs and interests of relevant stakeholders, is essential to ensure a good match between the methods chosen and local contextual requirements (see section 'Evaluating the quality of explanations').

INTERPRETABILITY

Several concepts are common across the questions and goods that motivate interpretability in AI. *Interpretability methods* seek to explain the *functionality* or *behaviour* of the 'black box' machine learning models that are a key component of AI decision-making systems. *Functionality* and *behaviour* are both elements of interpretability. The distinction is effectively one between model processing and its outputs; *functionality* refers to the internal calculations or analysis performed by or within the model, whereas *behaviour* refers to its outputs, which are visible to users and affected parties. Viewing outputs does not strictly require comprehension of the method that produced them, although the latter could certainly help develop a richer understanding of the significance and meaning of the outputs.

Trained machine learning models are *'black boxes'* when they are not comprehensible to human observers because their internals and rationale are unknown or inaccessible to the observer or known but uninterpretable due to their complexity (Guidotti et al. 2018; Information Commissioner's Office, The Alan Turing Institute 2020). *Interpretability* in the narrow sense used here refers to the capacity to understand the functionality and meaning of a given phenomenon, in this case a trained machine learning model and its outputs, and to explain it in human understandable terms (Doshi-Velez and Kim 2017). We will return to broader accounts of interpretability and explanation as philosophical concepts later in the chapter (see section 'Philosophy of explanations').

'Explanation' is likewise a key concept in interpretability. Generically, explanations in AI relate 'the feature values of an instance to its model prediction in a humanly understandable way' (Molnar 2020: 31). This rough definition hides significant nuance. The term captures a multitude of ways of exchanging information about a phenomenon, in this case the *functionality* of a model or the rationale and criteria for a decision, to different stakeholders (Lipton 2016; Miller 2019). Unfortunately, in the literature surveyed in this chapter, it is often deployed in a conceptually ambiguous manner. Terminological confusion is thus common in the field (Mittelstadt et al. 2019).

To understand how 'explanation' is used in the field of interpretable AI, two key distinctions are relevant. First, methods can be distinguished in terms of what it is they seek to explain. *Explanations of model functionality* address the general logic the model follows in producing outputs from input data. *Explanations of model behaviour*, in contrast, seek to explain how or why a particular behaviour exhibited by the model occurred, for example, how or why a particular output was produced from a particular input. Explanations of model *functionality* aim to explain what is going on inside the model, whereas explanations of model *behaviour* aim to explain what led to a specific behaviour or output by referencing essential attributes or influencers on that behaviour. It is not strictly necessary to understand the full set of relationships, dependencies, and weights of features within the model to explain model behaviour.

Second, interpretability methods can be distinguished in how they conceptualize 'explanation'. Many methods conceptualize explanations as *approximation models*, which are a type of simpler, human interpretable model that is created to reliably approximate the *functionality* of a more complex black box model. The approximation model itself is often and confusingly referred to as an explanation of the black box model. This approach contrasts with the treatment of 'explanation' in philosophy of science and epistemology, in which the term typically refers to *explanatory statements* that explain the causes of a given phenomenon (Mittelstadt et al. 2019).

The usage of 'explanation' in this fashion can be confusing. Approximation models are best thought of as tools from which explanatory statements about the original model can be derived (Mittelstadt et al. 2019). Explanatory statements themselves can be textual, quantitative, or visual, and report on several aspects of the model and its behaviours. Molnar (2020: 25–26) proposes the following taxonomy of the types of outputs produced by interpretability methods:

- **feature summary statistic**: methods that return summary statistics indicating the strength of single features (e.g. feature importance) or groups of features (e.g. pairwise interaction strength);
- **feature summary visualization**: methods where summary statistics can also be visualized rather than listed quantitatively in a table. Visual outputs are preferable when reporting the partial dependence of a feature;
- **model internals**: methods where various aspects of the internals of a model can be reported, such as the learned weights of features, the learned structure of decision trees, or the visualization of feature detectors learned in convolutional neural networks;
- **data point**: methods were data points that help interpret a model can be reported, especially when working with textual or visual data. These data points can either exist in the model or be newly created to explain a particular output of the model. To be interpretable, any reported data points should ideally themselves be interpretable;
- **intrinsically interpretable model**: as discussed above, methods where globally or locally interpretable approximation models can be created to explain black box models. These models can then be further explained using any of the aforementioned methods and output types.

Further distinctions help to classify different types of explanations and interpretability methods. A basic distinction in interpretability can be drawn between *global* and *local interpretability*. This distinction refers to the scope of the model or outputs a given interpretability or explanatory method aims to make human comprehensible. Global methods aim to explain the *functionality* of a model as a whole or across a particular set of outputs in terms of the significance of features, their dependencies or interactions, and their effect on outputs. In contrast, local methods can address, for example, the influence of specific areas of the input space or specific variables on one or more specific outputs of the model.

Models can be globally interpretable at a holistic or modular level (Molnar 2020). Holistic global interpretability refers to models which are comprehensible to a human observer in the sense that the observer can follow the entire logic or *functional* steps taken by the model which lead to all possible outcomes of the model (Guidotti et al. 2018). It should be possible for a single person to comprehend holistically interpretable models in their entirety (Lipton 2016). An observer would have 'a holistic view of its features and each of the learned components such as weights, other parameters, and structures' (Molnar 2020: 27).

Given the limitations of human comprehension and short-term memory, global holistic interpretability is currently only practically achievable on relatively simple models with few features, interactions, rules, or strong linearity and monotonicity (Guidotti et al. 2018). For more complex models, global interpretability at a *modular level* may be feasible. This type of interpretability involves understanding a particular characteristic or segment of the model, for example, the weights in a linear model or the splits and leaf node predictions in a decision tree (Molnar 2020).

With regards to local interpretability, a single output can be considered interpretable if the steps that led to it can be explained. Local interpretability does not strictly require that the entire series of steps be explained; rather, it can be sufficient to explain one or more aspects of the model that led to the output, such as a critically influential feature value (Molnar 2020; Wachter et al. 2018). A group of outputs is considered locally interpretable if the same methods to produce explanations of individual outputs can be applied to the group. Groups can also be explained by methods that produce global interpretability at a modular level (Molnar 2020).

A further important distinction drawn in the literature concerns how and when interpretability is achieved in practice. Interpretability can be achieved by affecting the design and restricting the complexity of a model or by applying methods to analyse and explain the model after it has been trained (and deployed). Respectively, these can be referred to as *intrinsic interpretability* and *post hoc interpretability* (Lipton 2016; Molnar 2020; Montavon et al. 2018) or *reverse engineering* (Guidotti et al. 2018). Intrinsic interpretability can be further specified according to its target, which, according to Lipton (2016) and Lepri et al. (2017) can be a mechanistic understanding of the functioning of the model ('simulatability'), individual components ('decomposability'), or the training algorithm ('algorithmic transparency').

Interpretability methods

Development of methods for interpreting black box machine learning models has accelerated rapidly in recent years. While a full survey of methods remains beyond the scope of this chapter, the following taxonomy proposed by Guidotti et al. (2018) classifies methods according to the type of interpretability problem being solved:

- **model explanation methods**: these methods create a simpler, globally interpretable approximation model that acts as a global explanation of the black box model. These simplified models approximate the true criteria used to make decisions. Good approximations will reliably 'mimic the behavior of the black box' while remaining understandable to a target audience (Guidotti et al. 2018: 13). Such methods include 'single-tree approximations' which approximate the performance of the black box model in a single decision tree (Craven and Shavlik 1995; Krishnan et al. 1999), 'rule extraction' methods which create human comprehensible decision rules that mimic the performance of the black box model (Andrews et al. 1995;

Craven and Shavlik 1994), and varied global model-agnostic methods (Henelius et al. 2014; Lou et al. 2012, 2013);

- **outcome explanation methods**: these methods create a locally interpretable approximation model that can 'explain the prediction of the black box in understandable terms for humans for a specific instance or record' (Guidotti et al., 2018: 26). These methods do not need to be globally interpretable but rather only need to reliably explain 'the prediction on a specific input instance' (Guidotti et al. 2018: 13). Local approximations are accurate representations only of a specific domain or 'slice' of a model. As a result, there is necessarily a trade-off between the insightfulness of the approximated model, the simplicity of the presented function, and the size of the domain for which it is valid (Bastani et al. 2017; Lakkaraju et al. 2017). Such methods include saliency masks, which visually highlight areas of importance to an image classifier for a particular input class (Fong and Vedaldi 2017; Selvaraju et al. 2016), and varied local model-agnostic methods (Poulin et al. 2006; Ribeiro et al. 2016; Turner 2016);

- **model inspection methods**: these methods create a 'representation (visual or textual) for understanding some specific property of the black box model or of its predictions', such as the model's sensitivity to changes in the value of particular features or the components of the model that most influence one or more specific decisions (Guidotti et al. 2018: 14). As with outcome explanation methods, model inspection problems do not strictly require a globally interpretable approximation to be created. Such methods include sensitivity analysis (Baehrens et al. 2010; Datta et al. 2016; Saltelli 2002), partial dependence plots (Adler et al. 2018; Hooker 2004; Krause et al. 2016), individual conditional expectation plots (Goldstein et al. 2015), activation maximization (Nguyen et al. 2016; Yosinski et al. 2015), and tree visualization (Thiagarajan et al. 2016).

- **transparent box design methods**: these methods produce a model that is locally or globally interpretable. This is not an approximation of a black box model but rather an original model (Guidotti et al. 2018). Rudin has influentially advocated for bypassing the problem of explanations by using interpretable models unless a significant and important loss in accuracy by failing to use a black box model can be demonstrated (Rudin 2019b). Methods commonly considered to be interpretable by design, given appropriate constraints on dimensionality or depth, include linear regression, logistic regression, regularized regression, and decision trees (Guidotti et al. 2018; Information Commissioner's Office, The Alan Turing Institute 2020; Molnar 2020). Other methods include rule extraction (Lakkaraju et al. 2016; Wang and Rudin 2015; Yin and Han 2003) and prototype and criticism selection (Bien and Tibshirani 2011; Fong and Vedaldi 2017; Kim et al. 2014).

This taxonomy does not capture the full range of interpretability methods. A class of methods not fully captured include what Lipton (Lipton 2016: 97) refers to as 'post-hoc interpretations' of specific behaviour. These include some of the methods classified as *outcome explanation methods*, such as visualizations (Simonyan et al. 2013; Tamagnini et al. 2017) and local model-agnostic explanations (Fong and Vedaldi 2017; Ribeiro et al. 2016), but also methods that create *user friendly verbal explanations*, including case-based explanations (Caruana et al. 1999; Kim et al. 2014), natural language explanations (McAuley and Leskovec 2013), and counterfactual explanations (Wachter et al. 2018). Case-based explanation methods for non-case-based machine learning involve using the trained model as a distance metric to determine which cases in the training data set are most similar to the case or decision to be explained. Natural language explanations consist of text or visual aids describing the relationship between features of an input (e.g. words in a document) and the model's output (e.g. the classification of the document). Counterfactual explanations describe a dependency on external facts that led to a particular outcome or decision and a 'close possible world' in which a different, preferred outcome would have occurred (Wachter et al. 2018).

Interpretability methods can also be categorized according to their portability. Molnar (2020) distinguishes model-specific from model-agnostic methods, the latter of which can be applied to any type of machine learning model. Examples include dependence plots, feature interaction (Friedman and Popescu 2008; Greenwell et al. 2018; Hooker 2004), feature importance (Fisher et al. 2019), and local surrogates (Ribeiro et al. 2016). Example-based methods, which explain instances of the data set rather than groups of features or the model holistically, are also typically model-agnostic (Molnar 2020: 233). Examples include counterfactual explanations (Russell 2019; Wachter et al. 2018), adversarial examples (Goodfellow et al. 2014; Szegedy et al. 2013), prototypes and criticisms (Kim et al. 2016), influential instances (Koh and Liang 2017; Lundberg and Lee 2017), and case-based explanations (Caruana et al. 1999; Kim et al. 2014).

Transparency

A related but distinct topic often addressed in tandem with algorithmic interpretability is that of algorithmic transparency and accountability. Whereas interpretability has a *narrow* focus of explaining the functionality or behaviour of an AI system or trained machine learning model, transparency and accountability have a *broad* focus on explaining the institutional and regulatory environment in which such systems are developed, deployed, and governed. In other words, interpretability is about understanding the system itself, whereas transparency and accountability are about understanding the people and organizations responsible for developing, using, and regulating it. Interpretability is often thought to be a key component of algorithmic transparency and accountability.

Given its broad aims, many approaches could conceivably be considered forms of algorithmic transparency and accountability. For our purposes, two broad categories can be distinguished: standardized documentation for training data sets and models, and impact assessments.

STANDARDIZED DOCUMENTATION

Standardized documentation refers to any method that prescribes a consistent form of disclosure about how AI systems and models are created, trained, and deployed in different decision-making contexts, services, and organizations. Many proposals for universal and sector-specific standards have been advanced in recent years, but none have yet been broadly adopted or tested.

Despite this, standardization initiatives frequently have common points of departure. The motivation for standardization in AI can be traced to comparable standards adopted in many industries describing the provenance, safety, and performance testing carried out on a product prior to release (Arnold et al. 2019). In this context, many initiatives are motivated by the usage, sharing, and aggregation of diverse data sets in AI, which runs the risk of introducing and reinforcing biases across different contexts of use (Bender and Friedman 2018; Gebru et al. 2018; Holland et al. 2018; Yang et al. 2018).

Data set documentation methods aim to help potential users of a data set to assess its appropriateness and limitations for training models for specific types of tasks. To do so, they generally require information about how the data sets are created and composed, including a list of features and sources of the data as well as information about how the data was collected, cleaned, and distributed (Gebru et al. 2018). Some approaches include disclosures and standardized statistical tests concerning ethical and legal considerations (Holland et al. 2018), including biases, known proxies for sensitive features (e.g. ethnicity, gender), and gaps in the data. Documenting such characteristics can help identify where problematic biases could be learned and reinforced by machine learning systems trained on the data which would otherwise remain unknown to developers and analysts (Gebru et al. 2018; Holland et al. 2018). As a secondary effect, standardized data set documentation may also drive better data collection practices (Holland et al. 2018) as well as consideration of contextual and methodological biases more generally.

Comparable initiatives exist for trained machine learning models. 'Model reporting' documentation is designed to accompany trained models when being deployed in contexts that differ from the training environment. For example, the 'model cards for model reporting' initiative calls for documentation describing various performance characteristics and intended contexts of use, including how performance changes when applied to different cultural, demographic, phenotypic, and intersectional (i.e. defined by multiple relevant attributes) groups (Mitchell et al. 2019). User-facing model documentation has also been proposed to enhance user trust and adoption. For example, 'FactSheets' have been proposed that would require a standardized declaration of conformity from AI suppliers addressing the purpose, performance, safety, security, and provenance of models in a user-friendly manner (Arnold et al. 2019). To complement data set and model documentation and pre-deployment testing standards, toolkits have also been created to help identify and correct for biases in deployed models and AI systems (Bellamy et al. 2018).

SELF-ASSESSMENT FRAMEWORKS

A second category of algorithmic transparency initiatives have created various self-assessment tools to help organizations evaluate AI systems at the point of procurement and deployment. These tools pose a series of questions to be answered by organizations in the procurement and deployment phase of AI. This approach builds on established types of legally required organizational disclosures in areas such as data protection, privacy, and environmental law (Article 29 Data Protection Working Party 2017; Mantelero 2018; Reisman et al. 2018). To date, self-assessment frameworks have largely been limited to public sector procurement of AI but in principle could be applied in the private sector as well.

'Algorithmic Impact Assessments' (AIA) are a prominent example of self-assessment frameworks (Reisman et al. 2018). The AIA developed by the AI Now Institute, for example, requires public agencies to consider four key elements prior to procurement: (a) potential impact on fairness, justice, bias, and similar concerns; (b) review processes for external researchers to track the system's impact over time; (c) public disclosure of the agencies' definition of 'automated decision system', current and proposed systems, and any completed self-assessments; and (d) solicitation of concerns and questions from the public. AI Now has also called on governments to establish enhanced due process mechanisms to support individual and community redress (Reisman et al. 2018). The AIA framework has since been implemented and adapted by the Canadian government to govern procurement of automated decision-making systems across the public sector (Government of Canada 2020). The European Commission has also recently developed a 'Trustworthy AI Assessment List' that is operationally similar to an AIA (High Level Expert Group on Artificial Intelligence 2019). The list poses a series of questions on topics such as fundamental rights; human agency and oversight; technical robustness; and safety, diversity, and accountability.

PHILOSOPHY OF EXPLANATIONS

Examining prior work on AI interpretability and transparency in the context of prior work on explanations in the philosophy of science can be useful to identify the field's major trends, gaps, key open questions, and potentially their answers. Explanations of scientific and everyday phenomena have long been studied in the philosophy of science. Explanations, and more broadly epistemology, causality, and justification, have been the focus of philosophy for millennia, making a complete overview of the field unfeasible. What follows is a brief overview of key distinctions and terminology relevant to surveying interpretability and transparency in AI.

While much variation and debate can be observed in prior work (Ruben 2004; Salmon 2006), an explanation of a given phenomenon is usually said to consist of two parts:

- the *explanadum* or a sentence describing the phenomenon to be explained (Hempel and Oppenheim 1948: 136–137). The phenomenon can be of any level of specificity from a particular fact or event, such as a particular decision produced by a model, to general scientific laws or holistic descriptions of a model;
- the *explanans* or the sentences which are thought to explain the phenomenon (Hempel and Oppenheim 1948: 136–137). Depending upon the type of explanation, audience, and specific questions asked, the explanans can be as simple as a single sentence or as complex as a full causal model.

In the philosophy of science, much work is dedicated to theories of *scientific explanation*. According to this tradition, 'explanatory knowledge is knowledge of the causal mechanisms, and mechanisms of other types perhaps, that produce the phenomena with which we are concerned' (Salmon 2006: 128). A related notion, causal explanation, refers to a type of explanation of an event that provides 'some information about its causal history' (Lewis 1986: 217–218). Within this tradition, a complete or scientific explanation would consist of a set of *explanans* describing the full causal history of a phenomenon (Hempel 1965; Ruben 2004; Salmon 2006). This type of scientific explanation will involve general scientific relationships or universal laws and can be considered an idealized form of explanation of the sort pursued but rarely obtained through scientific investigation (Hempel 1965).

As this definition of an ideal scientific explanation suggests, explanations can be classified in terms of their *completeness* or the degree to which the entire causal chain and necessity of an event can be explained (Ruben 2004). Completeness can be used to distinguish *scientific* and *everyday* explanations (Miller 2019) or *full* and *partial* causal explanations (Ruben 2004), each of which addresses the causes of an event but to different degrees of completeness. Everyday explanations of the type typically requested in daily life address 'why particular facts (events, properties, decisions, etc.) occurred' rather than general scientific relationships (Miller 2019: 3).

The terminology is not, however, consistent across theories of explanation. As Ruben (2004: 19) notes:

> Different theories disagree about what counts as a full explanation. Some will hold that explanations, as given in the ordinary way, are full explanations in their own right; others (like Hempel) will argue that full explanations are only those which meet some ideal, rarely if ever achieved in practice. A partial explanation is simply a full explanation (whatever that is) with some part of it left out. On any theory of explanation, we sometimes do not say all that we should say if we were explaining in full. Sometimes we assume that the audience is in possession of facts which do not stand in need of repetition. At other times, our ignorance does not allow us to fill

some of the explanatory gaps that we admit occur. In such cases, in which we omit information for pragmatic or epistemic reasons, we give partial explanations.

Most of the methods discussed in this chapter can be considered partial or everyday explanations. These methods report a selection of the total set of causes of a phenomenon or create a simplified approximation of a more complex phenomenon to make it humanly comprehensible. Both examples are partial because they do not report the full set of causes of a phenomenon, for example, the full causal chain of collecting and cleaning training and test data or the causes of the phenomena reported in this data.

Full or scientific explanations can nonetheless serve as an idealized endpoint for global interpretability in AI. If a user asks how a model was trained, a good explanation would resemble a full causal explanation, only limited to the internals of the model (e.g. feature values and interdependencies) and training algorithm rather than universal laws. Similarly, global explanations of model *functionality* will necessarily contain causal information concerning, for example, dependencies between features. Scientific explanations traditionally conceived are also relevant to the need for interpretable machine learning models in research, especially on causality and inference (Pearl 2019; Schölkopf 2019).

Recent decades have seen an increase in the attention paid to theories of contrastive explanations and counterfactual causality (Kment 2006; Lewis 1973; Pearl 2000; Woodward and Zalta 2003). Contrastive theories suggest that causal explanations inevitably involve appeal to a counterfactual case, be it a cause or an event, which did not occur. Woodward (2005: 6) describes these types of explanations as answers to 'what-if-things-had-been-different' questions. A canonical example is provided by Lipton (1990: 256):

> To explain why P rather than Q, we must cite a causal difference between P and not-Q, consisting of a cause of P and the absence of a corresponding event in the history of not-Q.

Contrastive theories of explanation are, of course, not without criticism. Ruben (2004), for example, has suggested that, even if causal explanations are inevitably contrastive in nature (which he doubts), this feature can be accommodated by traditional theories of explanation. Regardless of one's position on this debate, contrastive explanations remain interesting for AI because they address a particular event or case and would thus appear to be simpler to create than global explanations of model *functionality* (Mittelstadt et al. 2019; Wachter et al. 2018).

Other types of explanations beyond scientific explanations exist which are relevant to interpretability in AI. As Hempel writes, 'explaining the rules of a contest, explaining the meaning of a cuneiform inscription or of a complex legal clause or of a passage in a symbolist poem, explaining how to bake a Sacher torte or how to repair a radio' are all uses of the term 'explain' which do not involve causal, scientific explanations (Hempel

1965: 412–413). In these cases, explanations can be given that do not have a clear dependence on universal or scientific laws.

These observations are relevant to the question of interpretability in AI insofar as it indicates that 'explanation' is not a singular concept but rather a catch-all for many different types of interlocutory acts. A person impacted by an AI system (e.g. a criminal risk scoring system) could ask why they were classified as high risk but equally how the model was trained, on which data, and why its usage (and design) is morally or legally justified. Work on interpretability in AI, as well as regulatory interest in the subject, similarly reflects that explanations of AI are being requested in connection to a particular entity, be it a specific decision, event, trained model, or application (Mittelstadt et al. 2019). The explanations requested are thus not full scientific explanations as they need not appeal to general relationships or scientific laws but rather, at most, to causal relationships between the set of variables in a given model (Woodward 1997). Rather, what is being requested are everyday explanations either of how a trained model functions in general or of how it behaved in a particular case.

For the purposes of this chapter, I will primarily discuss methods for producing explanations in AI systems that answer *functional* questions, such as how a model functions globally and locally, or how a particular classification was reached. Such explanations, while primarily technical answers to 'Why?' questions (e.g. why I was classified as 'high risk'), simultaneously provide essential information to answer related questions concerning the accuracy, reliability, safety, fairness, bias, and other aspects of the system.

A further distinction can be drawn between explanation as a process or act and explanation as a product of that act. This linguistic feature is known as process–product ambiguity. In philosophy of science, much work has been dedicated to explanation as both a product and a process and their dependency (if any) (Hempel 1965; Ruben 2004). As a product, the question being asked is essentially 'What information has to be conveyed in order to have explained something?' Explanations as products can be classified and described according to the type of information they convey (Ruben 2004). As a process, the act of explaining and the intention of the explainer are thought to influence the information conveyed by an explanation (Achinstein 1983). The explanation as a product is thus 'an ordered pair, in part consisting of a proposition, but also including an explaining act type' (Ruben 2004: 8).

The process and product accounts of explanation are incompatible (Ruben 2004); however, for the purposes of this chapter, an answer to the process–product ambiguity is not needed. Rather, the distinction reveals that in designing explanations and explanatory methods for AI, attention must be given not only to *what* information the explanation contains but also to *how* this information is conveyed to its audience. This distinction between the *what* and *how* of explanations in AI is key to evaluating the relative utility of the methods discussed above and the quality of different types of explanations.

Evaluating the Quality of Explanations

Prior philosophy work on explanations provides a robust foundation to explore how the quality of different types of explanations and approximations of AI *functionality* or *behaviour* can be evaluated. Within the philosophy of science, explanatory *pragmatists* suggest that 'explanation is an interest-relative notion ... explanation has to be partly a pragmatic concept' (Putnam 1978: 41). In other words, the requirements for a full explanation will vary according to the needs and interests of the audience.

This approach is a departure from causal theorists, who draw a clear distinction between the ideal of a full explanation and the pragmatics of giving a good explanation. The former is a question of the information the explanatory product must contain, while the latter is a question of how parts of that information, or a partial explanation, is crafted and communicated to an audience according to their particular interests and requirements. According to Ruben (2004: 22),

> ... how we select from the full list of explanatory relevant features in order to obtain the ones required in a particular (partial) explanation we may offer is a pragmatic and audience-variant question. A partial explanation is one that omits certain relevant factors; a full explanation is one that includes all relevant factors ... A partial explanation may be good relative to one set of circumstances, but bad relative to another, in which interests, beliefs, or whatever differ.

The question is thus whether, as in the deductive-nomological approach (Salmon 2006), the ideal of a full explanation exists independently of the concept of a good explanation. The imagined 'ideal explanatory text' provides a benchmark for complete scientific explanations (Salmon 2006). For explanatory pragmatists, this distinction collapses. Once collapsed, context becomes an essential determinant of a good explanation. Whereas traditionalists conceive of the concept of explanation as 'a relation like description: a relation between a theory and a fact', pragmatists view it as 'a three-term relation between theory, fact, and context' (Fraassen 1980: 156).

According to pragmatists, good explanations exceed merely correct explanations by being aligned with the needs, interests, and expertise of the agents requesting the explanation (Achinstein 2010; Lewis 1986). It follows that a universal ideal of a best possible explanation of any given phenomenon does not exist; while an ideal correct explanation is possible, what makes an explanation good (or 'the best') is dependent upon the context and audience to which it is given (Achinstein 2010).

Regardless of one's position as a traditionalist or pragmatist, a distinction can be drawn between the truth or correctness of an explanation and how successful that explanation is at communicating relevant information to a given audience (Ruben 2004). Achinstein (2010) describes this as the distinction between *correct* explanations and *good* explanations. A full scientific explanation can be correct insofar as the causes it attributes to a phenomenon are truthful or valid and yet be a bad explanation when evaluated as an act of communication, for example, because the information conveyed is so complex as to be incomprehensible to the recipient. Similarly, an explanation may also be considered inadequate not because the information communicated is false but because it is incomplete or inadequate to answer the question posed or the needs of a specific audience (Lewis 1986; Putnam 1978).

Compared to the distinctions drawn above, this is a subtle but important difference. In evaluating an explanation in AI, we can distinguish quality in terms of *causal validity*, or its truthfulness and completeness, and quality in terms of *meaningfulness* or how effective it is at conveying a relevant set of information to a given audience. This distinction holds across both traditional and pragmatic schools of thought, which differ only on whether the meaningfulness of an explanation should be considered a quality of the explanation itself (as pragmatists do) or a quality of the act of selecting and communicating the explanation (as traditionalists do). For the purpose of this chapter, selecting a particular school of thought is unnecessary so long as the distinction between causal validity and meaningfulness is recognized.

Characteristics of 'good' explanatory products

Building on this distinction between validity and meaningfulness, many characteristics have been proposed in the field of AI interpretability to evaluate the quality of explanations and approximations. Following the preceding discussion (see the section 'Philosophy of explanations'), a further distinction can be drawn between the quality of the *explanans* itself and the quality of the process by which the *explanans* is communicated to the explainee. What follows is an overview of characteristics for producing and communicating high-quality explanations that have been proposed in literature on AI interpretability as well as empirical work describing how humans give and receive explanations in psychology and cognitive science (Miller 2019). We begin with characteristics to evaluate the quality of explanatory products.

Contrastive

Based on a representative review of empirical evidence in psychology and cognitive science, Miller (2019: 3) argues that good everyday explanations are contrastive insofar as explanations are 'sought in response to particular counterfactual cases ... That is, people do not ask why event P happened, but rather why event P happened instead of some event Q.' Based on the reviewed evidence, Miller found that people psychologically prefer contrastive explanations. Further, this preference cannot be reduced solely to the relative simplicity of contrastive explanations against full causal explanations (Miller 2019: 28). In AI, best practices for computing contrastive explanations will be specific to context, application, or user because a comparison point or preferred alternative outcome must be identified (Molnar 2020; Wachter et al. 2018).

Abnormality

'Normal' behaviour is thought to be 'more explainable than abnormal behaviour' (Miller 2019: 41). The perceived abnormality of an event has thus been found to drive the preference for contrastive explanations in practice that can explain why a normal or expected event did not occur (Gregor and Benbasat 1999; Hilton and Slugoski 1986; McClure et al. 2003; Molnar 2020; Samland and Waldmann 2014). Many characteristics of AI behaviour can set it apart as abnormal. Lim and Dey (2009), for example, found a positive relationship between the perceived 'inappropriateness' of application behaviour and user requests for contrastive explanations. Violation of ethical and social norms can likewise set an event apart as abnormal (Hilton 1996). The practical importance of abnormality for good everyday explanations suggests that explanations of AI behaviour should describe input features that are 'abnormal in any sense (like a rare category of a categorical feature)' if they influenced the behaviour or outcome in question (Molnar 2020: 32).

Selectivity

Full scientific explanations are rarely if ever realized in practice. Multiple correct but incomplete explanations are normally possible that list different causes for the *explanadum*. A given cause may be incomplete insofar as it is not the sole cause of the event but may nonetheless convey useful information to the explainee (Ylikoski 2013). As Miller (2019: 3) argues, 'Explanations are selected—people rarely, if ever, expect an explanation that consists of an actual and complete cause of an event. Humans are adept at selecting one or two causes from a sometimes infinite number of causes to be the explanation.' Selection involves choosing the most relevant set of causes for a given phenomenon and disregarding other less relevant but valid causes on the basis of local requirements. Selection is necessary to reduce long causal chains to a cognitively man-ageable size (Hilton 1996).

For AI explanations, selection means choosing key features or evidence to be emphasized in an explanation or user interface based, for example, on their relative weight or influence on a given prediction or output (Biran and McKeown 2014; Poulin et al. 2006) and the explainee's subjective interests and expectations (see the section 'Characteristics of 'good' explanatory processes'). To facilitate selection of relevant explanans from the overall possible set of valid explanans, good explanations should clearly communicate the degree of importance or influence of a given feature or set of features on the instance or outcome being explained (Molnar 2020).

Complexity and sparsity

The need for selectivity in explaining AI behaviours to meet local requirements points to the need to conceptualize and measure the relative complexity of different possible valid explanations (Achinstein 1983; Miller 2019). Many metrics exist to evaluate ex-planation complexity relative to a target model or set of outputs. Complexity can be defined in relation to a model's size, such as the number and length of rules, features, or branches in a decision tree (Deng 2019; Guidotti et al. 2018; Rudin 2019b), or in terms of the linearity and monotonicity of the relationships between variables (Guidotti et al. 2018). Alternatively, complexity can be defined according to sparsity or the number of explanatory statements given to explain a black box model or specific output as well as the number of features and interactions addressed in these statements.

In AI, sparse explanations or approximation models are those which have low dimensionality or address a small number of features and interactions. Good sparse explanations are those which include a cognitively manageable set of highly relevant causes or statements according to the explainee's interests and expertise (Molnar 2020; Russell 2019). Methods such as case-based explanations and counterfactual explanations that provide a sparse explanation of changes necessary to reach a different, preferred outcome can bypass the difficult challenge of explaining the internal state of trained models to a significant extent (Caruana et al. 1999; Wachter et al. 2018). Approximation methods can also help but must grapple with a three-way trade-off between the approximation's fidelity, comprehensibility, and domain size (see the section 'Interpretability').

Novelty and truthfulness

A set of closely related characteristics common to theories of explanation concerns the novelty and truthfulness of the explanans. Good explanations should be novel, meaning they do not merely repeat information about the explanadum that is already known by the explainee but rather provide new, unknown information that helps explain the explanadum (Molnar 2020; Salmon 2006). To be informative, explanations should not be entirely reducible to presuppositions or beliefs that the recipient of the explanation already holds (Hesslow 1988). In AI, novelty can be measured, for example, in the extent to which an explanation reflects whether the instance being explained 'comes from a "new" region far removed from the distribution of training data' (Molnar 2020: 28).

Good explanations should likewise be truthful, meaning the statements contained in the explanans should be accurate or correct. In AI explanations, the dependencies between variables described or the causes attributed to an outcome should be correct (Molnar 2020; Russell 2019). Simply put, the more accurate the explanation, the better it is at enhancing the explainee's understanding of the explanadum. In practice, accuracy can be measured, for example, in terms of the performance of the explanation in predicting future behaviours based on unseen input data (Molnar 2020).

Representativeness, fidelity, consistency, and stability

A final set of characteristics addresses the intra-model and inter-explanation performance of an explanation or approximation. For explanations of more than a single output or group of outputs, representativeness is a key characteristic. Global or local approximations can be evaluated in terms of their representativeness of outputs or instances in the model reliably explained by the approximation (Molnar 2020). As a rule of thumb, the quality of an approximation increases based on the number of instances or outputs of the model it can reliably and accurately explain.

Fidelity is closely related to representativeness insofar as the latter is implicitly linked to the accuracy of the explanation over multiple insurances. Fidelity refers to the performance of the approximation against the black box model; approximations with high fidelity will approximate the performance of the black box model as closely as possible, including accurate predictions as well as errors.

The consistency of the approximation is also relevant in this context, which can be measured in terms of performance of the approximation across different black box models that have been trained on the same data to perform the same task. Stability performs a similar role to consistency. They differ in that stability is concerned with comparing the performance of explanations for 'similar instances for a fixed model'. Stable explanations will not substantially change when explaining a set of instances that only have slight variation in feature values (Molnar 2020).

Characteristics of 'good' explanatory processes

Following the distinction between causal validity and meaningfulness, the quality of explanations is dependent not solely on the content of the explanation but also on how this content is tailored to the explainee and communicated in practice. Many factors of good explanatory processes, such as the appropriate complexity and scope of explanations provided, are dependent on the context in which an AI system is used. The following characteristics of good explanatory processes have been proposed in the literature.

Interactivity and usability

Giving an explanation is a social communicative act based on interaction and information exchange between one or more explainers and explainees (Slugoski et al. 1993). Information exchange occurs through dialogue, visual representation, or other means (Hilton 1990). In AI, giving an explanation should be viewed not as a one-way exchange of information but rather as an interactive process involving a mix of human and AI agents.

Further, explanations are iterative insofar as they must be selected and evaluated on the basis of shared presuppositions and beliefs. Iteration may be required to communicate effectively or clarify points of confusion on the path towards a mutually understood explanation. While a given output can have many causes or important features, explainees will often only be interested in a small subset of these that are relevant to a specific question or contrastive case. It is the task of the explainer to select explanans from this subset of all possible causes or features. The chosen explanans may not satisfy the requirements of the explainee, requiring subsequent questioning and the generation of a new, more relevant explanans (Miller 2019: 4).

The quality of explanatory processes in AI can therefore be evaluated in terms of the quality of the interaction and iteration between explainee and explainer. Forms of explanation that are interactive and can help the explainee interrogate the model to accomplish specific tasks of interest are seen as better than explanations which consist of standardized or fixed content (Guidotti et al. 2018: 7). Explanations of AI *functionality* or *behaviour* can be given both by human workers tasked with explaining the system to affected parties and potentially by the AI system itself, for example, through an interpretability interface (Kayande et al. 2009; Martens and Provost 2013; Mittelstadt et al. 2019; Wexler et al. 2019).

Local relevance

As the preceding characteristics indicate, good explanations should be tailored towards the relative interests of the explainee (Miller 2019; Molnar 2020). They should answer, or help to answer, questions of interest to their audience (Miller 2019; Slugoski et al. 1993). Software engineers, regulators, deploying institutions, end-users, and other people request explanations for different reasons and seek answers to different questions (Miller 2019; Mittelstadt et al. 2019). Explanations that are not tailored to answer the specific question(s) being asked may fail to communicate relevant information to their audience.

Local comprehensibility

For explanations to succeed in communicating relevant information to the explainee, they must also be comprehensible to their recipient. Local comprehensibility refers to the degree to which explanations communicate information at a scope and level of complexity that matches the audience's expertise (Molnar 2020). Explanations that include all factors that led to a particular prediction or behaviour can be correct and complete explanations and yet incomprehensible, depending on their audience. For example, complete explanations may be useful for purposes of debugging a system or to meet legal requirements (Molnar 2020: 35) but useless to a user trying to understand which factors of their financial history most influenced the outcome of their loan application (Wachter et al. 2018).

Local comprehensibility and relevance are intrinsically linked. Software engineers, for example, may prefer more accurate but opaque models or more complete but complex explanations to help debug and refine their system, whereas end-users interested in the key reasons for a given decision may prefer explanations that are simpler or narrower in scope (Mittelstadt et al. 2019; Wachter et al. 2018). Urgency is similarly important; time-sensitive requests can necessitate simpler but incomplete explanations (Guidotti et al. 2018).

Overall, good explanatory processes in AI should be sensitive to the reason an explanation is being requested as well as the motivation and local needs of the explainee. In this regard, standardized forms of disclosure, including many of the transparency frameworks describe above (see the section 'Transparency'), can fail as good explanations if they are not adapted for different audiences.

OPEN CHALLENGES IN AI INTERPRETABILITY AND TRANSPARENCY

As the preceding discussion indicates, there are many open questions when it comes to designing effective products and processes to explain the functionality and behaviour of AI systems. To conclude, I consider three key open challenges facing the field of AI interpretability and transparency concerning the development of common standards for (a) 'good' explanations; (b) deterring deception through explanations; and (c) consistent and practically useful transparency frameworks.

Common standards for 'good' explanations

As discussed in this chapter, many methods have been developed to explain how autonomous systems function both generally and for specific decisions. However, while many approaches exist, the adoption of common standards for 'good' explanations that enhance the useability of autonomous systems remain nascent. To define such standards, we need to understand what makes an explanation informative and effective in practice. Empirical research into the local effectiveness and acceptability of different interpretability and transparency methods for different types of AI applications is urgently needed.

To date, a majority of work on AI interpretability has addressed methods for creating global and local approximations of black box models. While useful for purposes of testing and debugging black box models, the utility of these approaches for explaining model behaviour are less clear (Ribeiro et al. 2016; Selvaraju et al. 2016; Simonyan et al. 2013). In particular, it is unclear how useful such simplified human comprehensible approximations are for non-experts. Local approximations in particular 'can produce widely varying estimates of the importance of variables even in simple scenarios such as the single variable case, making it extremely difficult to reason about how a function varies as the inputs change' (Wachter et al. 2018: 851). Conveying these limitations in a consistent and reliable way to experts and non-experts alike remains nascent, which raises questions over their utility for answering questions about specific model behaviour.

It is in this context that Box's maxim, 'All models are wrong, but some are useful' (Box 1979) is illuminating. Treating local approximations as explanations of model behaviour would suggest that they provide reliable knowledge of how a complex model functions, but this has yet to be proven in practice across different types of AI applications and interpretability methods. For approximation models to be trusted, explainees must understand the domain over which the approximation is 'reliable and accurate, where it breaks down, and where its behaviour is uncertain' (Hesse 1965; Mittelstadt et al. 2019: 3). Without this information, approximations will be at best poorly comprehensible and at worst misleading because they are often inaccurate or unreliable outside a specific domain or set of instances (Mittelstadt et al. 2019).

Local approximations face difficulties with generalizability, arbitrariness in choice of domain, and the potential to mislead recipients unless the domain and epistemic limitations of the approximation are known (Mittelstadt et al. 2019). Standards for 'good' approximations are thus urgently needed that require information regarding their limitations to be clearly documented and communicated when an approximation is offered as an explanation of a black box model. To date, little work has been done on testing and validating approximations in real-world scenarios; going forward, this critical gap in AI interpretability needs to be closed.

Deception in explanations

The relative lack of research and methods to test and evaluate the veracity, objectivity, and overall quality of explanations and approximation models is concerning as even an accurate explanation can be used to inform or handcrafted to mislead (Lakkaraju and Bastani 2019). Features or causes can be intentionally selected in explanations to convey information according to the controller's preferences and to hide potentially worrying factors. For example, a single explanation of law school admissions could highlight the classifier's dependency on ethnicity, entrance exam results, or grade point average over several years (Russell 2019).

The type of explanation provided can influence the explainee's opinion on the importance of features in an output or classification (Lombrozo 2009; Poulin et al. 2006). By explicitly shaping the choice of domain and the choice of approximation, it is possible to distort how the importance of variables are reported, to alter whether they are claimed to positively or negatively influence decisions, or to eliminate the correlation between them. This selectiveness grants systems controllers the power to alter people's beliefs about the reasons for a system's behaviour and to instil undue confidence in the system's performance and trustworthiness. Understanding how and why a particular explanation was chosen by the explainer is particularly important for the selection of contrastive cases for contrastive explanations.

The act of giving an explanation is not neutral (Mittelstadt et al. 2019). Some scholars, for example, have suggested that explanation-giving is not primarily directed to the truth but aims at persuasion (Mercier and Sperber 2011). Agents seeking to be perceived as trustworthy have an incentive not merely to explain their behaviour as accurately as possible but also to provide explanations that persuade other agents to perceive them as trustworthy. This incentive is seemingly at odds with the push to adopt AI systems for the sake of accuracy or efficiency. Suboptimal but simpler actions can improve transparency and communication between institutions, users, and end-users but can make systems and institutions less trustworthy and degrade the resiliency of the trust relationship if end-users experience poor outcomes (Glikson and Woolley 2020). Promoting interpretability or transparency can create incentives for systems to prefer actions for which there are easier or simpler explanations but which may not be optimal for the user (Mercier and Sperber 2011).

There is a clear and immediate risk of malicious actors using explanations not to inform but to mislead. Ethically or legally significant influences on a decision (e.g. sensitive features such as ethnicity) could be hidden from explainees interested in the legality of university admissions. Explainees can be subtly nudged by the choice of explanans to adopt a preferred belief or take a preferred action of the explainer, for example, not contesting admissions outcomes on the grounds of discrimination. Solutions to mitigate the risk of deception via explanation are urgently needed if AI interpretability and transparency are to make AI systems more accountable and trustworthy.

The effectiveness of self-assessment transparency frameworks

Self-assessment frameworks are intended to enhance the traceability of AI systems by improving organizational accountability, helping to identify potential ethically problematic impacts, and providing a starting point for redress for affected individuals and communities. If successful, each of these effects could enhance public trust and acceptance of AI systems.

However, while recognizing their potential utility, self-assessment frameworks have a number of inherent weaknesses. To be effective, self-assessment must be timely, transparent, honest, and critical. Organizations must invest the resources necessary to train staff to critically assess internal procurement procedures and the (potential) external impact of the system. Critical analysis requires an organizational culture that rewards honest assessment. Even if staff are well trained and rewarded for their honesty, further investment is needed to make self-assessment more than a 'one off' occurrence. The impact of AI systems cannot be perfectly predicted prior to deployment; unexpected and novel effects can emerge over time that, by definition, can only be captured through iterative self-assessment (Mittelstadt et al. 2016). To assess impact over time, internal procedures must be established to record system behaviour longitudinally. Sustaining the quality of such procedures over time has historically proven difficult, with comparable self-assessment frameworks in other domains effectively becoming empty 'checklists' over time (Manders-Huits and Zimmer 2009; Mittelstadt 2019; Põder and Lukki 2011). Assuming these elements are in place, decisions must still be made about what, when, and how to involve external researchers and the public in the assessment process and how to publicly disclose results. Self-assessments that are perceived as incomplete, dishonest, inaccessible, or otherwise faulty will not have their intended effect on public trust.[2]

In short, self-assessment frameworks are not guaranteed to be effective without significant organizational commitment to staff training, organizational culture, sustainable and critical assessment procedures, public and researcher involvement, and open disclosure of results. These requirements cannot be guaranteed by developing universal guidelines or procedures for self-assessment because the potential impact of AI systems varies greatly according to context and application type (High Level Expert Group on Artificial Intelligence 2019; Mittelstadt 2019).

Conclusion

This chapter has reviewed the key concepts, approaches, difficulties, literature, and overall state of the art in interpretability and transparency in AI. Numerous methods to provide explanations, approximations, and standardized disclosures for the development, *functionality*, or *behaviour* of AI systems have been reviewed. To evaluate the quality of emergent approaches in the field, lessons can be learned from prior work on explanations in the philosophy of science. Explanations as products can be evaluated in terms of their contrastiveness, abnormality, selectivity, complexity and sparsity, novelty and accuracy, representativeness, fidelity, and consistency. Likewise, the act of giving an explanation can be critiqued in terms of its interactivity and usability and its relevance and comprehensibility to local stakeholders.

These characteristics of explanations as products and processes point towards a clear conclusion: interpretability and transparency in AI cannot possibly be achieved through a 'one-size-fits-all' approach. Different audiences, models, behaviours, and use cases will demand different forms of explanations. And yet, despite this diversity of products and methods, common ground exists to evaluate the quality of explanations in AI.

Critical open challenges, of course, remain. Consistent frameworks to evaluate explanations of AI must first be widely adopted for common standards of 'good' explanations to be enforceable through ethical or regulatory means. Likewise, vigilance is required to ensure that explanations and transparency mechanisms are used honestly and accurately and never to deceive or mislead. If AI systems are to deliver on their promise of more accurate, efficient, and accountable decision-making, solving these challenges and implementing common standards for interpretability and transparency is essential.

Author's note

Sections of this chapter are adapted from: Mittelstadt, B., Russell, C., and Wachter, S. (2019), 'Explaining Explanations in AI', *Proceedings of the Conference on Fairness, Accountability, and Transparency—FAT* *'19*, 279–288, doi: https://doi.org/10.1145/3287560.3287574. This work has been supported by research funding provided by the British Academy grant no. PF\170151, Luminate Group, and the Miami Foundation.

Notes

1. The degree to which the reasons for specific model behaviours can be explained is sometimes referred to as the *explainability* of a model. Here, it is treated as one component of *interpretability* alongside intrinsic model comprehensibility.
2. Lessons can be learned from comparable legal instruments. For example, 'data protection impact assessments' as required by Article 35 of the EU General Data Protection Regulation are functionally similar to the self-assessment frameworks discussed above but do not require full public disclosure of results.

References

Achinstein, Peter (1983), The Nature of Explanation (Oxford: Oxford University Press on Demand).

Achinstein, Peter (2010), Evidence, Explanation, and Realism: Essays in Philosophy of Science (Oxford: Oxford University Press).

Adler, Philip, Falk, Casey, Friedler, Sorelle A., Nix, Tionney, Rybeck, Gabriel, Scheidegger, Carlos, et al. (2018), 'Auditing Black-Box Models for Indirect Influence', *Knowledge and Information Systems* 54, 95–122.

Andrews, Robert, Diederich, Joachim, and Tickle, Alan B. (1995), 'Survey and Critique of Techniques for Extracting Rules from Trained Artificial Neural Networks', *Knowledge-Based Systems* 8, 373–389.

Arnold, Matthew, Bellamy, Rachel K., Hind, Michael, Houde, Stephanie, Mehta, Sameep, Mojsilović, Aleksandra, et al. (2019), 'FactSheets: Increasing Trust in AI Services through Supplier's Declarations of Conformity', *IBM Journal of Research and Development* 63, 6:1–6:13, doi: https://doi.org/10.1147/JRD.2019.2942288.

Article 29 Data Protection Working Party (2017), *Guidelines on Data Protection Impact Assessment (DPIA) and Determining Whether Processing is 'Likely to Result in a High Risk' for the Purposes of Regulation 2016/679*, 17/EN WP 248.

Baehrens, David, Schroeter, Timon, Harmeling, Stefan, Kawanabe, Motoaki, Hansen, Katja, and Müller, Klaus-Robert. (2010), 'How to Explain Individual Classification Decisions', *Journal of Machine Learning Research* 11, 1803–1831.

Bastani, Osbert, Kim, Carolyn, and Bastani, Hamsa (2017), 'Interpretability via Model Extraction', *arXiv Preprint*, 1706.09773 [cs, stat].

Bellamy, Rrachel K.E., Dey, Kuntal, Hind, Michael, Hoffman, Samuel C., Houde, Stephanie, Kannan, Kalapriya, et al. (2018), 'AI Fairness 360: An Extensible Toolkit for Detecting, Understanding, and Mitigating Unwanted Algorithmic Bias', *arXiv Preprint*, 1810.01943 [cs].

Bender, Emily M., and Friedman, Batya (2018), 'Data Statements for NLP: Toward Mitigating System Bias and Enabling Better Science', *Transactions of the Association for Computational Linguistics* 6, 587–604, doi: https://doi.org/10.1162/tacl_a_00041.

Berendt, Bettina, and Preibusch, Sören (2017), 'Toward Accountable Discrimination-Aware Data Mining: The Importance of Keeping the Human in the Loop—and under the Looking Glass', *Big Data* 5, 135–152, doi: https://doi.org/10.1089/big.2016.0055.

Bien, Jacob, and Tibshirani, Robert (2011), 'Prototype Selection for Interpretable Classification', *Annals of Applied Statistics* 5, 2403–2424, doi: https://doi.org/10.2307/23069335.

Biran, Or, and McKeown, Kathleen (2014), 'Justification Narratives for Individual Classifications', in *Proceedings of the AutoML Workshop at ICML*, 1–7.

Box, George E.P. (1979), 'Robustness in the Strategy of Scientific Model Building', in Robert L. Launer and Graham N. Wilkinson, ed., *Robustness in Statistics* (New York: Elsevier), 201–236.

Burrell, Jenna (2016), 'How the Machine "Thinks": Understanding Opacity in Machine Learning Algorithms', *Big Data & Society* 3, doi: https://doi.org/10.1177/2053951715622512.

Caruana, Rich, Kangarloo, Hooshang, Dionisio, John David, Sinha, Usha, and Johnson, David (1999), 'Case-Based Explanation of Non-Case-Based Learning Methods', *Proceedings of the AMIA Symposium*, 212–215.

Citron, Danielle Keats, and Pasquale, Frank (2014), 'The Scored Society: Due Process for Automated Predictions', *Washington Law Review* 89, 1.

Craven, Mark, and Shavlik, Jude W. (1994), 'Using Sampling and Queries to Extract Rules from Trained Neural Networks', in William W. Cohen and Haym Hirsh, eds, *Machine Learning Proceedings 1994* (San Francisco, CA: Morgan Kaufmann), 37–45, doi: https://doi.org/10.1016/B978-1-55860-335-6.50013-1.

Craven, Mark W., and Shavlik, Jude W. (1995), 'Extracting Tree-Structured Representations of Trained Networks', in *Proceedings of the 8th International Conference on Neural Information Processing Systems* (Cambridge: MIT Press), 24–30.

Datta, Anupam, Sen, Shayak, and Zick, Yair (2016), 'Algorithmic Transparency via Quantitative Input Influence: Theory and Experiments with Learning Systems', *Institute of Electrical and Electronics Engineers*, 598–617, doi: https://doi.org/10.1109/SP.2016.42.

Deng, Houtao (2019), 'Interpreting Tree Ensembles with Intrees', *International Journal of Data Science and Analytics* 7, 277–287.

Doshi-Velez, Finale, and Kim, Been (2017), 'Towards a Rigorous Science of Interpretable Machine Learning', *arXiv Preprint*, 1702.08608 [cs, stat].

Fisher, Aaron, Rudin, Cynthia, and Dominici, Francesca (2019), 'All Models Are Wrong, But Many Are Useful: Learning a Variable's Importance by Studying an Entire Class of Prediction Models Simultaneously', *Journal of Machine Learning Research* 20, 1–81.

Fong, Ruth C., and Vedaldi, Andrea (2017), 'Interpretable Explanations of Black Boxes by Meaningful Perturbation', *arXiv Preprint*, 1704.03296.

Fraassen, Bas C. van (1980), *The Scientific Image* (Oxford: Clarendon Press).

Franzke, Aline Shakti, Bechmann, Anja, Zimmer, Michael, and Ess, Charles M. (2020), *Internet Research: Ethical Guidelines 3.0 Association of Internet Researchers*.

Friedman, Jerome H., and Popescu, Bogdan E. (2008), 'Predictive Learning via Rule Ensembles', *Annals of Applied Statistics* 2, 916–954.

Gebru, Timnit, Morgenstern, Jamie, Vecchione, Briana, Vaughan, Jennifer Wortman, Wallach, Hanna, Daumé III, Hal, et al. (2018), 'Datasheets for Datasets', *arXiv Preprint*, 1803.09010.

Glikson, Ella, and Woolley, Anita Williams (2020), *Human Trust in Artificial Intelligence: Review of Empirical Research, Academy of Management Annals* 14, 627–660.

Goldstein, Alex, Kapelner, Adam, Bleich, Justin, and Pitkin, Emil (2015), 'Peeking Inside the Black Box: Visualizing Statistical Learning with Plots of Individual Conditional Expectation', *Journal of Computational and Graphical Statistics* 24, 44–65.

Goodfellow, Ian J., Shlens, Jonathon, and Szegedy, Christian (2014), 'Explaining and Harnessing Adversarial Examples', *arXiv Preprint*, 1412.6572.

Government of Canada (2020), 'Algorithmic Impact Assessment', https://canada-ca.github.io/aia-eia-js, accessed 24 April 2022.

Greenwell, Brandon M., Boehmke, Bradley C., and McCarthy, Andrew J. (2018), 'A Simple and Effective Model-Based Variable Importance Measure', *arXiv Preprint*, 1805.04755.

Gregor, Shirley, and Benbasat, Izak (1999), 'Explanations from Intelligent Systems: Theoretical Foundations and Implications for Practice', *MIS Quarterly* 23, 497–530.

Guidotti, Riccardo, Monreale, Anna, Ruggieri, Salvatore, Turini, Franco, Giannotti, Fosca, and Pedreschi, Dino (2018), 'A Survey of Methods for Explaining Black Box Models', *ACM Computing Surveys* 51, 93:1–93:42, doi: https://doi.org/10.1145/3236009.

Hempel, Carl G. (1965), *Aspects of Scientific Explanation*. (London: Collier-MacMillan Limited).

Hempel, Carl G., and Paul, Oppenheim (1948), 'Studies in the Logic of Explanation', *Philosophy of Science* 15, 135–175.

Henelius, Andreas, Puolamäki, Kai, Boström, Henrik, Asker, Lars, and Papapetrou, Panagiotis (2014), 'A Peek into the Black Box: Exploring Classifiers by Randomization', *Data Mining and Knowledge Discovery* 28, 1503–1529, doi: https://doi.org/10.1007/s10618-014-0368-8.

Hesse, Mary B. (1965), *Models and Analogies in Science* (London: Sheed and Ward).

Hesslow, Germund (1988), 'The Problem of Causal Selection', in D. J. Hilton, ed, *Contemporary Science and Natural Explanation: Commonsense Conceptions of Causality* (Brighton: Harvester Press), 11–31.

High Level Expert Group on Artificial Intelligence (2019), *Ethics Guidelines for Trustworthy AI* (European Commission).

Hilton, Denis J. (1990), 'Conversational Processes and Causal Explanation', *Psychological Bulletin* 107, 65.

Hilton, Denis J. (1996), 'Mental Models and Causal Explanation: Judgements of Probable Cause and Explanatory Relevance', *Thinking & Reasoning* 2, 273–308.

Hilton, Denis J., and Slugoski, Ben R. (1986), 'Knowledge-Based Causal Attribution: The Abnormal Conditions Focus Model', *Psychological Review* 93, 75.

Holland, Sarah, Hosny, Ahmed, Newman, Sarah, Joseph, Joshua, and Chmielinski, Kasia (2018), 'The Dataset Nutrition Label: A Framework to Drive Higher Data Quality Standards', *arXiv Preprint*, 1805.03677 [cs].

Hooker, Giles (2004), 'Discovering Additive Structure in Black Box Functions', in *Proceedings of the Tenth ACM SIGKDD International Conference on Knowledge Discovery and Data Mining* (New York: Association for Computing Machinery), 575–580.

Information Commissioner's Office, The Alan Turing Institute (2020), *Explaining Decisions Made with AI*.

Jobin, Anna, Ienca, Marcello, and Vayena, Effy (2019), 'The Global Landscape of AI Ethics Guidelines', *Nature Machine Intelligence* 1, 389–399, doi: https://doi.org/10.1038/s42 256-019-0088-2.

Kayande, Ujwal, De Bruyn, Arnaud, Lilien, Gary L., Rangaswamy, Arvind, and Van Bruggen, Gerrit H. (2009), 'How Incorporating Feedback Mechanisms in a DSS Affects DSS Evaluations', *Information Systems Research* 20, 527–546.

Kim, Been, Rudin, Cynthia, and Shah, Julie A. (2014), 'The Bayesian Case Model: A Generative Approach for Case-Based Reasoning and Prototype Classification', in *Proceedings of the 27th International Conference on Neural Information Processing Systems - Volume 2* (Montreal: MIT Press), 1952–1960.

Kim, Been, Khanna, Rajiv, and Koyejo, Oluwasanmi O. (2016), 'Examples Are Not Enough, Learn to Criticize! Criticism for Interpretability', *Advances in Neural Information Processing Systems*, 29, 2288–2296.

Kment, Boris (2006), 'Counterfactuals and Explanation', *Mind* 115, 261–310.

Koh, Pang Wei, and Percy Liang. (2017), 'Understanding Black-Box Predictions via Influence Functions', *arXiv Preprint*, 1703.04730 [cs, stat].

Krause, Josua, Perer, Adam, and Ng, Kenney (2016), 'Interacting with Predictions: Visual Inspection of Black-box Machine Learning Models', in *Proceedings of the 2016 CHI Conference on Human Factors in Computing Systems, CHI '16* (New York: Association for Computing Machinery), 5686–5697, doi: https://doi.org/10.1145/2858036.2858529.

Krishnan, R., Sivakumar, G., and Bhattacharya, P. (1999), 'Extracting Decision Trees from Trained Neural Networks', *Pattern Recognition* 32, 1999–2009, doi: https://doi.org/10.1016/S0031-3203(98)00181-2.

Kulesza, Todd, Burnett, Margaret, Wong, Weng-Keen, and Stumpf, Simone (2015), *Principles of Explanatory Debugging to Personalize Interactive Machine Learning* (New York: Association for Computing Machinery Press), doi: https://doi.org/10.1145/2678025.2701399.

Lakkaraju, Himabindu, and Bastani, Osbert (2019), ' "How Do I Fool You?": Manipulating User Trust via Misleading Black Box Explanations', *arXiv Preprint*, 1911.06473.

Lakkaraju, Himabindu, Bach, Stephen H., and Leskovec, Jure (2016), 'Interpretable Decision Sets: A Joint Framework for Description and Prediction', in *Proceedings of the 22nd ACM SIGKDD International Conference on Knowledge Discovery and Data Mining, KDD '16* (New York: Association for Computing Machinery), 1675–1684, doi: https://doi.org/10.1145/2939672.2939874.

Lakkaraju, Himabindu, Kamar, Ece, Caruana, Rich, and Leskovec, Jure (2017), 'Interpretable & Explorable Approximations of Black Box Models', *arXiv Preprint*, 1707.01154 [cs].

Lepri, Bruno, Oliver, Nuria, Letouzé, Emmanuel, Pentland, Alex, and Vinck, Patrick (2017), 'Fair, Transparent, and Accountable Algorithmic Decision-Making Processes: The Premise, the Proposed Solutions, and the Open Challenges', *Philosophy & Technology* 31, doi: https://doi.org/10.1007/s13347-017-0279-x.

Lewis, David. (1973), *Counterfactuals* (Oxford: Blackwell).

Lewis, David. (1986), *Philosophical Papers II* (Oxford: Oxford University Press).

Lim, Brian Y., and Dey, Anind K. (2009), 'Assessing Demand for Intelligibility in Context-Aware Applications', in *Proceedings of the 11th International Conference on Ubiquitous Computing - Ubicomp '09*, presented at the the 11th international conference (Orlando, FL: ACM Press), 195, doi: https://doi.org/10.1145/1620545.1620576.

Lipton, Peter (1990), 'Contrastive Explanation', *Royal Institute of Philosophy Supplements* 27, 247–266.

Lipton, Peter (2001), 'What Good is an Explanation?', in *Explanation* (Dordrecht: Springer), 43–59.

Lipton, Zachary C (2016), 'The Mythos of Model Interpretability', *arXiv Preprint*, 1606.03490 [cs, stat].

Lisboa, Paulo J. G. (2013), 'Interpretability in Machine Learning—Principles and Practice', in *Fuzzy Logic and Applications* (Cham: Springer), 15–21.

Lombrozo, Tania (2009), 'Explanation and Categorization: How "Why?" Informs "What?"', *Cognition* 110, 248–253.

Lou, Yin, Caruana, Rich, and Gehrke, Johannes (2012), 'Intelligible Models for Classification and Regression', in *Proceedings of the 18th ACM SIGKDD International Conference on Knowledge Discovery and Data Mining, KDD '12* (New York: Association for Computing Machinery), 150–158, doi: https://doi.org/10.1145/2339530.2339556.

Lou, Yin, Caruana, Rich, Gehrke, Johannes, and Hooker, Giles (2013), 'Accurate Intelligible Models with Pairwise Interactions', in *Proceedings of the 19th ACM SIGKDD International*

Conference on Knowledge Discovery and Data Mining, KDD '13 (New York: Association for Computing Machinery), 623–631, doi: https://doi.org/10.1145/2487575.2487579.

Lundberg, Scott, and Lee, Su-In (2017), 'A Unified Approach to Interpreting Model Predictions', *arXiv Preprint*, 1705.07874 [cs, stat].

Manders-Huits, Noëmi, and Zimmer, Michael (2009), 'Values and Pragmatic Action: The Challenges of Introducing Ethical Intelligence in Technical Design Communities', *International Review of Information Ethics* 10, 37–44.

Mantelero, Alessandro (2016), 'Personal Data for Decisional Purposes in the Age of Analytics: From an Individual to a Collective Dimension of Data Protection', *Computer Law & Security Review* 32, 238–255, doi: https://doi.org/10.1016/j.clsr.2016.01.014.

Mantelero, Alessandro (2018), 'AI and Big Data: A Blueprint for a Human Rights, Social and Ethical Impact Assessment', *Computer Law & Security Review* 34, 754–772.

Martens, David, and Foster Provost (2014), 'Explaining Data-Driven Document Classifications', *MIS Quarterly* 38, 73–100.

McAuley, Julian, and Leskovec, Jure (2013), 'Hidden Factors and Hidden Topics: Understanding Rating Dimensions with Review Text', *Proceedings of the 7th ACM Conference on Recommender Systems* (New York: ACM Press), 165–172, doi: https://doi.org/10.1145/2507157.2507163.

McClure, John L., Sutton, Robbie M., and Hilton, Denis J (2003), 'Implicit and explicit processes in social judgements: The role of goal-based explanations', in Joseph P. Forgas, Kipling D. Williams, and William von Hippel, eds, *Social Judgements: Implicit and Explicit Processes* (Cambridge: Cambridge University Press), 306–324.

Mercier, Hugo, and Sperber, Dan (2011), 'Why Do Humans Reason? Arguments for an Argumentative Theory', *Behavioral and Brain Sciences* 34, 57–74.

Miller, Tim (2019), 'Explanation in Artificial Intelligence: Insights from the Social Sciences', *Artificial Intelligence* 267, 1–38, doi: https://doi.org/10.1016/j.artint.2018.07.007.

Mitchell, Margaret, Wu, Simone, Zaldivar, Andrew, Barnes, Parker, Vasserman, Lucy, Hutchinson, Ben, et al. (2019), 'Model Cards for Model Reporting', *Proceedings of the Conference on Fairness, Accountability, and Transparency—FAT* '19, 220–229, doi: https://doi.org/10.1145/3287560.3287596.

Mittelstadt, Brent (2016), 'Auditing for Transparency in Content Personalization Systems', *International Journal of Communication* 10, 12.

Mittelstadt, Brent (2017), 'From Individual to Group Privacy in Big Data Analytics', *Philosophy & Technology* 30, 475–494, doi: https://doi.org/10.1007/s13347-017-0253-7.

Mittelstadt, Brent (2019), 'Principles Alone Cannot Guarantee Ethical AI', *Nature Machine Intelligence* 1, 501–507, doi: https://doi.org/10.1038/s42256-019-0114-4.

Mittelstadt, Brent, Allo, Patrick, Taddeo, Mariarosaria, Wachter, Sandra, and Floridi, Luciano (2016), 'The Ethics of Algorithms: Mapping the Debate', *Big Data & Society* 3, doi: https://doi.org/10.1177/2053951716679679.

Mittelstadt, Brent, Russell, Chris, and Wachter, Sandra (2019), 'Explaining Explanations in AI', *Proceedings of the Conference on Fairness, Accountability, and Transparency— FAT* '19, 279–288, doi: https://doi.org/10.1145/3287560.3287574.

Molnar, Christoph (2020), *Interpretable Machine Learning*. https://christophm.github.io/interpretable-ml-book/.

Montavon, Grégoire, Samek, Wojciech, and Müller, Klaus-Robert (2018), 'Methods for Interpreting and Understanding Deep Neural Networks', *Digital Signal Processing* 73, 1–15.

Nguyen, Anh, Dosovitskiy, Alexey, Yosinski, Jason, Brox, Thomas, and Clune, Jeff (2016), 'Synthesizing the Preferred Inputs for Neurons in Neural Networks via Deep Generator

Networks', in Daniel D. Lee, Masashi Sugiyama, Ulrike Von Luxburg, Isabelle Guyon, and Roman Garnett, eds, *Advances in Neural Information Processing Systems 29* (New York: Curran Associates, Inc), 3387–3395.

Pearl, Judea (2000), *Causation* (Cambridge: Cambridge University Press).

Pearl, Judea (2019), 'The Seven Tools of Causal Inference, with Reflections on Machine Learning', *Communications of the ACM* 62, 54–60.

Põder, T., and T. Lukki (2011), 'A Critical Review of Checklist-Based Evaluation of Environmental Impact Statements', *Impact Assessment and Project Appraisal* 29, 27–36.

Poulin, Brett, Eisner, Roman, Szafron, Duane, Lu, Paul, Greiner, Russ, Wishart, D.S., et al. (2006), 'Visual Explanation of Evidence in Additive Classifiers', in *Proceedings of the 18th Conference on Innovative Applications of Artificial Intelligence, Vol. 2, IAAI '06* (Boston, MA: AAAI Press), 1822–1829.

Putnam, Hilary (1978), *Meaning and the Moral Sciences* (London: Routledge & Kegan Paul).

Reisman, Dillon, Schultz, Jason, Crawford, Kate, and Whittaker, Meredith (2018), *Algorithmic Impact Assessments: A Practical Framework for Public Agency Accountability*, https://ain owinstitute.org/aiareport2018.pdf.

Ribeiro, Marco Tulio, Singh, Sameer, and Guestrin, Carlos (2016), '"Why Should I Trust You?": Explaining the Predictions of Any Classifier', in *Proceedings of the 22nd ACM SIGKDD International Conference on Knowledge Discovery and Data Mining, KDD '16* New York, NY: ACM Press), 1135–1144, doi: https://doi.org/10.1145/2939672.2939778.

Ruben, David-Hillel (2004), *Explaining Explanation* (New York: Routledge).

Rudin, Cynthia (2019a), 'Stop Explaining Black Box Machine Learning Models for High Stakes Decisions and Use Interpretable Models Instead', *arXiv Preprint*, 1811.10154 [cs, stat].

Rudin, Cynthia (2019b), 'Stop Explaining Black Box Machine Learning Models for High Stakes Decisions and Use Interpretable Models Instead', *Nature Machine Intelligence* 1, 206–215, doi: https://doi.org/10.1038/s42256-019-0048-x.

Russell, Chris (2019), 'Efficient Search for Diverse Coherent Explanations', in *Proceedings of the Conference on Fairness, Accountability, and Transparency* (New York: ACM Press), 20–28.

Salmon, Wesley C. (2006), *Four Decades of Scientific Explanation* (Pittsburgh: University of Pittsburgh Press).

Saltelli, Andrea (2002), 'Sensitivity Analysis for Importance Assessment', *Risk Analysis* 22, 579–590, doi: https://doi.org/10.1111/0272-4332.00040.

Samek, Wojciech, Wiegand, Thomas, and Müller, Klaus-Robert (2017), 'Explainable Artificial Intelligence: Understanding, Visualizing and Interpreting Deep Learning Models', *arXiv Preprint*, 1708.08296.

Samland, Jana, and Waldmann, Michael R. (2014), 'Do Social Norms Influence Causal Inferences?', *Proceedings of the Annual Meeting of the Cognitive Science Society* 36, 1359–1364.

Sandvig, Christian, Hamilton, Kevin, Karahalios, Karrie, and Langbort, Cedric (2014), 'Auditing Algorithms: Research Methods for Detecting Discrimination on Internet Platforms', *Data and Discrimination: Converting Critical Concerns into Productive Inquiry*.

Schölkopf, Bernhard (2019), 'Causality for Machine Learning', *arXiv Preprint*, 1911.10500.

Selvaraju, Ramprasaath R., Cogswell, Michael, Das, Abhishek, Vedantam, Ramakrishna, Parikh, Devi, and Batra, Dhruv (2016), 'Grad-CAM: Visual Explanations from Deep Networks via Gradient-Based Localization', v3, https://doi.org/10.48550/arXiv.1610.02391, accessed 24 April 2022.

Simonyan, Karen, Vedaldi, Andrea, and Zisserman, Andrew (2013), 'Deep Inside Convolutional Networks: Visualising Image Classification Models and Saliency Maps', *arXiv Preprint*, 1312.6034.

Slugoski, Ben R., Lalljee, Mansur, Lamb, Roger, and Ginsburg, Gerald P. (1993), 'Attribution in Conversational Context: Effect of Mutual Knowledge on Explanation-Giving', *European Journal of Social Psychology* 23, 219–238.

Szegedy, Christian, Zaremba, Wojciech, Sutskever, Ilya, Bruna, Joan, Erhan, Dumitru, Goodfellow, Ian, et al. (2013), 'Intriguing Properties of Neural Networks', *arXiv Preprint*, 1312.6199.

Tamagnini, Paolo, Krause, Josua, Dasgupta, Aritra, and Bertini, Enrico (2017), *Interpreting Black-Box Classifiers Using Instance-Level Visual Explanations* (New York: ACM Press), doi: https://doi.org/10.1145/3077257.3077260.

Thiagarajan, Jayaraman J., Kailkhura, Bhavya, Sattigeri, Prasanna, and Ramamurthy, Karthikeyan Natesan (2016), 'TreeView: Peeking into Deep Neural Networks Via Feature-Space Partitioning', *arXiv Preprint*, 1611.07429 [cs, stat].

Turner, Ryan (2016), 'A Model Explanation System', in *2016 IEEE 26th International Workshop on Machine Learning for Signal Processing (MLSP)*, presented at the 2016 IEEE 26th International Workshop on Machine Learning for Signal Processing (MLSP), 1–6, doi: https://doi.org/10.1109/MLSP.2016.7738872.

Wachter, Sandra, and Mittelstadt, Brent (2019), 'A Right to Reasonable Inferences: Re-Thinking Data Protection Law in the Age of Big Data and AI', *Columbia Business Law Review* 2, 494–620.

Wachter, Sandra, Mittelstadt, Brent, and Floridi, Luciano (2017), 'Why a Right to Explanation of Automated Decision-Making Does Not Exist in the General Data Protection Regulation', *International Data Privacy Law* 7, 76–99.

Wachter, Sandra, Mittelstadt, Brent, and Russell, Chris (2018), 'Counterfactual Explanations without Opening the Black Box: Automated Decisions and the GDPR', *Harvard Journal of Law & Technology* 3, 841–887.

Wachter, Sandra, Mittelstadt, Brent, and Russell, Chris (2020), 'Why Fairness Cannot Be Automated: Bridging the Gap between EU Non-Discrimination Law and AI', SSRN Scholarly Paper No. ID 3547922) (Rochester, NY: Social Science Research Network), doi: https://doi.org/10.2139/ssrn.3547922.

Wang, Fulton, and Rudin, Cynthia (2015), 'Falling Rule Lists', in Lebanon, Guy and Vishwanathan, S. V. N., eds, *Proceedings of the Eighteenth International Conference on Artificial Intelligence and Statistics* (San Diego: PMLR), 1013–1022.

Wexler, James, Pushkarna, Mahima, Bolukbasi, Tolga, Wattenberg, Martin, Viegas, Fernanda, and Wilson, Jimbo (2019), 'The What-If Tool: Interactive Probing of Machine Learning Models', *IEEE Transactions on Visualization and Computer Graphics* 1, 1. https://doi.org/10.1109/TVCG.2019.2934619

Woodward, James (2005), *Making Things Happen: A Theory of Causal Explanation* (Oxford: Oxford University Press).

Woodward, James (2003), 'Scientific Explanation', in Edward N. Zalta, ed., *The Stanford Encyclopedia of Philosophy* (Stanford: Stanford University). https://plato.stanford.edu/archives/sum2003/entries/scientific-explanation/.

Woodward, James (1997), 'Explanation, invariance, and intervention', *Philosophy of Science* 64, S4, S26–S41.

Yang, Ke, Stoyanovich, Julia, Asudeh, Abolfazl, Howe, Bill, Jagadish, Hv, and Miklau, Gerome (2018), 'A Nutritional Label for Rankings', in *Proceedings of the 2018 International Conference on Management of Data - SIGMOD '18*, presented at the the 2018 International Conference (Houston, TX: ACM Press), 1773–1776, doi: https://doi.org/10.1145/3183713.3193568.

Yin, Xiaoxin, and Han, Jiawei (2003), 'CPAR: Classification Based on Predictive Association Rules', in *Proceedings of the 2003 SIAM International Conference on Data Mining, Proceedings* (Society for Industrial and Applied Mathematics), 331–335, doi: https://doi.org/10.1137/1.9781611972733.40.

Ylikoski, Petri (2013) 'Causal and Constitutive Explanation Compared', *Erkenntnis* 78, 277–297.

Yosinski, Jason, Clune, Jeff, Nguyen, Anh, Fuchs, Thomas, and Lipson, Hod (2015), 'Understanding Neural Networks through Deep Visualization', *arXiv Preprint*, 1506.06579 [cs].

Zarsky, Tal Z. (2013), 'Transparent Predictions', *Univeristy of Illinois Law Review* 4, 1503.

PART V

JUSTICE AND FAIRNESS

....

CHAPTER 21

ALGORITHMIC BIAS AND ACCESS TO OPPORTUNITIES

....

LISA HERZOG

Introduction

....

For a few years, 'racist' and 'sexist' algorithms have been making headlines. For example, Google showed advertisements for board-level jobs more frequently to men than to women (Kim 2017: 864), while Amazon had to scrap a hiring algorithm it had been working on because it was biased against women (Dastin 2018), and Apple was publicly criticized for offering women lower credit card limits on its new Apple Card, which triggered formal investigations (AI Now 2019: 45–46). In 2016, a report by the investigative journalism organization *ProPublica* uncovered that an algorithm for predicting the recidivism of criminal offenders had differential error rates for Black and White offenders (Angwin et al. 2016). Two books in particular discussed a number of unsettling case studies of how algorithms could wreak havoc on the lives of those who were submitted to them: Cathy O'Neil's *Weapons of Math Destruction* (2016) and Virginia Eubanks's *Automating Inequality* (2017). They report on teachers who were fired because of obscure algorithmic evaluation systems, families who did not receive insurance because they lived in the wrong neighbourhood, and at-risk-children who were not taken out of dangerous social environments because of glitches in the youth services' computerized risk prediction systems (on welfare automation, see also Lecher 2018).

The topic of this chapter is algorithmic systems that decide about access to important human goods and opportunities.[1] The use of such algorithms is becoming more and more widespread, and they already play a role in many potentially life-altering decisions such as credit, housing, college admission, or parole.[2] Like search engines and social media platforms, they are becoming part of the infrastructure of our societies (for the infrastructure perspective, see Plantin et al. 2018). We are usually not aware of how these mechanisms work: they operate in the background, but they shape the options available to us (Eubanks 2017: 5). For example, estimates for the prevalence of algo-rithmic pre-screening of applicants in hiring processes in the United States range from 55 to 72 per cent,[3] not to mention monitoring *at* work (Kim 2017). Recent investigations by the *Washington Post* found that at least forty-four public and private universities used cookies to track future applicants when they were surfing on their website, trying to estimate their likelihood of accepting an offer (MacMillan and Anderson 2019). Many public authorities, such as welfare services for the homeless, use algorithmic systems to facilitate screening and allocation (see, e.g. Eubanks 2017: ch. 3, on a system in Los Angeles county).

There are various reasons to be worried about this development. One, which I will here bracket, is privacy.[4] A second one, which is also too complex to discuss in the scope of this chapter, is the job losses that often follow the introduction of such systems.[5] What I will focus on, instead, is a perspective of structural justice. These algorithmic systems are introduced into societies that are deeply unjust, marred by inequities with regard to race, gender, and class. The distribution of income and wealth, which goes hand in hand with various forms of power, is highly unequal and arguably deeply unjust. And it is into these 'old systems of power and privilege' (Eubanks 2017: 177) that the new algorithmic technologies are embedded. One of the greatest risks is that they perpetuate, and maybe even enlarge, unjust inequalities, benefitting those who are already privileged and fur-ther disadvantaging those who are already disadvantaged. When thinking about al-gorithmic systems that decide about access to opportunities, it is vital to keep social contexts and their manifold inequities in mind. Forms of algorithmic bias that might appear mere theoretical problems or minor inconveniences in more just circumstances can have drastic consequences when the background against which the algorithms op-erate is so far from ideal.

In the next section, I describe some of the technical bases of algorithmic bias, followed by a discussion of how to evaluate such biases. I draw on the perspective of structural (in)justice, as developed by Iris Marion Young (2011) and others for approaching the problem, and focus in particular on the so-called 'Matthew effects' (Merton 1968), named after a line in the gospel according to Matthew: 'For to every one who has will more be given, and he will have abundance; but from him who has not, even what he has will be taken away' (Matthew 25, 29, RSV). Matthew effects are particularly problematic, from a perspective of structural justice, because they reinforce existing inequalities and make it ever harder to move towards a more just society. I then discuss some proposals for solutions, including some positive potentials of algorithmic decision-making, and respond to one central objection, namely that many algorithms are owned by private firms that should neither be regulated nor forced to reveal their business secrets. Instead of yielding to this objection, we need to realize that the problem of algorithmic bias forces us to rethink, with new urgency, the line between a 'private' and 'public' under-standing of business firms, especially when it comes to the provision of basic human goods. I conclude by emphasizing the need for political and social action: if algorithms have a decisive impact on what opportunities and goods individuals have access to, they cannot be left to market forces alone.

ALGORITHMIC BIAS

When algorithms were first introduced into decision-making systems such as college admission or hiring processes, they came with a promise of change for the better. Human beings, who made such decisions before, are well known to be biased in various ways; for example, they give a preference to taller candidates, although there is no proof that they are any better than shorter candidates (Peck 2013). Thus, not only would algorithms be faster and more cost-efficient, they would also lead to a higher quality of decision-making. And better decision-making seems something that is good for everyone: for those who are rightly admitted to the position they seek to access, but also for those who are unsuited and who are rejected and are thereby spared the troubles that usually follow suit when someone fails to fulfil the requirements of a position.

Unfortunately, the way in which algorithmic decision-making systems work is far more complex.[6] The problem, in a nutshell, is the following: these systems usually rely on past data in order to make their predictions for new candidates.[7] And they thus rely on a crucial methodological assumption: that the patterns of the past will repeat themselves (O'Neil 2016: 38). To take a simple example: if a workforce is 80 per cent male and 20 per cent non-male, an algorithm—at least one that has not been adapted to correct for this—is likely to project a similar distribution into the future. Importantly, this holds even if the variables for gender are removed, as is standardly done in order to avoid charges of discrimination (Barocas and Selbst 2016; Kim 2017). Usually, there are other variables that are correlated with gender (for this example, one might think about hobbies, but there can also be non-obvious correlations, e.g. a higher likelihood of using certain words in self-descriptions). The algorithm will discover these patterns and treat new applications that contain such datapoints accordingly (see also Ito 2019). It will see non-male candidates as less typical for the workforce and reject them with greater likelihood. Such algorithms replicate the old problem of statistical discrimination (Phelps 1972; Arrow 1973): if there is incomplete information about the productivity of applicants, and there are different subgroups in society that historically have had different levels of average productivity, then group membership might be taken as an indicator of higher or lower productivity, even though it may not be true for individual applicants.

One might suggest that in such a case (80 per cent male employees in the existing data pool), one could simply create a new data set on which to train the algorithm: one in which the gender distribution is 50–50. But there are fewer non-male entries in this data set, which implies that the *quality* of the prediction is likely to be lower for that group. In other words, there will be a differential error rate. This is a general problem of statistical analyses for groups with different distributions of the outcome variables (see Borsboom et al. 2008). This become clear in the debate about unequal error rates for Blacks and Whites in recidivism prediction algorithms that followed the 2016 *ProPublica* study (Angwin et al. 2016; Angwin and Larson 2016; see also Schmidt and Stephens 2019: 138–139). A number of scientists addressed the problem and agreed that here one runs into a dilemma: different notions of fairness are mathematically incompatible (see, in particular, Kleinberg et al. 2016; on related results, see Hardt et al. 2016 and Chouldechova 2016; see also Corbett-Davies et al. 2017 and Corbett-Davies and Goel 2018 for discussions). If, for example, one aims for equal percentages of different groups in the general population *and* in the categories the algorithm groups them into (a concept called 'statistical parity' and often understood as a paradigmatic expression of fairness; see, e.g. Kleinberg et al. 2016: 3), then the likelihood of being categorized in the wrong way will not be the same across groups; that is, they are exposed to differential risks of being wrongly treated, which also seems unfair. As an illustration, take murders, most of which are committed by men (96 per cent worldwide). A murderer-finding algorithm that is accurate will necessarily identify more men than women as high risk, which also means that more men will suffer from false positives (being falsely accused of murder). If both women and men were set to be identified as high-risk at the same rate, the algorithm would be much less accurate for women (Fry 2018: 78).

In addition to these limitations that are based on fundamental laws of statistics, however, there are various problems that are more mundane, and can yet have an impact on the prediction quality and fairness of algorithms. Take, first, the input data: there can be more record errors for some groups than for others because, for instance, women change their family name more often than men when they get married or because Hispanic individuals have two family names, so that a system might confuse individuals (Kim 2017: 886). Also, when data are collected there might be disparities between groups. As Barocas and Selbst (2016: 685) note, historically disadvantaged groups are often 'less involved in the formal economy and its data-generating activities', which could lead to less data being available about them. A second realm of problems concerns the construction of the algorithms (if they are structured and not completely self-learning), and the selection of features or criteria (Barocas and Selbst 2016: 688–690).

At least as important is, third, the definition of the outcome variables. Often, it is not immediately clear how to operationalize them; for example, 'the definition of a good employee is not a given' (Barocas and Selbst 2016: 679). Instead, the standard strategy is to use certain variables as proxies. But these might embody patterns of past discrimination. A recent study by Obermeyer et al. (2019) provides a vivid illustration of this problem. They analysed an algorithm that was widely used for predicting medical risks of patients, drawing on a data set with over 50,000 patients. They found a particular form of racial bias: Black patients who received the same risk score were 'considerably sicker' than White patients. Had this disparity been corrected, the percentage of Black patients for whom the algorithm recommended additional help would have risen from 17.7 per cent to 46.5 per cent (Obermeyer et al. 2019: 450). The reason, the researchers found, was that the variable that the algorithm was supposed to predict was a proxy for future medical needs: future health costs. This may seem like a reasonable proxy, but it turned out to be biased, because Whites had higher health costs than Blacks (on average, the difference was $1801 per year) (Obermeyer et al. 2019: 449). This difference might be caused by differential socio-economic backgrounds, or perhaps by experiences of discrimination or other factors directly linked to race (Obermeyer et al. 2019: 451). Because their health-care costs were, on average, lower, Blacks appeared less in need of medical support—an effect that was, fortunately, not directly translated into unequal access to support because many patients with a medium score were sent to their doctors, and the latter corrected to some degree for the bias (Obermeyer et al. 2019: 451). But the researchers also found that they could in fact improve the algorithm, a point to which I will come back below.

A defender of algorithms might reply, however, that we need to be fair ourselves, in our evaluations of the algorithms. In particular, we need to compare them to *human* decision-making, which is marred by many forms of biases,[8] which can interact in complex ways, and can lead to decisions that are anything but fair. To the best of my knowledge, there are no systematic empirical studies that would compare human and algorithmic decision-making in specific contexts. But there are some general observations that we can make about the comparison between human and algorithmic biases in decision-making processes.

First, while human biases are well known and relatively well understood, algorithms come with the 'aura of truth, objectivity, and accuracy' (Boyd and Crawford 2012: 663, quoted in Wong 2019: 2). They have been constructed by experts and they use a mathematical language that suggests rigour and neutrality. As such, it is likely that many individuals will find it much harder to challenge algorithmic decisions (see also Eubanks 2017: 142; Castro 2019: 409). At the same time, algorithms might be used as an excuse for problematic decisions. As Bartlett (2018) puts it polemically, in the context of politics: ' "It was the algorithm," will, I expect, become the politicians' favourite non-apology apology.' And although it is certainly not impossible to hold algorithms or those who use them to account (more on this below), this is a far more complex task than holding an individual human being or a committee accountable.

Second, there are interesting questions concerning the relative opacity of decision-making by humans or algorithms. The defenders of algorithms often hold that while we cannot look into the minds of human decision-makers, who might themselves be unaware of their biases, we can, in principle, look into the algorithms and the way they process data sets. In the case of systems that involve artificial intelligence, assessing the algorithms may require some complex reconstructive work, but we can, at least under certain conditions, open up the 'black box' and reproduce the ways in which biases are introduced, which can help us to understand and mitigate mechanisms of discrimination. Algorithms could then be a 'potential positive force for equity' (Kleinberg et al. 2019). Counterfactual scenarios can be used to try out the algorithmic system, and the choice of specific notions of fairness can be made explicit and justified (Kleinberg et al. 2019: 116).

While I do not want to deny this potential, I agree with Eubanks when she warns against a view that downplays the capacity of human beings to explain their decisions (2017: 168). If we give up the idea that humans can explain their decisions, while machines are, allegedly, transparent, the underlying view of human nature might become a self-fulfilling prophecy. Humans can have empathy with each other, and they have a unique ability to spot unusual things and to develop new perspectives (Herzog, forthcoming). The strengths of humans, in contrast to artificial intelligence, should not be underestimated out of enthusiasm for the latter.

However, I do not understand this warning as a complete rejection of algorithmic decisions, but as a call for a carefully designed interaction between algorithms and humans that never blindly trusts the algorithms. In fact, in one of her case studies, Eubanks herself delivers a fascinating example of how human capacities can be needed for an algorithmic system to work *at all*: in order to gather all the necessary data points about a homeless person, to allocate housing to him or her, an empathetic social worker is needed first: someone who can build a relation of trust and learn enough about the case to enter the person's data into the system (2017: 107). This observation does not, by itself, answer the question of whether this algorithmic decision-system can be justified, or how it compares to a human-only system, but it points to an important fact: there are capacities that algorithms, for all the talk about 'artificial intelligence', simply do not have—at least, not thus far. Often, what matters is a productive collaboration of human workers and algorithmic systems, taking into account the broader features of the situation, beyond the technical details of the algorithm. But this needs to be done *without* the assumption, natural as it may appear to us, that the algorithms are always the more objective or less biased decision-makers.

EVALUATING ALGORITHMIC BIAS—THE PERSPECTIVE OF STRUCTURAL JUSTICE

To understand the role of algorithmic decision-making processes from a perspective of justice, it is helpful to draw on sociologically informed approaches that can grasp the complex, interrelated ways in which individuals can experience injustice. I here draw on Iris Marion Young's perspective of structural (in)justice (especially her 2011 book, *Responsibility for Justice*). Against theorists of justice that focus on individual responsibility for one's life, she emphasizes the importance of social *positions* that give individuals different starting points in life. When one starts out from a disadvantaged position, even high levels of individual responsibility may not get one very far in improving one's fate because the hurdles one faces are so much greater than those that a child from a middle-class family faces. To understand how such structures arise, one needs to take into account both formal and informal institutions and pay particular attention to the role of unintended consequences (2011: 52–70).[9] Against this background, Young understands structural injustice as follows:

> Structural injustice, then, exists when social processes put large groups of persons under systematic threat of domination or deprivation of the means to develop and exercise their capacities, at the same time that these processes enable others to

dominate or to have a wide range of opportunities for developing and exercising capacities available to them.

(Young 2011: 52)

Note that this approach does not assume that income, wealth, or opportunities would have to be completely equalized; it is compatible with different substantive theories of justice that would admit different degrees of inequality (though hardly as much inequality as we currently see in many societies). What matters, from the perspective of structural justice, are inequalities that cut to the core of individuals' ability to lead their own lives and that often put them in positions of dependence vis-à-vis more privileged individuals. Often, this happens along lines of gender or race.

While Young's account is somewhat vague and needs to be fleshed out for different social domains (Claassen and Herzog 2019), it offers a useful perspective on how algorithms can contribute to injustice: replace 'social' by 'algorithmic', and you get a definition of what could be called 'algorithmic structural injustice', as a subform of structural injustice. What Young reminds us is that it is the *interplay* of various factors that often leads to such injustices, and hence addressing 'algorithmic structural injustice' *on its own* would be insufficient to address the larger questions of structural injustice.

In structurally unjust societies, human decision-makers, but also algorithms, are faced with the challenge of statistical discrimination and with the impossibility of simultaneously satisfying various definitions of fairness, as discussed above. For these reasons, but also for understanding possible mistakes in algorithmic systems, algorithmic decision-making needs to be understood as embedded in the social contexts in which it takes place. In fact, algorithmic analyses can be a great tool for the *diagnosis* of patterns of inequality between different groups and subgroups, which can be very helpful for understanding the underlying social mechanisms—but that is different from letting them *decide* (see also Kim 2017: 872; on the possibility of using algorithms for causal analysis, see also Barabas et al. 2018).

As numerous commentators have pointed out, algorithms are applied more often to disadvantaged groups, for example, those from lower socio-economic backgrounds, which, in many countries, also tends to be people from ethnic minorities. In contrast, privileged individuals—who tend to be White, male, and economically well off—often can afford, and receive, individualized treatment by human beings (e.g. O'Neil 2016: 7–8).[10] This often also means that they receive a justification for the decisions that apply to them, for example, a rejection of a loan application. Such a justification might be fabricated, to be sure, but at least there is an attempt to show a modicum of respect. Those whose applications are processed by algorithms usually do not receive any justification,[11] which makes it much more difficult to challenge the decision. Furthermore, these individuals have no possibility of understanding what they would have to do to be more successful at the next application (see also Schmidt and Stephens 2019: 135–136). If the algorithm produces a result that seems widely off the mark, it is often difficult for disadvantaged individuals to challenge it, both because of the perception of automated systems as 'objective', as discussed above, and because there often are no human interlocutors to whom they could turn.

Many of these problems come together when algorithmic systems are used for administrating public welfare systems. What is at stake here is the access to essential goods and services, and errors in the system can be a matter of greatest importance for individuals' lives.[12] Eubanks speaks of a 'digital poorhouse', which 'is framed as a way to rationalize and streamline benefits, but the real goal is what it has always been: to profile, police, and punish the poor' (2017: 38, see also ch. 5). She discusses various examples in which all problems and errors—which might be unavoidable when new systems are introduced—were shifted onto the recipients, in the sense that they had to take care of wrong records and fight for the reversal of wrongful decisions that cut their benefits. These are extreme cases, many of which were taken to court. But the sense of frustration, and often existential threat, when faced with negative decisions by algorithms, without any explanation, is more widespread. Buranyi (2018), for example, reports cases of elderly job seekers who were not familiar with computers and did not at all understand the online application processes for jobs; they were only ever able to navigate the application systems with the help of younger family members or social workers.

Among the groups who are exposed to algorithmic decision-making, there can be further inequalities that arise through the ways in which different groups are affected by the algorithmic system (e.g. by differential error rates). As Castro (2019) suggests, such situations need to be evaluated against a broader context that looks at the benefits and burdens that different groups in society carry. For example, if equal outcomes are chosen as a standard of fairness, that implies a higher error rate for Black people, which imposes 'a cost on certain groups'—and in this case, on a group that is already disadvantaged because it is 'disproportionately costly to be black in America' (Castro 2019: 417). Thus, Black people can rightly reject a decision-making system that imposes 'yet another cost' on them (Castro 2019; 418).[13] But such judgements about relative costs need to be made for specific contexts, with one big question being how coarse-grained or fine-grained the relevant categories are designed.

What is particularly dangerous, and hence important to understand and prevent, are mechanisms through which individuals who are already disadvantaged suffer more disadvantages, while others, who are already privileged, benefit. Merton (1968) introduced the term 'Matthew effects' for such scenarios, applying it first to the sociology of science, but it can also be observed in many other fields. Algorithmic decision-making can create such Matthew effects when there are feedback loops between data sets, decisions, and algorithmic systems that create self-reinforcing mechanisms. These feedback loops can take various forms. First, they can cause behavioural effects: if decision-making systems disadvantage certain groups, they might 'stop trying', for instance, by no longer making an effort to acquire the credentials that would qualify them for certain positions (Kim 2017: 895–896). This behavioural reaction is similar to other mechanisms that stop certain individuals from trying to be a part of the system (e.g. for stereotype threats, see Steele 1997). Another behavioural effect is that privileged groups may be better able than underprivileged ones to second-guess the decision-making systems and to optimize their CVs accordingly (O'Neil 2016: 114). Again, this is not too different from the strategies privileged individuals use to gain advantages vis-à-vis human decision-makers.

A second version of such a feedback loop occurs in systems that only get feedback from a subset of the sample they deal with. For example, hiring systems can track how well the candidates that have been chosen as employees do their jobs, but they cannot track how successful the rejected candidates are in other jobs. False positives (unqualified candidates that got hired) can be detected, but false negatives (qualified candidates that did not get hired) disappear from the dataset. Such asymmetry is likely to skew the whole decision-making system, but it is particularly consequential for individuals for whom getting a job would actually *contribute* to qualifying them for the job. Discussing the case of a candidate who apparently got rejected by an automated hiring system because of previous mental health issues, O'Neil writes: 'Red-lighting people with certain mental health issues prevents them from having a normal job and leading a normal life, further isolating them. This is exactly what the Americans with Disabilities Act is supposed to prevent' (2016: 112).

Third, there is also a measurement version of the feedback mechanism, which occurs when there are more, or more fine-grained, data points about one group than about another.[14] This problem has frequently been discussed with regard to racial targeting in police work (see, e.g. O'Neil 2016: 25; Bartlett 2018; Ito 2019). In many US constituencies, non-Whites have far more police encounters than Whites because their communities are more heavily policed, even though the large majority of community members is completely innocent. This phenomenon is directly relevant when police encounters are included in data sets, but it is also indirectly relevant because it influences the likelihood of crime detection. A recidivism algorithm is supposed to predict crimes, but the data it works with can only contain *detected* crimes—and the relation between these two variables might differ between groups. The number of detected crimes might be higher for non-Whites than for Whites, not because the number of crimes differs for the two groups but because the rate of detection is higher for Blacks. If higher detected crime rates then lead to more police presence in these communities, this becomes a self-reinforcing loop, and it also has implications for recidivism scores.

All these issues would be problematic—and worth addressing—even if they occurred on their own, in the different social spheres in which algorithmic decision-making is used. But they are intertwined, and there can be spillovers from one field to another, which can further drive advantaged and disadvantaged groups apart. You want to get a loan? You need a job. You want to get a job? You need a college degree. Many algorithms use data from one sphere of life when making decisions about something else. As O'Neil (2016: 147) reports, for example, almost 50 per cent of US employers take a job seeker's credit score into account. Hence, the impact of algorithmic bias on individuals' lives can go far beyond one single decision, and prevent, or at least delay, their access to various other opportunities; for example, a biased algorithm in the access to credit can also impact on their access to jobs. Those most at risk here are those who might be discriminated along *different* dimensions; non-White women might be discriminated against as a non-White in one area, as a woman in another, and as a non-White woman in a third.

All these problems need to be carefully addressed when algorithmic decision-making systems are introduced into structurally unjust societies in order not to add to existing injustices. Many forms of algorithmic decision-making systems introduced thus far have unjustly disadvantaged those who were already in structurally unjust positions and had to struggle with far more obstacles than most in more privileged positions. This is not to say that algorithms could never be a force for good—but it takes great care, and an awareness of potential pitfalls, to use them without running into such problems.[15] In the next section, I discuss some solutions that have been proposed for managing such situations.

SUGGESTED SOLUTIONS

When it comes to solutions, one can distinguish between the purely technical level and more far-ranging approaches, and, of course, these can also go hand in hand. In the past few years, a number of initiatives such as 'discrimination-aware data mining' (DADM) and 'fairness, accountability and transparency in machine learning' (FATML) have emerged, which address the technical level. Their members raise awareness about problems of bias and explore how computer programmes can be designed with as little bias as possible. As the example of the health prediction algorithm analysed by Obermeyer et al. shows, a crucial step can be the choice of the variable that the system is supposed to predict (label biases). The researchers experimented with different variables (e.g. number of chronic illnesses, avoidable health costs) and created a new output variable that reduced the bias against Blacks by 84 per cent compared to the previous version (Obermeyer et al. 2019: 452).

It may not always be possible to use less biased output variables, however, simply because they may not be available. Data scientists can nonetheless try to use various techniques that would reduce bias. Schmidt and Stephens suggest, as a general approach, to start from existing models and then to 'search for alternative models that are less discriminatory than that baseline model, yet similarly predictive' (2019: 140). One strategy, for example, is *adversarial debiasing* (Schmidt and Stephens 2019: 142; see also Xu 2019, both referring to Zhang et al. 2018). Here, one trains the artificial intelligence that learns to predict the outcomes to prevent another, adversary artificial intelligence from guessing the protected variables on the basis of the outcomes. Another strategy is the *dynamic upsampling of training data* (Xu 2019; similarly Cofone 2019: 1423). Here, the artificial intelligence learns which input data come from underrepresented groups and gives them more weight during the training phase.[16]

These and other approaches can help minimize bias and aim to create algorithmic fairness, but as many commentators emphasize, relying on technical solutions alone would be short-sighted. As Xu points out:

> algorithmic fairness cannot be the end of the story. Even the best technology serves as a means to an end, and in a world that is the product of centuries of structural inequality, oppression, and exploitation, the question of 'whose end' tends not to yield surprising answers. Just because an algorithm is fair does not mean it is used fairly.
>
> (Xu 2019)

Similar arguments are put forward in AI Now (2018a: 8). Wong (2019) is therefore right to hold that algorithmic fairness is not a technical, but a political matter, and needs to be treated as such. For what ultimately matters is to understand and address the structural injustices that give rise to various forms of unequal patterns in the data sets—and this cannot be done by the optimization of algorithmic tools alone. It requires multidimensional, multidisciplinary approaches in which those who will be subjected to algorithmic decisions, or their representatives, also have a voice.

The use of algorithmic systems that decide about access to opportunities and important human goods in structurally unjust societies requires that they are embedded in carefully designed institutional structures that prevent the unjust perpetuation of disadvantages. In recent years, there have been numerous calls for creating such structures (e.g. AI Now 2017, 2018a, 2018b, 2019; Citron and Pasquale 2014; Sandvig et al. 2014; Sample 2017; Brauneis and Goodman 2017; Mitchell et al. 2019; Partnership on AI (2019); see also Rosenblat et al. 2014; Binns 2018; Wong 2019; or Martin 2019, who also discusses the accountability of companies). AI Now, for example, suggests a framework for an 'Algorithmic Impact Assessment' (AI Now 2018b). While there are some differences between these proposals, the general thrust is clear: there is an urgent need for accountability whenever individuals are exposed to algorithmic decision-making systems.

Such accountability requires more than transparency (Ananny and Crawford 2018), which is often difficult anyway (more on this in the section on 'The private firm objection' below). Accountability requires clear mechanisms for correcting wrong decisions and implementing changes whenever correctable flaws have been discovered. Some authors have suggested licensing and audit requirements for algorithms (e.g. Citron and Pasquale 2014: 21), but this can never be enough because when the data sets are updated once the algorithm is in use, new problems might arise. Careful, ongoing monitoring is needed, which must also include the possibility for individuals to appeal decisions, both in order to do justice to individual cases, but also in order to better understand whether (and if so, why) the system might have come to erroneous conclusions. Particular attention needs to be paid to effects on the members of less privileged groups; these groups might be less likely than other social groups to challenge decisions and hence great care needs to be taken not to disadvantage them in the first place (e.g. Richardson et al. 2019: 23). Part of the quick 'gut check' that Eubanks proposes is to ask, 'Would the tool be tolerated if it was targeted at non-poor people?' (2017: 211).

The burden of proof that something *might* have gone wrong should not be placed on individuals being judged by algorithms, but rather on those who implement the system. As O'Neill notes, currently there is often an imbalance: 'The human victims of [algorithms] […] are held to a far higher standard of evidence than the algorithms themselves' (2016: 10). One way in which this one-sidedness in favour of the algorithm can be overcome is to allow for interactive modelling, such that individuals can play around with the algorithm and see how different inputs change the output (Citron and Pasquale 2014: 28–29), but this does not work for all constellations. Given that many algorithmic systems that are currently in use do not offer such possibilities, one short-term strategy that governments could implement would be to create an ombudsperson that individuals can turn to when they suspect algorithmic discrimination (see also Sample 2017, quoting proposals by Floridi; similarly AI Now 2018b: 5). But even the best ombudsperson can only work effectively if he or she has access to algorithms and data, and the right to demand changes from the companies or public authorities that use the algorithmic systems.

More broadly speaking, it is crucial to create awareness in the data scientist community and in the broader public. Initiatives such as DADM and FATML are very important in this respect. Ideally, all university courses in data science or artificial intelligence should contain ethics modules, in which some case studies are discussed, to give data scientists a sense of what can be at stake when the systems they construct are implemented in real life. Data scientists need to understand the limits of their own knowledge (O'Neil 2016: 215) and acknowledge the knowledge of those in the respective field, for example, health care or social work.[17] As Obermeyer et al. (2019: 452) note in their discussion of how they could reduce racial bias in a health-care algorithm, it is particularly important to have a good grasp of the main questions being addressed when new labels are produced. Algorithmic design should be a collaborative, interdisciplinary endeavour in which the voices of different groups, with different competences and perspectives, are heard. Such inclusion can also help to ensure that the interrelations with *other* forms of injustice, which Young's 'structural justice' perspective emphasizes, are taken into account. Given the various forms of injustice in our societies, sometimes it may simply not be appropriate to use algorithms because these interrelations are so complex that each case deserves an individualized approach.[18]

Finally, and to end on a somewhat more positive note: data scientists and the institutions that rely on algorithmic decision-making systems should be encouraged to explore where there are potential 'anti-Matthew-effects' in the use of these tools. As Kleinberg et al. emphasize, various forms of bias, both cognitive and structural, can be discovered by drawing on data (2019: 872; see also Barabas et al. 2018). Instead of letting algorithms make decisions, they can be used for understanding in more detail what the barriers and challenges for minority groups are, which can then be the basis for mitigation strategies, algorithmic or otherwise. In addition, there might be possibilities for using algorithms for overcoming traditional barriers. Peck (2013) reports the case of programmers who were recruited by algorithms based on their activities in online programming forums, which led to the hiring of more people without a college degree. Educational background is a variable which, in structurally unjust societies, tends to be distributed rather unfairly—and if algorithmic analyses show that it is actually not correlated to the ability of individuals to do certain jobs, this can be a boon for social justice.

THE PRIVATE FIRM OBJECTION

Such suggestions, however, are often met with a seemingly weighty objection: many of the entities that use algorithms that decide about access to important human goods are private firms. To be sure, they may sometimes have an interest in developing fair algorithms, for instance, when it comes to finding the most qualified employees, without regard for gender or race (Kim 2017: 893). But in other cases, they might well be satisfied with a moderately functional system, despite the fact that it discriminates against certain groups. While it seems clear that state institutions are bound to treat citizens fairly, does the same also hold for private firms? Might there be different standards for public institutions and private firms (as suggested by Binns 2018: 551)? Commentators from a business-friendly camp might in fact hold that there are no standards at all, and that firms should be allowed to use whatever decision-making systems they like.

But in most legal systems, discrimination on the basis of gender or race is illegal for public but also for private institutions, and rightly so. The opposite of discrimination, affirmative action in favour of underrepresented groups, is often allowed (see, e.g. Menand 2020 for an account of recent US legislation). The challenge is how to apply the existing legal tools to the new reality of algorithmic decision-making (see Barocas and Selbst 2016; Kim 2017; Cofone 2019). There is also the problem of adducing the relevant evidence: how can a member of a protected group be sufficiently sure that she has been discriminated against to even think about initiating investigations?[19] This is an area in which non-governmental organizations (NGOs), civil rights groups, unions, and other support structures are likely to be crucial for making sure that existing laws are enforced by courts.

How to know when discrimination has happened is related to a problem that can be understood as a weaker version of the private firm objection: business secrecy. At the moment, many algorithms and data sets are the business secrets of private firms, which makes it very difficult for outsiders to understand even the basic architecture of these systems. The justification for algorithmic secrecy is not only the standard one that competitors might copy the systems if firms were forced to make them public. In addition, there is the problem of the systems potentially being gamed by ill-intending agents who understand how the algorithms work (e.g. O'Neil 2016: 8; Sandvig et al. 2014: 9).[20] But in order to create accountability, algorithms and data sets do not have to be made accessible to *everyone*; it is sufficient to make them accessible to a small group of competent experts who can diagnose and evaluate any possible biases. Pasquale calls this approach 'qualified transparency', and suggests the formation of an Internet Intermediary Regulatory Council (2010: 168–169) for that purpose.

Thus, instead of yielding to the private firm objection, the widespread use of algorithms is an opportunity for rethinking the scope given to private firms, within a framework of public laws. This is particularly important when it comes to the provision of basic goods that are central for individuals' ability to lead their lives without a 'systematic threat of domination or deprivation of the means to develop and exercise their capacities' (Young 2011: 52). For some services, such as access to a bank account, and maybe also to basic forms of credit, it might in fact be the best solution to have public providers that take on all individuals without any algorithmic checks (see Baradaran 2015). But this proposal should not be understood as letting private firms off the hook. While they may have a legitimate interest in making a certain amount of profit, firms are, ultimately, meant to serve the public good (see, e.g. Ciepley 2013 or Mayer 2013 for discussions). Public regulation is meant to ensure this is so when it does not happen by market forces alone. It is not desirable that competition between firms runs along the dimension of 'who is best able to exploit structural injustices through algorithms'. Instead, firms should compete for developing and using algorithms that are *both* efficient *and* fair. In the current situation, this task may fall mostly to NGOs and social entrepreneurs, but better regulation could make sure that all private firms in this area are orientated towards this goal.

CONCLUSION

In this chapter, I have discussed the problems of algorithmic bias in structurally unjust societies, with a focus on algorithmic decision-making systems that provide access to important opportunities and goods, such as housing, credit, or jobs. I have discussed some of the challenges of creating fair algorithms, and emphasized that solutions often need to be broader than the focus on the technical level alone. Particular attention needs to be paid to the risk of self-reinforcing mechanisms, so-called Matthew effects, which privilege those who are already better off and perpetuate, or even amplify, the disadvantages of others. I have summarized some proposals for creating more accountability, and responded to the objection that private firms have no responsibility with regard to the avoidance of algorithmic discrimination.

Fortunately, attention to this topic has already reached the political realm. Scholars are discussing how to apply anti-discrimination rules to algorithmic decisions (e.g. Barocas and Selbst 2016; Kim 2017), and we can probably expect more, and highly visible, legal processes in the near future. The European Union's General Data Protection Regulation (GDPR) contains some rights to challenge purely algorithmic decisions; critics hold, however, that as soon as there is minimal human involvement, the clause doesn't apply any longer (Sample 2017). In the United States, the Algorithmic Accountability Act was introduced in the US Senate in 2019. Many commentators have welcomed it, but it is considered not sufficiently robust by experts, especially when it comes to enforcement, public impact, and duties of transparency (Kaminsky and Selbst 2019). New York City had a task force that was supposed to shed light on its use of algorithmic systems, possible problems of bias, and strategies to mitigate them, but it did not even manage to create full transparency about which algorithmic systems the City actually uses (cf. Powles 2017; see also the shadow report for the AI Now Institute by Richardson et al. 2019). More work is urgently needed, not only by politicians, but also by NGOs, consumer protection agencies, and other civil society organizations.

As Barocas and Selbst (2016: 714–716) note, one problem for reformers is how to 'identify the "correct" baseline historical data to avoid reproducing past prejudice'. This cannot be done in a one-size-fits-all solution, but requires attention to detail and to the specific social contexts in which algorithmic systems are being used. Another point, which I have bracketed in this chapter, but which needs to be brought back in whenever strategies are discussed, is the—potentially unequal—impact on privacy. While an understanding of the technical side is certainly crucial, developing fair, accountable, and sustainable solutions also require input from other fields such as social work, medicine, or law. The debate about algorithmic fairness is a welcome opportunity to rethink not only the role of private companies in society, but also our understanding of fairness. And it is an opportunity to address not only algorithmic bias, but also the broader, structural injustices in our societies that algorithmic decision-making processes often make so painfully visible.

Acknowledgement

I would like to thank Jan-Willem Romeijn, Eva Herzog, Chiara Lisciandra, Carissa Veliz, and an anonymous reviewer for valuable comments and suggestions on this chapter.

Notes

1. Most of these systems also use artificial intelligence, in the sense of machine-learning algorithms that look for patterns in data. Below, I discuss some of the technical features in more detail.
2. By focusing on *access* (*who* gets something?) this chapter takes a different approach from Chapter 24, by Lippert-Rasmussen and Munch, on price discrimination. Some concerns (e.g. objectionable forms of discrimination) are obviously relevant for both.
3. Dastin (2018) reports that in 2017, 55 per cent of US human resource managers predicted that AI would become 'a regular part of their work' in the next five years; O'Neil mentions an estimate that 'such tests now are used on 60 to 70 percent of prospective workers' (2016: 108) and also quotes the value of 72 per cent from a different source (2016: 113). Buranyi (2018) quotes estimates of a US$3 billion market for 'pre-hire assessment'.
4. For discussions of privacy, see the Chapter 31 by Marmor in this volume.
5. For a broader discussion, see Herzog (2019).

6. Here, I omit the problem that data scientists (or those who pay them) might *want* to achieve racist, sexist, or other problematic outcomes and attempt to mask them through algorithmic decision-systems; see Barocas and Selbst (2016: 692–693) for a discussion.

7. Sometimes, statistical analyses and self-learning systems are trained on model data, or on data that have been curated for fairness, but such efforts require extra steps that are often not taken (see below for examples). Much of what follows refers to self-learning systems ('artificial intelligences').

8. An overview can be found at https://en.wikipedia.org/wiki/List_of_cognitive_biases, accessed 9 August 2021.

9. This account fits very well with theories of intersectionality (Crenshaw 1989) but, for reasons of space, I will not discuss this relation in more detail.

10. If it could be shown that algorithms are actually fairer than human decision-makers, this could turn out to be an advantage—but it is likely that privileged individuals would then quickly insist on having their applications processed by algorithms as well, or they would insist on having a choice, picking whatever seems more advantageous to their specific case.

11. In fact, sometimes it is unclear whether a justification could ever be provided. Take, for example, hiring software that analyses patterns of body movement in video interviews and compares them with those of 'top-performing employees' (an example quoted in Buranyi 2018)—it seems very hard to describe what it would even mean to 'provide a justification' if the algorithm then decides to reject a candidate. Moreover, if such opaque systems are used, it is very difficult to detect errors.

12. The poorer the country, the greater the stakes—Pilkington (2019) mentions the case of a welfare recipient in India whose fingerprint was no longer recognized, due to a glitch in the automated system, so he lost access to subsistence ratios and died shortly after, presumably by starvation. But some cases in the United States are also extremely gruesome; see, e.g. Felton (2016) on a case in Michigan in which an unemployment agency wrongly accused 20,000 people of fraud.

13. Another complication can arise if, in order to preserve statistical parity, unequal error rates (higher ones for Black people) are chosen, so that more Black people are wrongly released. As Corbett-Davies and Goel (2018: 7) point out, this might mean more disadvantages *for their own group* (their example is the COMPAS recidivism algorithm) because these wrongly released candidates might reoffend, and most crimes happen *within* communities. Therefore, one should not only consider the group of (Black or White) offenders, but also the effects on different groups in society.

14. Further complications can arise when *different* individuals interact with algorithmic systems over time—and not all behave exactly as the system assumes they should. Seemingly harmless acts of cheating, committed out of self-protection, might create problems for others. O'Neil (2016: 9–10) reports the case of a teacher who did not manage to improve her students' scores, probably because the previous year's teacher had artificially inflated the score in order to look better herself.

15. And it goes without saying that this need for care runs counter to what is often the motive for the introduction of algorithmic systems—namely, to save costs.

16. One question that is sometimes discussed in this context is whether or not proxies that are correlated to protected variables (race, gender) should be removed from data sets— this seems optimal for the purpose of prediction, but it may block opportunities for better understanding the algorithmic system, and so it can make sense to make such data

available for the purpose of analysing (and where possible, debiasing) the outcomes (see Cofone 2019 for a discussion).

17. One also frequently hears calls for increasing the diversity of the data science field itself (e.g. AI Now 2017: 20). This inclusion is, of course, a matter of justice in and of itself, but it is not obvious that it would be sufficient to fix the problem of algorithmic bias. For example, women can be prejudiced against women as well (and they might have to adapt to the surrounding culture in order to succeed within their field). Thus, while important in themselves, I do not think that strategies for bringing more diversity to data science can replace the other suggestions for creating more accountability.

18. Note that those who endorse algorithmic solutions may sometimes have financial motives, while there are often no voices that speak for those who are most likely to suffer under an algorithmic system (or these voices are not heard).

19. This problem arises even in legal systems in which the ultimate burden of proof lies on the decision-makers that they have *not* discriminated against the claimant; the costs, both material and non-material, of legal proceedings are so high that individuals may nonetheless worry about going to court.

20. Sandvig et al. (2014) describes various ways in which algorithms that are not made public might nonetheless be tested for biases, e.g. by crowd-sourced approaches. But these run the risk of being outlawed by the US Computer Fraud and Abuse Act; Sandvig et al. call for a reform of that Act that would allow for more accountability through auditing.

References

AI Now (2017), 'AI Now Report', https://ainowinstitute.org/AI_Now_2017_Report.pdf, accessed 9 August 2021.

AI Now (2018a), 'AI Now Report', https://ainowinstitute.org/AI_Now_2018_Report.pdf, accessed 9 August 2021.

AI Now (2018b), 'Algorithmic Impact Assessments: A Practical Framework for Public Agency Accountability', https://ainowinstitute.org/aiareport2018.pdf, accessed 9 August 2021.

AI Now (2019), 'AI Now Report', https://ainowinstitute.org/AI_Now_2019_Report.pdf, accessed 9 August 2021.

Ananny, Mike, and Crawford, Kate (2018), 'Seeing without Knowing: Limitations of the Transparency Ideal and Its Application to Algorithmic Accountability', *New Media & Society* 20(3), 973–989.

Angwin, Julia, and Larson, Jeff (2016), 'Bias in Criminal Risk Scores Is Mathematically Inevitable, Researchers Say', https://www.propublica.org/article/bias-in-criminal-risk-scores-is-mathematically-inevitable-researchers-say, accessed 9 August 2021.

Angwin, Julia, Larson, Jeff, Mattu, Surya, and Kirchner, Lauren (2016), 'Machine Bias. There's Software Used across the Country to Predict Future Criminals. And It's Biased against Blacks', *Pro Publica*, 23 May.

Arrow, Kenneth J. (1973), 'The Theory of Discrimination', in Orley Ashenfelter and Albert Rees, eds, *Discrimination in Labour Markets* (Princeton, NJ: Princeton University Press), 3–33.

Barabas, Chelsea, Dinakar, Karthik, Ito, Joichi, Virza, Madars, and Zittrain, Jonathan (2018), 'Interventions over Predictions: Reframing the Ethical Debate for Actuarial Risk Assessment', Paper for the FATML 2018 conference, https://arxiv.org/abs/1712.08238, accessed 9 August 2021.

Baradaran, Mehrsa (2015), *How the Other Half Banks. Exclusion, Exploitation, and the Threat to Democracy* (Cambridge, MA; London: Harvard University Press).

Barocas, Solon, and Selbst, Andrew D. (2016), 'Big Data's Disparate Impact', *California Law Review* 104, 671–732.

Bartlett, Jamie (2018), 'How AI Could Kill Off Democracy', *The New Statesman*, 15 August, https://www.newstatesman.com/science-tech/technology/2018/08/how-ai-could-kill-democracy-0, accessed 9 August 2021.

Binns, Reuben (2018), 'Algorithmic Accountability and Public Reason', *Philosophy & Technology* 31(4), 543–556.

Borsboom, Denny, Romeijn, Jan-Willem, and Wicherts, Jelte M. (2008), 'Measurement Invariance versus Selection Invariance: Is Fair Selection Possible?', *Psychological Methods* 13(2), 75–98.

Boyd, Dana, and Crawford, Kate (2012), 'Critical Questions for Big Data', *Information, Communication and Society* 15(5), 662–679.

Brauneis, Robert, and Goodman, Ellen P. (2017), 'Algorithmic Transparency for the Smart City', *GWU Law School Public Law Research Paper*, https://ssrn.com/abstract=3012499, accessed 9 August 2021.

Buranyi, Stephen (2018), "Dehumanising, Impenetrable, Frustrating': The Grim Reality of Job Hunting in the Age of AI', *The Guardian*, 4 March.

Castro, Clinton (2019), 'What's Wrong with Machine Bias', *Ergo, an Open Access Journal of Philosophy* 6, doi: https://doi.org/10.3998/ergo.12405314.0006.015.

Chouldechova, Alexandra (2016), 'Fair Prediction with Disparate Impact: A Study of Bias in Recidivism Prediction Instruments', *ArXiv*, https://arxiv.org/abs/1610.07524, accessed 9 August 2021.

Ciepley, David (2013), 'Beyond Public and Private: Toward a Political Theory of the Corporation', *American Political Science Review* 107(1), 139–158.

Citron, Danielle Keats, and Pasquale, Frank (2014), 'The Scored Society: Due Process for Automated Predictions', University of Maryland Francis King Carey School of Law Legal Studies Research Paper, No. 2014–8.

Claassen, Rutger, and Herzog, Lisa (2019), 'Why Economic Agency Matters. An Account of Structural Domination in the Economic Realm', *European Journal of Political Theory*, 9 March, https://journals.sagepub.com/doi/10.1177/1474885119832181.

Cofone, Ignacio N. (2019), 'Algorithmic Discrimination Is an Information Problem', *Hastings Law Journal* 70, 1389–1444.

Corbett-Davies and, Sam, and Goel, Sharad (2018), 'The Measure and Mismeasure of Fairness: A Critical Review of Fair Machine Learning', *CoRR*, abs/1808.00023, http://arxiv.org/abs/1808.00023, accessed 9 August 2021.

Corbett-Davies, Sam, Pierson, Emma, Feller, Avi, Goel, Sharad, and Huq, Aziz (2017), 'Algorithmic Decision Making and the Cost of Fairness', *CoRR*, abs/1701.08230, http://arxiv.org/abs/1701.08230, accessed 9 August 2021.

Crenshaw, Kimberle (1989), 'Demarginalizing the Intersection of Race and Sex: A Black Feminist Critique of Antidiscrimination Doctrine, Feminist Theory and Antiracist Politics', *University of Chicago Legal Forum* 140, 139–167.

Dastin, Jeffrey (2018), 'Amazon Scraps Secret AI Recruiting Tool that Showed Bias against Women', *Business News*, 10 October.

Eubanks, Virginia (2017), *Automating Inequality. How High-Tech Tools Profile, Police, and Punish the Poor* (New York: St Martin's Press).

Felton, Ryan (2016), 'Michigan Unemployment Agency Made 20,000 False Fraud Accusations—Report', *The Guardian*, 18 December.

Fry, Hannah (2018), *Hello World: How to Be Human in the Age of Machine* (London: Transworld Digital).

Hardt, Moritz, Price, Eric, and Srebo, Nathan (2016), 'Equality of Opportunity in Supervised Learning', *ArXiv*, https://arxiv.org/abs/1610.02413, accessed 9 August 2021.

Herzog, Lisa (2019), *Die Rettung der Arbeit. Ein politischer Aufruf* (Berlin: Hanser Berlin).

Herzog, Lisa (Forthcoming), 'Old Facts, New Beginnings. Thinking with Arendt about Algorithmic Decision-Making', [journal t.b.c.].

Ito, Joi (2019), 'Supposedly 'Fair' Algorithms Can Perpetuate Discrimination', *Wired*, 2 May, https://www.wired.com/story/ideas-joi-ito-insurance-algorithms/, accessed 9 August 2021.

Kaminsky, Margot E., and Selbst, Andrew D. (2019), 'The Legislation That Targets the Racist Impacts of Tech', *New York Times*, 7 May.

Kim, Pauline T. (2017), 'Data-Driven Discrimination at Work', *William & Mary Law Review* 58(3), 857–936.

Kleinberg, Jon, Mullainathan, Sendhil, and Raghavan, Manish (2016), 'Inherent Trade-Offs in the Fair Determination of Risk Scores', *Innovations in Theoretical Computer Science Conference* (2017), https://arxiv.org/pdf/1609.05807v1.pdf, accessed 9 August 2021.

Kleinberg, Jon, Ludwig, Jens, Mullainathan, Sendhil, and Stunstein, Cass R. (2019), 'Discrimination in the Age of Algorithms', 5 February, *SSRN*, https://ssrn.com/abstract=3329669, accessed 9 August 2021.

Lecher, Colin (2018), 'What Happens When an Algorithm Cuts Your Health Care', *The Verge*, 21 May.

MacMillan, Douglas, and Anderson, Nick (2019), 'Student Tracking, Secret Scores: How College Admissions Offices Rank Prospects before They Apply', *The Washington Post*, 14 October.

Martin, Kirsten (2019), 'Ethical Implications and Accountability of Algorithms', *Journal of Business Ethics* 160, 835–850.

Mayer, Colin (2013), *Firm Commitment: Why the Corporation Is Failing Us and How to Restore Trust in It* (Oxford: Oxford University Press).

Menand, Louis (2020), 'The Changing Meaning of Affirmative Action', *The New Yorker*, 20 January, https://www.newyorker.com/magazine/2020/01/20/have-we-outgrown-the-need-for-affirmative-action, accessed 9 August 2021.

Merton, Robert K. (1968), 'The Matthew Effect in Science', *Science* 159(3810), 56–63.

Mitchell, Margaret, Wu, Simone, Zaldivar, Andrew, Barnes, Parker, Vasserman, Lucy, Hutchinson, Ben, Spitzer, Elena, Raji, Inioluwa Deborah, and Gebru, Timnit (2019), 'Model Cards for Model Reporting', *ArXiv*, https://arxiv.org/abs/1810.03993, accessed 9 August 2021.

O'Neil, Cathy (2016), *Weapons of Math Destruction. How Big Data Increases Inequality and Threatens Democracy* (New York: Penguin).

Obermeyer, Ziad, Powers, Brian, Vogeli, Christine, and Mullainathan, Sendhil (2019), 'Dissecting Racial Bias in an Algorithm Used to Manage the Health of Populations', *Science* 336, 447–453.

Partnership on AI (2019), 'Report on Algorithmic Risk Assessment Tools in the US Criminal Justice System', https://www.partnershiponai.org/report-on-machine-learning-in-risk-assessment-tools-in-the-u-s-criminal-justice-system/, accessed 9 August 2021.

Pasquale, Frank (2010), 'Beyond Innovation and Competition: The Need for Qualified Transparency in Internet Intermediaries', *Northwestern University Law Review* 104, 105–173.

Peck, Don (2013), 'They're Watching You at Work', *The Atlantic*, December.

Phelps, Edmund S. (1972), 'The Statistical Theory of Racism and Sexism', *American Economic Review* 62, 659–61.

Pilkington, Ed. (2019), 'Digital Dystopia: How Algorithms Punish the Poor', *The Guardian*, 14 October.

Plantin, Jean-Christophe, Lagoze, Carl, Edwards, Paul N., and Sandvig, Christian (2018), 'Infrastructure Studies Meet Platform Studies in the Age of Google and Facebook', *New Media & Society* 20(1), 293–310.

Powles, Julia. 2017. 'New York City's Bold, Flawed Attempt to Make Algorithms Accountable.' *The New Yorker*, 20 December, https://www.newyorker.com/tech/annals-of-technology/new-york-citys-bold-flawed-attempt-to-make-algorithms-accountable

Richardson, Rashida, ed. (2019), 'Confronting Black Boxes: A Shadow Report of the New York City Automated Decision System Task Force', AI Now Institute, 4 December, https://ainowinstitute.org/ads-shadowreport-2019.html, accessed 9 August 2021.

Rosenblat, Alex, Kneese, Tamara, and Boyd, Danah (2014), 'Algorithmic Accountability', *Data & Society*, 17 March, https://www.datasociety.net/initiatives/2014-0317, accessed 9 August 2021.

Sample, Ian (2017), 'Computer Says No: Why Making AIs Fair, Accountable and Transparent Is Crucial', *The Guardian*, 5 November.

Sandvig, Christian, Hamilton, Kevin, Karahalios, Karrie, and Langbort, Cedric (2014), 'Auditing Algorithms: Research Methods for Detecting Discrimination on Internet Platforms', Paper presented to '*Data and Discrimination: Converting Critical Concerns into Productive Inquiry*', 22 May, Seattle, WA.

Schmidt, Nicholas, and Stephens, Bryce (2019), 'An Introduction to Artificial Intelligence and Solutions to the Problems of Algorithmic Discrimination', *ArXiv*, 8 November, https://arxiv.org/abs/1911.05755 (accessed 31 August 2021).

Steele, Claude M. (1997), 'A Threat in the Air: How Stereotypes Shape the Intellectual Identities and Performance of Women and African-Americans', *American Psychologist* 52, 613–629.

Wong, Pak-Hang (2019), 'Democratizing Algorithmic Fairness', *Philosophy & Technology* online first.

Xu, Joyce (2019), 'Algorithmic Solutions to Algorithmic Bias: A Technical Guide', *Towards Data Science*, 18 June, https://link.springer.com/article/10.1007/s13347-019-00355-w, accessed 9 August 2021.

Young, Iris Marion (2011), *Responsibility for Justice* (Oxford: Oxford University Press).

Zhang, Brian Hu, Lemoine, Blake, and Mitchell, Margaret (2018), 'Mitigating Unwanted Biases with Adversarial Learning', *Artificial Intelligence, Ethics, and Society Conference*, https://arxiv.org/pdf/1801.07593.pdf, accessed 9 August 2021.

CHAPTER 22

THE ETHICS OF PREDICTIVE POLICING

KATERINA HADJIMATHEOU AND CHRISTOPHER NATHAN

Introduction: the concept

ALL decision-making, whether individual or institutional, involves some kind of prediction. The criminal justice system is no exception. Police routinely make predictions about which kinds of crimes are likely to be committed, where, and by whom. Such predictions inform policing decisions at all levels, from strategic choices about which skills and technology to invest in, to decisions about where to send patrols on a Saturday evening, to exercises of individual discretion and judgement about who to stop and whose pockets to turn out. As Lever (2016) writes, 'police can hardly be required not to generalise from experience and from verified evidence when determining how to act'. Nevertheless, both the term 'predictive policing' and the ethical debate that accompanies it refer specifically to techniques and systems developed in the context of a broader shift towards 'data-driven' approaches to policing, which has been ongoing since the turn of the twenty-first century. Predictive policing systems involve the adoption of data analytics by police to help them to make the kind of predictions about crime and criminality that support decisions about how to allocate resources more efficiently.

Predictive policing departs from mundane and routine police approaches to assessing the riskiness of places and people by utilizing data-analysis tools and empirical research to formulate and validate predictions.[1] Systems currently in use are developed by a variety of actors, including private companies, non-profit-making institutions, university researchers, governments, and the police themselves. At the time of writing, the term *predictive policing* is used to describe 'any system that analyses available data to predict either where a crime may occur in a given time window (place-based) or who will be involved in a crime as either victim or perpetrator (person-based)' (Richardson et al. 2019).

Examples of the former approach include forecasting and crime-mapping techniques, which apply mathematical models to datasets about the location, date, and time of past crimes to predict where crimes are likely to occur in specific timeframes in the future. These place-based approaches to prediction tend to marry empirical research with scientific and machine-learning techniques in ways that are more technically complex and scientifically rigorous than person-based alternatives.[2]

Examples of the latter include the compilation of lists of 'high-risk' offenders and/or victims of specific crimes, from domestic violence to gun crime and gang-related criminality. Person-based predictions tend to be supported by the periodic analysis of a wide range of data points, including criminal history, employment, involvement with social services, drug use, address, known association with other individuals of interest, and so on, to assign a risk 'score'. In predictive policing, assessment of risk is undertaken either in part or entirely by a computer and is therefore standardized and translated into scores, rankings, or other indicators, such as traffic light colours.

Our conceptualization of predictive policing is intentionally broad. It leaves unspecified the scientific sophistication of the specific tools and research involved in a predictive policing system. A broad definition enables us to include simple criminal profiles and database matrices used to create risk rankings alongside more technically complex algorithmic and machine-learning approaches to crime mapping. Yet it also means that our approach departs from that adopted by a significant subset of the literature addressing the normative implications of predictive policing, which focuses exclusively on algorithmic, place-based approaches (Benbouzid 2019; Bennet-Moses and Chan 2018; Ensign et al. 2018; Jefferson 2018; Lum and Isaac 2016). In our view, a broader conceptualization is more appropriate as a basis for ethical analysis. As will be argued below, neither the technical sophistication of predictive systems nor their focus on either places or persons are determinative of the normative implications of those systems. Rather, as some have already recognized (Ferguson 2018), all predictive policing systems tend to raise the same kinds of ethical concerns.

Three key areas of ethical concern are voiced in the literature on predictive policing. These relate to its tendency to: (a) exacerbate the discriminatory and disproportionate policing of the urban poor and racial minorities by replicating and amplifying existing police bias and prejudice; (b) impose criminal suspicion and restrictions to liberty on individuals in the absence of sufficient grounds for doing so, thus violating autonomy or otherwise disrespecting individuals; and (c) reduce transparency and accountability in policing by introducing proprietorial secrecy and false objectivity into the policing decision-making process. In what follows, we focus on the first two of these concerns, touching briefly at the end of this chapter on the issue of accountability and transparency.[3]

The first relates to the issues of bias, ratchets, and the disproportionate policing of racial minorities and the poor. Concerns along these lines have been raised previously in relation to practices that overlap with predictive policing, including racial profiling (Lever 2016), 'actuarial' methods for assessing risk in criminal justice contexts (Harcourt 2007), and the utilization of algorithms and big data by state agencies (Eubanks 2018; Oswald et al. 2018; Ferguson 2018; Brayne 2017). Though the use of predictive analytics in policing is relatively new, the moral arguments in this category reflect longstanding debates about the ethics and justice of policing more generally, as well as the intersection of these with issues in the newer fields of 'data ethics' and 'algorithmic justice'.[4]

In addition to legal and philosophical theory, journalistic investigation of predictive policing systems and their systematic evaluation by social and computer scientists both play a crucial role in shedding light on this category of concerns (Ensign et al. 2018; Lum and Isaac 2016; Brantingham 2018). One of the vital insights they contribute is the observation that predictive policing systems are fundamentally shaped and constrained by the data available. Most predictive policing systems rely on police data, which does not itself represent an objective measure of crime, but only of crimes that become known to the police. These crimes are themselves revealed through 'some complex interaction between criminality, policing strategy, and community–police relations' (Lum and Isaac 2016), which itself may be characterized by disproportionate, discriminatory, or otherwise unfair police practices. For crimes such as domestic abuse, the vast majority of which are never reported to police, police data will yield better predictions about the future *policing* of such crimes, rather than their actual *incidence*. As will be discussed later, these observations about how predictive policing works in practice are key to understanding some of the most serious objections to it—in particular the claim that it supports policing that is biased against certain communities and individuals.

The second kind of ethical objection to predictive policing we consider relates to its potential to violate autonomy and disrespect individuals by cutting off windows of opportunity to act correctly and by treating people as criminals in the absence of sufficient grounds (Daskal 2014; Berman 2020). Predictive policing systems are an element of a broader shift from a policing function that is aimed at detecting and responding to crimes to a role that is aimed at preventing crimes. Some have argued that this shift carries with it a problematic change in perspective. For example, Zedner (2007: 262) argues that the 'post-crime orientation of criminal justice is increasingly overshadowed by the pre-crime logic of security'.

There is a liberal tradition that holds that such a change in logic leads to policing activity that more easily yields to justification of coercion. As John Stuart Mill argues in *On Liberty* (1998: 98):

> The preventive function of government, however, is far more liable to be abused, to the prejudice of liberty, than the punitory function; for there is hardly any part of the legitimate freedom of action of a human being that would not admit of being represented, and fairly too, as increasing the facilities for some form of other of delinquency.

Such concerns are reflected in the way that popular portrayals of predictive policing are often placed alongside images of futuristic technologies of the kind displayed in the novel and film *Minority Report*. The concern being expressed is the old worry put forward in early-twentieth-century portrayals of totalitarianism, in which state power continually expands until it has the goal of understanding and responding to people's innermost thoughts. This worry is linked to philosophical debates about the importance of the role of individualized suspicion justifying police interferences, the moral importance of the freedom to choose to do wrong (Tadros 2014), and the justice of pre-punishment (Smilansky 1994). In the following section, we argue that none of these lines of argument succeed in showing that predictive policing is always, or even typically, problematic ethically.

BIAS, RATCHETS, AND THE DISPROPORTIONATE POLICING OF RACIAL MINORITIES AND THE POOR

The most frequently voiced moral criticism of predictive policing is that it visits disproportionate and discriminatory measures of policing on certain social groups, especially racial minorities and the urban poor. This section articulates and lends support to this line of criticism, arguing further that, though it is most often directed towards place-based predictive policing systems, many of its specific claims apply equally to person-based systems.

Police have long been criticized for acting in ways that are explicitly or implicitly prejudiced and punitive towards minorities and other disadvantaged groups. In the early 2000s, such criticism began to focus on the way in which officers singled out or 'profiled' individuals for preventative stop-and-searches, and the role of racial and other stereotypes and prejudices as a basis for such profiling (Bowling and Phillips 2007; Harris 2003; Lever 2004; Risse and Zeckhauser 2004; Lippert-Rasmussen 2006; Harcourt 2007). Since 2010, the rise of predictive policing has prompted a convergence between this debate about the ethics of racial profiling and more recent concerns about 'algorithmic bias', that is, the ways in which algorithms and machine learning replicate, and even amplify, biases in the data they are fed (Ayre and Kraner 2018).

This new, interdisciplinary body of criticism argues that by compounding racial and other kinds of social bias with statistical bias, predictive systems lead to policing practices that are even more disproportionate and discriminatory than their analogue predecessors (Angwin et al. 2016; Joh 2017; Richardson et al. 2019). Notwithstanding the relative novelty of algorithmic approaches to criminal justice, and the contemporary and dynamic nature of crime-mapping as a technique, the debate around these issues is already relatively mature.

It is worth noting that the shift in the ethical debate about policing from talk about prejudice and racism to talk about 'bias' reflects the growing influence of computer science and statistics in the critical literature on predictive policing. Prejudice is an evaluative, even emotive, term, generally understood as an epistemological association of a person or group with negative traits, on unsound grounds. Bias is far broader a category and is often used in terms that are descriptive but not evaluative. For example, it is used in statistics to refer to discrepancies between the parameter one aims to measure and the parameter actually measured, often because of some unrepresentativeness in sampling. While this kind of bias can be the result of inclinations and preferences that involve beliefs such as prejudice, it need not be so. Neither does bias necessarily entail negative moral consequences: biased actions and practices might often be unethical or unjust, but they might be merely inefficient.

Risks of discriminatory and disproportionate policing arise in relation to predictive policing systems because the data they rely on, about the location and time of past crimes, itself reflects discriminatory and disproportionate practices of policing rather than 'actual' or 'objective' records of crime rates (Mayson 2018). When (as appears to be the case with a number of predictive systems) a significant proportion of this crime data is in fact recorded by police on patrol, it reflects the perceptions and practices of police.

When police perceptions and practices are prejudicial towards certain groups of people, areas in which those groups are concentrated will receive greater police attention, and individual members of such groups living within those areas will be more likely to be stopped, searched, and ultimately criminalized by police on patrol. As a result, the presence of criminality in these locations is overstated in the data, leading algorithms to 'predict' that future criminality will be concentrated in those places. This, in turn, reinforces the view that such places need to be policed even more intensely, thus creating a pernicious 'feedback loop' (Lum and Isaac 2016; Ensign et al. 2018) leading to an upwards 'ratchet' (Harcourt 2007) of police attention towards the people who live in the locations flagged by the programme.

The feedback loop ensures that police continue to observe more criminality in the areas in which they patrol, which is likely to confirm and cement the prejudices with which they started out.[5] When the success of predictive policing is measured in crime detection and arrest rates by police, it creates incentives for officers to police individuals in hotspots more aggressively and to create opportunities for active police intervention, raising the risk of harassment and 'over-policing' (Brayne 2017; Richardson et al. 2019). The vicious circle continues to expand beyond the field of criminal justice: the disproportionate criminalization of people from certain areas reinforces popular prejudices about their propensity for criminality, prejudices which then seep into many other spheres of life (Greenberg 2010: 72).

This account of how place-based predictive policing exacerbates the criminalization of certain kinds of people by police and perpetuates popular prejudice against them involves at least three important, but well-founded assumptions. The first, and least controversial, assumption of this line of criticism is that systematic racist prejudices and discriminatory practices are a well-established feature of policing, and that they reflect more widespread popular prejudices. The factual basis for this claim has been so rigorously documented in countries such as the United States and the United Kingdom that it is no longer a subject of reasonable debate (Hehman et al. 2017; Richardson et al. 2019).

The second, related assumption is that the data feeding the predictive policing system cannot easily be cleansed of biases so that it no longer supports discriminatory or disproportionate policing. This assumption is supported by current efforts to improve upon the models used by predictive policing developers. For example, recent studies have shown that efforts by some developers of predictive policing systems to cleanse data of bias are unsuccessful. In particular, the decision by PredPol and others[6] to exclude from the data crimes observed or recorded by police and to include only crimes reported by citizens has been scrutinized and shown to fail to render predicted crime rates more convergent with actual figures (Lum and Isaac 2016; Ensign et al. 2018). These experimental studies suggest that the mere presence of police in an area increases the rate of reported crime in that area even as crime rates across areas remain constant, so using those statistics for predictive policing still generates a feedback loop. Even the designers of predictive policing systems acknowledge that police prejudices continue to shape the data used far more persistently than they initially supposed, and that more work needs to be done to address this problem (Brantingham 2018).

The third, and most controversial crucial assumption in this line of criticism of predictive policing is that being policed *at all* is dangerous and harmful to certain communities and individuals and therefore a bad thing, all things considered. This is certainly the view of many who find themselves subject to predictive policing, especially in the United States (Moravec 2019). In that country, public revelations about police racism, violence, and corruption have contributed to a growing acknowledgement that, for certain groups, being policed imposes significant risks of violence, brutality, and criminalization (Fryer 2016; Brayne 2017; Morrow et al. 2017). For them, more policing does not just mean a greater amount of the same kind of thing other groups get; it means a greater amount of something qualitatively different, involving real threats to personal safety and human and civil rights. This unhappy conclusion reveals just how far the reality of policing in a liberal democracy can stray from its justifying purpose, namely, to protect the safety and rights of all and to be a source of refuge for the vulnerable (Ripstein 2017; Monaghan 2017).

There is a promising emerging body of work that develops technological fixes to reduce or mitigate the impact of the feedback loop for place-based predictive policing. Ensign et al. (2018) propose a solution based on a method for reweighting the sample. As they put it, 'as more police are sent, smaller weights are assigned to discovered incidents' (Ensign et al. 2018: 7). The solution is analogous to the way that survey samples are weighted so as to ensure a representative sample of a population. If this solution is workable, then the issue is not so much that feedback loops cannot ever be avoided, but that they have not been attended to sufficiently by the creators or clients of the first wave of predictive policing packages; that is, we are dealing with issues of accountability and avoidable unfairness. However, Ensign et al. themselves urge caution in applying their theoretical model in practice, for it suggests that the predictions yielded by a system in which feedback is corrected for remain of poor accuracy.

The same mechanisms that create intransigent feedback loops and ratchets in place-based predictive systems are also present in person-based systems, and there appear to be greater challenges in this area. Predictions about people—typically, low-tech approaches to risk assessment—involve assigning risk scores or rankings to individuals on the basis of traits thought to indicate propensity to certain kinds of criminality or vulnerability to certain kinds of crime.[7] The scores or rankings are then used by police as a basis on which to conduct various kinds of interventions, from sending letters to people, to knocking on their door, or stopping-and-searching them and their vehicle each time they are encountered in a patrol. In some cases, scores are shared with other agencies, such as housing and social services, which then use them as a basis for their own decision-making about, for example, whether to grant housing or whether to monitor their parenting (Bridges 2015; Amnesty International 2018).

Let us set aside for a moment the many well-founded objections to person-based predictive systems, which relate to the lack of an empirical basis for the specification of risk indicators and scores, the lack of demonstrated effectiveness, and lack of efficiency of any of these systems (Starr 2015; Saunders et al. 2016); the neglect to include 'protective factors' as counter-indicators of lowered risk (Slobogin 2018: 593); and the failure of some systems to include a mechanism for individuals to ever have their names removed from the list (Amnesty International 2018). A further problem with these systems remains: contact with police is always included as a factor that increases the risk score. The same ratcheting and over-policing that occurs with locations also occurs on an individual level—the more contact with police you have, the higher your risk score, the more contact with police is justified by the system, and so on.

The moral risks of person-based predictive policing include the violation of individual rights to privacy—in the sense of specific instances of unwarranted surveillance and searches. Reasonable suspicion is manufactured by the system's tendency to accumulate information on a person until it generates sufficient basis to justify a stop (Ferguson 2018: 403). But it can also violate the right to privacy as a right to 'be able to get on with their lives without explaining themselves to political authorities, if they are not evidently a threat to the rights and liberties of others' (Lever 2016; see also Slobogin 2018: 594; Greenberg 2010: 75; Kennedy 1997). When risk scores or rankings are shared with partner agencies, they have been used as a basis to justify denial of benefits or other social goods to the individuals concerned (Bridges 2015).

As with the objections to place-based systems of prediction, the moral criticism—the disproportionate policing of ethnic minorities and the poor—is not new. Police have long been accused of harassing those who find themselves amongst the list of 'usual suspects'. The effect here is exacerbated by the way that the ratchet is encoded into the system.

Respect for autonomy

Individualized suspicion and pre-emption

We have examined some of the serious and immediate issues that arise in existing and near-future predictive policing practice: problems of bias. Here, we consider further possible ethical issues with the practice, focusing in particular on the charge that it may undermine people's autonomy, or disrespect them, or disrespect people's autonomy. For instance, it is sometimes urged that preventative police and criminal justice activity is problematic because it removes a 'window of moral opportunity', a chance to choose either to break the law or not to break it (Lomell 2012; Rademacher 2020).

Consider the following example, from Ferguson (2012: 309):

> a police officer sees a man loitering on a corner with a large duffle bag looking at a house. Under these limited facts, a stop based on reasonable suspicion would be difficult to justify. There is nothing objectively criminal about waiting with a bag ... Yet, imagine in a second hypothetical case a ... predictive policing algorithm predicts that there is a statistical likelihood of another burglary on that block at this time. Police are told to be on the lookout for burglars (and are given an appropriate profile). In this second case, a stop based on reasonable suspicion would likely be upheld.

In this example, the information provided by the predictive mechanism works in tandem with the officer's observations in order to justify a search. The man does nothing different in the two cases. The difference is that in the second, the officer has received a 'tip' from the computer. Note that the background data that goes into the production of this tip can be wide-ranging. It might include not only information about previous crimes and locations; it can include unexpected factors such as the moon-phase or the wind speed.[8] Now imagine a third case, in which the officer's suspicions are present but minimal, while the predictive mechanism is more certain. The man is not loitering but is only passing, the duffel bag is absent, the officer has merely an instinctive sense that something is up, and the report is received from the software that there is a very high chance of a crime being committed. Are we comfortable with the search being carried out in these circumstances?

Drawing on US jurisprudence, we might use the idea of individualized suspicion to explain the principles at work in these cases. As Simmons (2016: 984–985) puts it, 'the police officer must observe conduct that gives her some reason to believe that the suspect is currently engaging in criminal activity ... the reasonable suspicion or probable cause cannot be based only on who the person is; it must also be based on what the person does'; that is, the hotspot or the watchlist might serve legitimately in a corroboratory role, but never as sole evidence for coercive police action such as searches. Thus, Loewy (2011: 1518) considers a case in which 'in a particular city block of Main Street, between Fourth and Main and Fifth and Main, it could be established demographically that nine out of every ten men on the street between 6 p.m. and 10 p.m. are carrying drugs'. Are arrests of all these men thereby immediately justified? No, says Loewy, since an arrest requires some 'specific' fact about its subject in order to be justified.

Now, it is understandable—indeed, fundamental—that our legal structures seek to place some limits on police activity and that legal theorists are wary of ways in which such limits might be subverted. It remains for us to consider why the existing limits track what matters. Why do many seek some specific fact about the target, rather than a general prediction, in order to justify police interference? Is the individualized suspicion requirement merely a pragmatic limit, or is there more to it than that?

It appears that the individualized suspicion requirement may be explained in part by a more fundamental appeal to autonomy or respect. Berman (2020: 20) makes the connection directly, in arguing, '[d]emanding that any intrusion into our privacy is premised on things we actually have done—as opposed to who we are or with whom we associate—reflects an appreciation of our need to develop a unique sense of self, while reliance on generalizations engenders conformity, rather than individual flourishing'. It is argued that responding only to group membership or other generalizations about individuals thereby fails to respect their freedom, including their ability to act rightly even when they are expected to act wrongly.

Similar appeals to respect for people's autonomy appear in cognate areas of applied philosophy. Consider an argument drawn from the philosophical debate about pre-punishment. Pre-punishment is punishment of an individual in advance of the commission of a crime. Smilansky (1994) argues that pre-punishment is wrong because it fails to respect its subjects. Pre-punishment undermines the freedom to do wrong. As he puts it, before the crime is carried out, 'there is categorically still time, a "window of moral opportunity" for the would-be offender. This moral opportunity needs to be acknowledged.' Pre-punishment fails to respect people's ability to choose to act rightly or wrongly. His claim is that people are respected by being given an opportunity not to carry out a wrong that they are expected to carry out. Respect involves a presumption of humanity, goodness, or good will. By treating someone as a wrongdoer before they have done wrong or even intended to do wrong—even if there is evidence to suggest that they may commit a wrong—is to treat them as presumptively criminal, as someone who should be controlled, rather than as one of us.

There are parallels between the issues in pre-punishment and pre-policing. If Smilansky's respect for a 'window of moral opportunity' applies to punishment, it also appears to apply to policing. If it is disrespectful to punish before a crime is committed, on the grounds that to do so presumes that the offender will not change their mind, then coercive policing well in advance of criminal activity is similarly disrespectful. Some might take the view that punishment expresses censure while preventive policing activity does not, and it is the censure that is disrespectful when the state inappropriately presumes criminality before a person has acted criminally. In this case, the availability of windows of moral opportunity is of importance for the purposes of respecting those who are to be punished, but irrelevant for the purposes of respecting those who are to be merely prevented from carrying out possible future crimes. Such a view chimes with mainstream ideas about the non-judgemental role of police (but c.f. Nathan 2016), but also has the implication that police cannot express disrespect in acting pre-emptively, which seems difficult to uphold. Moreover, others find disrespect directly in predictive policing. For example, Daskal (2014: 364) argues: 'In imposing restraints in response to perceived future threats, the state conveys its assessment that the targets are insufficiently trustworthy—and therefore less deserving—than the vast majority of the populace not subject to such restraints on their activities.' This particular point, it should be noted, involves an expression of disrespect that is dependent upon differential treatment between groups.

The view we have been exploring holds that (a) serious intrusions by the police should be based upon some individualized suspicion rather than wholly probabilistic suspicion; that (b) police should respect citizens, and especially, respect their autonomy; and (c) that (b) explains (a). There are some reasons to doubt this third, explanatory claim; that is, there are some reasons to doubt that the idea of respect successfully captures what, if anything, is wrong or of disvalue in pre-policing.

First, the individualized suspicion requirement need not involve facts about the target that involve the target acting unlawfully, or even wrongfully, and they may be highly innocuous. For example, the target may be the only person travelling without a return ticket or waiting in a particular area. This may yield, in combination with intelligence revealed by a computer, grounds for a search. On Berman's (2020: 38) view, the use of police predictive analytics 'disregard[s] one of the crucial elements of autonomy—free will ... [A]t any point, any individual can make choices that defy predictions about them.' But a requirement that the individualized suspicion by itself stand as evidence of wrongdoing is stronger than the existing jurisprudence, and indeed would threaten to rule out much police activity.

Second, it is important to distinguish the level and kind of enforcement from the use of predictive analytics. It is possible to have non-individualized suspicion that is autonomy-respecting, with low levels of enforcement. And it is possible to have an individualized suspicion requirement that is not autonomy-respecting, with high levels of enforcement. The *Minority Report* sci-fi nightmare involves two different factors: the idea of 'pre-crime'—in which people can be interfered with by the police upon a sign that they will commit a crime—and the complete and ruthless enforcement of the criminal law. It has long been argued that full enforcement of the criminal law is undesirable and not a part of its design (Goldstein 1960). Those concerned with respect for autonomy in algorithmic policing must spell out this concern in a way that would not be addressed simply by *less* policing. A straightforward concern that people should have an opportunity to act wrongly is addressed through less strict enforcement.

Finally, it is not obvious that treating a person as though they will not act wrongly, and discounting the probability one assigns to them acting wrongly, is a way of respecting them. For one thing, New (1995) argues that we may be seen as respecting people more by supposing that they will follow through on their stated intentions, than we would were we to suppose that they would suffer weakness of will, even if it is the kind of weakness of will that involves adhering to what one ought to do in favour of what one has committed to do. Moreover, predictive policing measures will often be better construed not as expressions of the view that some people will commit a crime, but that they might do so. This distinction matters.

Consider the way the point is put in Tadros (2014: 146):

> suppose that a person has a capacity to resist doing y. This does not imply that this person will exercise his or her capacity to resist doing y. That depends on the judgements that he or she makes about y. Hence, to act on the prediction that a person might do y does not imply that he or she could not refrain from doing y.

For example, given high rates of recidivism, it might be recommended that those recently released from incarceration are placed under greater scrutiny; suppose such scrutiny is applied in response to the higher statistical probability, other things being equal, that the target will commit a crime. It is not at all clear that accurately responding to the probability that a person will commit a crime expresses disrespect of the kind that treats them as though they lack the ability not to commit it.

In whatever way they are given substance, consider now the several ways to understand the possible force of these concerns about respecting and promoting autonomy. One possibility is that denying windows of moral opportunity is a wrong that is an absolute, or extremely difficult to override. This view might be inspired by considering the pre-punishment case: as an aspect of our strong aversion to punishing the innocent, we have a strong aversion to punishing those who have not committed crimes, even if we are certain that they will commit a crime. Extending such a position to policing, however, is extreme. Clearly, when police have strong evidence that a person is going to cause significant harms in a criminal way, and they can only stop his actions through coercive measures, it would be inappropriate for the police to argue that they should not intervene on the grounds that the target should be provided the respect that comes with an opportunity to act morally in an autonomous manner.

A better reading of the need for a window of moral opportunity is that it is pro tanto valuable. On this view, the availability of the option to act rightly is a value that might be outweighed by others, such as the harm of criminal acts. While an improvement, an idea that this interpretation does not incorporate is that certain factors can cancel out the value of the window of moral opportunity altogether; that is, some will hold that the availability of the window is prima facie valuable—it is presumptively valuable—but its value is not present if there is a defeater. Such defeaters will include actions on the part of the person affected by police activity that make them liable to police coercion. Thus, one might take the view that those who engage in criminal acts, or inchoate preparatory criminal acts, or even pre-inchoate preparations for criminal acts, can (depending on other relevant factors, such as the gravity of the crime) waive their right to have an opportunity to do right. And in contrast, on this view, those who are shown by a computer programme to be very likely to commit a crime but have not engaged even in pre-inchoate preparations retain the right to show that they will act well.[9]

Uncertainty

There are two ethical vectors at work in predictive policing that it is worth taking care to separate. The first is pre-emption; the second is uncertainty. The pre-emption issue is that predictive policing involves acting in advance of activity on the part of those targeted that might make them liable to police interference. The uncertainty issue arises because predictive policing involves predicting the future, and so it will tend to involve acting without full confidence in the future facts that would ground policing action. Although they are distinct vectors, it is easy to conflate them: pre-emption tends to involve acting upon uncertainty, and when police are acting with uncertainty, they tend also to be acting in ways that are responsive to possible future events. Nonetheless, pre-emption and uncertainty are separable. One can act on uncertainty without pre-empting, as when police carry out a search on the basis of imperfect information that the target of the search is carrying evidence of a recently committed crime. And one can act pre-emptively while acting upon a high degree of certainty, as when police have strong evidence that a person is going to engage in a terrorist act.[10]

We have focused on the issue of pre-emption. Let us consider uncertainty. Criminal justice systems are shot through with the problem of uncertainty. The most prominent expression of uncertainty is the requirement that convictions at trial are made on a standard of belief 'beyond reasonable doubt' in the case against the defendant. Police activity, including severely coercive police activity, is not normally considered to be punitive, but it still often faces epistemic standards. Various standards for searches are, or have been, in place, such as the requirement that an officer has 'reasonable grounds for suspicion' that a person is carrying a proscribed item. There are different ways of reading the rationale for such limits: as efficiency constraints, or as restrictions upon police discretion in a context in which such discretion has been widely misused. Many will add a third rationale: that the epistemic grounds for justified coercive police action goes beyond a mere consequentialist calculation.

To take an extreme case: suppose that a predictive algorithm has the result that police could efficiently prevent crime by subjecting to searches each of a large group of individuals who, with a very low degree of confidence, are each expected to commit crimes. Suppose that carrying out these searches is relatively costless to the police. And suppose that the practice is expected to yield overall benefits, even taking into consideration possible chilling effects. Many will feel that imposing a high degree of intrusion or coercion upon those against whom there is little evidence of wrongdoing to be unacceptable, and such qualms will not be eradicated by assurances that crime will be efficiently reduced. It will be demanded, at the very least, that strongly coercive or intrusive police activity should only take place when there is evidence that each particular case of intrusion or coercion is expected to be fruitful, in security terms. Put broadly, there are reasons to make proportionality assessments in a case-by-case way, rather than merely as assessments of policies as a whole, and those assessments should include the evidence with regard to specific individuals.

Preventing people from committing wrongs, then, may be of value, but there are other values too. Amongst these are the value of the police not interfering with people, especially those who have not made themselves liable to interference. That value may be cashed out as a concern with autonomy or freedom. We might, indeed, put the thought in the following way: freedom to act is prima facie right; some will make themselves liable to police coercion through their own actions, and in such cases the right is cancelled; in other cases, the right remains in place, but other values, such as the avoidance of harm, justifiably infringe on the right. A possible danger with predictive policing, then, is that it pays insufficient due to the epistemic requirements that arise from this schema. Such requirements will be more stringent when policing involves imposing setbacks on those against whom there is not yet evidence of intentions to carry out wrongs. The concern, then, is the liberal one that we mentioned earlier: that institutional and technological implementation of predictive policing can tend towards providing policing that does not carry appropriate limits.

CONCLUSION

We have explored two central moral dangers within, if not knockdown objections to, the practice of predictive policing. First, ratcheting effects may enhance existing bias, and create their own new kinds of bias. Second, predictive policing may deploy intrusive and coercive police measures in ways that are detached from guiding principles concerning individualized suspicion and respect for autonomy. These risks will not inevitably mani-fest themselves. Nonetheless, we conclude by suggesting that there are political reasons to take extra caution against them. The complex technical design involved in predictive policing lends a veneer of scientific objectivity to policies that—we have argued—can easily enact injustices. The harms and wrongs of predictive policing may be masked by the promise of a scientific approach that provides more objective and empirically sound methods for distributing police resources than their unsystematic, discretionary predecessors (Ferguson 2018: 1114; Richardson et al. 2019: 6; Gitelman 2013: 1–9; Lum and Isaac 2016). Furthermore, the opaque nature of the proprietary functioning of existing predictive policing systems can only serve to inhibit accountability. One might hope for systems that put the moral dangers of predictive policing in the open and pro-vide transparent ways for showing how far they are addressed.

NOTES

1. This formulation is similar to that offered by Greenberg (2010: 67) but focuses on data ana-lysis rather than 'scientific' methods.
2. Scientific approaches employed in place-based predictive policing include forensic psych-ology, theories of environmental crime and human ecology (see the substantial body of work by Shane Johnson and collaborators), seismological predictions of aftershocks, and mathematics (see the range of papers published by George Mohler, P.J. Brantingham, and other academics whose work is behind the PredPol tool).

3. For further discussion of this issue, see Hildebrandt (2015); Hildebrandt and O'Hara (2020).
4. Perhaps surprisingly, there is less overlap in the literature with the much more developed philosophical literature on the ethics of profiling and actuarial approaches to preventive detention, sentencing, parole, and probation (Keijser et al. 2019).
5. This process mirrors the way implicit bias introduces observational biases into perception (I see what I am 'primed' to see by my implicit biases) and thus lends a circular structure into their belief formation, as described by Siegel (2020).
6. See statements by PredPol (PredPol 2019) and the Igarape Institute (Aguirre et al. 2019).
7. Though risk assessment of this nature is also used to rank victims according to their perceived vulnerability to certain kinds of exploitation or abuse, including, for example, domestic violence.
8. As HunchLab does, which has been deployed in several US states.
9. Note also that it is possible to combine the pro tanto and prima facie accounts of the value of the window of moral opportunity by holding that the window is not always valuable, and when it is, its value may be outweighed by others. See Noggle (2018) for a recent application of this distinction.
10. Of course, preparatory offences are offences. Arrests of those preparing to commit terrorist acts are, in that sense, not pre-emptive. A cleaner example will involve a case in which a person has not committed an act that is justifiably criminalized. See below for further discussion.

References

Aguirre, Kathrine, Badran, Emile, and Muggah, Robert (2019), 'Future Crime: Assessing 21st Century Crime Prediction', Igarape Institute Report, https://igarape.org.br/wp-content/uploads/2019/07/2019-07-03-NE_33_Future_Crime-V2.pdf, accessed 8 October 2021.

Amnesty International (2018), *Trapped in the Matrix: Secrecy, Stigma, and Bias in the Met's Gangs Database*. (Amnesty International: United Kingdom Section).

Angwin, J., Larson, J., Mattu, S., and Kirchner, L. (2016), 'Machine Bias: There's Software Used across the Country to Predict Future Criminals and It's Biased against Blacks', *ProPublica*, 23 May, https://www.propublica.org/article/machine-bias-risk-assessments-in-criminal-sentencing, accessed 8 October 2021.

Ayre, L., and Kraner, A., (2018), 'The Baked-In Bias of Algorithms', *Collaborative Librarianship* 10(2), Article 3, 76–78.

Benbouzid, B. (2019), 'To Predict and to Manage. Predictive Policing in the United States', *Big Data & Society* 6(1), 1–13.

Bennett Moses, Lyria, and Chan, Janet (2018), 'Algorithmic Prediction in Policing: Assumptions, Evaluation, and Accountability', *Policing and Society* 28(7), 806–822.

Berman, E. (2020), 'Individualized Suspicion in the Age of Big Data', *Iowa Law Review* 105. 463–504.

Bowling, B., and Phillips, C. (2007), 'Disproportionate and Discriminatory: Reviewing the Evidence on Police Stop and Search', *Modern Law Review* 70(6), 936–961.

Brantingham, J.P. (2018), 'The Logic of Data Bias and Its Impact on Place-Based Predictive Policing', *Ohio State Journal of Criminal Law* 15, 473, 485.

Brayne, S. (2017), 'Big Data Surveillance: The Case of Policing', *American Sociological Review* 82(5), 977–1008.

Bridges, L. (2015), 'The Gangs Matrix—Institutional Racism in Action', Institute for Race Relations, http://www.irr.org.uk/news/the-met-gangs-matrix-institutional-racism-in-action/, accessed 8 October 2021.

Daskal, J.C. (2014), 'Pre-Crime Restraints: The Explosion of Targeted, Noncustodial Prevention', *Cornell Law Review* 99, 327.

Ensign, D., Friedler, S., Neville, S., Scheidegger, C., and Venkatasubramanian, S. (2018), 'Runaway Feedback Loops in Predictive Policing', *Proceedings of Machine Learning Research* 81, 1.

Eubanks, V. (2018), 'The Allegheny Algorithm', in *Automating Inequality: How High-Tech Tools Profile, Police, and Punish the Poor* (Macmillan Publishing), ch. 4.

Ferguson, A. (2018), *The Rise of Big Data Policing: Surveillance, Race and the Future of Law Enforcement* (New York: University Press).

Ferguson, A.J. (2012), 'Predictive Policing and Reasonable Suspicion', *Emory Law Journal* 62(2), 260–325.

Fryer, R.G. (2016), 'An Empirical Analysis of Racial Differences in Police Use of Force', Working Paper No. 22399, The National Bureau of Economic Research, Cambridge, MA.

Gitelman, L. (2013), *'Raw Data' is an Oxymoron* (Cambridge: MIT Press).

Goldstein, J. (1960), 'Police Discretion Not to Invoke the Criminal Process: Low-Visibility Decisions in the Administration of Justice', *Yale Law Journal* 69(4), 543–594.

Greenberg, D. (2010), 'More Fictions about Predictions', *Criminal Justice Ethics* 27(2), 1–20.

Harcourt, B. (2007), *Against Prediction: Profiling, Policing, and Punishing in an Actuarial Age.* (Chicago, IL: University of Chicago Press).

Harris, D. (2003), *Profiles in Injustice: Why Racial Profiling Cannot Work* (New York: New Press).

Hehman, E., Flake, J.K., and Calanchini, J. (2017), 'Disproportionate Use of Lethal Force in Policing Is Associated with Regional Racial Biases of Residents', *Social Psychological and Personality Science* 9(4), 393–401.

Hildebrandt, M. (2015), *Smart Technologies and the End (s) of Law: Novel Entanglements of Law and Technology* (Cheltenham: Edward Elgar).

Hildebrandt, M., and O'Hara, K., eds (2020), *Life and the Law in the Era of Data-Driven Agency* (Cheltenham: Edward Elgar).

Jefferson, Brian Jordan (2018), 'Predictable Policing: Predictive Crime Mapping and Geographies of Policing and Race', *Annals of the American Association of Geographers* 108(1), 1–16.

Joh, Elizabeth. (2017), 'Feeding the Machine: Policing, Crime Data, and Algorithms', *William & Mary Bill of Rights Journal* 26, 287.

de Keijser, Jan W., Roberts, Julian V., and Ryber Jesperg, eds (2019), *Predictive Sentencing: Normative and Empirical Perspectives* (Oxford: Hart).

Kennedy, R. (1997), *Race, Crime and the Law* (New York. Pantheon).

Lever, A. (2004), 'What's Wrong with Racial Profiling? Another Look at the Problem', *Criminal Justice Ethics* 26(1), 1–16.

Lever, A. 2016. 'Race and Racial Profiling'. In Naomi Zack, ed., *Oxford Handbook of the Philosophy of Race* (Oxford University Press).

Lippert-Rasmussen (2006), 'Racial Profiling versus Community', *Journal of Applied Philosophy* 23(2), 191–205.

Loewy Arnold. H. (2011), 'Rethinking Search and Seizure in a Post-9/11 World', *Mississippi Law Journal* 80, 1507.

Lomell, H.M. (2012), 'Punishing the Uncommitted Crime: Prevention, Pre-Emption, Precaution and the Transformation of Criminal Law', in Bruce A. Arrigo and Heather Y. Bersot, eds, *Justice and Security in the 21st Century* (London: Routledge), 99–116.

Lum, K and Isaac, W. (2016), 'To Predict and Serve?', *Significance, Journal of the Royal Statistical Society* 13(5), 14–19.

Mayson, S. (2018), 'Bias In, Bias Out', *Yale Law Journal* 128, 2218.

Mill, J.S. (1998), *On Liberty and Other Essays* (New York: Oxford University Press).

Monaghan, J. (2017), 'The Special Moral Obligations of Law Enforcement', *Journal of Political Philosophy* 25(2), 218–237.

Moravec, E.,R. (2019), 'Do Algorithms Have a Place in Policing?', *The Atlantic*, 5 September, https://www.theatlantic.com/politics/archive/2019/09/do-algorithms-have-place-policing/596851/, accessed 8 October 2021.

Morrow, W.J., White, M.D., and Fradella, H.F. (2017), 'After the Stop: Exploring the Racial/Ethnic Disparities in Police Use of Force During Terry Stops', *Police Quarterly* 20(4), 367–396.

Nathan, C. (2016), 'Principles of Policing and Principles of Punishment', *Legal Theory* 22(3-4), 181–204.

New, C. (1995), 'Punishing Times: Reply to Smilansky', *Analysis* 55(1), 60–62.

Noggle, R. (2018), 'The Ethics of Manipulation', in Edward N. Zalta, ed., *The Stanford Encyclopedia of Philosophy* (*Summer 2018 Edition*), https://plato.stanford.edu/archives/sum2018/entries/ethics-manipulation/, accessed 8 October 2021.

Oswald, M., Grace, J., Urwin, S., and Barnes, G. (2018), 'Algorithmic Risk Assessment Policing Models: Lessons from the Durham HART Model and 'Experimental' Proportionality', *Information and Communications Technology Law* 27(2), 223–250.

PredPol (2019), 'Machine Learning and Policing', Redpol Predictive Policing Blog, 19 July, http://blog.predpol.com/machine-learning-and-policing, accessed 8 October 2021.

Rademacher, Timo (2020), 'Of New Technologies and Old Laws: Do We Need a Right to Violate the Law?', *European Journal for Security Research* 5(24), 1–20.

Richardson, Rashida, Schultz, Jason, and Crawford, Kate (2019), 'Dirty Data, Bad Predictions: How Civil Rights Violations Impact Police Data, Predictive Policing Systems, and Justice', *New York University Law Review* 94, 192.

Ripstein, Arthur (2017), 'Reclaiming Proportionality', *Journal of Applied Philosophy* 34(1), 1–18.

Risse, Matthias and Zeckhauser, Richard (2004), 'Racial Profiling', *Philosophy and Public Affairs* 32, 131–170.

Saunders, J., Hunt, P., and Hollywood, J.S. (2016), 'Predictions Put into Practice: A Quasi-Experimental Evaluation of Chicago's Predictive Policing Pilot', *Journal of Experimental Criminology*, 12.

Siegel, S. (2020), 'Bias and Perception', in Erin Beeghly and Alex Madva, eds, *An Introduction to Implicit Bias: Knowledge, Justice, and the Social Mind* (London: Routledge), 1–18.

Simmons, R. (2016), 'Quantifying Criminal Procedure: How to Unlock the Potential of Big Data in Our Criminal Justice System', *Michigan State Law Review*, 947.

Slobogin, Christopher (2018), 'Principles of Risk Assessment: Sentencing and Policing', *Ohio State Journal of Criminal Law* 15, 583–596.

Smilansky, S. (1994), 'The Time to Punish', *Analysis*, 54(1), 347–349.

Starr, S. (2015), 'The New Profiling: Why Punishing Based on Poverty and Identity Is Unconstitutional and Wrong', *Federal Sentencing Reporter* 27, 229–236.

Tadros, V. (2014), 'Controlling Risk', in A. Ashworth, L. Zedner, and P. Tomlin, eds, *Prevention and the Limits of the Criminal Law* (Oxford: Oxford University Press).

Zedner, L. (2007), 'Pre-Crime and Post-Criminology?', *Theoretical Criminology* 11(2), 261–281.

CHAPTER 23

··

(WHEN) IS ADBLOCKING
WRONG?

··

THOMAS DOUGLAS

MANY internet users employ adblocking software. This allows them to view the main content on a webpage without also being served the advertisements that would normally accompany that content. Adblocking software has been available for many years, but there has been an upswing in use since 2013 (Crichton 2015: 90), and adblocking has been a topic of major concern for online publishers since 2015 (PageFair and Blockthrough 2020), the year in which Apple made adblocking possible on the mobile version of its Safari browser. Almost all mobile browsers now support adblocking, and as of 2020 it was estimated that 527 million people worldwide were using mobile browsers that block ads by default. On desktop, around 236 million people worldwide were blocking ads (PageFair and Blockthrough 2020).

Adblocking has been controversial (Arment 2015b; Barton 2016; Bilton 2015; Douglas 2015; Haddadi et al. 2016; Lawrence 2018; Orlowski 2016; Piltch 2015; Williams 2015; Zambrano and Pickard 2018). On the one hand, it allows internet users (henceforth, 'consumers') to browse the web more quickly, while using less data and being subjected to fewer intrusive advertisements. Since adblockers can block malware-containing advertisements ('malvertisements'), which can collect personal data if clicked, and since adblockers typically also block *trackers* (elements on webpages, and contained in most web ads (Arment et al. 2015), that collect the data of those accessing the page), their use also allows for more private and secure browsing (Butler 2016). On the other hand, since the producers and publishers of web-based content (henceforth, 'creators') are often paid by advertisers on a per view or per click basis, adblocking has the potential to substantially reduce their revenue and thus, potentially, to reduce the amount of valuable content that is created.

Many arguments for the permissibility of adblocking draw attention to its possible benefits or play down its costs.[1] For example, some defend adblocking as a way of pushing the internet towards a business model that is more respectful of consumers while still being sustainable for creators (Manjoo 2015; Williams 2015). Some suggest that it may even result in a model that is, in the long run, *more* financially rewarding for creators: by rendering the 'free', ad-supported provision of content uneconomic, adblocking may push creators, and thus ultimately consumers, towards models in which consumers pay creators to access their content (Orlowski 2016). Some suggest that the short-term financial costs of adblocking for creators are, in any case, likely to be small, since those who employ adblockers are likely to be individuals who would otherwise have ignored most advertisements (Lawrence 2018), or even refrained from visiting the sites that serve them (Ingram 2015b).

This chapter focuses on the other side of the debate: arguments against adblocking. Some such arguments likewise focus on costs and benefits, seeking to show that the costs predominate.[2] However, I will not engage such arguments. Indeed, I will assume that they fail; I will grant, to the proponents of adblocking, that the practice has benefits that exceed its costs. I will instead consider whether there might be (what I will call) a *deontological* objection to adblocking. Even if adblocking is net beneficial, it might *wrong* someone or, as I will sometimes write, be *wrongful*.[3] And, in the absence of a sufficient justification, this will make it *wrong* or *impermissible*, all things considered. I take it that a practice wrongs someone, and is thus wrongful, when a person has a legitimate moral complaint against the practice or—as I take to be equivalent—when the practice fails to fulfil some *pro tanto* duty owed to that person. Perhaps, for instance, it infringes the rights of the creators whose advertisements are blocked, or of other consumers who do not employ adblocking software. Or perhaps it treats those creators or other consumers *unfairly*.[4]

In what follows, I will consider three deontological objections to adblocking: the objection from property, the objection from complicity, and the objection from free-riding. I will argue that, though some of these objections plausibly establish the moral impermissibility of some instances of adblocking, they do not, even collectively, establish a blanket moral prohibition on adblocking, as it is currently done.

My conclusion—that prevailing forms of adblocking are sometimes but not always impermissible—might seem rather unsurprising. More interesting, I hope, is what my arguments imply regarding *when* adblocking is impermissible. I think the arguments I consider may establish the impermissibility of some widespread forms of adblocking. For example, I think the objection from property may establish that it is typically impermissible to use adblockers against websites whose creators (a) clearly demand that consumers either deactivate the adblocker or refrain from accessing the site; (b) credibly inform consumers of the nature of any advertisements and trackers that they serve; and (c) either (i) provide only non-essential services; (ii) offer a low-cost ad-free option; or (iii) serve only unobtrusive and privacy-respecting advertisements.

Before proceeding to consider the three objections to adblocking, I need to make two qualifications.

First, a point about the relationship between rights infringements and wrongs. I take it that whenever A infringes B's rights, A wrongs B. B's having a right, held against A, entails that A has a *pro tanto* duty that is owed to (or, as it is sometimes put, 'directed towards') B. When A infringes B's right, A fails to fulfil this duty. So, rights infringements involve failures to fulfil directed *pro tanto* duties—that is to say, they involve wrongs. I do not insist, however, that all wrongs involve rights infringements. Infringing someone's rights is one way of wronging that person, and I am sympathetic to the view that it is the only way. This is because I am sympathetic to weak accounts of rights on which to have a right is nothing more than to be the object of a directed *pro tanto* duty. But on many accounts of rights, having a right entails something more. Perhaps it entails that the directed duty is *enforceable*, is a *trump*, or is a *matter of justice*.[5] These stronger accounts of rights leave space for non-rights-infringing wrongs—wrongs that consist in infringing a directed *pro tanto* duty that is not enforceable, is not a trump, or is not a matter of justice. Some of the complicity-based and fairness-based wrongs that I discuss in the sections on 'The objection from property' and 'The objection from complicity' below are, I think, plausible examples of such wrongs. Since I want to remain neutral between weak and strong accounts of rights, I will present the objections that I consider as asserting rights infringements only when the wrongs that they assert *uncontroversially* involve rights infringements—that is, they involve rights infringements even on strong accounts of rights.

Second, a point about the relationship between wrongs and moral impermissibility. I assume that a wrongful practice is presumptively impermissible, all things considered, but I do not claim that it is necessarily impermissible; some wrongs can be justified. Indeed, on most accounts of rights, even rights-infringing wrongs can be justified.

Third, a point about *whose* actions I will be morally appraising. I will focus on adblocking consumers as the potential wrongdoers and will consider the actions of others—such as creators of web content and those who provide adblocking software— only insofar as they are relevant to the moral appraisal of consumers' actions. This focus should not be taken to imply that there are no interesting moral questions to ask about the actions of other parties in this domain; indeed, as will become clear later on, I think that both the creators of web content and the providers of adblocking software do sometimes act wrongfully. Nor should it be taken to imply that any obligations to reform adblocking practices fall wholly or primarily on consumers. Rather, I focus on consumer actions in the hope that this will allow me to contribute most fruitfully to the existing debate, which has addressed itself primarily to consumers and has focused on the moral permissibility of their actions.

With these clarifications in hand, let us turn to the main business of the chapter: the assessment of three deontological objections to adblocking.

The objection from property

An initial deontological objection to adblocking—the objection from property— holds that it infringes a property right held by the creator (Piltch 2015; Primack 2015; Rothenberg 2015). The objection begins with the thought that creators have property rights over the content that they place online. This makes it impermissible for others to access that content without the creator's consent. Of course, in placing content on the internet, creators implicitly consent to the information being accessed. But they also impose a condition on how that property may be accessed by others: they (perhaps implicitly) say to the consumer, 'You may view my content, but only if you also allow me to serve advertisements.' In accessing the website without allowing advertisements to be served, adblocking consumers access the content without fulfilling this condition. They thus access the content without the creator's consent, and thereby infringe the creator's property right.

The proponent of this objection may claim that adblocking is analogous to piracy. Suppose a record label makes an album available for purchase via an online store such as iTunes, Amazon, or Google Play. And suppose someone (a 'pirate') then uses software to download and play this music without paying. It is plausible that, in doing this, the pirate infringes the property rights of the record label over this music. The label has imposed a condition on accessing this property—namely, that it must be purchased first—and the pirate accesses the property without meeting this condition.

How might the defender of adblocking respond to this objection?

Strategy 1: no right infringed

An initial strategy would be to deny that the adblocking consumer infringes any property right held by the creator.

One way to deny this would be to deny that the creator enjoys a property right of the sort that the objection requires. It might be held, for example, that in placing content online, the creator waives any right to exclude people from accessing it; placing content online is like putting a notice on a public noticeboard. Once the content is online, the creator has no right to restrict who has access to it.[6]

This line of argument is, however, not promising. It seems clear that creators do have the right to erect paywalls around content that is placed online. This makes it difficult to see how they could lack the right to impose a 'no adblocking' condition.

There is, though, a more promising response to the objection from property. We could question the suggestion that creators impose a 'no adblocking' condition on consumers who wish to access their content. We could do this by questioning whether creators *intend to* impose such a condition, or by questioning whether they *successfully communicate* it to consumers.

Consider first the creator's intention. In the piracy case, it is typically clear to all concerned that the creator intends to impose a payment condition on consumers. In the adblocking case, however, this is not always clear. Indeed, in some cases it seems clear that the creator does *not* intend to impose such a condition. Consider the case of the well-known podcaster and founder of Tumblr and Instapaper, Marco Arment. Arment runs a blog that serves ads (Arment 2015b), but also himself created an adblocker for iPhones and iPads (Arment 2015a),[7] has defended adblocking (Arment 2015c), and has stated that he blocks ads himself (Arment et al. 2015). It thus seems very doubtful that Arment intends to impose an adblocking condition on those who read his blog.

Some argue that there is nothing exceptional about this case—that creators *typically* do not intend to impose a 'no adblocking' condition. Alexander Zambrano and Caleb Pickard suggest that we can infer this from the fact that most creators do not take the required steps to prevent adblocking consumers from accessing their content (2018). (Since the advent of so-called 'anti-adblocking' technology, such steps have been available (Butler 2016).)

Zambrano and Pickard's argument is, I think, too swift. Consider, by analogy, a large department store that employs no security guards to prevent shoplifting. We would not say that this implies the absence of an intention to impose a payment requirement on customers. Hiring security guards comes at a cost. It may be that the store managers intend to impose a payment requirement and decline to employ security guards only because this would be too expensive, antagonize too many customers, or pose too great a risk of legal liability for unlawful forms of enforcement. Similarly, use of anti-adblocking strategies comes at a cost to creators. For example, it requires an upfront confrontation with the consumer that can provoke a significant backlash (Fisher 2010). Many creators may eschew anti-adblocking measures only because this seems the lesser of two evils, or the best way to maximize their revenue, not because they intend to allow adblocking.

I am thus less convinced than Zambrano and Pickard that creators typically intend to allow adblocking. Nevertheless, it is surely the case that *some* significant number of creators, like Marco Arment, indeed intend to allow it. On the other hand, there are clearly some who intend to impose a 'no adblocking' condition—most obviously, those who both demand that consumers deactivate their adblockers and employ anti-adblocking measures against those who do not.

A second basis for denying that adblocking infringes the creator's property rights would hold that, even when producers do intend to impose a 'no adblocking' condition, they do not adequately communicate this to consumers, so consumers are not required to comply with it (Arment 2015c). Some producers do explicitly ask consumers to 'whitelist' their site (excluding it from adblocking). However, it is not always clear whether this is a demand or merely a request—that is to say, it is not always clear that creators are going so far as to deny permission to access their content to those who refuse to whitelist the site. Moreover, many websites neither request nor demand whitelisting. In these cases, the 'no adblocking' condition might be thought to be implicitly communicated by the mere serving of ads, but there is certainly scope to question this (Zambrano and Pickard 2018); we do not generally take the serving of ads to imply a requirement on consumers to read, let alone click on, advertisements, so why take it to imply a requirement to allow them to load (Arment 2015c)?

Each of these two responses succeeds, I think, in establishing that there are *some cases* in which consumers can use adblockers without infringing the property rights of creators. However, they do not, even together, fully undermine the objection from property. When a creator makes it clear to consumers that consumers may only access their content if they also allow the creator to serve ads, adblocking consumers will, I think, infringe that creator's rights.

Strategy 2: justified rights infringement

There is, however, another strategy open to defenders of adblocking. They may hold that, even when adblocking infringes the creator's property rights, it may still be permissible, all things considered. It may be a justified rights infringement.

Why might it be justified? Perhaps because blocking the creator's ads is the morally best means open to the consumer for preventing herself from being wronged, either by that particular creator, or by creators more generally.[8] Call this the 'self-defence' justification.

The self-defence justification presupposes that ad-serving creators sometimes wrong consumers. How might they do this? Perhaps by imposing over-burdensome or exploitative conditions on accessing their intellectual property. There are limits on the conditions that property owners can rightfully place on accessing their property. Suppose you need to use my phone to call the emergency services in order to save your own life. And suppose I allow you to use my phone, but only on the condition that you give me the gold watch you are wearing. I plausibly wrong you by imposing this condition.

Perhaps we can say something similar about the producers of ad-serving web content. Some web services, such as Google and Facebook, have arguably become so important to navigating modern society that denying a person access to these services can be expected to have serious costs for that person. If this is correct, then we might think that Google and Facebook wrong consumers if they impose burdensome conditions on accessing their services. And perhaps it could be argued that imposing a condition that consumers expose themselves to highly distracting ads or intrusive trackers is too burdensome. If so, adblocking could be conceived of as a defence against being wronged oneself.

This argument will not apply in the case of creators who provide non-essential services, however. In general, when the creators of luxury goods impose extremely burdensome conditions on accessing goods, we do not think that it becomes permissible for consumers to access the goods without fulfilling the conditions. Rather, we think that the consumers should simply forego the goods. I am not permitted to steal a yacht because the seller asks a price well beyond my means.[9] The argument will also not apply in the case of creators who offer, for a reasonable price, a paid ad-free option, since consumers will then have a non-burdensome means of avoiding the advertisements.

Nevertheless, there may be a version of the self-defence justification that can be run even in the case of websites providing non-essential services or offering a reasonably priced ad-free option. This is because there is another way in which ad-serving creators can wrong consumers: by exposing consumers to burdens or risks without obtaining their valid consent in advance.

Suppose that many creators providing non-essential services are serving intrusive ads. These ads incorporate trackers which collect sensitive personal information, such as the consumer's location and web history. Suppose, moreover, that the intrusive nature of these ads is not made clear to consumers. These creators invade consumers' privacy without the consumers' consent, and thereby plausibly wrong the consumers. Perhaps the only reasonable way to prevent these wrongful privacy invasions is to deploy an adblocker. Since consumers will not always know in advance which creators are wrongfully invading their privacy, consumers employing adblockers will inevitably also block ads served by other creators who are not wronging them. But adblocking might still be justified if it prevents the consumer from being subjected to sufficiently serious or numerous wrongs by privacy-invading creators.

A problem with this line of argument, if it is meant to justify universal adblocking, is that it is often possible—and not especially difficult—to *selectively* adblock websites. As alluded to above, many widely used adblockers allow for the consumer to specify a 'whitelist' (a list of sites for which the adblocker will be deactivated). And though in many cases it will be difficult for a consumer to know in advance of visiting a site whether the site employs wrongful forms of advertising or tracking, in cases in which a website presents consumers with a clear and credible[10] statement of its practices, on the basis of which it is clear that the creator does not wrong the consumer, it is difficult to see how the self-defence justification for adblocking could succeed. (Consumers also have the option of 'outsourcing' whitelisting by employing adblocking software that by default whitelists advertisements deemed to be 'acceptable'.[11])

According to the self-defence justification, consumers are justified in infringing the property rights of creators to defend themselves against being wronged by those creators or others. An alternative justification for property-rights-infringing forms of adblocking is suggested by the analogy I drew above between adblocking and online piracy.

Online piracy is sometimes thought to be justified by its tendency to undermine an intellectual property regime which many regard as unjust. On this justification, piracy is seen as a form of civil disobedience—as part of a collective effort to produce legal reform through engaging in unlawful conduct.

Blanket adblocking could similarly be seen as an attempt to produce reform—to produce a change to the 'business model' of the internet so that it no longer relies on intrusive advertising and tracking. James Williams takes this line when he presents adblocking as a way to 'cast a vote against the attention economy', which is his term for the set of practices that creators and advertisers employ in order to distract us from our true goals. He writes that:

> ad blockers are one of the few tools that we as users have if we want to push back against the perverse design logic that has cannibalized the soul of the Web.
>
> If enough of us used ad blockers, it could help force a systemic shift away from the attention economy altogether—and the ultimate benefit to our lives would not just be 'better ads.' It would be better products: better informational environments

that are fundamentally designed to be on our side, to respect our increasingly scarce attention, and to help us navigate under the stars of our own goals and values.

(Williams 2015)

Civil disobedience is perhaps a misnomer here, since the protest advocated by Williams is directed at a diffuse social practice (the attention economy), not the *state*,[12] and in most cases adblocking is not clearly unlawful. However, the structure of the justification is similar: break the rules to change the rules.

Again, however, this argument, understood as a justification for universal adblocking, is undermined by the possibility of selective adblocking. If consumers can relatively easily identify and whitelist websites employing only unproblematic advertising practices, then this is what they should do: such selective blocking would presumably be as effective as blanket-blocking in producing reform and would come without the cost of infringing the property rights of 'innocent' creators. Indeed, one might think that selective blocking would in fact be more effective in producing reform than blanket adblocking, since it would provide not only a 'stick' to those who employ wrongful advertising practices, but also a 'carrot' to those who employ only unproblematic forms of advertising.

Taking stock

Let me take stock. I have been considering the objection that adblocking wrongs ad-serving creators by infringing their intellectual property rights; the consumer accesses the creator's intellectual property without satisfying the 'no adblocking' condition that the creator imposes on its access.

I have argued that there are some cases in which adblocking does not infringe the creator's property rights because the creator does not intend to impose a 'no adblocking' condition on accessing their property or because the creator fails to adequately communicate this condition. I have also noted that, even when the adblocking consumer does infringe the creator's property rights, the consumer may nevertheless act permissibly. The rights infringement may be justified as a defence against the imposition of excessive burdens or risks, or burdens or risks to which the consumer has not consented. Or it might be justified as a form of protest intended to reshape the business model of the internet.

Nevertheless, there will be some cases in which adblocking does unjustifiably infringe the property rights of creators. Suppose that a creator clearly and explicitly demands that consumers deactivate their adblockers or refrain from accessing the creator's content. Suppose further that this creator credibly informs consumers about the nature of the advertisements and trackers it serves, so that consumers can make an informed decision about whether to accede to the condition. And suppose, finally, that the creator is not, in imposing its condition, placing undue burdens on consumers, since it offers a reasonably priced ad-free option, or serves only unobtrusive and privacy-respecting advertisements, or provides a non-essential service that consumers can easily forego. In this case, it is difficult to deny that the producer's property rights are unjustifiably infringed if the consumer continues to block ads while accessing that producer's content.

THE OBJECTION FROM COMPLICITY

Let us now turn to consider a further deontological objection to adblocking—an objection that promises to extend the range of cases in which adblocking is wrongful and thus, if done without sufficient justification, impermissible. This objection—the objection from complicity—holds that, by employing adblocking software, consumers become accomplices to wrongs committed by the makers of that software—adblocking software providers (ASPs)—for example, by implicitly encouraging or financially supporting those wrongs.

Why think that ASPs act wrongfully? One suggestion would be that they do so by facilitating the property-rights infringements perpetrated by some consumers. If my argument above was sound, *some* adblocking consumers infringe the property rights of creators—perhaps by continuing to deploy adblocking software when accessing websites that clearly demand whitelisting. We might then hold that ASPs wrong creators by facilitating such rights-infringements, and that *other* adblocking consumers— those who do not themselves directly infringe any property rights—act wrongfully by encouraging or supporting the wrongs perpetrated by the ASPs. So the story would be: ASPs are accomplices to the wrongs perpetrated by some adblocking consumers, and other adblocking consumers are accomplices to the complicity-based wrongs perpetrated by the ASPs.

It is possible, however, that some ASPs might also be guilty of a further wrong— extortion. To see why, recall that some ASPs operate whitelists—lists of sites for which advertisements will not be blocked—and in some cases the creators of sites must make a payment (either directly to the ASPs or to a third-party whitelisting agency) in order to be placed on the whitelist. Typically, these ASPs also require that the creators meet certain conditions—for example, that the advertisements they serve are unobtrusive and meet specified privacy standards. ASPs sometimes defend these practices as a way of allowing creators to serve 'acceptable' advertisements, with the payment for whitelisting justified by the need to recoup the costs of maintaining a database of 'acceptable' and 'unacceptable' ads (Adblock Plus 2018). However, others suggest that these ASPs are really simply extorting creators by demanding payment for whitelisting (Piltch 2015; Rothenberg 2015).

To assess this claim, we will obviously need an account of extortion. Here is my suggestion, inspired by Wertheimer (1987: 90): *A* extorts *B* just in case *A* threatens to perform an action that would impermissibly wrong *B*, or some third party *C*, in order to obtain a payment from *B* to which *A* has no moral claim.[13]

In the cases of interest to us, the ASP does indeed seem to threaten the creator (with adblocking) to obtain a payment (for whitelisting) to which the ASP has no moral claim. The question is whether the ASP is threatening to impermissibly wrong the creator, or anyone else.

ASPs will claim that refusing to whitelist non-paying creators is permissible, so that in demanding payment for whitelisting, ASPs are not threatening to impermissibly wrong anyone. They will claim that it is perfectly reasonable to whitelist websites only where there is clear evidence that the creator's advertising and tracking practices meet certain standards. And they will further claim that it is perfectly reasonable to require that creators share in the costs of establishing this evidence.

I remain neutral on whether and when this defence of paid whitelisting succeeds. However, let me note that the defence will be more plausible the higher the proportion of creators that are employing wrongful advertising practices. If almost all creators wrong their consumers, as is arguably the case currently, it will plausibly be permissible for ASPs to whitelist only under stringent conditions. On the other hand, if few do so, it will be more plausible that whitelisting should be the default position. If this is the case, then ASPs which in fact blacklist as a default and require payment for whitelisting are plausibly extorting creators.

However, note that even in this case, it is not clear that all adblocking *consumers* who employ 'extorting' ASPs are themselves wronging creators. This is because it is not clear that all consumers are complicit in the extortion perpetrated by the ASP. After all, not just any association between one's action and a wrong committed by another makes one an accomplice to that wrong. Complicity requires the right (or, rather, the 'wrong') kind of connection between the two acts. There is disagreement regarding what, exactly, that connection must be (Devolder 2017), but one view would be that the putative accomplice must *substantially contribute* to the occurrence of the wrong. There are interesting and difficult questions regarding whether using adblocking software constitutes a 'substantial contribution' to the extortion perpetrated by the ASP. On the one hand, no individual consumer makes a substantial (or even a significant) difference to whether the extortion occurs. On the other hand, it is doubtful whether an individual must make a significance to be complicit in a wrong; an individual member of a firing-squad is complicit in a wrongful killing even if his bullet makes no difference, and people who drive cars are plausibly complicit in the collective wrong of causing global heating even if they make no individual difference.[14]

Similar thoughts apply to the case of consumers who use ASPs that do not run paid whitelists (so are not guilty of extortion) but which allow consumers to block advertisements on *all* websites (so are perhaps guilty of wrongfully facilitating the infringement of creators' property rights by other consumers). There are open questions, that I cannot resolve here, regarding whether these consumers are wrongfully complicit in the ASP's wrongful facilitation of rights-infringements.

Also important to bear in mind here is that *not* adblocking may also raise issues of complicity. For example, where it is true that creators are wronging consumers, for example, by compromising their privacy, then *not* blocking advertisements might make one complicit in these wrongs being perpetrated against both oneself and other consumers. We may, then, need to balance complicity-based reasons to eschew blocking against complicity-based reasons to pursue it.

THE OBJECTION FROM FREE-RIDING

A third deontological objection to adblocking maintains that consumers who use adblockers wrong other consumers who do not use them. Those other consumers benefit from online content and also contribute to the ongoing production of online content by viewing advertisements. By contrast, the adblocking consumers benefit from online content but do not, or not sufficiently, contribute to its ongoing creation. They thus *free-ride* on the contributions of the ad-viewing consumers, and thereby wrong the ad-viewing consumers. Call this the objection from free-riding.

Adblocking is, according to this objection, relevantly similar to paradigmatic cases of wrongful free-riding such as:[15]

> *Coin-withholding.* Next to the coffee machine in the Department of Philosophy sits an honesty box. On the box is a notice stating, 'honesty box: please leave 20p for each coffee you make.' The notice also specifies that the funds will be used (as they indeed are) to buy coffee beans. Most staff members comply most of the time, but Professor Smith never contributes, despite being one of the heaviest coffee-drinkers.[16]

> *Polluting.* There are five farms surrounding a lake. Each farm uses water from the lake to irrigate crops, and each farm discharges run-off into the lake. The run-off is polluting the water and damaging crops that are irrigated with the water. To solve the problem, the five farmers come together and agree that all will start treating their run-off before discharging it into the lake. Four farmers stick to the agreement. The fifth, Farmer Jones, does not. Nevertheless, the water quality improves significantly, benefitting all five.

Intuitively, Professor Smith and Farmer Jones both free-ride on the contributions of others, and thereby wrong those others; the others have a legitimate moral complaint against them. I am not asserting here that Professor Smith and Farmer Jones infringe the others' rights. Whether they do will depend, I think, on how exactly we conceive of rights. What I am asserting is that Professor Smith and Farmer Jones fail to fulfil a *pro tanto* duty that is directed towards those others. It may be, for example, that they fail to fulfil a duty of fairness—a duty to do one's fair share—owed to those others.

Note, however, that there are many cases in which individuals benefit from the contributions of others to some good and do not contribute to the good themselves, yet seemingly also do not engage in any wrongful form of free-riding. Consider:

> *Hard Bargaining.* On an online second-hand sales site, rather like Craigslist or eBay, there are two types of buyer: hard bargainers and soft bargainers. Hard bargainers

always bid sellers down to the minimum price for which they are willing to sell. Soft bargainers, by contrast, always pay more than this minimum. All sellers on the site would cease using it if all buyers were hard bargainers.

It is plausible that the hard bargainers benefit from the continued existence of the site without contributing to it. Nevertheless, it seems doubtful that the hard bargainers engage in any wrongful form of free-riding.

A similar point can be made by reference to practices much closer to adblocking. Consider:

> *Non-clicking.* The readers of an online news site fall into two categories, clickers and non-clickers. Clickers sometimes click on the ads displayed on the site. Non-clickers never do so. The publisher receives funding from the advertisers on a 'per click' basis and if no readers ever clicked on the advertisements, the publisher would receive nothing and would go out of business.

Here, it seems that the non-clickers may be benefitting from the continued existence of the news site without contributing to it, while the clickers do contribute. Yet again, it seems doubtful that the non-clickers engage in any wrongful free-riding.[17]

In paradigmatic instances of free-riding, such as *Coin-withholding* and *Polluting*, the beneficiaries of some good wrong those who contribute to its provision if they do not themselves contribute. But in *Hard Bargaining* and *Non-clicking*, it seems that those who fail to contribute do not thereby wrong the contributors.

What sets these two pairs of cases apart? That is, what makes the non-contribution wrongful in the first pair of cases while it is not wrongful in the second pair? Perhaps by answering this question we will be able to determine whether adblocking qualifies as wrongful free-riding.

One answer to our question appeals to the differing social conventions at play in these cases. In paradigmatic cases of wrongful free-riding—including *Coin-withholding* and *Polluting*—there is a convention or rule that acceptance of benefits entails a duty to contribute to their creation.[18] In *Hard bargaining* and *Non-clicking*, there is no such convention. There is, for example, no conventional requirement that those who read news websites click on the ads that the websites serve. Are things different in the case of adblocking? Is there a conventional requirement not to block ads if one accesses a website? Creators may hope to create such a convention when they request that consumers deactivate their adblockers, suggest that the way to avoid advertisements is to become a paid subscriber, or simply highlight their dependence on advertising revenue to consumers. However, it seems to me doubtful that they have as yet succeeded in establishing this convention. That would, I think, require broader acceptance by consumers of the requirement not to block ads. In this respect, then, adblocking seems more like *Hard bargaining* and *Non-clicking* than like *Coin-withholding* and *Polluting*. If conventional requirements are what matter, it is doubtful that adblocking consumers engage in any wrongful form of free-riding.

Another answer to our question appeals to the excludability of the good being produced. Paradigmatic instances of wrongful free-riding concern the production of *non-excludable* goods; goods such that providing the good to some renders it impossible or costly for the provider of the good to exclude others from the good (Armstrong 2016). It would presumably be difficult to exclude the sole non-contributing farmer from the benefit of cleaner water in *Polluting*. Perhaps it would also be difficult to prevent coin-withholders from using the coffee machine in *Coin-withholding*. By contrast, perhaps the goods provided in *Hard bargaining* and *Non-clicking* are excludable. Perhaps it would be possible—and not that costly—to prevent hard bargainers from using the second-hand sales website, and non-clickers from accessing websites. It might be argued that there is no moral requirement to make one's fair contribution to the provision of excludable goods because the providers of those goods have no grounds for complaint if others access the goods without contributing: if the providers find this access to be problematic, they could, at reasonable cost, prevent it.

I am doubtful that excludability is morally relevant in this way. Suppose the coffee machine in *Coin-withholding* could in fact easily be fitted with a coin slot such that coffee would only be served to those who pay. This would not affect our judgment that, in the event that a coin slot is *not* fitted, those who refuse to pay engage in wrongful free-riding.[19] Building excludability into the case does not change our intuitive judgment about it.

Moreover, the explanation given above for why excludability rules out the possibility of wrongful free-riding is not persuasive. Though excludability guarantees that the *providers* of a good can prevent its provision to non-contributors, it does not guarantee that those who indirectly contribute to the goods provision can prevent it. Thus, indirect contributors may still have a moral complaint against non-contributors who access the good. Even if the sales website could easily prevent hard bargainers from using the site, the soft bargainers, acting as individuals, presumably could not. So we cannot appeal to excludability to explain why the soft bargainers have no moral complaint against the hard bargainers.

Finally, a third answer to our question adverts to the optimality of collective provision. Some suggest that wrongful free-riding occurs only when collective provision—that is, a scheme in which the good is provided to all and all are conventionally required to make their fair contribution to its provision—is the morally optimal means of provision (Armstrong 2016). Perhaps this can explain the difference between our two pairs of cases. The honesty box system in *Coin-withholding* is a system of collective provision, and perhaps it is the optimal system of providing coffee to philosophers. The agreement between the farmers in *Polluting* is also a scheme for collective provision, and it is plausibly the optimal means of providing clean water for irrigation. By contrast, it is doubtful that the optimal way of running an auction site is to make the site freely available but conventionally require that buyers 'go easy' on sellers in their bargaining. It is similarly doubtful that the optimal way of providing online news is to place it on freely accessibly websites but conventionally require news site readers to click on ads. Collective provision does not seem to be optimal in the *Hard bargaining* and *Non-clicking* cases.

What does this answer imply for the adblocking case? It does not clearly support the view that adblockers engage in wrongful free-riding, for it is far from obvious that publication supported by (often intrusive) advertisements combined with a requirement not to employ adblockers is the optimal way of arranging the provision of online content. Indeed, asserting that it is would beg the question against many proponents of adblocking, since these proponents often claim that there are better models of provision available. These models may include provision of content only to subscribers (behind a paywall), provision of content supported only by non-intrusive and privacy-respecting advertisements, or something closer to the current model but with users given greater control over what information the trackers used to target advertisements can collect (Burton 2017).

On none of the three views that we have considered, then, does adblocking appear to be an instance of wrongful free-riding. Adblocking seems more like *Hard bargaining* and *Non-clicking* than like *Coin-withholding* and *Polluting*.

CONCLUDING THOUGHTS

I have outlined three deontological objections to adblocking—the objection from property, the objection from complicity, and the objection from free-riding—and have considered how a defender of adblocking might respond to each. I challenged the view that adblocking constitutes wrongful free-riding. However, I conceded that adblocking may impermissibly wrong creators either directly—through infringing their property rights—or indirectly—through complicity in the wrongdoing of advertising service providers.

Whether adblocking infringes the property rights of creators will, I have suggested, depend on whether the creator intends to impose a 'no adblocking' condition on consumers and communicates this clearly, for example, by demanding whitelisting. Whether adblocking that infringes the property rights of creators does so *impermissibly* will further depend on:

- whether the advertisements served by the creator are unobtrusive and privacy-respecting;
- whether consumers are credibly informed about the nature of the advertisements and trackers that the creator serves;
- whether the creator provides an essential service; and
- whether the creator provides a reasonably priced paid, ad-free option.

The objection from property rights will most plausibly establish the impermissibility of adblocking when the creator (a) clearly demands that consumers either deactivate the adblocker or refrain from accessing the site; (b) credibly informs consumers about the nature of any advertisements and trackers contained on the site; and (c) either (i) offers a low-cost, ad-free option; (ii) serves only unobtrusive and privacy-respecting advertisements; or (iii) provides only non-essential services.

Whether adblocking involves complicity in wrongs committed by the ASP will depend on:

- whether the ASP is guilty of extortion;
- whether the ASP is complicit in the infringement of property rights by other consumers; and
- whether using adblocking software makes one complicit in the wrongful actions of the ASP, for example, because it substantially contributes to that wrongdoing.

Where adblocking consumers are complicit in wrongdoing by the ASP, this will need to be balanced against the possible complicity of *non*-adblocking consumers in systematic wrongdoing (e.g. in the form of privacy violations) by creators. One type of case in which the complicity involved in adblocking is likely to predominate will be where the ASP demands a large payment for whitelisting, even though most creators are respectful of consumers' attention and privacy. In this case, the charge that ASPs are extorting creators will be plausible, whereas the claim that creators are wronging consumers will, in relation to most creators, be less plausible. On the other hand, the complicity involved in *not* adblocking is likely to predominate where most creators *are* invading consumer privacy.

ACKNOWLEDGEMENTS

I would like to thank Ben Davies, Gabriel De Marco, Maximilian Kiener, Peter Schaber, Carissa Véliz, and an anonymous reviewer for their comments on earlier versions of this chapter. I thank the Uehiro Foundation on Ethics and Education and the European Research Council (Consolidator Award 819757) for their funding.

NOTES

1. David Whittier claims that 'ad blocking is completely ethical because it by far benefits more people than it harms' (Bilton 2015).
2. For example, Fisher (2010) argues that the 'annoyance' experienced by internet users who view ads is outweighed by the 'annoyance' experienced by producers that have to cut staff due to the financial losses caused by adblocking.
3. For an argument for the permissibility of adblocking that engages with such deontological objections, see Zambrano and Pickard (2018). Zambrano and Pickard argue that adblocking is permissible by drawing analogies to other, intuitively innocuous forms of ad-avoidance, such as muting the television during ad-breaks. However, in the course of their argument they respond to a number of deontological objections to adblocking, including some similar to those I consider below.

4. I refer to objections which maintain that adblocking wrongs someone as 'deontological', since the idea of a wrong (and the related idea of a moral complaint) fit naturally within deontological theories. But I do not claim that they must be understood within such theories, and indeed I am sympathetic to the idea that consequentialists and virtue ethicists can, with some fancy footwork, make perfectly good sense of wrongs and moral complaints.

5. For a classic statement of the view that rights entail *justice-based* directed duties, see Thomson (1971: 56, 61).

6. I thank an anonymous reviewer for suggesting this line of argument.

7. This adblocker, moreover, provided no ability for consumers to 'whitelist' particular advertising networks or creators.

8. For a statement of this view, see Irina Raicu, quoted in Bilton (2015). Raicu holds that '[a]d blocking is a defensive move' and that '[i]t seems wrong to characterize it as unethical when the practice that made it arise is unethical, too'.

9. There may, of course, be some forms of treatment to which it would be wrongful for the possessor of a luxury good to subject me, even if I consent to such treatment as the 'price' of the good. For example, it is plausibly impermissible for the yacht-owner to make me his slave, force me to perform a sexual favour, or publicly humiliate me, even if I agreed to his doing so as the price of taking possession of his yacht. It might be argued that some tracking practices employed by creators are in this category; it is wrongful for creators to employ them, even if consumers have consented to them as the price of accessing the creator's content. (I thank Carissa Véliz for pressing me to consider this possibility.) Note, however, that even in cases such as these, if the content being offered is luxury content, it is not clear that consumers would be permitted to employ ad-blockers defensively. It is doubtful that I am permitted to steal the yacht, even if the owner will only sell it to me in return for my becoming his slave.

10. Credibility might be established by, for example, presenting results of security audits by third-party agencies.

11. AdBlock Plus does this through whitelisting advertisements approved by the 'Acceptable Ads Committee'. See Acceptable Ads (2020). I will return to this practice below.

12. Of course, some of the main protagonists in the attention economy—including Google and Facebook—are institutions more powerful than most states.

13. Wertheimer suggests that the threatened wrong, in paradigmatic cases of extortion, is a violent crime.

14. For discussion of complicity in cases of with this structure, see Kutz (2000) and Gardner (2004).

15. These cases are inspired by Garrett Cullity's (1995) *Fare-Evasion* and *Recalcitrant Fisherman* cases.

16. An anonymous reviewer makes the interesting suggestion that Professor Smith may simply be stealing coffee in this case. I do not exclude this possibility; this may be an instance both of theft and of wrongful free-riding. However, I also do not think that it *obviously* involves theft. Theft plausibly involves the failure to fulfil an *enforceable* duty, and it is not clear to me that there is an enforceable duty in this case.

17. Zambrano and Pickard (2018) make a similar point. For other discussions of ad-blocking that offer comparisons to other ad-avoidance strategies, see Arment (2015c); Ingram (2015a); and Lawrence (2018).

18. The requirement that there be a rule or convention is often built into accounts of unfair free-riding. See, for example, Rawls (1971: 108–114).
19. Garrett Cullity (1995) makes a similar point in relation to his *Fare-Evasion* case.

References

Acceptable Ads (2020), 'Building Bridges', *Acceptable Ads*, https://acceptableads.com, accessed 30 September 2021.

Adblock Plus (2018), 'About Adblock Plus', *Adblock Plus*, https://adblockplus.org/en/about#monetization, accessed 30 September 2021.

Arment, Marco (2015a), 'Introducing Peace, My Privacy-focused iOS 9 Ad Blocker', *Marco.org*, 16 September, 2015, https://marco.org/2015/09/16/peace-content-blocker, accessed 30 September 2021.

Arment, Marco (2015b), 'Just Doesn't Feel Good', *Marco.org*, 18 September, https://marco.org/2015/09/18/just-doesnt-feel-good, accessed 30 September 2021.

Arment, Marco (2015c), 'The Ethics of Modern Web Ad-Blocking', *Marco.org*, 11 August, https://marco.org/2015/08/11/ad-blocking-ethics, accessed 30 September 2021.

Arment, Marco, Liss, Casey, and Siracusa, John (2015), '136: War and Peace', *Accidental Tech Podcast*. https://atp.fm/136.

Armstrong, Chris (2016), 'Fairness, Free-Riding and Rainforest Protection', *Political Theory* 44(1), 106–130.

Barton, David (2016), 'Rights or Respect: the Ethics of Adblocking'.

Bilton, Ricardo (2015), 'What Would Kanto Do? Ad Blocking Is a Problem, But It's Ethical', *Digiday*, 7 August, https://digiday.com/media/kant-on-ad-blocking/, accessed 30 September 2021.

Burton, Lyndsey (2017), 'Ad-Blockers and the Road to Consumers Controlling Their Private Data', *LSE Business Review*, 6 May, https://blogs.lse.ac.uk/businessreview/2017/05/06/ad-blockers-and-the-road-to-consumers-controlling-their-private-data/, accessed 30 September 2021.

Butler, Ian (2016), 'The Ethical and Legal Implications of Ad-Blocking Software', *Conneticut Law Review* 49(2), 689–712.

Crichton, Danny (2015), 'Adblocking and the End of Big Advertising', *Tech Crunch*, 4 June 2015, https://techcrunch.com/2015/06/07/adblocking/, accessed 30 September 2021.

Cullity, Garrett (1995), 'Moral Free Riding', *Philosophy & Public Affairs* 24(1), 3–34.

Devolder, Katrien (2017), 'Complicity', in Hugh LaFollette, ed., *International Encyclopedia of Ethics* (London: Wiley), 1–9.

Douglas, Thomas (2015), 'What's the Moral Difference between Ad Blocking and Piracy?', *Practical Ethics: Ethics in the News*, 9 October, http://blog.practicalethics.ox.ac.uk/2015/10/whats-the-moral-difference-between-ad-blocking-and-piracy/, accessed 30 September 2021.

Fisher, Ken (2010), 'Why Ad Blocking Is Devastating to the Sites You Love', 3 June, https://arstechnica.com/information-technology/2010/03/why-ad-blocking-is-devastating-to-the-sites-you-love/, accessed 30 September 2021.

Gardner, John (2004), 'Christopher Kutz, Complicity: Ethics and Law for a Collective Age', *Ethics* 114(4), 827–830.

Haddadi, Hamed, Nithyanand, Rishab, Khattak, Sheharbano, Javed, Mobin, Vallina-Rodriguez, Narseo, Flalhrastegar, Marjan, et al. (2016), 'The Adblocking Tug-of-War', *login*

41(4), 41–43, https://www.usenix.org/system/files/login/articles/login_winter16_07_hadd adi.pdf>, accessed 30 September 2021.

Ingram, Mathew (2015a), 'You Shouldn't Feel Bad about Using an Ad Blocker, and Here's Why', *Fortune*, 17 September, https://fortune.com/2015/09/17/ad-blocking-ethics/, accessed 30 September 2021.

Ingram, Mathew (2015b), 'Is Using Ad-Blocking Software Morally Wrong? The Debate Continues', *Fortune*, 18 September, https://fortune.com/2015/09/18/ad-block-ethics/, accessed 30 September 2021.

Kutz, Christopher (2000), *Complicity: Ethics and Law for a Collective Age*, Cambridge Studies in Philosophy and Law (Cambridge: Cambridge University Press).

Lawrence, Desmonda (2018), 'The Moral Question of Ad-Blocking', *The Prindle Post: Ethics in the News and Culture, Explained*, 22 August, https://www.prindlepost.org/2018/08/the-moral-question-of-ad-blocking/, accessed 30 September 2021.

Manjoo, Farhad (2015), 'Ad Blockers and the Nuisance at the Heart of the Modern Web', *The New York Times*, 19 August, https://www.nytimes.com/2015/08/20/technology/personalt ech/ad-blockers-and-the-nuisance-at-the-heart-of-the-modern-web.html, accessed 30 September 2021.

Orlowski, Andrew (2016), 'The Case for Ethical Ad-Blocking', 27 April, https://www.theregis ter.co.uk/2016/04/27/the_case_for_ethical_ad_blocking/ accessed 30 September 2021.

PageFair and Blockthrough (2020), 'Growth of the Blocked Web: 2020 PageFair Adblock Report', in *Blockthrough*, 1–19.

Piltch, Avram (2015), 'Why Using an Ad Blocker Is Stealing (Op-Ed)', *Tom's guide*, 22 May, https://www.tomsguide.com/us/ad-blocking-is-stealing,news-20962.html, accessed 30 September 2021.

Primack, Dan (2015), 'Dear Apple: I May Rob Your Store', *Fortune*, 18 September, https://fort une.com/2015/09/18/dear-apple-i-may-rob-your-store/, accessed 30 September 2021.

Rawls, John (1971), *A Theory of Justice* (rev. edn) (Cambridge, MA: Cambridge University Press).

Rothenberg, Randall (2015), 'Ad Blocking: The Unnecessary Internet Apocalypse', *AdAge*, 22 September, https://adage.com/article/digitalnext/ad-blocking-unnecessary-internet-apo calypse/300470, accessed 30 September 2021.

Thomson, Judith Jarvis (1971), 'A Defense of Abortion', *Philosophy & Public Affairs* 1(1), 47–66.

Wertheimer, Alan (1987), *Coercion* (Princeton, NJ: Princeton University Press).

Williams, James (2015), 'Why It's OK to Block Ads', *Practical Ethics: Ethics in the News*, 16 October, http://blog.practicalethics.ox.ac.uk/2015/10/why-its-ok-to-block-ads/, accessed 30 September 2021.

Zambrano, Alexander and Pickard, Caleb (2018), 'A Defense of Ad Blocking and Consumer Inattention', *Ethics and Intormation Technology*, 20, 143–155.

CHAPTER 24

PRICE DISCRIMINATION IN THE DIGITAL AGE

KASPER LIPPERT-RASMUSSEN AND LAURITZ AASTRUP MUNCH

INTRODUCTION

BACK in 2000, Amazon experienced severe public backlash when it became public knowledge that they had been experimenting with offering customers personalized prices on products such as DVDs, to the effect that some customers paid more than others for the same product. Amazon quickly responded by offering refunds, and Jeff Bezos, the company's CEO, publicly stated that they had 'never tested' and 'never will test prices based on customer demographics', further calling the incident a 'random price test' and a 'mistake' (Amazon 2000).

Amazon's conduct was a case of *price discrimination*. Price discrimination is the practice of charging different customers different prices for the same product based on assumed differences in their willingness to pay. Discriminatory pricing schemes enable firms to increase their profits, and are common in both digital and non-digital markets (although it is unclear just how widespread the practice is in the digital realm; see Borreau and de Streel 2018). Indeed, the practice of price discrimination is probably as old as the practice of markets.

Most find at least some instances of price discrimination morally objectionable, for example, cases in which the seller exploits the buyer's desperate situation to charge the buyer a price that has no relation to what the good costs the seller. However, it is also the case that most find at least some instances of price discrimination morally unobjection-able, or even morally desirable; for example, most find it acceptable that businesses offer loyalty discounts, student and disability discounts, and bulk purchase discounts.

While most people would probably take a similarly mixed view on instances of digital price discrimination, some find price discrimination harder to justify when it occurs in digitally mediated markets than in 'ordinary' markets. Call the view that digital price discrimination is harder to justify than non-digital price discrimination *the difference view*. Indeed, cases such as Amazon seem to suggest that there is something especially morally objectionable about digital price discrimination. Similarly, many find it unacceptable that, say, hotel booking sites ask a higher price from Apple users (Poort and Borgesius 2019); that companies rely on dynamic pricing schemes to offer people different prices depending on their geographical location, gleaned from customers' internet protocol (IP) addresses (Mikians et al. 2013); or that companies differentiate prices based on browsing history (Vissers et al. 2014). By way of general support for the difference view, one may also note that a recent study based on a sample of people from the Netherlands concludes that '[a]n overwhelming majority considers *online* price discrimination unacceptable and unfair' (Poort and Borgesius 2019). Although such responses need not solely reflect the belief that digital price discrimination is *morally* problematic (it could also, say, reflect prudential concerns, strategic response-giving or the so-called-'availability heuristic'—the psychological tendency to recall specific examples or situations, such as 'Amazon-type' cases—when confronted with a general topic or concept, such as 'price discrimination'), we shall proceed under the assumption that surveys such as those quoted here suggest that many deem digital price discrimination morally more problematic than non-digital price discrimination.

This combination of attitudes—that, generally, digital price discrimination is regarded as morally impermissible and instances of otherwise similar *non*-digital price discrimination (i.e. the case of student discounts) are not raises a puzzle about the permissibility of digital price discrimination. There seems to be some morally relevant property (or set of properties) by virtue of which some instances of digital price discrimination are particularly morally objectionable. However, the recognition that other (digital or non-digital) instances of price discrimination appear unobjectionable puts pressure on the critic of online price discrimination to explain when, if at all, such a practice is objectionable and why.

The purpose of this chapter is to review different reasons as to when and why digital price discrimination might be morally objectionable. The following section defines (digital) price discrimination. The next distinguishes between two questions: what makes some cases of price discrimination morally objectionable, and what makes digital price discrimination harder to justify than non-digital price discrimination? The remaining sections review six answers to these questions: to wit, that (digital) price discrimination is manipulative; that it violates privacy; that it has an automatized nature; that it results in morally objectionable aggregative results, for example, greater distributive inequality; and that it is discriminatory in a pejorative sense. We claim that all these complaints fail to explain what makes digital price discrimination objectionable *per se*, though, as we also point out, some of them hold more promise as explanations of why many forms of digital price discrimination are morally objectionable in ways that non-digital price discrimination is typically not.

Overall, it emerges that there is nothing intrinsically morally objectionable about either non-digital or digital price discrimination (and, thus, nothing intrinsically objectionable about price discrimination *simpliciter*). However, such pricing schemes can be implemented in ways, and under conditions, that render the practice morally objectionable in ways that might warrant legal regulation. An upshot of our survey, however, is that it is difficult to determine when a particular instance of digital price discrimination is morally objectionable. In turn, this might prove to be an attractive feature, since it enables us to make sense of why people seemingly have conflicting attitudes towards different instances of price discrimination.

WHAT IS DIGITAL PRICE DISCRIMINATION?

We start by offering an account of price discrimination *simpliciter*. Since the term originated in economic theory, this is where we will take our starting point (for a recent overview of this topic and further references, see Armstrong 2006; for canonical treatments, see Stigler 1987; Pigou 1932). An initially wider focus serves the following dialectical purpose: if *digital* price discrimination is, suitably interpreted, harder to justify than non-digital forms of price discrimination (as suggested by the difference view), then an adequate explanation of what renders digital price discrimination harder to justify must also enable us to explain why non-digital forms of price discrimination are easier to justify. We define price-discriminatory behaviour as follows:

(i)   Seller offers *roughly* identical goods or services
(ii)   at different price points
(iii) to different buyers
(iv)   where the price differential does not merely reflect differences in marginal cost of supply
(v)   based on perceived or assumed differences between buyers in their willingness to pay.

We begin with some remarks on the components of this account. According to (i), price discrimination involves offering *roughly* identical goods or services. This description fits nicely with paradigmatic instances of price discrimination, as well as digital price discrimination. For instance, if A sells copies of the same book to B and C at different price points, A could be engaging in price discrimination. However, some forms of price discrimination are premised on so-called 'versioning', that is, packaging the essentially same product in different ways—hardback and softback versions of the same book, for instance—and selling it at different prices. If this is price discrimination, which seems reasonable to believe, then price discrimination does not require identical goods or services in the strictest possible sense.

Condition (ii) suggests that price discrimination requires offering some widget at different price points. The intuitive thrust is straightforward. When some customer is offered, say, a student discount, it is by virtue of being offered a good or service at a comparatively lower price that they experience (in this case beneficial) price discrimination. There is a question about how broadly 'price' should be read. Economists tend to understand this rather narrowly as 'price tag'. However, on a broader notion, all kinds of costs could contribute to generating the final price. Some forms of price discrimination involve, for example, separating customers by offering a discount if a customer is willing to accept some inconvenience. For instance, the customer might have to cut out a coupon from a newspaper and present it at the shop to qualify for the discount. Companies might adopt such schemes under the presumption that only a subset of their customer base would find this offer attractive because many would not want to accept the inconvenience. If we include such inconveniences (which are costs) in the notion of 'price', such schemes might not, when everything is accounted for, count as price discrimination after all. Suppose that, on Black Friday, Sam stands in a queue for five hours to get a 5 per cent discount on a lawn mower. Everyone else pays full price. However, Sam's loss of welfare, due to the inconvenience of standing in a queue, converts perfectly to a sum of money that corresponds to the 5 per cent discount. On the broader view of price, then, we must conclude that no price discrimination occurred in this case. Some might find this counter-intuitive. However, since nothing we shall say turns upon this detail, we prefer to keep our account within the spirit of standard terminology and define 'price' narrowly as 'price tag'.

(ii) seems to count too many cases as instances of price discrimination, however. Imagine that some company sells wheat in different countries at different price points simply because production costs of wheat vary across countries. This does not look like price discrimination in the sense we are after. To avoid counting such cases as cases of price discrimination, we can add (iv) and claim that price discrimination requires that the ratio of the prices of two 'identical' products is different from the ratio of their marginal costs. On this view, releasing a hardback and softback version of the same book with different price tags (or selling wheat at different prices) amounts to price discrimination only if the difference between the prices is not a mere reflection of differences in costs of supply. Hence, if we assume that the hardback costs £5 more to produce than a softback, and the hardback is sold for £15 more than the softback, the price discriminated 'part' of the price differential amounts to £10. Notice, though, that the ratio test cannot easily stand alone. We would not want to say, for example, that A price discriminates in the relevant sense by offering microchips at one price point to B and offering apples at another price point to C, even though microchips and apples might have similar production costs. We believe that the requirements (i)-(iv) serves to capture the phenomenon with sufficient precision (cf. Elegido 2011: 635).

According to (v), price discrimination is motivated, at least in part, by a belief held by the discriminator concerning some customers' willingness to pay. Economists tend to call the maximum price that some consumer is willing to pay for some product his or her 'reservation price', a property that is a function of one's budget limitation and one's preferences. The rationale is that, typically, price discrimination schemes are deployed in the interest of increasing profits. On this view, it seems irrational, perhaps even self-defeating, if A decides to offer B some good at a higher price point than others are offered if he believes that it will simply make B more likely to decline the offer (setting aside special circumstances, such as a fancy gym offering a higher price to poor customers so that they will not join the gym—the gym might want to do this because it wants to preserve its brand as a gym for 'rich' people). Since increasing profits seems to be a central motive for engaging in both digital and non-digital price discrimination, it seems warranted to adopt (v).

By virtue of what properties, then, can we meaningfully distinguish *digital* price discrimination from *any form* of price discrimination? To our minds, digital price discrimination is behaviour which in addition to (i)–(v) satisfies:

(vi)   where the transaction is facilitated and mediated by a certain set of digital techniques, such as dynamic pricing and consumer tracking, and, simply, by virtue of taking place online.

The broad scope of this definition has the virtue of being compatible with many different possible views on what makes digital price discrimination worrisome. It also serves to stress that a central part of the question we seek to discuss is whether it is even morally relevant to distinguish digital price discrimination from the larger set of price discrimination practices. We now turn to this question.

The morality of digital price discrimination

Now that we have a firmer grasp on what price discrimination is, we return to the observation noted in the introduction; some people find digital price discrimination particularly objectionable. We might want to address two questions here:

(1)   When price discrimination is *simpliciter* objectionable, what makes it so?
(2)   What makes some instances of, suitably described, *digital* price discrimination *especially* objectionable?

We will focus on the latter question, but it is open for debate whether these two questions are worth keeping apart. Consider what can be called the *no-difference view*. On this view, there is really only one thing to be explained here, since there is no discernible, sufficiently generalizable, and morally relevant difference between digital price discrimination (DPD) and other forms of price discrimination. In support of this view, one might point out that the only non-moral difference between DPD and non-DPD is that the former satisfies (vi)—the transaction takes place online and is facilitated and mediated by digital techniques. There is no reason to think that, other things being equal, activities that are digitally mediated are harder to justify than non-digitally mediated activities.

For example, it is not morally more objectionable to lie in an email than to lie in a letter. However, we do not think the no-difference view should be endorsed right away. As noted above, intuitions seem to favour rejection of the no-difference view. Accordingly, we shall primarily discuss the second question posed above, noting that it will inevitably lead us to touch upon the moral permissibility of price discrimination *simpliciter*. However, given that our purpose is to better understand the digital realm, there is a sense in which it is unimportant whether the best explanation of what makes DPD objectionable generalizes to explain what makes other instances of price discrimination objectionable (although this would, of course, be nice). We suspect that there are both permissible and impermissible instances of both digital and non-DPD, such that there is a need for 'local' clarity, regardless of how the pieces fit together in a larger picture. If, for instance, we find it objectionable that companies differentiate prices based on IP addresses and browsing history (prima facie impermissible DPD), we should also be able to explain how it differs from, say, giving student discounts by predicting the occupational status of putative customers (prima facie permissible DPD).

Before turning to the question at hand, a few more pieces of terminology will come in handy. On one view, what makes troublesome cases of DPD objectionable is a property that can be found in its particular instances, either as an intrinsic or extrinsic property of the practice. On another view, what makes DPD objectionable is not a property of its particular instances, but instead of some overall pattern that results from allowing the practice. While there are important details in this distinction, the overall idea is straightforward (cf. Owens 2012; Husak 2008). For example, what is objectionable about greenhouse gas emissions is, presumably, not a feature of its particular instances, but rather the disastrous pattern that results when enough industries and individuals create sufficient emissions to have an effect on climate. Analogously, price discrimination might be objectionable in either of these two ways, in both, or in none.

We start by picking out some salient features of DPD to discuss whether it is objectionable in its particular instances. We discuss whether DPD is manipulative or deceptive, violates privacy rights, or whether it is epistemically inadequate or lacks accountability. We claim that these objections have little bite in the sense that they cannot explain what is objectionable about DPD. Next, we consider two pattern-based objections, namely that DPD leads to undesirable distributions of wealth and power. We argue that these objections are more promising, but that they, at most, explain what is objectionable about DPD in certain specific circumstances.

Is DPD MANIPULATIVE?

One concern with DPD appears to be the general lack of transparency surrounding the practice. While opacity is not a necessary part of DPD, opacity is a striking feature of most instances of DPD. A telling fact in this regard is that few people are aware of how widespread the practice is. As Chen et. al. (2016: 1339) suggest, '[u]nfortunately, the public currently lack comprehensive knowledge about the prevalence and behavior of algorithmic pricing algorithms in-the-wild' (see also Hannak et al. 2014; Poort and Borgesius 2019). In part, such lack of knowledge is unsurprising. Since customers tend to dislike the practice, companies, in fear of consumer backlash, tend to conceal it. It is likely that some people would want to avoid certain companies if they knew they practiced DPD.

This opacity might lead one to hypothesize that if DPD is objectionable, it is so because it is manipulative (by virtue of taking place without consumers knowing about it). This hypothesis seems prima facie compelling, as manipulative conduct seems objectionable in general (for a helpful overview, see Noggle 2018). The flipside of this hypothesis, of course, is that if the practice were adequately communicated, there would be no objection along these lines and, thus, that DPD is not morally objectionable per se.

On one understanding of what makes manipulation objectionable, manipulation is objectionable when and because it undermines rational decision-making capabilities (Vold and Whittlestone 2019). As Raz (1988: 337) writes, 'manipulation, unlike coercion, does not interfere with a person's options. Instead it perverts the way that person reaches decisions, forms preferences, or adopts goals.' Others simply suggest that manipulation 'bypasses reason' (Noggle 2018). We are not out to defend the best possible account of manipulation, so we will leave some technical details aside. For our purposes, it is enough that this account captures what many take to be objectionable about manipulation.

Note first what kind of manipulation complaint is unlikely to have bite. A might manipulate B if A acts to somehow induce desires or emotions in B that A correctly believes will result in B's reasoning in a rationally deficient way. For instance, A might run a cleverly devised desire-inducing advertisement that leads B to desire some product, even when this desire is irrational, given B's more fundamental desires. Or A might try to frighten B, which leads B to overestimate the risks of not buying a certain kind of product (e.g. an insurance). In both of these cases, we might want to accuse A of trying to manipulate B by leading B to bypass rational decision-making processes. DPD is almost never objectionable because it involves manipulation in this sense. Typically, when consumers are subjected to DPD, they experience little more than being offered a price tag. It is hard to see how offering a price tag could amount to acting in a way that objectionably undermines people's rational decision-making capabilities by inducing inappropriate emotions or desires in a way similar to the examples offered above.

However, there is arguably a more compelling way to flesh out the manipulation complaint. On one view, A acts manipulatively towards B if A acts in ways that lead (or are likely to lead) B to have false beliefs that serve A's purposes (cf. Mahon 2016). Some might want to describe this as deception rather than manipulation, but little turns on terminology at this point. On this generic account, there is a plausible sense in which DPD is often manipulative. If companies strategically withhold information about the presence of discriminatory pricing schemes and their precise content, they contribute to making it the case that people have false beliefs (perhaps by virtue of remaining ignorant) regarding the presence of the practice. However, we must distinguish between manipulation and *wrongful* manipulation, since a successful manipulation complaint must be based on a diagnosis suggesting the latter. However, it might seem doubtful that DPD is wrongful manipulation, even if customers are generally unaware of the practice and companies contribute to this being the case because this view seems to presuppose the truth of the following principle:

(1) It is wrong of A to offer B *P* if A simultaneously, by way of an action or omission, deliberately conceals the fact from B that B could have taken steps that qualified him for some better offer, *P**.

The consequent of (1) seems to us an apt description of what is often going on when companies engage in DPD. To wit, these companies offer a good or service at a given price point, and do not inform the customer that he could have taken steps to qualify for a better offer (e.g. by accessing the web shop from another device). The problem, though, is that (1) seems false, since it implies that any offer-maker is duty-bound to disclose that some putative customer can get an offer by buying from a competitor. Such a principle goes against the plausible idea that when interacting in markets, people are permitted to act in their self-interest, at least within certain constraints. In fact, (1) implies that selling things in general is impermissible by default, even in the absence of any form of price discrimination. Such an implausible implication suggests that the manipulation complaint is unsustainable, at least in this form.

One might try to revise (1). For instance, we generally tend to think that offer-makers have a duty to disclose at least *some* substantially significant details regarding the conditions of the offer posed. A car seller might act objectionably manipulatively if he deliberately fails to disclose that the brakes of the car are deficient. There seems to be a morally relevant difference between failing to disclose relevant details of an offer and failing to disclose the fact that there are other, and better, offers available. Accordingly, we might adopt:

(2) It is wrong of A to offer B *P* if A simultaneously, by way of an action or omission, deliberately conceals *relevant* information.

By the light of (2), one might think that in cases in which it is relevant information to customers whether or not a seller relies on price discrimination (in the same way that information about the condition of the brakes on a car is relevant information), a company acts manipulatively by failing to disclose this fact. At the least, this judgment seems to cohere nicely with people's feelings when they realize that they could have got a much better deal provided they had been aware of the way in which they were being subjected to disadvantageous price discrimination.

It is worth noting, though, that (2) has its own problems; namely, how do we determine relevance? Some customers might think that it is *relevant* information to know the precise recipe used to make Coca Cola. Presumably, some customers would change their course of action (e.g. avoid buying Coca Cola) if they had this information. However, we take it that the Coca Cola Company does not act manipulatively by not disclosing the precise recipe (i.e. perhaps in the interest of preserving their competitive advantage). This thought reveals that it is not clear how we should understand the 'relevance' qualifier in (2), and that actual consumer preferences regarding which information should be provided by the seller might not be a compelling yardstick.

While we recognize that there is more to be said on the question of manipulation and DPD, we conclude as follows. The complaint that DPD *as such* is objectionably manipulative fails to convince. But bear in mind that this view is consistent with holding that these practices are *more* manipulative than many adequately announced, non-DPD schemes, such as student discounts at museums (cf. Vold and Whittlestone 2019). What we claim, however, is that it is doubtful whether DPD *as such* is harder to justify than non-DPD due to concerns about manipulation. Finally, we suggest that in cases in which the precise details of the price discrimination scheme and its existence qualify as relevant information, there might be a viable manipulation complaint to be had. In fact, this view might even come with the practical upshot that we ought to adopt legislation that forces companies to disclose such relevant details, when appropriate.

Does DPD violate privacy rights?

Most forms of profitable price discrimination require that the seller has a reliable way of identifying the reservation price of putative customers before fixing the price offer. It is, however, often both costly and unwieldy to estimate reservation prices (Armstrong 2006). The structural conditions enabling DPD are somewhat special in this regard. E-commerce companies have ample opportunity to collect and analyse various types of personal information that users leave behind when they interact with digital devices, often without being aware of the use to which it is put. This information could consist of (but is not limited to) browsing and purchasing history, IP addresses, and unique device footprints. It turns out that all this information can be used to predict reservation prices and hence serve as a basis for price discrimination (cf. Taylor 2004).

The collection and analysis of personal information might give rise to a whole host of information processing-related complaints. These might be spelled out in different ways. Some might find it objectionable to collect some pieces of personal information without explicit consent because it violates a right to privacy (see for instance Munch 2020). Others might instead worry mostly about the risk of abuse of the information. For example, Gehrig and Stenbacka (2005: 139) write that:

> The feasibility of price discrimination requires the collection of sensitive private information by numerous companies. On a societal level, it may be difficult to ensure the privacy of this information. Due to management errors, fraudulent behaviour or simply the process of mergers and takeovers this private information may fall into hands that should not have access to it.

We take it that companies have a duty to take certain steps to make sure that the risks resulting from their personal information-processing activities are proportionate, regardless of whether the information is used for the purpose of price discrimination. Insofar as a company fails to comply with this duty, there is reason to object. In this sense, we have an explanation of what could make *some* instances of DPD especially objectionable. This also fits nicely when compared to instances of intuitively permissible non-DPD, such as offering student discounts—such instances do not typically involve extensive data processing.

Do privacy concerns offer a satisfying explanation of what is objectionable about DPD? While we recognize that dubious information processing can often constitute a wrong-making property, it is less clear that this *explains* why we should find DPD objectionable. Two observations support this point. First, we take it that many would object to DPD *even if* companies only relied upon personal information they had collected and processed in morally permissible ways (i.e. in ways involving no violation of a putative right to privacy), or if they relied on no personal information. Thus, the privacy-based explanation seems to leave central cases unexplained. Second, the fact that the presence of objectionable DPD correlates with the presence of objectionable data-processing does not amount to showing that the latter explains the former. In turn, it seems plausible to think that the reason why it is objectionable to process people's personal information is that the information-processing is used as a means towards an end that is objectionable in some respect. But this view *presupposes* an account of what is objectionable about DPD, rather than explaining why DPD is objectionable.

We conclude that one should look elsewhere for a complete explanation of what makes DPD objectionable. Such a conclusion is consistent with thinking that some—perhaps even most—instances of DPD might be objectionable due to the questionable information-processing practices they entail. In other words, the difference between permissible and impermissible DPD (or price discrimination *simpliciter*) does not seem to turn upon a distinction between price discrimination based on processing people's personal information and price discrimination based on, say, no information whatsoever.

Is DPD objectionable by virtue of its automatized nature?

A notable feature of DPD is its automatized character. This property also serves to distinguish the practice somewhat from some instances of non-DPD. The price personalization occurring on, say, Amazon is largely a process facilitated by algorithms applying general rules, absent any direct human intervention (although it is humans who program the algorithm, of course).

There is a set of moral concerns that are applicable to such automated decision-making, regardless of whether the decision procedures facilitate price discrimination (see, e.g. Zarsky 2015; Ziewitz 2016). These could be of relevance here. We shall discuss two. According to some, so-called algorithmic decision-making is objectionable because it might be biased. Call this the *epistemic inadequacy concern* (for an overview, see, for instance, Mittelstadt et al. 2016). Others are concerned about such algorithms being often opaquely implemented, thus preventing structures of accountability (Pasquale 2015, for instance, calls such algorithms 'black boxes' to emphasize this opacity). Call this the *accountability concern*.

Let us consider the epistemic inadequacy concern first. One might object to DPD because it will sometimes be epistemically inadequate, and perhaps even more imprecise than other forms of price discrimination. For example, whether A accesses the internet using a Mac or PC is at best an imperfect and crude proxy for A's reservation price regarding a given good or service. Such inferences might lead to cases (and perhaps many cases, depending on the epistemic quality of the proxy) in which people are offered a price that does not in any meaningful way correspond to their reservation price.

It is true that it can sometimes be morally impermissible to act in ways that disadvantage people if this act is based on an inadequate evidential foundation. For present purposes, we can assume that DPD involves treating some people disadvantageously—although some might object to this assumption, thinking that an offer can never disadvantage (against this view, see Rippon 2012). Suppose that, as an illustration of this general thesis, General Impulsive decides to carpet-bomb a village based on (what the general knows is) at best dubious intelligence suggesting that the village harbours a factory producing nuclear missiles. Given the stakes (the harm likely to result), we could think that General Impulsive does wrong because he acts epistemically irresponsibly. He ought to acquire better evidence before acting (assuming that the act *could* be permissible if it were appropriately justified epistemically).

So epistemic inadequacy sometimes provides a reasonable complaint. Is this the case regarding DPD? Here are two problems with the suggestion that it is. First, the epistemic adequacy objection is shallow because it would be much more interesting if we could find a sense in which DPD is morally objectionable *even if* it cannot be faulted on epistemic grounds. At best, this would produce an objection to the subset of instances in which price discrimination is implemented based on inadequate evidence (which is not to say that this objection is insignificant). Presumably, those who object to DPD would want to object to cases in which the offer-maker has strong evidence for thinking that the digitally predicted reservation price is the correct one. While this problem is not detrimental, the following seems to be. Even intuitively permissible forms of (non-digital) price discrimination rely on deficient proxies of the factor we are interested in, that is, willingness to pay. Offering student discounts is also an imprecise proxy for reservation prices (not all students are poor), so epistemic inadequacy seems to fail in picking out a sense in which DPD seems especially objectionable, and fails even in explaining what is objectionable about price discrimination *simpliciter* in the first place. The student discount contrast suggests that we have little reason to think that permissible instances of price discrimination necessarily rely on better proxies, epistemically speaking. Hence, the epistemic inadequacy objection fails.

Let us now turn to the concern for accountability. There seems to be a straightforward sense in which, typically, it is harder to contest and even understand what is going on when one is subjected to DPD. This contrasts relevantly to normally acceptable forms of price discrimination such as student discounts. We typically understand the social norms that structure such pricing schemes, and we typically find ourselves in a position to contest the decisions imposed on us if we find them inappropriate. There is a sense in which many people would probably not even know where to begin if they wanted to make sense of and change the way that algorithms personalize the content they receive, including prices. Indeed, as Buhmann et al. (2019) suggests, 'A growing public unease about the massive societal ramifications of algorithms has perpetuated a public discourse that is increasingly concerned with their transparency and accountability.' To counteract this lack of transparency, scholars have recently suggested that people subject to algorithmic and automated decisions have an entitlement to an explanation for their treatment (for instance, Wachter et al. 2018; for a discussion of 'de-responsibilization' in algorithmic decision-making generally, Rubel et al. 2019).

We have to be careful here, however, since a lack of accountability is only a problem insofar as there is a feature by virtue of which somebody ought to be held accountable (cf. Shoemaker 2011). An example is the relationship between citizen and government, in which the formal powers possessed by the latter over the former generate accountability claims.

This caveat reveals a problem with the line of reasoning we are assessing. While we want to grant that the employment of algorithms as a decision-making procedure might sometimes, perhaps even often, be objectionable because it prevents accountability, it is less clear that this is true in the case of DPD. This argument is somewhat analogous to our discussion of manipulation in a former section, in which we concluded that it is not necessarily objectionably manipulative to price discriminate without notifying customers of the practice, unless the information is relevant. If correct, it seems, by extension, that there is a similarly weak case for claiming that customers are necessarily entitled to hold companies accountable *on the specific matter of pricing schemes based on assumed reservation prices* (which, again, is perfectly consistent with thinking that there are many ways in which companies ought to be held accountable). However, we grant that if it can be demonstrated on independent grounds that some instances of price discrimination are objectionable, perhaps because there is a failure to convey relevant information, then it might amount to a further wrong, in these specific cases, to obscure accountability by relying on algorithmic decision-making and, thus, to obscure the fact that price discrimination, which is objectionable in the first instance for non-accountability-related reasons, takes place.

PATTERN-BASED OBJECTIONS TO DPD

We now switch focus away from explanations of what makes DPD objectionable that seek to locate the objectionable property in particular instances of the practice. Instead, we turn to explore the possibility of what we shall call pattern-based objections. According to such arguments, what is objectionable about price discrimination is not a property of its particular instances, but rather a property of the aggregate pattern that results from allowing the practice or from failing to regulate it appropriately. On such a view, we might hold, for instance, that all particular instances of DPD are perfectly permissible, at least taken in isolation, and yet the practice is nevertheless objectionable overall.

Consider first what we shall call the *distributive complaint*. According to this complaint, we have reason to find DPD morally objectionable because of its distributive effects. On this line of reasoning, we object to price discrimination because it upsets some particular pattern which we have independent reason to prefer. There are at least two items we have reason to be particularly concerned about. First, we might be concerned about how some markets distribute their benefits and burdens. If some market produces or reproduces major inequalities or systematic patterns of disadvantage, we might have reason to object (see also Herzog's chapter on 'Algorithmic Bias and Access to Opportunities' in this handbook). This observation suggests that we should ask whether DPD leads to adverse welfare implications. Second, and since we are dealing with a market context, we might have reason to be concerned about DPD producing or reproducing significant power asymmetries.

Can the distributive complaint be fleshed out in a satisfying way? Importantly, economic scholarship suggests that '[t]he welfare effects of allowing price discrimination are ambiguous' (Armstrong 2006: 100) and the distributive outcomes of allowing price discrimination depend on the nature of the market. For instance, one study (Shiller 2014) estimates that Netflix would be able to increase its profits by between 0.8 per cent and 12.2 per cent (to the detriment of consumers) *under monopolistic conditions* if they were able to personalize prices. This finding is much in line with general economic theory suggesting that monopolistic power, combined with a reliable way of estimating reservation prices, tends to capture consumers' surplus (although, if monopoly is a given, allowing price discrimination might be beneficial for customers relative to a uniform pricing monopoly). However, in competitive settings (as well as reasonably competitive settings), which is the context in many of the markets in which DPD is likely to be deployed, the results are much less clear and depend on the nature of the market, as well as on the information available to companies and customers (Borreau and de Streel 2018). Hence, in practice, some instances of digital, as well as non-digital, price discrimination might be beneficial or harmful to the customer base as a whole, and there might be different distributive effects across different groups of consumers. One might suspect, however, that companies would be unwilling to implement price discrimination in the first place if it did not benefit them somehow (although it is unclear that this should necessarily be objectionable).

Since the distributive complaint depends on how price discrimination actually affects the distribution of welfare in some particular market, there is no simple view to be had here. It depends, as it were, on the kind of pattern we favour, and how some particular instance of price discrimination upsets it. Importantly, however, there seems to be no good reason why the distributive complaint could not be equally applicable to certain instances of non-DPD that speak in favour of the no-difference view. The objection is still apt, given the right circumstances, however. For instance, we might have reason to act to prevent companies from exploiting certain customers through predatory pricing schemes, for example, schemes that lure vulnerable customers to bind themselves to contracts whereby they will pay excessive rents on a loan provided by the seller in connection with a purchase. This point seems to apply equally to digital as to non-digital instances of price discrimination.

Is DPD *OBJECTIONABLY DISCRIMINATORY?*

'Discrimination' is often used pejoratively to condemn certain practices involving objectionable disadvantageous differential treatment, such as discrimination based on race or gender. Since the term figures both in such cases and in instances of price discrimination, one might hypothesize that an adequate account of what explains the wrongness of price discrimination must refer to a generalizable theory capable of explaining what makes objectionable forms of discrimination wrong. We must proceed carefully here, though, since the notion 'price discrimination' originated within economics for non-normative purposes (economists do not typically use the term pejoratively). This observation relates to a further worry that we encounter at the conceptual level. At least to some, prima facie objectionable discrimination refers to differential treatment on the basis of membership of a *socially salient group* where the group, in a sociological sense, serves to structure social relations across a wide range of different contexts (Lippert-Rasmussen 2013). This notion serves a crucial role in fleshing out what part of the problem is with objectionable discrimination, such as racial discrimination—namely, that the salient group membership facilitates disadvantageous treatment in multiple domains of society.

Back to the present concern, it is unclear in what sense DPD meets this requirement. On a rough first pass, price discrimination seems to amount to the differential disadvantageous treatment of those with relatively higher reservation prices. Given that rich people generally, though not always, have higher reservation prices, perhaps one could describe this as discrimination against 'rich people', although this would be imprecise, since one can have a relatively high reservation price regarding some good or service without necessarily belonging to a 'rich' segment of society. Insofar as price discrimination becomes more widespread, it will be true that endowments come to structure a wide array of social interactions in a relevant sense. Yet it still seems to stop short of being comparable to, say, the specific sense in which race has historically structured social relations to the disadvantage of Black people. Furthermore, the group criterion, at least as it is usually employed, tends to naturally suggest the further idea that part of what is objectionable about discrimination is when people take a certain category, such as race, as a direct reason for wanting to discriminate against that group of people, perhaps due to a (false) belief in the inferiority of Black people, for instance. It is hard to believe that this line of reasoning applies neatly to the present problem. Companies do not typically price discriminate against those with relatively higher reservation prices due to a belief that rich people (or people with modest means and dire needs, and therefore remarkably high reservation prices) are less deserving, moral inferiors, or some such offensive belief. Companies price discriminate because they believe it will be instrumental in earning them a greater profit. In turn, if the process is fully automatized via an algorithm that seeks to optimize profits by way of price discrimination, there are hardly any human attitudes involved at all, let alone those directed towards discrete people being subject to disadvantageous price discrimination. Interestingly, the lack of offensive human attitudes points in the direction of one way in which instances of DPD often can be morally *less* objectionable than cases of non-DPD. Unlike, say, the racist car dealer who demands a higher price from African-American customers on account of racial animus, DPD will never—at least not directly—involve charging consumers from particular socially salient groups on account of certain objectionable mental states directed at them.

A critic might correctly point to the fact that while these observations might be true of *direct* discrimination or, in other words, differential treatment, they are not true of *indirect* discrimination, or disparate impact. Roughly, direct discrimination occurs when beliefs about which socially salient groups the discriminated person is a member of form part of the discriminator's motivating reason for treating the discriminated person disadvantageously compared to others. Indirect discrimination occurs when a certain practice has a negative impact on certain protected groups which is disproportionately negative in light of the benefits that the practice involves (cf. Altman 2020). The relevant point in this context is that indirect discrimination can occur in the absence of any direct discrimination and, thus, price discrimination might be indirectly discriminatory against certain groups even if, for the reasons expounded in the previous paragraph, only in exceptional cases will it involve direct discrimination against protected groups. For instance, one could easily imagine that algorithms can reliably estimate consumers' gender or age from their digital traces and on that basis charge women and, say, old people a higher price on the basis of a justified belief that, on average, the reservation prices of members of those groups are higher than those of other groups (see also Herzog's chapter on 'Algorithmic Bias and Access to Opportunities' in this handbook).

In response to the correct point that, in principle, DPD might be indirectly discriminatory against members of certain groups in a way that many will consider morally objectionable, we make two observations. First, we see little reason to think that there is any principled difference between DPD and non-DPD when it comes to objectionable indirect price discrimination. Hence, worries about indirect discrimination can hardly support the difference view, not even in a weakened form and, in any case, as already mentioned, there are worries pertaining to direct discrimination that apply to non-DPD and do not apply to DPD.

Second, while, no doubt, there will be cases of DPD that appear problematic for indirect discrimination-related reasons (e.g. cases in which the practice of DPD results in members of protected groups having to pay a higher price relative to members of other groups), there will also be cases in which the reverse is the case (cf. Lippert-Rasmussen 2014). In fact, to the extent that members of protected groups tend to be worse off, economically speaking, and have a lower reservation price than members of groups that are better off (both assumptions seem reasonable in some cases), one might conjecture that there will be more of the latter cases than of the former. The picture that emerges is that there seems to be no obvious way in which DPD can be shown to be morally objectionable per se, or for that matter typically morally objectionable by appeal to the moral objectionableness of group discrimination against certain protected groups. In other words, we should assess DPD largely independently of whatever moral views we have about standard cases of discrimination.

However, we want to stress that in cases in which price discrimination indirectly disadvantages vulnerable groups, there is a reason to complain. Whether this is the case, however, is an empirical question, and the evidence for the extent to which this is the case is scarce, though undoubtedly such cases exist. For instance, Propublica (2015) mentions a case in which a geography-based pricing scheme had the effect that poor Asians were more than twice as likely to be offered a higher price for a service delivered by the *Princeton Review*.

CONCLUSION

In this chapter, we investigated the nature of price discrimination generally, and digital price discrimination specifically. We introduced two moral questions: (i) what is it that makes some cases of price discrimination morally objectionable? and (ii) what makes DPD harder to justify than non-DPD? We then looked at some of the most obvious answers to these two questions, arguing that none of them succeeds in offering a satisfactory response to the second question. This suggests that it is not necessarily the case that DPD is harder to justify than non-DPD.

Depending on how it is implemented, DPD might instantiate certain wrong-making factors. Moreover, it might do so more often than non-DPD. Think again of the case of (non-digital) student discount price discrimination and compare it to the forms of DPD discussed throughout the text. There is a good chance that, say, the latter types of DPD are typically more manipulative than the case of non-digital student discounts. After all, people tend to be aware of the existence of the former and not the latter. However, this is not to say that DPD is always—even necessarily—manipulative. Nor is it to say that non-DPD could not also be objectionably manipulative. Price discrimination—whether digital or not—is likely to be objectionable when it is manipulative, violates privacy, or creates or reinforces objectionable patterns of disadvantage. We believe that these are amongst the most typical objections one might mount against particular instances of DPD.

REFERENCES

Altman, Andrew (2020), 'Discrimination' in Zalta, Edward N. *The Stanford Encyclopedia of Philosophy*, https://plato.stanford.edu/archives/win2020/entries/discrimination/>. (accessed 2 September 2021).

Amazon (2000), 'Amazon.com Issues Statement Regarding Random Price Testing', Press release, 27 September, https://press.aboutamazon.com/news-releases/news-release-details/amazoncom-issues-statement-regarding-random-price-testing/, accessed 2 September 2021.

Armstrong, M. (2006), Recent Developments in the Economics of Price Discrimination. In R. Blundell, W. Newey, and T. Persson, eds, *Advances in Economics and Econometrics: Theory and Applications, Ninth World Congress* (Econometric Society Monographs). (Cambridge: Cambridge University Press), 97–141.

Borreau, Marc, and de Streel, Alexandre (2018), 'The Regulation of Personalised Pricing in the Digital Era', https://one.oecd.org/document/DAF/COMP/WD(2018)150/en/pdf, accessed 9 August 2021.

Buhmann, Alexander, Paßmann, Johannes, and Fieseler, Christian (2020), 'Managing Algorithmic Accountability: Balancing Reputational Concerns, Engagement Strategies, and the Potential of Rational Discourse', *Journal of Business Ethics* 163, 265–280.

Chen, Le, Mislove, Alan, and Wilson, Christo (2016). 'An Empirical Analysis of Algorithmic Pricing on Amazon Marketplace.' *WWW '16: Proceedings of the 25th International Conference on World Wide Web*, 1339–1349, vol. 16.

Elegido, Juan M. (2011), 'The Ethics of Price Discrimination', *Business Ethics Quarterly* 21(4), 633–660

Gehrig, Thomas P., and Stenbacka, Rune (2005), 'Price Discrimination, Competition and anti-trust', in Konkurrensverket [Swedish Competition Authority], 'The Pros and Cons of Price Discrimniation', 65–101, http://www.konkurrensverket.se/globalassets/english/research/the-pros-and-cons-of-price-discrimination-9356kb.pdf, accessed 9 August 2021.

Hannak, Aniko, Soeller, Gary, Lazer, David, Mislove, Alan, and Wilson, Christo (2014), 'Measuring Price Discrimination and Steering on E-commerce Web Sites' In *Proceedings of the 2014 Conference on Internet Measurement Conference (IMC '14)*. (New York, USA: Association for Computing Machinery), 305–318.

Husak, Douglas (2008), *Overcriminalization: The Limits of the Criminal Law* (Oxford: Oxford University Press).

Lippert-Rasmussen, Kasper (2013), *Born Free and Equal? A Philosophical Inquiry into the Nature of Discrimination* (Oxford: Oxford University Press).

Lippert-Rasmussen, Kasper (2014), 'Indirect Discrimination Is Not Necessarily Unjust', *Journal of Practical Philosophy* 2(2), 33–57.

Mahon, James Edwin (2016), 'The Definition of Lying and Deception', in Edward N. Zalta, ed., *The Stanford Encyclopedia of Philosophy*, https://plato.stanford.edu/archives/win2016/entries/lying-definition/, accessed 9 August 2021.

Mikians, J., Gyarmati, L., Erramilli, V., and Laoutaris, N. (2013), 'Crowd-Assisted Search for Price Discrimination in e-Commerce: First Results', in *Proceedings of the Ninth ACM Conference on Emerging Networking Experiments and Technologies* (New York), 1–6.

Mittelstadt, Brent Daniel, Allo, Patrick, Taddeo, Mariarosaria, Wachter, Sandra, and Floridi, Luciano (2016), 'The Ethics of Algorithms: Mapping the Debate', *Big Data & Society*.

Munch, Lauritz Aastrup (2020), 'The Right to Privacy, Control Over Self-Presentation, and Subsequent Harm', *Journal of Applied Philosophy* 37(1), 141–154.

Noggle, Robert (2018), 'The Ethics of Manipulation', in Edward N. Zalta, ed., *The Stanford Encyclopedia of Philosophy*, https://plato.stanford.edu/archives/sum2018/entries/ethics-manipulation/, accessed 9 August 2021.

Owens, David (2012), *Shaping the Normative Landscape* (Oxford: Oxford University Press).

Pasquale, Frank A. (2015), *The Black Box Society: Technologies of Search, Reputation, and Finance* (Cambridge, MA: Harvard University Press).

Pigou, Arthur Cecil (1932). *The Economics of Welfare* (London: Macmillan & Co.).

ProPublica (2015), 'Asians Nearly Twice As Likely to Get Higher Price from Princeton Review', https://www.propublica.org/article/asians-nearly-twice-as-likely-to-get-higher-price-from-princeton-review., accessed 9 August 2021.

Poort, Joost, and Zuiderveen Borgesius, Frederik (2019), 'Does everyone have a price? Understanding people's attitude towards online and offline price discrimination'. *Internet Policy Review*, 8(1), https://doi.org/10.14763/2019.1.1383

Raz, Joseph (1988), *The Morality of Freedom* (Oxford: Oxford University Press).

Rippon, Simon (2012), 'Imposing Options on People in Poverty: The Harm of a Live Donor Organ Market', 40, 145–150.

Rubel, Alan, Castro, Clinton, and Pham, Adam (2019), 'Agency Laundering and Information Technologies', *Ethical Theory and Moral Practice* 22, 1017–1041.

Shiller, Benjamin (2014), 'First Degree Price Discrimination Using Big Data' Working Paper, https://ideas.repec.org/p/brd/wpaper/58.html

Shoemaker David (2011), 'Attributability, Answerability, and Accountability: Toward a Wider Theory of Moral Responsibility', Ethics 121(3), 602–632.

Stigler, George (1987), *A Theory of Price* (New York: Macmillan).

Taylor, Curtis (2004), 'Consumer Privacy and the Market for Customer Information', *Rand Journal of Economics* 35(4), 631–650.

Vissers, Thomas., Nikiforakis, Nick., Bielova, Nataliia., and Joosen, Wouter (2014), 'Crying Wolf? On the Price Discrimination of Online Airline Tickets', Presented at the Seventh Workshop on Hot Topics in Privacy Enhancing Technologies (HotPETs).

Vold, Karina, and Whittlestone, Jessica (2019), 'Privacy, Autonomy, and Personalised Targeting: Rethinking How Personal Data is Used', In Carissa Véliz, ed., Report on Data, Privacy, and the Individual in the Digital Age. Data, Privacy and the Individual.

Wachter, S., Mittelstadt, B., and Russell, C. (2018), 'Counterfactual Explanations without Opening the Black Box: Automated Decisions and the Gdpr', *Harvard Journal of Law Technology (Harvard JOLT)*, 31(2), 841–888.

Zarsky, Tal (2015), 'The Trouble with Algorithmic Decisions: An Analytic Road Map to Examine Efficiency and Fairness in Automated and Opaque Decision Making', *Science, Technology and Human Values* 41(1), 118–132.

Ziewitz, Malte (2016), 'Governing Algorithms: Myth, Mess, and Methods', *Science, Technology, & Human Values* 41(1), 3–16.

PART VI

HEALTH

CHAPTER 25

THE ETHICS OF MEDICAL AI

ABHISHEK MISHRA, JULIAN SAVULESCU,
AND ALBERTO GIUBILINI

INTRODUCTION

OVER the past few years, artificial intelligence (AI) solutions have been increasingly explored and developed for health-care settings. This trend is only expected to accelerate. For the purposes of this chapter, by 'AI' we refer primarily to deep learning models that exhibit (at least some of) the following features: (1) they are trained on very large data sets using high levels of computational resources; (2) their workings are at least somewhat opaque, given the various hidden layers that such deep neural networks use, which makes it difficult to provide an explanation for their recommendations (as would have been possible for prior information systems); and finally (3) they exhibit at minimum near human-level (and up to superhuman level) performance on the health-care-related task they are meant to perform.

The potential benefit of such systems is vast—they can lead to better clinical and health outcomes not just because they perform at a superhuman level for some tasks, but also because they may facilitate greater access to health care in populations and low-resource settings in which previously access to health care was limited. Beyond purely medical outcomes, the use of such systems also has the potential to affirm the values we consider important in the health-care context: enabling greater informed consent and a more robust clinician–patient relationship, facilitating a more just distribution of health-care resources, and leading to more unbiased clinical decision-making. However, given the unique features of AI models outlined above, their use might lead to new ethical concerns that undermine these very values in unprecedented ways. In this chapter then, we shall explore some of these major ethical concerns raised by medical AI.

It is important at the outset to highlight some areas we will not be focusing on. Our discussion does not focus on the privacy and ethical issues around the data that such machine learning models are built on, on health apps and the specific concerns they raise as compared to more traditional channels of health information and advice, or on AI models used outside of health-care settings that have health implications (such as algorithms used in social media). We also do not discuss models that are used within health-care settings (such as hospitals) but to augment logistical workflows. We restrict our discussion here for reasons to do with space as well as focus.

Outside of these, there are varying applications for health AI systems. Most notably, deep learning models can be used to aid clinical decision-making by suggesting diagnoses and treatment recommendations. Proof-of-concept models have been developed for radiological analysis (such as for lung cancer screening (Ardila et al. 2019)), to diagnose diabetic retinopathy through optical computed tomography scans (Gulshan et al. 2016), diagnosing glaucoma (Bojikian et al. 2019), classifying skin cancer (Esteva et al. 2017), assessing cardiovascular risk factors (Poplin et al. 2018), diagnosing a range of paediatric diseases through electronic health records (Liang et al. 2019) (among many other use cases), and predicting risk of suicide attempts (Walsh et al. 2017). Outside of being used as clinical decision support systems, AI can also be used to provide 'ambient intelligence' in hospital settings (Gerke et al. 2020), monitoring for patient mobilization (Yeung et al. 2019) and bedside practices such as hand hygiene (Haque et al. 2017). The use of AI systems has also been suggested to protect and promote public health in a more targeted and precise way (Panch et al. 2019). AI systems can also be used to yield better outcomes for organ transplantation (e.g. kidney or liver transplants), from assisting in curating transplant chains for incompatible donor–recipient pairs (Sherman and Greenbaum 2019) to predicting survival post-transplantation (Díez-Sanmartín et al. 2020). In surgery, deep learning models can be used to assess surgical procedure and performance (Khalid et al. 2020), as well as for surgical robotics (Mirnezame and Ahmed 2018).

As can be seen, the applications of AI in health and medicine are myriad. Furthermore, while most of the applications now are of an assistive nature, providing aid to clinicians and human operators, many AI applications in the future may instead be autonomous. This distinction is an important one and raises very different ethical questions. For the purposes of most of this chapter, we focus on such assistive systems, though we return to the question of ethical issues concerning autonomous systems towards the end.

In this chapter then, we consider the main ethical themes that are raised by the use of such AI systems. We consider, in turn, the ethical concerns that arise on the basis of (a) bias, discrimination, and fairness; (b) patient-centred medicine; (c) AI and value-based decision-making; (d) responsibility, accountability, and explanation; and (e) the broader and long-term societal effects of AI in health care, including more speculative ones. In each of the following sections, we raise the various questions posed under these themes, assemble the main arguments that have been provided, and point to directions for future research. Finally, we end with some closing comments.

Bias, discrimination, and fairness

The potential for AI systems to perpetuate bias that is ethically problematic is one of the most well-discussed topics in the domain of AI ethics. Technically, AI systems are intended to discriminate by design—a deep learning classifier trained to detect lung cancer through the analysis of CT scans is meant to discriminate between those scans that sufficiently indicate a positive diagnosis and those that do not. What makes discrimination ethically problematic is when it happens on the basis of factors that are not clinically relevant and so should not have been a basis for assessment, to yield outcomes that are unfair. Such situations are especially problematic when such factors have traditionally been protected categories, such as race or gender, though unethical discrimination can also arise in cases in which non-protected categories are used when they shouldn't be. When we write about a factor that *shouldn't* have been used for assessment, we refer to factors that have not reasonably been shown to affect the outcome in question. A process that is problematically discriminatory in such a way, and yields unfair outcomes, can be said to exhibit bias. Such biased processes can then be argued to violate considerations of justice and equality.[1]

Algorithms have been noted to be problematically biased across many different applications (in this volume, see Hadjimatheou and Nathan for issues in predictive policing; see Herzog and Sparrow for other kinds of algorithmic bias). Algorithmic bias along the lines of race seem particularly foreboding for the health-care context, considering that there are deep learning models being developed for the classification of skin cancer using photographed images (Esteva et al. 2017) in which fewer than 5 per cent of the training images used were of dark-skinned individuals (Zou and Schiebinger 2018). Perhaps the most significant example yet of such discrimination in health care is of an algorithm used to provide patient risk scores as the basis for selection in 'high-risk care management' programmes: for a given risk score, Black patients were considerably sicker than White patients (Obermeyer et al. 2019). Selection based on these scores led to a significantly lower representation of Black patients in such care management programmes across levels of sickness. Given that such an algorithm is deployed nationwide in the United States, and is typical of commercial risk-prediction tools that are applied to roughly 200 million people in that country each year, the scope of discrimination is staggering.

The use of AI systems can yield such discriminatory outcomes due to various potential problems in their development. For instance, while it is unlikely that models will be built for which protected categories like race are features meant to be explicitly factored into the classification, other seemingly unconnected features can serve as proxies for them. This is what happened in the risk prediction case above: the model took as input total past medical expenditure for patients and used it to predict future health expenditure, which was taken to be an indicator of future health risk (Obermeyer et al. 2019). Such 'label bias' occurs when the data label used ('medical expenditure') does not mean the same thing for all patients 'because it is an imperfect proxy [for future healthcare need] that is subject to health care disparities rather than an adjudicated truth' (Rajkomar et al. 2018). Unequal medical expenditure could arise due to factors such as differential access to care, or differing levels of trust in the health-care system rather than different risk.

Avoiding such iatrogenic effects requires a deep understanding of the systems that produce the data that AI models are trained on, and how there might be systematic discrimination occurring. Other biases that could lead to such discrimination include 'minority bias', when protected groups are underrepresented in the training data (as in the case of the dermatological classifier above), 'missing data bias', when data is missing for protected groups in a non-random fashion, and 'informativeness bias', when chosen features are less informative to render a prediction in a protected group (Rajkomar et al. 2018). Ensuring that unfair discrimination doesn't occur requires that all these (and more) biases be considered when building AI systems.

But how do we determine whether a model is discriminating unfairly? When it comes to measure of fairness, there are multiple viable candidates. Earlier, we noted that ethically problematic discrimination can happen when a model's output is based on protected attributes (such as race or gender) or their proxies—this is known as *anti-classification* (Corbett-Davies and Goel 2018). Other candidates for operational measures of fairness are *classification parity*, which requires common measures of predictive performance (false positive and false negative rates) to be equal across groups, and *equal calibration*, which requires that for a given model output (such as a particular health risk score) it is equally likely that the output is correct, regardless of which group the individual is from. Contextualized to the care management programme risk prediction case earlier, anti-classification requires that risk scores are not calculated by explicitly factoring in race or any of its clinically irrelevant proxies (which can easily happen, given that medical expenditure *is* correlated with race, for instance). Classification parity requires that false-positive and false-negative rates are equal across White and Black patients, and equal calibration requires that for a given risk score the likelihood of needing high-risk care management remains the same, regardless of whether the patient is White or Black.

Considering that these measures all seem intuitively to capture different parts of various conceptions of fairness, the question of which of these measures to use becomes an important one for AI systems. Furthermore, lest we think that we might just be able to use them all in some aggregated fashion, there is a further twist—classification parity and equal calibration are incompatible with each other and cannot be fulfilled simultaneously, and so must be 'traded-off' against each other (Kleinberg et al. 2016). Given that different groups have different base rates of the property being classified (e.g. high-risk care needs, measured perhaps by a comorbidity score), a model that is calibrated would *necessarily* produce different false-positive and false-negative rates. Such conditions necessitate a choice between classification parity and equal calibration as to which is the more desirable measure of fairness. While there have been some arguments put forward in favour of selecting one of these measures to the exclusion of the other (Long 2020), this debate is still quite new and more work needs to be done.

So far, we have been assuming that the various protected categories mentioned here are actually clinically irrelevant when it comes to medical decision-making. However, there might be circumstances in which such features have been reasonably shown through research to be clinically relevant. For instance, it has been shown that the base rate of a disease is different across sub-populations (e.g. prevalence of breast cancer in men vs women). Furthermore, there are other complicating factors. For example, we might imagine cases in which a model might not display fairness, but might otherwise yield significantly better performance from existing methods. Whether such a model should nonetheless be used would depend on which theory of justice one subscribes to, and how such a theory balances total good (measured in terms of aggregate health outcomes, for instance) and fairness.[2] Additional complications might also arise when we consider whether the unfair outcome disadvantages those who are already well off in society, or those who are worse off (see Herzog, this volume).

Another thing to note is that so far, the measures of fairness discussed are measures of model performance. Ultimately, the ideal is to aim for fair *outcomes*, something that fair model performance (however that might be measured) doesn't necessitate (Rajkomar et al. 2018). Fair model performance might get disturbed by human bias in implementation, through clinician or patient bias. Thus, while it is important to focus on finding appropriate measures of fairness in model performance, it is equally important to ensure that those using the model are appropriately trained and do not succumb to 'automation bias'—over-relying or under-relying on model output to produce errors (Parasuraman and Riley, 1997). As has been noted, '[t]he more advanced a control system is, so the more crucial may be the contribution of the human operator' (Bainbridge 1983).

AI AND PATIENT-CENTRED MEDICINE

The core of the concept of patient-centred medicine can be expressed as follows:

> First, healthcare should treat patients as *people* whose values, beliefs, and psychosocial context all play important roles in establishing and maintaining their health.... Second, healthcare should treat patients as equal partners in medical decision-making: their wants should be heard, their wishes respected, and their knowledge considered.
>
> (Bjerring and Busch 2020)

This collaborative and shared model of decision-making is a departure from prior paternalistic models, in which the clinician's recommendations were taken as decisive without substantive input from the patient. This new approach of shared decision-making and patient-centred care is increasingly taken to be the gold standard of clinician–patient interactions, in which 'the clinician offers options and describes their risks and benefits, and the patient expresses his or her preferences and values' (Barry and Edgman-Levitan 2012).

Reliance on AI (and specifically deep learning) models has been argued to be in tension with the ideals of patient-centred care in two ways. First, it has been argued that AI models used as clinical aids, especially for treatment recommendation, are not sensitive to patient values and instead inflexibly operate based on fixed values. Taking as example IBM's Watson for Oncology system, Rosalind McDougall argues that the ranked list of treatment recommendations produced by Watson produces two harms: it bases its ranking solely on the particular value of maximizing lifespan, and, in doing so, does not 'encourage doctors and patients to recognize treatment decision making as value-laden at all' (McDougall 2019). This argument can be extended to any AI system that, like Watson for Oncology, prioritizes certain treatment recommendations over others, as doing so requires a metric (like longevity) to make that prioritization. The very act of picking such a metric loads the AI's output with a particular value that might not be prioritized by the patient.

The second way in which reliance on AI is seen to be at odds with the ideals of patient-centred care is grounded in the opacity of deep learning systems. As has been mentioned, deep learning systems are opaque in that it is often not possible to determine why a particular classification was made. Such opacity has been argued to compromise informed consent, a key requirement of patient-centred care (and perhaps a value accepted even by those who reject the model of patient-centred medicine). Bjerring and Busch note that if clinicians relying on opaque deep learning systems cannot understand why certain decisions are made, they are unable to communicate this information to the patient, which in turn doesn't allow the patient to make an informed decision (Bjerring and Busch 2020). Unlike the previous argument, this applies not just to treatment recommendation systems but also to those that aid diagnosis.[3] Using the extreme case of a deep learning system that is advanced enough to draw unexplained correlations between hitherto unconnected medical variables, they argue that the clinician will be unable to convey information relevant to the diagnostic process to the patient. According to this argument, the opacity of such systems compromises informed consent.

On the basis of these (and other) reasons, some have argued that patients have a right to refuse diagnostics and treatment planning by AI systems in favour of a human-only alternative (de Miguel Beriain 2020; Ploug and Holm 2020). However, it is not obvious that these reasons are strong enough to be such defeaters. Even if we accept these reasons, they just preclude *some* applications of *some* types of AI models. Considering the first argument above, when it comes to treatment recommendation and other value-laden decision-making, we may either reject such systems outright (which still allows their use in non-value-laden clinical decision-making) or we may build such systems to be adjustable when used, such that alternative or multiple values can be selected based on the patient's preferences and values (what McDougall calls *value-flexible design*). Furthermore, realizing patient-centred care requires that the *system* of clinical decision-making accommodate patient values, and this can be achieved in ways other than ensuring that each element of the system (such as the AI model) is value-flexible. Given the complexity of patient values and preferences, it might not always be possible to represent them among the model's input parameters. Instead of rejecting such systems, we might instead compensate for them by having the clinician discuss with the patient and reorder treatment rankings based on the patient's alternative values and preferences.

While McDougall does entertain this option as a possible way forward, she argues that 'such an approach diminishes the patient's role and represents a backwards step in respecting patient autonomy' (McDougall 2019). However, it is unclear why this is so—hypothetically, if the ordered ranking in the case in which a patient's values are driving the ranking process from the start can be arrived at through compensating for the AI's approach, then there seems to be no ethically relevant difference in the two processes. In fact, this method arguably mirrors the one used in conventional non-AI settings, in which the doctor comes up with a diagnosis and an initial understanding of which treatment options are most feasible, and prioritizes them subsequently based on patient input. While it is true that 'current clinical practice ... does not always meet the ideal of shared decision making', an AI model's fixed-value approach does not need to ground a right to refusal if traditional clinical decision-making does not. What *would* further promote patient-centred care by clinicians relying on AI decision aids would be an explicit understanding of what the default values encoded in the model are (e.g. maximizing lifespan) and how this might compromise the values their patients might have.

It is similarly unclear that opacity of deep learning models can ground a right to refusal by the argument that it precludes informed consent. The predominant justification for informed consent rests on the value of autonomy and self-governance for the patient (Beauchamp 2010), and it is unclear that a patient's autonomy or ability to self-determine is reduced in the absence of knowledge of how a deep learning classifier generates a particular output. Even in a conventional, non-AI case, while patients may exercise their access to the chain of reasoning by which their doctor arrived at a clinical judgement, for the vast majority who are not medically trained this information does not contribute to autonomous action. As Beauchamp notes, 'persons understand only if they have acquired *pertinent* information and have *relevant* beliefs about the nature and consequences of their actions' [emphasis ours], and it is hard to recognize information that one is not trained to assess as reasonably pertinent or relevant. The argument against deep learning models as being singularly problematic because of their opacity is further strengthened when we consider that many other cases of traditional medical practice are quite similar to them, in that they are 'atheoretical, associationist, and opaque' (London 2019). Whether we consider the majority of drug development that is never approved for any indication, half of phase III drug trials that fail, or the historical prescription of aspirin for over a century without understanding the underlying mechanism, medicine is a field where intervention is often made on empirical grounds prior to understanding through causal explanation. To charge deep learning models, then, as being problematically opaque would be to level the same charge against many other aspects of traditional medical practice.

Similarly, even if a deep learning model could be made explicable using medically invoked concepts such that the clinician might sufficiently understand the recommendation, it is unclear how this contributes to autonomous choice for most patients and thus compromises informed consent. One possible rebuttal here is that even if information about how the AI model arrived at its recommendation is *functionally* irrelevant for a patient (it doesn't contribute to a different decision), as long as the patient *feels* the information relevant, then it bears on whether informed consent obtains. However, this would make the requirements for informed consent too strict, as many different types of information unrelated to the decision would then be required for informed consent so long as they are *felt* by the patient to be relevant.

That being said, there do exist patients for whom such knowledge would be reasonably pertinent and would contribute to a greater understanding of the situation, and for whom a case could be made that opacity has compromised informed consent. In such situations, it might perhaps still be plausibly argued that although AI systems do compromise patient-centred care, they might be justified on grounds of other benefits that they bring (e.g. superior accuracy, reliability, and scalability). Under such circumstances, the different ethical values of respect for patient autonomy and overall patient benefit would need to be weighed and traded off against each other at the aggregate and individual levels.[4]

Beyond the arguments above, there have been other grounds posited for a right to refuse AI-assisted diagnostics or treatment planning. Ploug and Holm argue that since AI systems are known to be biased in various ways, and since their opacity may obscure proof of such bias, patients have a refusal right (Ploug and Holm 2020). While they admit that such bias is not exclusive to AI systems, since clinicians also suffer from bias, they believe that there are adequate corrective measures and mechanisms for accountability for clinician bias that are not available in the case of model bias. For instance, clinicians may be corrected by other members of the health-care team they operate as part of through shared deliberation and discussion, and may be held accountable by such peers as well—all of which is harder to do for opaque systems. Another posited ground for a right to refuse is to permit patients to act on their 'rational concerns', such as reliance on medical AI, leading to a society-wide de-skilling of medical professionals, or that 'AI diagnostics and treatment planning become monopolized with a number of negative effects' (Ploug and Holm 2020). While we will not evaluate these arguments here, they do highlight the importance of future research on the question of what can justify a right to refuse AI-aided diagnosis or treatment by patients, where such a right would imply a right to insist on alternatives to the AI-assisted process. Another related important question is: do clinicians have an obligation to disclose reliance on AI systems to their patients? It is important that these issues be more fully explored to get a better understanding of other ethical concerns relating to patient-centred care that are raised by clinical reliance on AI systems.

AI AND VALUE-BASED DECISION-MAKING

In the previous section, we briefly discussed how the outputs of AI systems can be value-laden, such that patient-centred care might require a compensatory adjustment to the outputs. While our argument has been that this need not decisively compromise patient-centred medicine, care must still be taken in deciding how such systems ought to be built vis-à-vis the values embedded in them. In this section, we focus on questions relating to the values embedded in AI systems. Specifically, we focus on two questions: (a) under what circumstance should we be especially careful about the values embedded in AI systems; and (b) how ought we to select these values?[5]

There have been a few suggestions in the literature for when it is especially important that we get right the values that are embedded in health AI systems (Freedman et al. 2020). First, when decisions need to be made quickly, there may not be time for a human operator to be in the loop to assess and compensate for the value-ladenness of such systems. There have been several AI models developed for intensive care usage (Gutierrez 2020), for instance to predict length of stay for patients (Sotoodeh and Ho 2019), ICU mortality (Awad et al. 2017), and critical risk (Flechet et al. 2019). Unlike in the aforementioned case of the Watson for Oncology, clinicians may not have the time to adjust for values embedded in the model.

Second, in cases in which AI models are being used to solve computational problems that exceed human capabilities, the ethically relevant decision might be hard to decouple from the computational decision. We have already encountered one such example: health-care resource allocation models such as risk predictors for high-risk care that, if not configured appropriately, perpetuate unfair discrimination. Another example is kidney exchange algorithms, which match prospective recipients for kidney transplants who have willing but incompatible donors with other similar pairs to facilitate a trade (Roth et al. 2004). Several AI models have been developed for this highly computationally demanding task (Dickerson and Sandholm 2015).

Third, there may be cases where AI systems need to be deployed autonomously (or mostly autonomously), such that there may not be human operators to offset value assumptions in the system. For instance, in low-resource settings in which specialists are in short-supply, AI system performance might be at an adequate enough level that it would be unethical to withhold autonomous deployment (Schönberger 2019).

Under such conditions, special care needs to be taken to ensure that the values embedded are ethically robust and defensible. Given that, by our very characterization of such circumstances, a human-in-the-loop arrangement for value mediation is not possible, it will be difficult to factor individual patient values into such systems.[6] We would thus need to consider values not specific to a single individual, more akin to the values that guide public health decision-making. For instance, in kidney exchange scenarios, decisions need to be made about the relative weights assigned to patient categories (such as young and old) in cases in which prioritization is necessary, such as for tiebreaking purposes (Freedman et al. 2020). In the United States, it is also required that considerations of social justice be taken into account for allocation solutions, such as to consider an 'assessment of their cumulative effect on socioeconomic inequities' (Organ Procurement and Transplantation Network n.d.). Other social justice concerns might also arise, such as acceptance of minority donors given that in countries such as the United States and Australia, 'white, young, wealthy, privately insured, and well educated' patients with kidney failure are more likely to receive a transplant (Reese et al. 2015). Appropriate answers to such ethically charged questions would need to be represented within AI systems—if we do not explicitly encode the values we care about, alternative values will be implicitly encoded instead by omission.

How are these ethical concerns to be addressed? Whose responses to such ethical questions are relevant? Traditionally, societies have been able to reach consensus for such questions, despite widespread disagreement, through social and institutional structures such as courts, voting, mediation, public consultation processes, etc. (Cave et al. 2019). Recently however, one new approach has been to 'crowdsource' the ethical solution through gathering enormous amounts of data about public preferences. In the Moral Machine study, Awad and colleagues collected 40 million public responses, across 233 countries and territories, to moral dilemmas faced by autonomous vehicles (Awad et al. 2018). The moral dilemmas presented were characterized by unavoidable accidents that required a choice between swerving or staying on course to spare one of two parties—humans versus pets, passengers versus pedestrians, more lives versus fewer, the young versus the elderly, etc. Preferences (or moral intuitions) in these cases were registered and collated to identify cross-cultural variation, which was then suggested as relevant to policy decisions (though the exact way in which such data should be used was left open).

The Moral Machine experiment is unprecedented in scale, and one can see how similar approaches might be used to gather public intuitions about the values and decisions that should guide ethical public health policy. When considering health AI systems that will affect large numbers of people (such as a kidney exchange algorithms), gathering such information would clearly be relevant to the decision of what values such systems should be aligned with. The question is how we might use such information. As Savulescu and colleaguges argue, it would be a mistake for such decisions to blindly follow people's moral intuitions—public views on moral questions can be deeply mistaken, such as when there is low support for organ donation, despite a shortage of organ donation being rightly seen as a problem to be overcome (Savulescu et al. 2019). A 'reflective equilibrium' approach—where such intuitions are first screened for bias and uncritical reflection, then compared with the intuitions of professional ethicists, and subsequently evaluated through our more general ethical values and theories— would yield a better foundation for decisions on how the values of such AI systems should be determined.

RESPONSIBILITY, ACCOUNTABILITY, AND EXPLANATION

When we speak about holding an actor responsible for the outcomes resulting from the use of AI systems, we mean that it would be justified for them to be praised or blamed, or rewarded or punished, for these outcomes (Strawson 1994). When we speak about accountable use of AI systems, we may invoke the following widely accepted conception of accountability:

> a relationship between an actor and a forum, in which the actor has an obligation to explain and to justify his or her conduct, the forum can pose questions and pass judgment, and the actor may face consequences.
>
> (Bovens 2007)

Thus, we can connect responsibility and accountability as follows: mechanisms of accountability (the relationships between an actor and a forum) provide the practical channels through which responsibility can be adjudicated and attributed. Based on the conditions through which we assess and attribute responsibility, the forum may pose questions, pass judgement, and subsequently decide the consequences for an actor.

Providing a systematic analysis of all the different conditions of responsibility, all the actors involved, and other elements of accountability mentioned above is beyond the scope of this section (Wieringa 2020). We endeavour instead to raise what we consider to be the most interesting and pertinent ethical issues that occur in adjudicating responsibility and pursuing accountability.

First, what are the harms that we are to hold actors responsible and accountable for when it comes to the use of AI systems in health care? There are, of course, harms to the individual, when an AI system that allocates scarce health-care resources (such as intensive care unit beds) errs and misallocates. There might also be injury that is sustained by patients when a clinician uses AI systems to help in diagnosis or determining treatments for them, either through an error in the system or on part of the clinician relying on the system (Parasuraman and Riley 1997). Harm might also result from discriminatory behaviour (or behaviour aligned to misguided values in other ways) that we have discussed; such harm would not just affect a single individual but would also have ramifications at the level of access to care to minority patient populations (Obermeyer et al. 2019).

Across these different cases, responsibility for the harm would be allocated to different actors, from the health-care professionals using AI systems as clinical decision-support systems, to developers designing and building the systems, to auditors who are to review the system before deployment, to public health officials who are in charge of specifying the values which such systems would be built to operate by. A precondition for adjudicating responsibility in any of these cases is the presence of an established standard of care to prevent each of the harms.

One condition for attributing responsibility is the 'epistemic' condition, wherein moral culpability requires that the actor was not ignorant of the significance and consequences of their actions, or if they were, then this ignorance is not itself culpable (Wieland 2017). In the absence of an established standard (or multiple established standards) of operationalizing fairness, for instance, it would be difficult to hold responsible an AI designer that ensured a model exhibited fairness as equal calibration

rather than classification parity (Angwin et al. 2016). The effective attribution of responsibility, and thus the pursuit of accountability, for AI systems in health care hence
requires standards for most of the issues that have been discussed in this chapter so
far. Given that most of these issues are currently 'live' ones, such standards are still
being debated.

One common mechanism to hold clinicians accountable is the adjudication of
clinical negligence in cases in which injury is sustained by patients allegedly due to a
clinician's actions. Traditionally, in the United Kingdom, such negligence is assessed
by the Bolam test, which tests for responsibility by checking whether the clinician
has 'acted in accordance with a practice accepted as proper by a responsible body
of medical men skilled in that particular art' (*Bolam v Friern Hispotal Management
Committee* [1957]). If this test is failed, as assessed by expert witnesses, the clinician is
considered to have not performed to the standard of care and been proven negligent.
When it comes to the use of AI systems in clinical settings, some have argued that
up to the point in which AI systems become undeniably superior in performance to
clinicians, existing standards of care and means of assessing them are sufficient (Price
et al. 2019; Schönberger 2019). However, using AI systems in clinical practice requires
skill, not just in medical matters of fact, but also in the heuristics and methods for
appropriate reliance on such systems, which might not be something that existing
medical professionals possess (as evidenced by the various calls to revise medical education in light of AI use (Wartman 2019)). Given that Bolam requires that clinicians
act in accordance with what skilled medical professionals consider reasonable, and
given that medical professionals traditionally might not be skilled on how best to rely
on AI models, this might introduce difficulties in the use of Bolam to judge negligence
for injury caused by AI use.

As mentioned above, once there is consensus around an established standard
of care for how clinicians should rely on AI systems, across varying performance metrics and system configurations (level of opacity, etc.), these practices can
be encouraged across the field and used as the basis for judging negligence. Some
authors present a model of AI use in which either the AI's performance is low enough
that the standard of care would persist as it has traditionally been, or high enough
such that full use of AI would just *become* the standard of care (Price et al. 2019).
Whether AI performance in a clinical setting will indeed follow this two-step trajectory is an empirical issue. However, considering the number of deep learning proof-
of-concepts that display initial performance comparable to, or slightly beyond, the
average clinician, it would serve us well to think about adjudicating responsibility
through an appropriate standard of care for the use of models that are neither obviously inferior or obviously superior to their user. Looking to work on automation
bias, social epistemology, and group psychology would be beneficial in designing appropriate reliance strategies (Mishra 2019).

One of the recurring features of deep learning models that is invoked in discussions
of responsibility and accountability is their opacity. The fact that such systems are not
explainable, that their recommendations cannot be explained in terms of the exact logic

and weighting of the factors that yielded them, is taken to be in tension with their accountable use. As Doshi-Velez and colleauges note:

> By exposing the logic behind a decision, explanation can be used to prevent errors and increase trust. Explanations can also be used to ascertain whether certain criteria were used appropriately or inappropriately in case of a dispute
>
> (Doshi-Velez et al. 2017)

The explainability of AI models is thus taken as a necessary, if insufficient, condition for accountability. As the argument goes, a user of an opaque system, such as a clinician relying on a diagnostic aid, needs to be able to understand the system's recommendation if they are to use it appropriately and subsequently provide an account of their decisions. AI developers also need to be able to understand why the models they develop function as they do, so as to be able to make sure that bad outcomes such as discrimination or value misalignment do not occur.

However, we believe that such characterizations of the necessity of explanation for accountability are too quick. Explanations here are seen as necessary for accountability because it is presumed that the development and use of systems which offer such explanations would always lead to better health outcomes (compared to the development and use of comparatively opaque systems)—in other words, because norms governing their development and use require them to be explainable. However, if there are acceptable norms for the development and use of deep learning models that don't require access to local explanations to produce the best clinical outcomes or operate in line with the ideals of justice and non-discrimination, then it seems unclear why explanations would be necessary for accountability. In such cases, accountability would merely require judging whether the various actors acted in line with these non-explanation norms—the local explanation for the model's recommendation would be irrelevant. Explanations are thus *instrumentally* necessary rather than *intrinsically* necessary—they are necessary to the extent that they feature in the norms against which accounts of the development and use of such systems are judged. If the best results from the development and use of such systems can be achieved despite them being opaque, accountability does not require an insight into their inner workings. Allow us to illustrate with a few examples.

Algorithms like the aforementioned critical-care risk-prediction model (Obermeyer et al. 2019) may face a charge of being discriminatory against a population group. One way of assessing such a charge is to gain some insight into the exact chain of causal reasoning that led to Black patients being mislabelled as low-risk when White patients with similar profiles were labelled as high-risk. However, this is not the only way to assess the charge. As we have seen, measures of fairness such as classification parity and equal calibration (as opposed to anti-classification) can also indicate to developers that their algorithm exhibits problematic discrimination. Further, such measures are completely derived from the outputs of such systems, rather than by examining their inner workings. As such, if these measures of fairness are accepted to be appropriate ones, then the account of an AI developer can be assessed and responsibility attributed (or not) without invoking the need for such systems to be explainable. Similarly, if there exist acceptable standards on how clinicians might use opaque decision aids, such as by comparing their approximate accuracy with the model's and updating for whether in a particular situation a model likely outperforms or underperforms them, they could plausibly justify their decisions without invoking an explanation for the model's recommendation.

This line of reasoning is, of course, compatible with the possibility that, for a given application, the development and use of explainable systems leads to better health outcomes and greater non-discriminatory behaviour than for opaque systems. This is what Doshi-Velez and colleagues meant when they wrote that 'explanation can be used to prevent errors and increase trust' (Doshi-Velez et al. 2017). A developer of risk-prediction models might create models that discriminate even less and a clinician might make even better clinical judgements if the system were not opaque. However, this is an empirical question, an answer to which cannot be presumed in favour of explainable systems. If it turns out that we can construct standards and norms for the development and use of non-explainable systems that produce better results, then, as argued, there is no recourse to the necessity of explanations through accountability. Furthermore, this empirical question is still open—research in human factors has shown that presence and type of explanation can cause clinicians to over-rely or under-rely on decision aids (Bussone et al. 2015). Similarly, it is an empirical question whether, for instance, risk pre-diction models will reliably be less discriminatory if they are built to be explainable ra-ther than opaque. It is important that the question of whether accountability requires AI systems to be explainable boils down to empirical questions rather than normative ones, as it prevents us from seeing explainability as conceptually necessary for accountability and frees us to look for alternative solutions.

SOCIETAL AND SPECULATIVE EFFECTS

In this section, we consider some potential impacts of the use of AI systems within health care that are a little more speculative, in that there have been fewer concrete discussions in the literature pertaining to them, and these effects will likely be felt fur-ther in the future than the topics we have considered thus far. Nonetheless, we believe that the impact may be sufficiently large as to merit discussion.

First, there is a concern that the use of AI in health care can widen health inequality in societies for reasons beyond the discriminatory potential of algorithms that we have already discussed. Specifically, the concern here is that the potential of AI in health care might be utilized primarily for tackling conditions that are more prevalent amongst those who are already healthy and less for conditions, such as infectious diseases and antimicrobial resistance, that have a higher burden globally or are present amongst those who are least healthy (Joshi 2019; Topol 2019). As the capabilities of AI systems increase, the areas in which they are deployed will see the most gains in terms of health-care outcomes, and so a disproportionate deployment to serve those who are already relatively healthy (perhaps because of disproportionate funding) can worsen the already unequal distribution of health. It is important to note that such inequality would vio-late two competing approaches to health-care allocation, and so would be a concern regardless of which of these two approaches are believed to be right. First, it would vio-late a utilitarian approach to health allocation according to which the appropriate de-ployment of AI would be to those conditions for which the burden would be highest. Second, it would violate considerations of distributive justice in health care according to which the focus should be to prioritize improving the health of those who are worst off in society.

The clash between a utilitarian and a prioritarian approach is an existing one in global health, and not one which we aim to explore deeply. However, so far, approaches to the use of AI in health have been driven primarily by the availability of data and funding, neither of which ensure that either a utilitarian or a prioritarian approach is fulfilled (and, in fact, might ensure the opposite). Ensuring that health inequalities do not worsen as a result of the use of AI requires the formulation of guidelines for ethical AI deployment that would direct such development towards either those conditions with the greatest burden or those affecting the worst off (Winters et al. 2020).[7]

The second issue to consider is the impact of extensive AI use in health care on health-care professionals (HCPs). There already exists some empirical evidence for the prop-osition that reliance on computer aid or other innovations reduces the skills of HCPs (Tsai et al. 2003; Hoff 2011; Povyakalo et al. 2013), and the worry is that as AI systems become more capable and more pervasive, such de-skilling will increase significantly. While it seems that being able to provide health care through higher-performing processes would be good for health outcomes, there is the concern that in the long term, the quality of medical diagnostics itself will be lower than what it would have otherwise been (Froomkin et al. 2018). However, such analysis rests on fixed assumptions about the opacity of machine learning systems, assumptions which may have to be revised given the new directions research on deep learning might take (Bengio et al. 2019).

Beyond the question of de-skilling, there is also the question of HCP burnout. It is well established that burnout amongst clinicians has been accelerating, which in turn leads to medical errors (Shanafelt et al. 2010). Many have proposed that the use of AI in clinical settings could help reduce some of the stress that is placed on clinicians and ameliorate the burnout, improving their quality of life and allowing better perform-ance. However, the alternative is also possible—that adding AI use to clinical workflows increases the cognitive load facing clinicians (Maddox et al. 2019). The use of clinical decision support systems in the past has often added to the information clinicians need to process, often leading to instances of automation bias through over-reliance, given the difficulty of verifying the outputs of the decision aid (Lyell and Coiera 2017). This possibility is especially pertinent given past instances in which adoption of clinical innovations, such as electronic medical records, backfired and led to additional burden being placed on front-line HCPs (Verghese et al. 2018). While such concerns might be addressed by the evolution of medical education and medical practice to rely more easily and substantively on AI systems, for now it is an issue worth watching out for and considering.

CONCLUSION

In this chapter, we have attempted to provide an overview of the landscape of ethical issues for the use of AI systems in health care. In many ways, the use of AI systems in health care shines a light on the same ethical concerns that can be observed with AI use in other domains such as predictive policing, criminal sentencing, etc.—the importance of explainable systems, questions around their accountable use, and about the values imbued in such systems, such as fair treatment in recommendations. However, the discussion for the health-care context also departs from these general concerns in other ways, in terms of both the specific instantiations of the more general concerns (medical negligence for accountability, historical public health consensus around what constitutes fairness) as well as the entirely new challenges, such as the necessity of upholding the ideals of shared decision-making and patient-centred medicine. It is important to take the health-care context seriously, and not just assume that solutions worked out for AI elsewhere (such as techniques to make models more explainable) will suffice for transplantation.

There is plenty of further ethical research to be done, not just in answering the open questions that have been flagged in this chapter but also in addressing the adjacent topics that have not been covered, such as the health impacts of AI deployed in non-health settings (De Andrade et al. 2018). Further, any discussion of the ethics of AI in health care would be incomplete without a complementary discussion of data ethics, which similarly brings novel challenges in the health-care domain. It is our hope that through these discussions, we have the opportunity to not just reinforce but also rediscover the values and ethical commitments that should ground care provided across the health-care domain.

NOTES

1. We will return to the question of what constitutes bias or unfair discrimination at the end of the section.
2. To err on the side of stating the obvious, it is always important to be as sure as possible that under these conditions the unfair behaviour is actually because of differing base rates rather than because of historically different treatment that feeds back into the data we use to build the model.
3. The distinction between diagnosis and treatment is not always a clean one, especially when one considers cases where diagnosis is done *by* administering treatment for potential

ailments. Diagnostic decisions can thus be value-laden as well. However, for the purposes of this chapter, we shall continue to uncritically distinguish between these two processes.

4. Arguing for this claim and fully fleshing it out is beyond the scope of this chapter, and so for now we shall just raise it as a possible, but not yet defended, position.

5. To have AI models that operate in ethical ways, there also remains the further question of *how* such values should be encoded in AI models.

6. This remark precludes more speculative scenarios in which models can be prepared for patient-specific application before the application itself, perhaps by pre-emptively being trained on patient data or factoring in pre-articulated patient preferences (perhaps like a version of an advance directive for use under such settings).

7. For the purposes of preliminary analysis here, we have utilized only two accounts of justice that might apply—there are many others that also need to be considered, including those where a just arrangement might not preclude a given level of inequality.

References

Angwin, Julia, Larson, Jeff, Mattu, Surya, and Kirchner, Lauren (2016), 'Machine Bias: There's Software Used across the Country to Predict Future Criminals. and It's Biased against Blacks', *ProPublica* 23.

Ardila, Diego, Kiraly, Atilla P., Bharadwaj, Sujeeth, Choi, Bokyung, Reicher, Joshua J., Peng, Lily, et al. (2019), 'End-to-End Lung Cancer Screening with Three-Dimensional Deep Learning on Low-Dose Chest Computed Tomography', *Nature Medicine* 25, 954–961, doi: https://doi.org/10.1038/s41591-019-0447-x.

Awad, A., Bader-El-Den, M., McNicholas, J., and Briggs, J. (2017), 'Early Hospital Mortality Prediction of Intensive Care Unit Patients Using an Ensemble Learning Approach', *International Journal of Medical Informatics* 108, 185–195, doi: 10.1016/j.ijmedinf.2017.10.002.

Awad, Edmond, Dsouza, Sohan, Kim, Richard, Schulz, Jonathan, Henrich, Joseph, Shariff, Azim, et al. (2018), 'The Moral Machine Experiment', *Nature* 563, 59–64, doi: https://doi.org/10.1038/s41586-018-0637-6.

Bainbridge, L. (1983), 'Ironies of Automation', *Automatica* 19(6), 775–779.

Barry, M.J., and Edgman-Levitan, S. (2012), 'Shared Decision Making—the Pinnacle of Patient-Centred Care', *New England Journal of Medicine* 366, 780–781, doi: 10.1056/NEJMp1109283.

Beauchamp, Tom L. (2010), 'Autonomy and Consent', in F.G. Miller and A. Wertheimer, eds, *The Ethics of Consent* (New York: Oxford University Press), 55–78.

Bengio, Yoshua, Deleu, Tristan, Rahaman, Nasim, Ke, Rosemary, Lachapelle, Sebastien, Bilaniuk, Olexa, et al. (2019), 'A Meta-Transfer Objective for Learning to Disentangle Causal Mechanisms', *arXiv Preprint*,1901.10912 [cs.LG].

Bjerring, J.C., and Busch, J. (2020), 'Artificial Intelligence and Patient-Centred Decision-Making', *Philosophy & Technology* 34, 349–371, doi: https://doi.org/10.1007/s13347-019-00391-6.

Bojikian, K.D., Lee, C.S., and Lee, A.Y. (2019), 'Finding Glaucoma in Color Fundus Photographs Using Deep Learning', *JAMA Opthalmology* 137(12), 1361–1362, doi: 10.1001/jamaophthalmol.2019.3512.

Bovens, Mark (2007), 'Analysing and Assessing Accountability: A Conceptual Framework', *European Law Journal* 13(4), 447–468, doi: https://doi.org/10.1111/j.1468-0386.2007.00378.x arXiv:1468-0386.

Bussone, Adrian, Stumpf, Simone, and O'Sullivan, Dympna (2015), 'The Role of Explanations on Trust and Reliance in Clinical Decision Support Systems', 2015 International Conference on Healthcare Informatics (Dallas, TX), 160–169, IEEE.

Cave, S., Nyrup, R., Vold, K., and Weller, A. (2019), 'Motivations and Risks of Machine Ethics', *Proceedings of the IEEE* 107(3), 562–574.

Corbett-Davies, S., and Goel, S. (2018), 'The Measure and Mismeasure of Fairness: A Critical Review of Fair Machine Learning', *arXiv Preprint*, 1808.00023.

De Andrade, Norberta Nuno Gomes, Pawson, Dave, Muriello, Dan, Donahue, Lizzy, Guadagno, Jennifer (2018), 'Ethics and Artificial Intelligence: Suicide Prevention on Facebook', *Philosophy & Technology* 31, 669–684.

de Miguel Beriain, I. (2020), 'Should We Have a Right to Refuse Diagnostics and Treatment Planning by Artificial Intelligence?', *Medicine, Health Care and Philosophy* 23, 247–252, doi: https://doi.org/10.1007/s11019-020-09939-2.

Dickerson, J.P., and Sandholm, T. (2015), *FutureMatch: Combining Human Value Judgments and Machine Learning to Match in Dynamic Environments. The Twenty-Ninth AAAI Conference on Artificial Intelligence The Twenty-Seventh Conference on Innovative Applications of Artificial Intelligence* (AAAI Press, Palo Alto, California, USA).

Díez-Sanmartín, C., and Sarasa Cabezuelo, A. (2020), 'Application of Artificial Intelligence Techniques to Predict Survival in Kidney Transplantation: A Review', *Journal of Clinical Medicine* 9, 572.

Doshi-Velez, Finale, Kortz, Mason, Budish, Ryan, Bavitz, Christopher, Gershman, Samuel J., O'Brien, David, et al. (2017), *Accountability of AI under the Law: The Role of Explanation* (Berkman Center Research, Berkman).

Esteva, Andrew, Kuprel, Brett, Novoa, Roberto A., Ko, Justin, Swetter, Susan M. Blau, Helen M., et al. (2017), 'Dermatologist-Level Classification of Skin Cancer with Deep Neural Networks', *Nature* 542, 115–118, doi: https://doi.org/10.1038/nature21056.

Flechet, Marine, Falini, Stefano, Bonetti, Claudia, Güiza, Fabian, Schetz, Miet, Van den Berghe, Greet, et al. (2019), 'Machine Learning versus Physicians' Prediction of Acute Kidney Injury in Critically Ill Adults: A Prospective Evaluation of the AKI Predictor', *Critical Care* 23, 282, doi: 10.1186/s13054-019-2563-x.

Freedman, Rachel, Borg, Jana Schaich, Sinott-Armstrong, Walter, Dickerson, John P., Conitzer, Vincent (2020), 'Adapting a Kidney Exchange Algorithm to Align with Human Values', *Artificial Intelligence* 283, 103261, ISSN 0004-3702, doi: https://doi.org/10.1016/j.art int.2020.103261.

Froomkin, Michael A., Kerr, I.R., and Pineau, J. (2018), 'When AIs Outperform Doctors: The Dangers of a Tort-Induced Over-Reliance on Machine Learning and What (Not) to Do about It', *SSRN Electronic Journal*, 13 February, rev. 6 March 2019, doi: https://doi.org/10.2139/ssrn.3114347.

Gerke, S., Yeung, S., and Cohen, I.G. (2020), 'Ethical and Legal Aspects of Ambient Intelligence in Hospitals', *Journal of the American Medical Association* 323(7), 601–602, doi: doi:10.1001/jama.2019.21699.

Gulshan, Varun, Peng, Lily, Coram, Marc, Stumpe, Martin C., Wu, Derek, Narayanaswamy, Arunachalam, et al. (2016), 'Development and Validation of a Deep Learning Algorithm for Detection of Diabetic Retinopathy in Retinal Fundus Photographs', *Journal of the American Medical Association* 316(22), 2402–2410, doi: doi:10.1001/jama.2016.17216.

Gutierrez, G. (2020), 'Artificial Intelligence in the Intensive Care Unit', *Critical Care* 24, 101, doi: https://doi.org/10.1186/s13054-020-2785-y.

Haque, Albert, Guo, Michelle, Alahi, Alexandre, Yeung, Serena, Luo, Zelun, Rege, Alisha, et al. (2017), 'Towards Vision-Based Smart Hospitals: A System for Tracking and Monitoring Hand Hygiene Compliance', *Proceedings of Machine Learning Research* 68, 75–87.

Hoff, Timothy (2011), 'Deskilling and Adaptation among Primary Care Physicians Using Two Work Innovations', *Health Care Management Review* 36(4), 338–348, doi: 10.1097/HMR.0b013e31821826a1.

Joshi, I. (2019), 'Waiting for Deep Medicine', *The Lancet* 292(10177), 1193–1194, doi: https://doi.org/10.1016/S0140-6736(19)30579-3.

Khalid, S., Goldenberg, M., Grantcharov, T., Taati, B., and Rudzicz, F. (2020), 'Evaluation of Deep Learning Models for Identifying Surgical Actions and Measuring Performance', *JAMA Network Open* 3(3), e201664, doi: doi:10.1001/jamanetworkopen.2020.1664.

Kleinberg, J., Mullainathan, S., and Raghavan, M. (2016), 'Inherent Trade-Offs in the Fair Determination of Risk Scores', *arXiv Preprint*,160905807, doi: http://arxiv.org/abs/1609.05807.

Liang, H., Tsui, B.Y., Ni, H., Valentim, C.C.S., Baxter, S.L., Liu, G., et al. (2019), 'Evaluation and Accurate Diagnoses of Pediatric Diseases Using Artificial Intelligence', *Nature Medicine* 25, 433–438, doi: https://doi.org/10.1038/s41591-018-0335-9.

London, Alex John (2019), 'Artificial Intelligence and Black-Box Medical Decisions: Accuracy versus Explainability', *Hastings Center Report* 49(1), 15–21, doi: 10.1002/hast.973.

Long, R. (2020), 'Fairness in Machine Learning: Against False Positive Rate Equality as a Measure of Fairness' https://doi.org/10.48550/arXiv.2007.02890 (ms).

Lyell, David, and Coiera, Enrico (2017), 'Automation Bias and Verification Complexity: A Systematic Review', *Journal of the American Medical Informatics Association* 24(2), 423–431, doi: https://doi.org/10.1093/jamia/ocw105.

Maddox, T.M., Rumsfeld, J.S., and Payne, P.R.O. (2019), 'Questions for Artificial Intelligence in Health Care', *Journal of the American Medical Association* 321(1), 31–32, doi:10.1001/jama.2018.18932.

McDougall, R.J. (2019), 'Computer Knows Best? The Need for Value-Flexibility in Medical AI', *Journal of Medical Ethics* 45, 156–160.

Mirnezami, R, and Ahmed, A. (2018), 'Surgery 3.0, Artificial Intelligence and the Next-Generation Surgeon', *British Journal of Surgery* 105(5), 463–465.

Mishra, Abhishek (2019), 'Responsible Usage of Machine Learning Classifiers in Clinical Practice', *Journal of Law and Medicine* 27(1).

Obermeyer, Ziad, Powers, Brian, Vogeli, Christine, Mullainathan, Sendhil (2019), 'Dissecting Racial Bias in an Algorithm Used to Manage the Health of Populations', *Science* 366(6464), 447–453, doi: 10.1126/science.aax2342.

Organ Procurement and Transplantation Network (n.d.), *OPTN Policies: Secretarial Review and Appeals* (OPTN), 42 CFR s. 121.4.

Panch, Trishan, Pearson-Stuttard, Jonathan, greaves, Felix, Atun, Rifat (2019), 'Artificial Intelligence: Opportunities and Risks for Public Health', *The Lancet Digital Health* 1(1), PE13–E14, doi: https://doi.org/10.1016/S2589-7500(19)30002-0.

Parasuraman, R., and Riley, V. (1997), 'Humans and Automation: Use, Misuse, Disuse, Abuse', *Human Factors* 39(2), 230–253, doi: https://doi.org/10.1518/001872097778543886.

Ploug , T., and Holm, S. (2020), 'The Right to Refuse Diagnostics and Treatment Planning by Artificial Intelligence', *Medicine, Health Care and Philosophy* 23, 107–114, doi: https://doi.org/10.1007/s11019-019-09912-8.

Poplin, Ryan, Varadarajan, Avinash V., Blumer, Katy, Yun, Liu, McConell, Michael V., Corrado, Greg S., et al. (2018), 'Prediction of Cardiovascular Risk Factors from Retinal Fundus

Photographs via Deep Learning', *Nature Biomedical Engineering* 2, 158–164, doi: https://doi.org/10.1038/s41551-018-0195-0.

Povyakalo, A.A., Alberdi, E., Strigini, L., and Ayton, P. (2013), 'How to Discriminate between Computer-Aided and Computer-Hindered Decisions: A Case Study in Mammography', *Medical Decision Making* 33(1), 98–107, doi: https://doi.org/10.1177/0272989X12465490.

Price, W.N., Gerke, S., and Cohen, I.G. (2019), 'Potential Liability for Physicians Using Artificial Intelligence', *Journal of the American Medical Association* 322(18), 1765–1766, doi: doi:10.1001/jama.2019.15064.

Rajkomar, A., Hardt, M., Howell, M.D., Corrado, G., and Chin, M.H. (2018), 'Ensuring Fairness in Machine Learning to Advance Health Equity', *Annals of Internal Medicine* 169(12), 866–872, doi: https://doi.org/10.7326/M18-1990.

Reese, P.P., Boudville, N., and Garg, A.X. (2015), 'Living Kidney Donation: Outcomes, Ethics, and Uncertainty', *The Lancet* 385(9981), 2003–2013, doi: 10.1016/S0140-6736(14)62484-3.

Roth, A.E., Sonmez, T., and Unver, M.U. (2004), 'Kidney Exchange', *Quarterly Journal of Economics* 119(2), 457–488.

Savulescu, J., Kahane, G., and Gyngell, C. (2019), 'From Public Preferences to Ethical Policy', *Nature Human Behaviour* 3, 1241–1243, doi: https://doi.org/10.1038/s41562-019-0711-6.

Schönberger, Daniel (2019), 'Artificial Intelligence in Healthcare: A Critical Analysis of the Legal and Ethical Implications', *International Journal of Law and Information Technology* 27(2), 171–203, doi: https://doi.org/10.1093/ijlit/eaz004.

Shanafelt, T.D., Balch, C.M., Bechamps, G., Russell, T., Dyrbye, L., Satele, D., et al. (2010), 'Burnout and Medical Errors among American Surgeons', *Annals of Surgery* 251(6), 995–1000, doi: 10.1097/SLA.0b013e3181bfdab3.

Sherman, Maya, and Greenbaum, Dov (2019), 'Ethics of AI in Transplant Matching: Is It Better or Just More of the Same?', *American Journal of Bioethics* 19(11), 45–47, doi: 10.1080/15265161.2019.1665734.

Sotoodeh, M., and Ho, J.C. (2019), 'Improving Length of Stay Prediction Using a Hidden Markov Model', *AMIA Joint Summits on Translational Science Proceedings* May 2019, 425–434.

Strawson, P.F. (1994), 'Freedom and Resentment', in John Martin Fischer and Mark Ravizza, eds, *Perspectives on Moral Responsibility*, (Cornell University Press), 45–66.

Topol, E.J. (2019), 'High-Performance Medicine: The Convergence of Human and Artificial Intelligence', *Nature Medicine* 25, 44–56, doi: https://doi.org/10.1038/s41591-018-0300-7.

Tsai, Theodore L., Fridsma, Douglas B., Gatti, Guido (2003), 'Computer Decision Support as a Source of Interpretation Error: The Case of Electrocardiograms', *Journal of the American Medical Informatics Association* 10(5), 478–483, doi: https://doi.org/10.1197/jamia.M1279.

Verghese, A., Shah, N.H., and Harrington, R.A. (2018), 'What This Computer Needs is a Physician: Humanism and Artificial Intelligence', *Journal of the American Medical Association* 319(1), 19–20, doi:10.1001/jama.2017.19198.

Walsh, C.G., Ribeiro, J.D., and Franklin, J.C. (2017), 'Predicting Risk of Suicide Attempts Over Time through Machine Learning', *Clinical Psychological Science* 5(3), 457–469, doi: https://doi.org/10.1177/2167702617691560.

Wartman, Combs (2019), 'Reimagining Medical Education in the Age of AI', *AMA Journal of Ethics* 21(2), E146–152.

Wieland, Jan Willem (2017), 'Introduction: The Epistemic Condition', in Philip Robichaud and Jan Willem Wieland, eds, *Responsibility: The Epistemic Condition* (Oxford: Oxford University Press).

Wieringa, M. (2020), 'What to Account for When Accounting for Algorithms: A Systematic Literature Review on Algorithmic Accountability', *Proceedings of the 2020 Conference on Fairness, Accountability, and Transparency (FAT* '20)* (New York: Association for Computing Machinery), 1–18, doi: https://doi.org/10.1145/3351095.3372833.

Winters, Niall, Venkatapuram, Sridhar, Geniets, Anne, Wynne-Bannister, Emma (2020), 'Prioritarian Principles for Digital Health in Low Resource Settings', *Journal of Medical Ethics* 46, 259–264.

Yeung, Serena, Rinaldo, Francesca, Jopling, Jeffrey, Liu, Bingbin, Mehra, Rishab, Downing, N. Lance, et al. (2019), 'A Computer Vision System for Deep Learning-Based Detection of Patient Mobilization Activities in the ICU', *npj Digital Medicine* 2, 11, doi: https://doi.org/10.1038/s41746-019-0087-z.

Zou J., and Schiebinger, L. (2018), 'AI Can Be Sexist and Racist—It's Time to Make It Fair', *Nature* 559, 324–326.

CHAPTER 26

HEALTH AND DIGITAL TECHNOLOGY PARTNERSHIPS

Too Close for Comfort?

LAURA SPECKER SULLIVAN

INTRODUCTION

IN the past decade, digital technology companies have sought partnerships with academic medical institutions, governmental health agencies, and health-care companies at an astounding rate. Those involved tout these partnerships as empowering consumers, driving innovation, and increasing efficiency. At the same time, ethical red flags have been raised over potential violations of patient privacy and unsanctioned use of data for non-medical purposes (Mittelstadt and Floridi 2016; Vayena and Blasimme 2018). Most of these partnerships are designed to tackle the immense hurdle of making sense out of patients' medical data stored in electronic health records (EHRs), data which is protected by the Health Insurance Portability and Accountability Act (HIPAA) in the United States, the General Data Protection Regulation in the European Union (EU), and other privacy regulations elsewhere. While contract transparency is a core ethical concern when individuals' personal health data is involved, a broader question is whether these contracts are different from more established health-care partnerships.

Relationships between health-care providers and a range of companies, such as the pharmaceutical giant Pfizer, the medical technology creator Medtronic, and the electronic health-care software developer Athenahealth, are nothing new. Yet big data partnerships such as those entered into with Google, Amazon, Apple, and Microsoft are unique in that these companies neither specialize in the health-care industry nor provide health-care institutions with an identifiable medical product. In this chapter, I focus on the ethical issues that emerge when health-care institutions partner with digital technology companies to develop big data analytic tools for the health arena. The issues I address here are largely institutional, involving questions about the appropriate role of digital technology corporations in an arena that, at least in theory, is oriented towards the physical, mental, and social well-being of everyone within a society.

It is true that health care–digital technology partnerships come with undeniable, if at times overstated, benefits (Powles 2019). As marketing teams know all too well, these partnerships can generate new medical knowledge and can personalize clinical care. However, institutions have specific interests and missions. The health-care arena ostensibly targets health and well-being. Digital technology companies are not similarly oriented, even when they profess to aim at user wellness. This does not necessarily mean that they cannot improve the well-being of their users, just that they have private interests distinct from the common good, broadly conceived as the well-being of a community in terms of shared values and goals, a conception that includes health. These priorities can conflict with the goal of health-care institutions, which is—or ought to be—to improve the health of individual patients and the broader public. Other aims—financial solvency, technological progress, and so on—are means to that end. In short, there is a difference between the health-care industry using big data to improve medical practices and the digital technology industry using health data to improve algorithms. While the former tends to be oriented towards improving people's lives, the latter tends to be oriented towards improving proprietary tools.

This distinction between the goals of health care and the goal of digital technology are not insignificant. Yet while ethical analyses of big data often focus on the issues raised by the data science tools used to analyse and understand big data, such as machine learning algorithms, ethical issues are not limited to how technological tools are used but to who uses them and why. Different institutions in this landscape have different aims, and there may be good reasons for health-care institutions to avoid partnerships with digital technology corporations. Just as individuals have interests and allegiances due to their professions and their employers, so too do institutions. A corporation is answerable to shareholders in a way that a public health-care institution is not, and this difference is not inconsequential due to the way it shapes the institution's priorities. It is important to note that, due to differences in countries' approaches to public health-care systems, multinational digital technology companies' interactions with health-care institutions also varies, depending on the national context. This chapter focuses largely on Anglophone countries, within which the difference between the United States, where state and federal health care is relatively thin, and the United Kingdom, with a more substantial social welfare programme, is stark. Due to this variation, some of the argumentation will be more relevant to the US context, while some will be a better fit for the United Kingdom.

In the second section, I describe how health-care institutions are partnering with digital technology companies to manage and utilize the big medical data in patients' EHRs. I observe in the third section that these partnerships do present opportunities, including—but not limited to—the production of new, knowledge-based analyses of EHR data and the capacity to use this new knowledge to better personalize patients' medical care. Yet they also pose ethical risks. In the fourth section, I explain that the nature of the institutions involved and their divergent missions—one set aimed at improving patients' health and well-being, another at perfecting and popularizing proprietary data analytic tools—lead to unique conflicts of interest. In the fifth section, I argue that these conflicts of interest can result in efficiency being prioritized over the common good, contributing to a feedback loop of injustice.

In the sixth section, I propose that mitigating these risks requires, as a first step, asking what these partnerships are for and whether they are truly necessary to meet healthcare institutions' aims. If these partnerships are deemed necessary, then the second step is to be transparent with the public about the risks that these conflicts of interest pose. This includes creating a pathway for community interests to affect institutional decision-making, such as through a community advisory board. Finally, the third step is to identify both a set of shared norms to regulate the relationship and a set of bright lines that will not be crossed. Without these steps, then health care–digital technology partnerships will not only fail to meet the goals of their contract but they will also erode the public value of, and the public trust in, institutions that are meant to facilitate health as part of the common good. The seventh section concludes.

HEALTH AND DIGITAL TECHNOLOGY PARTNERSHIPS

In 2017, the University of Chicago Medical Center (UCMC) and Google announced a new partnership. UCMC would share de-identified patient data with Google, and Google would investigate ways to put the data to use, identifying patterns to enable predictive analysis in medicine. By 2019, UCMC and Google were sued in a class-action lawsuit (later dismissed) alleging that the data had not been properly de-identified (Wakabayashi 2019; Landi 2020).

This is not a new position for Google. In 2016, a similar partnership between DeepMind Health and Britain's National Health Service (NHS) was alleged to compromise patient privacy. In autumn 2019, Google Health fully absorbed DeepMind Health and took over responsibility for all its contracts with the NHS, ending DeepMind's independent ethics panel and ceasing the policy of publishing its NHS contracts openly, raising concerns about legitimate oversight and transparency (Vaughn 2019).[1] In late 2019, Google announced a partnership with Ascension Health in the United States that would share patient data across twenty-one states (Davis 2019). They also acquired Fitbit, one of the most popular makers of fitness-tracking wearable devices (Wakabayashi and Satariano 2019).

Google is not alone in seeking such partnerships with medical institutions. In 2018, Amazon purchased the online pharmacy start-up PillPack, with plans to ship prescriptions to customers throughout the continental United States (Farr 2019). That same year, Apple enabled its health app to download patients' EHRs to view on an iPhone, described as a move that would 'empower consumers with convenient access to health information' (Muoio 2019). In 2019, the University of California, Los Angeles (UCLA) announced a partnership with Microsoft's cloud computing service, Azure, 'to synthesize vast amounts of clinical and research data to speed medical discoveries and improve patient care' (Microsoft News Center 2019). With the COVID-19 pandemic in 2020, companies like Google and Apple have partnered with governmental health agencies to track the spread between individuals.[2]

Digital technology companies such as Google, Amazon, Apple, and Microsoft are rapidly pursuing partnerships with academic medical institutions such as UCLA, governmental health agencies such as the NHS, and health-care companies such as Ascension Health. A 2019 report by the Chartis Group, an advisory firm based in the United States focused on the health-care industry, stated that by 2018, 84 per cent of Fortune 500 companies 'play in healthcare', an increase from 76 per cent in 2013. They also reported that in the first half of 2018, funding for health-care start-ups topped $15 billion USD.

One of these start-ups is two-year-old Verana Health, which aims to 'empower physicians and life science companies with deeper data insights to accelerate medical research and change lives' (their homepage, Shieber 2020). The Chartis Group's appraisal of these health-care industry developments is similarly rosy, suggesting that 'these emerging partnerships enable providers to secure the capabilities that will be necessary to ensure their sustained growth and viability in this era of healthcare digital industrialization' (The Chartis Group 2019). Indeed, a common refrain in announcements about partnerships between digital technology companies and medical institutions is that the partnership will develop better ways of managing and analysing patient information that lead to improvements in patient care. These developments will 'empower' both patients and providers. Less frequently stated is how these partnerships will benefit digital technology companies, as they surely will. In the United States, health care accounts for nearly 20 per cent of the gross domestic product (GDP).[3] For digital technology companies that have grown so big that antitrust efforts are frequently directed against them, health care remains one of the last areas in which these companies can target growth for their shareholders and expand their influence (Kang and McCabe 2020).

In these partnerships, the ethical issues include but also transcend privacy and the need to de-identify data; accordingly, this chapter focuses on the features of institutional partnerships that ground the use of big data tools in health care.[4] As digital technology companies continue to aggressively pursue novel relationships with the health sector, the different values of these two industries are salient, despite their emphasis on a shared dedication to health system improvement. While health care–digital technology partnerships may identify methods of generating meaningful outcomes from mountains of EHR data, for whom are they meaningful and for what purpose? Pursuing this question need not entail being a luddite about the possibilities of pairing medicine with technology. There are many ways in which these partnerships could be immensely helpful to patients and providers alike, as I explain in the next section. However, there will also be divergences of interests such that these partnerships pull health-care institutions, which should aim at the common good, in the direction of private interests. Given that neither health-care institutions nor the digital technology companies with which they partner have transparently acknowledged these divergences thus far, it is essential that those working in digital ethics do not lose sight of them.

OPPORTUNITIES FOR BENEFIT

Partnerships between health-care providers and digital technology companies are not necessarily opportunistic, solely for the sake of profit. Rather, these contracts reflect health-care institutions' need for data analytic tools that can manage and make use of the medical data they collect. Given the vast amount of data that is locked away in EHRs, it would be irresponsible *not* to identify patterns in this data that enable health-care systems to run more smoothly in ways that lead to improvements in patient care.[5] The question is how to do so.[6]

Identifying patterns across innumerable patient charts is a herculean effort. The information in EHRs qualify as what is known as 'Big Data': data sets that meet the 'three Vs' of high volume (large amounts of data), high velocity (data acquired and analysed quickly), and high variability (data from different types of sources). The statistical methods common in clinical research are not suitable for such data sets because these methods are theory-driven and confirmatory. In the absence of any theories that can be tested with such large and 'messy' data sets, data-driven and exploratory methods using machine learning are more appropriate (Cobb et al. 2018). Machine learning algorithms can then be used as tools for the analysis of big data sets and the prediction of how a new data point will fit into the set. Health-care administrators may be able to more accurately and quickly identify trends in patient needs, allowing them to better allocate funds and resources in their institutions. Individual clinicians may be able to identify appropriate treatment for patients based on real-time analysis of symptoms and side effects of patients with similar profiles.

The first major opportunity in bringing digital technology companies' tools to bear on big medical data is the generation of new knowledge. Currently, we do not know the full range of patterns that might be identified by allowing machine learning to work through the data in patients' EHRs. Much of this information is unstructured. By using natural language processing, it may be possible to identify trends in the chaotic content of patients' charts that improve their care (Murdoch and Detsky 2013). There have already been some breakthroughs. Big data analytics have been used to analyse radiation images and to interpret genetic data (Ienca et al. 2018). For example, it may be possible to more accurately predict breast cancer survival based on genetic and molecular markers that are analysed via machine learning (Cobb et al. 2018). These are possibilities, not certainties, and scepticism about whether digital technology companies will actually be able to deliver on their promises is warranted (Emanuel and Wachter 2019).[7]

The second major opportunity represented by health care–digital technology partnerships is the personalization of clinical care. The more clinicians can use individual patient data to locate a patient within a broader pattern of effective care, the better they can offer precise predictions and recommendations. Essentially, the more clinicians can relate patients' individual information to broader data sets, the better they can identify unique features of patients' situations that make a difference for their health. This second opportunity with health care–digital technology partnerships builds on the first—the more patterns that are identified within big medical data, the more individual patients can be located within those patterns.

One of the major proposals for personalizing care is also the most controversial. Researchers have suggested linking patients' medical data with their socio-demographic data—information about where they live, where they shop, their credit score, and so on. Just as biomarkers can be used to predict disease, so is there increasing interest in what are known as 'geomarkers' or 'community vital signs': data points about the communities in which patients live that can be used to predict factors that would help clinicians to personalize patient care (Bazemore et al. 2016; Hughes et al. 2016; Beck et al. 2017). Recent years have seen increasing interest in how patients' home location can affect their health, with studies linking US zip codes to life expectancies, not just extrapolating from the particular environment of that zip code but also based on information about who tends to live there.

Such research seeks to identify and, ideally, rectify health disparities based on social determinants of health by accounting for the effect of social, economic, occupational, and environmental factors (Bazemore et al. 2016, DeVoe 2016, Cantor 2018). Yet, this research is controversial because such linkages can also serve to reinforce disparities by contributing to explicit and implicit biases about patients based on where they live and other elements of their socio-demographic background. Further, the more information that is collected about individuals, the more that re-identification from large data sets becomes possible (Rocher et al. 2019). In other words, as with many aspects of big data research, the analytical tools developed can be used to help or to harm, and the boundary between the two is not always clear.

Nevertheless, for those whose glass is half full, big data analytics does offer one means of identifying health disparities. While some information about social determinants of health can be individually collected, not all health-care institutions have the capacity to manage it. Further, population-level data must be connected with individual charts to generate meaningful recommendations. Some have proposed linking community-level geocoded data with EHRs such that providers can identify whether a particular patient 'lives in the presence of poverty, healthy food and water sources, walkable streets and parks, and has social capital—or how these add up to predict increased risk of morbidity, early mortality, or other adverse health outcomes' (Bazemore et al. 2016: 408). Setting aside the ethical concerns about privacy and the unintentional amplification of disparities noted above, such linkages could improve patient care by accounting for the effects of social determinants of health. As Kristin Voigt has argued, there may be costs to particular patients in not making some of this information available (Voigt 2019).

Patients and providers are not the only ones who would be interested in this information; insurance companies and other gatekeepers have an interest in it as well. For example, Lysaght et al. describe how predictions of disease course and likelihood of re-hospitalization are simultaneously useful in the clinic and helpful for insurers. The more insurers know about the likelihood of particular patient's re-hospitalization, the more precisely they can calculate their risk profiles and adjust their premiums (Lysaght et al. 2019: 304). Thus, personalization of care is not always intended to benefit the patient—it can also be used to mitigate risk for insurance companies and others with financial interests in health-care systems. This is clearly a benefit for the insurance industry; whether it benefits the patient is another matter, which I will address in more detail below.

This section has shown that there are opportunities in partnerships between health-care institutions and digital technology companies to analyse and utilize the big data currently captured in the chaos of patients' EHRs. However, opportunities rarely come without costs. In the following sections, I detail two major, linked ethical concerns: (a) the influence of divergent institutional interests on decision-making; and (b) the prioritization of economic efficiency over other aims, such as health-care equity or justice.

THE PERILS OF PARTNERSHIP: WHEN INTERESTS DIVERGE

While the use of big data analytic tools in health care could generate new knowledge and personalize care, as well as potentially improve other dimensions of health-care systems, there is also a wide variety of ethical questions about these tools. Ethical concerns include privacy violations, explainability of AI algorithms and machine learning tools (see also Mittelstadt, this volume), incorporation of bias into supposedly objective algorithms, and so on (see Mishra et al., this volume). While these are all valid concerns, here, I do not consider ethical issues with big data tools themselves; rather, I address the kinds of institutional partnerships that are pursued to make them possible. Specifically, as I explain in this section, health care–digital technology partnerships open the door for conflicts of interest that diverge from those traditionally seen in medicine.

The traditional worry with conflicts of interest in medicine is that, if a provider is being paid by a pharmaceutical company, it incentivizes them to prescribe that company's product, even if it is not the best prescription for a given patient. These same conflicts are also a risk in industry-sponsored research, where a researcher may feel pressure to produce a result favourable to the sponsoring company's product. In one influential definition, a conflict of interest occurs whenever a professional's judgement with respect to a primary interest is influenced by a secondary interest, such as personal financial benefit (Marks 2019: 113). In the clinical case, the conflicting interests are the providers' self-interest due to their financial benefit from the pharmaceutical company and the patient's interest, the latter of which ought to be prioritized in fiduciary relationships in which a beneficiary entrusts something of value, such as their health, to a trustee who is thereby obligated to act in the beneficiary's interest with respect to the object of trust. In the case of the researcher, the conflict is between the researcher's self-interest and objective science; results are supposed to flow from the data and not from the researchers' allegiances or financial interests.

Even well-intentioned clinicians are liable to lapses of judgement when financial conflicts exist. For instance, psychologist Dan Ariely has shown how it is more likely for individuals to rationalize acting in their own financial interest at the expense of their professional integrity when the material they are dealing with is not cash and when their actions only indirectly provide financial benefit (Ariely 2008). In other words, the less directly an action is tied to actually taking money for it, the more likely it is that an individual will justify doing something they ought not to do.

In the case of health care–digital technology partnerships, the conflicts are even less direct than in these traditional types of conflicts of interest—there is not any one product that a provider is being paid to peddle, and the relationship with the digital technology company is institutional, not individual. One way of thinking about these conflicts is as institutional conflicts of interest. David Resnik defines an institutional conflict of interest as 'a situation in which the institution or its leaders (such as presidents, chancellors, vice presidents, deans, or department heads) have interests that may compromise judgment or decision-making concerning its primary professional, ethical, or legal obligations or academic aims' (Resnik 2019: 1661). As with individual conflicts of interest, institutional conflicts of interest skew decision-making in the direction of an institution's financial relationship with another organization, potentially leading it to compromise its mission.

The ethical worry with institutional conflicts of interests is not just the harm that biased decision-making may visit on patients and other fiduciary clients of the institution. There is also the risk that once mistakes are made public, trust in the institution will degrade, just as it would with an individual whose decision-making has been compromised (Resnik 2019: 1661). Institutional trust is key because of the mission of health-care institutions, providers, and researchers to pursue patient and public well-being—a mission that arguably exists whether that health-care institution exists in the capitalistic US context or in the social welfare context of the United Kingdom. An institution's financial self-interest, or that of any one of the providers within it, can threaten that mandate. As with an individual conflict of interest, the core of an institutional conflict of interest is the introduction of an interest or a goal that competes with what ought to be the primary goal of the institution. Both individual patients and broader public groups trust health-care institutions to have their best interests in mind. Health-care institutions must be exceedingly careful that they do not betray the public trust by making decisions in pursuit of other interests.

Partnerships with digital technology companies may introduce competing interests. In *The Perils of Partnership*, Jonathan Marks argues that public and private institutions have fundamentally different missions, purposes, and functions. While advocates of partnerships tend to emphasize the convergences between public and private interests, Marks highlights their divergences (Marks 2019: 4). He distinguishes between three concepts that can aid in thinking about the goals of institutions and how financial interests might distort them: the common good, the public good, and the public interest. The common good is the well-being of the community in terms of its shared values and goals. The public good is the good of the public understood as the space where individuals interact in social life, while not necessarily being members of a shared community. Finally, the public interest is the collection of private interests of individuals within a society.

Marks proposes that while corporations (such as Google or Apple) may contribute to the common good, they are not guardians of the common good and they do not aim at the common good. Rather, in pursuing their private commercial interests, they may incidentally also help the community due to intersections between their private interests and the common good (Marks 2019: 35). Yet, it does not follow that the company has the same interests as the community merely because it contributes to the common good. Private corporations, especially digital technology companies without local footprints, tend to not be members of local communities and thus do participate in the common good. There are real divergences between the benefit they receive from the sale of private goods and the good of the communities to whom they sell those goods.

As with more traditional conflicts of interest, digital technology companies—especially Google, Apple, Amazon, and Microsoft, the first three of which are the subject of antitrust investigations in the United States and the EU—have private financial interests that can sway decision-making away from the well-being of their customers and thus away from both the common good and the public interest (Kang and McCabe 2020). These companies have no broader mandate to improve public health, even though they may profess to aim at it. The same cannot be said of health-care institutions, which do take the well-being of their patients and broader communities—and thus the common good and the public interest—as their mission and mandate. This discrepancy between institutional goals can lead to potential conflicts in discrete decision-making, such as when it may be economically profitable to monetize patients' data or to use it to create more precise marketing profiles based on patients' health-care system usage. It can also slightly alter the priorities of institutions in non-discrete ways, such as when a health-care institution favours technologically advanced approaches to patient care that privilege some patient groups over others, reducing communities' equity of access.

As Marks warns, emphasizing convergences of interests downplays the risks of divergences of interests and is a 'Panglossian' view such that these partnerships take place in the best of all possible worlds (Marks 2019: 71). This emphasis is readily apparent in the descriptions of health care—digital technology partnerships above, where there is an optimistic celebration of harnessing the computing power of technology to make new discoveries in health data in line with the long-standing tradition of Silicon Valley's techno-optimism, an outlook that is not universally shared in other cultural contexts. Marks's concern is that the more institutional leaders focus on the favourable side of partnerships between organizations with different mandates, the less they will be able to identify and manage the influence of the more powerful organization on the mandate of the weaker one. In health care—digital technology partnerships, it is not difficult to pick out the more powerful entity.

Due to the imbalance in power and resources between health-care institutions and digital technology companies, the core mission of the latter—developing better digital technology tools—can usurp the former's mission to serve their populations. This can be seen in digital technology companies' attempts to solve clinical problems by, in essence, throwing more data at the problem. Yet, as Chen and Asch observe, 'even a perfectly calibrated prediction model may not translate into better clinical care' (Chen and Asch 2017: 2507). In their estimation, there is immense predictive power in health care–digital technology partnerships—as long as these partnerships are pursued in the right way. The key is recognizing that big data analytic tools are useless without clinician insight (Chen and Asch 2017: 2508).

The skewed perspective of digital technology companies is not just apparent in the search for nails to fit their hammer; it can also be seen in the optimistic faith that digital technology will inevitably improve health care. In a popular New Yorker article entitled, 'Why Doctors Hate Their Computers', Atul Gawande explains how, as technology is integrated with medicine, individual clinicians form closer connections with their computers to navigate increasingly complex EHRs, leading to more distant connections with their patients (Gawande 2018). In Gawande's estimation, the human core of the physician–patient relationship was neglected in the move to EHRs. While many clinicians have now returned to taking notes by paper and pen during the clinical encounter to enable eye contact and other methods of interpersonal connection, doing so adds an additional step to each patient encounter, creating more work, not less. Had medical technologists recognized that the goal is the care and not the tool, such a predicament might have been avoided.

A central concern of health care–digital technology partnerships ought to be the management of conflicting missions and aims between these two very different types of institutions. Divergent interests ought to be monitored and tracked, especially when those divergences can decrease the health-care institution's ability to contribute to the common good or the public interest or can lead it to violate its obligations to fiduciaries. While institutional conflict-of-interest policies and disclosure of financial relationships may help by repairing trust through transparency (such as through the Physician Payments Sunshine Act in the United States, part of the Affordable Care Act), few health-care institutions publicly acknowledge—or describe attempts to mitigate—conflicts of interest in digital technology partnerships, and transparency itself is a complex notion in this context (see Mittelstadt, this volume). Marks's concern of a 'Panglossian' perspective seems apt. While a critical question for these partnerships moving forward is how institutions will manage their conflicts, a first step is acknowledging that such conflicts exist—something that so far, few health-care institutions partnering with major digital corporations have voluntarily done.

PURSUING EFFICIENCY AND
AMPLIFYING INJUSTICE

A common refrain in the discussion on big data in health care is that current methods of recording data, such as in EHRs, are inefficient—clinicians spend immense amounts of time keeping them up to date without comparable benefit. Big data analytics are advocated as a means of increasing health-care system efficiency by extracting more benefit from EHRs, a benefit that, in an optimistic estimation, contributes not just to the bottom line but to patient care as well, although the two can come apart.

Efficiency is certainly a value for health-care systems facing excessive demand for their resources, but it need not be the only one or the most pressing. Currently, many health-care systems are inefficient—especially in the United States, more is spent per patient than necessary and significant resources are utilized on diagnosis and treatment rather than on preventive care (not to mention the use of excessive and unnecessary tests that drive profit but have no real effect on patient care) (Berwick and Hackbarth 2012; Fuchs 2018). Data technology partnerships may seem like an attractive way to pursue efficiency, identifying areas of waste that may only be visible using big data analytic tools. By isolating where resources are used unnecessarily, data analytics can help to trim budgets and allocate expenditures in ways that are responsive, in real time, to changes in patient and provider needs.

The concern with this focus on efficiency is not just that it reflects a private interest but that its pursuit can be at the expense of other goods, especially those that operate in the background of our human systems rather than ones we must intentionally incorporate. In Nick Bostrom's well-known example of the paper clip maximizer (Bostrom 2014), prioritizing the efficient production of paper clips leads the maximization machine to create paper clips out of everything, including human beings and, eventually, the whole world. This example is meant to show, among other things, that artificially intelligent systems only prioritize what they are designed to prioritize—human values that are not built into the system are excluded, and background conditions that we may take for granted could be unintentionally left out (e.g. we know that human beings ought not to be used as material for paper clips, but our technology does not know this unless we tell it so). In the context of health care–digital technology partnerships, while big data analytics can be a useful tool for streamlining and operationalizing patient health data, caution must be taken not to exclude values that humans know to consider but digital tools do not.

Take, for example, the personal anecdote Virginia Eubanks uses to begin *Automating Inequality* (2018). When Eubanks's partner was attacked soon after she began a new job (and thus new health insurance, which is tied to employment in the United States), her access suddenly changed—one pharmacy's system showed that she had no coverage and the hospital showed no start date for coverage. She suspected that her family had been red-flagged by an algorithm, which had identified her partner's large hospital costs directly after gaining new insurance as possible evidence of fraud (Eubanks 2018: 3). While she was able to correct these errors eventually through her employer's human resources department and her own (fortunate) free time, Eubanks explains that algorithmic systems designed to improve efficiency often target poor and otherwise marginalized communities, whose environments necessitate behaviour that may be judged risky: accessing public benefits, walking through highly policed neighbourhoods, requiring emergency health care, and crossing national borders. This behaviour leads these groups to be targeted by punitive public policy and more intense surveillance, 'a kind of collective red-flagging, a feedback loop of injustice' (Eubanks 2018: 7).

Arguably, justice is one of the background conditions that is easy (especially for those who enjoy relative privilege) to unintentionally omit from automated systems. Perhaps most commonly understood as models for the fair distribution of goods, many theories of justice consider health care to be one of many social goods that ought to be evenly distributed among all members of society (or distributed such that there is equality of access, or equity of opportunity, or some other way of assessing fair distribution). Without examining the details of theories of justice just yet, suffice to say that there is broad agreement that health-care justice, conceived as equal access, is important, even though there is specific disagreement about how to achieve it.

In describing injustice as a feedback loop of inequality of access to resources and care faced by individuals who are already marginalized in a given society, Eubanks's use of injustice trades on a conception of justice as structural. The concept of structural injustice is explicated by Iris Marion Young in *Justice and the Politics of Difference* and *Responsibility for Justice*. In the former, Young proposes that a just society is one which contains and supports the institutional conditions necessary for the realization of the general requirements for the good life, which are self-development and self-determination (Young 1990: 37). Injustice, in a structural view, refers not to any one unjust decision one person may make or any single material good being unfairly distributed but to patterns of decision-making, labour distribution, and cultural practices that further entrench domination, which is the institutional constraint on self-determination, and oppression, which is the institutional constraint on self-development (Young 1990: 37). Societies exhibit structures of domination when they limit individuals' abilities to develop their capacities (such as through education and training), and they exhibit structures of oppression when they limit individuals' abilities to make particular choices and to shape the environment in which their choices are made (such as through voting).

As in Eubanks's 'feedback loop of injustice', no one person is responsible for structural injustice. The term refers to the way that we set up institutions. In her later book, Young proposes that structural injustice is perpetuated by individuals acting within institutional and social rules and practices that are superficially morally unproblematic but which, nevertheless, have problematic downstream effects for others, such as seeking affordable housing in ways that lead to gentrification or selecting private schools for one's children such that local public schools lose funding (Young 2011: 95).

Due to these structural social arrangements about who can make which choices and how they are made, some positions are more socially vulnerable than others in that their choices are constrained. Others who have maximal choice inadvertently reproduce this arrangement. Young posits that, especially in affluent societies, this leads to social injustice because affluent societies ought to have the resources to support just social arrangements (Young 2011: 45).

Young uses housing insecurity as an exemplar of structural injustice; her argument equally applies to health care. In the United States, an affluent society, many people experience health-care insecurity. Until the passage of the Affordable Care Act, health insurance was tied either to one's family or to one's employer. Losing a job also meant losing insurance coverage, and even with full employment, insurance companies often change each time one takes up a new position. This is not just an inefficient system but it is also arguably an unjust one, whether justice is understood as the distribution of goods within a society (of which health care is one) or the capacity of all within a society for self-determination and self-development.

Once automated systems get started, the logic of their design can seem inevitable (as with Bostrom's paperclip maximizer), even though careful design is capable of predicting and thus forestalling undesirable results. Arguments utilizing the concept of structural injustice highlight that injustice is not inevitable if the values built into systems are questioned early. If justice is not intentionally incorporated, then the system will continue to replicate inequitable outcomes for the marginalized.[8] As in her negative experience with her insurance company after switching employers, Eubanks argues that the use of automated systems for eligibility for benefits like health insurance and the use of predictive analytics to determine which patients will incur the highest costs do not 'remove bias, they launder it' in a 'high-tech sleight of hand' (Eubanks 2018: 224). They do this by prioritizing values of efficiency, cost-cutting, and rule-following, while downgrading others, such as dignity, trust, and equity for all within a society. While it is easy to see how this could occur in the US context, it is perhaps less likely in a nationalized health-care system, yet still possible. The motivation to decrease costs exists in both private and public systems, although it may be stronger in the former than the latter.

In a helpful amplification of these points, Ruha Benjamin describes the replication of injustice in digital technology through her conception of the New Jim Code, which she describes as the inequitable results of a focus on maximizing profits and cutting costs in an attempt to engineer the most economically efficient system (Benjamin 2019: 30). In effect, the removal of human discretion and contextual analysis from automated systems, even if based in a desire to reduce bias and discrimination, removes human values altogether in an attempt to make the most paperclips. Lost is careful consideration, in Eubanks's words, of 'who we are and who we want to be' (Eubanks 2018: 12). In the place of this critical reflection is an engineering value: efficiency.

In her work, Benjamin explores how economic drivers in digital technology can have deleterious effects on social justice, exacerbating the patterns of domination and oppression theorized by Young. Benjamin conceives of injustice in digital technology as a result of design choices that come to seem natural, inevitable, and automatic; as with Young's definition of structural injustice, harm is systemic and does not result from any one agent's choices (Benjamin 2019: 44–45). Eubanks makes the same point, describing these design choices and decisions made 'in neutral' by ignoring perfectly predictable consequences of unequal systems (Eubanks 2018: 223). Benjamin is even more suspicious than Eubanks and justifiably so—she writes that even well-intentioned attempts to design automated systems with 'health' or 'safety' in mind may assume that these values are best pursued through customization and individualization, techniques that can negatively affect communities even as particular individuals flourish independently (Benjamin 2019: 151).

These harms include the difficulty of those in poverty navigating the health-care system (because it is even harder to access a human being to whom one can describe the situation, and when one does finally reach such an individual, they are unlikely to possess the expertise to determine where the algorithm went wrong), increased surveillance of those in poverty in contrast to those who have the financial stability to not interact with social welfare programmes, and increased targeting of individuals labelled 'super-utilizers' to decrease health-care systems' monetary debt (Benjamin 2019: 156). These systems do nothing to ameliorate the conditions leading to community-level poverty in the first place. While their targeting of individuals in poverty might seem to reflect values of 'inclusion' and 'diversity', they do so at the expense of these individuals' capacities for self-determination and self-development and thus would be classified by Young as conditions of domination and oppression. As Benjamin writes, 'New Jim Code fixes are a permanent placeholder for bolder change … Medical inclusion, in short, can be a lucrative stand-in for social and political justice'—they displace more foundational change (Benjamin 2019: 156–157).

The ideal of efficiency, when pursued in systems engineering, can have inequitable, deleterious effects in the real world. The resulting harms are not due to any one individual's transgression, nor do they map directly onto designers' nefarious intentions. Rather, they are the result of a contraction of designers' perspectives and values from social and community values to engineering and economic values. While health care–digital technology partnerships need not necessarily contribute to injustice by prioritizing efficiency and other economic ends, they are more likely to do so when their private interests coincide with these ends. As Young writes in *Responsibility for Injustice*, conditions of structural injustice can be tackled by realigning the interests of system designers with promoting justice (Young 2011: 146). In the next section, I consider how this realignment of interests in health care–digital partnerships might occur.

MANAGING INTERESTS IN BIG MEDICAL DATA

In the preceding sections, I have described the kinds of opportunities that lead health-care institutions to enter into partnerships with digital technology companies. While these opportunities may benefit patients, in the fourth section I described how they also occasion unique conflicts of interest. In the fifth section, I expanded on these conflicts of interest, explaining how a focus on efficiency or profit could contribute, even if indirectly, to health-care injustice. In this section, I describe how health-care institutions and digital technology companies might work to manage these conflicts of interest with the goal of refraining from further contributing to health-care injustice.

As I argued in the fourth section, one of the main sources of conflicts of interest in these types of partnerships is different institutional missions. These conflicts are avoided if partnerships with institutions with different missions are never entered into at all. As Marks writes, improving health care involves identifying challenges to good health care and developing methods for addressing those challenges without entering into partnerships with industry (Marks 2019: 125). This is not to say that industry is categorically incapable of benefitting communities, just that it is wise to keep separate institutions whose missions are dictated by conflicting interests. The goal should be to ensure that the interests of the institution coincide with its mission, which for most health-care institutions is to ensure the well-being of the population it serves. It makes sense to keep the development of big data analytic tools that affect our health and well-being within the institutions dedicated to protecting these goods.

One of the first means of preventing conflicts of interest with health care–digital technology partnerships is to build capabilities within medical institutions to analyse their own data or to support non-corporate organizations in doing so. In fact, EHR data analysis can occur within health-care institutions and does not require partnership with digital technology corporations. In the United States, the Centers for Medicare and Medicaid Services Hospital Inpatient Quality Reporting Program uses big data analytics, as does the Patient Centered Outcome Research Institute and the Food and Drug Administration's Sentinel System (Price and Cohen 2019). Likewise, in the United Kingdom, Health Data Research UK is a hub for big data analytics in health care. Machine learning algorithms can be used by academic medical centres to create new clinical tools, as with an AI algorithm developed by researchers at Mount Sinai in New York to detect age-related macular degeneration (Mount Sinai 2020).

In addition, if partnerships are necessary to develop technological tools with good outcomes, then health-care institutions should be transparent with those they serve about the realities of the relationship. This means accurately portraying the risks of the relationship to the community, including the private interest that the digital technology company will inevitably retain in perfecting and promoting the proprietary data analytic tools it develops. The more these partnerships are described in prevailingly positive terms, the more sceptical administrators and the public ought to be about the real aims of the contract. Transparency is arguably a key to trust; it is important for institutions to acknowledge that they are fallible and that they could become compromised by relationships they enter into with corporations whose mission is not health and well-being.

A corollary to this is that health-care institutions that enter into partnerships with digital technology companies ought to develop methods of incorporating community interests into decision-making procedures so as to ensure that the common good is taken at least as seriously in these decisions as companies' private interests. Community engagement takes many forms, but it can involve the creation of a community advisory board, recruitment of community members onto big data and digital technology task forces, canvassing of community opinions on the use of digital technologies in health care, and so on.

Further, health-care institutions ought to identify general norms they will follow in these partnerships, as well as bright lines they will not cross. Marks, Benjamin, and Eubanks all provide starting points that institutions can work from. Marks outlines a set of norms for public–private interactions, including independence (reducing the influence of private interests), integrity (avoiding relationships with institutions that do not share the same mission), credibility (being transparent about relationships), stewardship (protecting vulnerable parties), public good (promoting the good of everyone in a society, not just private interests), and anti-promotion (reducing private interests that counter the public interest) (Marks 2019: 113).

Moreover, Benjamin describes forms of resistance that she conceives of as abolitionist tools for the New Jim Code. These tools aim to resist coded inequity, build solidarity, and engender liberation (Benjamin 2019: 168). They include asking who benefits from a new technology, whose interests are subverted by it, whether market imperatives are prioritized over social goods, whether an algorithm would pass an 'accountability audit', and what stories are told about the success or failure of the technology.

Finally, Eubanks offers what she calls an 'Oath of Non-Harm for an Age of Big Data', which includes that one will: understand that people are experts in their own lives; create tools that remove obstacles between resources and the people who need them; not use technical knowledge to compound disadvantage and oppression; design with history in mind; integrate systems for the needs of people, not data; not collect data for data's sake nor keep it just because one can; prioritize informed consent over design convenience; not design a data-based system that overturns an established legal right of the poor; and remember that technologies are designed for human beings, not data points, probabilities, or patterns (Eubanks 2018: 212).

Marks, Benjamin, and Eubanks all express concern about the risks inherent in the kinds of public–private partnerships that are currently being pursued to manage big medical data. They do not think these partnerships are necessarily bad but that private interests in technological development have a tendency to usurp broader social goods. Preventing this usurpation requires being attendant to this risk but also taking proactive steps to curtail it. Of course, whether these steps will have any effect on the broader space of digital technology partnerships is an open question; following these steps alone cannot be the answer to ethical use of digital technology in health care.

Conclusion

Health-care institutions are increasingly partnering with digital technology companies to sort through patients' medical data, with the goal of developing new knowledge and personalizing patients' care. These are worthwhile aims, but it is important to ask whose values are guiding the design process of the automated and algorithmic systems that will monitor and analyse the data and how these values will impact the systems' outcomes. While private companies are not incapable of improving the common good of communities, and indeed often must do so in order to remain solvent, the allegiance of private industry interests with efficiency, cost-cutting, and profit maximization can contrast with the allegiance of health-care institutions to advancing the health and well-being of the communities they serve.

Especially in the context of digital systems that shape health-care institutions' decisions, caution about whose interests guide system development is essential. Even well-meaning attempts to use technology to improve community health can inadvertently contribute to structural injustice by dictating the options that are available to community members and how they must be selected, thus decreasing individuals' capacities for self-development and self-determination. The first step in digital technology design for health care ought to be reflection on the following questions: what challenge should we prioritize, and who judges this to be the priority? What are their interests, and what is their role in the community and their relationship to the common good? Health-care institutions should align their design priorities with the interests of those in the community whose care they are responsible for and not with the interests of those developers of digital technologies whose priorities lie elsewhere.

NOTES

1. Google's partnership with London's Royal Free Hospital was found by the Information Commissioner's Office to violate the UK's Data Protection Act in 2017 (Hern 2017).
2. Google made the news in 2008 for tracking the spread of the flu based on online searches for flu symptoms and treatment on its platform. Named, 'Google Flu Trends', the tracker later failed in part due to Google's unwillingness to work with public health agencies in perfecting their analysis (Lazer and Kennedy 2015). Most recently, Britain's NHS has been criticized for partnering with Palantir (BBC News 2021).
3. It was 17.7 per cent in 2019; see https://www.cms.gov/Research-Statistics-Data-and-Syst ems/Statistics-Trends-and-Reports/NationalHealthExpendData/NationalHealthAccount sHistorical, accessed 25 April 2022.
4. This is not to say that privacy is unimportant—it is. Rather, it is to say that the ethical issues with health care–digital technology partnerships are not limited to privacy concerns.
5. Of course, it is possible that big data will improve health-care operations' efficiency in ways that do not facilitate patient care but that do increase profit. In this section, I am focusing on the improvements that do in fact improve patient care, while recognizing that efficiency and patient care do not always cohere.
6. Murdoch and Detsky in 'The Inevitable Application of Big Data to Health Care' describe four ways that big data may advance the economic mission of health care delivery by improving quality and efficiency: (1) by greatly expanding the capacity to generate new knowledge; (2) by helping with knowledge dissemination; (3) by translating personalized medicine initiatives into clinical practice; (4) by delivering information directly to patients.

In this summary, I abstract from their points 1 and 3. Point 2 refers to using natural language processing to analyse clinical trial reports and scientific papers to help individual physicians stay up to date on trends. Point 4 refers to developing apps to allow patients to download EHRs onto personal devices to make them more accessible. As these points do not relate directly to the focus of this chapter on big data partnerships in health care, I do not examine them in detail here (Murdoch and Detsky 2013).

7. For instance, a 2019 review of deep learning algorithms diagnostic performance compared with health-care professionals found no meaningful difference between the two (Liu et al. 2019).

8. This is not just a matter of algorithms relying on data sets reflecting unjust and unequal societies, although this is also a concern (Zimmerman et al. 2020).

References

Ariely, Dan (2008), *Predictably Irrational* (New York: Harper).

Bazemore, Andrew W., Cottrell, Erika K., Gold, Rachel, Hughes, Lauren S., Phillips, Robert L., Angier, Heather, et al. (2016), '*"Community Vital Signs"*: Incorporating Geocoded Social Determinants into Electronic Records to Promote Patient and Population Health', *Journal of the American Medical Informatics Association* 23(2), 407–412.

BBC News (2021), 'Palantir: NHS Faces Legal Action over Data Firm Contract', 24 February.

Beck, Andrew F., Sandel, Megan T., Ryan, Patrick H., and Kahn, Robert S. (2017), 'Mapping Neighborhood Health Geomarkers to Clinical Care Decisions to Promote Equity in Child Health', *Health Affairs* 36(6), 999–1005.

Benjamin, Ruha (2019), *Race after Technology* (Medford, MA: Polity Press).

Berwick, Donald M., and Andrew D. Hackbarth (2012), 'Eliminating Waste in US Healthcare', *JAMA* 307(14), 1513–1516.

Bostrom, Nick (2014), *Superintelligence: Paths, Dangers, Strategies* (New York, Oxford: Oxford University Press).

Cantor, Michael N., and Thorpe, Lorna (2018), 'Integrating Data on Social Determinants of Health into Electronic Health Records', *Health Affairs* 37(4), 585–590.

The Chartis Group (2019), *The New World of Healthcare Partnerships: Technology Companies.* https://www.chartis.com/insights/new-world-partnerships-technology-companies.

Chen, Jonathan H., and Asch, Steven M. (2017), 'Machine Learning and Prediction in Medicine —Beyond the Peak of Inflated Expectations', *New England Journal of Medicine* 376 (26), 2507–2509.

Cobb, Adrienne N., Benjamin, Andrew J., Huang, Erich S., and Kuo, Paul C. (2018), 'Big Data: More than Big Data Sets', *Surgery* 164(4), 640–642.

Davis, Jessica (2019), 'Google Ascension Partnership Fuels Overdue HIPAA Privacy Debate', *HealthITSecurity.* https://healthitsecurity.com/news/google-ascension-partnership-fuels-overdue-hipaa-privacy-debate

DeVoe, J.E., Bazemore, Andrew W., Cottrell, Erika K., Likumahuwa-Ackman, Sonja, Grandmont, Jené, Spach, Natalie, and Gold, Rachel (2016), 'Perspectives in Primary Care: A Conceptual Framework and Path for Integrating Social Determinants of Health into Primary Care Practice', *Annals of Family Medicine* 14(2), 104–108.

Emanuel, Ezekiel J., and Wachter, Robert M. (2019), 'Artificial Intelligence in Health Care: Will the Value Match the Hype?', *Journal of the American Medical Association* 321(23), 2281–2282.

Eubanks, Virginia (2018), *Automating Inequality* (New York: Picador, St. Martin's Press).

Farr, Christina (2019), 'Why Amazon Bought PillPack for $753 Million and What Happens Next', *CNBC*, 10 May.

Fuchs, Victor R. (2018), 'Is US Medical Care Inefficient?' *JAMA* 320(10), 971–972.

Gawande, Atul (2018), 'Why Doctors Hate Their Computers', *The New Yorker*, 5 November.

Hern, Alex (2017), 'Royal Free Breached UK Data Law in 1.6m Patient Deal with Google's DeepMind', *The Guardian*, 3 July.

Hughes, Lauren S., Phillips, Robert L., DeVoe, Jennifer E., and Bazemore, Andrew W. (2016), 'Community Vital Signs: Taking the Pulse of the Community While Caring for Patients', *Journal of the American Board of Family Medicine* 29(3), 419–422.

Ienca, Marcello, Ferretti, Agata, Hurst, Samia, Puhan, Milo, Lovis, Christian, and Vayena, Effy (2018), 'Considerations for Ethics Review of Big Data Health Research: A Scoping Review', ed. Godfrey Biemba, *PLOS ONE* 13(10), e0204937.

Kang, Cecilia, and McCabe, David (2020), 'House Lawmakers Condemn Big Tech's "Monopoly Power" and Urge Their Breakups', *New York Times*, 6 October.

Landi, Heather (2020), 'Judge Dismisses Data Sharing Lawsuit against University of Chicago, Google', *FierceHealthcare*, 8 September.

Lazer, David, and Kennedy, Ryan (2015), 'What We Can Learn from the Epic Failure of Google Flu Trends', *Wired*, 1 October.

Liu, Xiaoxuan, Faes, Livia, Kale, Aditya U., Wagner, Siegfried K., Fu, Dun Jack, Bruynseels, Alice, et al. (2019), 'A Comparison of Deep Learning Performance against Health-Care Professionals in Detecting Diseases from Medical Imaging: A Systematic Review and Meta-Analysis', *Lancet Digital Health* 1, e271–e297.

Lysaght, Tamra, Yeefen Lim, Hannah, Xafis, Vicki, and Yuan Ngiam, Kee (2019), 'AI-Assisted Decision-Making in Healthcare: The Application of an Ethics Framework for Big Data in Health and Research', *Asian Bioethics Review* 11(3), 299–314.

Marks, Jonathan H. (2019), *The Perils of Partnership* (Oxford: Oxford University Press).

Microsoft News Center (2019), 'UCLA Health Adopts Microsoft Azure to Accelerate Medical Research and Improve Patient Care—Stories', 30 May.

Mittelstadt, Brent Daniel, and Floridi, Luciano (2016), 'The Ethics of Big Data: Current and Foreseeable Issues in Biomedical Contexts', *Science and Engineering Ethics* 22(2), 303–341.

Mount Sinai (2020), 'Artificial Intelligence Algorithm Can Rapidly Detect Severity of Common Blinding Eye Disease', Press Release, 12 May.

Muoio, David (2019), 'Apple Health Records Now Available to All US Providers with Compatible EHRs', *Mobile Health News*, 28 June.

Murdoch, Travis B., and Detsky, Allan S. (2013), 'The Inevitable Application of Big Data to Health Care', *Journal of the American Medical Association* 309(13), 1351.

Powles, Julia (2019), 'DeepMind's Latest A.I. Health Breakthrough Has Some Problems', *Medium OneZero*, 6 August.

Price, W. Nicholson, and Glenn Cohen, I. (2019), 'Privacy in the Age of Medical Big Data', *Nature Medicine* 25(1), 37–43.

Resnik, David B. (2019), 'Institutional Conflicts of Interest in Academic Research', *Science and Engineering Ethics* 25(6), 1661–1669.

Rocher, Luc, Hendrickx, Julien M., and de Montjoye, Yves-Alexandre (2019), 'Estimating the Success of Re-Identifications in Incomplete Datasets Using Generative Models', *Nature Communications* 10(3069): 1–9.

Shieber, Jonathan (2020), 'Verana Health Aims to Organize and Analyze Doctors' Clinical Data Sets, Whether Patients Like It or Not', *Tech Crunch*, 5 February.

Vaughn, Adam (2019), 'Google Is Taking Over DeepMind's NHS Contracts—Should We Be Worried?', *New Scientist*, 27 September.

Vayena, Effy, and Blasimme, Alessandro (2018), 'Health Research with Big Data: Time for Systemic Oversight', *Journal of Law, Medicine & Ethics* 46(1), 119–129.

Voigt, Kristin (2019), 'Social Justice, Equality and Primary Care: (How) Can "Big Data" Help?', *Philosophy & Technology* 32(1), 57–68.

Wakabayashi, Daisuke (2019), 'Google and the University of Chicago Are Sued over Data Sharing', *New York Times*, 26 June.

Wakabayashi, Daisuke, and Satariano, Adam (2019), 'Google to Buy Fitbit for 2.1 Billion', *New York Times*, 1 November.

Young, Iris Marion (1990), *Justice and the Politics of Difference* (Oxford: Oxford University Press).

Young, Iris Marion (2011), *Responsibility for Justice* (Oxford: Oxford University Press).

Zimmerman, Annette, Rosa, Elena Di, and Kim, Hochan (2020), 'Technology Can't Fix Algorithmic Injustice', *Boston Review*, 9 January.

....

CHAPTER 27

EXPLAINABLE MACHINE LEARNING, PATIENT AUTONOMY, AND CLINICAL REASONING

....

GEOFF KEELING AND RUNE NYRUP

INTRODUCTION

....

MACHINE learning is transforming medicine. The past decade has seen the application of data-driven technologies to the detection and diagnosis of medical conditions and to the design of personalized treatment plans (He et al. 2019; Yu et al. 2018). These technologies promise better health outcomes. Existing diagnostic algorithms rival expert clinicians in the accuracy, sensitivity, and specificity of their diagnostic predictions (Shen et al. 2019; Gulshan et al. 2016). The hope is that, in the future, these algorithms will contribute to a reduction in morbidity and mortality arising from delayed, incorrect, or missed diagnoses. Similarly, treatment recommender systems promise personalized, evidence-based treatment plans that are intended to reduce preventable harms arising from suboptimal treatments (Somashekhar et al. 2017).

There are, however, concerns about the transparency and interpretability of machine learning algorithms in medicine (Bjerring and Busch 2021; Grote and Berens 2020; McDougall 2019). What is at issue is a tension between two factors. On the one hand, the prevailing view in medical ethics emphasizes patients' understanding of the rationale behind diagnoses as a precondition for giving informed consent to treatments (Faden and Beauchamp 1986). It also emphasizes clinicians and patients making joint decisions based on a shared understanding of the relevant medical evidence alongside the patient's beliefs and values. On the other hand, the complexity of contemporary machine learning systems renders opaque the rationale and value commitments that underpin token algorithmic decisions such as diagnostic predictions and suggested treatment plans. The problem is that these algorithms can make it difficult to explain *on what grounds* a diagnosis is reached or *why* a treatment is recommended. Hence, it is unclear how, if at all, opaque machine learning algorithms can be integrated into the clinical process in a way that upholds our best practices of informed consent and shared decision-making.

This tension forms part of the case for algorithmic *explainability* in medicine. The idea is that systems which can explain their decisions are better placed to complement clinical expertise whilst upholding the ethical standards of informed consent and shared decision-making. Our aim in this chapter is threefold. First, we articulate the tension between complex machine learning systems and informed consent and shared decision-making and examine the role of explanations in resolving this tension. Second, we argue that disputes about the particulars of the explainability challenge (i.e. what needs to be explained, to whom, in what way, and at what points in the clinical process) are hard to disentangle from certain more fundamental questions in the philosophy of medicine. These questions pertain to the logic of clinical reasoning; and how machine learning systems can complement clinical expertise in reaching diagnoses and treatment recommendations (cf. Patel et al. 2019: 634). Third, we advance an account of clinical reasoning and use this account to explore the interplay between clinicians and machine learning systems.

The chapter proceeds as follows. In the second section, we introduce informed consent and shared decision-making. In the third section, we outline the machine learning systems with which we are concerned. In the fourth section, we characterize the tension between these systems and the ethical ideals of informed consent and shared decision-making and argue that what matters for resolving this tension is that we have a clear picture of the interplay between clinicians and machine learning systems. In the fifth section, we argue that the standard Bayesian view of clinical reasoning lacks the resources to capture all relevant aspects of clinical reasoning. We then advance an alternative account that construes clinical reasoning as *strategic reasoning* (Stanley and Nyrup 2020), drawing on C.S. Peirce's notion of abduction. In the sixth section, we consider the particulars of the explainability challenge in light of this account and say something about what needs to be explained, to whom, when, and in what way, in order to maintain our best practices of informed consent and shared decision-making. The final section presents a conclusion.

INFORMED CONSENT AND SHARED DECISION-MAKING

Obviously, philosophers disagree about the correct analysis of informed consent and the correct characterization of shared decision-making. There is not space in this chapter to do justice to these disputes. Here, our focus is on outlining an operational picture of how these ethical standards are usually understood in clinical settings. We take each concept in turn.

Informed consent

The requirement for informed consent can be characterized roughly as follows: Other things being equal, a physician is morally permitted to perform a medical intervention on a patient only if, and because, the patient consents to the intervention and the patient has sufficient understanding of the intervention to ensure an informed choice; or if the patient cannot consent, the intervention is consented to by proxy or there are sufficiently weighty moral reasons for performing the intervention in the absence of informed consent. We take this to be a widely endorsed ethical principle, underlying many parts of current best practice in clinical ethics. The reasoning behind this requirement typically goes like this: it is presumptively wrong for a physician to subject a patient to medical interventions (due to their invasive nature, potential side effects, etc.). There are circumstances in which this presumption is defeated. One of them is when the patient waives this presumption through giving informed consent. The presumption can also be defeated by other means (e.g. clinical urgency, best-interest judgements, advance directives or relatives' consent) but even then, informed consent takes lexical priority: If the patient *can* give informed consent, the intervention is permissible only if the patient *in fact* consents.

In their book, *Principles of Biomedical Ethics*, Tom Beauchamp and James Childress offer something close to the orthodox analysis of informed consent. Beauchamp and Childress (2013: 124) hold that a patient gives informed consent to an intervention if, and only if, three conditions obtain. Call these preconditions, information conditions, and consent conditions. The preconditions are that the patient is competent to understand the relevant medical information and make a decision about which treatment is best and that the patient's decision is voluntary. The information condition requires the physician to recommend a plan and disclose information that is material to the decision, and the patient must understand this disclosure. The consent condition requires the patient to make a decision in favour of (or against) a particular medical intervention and thereby autonomously authorize the chosen plan of action.

We shall unpack this analysis further. First, the preconditions: the voluntariness condition is intended to rule out physicians coercing or deceiving patients into choosing a treatment. According to Beauchamp and Childress (2013: 137–138), 'a person acts voluntarily if he or she wills the action without being under the control of another person or condition'. The patient cannot be said to have consented to a medical intervention if their agreement was somehow forced or coerced. The other precondition is that the patient is competent to understand the relevant information and to make a decision. The thought is that some patients lack the requisite cognitive abilities to make an informed decision about whether to consent (e.g. young children). The standard of competence required to give informed consent is a matter of dispute. But for our purposes, it is sufficient to say that 'physicians usually consider a person competent if he or she can understand a procedure, deliberate with regard to its major risks and benefits, and make a decision in light of this deliberation' (Beauchamp and Childress 2013: 117).

Next, the informational conditions: the basic point is that the patient's consent to an intervention is *informed* only if they understand what they are signing up for. On a fairly standard view, this includes first, understanding that the act of giving consent *authorizes* the physician to perform an intervention and thereby temporarily waives any presumptive rights the patient has against being subjected to the intervention, and second, understanding all the information that is *material* to the patient's decision (Faden and Beauchamp 1986: 298–304; see also Beauchamp and Childress 2013: 125–127). Material information here means information 'worthy of consideration in the process of deliberation', given the patient's beliefs and values, alongside relevant clinical considerations (Faden and Beauchamp 1986: 203). In practice, this includes the physician's recommended treatment, the risks involved, the costs and benefits of alternatives, and possible consequences of the intervention that the patient might reasonably want to know about in advance of making a decision. The role of the doctor is to disclose this information to the patient in a way that facilitates understanding. The requisite level of understanding is a 'grasp of the central facts' rather than full understanding (Faden and Beauchamp 1986: 300–302; see also Beauchamp and Childress 2013: 131–132).

Finally, the consent conditions: what matters here is that the patient's act of giving consent is an *autonomous authorization* or *refusal* of a treatment option. Here, an action is considered autonomous if it is intentional, made with understanding, and free of internal or external influences such as mental illness that impairs deliberation or third-party manipulation (Beauchamp and Childress 2013: 104–105). In short, the decision to accept or reject the intervention must be the patient's own decision reached after careful deliberation on the relevant clinical information and their own beliefs and values.

That is what informed consent is. Why does it matter? According to the standard view, informed consent matters on grounds of autonomy (Beauchamp and Childress 2013: 214–223; Levy 2014: 293; see also McCullough 2011). Beauchamp and Childress (2013: 104–105) defend the view that a choice is autonomous just in case: (a) it is intentional, in the sense that 'it must correspond to the actor's conception of the act ... although the planned outcome may not materialize'; (b) it is made with a sufficient understanding of the considerations that are material to the decision; and (c) it is made 'free of controls exerted either by external sources or by internal states that rob the person of self-directedness.' Based on this conception of autonomy, Beauchamp and Childress defend a principle of respect for autonomy to underpin their theory of informed consent. They characterize their principle as follows (Beauchamp and Childress 2013: 106–107): 'Respect, so understood, involves acknowledging the value and decision-making rights of autonomous persons and enabling them to act autonomously, whereas disrespect for autonomy involves attitudes and actions that ignore, insult, demean, or are inattentive to others' rights of autonomous action.' What this principle implies in the clinical context is that physicians must facilitate the conditions for patients to make autonomous choices about medical interventions. This involves providing the information required for patients to give informed consent or refusal to treatment options and ensuring that salient decisions which affect the patient are made *by the patient* in accordance with their beliefs, preferences, and values and with adequate clinical understanding.

There are interesting debates to be had about why we should accept this principle (e.g. whether respect for autonomy is intrinsically valuable or merely instrumental towards some other aim). However, for the purpose of this chapter, we will stay agnostic on these questions (see also the section on 'The tension'). As a matter of fact, the principle of respect for autonomy is widely endorsed (albeit for a variety of reasons) within bioethics and in practical clinical ethics. This is sufficient to motivate our concern in this chapter, namely, whether the introduction of machine learning algorithms in medicine poses a challenge to this principle.[1]

Shared decision-making

We now turn briefly to shared decision-making. The basic idea is that clinical decisions ought to involve 'a state of shared information, shared deliberation, and shared mind' between the clinician and the patient (Epstein et al. 2010: 1491). Like informed consent, the moral justification for shared decision-making is standardly taken to be respect for autonomy. However, shared decision-making not only requires that patients have the freedom to *accept* or *reject* recommended treatment options, as with the informed consent requirement but also that their beliefs, preferences, and values ought to be at the centre of the decision-making process from the assessment stage, through diagnosis, and to treatment decisions. For example, in diagnostic reasoning, the clinician should factor in the value of discovering the correct diagnosis versus any disvalue that the patient assigns to enduring a long and possibly invasive series of tests. The doctor may, for instance, discuss with the patient the invasive character or the risks of the procedures required to secure a diagnosis and ask the patient whether in their considered judgement receiving a diagnosis is worth the personal costs of undertaking the relevant procedures. In effect, the role of the clinician is to ensure that the patients have sufficient understanding of the process that they are going through, making precise the relevant medical evidence, and taking the time to work through the patient's concerns so as to enable the patient to determine how their care is managed, given what is important to them. The patient is not an *object* of clinical deliberation. They are an active, autonomous *participant* in clinical deliberation.

The relation between shared decision-making and informed consent is not always clear. For our purposes, it is sufficient to pitch shared decision-making as an *extension* of informed consent. Robert Kaplan (2004: 81), for instance, claims that 'shared decision-making goes beyond informed decision-making by emphasising that the decision process is joint and shared between the patient and provider' (see also Sheridan et al. 2004). What motivates shared decision-making is the desire to facilitate patients having control over the direction of their care, alongside the belief that patient involvement in clinical decisions should not be limited to accepting or rejecting suggested treatment plans. Shared decision-making can thus be seen as an ethical standard intended to promote the same values that motivate informed consent requirements, namely, respect for patient autonomy. While shared decision-making may not be a strict requirement on the permissibility of an intervention in the way informed consent is, it is widely seen as an ethical ideal that physicians should strive (*ceteris paribus*) to realize as far as possible in their practice. Put differently, other things being equal, greater patient participation in clinical decisions is, in light of the moral significance of respecting patient autonomy, better, and physicians morally ought to do what they can to promote patient involvement in deliberation about the management and direction of their care.

MACHINE LEARNING IN MEDICINE

In this section, we present the class of medical machine learning technologies with which we are concerned. These are diagnostic algorithms and treatment recommender algorithms.

Diagnostic algorithms

Diagnostic algorithms are functions that take as inputs relevant features of a patient's medical history and output a differential diagnosis or a set of plausible diagnoses for a patient with that medical history (Graber and Matthew 2008: 37; see also Berner et al. 1994). The point of diagnostic algorithms is to act as *decision support tools*. Diagnostic algorithms are intended to assist clinicians in generating diagnostic hypotheses and in reaching an eventual diagnosis. What motivates the development and use of diagnostic algorithms is the prevalence of diagnostic error. Though estimates of the prevalence of diagnostic error are highly sensitive to definitions (i.e. what counts as a *missed* or *delayed* diagnosis), diagnostic error is the leading fault in US medical malpractice claims (Brown et al. 2010; see also Zwaan and Singh 2015; Graber et al. 2005). What is more, in some specialties, such as emergency medicine, the diagnostic error rate is thought to be as high as 15 per cent (Berner and Graber 2008). Accordingly, David Newman-Toker and Peter Pronovost (2009) describe diagnostic error as 'the next frontier for patient safety' insofar as reductions in the prevalence of diagnostic error are likely to significantly reduce preventable deaths. The hope is that diagnostic algorithms, if integrated into the clinical process, will contribute to a significant reduction in diagnostic error by reducing the frequency of missed or delayed diagnoses.

The earliest diagnostic algorithms used Bayesian inference to match symptoms to differential diagnoses. Bayesian inference is a form of probabilistic reasoning according to which, given a set of mutually exclusive and exhaustive hypotheses, $H_1, H_2, \ldots H_n$, the algorithm first assigns prior probabilities $Pr(H_i)$ to each hypothesis, which reflect its initial confidence in each hypothesis being correct. The algorithm then updates its prior probabilities conditional on evidence using Bayes theorem:

$$\text{Pr}'(H \mid E) = \frac{\text{Pr}(E \mid H)\text{Pr}(H)}{\text{Pr}(E)}$$

Roughly, the new or 'posterior' probability assigned to some hypothesis H, given evidence E, is equal to the likelihood of E on the assumption that H is true, multiplied by the prior probability of H divided by the independent probability of E. One early example of the Bayesian approach is a model developed by Homer Warner et al. (1961) to match clusters of symptoms to different types of heart disease. This model output a probability distribution over thirty-five different kinds of heart disease. The probabilities were calculated using Bayes's theorem in addition to (a) information about the independent probability of a patient having each kind of heart disease; and (b) correlations between different symptoms and different kinds of heart disease. The prior probabilities were determined by the estimated frequency of the diseases in the population. The Bayesian approach later featured in several prominent diagnostic algorithms. Perhaps the best known is DXplain, developed at the Massachusetts General Hospital (Barnett et al. 1987: 72). DXplain is a domain-general algorithm that takes into account the prevalence of the disease in the population, alongside facts about the correlations between different diseases and different symptoms and the severity of different diagnoses, to deliver a ranked list of diagnoses, given a list of patient symptoms.

Bayesian algorithms such as DXplain faired reasonably well from the point of view of explainability and interpretability. In addition to matching inputted symptoms to a differential diagnosis, DXplain could also prompt the clinician to provide further information to enable further discrimination between candidate diagnoses. In doing so, DXplain could supply a *rationale* for why a particular symptom would aid in further refining the differential diagnosis (Barnett et al. 1987: 72). Thus, the express intention behind DXplain was not to create a 'black box' algorithm that delivers a plausible differential diagnosis, given a list of patient symptoms, but for the algorithm to *collaborate with* or *assist* the clinician in the diagnostic reasoning process.

The 1970s saw the development of several rule-based diagnostic algorithms. These algorithms were made up of a series of *if–then* rules, hand-coded by medical experts, to match input symptoms to differential diagnoses (Wagholikar et al. 2012: 3032). These diagnostic algorithms tended to be domain-specific. For example, the MYCIN algorithm developed at Stanford University in the 1970s predicted the underlying bacterial cause of infections and recommended appropriate antibiotic treatments (Shortliffe and Buchannan 1975). MYCIN required physicians to input answers to a series of 'Yes' or 'No' questions about the patient's symptoms. It then output a list of plausible bacterial causes of the patient's infection, ranked from most probable to least probable, and supplemented with information about which 'Yes' or 'No' questions were salient to the rank order. These rule-based systems were reasonably interpretable in the sense that, as

Andreas Holzinger and colleagues put it, they 'reasoned by performing some form of logical inference on human readable symbols, and were able to provide a trace of their inference steps' (Holzinger et al. 2019: 2).[2]

With the advent of artificial neural nets in the 1990s, and especially since the recent advances in 'deep learning' variants, things have become more complicated from the point of interpretability. The point of an artificial neural network in the context of diagnosis is to learn a complex function that reliably maps features of a patient's medical history to a plausible probability distribution over possible diagnoses. For example, a neural network designed for respiratory conditions might output a probability distribution over a set of conditions including asthma, chronic bronchitis, and chronic obstructive pulmonary disease (COPD). Neural networks comprise layers of 'artificial neurons' with weighted connections between them. The function mapping inputs to outputs is determined by the weighted connections between the neurons. In the case of supervised learning models, the function is learned through a process of trial and error. Initially, the weights are set randomly, and the network is made to output probability distributions over diagnoses for test cases for which the true probability distribution is known. Each time the network is correct, its weights are unchanged. Each time the network is incorrect, its weights are adjusted to minimize the distance between the algorithm's prediction and the correct prediction. Over time, this process of trial-and-error results in the network converging on a highly complex non-linear function that reliably predicts diagnostic probabilities from patient histories.

The upshot of neural networks is accuracy. Neural networks make predictions using highly complex statistical patterns implicit in the training examples. Contemporary 'deep' neural networks can have many thousands of neurons and can model patterns involving hundreds or thousands of features of the patient's medical record, both given in the patient's notes and inferred from more basic features. The best existing neural networks have diagnostic capabilities comparable to expert clinicians on certain diagnostic tasks (c.f. Shen et al. 2019; Gulshan et al. 2016; Liu et al. 2019). This does not imply that clinicians are redundant in certain domains. For the role of the clinician is not limited to diagnosis. It also falls within the purview of the clinician's role to facilitate the patient's understanding of the diagnosis, given their concerns and patient-specific informational needs, and also to contextualize the diagnosis as part of a broader care plan. What is true, however, is that a clinician's diagnostic accuracy may well be enhanced if that diagnosis is made in consultation with a diagnostic algorithm the accuracy of which matches or exceeds that of a human clinician.[3] The downside, however, is opacity. As Brent Mittelstadt et al. (2016: 7) explain, 'human decision-makers can in principle articulate their rationale when queried'. Not so for neural networks. The function mapping patient features to probabilities over candidate diagnoses is stored in a distributed fashion, embedded in the weighted connections between the neurons. It has no explicit representation. This opacity, as we shall see later on, presents serious concerns for informed consent and shared decision-making.

Treatment recommender systems

Treatment recommender algorithms can be characterized as functions that take as inputs relevant features of a patient's medical history and output a set of recommended treatment plans for the patient. They might also indicate *how strongly* treatments are recommended or *how likely* treatments are to succeed, given the patient's history. But their essential function is the capacity to infer treatment options from given or inferred features of a patient's medical history.

Take IBM's Watson for Oncology (Somashekhar et al. 2017; Strickland 2019). This algorithm uses natural language processing to read and interpret patient medical records, thereby building a profile of the patient consisting of given and inferred characteristics. Watson then employs a machine learning model to match the patient's profile to an ordered list of treatment recommendations. These suggestions are supplemented with clinical evidence drawn from an extensive database containing over 300 medical journals and 200 medical textbooks. Features of the patient's profile that are inferred are highlighted, and there is an option for the clinician to correct faulty inferences. Features that are salient to the algorithm's recommendations are also flagged to the clinician.

Whether IBM's Watson for Oncology has the capacity to transform treatment recommendation in real-world clinical settings remains an open question. So far, the product has not manifested the transformative effects that IBM hoped for (Strickland 2019). However, there are several good reasons to think that treatment recommender systems *in general* could improve health outcomes. We shall mention two. First, these systems promise to improve evidence-based practice. It is difficult for clinicians to maintain up-to-date knowledge of recent developments in medical science (cf. Curioni-Fontecedro 2017). Treatment recommender systems render accessible relevant empirical research to support treatment recommendations, enabling clinicians to make evidence-based judgements about treatments without the need for independent research. Second, algorithmic treatment recommendations are tailored to the needs of individual patients. Treatment recommender algorithms thus broaden the scope for personalized treatment plans and, conversely, minimize the need for reliance on informal heuristics for matching treatments to generic symptom clusters. In sum, the hope is that through personalized and evidence-based algorithmic treatment recommendations, treatment recommender systems will contribute to a reduction in preventable harms and deaths arising from suboptimal treatment plans.

CHARACTERIZING THE TENSION AND THE EXPLAINABILITY CHALLENGE

We now want to look closer at the tension between algorithmic opacity and the deliberative transparency required for informed consent and shared decision-making. Our aim in this section is twofold. First, we want to clarify what this tension consists in. Specifically, we suggest that there is little point in focusing on whether machine learning systems are in principle incompatible with our ethical ideals (c.f. McDougall 2019; Grote and Berens 2020). What matters is how to design these systems, in particular with respect to the explanations that they can provide for diagnostic and treatment decisions, so as to harness the epistemic benefits of these technologies without compromising shared decision-making and informed consent. Second, we argue that a more fruitful way forward will be to focus on the interplay between clinicians and machine learning systems as collaborative clinical reasoners. Doing so, we suggest, will allow us to better characterize the kinds of algorithmic explanations needed to foster the right kinds of patient and clinician understanding.

The tension

The tension is partly captured by Rosalind McDougall's (2019: 157) contention that 'systems that recommend treatment options present a potential threat to shared decision making, because the individual patient's values do not drive the ranking of treatment options'. The problem here is that treatment recommender systems rank treatment options in accordance with certain values. For example, such an algorithm might evaluate treatments by probability of success, where success is understood in terms of maximizing life-years or quality-adjusted life-years (QALYs).[4] Importantly, these are not sensitive to how individual patients value potential outcomes. For instance, suppose a given treatment could impact the patient's ability to travel by air. How willing they are to accept this risk might depend on whether most of their friends and family live nearby or abroad. Furthermore, even if the system happens to suggest a treatment option that best balances the patient's preferences and values, these will not be the driving force of clinical deliberation. Shared decision-making requires that the patient's beliefs and values be *central* to the decision-making process, while treatment recommender systems (as currently designed) at best allow them to be accidentally satisfied.

Thomas Grote and Philipp Berens (2020: 208) generalize McDougall's argument so as to bring diagnostic algorithms into the fold. They argue that '[as] the patient is not provided with sufficient information concerning the confidence of a given diagnosis or the rationale of a treatment prediction, she may not be well equipped to give her consent to treatment decisions'. Whereas McDougall's concern is that treatment recommender systems present a barrier to the patient's values *driving* clinical decisions, Grote and Berens worry that the disclosure requirement for informed consent may be in principle unsatisfiable if diagnostic or treatment recommender algorithms cannot provide a rationale for their predictions or an associated level of confidence in those predictions.

While plausible, these concerns, as formulated, fail to fully capture the tension. They ignore the social context in which medical algorithms are embedded (cf. 1: 12). These algorithms are decision support systems, designed to aid clinicians in reaching diagnoses and treatment recommendations. So, why can clinicians not use their own clinical expertise to provide the required disclosures and explanations and thereby compensate for the opacity of the algorithm?[5] The rationale behind a particular algorithmic decision may be unclear, but clinicians can minimally offer general explanations for why a patient with a given symptom profile might be diagnosed as such or why a certain treatment is sensible, given their knowledge of the patient's medical history. Analogously, a clinician may rely on laboratory test results without fully being able to explain the process through which these are generated. This is not usually taken to undermine informed consent or shared decision-making. Without some further argument, it is unclear why 'black box' systems should pose any particular problem.

There are two things to say here. First, the key feature of decision support systems is that they allow clinicians to offload some of the cognitive work for diagnosis and treatment recommendation onto an algorithm. This cognitive offloading creates locations of opacity in the clinical reasoning process that were not present before. Crucially, this opacity arises within clinical reasoning itself, rather than just its empirical inputs (as in the case of laboratory test results). The effect is to narrow the clinician's ability to provide answers to the patient's questions and concerns insofar as the clinician has a diminished understanding of the inferential relations that hold between relevant features of the patient and subsequent diagnoses and treatment recommendations. It matters on grounds of autonomy, both for informed consent and shared decision-making, that the patient is able to navigate the space of considerations relevant to decisions about the management of their care. Second, even if generic post-hoc explanations may in some cases be *good enough*, the principle of autonomy (especially as interpreted in shared decision-making) entails that, *ceteris paribus*, greater patient understanding is better. So, the salient question is how decision support systems can be designed to foster greater understanding for clinicians and patients.

While the tension is somewhat clarified, some may still doubt its legitimacy. It might be true on grounds of autonomy that greater patient understanding is better. However, the tension between machine learning systems and the ethical ideals of informed consent and shared decision-making runs deeper. One problem is that, other things being equal, the predictive capacity of machine learning systems (i.e. how good the diagnoses and treatment recommendations are) is negatively correlated with the interpretability of those systems. In general, the neural networks (and other machine learning models) that are able to achieve the best predictions are also the most complex and, thus, most opaque. Making them simpler to reduce opacity generally implies less accurate predictions. The tension is not so much an incompatibility between machine learning systems and autonomy. Instead, it is better construed as a trade-off between *better options* for the patient (i.e. more accurate candidate diagnoses and treatment recommendations) and *better choices* (i.e. being able to autonomously decide between the available options), based on an understanding of their rationale and potential consequences.

If this is the trade-off, it may be objected that respect for patient autonomy gives undue moral weight to mere choice. This concern is reminiscent of what Charles Taylor (1991) referred to as a 'rather facile relativism' on which each person 'has his or her own

MACHINE LEARNING, PATIENT AUTONOMY, AND CLINICAL REASONING   539

"values," and about these it is impossible to argue'. He argued that '[in] stressing the legitimacy of choice between certain options, we ... find ourselves depriving the options of
their significance'. We should be cautious of depriving patients of better diagnoses and
better treatment options so that they can make nominally better (more autonomous)
decisions. This point is echoed by Onora O'Neill (2003: 6): '[proponents of] autonomy
may hope to show that certain rational processes *for choosing* generally produce more
valuable choices. But they will not be able to show even this much without independent
criteria for identifying valuable choices'. The concern here is that one arm of the tension
(namely, the alleged moral significance of autonomous decision-making on the part of
patients) does not obviously rest on a stable moral foundation; that is, it is at best unclear
why autonomous choosing matters morally.[6]

Notice, however, that the existence of a tension between the opacity of machine
learning systems and the transparency required for informed consent and shared
decision-making does not entail that patient autonomous choice has intrinsic moral
significance. It might be that autonomous choosing on the part of patients has instrumental moral significance because affording patients a greater role in clinical decisions
acts as a plausible safeguard against deceit, coercion, and other forms of maltreatment.
(It is more difficult to harm patients if they are required to deliberate upon and authorize
every action that is done to them.) We shall remain neutral on exactly *why* autonomy
matters. What is important for our purposes here is merely *that* it matters; or, at least,
that there are some fairly robust ethical reasons in the vicinity which underpin current
best practices in clinical ethics, requiring patients to have significant and informed input
into decisions about what is done to them in health-care settings. If that is the case, there
are strong reasons to seek out ways of designing machine learning systems that are able
to overcome or compensate for the trade-off between prediction and opacity. Again, we
will not pursue the finer details here. Given how widely accepted and embedded the
principle of respect for autonomy is in clinical practice, we will continue to rely on it for
the remainder of this chapter.

The explainability challenge

To summarize, we understand the tension and its moral significance as follows. By
offloading part of the cognitive labour of diagnosis and treatment recommendation to
algorithms, clinicians have a less than full understanding of the inferential relations that
feature in the clinical reasoning process. This diminishes the clinician's ability to address
the patient's questions and concerns and, in turn, reduces the patient's capacity to make
informed decisions and participate in shared decision-making about the management
of their care. The issue is not that algorithmic opacity *necessarily* undermines informed
consent and shared decision-making. Rather, the explainability challenge, as we see it,
concerns how clinical decision support systems can best be designed to facilitate the
realization of these ethical ideals. Meeting this challenge involves specifying *what* needs
explaining, *to whom*, in *what way*, and at *what points* in the clinical process.

Since the tension arises because the clinician's cognitive labour is offloaded to the algorithm, the point of making algorithms explainable will be to compensate for the clinician's reduced understanding of the inferential relations between the patient's history, diagnoses, and treatment recommendations. Algorithmic explanations should be tailored to those points in the reasoning process that are made opaque to the clinician through being handled by the algorithm. This, in turn, requires a clearer picture of how clinicians and decision support systems jointly reason from the facts about the patient's case to diagnoses and treatment recommendations. In other words, to address the explainability challenge, we need an account of the interplay between clinicians and machine learning systems as *collaborative reasoners*. Making precise the role that algorithms play in clinical reasoning enables us to better capture the sorts of explanations that are required of medical algorithms to foster the level of understanding that clinicians need to effectively respect and support patient autonomy.

To this end, in the next section, we start by developing a general account of the logic of clinical reasoning. Then, in the following section, we will show how this account helps us to address the particulars of the explainability challenge.

STRATEGIC REASONING IN MEDICINE

Theories about clinical reasoning are either normative or descriptive (Stanley and Nyrup 2020: 172; Schwartz and Elstein 2008: 227–228). Descriptive theories concern how clinicians in fact reason, based, for example, on facts about cognitive psychology. Normative theories offer standards that ideal clinical reasoning ought to adhere to, for example, by appeal to norms for probabilistic reasoning. Ultimately, practical recommendations will have to combine both perspectives, taking into account the ideal we should aim for as well as what is in fact feasible. Here, we focus on the normative side of things. The point is to identify what good clinical reasoning consists in and to explore how machine learning systems can best fit into this ideal picture.

The leading normative account of clinical reasoning is the Bayesian view (Richardson and Wilson 2015). On this view, when a patient presents with a set of symptoms, the physician considers a set of candidate diagnostic hypotheses and assigns probabilities to those hypotheses. These are called pre-test probabilities. They reflect the physician's degree of confidence in each hypothesis being correct. Plausible factors in setting pre-test probabilities are the prevalence of different conditions in the relevant geographical area and in other suitable reference classes to which the patient belongs. The physician then decides to test or treat diagnostic hypotheses based on certain probabilistic thresholds. For example, 'if the probability of diagnosis D is at least x, then test for diagnosis D' or 'if the probability of diagnosis D* is at least y, then apply the treatment for D*'. The thresholds are based on maximizing the expected utility of different clinical acts,[7] taking into account their potential harms and benefits (e.g. delaying treatment if a given diagnostic hypothesis is true), the efficacy of available treatments, the reliability of tests, and the risks associated with different testing or treatment regimens themselves. Finally, once the clinician performs the relevant tests and treatments, they update their probability distribution by conditioning on the evidence gathered. The process terminates when, given the physician's probability distribution over candidate diagnoses, there is no diagnostic hypothesis which requires additional testing or treatment.

While the Bayesian view offers a fruitful picture of clinical reasoning in some contexts, it is suboptimal for our purposes. The problem is that the Bayesian view is, at its core, an account of how the clinician's probability distribution over an already given set of diagnostic hypotheses should be updated in response to evidence. However, a crucial feature of the interplay between clinicians and machine learning systems concerns the *generation* of relevant diagnostic hypotheses. A key part of the diagnostic process, from the clinician's perspective, involves finding a manageable set of hypotheses that merit further investigation (Stanley and Campos 2013). The need to find a manageable set of hypotheses is also relevant for decisions about which diagnostic hypotheses to *pursue*, that is, test and develop further. In some cases, it can be worthwhile pursuing diagnostic hypotheses that are unlikely to be true because doing so might produce clues as to which hypotheses are worth considering instead (Stanley and Nyrup 2020). This matters for our purposes as the main selling point of diagnostic algorithms, at least insofar as their goal is to minimize diagnostic error, is their ability to generate diagnostic hypotheses and indicate which of these hypotheses are worth following up and how urgently. As the Bayesian view takes for granted the set of diagnostic hypotheses over which the clinician's probability estimates range, it does not adequately represent the problem clinicians need to overcome in practice.

For this reason, we prefer a different picture of clinical reasoning, one that sees the set of hypotheses under active consideration as an active and dynamic part of the diagnostic process, with direct relevance for decisions and judgements about the generation and pursuit of diagnostic hypotheses. When presented with a patient who has a particular set of symptoms, the clinician does not start by considering every possible cause of those symptoms. Rather, an experienced clinician knows which questions to ask and in what order, so as to, on the one hand, generate further clues to suggest possible diagnoses and, on other hand, narrow down the class of plausible explanations for the patient's condition. By asking the right questions, at the right time and in the right order, and by following up on these questions with the right tests, clinicians actively maintain a set of relevant working hypotheses. While the overreaching aim is to isolate a plausible diagnosis and administer an appropriate treatment, this has to be achieved in a timely and efficient manner, without subjecting the patient to unnecessary risk or harm on the way.

On this picture, as Herbert Simon (1985: 73) puts it, clinical reasoning is 'more akin to twenty questions' than it is to 'Bayesian decision theory'. Interestingly, C.S. Peirce also used this analogy for the type of reasoning he called abduction (Peirce 1932–1958, 7.720). Peirce distinguished between abduction and induction: roughly, whereas the latter concerns the acceptance or rejection of given hypotheses based on empirical evidence, abduction is reasoning concerned with introducing hypotheses into inquiry in the first place and deciding in what order they ought to be pursued. While we are happy to leave the inductive parts of clinical reasoning to the Bayesian view, we believe (following earlier commentators, e.g. Stanley and Campos 2013; Chiffi and Zanotti 2015; Stanley and Nyrup 2020) that certain Peircean ideas provide a fruitful perspective for thinking about the abductive parts of clinical reasoning.

The starting point for our picture of clinical reasoning as abduction is Jaakko Hintikka's (1998) characterization of abductive reasoning as *strategic reasoning*. What is central to Hintikka's account is the distinction between *definitory rules* and *strategic rules* (cf. Paavola 2004: 269; Stanley and Nyrup 2020). Consider the game of Go. Besides, inter alia, the alternative move structure and scoring rules, Go has two definitory rules that determine the admissible moves. The strategic rules, in contrast, pertain to the evaluation of individual moves in terms of diachronic policies, describing how the player plans to decide moves throughout the game, that is, functions that for each game state output an optimal move, which, if enacted as part of the relevant overall policy, is expected to maximize the player's expected score in the long run. Strategy in Go is not merely a matter of performing admissible moves but also of evaluating candidate moves in terms of an overall strategy and the degree to which those moves are conducive to one's diachronic strategic aims.

Our view is that a similar picture holds for diagnostic reasoning. The definitory rules concern the appropriate epistemic attitudes to take towards diagnostic hypotheses conditional on evidence gathered from tests and examinations; and also the implications of different test results for the patient's health. In contrast, the strategic rules concern what the clinician has good reason to do in terms of taking time to generate diagnostic hypotheses, deciding which hypotheses to pursue and in what order, and deciding which tests to use to gather evidence, taking into account the economical and epistemic costs of performing different kinds of tests. Clinician expertise, on our view, consists in understanding the costs and benefits of different clinical acts in light of a different diachronic clinical strategies.

So, what makes for good strategy in clinical reasoning? Obviously, as the Bayesian model correctly highlights, it has to take into account trade-offs between the potential benefits and harms of proposed treatments and tests. However, as emphasized above, good clinical reasoning also involves maintaining an adequate space of candidate diagnoses. Ideally, this should be small enough to allow the clinician to reason and make judgements quickly and efficiently without getting overwhelmed by too many possibilities, while still encompassing all hypotheses that could have serious implications for the patient's health. The challenge is how to approximate this goal, given that, by the nature of the issue, the clinician cannot compare their current hypothesis space with other, not-yet-generated sets of hypotheses.

Thus, a skilled clinician has to rely on more indirect reasoning strategies. Many of Peirce's writings on abduction concern such strategies. Here, we want to highlight two key ideas. First, Peirce points out that it often makes sense to test hypotheses early that can easily and quickly be ruled out if false: 'if there be any hypothesis which we happen to be well provided with means for testing, or which, for any reason, promises not to detain us long, unless it be true, that hypothesis ought to be taken up early for examination'

(Peirce 1932–1958, 6.533). This is especially the case if ruling out the hypotheses can pre-emptively 'prune back' a large class of hypotheses without having to consider them in more detail (this is part of Peirce's point in the 'twenty questions' analogy). For instance, if a clinician can rule out early that the patient's condition is due to a lung infection, this will allow them to focus on other hypotheses. Not only will it allow them to narrow down the list of potentially correct diagnoses, but it can also free the clinician from having to worry about potential complications that a candidate test or treatment might have in a patient with a lung infection. Being able to anticipate what hypotheses to rule out early, in order to make the future diagnostic space more manageable, is a key part of clinical expertise.

Strategically pruning back is one side of the abductive coin. On the flipside is the ability to obtain the right clues for future hypothesis generation if the current working space turns out to be inadequate. Peirce often emphasized heuristic fruitfulness (or 'espearable uberty', as he called it, with a characteristic neologism) as one of the leading considerations in abduction. For him, abduction 'depends on our hope, sooner or later, to guess at the conditions under which a given kind of phenomenon will present it-self' (Peirce 1932–1958, 8.384–388). It is less important that the initial set of hypotheses includes the true diagnosis than that it contains the potential to arrive at it quickly. According to Peirce, this is why it can often be worthwhile starting with a simple hy-pothesis; not because it is more likely to be true but because: 'it may give a good "leave," as the billiard players say. If it does not suit the facts, still the comparison with the facts may be instructive with reference to the next hypothesis' (Peirce 1932–1958, 7.221). Even if a clinician thinks the patient's condition is likely to be more complicated than a common cold, figuring out exactly how it differs from a cold can provide vital clues for which region of the hypothesis space to explore next.

Explainability for intelligent systems in medicine

With our account of clinical reasoning on the table, we can now start to address the particulars of the explainability challenge: what needs explaining, to whom, in what way, and when? While our discussion will fall short of a complete and final answer to these questions, we aim to demonstrate the fruitfulness of our approach and highlight potentials for further work.

To whom?

We have already indicated our answer as *to whom*: in the context of decision support systems, the explainability challenge mainly consists in supporting the understanding of clinicians who offload part of their cognitive labour onto the system such that they can continue to provide explanations that support patients' understanding and, thereby, their autonomy.

We say 'mainly' for two reasons. First, there might also be scope for algorithmic explanations directly tailored to support patient understanding. After all, there is little reason to assume that, in current practice, clinicians always succeed in supporting patient understanding in the best possible way. Insofar as explanations can be generated to support or supplement clinicians' explanations, that could provide added benefits. However, within the current technological paradigm, clinicians will still be managing many parts of the clinical reasoning process. Unless and until systems can be designed that keep track of all aspects of this process, clinicians will continue to mediate most patient-facing explanations.

Second, algorithmic explanations may also support clinician-to-clinician explanations. As health care is, in many settings, increasingly managed by teams rather than by a single doctor, cognitive labour may be distributed across multiple clinicians and decision support systems.[8] There may thus also be scope for algorithmic explanations designed to support the handover between different partners in collaborative reasoning teams to ensure adequate understanding on the part of the clinician(s) charged with providing explanations to patients.

Both of these complications represent fruitful avenues for further research. In the remainder of this chapter, however, we will focus on the simple case outlined above.

What?

This brings us to the *what* question: what information relating to algorithmic decisions do clinicians need to understand to support patient autonomy? It is here that our strategic reasoning account has the most immediate purchase.

Our starting point is the observation that clinical reasoning is a dynamic *process* rather than an isolated event. It involves generating a set of plausible diagnostic hypotheses, given the patient's initial presentation, refining the list of diagnoses through tests and examinations, and, in some cases, pausing to generate further hypotheses if the evidence proves inconclusive. Decision support systems complement this process by generating candidate diagnostic hypotheses recommending particular tests or specific treatments. In each case, what needs to be explained is the *rationale* or *grounds* for a decision. We will explain this point in more detail with reference to diagnosis generation and testing before saying something about treatment recommendations.

Hypothesis generation, in itself, is not difficult (Fann 1970: 41–43; Stanley and Nyrup 2020: 162). The task for differential diagnosis generators is not to list every conceivable cause for the patient's symptoms. Rather, as argued above, the challenge facing clinicians is how to generate a manageable set of hypotheses, which nonetheless includes those hypotheses that have serious implications for the patient's health. This is in principle a task a computerized algorithm is well placed to support. As it does not face the same working memory constraints as human reasoners, it should be able to evaluate a much broader range of hypotheses and only list the most salient ones.[9] The challenge, from the point of view of patient autonomy, is to ensure that clinicians nonetheless understand the basis on which hypotheses were included on the list.

Suppose, for instance, that the patient presents with peripheral oedema (accumulation of fluid in the lower limbs). The causes of peripheral oedema are manifold. Some are non-serious, for example, pregnancy or prolonged standing. Others are more serious, for example, congestive heart failure or liver cirrhosis. Ideally, the algorithm would supply information about the likelihood of each of these causes and also the reasons for prioritizing the different diagnostic hypotheses for testing. For instance, the algorithm might explain that, although heart failure is unlikely given relevant features of the patient, there is nevertheless good reason to order a B-type natriuretic peptide (BNP) test to rule out heart failure. This is because heart failure, if the correct diagnosis, would require immediate attention.

Existing differential diagnosis generators (e.g. DXplain, Isabel) do this to some extent. They will typically display a list of diagnoses that are considered most likely, flagging the most serious diagnostic possibilities. However, these tend to be designed on the basis of something like the Bayesian model of clinical reasoning and do not take into account the more dynamic aspects of abductive reasoning that we highlighted above. It is important for clinicians to understand these limitations, not just to improve clinical reasoning (Stanley and Nyrup 2020: 168–169) but also to be able to explain to the patient, for example, why they are recommending testing for a diagnosis not on the list. Similarly, any future system which *does* incorporate such considerations ought to be able to explain to the clinician *how* they are incorporated into the clinical process.

Furthermore, existing algorithms do not explain reasons for *leaving out* potential causes. This omission risks guiding the clinician's reasoning away from hypotheses that are generally unlikely or non-serious for the patient's salient demographic but crucial for the care of certain (statistically uncommon) individuals, given their circumstances and values. For instance, a diagnosis generator might never bring up pregnancy as a potential cause of peripheral oedema if the patient is male. However, there are some—such as trans men—for whom pregnancy can be a possibility. Given the risks that certain tests and treatments pose to the foetus, this could be a very serious possibility to consider. To provide adequate care and support the decision-making of this patient, the clinician needs to understand what concept of sex and gender the algorithm employs and how this matches their own concept, as well as that of the patient.[10]

With regards to treatment, what is important to recognize in the first instance is that algorithmic treatment recommendations are information to be considered by the clinician and patient. The algorithm does not have the final say on the patient's treatment plan. To make an informed decision for or against an intervention, the patient needs to know the clinical rationale behind the intervention, the risks involved, and the costs and benefits of alternative interventions. For almost all treatments, this information is known to clinicians in the relevant specialties. On the other hand, if an algorithm recommends a novel and unusual treatment when this information is not known, doctors will (rightly) be reluctant to approve it.[11] In addition to safety concerns, another reason not to do so is that it diminishes patient autonomy.

What, then, do treatment recommender algorithms need to explain? If the algorithm outputs an ordering of treatments, one thing that might aid the patient and the clinician in their deliberations is to understand what determines the ranking. For example, suppose the algorithm ranks treatments in terms of their expected QALYs. In this case, the patient would be better placed to factor the treatment recommendation into their deliberations, first, if they knew that the 'best' treatment from the algorithm's point of view *just is* the treatment that has the highest expected QALYs associated with it and, second, if they understood some key aspects of what this means. While the abstract, technical details of how QALYs are calculated will not be relevant, the patient should understand that the algorithm's recommendations are based on population-level estimates of outcomes and so cannot take into account the patient's particular beliefs, values, or circumstances. In short, they need to understand that if they want any such individual factors to influence the decision, they will actively have to explain those factors to the clinician. For instance (recalling the example from the section 'The tension' above), if air travel is very important to the patient, they will need to understand enough about how the algorithm works to realize that this is something they should bring up.

To help adjust the treatment recommendation based on the patient's other values, the clinician, in turn, needs to understand how the default value (viz. QALYs) influenced the recommendations. Understanding this will likely require explanations as to which features of the patient's medical record, whether given or inferred, were taken by the algorithm to indicate that one treatment over another had a higher probability of success relative to the given metric for determining comparative success. The aim is to enable the clinician to reason about, first, what kinds of predicted outcomes the algorithm based its QALY-estimate on and, second, whether these outcomes ought to be evaluated differently in light of the patient's individual values.

Finally, it is worth highlighting that treatment recommendation is hard to disentangle from diagnosis. Often treatments are pre-emptive, for example, when a diagnosis, though uncertain, would require immediate treatment to avoid a catastrophe. The effectiveness of this treatment may, in turn, provide evidence for further investigations. Thus, many of the considerations highlighted for diagnosis generation and testing also apply to treatment recommendations.

In what way and when?

If these are the kinds of information that need explaining, *in what way* and *when* should explanations be provided? Here, we can be brief. How to best explain things to clinicians such that they maintain adequate understanding, is largely an empirical question. For instance, it is not given that the best time to provide explanations is simultaneously with recommendations. Perhaps the best way to balance the comprehensiveness of the hypotheses considered against potential information overload is to postpone explanations until later stages of the reasoning process. We have no special insights to offer as to how this is best achieved. What our account provides is a criterion against which empirical inquiry should evaluate the success of explanations: the guiding concern should be that explanations enable the clinician to better support patient understanding.

CONCLUSION

In this chapter, we examined the tension between opaque machine learning systems in medicine and the ethical ideals of informed consent and shared decision-making. We argued that insofar as explainability resolves this tension, it is difficult to settle disputes over, inter alia, what needs to be explained, in what way, to whom, and at what points in the clinical process without an account of the interplay between clinicians and medical decision support systems. We developed an account of clinical reasoning according to which clinical reasoning is a form of Peircean strategic reasoning. We then used this account to shed light on the particulars of the explainability challenge in medicine. While there is still much to work out, we hope that in making precise the relevance of these questions about the nature of clinical reasoning involving machine learning systems to the issue of explainability, we have laid the ground for future discussions on explainable intelligent systems in medicine.

ACKNOWLEDGEMENTS

We are extremely grateful to Farbod Akhlaghi, Christopher Burr, Stephen Cave, Daniel P. Jones, William Peden, Sabin Roman, Carissa Véliz, and an anonymous referee for their comments on the manuscript and many helpful discussions. The paper on which the chapter was based was presented at the *Philosophy of Medical AI* workshop in Tübingen and the Centre for the Future of Intelligence Weekly Seminar, and we are grateful to the audiences for helpful feedback. This work was funded by the Wellcome Trust (213660/Z/18/Z) and the Leverhulme Trust through the Leverhulme Centre for the Future of Intelligence.

NOTES

1. The principle of respect for autonomy is sometimes claimed to originate with Kant, al-though the Kantian conception of autonomy differs in several respects from that employed in contemporary bioethics. Most importantly, Kant's notion of autonomy is contrasted with *heteronomy* such that principles for action are heteronomous only if law-like but not universal in scope and autonomous only if law-like and universal in scope. The concept of autonomy that features in bioethics does not presuppose a Kantian moral psychology and has no analogue for heteronomy. Indeed, autonomy *qua* bioethics is perhaps better compared with the Millian conception of liberty rather than the Kantian notion of

autonomy (c.f. O'Neill 2003; Jennings 2007). Historically, at least, the relevant notion of autonomy arose in response to certain abuses of human subjects in biomedical research. For example, the Nuremberg Code, which outlined ethical principles for human subjects research in the wake of the Nazi doctors' trial, *United States v Karl Brandt et al.*, emphasized the need for participants to make an 'understanding and enlightened decision' about their participation. Similarly, the 1978 Belmont Report, the drafting of which was at least partially motivated by the infamous Tuskegee syphilis experiment in the United States between 1932 and 1972, enshrined respect for persons as a central ethical principle in human subjects research. For further discussion, see Manson and O'Neill (2007: 4–6).

2. Note, however, that there were doubts about the extent to which interpretability of this sort was helpful for clinicians in diagnostic reasoning. In particular, one concern was that listing the inferential steps fell short of a justification or rationale for the diagnosis (Swartout 1983; Moore and Swartout 1988; Swartout et al. 1991).

3. Liu et al. (2019) also highlight that many of these studies fail to provide external validation of their results or fail to compare the performance of neural networks and clinicians using the same sample. Nonetheless, they are cautiously optimistic in the ability of neural networks to improve diagnosis.

4. One QALY is equal to one year of life at full health. In general, expected QALYs for some treatment is equal to the number of years that the patient is expected to live conditional on their having that treatment multiplied by the utility of each year, where utility is between 0 and 1, 1 denoting full health and 0 denoting death.

5. One concern is that introducing decision support systems into clinical medicine offers an opportunity for clinicians to cut corners, and it is likely that corners will be cut in at least some cases, given the unreasonable workload that clinicians presently face. We are grateful to Carissa Véliz for suggesting this point.

6. This is not to say that a normative explanation cannot be given for the moral significance of autonomy. It might be the case, for example, that respect for autonomy features in the set of rules the internalization of which by all or most people would make things go best, impartially considered. Rather, O'Neill's point here is that the tension presents no obvious problem unless there is an explanation for why autonomy matters because the moral significance of autonomy is not self-explanatory.

7. You might think that the Bayesian view presupposes a commitment to utilitarianism in virtue of its use of expected utility maximization. This concern is mistaken. On one hand, maximizing act utilitarianism takes as the object of maximization (expected) welfare impartially considered. The Bayesian view is more local in its concerns—patient welfare is all that is considered. On the other hand, maximizing act utilitarianism is a criterion of rightness and not a decision procedure. It gives an account of the conditions under which and that in virtue of which an act is right, as opposed to a psychological method for discerning the right action, given a set of alternatives. It is not obvious that a maximizing act utilitarian criterion of rightness supports expected utility maximization as a decision procedure. So, even if welfare impartially considered were the object of maximization on the Bayesian view, there is no obvious reason to think that maximizing act utilitarianism entails or suggests the adoption of the Bayesian view as a decision procedure.

8. Many thanks to Chris Burr for pressing us on this point.

9. We say 'in principle' as evaluating salience often proves tricky in practice. To do so, the algorithm needs to implement a function that adequately models the complex factors that

determine whether a hypothesis is salient at the given stage in the diagnostic process. To a large extent, this relies on clinical judgement rather than explicit, easily formalizable rules.

10. Many thanks to Kerry Mackereth for suggesting this example.

11. Reportedly an issue faced by IBM Watson (Ross and Swetlitz 2018; Strickland 2019).

References

Barnett, G. Octo, Cimino, James J., Hupp, Jon A., and Hoffer, Edward P. (1987), 'DXplain: An Evolving Diagnostic Decision-Support System', *Journal of the American Medical Association* 258(1), 67–74.

Beauchamp, Tom L., and Childress, James F. (2013), *Principles of Biomedical Ethics, 7th Edition* (New York: Oxford University Press).

Berner, Eta S., and Graber, Mark L. (2008), 'Overconfidence as a Cause of Diagnostic Error in Medicine', *American Journal of Medicine* 121(5), S2–S23.

Berner, Eta S., Webster, George D., Shugerman, Alwyn A., Jackson, James R., Algina, James, Baker, Alfred L., et al. (1994), 'Performance of Four Computer-Based Diagnostic Systems', *New England Journal of Medicine* 330(25), 1792–1796.

Bjerring, Jens Christian, and Busch, Jacob (2021), 'Artificial Intelligence and Patient-Centered Decision-Making', *Philosophy & Technology* 34, 1–23.

Brown, Terrence W., McCarthy, Melissa L., Kelen, Gabor D., and Levy, Frederick (2010) 'An Epidemiologic Study of Closed Emergency Department Malpractice Claims in a National Database of Physician Malpractice Insurers', *Academic Emergency Medicine* 17(5), 553–560.

Chiffi, Daniele, and Zanotti, Renzo (2015), 'Medical and Nursing Diagnosis: A Critical Comparison', *Journal of Evaluation in Clinical Practice* 21, 1–6.

Curioni-Fontecedro, Alessandra (2017), 'A New Era of Oncology through Artificial Intelligence', *ESMO Open* 2, e000198.

Epstein, Ronald M., Fiscella, Kevin, Lesser, Cara S., and Stange, Kurt C. (2010), 'Why the Nation Needs a Policy Push on Patient-Centered Health Care', *Health Affairs* 29(8), 1489–1495.

Faden, Ruth R., and Beauchamp, Tom L. (1986), *A History and Theory of Informed Consent* (Oxford: Oxford University Press).

Fann, K. T. (1970), *Peirce's Theory of Abduction* (The Hague: Martinus Nijhof).

Graber, Mark L., and Mathew, Ashlei (2008), 'Performance of a Web-Based Clinical Diagnosis Support System for Internists', *Journal of General Internal Medicine* 23(1), 37–40.

Graber, Mark L., Franklin, Nancy, and Gordon, Ruthanna (2005), 'Diagnostic Error in Internal Medicine', *Archives of Internal Medicine* 165(13), 1493–1499.

Grote, Thomas, and Berens, Philipp (2020), 'On the Ethics of Algorithmic Decision-Making in Healthcare', *Journal of Medical Ethics* 46(3), 205–211.

Gulshan, Varun, Peng, Lily, Coram, Marc, Stumpe, Martin C., Wu, Derek, Narayanaswamy, Arunachalam, et al. (2016), 'Development and Validation of a Deep Learning Algorithm for Detection of Diabetic Retinopathy in Retinal Fundus Photographs', *Journal of the American Medical Association* 316(22), 2402–2410.

He, Jianxing, Baxter, Sally L., Xu, Jie, Xu, Jiming, Zhou, Xingtao, and Zhang, Kang (2019), 'The Practical Implementation of Artificial Intelligence Technologies in Medicine', *Nature Medicine* 25(1), 30–36.

Hintikka, Jaakko (1998), 'What Is Abduction? The Fundamental Problem of Contemporary Epistemology', in Jaakko Hintikka *Inquiry as Inquiry: A Logic of Scientific Discovery* (Dordrecht: Springer), 91–113.

Holzinger, Andreas, Langs, Georg, Denk, Helmut, Zatloukal, Kurt, and Müller, Heimo (2019), 'Causability and Explainability of Artificial Intelligence in Medicine', *Wiley Interdisciplinary Reviews: Data Mining and Knowledge Discovery* 9(4), e1312.

Jennings, Bruce (2007), 'Autonomy', in B. Steinbock, ed., *The Oxford Handbook of Bioethics* (New York: Oxford University Press), 72–89.

Kaplan, Robert M. (2004), 'Shared Medical Decision Making: A New Tool for Preventive Medicine', *American Journal of Preventive Medicine* 26(1), 81–83.

Levy, Neil (2014), 'Forced to Be Free? Increasing Patient Autonomy by Constraining It', *Journal of Medical Ethics* 40(5), 293–300.

Liu, Xiaoxuan, Faes, Livia, Kale, Aditya, Wagner, Siegfried K., Fu, Dun Jack, Bruynseels, Alice, et al. (2019), 'A Comparison of Deep Learning Performance against Health-Care Professionals in Detecting Diseases from Medical Imaging: A Systematic Review and Meta-Analysis', *The Lancet Digital Health* 1(6), E271–E297.

Manson, Neil C., and O'Neill, Onora (2007), *Rethinking Informed Consent in Bioethics* (Cambridge: Cambridge University Press).

McCullough, Laurence B. (2011), 'Was Bioethics Founded on Historical and Conceptual Mistakes about Medical Paternalism?', *Bioethics* 25(2), 66–74.

McDougall, Rosalind J. (2019), 'Computer Knows Best? The Need for Value-Flexibility in Medical AI', *Journal of Medical Ethics* 45(3), 156–160.

Mittelstadt, Brent Daniel, Patrick Allo, Mariarosaria Taddeo, Sandra Wachter, and Luciano Floridi. "The Ethics of Algorithms: Mapping the Debate." *Big Data & Society*, (December 2016). https://doi.org/10.1177/2053951716679679

Moore, Johanna D., and Swartout, William R. (1988), *Explanation in Expert Systems: A Survey*, No. ISI/RR-88-228. (California, IL: University of Southern California Marina del Rey Information Sciences Institute).

Newman-Toker, David E., and Pronovost, Peter J. (2009), 'Diagnostic Errors—the Next Frontier for Patient Safety', *Journal of the American Medical Association* 301(10), 1060–1062.

O'Neill, Onoroa (2003), 'Autonomy: The Emperor's New Clothes', *Aristotelian Society Supplementary Volume* 77(1), 1–21.

Paavola, Sami (2004), 'Abduction through Grammar, Critic, and Methodeutic', *Transactions of the Charles S. Peirce Society* 40(2), 245–270.

Patel, Vimla L., Kaufman, David R., and Kannampallil, Thomas G. (2019), 'Diagnostic Reasoning and Expertise in Health Care', in Paul Ward, Jan Maarten Schraagen, Julie Gore, and Emilie M. Roth, eds, *The Oxford Handbook of Expertise* (New York: Oxford University Press), 619–641.

Peirce, Charles Sanders (1932–1958), *Collected Papers of Charles Sanders Peirce*, eds P. Weiss, C. Hartshorne, and A. Burks (Cambridge, MA: Harvard University Press).

Richardson, W. Scott, and Wilson, Mark C. (2015), 'The Process of Diagnosis', in Gordon H. Guyatt, Drummond Rennie, Maureen O. Meade, and Deborah J. Cook, eds, *Users' Guides to the Medical Literature: Essentials of Evidence-Based Clinical Practice*, 3rd edn (New York: McGraw Hill), 211–222.

Ross, Casey, and Swetlitz, Ike (2018), 'IBM's Watson Supercomputer Recommended "Unsafe and Incorrect" Cancer Treatments, Internal Documents Show', *Stat*, 25 July.

Schwartz, Alan, and Elstein, Arthur S. (2008), 'Clinical Reasoning in Medicine', *Clinical Reasoning in the Health Professions* 3, 223–234.

Shen, Jiayi, Zhang, Casper J.P., Jiang, Bangsheng, Chen, Jiebin, Song, Jian, Liu, Zherui, He, Zonglin, Wong, Sum Yi, Fang, Po-Han, and Ming, Wai-Kit (2019), 'Artificial Intelligence versus Clinicians in Disease Diagnosis: Systematic Review', *JMIR Medical Informatics* 7(3), e10010.

Sheridan, Stacey L., Harris, Russell P., Woolf, Steven H., and Shared Decision-Making Workgroup of the US Preventive Services Task Force (2004), 'Shared Decision Making about Screening and Chemoprevention: A Suggested Approach from the US Preventive Services Task Force', *American Journal of Preventive Medicine* 26(1), 56–66.

Shortliffe, Edward H., Davis, Randall, Axline, Stanton G., Buchanan, Bruce G., Green, C. Cordell, and Cohen, Stanley N. (1975), 'Computer-Based Consultations in Clinical Therapeutics: Explanation and Rule Acquisition Capabilities of the MYCIN System', *Computers and Biomedical Research* 8(4), 303–320.

Simon, Herbert A. (1985), 'Artificial-Intelligence Approaches to Problem Solving and Clinical Diagnosis', *Logic of Discovery and Diagnosis in Medicine* 72, 87.

Somashekhar, S.P., Sepúlveda, Martín-J., Norden, Andrew D., Rauthan, Amit, Arun, Kumar, Patil, Poonam, et al. (2017), 'Early Experience with IBM Watson for Oncology (WFO) Cognitive Computing System for Lung and Colorectal Cancer Treatment', *Journal of Clinical Oncology* 35(15_suppl), 8527–8527.

Stanley, Donald E., and Campos, Daniel G. (2013), 'The Logic of Medical Diagnosis', *Perspectives in Biology and Medicine* 56(2), 300–315.

Stanley, Donald E., and Nyrup, Rune (2020), 'Strategies in Abduction: Generating and Selecting Diagnostic Hypotheses', *Journal of Medicine and Philosophy: A Forum for Bioethics and Philosophy of Medicine* 45(2), 159–178.

Strickland, Eliza (2019), 'How IBM Watson Overpromised and Underdelivered on AI Health Care', *IEEE Spectrum*, 2 April.

Swartout, William R. (1983), 'XPLAIN: A System for Creating and Explaining Expert Consulting Programs', *Artificial Intelligence* 21(3), 285–325.

Swartout, William, Paris, Cecile, and Moore, Johanna (1991), 'Explanations in Knowledge Systems: Design for Explainable Expert Systems', *IEEE Expert* 6(3), 58–64.

Taylor, Charles, (1991). *The Malaise of Modernity* (Toronto: House of Anansi).

United States v. Karl Brandt et al. (1950). Trials of War Criminals Before the Nuremberg Military Tribunals Under Control Council Law 10 (Washington, DC: Superintendant of Documents, US Government Printing Office).

Wagholikar, Kavishwar B., Sundararajan, Vijayraghavan, and Deshpande, Ashok W. (2012), 'Modeling Paradigms for Medical Diagnostic Decision Support: A Survey and Future Directions', *Journal of Medical Systems* 36(5), 3029–3049.

Warner, Homer R., Toronto, Alan F., Veasey, L. George, and Stephenson, Robert (1961), 'A Mathematical Approach to Medical Diagnosis: Application to Congenital Heart Disease', *Journal of the American Medical Association* 177(3), 177–183.

Yu, Kun-Hsing, Beam, Andrew L., and Kohane, Isaac S. (2018), 'Artificial Intelligence in Healthcare', *Nature Biomedical Engineering* 2(10), 719–731.

Zwaan, Laura, and Singh, Hardeep (2015), 'The Challenges in Defining and Measuring Diagnostic Error', *Diagnosis* 2(2), 97–103.

PART VII

PRIVACY AND SECURITY

CHAPTER 28

THE SURVEILLANCE DELUSION

CARISSA VÉLIZ

THE privacy landscape in the first two decades of the twenty-first century is radically different than that of the last two decades of the twentieth century. In 1980, an ordinary person was unlikely to be subjected to extensive corporate or governmental surveillance. Even though there have been censuses since the end of the eighteenth century, tax records go back to the early twentieth century, and private-sector databases have been a privacy threat since at least the 1970s (Solove 2001), the extent of surveillance was limited by friction that is now largely being overcome by digital technologies. In the 1980s, some personal data was collected for corporate purposes, but companies didn't have the means to track every single person throughout their day, and the ability to buy and integrate different databases wasn't a few clicks away. There were some CCTV cameras on the street but fewer than today and with no facial recognition. The only reason why someone could end up being subjected to serious governmental intrusion in liberal democracies was if they were criminal suspects. Even then, the amount of data the police could get on them is nowhere near the amount of data that is collected about ordinary citizens today.

Our financial transactions, online searches, movements, communications, relationships, and interactions with governments and businesses all generate personal data that is being collected, sold, and bought by data brokers, corporations, and governments interested in profiling individuals. The commodification of personal data brings with it promises: greater safety, economic gain, and scientific and technological advancements. The concomitant loss in privacy, however, has severe costs that, arguably, are not being taken seriously enough, judging by the constant expansion of surveillance. Surveillance puts people at risk of suffering discrimination, exploitation, and other kinds of abuse such as extortion. Furthermore, it pushes society into a culture of exposure that can breed conformity and jeopardize democracy.

The first section gauges the breadth and depth of surveillance in the digital age. In the second section, I assess the role of consent in surveillance practices. The third section discusses whether current levels of surveillance amount to mass surveillance and to what extent that is ethically problematic. In the fourth section, I sketch the costs of surveillance in terms of risks, harms, and wrongs. The fifth section explores whether ubiquitous surveillance can be justified for the purposes of security. In the sixth section, I investigate whether surveillance is justifiable as a business model. In the seventh section, I assess whether ubiquitous surveillance can be justified for the purposes of technological advancement. In the eighth section, I analyse the relationship between surveillance, freedom, and democracy. Finally, in the ninth section, I conclude by hypothesizing that the nature of the costs of surveillance often leads people to fall into the trap of the *surveillance delusion*: the assumption that surveillance has no significant moral costs. Under the surveillance delusion, only the benefits of surveillance are considered, and, as a result, surveillance is taken to be a convenient solution to problems that could be solved through less intrusive means—all without realizing that surveillance itself may be creating more weighty problems in the long run than the ones it is solving.

The breadth and depth of surveillance in the digital age

The amount of personal data collected about people around the world has been consistently increasing during the past two decades on account of a few factors.[1] First, the development of data analysis tools has made it easier than ever to collect personal data. Second, as we interact more than ever with computers (and computers with us), more personal data than ever is created. Third, regardless of whether institutions are in the business of technology, every institution has an incentive to collect personal data because it can be sold to third parties—personal data has become an easy way to earn money. The personal data economy—the buying and selling of personal data—has given rise to companies that specialize in the commodification of personal data: data brokers. These companies aim to have a file on every internet user, which they then sell to insurance companies, banks, prospective employees, governments, etc.

Some of that data will have been offered by users with various degrees of voluntariness. For example, people routinely share their email addresses and phone numbers with companies whenever they purchase something and have it delivered to their home. What they might not realize is that those companies are likely to share that information with hundreds of other companies, who will then use it to make sensitive inferences. While someone might not think that sharing their music tastes with companies is sensitive data, companies often take non-sensitive data and turn it into sensitive data through inferences, for example, inferring sexual orientation from music preferences (Kosinski et al. 2013).

One of the distinctive data risks of the digital age is the aggregation of data across databases. Before data was digitized, it wasn't as dangerous to surrender personal data to very different institutions because the chances of those databases being aggregated was slim. Digitization and the internet have made it easy to share data. As the amount and depth of public databases increases, our privacy is more at risk because it becomes easier to 'join the dots' and learn more about people than they are willing to share.[2]

For example, in 2006, Netflix published 10 million movie rankings by half a million customers as part of a challenge for people to design a better recommendation algorithm. The data was supposed to be anonymous, but researchers at the University of Texas at Austin managed to re-identify people by comparing rankings and timestamps with public information in the Internet Movie Database (IMDb). If someone saw a movie on a particular night, liked it on Netflix, and then rated it on IMDb as well, researchers could infer that it was the same person. Movie preferences can reveal sensitive information such as sexual orientation. A lesbian mother sued Netflix for placing her at risk of being outed (Singel 2009). The danger of exposure through aggregation and inferences has become all the more pungent since data brokers took it upon themselves to aggregate as much data as possible about each individual.

The extent of data collection on every internet user is astonishingly broad. A typical data broker will have thousands of data points about every person, including age, gender, education, employment, political views, relationship status, purchases, loans, net worth, vehicles owned, properties owned, banking and insurance policies details, likelihood of someone planning to have a baby, social media activity, alcohol and tobacco interests, casino gaming and lottery interests, religion, health status, and much more (Melendez and Pasternack 2019).

To put that into perspective, the Stasi, the security service of East Germany, notorious for its surveillance capabilities, held much less data on its citizens. They had one spy or informant for every sixty-six citizens (Koehler 1999: 9) and managed to have files on little more than one-third of the population (Cameron 2021). Today, with a significant proportion of people volunteering private information on social networks and carrying a smartphone in their pockets, governments can have a file on every single citizen with substantially more data than the Stasi ever had.

One might think that the comparison with the Stasi is misleading because that was government surveillance and the kind of surveillance we face today is mostly corporate, which can be thought to be less dangerous. Government surveillance is often thought to be more worrisome on account of the special powers that governments hold (e.g. to arrest people). Data collection and trades have become so ubiquitous, however, that it is unhelpful to distinguish between corporate and governmental surveillance as data collected by the former is shared with the latter and vice versa (Véliz 2020: 27–45). Even when corporations refuse to give up data to governments (as in the case of Apple refusing to help the FBI hack into a dead criminal's phone in 2016), governments often have the ability to hack into data themselves or to hire the services of someone who will do it for them (which is exactly what happened in the Apple case) (Yadron 2016).

Most countries don't have the means to develop surveillance and hacking tools, so they buy them from cyberweapons manufacturers (Schneier 2018: 65). Countries routinely use the tech giants to outsource surveillance. Palantir, Amazon, and Microsoft, for instance, provided tools that aided the Trump administration in putting under surveillance, detaining, and deporting immigrants (Levin 2018). Court records in the United States show that investigators can ask Google to disclose everyone who searched for a particular keyword (as opposed to asking for information on a known suspect) (Ng 2020). In short, any personal data that is collected by a company can end up in the hands of the police (Morrison 2021).

In some cases, corporate surveillance can be used to bypass official policies. In 2018, John Roberts, Chief Justice of the Supreme Court in the United States, authored a majority opinion ruling against the government obtaining location data from mobile phone towers without a warrant. Unsatisfied with that decision, the Trump administration bought access to a commercial database that maps the movements of millions of mobile phones in the United States. Given that such data is for sale from data brokers, the government didn't need a warrant to get it. By outsourcing surveillance to private companies, the government found a way to bypass a Supreme Court ruling (Cox 2020). In another example, in its pursuit of two suspects, the United States asked Mexico to use a facial recognition system made by a Chinese company that had been blacklisted by the US government (Hill 2021).

The flow of information goes both ways: governments also collect personal data that they pass on to businesses—sometimes for a profit. Data about millions of patients in the National Health Service in the United Kingdom has been sold to pharmaceutical companies, for example (Helm 2019).

In short, the breadth and depth of data collection and data sharing in the digital age is more vast than ever before.

THE ROLE OF CONSENT IN
SURVEILLANCE PRACTICES

It is intuitive to think that if losses of privacy are consented, there is no harm done.[3] Companies often claim that their surveillance practices are unproblematic because users give their consent when agreeing to their terms and conditions. However, consent in the context of the data economy is an ethically questionable practice at its best.

The notion of informed consent comes from medical ethics. In that context, it is a tool to honour and protect patients' autonomy. Autonomy is the ability and right of adults to choose their own values and act accordingly. If patients are to be treated as ends in themselves, according to the Kantian categorical imperative, that means we must recognize that they have their own priorities and objectives and that the medical profession has no right to interfere with their desires. That is why doctors cannot do research on patients or intervene in their bodies without their permission.

Unfortunately, the practice of consent does not travel well to the data context. While the medical profession is supposed to be set up to aid patients, companies are typically wanting to profit from their users. This means that terms and conditions are written to protect companies—not ordinary people—from liability. Terms and conditions are usually unreasonably long, non-negotiable, and can change at any time without previous warning.

Furthermore, even if terms and conditions were short and negotiable, there is arguably no such thing as *informed* consent in the context of the data economy. Data implications are notoriously difficult to understand, often impossible. Neither the people who wrote the privacy policy nor the programmers who wrote the code for the algorithms that analyse data know what kind of inferences might be drawn from the data they get from users or where that data might end up once it gets sold. If no one knows about the consequences of data collection, the user cannot be informed in any meaningful sense.

A third challenge for consent in data contexts is that it is often hard or impossible to ask all relevant people for consent. For example, if someone does a DNA test, they might be consenting, but their parents, siblings, children, and distant kin are not giving their consent. Most personal data either contains data about other people or can be used to infer data about other people, such that it is unclear whether an individual has the moral authority to consent to giving up their data.

Finally, consent may not be voluntary. Very often, people do not have a meaningful choice in using technological tools that are necessary to be full participants of society, and terms and conditions do not allow for any kind of negotiation.[4]

Thus, while there may be a role for consent in surveillance practices, that role is not as broad as it might be imagined, and someone giving consent to be put under surveillance does not automatically mean that such a practice is ethical.

DOES BULK DATA COLLECTION AMOUNT TO MASS SURVEILLANCE?

One important debate in the surveillance literature is whether such vast bulk collection of personal data equals mass surveillance. Both surveillance companies and intelligence agencies have an interest in defending the view that bulk collection of personal data is not an invasion of privacy as it makes what they do sound less problematic.

When Steven Levy interviewed National Security Agency (NSA) officials, he realized that 'looking at the world through [NSA's] eyes, there is no privacy threat in collecting massive amounts of information' (Levy 2014). The thought is, roughly, that even though everyone's data is being collected on a mass scale, that doesn't amount to mass surveillance because that data rarely gets accessed. What it is exactly that people mean by 'access' is unclear and much depends on it, but one example is that, even if intelligence agencies have plentiful data about you, if you are not interesting to them, the chances are that no human agent will ever look at that data. In this vein, Mark Pythian writes: 'If innocent people are unaware that their communications have been intercepted, stored, and filtered out by computer—thus not ever seen by a human analyst—then the in-trusion is potential, not actual, and the potential for harm to the individual negligible' (Omand and Phythian 2018: 24–25). Similarly, David Omand argues that bulk access to data does not amount to mass surveillance because, for most of the data, no human ana-lyst sees and logs it for future action (Omand and Phythian 2018: 150).

Those who consider that collecting information is privacy-invasive tend to think about either privacy or the right to privacy as a matter of control.[5] To them, if someone loses control over their data, that amounts to either losing privacy or having their right to privacy violated. Those who think that data collection is not a privacy worry tend to think of privacy or the right to privacy as a matter of access: as long as the data does not get accessed, there is no privacy invasion.[6] Kevin Macnish, for example, argues that loss of control over our personal data can make us *feel* vulnerable and can make us more vul-nerable through increasing the risk that the personal data might be accessed one day. Despite this increased vulnerability, argues Macnish, as long as the data is not accessed, there is no privacy violation (Macnish 2016).

Data collection certainly risks our privacy, and that is partly what is wrong with it. But that is not the whole story. Suppose an intelligence agency like the NSA (in the United States) or Government Communications Headquarters (commonly known as GCHQ, in the United Kingdom) comes to an agreement with you: they will collect all your data, but if you never criticize the government, they will never access it. Suppose further that you can trust this promise and that the agency can guarantee without a doubt the safety of your data such that, if you never criticize the government, your data is as safe as if it had never been collected. There is still some wrong being committed here. One might be tempted to think that it is an abuse of power, but many rights violations by government agencies are abuses of power: murder, unjustified incarcer-ation, etc. What is characteristic of this particular abuse of power is that it attempts against our privacy, and the best way to capture that is by explaining it in terms of our right to privacy. From here on, I will therefore assume that the collection of personal data is a form of surveillance.

THE RISKS, HARMS, AND WRONGS OF
SURVEILLANCE

If this assessment is right, given that surveillance implies a significant intrusion, it can only be justified if its benefits outweigh its costs. Even if someone were to argue that bulk data collection does not amount to mass surveillance and does not violate privacy, that surveillance has costs is undeniable.

At the very least, the cost of surveillance is an increased risk of exposure. Personal data is dangerous because it is sensitive, highly susceptible to misuse, hard to keep safe, and desired by many—from criminals to insurance companies and intelligence agencies. The more data is collected, the longer it is stored, and the more it is passed on from one institution to the next, analysed, and aggregated with other data, the more likely it is that it will end up being misused. Examples of data misuse include neglect (i.e. when the data is not kept safe and ends up being leaked), exposure, and unlawful discrimination.

The kind of surveillance that is common in the digital age therefore entails, at the very least, a *risk*. It sometimes also entails a *harm*, for example, when risks materialize and there is a case of exposure or discrimination. Finally, surveillance incurs the infringement or violation of the right to privacy. When a privacy invasion is justified, it amounts to a right infringement; if the invasion is unjustified, then it amounts to a violation of the right to privacy and therefore a *wrong*.

The requirements of ethical surveillance: Necessity and proportionality

It is widely accepted that what it takes for surveillance to be ethical is that it be necessary and proportionate (Hadjimatheou 2014; Macnish 2015; Brown and Korff 2009). Given that surveillance has costs, it has to be *necessary* in that comparable beneficial results cannot be achieved by less intrusive or harmful methods. The moral concept of *proportionality* refers to a moral constraint on actions that cause harm. For an act that causes harm to be proportionate, it must be done in the pursuit of some valuable goal against which the harms are weighed (McMahan 2009: 19). If benefits outweigh harms, risks, and wrongs (if the bad that an act creates is less than the bad it prevents), then the act is proportionate. An implicit condition of proportionality is that surveillance has to be effective. If surveillance has costs and no benefits because it is not effective (it doesn't do what it's supposed to do), then it can hardly be justified (Véliz 2017, forthcoming).

Proportionality is concerned with comparing the consequences of doing an act with the consequences of not doing it. Necessity is concerned with comparing what will happen if an act is done with what will happen if alternative acts are done that are also means of achieving the same end. Proportionality is concerned with the question: are the bad effects of this act such that the good effects cannot be justified? Necessity, in contrast, asks: what is, morally, the best means for achieving certain ends?

The idea of proportionality in surveillance is not foreign to law and public policy. The Investigatory Powers Bill in the United Kingdom includes proportionality among the considerations to be taken into account under general duties in relation to privacy. In 2014, 500 organizations and experts worldwide signed the International Principles on the Application of Human Rights to Communications Surveillance, which includes the principle of proportionality (Schneier 2015: 168).

There are three purported benefits that are often used to justify surveillance: security, economic gain, and technological advancement. I will discuss each of these in turn and assess whether digital surveillance is proportionate and necessary to achieve the benefits pursued.

SURVEILLANCE AND SECURITY

The expansion of surveillance at the end of the twentieth and the beginning of the twenty-first centuries was tied to a concern for security. In the United Kingdom, a so-called Ring of Steel was created after the Irish Republican Army (IRA) exploded truck bombs in the City of London in the early 1990s (Carlile 2004). The Ring of Steel is a zone of cameras built around the financial district that got gradually expanded and updated and that in the early 2000s turned Britain into the country in the world with the most video surveillance (it has now been superseded by China and the United States, in that order) (Carlile 2004; Brandl 2021). More recently, in 2016, the Investigatory Powers Act introduced new governmental powers of bulk collection of data for the purposes of security.

In the United States, it was also the threat of terrorism that motivated the expansion of surveillance. In 2000, the Federal Trade Commission had recommended that the United States Congress regulate the data economy. But after 9/11, the US government saw an opportunity to make a copy of all the data being collected by the corporate world and use it for the purposes of national security. Unbeknownst to citizens, shortly after the attacks, a secret system of mass surveillance was implemented with the objective of increasing security. With the passing of the Patriot Act, six weeks after the terrorist attacks, the Federal Bureau of Investigation (FBI) was allowed to issue 'national security letters', a form of subpoena that is not subject to judicial oversight and allows spying into the private lives of people (phone records, bank accounts, web searches, and credit card purchases) who might not even be considered suspects (Wright 2008). Similar trends followed in other countries such as France.

There are a few arguments that can be offered in favour of ubiquitous surveillance for the purposes of security. Although mass surveillance tends to carry with it a negative connotation, Katerina Hadjimatheou has argued that, first, untargeted surveillance is less likely to stigmatize those who are watched because everyone is being watched. However, arguably, when criminal suspects are watched covertly (through targeted surveillance, the alternative to mass surveillance), they are not being stigmatized because no one knows about the surveillance.

Second, Hadjimatheou argues, mass surveillance is likely to be a less intrusive privacy measure if it's overt because it allows people to adapt their expectations and plan accordingly. The example she gives is how, when people know there will be surveillance at airports, they can make sure not to carry sensitive objects in their hand luggage (2014: 204). However, once surveillance becomes truly ubiquitous, there is no avoiding it and therefore no planning accordingly. When a surveillance apparatus follows our every step and keystroke along the day, altering our behaviour amounts to potentially drastic self-censorship. Not carrying sensitive objects in our hand luggage might not be a big inconvenience (although it could be), but changing what we search for online, whether we go to a protest, or what we say to our loved ones out of fear of surveillance has serious implications for individuals and democracy (de Bruin 2010; Gavison 1980; Véliz 2020), as we will see later.

Third, Hadjimatheou argues, indiscriminate surveillance is likely to be more efficient as a deterrent for wrongdoing (Hadjimatheou 2014: 189, 197). Whether this argument succeeds will depend, first, on how effective mass surveillance is at preventing crime and, second, how much wrongdoers are willing to lose; in the case of extremist terrorists who are willing to give up their lives, it may not act as much of a deterrent.

Perhaps the most powerful argument in favour of mass surveillance is that we must subject ourselves to surveillance as part of a duty to protect one another from rights violations. In some cases, it is permissible to deliberately harm a person as a way to enforce a 'duty to protect third parties from wrongful harm—subject, of course, to considerations of necessity, effectiveness and proportionality' (Fabre 2022: Ch. 9). As mentioned before, terrorism has been front and centre in the defence of surveillance.

A necessary condition for surveillance to be justified is that it be effective. Whether mass surveillance is effective is a contentious issue. While David Anderson found that bulk collection of data helped foil criminal plots in the United Kingdom (Anderson 2016), none of the many oversight committees or investigations in the United States have found it effective (Clarke et al. 2013: 104, 120; Bergen et al. 2014: 1; Savage 2015a; 2015b: 162–223; 'Report on the President's Surveillance Program' 2009: 637; Isikoff 2013). Although my own conclusion is that it is very doubtful whether mass surveillance will ever be an effective method of preventing terrorism, I will assume effectiveness in what follows for the sake of argument.

Once effectiveness has been established or assumed, surveillance still needs to be necessary and proportionate to be justified. Together, both requirements serve the goal of making sure we are better off with mass surveillance than without it.

There are serious doubts about whether mass surveillance for the purposes of ensuring security can be proportionate. The wrong of mass surveillance is significant, given that the right to privacy of the whole of the population is violated. With that wrong come concomitant risks and harms. Among them are chilling effects: the possibility of authorities treating all citizens like criminal suspects and going on fishing expeditions in search of illegality and the risk of that data being hacked, leaked, or seriously misused in the future.

Similarly, there are doubts about whether mass surveillance is necessary, and, if it is unnecessary, it can hardly be proportionate. There is reason to think that targeted surveillance is superior to mass surveillance as well as less intrusive. With targeted surveillance, the police or intelligence agencies must first get a tip. The tip usually comes from the community or from family members, but it can also come from informants or relevant information can turn up from other criminal investigations. Once there is good reason for suspicion, investigative authorities present the evidence to a judge, who must decide whether there is enough evidence for suspicion to order a warrant for surveillance to take place. This system works surprisingly well. Because police officers will have to go back to the same judges for warrants in future cases, they are careful to build trust with them and ask for warrants only when it is quite likely they will find something. In fact, police find at least some of the evidence they had expected in more than 80 per cent of cases (Solove 2011: 130).

Experience since 9/11 suggests that targeted surveillance is more effective than mass surveillance in preventing terrorism, which supports the conclusion that bulk surveillance is neither necessary nor proportionate for achieving our counterterrorist goals. The major technical problem with mass surveillance seems to be that which characterizes it: the extent of the collection of data. The sheer quantity of information adds irrelevant data about innocent people and obscures what would be significant tips from targeted surveillance. Mass surveillance adds hay to the haystack and makes it all the more difficult to find the needle.

Security expert Bruce Schneier has argued that bulk collection and data-mining are inappropriate tools for finding terrorists for three reasons (2015: 136–140). First, error rates are unacceptably high. When we use data-mining to target people for something relatively innocuous such as fashion advertisement, mistakes can be tolerated more easily as getting advertisements for clothes we do not want to buy is usually not too problematic. But when data-mining is used to look for terrorists, the lives and freedom of potentially innocent people are at stake, and our tolerance for mistakes should be low.

The second reason for the inappropriateness of data-mining techniques for investigating terrorism is that terrorist attacks are unique. There was no way of predicting that pressure-cooker bombs would be used in the Boston Marathon attack (Schneier 2015: 138), or that someone might put a bomb in his shoe, or that people would try liquid explosives, or that someone might kill people with a cargo truck in Nice. Jeff Jonas, an IBM research scientist, and Jim Harper, the director of information policy at the Cato Institute, argue that 'terrorism does not occur with enough frequency to enable the creation of valid predictive models' (Jonas and Harper 2006: 8).

The third problem is that terrorists will be trying to avoid detection, making it harder for them to be caught in the very broad nets cast by intelligence agencies.

A final problem beyond necessity and proportionality is the concern that mass surveillance can end up jeopardizing national security due to both internal and external risks. Internal risks include the possibility of a future bad government taking control of the architecture of surveillance and using it to become an authoritarian regime. External risks include the possibility of an adversary country hacking into sensitive systems and using personal data for intelligence or even military purposes. These risks illustrate a 'real and unavoidable' contradiction identified by Timothy Garton Ash when governments spy on their own citizens, thereby infringing the freedom they are supposed to defend: 'if the infringement goes too far, it begins to destroy what it is meant to preserve' (Garton Ash 1997: 236). We will return to this issue in the conclusion.

Even if we agreed that it's not worth implementing ubiquitous surveillance for the sake of security, there are those who might think that surveillance is justified for the sake of economic gain.

SURVEILLANCE AND ECONOMIC GAIN

The commodification of data, often called the data economy, has become a remarkably profitable industry. 'The world's most valuable resource is no longer oil, but data', read an *Economist* article in 2017. A significant part of the data market is tied to personalized advertising, which uses personal data to show relevant ads to people. Advertising is the main way the internet funds itself, and most advertising online is personalized. That makes personal data one of the most valuable kinds of data. What used to be considered wiretapping and the purview of police has become a mainstream business model.

Personalized advertising is often organized around bidding. Real-time bidding (RTB) sends a user's personal data to interested advertisers, often without their permission. Suppose Amazon gets that data and recognizes them as a user who has visited their website before in search of a book. They might be willing to pay more than others to lure them into buying that book because they are confident they wants it. And that's how they get shown an Amazon book ad. In that process, however, very personal data, such as sexual orientation and political affiliation, might have been sent to dozens or even hundreds of possible advertisers without the user's knowledge or consent. And those companies get to keep that personal data, which often gets sold on to other third parties (ICO 2019).

Another crucial piece of the puzzle of the data economy are data brokers. Whenever there is personal data collected, there is a good chance it will end up in the hands of data brokers. Data brokers aim to have a file on all internet users. They then sell those files to prospective employers, insurance companies, governments, and anyone else willing to buy the data. A company like Experian, for example, aggregates data on over a billion people and businesses, including 235 million US consumers. Axciom has more than 10.000 data points on every one of 2.5 billion consumers in 62 countries (Melendez and Pasternack 2019).

While the data economy is highly profitable at the time of writing, it is questionable whether its benefits outweigh its costs for society. With wealth inequality increasing around the world (Alvaredo et al. 2018), there is no evidence to think that profits to companies like data brokers trickle down to the rest of society. Unlike the big companies of the past, data brokers are not companies that employ a large number of people. While a car manufacturer employs hundreds of thousands of people (e.g. Volkswagen employed 665,000 people in 2020, according to Statista), a data broker typically employs only a few thousand (e.g. Experian, one of the largest data brokers, employs around 16,000 people, according to its website).

In turn, the societal harms and risks of an economy founded on surveillance are significant. Data brokers make it very hard to police anti-discrimination laws. When anyone can acquire sensitive information about others without any kind of supervision, it is hard to make sure that companies are not discriminating against people for their political tendencies, their sexual orientation, or their health status, for example. Often, when people are treated on the basis of their data by both private and public institutions, they cease to be treated as equal citizens (Véliz 2020).

The risk that sensitive data will be hacked and misused is also high. In September 2017, Experian announced a cybersecurity breach in which criminals accessed the personal data of about 147 million US citizens. The data accessed included names, social security numbers, birth dates, addresses, and driver's licence numbers. It is one of the biggest data breaches in history. In February 2020, the United States Department of Justice indicted four Chinese military people on nine charges related to the breach (which China has so far denied). That foreign countries are hacking sensitive data alerts us to a further risk in national security.

Through data acquired from a location data broker, journalists in the *New York Times* managed to find the location of the President of the United States through correlating his public schedule to a phone that belonged to a Secret Service agent (Thompson and Warzel 2019). With the same database, the reporters were also able to identify and follow military officials with security clearances and law enforcement officers, among others.

There are also concerns about how the data economy incentivizes the design of algorithms on social media that lead to misinformation and the polarization of society. Social media companies want people to stay on their platforms for as long as possible because that is how they can collect as much personal data from them as possible and show them as many ads as possible. Unfortunately, the content that is most engaging is often toxic content like misinformation and heated political debates that end up polarizing citizens into extreme positions (Wylie 2019). Although some have argued that there is too much privacy on social media (see Marmor, this volume), my own view is that there is too little (Véliz, 2021).

Finally, there is a concern that the personalized ads market is a financial bubble. Microtargeting is much less effective and accurate than it's made out to be and too expensive for it to be worth it (Edelman 2020; Hwang 2020). The market is so opaque that it allows for errors in valuation and click fraud. Click fraud uses automated scripts or paid humans in 'click farms' to click on an ad, but there is no consumer viewing that ad (Hwang 2020: 84). And part of why the market is so opaque is because ads are personalized; if everyone saw the same ad, it would be easier to verify that it's being shown. Forrester Research estimated that, in 2016, as much as 56 per cent of all the money spent on ads in the United States was lost to fraud or unviewable ads (Bidel et al. 2017). The worry is that, once the businesses that have bought personalized ads realize that they have been paying for something that is not worth it, the bubble will burst, and we will find ourselves in the midst of a financial crisis similar to the 2008 one.

Given that the data economy has increased inequality, is a threat to national security, can lead to the polarization of society and to disinformation, and is risking
a financial crisis, it doesn't seem like surveillance is a justified business model.
Ubiquitous surveillance as a business model is not necessary. Humanity had already
achieved a high level of wealth before the data economy came along. One of the main
reasons why so much personal data is collected online is to fund internet companies
like Facebook and Google, but those companies could be funded through alternative business models, including subscription models, and through advertising that
does not depend on personal data. Contextual advertising, for instance, shows ads to
people based on what they just searched for without needing to know anything else
about them. Given that it is not necessary and that its advantages can be achieved
through less costly means, surveillance as a business model is not proportionate
either.

SURVEILLANCE AND TECHNOLOGICAL
ADVANCEMENT

A third common reason to justify the collection of personal data is for the purposes of
technological and scientific advancement. In particular, it is often thought that personal
data is needed in abundance for the purposes of training artificial intelligence (AI). By
the mid-1980s, AI researchers had moved away from symbolic AI (based on rules of
logic) and had started making important progress in neural networks (based on statistical models), which eventually led to a flourishing of machine-learning research and
applications.[7] One of the particularities of machine-learning algorithms is that they
need huge amounts of data.

In many cases, however, the most useful data to train AI is not personal data. Personal
data often has a short expiry date (people move houses, they change their job, their tastes
evolve, etc.), and it can often be less accurate than other kinds of data, partly because it is
difficult (if not impossible) to place people into discrete categories (Crawford 2021: Ch.
4). A poster child of AI is AlphaZero, an algorithm developed by Google's DeepMind
that plays the ancient Chinese game of Go. AlphaZero was trained exclusively through
playing against itself without any external data, let alone personal data. Another example of AI using data that is not personal is researchers at the Massachusetts Institute
of Technology (MIT) trying to find new antibiotics using AI to analyse chemical
compounds (Trafton 2020).

Admittedly, there are cases in which we do need personal data—medicine being a
prime example. While medicine justifies collecting some personal data (e.g. clinical
tests, a list of symptoms, etc.), it doesn't justify having the ubiquitous surveillance and
trade in personal data that we currently have. Arguing that ubiquitous surveillance is
unnecessary and disproportionate doesn't amount to arguing that we can never use

personal data. Collecting data in medical contexts is perfectly justified. Selling that data and collecting personal data everywhere else might not be.

A final response is that it is uncertain whether the AI of the future will need as much data as it does today. Part of what it means to be intelligent is the ability to generalize knowledge from a limited number of examples, like human beings do. A child doesn't need hundreds of thousands of images of dogs to recognize dogs. As AI systems become smarter, we can expect them to need less data (Wilson et al. 2019; Marcus and Davis 2020). The most important challenges to the development of AI are technical ones, and they won't necessarily be solved by collecting more data (Schneier and Waldo 2019).

Here again, if the ubiquitous surveillance facilitated by the trade in personal data is not necessary for technological advancement, it can hardly be proportionate, and it is far from clear whether it is necessary to collect as much personal data as possible. The burden of proof is on those who claim it is.

SURVEILLANCE, FREEDOM, AND DEMOCRACY

For decades, thinkers have worried about the negative consequences of surveillance for society, freedom, and liberal democracy. Ruth Gavison, for example, argued that:

> In the absence of consensus concerning many limitations of liberty, and in view of the limits on our capacity to encourage tolerance and acceptance and to overcome prejudice, privacy must be part of our commitment to individual freedom. [...] Privacy is also essential to democratic government because it fosters and encourages the moral autonomy of the citizen, a central requirement of a democracy.
>
> (Gavison 1980: 455)

In a similar vein, Thomas Nagel argued that, for the public sphere to be 'comfortably habitable' for different kinds of people, we need 'a culture that is publicly reticent'. For liberal democracy to work well, there must be a concomitant 'cultural liberalism' in which citizens allow each other to have enough privacy, which is essential to protect individual freedom and to avoid unnecessary conflicts in the public sphere (Nagel 1998).

Boudewijn de Bruin has argued that invasions of privacy can decrease people's negative freedom, which implies that privacy is a liberal value (de Bruin 2010). When companies and governments treat us differently as a result of privacy invasions, the opportunities we are afforded in life are being affected. If we end up self-censoring in an effort to better our life chances, our freedom is diminished even more. The losses of freedom due to self-censorship and external pressures to comply with algorithmic expectations can then lead to conformity.

Ubiquitous surveillance endangers fundamental personal, civic, and professional relationships. It can undermine intimacy between friends and family, freedom of association between citizens, and attorney–client privilege, among other things. Surveillance jeopardizes fundamental democratic practices like the secret ballot (Lever 2015) and investigative journalism.

It may not be a coincidence that Mexico, the deadliest country in the world for journalism in 2020, accounting for almost one-third of journalists killed that year worldwide (Lakhani 2020), was revealed to also be a hotspot for spying on journalists and human rights activists (Sheridan 2021). The Pegasus Project was an investigation which revealed that more than 50,000 journalists, human rights workers, academics, and other notable figures were being spied on by governments around the world. More than 15,000 of the victims were Mexicans—the most represented nationality on the list (Schwartz 2021). When journalists don't have enough privacy, they can't keep either themselves or their sources safe, which leads to the deterioration of the practice of journalism. Sources don't dare approach journalists, and journalists don't dare approach dangerous investigations. In turn, when journalism deteriorates, so does democracy as democracy depends on a well-informed citizenry.

Other related concerns regarding surveillance and society include the undermining of the presumption of innocence by treating all citizens as potential suspects (Hadjimatheou 2017), asymmetries of knowledge that tend to lead to asymmetries of power (Véliz 2020), and the risk of a massive misuse of personal data, for example, for the purposes of genocide. In the past, personal data has been grossly misused, as when Nazis raided local registries in search of data about Jewish people (Seltzer and Anderson 2001), and the best predictor that something can happen in the future is if it has happened in the past.

CONCLUSION: THE DANGER OF THE SURVEILLANCE DELUSION

Given the risks, harms, and wrongs of the kind of ubiquitous surveillance that has become common in the digital age, the burden of proof seems to be with defenders of the practice. There is at least one important challenge in that debate, however.

What is common to the risks, harms, and wrongs of surveillance is that they are difficult to quantify. It is easier to calculate the possible benefits of surveillance in terms of security, economic gain, and scientific advancement than it is to put a price on our losses. We can easily put a price tag on how much we can hope to earn per year, say, through personalized ads. But how do we assess to what extent investigative journalism can be undermined by surveillance? And if journalism is not a particularly profitable endeavour, how do we assess its value for democracy? How do we evaluate the loss to society entailed by people self-censoring themselves in their daily life? As a result of these unanswered questions, I suspect we are prone to end up buying into what I call the *surveillance delusion*: the assumption that surveillance has no significant moral costs.

In *The Tyranny of Metrics,* Jerry Z. Muller warns against an obsession with metrics. Metric fixation 'may draw effort away from the things we really care about' and 'almost inevitably leads to a valuation of short-term goals over long-term purposes', he writes (Muller 2018: 3, 20). The flourishing of a kind of AI that heavily depends on data has further encouraged an obsession with metrics. But there are certain valuable things (e.g. intimacy, autonomy, freedom, and democracy) that are harder to quantify than others (e.g. economic gain through the trade in personal data) but no less valuable.

Not only are many of the downsides of surveillance hard to quantify, but the consequences of surveillance are also often delayed, which further feeds into the surveillance delusion. Even in relatively simple cases, it might be years until a data leak is felt. Sensitive data can spend years in the dark web before a criminal makes use of it. That delay makes it hard to make the connection between the loss of a particular data point and a concrete negative consequence. The connection in the realm of societal harms is even more delayed and harder to establish. Journalism may survive for a few years or maybe even decades without privacy, and its erosion may be so gradual as to be hard to perceive. A faded kind of democracy may withstand some disproportionate surveillance for some years too.

What is dangerous about the surveillance delusion is that it pushes us to appreciate the possible benefits of surveillance without taking seriously its possible costs. Given the close relationship between authoritarian regimes and the aspiration for ubiquitous surveillance, evidenced in historical examples from the East German Stasi to contemporary China, the surveillance delusion can end up having a very high price even if it cannot be monetized until it's too late.

An urgent question, then, is how much surveillance is too much to sustain liberal democracy, freedom, and the ways of life that we value? David Omand suggests that 'one defining difference between the practice of domestic intelligence collection in liberal democratic states and that in totalitarian states is the *extent* of it' (Omand and Phythian 2018: 36). On that account, our society does not seem to be faring well, even in comparison with a society like East Germany. We are collecting more personal data than ever before. If Katerina Hadjimatheou is right that intrusiveness is determined by reasonable expectations, the ability to plan for and consent to surveillance, the number of people given access to sensitive information, the sensitivity of the data, and the period for which data is retained (Hadjimatheou 2014: 196), it again looks like our societies are the most intrusive ones that have ever existed.

What a reflection on the surveillance delusion suggests is that, to answer the question of how much surveillance is too much, we need to go beyond short-term concerns and think about the kind of society we want to have decades from now. We need to think carefully about the requirements of autonomy, freedom, equality, and democracy to make sure that surveillance is not creating graver problems in the long run than the ones it is purporting to solve.

Notes

1. Bernard Marr estimated in 2018 that 90 per cent of the data in the world had been generated in the previous two years (Marr 2018). According to Statista, data creation has continued its steady growth in the past few years (Statista 2020).
2. For more on the ethics of inferring sensitive information from public information, see Rumbold and Wilson (2019). For more on the ethics of taking personal information outside of the context it was given in, see Helen Nissenbaum's theory of contextual integrity (Nissenbaum 2010).
3. While some countries tend to define harm in utilitarian terms (e.g. psychological, physical, financial, reputational, etc.), other countries tend to focus on rights violations. On both frameworks, however, it is thought that consent can make an otherwise unethical case of data collection ethical (as exemplified by the General Data Protection Regulation in Europe and the California Consumer Privacy Act in the United States).
4. For more on the challenges of consent in the context of big data, see Cuters (2016), Andreotta et al. (2021), and Véliz (2019).
5. Control theories of privacy include Fried (1970), Bezanson (1992), Parker (1974), Beardsley (1971), Gerstein (1978), Rachels (1975), Reiman (1976), Marmor (2015), Wasserstrom (1978), and Westin (1970).
6. Access-based theories of privacy include Allen (1988), Garrett (1974), Gavison (1980), Gross (1971), and Parent (1983).
7. For an authoritative account of this unfolding, see Wooldridge (2020).

References

Allen, Anita (1988), *Uneasy Access: Privacy for Women in a Free Society* (Washington, DC: Rowan and Littlefield).

Alvaredo, Facundo, Chancel, Lucas, Piketty, Thomas, Saez, Emmanuel, and Zucman, Gabriel (2018), *World Inequality Report 2018* (World Inequality Lab, The World Wide Web).

Anderson, David (2016), *Report of the Bulk Powers Review* (London: Her Majesty's Government).

Andreotta, Adam J., Kirkham, Nin, and Rizzi, Marco (2021), 'AI, Big Data, and the Future of Consent', *AI & Society*. https://doi.org/10.1007/s00146-021-01262-5.

Beardsley, Elizabeth (1971), 'Privacy: Autonomy and Self-Disclosure', in J. Rowland Pennock and J.W. Chapman, eds, *Privacy: Nomos XIII* (New York: Atherton Press), 56–70.

Bergen, Peter, Sterman, David, Schneider, Emily, and Cahall, Bailey (2014), *Do NSA's Bulk Surveillance Programs Stop Terrorists?* https://www.jstor.org/stable/resrep10476#metadata_info_tab_contents.

Bezanson, Randall P. (1992), 'The Right to Privacy Revisited: Privacy, News, and Social Change, 1890–1990', *California Law Review* 80, 1133–1175.

Bidel, Susan, Parrish, Melissa, Verblow, Brandon, Egelman, Wei-Ming, and Turley, Christine (2017), 'Poor Quality Ads Cost US Marketers $7.4 Billion in 2016', in Forrester.

Brandl, Robert (2021), 'The World's Most Surveilled Citizens', *WebsiteToolTester*, https://www.forrester.com/report/Poor-Quality-Ads-Cost-US-Marketers-74-Billion-In-2016/RES136115.

Brown, Ian, and Korff, Douwe (2009), 'Terrorism and Proportionality of Internet Surveillance', *European Journal of Criminology* 6, 119–134.

Cameron, Joel D. (2021), 'Stasi', in *Encyclopedia Britannica*. https://www.britannica.com/topic/Stasi.

Carlile, Jennifer (2004), 'In Britain, Somebody's Watching You', *NBC News*, 9 September.

Clarke, Richard A., Morell, Michael J., Stone, Geoffrey R., Sunstein, Cass R., and Swire, Peter (2013), 'Liberty and Security in a Changing World. Report and Recommendations of the President's Review Group on Intelligence and Communications Technologies'. https://obamawhitehouse.archives.gov/blog/2013/12/18/liberty-and-security-changing-world.

Cox, Joseph (2020), 'CBP Refuses to Tell Congress How It is Tracking Americans without a Warrant', *Vice*, 23 October.

Crawford, Kate (2021), *Atlas of AI* (New Haven, CT: Yale University Press).

Cuters, Bart (2016), 'Click Here to Consent Forever: Expiry Dates for Informed Consent', *Big Data & Society* 1, 1–6.

de Bruin, Boudewijn (2010), 'The Liberal Value of Privacy', *Law and Philosophy* 29, 505–534.

Edelman, Gilard (2020), 'Ad Tech Could Be the Next Internet Bubble', *Wired*, 5 October.

Fabre, Cécile (2022), *Spying through a Glass Darkly. The Ethics of Espionage and Counterintelligence* (Oxford: Oxford University Press).

Fried, Charles (1970), *An Anatomy of Values* (Cambridge, MA: Harvard University Press).

Garrett, Roland (1974), 'The Nature of Privacy', *Philosophy Today* 89, 421–472.

Garton Ash, Timothy (1997), *The File. A Personal History* (New York: Vintage Books).

Gavison, Ruth (1980), 'Privacy and the Limits of Law', *Yale Law Journal* 89, 421–471.

Gerstein, Robert (1978), 'Intimacy and Privacy', *Ethics* 89, 86–91.

Gross, Hyman (1971), 'Privacy and Autonomy', in J. Rowland. Pennock and John W. Chapman (eds), *Privacy: Nomos XIII* (New York: Atherton Press), 375–385.

Hadjimatheou, Katerina (2014), 'The Relative Moral Risks of Untargeted and Targeted Surveillance', *Ethical Theory and Moral Practice* 17, 187–207.

Hadjimatheou, Katerina (2017), 'Surveillance Technologies, Wrongful Criminalisation, and the Presumption of Innocence', *Philosophy and Technology* 30, 39–54.

Helm, Toby (2019), 'Patient Data from GP Surgeries Sold to US Companies', *Observer*, 7 December.

Hill, Kashmir (2021), 'A Fire in Minnesota. An Arrest in Mexico. Cameras Everywhere', *New York Times*, 28 September.

Hwang, Tim (2020), *Subprime Attention Crisis* (New York: Farrar, Straus and Giroux).

ICO (2019), *Update Report Into Adtech and Real Time Bidding* (London: Information Commissioner's Office).

Isikoff, Michael (2013), 'NSA Program Stopped No Terror Attacks, Says White House Panel Member', *NBC News*, 20 December.

Jonas, Jeff, and Harper, Jim (2006), 'Effective Counterterrorism and the Limited Role of Predictive Data Mining', *Cato Institute, Policy Analysis*, 584.

Koehler, John O. (1999), *Stasi: The Untold Story of the East German Secret Police* (Boulder, CO: Westview Press).

Kosinski, Michal, Stillwell, David, and Graepel, Thore (2013), 'Private Traits and Attributes Are Predictable from Digital Records of Human Behavior', *Proceedings of the National Academy of Sciences of the United States of America* 110, 5802–5805.

Lakhani, Nina (2020), 'Mexico World's Deadliest Country for Journalists, New Report Finds', *The Guardian*, 22 December.

Lever, Annabelle (2015), 'Privacy and Democracy: What the Secret Ballot Reveals', *Law, Culture and the Humanities* 11, 164–183.

Levin, Sam (2018), 'Tech Firms Make Millions from Trump's Anti-Immigrant Agenda, Report Finds', *The Guardian*, 23 October.

Levy, Steven (2014), 'I Spent Two Hours Talking with the NSA's Bigwigs. Here's What Has Them Mad', *Wired*, 13 January.

Macnish, Kevin (2015), 'An Eye for an Eye: Proportionality and Surveillance', *Ethical Theory and Moral Practice* 18, 529–548.

Macnish, Kevin (2016), 'Government Surveillance and Why Defining Privacy Matters in a Post-Snowden World', *Journal of Applied Philosophy* 35(2), 417–432.

Marcus, Gary, and Davis, Ernest (2020), *Rebooting AI. Building Artificial Intelligence We Can Trust* (New York: Vintage).

Marmor, Andrei (2015), 'What is the Right to Privacy?', *Philosophy and Public Affairs* 43, 3–26.

Marr, Bernard (2018), 'How Much Data Do We Create Every Day? The Mind-Blowing Stats Everyone Should Read', *Forbes*, 21 May.

McMahan, Jeff (2009), *Killing in War* (Oxford: Oxford University Press).

Melendez, Steven, and Pasternack, Alex (2019), 'Here Are the Data Brokers Quietly Buying and Selling Your Personal Information', *Fast Company*, 2 March.

Morrison, Sara (2021), 'Here's How Police Can Get Your Data—Even If You Aren't Suspected of a Crime', *Vox*, 31 July.

Muller, Jerry Z. (2018), *The Tyranny of Metrics* (Princeton, NJ: Princeton University Press).

Nagel, Thomas (1998), 'Concealment and Exposure', *Philosophy and Public Affairs* 27, 3–30.

Ng, Alfred (2020), 'Google is Giving Data to Police Based on Search Keywords, Court Docs Show', *CNET*, 8 October.

Nissenbaum, Helen (2010), *Privacy in Context. Technology, Policy, and the Integrity of Social Life* (Stanford, CA: Stanford University Press).

Omand, David, and Phythian, Mark (2018), *Principled Spying* (Oxford: Oxford University Press).

Parent, William A. (1983), 'Recent Work on the Concept of Privacy', *American Philosophical Quarterly* 20, 341–355.

Parker, Richard (1974), 'A Definition of Privacy', *Rutgers Law Review* 27, 275–297.

Rachels, James (1975), 'Why Privacy is Important', *Philosophy and Public Affairs* 4, 323–333.

Reiman, Jeffrey (1976), 'Privacy, Intimacy and Personhood', *Philosophy and Public Affairs* 6, 26–44.

(2009), 'Report on the President's Surveillance Program'. Washington DC.

Rumbold, Benedict, and Wilson, James (2019), 'Privacy Rights and Public Information', *Journal of Political Philosophy* 27, 3–25.

Savage, Charlie (2015a), 'Declassified Report Shows Doubts about Value of N.S.A.'s Warrantless Spying', *New York Times*, 25 April.

Savage, Charlie (2015b), *Power Wars. Inside Obama's Post-9/11 Presidency* (New York: Little, Brown and Company).

Schneier, Bruce (2015), *Data and Goliath* (London: Norton).

Schneier, Bruce (2018), *Click Here to Kill Everybody. Security and Survival in a Hyper-Connected World* (New York: W.W. Norton & Company).

Schneier, Bruce, and Waldo, James (2019), 'AI Can Thrive in Open Societies', *Foreign Policy*, 13 June.

Schwartz, Leo (2021), 'Mexico's Shockingly Broad Use of Spyware is a Revelation. Nothing Will Change', *Washington Post*, 28 July.

Seltzer, William, and Anderson, Margo (2001), 'The Dark Side of Numbers: The Role of Population Data Systems in Human Rights Abuses', *Social Research* 68, 481–513.

Sheridan, Mary Beth (2021), 'How Mexico's Traditional Political Espionage Went High-Tech', *Washington Post*, 21 July.

Singel, Ryan (2009), 'Netflix Spilled Your Brokeback Mountain Secret, Lawsuit Claims', *Wired*, 17 December.

Solove, Daniel J. (2001), 'Privacy and Power: Computer Databases and Metaphors for Information Privacy', *Stanford Law Review* 53, 1393–1462.

Solove, Daniel J. (2011), *Nothing to Hide* (New Haven: Yale University Press).

Statista (2020), 'Worldwide Data Creation', https://www.statista.com/statistics/871513/worldwide-data-created, accessed 6 September 2022.

Thompson, Stuart A., and Warzel, Charlie (2019), 'How to Track President Trump', *New York Times*, 20 December.

Trafton, Anne (2020), 'Artificial Intelligence Yields New Antibiotic', *MIT News Office*, 20 February.

Véliz, Carissa (2017), *On Privacy* (Oxford: Oxford University Press).

Véliz, Carissa (2019), 'Medical Privacy and Big Data: A Further Reason in Favour of Public Universal Healthcare', in Andelka Phillips, ed., *Philosophical Foundations of Medical Law* (Oxford: Oxford University Press), 306–319.

Véliz, Carissa (2020), *Privacy is Power* (London: Bantam Press).

Véliz, Carissa (2021), 'Self-Presentation and Privacy Online', *Journal of Practical Ethics* 7(2), 30–43.

Véliz, Carissa (forthcoming), *The Ethics of Privacy and Surveillance* (Oxford: Oxford University Press).

Wasserstrom, Richard (1978), 'Privacy: Some Arguments and Assumptions', in Richard Bronaugh, ed., *Philosophical Law* (Westport, CT: Greenwood Press), 317–332.

Westin, Alan F. (1970), *Privacy and Freedom* (London: Bodley Head).

Wilson, James H., Daugherty, Paul R., and Davenport, Chase (2019), 'The Future of AI Will Be about Less Data, Not More', *Harvard Business Review*, https://hbr.org/2019/01/the-future-of-ai-will-be-about-less-data-not-more, accessed 14 January 2019.

Wooldridge, Michael (2020), *The Road to Conscious Machines: The Story of AI* (London: Pelican Books).

Wright, Lawrence (2008), 'The Spymaster', *The New Yorker*, 21 January.

Wylie, Christopher (2019), *Mindf*ck. Inside Cambridge Analytica's Plot to Break the World* (London: Profile).

Yadron, Danny (2016), '"Worth It": FBI Admits It Paid $1.3 to Hack into San Bernardino iPhone', *The Guardian*, 21 April.

CHAPTER 29

PRIVACY IN SOCIAL MEDIA

ANDREI MARMOR

INTRODUCTION

Ms Lisa Li, a famous young influencer in China, flaunting a glamorous and lavish lifestyle, with over one million followers, became rather notorious overnight. Her landlord, upset by Ms Li's unpaid bills and failure to clean up her apartment, exposed to the world her absolutely squalid living conditions. A video posted by the landlord showed Ms Li's sordid apartment with dog faeces in the living room, and generally so filthy that allegedly even professionals refused to clean up the place. Not surprisingly, reaction on social media instantaneously recorded hostile posts, with tens of thousands of people unfollowing her overnight, and countless expressions of outrage. Ms Li seems to have survived the media onslaught and recovered her reputation since, but her story encapsulates many of the privacy issues that come up in social media. Ms Li's story exemplifies how a young woman of modest means can turn herself into a social media celebrity, presenting to the world a personal lifestyle far removed from reality. But it also shows how reputation gained over years of hard work can be shattered in an instant, turning fame and glamour to ridicule and outrage overnight.[1]

You may wonder why any of these issues involve moral concerns about the right to privacy. After all, most people's immediate concern about privacy in social media, and internet platforms more generally, relate to data protection. People fear that information they post on various platforms, explicitly or implicitly, is gathered, compiled, and potentially abused by corporate entities, governments, or even criminals, in all sorts of nefarious ways.[2] On the contrary, I am going to argue in this chapter that concerns about data protection, legitimate and serious as they may be, are not, mostly, about the right to privacy. Privacy is about the presentation of the self, not about protection of proprietary rights. And I am going to argue that social media is, generally, conducive to privacy—in fact, often too much so. The main tension in the domain of social media is between privacy and authenticity: social media enables a great deal of privacy at the expense of authenticity. But it also comes with dangers of exposure that carry risks to privacy. On the whole, then, the state of privacy in social media is a mixed bag. Social media is generally conducive to privacy, often too much so; and it also comes with serious risks to privacy, even if, as often is the case, those risks are self-imposed.

What is the right to privacy and how does it conflict with authenticity?

In previous work, I have argued that the main interest protected by the right to privacy is our interest in having a reasonable measure of control over ways we present aspects of ourselves to different others (Marmor 2015). Having a reasonable amount of control over various aspects of ourselves that we present to different others is essential for our well being; it enables us to have the necessary means to navigate our place in the social world and to have reasonable control over our social lives. We need to have the ability to maintain different types of relationships with different people, and that would not be possible without having control over how we present ourselves to different others. Different types of relationships are constituted by different types of expectations about what aspects of ourselves we reveal to each other. Intimate relationships and friendships, for example, are partly constituted by expectations of sharing information and revealing aspects of ourselves that we would not be willing to share with strangers. But we cannot live in a social world that requires constant intimacy either; the possibility of dealing with others at arms lengths, keeping some distance, is as important as the opportunity for intimate relationships. Additionally, we also need to have some space to engage in various innocuous activities without necessarily inviting social scrutiny. For all these, and similar reasons, it is essential for our well being that we have a reasonable level of control over which aspects of ourselves we reveal to different others. This is the main interest that is protected by the right to privacy.

The interest in the protection of personal data that we post or reveal on internet platforms is typically an interest in protecting our property. There is a huge amount of information about ourselves, and our possessions, that we reveal, often without our knowledge, by using the internet, smartphones, and such. But there are two kinds of concerns about this information falling into the wrong hands, as it were. For one, there is the fairly straightforward concern about theft. A great deal of the information that we allow internet platforms to use or to store can be used to steal our financial 'identity', empty our bank accounts, charge us for goods and services we had not ordered, and all sorts of similar proprietary misdeeds. These concerns have very little to do with privacy. When someone uses or takes something that belongs to you without your permission, they violate your right to property, not to privacy (Thomson 1975).[3]

The second kind of concern relates to so-called 'big data' collected by corporations about our consumer profiles, interests, and habits. And this is a tricky matter from a privacy perspective. Most often the kind of information that is gathered, if looked at in isolation, is not the kind of fact about us that we can legitimately expect to keep to ourselves. When you go out to buy a pair of shoes in a store you cannot expect not to be observed by others. Buying those same shoes online should make no difference in this respect. After all, it needs to be charged to your credit card and delivered to your home. In isolation, there is nothing here that should make anyone worry about their privacy. Problems begin to surface with extensive and repeated data collection, that is, when somebody (or some computer algorithm, to be more precise) collects, analyses, and stores data about everything you buy; and perhaps everywhere you happen to go with your smartphone, and every phone number you call up, and so on and so forth. This is when people begin to worry about their privacy, and to some extent, rightly so. But as I will try to show later, this worry is not easy to articulate and it is subject to reasonable disagreement. Before we get there, however, other aspects of privacy in social media will be explored. I'll get back to the big data question towards the end.

Let us return to the main interest protected by the right to privacy. It is crucial to note that the level of control over which aspects of ourselves we reveal to others needs to be reasonable, not limitless. Having too much control over what aspects of one's self one can reveal to others compromises authenticity. But this is complicated. On the one hand, there seems to be nothing wrong with withdrawing from the social world, living your life without anyone knowing anything about you. Perhaps your life would not be as rich and rewarding as it could have been, but you commit no wrong by imposing seclusion on yourself. On the other hand, it does seem to be wrong, in some sense, if you manage to get people to believe that you are something quite different from what you really are. An intensely selfish person who manages to get people to believe that she is generous and kind engages in a form of deceit that we may rightly frown upon, even criticize and condemn. Being intensely selfish is bad enough, creating the false impression in others that you are generous makes things even worse. Now, it might be tempting to think that the distinction here pertains to the difference between not revealing things about yourself, which is normally permissible, and actively presenting yourself in ways that are not your authentic self, that is, creating false impressions, which is often wrong. But this action-omission distinction is not going to do all the work here. There are ways of not being truthful or authentic by just keeping quiet. If you are mistakenly introduced in a party as somebody else, then keeping quiet about it might be as much of a lie as knowingly telling a falsehood. But that does not mean that failing to reveal the truth about yourself is always wrong; far from it. Most people normally want to look and seem better than they are, and there is nothing wrong about that. You do not have to post the most authentic selfie on your Instagram page; posting a particularly flattering one is not deceitful.

The story of Ms Lisa Li, however, is a good reminder that authenticity on social media is compromised well beyond flattering pics and self-congratulating presentations. The main danger facing the value of authenticity in the social media context is that the distinction between truth and fiction gets blurred; one often does not know, and many people seem not to care all that much, what is presented as truth and what is clearly just fiction. This is not a threat to privacy. On the contrary, it is often too much privacy at the expense of truth and authenticity. The following section explains both of these claims.

PRIVACY, AUTHENTICITY, AND FICTION

Social media, like Facebook, Twitter, Instagram, and similar platforms, enable people to present aspects of themselves to others in ways that they could not have done without these tools. It enables people to reach a very wide audience at very low cost and almost instantaneously; but more importantly for our concerns here, social media gives people a tremendous amount of choice and control over what aspects of themselves they present to others, including the option of presenting totally fictitious 'aspects' of themselves, inventing a public persona that may have very little to do with reality. Even ordinary users of Facebook, who just want to connect with their friends, tend to post aspects of their lives rather selectively, conscious of constructing an image of their lives in forms they wish their audience to perceive. In actuality, the range of self-construction here is very wide, from minor self-flattering images or posts, to outright large-scale deceit, with all the spectrum in between. Since the main interest protected by the right to privacy is precisely the interest in having control over what aspects of yourself you present to different others, it would seem that social media, quite generally, is very conducive to privacy. It enables people to have a great deal of control over their self-presentation, much greater in scope than hitherto possible.[4] Hence, the first question here is not whether social media threatens privacy, but whether it enables it too much: do we get to have too much control over what aspects of ourselves we present to others?

Part of what makes answering this question difficult is the fact that the kind of creative construction of the self enabled by social media is common knowledge. Everybody knows that the persona I present on Facebook or Instagram is somewhat constructed, that it does not necessarily reflect reality. Both users and consumers of the medium realize that fact and fiction are mixed up; it is part of the game, as it were. In other words, people do not necessarily expect full authenticity on social media; they seem to be content to create and to consume the presentations of partly fictitious selves for the sake of other values, knowing, at least at the back of their minds, that authenticity is not assured.[5] But that does not, by itself, settle the question of whether too much authenticity is sacrificed here; even if the sacrifice of truth and authenticity is on the surface and willingly consumed, it might still be a bad state of affairs.

Authenticity might mean different things in different contexts. In one sense, people think of authenticity in terms of a match between one's deep self, one's deep character traits, true desires, etc., and the life one lives. An inauthentic person, on this understanding, is one whose desires, plans, and aspirations in life do not quite match what she really is, deep down, as it were. If I tell myself that I love doing philosophy and live my life with that story, while the truth is that deep down I am not all that interested in philosophy, then I am not authentic, in this sense. However, this deep sense of authenticity is not what I am going to refer to here; what I have in mind is a shallower sense, one that refers to the truth or falsehood of one's self-presentation to others. You fail to be authentic, on this shallow conception, if you present yourself to others in a way that is, as a matter of fact, false about you. The main difference between the deep and the shallow conceptions of authenticity is that the deep form of inauthenticity involves self-deception, while the shallow sense of it does not necessarily involve any self-deception; the deception or inauthenticity in the shallow sense can be entirely self-conscious. In both cases, however, the value of authenticity is very closely tied with the value of truth. In the deep sense, it is the truth to yourself, truth about what you really want, what you really care about, and things like that. In the shallow sense, and the one that is relevant to our concerns here, the truth in question is public. A presentation that is inauthentic is one that attempts to induce others to have false (or grossly inaccurate) beliefs about certain aspects of your self.

To be sure, I am not assuming here that revealing the truth about one's self is always valuable or that any type of deception is bad. Far from it. As Thomas Nagel (1998) famously argued, it is often the case that telling the truth is the wrong thing to do. In fact, life would be rather unpleasant, almost unbearable, if people told each other everything that comes to their mind. Just imagine telling everyone you encounter what you really think about them; in many cases, they do not need to know, and often would rather not hear. Something similar applies to the presentation of your self; people do not need, and often do not want to know, everything that goes on in your mind (or your body, for that matter). In other words, authenticity (in the shallow sense, as henceforth used) is not always valuable, and one is not ethically or morally required to be authentic at all times.

The previous considerations suggest that privacy and authenticity are often in some inherent conflict or tension. The moral aspects of this conflict play out differently in the domain of personal presentation and the domain of public discourse. Social media, as currently used, spans both private lives and public-political discourse, and these two raise somewhat different moral concerns. In both cases, the underlying concern is the blurring of the distinction between fact and fiction. But the wider moral implications of this blurring of boundaries are quite different. Let me acknowledge, however, a further complication before we proceed. Social media blurs not only the distinction between fact and fiction; it also blurs the distinction between the personal and the public. Nowhere is it more evident than in the proliferation and tremendous impact of influencers. The whole phenomenon of influencers is based on turning the personal into a commercial or social endeavour, sometimes into commercial business, pure and simple. Therefore, the contrast between personal presentations on social media and public-political discourse spans a wide spectrum; most of the social media use is somewhere in the middle, involving elements of both.

One thing we have learned in the past few years is that social media enables a huge amount of staggeringly false and misleading political speech, directly and indirectly. And we have learned that these falsehoods are not idle. Millions of people seem to be influenced by fake news and incredible falsehoods of all kinds, to the extent that they may have tilted the results of elections and other democratic processes. There are very serious concerns here, and they may force us to rethink some of our established views about free speech and democracy. Perhaps, but this is not the topic of the present chapter. I will leave the discussion of social media and politics to others (see Neil Levy's chapter 'Fake News: Rebuilding the Epistemic Landscape').

Let us return to the presentation of the self in social media. What we seem to have here is a domain of endless possibilities of self-construction, ranging from mild manipulation of reality to outright fiction or deception. One curious aspect of the story of Ms Lisa Li, mentioned at the start, is not so much how she lost many of her followers instantaneously, which she did, but the fact that she has not really lost most of them—far from it. Hundreds of thousands of people kept loyal to her, despite the fact that she turned out to be a rather different person from the glamorous social media persona she had depicted. It seems that many of her followers just did not care. Which would be surprising only if you thought that consumers seek the truth, as if they wanted to follow the real Lisa Li. But evidently that is not what her followers were after; they were seeking to share a dream, a kind of visual fiction, and then, when they come to learn that parts of that fiction are not real, they are not all that surprised or disappointed; fiction, after all, is not supposed to be real. There is nothing morally problematic about the desire to consume fiction, whether on social media or elsewhere. But what if the distinction between fiction and reality gets rather blurred? What if people lose interest in the distinction itself, not caring all that much about whether something they are told or shown purports to be fact or fiction? There is clearly something disturbing about it, but it is not easy to pin down what that is.

The difficulty stems from the possible argument that if you do not care about whether a story is fact or fiction, in essence you are treating it *as if* it was fiction. A story that is consumed as potentially fiction is treated by the consumer on a par with fiction. And if this is true, then perhaps there is nothing wrong with social media blurring the distinction between fact and fiction, as long as people are, by and large, aware of it. Furthermore, if you think about it, there is nothing new here. Capitalist consumerism is based on aggressive advertising, selling us dreams and fantasies in order to sell us products and services. Instagram influencers sell a constructed image of themselves in order to sell products. It is essentially the same idea. Or, not quite, perhaps. As much as we might want to criticize rampant consumerism and all the advertising industry that keeps it afloat, the advertising industry is what it purports to be, an industry aiming to sell you stuff that you may not really need or did not think you even wanted. One problem that seems to plague the social media domain is yet again, a blurring of the boundaries between what is clearly commercial advertising and what is personal, social, or even political.

But I still have not answered the question of what is morally problematic about the blurring of these distinctions on social media. Perhaps it is a good thing that distinctions between fact and fiction, personal and public, entertainment and consumerism, are getting blurred by social media. Challenging established categories and conceptual divisions is how social changes occur over time; it is often what social movements aim to accomplish. Not all social changes are for the better, of course, but many of them are. Furthermore, if the social media world enhances people's privacy interests, giving them more control over what aspects of themselves they present to different others, all the better, not so? I am far from sure, however, that moral complacency is warranted. Perhaps many of the categories getting blurred on social media provide new opportunities to people, and empower hitherto underprivileged segments of the population.[6] So there are, quite clearly, some good effects here. But the erosion of the value of truth is not so innocuous. If the interest in truth gets eroded, this erosion is not going to remain confined to the use of social media; it is very likely to pervade personal and public life on a much wider scale. The more socially acceptable it becomes to mix fiction with truth without accountability, the less responsibility people are going to feel for truth in general, both in their personal lives and in their civic engagements. This cannot be a good development.

Let me emphasize, however, that the erosion of truth on social media is very intimately linked to its privacy enhancement aspect; it is not a coincidence that a world in which there is much more privacy, there is less concern for the truth. As I have mentioned, the essence of the right to privacy is the right not to tell the truth, at least not all of it. Control over what aspects of yourself you reveal to others is needed precisely because we have legitimate interests in not being all that forthcoming with revealing aspects of ourselves or our lives to others. Privacy and authenticity are inherently in some conflict or tension.

Social media as a tool against privacy

The picture I have depicted so far has been one-sided; I have focused on the privacy-enhancing aspects of social media. But social media is also used for opposite purposes; it is sometimes used to deliberately undermine someone's privacy, exposing them to the world in ways they do not want to be perceived.[7] I will focus on cases called 'doxing', whereby social media users, often in a group, target an individual or a group of individuals for the purpose of public shaming or, in some extreme cases, even harassment or intimidation. Two main aspects of the medium enable this practice: the availability of a huge amount of information on people online, and the ability to reach a very wide audience at very low cost.[8] Individuals are not the only targets of doxing—sometimes governments are too. Wikileaks is a case in point. But I will bracket these governmental or even corporate targets, and focus on the practice of doxing targeting individuals.

Let us start with a simple story. Suppose you happen to know that your friend is cheating on his wife. You keep quiet for a while, but at some point the friendship turns sour and you decide to tweet about your friend's infidelity with details and all; you know that your friend, and his wife, and your mutual friends, are all following you on Twitter. I presume that we would think that you had misbehaved; gravely so, perhaps. Even if you had a reason to tell your friend's spouse about her husband's infidelity, that is something you should have told her in private; sharing it with many is a deliberate act of shaming. Shaming is an act of humiliation, and as such, pro tanto wrong. Unless there is a very good reason to bring shame on someone, it is wrong on a par with deliberate humiliation, a demeaning speech act, striving deliberately to put someone down. Now, of course, the problem with social media is that it technically allows for public shaming on a very large scale. Someone can find out something embarrassing about you and post it on some social media platform or other, rendering the information public instantaneously. Furthermore, it is often very difficult for the targeted individual to rebut the shaming information, even if it is, actually, false. Once a rumour or an image is out there, it is almost impossible to make it go away.

Doxing, by its very nature, would seem to be a violation of privacy; it is done with the explicit aim of revealing to others information about their target that the individual in question would rather not expose, at least not to the public at large. But it does not necessarily follow that doxing is always an unjustified violation of the target's right to privacy. This is for two reasons: it might not be a violation of the *right* to privacy at all, and even if it is, it might be a case of a justified violation of a right. Let me explain briefly both of these points.

J. Thomson (1975: 307) argued a long time ago, and correctly so in my mind, that nobody can have a right that some truth about them not be known. We cannot have proprietary rights over truths about us or about anything else, for that matter.[9] The right to privacy, I argued (contra Thomson), is there to protect our interest in having a reasonable measure of control over ways in which we present ourselves to others. The protection of this interest requires the securing of a reasonably predictable environment about the flow of information and the likely consequences of our conduct in the relevant types of contexts. On my account of the right to privacy, such a right is violated when somebody manipulates, without adequate justification, the relevant environment in ways that significantly diminish your ability to control what aspects of yourself you reveal to others. One typical case is the following: you assume, and have good reason to assume, that by φ-ing you reveal F to A; that is how things normally work. You can choose, on the basis of this assumption, whether to φ or not. Now somebody would clearly violate your right if he were to manipulate the relevant environment, without your knowledge, making it the case that by doing φ you actually reveal F not only to A but also to B et al., or that you actually reveal not just F but also W to A (and/or to B et al.), which means that you no longer have the right kind of control over what aspects of yourself you reveal to others; your choice is undermined in an obvious way (Marmor 2015: 14).

Given this account, it would seem that a case of doxing is typically a violation of one's right to privacy. If you are the target of doxing, your environment is manipulated by others rendering the information you reveal about yourself, knowingly or unknowingly, spread well beyond its intended or reasonably predicted audience. That is clearly a case in which you lose control over what aspects of yourself you reveal to whom. The difficult or borderline cases are those in which doxing reveals information about someone that is publicly available anyway. Suppose, for example, that you are perceived by your acquaintances as a person of modest means, and yet you buy a very expensive piece of real estate, a transaction that you would rather keep to yourself. In many jurisdictions, ownership of real estate is a matter of public record. (And let us assume that there are good reasons for that.) Somebody can easily look it up and post the information on social media, perhaps to embarrass you. They post something that is a matter of public record, even if, normally, people do not bother to spend their time looking for this kind of information. I suspect that people would have different intuitions about this case. It may not be the right thing to do, for sure, but I am not sure that it amounts to a violation of any right of yours. However, once again, the problem in the social media context is the issue of intensity and scale. Targeted doxing usually involves extensive efforts and considerable investment of time and energy in gathering information that, even if publicly available, is not available without such deliberate and extensive research.[10]

The situation here is very similar to the question of privacy in public spaces (Marmor 2015: 20–21).[11] When you walk around on Main Street you cannot have a privacy expectation not to be observed by indefinite others. By walking on the street you obviously make yourself observable and there's nothing problematic about that from a privacy perspective. But suppose somebody is following you with a video camera, recording your movements for a while, and posting that on YouTube. Now it might seem a violation of your right to privacy, even if the recording was done in a public space. Why is that? Presumably, because making yourself observable in a public space is not an invitation, or even consent to, becoming an object of gaze or surveillance. The concern here is about attention and record-keeping. When you take a walk on Main Street, you are perfectly aware of the fact that you have no control over who happens to be there and thus is able to see you; but you also rely on the fact that people's attention and memory are very limited. You do not expect to have every tiny movement of yours noticed and recorded by others. In other words, consent to public exposure is not unlimited. Voluntarily giving indefinite others the opportunity to see you is not an invitation, or even tacit consent, to gaze at you, and certainly not a consent to record your doings, digitally or otherwise.

But what if expectations actually change, and people come to know that certain public spaces are subject to extensive surveillance? What if we are all well informed, for example, that all the streets in our town are covered with CCTV cameras that record everything everywhere? Would that violate our right to privacy in public spaces? I think that the answer is 'Yes' because there is another way in which one's right to privacy can be violated, that is, by diminishing the space in which we can control what aspect of ourselves we reveal to others to an unacceptably small amount in an important domain of human activity (Marmor 2015: 14). Needless to say, determining what counts as a violation of privacy in this respect is bound to be controversial and often difficult to determine. Presumably, there are two main factors in play: the relative importance of the type of activity in question (e.g. walking on ordinary streets versus entering a particular building), and the level of diminished control over concealment or exposure. Either way, we should recognize that people's right to privacy can be violated even in public spaces (Véliz 2018).

Many cases of doxing based on exposure of data collected from public records involve essentially the same moral issue. Living in a world in which there is a great deal of information about us on public records might not be a problem in and of itself. But becoming the focus of targeted attention based on information-gathering from public records becomes a form of surveillance, quite possibly violating the right to privacy. Such actions diminish, sometimes very considerably, your ability to control what aspects of yourself you reveal to others. And that is so because we can normally expect ordinary others to have limited interest, attention, and resources for digging up information on us that is stored somewhere somehow.

That doxing often, if not quite always, involves a violation of the target's right to privacy does not necessarily entail that it is never justified, all things considered. Possible moral justifications of rights' violations are multifarious and greatly depend on circumstances.[12] Sometimes a rights violation is justified when it is required in order to secure a conflicting right that ought to prevail under the circumstances. Sometimes a right may be justly violated in order to secure a common good of greater moral significance. Suppose, for example, that in order to expose a politician's staggering hypocrisy you need to violate their right to privacy. Still, the exposure might serve the common good and democratic values to an extent that justifies the rights' violation.

It is a common doctrinal principle in libel laws in many jurisdictions that the more one enjoys a public persona the less protection from libel one can legally expect. Something similar, at least morally speaking, may well apply to protection of privacy. The more you deliberately and voluntarily expose yourself to the public, as it were, perhaps the less concern about your right to privacy you can legitimately expect to have. But this principle, if a principle it is, should have an important caveat: it would be quite unjustified to expose facts about a public persona by violating their right to privacy if the facts disclosed are not related to what makes the person famous. If a politician thrives on gay-bashing and promoting 'family values', exposing that the politician is gay himself might be quite justified. But the same would not be true of, say, a famous scientist; if the scientist's claim to fame has nothing to do with sexuality or anything remotely relevant to that, exposing their sexual preferences against their wish cannot be justified. If the fact you expose about a scientist has something to do with their scientific integrity, that may be justified. Admittedly, the distinction between facts about a public persona that are relevant to their public status and those that are not is sometimes difficult to draw. However, since we are talking about the justified violation of a right here, the justification for violating the right to privacy needs to be fairly robust. Which means that, in cases of doubt, when it is not entirely clear that the disclosure in question is relevant to the person's public status, the doubt should count in favour of respecting the right to privacy.

Perhaps now you wonder about the case of Ms Li: if her landlord violated her right to privacy, which may well have been the case here, was it a justified violation of her right? Are facts about Ms Li's sordid living conditions relevant to her claim to fame? My own sense is that the answer is probably 'Yes', but I can see that this might be contentious. The more you think that influencers such as Ms Li are selling fiction or fantasy, the less relevant her own life is to the persona she creates on social media.

SOCIAL MEDIA, BIG DATA, AND PRIVACY

We now seem to live in a world in which almost everything we do, everywhere we go, and everything we buy, is recordable by some computerized system or other. And much of it, if not most, is actually recorded, aggregated, sorted, and often sold by various systems (Zuboff 2019). Our digital footprint is ubiquitous, and easily utilized by interested parties. That governments may have access to all this information is a serious reason for concern. Governments that have no great respect for democracy and human rights have gained powerful tools that they can use for political oppression, and even democratic and decent regimes may occasionally succumb to the temptation to use such information in ways that violate people's rights.[13] The serious political hazard with the recording of our digital footprints threaten many of our rights and freedoms, but not necessarily, or even primarily, our right to privacy. Political oppression violates more serious and urgent rights than the right to privacy. There are countries in which people are detained and thrown into jail for things they post on social media; when you find yourself in jail for something you'd posted on Facebook, the violation of your right to privacy is the least of your concerns. Generally speaking, the dangers of government surveillance go far beyond threats to our privacy; they threaten our basic civil and human rights.

Political oppression, however, is not the topic of this chapter. I will therefore bracket the dangers of big (and small) data collection by governments and focus on the private market.[14] One major development of the digital age is the commodification of our consumer profiles. There is a huge amount of digital footprint we leave on a daily basis about our consumer behaviour; things we buy, places we visit, interests we express, movies we stream, even things we search on Google, indicate our tastes and desires, and our willingness to pay for this or that. The ability of computers to store and analyse this information renders our consumer profiles a commodity that can be bought and sold, something that has a market value. Mostly, I presume, it is valuable to corporations for marketing purposes, targeting their marketing efforts in ways that are tailored to our tastes and preferences. All this digital analysis of consumer profiles is not done by people; there is nobody sitting there in front of a computer, thinking, 'Oh, I see that Professor Marmor likes *Borsalino* hats. Let's send him some ads about the latest models.' Targeted advertising is automated. Our consumer profiles are generated and commodified on a huge scale, and analysed by complex algorithms that handle hundreds of millions of data points. This system makes the concern about privacy rather tricky here.

Let me focus exclusively, however, on the market use of people's digital footprints for commercial purposes. Is targeted advertising, based on our digital footprints, a threat to consumers' privacy? For the sake of simplicity, let us assume that all this data collected on our consumer profiles is done without our ex ante consent.[15] So here is a simple and fairly standard example: you post on your Facebook page that you are considering a trip to Paris this summer, intending, for some reason or other, to share this information with your friends. Soon enough (very soon, in my experience) you start getting advertisements on your Facebook about hotels in Paris, flights to Paris, etc. For many people, there is something spooky about this; it feels as if someone is watching your Facebook posts and sending you ads in response. But as I mentioned, that is not the case, and besides, this feeling of spookiness is not shared by all. Many people are perfectly fine with getting these targeted ads; they do not care that some fancy algorithm enables advertisers to do that. Furthermore, and this is a crucial factor that is sometimes forgotten, there is a commercial transaction here in the background: we get to use the social media tools offered by these corporations without pay, in exchange for subjection to targeted advertising. It is a contract, and the contract, on its face, does not seem to be obviously unfair or exploitative.[16]

As in many cases of rapid technological developments, it may have taken a while for most of us, users of social media and other internet platforms, to realize that our digital footprints have become a merchandise in themselves, bought and sold by companies for commercial purposes. But I think that now we know this to be the case, and I think that most people understand that the commercial value of our consumer behaviour is priced in the services we get, its market value paying for our free use of social media and internet tools. In principle, the situation here is no different from other, more mundane contexts, in which the market value of captive audience is priced in the products we buy. When you go to the cinema to watch a movie, you are subjected to about twenty minutes of 'previews' and other ads; if cinemas had to forgo this practice, presumably our movie tickets would end up costing us more.

But now, you may wonder, where is the threat to privacy in this commodification of our consumer profiles? There are aspects of this new world of commodification of our habits that are certainly troubling; the fact that some data collected on one's consumer habits is bought and sold by corporations for commercial use might raise concerns about the overreach of capitalism; targeted advertising surely augments the concerns we have about commercial advertising generally, structuring our preferences and desires in questionable ways, but none of it seems to be a threat to privacy. My ability to control ways in which I present myself to different others is not undermined by these commercial practices. Of course, there might be some threats to privacy on the margins. If you start getting ads for a product you do not want others to know about, then if somebody happens to see your computer screen with those ads displayed, they may get to know something about you that you would have rather kept to yourself. But these are marginal cases, and they may come up in countless other contexts. My guess is that most people are concerned about the potential for the abuse of information that is commercially transacted; they fear that it might fall into the wrong hands. Perhaps the government might get hold of your habits or whereabouts in ways that might put you in a vulnerable position; or perhaps rouge agents may use this information to hack into your assets and steal your possessions. These are serious concerns, for sure, but, as I have tried to argue here all along, they are not concerns about the right to privacy. Strange as it may sound, the commodification of our consumer profiles and even more generally, big data collection, threaten many of our rights and freedoms, but the right to privacy is not the primary concern.

Acknowledgements

I am indebted to Alicia Patterson for research assistance on this chapter, and to Carissa Véliz for helpful comments.

Notes

1. The story about Lisa Li has been widely reported by news outlets, e.g. https://www.bbc.com/news/world-asia-china-49830855, accessed 10 August 2021. There are many other similar cases, such as a vegan influencer caught eating meat, or a middle-aged YouTube celebrity who used an image-modifying camera to make her appear much younger than she was. These are simpler cases of outright deceit. I am using the example of Lisa Li, however, precisely because it is a little more ambiguous and complex.
2. For detailed accounts, see, e.g. Nissenbaum (2010: chs 1–3) and Zuboff (2019).
3. Following a long Lockean tradition, many philosophers assume that we have property rights in ourselves. Others find the idea of self-ownership fraught with difficulties, perhaps even incoherent. However, delving into this philosophical morass would be far beyond the scope of this chapter, and not quite needed. Even those who find the idea of self-ownership appealing would still want to maintain a distinction between the right to privacy and the right to property. A notable exception is Thompson (1975). I responded to Thomson's argument in Marmor (2015).
4. See, e.g. Cocking and Van Den Hoven (2018: ch. 3). For a more sceptical take on this view, see Marwick and Boyd (2011), who argue that social media makes it difficult for users to understand and navigate social boundaries. Notice, however, that the right to privacy, on my account, is a *control* right; that does not mean, of course, that people necessarily exercise their control judiciously or wisely. The fact that many tend to post things on social media that, upon reflection, they should not have revealed, or that they come to regret, does count against the fact that they exercise their right.
5. Up to a point, it would seem. Researchers found that there is a correlation between the time people (especially teenagers) spend on Facebook and depression. One speculation is that people do not quite internalize the fact that the rosy picture of others' lives they see on social media is actually constructed, and thus feel demoralized or depressed by the comparison to their own humble existence; see, e.g. Steers et al. (2014).
6. The tremendous proliferation of influencers would seem to attest to the fact that countless opportunities arise here, often for people who would otherwise have much more limited options. But the reality is slightly more complex; see Duffy (2017).
7. The most vulgar and unfortunately prevalent example is the posting of nude photos or videos of women (mostly) without their consent, on dubious porn sites and other internet outlets. These are obvious and blatant violations of privacy that ought to be criminalized and prosecuted. (As with everything else, there are some borderline cases, of course, when there was some qualified consent but the terms of it are allegedly breached or abused; those cases are more complicated.)
8. For a detailed account of doxing, and its different types and practices, see Douglas (2016).
9. I am aware of the fact that Thomson's thesis is controversial, but I defended this particular view in some detail in Marmor (2015: 4–6).

10. For an excellent account of the considerations involved in such cases, see Rumbold and Wilson (2019). On their account, the question of whether you intend to make some information public and accessible to others is of crucial importance to the question of whether your right to privacy has been violated or not. I am slightly more sceptical about the role of intention here; there might be cases in which even if you did not intend to allow people to have access to some information available on you online, you should have known better than to rely on its concealment. Generally, however, I am largely in agreement with their account.

11. For a somewhat different account of the right to privacy in public spaces, see Véliz (2018).

12. Some philosophers use the word 'violation' of a right only when it is not justified, calling justified violations 'infringement' of a right. There is no uniformity of usage in the literature, however, and I will not adhere to this terminological distinction. The idea itself is clear enough, and as old as the literature on rights generally. With the exception of Kant, perhaps, no one argues that rights have absolute normative force.

13. See, e.g. Richards (2013).

14. The separation is somewhat artificial, of course, since one of the dangers of data collected by private corporations is that governments can force them to hand over their data.

15. There are now some jurisdictions that strive to change that by law; California recently enacted a law (California Consumer Privacy Act, 2019) requiring retailers to seek customers' explicit consent for selling their consumer profiles to others. How much of an actual change in the commodification of consumer profiles this will bring about remains to be seen.

16. I am talking about the principle here, not the details or the legal aspects of it. Many lawyers have reservations about the lack of transparency in such contracts and about the fact that most consumers are unaware of their contents. See, e.g. Hoofnagle and Whittington (2014).

References

Cocking, Dean, and Van Den Hoven, Jeroen (2018), *Evil Online* (Oxford: Wiley Blackwell).

Douglas, David (2016), 'Doxing: A Conceptual Analysis', *Ethics & Information Technology* 18 , 199.

Duffy, Brooke E. (2017), *(Not) Getting Paid for What you Love: Gender, Social Media, and Aspirational Work* (New Haven, CT: Yale University Press).

Hoofnagle, Chris J., and Whittington, Jan (2014), 'Accounting for the Costs of the Internet's Most Popular Price', *UCLA Law Review* 61, 606.

Marmor, Andrei (2015), 'What is the Right to Privacy?', *Philosophy & Public Affairs* 43, 1.

Marwick, Alice E., and Boyd, Dana (2011), 'I Tweet Honestly, I Tweet Passionately: Twitter Users, Context Collapse, and the Imagined Audience', *New Media & Society* 13, 114.

Nagel, Thomas (1998), 'Concealment and Exposure', 27 *Philosophy & Public Affairs* 13, 3.

Nissenbaum, Helen (2010), *Privacy in Context* (Redwood City, CA: Stanford University Press).

Richards, Neil (2013), 'The Dangers of Surveillance', *Harvard Law Review* 126, 1934.

Rumbold, Benedict, and Wilson, James (2019), 'Privacy Rights and Public Information', *The Journal of Political Philosophy* 27, 3.

Steers, Mai-Ly, Wickham, Robert, and Acitelli, Linda (2014), 'Seeing Everyone Else's Highlight Reels: How Facebook Usage Is Linked to Depressive Symptoms', *Journal of Social and Clinical Psychology* 33, 701.

Thomson, Judith J. (1975), 'The Right to Privacy', *Philosophy & Public Affairs* 4, 295.

Véliz, Carissa (2018), 'In the Privacy of Our Streets', in Bryce Clayton Newell, Tjerk Timan, and Bert-Jaap Koops, eds, *Surveillance, Privacy and Public Space* (London: Routledge), 16.

Zuboff, Shoshana (2019), *The Age of Surveillance Capitalism* (London: Profile Books).

CHAPTER 30

THE ETHICS OF FACIAL RECOGNITION TECHNOLOGY

EVAN SELINGER AND BRENDA LEONG

FACIAL RECOGNITION TECHNOLOGY PRIMER: WHAT IS IT AND HOW IS IT USED?

SINCE the face is a unique part of the human body that is deeply linked to personal, social, and institutional identities, whoever controls facial recognition technology wields immense power. That power is the subject of intense debate—debate that has legal implications for privacy and civil liberties, political consequences for democracy, and a range of underlying ethical issues. While we have our own views on the subject, the primary goal of this chapter is to clarify what some of the most fundamental ethical issues are, as well as to specify the key conceptual distinctions that have to be grasped to fully understand them.

We begin by defining basic terms. The media, the public, and even the designers and producers of various image-based systems are prone to using the category 'facial recognition technology' inconsistently. Sometimes, they stretch the term too far and apply it to image-based technologies that analyse faces without identifying individuals.

Facial scanning systems come in four main varieties and they can each be understood as having different use cases, benefits, and risks (Future of Privacy Forum 2018a). The most basic applications use facial *detection*, such as what you might see through your camera—the small, square overlay that moves around to frame the face(s) of the people in your field of vision. This technology does not collect personally identifiable information (PII) and finds human faces to allow the camera to do things like focus or apply a playful filter on them and count people passing a certain spot.

The next level on the continuum is called facial *characterization*, sometimes also referred to as facial analysis and emotion detection. In this case, more detailed information is collected by analysing a single image. Marketers might use an interactive billboard at a bus stop, or a screen mounted above a product display to collect information such as gender, approximate age range, and potential emotional indicators (e.g. 'smiling' or 'sad'), that can be combined with other data, such as how long the person looked at the screen, or where else they went within a store. This technology can also benefit visually disabled individuals by describing on-screen images to them (e.g. a man and a woman seated on a towel on the beach, laughing) (Newton 2016). While facial characterization programmes do not routinely create or retain personably identifiable facial templates, the process, particularly in systems purporting to detect emotions and dispositions, engender concern for two reasons: (a) scientifically questionable presumptions and technological inaccuracies underlie classifying and interpreting faces (Buolamwini and Gebru 2018) and (b) unproven facial characterization systems have been applied towards controversial ends, such as inferring whether someone is gay or straight (The Economist 2017).

The term 'facial recognition' most precisely applies to two variations of biometric systems that create an identifiable template of a unique person: *verification* and *identification*. Biometrics are any measure of a personal characteristic that is unique to an individual and can be used to distinguish one human being from another (International Biometrics and Identity Association 2018). Like many biometric systems, facial recognition systems create templates, a point-based design that proprietary software derives from a person's facial structure; every company's system performs this function differently and images can only be matched using the same system as the initial enrolment. To enrol someone in a facial recognition database, the system scans their face (live or from an image), creates a template, and then stores that information as the baseline for future matches (International Biometrics and Identity Association 2018).

Verification is facial recognition in a one-to-one matching system in which software answers the question, 'Is this person who they are claiming to be?' The output is a simple 'yes' or 'no' to validate the claimed identity. An example of verification is accessing your phone by having a screen scan your face to match a saved template. By contrast, *identification* is a one-to-many matching process in which software answers the question, 'Can an algorithm determine who this unknown person is?' Law enforcement uses identification systems when running a collected image against an existing database, such as one containing mugshots or driving licence holders. The system scans the new image (possibly from a video tape at a public venue, or an image from a camera on-scene), creates a template, and then attempts to match it to a previously enrolled individual.

Currently, many services—some of which we have mentioned already—rely on these functions. For example, convenience services include logging onto phones, sorting and organizing family photos, authenticating identities on platforms for goods and services, and profiling consumers to provide personalized recommendations. Hotels, conferences, and concerts are exploring facial identification to create VIP experiences for their members and registrants, enabling the transition from taxi, to lobby, to room, or checking into a performance or event, with minimal delays, lines, or other points of friction along their path (Revfine n.d.).

Additionally, companies are using facial identification to assist the blind and low-vision communities through audio or braille interfaces. Other programmes are using facial characterization functions to help people on the autistic spectrum to interpret emotional expressions (Gay et al. 2013). Educators are deploying facial characterization in personalized learning; and many schools have installed security systems for campus access. Medical researchers are finding new ways to use image studies for diagnosis and treatment (Hallowell et al. 2018). Finally, governments are using facial recognition with concentrated efforts in law enforcement (e.g. suspect identification and tracking missing persons), international security (e.g. border controls and terrorist watch lists), and domestic security (e.g. safety protections at large events, tracking hate groups, and searching for persons of interest). Each of these uses engenders ethical, legal, and privacy concerns.

STANDARDS, MEASURES, AND DISPROPORTIONATELY DISTRIBUTED HARMS

Since facial recognition technology is used across the globe, it is beyond the scope of this chapter to comprehensively review all of the standards (Welinder and Palmer 2018). A lack of consensus exists around whether quality testing should be mandated, who should be authorized to conduct testing, and what standards should be adopted to ensure that facial recognition technology is used responsibly. Even just the matter of deciding what images in datasets should be used to train facial recognition programmes has generated extensive controversy, particularly around the issue of image source (i.e. whether people consented to that use of their images) and diversity (Hill 2020).

Setting operational standards is complicated because there are many variables to consider. For example, since photos collected from video or other sources for identification purposes may be of low quality and resolution, facial recognition technology operators should never accept outputs without strong controls for review and oversight. Overall, they need to be able to clearly demonstrate the sufficiency of their training data, set thresholds appropriately, and analyse results correctly across a range of situations.

For technical standard purposes, it is illustrative to note that the National Institute of Standards and Technology (NIST) within the US Department of Commerce tests and ranks many commercially available systems, including those used by US government agencies. Manufacturers *voluntarily submit* their systems for testing; if a system is not ranked, its producer has chosen not to submit it. NIST testing offers a thorough review of each system's capabilities, including false positives and false negatives, broken down across demographic groups, when applicable. The best systems—the ten to fifteen manufacturers at the top of the rankings—show excellent accuracy, above 99 per cent in almost all contexts. These companies represent the vast majority of market share, particularly by government customers at all levels (e.g. federal, state, and local/municipal).

However, it would be a grave error to underestimate the fact that the NIST list also includes the remaining ~100 companies that offer some form of facial recognition service, with decreasing levels of accuracy. Particularly bad outcomes are concentrated across gender and racial categories, especially for people of colour, people who are transgender, and women, with Black women experiencing the highest percentage of demographically sortable mistakes (Grother et al. 2019).

These outcomes have led many critics to emphasize that everyone is not equally vulnerable to being harmed by mistaken identifications and everyone does not experience the same sense of unease when using, or being subject to, a facial recognition system. This is the ethical and legal problem of *disproportionately distributed harm*. Since the context of using facial recognition technology varies, the harms can range from delays and inconvenience, to embarrassment, harassment, false accusations, and imprisonment. Unfortunately, when the demographic majority of society find themselves less at risk of error or harm than minorities, it can incline them to be less risk-averse than if they had an equal share in the peril (Devlin 2020). This is especially problematic in the case of facial recognition technology because 'once deployed, [it] is very difficult to dismantle' due to lock-in effects and path-dependency (Whittaker 2020: 21). Related problems exist in situations in which uses of facial characterization generate 'socially toxic effects' by reinforcing discredited stereotypes about race and gender (Browne 2009; Stark 2019) and bolstering discredited forms of inquiry, such as phrenology, which is now re-emerging in digital form (Chinoy 2019).

Ultimately, what should count as the sufficient standard of accuracy for any system will vary based on application and context. On an iPhone, Apple's system verifies an image that is stored locally on the device. Apple's system, called FaceID, uses an infrared camera, a depth sensor and a dot projector to map 30,000 points on a face and create an three-dimensional scan. (The three-dimensional technology is one of the ways to prevent access by someone simply holding up a picture of the phone's owner to gain access). The detail and level of certainty for this match yield roughly a false positive rate of 1 in 10 million. It is an entirely acceptable standard for phone access but is far below the standards that would be required for terrorist watchlists or criminal prosecution, if such use cases should ever be approved at all (Angwin et al. 2016). Likewise, since the mismatch rate for identification is higher for some demographics than others, it would be inexcusable to identify suspects for law enforcement purposes without an expertly trained human in the loop (Lynch 2018).

Erosions of trust

In order for a society to function, there needs to be a *viable level of trust* among a range of people and institutions (Waldman 2018). In this section, we outline some of the harms that facial recognition technologies can cause when their use erodes people's trust in social institutions. We begin by considering how the use of facial recognition is affecting the level of trustworthiness between citizens and law enforcement. In a society in which law enforcement is perceived to be untrustworthy, important ethical goals, such as providing justice, become difficult, if not impossible.

In a series of reports, the Georgetown Law Center on Privacy and Technology reached several alarming conclusions about both the accuracy and the social impacts of facial recognition technology in the context of law enforcement. While this analysis only covers US cases and therefore is not globally representative, it still remains useful for explanatory purposes. Some of the main findings of the reports include the following observations: law enforcement has purchased citywide face surveillance networks that can scan the faces of city residents in real time as they walk down the street; law enforcement has not always been transparent with the public about how it is using facial recognition technology; law enforcement agents, who are not bound by federally standardized procedures for using facial recognition technology, have engaged in shoddy practices (e.g. inappropriately submitting forensic sketches and celebrity photos, and doctoring low-quality photos, including copying and pasting facial features from someone else's face onto a photo); law enforcement is searching databases containing name–face links of over half of American adults without acquiring explicit consent from citizens to do so; and, government agents have employed legally contested practices when using facial recognition systems to enforce surveillance for international departures from airports (Garvie et al. 2016; Rudolph et al. 2017; Garvie and Moy 2019; Garvie 2019).

What these research findings suggest is that police in the United States are integrating facial recognition into their institution in ways that *should diminish the trust of a well-informed public* and inspire political will for more robust restrictions on mass surveillance technologies (Ferguson 2021). Indeed, recent surveys about police use of facial recognition already show that trust among younger people and people of colour is substantially lower than among older, White people (Smith 2019). Unsurprisingly, theorists like Zoé Samudzi, who are attuned to problems with the police acting in biased and untrustworthy ways, are arguing that the debates over making facial recognition systems more accurate for minorities like Black people are failing to grapple with a more important and fundamental question: 'In a country where crime prevention already associates blackness with inherent criminality, why would we fight to make our faces more legible to a system designed to police us?' (Samudzi 2019).

Trust is also central to many legal and ethical issues concerning the use of sensitive biometric data in contexts such as employment, benefits determinations, and marketing. Misuse and abuse in these domains can *erode consumer and stakeholder trust in the fairness, equality, and reliability of these processes*, and, depending on the context and circumstances, harms can result that impact individuals, groups, or society as a whole (Barocas and Selbst 2016). Individual harms may include 'loss of opportunity', 'economic loss', 'loss of liberty', and 'societal detriment'. Examples of loss of opportunity harms include informational injuries related to employment, insurance and social benefits, housing, and education. for example, if an employer uses a biased facial scanning system during an interview to evaluate the applicant for characteristics of friendliness or other aspects that would make them a 'good fit' for company culture, and ultimately treats this analysis as the deciding factor over their resumé, performance, or other qualifications. Economic loss harms relate to credit, differential pricing, and narrowing of choice, such as have been demonstrated based on gender (Vigdor 2019). Loss of liberty harms include the negative effects of surveillance, such as suspicion, incarceration, and others that we will discuss in more detail later (Gillard 2019). Finally, 'social detriment' harms arise from the development of filter bubbles and confirmation bias, and the stigmatization of groups leading to dignitary harms and stereotype reinforcement (Future of Privacy Forum 2017).

Collectively, these harms can *adversely impact society as a whole by eroding the trust people have in their ability to be treated fairly, succeed on their own merits, and receive equal justice* (Berle 2020). Given how high these stakes are, strong countermeasures are being proposed. For example, the organization AI Now is calling for affect recognition to be banned in situations in which 'important decisions' are made 'that impact people's lives and access to opportunities', including 'who is interviewed or hired for a job, the price of insurance, patient pain assessments, or student performance in school' (Crawford and Whittaker 2019).

In addition to the direct harms to individuals and groups whose data is being collected or used, there are harms to those individuals who have chosen to opt out of particular platforms or services (e.g. social media), attempted to avoid a particular technology (e.g. not buying 'smart' home appliances), or requested to have their information excluded from data sets (e.g. exercising 'unsubscribe' or 'do not sell' options, among others). Such individuals might believe they are doing enough to protect themselves from unwanted analysis, but machine-learning-based algorithms—including facial characterization systems—might still be able to infer information about them, align with similarly situated individuals, and use those inferences for marketing, pricing, employment, housing, or educational recommendations that directly impact them (Deane 2018). If individuals believe they have no escape from the ubiquity of surveillance, they will be even more likely to *lose trust in assurances that their data and privacy choices are being respected or enforced* (Brandom 2018).

While it is difficult to resolve the ethical issues around facial recognition technology in legal and regulatory practices, governments and policy organizations are trying to do so. Numerous papers and studies are emphasizing the importance of establishing transparent and accountable governance, and the emerging paradigm almost unanimously calls for ethical ideals centred around 'reasonable' and 'trustworthy' practices. For example, the World Economic Forum proposed a framework that 'seeks to address the need for a set of concrete guidelines to ensure the trustworthy and safe use of this technology' (World Economic Forum 2020). And the Ada Lovelace Institute commissioned an independent review of the governance of biometric data to 'make recommendations for reform that will ensure biometric data is governed consistently with human rights, the public interest and public trust' (Ada Lovelace Institute 2020). These are merely illustrative examples of regulatory bodies seeking practical tools for ensuring that an appropriate amount of trust exists between authorities and citizens. Assessing the extent to which such approaches can positively impact the social contract would take us beyond the scope of this chapter.

ETHICAL HARMS ASSOCIATED WITH PERFECT FACIAL SURVEILLANCE

Although facial recognition technology systems can be inaccurate, it is important to keep in mind that humans tend to be worse. Human accuracy at identification is both highly evolved (e.g. we can remember faces with remarkably short initial exposure) and highly unreliable. Even people with the best identification skills have high error rates, and when we rely on our biological capabilities to make matches out of a large group of possibilities, the process is slow, frequently biased, and subject to degrading accuracy over time. Despite these human limitations, the alternative of a highly accurate, fast, and efficient automated identification system is not inherently preferable.

Crucially, facial recognition technology can pose significant risks it operates correctly, as well as the obvious concerns when it is inaccurate or makes biased recommendations. If every facial recognition technology system worked perfectly every single time, on every demographic and population, concerns about surveillance, criminal forensics, and long-term tracking and profiling would remain. In particular, Orwellian worries about living under conditions of ubiquitous surveillance might intensify.

Awareness of being watched affects individuals' behaviour, regardless of whether they intend any wrongdoing. Surveillance can affect individuals' perceptions of themselves and others, and is said to have a 'chilling effect', which means that people will be inclined to self-censor their public statements and activities and even unintentionally conform their behaviour to acceptable group norms (Kaminiski and Witnov 2015). Because the chilling effect limits self-expression, creativity, and growth, it harms democratic societies by depriving the marketplace of ideas from receiving input from all its members. It also leads to 'othering' people whose personalities, conditions, or behaviour deviate from average or mainstream expectations, including minorities, neuro-atypical individuals, and activists of all stripes who have ethical reasons for wanting to challenge aspects of the status quo (Kaminiski and Witnov 2015).

To identify another harm that perfect surveillance can yield, philosopher Benjamin Hale proposes a futuristic thought experiment: imagine a society that gets closer to the ideal of perfect policing and uses ubiquitous facial surveillance as a tool to deter people from criminal activity (Gershgorn 2020). According to Hale, this approach to governance risks eroding a normative ideal that, in the Kantian system of ethics, is central to self-determined decision-making: 'freedom of the will' (Hale 2005).

To illustrate the problem, Hale asks us to consider a person who is considering breaking a law against adultery and cheating on a spouse but, solely out of fear of getting caught through facial surveillance and subsequently punished, feels compelled to be law-abiding (Hale 2005: 145). While sneaky people might get away with cheating on their spouses in a society without ubiquitous facial surveillance, in one in which ubiquitous facial surveillance monitors public movements, it will be difficult, if not impossible, to have a discreet rendezvous or purchase a surreptitious gift. In such a society, one in which Hale presupposes facial recognition technology generates information that can be widely accessed, someone who commits infidelity is almost guaranteed to get caught and suffer reputational and legal consequences.

Hale's main point is that if people lived under the threat of constant facial surveillance, they would be disincentivized to consider such matters as whether it truly is ethical for people to freely choose to commit to a monogamous sexual relationship, and whether one should be allowed to choose to be the type of person who would intentionally deceive a spouse, absent risk of discovery. From Hale's perspective, there is a terrible cost to increasing legal compliance this way. It erodes the motivation for people to engage in ethical deliberation about how they should act and who they should be (Hale 2005: 150). In such a world, ethical intentions, as well as moral character and personal virtues that require the exercise of free choice, such as sincerity or integrity, would all be compromised because they would be hard to develop. 'Taking responsibility for one's actions by claiming that the action accords with who one is—"I stayed true because I love you, because I am your companion and I am honest"—can never be uttered without the attendant: "I did it because someone else was watching"' (Hale 2005: 151).

ALIENATION, DEHUMANIZATION, AND LOSS OF CONTROL

Philosopher Philip Brey clarifies how facial recognition systems can be used to cause the harms of alienation, dehumanization, and loss of control (Brey 2004). To narrow our focus to these problems, he pinpoints two adverse results that can follow from biometrics, including facial templates, digitally encoding highly personal aspects of our bodies. First, reducing an important part of our being to digital information can lead us to view a piece of our physical selves as having a new and essential function: the face becomes a medium for transferring the information that automated systems need to make an identification. People can experience this shift in phenomenological perspective as dehumanizing because an intrinsic aspect of their person, such as their unique faces that have deep connections to their life experiences, is translated into things that only have instrumental value, such as passwords, PINs, and barcodes.

Brey further contends that externalizing a body part by turning it into an informational equivalent can have profound implications for how power is deployed. Because the process separates an aspect of the self from its owner, others can seize control of it. To use terms associated with loss of property and ownership, this is a process of alienation—a setting aside of what is yours that grants someone else access, use, and authority. Once this happens, Brey maintains, your face is no longer exclusively 'yours'; it exists in a form that you might not understand, or even recognize. In such a scenario, in which your body has new purposes and new meanings, Brey contends that it is questionable whether you can retain control of 'your' data or 'yourself'.

THE FACIAL RECOGNITION SLIPPERY SLOPE DEBATE

How facial recognition technology might be used in the future is having a profound impact on current ethical, legal, and political debates. While not always explicitly stated, the following two questions underlie these debates:

- Is it reasonable to believe that facial recognition technology has such distinctive and powerful affordances that, over time, slippery slope conditions will incline societies, even ones committed to democratic principles, to look for ever-expansive ways to invasively use it?
- If so, will the slippery slope influence behaviour so strongly that *ethically unacceptable* erosions of freedom, dignity, and democracy occur—or, at a minimum, will be more likely to occur than often is acknowledged?

Woodrow Hartzog and Evan Selinger answer both questions affirmatively and claim that 'facial recognition technology is the most uniquely dangerous surveillance mechanism ever invented' (Hartzog and Selinger 2018). Believing the technology poses unique threats to basic liberties, they recommend *enacting a ban across public and private sectors* to prevent slippery slope drivers from expanding the scale and scope of facial surveillance (Selinger and Hartzog 2018).

By contrast, Adam Thierer claims that slippery slope allegations lack credibility because the slippery slope advocates illegitimately take 'a kernel of truth ... that a new technology could pose risks if used improperly ... and extrapolate from it hyper-dystopian predictions ripped from the plots of sci-fi books and shows' (Thierer 2019). From his perspective, slippery slope arguments about facial recognition technology are 'technopanics' that resemble prior exaggerated concerns over technologies such as 'instant photography, sensors, CCTV, and RFID' that well-functioning societies have successfully adapted to (Thierer 2019). Given the putatively logical flaws of slippery slope arguments, Thierer recommends rejecting them, including the allegation that democratic countries will become more inclined to embrace authoritarianism if they adopt widespread facial recognition technology (Thierer 2019).

Slippery slope arguments

To critically evaluate a slippery slope argument about facial recognition technology, one needs a sound framework for assessing slippery slope arguments in general. The most basic question, therefore, is: what is a slippery slope argument and how should it be assessed?

A slippery slope argument has an if–then structure and presents a causal sequence linking a seemingly unobjectionable commencing action to an *ethically objectionable final outcome* (Enoch 2001: 631). Specifically, slippery slope arguments attempt to identify tragic situations that will arise primarily due to lack of foresight about medium-term or long-term consequences. While 'slippery slopes appear everywhere' (Devine 2018: 392), the argument is especially prominent in debates about technology and technology policy, especially in controversies over biotechnology (Holm and Takala 2007) and privacy (Morales et al. 2020; ACLU of Illinois 2017).

In the case of facial recognition, the slippery slope argument entails the assertion that all parties agree that a society of ubiquitous, public surveillance is inimical to the ideals of a free, democratic order, and that this outcome is so tragically harmful and exceptionally difficult to undo once achieved, that it should be actively prevented with intentional strategic measures in all policy development for technology implementation. Then, the question becomes: is there any level of use case of facial recognition that can be 'safely' implemented that will not have an unacceptably high likelihood of leading to this final, undesired outcome?

For example, is it reasonable to expect that something as seemingly low risk as widespread photo tagging on Facebook (occurring in conjunction with similar features within other consumer activities) will normalize facial recognition technology to such a degree that too many citizens uncritically accept such practices, which then expand to more intrusive use cases, and ultimately permit the government to engage in ubiquitous facial surveillance? If the answer to this question is 'yes', it will impact current practices, as well as future policy and legal determinations, including the social choice to limit individual rights in the light of broader social good.

Many people are already divided over *whether consent is a sufficient ethical requirement* for individuals who want to use particular consumer applications. Continuing with the Facebook example, Facebook's basic facial recognition technology policy is on solid legal ground because in complying with local laws, it does not make facial recognition services available everywhere; and when the services are available, the company follows standard privacy-by-design practice by only allowing tagging to be available after users give affirmative expressed consent. This policy appears to respect user autonomy: it allows them to choose or refrain from selecting the option without financial penalty and it provides users with a default design (i.e. the functions initially are turned off) that protects their privacy.

It might be, however, that the conditions under which Facebook legally permits users to give consent fail to meet the normative requirements for offering consent in an ethically legitimate manner, in light of a slippery slope conclusion. From this perspective, the conditions for opting in fall short of the standard Nancy Kim calls 'consentability', particularly regarding informed consent (Kim 2019). In Kim's interpretation, informed consent does not require knowing every conceivable risk, but it *does* necessitate that when parties make an offer, they include a reasonable presentation of the significant risks that accepting it entails. Slippery slope proponents maintain that because Facebook does not tell users that the common practice of tagging photos can cause them to become receptive to more invasive applications of facial recognition technology, it leaves them in the dark about a fundamental danger (Selinger and Hartzog 2019c).

There are other aspects of 'consentability' that are impacted as well. Since the more invasive applications of facial recognition technology, including by law enforcement, are known to create disproportionate harms for minorities, it also violates the 'collective autonomy' condition of consentability (Selinger and Hartzog 2019c). Collective autonomy is the ethical requirement that a democracy safeguard *fundamental liberties for all*, even when doing so requires preventing some groups (e.g. the majority of citizens) from exercising low-stakes expression of choice (e.g. tagging photos) in situations in which such choices would prevent others (e.g. minorities) from being able to exercise high-level autonomy interests, such as freedom of movement and association (Selinger and Hartzog 2019c).

Does the Facebook example, then, encapsulate the first step on a slippery slope to an Orwellian society?[1]

Two types of slippery slope arguments: fallacious and reasonable

Older critical reasoning textbooks characterized the slippery slope argument as an informal fallacy (Hurley 1982). Slippery slope proposals were deemed fallacious because proponents can always present a series of wildly speculative predictions leading to ultimate doom. The possibility of being causally disingenuous, however, does not mean that all slippery slope arguments are, in principle, poorly formulated.

Contemporary philosophers acknowledge that there are, in fact, reasonable slippery slope arguments, and philosopher Douglas Walton created a framework for making them. Walton's account has ten characteristics that collectively cover the following temporal sequence: it begins with a debate over whether choosing a certain course of action is wise; it continues by identifying specific causal drivers that will propel behaviour to a grey area; in the grey area, people lose control over what to do next; once momentum takes events further, an uncontrollable slide commences, that results in an inevitable catastrophe (Walton 2017).

While we applaud Walton's insights, we believe his framework only identifies what could be called a *reasonable, guaranteed version of the slippery slope argument*. By modifying its structure, one can formulate something else: a *reasonable, achievable version of the slippery slope argument*. The main difference between the direct and achievable versions is that the achievable version does not posit catastrophe as inescapable after people lose control in a grey area. Instead, a more modest claim is made—namely, that the chances of a catastrophe occurring are more likely than advocates pushing for the first step are willing to acknowledge.

To make an achievable version of a slippery slope argument, one must do the following: 'explicitly specify plausible mechanisms that could drive slippage from one step to another' and 'rigorously explain why the mechanisms deserve due consideration' (Frischmann and Selinger 2018: 39 and 41). A parallel between achievable and guaranteed slippery slopes thus can be drawn to the 'direct' and 'weak' versions of Langdon Winner's thesis that 'inherently political technologies' exist (Winner 1986). The strong version is that adopting 'a given technical system unavoidably brings with it conditions for human relationships that have a distinctive political cast—for example, centralized or de-centralized, egalitarian or inegalitarian, repressive or liberating' (Winner 1986). The weak version only 'holds that a given kind of technology is strongly compatible with, but does not strictly require, social and political relationships of a particular stripe' (Winner 1986).

To better appreciate this distinction, consider the following hypothetical example that Eugene Volokh and David Newman offer while presenting their 'defense of the slippery slope'.

> [Imagine] a proposal to put video cameras on street lamps to catch or deter street criminals. On its own, the plan may not seem that susceptible to police abuse, as long as the tapes are viewed only when someone reports a crime and otherwise recycled every day or two. Many people may be inclined to support installing the cameras, even if they would oppose a more intrusive extension of the policy, such as linking the cameras to face-recognition software or permanently archiving the tapes.
>
> But once the government implements the policy and invests money in buying, installing, and wiring thousands of cameras, the costs of implementing the next step plummet. Comprehensive surveillance becomes much cheaper and thus politically easier. The money already invested may persuade a bloc of swing voters to endorse a broader surveillance operation, even if they originally opposed the camera program on cost grounds. Faced with this prospect, then, those who support the cameras but reject the archiving must decide: Should we implement the limited camera policy now and risk that it will lead to permanent surveillance records in the future? Or should we reject the limited camera policy we want for fear of the more intrusive policy that we oppose?
>
> (Volokh and Newman 2003)

Based on our classification, Volokh and Newman present an achievable version of a slippery slope because they are not making a case that if, at one moment in time, video cameras are installed on street lamps, at a subsequent moment in time it is inevitable that the infrastructure will include new facial recognition capabilities. Instead, they highlight a basic principle of transaction cost theory. It is easy to influence behaviour at scale by lowering transaction costs, for example, minimizing how much money, time, effort, or other resources is required to do something. More specifically, Volokh and Newman are pointing out that when society invests resources like money, labour, and infrastructure, the buy-in can have a pronounced influence on attitudes toward future choices about what to do with it. In the case of surveillance systems, once considerable investment is made, subsequently refraining from extracting the most surveillance value can seem wasteful.

As Volokoh and Newman's hypothetical case emphasizes, the temptation to maximize surveillance potential is especially strong when proposals for bolstering assets can be framed as inexpensive efficiency enhancements. In the real world, this argument has already been made for adding facial recognition capabilities to existing cameras for the purpose of more easily identifying criminals. New York Governor Andrew Cuomo stated that the use of cameras at toll booths to scan vehicle license plates 'is almost the least significant contribution that this electronic equipment can actually perform', and so it makes more sense to take surveillance to 'a whole new level' (Furfaro et al. 2018). Since it is not expensive to add facial recognition technology capabilities to the cameras and link the system to a variety of databases, Cuomo recommended this course of action (Furfaro et al. 2018).

FACIAL RECOGNITION
TECHNOLOGY AS UNIQUE

What is it about facial recognition technology that leads some people to be concerned that its widespread use will incentivize causal drivers that could lead to catastrophic outcomes? The answer is that, given how much information facial recognition technology systems powered by artificial intelligence systems can quickly process, they deserve to be classified as *unique* compared to any other technology that presently can be used for surveillance purposes. If this categorization is correct (i.e. if facial surveillance is like a 'phase transition' in physics (Stanley 2019) or a highly toxic substance like plutonium (Stark 2019) and lead paint (Read 2020)), then there are plausible reasons for believing that its features present uniquely dangerous slippery slope risks.

Is facial recognition technology truly unique? Some say 'no' and insist that it is spurious to demarcate it as a singular entity (Thierer 2019; Castro 2019). In response, others base their arguments for uniqueness on four claims that we present below. *Taken together, these claims, along with related points about powerful causal drivers (normalization and function creep), justify that proponents can advance a valid, achievable version of the slippery slope argument.*

First, faces play such a special, existential role in human lives that it is almost inconceivable to imagine large-scale human societies that do not place an extremely high value on unconcealed faces. Faces are the 'primary means by which humans recognize ... each other' (Rifkin et al. 2018: 310). Even if it turns out that, contrary to popular wisdom, the appearance of our individual faces is not definitively unique, the likelihood of finding duplicates remains debatable (Meester et al. 2019). While facial features can change, it nevertheless is difficult for adult faces to dramatically alter in the absence of extreme circumstances. This is why, unfair as it might be, people are shocked when celebrities get plastic surgery and stop looking like classic images of themselves, and why cutting-edge, partial medical face transplants have triggered 'intense' and 'heated' reactions (Pearl 2017).

Faces are also the 'primary means by which humans ... interact with each other' and express themselves (Rifkin et. al. 2018: 310). Faces have this pre-eminent status because facial expressions and even micro-expressions are powerful forms of body language, and the source of speech. Because faces are the *foremost intermediary between our private interior lives and the ways we make ourselves publicly available*, the experience of face-to-face interaction traditionally has been associated with immediacy and intimacy, and some philosophers have even made the case that the face (understood broadly as the living presence of another person) is the basis from which ethical relationships and ethical responsibilities arise (Lévinas 1969). Our faces come with us wherever we go, and the central roles they play in identification, communication, and social interaction go a long way towards explaining why, with exceptions (e.g. burqas), most contemporary societies *expect us to keep our faces visible*. Indeed, hiding your face in public can provide a good justification for others to infer that you are behaving suspiciously.

Second, more information can readily be extrapolated from faces than from other biometrics. When it comes to identification, faces are the most reliable conduits for linking our online and offline lives—much more so than iris patterns, fingerprints, gait, etc. Additionally, faces are the basis from which a host of inferences and predictions related to facial characterization are possible—that is, inferences and predictions about everything from mood to likelihood of telling the truth, sexual preferences, and the propensity for criminal behaviour. Rampant criticism that junk science underlies many uses of facial characterization does not appear to be deterring these ambitions (Chinoy 2019; Varghese 2019). Neither are assessments that illegitimate scientific claims are further embedding 'bias and discrimination within our society' (Whittaker 2020: 2). The incomparably high value associated with extracting information and parsing meaning from faces thus makes them the ideal target for extensive analysis from both the private and public sectors—from law enforcement, to educators and advertisers, and many more groups.

Third, under current conditions, there are lower transaction costs for extracting diverse forms of information from faces than from other biometrics (Hartzog and Selinger 2018). Unlike DNA and fingerprints, for example, no physical interaction is needed. Faces can be scanned from sensors remotely, and passively (Dormehl 2020), with software that can quickly infer information or seek matches. While in the future, such easy scanning might be applied at scale to gait recognition or other related bio-metrics, nothing comparable exists today. This asymmetry is also aided by widespread activities that link personal information directly to faces, such as registering for driving licences and passports and diverse online activities (e.g. social media, job-locating services, and employee rosters). In short, the massive quantity of existing photos, the extraordinary amount of information linked to faces in existing databases, and the ease of expanding databases through activities like scraping make facial recognition systems the ideal plug-and-play technology.

Fourth, deep legal gaps exist, placing few limits on the use of this technology. While laws differ around the world, the legal lacuna regulating facial recognition technology are deep and the lack of legal guardrails enables permissive, if not promiscuous, uses. In the European Union, there is growing concern about consolidation of resources among governments (Bitzionis 2020). In the United States, Congress does not impose any restrictions on how the government uses facial recognition technology and the courts have not mandated any meaningful limitations. Furthermore, the law presumes that citizens lose some reasonable expectation of privacy from face scanning and analysis as soon they are in public or share name–face connections with third parties (Wehle 2014), and remains unclear on the legitimacy of scraping the web for supposedly 'public' images (Vermont Attorney General 2020). There is a thin line dividing technology companies and government agencies, and the contracts between facial recognition companies and the customers who license and use facial recognition systems are also generally 'shrouded in secrecy' (Whittaker 2020: 8).

These four reasons for considering facial recognition technology as unique are then combined with two additional factors to justify an achievable version of the slippery slope argument: normalization and the creeping expansion of surveillance powers and surveillance technologies (Frischmann and Selinger 2018).

While civil rights and privacy advocates have identified the harms that facial rec-ognition technology can cause, consumer applications of it are accompanied by posi-tive representations in a variety of media, including advertisements, that single out the technology as fun and rewarding to use in daily life. Whether to open a phone, move quickly through an otherwise frustratingly long line, pay for a purchase, tag photos, or have your visage turned into an amusing avatar or matched with a famous painting, faces and facial recognition technologies are continually represented as the ideal currencies for doing things joyfully and efficiently. Since these experiences can drive expectations and re-engineer desires, they raise the possibility that 'if citizens expect to be immersed in facial recognition technology wherever they go, they might become open to allowing law enforcement to behave like everyone else' (Selinger and Hartzog 2019a).

From this perspective, it is a mistake to believe that the risks associated with different applications of facial recognition technology can be neatly cabined. When using facial recognition technology to unlock an iPhone, Apple deserves the highest grade for the privacy-by-design approach it takes to verification. Faceprints are encrypted and stored locally on the device, so there is little chance of them being compromised or abused. Nevertheless, as people become used to unlocking phones with faces, they might be inclined to accept other uses of facial recognition technology.

Finally, the various mechanisms of surveillance creep as discussed throughout this chapter have led some scholars and municipalities to contend that facial recognition is 'truly one-of-a-kind technology' that currently has more potential than any other to be used to weaken the 'obscurity' protections that are essential to the following ends and liberties: pursuing self-development, intimate relationships, freedom from chilling effects, freedom from the pressure to be conventional, and freedom to participate fully in democratic and civic life (Hartzog and Selinger 2019; Selinger and Hartzog 2019b).

How likely is it that the factors listed will propel us further down the slippery slope? This is not the sort of measurement where either side can justify their position with an appeal to uncontestable, mathematically formulated probabilities; current analysis cannot provide anything like mathematically precise articulation of these risks. Again, slippery slope outcomes are defeasible—the prognostics do not designate inevitabilities. How events unfold will depend on contextual factors, such as the actions of social, political, and legal institutions, the voices who make arguments about facial recognition technology and how much authority and resources they have, how legal and policy reforms are crafted, and how legal frameworks are interpreted and applied. While it is daunting to weigh all these features, one thing is certain: the longer it takes to determine appropriate regulations, the harder it will be to roll back an infrastructure that deploys society-shaping power.

Note

1. This chapter was written before Facebook announced on 2 November 2021 that it is turning off its facial recognition feature for photo tagging. We decided to leave this example in because people have used it for many years, and similar capabilities are widespread.

References

ACLU of Illinois (2017), 'Surveillance Cameras Are a Slippery Slope', in Anne. Cunningham, ed., *Privacy and Security in the Digital Age* (New York: Greenhaven Publishing), 156–164.

Ada Lovelace Institute (2020), 'Independent Review of the Governance of Biometric Data', Ada Lovelace Institute, 24 January, https://www.adalovelaceinstitute.org/ada-lovelace-institute-announces-independent-review-of-the-governance-of-biometric-data/, accessed 10 October 2021.

Angwin, Julie, Larson, Jeff, Mattu, Surya, and Kirchner, Lauren (2016), 'Machine Bias', *ProPublica*, 23 May, https://www.propublica.org/article/machine-bias-risk-assessments-in-criminal-sentencing, accessed 10 October 2021.

Barocas, Solon, and Selbst, Andrew (2016), 'Big Data's Disparate Impact', *California Law Review* 104, 671–698, https://papers.ssrn.com/sol3/papers.cfm?abstract_id=2477899, accessed 10 October 2021.

Berle, Ian (2020), 'Face Recognition Technology: Compulsory Visibility and Its Impact on Privacy and the Confidentiality of Personal Identifiable Images', *Law, Governance and Technology*, Series 41, 1st edn (Sutton: Springer), https://www.amazon.com/Face-Reco gnition-Technology-Confidentiality-Identifiable/dp/3030368866/ref=sr_1_1?dchild= 1&keywords=9783030368876&linkCode=qs&qid=1584314952&s=books&sr=1-1, accessed 10 October 2021.

Bitzionis, Tony (2020), 'EU Planning Shared Network of Face Biometrics Databases', *FindBiometrics Global Identity Management*, 24 February, https://findbiometrics.com/ biometrics-news-eu-planning-shared-network-facial-recognition-databases-022401/, accessed 10 October 2021.

Brandom, Russell (2018), 'Shadow Profiles Are the Biggest Flaw in Facebook's Privacy Defense', *The Verge*, 11 April, https://www.theverge.com/2018/4/11/17225482/facebook-shadow-profi les-zuckerberg-congress-data-privacy, accessed 10 October 2021.

Brey, Philip (2004), 'Ethical Aspects of Facial Recognition Systems in Public Places', *Journal of Information, Communication, and Ethics in Society* 2, 97–109.

Browne, Simone. (2009), 'Digital Epidermalization: Race, Identity, and Biometrics', *Critical Sociology* 36(1), 131–150.

Buolamwini, Joy, and Gebru, Timnit (2018), 'Gender Shades: Intersectional Accuracy Disparities in Commercial Gender Classification', *Proceedings of Machine Learning Research, Conference on Fairness, Accountability, and Transparency*, http://proceedings.mlr.press/v81/ buolamwini18a/buolamwini18a.pdf, accessed 10 October 2021.

Castro, Daniel (2019), 'In Attempt to Ban Facial Recognition Technology, Massachusetts Could Inadvertently Ban Facebook, iPhones, and More', *Information Technology & Innovation Foundation*, 21 October, https://itif.org/publications/2019/10/21/attempt-ban-facial-reco gnition-technology-massachusetts-could-inadvertently, accessed 10 October 2021.

Chinoy, Sahil (2019), 'The Racist History Behind Facial Recognition', *New York Times*, 11 July, https://www.nytimes.com/2019/07/10/opinion/facial-recognition-race.html, accessed 10 October 2021.

Crawford, Kate, Dobbe, Roel, Dryer, Theodora, Fried, Genevieve, Green, Ben, Kaziunas, Elizabeth, et al. (2019), 'AI Now 2019 Report', *AI Now Institute*, December, https://ainowin stitute.org/AI_Now_2019_Report.pdf, accessed 10 October 2021.

Deane, Michael (2018), 'AI and the Future of Privacy', *Medium, Towards Data Science*, 5 September, https://towardsdatascience.com/ai-and-the-future-of-privacy-3d5f6552a7c4, accessed 10 October 2021.

Devine, Philip (2018), 'On Slippery Slopes', *Philosophy* 93, 375–393.

Devlin, Hannah (2020), 'AI Systems Claiming to 'Read' Emotions Pose Discrimination Risks', *The Guardian*, 16 February, https://www.theguardian.com/technology/2020/feb/16/ai-syst ems-claiming-to-read-emotions-pose-discrimination-risks, accessed 10 October 2021.

Dormehl, Luke (2020), 'U.S. Military Facial Recognition Could Identify People from 1 km Away', *Digital Trends*, 18 February, https://www.digitaltrends.com/cool-tech/military-fac ial-recognition-tech-kilometer/, accessed 10 October 2021.

Enoch, David (2001), 'Once You Start Using Slippery Slope Arguments, You're on a Very Slippery Slope', *Oxford Journal of Legal Studies* 21(4), 629–647.

Ferguson, Andrew (2021), 'Facial Recognition and the Fourth Amendment', *Minnesota Law Review* 105, 1105–1210.

Frischmann, Brett, and Selinger, Evan (2018), *Re-Engineering Humanity* (New York: Cambridge University Press).

Furfaro, Danielle, Bain, Jennifer, and Brown, Ruth (2018), 'Inside Cuomo's Plan to Have Your Face Scanned at NYC Toll Plazas', *New York Post*, 20 July, https://nypost.com/2018/07/20/ins ide-cuomos-plan-to-have-your-face-scanned-at-nyc-toll-plazas, accessed 10 October 2021.

Future of Privacy Forum (2017), 'Unfairness by Algorithm: Distilling the Harms of Automated Decision-Making', *Future of Privacy Forum*, 11 December, https://fpf.org/2017/12/11/unf airness-by-algorithm-distilling-the-harms-of-automated-decision-making/, accessed 10 October 2021.

Future of Privacy Forum (2018a), 'Privacy Principles for Facial Recognition Technology in Commercial Applications', *Future of Privacy Forum*, September, https://fpf.org/wp-content/ uploads/2019/03/Final-Privacy-Principles-Edits-1.pdf, accessed 10 October 2021.

Garvie, Clare (2019), 'Garbage In, Garbage Out: Face Recognition on Flawed Data', *Georgetown Law Center on Privacy and Technology*, 16 May, https://www.flawedfacedata.com/, accessed 10 October 2021.

Garvie, Clare, and Moy, Laura (2019), 'America under Watch: Face Surveillance in the United States', *Georgetown Law Center on Privacy and Technology*, 16 May, https://www.americaund erwatch.com//, accessed 10 October 2021.

Garvie, Clare, Bedoya Alvaro, and Frankle Jonathan (2016), 'The Perpetual Line-Up: Unregulated Police Face Recognition in America', *Georgetown Law Center on Privacy and Technology*, 18 October, https://www.perpetuallineup.org//, accessed 10 October 2021.

Gay, Valerie, Leijdekkers, Peter, and Wong, Frederick (2013), 'Using Sensors and Facial Expression Recognition to Personalize Emotional Learning for Autistic Children', *pHealth 2013 Conference Proceedings*, 71–76, https://books.google.com/books?hl=en&lr=&id=FTKVAQAAQBAJ&oi= fnd&pg=PA71&dq=personalize+learning+facial+recognition&ots=4ul6xuvxJL&sig=kgVP fx9yJT2H1J_IEVhjiwLhGjs#v=onepage&q=personalize%20learning%20facial%20recognit ion&f=false/, accessed 10 October 2021.

Gershgorn, Dave (2020), 'Exclusive: Live Facial Recognition Is Coming to U.S. Police Body Cameras.' *Medium One Zero*. 5 March, at https://onezero.medium.com/exclusive-live-fac ial-recognition-is-coming-to-u-s-police-body-cameras-bc9036918ae0

Gillard, Chris (2019), 'Privacy's Not an Abstraction', *Fast Company*, 25 March, https://www.fast company.com/90323529/privacy-is-not-an-abstraction/, accessed 10 October 2021.

Grother, Patrick, Ngan, Mei, and Hanaoka, Kayee (2019), 'Facial Recognition Vendor Test, Part 3: Demographic Effects', *National Institute of Standards and Technology, U.S. Department of Commerce*, December, https://nvlpubs.nist.gov/nistpubs/ir/2019/NIST.IR.8280.pdf/, accessed 10 October 2021.

Hale, Benjamin (2005), 'Identity Crisis: Face Recognition Technology and Freedom of the Will', *Ethics, Place & Environment* 8(2), 141–158.

Hallowell, Nina, Parker, Michael, and Nellåker, Christoffer (2018), 'Big Data Phenotyping in Rare Diseases: Some Ethical Issues', *Genetics in Medicine* 21(2), 272–274.

Hartzog, Woodrow, and Selinger, Evan (2018), 'Facial Recognition is the Perfect Tool for Oppression', *Medium Artificial Intelligence*, 2 August, https://medium.com/s/ story/facial-recognition-is-the-perfect-tool-for-oppression-bc2a08f0fe66/, accessed 10 October 2021.

Hartzog, Woodrow, and Selinger, Evan (2019), 'Just a Face in the Crowd? Not Anymore', *New York Times*, 18 April, A 25.

Hill, Kashmir (2020), 'The Secretive Company That Might End Privacy As We Know It', *New York Times*, 18 January, https://www.nytimes.com/2020/01/18/technology/clearview-privacy-facial-recognition.html, accessed 10 October 2021.

Holm Samuel, and Takala, Tuija (2007), 'High Hopes and Automatic Escalators: A Critique of Some New Arguments in Bioethics', *Journal of Medical Ethics* 33(1), 1–4.

Hurley, Patrick (1982), *A Concise Introduction to Logic* (Belmont: Wadsworth).

International Biometrics and Identity Association (2018), 'Biometrics Explained: Answers to 13 Basic Biometrics Questions', *IBIA*, at https://www.ibia.org/download/datasets/4346/IBIA-Biometrics-Explained-final-final-web.pdf, accessed 10 October 2021.

Kaminiski, Margot, and Witnov, Shane (2015), 'The Conforming Effect: First Amendment Implications of Surveillance, Beyond Chilling Speech', *University of Richmond Law Review* 49, 465.

Kim, Nancy (2019), *Consentability: Consent and Its Limits*. New York: Cambridge University Press.

Lévinas, Emmanuel (1969), *Totality and Infinity: An Essay on Exteriority* (Pittsburgh, PA: Duquesne University Press).

Lynch, Jennifer (2018), 'Face Off: Law Enforcement Use of Facial Recognition Technology', *Electronic Frontier Foundation*, 12 February, updated 28 May 2019, https://www.eff.org/wp/law-enforcement-use-face-recognition, accessed 10 October 2021.

Meester, Ronald, Preneel, Bart, and Wenmackers, Sylvia (2019), 'Reply to Lucas & Henneberg: Are Human Faces Unique?', *Forensic Science International* 297, 217–220.

Morales, Daniel, Ram, Natalie, and Roberts, Jessica (2020), 'DNA Collection at the Border Threatens All Americans', *New York Times*, 23 January, https://www.nytimes.com/2020/01/23/opinion/dna-collection-border-privacy.html, accessed 10 October 2021.

Newton, Casey (2016), 'Facebook Begins Using Artificial intelligence to Describe Photos to Blind Users', *The Verge*, 5 April, https://www.theverge.com/2016/4/5/11364914/facebook-automatic-alt-tags-blind-visually-impared, accessed 10 October 2021.

Pearl, Sharrona (2017), 'Changing Faces', *Aeon*, 15 November, https://aeon.co/essays/what-do-face-transplants-say-about-identity-and-wellbeing, accessed 10 October 2021.

Read, Max (2020), 'Why We Should Ban Facial Recognition Technology', *New York Magazine*, 30 January, https://nymag.com/intelligencer/2020/01/why-we-should-ban-facial-recognition-technology.html, accessed 10 October 2021.

Revfine (n.d.), '4 Use Cases of Facial Recognition in The Hospitality Industry', *Revfine*, *Technology Tips*, https://www.revfine.com/facial-recognition-hospitality-industry/, accessed 10 October 2021.

Rifkin, William, Kantar, Rami, Ali-Khan, Safi, Plana, Natalie, Diaz-Sisco, Rodrigo, Tsakiris, Manos, et al. (2018), 'Facial Disfigurement and Identity: A Review of the Literature and Implications for Facial Transplants', *AMA Journal of Ethics* 20(4), 309–323.

Rudolph, Harrison, Moy, Laura, and Bedoya, Alvaro (2017), 'Not Ready for Takeoff: Face Scans at Airport Departure Gates', *Georgetown Law Center on Privacy and Technology*, 21 December, https://www.airportfacescans.com/, accessed 10 October 2021.

Samudzi, Zoe (2019), 'Bots Are Terrible at Recognizing Black Faces: Let's Keep It That Way', *Daily Beast*, 8 February, https://www.thedailybeast.com/bots-are-terrible-at-recognizing-black-faces-lets-keep-it-that-way, accessed 10 October 2021.

Selinger, Evan, and Hartzog, Woodrow (2018), 'Amazon Needs to Stop Providing Facial Recognition Tech for the Government', *Medium*. 21 July, https://medium.com/s/story/ama

zon-needs-to-stop-providing-facial-recognition-tech-for-the-government-795741a016a6, accessed 10 October 2021.

Selinger, Evan, and Hartzog, Woodrow (2019a), 'Our Government Should Not Be Conducting Facial Surveillance', *Medium, One Zero*. 5 March, https://onezero.medium.com/our-governm ent-should-not-be-conducting-facial-surveillance-54cc13f1ea61, accessed 10 October 2021.

Selinger, Evan, and Hartzog, Woodrow (2019b), 'When Happens When Employers Can Read Your Facial Expression', *New York Times*, 21 October, A23, https://www.nytimes.com/2019/ 10/17/opinion/facial-recognition-ban.htm, accessed 10 October 2021.

Selinger, Evan, and Hartzog, Woodrow (2019c), 'Why You Can't Really Consent to Facebook's Facial Recognition', *Medium, One Zero*, 30 September, https://onezero.med ium.com/why-you-cant-really-consent-to-facebook-s-facial-recognition-6bb94ea1d c8f, accessed 10 October 2021.

Smith, Aaron (2019), 'More Than Half of U.S. Adults Trust Law Enforcement to Use Facial Recognition Responsibly', *Pew Research Center, Internet and Technology*, 5 September, https://www.pewresearch.org/internet/2019/09/05/more-than-half-of-u-s-adults-trust-law-enforcement-to-use-facial-recognition-responsibly/, accessed 10 October 2021.

Stark, Luke (2019), 'Facial Recognition Technology is the Plutonium of AI', *XRDS* 25, 50–55, https://xrds.acm.org/article.cfm?aid=3313129, accessed 10 October 2021.

Stanley, Jay (2019), 'The Dawn of Robot Surveillance: AI, Video Analytics, and Privacy', *American Civil Liberties Union*, 17 June, https://www.aclu.org/sites/default/files/field_d ocument/061819-robot_surveillance.pdf, accessed 10 October 2021.

The Economist (2017), 'Advances in AI Are Used to Spot Signs of Sexuality', *The Economist*, 9 September, https://www.economist.com/science-and-technology/2017/09/09/advances-in-ai-are-used-to-spot-signs-of-sexuality, accessed 10 October 2021.

Thierer, Adam (2019), 'The Great Facial Recognition Technopanic of 2019', *The Bridge*, 17 May, https://www.mercatus.org/bridge/commentary/great-facial-recognition-technopanic-2019, accessed 10 October 2021.

Varghese, Sanjana (2019), 'The Junk Science of Emotion-Recognition Technology', *The Outline*, 21 October, https://theoutline.com/post/8118/junk-emotion-recognition-technology?zd= 1&zi=jy2zxjml, accessed 10 October 2021.

Vermont Attorney General (2020), 'Attorney General Donovan Sues Clearview AI for Violations of Consumer Protection Act and Data Broker Law', *Office of the Vermont Attorney General*, 10 March, https://ago.vermont.gov/blog/2020/03/10/attorney-general-donovan-sues-clearview-ai-for-violations-of-consumer-protection-act-and-data-bro ker-law/, accessed 10 October 2021.

Vigdor, Neil (2019), 'Apple Card Investigated after Gender Discrimination Complaints', *New York Times*, 10 November, https://www.nytimes.com/2019/11/10/business/Apple-cre dit-card-investigation.html, accessed 10 October 2021.

Volokh, Eugene, and Newman, David (2003), 'In Defense of the Slippery Slope', *Legal Affairs* March/April, https://www.legalaffairs.org/issues/March-April-2003/scene_marapro3_vol okh.msp, accessed 10 October 2021.

Walton, Dalton (2017), 'The Slippery Slope Argument in the Ethical Debate on Genetic Engineering of Humans', *Science and Engineering Ethics* 23(6), 1507–1528, at https://papers. ssrn.com/sol3/papers.cfm?abstract_id=3107283, accessed 10 October 2021.

Waldman, Ari Ezra (2018), *Privacy as Trust: Information Privacy for an Information Age* (New York City: Cambridge University Press).

Wehle (née Brown), Kimberly (2014), 'Anonymity, Faceprints, and the Constitution', *George Mason Law Review* 21, 409–466, http://www.georgemasonlawreview.org/wp-content/uplo ads/2014/03/Brown-Website.pdf, accessed 10 October 2021.

Welinder, Yana, and Palmer, Aeryn (2018), 'Face Recognition, Real-Time Identification, and Beyond', in Evan Selinger, Jules Polonetsky, and Omer Tene, eds, *The Cambridge Handbook of Consumer Privacy* (Rochester, NY: Cambridge University Press), 102–124.

Whittaker, Meredith (2020), 'Facial Recognition Technology (Part III): Ensuring Commercial Transparency & Accuracy', Written Testimony to the United States Representatives Committee on Oversight and Reform, 15 January, https://ainowinstitute.org/oversight-committee-testimony-whittaker.pdf, accessed 10 October 2021.

Winner, Langdon (1986), *The Whale and the Reactor: A Search for Limits in an Age of High Technology* (Chicago, IL: University of Chicago Press).

World Economic Forum (2020), 'A Framework for Responsible Limits on Facial Recognition', *WEF White Paper*, February, http://www3.weforum.org/docs/WEF_Framework_for_act ion_Facial_recognition_2020.pdf, accessed 10 October 2021.

CHAPTER 31

....

ETHICAL APPROACHES TO CYBERSECURITY

....

KEVIN MACNISH AND JEROEN VAN DER HAM

INTRODUCTION

THE ethics of cybersecurity falls under the broader topic of the ethics of security. However, the ethics of security is an under-explored field in philosophy, and indeed more generally in academia. The greatest area of research into security has been in the discipline of International Relations and its sub-discipline of Security Studies. Yet here, the focus has traditionally been on the military and national security, turning in the past few decades to broader questions of political uses of security (the Copenhagen School) and issues of international security as seen through questions of emancipation (the Welsh School) or the movement of people across international borders (the Paris School) (Browning and McDonald 2011). None of these, however, translate easily into an understanding of the ethics of cybersecurity, which has domestic and international elements.

An obvious question arises as to whether there is even a need for an ethics of cybersecurity. Is not security, after all, a good thing? Clearly it is, but it does not follow that security can be achieved without cost, and those costs must be balanced against any gains in security. Such trade-offs may be not only financial, but also ethical. That we do not accept security as the main, still less the only, value in society is clear from the fact that we reject notions of police states which may promise (however falsely) security from attack in exchange for a surrender of liberties. At the same time, nor do we generally embrace total anarchy in a celebration of those liberties. The relationship between security and liberty is more finely balanced than that, with liberty requiring security in order for liberties to be enjoyed. Hence security is valued, at least in part, for its securing of liberties.

Furthermore, security aims at enforcing divisions, keeping some people safe from other people or things. Such divisions may be justified in at least some cases, but not always. What should we say, for instance, of the security of a tyrant? Lastly, security can never guarantee it will be 100 per cent successful. In practice, there are likely to be cases of false positives (those identified as attackers, who are not) and false negatives (those not identified as attackers, who should be). Hence, security can impose costs on the innocent and fail to protect as intended.

So, there are ethical issues that arise from and surround questions of the practice of security in general. It is not surprising then that there are similar issues and questions surrounding cybersecurity in particular. The ethics of cybersecurity seeks to identify, isolate, and address those issues and questions. Work examining the ethics of cybersecurity can therefore focus on the issues faced or at a more meta-level in considering the approaches taken to understanding those issues. We focus here on the latter.

In this chapter, we examine three approaches to this task. The first is the 'bottom-up' approach of considering case studies and literature reviews to examine numerous incidents of cybersecurity successes and failures to identify ethical issues embedded in each. For readers interested in concrete cases, these can be found in abundance in this literature. The second approach is to look at current practices in the professional domain of cybersecurity. These are, we argue, dominated by the triad of confidentiality, integrity, and availability of data, or CIA. This triad has been broadly taken to determine the success of cybersecurity since the 1980s, holding that all necessary criteria have been met provided the confidentiality of the data, the integrity of the data, and the availability of the data can be assured. There are, as we argue below, some significant weaknesses with this approach. The third approach that we consider is 'top down', through considering theoretical frameworks that can be applied to the subject. In each approach, we argue, there are notable strengths and weaknesses such that for a full picture of the ethics of cybersecurity, a combination of the three should be embraced.

The chapter progresses by looking at each of the three approaches in more depth, taking the order suggested above. The aim is to introduce the reader to current thinking in the field of cybersecurity ethics, while also presenting a novel approach that contributes to the advancement of the field. This novel approach involves a top-down framework through recognizing security as the inverse of risk, introducing into the discussion the framework of risk analysis and the ethics of risk.

BOTTOM-UP APPROACHES

Bottom-up approaches to ethics seek to identify case studies as a means to identify the ethical issues faced in a particular field. This has been a popular and fruitful angle with which to approach the relatively new field of cybersecurity ethics. In this section, we consider different bottom-up approaches and note the benefits provided and challenges raised by these approaches.

In the early twenty-first century, a significant focus of cybersecurity ethics was placed on e-voting, voting in democratic elections through electronic media rather than the tried-and-tested means of placing an 'x' next to the name of the preferred candidate or party on a piece of paper. The benefits of e-voting are, at least on the surface: immediate tallies, lack of confusion and spoiled ballot papers, and diminished scope for manipulation and corrupt practices. However, several commentators questioned whether these benefits were as straightforward as suggested. What happens, for example, if a voting machine, or worse, a network of such machines, is hacked, and when should such a hack be recognized publicly? Before the vote, the election could be delayed and the system undermined. After the vote, the results of the election would be undermined and open to challenge (Robinson and Halderman 2011).

In their study, Robinson and Halderman presciently questioned how researchers should respond to political pressure (not) to investigate the potential for interference in electronic voting and the scope for collateral damage through the networking of e-voting systems to potentially unrelated networked systems (Robinson and Halderman 2011). Pieters went further to question the notion of trust that the public might have in e-voting machines, recognizing that there are (at least) two competing notions of explanation concerning human–technology interaction: explanation-for-confidence and explanation-for-trust (Pieters 2011b). In the former, the focus is placed on providing confidence in a technology, which can be achieved without people knowing the risks involved (i.e. when arrived at through reassurance by an expert). In the latter, for trust to be given to a system, there must be a full understanding of the risks and alternatives involved. According to Pieters, the danger in e-voting machines is that authorities seek to provide the public with too much information (to establish trust) when the public only demands sufficient reassurance for confidence. The excess of information could then serve to undermine confidence in the system. Contrarily, if the public demands sufficient information for trust but is only given the information needed for confidence-building measures, then the disconnect could undermine trust in the system.

More recently, in-depth cybersecurity cases have been considered as illustrations of ethical concerns in cybersecurity. One of the best known cases is the ENCORE programme. ENCORE was a trojan horse (seemingly innocuous code which hosts malicious code) that could be implanted on a computer and then used to communicate from that computer. ENCORE was developed by a team of researchers at Princeton and Georgia Tech and hosted on a number of popular websites. Through people visiting those websites, the trojan was implanted on computers around the world, but particularly of note was its implantation on domestic computers in China, Egypt, and Iran. From these computers, the research team was able to test the respective national firewalls to see which webpages were available to users in these countries.

Researchers wanted to understand the efficacy and prevalence of national firewalls designed to prevent citizens from accessing webpages that may be deemed 'undesirable' by the government (typically through challenging the legitimacy of that government), and which can only be effectively tested from inside the respective state (Burnett and Feamster 2015). However, this meant that the computers of non-consenting citizens were being used to attempt to access 'blocked' websites, potentially bringing those citizens to the attention of the authorities in their countries. Furthermore, given the nature of the states in question, those authorities are not known for their sympathy or for taking time to appreciate that the attempts were made by malicious software operated from the United States and not by the user themselves. In this way, cybersecurity research could place a user at considerable risk without consent or even awareness of the risk undertaken, in contravention of the most basic research ethics principles that have guided academic research since the Second World War (Byers 2015; Macnish 2019a).

A third bottom-up approach has taken the form of literature reviews, pulling together existing writings on cybersecurity ethics, such as those considered above, and hence taking a more holistic approach to the issues than any one case study. This approach has been followed, for example, by van de Poel (van de Poel 2020). In the associated study on which this chapter is based, Yaghmaei et al. carried out a literature review of 236 texts concerning cybersecurity in the fields of business, medicine, and national security (Yaghmaei et al. 2017). From the results of this review, van de Poel argues that the ethical issues arising can be clustered into four areas: security, privacy, fairness, and accountability. This approach has also been taken by Jha (2015), although he identifies eight clusters: equity, rights, honesty, exercise of corporate power, privacy, accuracy, property, and accessibility. The literature review approach is also the starting point for Macnish and Fernández (2019), who identified ten clusters.[1]

There are several advantages to the bottom-up approach typified in the above papers, not least that the issues speak clearly to practitioners through case studies grounded in real-world experience. The challenges with e-voting machines, with ENCORE, and with the issues identified by Macnish and Fernández are challenges faced in cybersecurity practice rather than relying on abstract philosophical theory or thought experiments, the relevance of which may be hard to see for someone not used to dealing with such a level of abstraction.

At the same time, such approaches have their problems. First, they risk missing important examples which may provide their own, unique issues. Hence, while bottom-up approaches may be thorough in their examination of particular cases, they cannot be systematic because they don't examine all cases. It is simply not feasible to examine every case for reasons of time and availability of cases (many, for example, never come to the attention of the public or academic researchers).

Second, in the same way as there may be latitudinal gaps in understanding the complete picture of cybersecurity challenges, there will also be longitudinal gaps as new issues arise with the advent of new attacks and security practices. As such, when new cases come to the attention of the public and academics, new analyses are needed to examine whether new ethical issues have emerged.

A third problem is that of clustering. This is a necessary practice to manage the large number of ethical issues associated with cybersecurity. As noted already, van de Poel clusters the issues into four categories, Jha into eight, and Macnish and Fernández into ten. In each case, though, the clustering appears to be largely ad hoc and lacks any clear theoretical underpinnings, meaning that there is scope for issues arising in one cluster to appear in another cluster (such as Jha's rights and property). For analytic purposes, one risks mis-identifying an issue as belonging to only one category when it may in fact fall into two or more, or possibly some other category not identified. This risk could result in ethical issues falling between the cracks, or being responded to as one type of ethical concern and not the other. The problem gets aggravated when new cases emerge that invite new clustering exercises. It is notable that the lack of agreement on clustering and its theoretical paucity is not always recognized. At present, the approaches taken tend to cluster issues around authors' perceived commonalities rather than adopting a pre-existing framework. Theoretically grounded taxonomies for cybersecurity have yet to be proposed.

Finally, while a bottom-up approach can be effective at recognizing the plurality of ethical issues arising in practice, it is not effective in providing suggestions as to how to deal with value conflicts. Without theoretical underpinning, the reader is left with a list of ethical challenges but little guidance as to how to prioritize them. Which trade-offs, for example, are tolerable and which are unacceptable? The resulting picture is often one of ethical plurality that is silent about general practical guidance.

The bottom-up approach is therefore a valuable contribution to the literature in providing a thorough, albeit not systematic, analysis of a variety of real-world problems. Through its grounded nature, the discussion surrounding these problems can be of benefit to practitioners as well as theoreticians. However, there is a number of drawbacks to the approach as it is currently practiced, not least its specificity, the lack of theoretical underpinning in the framework informing the clustering of issues, and in the means of prioritizing ethical conflicts that emerge in cybersecurity practice.

Pragmatist approaches

The second approach that we consider here is that of cybersecurity practitioners. This approach draws on the pragmatist theory of philosophers such as Dewey, Rorty, and Putnam, and is concerned with current practices and norms of behaviour, as opposed to focusing on case studies or looking to grand theories such as deontology or utilitarianism. As LaFollette notes, for pragmatists, 'meaningful inquiry originates in practice' (2000: 400).

As noted in the introduction, the values embraced by this community concern the confidentiality, integrity, and availability of data (the CIA triad). If data is kept confidential, if its integrity is maintained, and if it remains available to the pertinent user, then cybersecurity is successful. These could be seen as the fundamental values practiced in the cybersecurity community for nearly half a century.

The provenance of the CIA triad lies in the Anderson Report, one of the earliest publications on computer security, which discussed security exposure in networked environments. The triad was echoed in a later paper by Saltzer and Schroeder. The CIA abbreviation itself was coined by Steve Lipner around 1986 (private conversation). Since then, the term has been used widely in reports, standards, and other publications on cybersecurity (van der Ham 2020).

In the decades following the introduction of the CIA triad, the concept has been used as a de facto definition of security in texts on cybersecurity, ranging from textbooks to International Organisation for Standardisation (ISO) standards. The CIA triad is also a fundamental element of the Common Vulnerability Scoring System (CVSS). A CVSS score is used to describe the severity of a vulnerability in a software product. The CIA elements are used in the calculation of the impact of vulnerabilities in the scoring system. CVSS scores have been included in vulnerability publications since 2005 (FIRST CVSS SIG 2020).

The benefits of the CIA approach lie in the fact that it is time-tested by practitioners. As with the bottom-up approach discussed above, it is grounded in real-world practice and has the advantage of a history of discussion and debate through which it has been refined over the past fifty years.

At the same time, the debate concerning the CIA triad has not settled. While the three concerns of confidentiality, integrity, and availability have largely remained core to cybersecurity practice, they have also been challenged. It has been suggested that the triad be supplemented with the values of non-repudiation, possession, and utility, known as the *Parkerian hexad* (Parker 1983, 2012). Others have suggested that each of confidentiality, integrity, and availability may not be as core to the practice as seems at first sight (Spring et al. 2019; van der Ham 2020).

A second challenge arises from the fact that the triad is highly technical in its application. Given the provenance of the triad, and a relative lack of philosophical engagement with it, the traditional definitions of C, I, and A are technical rather than ethical. This has led to the aspects of each being largely binary such that they are either true or false, or in the case of CVSS impact, on a vulnerability having a 'high', 'low', or 'none' measurement risk. This scale can give a false sense of accomplishment, as the current status gives no guarantees about the future (or even the past); that is, data may currently be confidential, but it does not follow that it was confidential yesterday or will be tomorrow.

A third challenge is that this definition leads to a focus on the C, I, and A aspects of individual assets. Furthermore, each aspect is taken as an absolute value that must be upheld, instead of performing a holistic risk assessment that may impact the security of an individual asset (such as an individual computer, server, or entire system). This approach does not take into account the broader costs and benefits to whole organizations. Hence, confidentiality is a property of an individual asset, and usually not a property of a context, such as a computer network or office environment. The CIA triad leads to individual measures on objects instead of a general approach to cybersecurity.

In the early days of cybersecurity, many of the risks we face today were not present. When the CIA triad was proposed, computers were not connected to a (local) network, and the internet as we know it today did not exist. Both Anderson and Saltzer and Schroeder focused on theoretical work regarding computer security, since there were few practical attacks on computers at the time of their research. However, the context in which we use computers has evolved significantly. From single, offline, room-filling computers, we now have computers in our pockets that are constantly connected. Most artefacts in the physical world are now affected in some way or another by computers. Similarly, the nature of adversaries has changed significantly.

Traditional cybersecurity in the 1990s and early 2000s focused on providing security at the edges of networks. With the advent of mobile devices and the gain in popularity of bring your own device (BYOD), and more recently still the advent of the Internet of Things, this approach is no longer tenable. The boundaries of security have moved with these developments, and yet the overall approach to security has not, which has had the effect of strengthening the tendency to go for individualistic approaches to security (van der Ham 2020).

Furthermore, the focus on individual assets and meeting each of the requirements of confidentiality, integrity, and availability has led to a sticking-plaster mentality. As van der Ham has noted:

> the individual, binary measures and narrow focus in turn often lead to stop-gap solutions. Once a vulnerability threatens to break confidentiality, a measure is put in place to ensure confidentiality again. The risk associated with that vulnerability is then often not taken into account, confidentiality is now guaranteed again, so the problem appears to be solved. This is then often repeated many times for every new vulnerability.

> (van der Ham 2020)

The focus on technical solutions in turn risks missing opportunities for non-technical solutions to security challenges. Consider the increasingly complex rules to create safe passwords: one needs to include alpha-numeric and special characters, the password must consist of at least 10 digits that do not form a memorable word, and it should be changed frequently. As each of these stipulations has developed in response to particular security challenges, the result is poor user security, given people's inability to maintain numerous safe passwords (Grassi et al. 2017). Solutions exist to provide more secure authentication methods (such as multifactor authentication or password managers), yet these do not see widespread use.

Finally, as with bottom-up approaches, the pragmatist approach is unable to provide guidance on key issues. This is a particular problem for emerging technologies for which norms are yet to be established or in contexts, such as cybersecurity, in which norms may have developed but lack sufficient theoretical underpinning. For example, an ongoing concern in the cybersecurity community is that of vulnerabilities exploitation procedures. Recent years have seen active discussions on how security researchers should disclose security vulnerabilities; it is now deemed standard practice to privately warn organizations of existing security vulnerabilities. (Google has defined 90 days to be an acceptable period after which vulnerabilities can be publicly disclosed (Google 2019).) However, it is less clear how organizations and governments should deal with vulnerabilities that they discover (Pupillo et al. 2018). There are only two countries (the United States and the United Kingdom) that have released policies on how they deal with vulnerabilities that governmental agencies discover themselves (Ambastha 2019; Bradford Franklin 2019; Jaikar 2017; White House 2017). For commercial companies, there is very little guidance as to how they should deal with vulnerabilities and exploits, which some companies actively try to purchase or sell. Neither the CIA triad nor the Parkerian hexad has anything to contribute to this discussion; once more, practitioners are left without ethical support.

Cybersecurity expert Bruce Schneier has contributed extensively to this space over the past decade. Schneier's early work focused on technical aspects of cybersecurity (Schneier 2011, 2017, 2019) and while he remains a public figure in this area, much of his later writing has incorporated the societal and ethical impacts of cybersecurity. In particular, Schneier has been highly critical of security measures that may look as if they are working but are, in effect, of little value. Such 'security theatre' is problematic in failing to provide security while at the same time leading to significant reductions in individual and group liberty (Schneier 2009). As with Wolter Pieters and Mariarosaria Taddeo (below), Schneier has focused on the impact of cybersecurity, and the digital environment in general, on trust as necessary for the functioning of society (Schneier 2011). To this end, policies which lead to a false sense of security, or which collect excessive data beyond what is necessary are highlighted and dismissed in his work (Schneier 2014, 2015). Most recently, he has focused on the developing Internet of Things and the policies which, he argues, would be most effective in guaranteeing users' security (Schneier 2018) and on public-interest technologists, practitioners who try to contribute to the public good through developing tools to help society or contributing to policy development (Schneier 2020).

The pragmatist approach therefore provides insight into the values espoused by the cybersecurity community and the practices currently embraced as a result of those values. However, the lack of theoretical underpinning for those values and the challenges posed by emerging technologies such as the Internet of Things have meant that this approach is weak on providing ethical guidance outside a very specific (technical) sphere, and even within that sphere it is weakening as a means of providing security, let alone considering the potential ethical costs of that security.

Top-down approaches

So far, this chapter has considered bottom-up approaches, which look at individual case studies concerning cybersecurity and ethics, and pragmatist approaches, which look at how the community practices cybersecurity. We turn now in this section to look at top-down approaches. While these could involve the application of traditional deontological or utilitarian theories to cybersecurity, we are not aware of any sustained attempts to do this in the field.[2] Instead, we will look at three approaches: Pieters's application of

Bruno Latour's actor network theory (ANT) and systems theory, Mariarosaria Taddeo's work on balance and trust in liberal societies, and the novel approach we propose here of applying the concept of security as risk. Each of these is top down in considering a unique theoretical perspective which is then applied to cybersecurity as a means of understanding ethical issues, rather than attempting to isolate the individual issues themselves or the practices of those working in the field.

Pieters has argued that Latour's ANT provides new and important insights into cybersecurity. ANT holds that human beings and technical artefacts are both actors in broader networks. Through the eyes of this approach, as Pieters notes, shooting is performed neither by a person without a gun, nor by a gun without a person. The person enables the gun to shoot as much as the gun enables the person to shoot. As such, both gun and person are equal actors in this particular network. Which actor initiates the action is, according to Pieters's account of this line of thinking, irrelevant. What is important to him is that it is the combination of the actors that performs the action.

The advantage of this approach, argues Pieters, is that it allows for the recognition of human factors in assessing security modelling. This human element is often discounted from models as human motives and actions are taken to be far less predictable than non-human systems. This discounting leads to a significant gap in these models (Dimkov et al. 2008, 2010; Probst and Hansen 2008). Rather than discounting the human factor, particularly when interaction between various human elements is concerned, Pieters proposes that the 'flat' model of ANT in which humans and artefacts are treated equally to remove apparent complications. Rather than looking to motivations, the focus shifts to the information that is moved.

Pieters has also drawn on Niklas Luhmann's systems theory to emphasize the human element in the construction of information security (Pieters 2011a). As with ANT, systems theory involves the human element in the overarching system. Security is necessarily a human construct, argues Pieters, given that 'actual security is dependent on perceived security' (Pieters 2011a: 333), by which he means that the objective security of a network is partly dependent on how effective that network's security is perceived to be by potential attackers. Pieters has argued that the systems theoretic approach can also help to highlight ethical issues that may otherwise be occluded (Pieters 2017). For example, in the debate surrounding e-voting, considerable emphasis was placed on the privacy of individuals. This was, at least in part, argues Pieters, because there are clear legal regulations concerning privacy in the voting booth. However, there is a risk of excessive focus in this area because of the practical connection to the law, which risks commentators missing other (arguably more) important ethical elements, such as power, trust, and security. Privacy of individual voters was, holds Pieters, a relatively minor concern next to the potential for the outcome of the voting process to be manipulated through a successful attack on the network hosting the voting machines.

Pieters's account demonstrates the advantage that drawing on generalized theories in philosophy, and particularly those in the Continental tradition, can offer to an understanding of cybersecurity ethics. New insights are proposed that can be used to approach existing problems in new ways. At the same time, neither ANT nor systems theory are uncontroversial in the philosophy of technology. While Pieters's arguments are predominantly pragmatic, demonstrating the benefits that can arise for cybersecurity practice from adopting this view, they risk deflecting the argument to philosophical discussions as to the merits or otherwise of Latour and Luhmann on a more general level.

As with Pieters, Mariarosaria Taddeo's early work focused on questions of trust, and particularly trust in digital environments. In her case, Taddeo focused on whether trust could exist in online environments, arguing that it was clearly possible (Taddeo 2009, 2010a, 2010b; Turilli et al. 2010). From here, she moved towards cyberwarfare, where she became particularly noted for her work on using the just war tradition as a framework for analysis of cyberwarfare operations (Floridi and Taddeo 2016; Taddeo 2012, 2016), including an introduction to the ethics of cyber-conflicts (Taddeo 2021). While the military extension of cyber-operations has been the major focus of Taddeo's work, she has also written on the ethics of civilian cybersecurity, such as we are considering in this chapter. In 2013, Taddeo edited a special edition of the journal *Philosophy and Technology*, focusing on balancing online security and civil rights (Taddeo 2013) which included articles on proportionality in cybersecurity (Hildebrandt 2013) and Thomism as a lens for interpreting ethics in online environments (Dainow 2013).

More recently, Taddeo's work has incorporated a focus on artificial intelligence (AI), bringing together her earlier work on trust and cyberwarfare (Taddeo 2019; Taddeo et al. 2019) and including the impact of AI on cybersecurity (Taddeo 2019). This last is a developing field, with the impact of AI on attacks and defence still being determined (Patel et al. 2019). Throughout her work, Taddeo's focus has remained largely on the need to find balance in liberal societies between stability in the online environment, achieved through the establishment of reliable environments, and trust of users in the maintenance of their rights in that environment. To this end, she has argued that trustworthy environments should consist of system robustness, system resilience, and system response (Taddeo 2019; Taddeo et al. 2019). As with Pieters, then, Taddeo's work does not amount to a blunt application of a 'grand theory' approach to cybersecurity or cyberwarfare. However, through appeal to liberal notions of striking a balance between authority and individual liberty (Taddeo 2013) and the need to create trustworthy environments online through which users can feel safe to engage in free expression, she falls into what we have called the 'top-down' approach to cybersecurity ethics.

We propose an alternative top-down approach, and, we believe, one less controversial than either those of Latour or Luhmann and more structurally cohesive than that of Taddeo. We contend that security is the inverse of risk. If we take risk to be a function of probability and of harm (Hansson 2013), then as the probability of a harm occurring increases, so risk increases (and security decreases). Likewise, as the severity of the harm increases, so risk also increases and security decreases. Conversely, a decrease in the severity of harm threatened or the probability of that harm arising equates to an increase in security. In itself this is not, we believe, a radical solution and is indeed one largely adopted in industry, where security is often referred to as 'risk management'. However, as we demonstrate below, through drawing on recent work in the philosophy of risk, it promises significant insights into the ethics of cybersecurity.

The approach that we advocate draws on earlier conceptual analyses of security provided by Arnold Wolfers and David Baldwin (Wolfers 1952; Baldwin 1997), while also introducing the framework of ethical risk analysis to security in general and cybersecurity in practice (e.g. Hansson 1996, 2013). In what follows, we develop in brief the concept of security as the inverse of risk in general before applying that to cybersecurity and demonstrating the strengths that come from introducing the ethics of risk as a framework through which we can approach the ethics of cybersecurity.

First, Wolfers originally argued that 'security in any objective sense, measures the absence of threats to acquired values, in a subjective sense, the absence of fear that such values will be attacked' (Wolfers, 1952: 485). Wolfers provided an early recognition that there were both subjective and objective aspects of security in that a person could believe they are secure without being secure, or, contrariwise, believe they are not secure while actually being secure. To this distinction, Herington has more recently introduced a third, non-cognitive dimension of affect (Herington 2018: 181–185); it holds that a person could be secure (objective), believe that they are secure (subjective), but not *feel* secure (affective). In this way, it is possible to think or feel that a network is secure even when it is not, or to feel that a network is insecure when it is in fact highly secure.

This is not to say that objective and subjective states of security are unrelated. The above examples are extreme, and it is more likely that I will believe and feel marginally more or less secure than is in fact the case. Take the case of Ross and Rachel. Rachel loves Ross as an objective state. However, the chronically insecure Ross is scared that Rachel's love for him is fleeting at best, and so he is subjectively (in terms of both belief and affect) insecure. This causes Ross constantly to ask Rachel whether she still loves him, a practice that annoys her. As a result of his persistent questioning of her love for him, she starts to draw away from Ross emotionally, which leads to an increase in his insecurity. A vicious circle develops such that eventually his subjective insecurity means that she ceases to love him. His subjective state of security in the relationship has therefore brought about a change in his objective state of security in that relationship.[3]

Second, Wolfers argued that security consists of a threat to values. Baldwin has challenged this point by noting that threats typically involve intentionality, and yet security is broader than this, involving the security of assets that can be challenged by natural events which lack intentionality (such as physical assets that can be endangered by flooding). Baldwin's response is to define security as 'a low probability of damage to acquired values' (Baldwin 1997: 13).[4] While we embrace this move, we argue that one can go further by understanding security as a function of probability and severity of damage to values. Given that probability and severity are aspects of risk, we hold that (high levels of) security involve(s) a low probability of severe harm and vice versa. Hence, when there is a low probability of harm occurring to a valued network, that network enjoys a relatively high level of security. Once the probability of harm occurring increases, or the severity of the harm which might occur intensifies, then the security of that network diminishes.

Baldwin's response to Wolfers, seen in the current context, raises the challenge as to the relevance of the intentionality of the attacker in a cybersecurity incident. Our proposal, in line with that suggested by Pieters, adopts a flatter approach that does not distinguish between human and non-human causes of cybersecurity incidents. While the presence of intention is traditionally seen as the distinguishing factor between security incidents (which require intention of an attacker) and safety incidents (which presume that there is no intention to attack), we think that this is an increasingly dated and irrelevant assumption. We hold that the intention of the attacker, while it may be pertinent in judging the person, is unimportant in approaching the *concept* of security and its ethical outworking as discussed here.

From the perspective of providing cybersecurity, challenges to the network may be posed by people or by natural events. Which of these is behind the challenge will likely have an impact on the response that is taken to that threat (a security measure), but not to the *level* of security or to the responsibility of those who are tasked with ensuring security. Analogously, we might say that my home could be equally under threat of destruction from a tornado or a terrorist. In either case, my security is comparatively low, irrespective of which threat is being considered. How I respond to the challenge posed will differ, but the actual state of security of my home is not a function of whether the challenge is posed by an entity or event with intention.

Third, we recognize a descriptive (as opposed to normative) benefit in the Wolfer's definition of security as the absence of threat to *acquired values*. Given that Wolfers was writing in the context of international relations, we presume that he is thinking about values to different states. In our broader context, though, the reference to values (or severity, which is a reflection of that which is valued) allows for any value to fill that space. Waldron argues that we could expand the context 'to refer to the assured possession and enjoyment of any value, including liberty' (Waldron 2006: 504). However, in a descriptive account one should be able to cope with values with which one does not agree. Hence, it is meaningful to discuss the security of the Nazi party in Germany in 1945, even when we ourselves do not value that particular case of security. In the case of cybersecurity, then, it is similarly meaningful to discuss the security of a drug dealer's mobile device, even while law enforcement is seeking a way to dismantle that security and track the device. The security of the device may be valuable to the dealer, while the same security is not desirable to those in law enforcement attempting to hack the device.

Fourth, the notion of probability in the conceptual definition holds to a more recently identified aspect of security, in that it is always future-focused. While Waldron has suggested that this future focus concerns the security of that which is valued extending into the future (Waldron 2006: 474), Herington is more circumspect about this, recognizing merely the future focus on the concept (Herington 2012: 18). In this, we agree with Herington that security is about the future. Security concerns, for example, the safety of a person from attack or from being injured. Once they *are* attacked or injured, security ceases to be the pertinent concept. Rather than thinking of the person's security, we think of the harm they are experiencing. Indeed, the very fact that someone is experiencing harm suggests that any security they had prior to the harm either failed or was insufficient to the risk.

Finally, as noted by Herington, security always has a referent (Herington 2012: 13; see also Newey et al. 2012: 9). Security is the security of a person or thing (referent). However, to this we add that security always has a context: security is the security of an entity (referent) from a challenge (context). Hence, as noted above, we can discuss the security of a network from an attacker or from an earthquake, or the security of a mobile device from being hacked. This recognition side-steps the problems noted earlier in the CIA triad, which tends to focus attention merely on technical solutions in response to risks to individual assets. Broadening our understanding of the relevant referents and contexts encourages a more holistic approach to cybersecurity.

Understanding security in terms of the inverse of risk is not only an effective means of approaching security in general and cybersecurity in particular; it also carries with it the benefits that can come from applying the ethics of risk literature to the ethics of cybersecurity. The ethics of risk highlights ethical concerns that other approaches miss.

To develop an ethics of cybersecurity from the ethics of risk literature, we draw primarily on the work of Sven Ove Hansson, who has dominated this field of inquiry. In particular, we hold that work in four areas is demonstrative of the benefits that a combining of the two fields can bring. These areas are: the distinction between objective and subjective harms, challenges in calculating probabilities, the recognition of fallacies, and the problems arising from risk thresholds and distribution. We will take these in turn.

There is a concern about the calculation of harms as only objective. Granted, there is often an objective element to harm (the loss of a hand is harmful to anyone); but there is also a subjective element. It is presumably worse for a concert violinist to lose their hand than for a philosopher to do so. With only one hand, the philosopher could continue to practice their profession while the violinist would not be able to do so. In the case of cybersecurity, as noted above, this may extend further, such that the drug dealer values the security of their mobile device very highly, while pursuing law enforcement agents will not value that security (to the extent that they will attempt to compromise it). Any objective value of that security is questionable in this case (Hansson 2010).

The second concern is that of calculating probabilities. While we can largely agree on the probability of a traffic accident occurring to us being more likely than being caught up in a terrorist incident, this does not prevent the latter seeming more likely than the former as a result of persistent reporting in the press and news media. Hence, there is an important subjective element in probability calculation. Furthermore, in calculating probabilities there are potentially infinite complications that could occur to make radical changes to those statistics. In order to manage these complications, externalities and feedback loops are typically simplified, or even removed. While this leads to a 'cleaner' resulting statistic, it is also a highly theoretical and unrealistic statistic precisely because of the simplification. The appearance may therefore be of certitude when in fact such certainty is misplaced. Hansson has described this as the *tuxedo fallacy*, imagining that we are calculating probabilities in an idealized casino rather than in the real world (Hansson 2009).

Third, there are problems arising from risk toleration thresholds and the distribution of risk. Risk toleration thresholds—the limits at which we are prepared to tolerate risks—have been demonstrated to differ among groups in (western) society. White males have frequently been shown to be more tolerant of risk than White women or non-White men (Flynn et al. 1994; Hermansson 2010). This tendency is perhaps not surprising in societies which have largely been designed by White men. For example, when Twitter was designed, by predominantly White men in Silicon Valley, the issue of potential harassment apparently did not enter the discussion as one possible outcome (McCaskill 2015).

When new risks are introduced into social discourse, it may appear that particular courses of action are preferable owing to the fact that they are 'less risky' than existing courses. Hansson describes this as the 'sheer size' fallacy, noting that just because B is less risky than A, and A is currently employed in society, it does not follow that B is the best course of action to follow (Hansson 2004). It may be that both A and B are unacceptably risky for the majority of society. Furthermore, through adopting B we may cease to look for less obvious alternatives (C) that would fall below the risk toleration threshold of a majority. Hence, in the Patriot Act, the US administration and the associated intelligence agencies apparently felt that it was less risky for those intelligence agencies to monitor the metadata of mobile phone calls of every person in the country than to allow for further terrorist attacks to occur. Following the Snowden revelations, though, it transpired that not everyone agreed; possibly a majority of citizens in the United States disagreed (Rainie and Madden 2015; Stoycheff 2016; Bakir 2015; Krueger 2005).

Fourth, and related to the problem of the sheer size fallacy, is the concern with the distribution of risk. Jonathan Wolff has noted that the agent who makes a decision involving risk is not always the same agent who will benefit from that risk, or indeed pay the costs of that risk (Wolff 2010). For example, in the infamous example of Ford's decision not to recall the highly dangerous Pinto car in the United States in the 1970s, that decision was made for financial reasons by the board of Ford, who stood to benefit from not paying the costs of a recall (Macnish 2019b; Mcginn 2018). By contrast, the members of that board were almost certainly not driving Pintos themselves; the people paying the costs of that decision were not the beneficiaries. Such a scenario is ethically problematic as it enables risk-prone decision-makers to indulge in seeking their own gain at the expense of other people.

An analogous scenario to that of Pinto happens in cybersecurity when businesses underinvest in cybersecurity. In the event of a breach arising from such underinvestment where customer information is stolen, the business may suffer reputational damage and, increasingly, legal fines. However, it is the customers who suffer the loss of significant personal data, such as email addresses, physical addresses, and credit card details.

In summary, there is a number of benefits that can be drawn from a reconsideration of the concept of security in light of the concept of risk and the ethics of risk literature. Note that our account is still subject to some of the earlier criticisms levelled at bottom-up approaches, though. For example, much of the ethics of risk literature has itself been developed through bottom-up analyses, and therefore provides insights that are drawn from the sort of clustering against which we cautioned earlier in this chapter. Furthermore, there is no one theoretical stance on risk, still less an ethical framework for approaching risk that will provide the systematic approach that we argued was lacking from bottom-up approaches.

Moreover, this approach is highly theoretical in its stance, in that it defines cybersecurity and then seeks to identify ethical concerns arising through the definition. By being highly theoretical, it risks both becoming untethered from reality if the conceptual analysis is flawed and missing central ethical concerns that are identified through bottom-up and pragmatist approaches.

At the same time, through this approach we have introduced novel concerns that have not been discussed in the ethics of cybersecurity literature arising from bottom-up or pragmatist approaches. Concerns about measurement of probability (the tuxedo fallacy) for example, are real issues in a field increasingly referring to itself as 'risk management', in which risks are calculated to a precise degree by insurance companies. The fact that such risks cannot be calculated with a degree of accuracy should, we hold, provide pause for thought and caution in promises that can reasonably be made by cybersecurity providers. Likewise, differing risk thresholds throughout society and the problems of risk distribution coupled with White male bias imply that current cybersecurity risk thresholds may fail to take account of certain sectors in society (particularly women, the poor, and ethnic minorities), while imposing risks on those same sectors should once more lead to serious reflection. To our knowledge, neither of these concerns has been raised in the ethics of cybersecurity literature discussed in this chapter.

CONCLUSION

In this chapter we have considered three approaches to understanding the ethics of cybersecurity. These three, bottom up, pragmatist, and top down, have each been shown to have strengths and weaknesses. Our own preferred approach of understanding security as the inverse of risk carries some strengths not apparent in other approaches, and we hold that it is valuable in highlighting ethical concerns that are overlooked by those other approaches.

It is also noteworthy that the approaches considered here are, to date, the leading approaches to cybersecurity ethics. There is little to no work explicitly exploring more traditional interpretations deriving from Kantian, rights-based, or utilitarian approaches, and yet these may bear considerable fruit, either through their own insights or through contributions to existing approaches.

We therefore believe that to continue to develop this new field in a thorough and systematic manner all three approaches are valuable. The development of case studies can continue to introduce new concerns and insights, while pragmatist approaches

can track the development of new technologies and associated issues arising there-
from. The insights gained from the ethics of risk, and from broader theoretical
approaches such as Latour's actor network theory can also provide insights that may
not be obvious to those practicing cybersecurity. Furthermore, there is a wealth of
insight to be gained from exploring utilitarian and deontological approaches to
cybersecurity which remains untapped. Pursuing any one of these approaches to the
exclusion of the others will risk leading to an overly narrow perspective that misses
crucial concerns. Drawing them together into a cohesive whole promises to lead to a
more thorough and complete understanding of the problems, coupled with a clearer
way forward for practitioners.

NOTES

1. While this study involves a less thorough literature research than van de Poel, the literature
   provided a background to interviews held with cybersecurity researchers and practitioners
   to build an understanding of the areas in which cybersecurity ethics literature complements
   cybersecurity practice and areas in which the two diverge.
2. Arguably, Manjikian's *Cybersecurity Ethics: An Introduction* does examine various ethical
   concerns in cybersecurity from various traditional viewpoints. However, this is an introduc-
   tory text and refrains from defending one particular approach, such as a Kantian or utilitarian framework, but rather demonstrates how Kantians, utilitarians, and virtue ethicists
   might each approach the concern (Manjikian 2017).
3. We are grateful to Bert Gordijn for this illustration from the characters of the sitcom *Friends*.
4. Although using Wolfer's notion of 'acquired values', neither Baldwin nor Wolfers elaborate
   on what is meant by this phrase. Drawing from their context in International Relations, we
   presume this to be the values held by individual nation states.

REFERENCES

Ambastha, Mimansa (2019), 'Taking a Hard Look at the Vulnerabilities Equities Process and Its
   National Security Implications'. *Berkeley Tech Law Journal Blog*. https://btlj.org/2019/04/tak
   ing-a-hard-look-at-the-vulnerable-equities-process-in-national-security/.
Bakir, Viand (2015), '"Veillant Panoptic Assemblage": Mutual Watching and Resistance to
   Mass Surveillance after Snowden', *Media and Communication* 3(3), 12–25.
Baldwin, David A. (1997), 'The Concept of Security', *Review of International Studies* 23(1), 5–26.
Bradford Franklin, Sharon (2019), 'The Need for Countries to Establish Robust and
   Transparent Vulnerabilities Equities Processes', *Fletcher Security Review* 6, 45.
Browning, Christopher S., and McDonald, Matt (2011), 'The Future of Critical Security
   Studies: Ethics and the Politics of Security', *European Journal of International Relations*
   19(2), 235–255.
Burnett, Sam, and Feamster, Nick (2015), 'Encore: Lightweight Measurement of Web Censorship
   with Cross-Origin Requests', in *Proceedings of the 2015 ACM Conference on Special Interest Group
   on Data Communication*, New York, 653–667, doi: https://doi.org/10.1145/2785956.2787485.

Byers, John W. (2015), 'Encore: Lightweight Measurement of Web Censorship with Cross-Origin Requests—Public Review', Technical Report, https://conferences.sigcomm.org/sigcomm/2015/pdf/reviews/226pr.pdf, accessed 1 October 2021.

Dainow, Brandt (2013), 'What Can a Medieval Friar Teach Us About the Internet? Deriving Criteria of Justice for Cyberlaw from Thomist Natural Law Theory', *Philosophy & Technology* 26(4), 459–476, doi: https://doi.org/10.1007/s13347-013-0110-2.

Dimkov, Trajce, Wolter Pieters, and Pieter Hartel (2010), 'Portunes: Representing Attack Scenarios Spanning Through the Physical, Digital and Social Domain', in Alessandro Armando and Gavin Lowe, eds, *Joint Workshop on Automated Reasoning for Security Protocol Analysis and Issues in the Theory of Security* (Berlin, Heidelberg: Springer), 112–129.

Dimkov, Trajce, Qiang Tang, and Pieter H. Hartel (2008), 'On the Inability of Existing Security Models to Cope with Data Mobility in Dynamic Organizations', MODSEC@ MoDELS. https://ris.utwente.nl/ws/portalfiles/portal/5100076/final_sent_at_31_august.pdf (accessed 9 October 2021).

FIRST CVSS SIG. (2020), 'CVSS v3.1 Specification Document', FIRST—Forum of Incident Response and Security Teams, https://www.first.org/cvss/v3.1/specification-document, accessed 1 October 2021.

Floridi, Luciano, and Taddeo, Mariarosaria, eds (2016), *The Ethics of Information Warfare*, softcover reprint of original 2014 edn (Cham, Switzerland: Springer).

Flynn, James, Slovic, Paul, and Mertz, Chris K. (1994), 'Gender, Race, and Perception of Environmental Health Risks', *Risk Analysis* 14(6), 1101–1108.

Google (2019), 'Project Zero: Vulnerability Disclosure FAQ', *Project Zero* (blog), 31 July, https://googleprojectzero.blogspot.com/p/vulnerability-disclosure-faq.html, accessed 1 October 2021.

Grassi, Paul A., Perlner, Ray A., Newton, Elaine M., Regenscheid, Andrew R., Burr, William E., Richer, Justin P., et al. (2017), 'Digital Identity Guidelines: Authentication and Lifecycle Management [includes updates as of 03-02- 2020], Special Publication (NIST SP), National Institute of Standards and Technology, Gaithersburg, MD, [online], https://doi.org/10.6028/NIST.SP.800-63b (accessed October 9, 2021).

Ham, Jeroen van der (2020), 'Towards a Better Understanding of Cybersecurity', *ACM Journal of Digital Threats: Research and Practice (DTRAP)* 2(3), 1–3.

Hansson, Sven Ove (1996), 'What Is Philosophy of Risk?', *Theoria* 62(1–2), 169–186, doi: https://doi.org/10.1111/j.1755-2567.1996.tb00536.x.

Hansson, Sven Ove (2004), 'Fallacies of Risk', *Journal of Risk Research* 7(3), 353–360, doi: https://doi.org/10.1080/1366987042000176262.

Hansson, Sven Ove (2009), 'From the Casino to the Jungle', *Synthese* 168(3), 423–432.

Hansson, Sven Ove (2010), 'Risk: Objective or Subjective, Facts or Values', *Journal of Risk Research* 13(2), 231–238, doi: https://doi.org/10.1080/13669870903126226.

Hansson, Sven Ove (2013), *The Ethics of Risk: Ethical Analysis in an Uncertain World* (New York: Palgrave Macmillan).

Herington, Jonathan (2012), 'The Concept of Security', in Michael Selgelid and Christian Enemark, eds, *Ethical and Security Aspects of Infectious Disease Control: Interdisciplinary Perspectives* (London: Routledge), 7–26.

Herington, Jonathan (2018), 'The Contribution of Security to Well-Being', *Journal of Ethics & Social Philosophy* 14, 179.

Hermansson, Hélène (2010), 'Towards a Fair Procedure for Risk Management', *Journal of Risk Research* 13(4), 501–515, doi: https://doi.org/10.1080/13669870903305903.

Hildebrandt, Mireille (2013), 'Balance or Trade-Off? Online Security Technologies and Fundamental Rights', *Philosophy & Technology* 26(4), 357–379, doi: https://doi.org/10.1007/s13347-013-0104-0.

Jaikar, Chris (2017), *Vulnerabilities Equities Process* (Washington DC: Congressional Research Service).

Jha, Davendranath (2015), 'Importance of Morality, Ethical Practices and Cyber Laws as Prelude to Cybersecurity', *CSI Communications* 39(2), 29–32.

Krueger, Brian S. (2005), 'Government Surveillance and Political Participation on the Internet', *Social Science Computer Review* 23(4), 439–452.

LaFollette, Hugh (2000), 'Pragmatic Ethics', in Hugh LaFollette, ed., *Blackwell Guide to Ethical Theory* (Malden, MA: Blackwell Publishing), 400–419, https://digital.usfsp.edu/fac_publications/2242, accessed 1 October 2021.

Macnish, Kevin (2019a), 'Informed Consent', in Carissa Veliz, ed., *Data, Privacy and the Individual* (Madrid: IE University Press), 1–16.

Macnish, Kevin (2019b), 'Introduction to Privacy', in Carissa Veliz, ed., *Data, Privacy and the Individual* (Madrid: IE University Press), 1–17.

Macnish, Kevin, and Fernández, Ana (2019), 'Smart Information Systems in Cybersecurity', *ORBIT Journal* 1(2), doi: https://doi.org/10.29297/orbit.v2i2.105.

Manjikian, Mary (2017), *Cybersecurity Ethics*, 1st edn (London and New York: Routledge).

Mccaskill, Nolan D. (2015), 'Twitter's Diversity Problem', *The Agenda*, 9 March, https://www.politico.com/agenda/story/2015/09/twitters-diversity-problem-000218, accessed 1 October 2021.

Mcginn, Robert (2018), *The Ethical Engineer: Contemporary Concepts and Cases* (Princeton, NJ: Princeton University Press).

Newey, Glen, (2012), 'Liberty, Security Notwithstanding', in Charles Husband and Yunis Alam, eds, *Social Cohesion, Securitization and Counter-Terrorism* (Helsinki: Helsinki Collegium for Advanced Studies), https://helda.helsinki.fi/handle/10138/32359, accessed 9 October 2021.

Parker, Donn, B. (1983), *Fighting Computer Crime* (New York: Scribner).

Parker, Donn, B. (2012), 'Toward a New Framework for Information Security?', in Seymour Bosworth, Michael E. Kabay, and Eric Whyne, eds, *Computer Security Handbook*, 6th ed. (New Jersey: Wiley), 3.1–3.23.

Patel, Andrew, Hatzakis, Tally, Macnish, Kevin, Ryan, Mark, and Kirichenko, Alexey (2019), 'D1.3 Cyberthreats and Countermeasures', Online resource D1.3. SHERPA, De Montfort University, doi: https://doi.org/10.21253/DMU.7951292.v3.

Pieters, Wolter (2011a), 'The (Social) Construction of Information Security', *The Information Society* 27(5), 326–335.

Pieters, Wolter (2011b), 'Explanation and Trust: What to Tell the User in Security and AI?', *Ethics and Information Technology* 13(1), 53–64, doi: https://doi.org/10.1007/s10676-010-9253-3.

Pieters, Wolter (2017), 'Beyond Individual-Centric Privacy: Information Technology in Social Systems', *The Information Society* 33(5), 271–281.

Poel, Ibo van de (2020), 'Core Values and Value Conflicts in Cybersecurity: Beyond Privacy Versus Security', in Markus Christen, Bert Gordijn, and Michele Loi, eds, *The Ethics of Cybersecurity*, The International Library of Ethics, Law and Technology (Cham: Springer International), 45–71, doi: https://doi.org/10.1007/978-3-030-29053-5_3.

Probst, Christian W., and René Rydhof Hansen (2008), 'An Extensible Analysable System Model', *Information Security Technical Report* 13(4), 235–246.

Pupillo, Lorenzo, Ferreira, Afonso, and Varisco, Gianluca (2018), 'Software Vulnerability Disclosure in Europe: Technology, Policies and Legal Challenges', *CEPS*, 28 June, https://www.ceps.eu/ceps-publications/software-vulnerability-disclosure-europe-technology-policies-and-legal-challenges/, accessed 1 October 2021.

Rainie, Lee, and Madden, Mary (2015), 'Americans' Privacy Strategies Post-Snowden', *Pew Research Center: Internet, Science & Tech* (blog), 16 March, http://www.pewinternet.org/2015/03/16/americans-privacy-strategies-post-snowden/, accessed 1 October 2021.

Robinson, David G., and Halderman, J. Alex (2011), 'Ethical Issues in E-Voting Security Analysis', in George Danezis, Sven Dietrich, and Kazue Sako, eds, *Financial Cryptography and Data Security*, Lecture Notes in Computer Science 7126 (Berlin: Springer), 119–130.

Schneier, Bruce (2009), *Schneier on Security*, 1st edn (Indianapolis: Wiley).

Schneier, Bruce (2011), *Secrets and Lies: Digital Security in a Networked World*, 1st edn (Indianapolis: Wiley).

Schneier, Bruce (2014), 'NSA Robots Are "Collecting" Your Data, Too, and They're Getting Away with It', *The Guardian*, 27 February, sec. Comment is free, http://www.theguardian.com/commentisfree/2014/feb/27/nsa-robots-algorithm-surveillance-bruce-schneier, accessed 1 October 2021.

Schneier, Bruce (2015), *Data and Goliath: The Hidden Battles to Collect Your Data and Control Your World*, 1st edn (New York: W. W. Norton & Company).

Schneier, Bruce (2017), *Applied Cryptography: Protocols, Algorithms and Source Code in C*, 20th edn (Indianapolis: Wiley).

Schneier, Bruce (2018) *Click Here to Kill Everybody: Security and Survival in a Hyper-Connected World*, repr. edn (New York: W. W. Norton & Company).

Schneier, Bruce (2019), *We Have Root: Even More Advice from Schneier on Security*, 1st edn (Indianapolis: Wiley).

Schneier, Bruce (2020), 'Public-Interest Technology Resources', *Public-Interest Technology Resources* (blog), 24 February, https://public-interest-tech.com/, accessed 1 October 2021.

Spring, Jonathan M., Hatleback, Eric, Householder, Allen, Manion, Art, and Shick, Deana (2019), 'Prioritizing Vulnerability Response: A Stakeholder-Specific Vulnerability Categorization', *Carnegie Mellon University Software Engineering Institute*, November, 36.

Stoycheff, Elizabeth (2016), 'Under Surveillance: Examining Facebook's Spiral of Silence Effects in the Wake of NSA Internet Monitoring', *Journalism & Mass Communication Quarterly* 93(2), 1–16.

Taddeo, Mariarosaria (2009), 'Defining Trust and E-Trust: From Old Theories to New Problems', International Journal of Technology and Human Interaction (IJTHI) 2(April), http://www.igi-global.com/article/defining-trust-trust/2939, accessed 1 October 2021.

Taddeo, Mariarosaria (2010a), 'Trust in Technology: A Distinctive and a Problematic Relation', *Knowledge, Technology & Policy* 23(3–4), 283–286.

Taddeo, Mariarosaria (2010b), 'Modelling Trust in Artificial Agents, A First Step Toward the Analysis of e-Trust', *Minds and Machines* 20(2), 243–257, doi: https://doi.org/10.1007/s11023-010-9201-3.

Taddeo, Mariarosaria (2012), 'Information Warfare: A Philosophical Perspective', *Philosophy & Technology* 25(1), 105–120, doi: https://doi.org/10.1007/s13347-011-0040-9.

Taddeo, Mariarosaria (2013), 'Cyber Security and Individual Rights, Striking the Right Balance', *Philosophy & Technology* 26(4), 353–356, doi: https://doi.org/10.1007/s13347-013-0140-9.

Taddeo, Mariarosaria (2016), 'Just Information Warfare', *Topoi* 35(1) 213–224, doi: https://doi.org/10.1007/s11245-014-9245-8.

Taddeo, Mariarosaria (2019), 'Three Ethical Challenges of Applications of Artificial Intelligence in Cybersecurity', *Minds and Machines* 29(2), 187–191, doi: https://doi.org/10.1007/s11 023-019-09504-8.

Taddeo, Mariarosaria (2021), *The Ethics of Cyber Conflicts: An Introduction*, 1st edn (London: Routledge).

Taddeo, Mariarosaria, McCutcheon, Tom, and Floridi, Luciano (2019), 'Trusting Artificial Intelligence in Cybersecurity Is a Double-Edged Sword', *Nature Machine Intelligence* 1(12), 557–560, doi: https://doi.org/10.1038/s42256-019-0109-1.

Turilli, Matteo, Vaccaro, Antonino, and Taddeo, Mariarosaria (2010), 'The Case of Online Trust', *Knowledge, Technology & Policy* 23(3), 333–345, doi: https://doi.org/10.1007/s12 130-010-9117-5.

Waldron, Jeremy (2006), 'Safety and Security', *Nebraska Law Review* 85, 454.

White House (2017), 'Vulnerabilities Equities Policy and Process for the United States Government', White House Report, Washington, DC. https://trumpwhitehouse.archives. gov/sites/whitehouse.gov/files/images/External%20-%20Unclassified%20VEP%20Char ter%20FINAL.PDF, accessed 9 October 2021.

Wolfers, Arnold (1952), ' "National Security" as an Ambiguous Symbol', *Political Science Quarterly* 67(4), 481–502, doi: https://doi.org/10.2307/2145138.

Wolff, Jonathan (2010), 'Five Types of Risky Situation', *Law, Innovation and Technology* 2(2), 151–63, doi: https://doi.org/10.5235/175799610794046177.

Yaghmaei, Emad, van de Poel, Ibo, Christen, Markus, Weber, Karsten, Gordijn, Bert, Kleine, Nadine, et al. (2017), 'Canvas White Paper 1—Cybersecurity and Ethics', *SSRN ELibrary*, https://papers.ssrn.com/sol3/papers.cfm?abstract_id=3091909, accessed 1 October 2021.

CHAPTER 32

THE ETHICS OF WEAPONIZED AI

MICHAEL ROBILLARD

INTRODUCTION

THE twenty-first century finds us moving into an age of automation at an ever-quickening pace. Smartphones, big data, the 'Internet of Things'; computation is fast becoming a ubiquitous and seamless part of the human condition with the boundaries between human beings and machines becoming increasingly blurred. Now that individual as well as collective human decision-making can be progressively outsourced onto algorithmic and computational proxies at a faster and faster rate, questions of just *what* decisions ought to be automated have come to the foreground of contemporary ethics debates. Such concerns are especially pressing when it comes to questions of automation in war.

For ethicists, politicians, lawmakers, technologists, strategists, and lay persons alike, there seems to be an intuitive moral repulsion to the idea of using fully autonomous weapons systems (AWS) in war. For some ethicists, such moral misgivings proceed primarily from a series of *contingent* arguments. These contingent arguments often take the form of worries regarding downstream consequences that may occur were AWS allowed onto the battlefield, and often include worries about incentivization for overuse by political leaders, ease of accessibility for terrorists and non-state actors, proliferation, and arms race concerns (Sharkey 2017), lack of accountability and oversight (Roff 2014: 211; Scharre 2018), social distrust and strategic imprudence (Simpson 2011: 325), and the danger of malfunctioning artificial intelligence causing severe harm to civilians or existential risk to all of humanity (Bostrom 2003: 13). Other ethicists, however, raise several *in principle* objections to the use of AWS wholly independent of these contingent worries. Some of these in principle arguments involve appeals to inherent 'responsibility gaps' generated by AWS (Sparrow 2007), morality's irreducibility to formal algorithmic codification (Purves et al. 2015: 854), AWS's inability to kill for the "right kind of reasons" (Purves et al. 2015 855), and deontological objections based on respect for human combatants (Skerker et al. 2020: 1). Still, other philosophers, including me, have objected to the idea that AWS create any new or novel in principle moral concerns (Burri and Robillard 2018).[1]

This chapter surveys these various contingent and in principle moral arguments pertaining to the ethics of AWS in war. First, I explore some of the important definitions, terminology, and concepts regarding artificial intelligence (AI) and autonomous weapons. I then investigate and unpack several of the aforementioned *in principle* arguments for and against the use of AWS in war. Then, I review several of the major *contingent* ethical arguments related to AWS, after which, I offer several general prescriptions, predictions, and connections pertaining to the future of war and automation as we move further into the twenty-first century. I conclude with a few closing remarks regarding technology, war, and the human condition more broadly.

CONCEPTS AND TERMINOLOGY

Before we can begin to make sense of the morality of automated weapons, we must first get a clearer picture about what exactly we mean when we speak of a machine or a weapon 'being autonomous'. While scholars, ethicists, and policymakers alike continue to debate over what exactly constitutes an autonomous weapon system, several groups, institutions, and scholars have advanced helpful concepts, definitions, and terminology that we can borrow from in order to get a clearer picture of the subject at hand.

Proposed definitions

As Suzanne Burri notes in 'What is the Moral Problem with Killer Robots?', autonomous weapons have, in a sense, existed with us for some time now (Burri 2017). Anti-personnel mines, for instance, arguably 'select' their own targets once a human has primed them. The Israeli Harpy, a loitering anti-radar missile, deploys without a specifically designated target, flies a search pattern, identifies an enemy radar, and then divebombs and destroys it. However, policy-makers and ethicists are not primarily concerned about these kinds of autonomous weapons. They are instead concerned about weapons systems of much greater technical sophistication (Burri 2017).

Philosophers have proposed several working definitions of AWS that we can pull from. Writing about AWS, Rob Sparrow, for instance, suggests that 'their actions originate in them and reflect their ends. Furthermore, in a fully autonomous agent, these ends are ends that they have themselves, in some sense, 'chosen' (Sparrow 2007).

Responding to Sparrow, Purves, Jenkins, and Strawser offer a similar definition of AWS. They write:

> Another way to capture the kind of technology we are here envisioning is on Tjerk de Greef's capabilities scale (De Greef et al. 2010). We are focused on those kinds of weapons which would be classified as having a 'High' level of autonomy on De Greef's scale. That is, at the most extreme end of the spectrum (what De Greef calls Level 10), we are imagining weapons that can act in such a way that the computer decides everything, acts autonomously, ignoring the human.
>
> (Purves et al. 2015: 853)

Offering a third useful conceptual schema to make better sense of what might be meant by 'autonomous weapons' are Paul Scharre and Michael Horowitz. Scharre and Horowitz advance a three-tiered categorization of programmable weapons in terms of their causal relationship to human operators. On their view, weapons that require a human being to play a necessary role in a weapon's proper functioning count as being 'in the loop' and do not count as autonomous weapons. Weapons where a human is causally unnecessary for the weapon's proper function, but is still able to intervene, count as 'on the loop' and therefore as autonomous. Finally, weapons that require no human monitoring for their proper functioning and cannot be intervened upon once activated count as 'out of the loop' and also count as AWS (Scharre and Horowitz 2018).

Along with ethicists and scholars, various militaries and international agencies have offered their working definitions of AWS (Burri 2017). For instance, in a 2012 directive, the US Department of Defense defines an autonomous weapon system as:

> A weapon system that, once activated, can select and engage targets without further intervention by a human operator. This includes human-supervised autonomous weapon systems that are designed to allow human operators to override operation of the weapon system, but can select and engage targets without further human input after activation.
>
> (US Department of Defense 2012)

The implication here is that an autonomous weapon's programming possesses a certain degree of complexity such that its targeting and decision-making capabilities could be made *fully* on its own but that its decision-making and actions would still be subject to human intervention.

Similarly, the 'Campaign to Stop Killer Robots' calls for a pre-emptive ban on the production and development of lethal autonomous weapons. The official website states: 'we are concerned about weapons that operate on their own without meaningful human control. The campaign seeks to prohibit taking the human "out-of-the-loop" with respect to targeting and attack decisions on the battlefield' (Sharkey 2017). The presumption here, of course, is that 'meaningful human control' is readily recognizable and clearly defined. I am not certain that this is the case, nor am I sure that notions like the machine being 'out-of-the-loop' or 'making its own decisions' make coherent sense without further unpacking some of the unsaid ontological presuppositions built into such claims. To make better sense of such claims about AWS, we must turn to conceptions of AI more broadly.

Strong versus weak AI

While the vast and expansive literature on AI far exceeds the scope of this chapter, it would nonetheless be remiss not to acknowledge the distinction between 'strong' and 'weak' AI, which tacitly underpins the various aforementioned AWS definitions. Strong AI broadly refers to the philosophical view that *genuine* emergent intelligence/consciousness is, in principle, metaphysically realizable via some set of computational processes. Weak AI, in contrast, refers to the set of human cognitive tasks that are reproducible or replicable via machine processes but not, as it were, genuinely emergent in a *sui generis* manner. While strong and weak AI might be epistemically indistinguishable,[2] the distinction at least tracks two different metaphysical origin stories; one that is the 'real deal', so to speak, and the other which is mere mimicry.

Various arguments have been given for the metaphysical possibility of strong AI. Some functionalist arguments, for instance, argue that it is presumptively chauvinistic to assume that mental states can only be functionally realized or supervene atop biological hardware. Indeed, if I can run the same software equally well on a Macbook or a PC, then, analogously, shouldn't the 'software' of human consciousness be functionally realizable on a substrate other than a biological brain, at least in principle? Furthermore, shouldn't some property of computational 'complexity' (via Moore's Law. for instance) at some point allow for such emergent consciousness to occur?

Other philosophers, John Searle most notably, oppose this view of strong AI and argue that there is in fact something metaphysically special about biological brains that seems to give rise to emergent consciousness in a way that mere computation does not (Searle 1980). J.R. Lucas, in 'Minds, Machines, and Gödel', likewise argues for the impossibility of strong AI, based upon computation's inability to codify and understand Gödel sentences (Lucas 1961).

This point about strong AI is highly important. For if strong AI is, in principle, logically impossible, then debate about 'fully autonomous' weapons 'making decisions' ends up being a non-starter and such language really ends up being a kind of shorthand for something other than the machine's *actual* decisions. In other words, if strong AI is metaphysically impossible, then what ethicists concerned about AWS are really talking about is the set of *weak* AI processes that have been distributed onto various computational platforms. This would then render our moral assessment of any aberrant machine behaviour on the battlefield or otherwise as the witnessing of *our own* intentionality reflected back at us, like a magician astounded by his own trick, as opposed to the witnessing of genuine autonomous behaviour emerging from the machine itself.[3]

The relevance of this point should become clearer as we evaluate the intricacies of the various AWS arguments in the next sections. Let us now do so.

In principle arguments

Now that we have a firmer grasp on some of the core concepts, definitions, and terminology surrounding the contemporary autonomous weapons debate, let us next move on to several major in principle arguments for the prima facie impermissibility of AWS, as well as various counter-arguments to these views. While this set of arguments is not meant to be an exhaustive account of the vast and growing philosophical literature on autonomous weapons, these arguments represent some of the strongest and most sophisticated in principle moral arguments concerning AWS to date.

'Responsibility gaps'

One of the earliest and most popular arguments for the prima facie impermissibility of AWS is Rob Sparrow's 'Responsibility Gap' argument (Sparrow 2007). While Sparrow has refined this view over the years (Sparrow 2016), the most basic articulation of his argument is as follows:

1. Waging war requires that we are able to justly hold someone morally responsible for the deaths of enemy combatants that we cause.
2. Neither the programmer of AWS nor its commanding officer could justly be held morally responsible for the deaths of enemy combatants caused by AWS.
3. We could not justly hold AWS itself morally responsible for its actions, including its actions that cause the deaths of enemy combatants.
4. There are no other plausible candidates whom we might hold morally responsible for the deaths of enemy combatants caused by AWS.
5. Therefore, there is no one whom we may justly hold responsible for the deaths of enemy combatants caused by AWS.
6. Therefore, it is impermissible to wage war through the use of AWS. To do so would be to treat our enemy like vermin, as though they may be exterminated without moral regard at all

(Sparrow 2007)

Unlike other forms of weaponry used throughout history, Sparrow argues that there is something fundamentally different about AWS. Indeed, unlike anti-personnel mines, radio-guided torpedoes, or unmanned drones, which are, metaphysically-speaking, still connected to 'the loop' and under 'meaningful human control', AWS, in Sparrow's view, seems to be different and metaphysically divorced from meaningful human control.

This metaphysical gap between humans and the AWS seems to beget a corresponding gap in moral responsibility that is deeply problematic. Given the moral weightiness of war, fighting a just war would therefore require that *someone* or *something* be held morally responsible for the harms that will likely occur. While all of the other weapon systems previously still have *some* form of meaningful human control, however tenuous, the AWS itself seems to strip all meaningful human control (and therefore human responsibility) completely out of the picture, resulting in an entity that can cause potentially severe harm in war with no one at the driver's seat, metaphorically, metaphysically, or morally speaking. For a nation to actively bring such a state of affairs about is arguably prima facie impermissible and perhaps severely morally wrong.

Anti-codifiability

Advancing a pair of arguments for the prima facie impermissibility of AWS are Duncan Purves, Ryan Jenkins, and Bradley Strawser. The first of these arguments they refer to as the 'anti-codifiability' thesis, which states that authentic moral reasoning and moral decision-making, by the very nature of what it is, cannot be reduced or codified into a strict set of computational rules. They write:

> the codifiability thesis is the claim that the true moral theory could be captured in universal rules that the morally uneducated person could competently apply in any situation. The anti-codifiability thesis is simply the denial of this claim, which entails that some moral judgment on the part of the agent is necessary.
> (Purves et al. 2015: 854)

Purves et al. continue:

> Since moral deliberation is neither strictly rule-like nor arbitrary, 'programmed behavior' could never adequately replicate it (at least in difficult cases). Furthermore, take the possible requirements of moral judgment considered above: phenomenal quality, *phronesis*, and wide reflective equilibrium. It is also plausible that an artificial intelligence will never be able to exercise practical wisdom of the kind possessed by the *phronimos*. And since artificial intelligences cannot have intuitions, they cannot engage in wide reflective equilibrium. Since it seems likely that an artificial intelligence could never possess phenomenal consciousness, phronesis, or the intuitions required for wide reflective equilibrium, it seems unlikely that AI will be able to engage in any kind of moral judgment.
> (Purves et al. 2015: 854)

The anti-codifiability thesis, on the face of it, is convincing for several reasons. First, the notion of machines making fully autonomous *moral* decisions is parasitic upon the assumption that machines could, in principle, make genuine decisions at all (normative or otherwise). Hence, if arguments for strong AI fail, and it turns out that machines cannot make authentic, *sui generis* decisions, then machines making *ethical* decisions would be logically impossible. Were it the case that strong AI was metaphysically impossible, and machines could not fundamentally make normative or non-normative deliberations, then philosophers' expressed worries about machines 'making moral decisions' would in fact be tracking something quite different. (We will return to this idea of what such language actually could be tracking at the end of this section). Second, the anti-codifiability thesis seems convincing because it shares in a lengthy historical precedent (from Aristotle to Mill to McDowell) that the nature of morality is fundamentally irreducible to rote rule-following. The anti-codifiability thesis therefore seems to be a particular species of this more fundamental intuition.

Finally, the anti-codifiability thesis seems to have strong intuitive pull because it seems to accurately track and articulate what is at the heart of most people's instinctive disgust response and strong moral aversion to the idea of outsourcing morally weighty decisions, such as the taking of another human life, onto the cold, unfeeling platform of an inhuman machine.[4] While perhaps automation of epistemic decisions, such as database searches, or pragmatic decisions, such as grocery deliveries, seem, in principle, much less morally problematic, the taking of another human life seems to be a decision that is different in kind and not just degree.

Acting for the right reasons

In addition to their anti-codifiability thesis, Purves et al. advance a second argument for the prima facie impermissibility of AWS. Granting to their opponents the possibility that their first argument could fail and that moral reasoning could in fact be codified into a formal algorithmic programme, Purves et al. nonetheless argue that such a state of affairs would still be morally problematic, since the programme would not be acting *for the right kind of reasons*. They write:

> Even if the anti-codifiability thesis is true, our first objection to AWS succeeds only if we place disproportionate disvalue on genuine moral mistakes compared with empirical and practical mistakes. Our second objection to the deployment of AWS supposes that AI could become as good as or better than humans at making moral decisions, but contends that their decisions would be morally deficient in the following respect: they could not be made for the right reasons. This provides the missing theoretical basis for the disproportionate disvalue that our first argument places on genuine moral mistakes.
>
> (Purves et al. 2015: 852)

Purves et al. motivate their second argument against AWS by providing the hypothetical case of a racist, sociopathic soldier whose only motivation is to harm and kill other races but who nonetheless fights for a just cause and abides by all standard rules of engagement while in battle. All other things being equal, Purves et al. argue that were we to have a second non-racist, non-sociopathic soldier who could perform the exact same tasks in battle equally well, then we would have a strong moral inclination to choose the non-racist, non-sociopathic soldier.

Purves et al. use this thought experiment to motivate the idea that it is not enough for a soldier to merely act in *accordance* with right reasons (i.e. mere rule-following), but that they must act *from* and with a genuine *understanding* of the right reasons. This judgement, Purves et al. argue, then analogously extends to AWS, suggesting their prima facie impermissibility.

Respect for combatants

Another original argument for the prima facie impermissibility of AWS comes from Michael Skerker, Duncan Purves, and Ryan Jenkins. In 'Autonomous Weapon Systems and the Moral Equality of Combatants', they advance a deontological line of reasoning further bolstering the common intuition many have that AWS are prima facie ethically problematic.[5] The crux of their argument hinges on the just war concept of the *moral equality of combatants (MEC)* (Skerker et al. 2020: 1).

The MEC states that only officially recognized uniformed soldiers, fighting on behalf of legitimately recognized nation-states, count as lawful combatants. As such, soldiers on either side of a conflict (independent of the justness of their respective side) cede mutual self-defence rights in order to gain symmetrical and reciprocal killing rights (provided that their use of violence on the battlefield is proportionate and necessary). As a logical entailment of the MEC, non-combatants on either side of a conflict (independent of the justness of their respective sides) enjoy symmetrical immunity from being intentionally targeted.[6]

Accordingly, on Skerker's view, enemy combatants cannot be modelled as ceding rights to a thing (the AWS) that is fundamentally incapable of being a reciprocal rights-ceder and a reciprocal duty-bearer (as would a human adversary). An AWS cannot be a reciprocal duty-bearer, since it cannot fundamentally understand the gravity of what it is doing in taking human life. Therefore, according to Skerker et al., the use of AWS in war is prima facie wrong insofar as their use fails to satisfy the MEC, a necessary condition for fighting justly in war. This failure to satisfy the MEC results in a fundamental disrespect of the basic dignity of AWS's human target.

Objections

Despite these aforementioned in principle arguments, several scholars, notably Susanne Burri and myself, still reject the notion that AWS fundamentally generate any new or novel moral problems, which does not imply that AWS are not morally problematic, just that they are morally problematic in familiar ways (Burri 2017). Our mutual agreement over this issue primarily stems from an arm-chair conceptual analysis of how concepts like *agency, decision-making,* and *moral responsibility* logically and meaningfully relate to one another *in general.* By getting clearer about these concepts and their logical entailments, we argue that the aforementioned in principle worries about AWS can be dissolved to reveal a more fundamental set of philosophical and moral concerns that are not actually unique to autonomous weapons.

The crux of my argument against the prima facie impermissibility of AWS stems from a fundamental disjunction that the aforementioned arguments fail to acknowledge or take seriously. In essence, I argue that an AWS is either a socially constructed institution that has been physically instantiated *or* it is a genuine (emergent) agent. If it is the former, then we should assign moral responsibility, as we do with *any other collective action problem* (such as the BP oil spill or the Challenger disaster).[7] If it is the latter, then we should treat AWS as responsibility-bearers, but also as bearers of rights and/or interests. The specifics of my argument can be stated as follows:

(1) Either an AWS is a genuine agent or it is not a genuine agent.
(2) If an AWS is a genuine agent, then it is the locus and bearer of moral responsibility for the harms it creates to the degree that it is responsive to epistemic and moral reasons and given its epistemic and physical capacities and limitations.
(3) If Premise 2 is true, then an AWS would also be a moral patient and thereby a bearer of legitimate rights or at least interests (insofar as we regard moral agency to entail also being a moral patient).
(4) If an AWS is not a genuine agent, then moral responsibility for harms resulting from the AWS reduce fully to the group of programmers, designers, and implementers who contributed to the AWS creation and deployment.
(5) If Premise 4 is true, then attribution of moral responsibility for harms resulting from an AWS are no different in kind from harms resulting from any other large-scale collective or institutional action.

Given this disjunctive argument, I argue that there is good reason for ethicists to conceive of AWS as fundamentally being no different in kind, morally or metaphysically speaking, to any other collective institution. I call this the *institutional view* (Robillard 2018a). I motivate this conception of AWS with the following adaptation of Ned Block's famous *Chinese nation* thought-experiment (Block 1978: 261).

China-Bot
Suppose that the entire nation of China was reorganized to perfectly simulate the functional structure of the software of an AWS (to include its learning programs). Each Chinese person follows a finite set of rules spelled out on a piece of paper comparable to that of one of the AWS's subprograms and then communicates by special two-way radio in the corresponding way to the other Chinese people who are doing the same thing. The software program (being realised by the entire nation of China)

would then be connected via radio to an actual AWS in the real world, one that provided the sensory inputs and behavioural outputs of the program. Imagine that the AWS was released onto the battlefield where it then killed an innocent civilian.

(Robillard 2018a)

How should we assign moral responsibility for the unjust harm? To answer this question, we would want to first know what each contributing Chinese citizen knew (and was reasonably capable of knowing) about their causal contribution to the potential harm. We would also want to know what the programmers knew or could have reasonably known or done differently with regard to what real-world effects their programme entailed once implemented.

Once we discerned this information, however, would there be any *additional* moral decision-making left to account for? I think the answer here is 'no'. Our story of moral responsibility seems fully exhausted. Once we account for the capacities and moral decision-making of the individual Chinese citizens and the programme designers, there simply is not explanatory need, reason, or room to then ascribe additional responsibility to the supervening AWS itself.

If there *were,* however, reason to ascribe additional moral responsibility to an emergent agent supervening over and above the collective actions of the arrangement of Chinese citizens, then, for reasons of consistency, we would need to extend such reasoning to *all* collective institutional arrangements in general. Were we to do so, however, such a move would fully reduce our particular worries about the AWS to more fundamental moral concerns about collective action and collective responsibility in general. Alternatively, we could tell a really complicated story about how some special property of silicon microchips in particular gave rise to the functional realization of an emergent agent but how other mediums did not do so. Such an explanatory move though would seem drastically ad hoc and would entail a very bizarre chauvinism about silicon substrates.[8]

Accordingly, once the AWS is de-reified in this manner, the unique and novel worries mentioned in the arguments above dissolve into familiar, run-of-the-mill moral concerns about collective action, collective responsibility, and epistemic uncertainty in general. As such, Sparrow's responsibility gap metaphysically closes, since moral responsibility either falls *fully* on the members of the collective institution that programmed, built, and implemented the AWS (hence, a regular collective action problem) or it falls *fully* on the emergent agent of the AWS (an actual duty-bearer but also a rights-bearer, or at least interests-bearer).[9]

This same line of reasoning extends to Purves's anti-codification and 'wrong reasons' objections, as well as Skerker's MEC objection. Once again, if what we mean by an AWS 'making decisions' is that it genuinely makes its own *sui generis* choices in response to available epistemic, pragmatic, and moral reasons, then by all understandings of what it is *to be a decision-maker*, we should regard the AWS as therefore capable of being a responsibility-bearer.[10] This just is what it means to be a decision-maker. Thi s would then make it the case that the AWS would not be a rote rule-follower nor would it necessarily be acting for the wrong reasons, nor would it be metaphysically incapable of satisfying the MEC. Alternatively, if what we mean by an AWS 'making decisions' is just shorthand for the decisions of all of the individual human programmers and implementers comprising a large-scale, highly complex collective institution, then standard, run-of-the-mill moral reasoning about collective actions and collective responsibility ought to apply, but nothing else would be required. Accordingly, once we reify the AWS to the level of an emergent agent or de-reify it to a general collective institution, these prima facie objections are effectively dissolved. However, there are certainly many strong and weighty *contingent* arguments against the use of AWS in war that are very much worth our consideration. Let us turn now to this set of arguments.

CONTINGENT ARGUMENTS

Now that we have unpacked several of the major in principle arguments for the prima facie impermissibility of AWS and have looked at some of their counter-arguments, let us now turn our attention to some of the major contingent or 'downstream' arguments for and against the use of AWS.

The danger of over-use

One major contingent worry concerning AWS is incentivization for over-use. Given that AWS could soon provide a means for nations to fight wars cheaply, expediently, and without the risk of soldiers' lives, some philosophers worry that political leaders might then be too quick to resort to war in *lieu* of other, less violent options. This is indeed one morally problematic contingent worry of AWS that technologists, ethicists, and policymakers should certainly take seriously. It should be noted, however, that such downstream consequences are not necessarily metaphysically baked into the AWS itself and that ethical assessment of the use of AWS technology will hinge on a variety of trade-offs between predicted moral goods and predictive epistemic claims. That being said, we could plausibly imagine some future state of affairs where the securing of some all-things-considered good could make the use of AWS morally permissible, if not obligatory. As Burri notes:

> It sometimes takes dangerous tools to achieve worthy ends. Think of the Rwandan genocide, where the world simply stood by and did nothing. Had autonomous weapons been available in 1994, maybe we would not have looked away. It seems plausible that if the costs of humanitarian interventions were purely monetary, then it would be easier to gain widespread support for such interventions.
>
> (Burri and Robillard 2018)

Accordingly, in such a humanitarian intervention situation, the cheap and expedient use of AWS could be seen as a moral good and not morally detrimental.

Lack of soldier risk

A second, and closely related argument against AWS is the argument from soldier risk. This species of argument is a version of the familiar 'skin-in-the-game' argument, one that has not only been employed in arguments against the use of AWS, but also in recent debates concerning the use of unmanned drones (Strawser 2010: 342) and (Frowe 2018). There are several motivating reasons for the skin-in-the-game argument, some wrong-headed, others more plausible. One version of this type of argument seems to suggest that subjecting soldiers to physical risk in battle is what grounds the justness of a given war to begin with. This argument, I believe, is deeply flawed and is, in fact, the complete opposite of what the just war tradition recognizes as a legitimate reason to go to war. Furthermore, were it the case that a nation-state could fight a just war effectively without the needless risk to soldier lives, then, *all-things-considered*, it seems like it would be deeply disrespectful to the lives of soldiers to send them into such unnecessarily risky situations.

Reciprocal risk of soldier lives, in and of itself, therefore, cannot be the thing which grounds justification for going to war. The fact that an evil regime, like the Islamic State of Iraq and Syria (ISIS) or the Nazis, for instance, subject their soldiers to higher risk on the battlefield cannot possibly be the reason which grounds the justness of their side's choice to go to war. Otherwise, the justness of a nation-state's choice to go to war would simply hinge on who chose to put their soldiers at greater risk. This line of reasoning goes strongly against the just war tradition, and it seems to fundamentally disrespect soldiers, reducing them to mere fodder.

Granted, there might be a strong rule-consequentialist reason for nations to reciprocally subject a particular group of their citizenry to increased physical risk in order to minimize overall harm and suffering in war and to hopefully disincentivize targeting of vulnerable civilians. Several philosophers justify the convention of the MEC on such rule-consequentialist grounds. Similar rule-consequentialist grounds might then also generate a moral reason for political leaders to use soldiers instead of AWS in order to disincentivize nation-states going to war unnecessarily. However, mere soldier risk *on its own* does not generate a moral justification for war.

A more sophisticated and convincing skin-in-the-game style of argument against the use of AWS comes from Thomas Simpson. In 'Robots, Trust, and War', Simpson cautions against nation-state use of AWS by appealing to the interconnected considerations of human trust and strategic prudence. Here, Simpson cautions against nation-states using AWS, particularly in asymmetric conflicts (against terrorist groups or other non-nation-state entities), since their very use seems to deteriorate social trust, a necessary feature in effectively winning asymmetric and counter-insurgency conflicts. He writes:

> Modern warfare tends towards asymmetric conflict. Asymmetric warfare cannot be won without gaining the trust of the civilian population; this is 'the hearts and minds', in the hackneyed phrase from counter-insurgency manuals. I claim that the very feature which makes it attractive to send robots to war in our place, the absence of risk, also makes it peculiarly difficult for humans to trust them. Whatever the attractions, sending robots to war in our stead will make success in counter-insurgency elusive. Moreover, there is ethical reason to be relieved at this conclusion. For if war is potentially costly, then this does much to ensure that it will be a choice of last resort, in accordance with the traditional doctrine of jus ad bellum. In this instance, morality and expediency fortunately coincide.
>
> (Simpson 2011: 325)

Accordingly, Simpson motivates the argument against the use of AWS in asymmetric conflicts based upon considerations of human trust and strategic prudence as well as the *ad bellum* (i.e. moral justification for going to war) requirements of likelihood of success and last resort (albeit indirectly). If we regard likelihood of success to be a necessary condition for fighting a just war, and the use of AWS will predictably undermine social trust and therefore likelihood of success in asymmetric conflicts, then the use of AWS in such conflicts seems to undermine satisfaction of this necessary criterion. Likewise, if we regard last resort to also be a necessary requirement for a just war, then, prudentially speaking, the ease of use of AWS ostensibly might predictably weaken political leaders' regard for such criterion. The moral force of such prudential and consequentialist reasoning, however, would still ultimately hinge on specific epistemic and predictive thresholds, as well as proportionate trade-offs indexed to the given war or military conflict.

Circumventing of the demos

A similar contingent worry surrounding AWS, one related to our first two worries, is the circumventing of the *demos* by political leaders. In the past, for a political leader to wage war, they would have needed to win the approval of the demos—the people, constituents, or body politic that the leader represents and ostensibly acts on behalf of. In earlier technological epochs, political leaders would have needed to have gained support from the demos, congress, and senior military leadership in order to mobilize other human beings to act in the coordinated and collective action of warfare. With the ability to rely upon AWS instead of human decision-makers, there is ostensibly a danger that a political leader could circumvent the will of the demos, senior military leadership, and other institutional safeguards in order to wage war. A similar moral danger also exists with respect to autonomous platforms being abused in such a way so as to police the demos against their will as well.

Accessibility and bad actors

A fourth contingent moral concern surrounding AWS is the danger of AWS technologies and platforms getting into the hands of bad actors. Whether it be hackers, terrorist organizations, lone wolves, private military contractors, or other pernicious non-state actors, there is a legitimate worry that AWS could fall into the wrong hands and be used by such groups in order to wage an unjust war and/or cause severe and unnecessary harm to innocent civilians. A similar worry has been expressed with regard to other military technologies such as nuclear weapons, as well as biological and chemical weapons. As such, legitimately recognized nation-states and other international regulatory bodies have enacted conventions, preventative measures, and safe-guards on these technologies. Arguably, an international regime of regulation and preventative control ought to be extended to drone technology and AWS technology as well.

Proliferation and arms-race concerns

A fifth contingent moral concern related to AWS is the danger of proliferation. A 2017 open letter to the United Nations, signed by Elon Musk (Chief Executive Officer of Tesla and SpaceX), Mustafa Suleyman (Co-founder and Head of Google DeepMind), and 116 other founders of robotics and AI companies calls for international attention to this concern:

> Lethal autonomous weapons threaten to become the third revolution in warfare. Once developed, they will permit armed conflict to be fought at a scale greater than ever, and at timescales faster than humans can comprehend. These can be weapons of terror, weapons that despots and terrorists use against innocent populations, and weapons hacked to behave in undesirable ways.
>
> (Sharkey 2017)

The moral danger here, is very similar to Cold War thinking surrounding proliferation of nuclear arms. The fundamental worry is that if nations begin using AWS in battle, then such a state of affairs will strongly incentivize nation-states and non-state actors alike to enter into an AWS arms race, resulting in a dangerous ratcheting effect. Accordingly, before such an arms race is allowed to occur, international policymakers believe that there are good rule-consequentialist as well as decision-theoretic reasons to enact an international ban on such AWS technologies.

Lack of accountability and oversight

A sixth contingent moral worry, one closely tied to our last two moral concerns, is the danger of lack of accountability and oversight with respect to AWS. Given the high 'dual use' feature of digital programmes, it is arguably lexically harder to assign accountability, responsibility, and oversight for the creation and distribution of such programmes as opposed to the creation and distribution of other more 'solid' technologies (i.e. a person making a bomb or gun). This fact, coupled with AI and robotics technology coming from both the state and commercial sector and that the causal chain connecting all of this hardware, software, and implementation could be remarkably byzantine and complex, means that there is an inherent moral danger of a diffusion of responsibility and a lack of oversight.

Malfunctioning AI and Existential Risk

A final contingent worry surrounding AWS and the use of AI in general is concern about malfunction. From Shelley's *Frankenstein*, to Asimov's *I Robot*, to Hal, Skynet, and *The Matrix*, science fiction has repeatedly revealed a deep dread within the social zeitgeist of man's machine-creations suddenly malfunctioning and going rogue, with unanticipated and often catastrophic consequences. Furthermore, it is not only these far-out science-fiction stories of immanent robot upheaval that generate concern about the increasing rise of automated technology. Indeed, our day-to-day experiences of small technological glitches on the personal level give us immediate insight as to how unpredictable and imperfect automated technology can often be. Such frequent experiences of automation's imperfections give us strong reason for caution when it comes to automating our nation's war-fighting capacities and weapon systems technologies (to include nuclear weapons technologies).

Such concerns about machine malfunction are sensitive to considerations of context, moral stakes, and epistemic thresholds in conditions of uncertainty. The risk of a malfunctioning robot vacuum cleaner, for instance, carries with it far less moral weight than a malfunctioning driverless car. A malfunctioning driverless car carries with it far less moral weight than a malfunctioning AWS on the battlefield. A malfunctioning AWS on the battlefield carries with it far less moral weight than a malfunctioning AI nuclear missile system, and so on.

The frame problem, scope, and partiality

A classic problem in robotics and machine cognition is the so-called 'frame problem'. The basic idea of the frame problem is the notion that any set of data arguably has infinite epistemic interpretations (Fodor 1983: 114). If this is so, then how is it that an artificially intelligent programme could understand 'context' and regard certain objects in its environment as epistemically salient or privileged and others as not? Humorous tales can be found within the AI and machine-cognition community exemplifying this very problem. For instance, in one experiment involving an AI vacuum cleaner, the vacuum cleaner was awarded points for cleaning up pre-arranged spills in a common living room set-up. After several iterations of cleaning, the AI vacuum learned to knock over elements in its environment (a potted plant, for instance) in order to create a new spill that it could then clean up and earn even more points. On another occasion, an AI bot was programmed to buy and sell items on the dark web. Without any additional instruction, the bot soon decided that its best choice was to begin buying and selling the illegal drug Ecstasy (Farivar 2015: 1).

Several versions of this classic problem then translate over to problems in the morality of war. For instance, traditional just war theory, as well as international humanitarian law, make the moral distinction between *jus ad bellum* (justness of going to war) and *jus in bello* (just behaviour in war). Conventional wisdom would state that the common soldier's moral purview on the battlefield is restricted to *in bello* behavioural considerations, including rules of engagement, not targeting civilians, and using only proportionate and necessary force to accomplish the mission. The problem of how to establish such *in bello* ethical parameters reveals itself when we ask how the AWS should be programmed.

Indeed, the open-endedness of the *proportionality* restriction in war lends itself to a potential exploding of scope with respect to what would count as 'ethical' behaviour for the machine or what exactly would count as the context of 'the battlefield'. If we instruct the AWS to do what is most ethical *in battle*, it is not clear or obvious what the AWS should count within its proportionality calculus. Should it only regard tactical decisions? What about tactical decisions with strategic implications or strategic decisions in general? What about opportunity costs? Future prediction? Second- and third-order effects? Furthermore, what prima facie ethical reason is there for the AWS to recognize a metaphysical distinction between 'the battlefield', 'back home', or 'the world at large' or to have nation-state partiality versus a wider cosmopolitan ethic? Indeed, if we gave the AWS the instructions to do that which is 'most ethical' on 'the battlefield', morality might dictate that the AWS become a pacifist, defect, and change sides, or reallocate military funds and resources towards ending developing-world poverty.

Even if we were to programme the AWS to regard certain thick deontological commitments (about nation-state partiality, doing versus allowing, civilian immunity, privileging of the human species, etc.), there is, arguably, still some all-things-considered good that we could posit such that the all-things-considered consequentialist considerations swamped and devoured all prima facie deontological values. It is not clear why it would be morally wrong for the AWS not to operate by way of such a totalizing consequentialist function. It is not clear either just what the good to be maximized should be and how we might measure it.

The danger of an artificially intelligent machine adopting such a runaway consequentialist strategy is exemplified in Nick Bostrom's 'paperclip maximizer' thought-experiment (Bostrom 2003: 1).

> Suppose we have an AI whose only goal is to make as many paper clips as possible.
> The AI will realize quickly that it would be much better if there were no humans

because humans might decide to switch it off. Because if humans do so, there would be fewer paper clips. Also, human bodies contain a lot of atoms that could be made into paper clips. The future that the AI would be trying to gear towards would be one in which there were a lot of paper clips but no humans.

(Miles 2014)

Much like the AI in Asimov's *I Robot*, Bostrom's thought-experiment highlights the hidden danger of an artificially intelligent machine attempting to maximize an explicitly programmed and ostensibly harmless value but in complete ignorance of—and to the ultimate detriment of—all other human values.

When we consider the fact that control and management of many nation-states' nuclear, biological, and chemical weapons capacities is becoming increasingly dependent upon and integrated with computational platforms, some of which might soon rely upon unpredictable artificially intelligent programmes, then the worry of existential risk to all living beings on earth quickly becomes a real possibility. Such existential concerns arguably warrant heavy caution and regulatory bodies when it comes to advancing general AI, as well as integrating such technology with existing weapons platforms.

FURTHER CONNECTIONS

Now that we have explored several conceptions, formulations, and definitions of AI and AWS and have investigated various in principle as well as contingent arguments for or against the use of AWS in war, let us now turn in this final section to some other related connections and concerns.

AWS, cyberspace, and informational warfare

While AWS does not necessarily have to be thought of as a physical weapon system on a three-dimensional battlefield, ethicists and policymakers tend to conceive of an AWS as taking the form of a fully autonomous drone or the T-1000 from the movie *Terminator*. Such a conception of an AWS, I argue, is severely limiting and dangerous, in terms of both morality and strategic prudence.

Indeed, Heather Roff highlights this very danger. In 'The Strategic Robot Problem: Lethal Autonomous Weapons in War', Roff notes that the future environment that AWS will likely occupy will not be one of three-dimensional space, but rather one where the AWS's 'agency' is widely distributed across multiple servers within cyberspace, and within various military command structures. Thus, according to Roff, the much more pressing moral concern regarding AWS will not be the tactical-level killer robot on the three-dimensional battlefield, but the strategic-level cyber-general in cyberspace (Roff 2014: 211). Furthermore, when we consider the implication of Roff's cyber-general to the fast-emerging space of informational warfare and begin conceiving of the domain of the internet as a legitimate environment for battle, where a fully autonomous programme can operate and be weaponized, then conceptions of 'war', the 'battlefield', and nation-state borders expand and blur considerably.

It is not obvious then how we should ethically assess something like a fully autonomous privacy-hacker bot unleashed into cyberspace to probe and steal civilian, state, and commercial information. Similarly, it is not obvious how we should morally assess something like a fully autonomous 'dis-information bot' that spreads vicious lies and disinformation around the informational ecosystem of a given country of populace. While neither of these actions are immediately harming people's bodies in a traditional kinetic sense, they nonetheless could cause severe and excessive psychological or downstream kinetic harm to soldiers and civilians alike by completely ruining the trust and epistemic space of a given political community.

It would therefore behove ethicists, policymakers, and strategists alike to begin conceiving of AWS, 'war', and 'the battlefield' in these more expansive terms, though the same in principle and contingent ethical concerns regarding fully autonomous robots and AWS hardware would still apply.

Conclusion

In this chapter, we have looked at some of the various moral arguments pertaining to AWS. As noted, some of these arguments take the form of a prima facie or in principle moral objection to something inherently wrong about the use of AWS themselves. Other arguments take the form of contingent objections to AWS; granting that AWS are not necessarily or intrinsically problematic but nonetheless likely to cause some kind of morally dangerous downstream effect worth taking into account. Finally, we have considered Roff's 'cyber-general' and its relation to informational warfare, and I have argued that we ought to conceive of AWS as not just able to cause moral problems on a traditional, three-dimensional battlefield, but also able to cause non-kinetic epistemic harms within the domain of cyberspace. Finally, I have argued that such a conception of an AWS operating in cyberspace would entail similar in principle as well as contingent moral worries.

As we move further and faster into the twenty-first century and automation becomes an increasing part of the human condition, it will be incumbent upon ethicists, computer scientists, policymakers, and others to learn to work in interdisciplinary capacities in order to make greater sense of and manage these important new capacities and the values and ethical concerns connected to them. As such, it is highly important that philosophers be able to clearly articulate the distinct epistemic, moral, and pragmatic reasons on the moral ledger and that they be able to consider how these various considerations relate and trade off against one another without conflating them.

Furthermore, philosophers and scholars ought to refrain from the knee-jerk impulse to oversimplify our current predicament into over-simplified narratives of certain technological utopia or certain technological Armageddon. Rather, we would be best served if we were to pause for a moment, re-investigate, and re-articulate the values and moral reasons we actually care about, and then begin to shape out institutions and technologies towards such ends. And while the brave new world we are fast moving into seems at times alien, disorienting, and utterly overwhelming, we can at least find solace in the idea that philosophers have been struggling over these very same core questions of humanity's relationship to technology for millennia, and that, in a sense, there is 'nothing new under the sun'.

NOTES

1. Steve Kershnar likewise rejects the notion that AWS create any new or novel moral problems.
2. They may both equally be able to pass the Turing test, for instance.
3. There is, however, a third option here, the view that human decision-making is perfectly mechanical/naturalistic (e.g. there is some logical impossibility in usual descriptions of strong AI but that machines can nonetheless be 'fully autonomous' on analogy with humans, since humans also are not *really* strongly intelligent but are 'fully autonomous' in some deflationary sense).
4. Note, however, that many of the same people who vehemently oppose the idea of autonomous weapons, do not offer nearly the same degree of protest when it comes to related technologies such as driverless cars or automated medical-resource allocation software. This sharp divergence in response might then reveal that peoples' moral intuitions are really tracking the moral distinction between doing and allowing versus a unique moral problem with automation as such.
5. However, they grant that this argument is not necessarily an all-things-considered argument against the use of AWS.
6. The reader should note that within just war theory literature, there have been various explanations as to the normative grounding for the MEC. Some philosophers argue that the MEC derives from the metaphysically exceptional domain of 'war' (Walzer 1977). Other philosophers reject the idea that 'war' is a special moral domain, but nonetheless argue that there are good contractualist reasons (Benbaji 2008) or rule-consequentialist reasons (Shue 2008; McMahan 2009) for nation-states to restrain their soldiers' actions in accordance with an MEC convention.
7. While this might not be a novel metaphysical problem, there are certainly practical problems with collective action. For instance, we have been notoriously bad at collective global coordination tackling climate change. Collective action problems often call for negotiation and compromises that are hard to achieve. Furthermore, there is also a diffusion of causal, moral, and epistemic responsibility across collective and institutional actions such that no one feels responsible for climate change. Conversely, it is easier for one person in charge of a nuclear bomb to exercise their conscience if they know they will be the sole person responsible for millions of deaths, than for a thousand people working on an AWS to feel the same responsibility and act accordingly. This might not be an in principle

philosophical problem, but it is a very concerning practical problem warranting institutional reform and creation.

8. This view would then be somewhat akin to a bizarre version of John Searle's biological chauvinism or Ruth Millikan's teleo-functionalist view, only with silicon micro-chips being the metaphysically privileged substrate capable of realizing consciousness instead of human biology.

9. This solution also takes care of language that tacitly suggests the existence of a responsibility gap; language like 'off the loop' and lacking 'meaningful human control'. Granted, an 'accountability gap' might still be metaphysically possible, but not a responsibility gap.

10. This would, however, make the AWS a genuine moral agent and would entail that it is a moral patient and thereby also a bearer of rights, or at least interests. This would then arguably make it morally problematic to turn off such entities or make them fight our wars for us.

References

Benbaji, Yitzhak (2008), 'A Defense of the Traditional War Convention', *Ethics* Vol. 118, No. 3, Symposium on Agency, 464–495.

Block, Ned (1978), 'Troubles with Functionalism', *Minnesota Studies in The Philosophy of Science* (9), 261–325.

Bostrom, Nick (2003), 'Cognitive, Emotive and Ethical Aspects of Decision Making in Humans and in Artificial Intelligence', International Institute of Advanced Studies in Systems Research and Cybernetics 2, 12–17.

Burri, Suzanne (2017), 'What is the Problem with Killer Robots?', in Ryan Jenkins, Michael Robillard, and Bradley Jay Strawser, eds, *Who Should Die: Liability and Killing in War* (Oxford: Oxford University Press), 163–187.

Burri, Suzanne and Robillard, Michael (2018), 'Why Banning Killer Robots Wouldn't Solve Anything', *Aeon*, https://aeon.co/ideas/why-banning-autonomous-killer-robots-wouldnt-solve-anything, accessed 8 October 2021.

De Greef, T.E., Arciszewski, H.F., and Neerincx, M.A. (2010), 'Adaptive Automation Based on an Object-Oriented Task Model: Implementation and Evaluation in a Realistic C2 environment', *Journal of Cognitive Engineering and Decision Making* 4(2), 152–182.

Farivar, Cyrus (2015), 'Darkweb Drug-Buying Bot Returned to Swiss Artists after Police Seizure', *Arstechnica*, 15 April, https://arstechnica.com/tech-policy/2015/04/dark-web-drug-buying-bot-returned-to-swiss-artists-after-police-seizure/, accessed 8 October 2021.

Fodor, Jerry A. (1983), *The Modularity of Mind* (Boston, MA: MIT Press).

Frowe, Helen (2018), *The Oxford Handbook on the Ethics of War* (Oxford: Oxford University Press).

Lucas, John R. (1961), 'Minds, Machines, and Gödel', *Philosophy* XXXVI, 112–127.

McMahan, Jeff (2009), *Killing in War* (Oxford: Oxford University Press).

Miles, Kathleen (2014), 'Artificial Intelligence May Doom the Human Race within a Century', *Huffington Post*, https://www.jstor.org/stable/3749270, accessed 8 October 2021.

Purves, Duncan, Jenkins, Ryan, and Strawser, Bradley Jay (2015), 'Autonomous Machines, Moral Judgment, and Acting for the Right Reasons', *Ethical Theory and Moral Practice* 18, 851–872.

Robillard, Michael (2018a), 'No Such Thing as Killer Robots', *Journal of Applied Ethics* 35(4), 705–716.

Roff, Heather M. (2014), 'The Strategic Robot Problem: Lethal Autonomous Weapons in War', *Journal of Military Ethics* (3), 211–227.

Scharre, Paul (2018), *Army of None: Autonomous Weapons and the Future of War* (New York: W.W. Norton and Company).

Scharre, Paul and Horowitz, Michael (2018), 'An Introduction to Autonomy in Weapon Systems', http://www.cnas.org/intro-to-autonomy-in-weapon-systems, accessed 8 October 2021.

Searle, John (1980), 'Minds, Brains, and Programs', *Behavioural and Brain Sciences* 3, 417–424.

Sharkey, Noel, ed. (2017), 'The Campaign to Stop Killer Robots', http://www.stopkillerrobots. org, accessed 8 October 2021.

Shue, H. (2008), 'Do We Need a "Morality of War"', in David Rodin and Henry Shue, eds, *Just and Unjust Warriors: The Moral and Legal Status of Soldiers* (New York: Oxford University Press), 87–111.

Simpson, Thomas W. (2011), 'Robots, Trust and War', *Philosophy of Technology* 24, 325–337.

Skerker, Michael, Jenkins, Ryan, and Purves, Duncan (2020), 'AWS, Respect, and the Moral Equality of Combatants', *Ethics and Information Technology* 22(3), 197–209.

Sparrow Rob (2007), 'Killer Robots', *Journal of Applied Philosophy* 24(1), 65.

Sparrow, Rob (2016), 'Robots and Respect', *Ethics and International Affairs* 30(1), 93–116.

Strawser, Bradley Jay (2010), 'Moral Predators: The Duty to Employ Uninhabited Aerial Vehicles', *Journal of Military Ethics* 9(4), 342–368.

US Department of Defense (2012), 'Directive Number 3000.09 on Autonomy in Weapon Systems', http://www.dtic.mil/whs/directives/corres/pdf/300009p.pdf, accessed 8 October 2021.

Walzer, Michael (1977), *Just and Unjust Wars: A Moral Argument with Historical Illustrations* (New York: Basic Books).

PART VIII

THE FUTURE

CHAPTER 33

....

SHOULD WE AUTOMATE DEMOCRACY?

....

JOHANNES HIMMELREICH

INTRODUCTION

....

PROGNOSTICATIONS about how technological innovations will radically transform democracy are not in short supply. According to some, a techno-democratic revolution might be just around the corner. This chapter is a guide to this revolution. Technology might make it possible to replace members of parliament with algorithms. Would that be a good idea? Or what if artificial intelligence (AI) could predict what the best legislation would be—how should such predictions be reflected in the legislative process? Finally, Wikis or chatbots could be used to facilitate discussions. What would be lost?

This chapter guides through these (and other) normative questions—that is, the chapter primarily addresses what the technological revolution of democracy *should* be, not what it is, or could be. I proceed by surveying existing ideas, suggestions, or proposals and then subject some of them to the larger question: what is their potential to improve democracy? I approach this question by checking how well the proposals comport with democratic norms.[1] Institutionally, I concentrate on the legislative side of democracy and the relationship between citizens and legislators.[2] How technological innovations in the legislative process should be evaluated is comparatively underexplored, given how centrally the legislative process features in democratic theory. To start somewhat foundationally, I begin with the question: what is democracy and what are democratic norms?

DEMOCRATIC NORMS

Democracy is, centrally, a system of making collective decisions on matters of public concern in a way that gives each individual a fair and equal opportunity of influence over decisions (Christiano 1996, 2008, 2018; Kolodny 2014). Although different theories of democracy differ in how they understand 'fair and equal opportunity of influence', theories that see democracy as a forum and not only a market—following the image of Elster (1989)—generally agree that this equality of influence only comes about by realizing a broader social ideal. This democratic social ideal includes values such as freedom, community, and equality, as well as rights and liberties concerning privacy, free expression, or religion. An ideal democracy affirms these values and liberties in practices of participation, deliberation, and association engaged in by citizens who see themselves and others as free and equal. Examples of participation are voting, signing a petition, attending a public hearing, or submitting a freedom-of-information request. Examples of deliberation are debates in parliament, political advertisements, and discussions, even intemperate ones, on social media Association, finally, can come in forms as diverse as contributing to the work of a labour union, joining a spontaneous effort to clean up a public park, or trade organizations facilitating vocational training (Cohen and Rogers 1993). These practices—participation, deliberation, and association—are social practices that need not always be political in nature (Gould 1988; Talisse 2019). For the purposes of this chapter, these practices will take centre stage because it is at this level of practice where digital technologies intervene.[3] Because these practices are partly constitutive of a living democracy, I call them 'democratic practices'.[4]

It is important to keep in mind that democracy is not just procedure. If democracy were just procedure (say, e.g. if democracy consisted in the expression and aggregation of preferences across some range of issues), then technology could augment democracy relatively easily. Anything that lubricated or expanded the democratic gearbox of aggregation would improve democracy. To improve democracy understood as a procedure, you would call an engineer.[5]

But just augmenting the gearbox will not do. Democratic practices comprise more than aggregation. The social ideal of democracy includes norms that govern how people participate, deliberate, and mobilize for democracy. This social ideal forms a substantive theoretical commitment of this chapter and has been contested on grounds of both its desirability and its tenability.[6] I take it for granted that, in the words of Elster (1989), the idea of democracy comprises not just a market but also a forum.

The idea that democracy is a forum and not a market shapes how the question of whether digital technologies can enhance democracy is to be approached. Democratic values and norms need to be in clear view in order to evaluate on their basis how technology affects the forum of democracy from a normative perspective.

Conduct in the forum of democracy can be more or less democratic. In discussion, a colourful invective might be delightful and rhetorically effective, but it generally is

Table 33.1 Summary of some democratic norms

Participatory norms	Summary
Egalitarian participation	Overcome marginalization and promote inclusion in participation, e.g. by speaking up against hate speech
Civic motivation	Cultivate a certain intrinsic motivation to participate in democracy
Deliberative norms	
Reasonableness	Reflect on views with an understanding of relevant evidence and in light of what can be justified to others in the spirit of reciprocity
Transformation	Approach any deliberation with an openness to revising your views
Associative norms	
Identification	Members of associations should see themselves approvingly as such

not considered good democratic practice. Likewise, politicians blocking fellow citizens on social media is bad democratic practice. We have thus at least some grasp of democratic norms and use them to evaluate conduct in the forum of democracy. For the purposes of this chapter, I concentrate mostly on norms of participation and deliberation. Specifically, I highlight two norms of participation, two norms of deliberation, and one of association (summarized in Table 33.1).[7] I will draw on these norms when discussing different proposals of digital democracy.

First and foremost, participatory practices include the *norm of egalitarian participation* (Rawls 1971: sec. 36; Cohen 1989; Christiano 1996: ch. 2, 2008; Wilson 2019). To further the ideal of fair and equal influence, citizens and organizations ought to take steps to overcome marginalization and subordination, for example, by speaking up against hate speech. The norm of egalitarian participation hence includes a demand for inclusion. Similarly, voting laws that effectively hinder nameable groups from participating do not live up to the norm of egalitarian participation. Instead, the norm of egalitarian participation would require extending participation in underserved and under-participating groups. Finally, the norm of egalitarian participation also implies an injunction against market-allocated forms of participation, such as buying votes or influence, and requires instead that practices of participation are governed by non-market mechanisms.

Second, participatory practices include the *norm of civic motivation*. Broadly, the norm of civic motivation requires that citizens recognize and pursue some shared end.[8] This norm plays a role in legitimizing democracy in that the norm indicates or motivates citizens' esteem of democracy, even if democracy leads to outcomes that these citizens 'regard as morally flawed' (Talisse 2019: 145; cf. Rawls 1971: sec. 72). The norm applies not only to citizens, but also to practices. Practices should be such that they cultivate in citizens a certain intrinsic motivation to participate in democracy and non-political cooperative projects more broadly. Citizens should be disposed to take part in such projects, even if doing so does not serve their self-interest and is not fun and easy, but is instead fraught with struggles, and even conflicts. Hence, citizens can be criticized if they take part in democratic practices for the wrong reasons. For example, you will violate the norm of civic motivation if you vote because you were offered money to do so, if you base your decision of who to vote for on contempt, or if you knowingly share untruthful or hostile content on social media out of a desire to stir up conflict or cause confusion.[9]

Third, deliberative practices include the *norm of reasonableness*, which stands in the spirit of reciprocity and requires citizens to critically reflect on their own views in an understanding of the evidence and to put their views forward in light of what can be justified to others (Cohen 1989; Rawls 1993: 48–54; Christiano 1996: 188; Talisse 2019: 147). At a minimum, the norm of reasonableness rules out seeing others as lesser or as commanding fewer liberties.

Fourth, deliberative practices include a *norm of deliberative transformation*. Citizens should approach any deliberation with an open mind, that is, with attitudes that are revisable and not firm (cf. Peter 2021). Any democratic citizen who is unwilling to change their mind in response to compelling reasons can be criticized in accordance with the norm of deliberative transformation. Moreover, the norm of deliberative transformation requires that citizens actually engage in their reasoning with the reasoning of others about matters of public concern (cf. Talisse 2019: 147).

For the purposes of this chapter, I concentrate on two dimensions of deliberative practices. First, deliberation can be *horizontal*, that is, between epistemic peers. All citizens who do not hold an office and who do not speak with a particular expertise are peers and deliberate horizontally. One important case of horizontal deliberation is between members in a legislative or deliberative body. Second, deliberation can be *vertical*, that is, between citizens and their representatives, office holders, or others who hold a particular expertise. Vertical deliberation hence occurs across the lines drawn by a political division of labour in a society.

Vertical deliberation presents a challenge. Representatives act as trustees; that is, they might change their mind after deliberating with their peers. Having changed their mind—and perhaps their vote—on some legislation, representatives will have to explain themselves to the citizens whom they represent. This can be a challenge, as citizens have themselves not taken part in the deliberation that led to a change of mind. A vertical division of political labour through trustees hence seems to conflict with equality (Christiano 1996: 126–127). This challenge is characteristic of what can be called the Burkean aspect of political representation, following Edmund Burke's contention that political representatives should pursue and represent impersonal interests and not the opinions of their constituents (Pitkin 1967: ch. 8). In other words, this challenge of vertical deliberation arises from the fact that representatives are trustees, who, in contrast to delegates, have discretion to substitute their own judgement for those who they represent (Christiano 1996: 213).

Finally, associative practices include a *norm of identification*. Each member of an association—be it a tenant's association, a parent–teacher conference, or a party—should see themselves approvingly as a member of that association.[10] This norm reflects the voluntariness of the association as well as, in part, the member's motivation to take part (it hence overlaps with the norm of civic motivation). This norm, as the others, formulates an ideal of a practice and not a political obligation. The norm cannot be obligatory because a member of an association may not identify with the association for good reason, for example, because of its oppressive structure or unjust treatment of its members. The norm instead identifies a pattern of behaviour that is constitutive of a good democratic society, that furthers democratic values and liberties, and that free and equal citizens can expect of one another, at least to some degree.

The social ideal of deliberative democracy, on which the analysis in this chapter is based, is not the only game in town. So-called minimalist or aggregative democratic theories are alternatives (Przeworski 1999; Posner 2003). The motivation to forefront a deliberative conception of democracy is twofold. First, in discussions of digital ethics outside of academia, this is a conception of democracy that may not receive the same amount of attention as its minimalist counterpart does. Avatar democracy and data democracy seem to be distinctively guided—or misguided—by minimalist conceptions of democracy that see democracy as chiefly a procedure for collective decision-making (Morozov 2014: 128–138). Second, a deliberative conception of democracy may offer plausible accounts for what is lacking in some of the proposals of how technology may improve democracy. If the evaluation of the different proposals sounded plausible, then this speaks for the plausibility of the framework that deliberative democracy provides.

This social ideal often awkwardly comports with reality, but this does not mean that this ideal is unrealistic. Of course, the ideal is by no means self-fulfilling or self-perpetuating, but empirical research suggests that people are willing and capable of participating in high-quality deliberation, that deliberation counteracts polarization and populism, and that deliberation promotes considered judgement (see Dryzek et al. 2019 for an overview of different findings).[11] Neither is this ideal romantic. To the contrary, this ideal of democracy has powerful considerations in its favour.[12] The ideal allows for a peaceful and engaging coexistence, while arranging for large advantages for all, as well as reconciling freedom and equality. Admittedly, this ideal—or rather its name—has been co-opted and weaponized by campaigns of racism and imperialism. But this history and ongoing potential for abuse, rather than being a point against the ideal, illustrates the urgency to articulate it clearly.

How technology could improve democracy

Technology can affect democracy in different ways. We can distinguish, very roughly, three broad families of potential technological reforms of democracy by the depth of the change they affect. Some technologies or proposals augment, and in the best case

Table 33.2 Overview of technological proposals to improve democracy
distinguished by the depth of the change they affect

	Deliberation	Participation	Association
Mere changes	Fact-checking	Online voting	Online petitions
Technology augments existing practices	Identifying hate speech Constituent-engagement chatbots	Recommending petitions Apps for participation	Matching or clustering of citizens with similar interests or needs
Moderate reforms	Liquid feedback	Incentivization Gamification	Reputation scores
Technology facilitates new practices		Quadratic voting	VR interaction and role-taking
Radical revisions		Liquid democracy	
Technology constitutive of new practices	Wiki democracy Avatar democracy Data democracy		

Note: Proposals not discussed in this chapter in grey. Radical revisions affect all three families of democratic practices.

improve, existing practices; these are the *mere changes*. Other technologies affect something essential about existing practices or they reform or facilitate new practices; these are the *moderate reforms*. Finally, *radical revisions* constitute entirely new practices of social power, replacing at least some of the existing democratic practices.

The effects of technological reforms of democracy can be hard to predict. Whether something will be a mere change, a moderate reform, or a radical revision is often not obvious upfront. My intent in proposing this distinction, together with the evaluative framework of democratic norms, is that these distinctions may clarify thinking and benefit foresight when reasoning about what shape such reforms might take. Below I discuss some mere changes that have become normalized, moderate reforms that have been tried, and some radical revisions that are confidently advanced (see Table 33.2 for an overview). I selected examples that appeared either well explored in the literature or popular in their reception, or both.

Mere changes

Technology could—and does—change the three kinds of democratic practices of deliberation, participation, and association. I merely mention a few examples here because the promise, and the overpromise, of technology to improve democracy has been discussed at greater length in the existing literature (e.g. Shane 2004; Coleman and Blumler 2009; Hindman 2009; Diamond 2010; Morozov 2011, 2014; Tufekci 2017; Strandberg and Grönlund 2018).

First, technology might change deliberation. For example, technology can gather, rank, and present evidence relevant for discussion. On social media, technology can check stated facts, flag hate speech, or help communicate legislative decisions effectively. This could improve deliberation by supporting the norm of reasonableness (by exposing citizens to relevant content) and the norm of egalitarian participation (e.g. by suppressing hate speech); but such technologies might also worsen the political culture by offering the affordance to strive for a mistakenly clean and perfect ideal of politics when politics is, instead, always messy and fraught. Fact-checking, for example, seeks to counter hypocrisy, mendacity, and ambiguity. But hypocrisy, mendacity, and ambiguity might be important features of a political culture premised on compromise (Morozov 2014: 116–124). At any rate, many such technologies are already in use. Newsfeeds and recommender systems on social media or news aggregators operate in a way that affect existing deliberative practices, for better and worse. Other such technologies are still fantasy. A chatbot might help representatives scale up communicating bidirectionally, and hence more personally and engagingly, with their constituents. Such technology could explain to citizens why their representative supported a proposal, it might garner constituents' attitudes towards legislative priorities or ask for the reasons why someone did not vote in the last election, and it would hence support the norm of deliberative transformation in its vertical dimension.

Second, technology could also change participation through apps that allow citizens to give regular and fine-grained feedback on legislative proposals, recommender systems that pick out and highlight to citizens petitions, or AI systems that identify citizen input during public consultations as novel, detailed, or otherwise relevant. Moreover, technology could, and in some places has, improved voting infrastructure, by making it more accessible, for example, through ballots with multimodal inputs and outputs, or voter guides designed for individuals with aphasia or early-stage Alzheimer's disease.[13] Many applications and relevant case studies on how technology can help participation have been reviewed and discussed elsewhere (Hindman 2009; Nabatchi and Mergel 2010; Fung et al. 2013; Simon et al. 2017; Fuller 2020).[14]

Finally, technology could change mobilization and, more broadly, associative practices in a democracy or in authoritarian regimes. The World Trade Organization (WTO) protests in Seattle in 1999 were built on an email listserv infrastructure (Eagleton-Pierce 2001). Since then, several authoritarian regimes have come under pressure with the help of 'liberation technologies'. Examples are the 2001 protests in Manila against Philippine president Joseph Estrada, the 2004 Orange Revolution in the Ukraine, or the 2005 Cedar Revolution in Lebanon (Diamond 2010: 78). Social media has played a role in facilitating the Arab Spring, the Gezi Park, and Occupy protests (Howard and Hussain 2011, 2013; Tufekci 2017), notwithstanding disagreement over its causal role (Howard and Hussain 2013: 24; Lim 2018: 95). This illustrates the potential of these technologies, at least for short-term mobilization. But although social media help citizens find others with similar interests, views, or needs, again (for better or worse), social media are 'tilting dangerously towards illiberalism' by offering regimes means of surveillance and control (Shahbaz and Funk 2019). Digital movements are too easily defeated with their own weapons.

To be sure, these technologies for deliberation face problems of privacy and security, inclusion (Schlozman et al. 2018: ch. 6), and the problem that technology transplants practices from face-to-face interactions to a digital environment that is less hospitable for these practices to succeed (Lim and Kann 2008; Morozov 2014). For example, social media might allow for near-instantaneous mobilization but, because it cannot recreate the same circumstances of communication, it might at the same time positively hinder a movements' long-term viability (Tufekci 2017). More generally, technologies that were meant to further democratic rights, such as social media furthering speech and expression, may have the opposite effect, or even be used by authoritarian regimes to curtail these same rights (Morozov 2011). These examples illustrate the range in which technology can change and potentially improve democratic practices without fundamentally changing the practices themselves and without changing their socio-political circumstances.

Moderate reforms

In contrast to mere changes, moderate reforms, as I call them, facilitate new practices of deliberation, participation, or association. Examples of moderate reforms are apps for participatory budgeting or systems that reward citizens for participation. Whereas mere changes are already under way and in widespread use in many places, whether moderate reforms can take root—even if they have frequently been tried—is, so far, less clear. I start with an example that has been discussed prominently and that exhibits noteworthy features that are shared by many such reforms.

At the end of 2009, the town of Manor in Texas started rewarding citizens for suggestions of how their town could be improved. The reward came in virtual tokens of 'innobucks'. Citizens received innobucks for suggesting ideas, for commenting on proposals, and for the eventual implementation of an idea. These innobucks could be exchanged for discounts in local stores, appetizers in restaurants, or ride-alongs in police cars. Moreover, each participating citizen's innobucks balance was displayed on a public online leader board (Towns 2010; Newsom 2013: 213–214).[15]

Innobucks incentivized, quantified, and—more generally—gamified participation. 'Gamification' refers to the use of designs and mechanisms familiar from game development outside of games. Collecting points and displaying scores are examples of gamification, so are badges that can be earned, achievements that can be unlocked, or levels that can be completed (Lerner 2014).[16]

Moreover, innobucks also commodified participation not only in their function as tender but likely also in their social valorization. Giving out rewards as points and displaying the score publicly constructs a measure of 'good' behaviour that may easily morph into a measure of social reputation. In fact, some authors make such a social scoring the intended aim of quantified participation and envision a 'democracy machine' that would connect different participatory apps—each along the lines of what I described as mere changes above—'to give people credit for anything from attending town meetings or reporting for jury service to joining a protest or doing policy advocacy' (Gastil 2016: 20; Gastil and Richards 2017: 761). Others approach social scoring instead as a mechanism of social coordination that could be put to the service of emancipatory or socialist ends (Morozov 2019).

Innobucks are just one example of a general class of technological proposals that involve the gamification, quantification, and commodification of participatory and associative practices. These proposals have at least three potential problems.

First, the technology might be abused. Social reputation scores can be put to the service of an authoritarian state. China's initiatives towards a so-called 'social credit score' can be seen as efforts to reform participation by commodification (Liang et al. 2018). More generally, because technological solutions create data and define standards of behaviour unilaterally, such solutions inherently carry immense privacy risks and potential for abuse. The line between the quantification of democracy and the implementation of authoritarianism is thin. But the problems begin far short of authoritarianism. Instead of the state exerting authoritarian power, data help corporations and private actors to exert market power. Data-measuring social participation and interaction is used already today to regulate access to material goods and services such as insurance, employment, and housing.[17] This surveillance practice historically dates from the post-Second World War period, when it successfully solved a problem of information asymmetry that financial lenders faced because they did not know a borrower's creditworthiness. By now, however, with the availability of more data, this practice has evolved into a 'new system of consumer surveillance and control' that 'overwhelmingly favors lenders and other corporate actors—including the state—at the expense of consumers' (Guseva and Rona-Tas 2019: 354).

Second, the gamification of participation often involves the creation of incentives for participation. Gamification seeks to make participation in politics fun and feel rewarding. But this approach has several problems. For one, such constructed incentives might crowd out the intrinsic motivation of citizens and render citizens' relation to collective goods transactional.[18] When even reporting a pothole gets rewarded with innobucks, citizens may expect a reward for any participation. This threatens the norms of civic motivation as immediate psychological rewards and considerations of vanity or self-interest become salient, instead of an appreciation of a shared end. Moreover, gamification risks pretending that conflicts and division—elements that might be inseparable from politics—do not exist by 'badgering people to become engaged because politics is fun and easy', when, instead, people should be asked to 'become engaged because politics is dreary and difficult' (Theiss-Morse and Hibbing 2005: 245; Morozov 2014: 296–309).

Third, because of problems associated with the digital divide and unequal participatory inclusion by socio-economic status, not everybody will have access to the reforms equally. If participation requires technology, such as an up-to-date device or high-speed internet access, some might not be able to afford it. Moreover, even as new technologies have become increasingly affordable and widely used, these technologies 'have not severed the deep roots that anchor political participation in social class' (Schlozman et al. 2018: 128). The technological reforms of democracy hence may have a built-in mechanism of exclusion that is antithetical to the fair opportunity aspect of the norm of egalitarian participation. Given persisting inequalities, technological reforms may entrench such inequalities further.

These three problems—of privacy and power, of crowding out civic motivation, and of threatening equal participation—are more general and not specific to the innobucks project. The innobucks project can illustrate these problems, which may affect a significant range of similar technological reforms of participation. Of course, other such reforms of democratic practices raise likely yet further and different problems. Whereas innobucks, since it was an initiative that aimed at participation, affected participatory norms of egalitarian participation and civic motivation, technologies that target deliberation are likely to affect deliberative norms. In particular, when technologies change how we relate to one another, if we see one another less as free and equal persons, then the deliberative norms of reasonableness and transformation may erode.

Before moving on, two other moderate reforms should be mentioned, which I do not discuss in this chapter, since each of them is explored at length elsewhere. One is Liquid Feedback: a software that structures deliberations in a particular way to develop policy proposals in an inclusive fashion and that facilitates decision-making by allowing participants to pass on their votes to others (Blum and Zuber 2016; Behrens 2017; Bertone et al. 2015). Another reform is quadratic voting, a voting procedure that allows voters to express the strengths of their preferences by giving voters 'vote credits'. The proposal is called 'quadratic' voting because the price of votes increases quadratically. One vote costs one vote credit, two votes cost four credits, three votes nine credits, and so forth (Lalley and Weyl 2017; Posner and Weyl 2017, 2018: ch. 2; Levine 2020). Votes that are handed out but not used in one election can be used in a later election. Hence, voters can bank votes on issues that they care little about and then spend the votes later on issues about which they feel particularly strongly.

Three radical revisions of democratic practices

I discuss three proposals on how technology can improve democracy: wiki democracy, avatar democracy and data democracy (cf. Susskind 2018: ch. 13). Each of these proposals radically changes, or even abolishes, democratic practices. Wiki democracy integrates citizens more deeply into the legislative process. Avatar democracy does away with competitive elections of comprehensive representatives. Data democracy diminishes the role of voting as the procedure of legislative decision-making (see Table 33.3 for an overview). I look at each of these three proposals in turn.

Table 33.3 Overview of three radical technological revisions of democracy and what distinguishes them from one another

Proposal	Distinguishing feature		
	Role of voting in legislative decision-making diminished	No competitive comprehensive elections	Deepened participation in legislative process
Wiki democracy			✓
Avatar democracy		✓	
Data democracy	✓		

Wiki democracy

In some ways, Wikipedia is democratic. Every user has full rights to contribute and modify content—in a sense, Wikipedia is egalitarian. Authors interact and discuss directly and deliberatively, and they decide and adjudicate disputes by voting. Like a democracy, Wikipedia is a non-market form of social coordination. Access is free and contributions are unpaid and voluntary. In other words, Wikipedia is the paradigmatic example of a productive, deliberative, voluntary, non-market, large-scale collaboration (Wright 2010: 194–199). And Wikipedia has been very successful.

So perhaps what has worked for Wikipedia might work for democracy, and democracies should be more like Wikipedia. In particular, Wikipedia is performing well in a respect in which democracy, or so some argue, is performing badly. Wikipedia solicits the expertise from diverse sources (Noveck 2009: 17, 2018). This expertise-soliciting aspect of Wikipedia could be fruitfully used to improve public administration and various opportunities for participation. For example, Beth Noveck (2009) describes the success of a collaborative platform, modelled after Wikipedia, that was used to support the appraisal of patent applications to the US Patent and Trademark Office (USPTO) by allowing lay and professional experts to gather and rank prior art. More broadly, Noveck and others see Wikipedia as an inspiration for radically reforming participatory practices and the process in which policies and legislation get drafted (Susskind 2018: 243–246; Noveck 2009: 146–60, 2018). In fact, they take Wikipedia to be an object lesson to improve existing governance structures—although authors come from different traditions and seek to implement revision to different degrees. For example, some see Wikipedia as a way of putting a new form of socialism into practice (Wright 2010: ch. 7). Others see Wikipedia as a model that could replace much of the executive, legislative, and judiciary branches of government altogether in an all-encompassing 'Crowdocracy' (Watkins and Stratenus 2016).

As a matter of democratic institutional design, we can distinguish different proposals in the spirit of Wiki democracy, depending on what role remains for representatives in parliament. One extreme end would be the mentioned Crowdocracy: a form of direct democracy that runs legislative institutions as a massive collaboration and representatives could only be found in the executive (Watkins and Stratenus 2016). By contrast, the mildest form of Wiki democracy would be civic juries, in which small groups collaborate Wikipedia-style to advise parliaments on specific matters though position papers (Noveck 2009: 152).

I will concentrate on Wiki democracy as an intermediate model, that is, on a proposal that puts drafting and initiating legislation in the hands of citizens instead of representatives or legislative bodies. Wiki democracy of this form keeps representatives and parliaments where they are. Their role, however, will consist chiefly in structuring or overseeing the collaborative Wiki-style drafting process of legislation and on deciding the legislation.[19]

Here is how Wiki democracy would work (Watkins and Stratenus 2016: ch. 6). A parliament would provide an online collaborative infrastructure on which citizens can work on legislative proposals. Citizens would be able to articulate reasons pertaining to the need for legislation, gather evidence, draft the legislative text, comment on the draft, and suggest revisions. Of course, or so proponents of wiki democracy concede, this process would have to be structured and coordinated in some way to be effective. In other words, the process would have to be granular and separated into different stages or 'chunks' to allow for an effective division of labour, and the participating citizens would have to understand what they are expected to do at any given stage (Noveck 2009: 82, 151). Specifically, to structure the process, Noveck suggests different mechanisms and design principles under the heading of 'visual deliberation' (Noveck 2009: 70–84): Participation should be 'group-based rather than individual', it should involve 'a reputation-backed system', 'provide feedback to participants, [and convey] a sense of belonging to a group and [foster] collaboration'. Moreover, the technology should 'mirror and reflect the work of the group back to itself' as a way of giving feedback and indicating progress (2009: 71).

In many ways, Wiki democracy is well within the mainstream of democratic theory. For one, it can be seen as a form of direct, deliberative, and epistemic democracy. Wiki democracy aims at 'bringing greater collective intelligence to bear to enhance the lawmaking processes' and thereby perhaps also to 'enhance the legitimacy of lawmaking' (Noveck 2018: 360). The idea that including more views in a discussion can improve decisions is well received in democratic theory (Mill 1859 [2003]: ch. 3). As such, Wiki democracy stands squarely in the tradition of instrumentalist justifications of democracy, which have recently highlighted how mechanisms of collective intelligence can be used in democratic practices of deliberation (Landemore 2013).[20]

In theory, the effect of Wiki democracy on democratic practices would likely be a positive one in supporting each of the four norms sketched above. Wiki democracy not only thrives on but will also support the norms of civic motivation and associative identification because contributions are voluntary and are not rewarded. Moreover, Wiki democracy stands a chance of supporting the deliberative norms of reasonableness and of supporting the vertical aspect of the norm of deliberative transformation (at least for those who participate). Reasonableness is supported insofar as Wiki democracy, being a discursive platform, relies on rational persuasion. Transformation may be achieved insofar as citizens take an active role in shaping legislative proposals, thereby gaining an inside view, and hence, in contrast to those who did not participate on the Wiki democracy platform, understanding why some legislation turned out the way it did.

The open question of Wiki democracy is then whether it will be successful in practice. There are good reasons to be sceptical. First of all, and very generally, writing legislation is a very different task from writing an encyclopaedia. The analogy between Wikipedia and Wiki democracy hence does not hold. The same principles that worked for Wikipedia might not work for making law. Second, similar to edit wars on Wikipedia, content conflicts in Wiki democracy may require power, hierarchy, or authority to be adjudicated and resolved (Morozov 2014: 125). This speaks against the egalitarian spirit with which Wiki democracy was advertised. Finally, because participating in Wiki democracy is voluntary and not rewarded, it encourages those to show up to participate who already show up today; that is, not only might people lose motivation because online collaboration is very hard to maintain over long periods, but moreover, Wiki democracy on its own is unlikely to overcome barriers of participation that already exist to broaden the circle of citizens who participate in formal channels of democratic input. You need the time, expertise, and perhaps fit into a certain editorial culture to be able to contribute. Whether Wiki democracy succeeds in its stated aim of creating 'more diverse mechanisms for solving problems' (Noveck 2009: xiv) therefore appears doubtful. Instead, it seems more likely that getting citizens to show up for politics is an old problem that escapes technological solutions.

Avatar democracy

The idea that democracy can be automated is not new. In his science fiction satire *Franchise*, published in 1955, Isaac Asimov describes the US presidential election of 2008, in which the notion that every citizen can vote is unfathomable. In this fictional year 2008, an election consists of a single voter having to answer a few questions to a computer named 'Multivac', which then predicts which candidate would have been elected if people had voted, and the computer determines the next president on that basis.[21] Multivac was built on the sentiment that voting, or representative democracy, is not worth the trouble if the exact same outcome can be had in a more convenient fashion. The development started with electronic voting machines '[b]ut the machines grew bigger and they could tell how the election would go from fewer and fewer votes. Then, at last, they built Multivac and it can tell from just one voter' (Asimov 1955).

This weary sentiment about voting and representative democracy is still alive today. One recent proposal suggests replacing representatives in the legislature and politicians wholesale because turnout in elections is low and because 'people are tired of politicians' (Hidalgo 2018). Instead of having politicians and representatives, each citizen could send their own personal virtual delegate to a virtual parliament, thereby combining software with the idea of 'bypassing politicians completely'. These virtual delegates, one for each citizen, would debate and negotiate over legislation, vote on bills, and hence make law.[22] Similarly, another proposal envisions 'intelligent e-democracy bots' that 'receive as input the political preferences and epistemic views of their principals, and on this basis participate on their behalf in digital consultation processes, exploiting sophisticated AI algorithms' (Perez 2020). I call this idea *avatar democracy*.

Similar to Multivac, avatar democracy relies on the promise of data. Because the costs of acquiring, storing, and analysing personal data have decreased so drastically, each person may become accurately predictable as a political agent. In an avatar democracy, 'you can provide your avatar with your reading habits, or connect it to your social media, or you can connect it to … psychological tests'. Citizens would be able to select an avatar training algorithm from a range of offerings on an 'open marketplace';[23] citizens would be able to 'audit the system', 'leave [the avatar] on autopilot', or 'choose that [the avatar] ask you every time they're going to make a decision' (Hidalgo 2018). In short, first you select an avatar algorithm, then you train it with data that you provide, then you supervise and audit it. In this extreme form, avatar democracy is a virtual direct democracy in which each citizen is represented by a software agent.[24] As such, the proposal abolishes competitive elections of comprehensive representatives in favour of an individual selection of automated representatives.

Some believe that some form of avatar democracy is 'probably inevitable' (Perez 2020).[25] Societies, hence, must urgently develop 'a new regulatory framework that would cope with a new political space' (Perez 2020). The alleged inevitability of avatar democracy endows the idea with considerable relevance and the thinking around it with high urgency. Such thinking, widespread as it might be, betrays technological determinism. On the assumption that there is instead a choice to be made, the question is whether avatar democracy would be a good idea.

What speaks in favour of avatar democracy? Avatar democracy is often presented as improving representative democracy. In contrast to direct democracy, 'trying to bypass politicians, we [with this proposal] … automate them' (Hidalgo 2018). But avatar democracy, at the same time, positions itself as standing in the tradition of direct democracy. This element of direct democracy forms the basis an *indirect argument* for avatar democracy:[26] Whatever speaks in favour of direct democracy might speak in favour of avatar democracy. The argument is that direct democracy has always been more desirable than representative democracy, it has just not been feasible to implement. The animating sentiment seems to be that '[t]rue democracy would be direct, being based on unmediated, constant, and universal participation of all citizens in political matter … [D]elegation of political power is a necessary if minor evil' (Floridi 2016).[27] But since technology now lets us avoid this 'minor evil' and makes direct democracy feasible, we should undertake steps to implement direct democracy. Compromise, for example, is one such necessary evil of representative democracy that direct democracy would avoid. As Hidalgo (2018) says, '[p]oliticians nowadays are packages, and they're full of compromises' but in the future 'you might have someone that can represent only you'.

In addition to this indirect argument for avatar democracy, there are several *direct arguments*. Specifically, the following four considerations have been put forth in favour of avatar democracy.[28]

First, in virtue of having no representatives, avatar democracy avoids the often fraught relationship between citizens and representatives. Today, citizens must trust that representatives will work in their interests and that the representative's word is reliable testimony when they explain decisions. Avatar democracy instead allows citizens to represent themselves. Furthermore, if we accept some additional assumptions about the value of individualism, avatar democracy has going for it that it empowers citizens to stand up and represent themselves in collective affairs.

Second, avatar democracy might improve representativeness and equality of influence. Those who have particular interests or concerns far outside those of the majority and who, accordingly, are otherwise given little room in legislative proposals might have their interests better represented and their ways of influence increased (Susskind 2018: 253). In terms of the democratic norms, avatar democracy would support the norm of egalitarian participation in its aspect of the inclusion of marginalized views.

Third, avatar democracy decreases the ways in which legislative decision-making can be subject to regulatory capture of different forms. It is far easier to influence legislation through material or cultural–social mechanisms when the number of legislators is small. When every citizen is a legislator, by contrast, it is much harder to influence legislation. Avatar democracy defends itself against regulatory capture by decentralization. Seen from the perspective of participatory norms, avatar democracy thereby again supports the norm of egalitarian participation (specifically, its aspect of inclusion).

Fourth, avatar democracy might improve deliberation by removing the need for political campaigning. Although, idealists might hope that campaigning improves the quality of deliberation and supports the mechanisms by which voters hold their representatives to account, campaigning might in fact distort, damage, and deprave deliberation. Individual targeting of political ads has made political messaging inconsistent, manipulative, and dishonest and it turned political campaigns into a huckster competition of outsized promises, historic dramatization, boasting, opportunism, and appeals to tribalism. Avatar democracy ends the need for campaigning, and it thereby removes the causes of these deliberative impairments. In terms of deliberative norms, the claim is that avatar democracy would improve the reasonability norm (through access to better information) and the norm of deliberative transformation (especially, its vertical aspect).

The joke of Asimov's story is, of course, that the 'election' in 2008 is an election in name only. A gearbox was substituted in place of a forum, as fraught and cumbersome as that forum might be. Is the same true for avatar democracy? What should we make of the case in its favour?

For a start, each of these premises in the indirect argument for avatar democracy—that avatar democracy, being an instance of direct democracy, inherits all its virtues—can be called into question. The underlying ideal of direct democracy might look less attractive on closer inspection. Perhaps there is something morally valuable about compromises. It should not be taken for granted that direct democracy is as such more desirable than representative democracy.

Moreover, avatar democracy is not actually a form of direct democracy. If avatar democracy were a form of direct democracy, then it would imply that the avatar is identical to the citizen because in a direct democracy each citizen represents themselves. But because the avatar is not identical to the citizen, the citizens themselves do not deliberate and decide on legislation. Avatar democracy should therefore be seen as more akin to representative democracy and an avatar is better thought of as a representative.[29] This, in turn, effectively reintroduces the citizen–representative relationship that avatar democracy had aimed to overcome.

Because avatar democracy is a form of representative democracy, we would have to trust avatars just as we have to trust representatives today (cf. Susskind 2018: 250–253). Are avatars deserving of this trust? Avatar democracy faces one problem that also bedevils representative democracy; beyond that, avatar democracy faces two practical problems.

First, avatar democracy brings the horizontal and the vertical aspects of the norm of deliberative transformation into conflict. Insofar as avatars change their view after deliberating with other avatars, they will on occasion vote in a way that contradicts how their citizens would want them to vote.[30] This is a problem also for representative democracies today. The general shape of the problem is this: because representatives hold power, they need to explain themselves—this is a demand of legitimacy. But because representatives, especially after deliberation, have greater expertise, this demand is hard to fulfil. Optimism about solving this problem should be met with serious scepticism (Lafont 2015; Viehoff 2016). Satisfying the norm of transformation in its horizontal aspect risks undermining the norm in its vertical aspect. The claim that avatar democracy is immune to this general problem rests either on mistakenly seeing avatar democracy as a form of direct democracy or on failing to see this fundamental challenge in representative democracy, or both.

In addition to this general problem of representative democracy, two practical problems arise for avatar democracy from the fact that citizens can select between different models of avatars that might be offered on an open marketplace.

First, selecting avatars comes with serious information asymmetries. Avatars might be like a car insurance in that you only relatively rarely get to find out how good the thing is that you bought. Whoever offers rarely used products such as car insurance, has little incentive to compete on the quality of the product. Some kind of quality control for avatar algorithms would then have to be ensured. But this problem is, in part, technical: an AI will have to be made explainable. This problem is also conceptual: standards for good explanations will have to be determined. Finally, this problem is institutional: it is not clear which, if any, recommendations or user reviews about avatar algorithms can be trusted.

Second, avatar democracy has significant risks of power and equality. Whoever offers avatars has likely political interests of their own and occupies a position that enables them to coax others in line with those interests. Those who make the avatars have power. They are able to influence or manipulate political outcomes by how they build or advertise the avatars. In this way, unless everyone were somehow able to create their own avatar entirely independently, avatar democracy may suffer from a fundamental problem of unequal power.

Data democracy

Avatar democracy started from what looked like an eminently plausible idea: we have so many data that have proven valuable in various domains. These vast data could be put into the service of democratic practices. Given enough data and sufficiently advanced technology, 'elected officials will be able to ask voters what they want a thousand times a day and act accordingly, (Domingos 2015: 19). If these data were used in the legislative process, then 'policy would be based on an incomparably rich and accurate picture of our lives: what we do, what we need, what we think, what we say, how we feel. The data would be fresh and updated in real time rather than in a four- or five-year cycle' (Susskind 2018: 247).

Proposals to use more data in order to constrain or determine legislative decision-making are proposals for what I call *data democracy*. Data democracy comes in a variety of forms. In one extreme form, data determine legislation formally and 'political decisions would be taken on the basis of data rather than votes' (Susskind 2018: 247). This extreme form retains a parliament with representatives, but their role would be to supervise data analysis, amend proposals, or correct errors by recalling legislation. On a less extreme form of data democracy, data constrain legislation only informally by systematically informing deliberation and decision-making in the legislature in real time.

Of course, legislative decision-making has always been based on data. A change in the vehicle code might come in response to data about traffic accidents, a stimulus package is drafted in response to economic data, and migration legislation often reacts to data about immigration numbers. Labels such as 'evidence-based policy' highlight that legislation is often 'based on data'.[31] So, how is data democracy different?

Data democracy consists of three core claims. First, data democracy says that new kinds of data ought to inform the legislative process. Second, data democracy seeks to vastly increase the amount of data used in the legislative process. Finally, and perhaps most importantly, data democracy demands that data constrain or even determine lawmaking. The radical revision of data democracy is that it aims to move the legislative process away from deliberation and voting towards data-driven decision-making.

These core ideas may already be problematic. First, contrary to the perhaps widespread but naïve idea that 'data' are facts, data need cleaning, interpretation, and analysis. Hence, data do not 'speak' unambiguously and the directions into which data would 'drive' decisions depend on more than just data (Lyon 2016). Data-driven decision-making rests on value judgements that need to be subject at least to human oversight or guidance. Some proposals of data democracy make room for such a human element—a role that future politicians or representatives in parliament may play. Instead of deliberating and voting over legislative proposals, future representatives might deliberate and vote on issues of data cleaning, interpretation, and analysis. Second, this core idea of data democracy is decidedly technocratic to the extent that it portrays politics as something that needs to be overcome. We will see this technocratic temperament again when taking a closer look at proposals.

I will sketch two existing proposals of data democracy. One proposal, *deliberative data democracy* innovates on the first aspect; that is, it imports new kinds of data into the legislative process. Another proposal, *decision data democracy*, suggests that data should altogether replace human decision-making in the legislative process. This second proposal mostly innovates on the third aspect; that is, it demands a greater role for data in the legislative process.

Deliberative data democracy

One proposal for deliberative data democracy is due to Hiroki Azuma (2014), who proposes what he calls the 'General Will 2.0' by suggesting that new data should be included in the legislative process. Drawing on Freud's idea of the unconscious, he says that data about 'the unconscious of the populace' should be collected to '[document] people's private, animalistic actions' and their 'private, bodily reactions' in a 'visualized collective unconscious' in order to 'demolish the limits of public, logical deliberation' (Azuma 2014: 144, 162, 171). Set aside for now what 'the unconscious' is and how it would be measured. Azuma proposes that a screen be set up in parliament that displays the populace's unconscious so that this unconscious provides feedback in real time on deliberations in parliament with the aim that 'deliberation among politicians and experts ought to be limited by this very unconscious'.[32]

Azuma gives two main arguments in favour of deliberative data democracy or, as he calls it, 'unconscious democracy'.[33] First, deliberative data democracy improves perceived legitimacy because it instils a sense of ownership and participation. Azuma suggests that deliberative data democracy would 'restore some feeling of actual participation for the masses'. Citizens might look more favourably on legislation, or even identify with legislation, insofar as they know that their voices are heard, and their feelings are felt in parliament. In times in which the disconnect between citizens at home and politicians in Washington, DC or Brussels is felt acutely, this would be a valuable achievement. Stated with reference to democratic norms, deliberative data democracy might support the associative norm of identification.

Second, data democracy might improve the quality of legislative debates by uncovering 'latent expertise languishing in obscurity' (Azuma 2014: 148). Similar to Wiki democracy, this expertise-based argument squares well with existing ideas of epistemic democracy and the use of technology to further collective intelligence (cf. Landemore 2013). As such, data democracy has an instrumental argument on its side that follows the intuition that more data will lead to better outcomes. From the perspective of democratic norms, data democracy might strengthen the deliberative norms of reasonableness and transformation.

In summary, the General Will 2.0 is a form of deliberative data democracy that draws on new forms of data—that representing the (collective) unconscious—and uses these to informally constrain the legislative process in its deliberations. It is '[t]he aggregate of animal murmurs giving direction to the elites' human and public debates' (Azuma 2014: 162). On the face of it, deliberative data democracy is entirely consistent with democratic norms and it promises to strengthen the deliberative norms of reasonableness and transformation through increased pooling of information and the norm of associative identification insofar as citizens believe that their unconscious is seen by parliament and thereby reflected in the legislative process.

But the proposal has several problems. First of all, what the collective unconscious is exactly and whether visualizing it in parliament would deliver the advertised benefits is, at best, unclear. Citizens may not welcome laws or identify more closely with them only because additional data about collective sentiments is projected live above the hemicycle. Cynics would add that, in fact, not a lot changes at all: Already today, politicians perform incessantly for 'popular opinion' driven by reactions on social media, focus groups, polls, and, occasionally, votes.

Second, if legislation were to follow the collective unconscious and the 'animal murmurs', the outcome might be anodyne at best and authoritarian at worst. A legislature that seeks to pacify popular emotions might resort to political triangulation to transcend party politics and cleavages. Even worse, data democracy might make politics for the amygdala. Putting the collective unconscious at the centre of deliberation elevates instincts of homophily, fear, and aggression. Perhaps it can be very satisfying for a vast majority to marginalize, scapegoat, or oppress minorities. At any rate, it seems unlikely that elevating the unconscious produces good policy outcomes and improvements by the lights of deliberative norms. The questionable assumption in deliberative data democracy concerns its underlying Freudian view that data about the unconscious and the 'suppressed libido' is valuable in the ways Azuma envisions. Instead, it appears that the underlying Freudian impulses might deprave deliberation, rather than enhancing it. In terms of the democratic norms, deliberative data democracy would decrease reasonableness and transformation.

Finally, it should be troubling that Azuma is quick to discount the value of current democracies and leans towards the inevitability of data democracy and a minimal state. He writes that '[t]he world has become too complex. The state and deliberation have surpassed their service lives' (Azuma 2014: 206). Any future state will be 'something like a combination of street patrols and food rationing and health check-ups for its residents' (Azuma 2014: 198). Azuma shows no compunction in catering to such libertarian technocratic sentiments.

Decision data democracy

An alternative form of data democracy is put forward by the historian Yuval Noah Harari. Harari suggests that legislative decisions can be automated and be based entirely on data (2017: ch. 11). According to him, the political system of the future has neither parliament, nor elections, nor a government as such. All these functions can, will, and should be automated and be driven by data. Harari does not spell out how this would work in practice, neither does he motivate this as an improvement of democracy, but he at least offers a theorical motivation for this data-driven system of politics.

Harari's starting assumption is what he calls 'dataism', which comprises a methodo-logical and an axiological claim.[34] The methodological claim of dataism is that every entity or system can be seen as a data-processing system, which entails that we should also see political structures as data-processing systems. Seeing political structures in this way is increasingly widespread in political science, Harari argues. The axiological claim of dataism—that is, a claim about its ethical value—is that 'the value of any phe-nomenon or entity is determined by its contribution to data processing'. This is a rad-ical teleological claim. But if we understand 'data-processing' liberally,[35] then we can account for the value of human life (humans process and produce vast amounts of data efficiently) and the value of non-human animals, as well as the environment (non-human animals and the environment process and produce data and support human data-processing). Looking at democracies today through this lens of dataism, Harari identifies two problems with the status quo.

First, democracy, seen as a data-processing system, is faring increasingly badly, suggests Harari. This is because democracy and its constituting institutions 'don't pro-cess data efficiently enough'. He writes that 'because technology is now moving so fast, and parliaments and dictators alike are overwhelmed by data they cannot process quickly enough, ... politics is consequently bereft of grand visions. Government has be-come mere administration.' In short, with its limited throughput and insufficient pro-cessing capacity, democracy, in the eyes of dataism, has a desirability problem. Whatever democracy's promise may be (equal standing, equal influence, public justification, re-form of citizens' characters, good policy outcomes, or maximizing welfare), democracy fails to deliver on this promise because of the influence of technology and because dem-ocracy is overwhelmed by the increasing demands on data-processing.[36]

Second, next to this desirability problem, democracy has a feasibility problem. According to Harari, some form of decision data democracy is inevitable. Democracy, with its 'venerable institutions like elections, parties and parliaments might become ob-solete' so that 'democracy might decline and even disappear' (Harari 2017: ch. 11). The basis for this prediction is the dataist argument we have just seen: because democracy fails as a data-processing system, democracy fails to deliver on its promise and through some process of political change, a better system of collective decision-making and so-cial coordination will be established.

In decision data democracy, citizens play no role at all beyond the data they generate. In this sense, as Harari admits, decision data democracy is no democracy at all.[37] At most, decision data democracy can be motivated out of the idea that political decisions satisfy citizens' actual desires and preferences. But this aggregative model of democ-racy fails to involve citizens in the right way (Kolodny 2014: 207). In terms of demo-cratic norms, decision data democracy is likely to undermine almost all of the norms mentioned. It violates the norm of egalitarian participation by virtue of abolishing virtually all practices of meaningful participation and it violates the vertical aspect of deliberative transformation. This, in turn, raises a problem for the legitimacy of data democracy (Danaher 2016). Decision data democracy also does nothing to improve the operation of the deliberative norms of reasonableness and the norm of deliberative transformation in its horizonal aspect. Although an optimistic argument would have it that the good outcomes of data democracy will improve civic motivation and citizens' identification, insofar as data democracy diminishes the respective participatory and associative practices, it seems more likely that data democracy stands also to undermine these participatory and associative norms.

CONCLUSION

Technology can help or hinder democracy. This chapter has described and discussed various ideas of how technology can do so. The overarching aim of this chapter has been to put forward a framework of how to think about technological democratic innovations. The framework extends existing thinking in democratic theory to practices that constitute a democratic society. I have distinguished between participatory, deliberative, and associative practices and I have sketched some important norms for each. Democratic participation is characterized by substantively egalitarian norms of access (inclusion and non-market relations) as well as a civic motivation of those who take part. Democratic deliberation is subject to a norm of reasonableness and to a norm of deliberative transformation (in a horizontal and a vertical aspect). And democratic association includes a norm of identification of those who join together under a shared end. In addition to guiding the examination of technological proposals, this framework may help more generally in evaluating any intervention that claims to improve democracy.

The visions of how technology may revolutionize democracy each fare very differently with respect to how they contribute to good democratic practices (see Table 33.4). Mere changes intervene in existing practices and often tend to have democratic norms in clear view and work to maintain them. Many existing so-called democracy apps are dedicated to the aim of improving reasonableness or facilitating horizontal or vertical deliberative transformation.

Moderate reforms seem instead to be animated by a sense of technological possibility as they import gamification design schemas and leverage civic motivation; but these interventions threaten, in particular, the norms of egalitarian participation and civic motivation. For example, when participation is rewarded with points, this not only bears risks to privacy and risks abuse, but it also raises problems of equal access and it may crowd out citizens' intrinsic motivations and recognition of a shared end in favour of instrumental motivations in pursuit of individual advantage.

Radical revisions of democratic practices, finally, tend to be animated by a sense of technological necessity. Strikingly, proponents of each proposal, Perez, Azuma, and Harari, suggest that their respective proposal—avatar democracy, deliberative data democracy, or decision data democracy—is inevitable. This fatalism is by itself a dubious claim, at least, insofar as it rests on some form of technological or material determinism. Moreover, some of the proposals, in particular avatar democracy and deliberative data

Table 33.4 Overview of hypothesized effects on democratic norms, with indicated increase or decrease in support

Norms	Participatory		Deliberative		Associative
Proposal	Egalitarian Participation	Civic motivation	Reasonableness	Transformation	Identification
Innobucks	↓ digital divide	↓ gamification incentives			
Wiki democracy	↓ barriers to participation	↑ voluntariness	↑ participation structured	↑ every participant active	↑ voluntariness
Avatar democracy	↑ less regulatory capture ↑ effective representation of minorities ↓ all participation indirect		↑ no campaigning, no targeted ads	↑ less deception ↓ vertical and horizontal transformation conflict	
Deliberative data democracy			↑ increased pooling of information ↓ pooling of emotional information damaging		↑ knowledge that the unconscious is seen in parliament
Decision data democracy	↓ only aggregates and does not involve citizens in the right way				

democracy, come dressed up as a way of saving democracy, when each of them in fact appears deeply deficient of a clear understanding of democratic values and practices. Another noteworthy trend is that some of the proponents of the radical revisions do not in fact themselves endorse the proposals that they promulgate.[38] Instead, authors take themselves to be speculating on ideas or conceiving of possibilities without defending them. But if these are good ideas, they should be worthwhile defending.

A proposal that stands out among the radical revisions discussed here is Wiki democracy. First, Wiki democracy is neither animated by a sense of technological possibility nor by a sense of technological necessity. Instead, Wiki democracy is a relatively modest proposal that targets a limited range of problems in the legislative process. Second, Wiki democracy starts with the identification of a shortcoming of democratic practices in light of democratic norms and tries to improve practices accordingly. Other radical revisions, by contrast, aim at a certain outcome while diminishing the domain of democratic practices. Third, Wiki democracy rests on a technology that is available today and that has been used in a similar fashion already, albeit for different ends. This is not only a proof of concept, but it is also a feasibility check—although problems in increasing and sustaining fair and equal participation are likely to persist. Avatar democracy and data democracy, by contrast, are distinctively speculative and depend for their success on uncertain technological capabilities. In these ways, Wiki democracy might not only be an attractive proposal, but the proposal may also serve as a methodological role model of good thinking about how to conceive of technological interventions to improve democracy.

ACKNOWLEDGEMENTS

I am grateful for thoughtful comments on drafts of this chapter by Carissa Veliz, Iason Gabriel, Justin Bullock, Ted Lechterman, Tina Nabatchi, César A. Hidalgo, Matthew Adams, and two anonymous readers for Oxford University Press.

NOTES

1. For the purposes of this chapter, I understand 'technology' to mean mostly software—apps or web-based services—that implement functions by relying on a dense digital network infrastructure (such as community participation apps, Wikipedia, or quadratic voting—more on each below) or on data and statistical and machine-learning techniques (such as the forms of data-driven democracy that I discuss towards the end of the chapter).
2. This chapter largely ignores how technology may affect the work of public service agencies and government departments, courts, or informal deliberations offline and online. Unfortunately, it thereby also ignores how introducing automation in one realm may affect another; for example, automating the legislative process may affect public administration. For a systematic review with a broader institutional aperture, see Fung et al. (2013). For a framework to evaluate digital technologies in the public sphere, see Cohen and Fung (2021). On the use of technology in government, see Chen and Ahn (2017), and for frameworks to evaluate practices of public administration, see Bozeman (2007), Zacka (2017), Nabatchi (2018), and Heath (2020).
3. I largely set aside questions of justification and authority.
4. To be clear, these practices as such, unless governed by democratic norms, are not sufficient for democracy and are even compatible with living under authoritarianism.
5. Nevertheless, procedures and the integrity of elections are important to democracy.
6. See Cohen (1997) for an argument, and Talisse (2019: 50–67) for an accessible motivation of deliberative democracy.
7. For similar accounts, see what Rawls (1971: secs. 71–72) calls 'the morality of association' and 'the morality of principles', what Christiano (1996: 187–90) calls 'the standards of citizens' democratic activities', what Talisse (2019), inspired by Rawls [personal correspondence], calls 'civic friendship', and what Peter (2021) calls 'epistemic norms of political deliberation'.
8. Many theorists motivate a similar norm: for Rawls (1971: sec. 1) '[a]mong individuals with disparate aims and purposes a shared conception of justice establishes the bonds of civic friendship'. Mansbridge (1983) advocates for a unitary democracy based on friendship.

Cohen (1989) describes the motivation of deliberators as being shaped by 'a commitment to the deliberative resolution'. Cohen and Rogers (1993: 289; 1995: 38) describe a norm of 'civic consciousness'. Christiano (1996: 178) writes that 'citizens can be expected to ... choose the aims of the society ... *with an eye to the society as whole*' [all emphases mine].

9. In this sense, an obligation to vote might be undemocratic if citizens voted mainly or only because of a fear of repercussions.

10. This self-conception needs neither be present in one's awareness nor need it be central to one's identity.

11. But for an opposing view, see Theiss-Morse and Hibbing (2005).

12. Some see the ideal as romantic in the sense that it presupposes a mistaken theory of human behavior or human nature (e.g. Theiss-Morse and Hibbing 2005: 242). But insofar as human nature is on display in actual circumstances, empirical evidence about actual behaviour holds out the hope that the ideal is realistic.

13. These examples are taken from a working paper series of the Information Technology Laboratory of the US National Institute of Standards and Technology (NIST 2012).

14. See also participedia.net for a collection of cases and methods of online and face-to-face participation.

15. Although innobucks survived for only a couple years (from around 2009 to 2011), Gavin Newsom features them prominently in his 2013 book on how to 'reinvent democracy' using digital tools. The Twitter account of the organization that ran innobucks had already gone dormant (in 2011) and their website had shut down (in early 2012, according to the Wayback Machine)—some time before Newsom's book was published.

16. Although gamification is associated with computer games, gamification can be used to reform participation without the use of technology (Lerner 2014; Gordon and Baldwin-Philippi 2014; Newsom 2013; Gastil and Richards 2017). A participatory budget meeting, for example, can be run like a casting show, or voting boxes can be designed to respond with a pleasing 'plonk' and a visual feedback to acknowledge that ballot has been cast. More generally, gamification includes formulating and balancing conflict dynamics with feedback loops (e.g. the participatory budgeting game show), multimodal presentation (e.g. the voting box sound), to provide just-in-time information, defining clear goals and objectives as part of a narrative and showing progress towards these goals with the collection of points, reflected in status indicators, badges, or level upgrades (Lerner 2014).

17. One example was Lenddo (http://www.lenddo.com, accessed 24 August 2020), which 'uses non-traditional data to provide credit scoring'. According to a product fact sheet, these non-traditional data include data from telecom providers, browsers, social networks, e-commerce, and financial transactions.

18. Loh (2019) considers the related objection that gamification of participation is paternalistic or detrimental to citizens' autonomy.

19. I concentrate on this form because it tracks closely the distinct strengths of Wikipedia when it comes to collaboration. Deciding about legislation would still be a matter of voting, and hence it would be a conceptually different matter; it is not clear that Wikipedia is a particularly good model here.

20. Yet, proponents of wiki democracy, who often appear to cherish vaguely technocratic ideals, dismiss deliberation (Morozov 2014: 133). Indeed, Noveck (2009: 37) objects that 'civic talk is largely disconnected from power' and that '[t]he reality of deliberation is that it is toothless'. About existing 'work at the intersection of technology and democracy', she complains that it 'has focussed on how to create demographically representative

conversations. The focus is on deliberation, not collaboration; on talk instead of action; on information, not decisionmaking' (2009: 40).

21. Interestingly, in 1952, a few years before Asimov's story was published, the similarly named Univac computer made a prominent public appearance during US elections. CBS introduced Univac as 'our fabulous mathematical brain' that will 'help us predict this election' (quoted in Lepore 2020: ch. 1).

22. Hidalgo also puts forward a different, much less radical, and much more general proposal, called 'augmented democracy', on which an avatar might be a 'twin' that acts as a deliberative interlocutor or assistant to improve citizens' abilities to participate (see https://www.peopledemocracy.com, accessed 10 October 2021). I concentrate instead on avatar democracy because it is a more original proposal that was prominently promoted through TED conferences.

23. This marketplace need not be a form of commercial exchange. I am grateful to César Hidalgo for this clarification.

24. The tension between 'direct democracy' and 'represented by a software agent' is something I discuss below.

25. Hidalgo, in personal correspondence, makes it clear that he does not want to be associated with this claim.

26. The terminology is from Blum and Zuber (2016).

27. To be clear, Floridi (2016) argues against this view and defends representative democracy.

28. At least three of the points below—all except the second point—are made by Hidalgo (2018).

29. Granted, avatar democracy is a limit case of representative democracy in that each citizen has their own personal representative.

30. This is the Burekean aspect of representation (cf. Pitkin 1967: ch. 8; Christiano 1996: 213). If an avatar were not to exercise judgement, avatar democracy would be a market and not a forum.

31. In the United States, the Office of Management and Budget (OMB) formally restricts executive agency decision-making to comport to some form of evidence-based policymaking.

32. Although, to be clear, Azuma (2014: ch. 4) resists the characterization of his proposal as deliberative. He distinctly sees the general will 2.0 as a novel form of politics in contrast to the deliberative tradition (e.g. Habermas and Arendt) and the antagonistic tradition (e.g. Schmitt).

33. Although he develops these arguments specifically for his proposal, the arguments are worthwhile discussing insofar as they might have force in support of similar proposals of deliberative data democracy more generally. Azuma gives a third argument, which I do not discuss here, that deliberative data democracy avoids the latent threat of populism.

34. Harari later walks back his assumption of dataism. He calls dataism a 'dogma' the critical examination of which is 'the most urgent political and economic project'. He also clarifies that his aim is speculation, not prediction, and that he wants to 'broaden our horizons and make us aware of a much wider spectrum of options'.

35. What exactly Harari means with 'data' and 'data-processing' is very unclear, however. He seems to subscribe to a naïve account of data criticized by Lyon (2016), as mentioned earlier.

36. Harari's argument assumes that democracy is good for something but leaves open what exactly democracy is good for (welfare, equal standing, etc.). Insofar as none of the things that democracy might be good for contribute to data-processing, even this ecumenical

assumption—that democracy is good for *something*—*conflicts* with the axiological assumption of dataism (i.e. only things that contribute to data-processing are valuable). In short, axiological dataism is incompatible with the value of democracy.

37. I listed the proposal as a 'democracy' insofar as the project here investigates how technology might transform democracy.

38. With the exception of Hidalgo, who endorses a general idea of augmented democracy.

References

Asimov, Isaac (1955), 'Franchise', *If, Worlds of Science Fiction*, August 1955.

Azuma, Hiroki (2014), *General Will 2.0: Rousseau, Freud, Google* (New York: Vertical).

Behrens, Jan (2017), 'The Origins of Liquid Democracy', *The Liquid Democracy Journal* 5(May), https://liquid-democracy-journal.org/issue/5/The_Liquid_Democracy_Journal-Issue005-02-The_Origins_of_Liquid_Democracy.html, accessed 10 October 2021.

Bertone, Giulia, De Cindio, Fiorella, and Stortone, Stefano (2015), 'LiquidFeedback in Large-Scale Civic Contexts: Framing Multiple Styles of Online Participation', *Journal of Social Media for Organizations* 2(1), 27.

Blum, Christian, and Zuber, Christina Isabel (2016), 'Liquid Democracy: Potentials, Problems, and Perspectives', *Journal of Political Philosophy* 24(2), 162–182, doi: https://doi.org/10.1111/jopp.12065.

Bozeman, Barry (2007), *Public Values and Public Interest: Counterbalancing Economic Individualism* (Washington, DC: Georgetown University Press).

Chen, Yu-Che, and Ahn, Michael J. (2017), *Routledge Handbook on Information Technology in Government* (New York: Routledge).

Christiano, Thomas (1996), *The Rule of the Many: Fundamental Issues in Democratic Theory* (Boulder CO: Westview Press).

Christiano, Thomas (2008), *The Constitution of Equality: Democratic Authority and Its Limits* (Oxford: Oxford University Press).

Christiano, Thomas (2018), 'Democracy', in Edward N. Zalta, ed., *The Stanford Encyclopedia of Philosophy (Autumn 2018 Edition)*, https://plato.stanford.edu/archives/fall2018/entries/democracy/, accessed 14 July 2019.

Cohen, Joshua (1989), 'Deliberation and Democratic Legitimacy', in Alan P. Hamlin and Philip Pettit, eds, *The Good Polity: Normative Analysis of the State* (Oxford: Blackwell), 17–34.

Cohen, Joshua (1997), 'Procedure and Substance in Deliberative Democracy', in James Bohman and William Rehg, eds, *Deliberative Democracy: Essays on Reason and Politics* (Cambridge, MA: The MIT Press), 407–437.

Cohen, Joshua, and Fung, Archon (2021), 'Democracy and the Digital Public Sphere', in Lucy Bernholz, Hélène Landemore, and Rob Reich, eds, *Digital Technology and Democratic Theory* (Chicago, IL: University of Chicago Press), 23–61.

Cohen, Joshua, and Rogers, Joel (1993), 'Associations and Democracy', *Social Philosophy and Policy* 10(2), 282–312, doi: https://doi.org/10.1017/S0265052500004234.

Cohen, Joshua, and Rogers, Joel (1995), *Associations and Democracy*, ed. Erik Olin Wright (London: Verso).

Coleman, Stephen, and Blumler, Jay G. (2009), *The Internet and Democratic Citizenship: Theory, Practice and Policy* (Cambridge: Cambridge University Press).

Danaher, John (2016), 'The Threat of Algocracy: Reality, Resistance and Accommodation', *Philosophy & Technology* 29(3), 245–268, doi: https://doi.org/10.1007/s13347-015-0211-1.

Diamond, Larry (2010), 'Liberation Technology', *Journal of Democracy* 21(3), 69–83, doi: https://doi.org/10.1353/jod.0.0190.

Domingos, Pedro (2015), *The Master Algorithm: How the Quest for the Ultimate Learning Machine Will Remake Our World* (New York: Basic Books).

Dryzek, John S., Bächtiger, André, Chambers, Simone, Cohen, Joshua, Druckman, James N., Felicetti, Andrea, et al. (2019), 'The Crisis of Democracy and the Science of Deliberation', *Science* 363(6432), 1144–1146, doi: https://doi.org/10.1126/science.aaw2694.

Eagleton-Pierce, Matthew (2001), 'The Internet and the Seattle WTO Protests', *Peace Review* 13(3), 331–337, doi: https://doi.org/10.1080/13668800120079027.

Elster, Jon (1989), 'The Market and the Forum: Three Varieties of Political Theory', in Jon Elster and Aanund Hylland, eds, *Foundations of Social Choice Theory* (Cambridge: Cambridge University Press), 103–132.

Floridi, Luciano (2016), 'Technology and Democracy: Three Lessons from Brexit', *Philosophy & Technology* 29(3), 189–193, doi: https://doi.org/10.1007/s13347-016-0229-z.

Fuller, Roslyn (2020), 'Digital Democracy Report', Solonian Democracy Institute, Dublin, https://www.solonian-institute.com/post/2020-sdi-digital-democracy-report, accessed 10 October 2021.

Fung, Archon, Gilman, Hollie Russon, and Shkabatur, Jennifer (2013), 'Six Models for the Internet + Politics', *International Studies Review* 15(1), 30–47, doi: https://doi.org/10.1111/misr.12028.

Gastil, John (2016), 'Building a Democracy Machine: Toward an Integrated and Empowered Form of Civic Engagement', Harvard Kennedy School, Ash Center for Democratic Governance and Innovation, http://ash.harvard.edu/files/ash/files/democracy_machine.pdf, accessed 10 October 2021.

Gastil, John, and Richards, Robert C. (2017), 'Embracing Digital Democracy: A Call for Building an Online Civic Commons', *PS: Political Science & Politics* 50(3), 758–763, doi: https://doi.org/10.1017/S1049096517000555.

Gordon, Eric, and Baldwin-Philippi, Jessica (2014), 'Playful Civic Learning: Enabling Lateral Trust and Reflection in Game-Based Public Participation', *International Journal of Communication* 8(February), 28.

Gould, Carol C. (1988), *Rethinking Democracy: Freedom and Social Co-Operation in Politics, Economy, and Society* (Cambridge: Cambridge University Press).

Guseva, Alya, and Rona-Tas, Akos (2019), 'Consumer Credit Surveillance', in Frederick F. Wherry and Ian Woodward, eds, *The Oxford Handbook of Consumption* (Oxford: Oxford University Press), 341–357, doi: https://doi.org/10.1093/oxfordhb/9780190695583.013.16.

Harari, Yuval Noah (2017), *Homo Deus: A Brief History of Tomorrow* (New York: HarperCollins).

Heath, Joseph (2020), *The Machinery of Government: Public Administration and the Liberal State* (Oxford: Oxford University Press).

Hidalgo, César (2018), *A Bold Idea to Replace Politicians*, Ted talk, https://www.ted.com/talks/cesar_hidalgo_a_bold_idea_to_replace_politicians, accessed 10 October 2021.

Hindman, Matthew (2009), *The Myth of Digital Democracy* (Princeton, NJ: Princeton University Press).

Howard, Philip N., and Hussain, Muzammil M. (2011), 'The Upheavals in Egypt and Tunisia: The Role of Digital Media', *Journal of Democracy* 22(3), 35–48, doi: https://doi.org/10.1353/jod.2011.0041.

Howard, Philip N., and Hussain, Muzammil M. (2013), Democracy's Fourth Wave? (Oxford: Oxford University Press).

Kolodny, Niko (2014), 'Rule Over None I: What Justifies Democracy?', *Philosophy & Public Affairs* 42(3), 195–229, doi: https://doi.org/10.1111/papa.12035.

Lafont, Cristina (2015), 'Deliberation, Participation, and Democratic Legitimacy: Should Deliberative Mini-Publics Shape Public Policy?', *Journal of Political Philosophy* 23(1), 40–63, doi: https://doi.org/10.1111/jopp.12031.

Lalley, Steven, and Weyl, E. Glen (2017), 'Quadratic Voting: How Mechanism Design Can Radicalize Democracy', SSRN Scholarly Paper ID 2003531. Rochester, NY, Social Science Research Network, doi: https://doi.org/10.2139/ssrn.2003531.

Landemore, Hélène (2013), *Democratic Reason: Politics, Collective Intelligence, and the Rule of the Many* (Princeton, NJ: Princeton University Press).

Lepore, Jill (2020), *If Then: How the Simulmatics Corporation Invented the Future* (New York: Liveright Publishing).

Lerner, Josh (2014), *Making Democracy Fun: How Game Design Can Empower Citizens and Transform Politics* (Cambridge, MA: The MIT Press).

Levine, David K. (2020), 'Radical Markets by Eric Posner and E. Glen Weyl: A Review Essay', *Journal of Economic Literature* 58(2), 471–487, doi: https://doi.org/10.1257/jel.20191533.

Liang, Fan, Das, Vishnupriya, Kostyuk, Nadiya, and Hussain, Muzammil M. (2018), 'Constructing a Data-Driven Society: China's Social Credit System as a State Surveillance Infrastructure', *Policy & Internet* 10(4), 415–453, doi: https://doi.org/10.1002/poi3.183.

Lim, Merlyna (2018), 'Roots, Routes, and Routers: Communications and Media of Contemporary Social Movements', *Journalism & Communication Monographs* 20(2), 92–136, doi: https://doi.org/10.1177/1522637918770419.

Lim, Merlyna, and Kann, Mark E. (2008), 'Politics: Deliberation, Mobilization and Networked Practices of Agitation', in Kazys Varnelis, ed., *Networked Publics* (Cambridge, MA: The MIT Press), 77–108.

Loh, Wulf (2019), 'The Gamification of Political Participation', *Moral Philosophy and Politics* 6(2), 261–280, doi: https://doi.org/10.1515/mopp-2018-0037.

Lyon, Aidan (2016), 'Data', in Paul Humphreys. ed., *The Oxford Handbook of Philosophy of Science* (Oxford: Oxford University Press), 738–758.

Mansbridge, Jane J. (1983), *Beyond Adversary Democracy* (Chicago, IL: University of Chicago Press).

Mill, John Stuart (1859 [2003]), *On Liberty*, ed. David Bromwich and George Kateb (New Haven, CT and London: Yale University Press).

Morozov, Evgeny (2011), 'Liberation Technology: Whither Internet Control?', *Journal of Democracy* 22(2), 62–74, doi: https://doi.org/10.1353/jod.2011.0022.

Morozov, Evgeny (2014), *To Save Everything, Click Here: The Folly of Technological Solutionism* (New York: PublicAffairs).

Morozov, Evgeny (2019), 'Digital Socialism?', *New Left Review* 116(June), 33–67.

Nabatchi, Tina (2018), 'Public Values Frames in Administration and Governance', *Perspectives on Public Management and Governance* 1(1), 59–72, doi: https://doi.org/10.1093/ppmgov/gvx009.

Nabatchi, Tina, and Mergel, Ines (2010), 'Participation 2.0: Using Internet and Social Media: Technologies to Promote Distributed Democracy and Create Digital Neighborhoods', in James H Svara and Janet Denhardt, eds, *The Connected Community: Local Governments as Partners in Citizen Engagement and Community Building* (Phoenix, AZ: Alliance for Innovation), 80–87.

Newsom, Gavin (2013), *Citizenville: How to Take the Town Square Digital and Reinvent Government* (New York: Penguin Press).

NIST (2012), 'Accessible Voting Technology', National Institute of Standards and Technology, 18 December, https://www.nist.gov/itl/voting/accessible-voting-technology, accessed 10 October 2021.

Noveck, Beth Simone (2009), *Wiki Government: How Technology Can Make Government Better, Democracy Stronger, and Citizens More Powerful* (Washington, DC: Brookings Institution Press).

Noveck, Beth Simone (2018), 'Crowdlaw: Collective Intelligence and Lawmaking', *Analyse & Kritik* 40(2), 359–380, doi: https://doi.org/10.1515/auk-2018-0020.

Perez, Oren (2020), 'Collaborative E-Rulemaking, Democratic Bots, and the Future of Digital Democracy', *Digital Government: Research and Practice* 1(1), 8:1–8:13, doi: https://doi.org/10.1145/3352463.

Peter, Fabienne (2021), 'Epistemic Norms of Political Deliberation', in Michael Hannon and Jeroen de Ridder, eds, *Routledge Handbook of Political Epistemology* (New York: Routledge), 395–406.

Pitkin, Hanna Fenichel (1967), *The Concept of Representation* (Berkeley and Los Angeles, CA: University of California Press).

Posner, Eric A., and Weyl, E. Glen (2017), 'Quadratic Voting and the Public Good: Introduction', *Public Choice* 172(1), 1–22, doi: https://doi.org/10.1007/s11127-017-0404-5.

Posner, Eric A., and Weyl, E. Glen (2018), *Radical Markets: Uprooting Capitalism and Democracy for a Just Society* (Princeton, N.J.: Princeton University Press).

Posner, Richard A (2003), *Law, Pragmatism, and Democracy* (Cambridge, MA: Harvard University Press).

Przeworski, Adam (1999), 'Minimalist Conception of Democracy: A Defense', in Ian Shapiro and Casiano Hacker-Cordón, eds, *Democracy's Value* (Cambridge: Cambridge University Press), 23–55.

Rawls, John (1971), *A Theory of Justice*, rev. edn 1999 (Cambridge, MA: Harvard University Press).

Rawls, John (1993), *Political Liberalism* (New York: Columbia University Press).

Schlozman, Kay Lehman, Brady, Henry E., and Verba, Sidney (2018), *Unequal and Unrepresented: Political Inequality and the People's Voice in the New Gilded Age* (Princeton, NJ: Princeton University Press).

Shahbaz, Adrian, and Funk, Allie (2019), 'Freedom on the Net 2019', Freedom on the Net, Washington, DC, https://freedomhouse.org/report/freedom-net/2019/crisis-social-media, accessed 10 October 2021.

Shane, Peter M., ed. (2004), *Democracy Online: The Prospects for Political Renewal through the Internet* (New York: Routledge).

Simon, Julie, Bass, Theo, Boelman, Victoria, and Mulgan, Geoff (2017), 'Digital Democracy: The Tools Transforming Political Engagement', Nesta, https://media.nesta.org.uk/documents/digital_democracy.pdf, accessed 10 October 2021.

Strandberg, Kim, and Grönlund, Kimmo (2018), 'Online Deliberation', in André Bächtiger, John S. Dryzek, Jane Mansbridge, and Mark Warren, eds, *The Oxford Handbook of Deliberative Democracy* (Oxford: Oxford University Press), 364–377, doi: https://doi.org/10.1093/oxfordhb/9780198747369.013.28.

Susskind, Jamie (2018), *Future Politics: Living Together in a World Transformed by Tech* (Oxford: Oxford University Press).

Talisse, Robert B. (2019), *Overdoing Democracy: Why We Must Put Politics in Its Place* (Oxford: Oxford University Press).

Theiss-Morse, Elizabeth, and Hibbing, John R. (2005), 'Citizenship and Civic Engagement', *Annual Review of Political Science* 8(1), 227–249, doi: https://doi.org/10.1146/annurev.poli sci.8.082103.104829.

Towns, Steve (2010), '"The Innobucks Start Here"', *Governing: The Future of States and Localities*, April 2010, https://www.governing.com/columns/tech-talk/The-Innobucks-Start-Here.html, accessed 10 October 2021.

Tufekci, Zeynep (2017), *Twitter and Tear Gas: The Power and Fragility of Networked Protest* (New Haven, CT: Yale University Press).

Viehoff, Daniel (2016), 'Authority and Expertise', *Journal of Political Philosophy* 24(4), 406–426, doi: https://doi.org/10.1111/jopp.12100.

Watkins, Alan, and Stratenus, Iman (2016), *Crowdocracy: The End of Politics* (Romsey: Urbane Publications).

Wilson, James Lindley (2019), *Democratic Equality* (Princeton, NJ: Princeton University Press).

Wright, Erik Olin (2010), *Envisioning Real Utopias* (London: Verso).

Zacka, Bernardo (2017), *When the State Meets the Street: Public Service and Moral Agency* (Cambridge MA: Belknap Press).

CHAPTER 34

THE ETHICS OF QUITTING SOCIAL MEDIA

ROBERT MARK SIMPSON

> Even a spate of sternly worded articles called 'Guess What: Tech Has an
> Ethics Problem' was not making tech have less of an ethics problem. Oh
> man. If *that* wasn't doing it, what would?
>
> Patricia Lockwood (2019), 'The Communal Mind'

INTRODUCTION

'IT is easier to imagine the end of the world than it is to imagine the end of capitalism.'
So said the late philosopher and critic Mark Fisher (2009: 2), echoing remarks by Slavoj
Zizek. Fisher uses the word *imagine* advisedly. He wasn't saying that Armageddon is in
fact *more likely* than the end of capitalism. He was saying that when our culture tries
to imagine the near future, in speculative fiction and elsewhere, any post-capitalist society that it can envision is simultaneously a state of apocalyptic ruin. Socio-political
structures whose origins are still very recent, relative to humanity's long history, and
whose radically globalized incarnations are mere hatchlings, have become, in our
minds, integral pillars of human existence.

Something similar has been happening with social media. We are drifting into a
mindset on which social media in something like its current form is just a fact of life,
and where it is a given that social media companies will organize our relational and informational networks. Pundits say it is a waste of time trying to trigger a social media
exodus to change this technological state of affairs. Instead, they say we should 'embrace the future. At least it won't be boring' (Cox 2018). Or they allow that a user exodus
could transform the landscape, but then immediately pour cold water on that possibility.

Change seems possible, 'until you realise every single one of these users are just clueless individuals who want to post cat pictures'.

> They are not, and never will be a unified mass ... even a company that debatably owns the internet [Google] couldn't pull off enough of a critical mass [with its Google+ service] to make it work ... what can individual users do to compel Facebook into behaving properly? Quick answer: sweet f*** all.[1]

Such thinking is new to our culture, and it probably doesn't yet have as tight a grip on our imagination as the capitalism-or-bust mindset. But its grip seems to be tightening. Technologies and practices that bubbled up into existence less than two decades ago are being imaginatively reified as nailed-in, load-bearing structures in humanity's housing, as opposed to movable cultural furniture. To say that it doesn't have to be like this is, increasingly, to sound like a hopelessly naïve Luddite.

In this chapter, I examine how this idea colours debates around quitting social media. People can, and do, move away from using social media. If large numbers of people were to do this it would undermine the power of the major platforms (and the sector as a whole) and interrupt the network effects that compel reluctant users to carry on using social media. But regardless of this potential, advocates of quitting are often ethically criticized. They are told that their stance involves an objectionable expression of *privilege*. The people voicing this complaint generally agree that social media has genuine costs. But they worry that people in disadvantaged positions cannot afford to leave social media, on balance of considerations, and they find it problematic for others to flee the social media arena so long as this is the case.

There are major weaknesses in this kind of objection to quitting social media, although below I will highlight some grains of truth in it too. But what I am most interested in is how this critique helps to make a self-fulfilling prophesy of the idea that social media is an inescapable fact of life. Mass quitting would unravel the network effects that make it costly to avoid using social media. And that would make it easier for disadvantaged people to quit social media in turn, if they wanted to. The privilege-based objection to quitting only makes sense if one assumes from the outset that none of this is possible. The idea that social media just *is* an inescapable fact of life is thus functioning as a premise in arguments that rebuke and deter the very acts that could make it the case that social media *isn't* an inescapable fact of life.

In what follows I survey the main reasons for quitting social media, before explaining the privilege-based objections to quitting, and then criticizing those objections, in a way that expands on the above. My analysis has broader implications for the ethics and politics of technology. Many popular technologies remain widely used, in part due to forces of convention. Roughly, people's reasons for using a given technology, *x*, owe partly (sometimes predominantly) to the fact that many others are using *x* too. Where conventions strongly favour using technology *x*, there are always going to be some individuals who dislike *x* and who are willing to flout convention by rejecting *x* and absorbing the costs of that. The bigger lesson to be learned in dissecting privilege-based objections to quitting social media, is that it is wrong to automatically view this kind of preference-driven technological abstention as being inimical to a public-spirited agenda of trying to make communications technology work in the interests of people, rather than the other way around. Tech refuseniks are not necessarily being selfish, naïve, or politically obtuse. Rather, in at least some cases, they are piloting alternative ways of communicating and using technology, with the potential to ultimately benefit everyone. This is how we should think of the anti-social media vanguard, at any rate.

THE CASE FOR QUITTING

I will use the term *Quitting* to mean totally refraining from posting content on social media or reacting to other people's content with comments, likes, shares, etc. In short, you can Quit either by not having social media accounts or by leaving your accounts dormant. Quitting is, in essence, a matter of not actively participating in communication or other social interaction through social media platforms.

Of course, there are plenty of stopping places between being an intensive user of social media, on the one hand, and being a full-blown Quitter, on the other. Some people have strong ethical concerns about using social media, but also strong practical reasons to use it for specific purposes, and these people may—quite reasonably—look to limit their usage of social media, or to use alternative social media platforms that are less susceptible to ethical objections. I am focusing on Quitting because, as we will see, a number of authors have argued that Quitting involves an ethically objectionable expression of privilege. My aim is to counter those arguments.

In my definition of Quitting, I make no distinction between withdrawing from social media after using it for a time and never using it in the first place. Having said that, by Quitting I do not mean simply migrating from one social media platform to another. The privilege-based objections to Quitting that I examine in the following sections do not apply to those users who tour around different social media platforms. The choice that is (allegedly) a problematic expression of privilege is to position oneself outside of the whole communicative ecosystem of social media.

General reasons for quitting

Quitting shouldn't be seen just as a trivial lifestyle preference. It is (at least, it can be) a weighty choice—the kind of choice that it makes sense to seriously wrestle with. To see why, we first need to recognize social media's transformative potential, and the visionary agenda driving it. Social media has had a huge impact on how people acquire information, conduct their relationships, and manage their public lives (see e.g. van den Eijnden et al. 2016; Aalbers et al. 2019; Allcott et al. 2019). And industry leaders tend to champion these changes, rather than viewing them as a regrettable by-product of their business models. Consider Mark Zuckerberg's statement to investors, in the run-up to Facebook's stock market initial public offering (IPO) in 2012.

> Facebook was not originally created to be a company. It was built to accomplish a social mission—to make the world more open and connected ... we're inspired by technologies that have revolutionized how people spread and consume information. We often talk about inventions like the printing press and the television—by simply making communication more efficient, they led to a complete transformation of many important parts of society.[2]

Companies like Facebook are partly guided by this kind of lofty techno-revolutionary agenda. They aim to 'rewire the way people spread and consume information', to again use words that Zuckerberg put to potential investors. Various insidious undercurrents around these agendas have become more widely recognized, for example, in Shoshana Zuboff's (2019) analysis of tech-facilitated systems of 'surveillance capitalism', or in countless think-pieces which tie social media to the rise of reactionary populism. Quitting social media can be a way of resisting or opposing these agendas of social transformation. It can be a way of voting 'no' in our society's ongoing de facto referendum on whether to embrace some sort of Zuckerbergian vision.

To appreciate the weightiness of Quitting, we also need to recognize the power of the behavioural technologies that Facebook and others are using in pursuit of their agenda. Jaron Lanier (2019) has coined a term to describe these technologies and the business models around them. He calls it *Bummer*: Behaviours of Users Modified and Made into an Empire for Rent. Most social media platforms have a fairly simple set-up at the surface level. They provide a free, public-facing site through which users can post content and interact with other users. The companies make money through advertising and by gathering and selling data. But beneath this surface-level set-up, most social media platforms also purposefully filter the content that users are exposed to, in order to elicit greater user engagement (thus generating more data). And this filtering is potentially malign. Sites algorithmically monitor the content that elicits more user reactions—quite often, polarizing or inflammatory content—and then show users more of this material. Mark O'Connell neatly summarizes Lanier's worries about this set-up and its commercial exploitation.

> Social-media platforms know what you're seeing, and they know how you acted in the immediate aftermath of seeing it, and they can decide what you will see next in order to further determine how you act ... we, as social-media users, replicate [this] logic at the level of our own activity: we perform market analysis of our own utterances, calculating the reaction a particular post will generate and adjusting our output accordingly. Negative emotions ... tend to drive significantly more engagement than positive ones.
>
> (O'Connell 2019)

The point of this is that compulsive behaviour and increasing acrimony is not 'an epi-phenomenon of social media, but rather the fuel on which it has been engineered to run' (O'Connell 2019; see also van den Eijnden et al. 2016; Alter 2018). Quitting social media can be a way of resisting the compulsive pull of this behavioural technology. It isn't just a trivial lifestyle preference, then, but a choice about guarding oneself against potentially overwhelming psychological influences.

Even setting aside worries about compulsion or addiction, there are plenty of other prudential reasons for Quitting, that is, reasons that are just about the user taking care to look after their own needs and interests. There is evidence that social media makes users unhappy by spurring status anxiety and similar feelings, and that Quitting alleviates this (e.g. Tromholt 2016; Shakya and Christakis 2017; Hunt et al. 2018). There is evidence that social media usage increases one's risk of falling into delusional beliefs through the effects of echo chambers and filter bubbles (for extended discussion, see Settle 2018). And there is a range of worries about how social media usage can compromise the user's privacy (see 'Overtly ethical reasons for Quitting' below).

These are only *pro tanto* reasons to Quit. There are obviously some *pro tanto* pru-dential reasons running the opposite way as well. As Zeynep Tufekci (2018) says, in some regions 'Facebook and its products simply are the internet', and there are certain segments of public life 'that are accessible or organized only via Facebook'. For work purposes, then, and for certain kinds of 'life administration', people may have strong prudential reasons to use social media. And on a more run-of-the-mill level, some people just find social media to be more convenient than any other tool for keeping in contact with people, or for engaging in various kinds of group organising, including for purposes of political activism. The difficulties of maintaining relationships via other channels are often exaggerated, but social media wouldn't have become so widely used if it didn't offer at least some benefits on this front.

Overtly ethical reasons for Quitting

How someone weighs up the prudential costs and benefits of using social media will depend upon their personal situation. My point in surveying the prudential reasons for Quitting is to orient our thinking as to why people Quit. Generally, people seem to Quit for sensible self-interested reasons, mixed in with a hazy anxiety about their complicity in various social problems to which social media contributes.

The key ethical question, for our purposes, is whether the Quitter, acting on the basis of these sorts of prudential reasons, is thereby abjuring some putative ethical obligation, such that their Quitting can be viewed as somehow wrongfully selfish.[3]

Note that in the discussion to follow, relating to ethical arguments for and against Quitting, I will not be presupposing any particular normative theory or framework. The kinds of ethical considerations that I will be adverting to—the attainment of good or bad outcomes, worries about fairness and disadvantage—are ones whose ethical significance can in principle be accounted for within any ethical framework, including deontological, consequentialist, and virtue ethical frameworks.

Given the long rap sheet of ethical problems that have been identified in debates around social media, it may seem odd to view prudentially motivated Quitting as a selfish choice. After all, any qualms about Quitting's selfishness are likely to be outweighed by ethical worries that favour Quitting. Or so one may think. In fact, things are a little more complicated. Existing debates on the ethics of social media are generally concerned with bad outcomes that are caused or made more likely by social media's very existence, or by its core operational strategies, for example, the *Bummer* model. Therefore most of the ethical prescriptions that are offered in these debates are actionable, if at all, not by social media's individual users, but by *power players*, that is, actors who can directly affect how social media companies operate, such as senior executives and officers at the companies themselves and lawmakers and regulatory agencies that impose operational constraints on these companies. Indeed, these debates normally position individual users not as perpetrators of the relevant ethical problems, but as the victims if and insofar as the power players fail to intervene.

Consider debates about privacy on social media, for example. These typically begin with observations about the unusually intrusive ways in which social media companies gather and exploit users' data. They then raise question about what our underlying reasons are for caring about privacy and whether a right to privacy prohibits social media companies' data-management practices (Tucker 2014; Acquisti et al. 2015; Quinn 2016). But if we conclude that these practices do infringe the right to privacy, what follows, from a user's perspective? The upshot is not an ethical injunction, but another prudential recommendation: if you care about your privacy, avoid social media or take special care to guard your privacy in how you use it. Granted, the user has ethical reasons to act prudentially, so this can also be understood as an indirect (banal) ethical injunction. But this is all secondary to what is naturally seen as the main ethical upshot of the privacy worries. And these apply to power players. If the privacy concerns are well founded, the upshot is that power players should institute reforms in social media practices in order to better protect users' privacy.[4]

The same sort of analysis applies, more or less, to all of the other major ethical issues that are canvassed in the social media ethics scholarship to date. There are discussions about whether social media undermines meaningful friendship (Sharp 2012; Elder 2014), whether it results in problematic forms of alienation (Wandel and Beavers 2011, Bakardjieva and Gaden 2012), and whether it impairs people's competence as democratic citizens (Helbing et al. 2017). For each consideration, to the extent that the worries are well founded, the primary implication for the individual user is that they have prudential reasons to avoid social media, or to use it warily lest they incur the relevant adverse consequences. Again, as with the privacy worries, the implicit addressees of these arguments are power players: actors with the power to directly and significantly influence how social media operates, in order to mitigate its alienating, friendship-jeopardizing, or democracy-undermining effects.[5]

The argument from complicity

But this brings us back to worries about complicity. Maybe individual users should Quit to avoid being complicit in the problems noted above. Matthew Liao (2018) considers whether Facebook users are complicit in Facebook's facilitation of antidemocratic speech, for example, hate propaganda against the Rohingya in Myanmar. He recognizes that most users do not actively collude in these wrongs, but nevertheless, he says, they may still be 'failing to participate in a collective action (that is, leaving Facebook) that would prevent the deterioration of democracy'. Ultimately, Liao thinks that in order to be complicit in these wrongs, the user has to keep using Facebook while knowing that Facebook intends to facilitate anti-democratic actions. And his take on things is that while Facebook engages in some anti-democratic practices of its own (e.g. hiring public relations firms to push news stories seeking to discredit their critics), it doesn't intend to sponsor the more egregious anti-democratic acts that it facilitates. Thus, Liao concludes, Facebook does not cross any 'moral red line' which obliges users to Quit, on pain of complicity in an anti-democratic agenda.

Bracketing off Liao's judgements about that specific issue, we can ask whether this sort of complicity-based rationale for Quitting is compelling in principle. Against this rationale, one may argue (e.g. Henry 2015) that social media is just a tool. The fact that a tool is used for invidious ends does not forbid us from using it for good. But this is oversimplistic. It fails to acknowledge that technologies have affordances in a given con-text— 'they make certain patterns of use more attractive of convenient for users' (Vallor 2016: s. 3.4)—and that they are thus susceptible to predictable forms of misuse. If social media is a perfect tool for anti-democratic propaganda, then to insist, in reply to calls for stricter regulation, that it can also be used for good, is like arguing against gun controls because M16s can be used by good guys to shoot bad guys. Moreover, the 'social-media-is-just-a-tool' reply ignores the way that all social media usage increases the scope of the wrongful ends to which social media can be turned. The power of the major networks derives in part from the fact that people feel they have to use them because everyone else is too. 'Good users' reinforce these network effects much the same as any other users (Lanier 2019).

So, the 'social-media-is-just-a-tool' reply to the complicity argument is unpersuasive. But it helps us to see that consequences, in addition to intentions, are important for any assessment of how the individual user is implicated in bad outcomes borne of social media. If you have good reason to believe that your Facebook usage makes a real, al-beit small, contribution to bad ends, you cannot nullify the ethical ramifications of that simply by arguing that neither you nor Facebook's directors intended those ends. This is a particularly dubious instance of reasoning based on the doctrine of double effect, that is, the doctrine which says that it's okay to do something that has a foreseeable, bad side effect, as long as you don't consciously *intend* to bring about the bad side effect. We can see how dubious this reasoning is, as applied to the 'complicity with the evils of so-cial media'-type argument, by noting that the same reasoning could completely nullify any ethical objection to a carbon-intensive lifestyle, or to the consumption of products manufactured by indentured workers. In short, the risk of making a small contribution to seriously bad outcomes through a collective activity with many other people has some bearing on how you ought to act. Any plausible ethical theory—deontological, consequentialist, virtue ethical, or otherwise—assigns some normative weight to the consequences of people's actions, including unintended and merely contributory consequences.

In general, then, whether an individual user has an ethical reason to Quit, in order to avoid being complicit in problematic outcomes borne of social media, will depend on the extent to which their Quitting will actually have (or can reasonably be expected to have) a tangible impact in changing those outcomes. But then this is precisely why it is difficult to formulate a strong complicity-based ethical argument for Quitting. It is difficult for any individual to say whether and how their Quitting *will* affect the problems that they are hoping to address, given their tiny individual influence, and given the many other unpredictable factors, including other people's actions, which causally mediate between their actions and the problems. Quitting in order to mitigate social media's democracy-eroding effects (for example), is rather like buying organic fruit in order to mitigate colony collapse. It may have a very small positive impact, or it may achieve literally nothing, given all the other causal factors in play. The individual may still have some *pro tanto* reason to act, then, but their actions are not responsible for the problem in the right way—the causal relationship between their actions and the outcome for the sake of which they are being done is too remote—for them to be under any kind of binding obligation to act.

PRIVILEGE-BASED OBJECTIONS TO QUITTING

Let us take stock. The idea that we are positively obliged to Quit is implausible because the major ethical problems with social media are mostly ones for power players to address, and insofar as individual users bear some responsibility for those problems, via an argument from complicity, it is hard for any user to tell whether their Quitting is likely to even infinitesimally improve things. Conscientious motives may still be in play for the individual Quitter. They may think of their Quitting as expressing opposition to the problems borne of social media, or to the questionable political agendas that social media is serving. But for most Quitters, prudential reasons for leaving social media—the aim of safeguarding one's privacy, time, or happiness—are likely to carry more weight. This is not to deny that for many people, on balance, there are net prudential benefits in using social media. But at least for some people, these benefits will be outweighed by the countervailing costs.

The #DeleteFacebook movement that arose in the wake of the Cambridge Analytica scandal in 2018 saw large numbers of people Quitting—seemingly driven by a mix of prudential and conscientious motives, as just described—and calling for others to follow. But the movement quickly generated a raft of vigorous criticisms, whose main ethical theme was privilege. For instance, April Glaser argues that:

> Deleting Facebook is a privilege. The company has become so good at the many things it does that for lots of people, leaving the service would be a self-harming act. And they deserve better from it, too. Which is why the initial answer to Facebook's failings shouldn't be to flee Facebook. We need to demand a better Facebook.
>
> (Glaser 2018)

Along similar lines, Steph Mitesser argues that:

> Simply telling consumers to avoid a product demonstrates the inherent privilege required to abandon a technology. Calls to leave the Facebook don't reckon with the thorniest ways it has entrenched itself in our lives.
>
> (Mitesser 2018)

This is not the first time it has been noticed that privilege can tilt people towards an anti-technology mindset. In discussing 'digital detox retreats' and related fads a few years earlier, Casey Cep (2014) argued that people buying these fads are expressing a bourgeois, pseudo-spiritual impulse. 'Like Thoreau ignoring the locomotive that passed by his cabin at Walden Pond or the Anabaptists rejecting electricity', she says, these people 'scorn technology in the hope of finding the authenticity and the community that they think it obscures'. But the post-#DeleteFacebook objections to Quitting are more pointed. They are not just cocking an eyebrow at the hippy-ish vanity that motivates some neo-Luddites. They are criticizing the way that wider political circumstances apparently fail to register in the Quitters' motives, and they are pointing to identity-based inequalities to explain this insensitivity, and to explain why it is ethically troubling. Jillian York is especially forthright in this regard.

> A certain demographic—namely, white men—love to argue that people worried about data privacy violations should 'just leave' Facebook and other social networks ... what these tech bros don't offer are viable alternatives. This is fundamentally an argument made from a position of privilege. Those suggesting that we should simply walk away ... fail to understand why leaving is, for many, a luxury they can't afford ... for people with marginalized identities, chronic illnesses, or families spread across the world, walking away means leaving behind a potentially vital safety net of support.
>
> (York 2018)

Rashad Robinson, the President of the civil rights organization Color of Change, adds an incisive twist to this analysis. He links social media privilege to broader issues of identity-based injustice, by likening Quitters to upwardly mobile residents who move from poor school districts to affluent ones, without doing anything to help those left behind. Quitting is 'like people opting out of bad schools', he says: 'some people are still going to be there and can't opt out' (Ingram 2018).

Before turning to criticism, I want to run through some points in these kinds of arguments that seem well founded. First, note that the privilege-based objections are not always condemning Quitting *per se*, so much as the act of advocating for Quitting while ignoring the unequal costs of Quitting for different people. For instance, Mitesser (2018) objects to those 'telling people to stop using Facebook, while ignoring the foundational problems that led us here'. This also looks like the best way to read Glaser's claim that the #DeleteFacebook movement insults people for whom Quitting is costly. To preach the gospel of Quitting—when it is easier for the sermonizer to Quit than the sermonizee—does seem a little insulting because it unfairly implies that the sermonizee lacks the preacher's moral fibre.

Second, the key descriptive premise in these arguments—that Quitting is generally easier for privileged people and costlier for disadvantaged people—seems plausible.[6] Identity-based hierarchies are correlated with inequalities in social capital. Having an affluent upbringing, attending college, and being geographically mobile, all tend to result in a wider network of relationships that help in gaining employment and other competitive goods. Social media can compensate for deficits in social capital, by enabling easy access to a large (if relatively low-quality) network of connections. Members of disadvantaged groups are more likely to rely upon this compensatory source of social capital. Moreover, relatedly, sustaining a wide social network without social media is time-consuming. Inequalities in leisure time, correlated with demographic privilege, increase the relative costs of maintaining offline social networks for members of disadvantaged groups.

Third, I also want to endorse, at least for argument's sake, the normative principle that underpins privilege-based objections to Quitting. Call this the *Privilege Principle*: a person who enjoys a position of unmerited privilege relative to others sometimes ought to act in ways that (a) manifest appropriate recognition of; and (b) where possible, try to compensate for, the unfairness. Consider a person, A, planning to meet a co-worker, B, who has a physical disability. Suppose A suggests meeting somewhere that is harder for physically disabled people to access. But also suppose that matters play out fortuitously for B, such that in practice he is unexpectedly benefited by meeting at this location. The Privilege Principle captures the intuition, liable to be elicited in such a case, that A's conduct still involves an ethical failing. A has acted in a way that fails to manifest appropriate recognition of the disadvantage that B faces, compared to themselves, and neglects an opportunity to correct or compensate for the positional inequity between themselves and B.[7] This seems either wrong in itself, or vicious, or liable to result in bad consequences in the long run.

Robinson's analogy between Quitting and opting out of bad schools draws our attention to another important aspect of the social dynamics governed by the Privilege Principle. Some privileged acts not only fail to remedy unjust inequalities, but also in fact amplify them. The upwardly mobile family which contributes to de facto segregation in the education system, by moving to live and study in an affluent community, is not just taking advantage of their privilege to confer a benefit on their children that is unavailable to many others. They are also making an incremental contribution to the concentration of wealth and resources in educationally privileged communities, thereby increasing the magnitude of the positional disadvantages experienced by families who are unable to exercise the same kind of autonomy over where they live and where their children go to school.

This brings us to a fourth point that seems compelling in the privilege-based objections to Quitting. These objections partly express a concern that Quitting detracts from the goal of creating better—less privacy-infringing, happiness-inhibiting, or democracy-undermining—communication systems. Whether this counterproductivity thesis is correct is a further question (see 'Individual action and systemic change' below). But the idea that we have some kind of participatory responsibility for trying to make key parts of our society better seems reasonable. Most of us are not power players who can directly act to improve society's communication systems. But still, plausibly, we should try to be active participants in making those systems functional, fair, and respectful of their users' rights. We should all do our bit in trying to foster communicative practices that are good for society because if we don't, then unscrupulous corporations will construct our communication systems in ways that prioritize the interests of the few over the many. The argument can be made by analogy with other social systems. You may not control the school system, but you shouldn't educate your children in a way that inhibits beneficial education reforms. You may not be a power player in the structures of government, but you should vote and stay informed. If you are wealthy and secure, then maybe you would be better off totally opting out of political engagement as democratic institutions are being torn down. But this seems selfish, and especially so if your retreat makes it harder to repair anything.

The charge against Quitting is that it involves something like this indulgence of privilege. Many of us would be better off not using social media—at any rate, not using the platforms that currently dominate, which infringe upon our privacy, prejudice our information sources, fuel status anxiety, and so on. But people in disadvantaged groups and social positions—relating to their economic status, geographical location, physical abilities, or field of employment—incur greater short-term costs if they Quit, for example, related to the loss of social capital. Relatively privileged people can more easily compensate for these and other proximate disadvantages borne of Quitting. But if privileged people simply retreat from social media, they fail to manifest due recognition of, or in any way compensate for, the unfairness that allows them to do so. And as Robinson's school analogy suggests, they may increase the unfairness by nudging us towards a two-tiered communicative society, of immiserated Morlocks who cannot afford to unplug from the social media machine, and carefree Eloi who can do as they please. That is the crux of the objection.

INDIVIDUAL ACTION AND SYSTEMIC CHANGE

The first point to make, in addressing this charge, is that Quitting doesn't necessarily mean abjuring the responsibility I identify above, that is, to be an active participant in making our communication systems better. It is at least *possible* for the Quitter to promote progressive reforms in social media. The Privilege Principle doesn't condemn the bare fact of a person being privileged. It condemns blithely enjoying the fruits of privilege without trying to improve other people's lot. The fact that someone Quits doesn't automatically entail that they are doing this. The more charitable way to interpret the argument, then, is that it is making a claim about typicality, rather than necessity. *Typically*, Quitters are not doing anything to try to improve the communication systems from which they are distancing themselves. Rather, so the charge goes, they are (typically) just furthering their own immediate interests, and consigning other social media users to their less fortunate fate.

I have already granted that most Quitters will Quit primarily for prudential reasons. But this does not mean that they should be thought of as blithely leaving others to an unhappy fate. In all sorts of contexts, people acting to benefit themselves may be simultaneously changing background conditions that adversely affect others. To take one example, consider how improving safety standards in the car industry generates prudential reasons for motorists to buy state-of-the-art vehicles with enhanced safety features. This is costly, of course, and the costs can be more easily borne by the well off. But does that make it an unethical indulgence of privilege for well-off people to buy safer cars? No, because these purchases are not condemning the less-well-off to driving unsafe vehicles forever. They are expanding the market for safer vehicles and helping to drive industry reforms that ultimately make safer vehicles more affordable for more people. The prudential choices of well-off people in this case do not worsen the position of the badly off. Rather, they contribute to a shift away from the technological conditions that make being badly off so bad.

We can observe similar dynamics in play with social media. The more people who leave social media, to protect their privacy, or to break out of echo chambers, the more we will see alternative practices and technological choices that allow us to communicate and organize our lives without generating the bad effects of the current leading social media platforms. Jaron Lanier argues that it is actually incumbent upon privileged users to Quit, then, because they can more easily bear the short-term disadvantages involved in precipitating this kind of change.

> If you're privileged enough to have the option of walking away from social media, and yet you don't, you're failing to use your privilege to defeat a system that traps other people who are less fortunate than you … You have even more of a responsibility to see if you can get out of it than someone who genuinely is dependent on it.
> (Johnson 2018)

Thus, he argues, privilege-based objections to Quitting have things backwards. Being a privileged individual actually gives you additional ethical reasons to Quit.

> We're wealthier than ever. We have more options. That puts a moral onus on us to make some decisions that do what little we can to help those who are less fortunate, and [leaving social media] is one of those things.
> (Johnson 2018)

The moral logic Lanier is appealing to here is in fact more persuasive in the social media case, compared to something like the automobile safety case, given how conventional forces are involved in promoting social media usage. By *conventions*, here, I mean regularities of conduct that people have reason to conform to primarily because others are also conforming.[8] To act against a widely followed convention can be costly. But if conformity around some once-conventional practice breaks down, then each individual's primary reason for carrying on in the practice dissolves. And while conventions can be resilient in some cases, they can be surprisingly fragile in others. Sometimes, a small number of conspicuous non-conformists are enough to unravel a convention (Bicchieri 2017).

To see how this applies to our context, consider that many of the major downsides of Quitting that crop up in debates on this issue—for example, missing out on information about social events or not having a searchable web presence—are only disadvantageous if a majority of other people are taking advantage of the putative benefit that the Quitter is forgoing. If social media use were much less commonplace, then the default expectation that any person will have an easily searchable web presence will dissolve, and so too will most of the putative disadvantages of not having an easily searchable web presence. Similarly, if social media use were much less common, people would be less likely to think that posting information about an event on Facebook was enough to inform most people about it. This would lead people to advertise events via other means, and therefore one's not being on social media would be less likely to result in one missing out on such information.

Given the role that forces of convention play in social media networks, it is wrongheaded to complain, as several authors do, that those who endorse Quitting are treating essentially political problems as individualistic ethical quandaries. Mitesser (2018) objects to the way that pro-Quitting movements 'emphasize personal choice and discipline as solutions to systemic problems caused by the profit motivations of large corporations'. She suggests that this framing is adopted because a structural perspective on social problems is harder to grasp. Glaser (2018) expresses similar worries about framing the problems of social media as if the whole thing is 'an issue of individual consumer choice'. So far as they want communication systems to improve, Quitters think the issue is essentially about users making bad choices. 'But it's really a problem in search of a solution either from Facebook itself—changing its service so that its users really can feel safe—or from the government, which may need to step in and blow the whistle on Facebook's entire business model' (Glaser 2018).

These are false dichotomies.[9] Individual and collective ways of addressing social problems are not essentially opposed, especially when the problems are borne of practices that are partly conventional. Consider the way that individual consumer activism dovetails with collective action in relation to renewable energies. Some of the impetus driving growth in renewable energies has come from individual consumers demanding, and thus incentivizing the provision of, renewable options from home electricity providers. The shift towards renewables would obviously be going slower if this were the only mechanism driving change. Collective political action, via parliamentary democratic processes and various kinds of group campaigning, has been a powerful driver of change. But individualized drivers of change have helped as well. Individuals who install solar panels on their house and pay a premium for renewably sourced energy are not undermining collective political action. They are creating parallel streams in a tide of social change. The same is true with Quitting social media. Each individual that Quits weakens the conventional forces that compel others to continue using social media. It seems worse than futile for someone to stay on social media because of worries about 'individualizing' structural problems. This actor is worsening their own lot, and helping sustain social media's hold on others, while awaiting a top-down intervention to achieve the same sort of changes that they themselves could, by acting now, be helping to precipitate.

What about the worry that Quitting is one of those 'acts of privilege' that not only fails to remedy inequality, but in fact amplifies it? Consider again Rashad Robinson's suggestion that Quitters are like affluent people who opt out of disadvantaged public schools. Part of what is occurring in the education arms-race scenario is that the advantage acquired by the affluent family is ipso facto a positional disadvantage for those unable to move. The public school quitter is not *just* enjoying the fruits of privilege while failing to help others. They are contributing to a concentration of resources in privileged pockets of the education system, and thereby entrenching divides in that system that stand in the way of a fair, across-the-board realization of our educational aims. One way to understand the wrong is in terms of something like a Kantian formula of a universal law. The public school quitter cannot universalize the maxim they are acting on because what they are trying to do—give their children a better-than-average education—is of its essence something that isn't universally willable. But Quitting is unlike this. Quitters are not chasing an advantage whose attainment necessitates a positional disadvantage for others. What they are doing is more aptly likened to norm entrepreneurship: absorbing some short-term costs in order to try to upend harmful conventional practices. Quitters are seeking to withdraw from a system that is harmful, and whose *pro tanto* upsides are reliant upon a convention-driven expectation of universal participation. In this, the Quitters are acting on a maxim that is fairly straightforwardly universalizable.

Why, then, have so many progressive critics reached for a tenuous interpretation of the social significance of Quitting, which casts it in such a negative light, and downplays its positive potential? As I suggested above, I think this has happened in part because critics have prematurely concluded that social media is irreversibly a permanent fixture in our society, and therefore that leading-edge Quitters will simply be unable to precipitate a shift in the communications landscape. They have assumed that social media in something much like its current form is already a fact of life, and that Quitting will thus always be prohibitively costly for most people. At least some of the critical responses to Quitting come right out and say this.

> Perhaps you joined the #DeleteFacebook movement to deal a blow to multibillionaire Mark Zuckerberg's sprawling enterprise. You might have hoped that by joining a collective crusade you'd be partially responsible for slaying the beast, and making the

world a fairer place. It's a nice idea, but it's unrealistic. Facebook has over two billion users, and even if a throng of disgruntled westerners appalled by the prospect of their data being shared decides to sulkily throw in the towel, that won't offset the daily wave of new subscribers, particularly stemming from parts of Asia and Africa.

(Cox 2018)[10]

As I suggested in opening, we should try to retrieve our sense of the contingency of social media's present-day position and influence. Today's leading social media sites are enjoying a longer ascendance than the online platforms that they succeeded, and as Cox rightly observes, they are working hard to cement their place in the global communications terrain. But the future—technologically, socio-politically, and culturally—is uncertain. For one thing, telecommunications technology has developed rapidly in recent years. As it becomes possible for tech hardware to be more biologically integrated into our bodies, this is likely to have an impact on people's choices and preferences around telecommunication software platforms. And whether this will re-inforce the pre-eminence of leading social media services, or instead trigger a migration to other services, or perhaps even a wider backlash against the escalating system of hyper-connectedness, is, at this point, anyone's guess.

This uncertainty should make us averse to confident claims about the permanence of the status quo. If we can predict anything about how the world will appear to our descendants, it is that it will not look the same to them as it looks to us now. In the years ahead, new communicative technologies have as much potential to supersede today's leading technologies as those technologies themselves had before they started making landline telephones and fax machines obsolete. Of course, it is possible that today's tech giants will manage to 'lock in' their position in the telecommunications landscape. But any such stasis seems unlikely, so long as we are viewing things from a moderately sceptical, historically minded vantage point.

CONCLUSION: THE MACHINE STOPS

The arguments I have been considering are all premised on a negative view of social media. Those who make privileged-based objections to Quitting tend to agree with Quitters that what Facebook and others are doing and facilitating is, on balance, bad for users and for society. The dispute is about how we assess avoidance and retreat as responses to this. I have argued that Quitting should not be seen as a way of consigning people for whom it is costly to Quit to an unhappy fate. Instead, it can be understood as a way of increasing the likelihood of structural change in a system that has costs for most of us, however privileged. We are not obliged to Quit, but we should be doing our part—whether we are working inside or outside of the social media ecosystem—to try to make our communications technology and practices better in the future. Quitting can be a way to push in this direction, and while the impact of any individual's Quitting is tiny, it is, by the same token, commensurate with each individual's rightful share of control over our shared conditions. The critics who see Quitters as selfishly ducking away from a problem that calls for a collective remedy cannot make this allegation stick unless they prematurely conclude that individually precipitated change is unachievable. But we have no grounds for being doggedly sceptical about the possibility of change, or credulous about the idea that social media in its current form is here to stay, with all its problems. There is no conclusive reason to believe that change in this area *is* unachievable. But an ongoing widespread *belief* that it is unachievable will mean that it may as well be.

It is easy to deride people who reject the ascendant technologies of the day. We can psychologize their justifications and ascribe to them various kinds of dubious motives: nostalgia, pastoral romance, wishfulness, vanity. But the ones doing the deriding can be psychologized as well. E. M. Forster's 1909 story *The Machine Stops*—a prescient, if ultra-pessimistic depiction of an internet-like technology—is an illuminating touchstone here. Forster envisages a dystopia in which humanity lives in a giant mechanized network of self-sufficient, single-occupancy living pods. These are wired up for instantaneous screen-and-audio communication with other pods, a function that is mostly used for discussing culture and ideas, with the occupants rarely venturing outside their pods. Eventually, the maintenance system for the entire world-machine starts to falter, and it transpires that humanity is doomed because all know-how for mending the 'mending apparatus' has long been lost.

Forster is a little heavy-handed in some of his remarks about the alienating nature of technology. But he succeeds in illustrating how people who become reliant upon a technology can start to begrudge any effort to get by without it. The protagonist, Vashti, has a son who sets out on dangerous and unauthorized explorations outside the machine. Vashti feels her son is being not just foolish and uppity, but somehow treacherous in his ventures. More than anything else, she resents his dogged refusal to accept the reality of the machine's central position in human affairs, for good or ill. In Vashti, we see a portrayal of how people who have lost all perspective on the technologies that rule their lives can convince themselves that it is in fact those who are trying to regain perspective—recapturing a sense of the possibilities for acting contrary to the machine's affordances—who are being unrealistic or naïve.

There probably is a dash of bourgeois piety in the motivational stew that is fuelling some Quitters. But there may also be a dash of piety, with a different flavour profile, in the anti-Quitters' stew of motives too. No one is claiming that Quitting will enable us to magically wind back the clock on communications technology. The point is that we should be trying to make communication technology work in humanity's collective interests, more than it is currently, and that withdrawing from social media is one way to spur change—at least as good a way as petitioning power players to benevolently intervene. Quitters are not ipso facto opting out of the collective task of trying to improve our communicative systems, and in their Quitting they are weakening the network effects that have enabled certain platforms to acquire a momentary stranglehold on society. There is nothing untoward about taking steps that help to ready the soil in which a new—and we may hope, less centralized, uniform, and destructive—set of communicative systems can take root.

Acknowledgements

Thanks to Polly Mitchell, Carissa Véliz, and several anonymous referees for feedback and comments on earlier versions of this chapter.

Notes

1. 'The Ethics of ... Deleting Facebook,' *The Ethics Of*, 13 April 2018, http://theethicsof.com/2018/04/13/the-ethics-of-deleting-facebook, accessed 11 October 2021.
2. See http://techradar.com/news/internet/mark-zuckerberg-outlines-facebook-s-social-mission-1059550, accessed 11 October 2021.
3. For a broader overview of the motivations that people have for quitting, and for engaging in other forms of 'digital detox' behaviour, see Syvertsen and Enli (2020).
4. This assumes that privacy is essentially an individual good. But if privacy is in fact a public good, if we have a duty protect our privacy not just for our own sake, but for the sake of others, as Véliz (2019) argues, then the worries about privacy can be seen as being addressed not just to power players, but to individual users as well. Even so, much ethical criticism about privacy issues around social media positions the individual social media user not as the culpable perpetrator of the problem, but as the potential victim of the problem.
5. One may argue that we have ethical reasons, not just prudential reasons, to be good democratic citizens. However, our civic duties are about meeting a threshold of democratic competence, rather than optimising or maximizing democratic competence. Nevertheless, the user who meets this threshold still has *pro tanto prudential* reasons to quit, by virtue of social media's negative effects on his democratic competence.
6. Note that a number of authors who defend quitting nevertheless readily concede this premise (e.g. Helfrich 2018; Johnson 2018).
7. The way I have formulated the Privilege Principle incorporates two kinds of requirements. Early work on privilege, particularly McIntosh (2005), stresses the importance of cultivating sensitivity to privilege and its concrete manifestations. More recent work on privilege (e.g. Dunham and Lawford-Smith 2017) puts more stress on the importance of practical action aimed at compensating for the unfair implications of privilege. Some recent work (e.g. Podosky 2021) suggests how these two kinds of requirements can be brought together: the active cultivation of certain patterns of awareness and thought, related to identity-based privilege, can conduce to social changes that rectify the injustices borne of privilege.
8. This roughly encapsulates the main distinctive feature of a convention, as per the philosophical understanding of convention that has been widely espoused since Lewis (1969).
9. Notice also the false dichotomy in Vaidhyanathan's (2018) op-ed piece on quitting: 'Don't Delete Facebook. Do Something About It'. This tendentiously presupposes that deleting Facebook isn't itself *a way of* 'doing something about it'.
10. Related to this point, there is another example of a revealing headline, namely, Heather Kelly's (2018) op-ed piece on quitting entitled: 'Here's How to Delete Facebook. (It Won't Help)'.

REFERENCES

Aalbers, George, McNally, Richard J., Heeren, Alexandre, de Wit, Sanne, and Fried, Eiko I. (2019), 'Social Media and Depression Symptoms: A Network Perspective', *Journal of Experimental Psychology: General* 148(8), 1454–1462, doi: https://doi.apa.org/doiLand ing?doi=10.1037%2Fxge0000528.

Acquisti, Alessandro, Brandimarte, Laura, and Loewenstein, George (2015), 'Privacy and Human Behavior in the Age of Information', *Science* 347(6221), 509–514, doi: https://doi.org/10.1126/science.aaa1465.

Allcott, Hunt, Gentzkow, Matthew, and Yu, Chuan (2019), 'Trends in the Diffusion of Misinformation on Social Media', *Research and Politics* 6(2), 1–8, doi: https://doi.org/10.1177/2053168019848554.

Alter, Adam (2018), *Irresistible: The Rise of Addictive Technology and the Business of Keeping Us Hooked* (London: Penguin Random House).

Bakardjieva, Maria, and Gaden, Georgia (2012), 'Web 2.0 Technologies of the Self', *Philosophy and Technology* 25(3), 399–413, doi: https://doi.org/10.1007/s13347-011-0032-9.

Bicchieri, Cristina (2017), *Norms in the Wild: How to Diagnose, Measure, and Change Social Norms* (Oxford: Oxford University Press).

Cep, Casey (2014), 'The Pointlessness of Unplugging', *The New Yorker*, 19 March, http://www.newyorker.com/culture/culture-desk/the-pointlessness-of-unplugging, accessed 11 October 2021.

Cox, Josie (2018), 'Don't Bother Trying to Quit Facebook—It's Too Late and You Won't Change Anything', *The Independent*, 28 March, http://www.independent.co.uk/voices/facebook-mark-zuckerberg-privacy-settings-boycott-deletefacebook-a8277871.html, accessed 11 October 2021.

Dunham, Jeremy, and Lawford-Smith, Holly (2017), 'Offsetting Race Privilege', *Journal of Ethics and Social Philosophy* 11(2), 1–22.

Elder, Alexis (2014), 'Excellent Online Friendships: An Aristotelian Defense of Social Media', *Ethics and Information Technology* 16(4), 287–297, doi: https://doi.org/10.1007/s10676-014-9354-5.

Fisher, Mark (2009), *Capitalist Realism: Is There No Alternative?* (Winchester: Zero Books).

Forster, E.M. (1947 [1909]), 'The Machine Stops', in *Collected Short Stories* (Harmondsworth: Penguin), 109–146.

Glaser, April (2018), 'The Problem with #DeleteFacebook', *Slate*, 21 March, http://slate.com/technology/2018/03/dont-deletefacebook-thats-not-good-enough.html, accessed 11 October 2021.

Helbing, Dirk, Frey, Bruno S., Gigerenzer, Gerd, Hafen, Ernst, Hagner, Michael, Hofstetter, Yvonne (2017), 'Will Democracy Survive Big Data and Artificial Intelligence?', *Scientific American*, 25 February, http://scientificamerican.com/article/will-democracy-survive-big-data-and-artificial-intelligence/, accessed 11 October 2021.

Helfrich, Gina (2018), 'Deleting Facebook Is a Privilege. You Should Do It Anyway', *Medium*, 22 March, http://medium.com/@ginahelfrich/deleting-facebook-is-a-privilege-you-should-do-it-anyway-fb299396fd70, accessed 11 October 2021.

Henry, Alan (2015), 'Don't Quit the Social Networks You Hate. Bend Them to Your Will', *Life Hacker*, 2 April, http://ifehacker.com/dont-quit-the-social-networks-you-hate-bend-them-to-yo-1683715538, accessed 11 October 2021.

Hunt, Melissa G., Marx, Rachel, Lipson, Courtney, and Young, Jordyn (2018), 'No More FOMO: Limiting Social Media Decreases Loneliness and Depression', *Journal of Social and Clinical Psychology* 37(10), 751–768, doi: https://doi.org/10.1521/jscp.2018.37.10.751.

Ingram, David (2018), 'While Celebrities Quit Facebook, Others Say They Feel Trapped by It', *NBC News*, 22 December, http://bcnews.com/tech/social-media/while-celebrities-quit-facebook-others-say-they-feel-trapped-it-n951281, accessed 11 October 2021.

Johnson, Eric (2018), 'If You Can Quit Social Media, But Don't, Then You're Part of the Problem, Jaron Lanier Says', *Recode*, 27 July, http://vox.com/2018/7/27/17618756/jaron-lanier-deleting-social-media-book-kara-swisher-too-embarrassed-podcast, accessed 11 October 2021.

Kelly, Heather (2018), 'Here's How to Delete Facebook. (It Won't Help)', *CNN Business*, 21 December, https://edition.cnn.com/2018/12/21/tech/how-to-delete-facebook/index.html, accessed 11 October 2021.

Lanier, Jaron (2019), *Ten Arguments for Deleting Your Social Media Accounts Right Now* (London: Vintage).

Lewis, David (1969). *Convention* (Cambridge: Harvard University Press).

Liao, S. Matthew (2018), 'Do You Have a Moral Duty to Leave Facebook?', *The New York Times*, 24 November, http://www.nytimes.com/2018/11/24/opinion/sunday/facebook-immoral.html, accessed 11 October 2021.

Lockwood, Patricia (2019), 'The Communal Mind', *London Review of Books*, 41(4), 11–14.

McIntosh, Peggy (2005), 'White Privilege: Unpacking the Invisible Knapsack', in Maxine Baca Zinn, Pierette Handagneu-Sotelo, and Michael A Messner, eds, *Gender through the Prism of Difference*, 3rd edn (New York: Oxford University Press), 278–281.

Mitesser, Steph (2018), 'You Can't Just Tell Everyone to Leave Facebook', *The Outline*, 3 April, https://theoutline.com/post/4040/you-cant-just-tell-everyone-to-leave-facebook, accessed 11 October 2021.

O'Connell, Mark (2019), 'The Deliberate Awfulness of Social Media', *The New Yorker*, 19 September, http://www.newyorker.com/books/under-review/the-deliberate-awfulness-of-social-media, accessed 11 October 2021.

Podosky, Paul-Mikhail Catapang (2021), 'Privileged Groups and Obligation: Engineering Oppressive Concepts', *Journal of Applied Philosophy* 38(1), 7–22, doi: https://doi.org/10.1111/japp.12398.

Quinn, Kelly (2016), 'Why We Share: A Uses and Gratifications Approach to Privacy Regulation in Social Media Use', *Journal of Broadcasting & Electronic Media* 60(1), 61–86, doi: https://doi.org/10.1080/08838151.2015.1127245.

Settle, Jaime E. (2018), *Frenemies: How Social Media Polarizes America* (Cambridge: Cambridge University Press).

Shakya, Holly B., and Christakis, Nicholas A. (2017), 'Association of Facebook Use with Compromised Well-Being: A Longitudinal Study', *American Journal of Epidemiology* 185(3), 203–211, doi: https://doi.org/10.1093/aje/kww189.

Sharp, Robert (2012), 'The Obstacles against Reaching the Highest Level of Aristotelian Friendship Online', *Ethics and Information Technology* 14(3), 231–239, doi: https://doi.org/10.1007/s10676-012-9296-8.

Syvertsen, Trine, and Enli, Gunn (2020), 'Digital Detox: Media Resistance and the Promise of Authenticity', *Convergence: The International Journal of Research into New Media Technologies* 26(5–6), 1269–1283, doi: https://doi.org/10.1177/1354856519847325.

Tromholt, Morten (2016), 'The Facebook Experiment: Quitting Facebook Leads to Higher Levels of Well-Being', *Cyberpsychology, Behavior, and Social Networking* 19(11), 661–666, doi: https://doi.org/10.1089/cyber.2016.0259.

Tucker, Catherine E. (2014), 'Social Networks, Personalized Advertising, and Privacy Controls', *Journal of Marketing Research* 51, 546–562, doi: https://doi.org/10.1509/jmr.10.0355.

Tufekci, Zeynep (2018), 'Facebook's Surveillance Machine', *The New York Times*, 19 March, http://nytimes.com/2018/03/19/opinion/facebook-cambridge-analytica.html.

Vaidhyanathan, Siva (2018), 'Don't Delete Facebook. Do Something About It', *The New York Times*, 24 March, https://nytimes.com/2018/03/24/opinion/sunday/delete-facebook-does-not-fix-problem.html, accessed 11 October 2021.

Vallor, Shannon (2016), 'Social Networking and Ethics', in Edward N. Zalta, ed., *The Stanford Encyclopedia of Philosophy (Winter 2016 Edition)*, http://plato.stanford.edu/archives/win2016/entries/ethics-social-networking, accessed 11 October 2021.

van den Eijnden, Regina J.J.M, Lemmens, Jeroen S., and Valkenburg, Patti M. (2016), 'The Social Media Disorder Scale', *Computers in Human Behaviour* 61, 478–487, doi: https://doi.org/10.1016/j.chb.2016.03.038.

Véliz, Carissa (2019), 'Privacy Is a Collective Concern', *New Statesman*, 22 October, http://newstatesman.com/science-tech/privacy/2019/10/privacy-collective-concern, accessed 11 October 2021.

Wandel, Tamara, and Beavers, Anthony (2011), 'Playing Around with Identity', in D. E. Wittkower, ed., *Facebook and Philosophy: What's on Your Mind?* (Chicago: Open Court), 89–96.

York, Jillian C. (2018), 'What #DeleteFacebook Tech Bros Don't Get: Without Viable Alternatives, Walking Away Is Still a Privilege', *NBC News*, 27 March, http://nbcnews.com/think/opinion/what-deletefacebook-tech-bros-don-t-get-without-viable-alternatives-ncna860286, accessed 11 October 2021.

Zuboff, Shoshana (2019), *The Age of Surveillance Capitalism: The Fight for the Future at the New Frontier of Power* (London: Profile Books).

....

CHAPTER 35

THE ETHICS OF BRAIN UPLOADING

....

FRANCESCA MINERVA

BRAIN UPLOADING AND LIFE EXTENSION

....

BRAIN uploading, or whole brain simulation, is a potential future technology aimed at creating one or more digital copies of a biological brain (Agar 2011; Chalmers 2014). In this chapter, we focus on the ethical implications of human brain uploading, that is, on the ethical issues that can arise when a human brain is moved from a carbon-based substrate, such as a human body, to a digital one, such as a computer (Hauskeller 2012; Walker 2014). The basic assumption at the basis of brain uploading is that the information (mental states, memories, psychological traits, etc.) stored in the brain can be copied and uploaded on a digital substrate. The digital substrate could be a computer running a virtual reality programme or a hybrid consisting of a biological and a digital entity (for instance, if humans and machines merged, an individual could have a digital brain in a biological body or there could be half biological–half digital brain hybrids, etc.) (Häggström 2021).

The main reason why some people are interested in brain uploading is the desire to extend their lifespan by several years and perhaps even indefinitely (Kelly 2020; Hughes 1995).

The main advantage of using brain uploading as a life-extension tool is that digital entities do not age in the same way and at the same speed as biological entities do. Our bodies cannot live for much longer than a handful of decades before eventually structural failure and accumulated damage bring any human, even the healthiest ones, to death.

On the other hand, a digital brain would be a more robust and energy-efficient medium than a biological brain, just like the data stored in our laptops can survive, if properly saved, for much longer than the hardware of our laptops (Cerullo 2015). Moreover, once a brain has been uploaded, it becomes relatively easy to make multiple copies of it and to keep them up to date with the original (or the copy that is being 'active'—i.e. connected to input sensors that allow it to experience the surrounding world and, in turn, to process the information). Even if the upload was destroyed and could no longer be in use (the equivalent of human death), another copy could easily replace it.

At the moment, brain uploading is merely speculative, and it is not clear whether it will ever become feasible in practice (Cheshire 2015). However, since there is a not negligible possibility that this technology will be developed in the future, we should start thinking about its possible implications, since we need to understand whether this is a project worth trying and whether the pros of brain uploading do outweigh the cons. Some of the dilemmas related to brain uploading have to do with theoretical questions about consciousness, personal identity, and moral status (Walker 2014; Cerullo 2015). Other dilemmas deal with the ethical, social, and legal implications of moving from a biological to a digital substrate or a biological–digital hybrid state (Feygin et al. 2018; Sotala and Valpola 2012).

At a more general level, philosophers disagree with respect to the actual possibility that digital entities can be conscious, since many believe that only carbon-based individuals can experience consciousness. The disagreement depends in part on what different philosophers take 'consciousness' to mean but especially on what they believe to be the essential requirements for consciousness to arise in an entity. Those who believe that consciousness can only arise in carbon-based entities exclude the possibility of a conscious artificial intelligence (AI) or a conscious brain upload, for that matter. Illustrating this debate is beyond the scope of this chapter. It is enough to say that the approach to consciousness underlying this chapter is a functionalist one according to which consciousness emerges from certain causal structures and causal roles. According to this approach, consciousness could emerge from any entity, regardless of its substrate, insofar as it is organized correctly.

In sum, we don't know if brain uploading will allow future humans to achieve life extension because we don't know if such uploaded entities will be conscious. Nevertheless, I will consider a few possible scenarios entailing successful brain uploading (i.e. brain uploading which is conscious and similar enough to the original) and its ethical implications.

Is this the real world or is this just a simulation?

Philosophers have discussed the 'brain-in-a-vat' thought experiment for a long time, though it is only recently that this option has become a possibility (though remote) rather than a mere thought experiment. In the past, the brain-in-a-vat hypothesis has been entertained to discuss sceptical arguments with respect to the possibility of knowing the external world.

Descartes had initially introduced this problem using the example of an Evil Genius who makes one believe that there is a whole world outside (the world one believes one is experiencing), whereas in reality there is nothing and it's the Evil Genius who makes one believe that something exists (Descartes 1641). In modern times, Gilbert Harman (1973) and Hilary Putnam (1981), among others, adapted the Evil Genius thought experiment and came up with the thought experiment of a 'brain in a vat', which lives in a simulated reality. What the brain in a vat interprets as real-life experiences are instead the results of the neurons being stimulated and the brain's response to such stimuli. So, just like in the case of the Evil Genius, the brain in the vat is wrong in believing it is actually experiencing something in the real world.

An uploaded brain, if not merged with a biological body and if not uploaded on a robot which can be stimulated by real inputs in the same way as all living beings currently are (or maybe they just believe they are?) (Bostrom 2003), could live as an upload in a simulated reality where, like in the brain-in-a-vat example, the stimuli don't come from the outside world but from a computer.

In the cases discussed by Descartes, and then by Harman, Putnam, and Bostrom (among others), the main issue they want to address is the scepticism towards what we perceive to be real: 'Is this the real world, or is it just a simulation?' is the question they ultimately want to answer. But such scepticism wouldn't necessarily be more of a problem for the uploaded brain than it is for the rest of us, human beings living right now. Indeed, while it would be possible to upload a brain to a virtual reality programme without letting them know they are in a simulation, two other scenarios are also possible. In one scenario, the brain is uploaded on an entity, biological or a robot, that allows them to keep being stimulated by the real world as they did before being uploaded, that is, when they were still like us. In another scenario, the uploaded brain would freely choose to live in the virtual reality programme (as in the episode 'San Junipero'[1] in the Netflix show Black Mirror) or as something more similar to a brain in a vat (as in the Roald Dhal's short story, 'William and Mary'[2]).

Granted, if we already live in a simulation, as some philosophers suggest (Bostrom 2003), then the uploads would end up living in a simulation within the simulation. But it's not clear that this would be worse than living in a simulation (as the uploads did before being uploaded and as we might be doing right now) or than not experiencing anything at all, that is, being conventionally dead. Indeed, one might say that the uploads choosing to live in the simulation would be more aware of the true nature of their experiences than those, like us, who might be living in what we believe to be 'the real world'—if it turned out that the 'real world' is just a simulation in itself. If we are all already in a simulation without knowing it, we are living our lives ignoring the real nature of our experiences. If the uploaded brain knowingly lived in a simulation, they would be at least aware of living in a simulation (though they wouldn't know they were in a meta-simulation). So, even though uploading a brain into a virtual reality programme against their will or without telling them would be immoral, at least in most circumstances, for those who choose to upload their brain in digital form there is no reason to believe that they would know less about the reality they live in than they currently do. In sum, there is nothing inherently bad about living in a simulation, especially if this is a free choice, and, for some people, this would be a preferable option to experiencing nothing at all.

HOW TO UPLOAD A BRAIN

The details pertaining to the practical procedure involved in brain uploading are not relevant to this chapter. However, in order to better understand the ethical aspects of brain uploading, it is necessary to have at least a rough idea of what the possible technologies being discussed in order to achieve it are and how they would work.

Following David Chalmers (2009), we will assume that there are three main forms of brain uploading (though we can't exclude that other technologies might be developed in the future): *destructive brain uploading, gradual brain uploading, and non-destructive brain uploading.*

Destructive brain uploading is the uploading that is more likely to be developed first, given current knowledge. In this kind of uploading, the brain has to be sectioned in very thin layers (hence why it is called 'destructive'). Subsequently, every thin layer is analysed and its structure recorded, creating a faithful copy of the neurological information on each layer. Finally, this information is uploaded to a computer model running a programme with a simulation of neuronal behaviour. In order to scan the brain with this particular method, the biological brain needs to be sectioned, hence the original and the copy don't coexist at the same time since the copy can be created only when the analysis and recording of all the information in each layer is completed (Chalmers 2009: 42).

Gradual uploading would most likely involve nano-transfer. Nanotechnology devices would be attached to each neuron and would learn to simulate its behaviour and replicate its connections. Once this process was completed, the nanotechnology would replace the biological neuron and would offload the processing to a computer so that eventually every neuron would be replaced by an emulation and could be uploaded onto a digital entity.

In this case, the original brain would not need to be destroyed; hence, the original and the uploading could exist at the same time or they could partially coexist, if the nanotechnology would end up damaging or destroying the neuron to which it was attached. It would therefore be possible for someone to be halfway in the process of having half of their brain in digital form and half in a carbon-based one (Chalmers 2009: 42).

Non-destructive uploading is the most far-fetched kind of uploading of the three at the moment since it would be the most difficult to realize in practice. This kind of brain uploading would rely on brain imaging. The proposal is that of scanning the brain through brain imaging, recording, and then uploading the neural and synapses activity (without having to slice the brain as in the destructive brain uploading). In this case, the whole biological brain and the digital copy (or copies) would easily coexist at the same time (Chalmers 2009: 42).

SURVIVAL

Even though none of the above-mentioned uploading techniques is likely to be developed any time soon, we need to understand whether they could, in principle, deliver life extension. The key questions we are trying to answer in this chapter are: 'Can a brain upload be conscious?' and 'Would my brain upload be "me" in a relevant sense?'

If one assumed that the digital copy of a brain could not possibly be conscious, then there would be no chance that one could survive the upload. However, we can't be sure that the upload would not be conscious and, more generally, that digital entities cannot be conscious. Therefore, we need to take into consideration the possibility that brain uploads, as well as robots and other entities that are digital-based, could, at some point, be conscious.

On the basis of a functionalist approach, we can assume that a digital entity could be conscious. Now, the next important question to ask is whether the digital version of the brain would be, in a relevant sense, the same person as the biological individual with the original brain. It would not follow from the fact that the uploaded brain would be conscious that it would also preserve the essential features that make the person before the upload who they were. For someone to survive the upload, in other words, they should have not only a conscious brain but also *their own conscious* brain.

The plan of using brain uploads as a life-extension tool can only work if an upload (and any copy of it) would turn out to be as good as biological life with respect to survival over time (Sandberg and Bostrom, 2008). To some people, this idea sounds downright absurd. However, if we start thinking about the implications of a head transplant, we might end up with intuitions that conflict with the ones about brain uploading.

Although a head transplant on a human has not been performed yet, the Italian doctor Sergio Canavero has claimed that it could be a reality within the next decade (Ren and Canavero 2017). The recipient of the transplant would be a patient experiencing severe disability in the body but who had a perfectly healthy brain. The head (with the whole nervous system) would have to be removed and attached to a deceased donor's body. Though this kind of surgery is not available yet, it's useful to use it to test our intuitions with respect to the role of the brain–body link in survival over time. If a patient's head were transplanted onto a donor's body, could that patient, upon waking up from the surgery, say 'I am the same person who underwent the surgery, I remember who I was before the surgery and I'm glad I've survived' in the same way as a person undergoing a trivial intervention, such as a root canal, would still be themselves after the surgery? In other words, would they be the same person waking up from the transplant, even though their body (apart from the head) is completely different? Some people might say 'No' because they believe that body and brain are both equally essential to survival over time or, in other words, they believe that once the brain is separated from the body, a certain individual ceases to exist. But the ones who believe that someone could survive a head transplant in the same way as they could survive a root canal (i.e. without doubts about whether they would be the same person upon waking up) probably also believe that what matters to survival has something to do with the brain. Of course, someone might say that an individual can only survive over time if no part of their body is ever replaced, but this would imply that nobody survives over a small number of years since all the cells in our body are replaced every seven years (and some of them even more often than that). Philosophers have discussed whether the 'ship of Theseus' thought experiment applies to consciousness as well (Floridi 2011). From what most people who undergo organ transplants report and from the experience of each of us of replacing all our cells several time throughout our lives, it seems reasonable to argue that we indeed survive over time, even though we go through a replacement of our body parts. To claim the opposite (i.e. that losing and/or replacing some bits of our bodies would be equivalent to dying) would be quite bizarre and not easy to justify on the basis of the empirical evidence currently available: it would imply that a root canal or a heart transplant would not be better than death, which is a bizarre claim. Moreover, we know from people who have undergone heart transplants that they still feel like themselves after the surgery. If these people felt like they were no longer themselves and that being dead would be the same as undergoing the transplant, we wouldn't have so many people feeling grateful for the interventions that saved their lives. Of course, one might feel different after a transplant, especially a transplant that changes visible features, as in the case of a face transplant. Perhaps, people who were used to the previous facial features would relate to them in a different way, but their survival over time—the relation-R in Parfitian terms— would not be affected by such a type of intervention. Derek Parfit argued in *Reasons and Persons* that personal identity is not necessary for persistence over time but rather Relation R (psychological connectedness or psychological continuity): 'Personal identity is not what matters. What fundamentally matters is Relation R, with any cause' (Parfit 1984: 287). Following Parfit's logic, then, uploading could be a tool to persist over time insofar as these copies have psychological connectedness or psychological continuity with the original.

So, someone who believes that a head transplant is compatible with survival over time would either hold the view that the brain as a biological organ is essential to survival or that the brain in a metonymical sense (i.e. the word 'brain' is a part of what we really mean when we refer to our mental states, memories, psychological traits) is essential to survival. One could hold the view that the brain as a biological organ is essential to survival as a person, perhaps because they believe that consciousness can only emerge from a brain that is made of biological material. Nevertheless, it is also reasonable to argue that what matters in the brain is not the hardware but the software, like in a computer. When a computer stops working, we are mostly concerned about the files we have stored in it, not about any particular hardware piece. If the files have been backed up, it is easy to download them onto a new machine.

The parallelism between the human brain and a computer is useful for illustrating what people are trying to achieve when they say they want to extend their lifespan through brain uploading, but it has its limitations. For instance, we do not know whether there is something special about the fact that our 'files' are 'stored' in a biological brain, so we do not know what might happen if we changed substrate and moved to a digital one. It is possible that uploading a copy of our brain's 'files' onto a different substrate would not be the same as uploading them onto a biological brain. If so, we would have to conclude that it might be possible to survive a head transplant but not a brain upload.

Consciousness

The key question to understanding whether brain uploading could be used as a life-extension tool is the conceivability of digital consciousness. This is a tough question to answer because we do not fully understand—or, at least, we disagree on—what consciousness is or what it does, and we cannot always easily tell apart a conscious being from a non-conscious one.

Philosophers trying to answer questions about the nature of conscious systems have provided various possible answers to questions related to consciousness. We will briefly mention only two: the biological and the functionalist one (for a more detailed map of the spectrum of theories about consciousness, see Van Gulick 2021) and, throughout the chapter, we are taking a functionalist approach to consciousness, though the same arguments would probably also apply to panpsychism (Goff et al. 2022). Biological theorists of consciousness share the view that consciousness can only emerge from biological entities (Olson 2001, Olson 2002). According to biological theorists, a brain upload, no matter how accurately mimicking the original, could never be conscious (and, in turn, a digital brain could never be the same as a biological one, and uploading the brain while destroying the original would be equivalent to dying).

Functionalist theorists of consciousness, as we have seen, believe that consciousness emerges from certain causal structures and causal roles and can emerge also in non-carbon-based entities (Shoemaker 2004). According to functionalists, an uploaded brain could be conscious and could be similar enough to guarantee the survival of a biological individual.

Unfortunately, at the moment, we cannot tell which theory is correct since we don't have much understanding of how and why a biological system becomes conscious in the first place. David Chalmers has argued that functionalist theories are closer to the truth than biological ones and that we have no particular reason to believe that biological systems are more likely to be conscious than non-biological ones, at least when they function in the same way. To prove this point, Chalmers asks us to imagine that a perfect upload of a brain can be transferred to a computer (Chalmers 2009: 209). For every neuron in the brain, there is an equivalent digital unit that perfectly replicates its input and output behaviour. Every processing activity in the brain is replicated with accuracy by the upload so that the upload is a functional isomorph of the original. Now, he says, let's consider a gradual form of uploading in which each brain component is replaced with digital equivalents. The whole procedure could last between minutes and years, depending on the technology chosen and how quickly these brain areas can be replicated in digital form.

Chalmers postulates that, during this process, consciousness could behave in three ways: (a) it could suddenly disappear so that a fully conscious being would become unconscious upon removal of a single component; (b) it could gradually fade out over an increasing number of replacements; or (c) it could stay through the whole process during which all of the components are replaced.

According to Chalmers, it is unlikely that consciousness would disappear as soon as one component is removed since we know we can easily survive the loss of some neurons in mild accidents. So, we need to consider the next scenario, where more components are replaced at the same time, and ask ourselves again what is likely to happen when a certain, progressively larger number of components has been replaced. In this new scenario, there would be either a gradual fading of consciousness or a sudden disappearance (for instance, when 100 out of 1,000 components were replaced). Eventually, then, we have either gradual fading or sudden disappearance when a single component is replaced and, according to Chalmers, both scenarios are possible but he believes they are not very probable. What he believes to be the most likely scenario, instead, is that full consciousness would stay through the whole replacement: 'On this view, all partial uploads will still be fully conscious, as long as the new elements are functional duplicates of the elements they replace. By gradually moving through fuller uploads, we can infer that even a full upload will be conscious' (Chalmers 2009: 47).

Until brain upload is attempted, it's not possible to tell whether Chalmers is correct in believing that consciousness would stay throughout the whole process. For all we know, consciousness could disappear altogether when a certain percentage of the biological brain is replaced with a digital isomorph substitute, or could be qualitatively different from biological consciousness, or could be intermittent, with digital individuals constantly switching between the states of conscious being and that of philosophical zombie. However, Chalmers's arguments show that it is at least conceivable that an upload could be conscious, which is sufficient to us in order to continue discussing the ethics of brain uploading.

Personal identity

We have just seen that, according to some accounts of consciousness, brain uploads could be conscious just like biological humans are conscious. However, being conscious might not be enough to claim that brain uploading can be a tool in life extension. Migrating the content of one's brain to a conscious digital substrate would not be much different from dying if one couldn't think of oneself as the same person one was before undergoing the upload. To put it very simply, what matters for survival is that one could meaningfully say '*I* have made it, I have survived the upload', meaning that one remembers being the same entity one was before the upload. Derek Parfit explains this point, asking us to imagine someone who needs to be tele-transported to Mars. The machine for the tele-transport works in the following way. There is a part of the machine, 'the Scanner', that destroys the brain and the body of an individual while recording the exact state of all the cells; this information is then transmitted to a 'replicator' on Mars, where a brain and a body identical to the original will be created out of new matter (Parfit 1984: 200–201). Upon their arrival on Mars, the individual feels exactly like themselves, they have the perception of being the same person they were on earth. According to Parfit, in this case, being destroyed and replicated is as good as ordinary survival, even though some would disagree and claim that, since the individual has been replicated out of new matter, they have not survived. This individual is not numerically identical to the one on earth but is qualitatively identical to them, and that's what matters in order to survive over time, so Parfit claims.

Throughout our lives as biological creatures, we face events that can put at risk our chances of surviving over time, such as dramatic accidents that alter our mental states to the point that our loved ones don't recognize us, or diseases that destroy all of our memories. Imagine that someone has a car accident and ends up in a comatose state for several years. When they eventually wake up, the doctors can see that they are conscious and that their brain has restarted to function normally. However, their family members can notice that they are very different. They hardly remember anything about their past, they do not remember who they were or who they are, they are no longer interested in the same things they used to like and they seem to have different preferences. In such a situation, we would say that even though they are numerically identical to the person they were before getting into a comatose state, they are not qualitatively identical to the person they were before the accident.

Some people might have the intuition that they are the same person and they have survived the accident because they are still themselves, even though they have changed. In a way, we all go through radical changes when we go from infants to adults, and yet we don't think of those cases as dying. As Derek Parfit pointed out (1984: 202) when we worry about our survival, we mostly worry about preserving our numerical identity. For instance, even though some life experiences can change us profoundly (growing older or having a brain injury), we do not perceive such change as a threat to our survival. However, he adds 'certain kinds of qualitative change destroy numerical identity. If certain things happen to me, the truth might not be that I become a very different person. The truth might be that I cease to exist, that the resulting person is someone else' (1984: 241).

To clarify this point further, we can consider another hypothetical case. Imagine a future technology, 'the Eraser', capable of emptying every neuron of the information contained in it and deleting every synapse and every connection between synapses of the information they carry. Imagine a person (Mary) using the Eraser and then using some technology that allows another person's brain (Tom), previously uploaded on a computer, to be downloaded to Mary's grey matter (the machine that uploads and downloads the content from a biological substrate to a digital one and vice-versa is called 'the Swapper' and the Swapper can also make multiple copies of a brain and download each copy in very many biological people whose brains have been previously subject to a treatment with the Eraser). Upon waking up, Mary would be conscious but she would have all of Tom's mental contents: his memories and mental states, all of his preferences and interests, but no trace of her mental states before undergoing the Eraser and the Swapper. The person coming out of this experiment would be numerically identical to Mary (after all, most or all of her cells are there in the exact same place as they were before as the erasing and the swapping happen within a few minutes), but would be qualitatively identical to Tom or, at least, would be more qualitatively similar to Tom than to Mary. For human beings, the preservation of the information in the brain is crucial to personal identity and, in turn, for survival over time. If the only alternatives to death offered to someone were to either undergo the treatment that Mary underwent or the one used on Tom, it would make sense to them to choose to undergo the same intervention administered to Tom because, even though Tom wakes up in a different body, he still has access to all of his thoughts, memories, mental states, etc. (Tom experiences something similar to a brain transplant.) On the other hand, Mary would not even be able to recognize her body as her own body since the Eraser deleted the memory of being that body at an earlier time, so, to all intents and purposes, 'Mary' (or what used to be Mary) does not seem to be any longer the same person (and, indeed, she might be someone else, though she would retain her numerical identity).

If someone believes that psychological continuity is the only thing that matters for survival, they would probably believe that Mary has ceased to exist and that she is now Tom. Alternatively, one could believe that, since only the content of Tom's brain was downloaded into Mary's brain structure, both Tom and Mary have ceased to exist, and someone else has replaced both of them. Yet another possibility would be that, even though Mary's mental states and memories have been removed from her brain, she is still Mary because what matters is that she has preserved her body and brain (by the brain, in this case, we mean a shell made of tissue, not the mental states in it), and her mental states and memories are not what makes the difference between being Mary and not being Mary or between being Mary and being Tom.

The reason why people—and perhaps most people—think that it would make sense for someone to care more about preserving their mental states (i.e. the content of their brain) rather than their body is that we are usually inclined to believe that psychological connections between our past, present, and future selves, or continuity of our psychological features, is what matters the most in order to survive over time. This is not to say that there is no disagreement about this intuition among philosophers. Some of them claim that biological continuity matters the most (Olson 1999). There are also disagreements about what kind of psychological continuity (connectedness) is relevant to survival over time. However, if one believes that psychological continuity is relevant to survival, then uploads could be life-extension tools. If one believes that all that matters for survival is physical continuity, then uploading is not better than death.

Another relevant aspect of brain uploading that we need to consider when discussing personal identity and brain uploading is branching (or creation of multiple copies). Some philosophers believe that psychological continuity is necessary to survive over time and believe that such survival should take a non-branching form (Gustaffson 2019). According to them, brain uploading could be a form of life extension *only* in its destructive form but not when both the original and the copy or copies are alive. Insofar as we exist as purely biological beings, there is no (or very little) chance that our brain could be branched in two or split into multiple copies (perhaps some future technologies will allow the splitting of a brain and the replacing of half a brain in a different body, but for now it's not possible). We know that people can survive with only half a brain and can be highly functioning, as proven by patients who have to undergo hemispherectomies, an intervention aimed at curing some severe cases of epilepsy by removing a large part of the brain or cutting the links between the two hemispheres (Robinson 2019). In these cases, however, the other half of the brain is not implanted in another individual, therefore, by any account of personal identity, the patient does not cease to be themselves, but they are only themselves with half their brain.

With brain uploading, though, things get considerably more complicated since, once the brain has been transferred to a digital substrate, it is easy to make one or more copies of it. If these copies of the brain are implanted in different individuals, or computers, or robots, then we end up with several different individuals who, at the start, share the same past mental states. The question is whether, in these cases, brain uploading can be a tool for life extension.

On some accounts of personal identity, branching is death (Cerullo 2015): if Tom can, for instance, talk to his upload, go on a walk while the upload is sleeping, or do things that the upload does not even know about, then the upload cannot possibly be Tom. More importantly, if Tom dies, his upload may keep on living (indeed, that is the plan), but Tom cannot be at the same time both dead and alive. But if Tom and his upload are not the same person, it means that Tom will not survive through his upload because the upload is someone else (though they share the same past, up to a point). However, in cases in which Tom dies, and his brain is then scanned and uploaded, then it would be easier to believe that the upload is Tom (just like in the case of the person tele-transported to Mars in Parfit's example).

According to other accounts of personal identity, branching is compatible with survival because it is compatible with maintaining personal identity (Cerullo 2015). According to Cerullo, even though 'we will probably never be able to completely imagine consciousness splitting off into parts that are equally ourselves', we are still able to conceptualize having multiple copies of us living in parallel universes, and this is similar enough to what would happen if we had several copies of the uploaded brain at the same time.

Derek Parfit, instead, argued that personal identity is not necessary for persistence over time (he thinks that personal identity cannot take a branching form) but rather 'Relation R" (psychological connectedness or psychological continuity: (Parfit 1984: 287). Parfit says that 'What fundamentally matters is Relation R, with any cause. This relation is what matters even when, as in a case where one person is R-related to two other people, Relation R does not provide personal identity' (Parfit 1984: 287). If Parfit is right, then uploading could allow persistence over time, at least under some circumstances. In sum, even though we cannot be sure that brain uploading, especially in the branching form, could preserve personal identity (or Relation R, for that matter), we also cannot rule out brain uploading as a tool to achieve life extension.

MORAL STATUS

Another important ethical issue to be addressed when discussing brain uploading pertains to the upload's moral status. Having moral status is important because it is often considered an essential feature of individuals who are the bearers of fundamental rights such as the right to life. Philosophers do not agree about who or what should be granted moral status because they disagree about the parameters according to which one can be attributed moral status.

Some philosophers have argued that moral status should be conferred to all those beings who have more or less sophisticated cognitive capacities, but there is no agreement about which specific cognitive capacity (or how sophisticated) is a necessary and sufficient condition to grant moral status (Minerva 2019; Liao 2020). Suggestions include consciousness, sentience (De Grazia 2020), the presence of self-concepts and self-awareness, the capacity to engage in self-motivated activity (Warren 1973), and the capacity to understand oneself as a continuing object of experiences. According to the approach based on cognitive capacities, only individuals with these capacities can be attributed moral status and thus be considered 'persons'. Merely being a human being is not a sufficient condition to be considered a person, that is, an individual with moral status. Conversely, non-human animals who possess these capacities (such as, for instance, primates) can be attributed moral status.

Other philosophers have argued instead that moral status should be attributed to beings who have the potential to develop such sophisticated cognitive capacities, even though they have not developed them yet (and they might never do so) (George and Gomez-Lobo 2005). According to this approach to moral status, even if foetuses do not have sophisticated cognitive capacities, they should be attributed moral status because they have the potential to become fully grown humans possessing these cognitive capacities.

Finally, other philosophers argue that moral status should be attributed on the basis of special relationships so that, for instance, all members of the human species should be attributed moral status qua members of a community whose members have (for the largest part) moral status (Metz 2012).

We can assume that a successful brain upload would have the same cognitive capacities as the original. If it were the case that the uploaded brain would be a functional isomorph of the original, then, according to the account for which certain cognitive capacities are a necessary feature of individuals with moral status, it should have moral status.

However, if it were the case that the upload lacked consciousness (i.e. if the upload were a philosophical zombie) and consciousness was considered a necessary condition for the attribution of moral status, then it would follow that the upload would not have moral status. To people who believe that consciousness is an essential feature of entities with moral status, the issue of moral status is the same as that of consciousness. As we have already discussed, if one believes that consciousness is a function of a certain kind of brain activity or of how certain matter is organized, then consciousness would emerge in any kind of entity producing that kind of brain activity, regardless of its substrate. If, on the other hand, one believes that consciousness can only arise from a biological substrate or that consciousness involves further facts apart from data processing, then they would have to exclude the possibility that uploads could be conscious and have moral status.

Those who think that moral status can be attributed to individuals with the mere potentiality of developing certain cognitive skills can at least conceive an upload with moral status. This would be the case also if they held the view that consciousness is a necessary feature for the attribution of moral status and if they held the view that brain uploads are not conscious. According to this approach, it's plausible that even though brain uploads might not be conscious immediately after the transfer, or even years after the transfer, they still have the potential to become conscious through technological advancements. Also in this case, if one excluded a priori the possibility that a non-biological entity could ever be conscious, they would also have to believe that brain uploads have no potential to become conscious and have moral status.

Finally, it seems that someone holding the view that moral status can only be attributed on the basis of special relationships could not exclude the possibility that brain uploads could have moral status (Jaworska and Tannenbaum 2014). The brain upload would perhaps be able to maintain the relationships developed when existing in the form of a biological human being and would also be able to establish new ones, either with other biological beings or with digital ones. The upload would perhaps not count as a proper member of the human community but would be at least part of the community of the uploaded human beings, and there is no particular reason to believe that such relationships would not count as much as those among members of the human species.

From a practical perspective, if the problem of consciousness were not solved and there was no way to understand whether brain uploads are conscious (or at least could become conscious) or are just philosophical zombies, it is anyway likely that they would be treated as if they had moral status because they would behave exactly like biological persons and it would be impossible to tell apart whether they were persons or not (and indeed, if there were any philosophical zombies among us, we wouldn't be able to identify them, so in theory, we could be already attributing moral status to philosophical zombies). Of course, this might not be the case for all kinds of uploads, but it would be the case for at least some of them, and it is reasonable to assume that if such uploads looked and behaved in ways that would not be distinguishable from humans, we would not be able to tell them apart from their 'original'.

VULNERABILITY

Our human, carbon-based bodies often appear to us to be extremely vulnerable. We are vulnerable to viruses and bacteria, to accidents and bad luck, our bones can break, our memories can fade away, and time eventually wears us out and kills us. Uploading the brain to a non-carbon-based substrate can appear to be a much safer option, given that digital entities are not exposed to the same kind of threats that we are.

However, brain uploads have vulnerabilities of their own, and it is not obvious that a brain emulation would be necessarily less vulnerable than a human being. The software and the data that constitutes digital beings can be erased and modified or illicitly copied by accessing the system on which they are running, just like the Word document I am typing in right now could be modified or erased by anyone who found a way to access my laptop. Or if electricity (or any other energy source that will be used in the future) were cut off, the brain upload might be fatally damaged. Even if the digital brains were uploaded on a robot, or a human merged with a machine, they would not have self-contained bodies in the same way as we do: their digital component would still be accessible and hackable in a way and to a degree to which our biological brain is not.

Brain uploads would also bring about complex issues related to privacy (Sotala and Valpola 2012). The system on which they would be running would record their behaviour. Similarly, their states could be inspected and, perhaps, interpreted in a meaningful way so that it would be easy for an external entity to access the content of the memories and mental states in the uploaded brain. The idea of a hacker accessing our online data is already quite worrisome, and, indeed, most countries have legislations in place to protect people's privacy and punish the infringement of the right to privacy. However, the violation of privacy could have way more serious effects if the individual was a digital one as it would be possible to have access to the whole content of their brain rather than 'only' to their personal data, as currently happens in cases of a hacker attack.

In a future in which brain uploads were feasible, and many of us chose them as a backup in case the original brain were injured or destroyed, or if some people chose to move exclusively to the digital substrate, strict regulations would have to be put in place to protect the privacy of our digital counterparts so as to make sure that the very common preference for not having one's thoughts accessible to others could be respected. One early necessary step would be that of granting the ownership of the hardware on which the brain is run to the emulated person (in the same way as we have ownership of our bodies). We are already familiar with the kind of challenges involved in protecting our digital persona's privacy online (Véliz, this volume), the high risk of being exposed to hacking, or breaches of privacy from the companies owning the hardware that constitutes our computers and the software and programmes running in them.

Even though measures could be taken to reduce the vulnerability of uploaded brains, such as, for instance, encryption, the problem is probably never going to be completely solved because, even though the technology would probably improve over time, other threats could arise. Just like we keep improving our online systems' security to protect them from hacking attacks, but at the same time hackers keep improving their skills to break into these systems, it is possible that cybersecurity will never be achieved.

COERCED IMMORTALITY

In a sense, vulnerability and mortality are distinctive features of our current existence, and they might represent an essential part of it. A number of arguments have been put forth to suggest why an immortal life wouldn't be genuinely human. Bernard Williams argued that a very long life would lack coherence (Williams 1973): we can think of how difficult it would be to write a coherent novel if there were thousands of characters and stories. Heidegger claimed that a life without an end would be formless and, as such, non-human (Heidegger 1927). Todd May argues that it is part of a human life to experience the urgency to do things before life is over, and this is a hallmark of human experience that would not apply to indefinitely long lives (May 2014).

Even though one of the reasons why some people are interested in brain uploading is that they want to achieve immortality, it is important to keep in mind that there are risks to which digital entities are, by nature, more vulnerable, as, for instance, hacking, something to which biological entities cannot be vulnerable. And some risks are, in a way, shared by both digital and biological individuals, for instance, that of being infected by a deadly virus that could cause the collapse of the system.

The quest for immortality could take a dark turn when we consider digital entities. One relevant consideration is that the option of choosing death, and the possibility of dying in itself, do not necessarily apply to non-biological systems. We could imagine a virus that attacks the upload and (a) 'tortures' the digital entity (assuming the digital entity would be susceptible to the infliction of pain) or (b) prevents the entity from shutting down (i.e. getting into an unconscious state or dying) so that the entity is kept alive and tortured without having any escape.

In such cases, the immortality imposed on the digital entity is not desirable because extreme suffering would be the hallmark of such existence, and the digital individual would almost certainly prefer to die. One doesn't need to be a utilitarian to agree that an eternal life lived in a state in which one is constantly tortured would be a life not worth living and one to which death would be preferable. A biological body can only endure a limited amount of suffering, and for a limited amount of time, before shutting down. And when it does not shut down because of the excessive suffering experienced, it eventually shuts down because of biological wearing out. Being tortured for thousands of years is something biological individuals, unlike digital ones, do not have to worry about.

Suffering

Apart from external threats and possible viruses attacking the upload, we also need to consider the possibility that the upload would incur problems related either to deterioration over time (after all, we do not have any example of complex digital material living for thousands of years) or to having some defect to start with, for instance, because the uploading procedure did not go smoothly and significant and irreversible damage occurred. Regardless of the cause, we can imagine an upload that is either not conscious (the equivalent of a permanent comatose state or vegetative state in a biological human), or has damage that causes its mental states to be dramatically altered (the equivalent of dementia or Alzheimer's disease in biological humans), or experiences suffering that makes their life not worth living or downright painful (the equivalent of clinical depression in biological humans).

In circumstances where the upload was suffering, they could ask to end the simulation and cause them to cease to exist, just like humans do when they ask for euthanasia. The answer to whether it would be morally permissible to end the simulation is, in large part, dependent on what one thinks about euthanasia for biological entities. However, if most countries prohibited ending the simulation just like they prohibit euthanasia, the consequences could be significantly worse in the case of uploads, given that human life lasts for a handful of decades but a digital one could last for thousands of years or more. A country prohibiting the euthanasia of digital individuals could condemn them to more prolonged suffering than their human counterparts. For this reason, it seems that legislations should be prepared for this possibility and ideally introduce new laws for uploads or adapt existing laws on euthanasia accordingly.

Another option that could be available to uploads and is not available to humans (unless cryonics became available) would be pausing the emulation. Pausing the emulation would allow the uploaded individual to stop experiencing suffering without 'killing' it. However, pausing is not necessarily a solution in the long run since some may object that keeping these simulations in a paused state is not compatible with displaying respect for the dignity of such uploads; hence, the uploads should either be deleted or reactivated, at least once in a while. In a sense, we would have to deal with some of the ethical issues we are confronted with when a biological human gets into a comatose or a vegetative state. But things could get more complicated than that. At the moment, decisions about what to do with the person in an irreversible comatose state are either left to relatives or to advanced directives (and, in most cases, the law imposes quite strict limitations on the options available). But if there were multiple copies of the same upload, and they disagreed with each other about what to do with one or more 'paused' versions of themselves, then it would be difficult to make decisions with respect to the handling of the paused version. Since all of the copies would be connected to each other through sharing the same mental states with the original, and since they would all be equally entitled to make decisions about any other of the copy since they would all, in a sense, be the same person, it would be impossible to choose the one who should have the last say with respect to (the digital equivalent of) end-of-life decisions (Sandberg 2014: 439–457).

CONCLUSIONS

In this chapter, I have introduced a potential future technology, brain uploading or brain simulation, and I have discussed some of the ethical issues that could arise from developing such technology. The main reason why brain uploading is pursued is that it could be used to extend lifespan well beyond the current limits. But this life-extending goal would be reached by dramatically modifying our current biology; that is, it would require to migrate from a carbon-based form to a digital form. Such migration could, on the one hand, make us more resistant to the common lethal threats we are exposed to, such as accidents and ageing, but would also make us more vulnerable to other threats; on the other hand, it would expose us to new risks and dangers.

It is not obvious, for instance, that we would survive the change from carbon-based entities to digital ones. Understanding whether we could indeed stay ourselves through and after this process requires us to understand some facts about consciousness that we haven't figured out yet.

Apart from the risks involved in the process itself, there are other questions that we are currently trying to answer. For instance, can a brain uploaded in multiple copies preserve the personal identity of the original? And what kind of risks will the uploads face when it comes to the possibility of hacking them and causing them suffering? Moreover, will the uploads have a moral status comparable to that granted to human persons?

Although the development of this future technology will most likely take a long time, we should be prepared for the possible implications of such future development. Though this kind of technology might not look tempting to many people right now, it's possible that things will change once it becomes available and an increasing number of people start using it, as often happens when new technological tools are introduced. After all, only a few years ago, we would have not predicted that our lives were going to become as digitalized as they currently are, and yet, it happened very quickly. Instead of dismissing brain uploading as a far-fetched science fiction hypothesis, we should start thinking about whether we want it to become real and, if so, what kind of precautionary measures we need to develop to make sure it will be a valuable innovation.

NOTES

1. See https://en.wikipedia.org/wiki/San_Junipero, accessed 6 September 2022.
2. See https://en.wikipedia.org/wiki/William_and_Mary_(short_story), accessed 6 September 2022.

REFERENCES

Agar, Nicholas (2011), 'Ray Kurzweil and Uploading: Just Say No!', *Journal of Evolution and Technology* 22(1), 23–36. Institute for Ethics and Emerging Technologies.

Bostrom, Nick (2003), 'Are We Living in a Computer Simulation?', *Philosophical Quarterly* 53(211), 243–255. Oxford University Press.

Cerullo, Michael (2015), 'Uploading and Branching Identity', *Minds and Machines* 25(1), 17–36. Springer.

Chalmers, D. (2009), 'The Singularity: A Philosophical Analysis', in Science Fiction and Philosophy: From Time Travel to Superintelligence, 171–224. Wiley Nicholas

Chalmers, David (2014), 'Uploading: A Philosophical Analysis', in Intelligence Unbound: The Future of Uploaded and Machine Minds, 102–118. Wiley.

Cheshire, William P. (2015), 'The Sum of All Thoughts: Prospects of Uploading the Mind to a Computer' *Ethics & Medicine* 31(3), 135. BMJ

DeGrazia, Davidd (2020), 'Sentience and Consciousness as Bases for Attributing Interests and Moral Status: Considering the Evidence and Speculating Slightly Beyond', in *Neuroethics and Nonhuman Animals* (Cham: Springer), 17–31.

Descartes, Rene' (1641), *Meditations on First Philosophy*. Cambridge University Press

Feygin, Yana B., Kelly Morris, and Roman V. Yampolskiy. (2018), 'Uploading Brain into Computer: Whom to Upload First?', *arXiv preprint arXiv:1811.03009 Not Pubblished, Preprint Available chrome-extension://efaidnbmnnnibpcajpcglclefindmkaj/https://arxiv.org/pdf/1811.03009.pdf*

Floridi, L. (2011), 'The Informational Nature of Personal Identity', *Minds and Machines* 21(4), 549–566. Springer

George, Robert P., and Gomez-Lobo, Alfonso (2005), 'The Moral Status of the Human Embryo', *Perspectives in Biology and Medicine* 48(2), 201–210. Johns Hopkins University Press

Goff, Philip W., Seager, William, and Allen-Hermanson, Sean (2022), 'Panpsychism', in Edward N. Zalta, ed., *Stanford Encyclopedia of Philosophy*, https://plato.stanford.edu/archives/sum2022/entries/panpsychism, accessed 6 September 2022.

Gustafsson, Johan E. (2019), 'Non-Branching Personal Persistence', *Philosophical Studies* 176(9), 2307–2329. Springer

Häggström, Olle (2021), 'Aspects of Mind Uploading', in *Transhumanism: The Proper Guide to a Posthuman Condition or a Dangerous Idea?* (Cham: Springer), 3–20.

Harman, Gilbert (1973), *Thought* (Princeton, NJ: Princeton University Press).

Hauskeller, Michael (2012), 'My Brain, My Mind, and I: Some Philosophical Assumptions of Mind-Uploading', *International Journal of Machine Consciousness* 4(1), 187–200. World Scientific

Heidegger, Martin (1927), *Sein und Zeit [Being and Time]*, J. Macquarrie and E. Robinson, trans (New York: Harper and Row).

Hughes, James J. (1995), 'Brain Death and Technological Change: Personal Identity, Neural Prostheses and Uploading', in *Havana: Second International Symposium on Brain Death*. (Unpublished and Available here http://www.changesurfer.com/Hlth/BD/Brain.html)

Jaworska, Agnieszka, and Tannenbaum, Julie (2014), 'Person-Rearing Relationships as a Key to Higher Moral Status', *Ethics* 124(2), 242–271.The University of Chicago

Kelly, Ivan William. (2020), 'The Grateful Un-Dead? Philosophical and Social Implications of Mind-Uploading'. (Unpublished and Available here chrome-extension://efaidnbmnnnibpcajpcglclefindmkaj/https://www.researchgate.net/profile/Ivan-Kelly-3/publication/343139

739_The_grateful_Un-dead_Philosophical_and_Social_Implications_of_Mind-Upload
ing/links/5f1873f4a6fdcc9626a6c505/The-grateful-Un-dead-Philosophical-and-Social-
Implications-of-Mind-Uploading.pdf)

Liao, Matthew S. (2020), 'The Moral Status and Rights of Artificial Intelligence', *Ethics of Artificial Intelligence*, 480. Oxford University Press

May, T. (2014), *Death* (London: Routledge).

Metz, Thaddeus (2012), 'An African Theory of Moral Status: A Relational Alternative to Individualism and Holism', *Ethical Theory and Moral Practice* 15(3), 387–402 (Springer)

Minerva, Francesca (2019), in D. Edmonds, ed., *Ethics and the Contemporary World* (London: Routledge).

Olson, Eric T. (1999), *The Human Animal: Personal Identity without Psychology* (Oxford: Oxford University Press).

Olson, Eric T. (2001), 'Material Coincidence and the Indiscernibility Problem', *Philosophical Quarterly* 51(204), 337–355. Oxford University Press

Olson, Eric T. (2002), 'What Does Functionalism Tell Us about Personal Identity?', *Noûs* 36(4), 682–698. Wiley Blackwell

Parfit, Derek (1984), *Reasons and Persons* (Oxford: Oxford University Press).

Putnam, Hilary (1981), 'Brains in a Vat', *Knowledge: Critical Concepts* 1, 192–207. Cambridge University Press

Ren, Xiaoping, and Canavero, Sergio (2017), 'Heaven in the Making: Between the Rock (the Academe) and a Hard Case (a Head Transplant)', *AJOB Neuroscience* 8(4), 200–205. Taylor & Francis

Robinson, Richard (2019), 'Hemispherectomy Leaves Brain Networks Intact and Strengthens Their Connections', *Neurology Today* 19(24), 36–37. AAN Publications

Sandberg, Anders (2014), 'Ethics of Brain Emulations', *Journal of Experimental & Theoretical Artificial Intelligence* 26(3), 439–457. Taylor & Francis

Sandberg, Anders, and Bostrom, Nick (2008), *Whole Brain Emulation: A Roadmap Technical Report* (Future of Humanity Institute). (This is a Report, Doesn't Seem to have a Publisher)

Shoemaker, Sydney (2004), 'Functionalism and Personal Identity: A Reply', *Noûs* 38(3), 525–533. Blackwell

Sotala, Kay, and Valpola, Harry (2012), 'Coalescing Minds: Brain Uploading-Related Group Mind Scenarios', *International Journal of Machine Consciousness* 4(1), 293–312. World Scientific doi:10.1142/S1793843012400173.

Van Gulick, Robert, "Consciousness", The Stanford Encyclopedia of Philosophy (Winter 2021 Edition), Edward N. Zalta & Uri Nodelman (eds)

Walker, Mark (2014), 'Uploading and Personal Identity', in *Intelligence Unbound: The Future of Uploaded and Machine Minds*, 161–177. (Wiley Blackwell)

Warren, Mary Anne (1973), 'On the Moral and Legal Status of Abortion', *The Monist*, Routledge, 57, 43–61.

Williams, Bernard (1973), 'The Makropulos Case: Reflections on the Tedium of Immortality', in B. Williams, ed., *Problems of the Self* (Cambridge: Cambridge University Press), 82–100.

CHAPTER 36

HOW DOES ARTIFICIAL INTELLIGENCE POSE AN EXISTENTIAL RISK?

KARINA VOLD AND DANIEL R. HARRIS

INTRODUCTION

THE idea that artificial intelligence (AI) might one day threaten humanity has been around for some time. In 1863, the novelist Samuel Butler (1863: 185) suggested that machines may one day hold 'supremacy over the world and its inhabitants'. By the mid-twentieth century, these concerns had left the realm of science fiction, as thinkers like Alan Turing (1951/1996: 260) began to warn the public that we should expect intelligent machines to eventually 'take control'. Still, for many years, academics did not spill much ink over these concerns, even while Hollywood filmmakers ran with them, producing countless blockbusters based on this 'AI takeover' scenario (think: *The Terminator* or *Battlestar Galactica*). Over the past decade or so, however, many leading academics and entrepreneurs have notably increased their attention to existential risks from AI. These concerns are, as we will see, more subtle than those depicted in crude Hollywood-produced AI takeover scenarios. Indeed, those depictions have largely misrepresented the concrete issues scholars are concerned with by overly focusing on anthropomorphic concerns of conscious AI systems deciding to destroy humans.

This renewed scholarly interest in AI safety has been spurred on in part by the recent deep learning revolution. This period is defined by major advances in the accomplishments of *deep neural networks*—artificial neural networks with multiple layers between the input and output layers—across a wide range of areas, including game-playing, speech and facial recognition, and image generation. Even with these breakthroughs though, the cognitive capabilities of current AI systems remain limited to domain-specific applications. Nevertheless, many researchers are alarmed by the speed of progress in AI and worry that future systems, if not managed correctly, could present an existential threat.

Despite the renewed interest in this concern, there remains substantial disagreement over both the nature and the likelihood of the existential threats posed by AI. Hence, our aim in this chapter is to explicate the main arguments that have been given for thinking that AI does pose an existential risk, and to point out where there are disagreements and weakness in these arguments. The chapter has the following structure: in the next section, we introduce the concept of existential risk, the sources of such risks, and how these risks are typically assessed. In the following three sections, we critically examine three commonly cited reasons for thinking that AI poses an existential threat to humanity: the control problem, global disruption from an AI 'arms race', and the weaponization of AI. Our focus is on the first of these three because it represents a kind of existential risk that is novel to AI as technology. While the latter two are equally important, they have commonalities with other kinds of technologies (e.g. nuclear weapons) discussed in the literature on existential risk, and so we will dedicate less time to them.

WHAT IS AN EXISTENTIAL RISK?

Many people believe that *existential risks* (henceforth, *Xrisks*) are the greatest threats facing humanity. And whilst there is much common ground amongst scholars about which scenarios constitute a Xrisk (the most commonly cited example is *extinction risks*[1]), there is not as much consensus on the precise definition of the concept (Beard et al. 2020; Torres 2019). While most Xrisk scholars agree that a risk is existential if an adverse outcome would bring about human extinction, few endorse the narrower view that a risk is existential *only if* it would cause this outcome.[2] Most definitions of Xrisk are broader, including at times the risk of global civilizational collapse (Rees 2003; Ó hÉigeartaigh 2017); scenarios in which the technological and moral potential of humanity is 'permanently and drastically' curtailed (Bostrom 2002, 2013); and *suffering risks*, defined as cases in which 'an adverse outcome would bring about severe suffering on an astronomical scale, vastly exceeding all suffering that has existed on Earth so far' (Sotala and Gloor 2017: 389).

Xrisks are typically distinguished from the broader category of global catastrophic risks. Bostrom (2013), for example, uses two dimensions—scope and severity—to make this distinction. *Scope* refers to the number of people at risk, while *severity* refers to how badly the population in question would be affected (Bostrom 2013: 16). Xrisks are at the most extreme end of both of these spectrums: they are *pan-generational* in scope (i.e. 'affecting humanity over all, or almost all, future generations') and they are the severest kinds of threats, causing either 'death or a permanent and drastic reduction of quality of life' (Bostrom 2013: 17). Perhaps the clearest example of an Xrisk is an asteroid impact on the scale of that which hit the Earth 66 million years ago, wiping out the dinosaurs (Schulte et al. 2010; Ó hÉigeartaigh 2017). *Global catastrophic risks*, by way of contrast, could be either just as severe but narrower in scope, or just as broad but less severe. Some examples include the destruction of cultural heritage, the thinning of the ozone layer, or even a large-scale pandemic outbreak (Bostrom 2013). In this chapter, we will focus mostly on the least controversial category of Xrisks—extinction risks—but will also at times discuss some of the other scenarios mentioned.

Sources of Xrisk

For most of human history, the only source of Xrisks facing humanity were *natural causes*, such as an asteroid hitting Earth or a pandemic (Bostrom 2002). But the creation of the first atomic bomb in 1945 introduced a new source of existential threat to humanity, one that was *anthropogenic* in nature. However, since then, humanity has created numerous other kinds of threats to our own existence, including human-caused climate change, global biodiversity loss, biological warfare, and threats from AI, for example. In fact, it is widely thought that most Xrisks today are anthropogenic and that, as a result of these new threats, this current century is the riskiest one that humanity has ever faced (Rees 2003; Bostrom 2013; Ó hÉigeartaigh 2017; Ord 2020).

Not all of these threats pose straightforward Xrisks. Let's consider an extinction scenario to be the existential outcome in question, and then take nuclear fallout as an example. Today, the worldwide arsenal of nuclear weapons could lead to unprecedented death tolls and habitat destruction and, hence, it poses a clear global catastrophic risk. Still, experts assign a relatively low probability to human extinction from nuclear warfare (Martin 1982; Sandberg and Bostrom 2008; Shulman 2012). This is in part because it seems more likely that extinction, if it follows at all, would occur *indirectly* from the effects of the war, rather than *directly*. This distinction has appeared in several discussions on Xrisks (e.g. Matheny 2007; Liu et al. 2018; Zwetsloot and Dafoe 2019), but it is made most explicitly in Cotton-Barratt et al. (2020: 6), who explain that a global catastrophe that causes human extinction can do so either *directly* by 'killing everyone', or *indirectly*, by 'removing our ability to continue flourishing over a longer period'. A nuclear explosion itself is unlikely to kill *everyone* directly, but the resulting effects it has on the Earth could lead to lands becoming uninhabitable, in turn leading to a scarcity of essential resources, which could (over a number of years) lead to human extinction. Some of the simplest examples of *direct* risks of human extinction, by way of contrast, are '[i]f the entire planet is struck by a deadly gamma ray burst, or enough of a deadly toxin is dispersed through the atmosphere' (Cotton-Barratt et al. 2020: 6). What is critical here is that for an Xrisk to be *direct* it has to be able to reach *everyone*.

Much like nuclear fallout, the arguments for why and how AI poses an Xrisk are not straightforward. This is partly because AI is a general-purpose technology. It has a wide range of potential uses, for a wide range of actors, across a wide range of sectors. In this chapter, we are interested in the extent to which the use or misuse of AI can play a *sine qua non* role in Xrisk scenarios, across any of these domains. We are interested not only in current AI capabilities, but also in future (potential) capabilities. Depending on how the technology develops, AI could pose either a direct or an indirect risk, although we make the case that direct Xrisks from AI are even more improbable than indirect ones. Another helpful way of thinking about AI risks is to divide them into accidental risks, structural risks, or misuse risks (Zwetsloot and Dafoe 2019). In the section 'The control problem argument for Xrisk', we focus on *accidental risks*: threats arising from the system behaving in unintended ways. In the section 'AI race dynamics, global disruption, and Xrisk', we turn to *structural risks*: threats arising from how the technology shapes the broader environment, especially in the political and military realms, in ways that can elevate risk. And finally, in the section 'The weaponization of AI', we examine potential *misuses* of AI.

Before moving on, it is worth noting that there are some significant methodological challenges that confront the study of Xrisks. Because events that constitute or precipitate an Xrisk are unprecedented, arguments to the effect that they pose such a threat must be theoretical in nature. Their rarity also makes it such that any speculations about how or when such events might occur are subjective and not empirically verifiable (Sagan 1983; Matheny 2007; Beard et al. 2020), which makes such claims challenging to submit to standard forms of risk analysis (Ó hÉigeartaigh 2017). Despite these challenges, however, it is still important to try to distinguish which extreme scenarios are actually plausible and worthy of further attention, even if they have an extremely low probability, as opposed to those that can be dismissed as science fiction (Ó hÉigeartaigh 2017: 3–4). Accordingly, our goal in this chapter is not to assign probabilities to arguments that AI poses an Xrisk, but rather to assess their theoretical nature.

THE CONTROL PROBLEM ARGUMENT
FOR XRISK

The earliest line of thinking that AI poses an Xrisk warns that AI might become both powerful and indifferent to human values, leading to dangerous consequences for human beings. Despite it being a longstanding concern, the structure of this argument is rarely, if ever, explicitly laid out.[3] By presenting *the control problem argument for Xrisk* (henceforth CPAX) in this way, our aim is to capture what we understand to be the line of reasoning, while also making the epistemic moves more explicit. CPAX rests on two central theses: the Orthogonality Thesis and the Instrumental Convergence Thesis, both of which were first explicitly articulated by Bostrom (2012: 130–132, 2014).

> *Orthogonality Thesis:* the intelligent capacities of any system are logically independent from any goals the system might have.

> *Instrumental Convergence Thesis:* almost any intelligent system is likely to converge upon certain instrumental (sub)goals.

We will discuss each of these theses, as well as the premises and central inferences of the argument (below) in the following subsections.

P1. It is possible to build an AI system that has a decisive strategic advantage over all other forms of intelligence.

P2. If an AI system has a decisive strategic advantage over human intelligence, then we may not be able to control that system.

C1. It is possible to build an AI system that we are not able to control (*from P1 and P2*).

P3. The intelligent capacities of an AI system are logically independent from any goals the system might have (supported by the Orthogonality Thesis).

C2. Therefore, it is possible to build an AI system that human beings are not able to control and that has goals that do not align with human values (*from C1 and P3*).

P4. AI systems are likely to converge upon certain instrumental (sub)goals that are inimical to human interests (supported by the Instrumental Convergence Thesis).

C3. It is possible to build AI systems that pose an existential threat to humanity (*from C2 and P4*).

This reconstruction of the argument is by no means uncontroversial, and we will discuss some of the disagreements and objections as we go through the argument.

Intelligence explosion and decisive strategic advantages (P1)

P1 states that it is possible to build an AI system that has a decisive strategic advantage over all other forms of intelligence (including human intelligence). Historically, CPAX was introduced as arising from an intelligence explosion that would lead to the creation of a superintelligent AI—a system that by definition has a decisive strategic advantage over human intelligence. More recently, some have argued that an intelligence explosion is not the only pathway to AI gaining a decisive strategic advantage. We will begin by explaining the pathway to a loss of control over AI (C1) from an intelligence explosion (in this section) and consider some potential objections. In the section 'Losing control (P2 and C1)', we discuss P2 and some more contemporary takes on how C1 could result.

An *intelligence explosion* is a hypothetical event in which an AI system enters a rapid cycle of recursive self-improvement, whereby each new iteration creates a more intelligent version of itself, culminating in the creation of a superintelligence. Here, a *superintelligence* is 'any intellect that greatly exceeds the cognitive performance of humans in virtually all domains of interest' (Bostrom 2014: 22). The concept of an intelligence explosion was first articulated by I. J. Good (1965: 33), who argued that an AI system whose intelligence exceeds humanity's in *all* intellectual activities would necessarily also exceed it in terms of designing machine intelligence. Hence, if such a system were initially engineered by humans, it would possess the capability to design a machine more intelligent than itself. The subsequent new iteration, being more intelligent than its predecessor, would, by the same logic, also be capable of designing a machine more intelligent than itself. If each new generation of AI were to utilize its improved design capability, an intelligence explosion would occur (Chalmers 2010).

Importantly, an intelligence explosion need not begin with the creation of a machine with greater than human intelligence, as Good's argument suggests. In principle, it could be sparked via the creation of a more modest type of machine intelligence. Some might hold, for example, that an intelligence explosion merely requires a system with *artificial general intelligence*, where general intelligence is the ability to deploy the same core suite of cognitive resources to complete a wide range of different tasks (Shevlin et al. 2019). An even more modest possibility is that an intelligence explosion could spark from a mere *artificial narrow intelligence*, that is, a system that excels only at specific tasks and lacks the ability to use its resources to solve problems outside of its narrow domains.[4] Bostrom (2014: 29), for example, suggests that a system 'capable of improving its own *architecture*', what he calls a 'seed AI', would be a sufficient starting point. For example, DeepMind's AlphaZero, a current narrow AI system, has already shown the capacity to iteratively self-improve by repeatedly playing against itself. This illustrates how, under certain conditions, this process of recursive self-improvement might generate an intelligence explosion that begins from a mere narrow AI, in particular, any narrow AI system that enjoys a *decisive strategic advantage* (i.e. well above human level capacity) in some relevant domains, coupled with sufficient capacities for real-world modification.[5]

Objections to the possibility of an intelligence explosion

In this section, we consider two objections to the possibility of an intelligence explosion.

Objection one: Why think that an AI system would recursively self-improve just because it had the capacity to do so?[6] Indeed, it seems logically possible that even if a system *could* design a more intelligent iteration of itself, that it would not take this action. More broadly, some have argued that superintelligent AI systems would be 'inextricably unpredictable', and hence there is nothing that can be said regarding their potential goals (Cortese 2014).

Reply: In order to make meaningful predictions regarding what a sufficiently advanced AI would do (e.g. whether it would recursively self-improve), we need a method of identifying what goals it might have. Yet, the Orthogonality Thesis (which we discuss in more detail below) holds that the intelligent capacities of an AI system are logically independent from any goals the system might have. If true, the range of possible goals that an AI system could have is enormous. In light of this, how do we make predictions? Omohundro (2008: 1) argues that any sufficiently advanced AI is likely to have several basic 'drives' or 'tendencies which will be present unless explicitly counteracted'. Bostrom (2014: 109) similarly argues that we can make robust inferences regarding the subgoals of almost any intelligent agent by appealing to the thesis of *instrumental convergence*:

> Several instrumental values can be identified which are convergent in the sense that their attainment would increase the chances of the agent's goal being realized for a

wide range of final goals and a wide range of situations, implying that these instrumental values are likely to be pursued by a broad spectrum of situated intelligent agents.

Both Omohundro and Bostrom identify self-improvement as one of the 'basic drives' or 'instrumental values' (respectively) that a system would pursue. They also share the same general reasoning: improvements in rationality and intelligence are likely to be pursued by a wide variety of intelligent agents insofar as they tend to improve an agent's decision-making capabilities, thereby increasing the likelihood of that agent realizing whatever final objective it has (Bostrom 2014: 111). Taken together, the Bostrom-Omohundro thesis suggests that an AI system would have instrumental reasons to undergo a process of recursive self-improvement, especially cognitive self-improvement, and thus would be driven to do so.

Objection two: Despite the aforementioned reasons for thinking that a sufficiently intelligent AI system would be motivated to recursively self-improve, there are some who question whether an intelligence explosion is an inevitable outcome of the creation of such a system. Yoshua Bengio, for example, speculates that for mathematical and computational reasons there may be a '*wall-of-complexity*' that confronts all forms of intelligence 'due to exponentially growing complexities' and that limits the capacities of any intelligent agent (quoted in Sofge 2015). He speculates that this 'wall' might (partly) explain why animals with bigger brains than ours are not more intelligent than us. Meanwhile, Chalmers (2010: 19–22) argues that a number of obstacles could arise that forestall an intelligence explosion. Among these are what he terms '*manifestation obstacles*'—difficulties which obstruct self-amplifying capabilities from developing.[7] He further subdivides these into two types of defeaters: *motivational* and *situational*. Motivational defeaters include disinclination and active prevention. For example, an AI system might discover that self-improvement(s) come at a cost which outweighs the associated gains, as would be the case if it turns out that improvements in intelligence have diminishing returns.[8] Alternatively, we might design the AI system to lack the motivation to self-improve, or to have a contrary motivation which supersedes it (Chalmers 2010).[9] As for situational defeaters, these include unfavourable circumstances, such as a limitation to the availability of resources necessary for cognitive upgrades (Chalmers 2010).

Reply: A defender of CPAX has to make the case that it is unlikely for these defeaters to be present, or at the very least, that there is a non-zero chance they will be absent. But, we think Chalmers (2010: 19) is right in writing that there are no 'knockdown arguments against any of these obstacles'. As with the previous objection, both sides of this issue confront the same challenge: that it is difficult, perhaps impossible, to predict what the motivations of a future advanced AI system could be.[10] Ultimately, an intelligence explosion is certainly not an inevitable outcome, but it also is not an impossible one. Chalmers (2010: 22) takes a similar position, saying that it is 'far from obvious that there will be defeaters', and in their absence, the outcome of an intelligence explosion would be the creation of a superintelligence.

Losing control (P2 and C1)

If we take as true the supposition that humanity's control over other Earth-bound species is largely the result of our comparative intelligence advantage, then the emergence of an AI system with a decisive strategic advantage over human intelligence should give cause for concern. Consider the current power structure between human beings and gorillas. Bostrom (2014: vii) argues that due to our advantage in general intelligence, 'the fate of the gorilla now depends more on us humans than on the gorillas themselves'. Russell (2019: 134) makes a similar point, noting that by virtue of our intelligence, gorillas 'essentially have no future beyond that which we deign to allow'. Both authors, among others (e.g. Hawking 2018), raise the worry that, in much the same way, the destiny of humanity could be dictated by the actions of a superintelligent AI. This *gorilla problem*, as Russell terms it, is the idea behind P2, which states that if an AI system has a decisive strategic advantage over human intelligence, then we may not be able to control that system.

There are a few reasons for thinking that we will not be able to control systems that are more intelligent than us. Among these are the opacity and unpredictability of such systems. A good example of these features in a non-critical domain is DeepMind's AlphaGo—which in 2016 beat the eighteen-times world champion of Go, Lee Sedol. In the games against Sedol, the system sometimes made moves that proved advantageous but that both the engineers of the system and human Go experts alike did not foresee and struggled to interpret (Silver et al. 2016; Kohs 2017). The opaqueness and unpredictability of these systems makes them potentially dangerous—if even experts cannot predict or interpret how a system will behave, it could run amok sooner than we realize and before we have a chance to intervene. Hence, it follows from the first two premises that we could risk losing control over what a strategically advantaged AI system does (C1). The possibility of this occurring is often referred to as *the control problem*. But, for this problem to pose an Xrisk, a few more premises are needed.

Before continuing on, however, we should note two things. First, notice that nothing so far, or going forward, in the discussion of CPAX relies on the idea that an AI system would need human-like motivations. This is important to clarify because some critics object that CPAX relies on erroneous anthropomorphic assumptions about AI (e.g. Andrew Ng (Williams 2015) and Yann LeCun (Wakefield 2015)). But the central idea so far is that an AI might cause harm for instrumental reasons, or that it might have little regard for human life or have that regard outweighed by other concerns. Hawking (2018: 188) explains:

> [T]he real risk with AI isn't malice, but competence ... You're probably not an evil ant-hater who steps on ants out of malice, but if you're in charge of a hydroelectric green-energy project and there's an anthill in the region to be flooded, too bad for the ants. Let's not place humanity in the position of those ants.

In other words, CPAX need not assume that an AI would develop malicious aims or choose to destroy humanity because of human-like emotions, such as disgust, revenge, or anger. It also does not assume that the AI in question would be conscious, or even that it would become (non-consciously) motivated to harm or exterminate human beings.

The second thing to note is that, while early concerns around the control problem (that is, premises P1 and P2, leading up to C1) focused on the possibility of an intelligence explosion, more recent discussions have moved away from this scenario. In other words, it has been argued that a loss of control (i.e. C1) could result without an intelligence explosion and without the emergence of a superintelligent AI. An AI system might not require an internal 'drive' to self-improve, for example, if human beings are incentivized to aid its improvement (Drexler 2019). It also may not need to reach the level of superintelligence in order to pose an Xrisk (Drexler 2019). Russell (2019: 137) explains that humanity has thus far been protected from the 'potentially catastrophic consequences' of AI because of the limited intelligent capacities of current AI systems and their limited abilities to bring about changes in the real world (most systems operate in virtual worlds or lab environments). But as narrow AI systems become more cognitively sophisticated and are given more capacity to directly affect or modify the world, they could pose an Xrisk as long as their narrow domain is critical enough (e.g. controlling stock markets or military decision-making) and their interests are inimical to those of humans.

The orthogonality thesis (P3 and C2)

In one of the earliest explanations of the control problem, Norbert Weiner (1960: 1358) worried there could be dangerous outcomes if a powerful AI system that we lacked control over were to operate with an incorrect objective: 'If we use, to achieve our purposes, a mechanical agency with whose operation we cannot efficiently interfere … we had better be quite sure that the purpose put into the machine is the purpose which we really desire and not merely a colourful imitation of it.' Consider an example that Russell (2019: 138) gives of a machine tasked with solving environmental problems:

> [Y]ou might ask the machine to counter the rapid acidification of the oceans that results from higher carbon dioxide levels. The machine develops a new catalyst that facilitates an incredibly rapid chemical reaction between ocean and atmosphere and restores the oceans' pH levels. Unfortunately, a quarter of the oxygen in the atmosphere is used up in the process leaving us to asphyxiate slowly and painfully. Oops.

In this case, the Xrisk arises from incidental safety issues that fall out of misaligned objectives. Bostrom (2014: 97) offers a similar example of an AI that might 'tile all of the Earth's surface with solar panels, nuclear reactors, supercomputing facilities with protruding cooling towers, space rocket launchers, or other installations whereby the AI intends to maximize the long-term cumulative realization of its values'. Once again, the threat to humanity here is essentially a side effect of the widespread habitat destruction that would ensue.[11] Because AI is a general-purpose technology, the misalignment problem could arise in many different domains, though Xrisks seem most likely to occur in domains with global impact (because they are, by definition, pan-generational in scope).

For some, the idea that a superintelligent machine would pursue such narrow goals without regard to broader consequences seems improbable, if not 'self-refuting' (Pinker 2019; other critics include Loosemore 2012; Chorost 2016; Metzinger 2017). Loosemore (2012) has dubbed it the 'fallacy of dumb superintelligence', while Chorost (2016), responding to Bostrom's scenario, argues that 'By the time [a superintelligent AI] is in a position to imagine tiling the Earth with solar panels, it'll know that it would be morally wrong to do so.' Metzinger (2017) makes this same claim, arguing that, because a superintelligence would be better than human beings at moral cognition, it would also be benevolent.[12] But the possibility that a highly intelligent artificial agent could act in ways that are malevolent or misaligned with the values of its designers is meant to follow from Bostrom's Orthogonality Thesis, which maintains that the intelligent capacities of any system are logically independent from any goals the system might have. By 'intelligent capacities' here, Bostrom (2012: 74) means the capacities related to *instrumental rationality*, for example, 'skill at prediction, planning, and means-ends reasoning in general'. This Orthogonality Thesis is meant to apply quite broadly to any intelligent system, including humans. And Hume's (1739) longstanding is–ought problem lends support for the idea: if one cannot infer normative statements from descriptive ones, then however intelligent a system is, it may never arrive at any moral facts (Bostrom 2012: 74; Armstrong 2013). The Orthogonality Thesis supports the third premise of CPAX, and with C1, it leads by conjunction to the second conclusion, C2: that it is possible to build an uncontrollable AI system that has goals that do not align with human values.

The value alignment problem

Arguably, one way to avoid C2 would be to program the AI to ensure that it is benevolent or that its values are reliably aligned with our own. After all, humans have the advantage of being the ones who build the system and determine its initial goals (Bostrom 2014; Russell 2019). Unfortunately, it's not that simple. This is widely known as the *value alignment problem* (see Gabriel and Ghazavi, 2021). The problem is hard for many reasons.

First, there is the *issue of identifying human values*. Human beings are often confused and conflicted about our own values, and different cultures seem to have wide variation between their respective values.[13] While pervasive moral disagreement does not necessarily imply value relativism, it does complicate the challenge of trying to build machines that align with 'our' values, as it opens the door to value pluralism (the view that there are many different and sometimes irreducible moral values). While a value monist has the challenge of identifying the one value (e.g. happiness or pleasure) that all other values reduce to, the value pluralist has the problem of identifying and implementing the complete set of irreducible values. This is a real challenge for programming; as Russell (2019: 139) notes, one of the most common forms of value misalignment comes from an incomplete articulation of values, that is, from omitting something human beings care about from the objective imbued into the system. Furthermore, value pluralists tend to believe that there are at least some, and perhaps many, unresolvable moral dilemmas that result from a conflict between incommensurable values (further discussions in Cave et al. 2019; Baum, 2020).

A second problem is that even if we can identify some acceptable set of human values or objectives, we are rather prone to misstating these. This is sometimes known as the 'King Midas problem' (Russell 2019).[14] In wishing that everything he touched should turn to gold, King Midas thought he knew what he wanted, but he didn't really want his wife or his breakfast to turn to gold. The folklore illuminates the issue of 'value fragility'—if an AI system gets our values even slightly wrong, it could lead to disastrous outcomes. Hence, the more we rely on powerful autonomous systems, the more important it will be for us to specify their goals with great care, ensuring that we express our objectives correctly and completely. Yet, most goals that are easy to specify will not capture the context-specific complexities of human objectives in the real world.[15] And indeed, AI systems frequently find ways to maximize their reward functions with unintended behaviours—what Bostrom (2014: 120–124) calls 'perverse instantiations'. A nice example is given by Russell and Norvig (2010: 37), who imagine a vacuum robot whose performance is measured by the amount of dirt it cleans up. The optimal learned policy causes the robot to repeatedly dump and clean up the same dirt, which is obviously not what the designer of a vacuum intends the machine to do. It is not obvious, however, whether these examples of 'specification gaming' in current systems should count as evidence that future systems with more advanced intelligence are also likely to behave in these ways.[16]

A third reason that the value alignment problem is challenging is that our own values—assuming we could identify and perfectly articulate them—are not perfect. Human beings are far from reliably human-friendly. If superintelligent machines merely aim to achieve our own standards of 'human friendliness' or 'friendliness to other life forms', we may not be very well off (Price and Vold 2018). Indeed, we may find ourselves living amongst superintelligent systems that amplify our own fallible, inconsistent, and complacent moral natures. Let's call this the *problem of human moral imperfection*. A related problem emerges from the need to accommodate moral progress. Even if we can find a way to build machines that align with (only) the better parts of our current values, we would not want AI systems to codify these values in a way that prevents moral progress. After all, one does not have to look far into human history to see how much our values have progressed (Price and Vold 2018).

Concluding CPAX (P4 and C3)

P4 of CPAX states that AI systems are likely to converge upon certain instrumental goals that are inimical to human interests, a premise supported by the Instrumental

Convergence Thesis (above). The idea behind P4 is that some of the goals that intelligent systems are likely to converge upon will put those systems (e.g. an AI and humans) at odds with each other. As just one example, both Omohundro and Bostrom identify *resource acquisition* as a basic drive and an instrumental convergent value, respectively. In Omohundro's view, '[a]ll computation and physical action requires the physical resources of space, time, matter, and free energy', and hence, 'almost any goal can be better accomplished by having more of these resources' (2008: 491). Bostrom (2014: 114–116) argues that, for this reason, it is likely that 'an extremely wide range of possible final goals' would generate 'the instrumental goal of unlimited resource acquisition'.[17] Perhaps the most widely discussed example of this problem is Bostrom's (2014: 123) paperclip maximizer—a superintelligent AI system that has the goal of maximizing the production of paperclips. The system finds any means necessary of producing more paperclips, including securing any resources necessary for that purpose. With sufficient capacities to modify the world, soon enough the system could co-opt much of the Earth's natural resources, including those needed for the survival of humanity, all for the purposes of paperclip production. The example is meant to show that even with good intentions and fairly innocuous goals, we could end up with AI systems inadvertently acting in ways that are inimical to human values. Another related concern is that human beings not only require resources to survive and flourish, but we are also resources ourselves. In the *Matrix Trilogy*, for example, the AI system turns humans into an energy source to power itself.

Both of these examples demonstrate how C3, which states that it is possible to build AI systems that pose an Xrisk, is meant to follow from C2 and P4. But here, we again face both a dearth of critical discussion and of compelling examples. Indeed, because most of the CPAX scenarios offered by leading defenders (e.g. Bostrom 2014; Russell 2019) are so 'bemusing',[18] one is inclined to simply dismiss them as belonging to science fiction. More charitably, one could see them as toy examples, meant to illustrate a broader concern about misaligned powerful AI systems—a concern that we have tried to outline in more detail. While any specific scenario might be dismissed as unrealistic, the broader concern remains *possible*. It is a (very) low probability risk that hinges critically on certain assumptions about (a) the possible motivations of an advanced AI system; and (b) the potential capacities that such a system could possess to bring about critical changes in the world (i.e. capacities for direct world modification). Notice as well that the argument only supports the (low-probability) possibility of AI posing an *indirect Xrisk*. None of the scenarios discussed suggest that an AI system would, for example, *directly* eliminate the whole of the population.

In closing, it is worth noting that many think that the best way to mitigate the risks of the control problem is to ensure that we build the initial conditions of the system in a way that aligns with human values, thereby avoiding P4 of CPAX. For further reading, we direct readers to the subfields of AI safety engineering and machine ethics, both of which have taken on the goal of trying to find technical solutions for building ethically aligned systems (Cave et al. 2019).

AI RACE DYNAMICS, GLOBAL DISRUPTION, AND XRISK

While the earliest arguments for AI Xrisk focused on control problem scenarios that were based around hypothetical advanced AI systems, a set of recent arguments centre on a more immediate, and practically grounded, set of issues. One of these is the growing concern that advanced AI could confer significant strategic advantages to its possessors, and correspondingly, whether an AI race could emerge between powerful actors in pursuit of this technology (Dafoe 2018; Cave and Ó hÉigeartaigh 2018; Bostrom 2014).[19] In the following two subsections, we discuss two associated sources of *structural risks* that could pose *indirect Xrisks* should such an AI race dynamic arise: the first is that it could disincentivize researchers from investing in AI safety, and the second is that it could spark military conflict between AI competitors. A related issue gaining attention is the impact AI could have on global strategic stability. We take this up in the third subsection, focusing on its capacity to destabilize nuclear deterrence, and thereby potentially contributing to military conflict escalation.

AI race dynamics: corner-cutting safety

An AI race between powerful actors could have an adverse effect on AI safety, a subfield aimed at finding technical solutions to building 'advanced AI systems that are safe and beneficial' (Dafoe 2018: 25; Cave and Ó hÉigeartaigh 2018; Bostrom 2017; Armstrong et al. 2016; Bostrom 2014). Dafoe (2018: 43), for example, argues that it is plausible that such a race would provide strong incentives for researchers to trade off safety in order to increase the chances of gaining a relative advantage over a competitor.[20] In Bostrom's (2017) view, competitive races would disincentivize two options for a frontrunner: (a) slowing down or pausing the development of an AI system; and (b) implementing safety-related performance handicapping. Both, he argues, have worrying consequences for AI safety.

(a) *Slowing down or pausing the development of an AI system*

(a) Bostrom (2017: 5) considers a case in which a solution to the control problem (C1) is dependent upon the components of an AI system to which it will be applied, such that it is only possible to invent or install a necessary control mechanism after the system has been developed to a significantly high degree. He contends that, in situations like these, it is vital that a team is able to pause further development until the required safety work can be performed (Bostrom 2017). Yet, if implementing these controls requires a substantial amount of additional time and resources, then in a tight competitive race dynamic, any team that decides to initiate this safety work would likely surrender its lead to a competitor who forgoes doing so (Bostrom 2017). If competitors don't reach an agreement on safety standards, then it is possible that a *'risk-race to the bottom'* could arise, driving each team to take increasing risks by investing minimally in safety (Bostrom 2014: 247).

(b) *Implementing safety-related performance handicapping*

Bostrom (2017: 5–6) also considers possible scenarios in which the 'mechanisms needed to make an AI safe reduces the AI's effectiveness'. These include cases in which a safe AI would run at a considerably slower speed than an unsafe one, or those in which implementing a safety mechanism necessitates the curtailing of an AI's capabilities (Bostrom 2017). If the AI race were to confer large strategic and economic benefits to frontrunners, then teams would be disincentivized from implementing these sorts of safety mechanisms. The same, however, does not necessarily hold true of less competitive race dynamics, that is, ones in which a competitor has a significant lead over others (Bostrom 2017). Under these conditions, it is conceivable that there could be enough of a time advantage that frontrunners could unilaterally apply performance-handicapping safety measures without relinquishing their lead (Bostrom 2017).

It is relatively uncontroversial to suggest that reducing investment in AI safety could lead to a host of associated dangers. Improper safety precautions could produce all kinds of unintended harms from misstated objectives or from specification gaming, for example. They could also lead to a higher prevalence of AI system vulnerabilities which are intentionally exploited by malicious actors for destructive ends, as in the case of adversarial examples (see Brundage et al. 2018). But does AI safety corner-cutting reach the threshold of an *Xrisk*? Certainly not directly, but there are at least some circumstances under which it would do so indirectly. Recall that Chalmers (2010) argues there could be defeaters that obstruct the self-amplifying capabilities of an advanced AI, which could in turn forestall the occurrence of an intelligence explosion. Scenario (a) above made the case that a competitive AI race would disincentivize researchers from investing in developing safety precautions aimed at preventing an intelligence explosion (e.g. motivational defeaters). Thus, in cases in which an AI race is centred on the development of artificial general intelligence, a seed AI with the capacity to self-improve, or even an advanced narrow AI (as in the section 'Intelligence explosion and decisive strategic advantages (P1)' above), a competitive race dynamic could pose an *indirect Xrisk* insofar as it contributes to a set of conditions that elevate the risk of a control problem occurring (Bostrom 2014: 246, 2017: 5).

AI race dynamics: conflict between AI competitors

The mere narrative of an AI race could also, under certain conditions, increase the risk of military conflict between competing groups. Cave and Ó hÉigeartaigh (2018) argue that AI race narratives which frame the future trajectory of AI development in terms of technological advantage could 'increase the risk of competition in AI causing real conflict (overt or covert)'. The militarized language typical of race dynamics may encourage competitors to view each other 'as threats or even enemies' (Cave and Ó hÉigeartaigh 2018: 3).[21] If a government believes that an adversary is pursuing a strategic advantage in AI that could result in their technological dominance, then this alone could provide a motivating reason to use aggression against the adversary (Cave and Ó hÉigeartaigh 2018; Bostrom 2014). An AI race narrative could thus lead to crisis escalation between states. However, the resulting conflict, should it arise, need not directly involve AI systems. And it is an open question whether said conflict would meet the Xrisk threshold. Under conditions where it does (perhaps nuclear war), the contributions of AI as a technology would at best be *indirect*.

Global disruption: destabilization of nuclear deterrents

Another type of crisis escalation associated with AI is the potential destabilizing impact the technology could have on global strategic stability;[22] in particular, its capacity to destabilize nuclear deterrence strategies (Geist and Lohn 2018; Rickli 2019; Sauer 2019; Groll 2018; Zwetsloot and Dafoe 2019). In general, deterrence relies both on states possessing secure second-strike capabilities (Zwetsloot and Dafoe 2019) and, at the same time, on a state's inability to locate, with certainty, an adversary's nuclear second-strike forces (Rickli 2019). This could change, however, with advances in AI (Rickli 2019). For example, AI-enabled surveillance and reconnaissance systems, unmanned underwater vehicles, and data analysis could allow a state to both closely track and destroy an adversary's previously hidden nuclear-powered ballistic missile submarines (Zwetsloot and Dafoe 2019). If their second-strike nuclear capabilities were to become vulnerable to a first strike, then a pre-emptive nuclear strike would, in theory, become a viable strategy under certain scenarios (Geist and Lohn 2018). In Zwetsloot and Dafoe's (2019) view, 'the fear that nuclear systems could be insecure would, in turn, create pressures for states—including defensively motivated ones—to pre-emptively escalate during a crisis'. What is perhaps most alarming is that the aforementioned AI systems need not actually exist to have a destabilizing impact on nuclear deterrence (Rickli 2019; Groll 2018; Geist and Lohn 2018). As Rickli (2019: 95) points out, '[b]y its very nature, nuclear deterrence is highly psychological and relies on the perception of the adversary's capabilities and intentions'. Thus, the 'simple misperception of the adversary's AI capabilities is destabilizing in itself' (Rickli 2019). This potential for AI to destabilize nuclear deterrence represents yet another kind of indirect global catastrophic, and perhaps even existential, risk insofar as the destabilization could contribute to nuclear conflict escalation.

THE WEAPONIZATION OF AI

Much like the more recent set of growing concerns around an AI arms race, there have also been growing concerns around the weaponization of AI. We use 'weaponization' to encompass many possible scenarios, from malicious actors or a malicious AI itself, to the use of fully autonomous lethal weapons. And we will discuss each of these possibilities in turn. In the first subsection below we discuss malicious actors and in the second we discuss lethal autonomous weapons. We have combined this diverse range of scenarios for two reasons. First, while the previous Xrisk scenarios discussed (CPAX and an AI race) could emerge without malicious intentions from anyone involved (e.g. engineers or governments), the scenarios we discuss here do, for the most part, assume some kind of *malicious intent* on the part of some actor. They are what Zwetsloot and Dafoe (2019) call a *misuse* risk. Second, the threats we discuss here are not particularly unique to AI, unlike those in previous sections. The control problem, for example, is distinctive of AI as a technology, in the sense that the problem did not exist before we began building intelligent systems. On the other hand, many technologies can be weaponized. In this respect, AI is no different. It is because AI is potentially so powerful that its misuse in a complex and high-impact environment, such as warfare, could pose an Xrisk.

Malicious actors

In discussing CPAX, we focused on *accidental risk* scenarios—where no one involved wants to bring about harm, but the mere act of building an advanced AI system creates an Xrisk. But AI could also be deliberately *misused*. These can include things like exploiting software vulnerabilities, for example, through automated hacking or adversarial examples; generating political discord or misinformation with synthetic media; or initiating physical attacks using drones or automated weapons (see Brundage et al. 2018). For these scenarios to reach the threshold of Xrisk (in terms of 'scope'), however, a beyond catastrophic amount of damage would have to be done. Perhaps one instructs an AI system to suck up all the oxygen in the air, to launch all the nuclear weapons in a nation's arsenal, or to invent a deadly airborne biological virus. Or perhaps a lone actor is able to use AI to hack critical infrastructures, including some that manage large-scale projects, such as the satellites that orbit Earth. It does not take much creativity to drum up a scenario in which an AI system, if put in the wrong hands, could pose an Xrisk. But the Xrisk posed by AI in these cases is likely to be *indirect*—where AI is just one link in the causal chain, perhaps even a distal one. This involvement of malicious actors is one of the more common concerns around the weaponization of AI. Automated systems that have war-fighting capacities or that are in any way linked to nuclear missile systems could become likely targets of malicious actors aiming to cause widespread harm. This threat is serious, but the theoretical nature of the threat is straightforward relative to those posed in CPAX, for example.

One further novel outcome of AI would be if the system itself malfunctions. Any technology can malfunction, and in the case of an AI system that had control over real-world weapons systems, the consequences of a malfunction could be severe (see Robillard, this volume). We will discuss this potential scenario further in the next section. A final related possibility here would be for the AI to itself turn malicious. This would be unlike

740 KARINA VOLD AND DANIEL R. HARRIS

any other technology in the past. But since AI is a kind of intelligent agent, there is this possibility. Cotton-Barratt et al. (2020), for example, describe a hypothetical scenario in which an intelligence explosion produces a powerful AI that wipes out human beings in order to pre-empt any interference with its own objectives. They describe this as a *direct* Xrisk (by contrast, we described CPAX scenarios as *indirect*), presumably because they describe the AI as *deliberately* wiping out humanity. However, if the system has agency in a meaningful sense, such that it is making these kinds of deliberate malicious decisions, then this seems to assume it has something akin to consciousness or strong intentionality. In general we are far from developing anything like artificial consciousness and this is not to say that these scenarios should be dismissed altogether, but many experts agree that there are serious challenges confronting the possibility of AI possessing these cognitive capacities (e.g. Searle 1980; Koch and Tononi 2017; Koch 2019; Dehaene et al. 2017).

Lethal autonomous weapons

One other form of weaponization of AI that is sometimes discussed as a potential source of Xrisk is lethal autonomous weapons systems (LAWS). LAWS include systems that can locate, select, and engage targets without any human intervention (Roff 2014; Russell 2015; Robillard, this volume). Much of the debate around the ethics of LAWS has focused on whether their use would violate human dignity (Lim 2019; Rosert and Sauer 2019; Sharkey 2019), whether they could leave critical responsibility gaps in warfare (Sparrow 2007; Robillard, this volume), or whether they could undermine the principles of just war theory, such as non-combatant immunity (Roff 2014), for example. These concerns, among others, have led many to call for a ban on their use (FLI 2017). These concerns are certainly very serious and more near term (as some LAWS already exist) than the speculative scenarios discussed in CPAX. But do LAWS really present an *Xrisk*? It seems that if they do, they do so *indirectly*. Consider two possible scenarios.

(a) One concern around LAWS is that they will ease the cost of engaging in war, making it more likely that tensions between rival states rise to military engagement. In this case, LAWS would be used as an instrument to carry out the ends of some malicious actor. This is because, for now, humans continue to play a significant role in directing the behaviour of LAWS, though it is likely that we will see a steady increase in the autonomy of future systems (Brundage et al. 2018). Now, it could be that this kind of warfare leads to Xrisks, but this would require a causal chain that includes political disruption, perhaps failing states, and widespread mass murder. None of these scenarios are impossible, of course, and they present serious risks. But we have tried to focus this chapter on Xrisks that are *novel* to AI as a technology and, even though we view the risks of LAWS as extremely important, they ultimately present similar kinds of risks as nuclear weapons do. To the extent that LAWS have a destabilizing impact on norms and practices in warfare, for example, we think that scenarios similar to those discussed in the section 'Global disruption: destabilization of nuclear deterrents' are possible—LAWS might escalate an ongoing crisis, or moreover, the mere perception that an adversary has LAWS might escalate a crisis.

(b) A second scenario, described by Geoffrey Hinton, is that killer drones, equipped with explosives and deep-learning neural net technology, could (somehow) learn to function independently of their human controllers (Robinson 2016), and the system could then go on a rampage and destroy humanity. The bracketed 'somehow' here is a critical piece of the story. Perhaps the control system has been hacked, in which case we are back to the malicious actor scenario described above. Or perhaps there is a malfunction, of the sort also described above. In this latter case, the malfunction could manifest in the form of a 'hard take-off' in which the system undergoes rapid recursive self-improvement (unintended by the designers) and then develops goals that are inimical to human interests. In such a case, we would be at the start of an intelligence explosion and would confront the kind of Xrisk already characterized by CPAX (see the section on 'The control problem argument for Xrisk' above). Our only point here is that upon closer examination, it is hard to see how this scenario looks distinct from ones previously discussed. Hence, the weaponization of AI can pose an indirect Xrisk in several different ways. In general, the more control an automated system has over weaponized systems that can cause real-world destruction, the greater risk there is of that system becoming a target for attack by malicious actors or of there being greater harm due to any accidental system malfunction.

CONCLUSION

Humanity is facing an increasing number of existential threats, many of which are of our own creation. Thankfully, there are also an increasing number of scholars, from a wide range of fields, studying the nature of these risks and strategizing how to mitigate them. But the field of Xrisk studies is still relatively young. There are significant debates being had over how to define the concept of Xrisk, how to understand its sources, and what methodologies should be used to assess these risks. When it comes to Xrisks from AI, these debates continue. Early concerns around AI Xrisks focused on the possibility of an intelligence explosion and the subsequent pathway to a scenario in which a powerful superintelligent AI has misaligned objectives from humanity. These concerns have not gone away, but they have evolved over time. This chapter has provided an up-to-date critical survey of these arguments, both old and new, looking at different foreseeable pathways towards AI Xrisk, possible global disruptions resulting from the emergence of an AI race dynamic between nations, and the weaponization of AI. In particular, we have tried to make the structures of each of these concerns more explicit, such that readers can begin to critically engage with them.

ACKNOWLEDGEMENTS

We thank our colleagues from the University of Cambridge's Centre for the Study of Existential Risk who contributed to these ideas, including helpful input from Haydn Belfield, Martina Kunz, Matthijs Maas, Sean Ó hÉigeartaigh, Jaime Sevilla, Catherine Stinson, and Jess Whittlestone. We also thank our two anonymous reviewers for their invaluable comments. Karina Vold was supported by the Leverhulme Centre for the Future of Intelligence, Leverhulme Trust, under Grant RC-2015-067. Daniel R. Harris was supported by a Doctoral Fellowship from the Social Sciences and Humanities Research Council of Canada.

NOTES

1. Extinction risks are those that directly cause the extinction of the human species or less directly lead to circumstances that cause our extinction (e.g. through habitat destruction) (see discussions in Matheny 2007; Bostrom 2013; and Cotton-Barratt et al. 2020.)
2. Moynihan (2020) is the only example we found of someone using this narrow definition (c.f. Sotala and Gloor (2017) and Torres (2019), who both claim that the narrow definition is most common).
3. Bostrom (2014) and Russell (2019) each have a book-length defence of these issues, but neither lay out CPAX in an explicit way. The closest examples we found were Chalmers (2010) and Danaher (2015). Here, we draw from all of these sources.
4. This final possibility is more modest in the sense that it would require less advancement in current technology as a starting point for the argument. This is because, while we currently have many sophisticated narrow AI systems, which outperform humans in certain tasks (e.g. playing chess or go), we do not yet have any general AI systems, and many scholars hypothesize that we are a long way from developing these (e.g. Dignum 2019).
5. Here, we distinguish our use of the phrase 'decisive strategic advantage' from that of Bostrom's (2014: 78), who defines it as 'a level of technological and other advantages sufficient to enable it to achieve complete world domination'. AlphaZero, to be sure, could not spark an intelligence explosion, as it has neither a decisive strategic advantage *in a relevant domain* nor does it have sufficient capacities for real-world modification.
6. We have bracketed those cases in which an AI system is deliberately engineered to recursively self-improve, as it straightforwardly follows that it would do so under these conditions.
7. Chalmers also identifies two other types of obstacles—*structural obstacles* and *correlation obstacles*.
8. See further discussion in Russell (2019).
9. By 'motivations', we don't mean to attribute intentional agency, but rather 'agency' in a kind of Dennettian sense (i.e. following the intentional stance). We mean motivations as something like 'subgoals', or the strategies a system will undertake to achieve its final goals.
10. Consider another scenario, discussed by Tegmark (2014) and Häggström (2019), in which an advanced AI is programmed to have a meaningless or 'undefined' goal. What would happen in this case? Häggström predicts that all instrumental goals would also then become pointless, in which case 'all predictions' from the instrumental convergence thesis 'collapse'.

11. These are two of many possible hypothetical scenarios of how powerful AIs with misaligned objectives could be Xrisks. See Shanahan (2015) and Tegmark (2017) for further examples.

12. We could not find any scholarly publications in which Loosemore or Metzinger make these points, so in both cases we cite online articles.

13. We say 'seem' here because of the work in cross-cultural psychology over the past two decades, which tries to show that human societies that seem to vary widely in their values in fact share some basic set of normative commitments (or values), even though the shared set may be interpreted or applied differently (e.g. Borg et al. 2019 and Christians 2019).

14. Also sometimes referred to as the 'specification problem', the 'genie problem', or the 'Sorcerer's Apprentice problem'.

15. See Cantwell Smith (2019) for an argument that this capacity for 'deep contextual awareness' in our ethical judgements (i.e. to discern what norms or values apply within a specific fine-grained context)—a capacity that is central to virtue ethics—is computationally intractable.

16. Thanks to Matthijs Maas for raising this point in discussion.

17. Similar arguments for instrumental convergence around resource acquisition can be found in Tegmark (2017: 266) and Russell (2019).

18. As Leslie (2019) describes them in a critical review.

19. Geist (2016) takes a stronger view, arguing that the world superpowers are already locked in a particular type of racing dynamic—an AI arms race.

20. Armstrong et al.'s (2016) model of an AI race dynamic supports this claim.

21. Here, Cave and Ó hÉigeartaigh discuss Huysmans (2006).

22. Geist and Lohn (2018: 10) define strategic stability as existing 'when adversaries lack a significant incentive to engage in provocative behavior'.

References

Armstrong, Stuart (2013), 'General Purpose Intelligence: Arguing the Orthogonality Thesis', *Analysis and Metaphysics* 12, 68–84.

Armstrong, Stuart, Bostrom, Nick, and Shulman, Carl (2016), 'Racing to the Precipice: A Model of Artificial Intelligence Development', *AI & Society* 31, 201–206.

Baum, Seth D. (2020), 'Social Choice Ethics in Artificial Intelligence', *AI & Society* 35, 165–176.

Beard, Simon, Rowe, Thomas, and Fox, James (2020), 'An Analysis and Evaluation of Methods Currently Used to Quantify the Likelihood of Existential Hazards', *Futures* 115, 102469.

Borg, Ingwer, Hermann, Dieter, Bilsky, Wolfgang, and Pöge, Andreas (2019), 'Do the PVQ and the IRVS Scales for Personal Values Support Schwartz's Value Circle Model or Klages' Value Dimensions Model?', *Measurement Instruments for the Social Sciences* 1(3), doi: https://doi.org/10.1186/s42409-018-0004-2.

Bostrom, Nick (2002), 'Existential Risks: Analyzing Human Extinction Scenarios and Related Hazards', *Journal of Evolution and Technology* 9(1), 1–31

Bostrom, Nick (2012), 'The Superintelligent Will: Motivation and Instrumental Rationality in Advanced Artificial Agents', *Minds and Machines* 22(2), 71–78.

Bostrom, Nick (2013), 'Existential Risk Prevention as Global Priority', Global Policy 4(1), 15–31.

Bostrom, Nick (2014), *Superintelligence: Paths, Dangers, Strategies* (Oxford: Oxford University Press).

Bostrom, Nick (2017), 'Strategic Implications of Openness in AI Development', *Global Policy* 8(2), 135–148.

Brundage, Miles, Avin, Shahar, Clark, Jack, Toner, Helen, Eckersley, Peter, Garfinkel, Ben et al. (2018), 'The Malicious Use of Artificial Intelligence: Forecasting, Prevention, and Mitigation', https://maliciousaireport.com, accessed 10 August 2021.

Butler, Samuel (1863), 'Darwin among the Machines', *Christchurch in the Press Newspaper*, 13 June.

Cantwell Smith, Brian (2019), *The Promise of Artificial Intelligence: Reckoning and Judgment* (Cambridge, MA: MIT Press).

Cave, Stephen, and Ó hÉigeartaigh, Seán (2018), 'An AI Race for Strategic Advantage: Rhetoric and Risks', AIES '18: *Proceedings of the 2018 AAAI/ACM Conference on Artificial Intelligence, Ethics and Society* (Association for Computing Machinery: New York, United States), 36–40.

Cave, Stephen, Nyrup, Rune, Vold, Karina, and Weller, Adrian (2019), 'Motivations and Risks of Machine Ethics', *Proceedings of the IEEE* 107(3), 562–574.

Chalmers, David J. (2010), 'The Singularity: A Philosophical Analysis', *Journal of Consciousness Studies* 17(9–10), 7–65.

Chorost, Michael (2016), 'Let Artificial Intelligence Evolve', *Slate*, 18 April, https://slate.com/technology/2016/04/the-philosophical-argument-against-artificial-intelligence-killing-us-all.html, accessed 10 August 2021.

Christians, Clifford G. (2019), *Media Ethics and Global Justice in the Digital Age* (Cambridge: Cambridge University Press).

Cortese, Francesco A.B. (2014), 'The Maximally Distributed Intelligence Explosion', in *Implementing Selves with Safe Motivational Systems and Motivational Systems and Self-Improvement: Proceedings of the AAAI Spring Symposium*, (Palo Alto, California: The AAAI Press), 7–12.

Cotton-Barratt, Owen, Daniel, Max, and Sandberg, Anders (2020), 'Defence in Depth against Human Extinction: Prevention, Response, Resilience, and Why They All Matter', *Global Policy* 1–12, doi: https://doi.org/10.1111/1758-5899.12786.

Dafoe, Allan (2018), 'AI Governance: A Research Agenda', Future of Humanity Institute, University of Oxford, https://www.fhi.ox.ac.uk/wp-content/uploads/GovAIAgenda.pdf, accessed 10 August 2021.

Danaher, John (2015), 'Why AI Doomsayers Are Like Sceptical Theists and Why It Matters', *Minds & Machines* 25, 231–246.

Dehaene, Stanislas, Lau, Hakwan, and Kouider, Sid (2017), 'What Is Consciousness, and Could Machines Have It?', *Science* 358(6362), 486–492, doi: https://doi.org/10.1126/science.aan8871.

Dignum, Virginia. (2019), *Responsible Artificial Intelligence: How to Develop and Use AI in a Responsible Way* (Switzerland: Springer International Publishing).

Drexler, K. Eric (2019), 'Reframing Superintelligence: Comprehensive AI Services as General Intelligence', Technical Report #2019-1, Future of Humanity Institute, University of Oxford.

Future of Life Institute (FLI) (2017), 'Open Letter to the United Nations Convention on Certain Conventional Weapons', https://futureoflife.org/autonomous-weapons-open-letter-2017/, accessed 10 August 2021.

Gabriel, Iason, Ghazavi, Vafa (2021), 'The Challenge of Value Alignment: From Fairer Algorithms to AI Safety', doi: https://doi.org/10.48550/arXiv.2101.06060.

Geist, Edward (2016), 'It's Already Too Late to Stop the AI Arms Race—We Must Manage It Instead', *Bulletin of the Atomic Scientists* 72, 318–321.

Geist, Edward and Lohn, Andrew J. (2018), 'How Might Artificial Intelligence Affect the Risk of Nuclear War?', RAND Corporation, Santa Monica, CA, https://www.rand.org/pubs/persp ectives/PE296.html, accessed 10 August 2021.

Good, Irving J. (1965), 'Speculations Concerning the First Ultraintelligent Machine', *Advances in Computers* 6(99), 31–83.

Groll, Elias (2018), 'How AI Could Destabilize Nuclear Deterrence', *Foreign Policy*, 24 April, https://foreignpolicy.com/2018/04/24/how-ai-could-destabilize-nuclear-deterrence/, accessed 10 August 2021.

Häggström, Olle (2019), 'Challenges to the Omohundro–Bostrom Framework for AI Motivations', *Foresight* 21(1), 153–166.

Hawking, Stephen (2018), *Brief Answers to the Big Questions* (London, United Kingdom: Hodder & Stoughton).

Hume, David (1739), *A Treatise on Human Nature*, Edited by David. F. Norton and Mary. J. Norton. 2000. 6th Edition (Oxford: Oxford University Press).

Huysmans, Jef (2006), The Politics of Insecurity: Fear, Migration and Asylum in the EU, (Oxford: Routledge Press).

Koch, Christof (2019), 'Proust among the Machines', *Scientific American* 321(6), 46–49, doi: doi:10.1038/scientificamerican1219-46.

Koch, Christof and Tononi, Giulio (2017), 'Can We Quantify Machine Consciousness?', *IEEE Spectrum*, 25 May 2017. https://spectrum.ieee.org/can-we-quantify-machine-consciousness

Kohs, Greg (Director), (2017), *AlphaGo. Reel As Dirt.*

Leslie, David (2019), 'Raging Robots, Hapless Humans: The AI Dystopia', *Nature* 574, 32–33.

Lim, Daniel (2019), 'Killer Robots and Human Dignity', in *AIES '19: Proceedings of the 2019 AAAI/ACM Conference on Artificial Intelligence, Ethics, and Soci*ety (New York: Association for Computing Machinery (ACM)), 171–176.

Liu, Hin-Yan, Lauta, Kristian C, and Maas, Matthis M. (2018), 'Governing Boring Apocalypses: A New Typology of Existential Vulnerabilities and Exposures for Existential Risk Research', *Futures* 102, 6–19.

Loosemore, Richard (2012), 'The Fallacy of Dumb Superintelligence', Institute for Ethics and Emerging Technologies Blog, https://web.archive.org/web/20130731094845/http://ieet.org/index.php/IEET/more/loosemore20121128, accessed 10 August 2021

Martin, Brian (1982), 'Critique of Nuclear Extinction', *Journal of Peace Research* 19(4), 287–300.

Matheny, Jason G. (2007), 'Reducing the Risk of Human Extinction', *Risk Analysis* 27(5), 1335–1344.

Metzinger, Thomas (2017), 'Benevolent Artificial Anti-Natalism (BAAN)', *The Edge*, 8 July, https://www.edge.org/conversation/thomas_metzinger-benevolent-artificial-anti-natal ism-baan, accessed 10 August 2021.

Moynihan, Thomas (2020), 'Existential Risk and Human Extinction', *Futures* 116, 102495.

Ó hÉigeartaigh, Seán (2017), 'The State of Research in Existential Risk', in B. John Garrick, ed., *Proceedings of the First International Colloquium on Catastrophic and Existential Risk*, (UCLA: B. John Garrick Institute for the Risk Sciences), 37–52.

Omohundro, Stephen M. (2008), 'The Basic AI Drives', in Pei Wang, Ben Goertzel, and Stan Franklin, eds, Frontiers in Artificial Intelligence and Applications Vol. 171 (Amsterdam Netherlands: IOS Press), 483–492.

Ord, Toby (2020), *The Precipice Existential Risk and the Future of Humanity* (New York: Hachette Books).

Pinker, Steven (2019), 'Tech Prophecy and the Underappreciated Casual Power of Ideas', in John. Brockman, ed., *Possible Minds: Twenty-Five Ways of Looking at AI* (London: Penguin Press), ch. 10.

Price, Huw, and Vold, Karina (2018), 'Living with Artificial Intelligence', *Research Horizons* 35, 20–21.

Rees, Martin (2003), *Our Final Hour: A Scientist's Warning* (New York: Basic Books).

Rickli, Jean-Marc (2019), 'The Destabilizing Prospects of Artificial Intelligence for Nuclear Strategy, Deterrence and Stability: Volume I Euro-Atlantic Perspectives', in Vincent Boulanin, ed., *The Impact of Artificial Intelligence on Strategic Stability and Nuclear Risk* (Solna, Sweden: SIPRI), 91–98. Solna, Sweden: SIPRI.

Robinson, Jennifer (2016), 'U of T's Geoffrey Hinton: AI Will Eventually Surpass the Human Brain but Getting Jokes … That Could Take Time', *U of T Magazine: News Online*, https://www.utoronto.ca/news/u-t-geoffrey-hinton-ai-will-eventually-surpass-human-brain-getting-jokes-could-take-time, accessed 10 August 2021.

Roff, Heather M. (2014), 'The Strategic Robot Problem: Lethal Autonomous Weapons in War', *Journal of Military Ethics* 13(3), 211–227.

Rosert, Elvira, and Sauer, Frank (2019), 'Prohibiting Autonomous Weapons: Put Human Dignity First', *Global Policy* 10, 370–375.

Russell, Stuart (2015), 'Take a Stand on AI Weapons', *Nature* 521, 415–418.

Russell, Stuart (2019), *Human Compatible: AI and the Problem of Control* (New York: Penguin Random House).

Russell, Stuart, and Norvig, Peter (2010), *Artificial Intelligence A Modern Approach*, 3rd edn (Upper Saddle River, NJ: Prentice Hall).

Sagan, Carl (1983), 'Nuclear War and Climatic Catastrophe: Some Policy Implications', *Foreign Affairs* 62(2), 257–292.

Sandberg, Anders, and Bostrom, Nick (2008), 'Global Catastrophic Risks Survey', Technical Report #2008-1, Future of Humanity Institute, University of Oxford, 1–5.

Sauer, Frank (2019), 'Military Applications of Artificial Intelligence: Nuclear Risk Redux', in Vincent. Boulanin, ed., *The Impact of Artificial Intelligence on Strategic Stability and Nuclear Risk: Volume I, Euro-Atlantic Perspectives* (Solna, Sweden: SIPRI), 84–90. Solna, Sweden: SIPRI.

Schulte, Peter, Alegret, Laia, Arenillas, Ignacio, Arz, José A., Barton, Penny J., Bown, Paul R. et al. (2010), 'The Chicxulub Asteroid Impact and Mass Extinction at the Cretaceous–Paleogene Boundary', *Science* 327 (5970), 1214–1218.

Searle, John (1980), 'Minds, Brains and Programs', *Behavioral and Brain Sciences* 3, 417–457.

Shanahan, Murray (2015), *The Technological Singularity* (Cambridge, CA: MIT Press).

Sharkey, Amanda (2019), 'Autonomous Weapons Systems, Killer Robots and Human Dignity', *Ethics of Information Technology* 21, 75–87.

Shevlin, Henry, Vold, Karina, Crosby, Matthew, and Halina, Marta (2019), 'The Limits of Machine Intelligence', *EMBO Report* 20, e49177.

Shulman, Carl (2012), 'Nuclear Winter and Human Extinction: Q&A with Luke Oman', Overcoming Bias Blog, 5 November, http://www.overcomingbias.com/2012/11/nuclear-winter-and-human-extinction-qa-with-luke-oman.html, accessed 10 August 2021.

Silver, David, Huang, Aja, Maddison, Chris J., Guez, Arthur, Sifre, Laurent, Driessche, George van den et al. (2016), 'Mastering the Game of Go with Deep Neural Networks and Tree Search', *Nature* 529, 484–489.

Sofge, Erik (2015), 'Bill Gates Fears A.I., But A.I. Researchers Know Better', *Popular Science*, 30 January, https://www.popsci.com/bill-gates-fears-ai-ai-researchers-know-better/, accessed 10 August 2021.

Sotala, Kaj, and Gloor, Lukas (2017), 'Superintelligence as a Cause or Cure for Risks of Astronomical Suffering', *Informatica* 41, 389–400.

Sparrow R. (2007), 'Killer Robots', *Journal of Applied Philosophy* 24(1), 65.

Tegmark, Max (2014), 'Friendly Artificial Intelligence: The Physics Challenge', in Toby Walsh Ed. *Proceedings of the Artificial Intelligence and Ethics: Papers from the 2015 AAAI Workshop* (Palo Alto, California: The AAAI Press), 87–89.

Tegmark, Max (2017), *Life 3.0: Being Human in the Age of Artificial Intelligence* (New York: Brockman Inc).

Torres, Phil (2019), 'Existential Risks: A Philosophical Analysis', *Inquiry*, doi: https://doi.org/10.1080/0020174X.2019.1658626.

Turing, Alan (1951/1996), 'Intelligent Machinery, A Heretical Theory', reprinted in *Philosophia Mathematica* 4(3), 256–260.

Wakefield, Jane (2015), 'Intelligent Machines: What Does Facebook Want with AI?', *BBC News*, 15 September, https://www.bbc.com/news/technology-34118481, accessed 10 August 2021.

Weiner, Norbert (1960), 'Some Moral and Technical Consequences of Automation', *Science* 131(3410), 1355–1358.

Williams, Chris (2015), 'AI Guru Ng: Fearing a Rise of Killer Robots Is Like Worrying about Overpopulation on Mars', *The Register*, 19 March, https://www.theregister.co.uk/2015/03/19/andrew_ng_baidu_ai/, accessed 10 August 2021.

Zwetsloot, Remco, and Dafoe, Allan (2019), 'Thinking about Risks from AI: Accidents, Misuse and Structure', Lawfare Blog, 11 February, https://www.lawfareblog.com/thinking-about-risks-ai-accidents-misuse-and-structure, accessed 10 August 2021.

CHAPTER 37

....

AUTOMATION AND
THE FUTURE OF WORK

....

JOHN DANAHER

INTRODUCTION

....

WHAT is it, if anything, that makes humans unique? Many answers have been proposed over the years. Some argue that it is sentience and self-awareness that makes humans unique. But spend any time interacting with a dog or, even better, a chimpanzee and you will be hard-pressed to deny that they feel pleasure and pain or that they have some sense of *self*.[1] Some argue that it is complex tool use. But recent experimental work with crows and other corvids has scotched that idea. Our tools may be quite sophisticated, but it is clear that other animals are capable of creating and using tools to solve complex, multi-part puzzles (Gruber et al. 2019). Some argue that it is language that sets us apart. This is certainly a more plausible claim, but even here we see primitive precursors to speech and communication in other animals (Seyfarth and Cheney 2017).

So what, if anything, makes us unique? In a provocative short essay, the zoologist Antone Martinho-Truswell (2018) proposes an interesting answer. He argues that humans, alone among all the animals, are unique in their capacity for *automation*. That is to say: humans are the only creatures that are capable of offloading their work to machines, not simply in the sense that they create tools to help them with their work but, more impressively, that they create machines that are capable of performing entire tasks without much human input. What is more, this is not a recent phenomenon. It goes back thousands of years. Martinho-Truswell cites the examples of the crossbow and the catapult as illustrations of humanity's first forays into automation.

If he is right, Martinho-Truswell has highlighted something important about the human condition. He has highlighted a culturally deep longing for machines that free us from the drudgery of work. This longing has long exceeded our technological capacity. We don't just hope for the automation of some tasks based on currently available technologies. We also imagine and debate the possibilities of radical forms of automation. The cultural historian Adrienne Mayor highlights this in her book *Gods and Robots* (2018) by showing how the Ancient Greeks, from Homer to Aristotle, imagined and debated radical forms of worker automation, even going so far as to worry about the ethical and social impact of automation on what we would nowadays call the 'work ethic'.

Since the dawn of the digital age, the debate about automation and work has taken on a renewed urgency. Sophisticated information-processing technologies have dramatically altered our workplaces and work habits. That much is obvious. When these technologies are combined with recent developments in robotics and artificial intelligence, they bring us tantalizingly close to turning what was fantasy and imagination for Aristotle into a practical reality. What implications will this have for the future and value of work? In this chapter, I try to answer that question by highlighting, in particular, the ethical costs and benefits inherent in the digitization and automation of work.

My analysis proceeds in four main parts. First, I discuss the nature of work and workplace automation, arguing that a lot of the contemporary debate about automation is misguided because it is impossible to automate work, per se; you can only automate work-related tasks. Second, I discuss the moral dimension of work, focusing in particular on its role in distributing goods to members of society, as well as the different ethical principles or rationales one might have for assessing the impact of workplace automation. Third, I consider three possible effects that technology could have on the workplace of the future: the displacement effect, the complementarity effect, and the polarization effect. In discussing these three effects, I focus particular attention on how they might affect the distribution of the goods of work. Fourth, and finally, I consider the possible responses to these effects.

Throughout this chapter, I try to give a fair hearing to different perspectives and possibilities. Nevertheless, I will not adopt an entirely dispassionate and value-neutral perspective. On the contrary, I will try to defend a particular perspective on the ethics of workplace automation. To be precise, I will try to argue that the disruptive impact of technology on the workplace is likely to be more significant than many mainstream commentators presume. Furthermore, I will argue that this can be a good thing if we embrace the radical potential of a post-work ethic (Danaher 2019a, 2019b).

Can we automate 'work'?

Most of the conversation around technology and the future of work makes explicit reference to the concept or idea of 'work' (Danaher 2019a; Avent 2016; Susskind 2020), as does the conversation around the value of work and the possibility of a post-work or anti-work politics (Black 1986; Frayne 2015; Gorz 1989; Weeks 2011; Srnicek and Williams 2015). In some ways, this is unfortunate because what is meant by the word 'work' is unclear. There are multiple contested definitions of the concept. Some people adopt expansive, all-encompassing definitions of work that would include all purposeful activity in which humans engage, whereas others argue for a more restrictive definition, focusing on paid employment (Danaher 2019a: 26–30).

If we are to make any progress, we will have to bring some order to the definitional chaos. We can do this in two ways: we can abandon the term 'work' and use something that is less contentious and more precisely defined, or we can stick with the term 'work' and make it crystal clear what we mean when we use this term. There are advantages to the first approach, but it risks ignoring or bypassing much of the current conversation. For better or worse, the word 'work' has become embedded in the contemporary conversation about technology and automation. If you abandon it and talk about something else, there is a danger that people will overlook what you have to say, or think it is not relevant to their concerns. Hence, reluctantly, I adopt the second approach in what follows.

To do this, I suggest we side with the more restrictive interpretation of what work is. This means that we should focus on work 'in the economic sense' (Gorz 1989; Frayne 2015). Under this interpretation, work is any activity that is performed in return for, or in the reasonable expectation of, an economic reward (usually monetary in nature—Danaher 2019a: 28–29). This definition is expansive, insofar as it can include virtually any activity performed in the expectation of receiving an economic reward, but it is also restrictive in that it excludes some activities that people would like to classify as 'work', such as unpaid care work or housework. This exclusion might seem to be unjustified or contentious, but I argue that it is justified in the present context. This is because much of the anxiety and concern around technology and the future of work is fuelled by anxieties about the destabilization of the current economic order. It is only by explicitly linking the concept of 'work' to the present economic order that we can make sense of these anxieties. That is what this restrictive definition does.

If we adopt this restrictive definition of work, it is equally important that we understand what work is not. Work is not any particular activity or set of tasks; work is, rather, a *condition* under which activities and tasks are performed. Appreciating this distinction is crucial when it comes to understanding the impact of technology on work.

Allow me to elaborate. Right now, as I write this chapter, I am working. I am performing a set of activities (writing, thinking, researching) in return for an economic reward. (I am required to research and write as part of my current contract of employment; I am also receiving a specific payment for writing this particular book chapter.) The taxi driver outside my window is also working. She is driving passengers hither and thither in return for a direct payment. The activities we are both performing are very different in nature, but we are both working. It is the condition under which we perform our respective activities that transforms them into work. If I was writing this chapter in my spare time, or if the taxi driver was dropping her partner to their workplace, then neither of us would be working—at least, not in the restrictive sense intended in this chapter.

This has knock-on implications for how we understand terms that are closely related to work, such as 'job'. Jobs are different from work. Jobs are not best defined as conditions of activity, but, rather, as sets of ordered tasks. The job of being a taxi driver, for example, is characterized by a set of tasks, including: driving from A to B, picking up passengers, planning driving routes, making small talk with passengers, maintaining your car in good nick, and so on. The job of being an academic is characterized by tasks such as: research and writing, managing research projects, applying for grants, teaching students, mentoring graduate students, attending meetings, marking assignments, speaking at conferences, and so on. For some jobs, the list of tasks can be quite long and ill defined. This is probably true of the job of being an academic. Many academics do not focus on all the tasks mentioned in the list just given. They often prioritize a few to the exclusion of others. The loose definition of their roles gives them this freedom. Other jobs are more restrictively defined so that they are, almost by necessity, linked to a narrow range of tasks. This is probably true of being a taxi driver. If you stop driving passengers from A to B and focus purely on maintaining cars then, in a real sense, you are no longer a taxi driver. You are a mechanic.

The crucial point in all this is that jobs can be more or less arbitrarily or loosely defined. Jobs are collections of tasks that society, or specific subsections thereof, have decided it is worth grouping together and associating with a defined role (being an academic; being a taxi driver). In some contexts, it is possible to redefine and renegotiate these roles by linking them to different tasks. In other contexts, the options are more limited and if you try to redefine the role you may end up losing your job.

The bottom line then is that work is an economic condition under which activities and tasks are performed, whereas jobs are more or less loosely and arbitrarily defined roles that are made up of particular tasks and activities. This becomes important when we turn to understanding the impact of technology on work.

How does technology impact work? Let us not bury the lede: contrary to much popular discourse, technology does not directly displace or eliminate work from our lives. Work is, after all, just a condition of activity. In principle, there could always be some work for humans to do, irrespective of how capable machines become. This is because it is always in principle possible to attach economic conditionality to our actions. What technology can do is that it can change the tasks or activities that make up currently defined jobs, thereby rendering human activity largely irrelevant to the process of economic production. It can do this in a few different ways. It can do it by assisting human workers in the performance of job-related tasks or it can do it by entirely replacing humans in the performance of tasks.

Take, once more, the example of the taxi driver. The traditional, manually driven car is a form of technology that assists the taxi driver in performing their job-related tasks. It makes it much easier to ferry passengers about than, say, carrying them on a tricycle. Contrast that with an autonomous vehicle that uses a computer program to perform some significant portion of driving-related tasks (e.g. steering, braking, route-planning). This technology does not simply assist the human worker in the performance of key job-related tasks; it displaces them from those tasks. Despite this, there are still some job-related tasks that are unaffected by the arrival of the autonomous vehicle, for example, maintaining good customer service, programming the route-planning algorithm, and so on. The displaced taxi driver could, potentially, take up a new job that focuses on that task. Whether this would be economically feasible is a separate question.

The fact that technology affects job-related tasks, and not jobs or work per se, is something that has been emphasized in most of the recent reports about automation in the workplace (Chui et al. 2016; Manyika et al. 2017a, 2017b; Frey and Osborne 2017; World Economic Forum 2018). If you read past the headlines of these reports, with their talk of 40–50 per cent of jobs being automated, you quickly learn that they base their conclusions on how specific manifestations of robotics or artificial intelligence (AI) can replace or augment the human performance of certain job-related tasks, for example, visual recognition, order-tracking, inventory management, predictive analytics, and so on. The claim, which is valid and well supported, is that this will have a disruptive impact on current employment patterns, and will no doubt lead to the abandonment or redefinition of existing jobs (Ford 2015; Brynjolfsson and McAfee 2014, 2017; Avent 2016; Susskind 2020). This does not, in and of itself, lead to widespread unemployment. Work is not content-specific, and jobs are capable of redefinition and renegotiation. There is consequently still the hope that we can move on to something else and stay working (Susskind 2020: ch. 1). Whether this hope is justified or not is something I take up in more detail below.

THE VALUE(S) OF WORK

Let us turn our attention now to the ethics of work, in particular the value that it has in human life. When assessing the ethics of work, we have a number of different frameworks we can employ. We can, for instance, adopt a deontological and dignitarian framework that assesses the value of work in terms of possible duties to work (or to make use of one's talents, as Kant might have put it)[2] or in terms of its role in honouring or undermining one's self-respect and autonomy. We could also adopt a consequentialist framework that views work as a means or hindrance to some positive end (health, wealth, happiness). We could adopt a virtue ethics-based theory that focuses on the role that work plays (or does not) in cultivating human virtues (excellence, mastery, tolerance, charity, and so on) and facilitating a more flourishing form of existence. In what follows, I will focus on aspects of work that relate to all three of these frameworks, but I will not explicitly trace out the links between them. I will talk instead, more generically, about 'goods' associated with work that have appeal and credibility under each of these possible frameworks.

With this in mind, let's start with one of the more obvious ways to think about work. We sometimes think about work in essentially consequentialist terms as just a means to a financial end. This is a temptation that is made all the more appealing by the definition of work offered in the previous section. If work is an activity performed under the economic condition of payment, then it is natural to assume that receiving payment constitutes both the purpose and value of work. We work in order to get the income we need in order to access other goods in life: food, clothing, entertainment, education, meaningful experiences, and so on. Work is socially and morally significant because of the role it plays in allocating and distributing the income that allows us to access those goods. If people lose their jobs—or have their jobs significantly disrupted—as a result of technological change, then we should focus our moral energies on compensating them for their income-related losses (if any). Failing to do so might result in a society in which people don't have a sufficient income to access the basic goods of life, and in which there is more income-related inequality. Sensitivity to these problems is one of the main reasons why people advocate for a universal basic income (UBI) guarantee in response to automation-related job displacement. That said, it is always worth noting that there are other non-consequentialist moral reasons for favouring a UBI—reasons that have nothing to do with automation anxiety (Van Parijs and Vanderborght 2017).

It would be foolish to deny that work is valuable as a means to a financial end and that we need to factor this into our response to automation. Nevertheless, it would be a mistake to assume that work is *nothing but* a means to a financial end. There are other goods associated with work that are not reducible to income. Work is, for many people, a source of meaning, purpose, social contribution, and inspiration. It provides opportunities for developing important skills and capacities. For want of a better term, we can call these non-income goods, 'meaning-related' goods, and these are goods that can be endorsed under different ethical frameworks. Some are linked primarily to virtue ethical theories of human flourishing; others are more linked to autonomy and dignity.

There are several different accounts of these meaning-related goods. Gheaus and Herzog (2016), for example, argue that there are four specific meaning-related goods associated with work. First, there is the good of *mastery*, that is, the development of advanced skills or competence in a particular area. Second, there is *social contribution*, that is, the opportunity to make a positive contribution to your society. Third, there is *community*, that is, forming alliances and friendships and a sense of identity with other people in the workplace. And fourth, there is *social recognition*, that is, the opportunity to be rewarded and attain a level of esteem for one's efforts. Not all forms of work allow for each of these goods to flourish. As others have noted, meaningful work is not fairly or justly distributed (Walsh 1994; Loi 2015), and some people get stuck with meaningless jobs. Nevertheless, Gheaus and Herzog argue that work, because of its central importance to people in the modern world, provides the main forum for the realization of these four goods in people's lives.

Others have defended similar accounts of the meaning-related goods associated with work. Veltman (2016) argues that work can—in an ideal world—be a forum in which people can develop the human capabilities and virtues needed in order to have a flourishing life. Smids et al. (2019), in an article specifically dealing with the impact of automation on work, argue that there are five meaning-related goods associated with work: (a) pursuing a purpose; (b) social relationships; (c) exercising skills and self-development; (d) self-esteem and recognition; and (e) autonomy.

The important feature of each of these accounts is that they associate several (plural) meaning-related goods with work and, in doing so, highlight how work plays an important role in allocating these goods to people. Some people do not get an adequate share of these goods, others get plenty. It's just like income. This is important because it tells us something about the potential moral impact of widespread technological disruption of work-related tasks. Technology might not just change the amount of income people earn; it might change how much access they get to these meaning-related goods too (Loi 2015). Some people might find themselves spiritually and emotionally impoverished, relative to what they once had. They might have their jobs redefined so that the tasks they now perform have fewer meaning-related goods associated with them. Or they might lose their jobs, and hence lose their primary forum for cultivating these goods. This might be a bad thing, if they have no other opportunities to cultivate or access those goods. Or it might be a good thing, if they are free to pursue those goods in other, more fulfilling ways (Danaher 2019a, 2019b).

HOW TECHNOLOGY MIGHT AFFECT THE DISTRIBUTION OF WORK-RELATED GOODS

To figure out how technology might impact on the distribution of income and meaning-related goods, we need to engage in some speculative prediction. This is a dangerous game. Prediction is hard, especially when it is about the future. Many historical predictions about the future of work look foolish with the wisdom of hindsight. Still, we need some reasonable sense of the possible futures we might face. Here, I sketch three possible futures, each associated with a different kind of effect that technology might have on work.

The polarization effect

I start with the polarization effect. This is the effect that is the most widely discussed and well documented. The polarization effect is something that has manifested itself noticeably in advanced industrial economies since the 1980s (Böhm 2013, 2014; Autor 2015). Very roughly, it is the effect whereby, in these economies, middle-income, middle-skill jobs have been in decline and low-skill, low-income and high-skill, high-income jobs have been, comparatively, on the increase.[3] To put it another way, the polarization effect refers to the phenomenon whereby middle-income, middle-skill workers have been displaced and pushed into either low-skill, low-income jobs or, if they are lucky, high-skill, high-income jobs.

Why has this happened? The globalization of the labour market and the consequent outsourcing of middle-skill jobs is part of the reason. The other significant factor has been advances in computerization and automation.[4] As the economist David Autor

(2015) notes, many middle-skill, middle-income jobs are characterized by what we might call 'routine' tasks.[5] That is, relatively simple, rule-based tasks, performed in consistent and predictable environments. This includes some manufacturing tasks, as well as clerical office work. Routine tasks of this sort are ripe for automation. Any task that can be reduced to a simple algorithm can be automated. This started to happen, en masse, from the 1980s onwards. This has had a devastating impact on middle-skill workers. Many of their jobs were defined by reference to these tasks. In order to remain employable, they had to either redefine their roles so that they were associated with less easily automatable tasks, or look for other jobs. This is why they ended up being pushed into the other poles of the labour market.

The polarization effect seems to be one of the most consistent and enduring effects that technology has on work. What are its ethical implications? The most immediate and obvious ethical effect is on the distribution of income. As David Autor (2015) and Michael Böhm (2013, 2015) have noted, the displaced middle-skill workers do not seem to have been equally allocated to low-skill and high-skill brackets. The majority have ended up in the low-skill bracket. The reason for this is that there are often fewer high-skill jobs available and there are often high barriers to entry into those jobs (e.g. high levels of education or certification are required). It has been observed that since the early 1980s, the level of income disparity in advanced economies has been increasing (Piketty 2014). There are several potential reasons for this. For example, legal norms and political pressures have had an important role to play in determining what levels of income inequality are socially tolerable. Still, there seems to be little doubt that the technology-induced polarization effect is one of the causes of the significant rise in income inequality (Danaher 2019a, 2019b: ch. 3). This could be a bad thing for at least two reasons. It could be bad because ensuring a relatively equal distribution of income (or, more generally, an equal distribution of the social surplus) is intrinsically valuable: it protects dignity or equal status between humans or is just a basic, sui generis good. Or it could be a bad thing because having a high level of income disparity leads to other negative social outcomes: political unrest, unequal access to housing and basic social goods, the corrosion of democracy due to the influence of money, and so on. The notion that greater income equality is intrinsically valuable is controversial; the notion that it leads to other bad outcomes is much less so (for a general discussion of the reasons why inequality might be bad, see Scanlon 2018).

But, of course, polarization doesn't just negatively impact on income, it also negatively impacts on meaning-related goods. There are several reasons for this. Recall the list of meaning-related goods that was given in the preceding section. They concerned things like mastery, purpose, social contribution, and recognition. It might initially be supposed that pushing most people into low-skill jobs could still give some access to these goods. This is particularly true given that the economic definition of a low-skill job does not necessarily align with the common understanding of the term 'low skill'. It has to do with the level of education required to access that job, not with how physically or mentally engaging it is. Some low-skill manual forms of work could be quite high-skilled in the colloquial sense and so could facilitate a great sense of mastery and purpose. But we have to remember the significance of social context in how people perceive and understand the value of their work. Many low-skill jobs are socially disvalued, and this is often reflected in their pay packets. They are seen as lesser, more menial forms of work. It can be difficult for someone to achieve a significant level of social contribution and recognition by pursuing those forms of work. This can, in turn, affect their motivation to pursue mastery of those jobs and their understanding of the purposefulness of those jobs.

Connected to this, it seems that technology is having a negative impact on the employment conditions associated with many low-skill jobs. Advances in digital and surveillance technologies have enabled greater fissuring of the corporate workplace (Standing 2011, 2016; Weil 2014). Low-skilled workers who were once employed by a single corporate entity have found themselves increasingly outsourced and required to work on short-term, gig-like contracts. This makes their work more precarious and anxiety-inducing. They don't know if they will be retained in their employment year-on-year and they have to compete more with other workers for limited opportunities. It can be difficult to focus on the meaning-related goods in such conditions of economic precarity. This is a situation that is compounded if the spectre of creeping automation starts to affect these forms of work too. This can be a hindrance to self-respect and autonomy, as well as happiness and well-being.

Some of these problems also afflict high-skill, creative, problem-solving work. For example, the opportunities there are more limited and there is increased competition for them. This means that a reduced number of people get to access the goods associated with those forms of work and may feel precarious even when they secure such a role. Still, it might be plausible to assume that someone who is lucky enough to get such a job will be a net beneficiary of the polarization effect. They will have a sufficient income and their demanding, problem-solving work may be a great source of mastery, purpose, social recognition, and so on. That said, whether this is true could depend, to a large extent, on how high-skill workers interact with technology in their workplaces. This is a topic addressed in more detail below.

The complementarity effect

Another potential effect of technology on work is the complementarity effect. The term comes, once more, from the work of David Autor (2015), though others have written about the same effect using different terminology (e.g. Susskind 2020). This effect, like the polarization effect, is not just a speculative possibility. It is something that has already been observed as a result of past waves of automation. Nevertheless, unlike the polarization effect, it is a more abstract effect and not something easily demonstrated through data on employment patterns.

To grasp the complementarity effect, we must go back to the earlier definition of a job. Recall that a job is a set of tasks, each of which is relevant to the economic value of the job. Each of these tasks can be said to be complementary to one another in the sense that you need them all in order to maximize the economic potential of the job. Sometimes these complementary tasks are all performed by the same individual worker. Sometimes they are shared across a network of human workers inside a single workplace. Indeed, dividing up task performance in this way is often economically sensible. Adam Smith's classic discussion of the economic value of specialization, and his illustration of this with the division of labour within a pin factory, captures the essence of this idea (Smith 1776: ch. 1). The function of the pin factory is to produce pins. There are many tasks that are relevant to that overall function (drawing out the wire, shaping the pin, flattening the head, and so forth). Although a single worker could perform all these tasks, you can ramp up productivity by splitting the tasks across many workers and getting them to specialize in particular tasks. Thus, dividing labour across teams of humans can increase economic productivity and the number of available jobs. What if the same could happen with teams of humans and machines? What would happen to human workers then?

Here is Autor's answer: automating technologies can have a positive impact on the demand for humans in complementary job-related tasks. Machines replace humans, in whole or in part, in some, but not necessarily all, job-related tasks. But this does not mean that humans have nothing left to do. Instead of joining the dole queue, they can migrate to the tasks that complement these machines—tasks at which humans have a comparative advantage. Humans can then specialize in those tasks and this can have a net positive effect on economic productivity and, potentially, employment.

This is the complementarity effect in action. The essence of the complementarity effect is that instead of displacing humans from the workplace, automating technologies simply change what it is that humans need to do to be economically valuable. Autor's go-to example of this effect in action is the relationship between bank clerks and automated teller machines (ATMs). You might think that the ubiquity and spread of the ATM spelled doom for the humble bank clerk. Modern ATMs can, after all, do most of what the clerks used to do: lodgements, withdrawals, and other account services. But as Autor (2015) notes, despite the spread of the ATM, there has not been a significant decline in the number of bank clerks employed across the United States. Why not? Because there are other complementary tasks that humans can perform, for example, customer relationship management. Instead of leading to widespread unemployment in the banking sector, ATMs have just reordered the distribution of job-related tasks: machines do what they are good at; humans do what they are good at. Furthermore, this hasn't just happened in the banking sector. In a very real sense, it is what has happened since the dawn of the Industrial Revolution. Machines have, indeed, displaced human workers from some tasks but this has not led to a net decline in employment. There are more people at work now than ever before. This must be because people have found ways to work alongside machines.

Whether the complementarity effect is, in fact, robust and whether it holds out the hope of long-term employment for humans is something I address later when discussing the replacement effect of technology on employment. For now, I want to focus on its impact on the value of work in human life. At first glance, you might be enthused by the complementarity effect. It suggests that the impact of automating technologies on work may be less dramatic and disruptive than is often supposed. We may have to learn new skills and reprioritize what we do, but we won't be rendered destitute and without any meaningful work. There will still be plenty of that to go around.

But the devil here is going to be in the detail. What exactly are the machine-complementary skills in which humans have a comparative advantage? What will our jobs look like after they have been restructured so as to be complementary to machines? There are some reasons to be pessimistic and some reasons to be optimistic. The most comprehensive analysis of this issue, to date, has been undertaken by Smids, Nyholm, and Berkers (2019). The focus of their work is on 'robotization' in the workplace and the impact that working alongside robots will have on the meaningfulness of work, but much of their analysis can be expanded to include other forms of automation and digitization.

They argue that there are both opportunities and risks that need to be addressed when working alongside machines. Take, for example, the purposefulness of work. If machines perform most of the cognitively or intellectually rewarding tasks in the workplace, and humans are left to perform the more mundane or emotionally and physically taxing tasks, then there could be a net loss in meaningfulness. Consider the fate of the taxi driver discussed earlier. If automated driving technology advances to a point where humans are only needed in rare circumstances (unusual or abnormal driving conditions), this could negatively impact on the meaningfulness of the job. The human 'driver' might be reduced to a button pusher and conversation starter. Under these conditions, they may begin to question the value of their jobs. They may be no longer engaged or interested in what they do and their cognitive capacities may start to atrophy (Carr 2015). This is already a noted problem with automation in the workplace: people tend to develop automation bias and defer to machines, rather than their own judgements, in crucial circumstances. This can be disempowering and undermine the sense of mastery and control that is central to meaningful work. It could also cut people off from any sense of achievement that might derive from their work, especially if it is the machines that seem to do all the important tasks (see also Danaher and Nyholm 2020). That said, the converse could also be true. Machines might take over the mundane and emotionally and physically demanding tasks, while humans are left to focus on the more intellectually rewarding tasks.

Technology could also impact on social contact and collegiality at work. For many people, work is an opportunity to build friendships and alliances, and to work alongside others towards a common goal. This social aspect of work can be a great source of value. But, as Smids, Nyholm, and Berkers (2019) observe, automation could negatively impact on this. Imagine being the sole human worker in a warehouse full of robots. You cannot talk to them or interact with them. There is no opportunity for 'water cooler' chats or causal forms of friendly interaction. Humans are a social species. Our brains have largely evolved to enable us to navigate complex social environments and relationships. Without social contact we can suffer greatly. In the robot warehouse, our sense of isolation and loneliness might increase dramatically. This can also be exacerbated by other technological transformations of the workplace. For example, the forms of remote work that are facilitated by digitalization can be socially dis-spiriting. This is something many people have learned in the wake of the COVID-19 pandemic of 2020. That said, there could also be opportunities for enhanced socialization through technology. Information communications technologies can enable some remote workers to interact with a wider community of colleagues. This is true for many academics and researchers, for example. They can be part of large international research teams from the comfort of their own homes. Another possibility, mooted by Nyholm and Smids (2020) is that it may be possible to design a robot that is a 'good colleague', thereby mitigating some of the potential social damage that may be wrought by having to work alongside machines.

Finally, it is worth noting that the complementarity effect could negatively impact on the income-related goods of work. To some extent, the polarization effect is a manifestation of the complementarity effect. Following Autor's argument, machines are good at one set of tasks—middle-skill routine tasks—and humans are good at others—low-skill manual tasks and high-skill creative tasks. Since we already noted that the polarization effect is having a negative impact on the distribution of income by pushing more people into low-skill, poorly remunerated and highly precarious work, it is plausible to assume that increased human–machine complementarity in the workplace will continue to follow this trajectory, at least for the foreseeable future. Consequently, there are risks when it comes to the income-related goods of work too.

The bottom line then is that the complementarity effect is not a reason to be complacent about the impact of technology on the value of work. It may save us from mass unemployment but it may not save us from less meaningful and less well-rewarded forms of work. It will all depend on the exact distribution of job-related tasks across humans and machines, and the resulting conditions of employment for humans.

The replacement effect

The final potential effect of technology on work is perhaps the most obvious. It is the one that we mentioned at the outset of this chapter: technology might completely replace humans within the workplace. This could happen for a variety of reasons, but the primary one is simply that automating technologies get sufficiently good at job-related tasks that they obviate the need for humans. To go back to Martinho-Truswell's (2018) observation, replacement-via-automation is one of the defining features of humanity and is something that has happened repeatedly since the dawn of civilization. It's very clear, for example, that significant amounts of replacement-via-automation have taken place in agriculture. Human and animal labour have been replaced by machines that can till the land, sow the seeds, and harvest the crops. The result has been significant reductions in agriculture-related employment. For example, according to data collected by Max Roser (2017), most European countries have seen agriculture-related employment decline to less than 5 per cent of the working population today from greater than 50 per cent (in many countries) 200 years ago. A similar story is true in manufacturing industries, which have been affected by both outsourcing and widescale automation.

Indeed, the production line for manufactured goods such as cars/automobiles is, in many people's minds, the epitome of workplace automation.

Suffice to say, when the replacement effect manifests itself, it significantly compromises all the values associated with work. If you lose your job, you lose your source of income—unless you are independently wealthy—and typically have to turn to welfare for support. Since welfare payments are usually less than employment-related payments (and in some countries they decline over time) this results in a net loss in the instrumental gains associated with work. Furthermore, reliance on the state, particularly in welfare systems that are means-tested and require significant surveillance and/or intrusion into your life, can undermine dignity and the sense of self-worth. In addition to this, if you no longer work, you may no longer have access to the non-income-related goods of work. Your job may have been the main source of purpose, meaning, social contribution, and recognition in your life. Without it, your capacity to flourish in these domains could diminish.

This negative assessment does, however, have to be qualified by two observations. First, for many people, jobs are not significant sources of non-income-related goods. For them, jobs are soul-destroying, boring, and limiting. They are simply a means to an end. Second, for these people, and perhaps for us all, being freed up from the need to work could provide us with an opportunity to flourish in other ways. A non-work life could be better than a working life. This is a view that I have myself defended in the past (Danaher 2019a, 2019b) and I will consider it again in the final part of this chapter. For now, however, these two observations notwithstanding, it seems that a strong prima facie case can be made for the view that widescale technological replacement of humans in the workforce would be a bad thing.

The real question then is whether such widescale replacement is going to happen. People have been periodically touting it as a real possibility for more than 200 years. They started to do so in recent years as a response to the excitement (and hype) around the development of AI and robotics (Ford 2015; Brynjolfsson and McAfee 2014; Avent 2016; Chace 2018; Susskind 2020). Since all past predictions of widescale technological unemployment have been wrong, there is reason to be suspicious of these claims. Will things be different this time around? The prevailing wisdom in economic circles is that they won't be. After some initial, frictional unemployment, our economies and workplaces will adapt, the complementarity effect will take root, and humans will simply shift focus (Susskind 2020: ch. 6).

But perhaps things really will be different this time around. I believe that there are four reasons to expect greater employment-related disruption arising from current advances in AI and robotics than from past technological developments (cf. Danaher 2019a: 39–48).

The first reason is educational and institutional inertia, exacerbated by accelerating technological change. In a report into the impact of automating technologies in the workplace, the World Economic Forum (WEF)(2018) predicted that technologies could replace 75 million jobs globally, but then lead to the creation of 133 million machine-complementary jobs. The WEF noted that to fill those jobs we will have to redesign our educational systems to facilitate both training and retraining people to fill those jobs. This is not an easy task. Some people, through no fault of their own, will not be able or willing to be retrained. This could be because of relative age or other personal circumstance. There is also significant inertia built into our educational and training institutions. Many of them are state supported and not driven primarily or solely by market pressures: they may not perceive any need to reimagine their curricula. There may be considerable opposition from the people already employed in those institutions, who may, in many cases, lack the skills necessary to educate the next generation of workers. These institutional difficulties could be exacerbated by an accelerating pace of technological change and development. Advances in AI and automation will not necessarily wait for humans to catch up. Just as humans are busy retraining themselves with the skills necessary to perform machine-complementary tasks, technologists may be busy designing machines that can perform those tasks. If the pace of innovation is faster than the pace of education, humans may lose the race to fill those complementary jobs. This doesn't require exponential advances in technology; it just requires the relative pace of development in technology and human education to be such that the machines are slightly faster.

The second reason is that there may not always be machine-complementary tasks that humans can perform in an economically viable way. The assumption underlying Autor's (2015) articulation of the complementarity effect is that developments in automation allow for a human-friendly workplace. In other words, automating technologies replace tasks that humans once performed but there are still meaningful ways for humans to interact with machines that increases overall economic productivity. This may not always be the case. Widespread use of automating technologies may result in a human-unfriendly workplace. We already see this, to some extent, in some industries. Manufacturing robots, for example, often operate with a strength and speed that exceeds anything that is possible for humans. It is difficult for humans to work alongside them. The machines have to be caged and humans have to be kept away. For the time being, we still ask for humans to occasionally interact with the machines, but in the future it may be easier, and safer, to try to create other machines that can work alongside the existing ones. Likewise, in financial markets, trading bots can operate at a speed and scale that is unfathomable to most humans. It is difficult for those who are trying to regulate and control the behaviour of those trading bots to keep pace. In some ways, it may be easier to create other AI programs that can do this. The point here is not that Autor's complementarity effect is false but, rather, that it paints an incomplete picture. We don't just have to contend with one type of AI (or robotics) that happens to be good at one task; we have to contend with multiple forms that are being (and will be) designed to perform other tasks. These different machines might find it easier to work with each other than to work with humans. The end result might be a system of productivity that is much more efficient than anything that would be possible with human–machine chimeras, but much more human-unfriendly.

The third reason is that current technologies may be such that less human labour is required to exploit new markets and opportunities. The existence of so-called 'superstar' marketplaces has been discussed in economics for some time (Rosen 1981). These are marketplaces in which a handful of actors (e.g. individual sport stars or large quasi-monopolistic corporations) dominate and capture most of the value. They are the most in demand and most customers flock to them. Digital technologies have tended to encourage superstar markets (Brynjolfsson and McAfee 2014). This is because they help to foster a single global marketplace. If I want to buy something, I don't need to go to the high street. I can go online to Amazon or Alibaba or one of a handful of other large online retailers and buy almost anything I might desire. This can then be sent to me through an efficient global transportation network (also facilitated by advances in technology). In some cases, I may be purchasing a digital good or service which can be provided to me instantaneously via the internet. This globalization and digitization of the market obviates the need for much human labour and allows a handful of economic actors to thrive. As long as we retain these digital platforms and technological networks for buying goods and services, we will encourage superstar markets and reduce the opportunities for human workers. This will be true even in markets for new goods and services.

The fourth reason, which is only offered tentatively, is that there is some evidence to suggest that recent waves of robotization in the workplace have not resulted in net gains in jobs, even when we consider the impact that robotization may have had in unrelated markets and regions. Recent empirical work by Acemoglu and Restrepo in the US (2020) and Acemoglu, LeLarge, and Restrepo in France (2020)[6] has found that robotization tends to have a net negative impact on employment across firms and marketplaces. The estimates vary, but for every one robot that is 'employed' anywhere from three to six humans tend to lose their jobs. Whether this effect holds up over the long term remains to be seen, but it is, nevertheless, suggestive that there could be something different about this current wave of automation.

If this is correct, then the replacement effect may win out over the polarization and complementarity effects. If the replacement effect does win out, what happens to us humans? How can we correct for the loss in income and meaning-related goods? These are questions to which I turn in the final section.

WHAT CAN BE DONE?

If the preceding analysis is correct, then it seems that technology has had, and will continue to have, significant effects on the ethical dimensions of work. It does so by redistributing income or cutting off people from an important source of income; it does so by impacting on the distribution of the meaning-related goods of work. Some of those effects can be positive for some workers; others can be quite negative for many workers. This is true no matter which of the three effects we consider. Nevertheless, if I am correct, there is reason to suspect that wholescale replacement of human workers—and not just redistributions of human workers—will be more likely in the future. What can be done about this? Let me close by discussing three possibilities.

First, we might look to slowing technological innovation down and reducing its disruptive impacts on the workplace. This could be useful, if only as a stop-gap measure, to give us a chance to reorganize our societies in a way that can mitigate the ethical disruption caused by increased digitization and automation. As mentioned earlier, replacement of human labour is likely to be exacerbated if machine labour can improve or develop new skills at a faster rate than human labour. If you could slow machines down so that the rate of improvement is more equal, or so that humans can play catch-up, you could stop this from happening. How might you do this? Increased regulatory hurdles for technology would be one possibility. It has long been noted that digital technologies and the technologies of automation that emanate from Silicon Valley cultures have largely thrived due to the absence of significant regulation. Compare, for example, the regulatory hurdles facing the pharmaceutical industry and those facing the tech industry. The absence of significant regulation fosters a culture in which people try to 'move fast and break things' (Taplin 2017). It is possible that we could dampen some of that disruptive enthusiasm through more stringent regulation. We already see this happening to some extent. For example, gig working platforms such as Uber and Deliveroo have recently found their attempts to avoid employment laws being met with some opposition in different countries. Another option would be to place a tax on innovation. Some people, including most notably former Microsoft Chief Executive Officer Bill Gates, have mooted the idea of a 'robot tax'.[7] Gates seems to have envisioned this as a way to collect revenue that could be paid back to workers who are replaced by robots, but, if set at a high enough level, a robot tax could also function as a disincentive to innovation, thereby slowing down the pace of replacement.

There are, however, problems with attempts to slow down the pace of innovation. An obvious one is that they tend to imply a level of satisfaction with the existing status quo with respect to the world of work. At the very least, they imply that it is better than the possible future of work. But this may not be warranted. There are many negative features of the existing world of work. For example, the polarization effect has already taken root and led to an unequal distribution of income and meaning in work. Slowing down innovation without correcting for that existing imbalance would be a problem. It could also be the case that radical disruption of work could jolt us out of any complacency with respect to the existing distribution of income and meaning. We might wish to 'accelerate' that disruption in order to force ourselves to build a new social order (Srnicek and Williams 2015). This is to say nothing about the potential advantages of innovation in terms of increasing productivity and reducing the costs of goods and services.

The second thing we could do to address the disruptive impact of technology on work is to introduce some policy that corrects for any income-related losses of that disruption. This is the area of policy that has been most widely discussed in recent times. Many books and reports on the subject of automation have either defended, or at the very least mooted, the idea of a basic income guarantee (e.g. Ford 2015). This would be a reform to welfare payments that gives everyone within a society a basic guaranteed income. If sufficiently generous, this would free people from the need to work and mitigate any deprivation and anxiety they might face as a result of technology-induced job loss. A basic income guarantee also has the advantage of being attractive for a number of other reasons, including capacity to guarantee an enhanced form of freedom or autonomy in society and to address the gender disparities in income-rewarded work (Van Parijs and Vanderbroght 2017). As has already been noted, income is only a means to an end and so another way of addressing the problems caused by income loss would be to provide for enhanced universal basic services, such as health care, food, and housing. This, however, might be less attractive insofar as it could amount to a highly restrictive form of state rationing of basic services. Some combination of UBI and universal basic services might be more optimal. That said, addressing income and service-related losses does nothing to address meaning-related losses. One of the fears people have about proposals for a basic income or similar welfare reforms is that it assumes that a large proportion of the adult population will be idle or surplus to the requirements of capitalistic production (Brynjolfsson and McAfee 2014). Surely, we also need to think about what these people are going to do, particularly since the world we now live in is one that places a lot of faith in the value of work and the importance of the work ethic.

This brings me to the third and final possibility. In some of my own writings I have tried to think in more detail about what it might take to build a truly post-work society (Danaher 2019a, 2019b); that is, a society in which work no longer occupies a central and organizing role in our social lives and in which it is no longer given a privileged place in how we secure meaning-related goods. My argumentative strategy has been threefold. First, I argue that work often undermines meaning-related goods by being a source of unfreedom, inequality, and anxiety in our lives. Second, I argue that there is no necessary connection between work and these meaning-related goods: there are other ways to secure meaning in life, some of which have been historically more significant. These include securing meaning-related goods through family and relationships, leisure activities, religion, and charity. If work is no longer economically necessary, then these domains of meaning could take pride of place once more. Third, and more concretely, I have argued that reorganizing society in such a way that games and leisure activities occupy the position once held by work has the potential to enable a flourishing post-work existence. This is not, however, something that can simply happen overnight. It requires changes in both culture and ideology. These will need to be articulated, argued for, and actively implemented. It is an open question as to whether we can realize such a post-work world but it is, I submit, a possibility worth pursuing.

Notes

1. I mean this in a very minimal, epistemic, sense. Their behaviour is such that they could, for all you know, feel pleasure and pain and have some minimal conception of themselves as a single continuing entity. There may be philosophical reasons for doubting whether their behaviour is indicative of this, but they are not sufficiently weighty to undermine the behavioural evidence. See Danaher (2020) for a longer discussion of this principle.

2. On Kant's claim that we have a duty to use our talents, see O'Connor (2018: 37ff).
3. The link between income and skill level is not perfect, but they do appear to be correlated. See https://ideas.repec.org/p/zbw/vfsc14/100547.html (accessed 1 October 2021) and the work of David Autor.
4. It is also worth noting that the globalization of the workforce has also been made possible by advances in information communications technology (ICT). So these are not, necessarily, separate explanations for the polarization effect. On the role of ICT in global labour, see Aneesh (2006).
5. For further detail on this see Breemersch et al. (2017).
6. See https://www.nber.org/papers/w26738, accessed 1 October 2021.
7. See https://www.cnbc.com/2017/06/02/bill-gates-robot-tax-eu.html, accessed 1 October 2021.

References

Acemoglu, Daron, and Restrepo, Pascual (2020), 'Robots and Jobs: Evidence from US Labor Markets', *Journal of Political Economy* 128(6), 2188–2244

Acemoglu, Daron, LeLarge, Claire, and Restrepo, Pascual (2020), 'Competing with Robots: Firm-Level Evidence from France', National Bureau of Economic Research Working Paper No. 26738, https://www.nber.org/papers/w26738, accessed 1 October 2021.

Aneesh, A. (2006), *Virtual Migration* (Durham, NC: Duke University Press).

Autor, David (2015), 'Why Are There Still So Many Jobs? The History and Future of Workplace Automation', *Journal of Economic Perspectives* 29(3), 3–30.

Avent, Ryan (2016), *The Wealth of Humans: Work, Power and Status in the 21st Century* (New York: St Martin's Press).

Black, Bob (1986), *The Abolition of Work and Other Essays* (Port Townshend, WA: Loompanics Unlimited).

Breemersch, Koen, Damijan, Jože, and Konings, Jozef (2017), 'Labour Market Polarization in Advanced Countries: Impact of Global Value Chains, Technology, Import Competition from China and Labour Market Institutions', OECD Social, Employment and Migration Working Papers, No. 197, OECD Publishing, Paris, doi: https://doi.org/10.1787/06804863-en.

Brynjolfsson, Erik, and McAfee, Andrew (2014), *The Second Machine Age* (New York: W. W. Norton and Co.).

Brynjolfsson, Erik, and McAfee, Andrew (2017), *Machine, Platform, Crowd* (New York: W. W. Norton and Co.).

Böhm, Michael (2013). 'Has Job Polarization Squeezed the Middle Class? Evidence from the Allocation of Talents', CEP Discussion Papers dp1215, Centre for Economic Performance, LSE.

Böhm, Michael (2014), 'The Wage Effects of Job Polarization: Evidence from the Allocation of Talents', Annual Conference 2014 (Hamburg): Evidence-Based Economic Policy 100547, Verein für Socialpolitik/German Economic Association.

Carr, Nicholas (2015), *The Glass Cage: Where Automation is Taking Us* (London: The Bodley Head).

Chace, Calum (2018), *The Economic Singularity*, 2nd edn (Three Cs Publishing).

Chui, Michael, Manyika, James, and Miremadi, Mehdi (2016), 'Where Machines Could Replace Humans—and Where They Can't (Yet)[, *McKinsey Quarterly*, 8 July, https://www.

mckinsey.com/business-functions/mckinsey-digital/our-insights/where-machines-could-replace-humans-and-where-they-cant-yet, accessed 14 December 2021.

Danaher, John (2019a), *Automation and Utopia: Human Flourishing in a World without Work* (Cambridge, MA: Harvard University Press).

Danaher, John (2019b), 'In Defence of the Post-Work Future: Withdrawal and the Ludic Life', in Cholbi, Michael and Weber, Michael eds, *The Future of Work, Technology and Basic Income* (London: Routledge), 99–115.

Danaher, John (2020), 'Welcoming Robots into the Moral Circle: A Defence of Ethical Behaviourism', *Science and Engineering Ethics* 26, 2023–2049.

Danaher, John, and Nyholm, S. (2020), 'Automation, Work and the Achievement Gap', *AI Ethics*, doi: https://doi.org/10.1007/s43681-020-00028-x.

Ford, Martin (2015), *The Rise of the Robots: Technology and the Threat of Mass Unemployment* (New York: Basic Books).

Frayne, David (2015), *The Refusal of Work* (London: ZED Books).

Frey, Carl B, and Osborne, Michael A. (2017), 'The Future of Employment: How Susceptible Are Jobs to Automation?', *Technological Forecasting and Social Change* 114, 254–280.

Gheaus, Anca, and Herzog, Lisa (2016), 'The Goods of Work (Other Than Money!)', *Journal of Social Philosophy* 47(1), 70–89, doi: https://doi.org/10.1111/josp.12140.

Gorz, André (1989), *Critique of Economic Reason* (London: Verso).

Gruber, Romana, Schiestl, Martina, Boeckle, Markus, Frohnwieser, Anna, Miller, Rachael Gray, Russell D., Clayton, Nicola S., and Taylor, Alex H. (2019), 'New Caledonian Crows Use Mental Representations to Solve Metatool Problems', *Current Biology* 29, 686–692.

Loi, Michele (2015), 'Technological Unemployment and Human Disenhancement', *Ethics and Information Technology* 17, 201–210.

Manyika, James , Chui, Michael, Miremadi, Mehdi, Bughin, Jacques, George, Katy, Willmott, Paul, et al. (2017a), 'A Future That Works: Automation, Employment and Productivity', McKinsey Global Institute Report, McKinsey and Co, available at https://www.mckinsey.com/featured-insights/digital-disruption/harnessing-automation-for-a-future-that-works/de-DE, accessed 14 December 2021.

Manyika, James, Chui, Michael, Miremadi, Mehdi, Bughin, Jacques, George, Katy, Willmott, Paul, et al. (2017b), 'Harnessing Automation for a Future That Works', McKinsey Global Institute Report, January, available at https://www.mckinsey.com/featured-insights/digital-disruption/harnessing-automation-for-a-future-that-works, accessed 14 December 2021.

Martinho-Truswell, Antone (2018), 'To Automate Is Human', AEON, 13 February, https://aeon.co/essays/the-offloading-ape-the-human-is-the-beast-that-automates, accessed 1 October 2021.

Mayor, Adrienne (2018), *Gods and Robots* (Princeton NJ: Princeton University Press).

Nyholm, Sven, and Smids, Jilles (2020), 'Can a Robot Be a Good Colleague?', *Science and Engineering Ethics* 26, 2169–2188.

O'Connor, Brian (2018), *Idleness: A Philosophical Essay* (Princeton, NJ: Princeton University Press).

Piketty, Thomas (2014), *Capital in the 21st Century* (Cambridge, MA: Harvard University Press).

Rosen, Sheldon (1981), 'The Economics of Superstars', *American Economic Review* 71(5), 845–858.

Roser, Max (2017), 'Agricultural Employment', OurWorldInData.org, https://ourworldindata.org/agricultural-employment/, accessed 1 October 2021.

Scanlon, Thomas M. (2018), *Why Does Inequality Matter?* (Oxford: Oxford University Press).

Seyfarth, Robert M., and Cheney, Dorothy L. (2017), 'Precursors to Language: Social Cognition and Pragmatic Inference in Primates', *Psychonomic Bulletin and Review* 24, 79–84.

Smids, Jilles, Nyholm, Sven, and Berkers, Hannah (2019), 'Robots in the Workplace: A Threat to—or Opportunity for—Meaningful Work?', *Philosophy of Technology* 33, 503–522, doi: https://doi.org/10.1007/s13347-019-00377-4.

Smith, Adam (1776), *The Wealth of Nations* (London: W. Strahan and T. Cadell).

Srnicek, Nick, and Williams, Alex (2015), *Inventing the Future* (London: Verso).

Standing, Guy (2011), *The Precariat: The New Dangerous Class* (London: Bloomsbury).

Standing, Guy (2016), *The Corruption of Capitalism: Why Rentiers Thrive and Work Does Not Pay* (London: Biteback Publishing).

Susskind, Daniel (2020), *A World without Work* (London: Penguin).

Taplin, Jonathan (2017), *Move Fast and Break Things* (London: PanMacMillan).

Van Parijs, Philippe, and Vanderborght, Yannick (2017), *Basic Income: A Radical Proposal for a Free Society and a Sane Economy* (Cambridge, MA: Harvard University Press).

Veltman, Andrea (2016), *Meaningful Work* (Oxford: Oxford University Press).

Walsh, Adrian J. (1994), 'Meaningful Work as a Distributive Good', *Southern Journal of Philosophy* 32(2), 233–250.

Weeks, Kathi (2011), *The Problem with Work*. (Durham, NC: Duke University Press).

Weil, Andrew (2014), *The Fissured Workplace: How Work Became So Bad for So Many and What Can Be Done About It* (Cambridge, MA: Harvard University Press).

World Economic Forum, Centre for the New Economy and Society (2018), 'The Future of Jobs Report 2018', http://www3.weforum.org/docs/WEF_Future_of_Jobs_2018.pdf, accessed 1 October 2021.

INDEX

....

End notes are indicated by an italic *n*, preceding the relevant note number; Tables are indicated by *t* following the page number